eading

90 0602137 7

The Economic Development of Italy since 1870

The Economic Development of Modern Europe since 1870

Series Editor: Charles Feinstein
Chichele Professor of Economic History
All Souls College, Oxford

1. The Economic Development of France since 1870 (Volumes I and II)
   François Crouzet

2. The Economic Development of Denmark and Norway since 1870
   Karl Gunnar Persson

3. The Economic Development of Italy since 1870
   Giovanni Federico

4. The Economic Development of Austria since 1870
   Herbert Matis

5. The Economic Development of Ireland since 1870 (Volumes I and II)
   Cormac Ó Gráda

Future titles will include:

The Economic Development of The Netherlands since 1870
Jan Luiten van Zanden

The Economic Development of Belgium since 1870
H. Van Der Wee and J. Blomme

The Economic Development of Germany since 1870
W. Fischer

The Economic Development of the United Kingdom since 1870
C. Feinstein

The Economic Development of Sweden since 1870
L. Jonung and R. Ohlsson

The Economic Development of Spain since 1870
P. Martín-Aceña and J. Simpson

The Economic Development of the European Community
R.T. Griffiths

The Economic Development of Italy since 1870

Edited by

Giovanni Federico

Life Fellow
Department of Modern and Contemporary History
University of Pisa, Italy

An Elgar Reference Collection

Published by
Edward Elgar Publishing Limited
Gower House
Croft Road
Aldershot
Hants GU11 3HR
England

Edward Elgar Publishing Company
Old Post Road
Brookfield
Vermont 05036
USA

British Library Cataloguing in Publication Data
Economic Development of Italy Since 1870.
– (Economic Development of Modern Europe
Since 1870; Vol. 3)
I. Federico, Giovanni II. Series
330.945

Library of Congress Cataloguing in Publication Data
The Economic development of Italy since 1870 / edited by Giovanni Federico.
p. cm. — (The Economic development of modern Europe since 1870; 3) (An Elgar reference collection)
1. Italy—Economic conditions. 2. Italy—Industries—History.
I. Federico, Giovanni. II. Series. III. Series: An Elgar reference collection.
HC303.E25 1994
330.945—dc20 93–49865
CIP

ISBN 1 85278 701 5

Printed in Great Britain at the University Press, Cambridge

Contents

Acknowledgements

The editor and publishers wish to thank the following who have kindly given permission for the use of copyright material.

Associazione Sindacale Intersind for article: Franco Bonelli (1984), 'The State and the Economy in the Industrialization of Italy from its Origins to the Welfare State', translated from 'Stato ed Economia nell'Industrializzazione Italiana dalle Origini al "Welfare State"', *Governare l'economia. Atti del Convegno "Stato Impresa Sindacato: i soggetti delle relazioni industriali nel governo dell'economia"*, Roma, 27–28 ottobre 1983, *Quaderni di industria e sindacato*, **12**.

Banca di Roma for article: Pierluigi Ciocca and Gianni Toniolo (1984), 'Industry and Finance in Italy, 1918–1940', *Journal of European Economic History*, Special issue on Banks and Industry in the Interwar Period, Fall, **13** (2), 113–36.

Basil Blackwell Ltd for articles: Jon S. Cohen (1988), 'Was Italian Fascism a Developmental Dictatorship? Some Evidence to the Contrary', *Economic History Review*, Second Series, **XLI** (1), 95–113; Nicola Rossi and Gianni Toniolo (1992), 'Catching Up or Falling Behind? Italy's Economic Growth, 1895–1947', *Economic History Review*, European Special Issue, August, **XLV** (3), 537–63; Jon S. Cohen and Francesco L. Galassi (1990), 'Sharecropping and Productivity: "Feudal Residues" in Italian Agriculture, 1911', *Economic History Review*, Second Series, **XLIII** (4), 646–56.

Berg Publishers Limited for article: V. Zamagni (1989), 'An International Comparison of Real Industrial Wages, 1890–1913: Methodological Issues and Results', in Peter Scholliers (ed.), *Real Wages in 19th and 20th Century Europe: Historical and Comparative Perspectives*, 107–39.

Cambridge University Press for articles: Stefano Fenoaltea (1988), 'International Resource Flows and Construction Movements in the Atlantic Economy: The Kuznets Cycle in Italy, 1861–1913', *Journal of Economic History*, **XLVIII** (3), September, 605–37; Richard S. Eckaus (1961), 'The North–South Differential in Italian Economic Development', *Journal of Economic History*, **XX** (3), September, 285–317.

Economic History Association for article: Alexander Gerschenkron (1962), 'Notes on the Rate of Industrial Growth in Italy, 1881–1913', in *Economic Backwardness in Historical Perspective: A Book of Essays*, 72–89.

Edizione Scientifiche Italiane for article: Alexander Gerschenkron (1968), 'The Industrial Development of Italy: A Debate with Rosario Romeo', in *Continuity in History and Other Essays*, 98–127.

Einaudi Editore S.p.A for articles: Franco Bonelli (1978), 'Italian Capitalism: General Interpretative Guidelines', translated by Brian Williams from 'Il Capitalismo Italiano. Linee Gerali di Interpretazione', in *Storia d'Italia. Annali I. Dal Feudalesimo al Capitalismo*, 1195–255; G. Federico (1986), 'Commercialization and Economic Development in Italy (1860–1940)', translated from 'Mercantilizzazione e sviluppo economico italiano (1860–1940)', *Rivista di Storia Economica*, Volume 3, 149–86.

Fondazione ASSI for article: Duccio Bigazzi (1990), 'Business History in Italy: A Provisional Review and Research Prospects', translated by John Donaldson from 'La Storia d'Impresa in Italia: Bilancio Provvisorio e Prospettive di Ricerca', *La Storia d'Impresa in Italia*, 7–54.

Fontana, an imprint of HarperCollins Publishers Limited, for article: Luciano Cafagna (1972), 'The Industrial Revolution in Italy 1830–1914', in Carlo M. Cipolla (ed.), *The Fontana Economic History of Europe: The Emergence of Industrial Societies, Part One*, Volume IV, 279–328.

Macmillan Ltd and St Martin's Press, Incorporated for article: Stefano Fenoaltea (1983), 'Italy', in Patrick O'Brien (ed.), *Railways and the Economic Development of Western Europe, 1830–1914*, 49–120.

Marsilio Editori for article: L. Cafagna (1989), 'Discussion of the Origins of Italian Economic Dualism', translated from 'La Questione delle Origini del Dualismo Economico Italiano', in *Dualismo e sviluppo nella storia d'Italia*, 187–220.

Manchester University Press for article: Patrick K. O'Brien and Gianni Toniolo (1991), 'The Poverty of Italy and the Backwardness of its Agriculture Before 1914', in Bruce M.S. Campbell and Mark Overton (eds), *Land, Labour and Livestock: Historical Studies in European Agricultural Productivity*, 385–409.

Routledge for article: Giovanni Federico and Gianni Toniolo (1991), 'Italy', in Richard Sylla and Gianni Toniolo (eds), *Patterns of European Industrialization: The Nineteenth Century*, 197–217.

Societá Editrice Il Mulino for article: Pierluigi Ciocca and A.M. Biscaini Cotula (1982), 'Italian Financial Structures: Long-Term Quantitative Profiles (1870–1970), translated from 'Le Strutture Finanziarie Italiane: Profili Quantitativi di Lungo Periodo (1870–1970)', in *Interesse e Profitto*, 61–136.

University of Chicago Press for article: Michele Fratianni and Franco Spinelli (1984), 'Italy in the Gold Standard Period, 1861–1914', in Michael D. Bordo and Anna J. Schwartz (eds), *A Retrospective on the Classical Gold Standard, 1821–1931*, 405–41.

Zentrum für historiche Sozialforschung, Zentralarchiv für Empirische Sozialforschung an der Universität zu Köln for article: Vera Zamagni (1987), 'A Century of Change: Trends in the Composition of the Italian Labour Force, 1881–1981', *Historical Social Research*, **44**, 36–97.

Every effort has been made to trace all the copyright holders but if any have been inadvertently overlooked the publishers will be pleased to make the necessary arrangement at the first opportunity.

In addition the publishers wish to thank the Library of the London School of Economics and Political Science, the Photographic Unit of the University of London Library, and the Marshall Library, Cambridge University, for their assistance in obtaining these articles.

Introduction*

1. Italy: A Little-Known Success Story

Interest in Italy's development is warranted by the size of the country, the level of income it has achieved and the lessons its particular story may contain. The relevant literature is extensive, and includes studies by social historians as well as by economic historians and economists. Though the number of works in English is growing, most of the literature is still in Italian. It is therefore accessible abroad only to a few specialists. So in the main the Italian case remains far less known overseas than it would seem to deserve. This introduction aims to provide the non-Italian reader with a general overview of the discussion that forms the background to the essays collected here.[1] The next section reviews the overall interpretations, and the following ones deal with various features of the development process. The first of these considers agriculture and its (supposed) shortcomings. The next two examine industrialization; one focuses on input use and technical progress, the other on industrial policy. The sixth section presents the macroeconomic framework and the last raises the issue of geographical and economic dualism as a peculiarity of Italian development. A brief conclusion follows.

The review emphasizes the more recent works that mark the state of the art: references to earlier studies can be found in the works cited here. Its primary concern is with issues of general interest from a developmental perspective. It will therefore pay little attention to works dealing with single areas, firms and/or entrepreneurs, which represent the overwhelming bulk of the literature. Nor will this review take into consideration the period after the Second World War. The war marked a clear political and economic watershed and – to some extent – the end of the process of development. The postwar years have been studied by economists rather than by economic historians, and the two literatures are in the main quite separate: a review of postwar growth would have needed a wholly different approach. In a way, this is unfortunate: the historians tend to underestimate the long-term Italian performance and the economists to forget the historical roots of the growth, which thus appears to be an unexpected 'Italian miracle'.

2. The Italian Development in the Long Run

2.1 The first signs of growth can be traced back to the first half of the nineteenth century but quantitative evidence on those years is extremely scarce. The macroeconomic series begin in 1861 (the year of the Unification of Italy into a single state). According to them, from 1870 to 1989 the aggregate GDP increased 21 times, and the per capita 9.5, from 1,210 (US 1985) dollars to 12,955 (Maddison 1991). Most of this growth was achieved after 1945. In the previous period, the Italian performance had been much less impressive: the aggregate increased 2.5 times, and the per capita income slightly more than doubled (to 2,630 dollars).

* The author thanks L. Cafagna, C. Feinstein, S. Fenoaltea and V. Zamagni for the useful comments and suggestions to earlier versions of this text. None of them is responsible for the remaining faults.

The growth seems to have been slow at the beginning, to have acquired some momentum towards the end of the nineteenth century during the so-called Giolitti years (named after the prime minister), and to have slowed down remarkably between the world wars.[2] These are of course national averages. For a country like Italy, it can be safely argued that they are not really representative because the regional disparities of income were very wide. The extent of the North–South gap in 1860 is uncertain, but it has surely been growing throughout the following one hundred years (Zamagni 1987; Esposto 1992; Federico and Toniolo [5]).[3] In fact until the Second World War, industry was concentrated in a 'small country' (Cafagna [3]), that is in the three regions of the North-West (Piedmont, Lombardy, Liguria), also known as the 'industrial triangle'.

The growth has been accompanied – as elsewhere in Europe (Kaelble 1989) by changes in the composition of GDP and of the active population – a decline of agriculture, an increase of industries and later of services (ISTAT 1957; Zamagni [8]). These changes have, however, been relatively slow: nationwide the agricultural sector still accounted for one-quarter of GDP and two-fifths of the total active population in 1951. The industrialization affected the composition of trade flows according to the well-known 'Kuznetsian' pattern (Kuznets 1967).[4] In the middle of the nineteenth century, Italy exported only primary products and imported industrial products. Since the 1880s imports of manufactured goods decreased and those of raw materials increased. The first substantial exports of industrial products began in the late 1890s, starting with labour-intensive ones such as textiles. Manufactures exceeded 50 per cent of the total value of Italian exports already in the 1920s, but their growth was, however, not impressive. The Italian share of the world market remained stable and low till 1937 (Maizels 1963).

While the existence of a long-term growth is beyond any doubt, its rates and time profile are uncertain, because the available macroeconomic series are regarded as unreliable by the overwhelming majority of scholars.[5] They suggest an implausibly high level of per capita income in the 1860s and they underestimate the GDP at the eve of the First World War and therefore the rate of growth in the first fifty years.[6] For the same period, no less than four indices of industrial output are available (Gerschenkron [1]; ISTAT 1956; Fenoaltea [15]; Carreras 1992). Each of them tells a different story – and none of them is faultless or even clearly superior to others (Federico and Toniolo [5]).

2.2 The overall assessments of Italy's economic performance appear to be heavily influenced by their author's attitude towards development. Many, perhaps most, scholars see development as the 'natural state' that all (European?) countries have to reach sooner or later. Comparing Italy with other countries, they find its development late, slow and partial: they therefore search for the causes of 'delays' and 'distortions' with respect to a norm, often identified with the British Industrial Revolution. Other authors start from the opposite assumption – that is, that development itself is an exception – and therefore try to pinpoint the causes of Italy's success. That success appears the more remarkable given such structural disadvantages as overpopulation, the limited supply of good farmland and a poor endowment of minerals and especially of coal.[7] To some extent the distinction between these two positions hinges on the sociopolitical climate and the political ideas of the authors. Broadly speaking, a negative evaluation of Italy's development prevailed during the years of economic slowdown (the 1970s) and among left-wing writers, while a more sanguine view prevailed during periods of economic growth (the 1960s and 1980s).

2.3 The debate on development is as old as the development itself: on some topics it seems to have remained much where it was in the late nineteenth century. The first historical narrations were published just before the Second World War (Morandi 1931; Tremelloni 1937; Golzio 1942). The modern discussion was opened in 1947 by the publication of E. Sereni's book (Sereni 1947, 1966). His opinion on Italy's industrialization was decisively negative: he regarded it as slow, uneven and biased towards heavy industry by the insufficient size of the market for consumption goods. He suggested that an alternative, more balanced, development pattern would have been feasible if the new Italian government after 1861 had accepted the peasants' claims to a redistribution of land. Such a policy would have wiped out the 'feudal heritage' in the countryside, increasing purchasing power of peasants and thus widening outlets for industrial products.[8] Sereni's views have been discussed at length (Caracciolo 1969a). The most important criticism came from Romeo (1958). He praised the government in the 1860s and 1870s precisely for its policy of high taxes on agricultural rents and on consumption. The proceeds were invested in social overhead capital (above all railways) which he took to be an indispensable prerequisite for industrialization. Not by chance, according to him, Italian economy 'took off' in the 1880s, soon after the completion of the main railway network.

A few years before, Gerschenkron had computed an index of Italian industrial output from 1881 to 1913 (Gerschenkron [1] as part of his own broader research on European industrialization. The performance of the Italian economy disappointed him: the big spurt was later (from 1896 to 1907) and weaker than Italy's serious relative backwardness had led him to expect. For that he blamed the government. In his opinion tariff policy had been misguided and the railways had been built too early.[9] The big spurt was therefore delayed until the creation of German-style mixed banks, the Banca Commerciale and the Credito Italiano, both established in 1894. Gerschenkron also criticized Romeo's very different interpretations and their discussion reached a climax in a public debate (see Gerschenkron [2]; Cafagna 1983b). Their disagreement focused the subsequent discussion and the broader issues raised by Sereni were left behind.

2.4 For all their differences, the interpretations of Romeo and Gerschenkron shared two essential features. Both assumed that development had begun with a clearly marked discontinuity in the growth rate of GDP (take-off) or of industrial production (big spurt) and both assumed that the growth was shaped by essentially domestic forces. These shared assumptions were challenged a few years later by Cafagna and Fenoaltea.

Cafagna (1961; [3]) suggested that Italy's development had been characterized by a succession of periods ('waves' as he called them) of faster growth and of slowdown or outright crisis. Each wave increased the per capita income and caused structural changes that set the stage for the following one. In a later work (Cafagna 1983a) he refined the concept, suggesting that each 'wave' was led by a different industrial sector: textiles in the first one (*c.* 1820–*c.* 1850), light engineering in the 1880s, and heavy industries (carmaking, iron and steel, electricity and so on) during the Giolitti years. These waves can also be seen very clearly in Fenoaltea's index of Italian industrial output from 1861 to 1913 (Fenoaltea [15]). It is obtained as a weighted sum of three different growth paths. Traditional industries (food and drug processing, textiles) grew at a slow, steadier pace throughout the whole period. The new industries of the second industrial revolution (electricity, rubber, modern chemicals) grew very quickly from the end of the nineteenth century onwards. The aggregate cyclical pattern was caused by fluctuations in engineering and building, which Fenoaltea attributes to cycles in investments.[10]

Cafagna's and Fenoaltea's ideas differed initially on the second point, that is the role of foreign relationhips. Cafagna ([3], 1989), later followed by Bonelli [4], suggested that the main cause of growth had been the growth of exports of primary products, through its dynamic effects on aggregate demand and on capital accumulation. Fenoaltea (1973a), on the contrary, attributed the investment cycle to changes in the internal 'political environment' – that is to expectations about the future economic policy towards industry. Later, however, he changed his mind (Fenoaltea [9]), and tied the Italian cycle in capital formation to fluctuations in the world supply of capital. Warglien (1985, 1987) put forward an alternative internal cause of business cycles, namely speculative fluctuations in the supply of short-term credit, which financed most of the industrial investments.

The idea of a cyclical pattern of development seems nowadays to be accepted by the majority of scholars (an exception is Pescosolido 1977). The discussion has moved to the search for its causes. There are four competing hypotheses: two domestic ones (political climate and financial instability), and two external ones (growth of exports and the inflow of capital).[11] They may not be mutually exclusive, if one drops the assumption of a common cause for all the observed cycles. Warglien's hypothesis concerns more precisely the mechanisms that triggered a crisis at the end of expansion.[12] Each of the others seems more suited to account for one of the waves of growth. Exports of primary products might have played a dynamic role in the first half of the nineteenth century (Federico 1991b) and those of manufactures immediately after the First World War (Ciocca 1976; Tattara and Toniolo 1976). Changes in capital flows seem consistent with Fenoaltea's model during the 1880s and perhaps the late 1920s.[13] The growth during the Giolitti years has perhaps to be explained by a lucky coincidence of different internal and external drives (Federico and Toniolo [5]; Toniolo 1988).

3. Agriculture, the Market and Economic Backwardness

3.1 According to the conventional wisdom, the performance of Italian agriculture was very poor. It was backward, technically stagnant and therefore the main culprit of the biases and shortcomings of Italian development.[14] This negative assessment rested on three stylized facts: the laggard growth of output; the dire poverty of the rural population; and the extremely slow diffusion of modern techniques.

The first two facts are still widely accepted. As already stressed, the ISTAT output series are largely unreliable (Federico 1982a; Pescosolido 1979), but they are the only ones presently available. The peasants' standard of living was further reduced by a remarkably skewed income distribution.[15] Quantitative evidence on the peasants' income and standard of living is limited to a few family budgets (Somogyi 1959) and to scattered data on the (very low) wages of day labourers (Arcari 1936). Qualitative evidence, from official and private enquiries, pamphlets, and the like is instead fairly abundant (for a large bibliography, including historical studies, see Vivarelli 1990), and it conveys an extremely dreary and dismal picture.[16]

According to the conventional wisdom, technical progress would have been fairly fast only in the large capitalistic estates of the Po Valley (for a case study see Banti 1989b). This statement is backed by the only quantitative estimate of the increase of total factor productivity (Orlando 1969a, b). The rate of progress significantly exceeds zero only in the North (and only in the years 1897–1925), while in other areas and on average it is nil or negligible. These results are however dubious, because the data Orlando uses are, to say the least, highly questionable.

The alleged technical stagnation of Italian agriculture seems at odds with the results of some recent research on the diffusion of innovations (Corona and Massullo 1989; Cohen and Galassi [11]; Galassi 1986; Petrusewicz 1990). Land-saving innovation such as fertilizers and, to a lesser extent, new varieties of seeds were quickly adopted throughout the whole country (Pezzati 1990; Porisini 1971). Also an expensive machine like the thresher was widely adopted from the 1850s, because it reduced the risks of losing the harvest. The conventional wisdom has until now understated the technical progress because it focused on only a few innovations like labour-saving machines and high-farming techniques. They actually diffused slowly and only in some areas, but this is because they were not suited to Italy's input endowment and to the Mediterranean soil and climate. Though plausible, this more sanguine view of progress still has to be confirmed by new quantitative estimates. Like every statement relying on qualitative evidence, it is hardly conclusive, because the source might be biased by the personal views of the author or it might refer only to outliers.

It can be argued that, no matter how fast it was, technical progress could have been faster if more innovations suited to the peculiar needs of Mediterranean agriculture had been made available. This was a typical task for the state, which could organize and fund the R and D effort better than any private firm (or farmers). It actually created a network of centres for technical assistance for farmers and financed some R and D, but the funds were largely insufficient. The whole public support to agricultural growth has been, according to most historians, insufficient, save perhaps for the first two decades of the twentieth century (Orlando 1984). The most effective measure for agriculture was the protection of wheat growing, which is controversial, to say the least (see below).

3.2 Recent research has challenged, even more than the backwardness and poor performance by themselves, their alleged causes. The conventional wisdom resorts largely to institutional factors – like the persistence of 'feudal heritage' and of traditional, inefficient tenancy systems – sharecropping in the Centre and latifundia in the South (Esposto 1990). Peasants and landlords are also supposed to have been conservative and 'irrational' (that is not profit-seeking), sticking on traditional farming practices and aiming at self-sufficiency, even if this behaviour caused them to lose potential gains from market exchange. All these features have been questioned.

Firstly, 'legal' imperfections stemming from the permanence of feudal legislation were on balance unimportant. Feudal rights had been abolished at the beginning of the nineteenth century in the South (in the North they had disappeared much earlier).[17] Property rights were strictly protected by French-type codes. If the legal system was rather slow and inefficient (but less so than nowadays), it nonetheless guaranteed the physical safety of markets and tolerably low transaction costs.[18] It also offered would-be investors the complete freedom of enterprise: the first effective legislation to protect industrial workers was enacted only in 1902 and the government adopted a strike-breaking policy till 1901 and again during the fascist period.

Secondly, the revisionists also highlight the rationality of traditional contractual arrangements. Sharecropping spread in the Middle Ages as the most efficient tenancy system for land reclamation to feed burgeoning cities because it reconciled the divergent interests of peasants and landlords (Anselmi 1990; Biagioli 1987; Galassi 1992).[19] In the nineteenth century it still may have been the most efficient way to tackle problems of supervision and risk (Cohen and Galassi [11]) and/or to engage in the very intensive mixed farming needed by the large capital stock embodied in the land (Biagioli 1981).[20] And even the latifundium, the bugbear of all agrarian reformers, can be upheld, given the adverse environment and the insufficient means of communication (Bevilacqua 1985, 1989; Petrusewicz 1990).[21] An econometric analysis has not found any statistically significant effect of tenancy systems on regional differences in input productivity (Galassi and Cohen 1992).

Thirdly, the alleged 'irrationality' of landlords' and peasants' behaviour seems disproved by the evidence. On the one hand, movements in relative prices seem to have been generally followed by changes in the output mix or by the quick growth of exports (as for cotton in the 1860s or wine in the 1880s, see De Felice 1971). On the other, market exchanges were very diffused: the aggregate self-sufficiency ratio probably did not exceed 25 per cent either in 1880 or in 1930 (Federico [10]). This extensive involvement in the market was a legacy of Italy's century-old civilization. Market demand was created by the fairly dense urban population and by the large number of landless labourers, while the supply consisted of surpluses of peasant farms, rents and the output of capitalistic estates.

Finally, there is also some evidence of a 'rational' choice of techniques and use of available inputs. As already suggested, technical progress was clearly aimed at saving the scarce input (land) and at using as much labour as possible. This is confirmed by interregional and international comparisons of factor productivity on the eve of the First World War (O'Brien and Toniolo [12]; Federico 1992b; O'Brien and Prados de la Escosura 1992). Besides, a microeconomic analysis of the peasants' behaviour suggests that they rationally chose their crop mix and the amount of outside work according to the land/labour ratio, irrespective of the consequent need of market transactions (Federico 1991a).[22]

These revisionist results suggest that Italian peasants were 'rational but poor' (Schultz 1964). Poverty would have been caused by a high labour/land ratio and by an insufficient specialized R and D effort. Italy's agriculture seems to have made significant contributions to the broader development process. It succeeded in feeding a growing population with an increasing per capita income and in earning a large, though declining, trade surplus; it remained for a long time the main outlet for manufactures; and, last but not least, it supplied industry with labour and capital, especially during the first phases of its growth.

4. Patterns of Industrialization: Input Endowment and Technical Progress

4.1 The innovative performance of Italian industry is, to say the least, not impressive. According to Rossi and Toniolo's [7] estimates, the rate of technical progress was very low in the long run and negative or even nil in some periods. Italy ranked only eleventh in 1890–92 and ninth in 1910–12 among European countries in the number of patents granted in the United States (Cantwell 1992). Most historians scold Italian industry for its alleged failure to adopt the most modern techniques, attributing it to lack of capital, conservatism and to the fear of the revolutionary potential of large concentrations of workers (Hunecke 1977, 1982). What seemed technical backwardness, however, might have been simply the outcome of a rational choice of the technologies best suited to Italy's input endowment. As in most underdeveloped countries, labour was abundant (the Italian population was rather dense and growing (Del Panta 1984) and capital and energy sources were scarce (Italy has practically no coal or oil). The appropriate technology was clearly a labour-intensive one, but it was not readily available on the world market because technological progress in more advanced countries was going in a quite opposite direction (Abramowitz 1989). So available technologies were very often too capital- and energy-intensive (especially in heavy industries). The development of an appropriate technology would have needed a specific R and D effort, as for agriculture. Such an effort was, however, not implemented: Italian innovations were rare, and the overwhelming majority were the result of individual endeavour.[23] Organized R and D activities began only in the 1930s in only a few large firms such as Montecatini, the largest chemical company (Zamagni 1991a). Possibly the average firm was too small to finance them, and the state did not lend any substantial support to R and D till the late 1930s. As a result, Italy imported nearly all the modern technology, through purchase of patents by engineering firms, imports of equipment (Davis 1990; Giannetti et al. forthcoming; Vasta 1990; Gianetti 1993) and, sometimes, direct investment, in particular from Germany (Hertner 1978, 1981, 1982, 1983, 1987). The techniques suitable to the input endowment spread very quickly, and Italy was second to none in their use, as the example of hydro-electric power clearly shows (Gianetti 1985; Bardini 1991; Bardini and Hertner 1992).[24] Other technologies were more difficult to use, though Italians proved to be very proficient in adapting imported equipment to their needs and in combining machines of different provenance and vintage. In many cases, however, this skill did not prevent them from being used in a suboptimal way from a purely technical point of view, at times with a loss of externalities and/or of possible scale or scope economies because of insufficient standardization (Giannetti 1992).

4.2 The characteristics of the machinery available made it less easy to achieve the best (or desired) input ratio in practice than in theory. The task was fairly easy in industries like textiles where equipment was highly divisible and scale economies not very relevant.[25] Their mechanization was therefore relatively early and complete. Spinning was already fully mechanized in the first half of the nineteenth century, and weaving at the beginning of the 1890s (Ramella 1984; Romano 1992).

In heavy industries such as iron and steel and chemicals, technical requirements about plant size and design were not so flexible and the standard foreign technology (often bought turnkey) was very capital-intensive (Mori 1978; Bonelli 1978; Zamagni 1978). In fact, in 1911 the HP/workers ratio (the only available proxy for capital intensity) was remarkably higher than average (Zamagni 1978). Some authors have suggested that the national equipment was even more capital-intensive than strictly necessary, because the capital price was kept below its opportunity cost by low-interest loans from mixed banks and/or by state subsidies (Farina 1976, 1980; Zamagni 1978).

Other industries, notably engineering, were somewhere in the middle. Mechanization began rather early (though later than in textiles), but it was slow and gradual. Till the First World War, the techniques actually in use were a mix of modern and traditional ones. The war changed the situation because the need for large quantities of weapons and ammunitions boosted the introduction of more advanced techniques of large-scale mass production (Caracciolo 1969b).

4.3 In Italy as in other countries, the industrial workforce was mostly recruited from the rural population, and from urban (and rural) craftsmen.[26] Technical progress was on the whole skill-saving. In fact, the modern equipment required a vast mass of unskilled and semi-skilled workers (who could easily be trained on the job) and small groups of specialists, often with a formal technical education.[27] Since the rural supply was largely the same, differences among industries have to be traced back to the demand side, that is, to the technologies they used. They can explain differences in the patterns of location of factories (Federico 1985a) and in the level of wages (Zamagni 1976, 1984a, [14]).

Modern textile technology needed neither physical strength nor skill, and therefore it could employ female and child labour. The latter was drawn from members of rural families, which sought a supplement to their family income (Serpieri 1910). It was very cheap, especially in certain areas of the North, because its agricultural opportunity cost was very low.[28] On the other hand women and children were hardly mobile, because they could not afford to sever the ties with their households for emotional, familiar and economic reasons (wages were too low to make ends meet). So capital went searching for manpower and water power, scattering factories in the countryside. Many historians single out this pattern of 'diffused industry' as an Italian peculiarity (Dewerpe 1985a, 1991; Romano 1978, 1992; Corner 1984, 1990).

In heavy industries the most advanced equipment required mainly male unskilled workers and few technicians (Busino 1977; Biffoli and Lungonelli 1985; Favilli 1974; Tattara and Piva 1983). The whole male rural population would be eligible and therefore the abundant supply kept wages low.[29] The existence of a potential pool of unskilled manpower is clearly shown by emigration, both abroad and in northern cities.[30] To some extent it is also shown by the diffusion of handicrafts and other non-agricultural activities as part-time jobs in the countryside.[31] The recruitment of unskilled local manpower was never really difficult for firms who wanted to build a modern plant far away from the existing industrial areas.[32]

In most cases, however, technical change in heavy industries was rather slow. For a long time unskilled and highly-skilled (the so-called 'operai di mestiere') workers laboured together in the same plants (Musso 1980; Donvito and Garbarini 1984, 1985; Dewerpe 1985b; Bigazzi 1988; Gigli Marchetti 1983; Marianelli 1983; Spinelli 1985). The share of unskilled workers had always been substantial and it was indeed rising, but companies were long unable to dispense with a core of (traditionally) skilled operatives. These latter were in short supply and therefore they earned relatively higher wages (at least by contemporary standards). They lived mainly in larger towns such as Milan, Turin and Genoa, where most factories were therefore located.

4.4 The impression of a dearth of capital clearly refers to funds for new industrial and agricultural investments. The existing capital stock, on the contrary, was probably rather large, as an outcome of centuries of wealth and investments.[33] Besides, according to macro-economic data, savings were not so scarce: according to available series, the average propensity to save always exceeded 8 per cent, and grew remarkably with time. Besides, though starting from a rather low level, Italy's financial sophistication was fast growing towards the level of the more advanced European countries (Fisher 1992).

The problem was the use of this cumulated capital. Italians preferred to invest in state bonds, which were perceived as being less risky and offered a reasonably high rate of interest, than in stocks.[34] The stock exchange was therefore very small, prone to speculation and nearly always useless as a means of raising long-term capital (Polsi 1993; Ciocca and Biscaini Cotula [16]; on the stock exchange see also Da Pozzo and Felloni 1964; Aleotti 1990).

Fixed investments were financed from two different sources of capital, private ones (ploughing back of profits, loans from friends and relatives, proceeds of commercial activities and so on) and bank credit. The former points to what in a Gerschenkronian taxonomy would be called the English way of financing industrialization (Giannetti et al. 1991; Angeli 1989–90). It was feasible if and when barriers to entry were low and gradual growth was possible, because the scale economies were not important. These conditions held steadily in the traditional light industries, such as textiles, where private sources of capital largely prevailed (Castronovo 1964, 1965; Pozzobon 1981; Romano 1992). They were used also by large companies in innovative industries like FIAT (Bottiglieri 1987) or Pirelli (Bigazzi 1981; Confalonieri 1982), especially at the beginning of their growth. The literature seems to underestimate the importance of this way of financing, possibly because of a lack of case studies.

The development of the Italian banking system was slow (as shown by Ciocca and Biscaini Cotula's quantitative work [16]), late and eventful. Still, in 1861 it consisted mainly of private banks and of savings and loans banks (Sannucci 1989). The growth of the joint-stock banks was marked by a succession of booms and crises (Polsi 1993). The worst of all happened in 1888–93, causing the failure of the two major banks, the Credito Mobiliare and the Banca Generale (Pantaleoni 1895). The following year they were replaced by two new large banks, the Banca Commerciale and the Credito Italiano, established by German capital on the model of German mixed banks. As noted, they were credited by Gerschenkron with having been the agents of Italy's big spurt (Gerschenkron [1]), and this idea is widely accepted (Cohen 1967, 1975; Mori 1981, 1992; Hertner 1983; Warglien 1987). No one would deny that they played an outstanding role in Italian development. Their growth has been impressive, though, as shown by the quantitative work by Ciocca and Biscaini Cotula [16], mainly substituting other banks and financial intermediaries. They financed most of the larger companies especially, but not necessarily, in heavy and new industries (Cohen 1977; Zamagni 1978). These facts are, however, not sufficient to demonstrate Gerschenkron's thesis. In fact it also implies that mixed banks actually represented a large improvement over previously existing ones and/or a new solution to old problems. In other words, they should have supplied not only funds, but also other scarce inputs such as managerial skill for firms and strategic planning for whole industries. Otherwise, mixed banks would at best have fulfilled only their institutional role within the development process, but they cannot be singled out as its prime mover as Gerschenkron did.

This question has stimulated some of the best archival researches on Italian economic history, notably a massive study by Confalonieri (1974–76, 1982).[35] They show that the Banca Commerciale and the Credito Italiano had a first-rate management (of German nationality and training) and close links with the international *haute banque*. The mixed banks also had the means to control the behaviour of the companies they financed as they has placed their own men on their boards of directors (Zamagni 1980; Pino Pongolino 1991). Confalonieri's study, however, lends little support to Gerschenkron's view. It stresses the continuity, in banking practices and staff, with the failed Italian banks, and it singles out short-term banking profit as the main interest of the mixed banks. They lent sums by separately assessing each project and not as a part of a larger industrial strategy.[36] The electrical industry was an exception, but it had so clearly brilliant perspectives that strategic planning did not require any particular foresight.[37] Bail-outs and large-scale rationalizations were more often suggested by the government than decided independently by the banks within their long-run strategy. Neither was permanent ownership of industrial firms intentional. The banks usually subscribed shares when floated in order to sell them afterwards to their clients, or they took them as a collateral for loans to firms. Permanent ownership was an undesired consequence of the industrial crisis after the First World War, which compelled the mixed banks to take on themselves companies unable to pay back their debts (Conti 1993; Ciocca and Toniolo [17]). Confalonieri's research, in other words, suggests that banks offered developmental assistance to the already strong (to quote Tilly 1986). The research is still going on, and the issue is still open.[38]

4.5 According to the conventional wisdom (Sereni 1947, 1966; Bonelli [4]), Italian industrialization was delayed by the insufficient 'size of the market' (that is, the aggregate level of demand) for mass manufactures. It would directly have hampered the growth of the consumer goods industry, and indirectly the whole industrialization. It is implicitly assumed that in a country like Italy it had to follow a 'Hirschmanian' pattern, proceeding backwards from production of consumer goods for the internal market to engineering and to heavy industries.

As has already been said, there is ample evidence of the low standard of living of peasants. The same applies to industrial workers. Only a small number of skilled workers could support a family with their wage alone. Life was made possible by the pooling of incomes, often from different activities. Foodstuffs absorbed the greater part of workers' budgets and the per capita consumption of manufactures was very low compared to the level achieved in other European countries, let alone the United States (Somogyi 1959; Zamagni 1990a). Even the spread of bicycles in northern cities at the beginning of the twentieth century was heralded as a great improvement (Piloni 1985). Industrialization did not improve the situation for a long time. Real wages remained stagnant till the end of the nineteenth century, rose in the Giolitti years and in the aftermath of the war and again remained stable – or even declined – in the interwar years (Zamagni 1976, 1991b, [14]). The fascist regime banned trade unions (from 1926) and used wage regulation as a tool of economic policy, forcibly reducing wages after the 1926 revaluation of the lira and during the Great Crisis (Acquarone 1965; Piva and Toniolo 1987). Even in the Giolitti years, the growth of wages seems to have trailed behind that of GDP per worker (Zamagni [14]). *A fortiori*, this holds true in the long run (Del Monte 1977; Fuà 1981; Lay and Pesante 1981). Many Italian historians attribute this widening gap to an unlimited or at least very abundant supply of labour, and some hypothesize a 'classical' model of growth. This feature is embodied by some econometric models tying investments to past profits (see Del Monte 1977; Filosa, Rey and Sitzia 1976; Ganugi 1989; for an alternative Keynesian approach see Niccoli 1969).

No matter how low the standard of living is, the idea of insufficient aggregate demand hampering development only has economic sense provided that three conditions hold. Income distribution has to be skewed (increasing savings and the consumption of luxury goods instead of mass manufactures), exports have to be ruled out and scale economies have to be substantial and widespread.[39] The first condition is – by and large – met, even if there are some signs of a decreasing inequality from 1875 to at least the First World War (Zamagni 1980). The other two seem hardly plausible for consumer industries, as plants were highly divisible and exports were substantial from the last years of the nineteenth century onwards. The situation may have been different in heavy industries: scale economies were larger and, at least in engineering, fluctuations of demand seem to have hampered the specialization of firms, worsening the quality of the output (Giannetti 1992; Doria 1989). On the other hand, Italy did actually export engineering goods to more backward countries like Argentina or the Balkans from the first year of the twentieth century onwards. Perhaps the conventional wisdom needs to be revised.

5. Patterns of Industrialization: The State

5.1 In the eighteenth century and the first years of the nineteenth century, most Italian governments tried to foster industrialization, but these mercantilistic policies were progressively abandoned. In the 1860s–70s, the new Italian state did not include industrialization among its targets. Like other European countries, it left any industrial growth to spontaneous market forces (Cafagna 1962). *Laissez-faire* was slowly abandoned from the end of the 1870s, as a consequence of the diffusion of imperialistic and nationalistic ideas and of the agrarian crisis. In the new political mood, industrial development was increasingly considered necessary to Italy if it wanted to occupy its 'right' position in the world (Lanaro 1979; De Rosa 1982). The crisis urged the owners of large wheat-producing estates to change sides and join industrialists in pressing for duties (the alliance was called by Gramsci the 'industrial–agrarian coalition'). The ensuing tariff is the symbol of a long-lasting change of economic policy. Since then, the state went on supporting industrialization with a wide range of tools (public procurements, bail-outs and, in the 1930s, market control and planning). This support is usually judged to have been instrumental for Italian industrialization: Bonelli [4] speaks of 'state capitalism'. Heavy industries like iron and steel, shipbuilding and some branches of engineering got more support than others. Tariffs on their output were the highest, they got the bulk of state orders and, if the worst came to the worst, these industries and the banks which financed them were sure to be bailed out. They received such preferential treatment because they were thought of as essential for military purposes – and much less able than others (like textiles) to survive without state help. In the long run, the rest of the economy (including other industries) had to pay for this support.

This policy has, not surprisingly, been heatedly debated both at the time by free-traders and nowadays by historians. Two different questions were raised: was (that type of) state support vital for the growth of these industries and was the growth itself worth the price the Italian economy had to pay for it?

5.2 Italian tariff history has drawn a lot of attention (see for general outlines IPSOA 1985; Zamagni 1990a; Calderoni 1961; Lombardi 1959; Pedone 1969a; and on specific issues Izzo 1965; Pegorari 1989; Del Vecchio 1978; Sereni 1958–59; Prodi 1965–66; Villari 1966; Are 1965; Calzavarini 1966). It closely resembles that of other Continental countries. At the beginning of the nineteenth century duties were very high and they were slowly reduced afterwards – the trend being led by Piedmont and Tuscany. After Unification, the Piedmontese free-trade policy was abruptly extended to the whole country. Italy switched back to protection gradually: a first, partial and very low tariff was issued in 1878, and a much higher one in 1887, together with a duty on wheat. Duties were high on textiles (especially cotton goods) and iron and steel products, while other industries were less protected. In retrospect, 1887 proved to be a historical watershed, probably exceeding the will of the parliament at that time. Duties have been changed many times since then, but the policy of protection and inward-looking industrialization was not to be overturned till the 1950s.[40]

Nominal Italian duties do not seem that high in comparative perspective, at least till 1913 (Capie 1983; Tattara 1980; Liepmann 1938).[41] However, they reached their target, that is they fostered the growth of the protected industries through import substitution and saved cereal production from overseas competition. Some historians argue that this growth was worth the price, and that protectionism has been, on balance, a wise choice, especially the more moderate one of the liberal Italy (Zamagni 1981; Sapelli 1991). The majority of historians do not agree, but for different reasons. Some criticize the difference in rates among industries which was caused by lobbying during drafting by the committee and even more during parliamentary debates, and was aggravated by subsequent changes. Are (1974) has argued that it would have been better to offer all industries the same effective rate. Many believe that protectionism has caused a too expensive misallocation of resources. In the nineteenth century a powerful lobby, backed by nearly all Italian economists (Cardini 1981), protested against the very idea of promoting industrial growth through protectionism, arguing that Italy had to be an exporter of primary products and of the output of 'natural' industries, if any.[42] Several historians concede that some protection might have been useful, but object to the selection of protected activities (Gerschenkron [1]). Wheat growing was wholly unsuited to Italian resource endowment, and its protection was particularly harmful to industrialization, because it supplied a basic wage good (Sylos-Labini 1973; Cohen 1979; Fenoaltea 1993). They also suggest that engineering, which was not protected at all (Toniolo 1977; Tattara 1980), deserved support more than other industries. Fenoaltea (1973a) goes as far as to argue that, without duties on steel, Italy could have started an export-led industrialization sixty years before it did so. In principle, all these statements imply some sort of testable counterfactual hypothesis, but none of the authors has explored them. The perspectives of Italy's exports of primary products would not seem particularly brilliant according to the available estimates of export elasticities (Balloni 1969; Glazier, Bandera and Berner 1975), but these latter are largely questionable (Federico 1988). According to Toniolo's estimates (1977), substituting the duty in iron and steel with a subsidy would have increased the total GDP by 1.5 per cent at most in 1906–8 (at a high cost for the state coffers). His estimate does not take into consideration the possibility of exports of engineering goods which, however, could have been hampered more by lack of know-how and skilled manpower than by the duty (Cafagna 1978).[43]

5.3 Most scholars think that protection alone would not have been sufficient to foster the development of the heavy industries. The state had also to substitute an inadequate private demand by public orders for railways and the military. This statement has been tested and partially put in doubt by Fenoaltea's careful study of railway expenditure (1973b, [15]). He shows that a large share of total investments was spent on construction works and that orders for goods represented a substantial but by no means decisive share of total value added of engineering and iron and steel industries.[44] This evidence cannot, however, be taken as conclusive without a similar study of military expenditures (some data in De Rosa 1969; Ferrari 1986; and for the 1930s Covino, Gallo and Mantovani 1976). The state expenditure for industrial products may have accounted for no more than 7–8 per cent of total industrial GDP in 1911 and 12–13 per cent in 1938.[45] The figures were higher for some products (weapons, steamships, locomotives) or those companies that produced rolling stocks of weapons like Ansaldo or Terni (Bonelli 1975; Doria 1989; Merger 1986; Federico 1982b).

5.4 Last but not least, the state offered entrepreneurs of strategic industries an informal but nevertheless reliable insurance against failure. Actually, bail-outs can be found throughout the whole economic history of liberal and fascist Italy. In some cases, industries were formally bailed-out by banks which, however, acted under the state's supervision and financial guarantee – as in the well-known case of the creation of the iron and steel cartel in 1911 (Confalonieri 1982). In other instances, the state acted directly, usually through *ad hoc* boards such as the CSVI for Ansaldo in 1922 (Carparelli 1982). In many cases, banks themselves had to be saved, having overstretched their resources in lending to industries – as in 1907 the Società bancaria Italiana (Bonelli 1971) or in 1922 the Banco di Roma (De Rosa 1982–83). The last and largest of these bail-outs was made necessary by the Great Crisis, which had driven many large companies and the mixed banks which owned them to the edge of failure. The government first tried to bail-out industries alone, and afterwards was compelled to rescue banks as well (Ciocca and Toniolo [17]; Roselli 1992; Cianci 1977; Toniolo 1980 Ch. 5). So, almost by chance, that system of public ownership was created that was to characterize – for good and evil – the Italian economy after the start of the Second World War.

5.5 The 1930s marked a discontinuity in the long tradition of state intervention, or at least this is the impression that the fascist regime wanted to give. It proclaimed self-sufficiency ('autarchia') as a vital necessity for Italy, to be pursued at any cost.[46] Moreover it implemented a wide range of new policies, ranging from extensive land reclamation to wage control, from incentives to investments in new industrial districts (Petri 1990) to market regulation through compulsory cartels, price control and a system of obligatory permission for new plants. This policy is highly controversial. Opinions range within two extremes. Some scholars argue that the regime imposed its own policy, either as the outcome of Mussolini's personal decisions (La Francesca 1973) or as the result of a coherent plan to prepare the country for war (Gregor 1979). Others suggest that it was the puppet of a coalition of landowners and big business (Rossi 1966; Fano Damascelli 1971; Grifone 1971). The truth probably lies somewhere half-way. The decisions were taken by making compromises between different lobbies and under the spur of circumstances (Cohen 1979; Toniolo 1980). In most cases, if cleansed of the fascist bombast and rhetoric, policies turned out to be very similar to those of other industrialized countries (Gualerni 1982). The results of these policies were on balance rather limited. Self-sufficiency was never approached (nor was it possible) and the overall efficiency of fascist planning was scarce if not nil – as shown by Italy's very poor industrial performance during the Second World War (Covino, Gallo and Mantovani 1976). During the 1930s the heavy industries grew substantially and modernized, but this has to be credited more to the management of single companies (including that of state-owned ones, which was very active and far-sighted) than to state planning.

6. The Macroeconomic Framework: Balance of Payments and Monetary Policy

6.1 As already said, exports probably drove development only in the first half of the nineteenth century and during the 1920s. This does not mean that foreign trade was irrelevant. Its very poor resource endowment compelled Italy to import all fuel (coal and later oil) and most raw materials (cotton, wool, later iron). Italy had therefore to be more open than other European economies at a comparable level of development, and the trade/output ratio was increasing with industrialization (Tena 1992). According to the conventional wisdom, the trade balance played a paramount role in macroeconomic adjustment through the balance of payments. The model adopts a 'Keynesian-absorption' approach: exports are assumed to be fixed by the world demand, imports by the level of internal activity.[47] The rate of growth of available foreign exchange (proceeds of exports and of possible loans) would have constrained the rate of growth of Italian economy. The constraint was loosened during the Giolitti years by the increase of earnings from emigrants' remittances and tourism (Cafagna [3], Bonelli [4]). It became tighter after the First World War (Ciocca 1976; Filosa, Rey and Sitzia 1976; Paradisi 1976): according to Gualerni (1982) the need of foreign exchange dictated the whole fascist economic policy. Bonelli [4] stresses that this constraint would have made Sereni's counterfactual unfeasible.[48]

This conventional wisdom has been recently challenged. It has been argued that the causal link between capital and trade balances was quite the opposite, the former causing the latter (a net inflow determining a deficit of trade balance). These new models suggest different causes of capital flows. Fratianni and Spinelli (Fratianni and Spinelli [18], 1985; Spinelli 1988) following the modern monetarist orthodoxy, emphasize the balance between demand and supply of money (that is a pull factor), Fenoaltea [9] emphasizes the exogenous movements of the world supply of capital (that is a push factor). Both hypotheses are tested through an econometric analysis. The results are not conclusive, and this is not surprising at all: the choice of one of the two competing models would need to test very complex causal links on the basis of rather unreliable data. In any case, capital flows came out to be heavily influenced by the foreign investors' assessment of the country-specific risk.[49]

6.2 Foreign investors assessed the risks of investing in a country mainly on the basis of its macroeconomic policy. Reputation rested mainly on its abiding by the guidelines of a 'sound' policy under the gold standard. From this point of view, the Italian performance has been far from brilliant. The budget remained in deficit for most years, the debt stock had been very high since the beginning of the new state and the lira was redeemable only for very short periods (Pedone 1969b; Brosio and Marchese 1987; Parravicini 1958; Zamagni 1988; De Cecco 1990; Marconi 1982). For several decades, the management of financial crises had been very poor because a unified central bank (Banca d'Italia) was established only in 1893, and it was given the monopoly of issue in 1926 and a clear right of supervision of commercial banks in 1936 (Di Nardi 1953; Sannucci 1989; Vitale 1972; Bonelli 1991; De Mattia 1990; Negri 1989; Toniolo 1989).[50] Therefore, the monetary policy was sternly criticized by economists at the time (Supino 1929; Jannaccone 1936).

Most historians recognize these shortcomings, but are ready to find some justification. For instance, the large budget deficits of the 1860s are justified by the urgent needs of building a new state and somewhat redeemed by the following years of very tight finance (Zamagni

1992). Under special circumstances (as in the war years and in the late 1930s) deficits are believed to have contributed substantially to aggregate demand (Tattara and Toniolo 1976; Covino, Gallo and Mantovani 1976; Toniolo 1980; Gualerni 1982).[51] Barone (1972) praises also the deficit of the 1880s as a sort of deficit spending *avant la lettre* (though he is alone in doing so). The currency devaluation in 1866 is thought to have given the battered Italian industry relief from competition by imports.[52] On the other hand an orthodox decision like the return to the gold standard in 1926 is criticized, albeit not in itself but for the too high exchange rate chosen (Cohen 1973; Marconi 1982; for a different view see Gualerni 1982). Many historians agree on the possible crowding-out effects of the issuing of state bonds and, to a lesser extent, of the sale of lands in the 1860s and 1870s (Lupo 1990b). In fact it is widely believed that the balanced budgets had substantially fostered economic growth during the Giolitti years (Bonelli 1968; Confalonieri 1974–76; Fisher 1992) and the 1920s (Toniolo 1980). Other scholars contest the very existence of this crowding-out, because state bonds might not have been close substitutes for other types of investment (Gerschenkron [1]; Warglien 1987) and capital might have come from abroad (Fenoaltea [9]).

The traditional monetarist approach has been recently revived by Fratianni and Spinelli in a series of articles and in a big book (1985, [18]; Spinelli and Fratianni 1990). They support their argument with some quantitative tests on the links between money supply, prices and real variables and on the demand for money. This latter proves to be stable in the long run, and money turns out to have Granger-caused inflation (and a declining exchange rate). Those ultimately responsible were the deficits, which had been financed mainly by the increase of the money supply. Another econometric work (about the period 1881–1936) by Ganugi (1989) adds that inflation, reducing the real remuneration of savings, could have damaged investments and therefore lowered the long-term growth rate (he implicitly rules out capital flows). The issue has very recently been reconsidered in the chapter on Italy in a book on the monetary macroeconomics of European development (Fisher 1992). The results of the same tests are somewhat different from those of Fratianni and Spinnelli. The money supply is found to have caused changes in prices only in 1861–90, while there is evidence of Granger-causality on real variables (income till 1890 and industrial production in 1881–1910). Not surprisingly, then, Fisher finds that money was not neutral (with a declining elasticity to income). These differences can partially be accounted for by the different data and ways of detrending, but anyway they highlight the need for further research, possibly using more reliable macroeconomic data.

7. A Dualistic Development?

7.1 The previous analysis has highlighted the existence of wide differences between light and heavy industries. The former adopted labour-intensive technologies, hired nearly exclusively low-skilled females and children, financed investments with their funds and exported a substantial share of their output, facing a highly competitive market both at home and abroad. By contrast, heavy industries used capital-intensive equipment, manned by males (in a different proportion between skilled and unskilled according to the industry), borrowed from banks most of the capital they needed and sold the output mainly on the (possibly oligopolistic) internal market.[53] Last but not least, the light industries received only protection from the state, while the heavy ones also got procurements and, if needed, were bailed-out. Therefore, the entrepreneurs of these latter were also more involved in politics, usually on the side of the ruling party (Amatori 1980; D'Angiolini 1972; De Rosa 1982; Baglioni 1974).

Most historians take a step forward, interpreting these differences as evidence of a dualism between a small core of giant oligopolistic companies and a large number of small competitive enterprises. Sapelli (1991) goes so far as to suggest that they followed two altogether different paths of development (calling them respectively 'Manchesterian' and 'oligopolistic'). The oligopolistic core is supposed to have grown in relative terms in the long run, peaking on the eve of the Second World War. The share of heavy industries in total GDP had increased (Tattara and Toniolo 1976), and the whole economy had been featured by a growing concentration and by the diffusion of oligopolistic behaviours (concentration, cartels, collusive behaviours and so on).

Historians show somewhat mixed feelings towards this feature. Many of them, perhaps the majority, see it as the congenital fault of Italian capitalism, caused by backwardness and a somewhat too hasty development policy. According to Bonelli [4], dualism caused Italy to lose the advantages of interdependence among industries. Most criticism focuses, however, on the collusion between the state and the larger companies. In the short run, it was a source of corruption and waste of resources (Mori 1992; Bigazzi 1981), in the long run it would have caused imperialism in the Mediterranean (Webster 1974a), fascism and war (Grifone 1971; Cardillo 1978). Other scholars consider it a necessary evil, because the heavy industries would not have developed otherwise, and the Italian industrialization would have been impossible or at least severely crippled. Sapelli (1991) is particularly sanguine about the role of large companies as the only importers of the badly needed advanced technology.

7.2 The decisive question is to what extent this dualistic scheme is supported by evidence. Two recent quantitative works could shed some light on the issue, but unfortunately they tell different stories. Rossi and Toniolo's [7] estimate of a sophisticated aggregate production function seems to give evidence of an oligopolistic development. They find a substantial mark-up on prices, relevant scale economies and an undercapitalization of the economy. All these features were remarkably less widespread in 1905–25 than in 1896–1905 or in 1925–47, possibly because of the more liberal economic policy. The values of the parameters seem, however, too high and the whole exercise is subject to the usual doubts about the reliability of the macroeconomic data.[54]

A wholly opposite picture comes out from microeconomic research on the size of joint-stock industrial companies from 1907 to 1936 (Giannetti et al. forthcoming). It is possible to compute Hirschman's indices of concentration, which on average come out to be very low, with few exceptions (e.g. artificial fibres). The concentration was low even in industries usually regarded as oligopolistic, such as iron and steel.[55] The indices are stable through time, rising only in 1936 (confirming the qualitative evidence on an increase of concentration during the 1930s). Moreover the survival rates of companies from one benchmark year to another are rather high. In other words, there was indeed a stable core of the Italian industry, but it was composed not of large companies but of medium-sized firms. What is usually believed to be a recent development would have been, on the contrary, a long-run constant of Italian industrial history. This evidence is not conclusive, either.[56] The issue is still open.

7.3 The income gap between North and South has been so wide and so stubbornly persistent for such a long time that geographical dualism (the so-called 'questione meridionale') is one of the best-known features of the Italian case (Zamagni 1987). The literature on it is extensive, but it has largely remained separated from that presented so far. Until very recently, it was assumed as a matter of fact that the South had remained stagnant and backward (Russo 1991). The debate focused on the causes of this allegedly disappointing performance. Broadly speaking, two competing hypotheses have been suggested. Most scholars have blamed the environment or the legacy of the past (as far back as the Middle Ages), attributing backwardness and stagnation to a long list of causes like the dry climate, the inferior endowment of natural resources (above all water), the scarce population (in comparison with the North), the very limited social overhead capital, the extremely low literacy rate and perhaps the 'feudal heritage' – that is the tenancy arrangements and social structure unfit for development (Zamagni 1987). Other scholars suggest on the contrary that the North–South gap was created after and by Unification by the economic policy and/or by the exploitation of the southern market by the northern industries. This latter hypothesis seems to be ruled out by some hard evidence. The North–South trade was very scarce before Unification, and it remained so at least until the First World War (Zamagni 1983). The railways system was rather inefficient and fares were high (Fenoaltea [15], but this was not the main reason. As convincingly argued by Cafagna [20], the production of the two parts of the country were not complementary in 1861, and they became so only much later, when northern industrialization was well ahead and the southern income was raised by state transfer. The issue of the role of the state is more difficult to settle. Capacelatro and Carlo (1972) argue that in the 1860s and 1870s the unified state had deliberately damaged the southern regions which previously had been growing thanks to an allegedly far-sighted Bourbonic policy.[57] Probably no one would nowadays subscribe to this thesis, but conventional wisdom agrees that the government has long sinned by omission. Since the beginning it enforced the same legislation throughout the whole country, whilst the South allegedly needed special treatment.[58] The first special law for Naples was approved only in 1904 (Petri 1990; Dell'Orefice 1980), and a systematic development policy was implemented only after the Second World War. It is, however, difficult to assess to what extent an earlier start (or more funds) of the same policy or a different one (such as an agrarian reform) would have changed the final outcome.[59]

Recent research by social historians has put in doubt the basic assumption of this conventional wisdom, that is that the South was homogeneous and stagnant (Pezzino 1987; Donzelli 1990; Bevilacqua 1993). On the contrary they stress the great differences among areas within the South and the extent of changes. They refer more to the whole process of modernization than to economic growth, but this latter is obviously an essential component of the overall transformation. The whole process is believed to have been started from the outside (a 'passive' modernization in Cafagna's words (1988)). So the economic growth in the South was started by the increase in exports of primary products (wine, oil, citrus fruit) and later by emigration. The former, however, is regarded as a somewhat missed opportunity because the southern agrarian producers were not able to innovate and remained dependent on foreign and domestic merchants (Salvemini 1984; Lupo 1990a). Emigration had very high human costs and caused the South to lose some of its best people.

8. Conclusions

The previous discussion shows that Italian historians have made substantial headway towards a better understanding of the Italian development on a large number of issues. Some topics – and above all the economic policies – have, however, attracted more attention than others. The role of the state, however, is so manifold that it is difficult to sum up opinions in a conventional wisdom. Clearly most scholars have a poor opinion of the economic policy. The government is blamed either for having done too little too late (for example for the South, for agriculture or for the welfare of working classes) or for having done too much (for the wheat-growing landowners and the military–industrial complex, or, possibly, for both at the same time. These charges cannot now (or probably ever) be assessed, but a word of caution is probably appropriate. The expenditure/GDP ratio was actually higher in Italy than elsewhere in Europe, but till 1940 it never exceeded (war years apart) 15 per cent (Brosio and Marchese 1987, table 3.1). Of course, such aggregate figures might conceal the real importance of the state at a micro level, but it cannot be excluded that the whole issue had been overemphasized. The historians' concern probably stems from a vision of the state's tasks as being rather larger than those current at the time.

As repeatedly remarked, many issues still remain open to research. Of course, it is very difficult to set an agenda of priorities. Probably, the most urgent task is the revision and increase of the existing quantitative series. Some work is in progress, for example on monetary and foreign trade statistics, but a revision of historical national accounts is badly needed. A large research project about industrial production has been going on for many years (Fenoaltea 1982, 1987, 1988a, 1988b), while the work on agriculture and services has begun only very recently (Rey 1992). It would also be necessary – though very difficult on the basis of available sources – to extend their coverage back in time towards the first half of the nineteenth century. Such a work of course will add a lot of new series about output and prices, and the increase in available data will surely stimulate further quantitative research and hypothesis testing. It is difficult to judge *a priori* their possible results and therefore their consequences on the traditional wisdom. In any case, the Italian case is far from being assessed: it still offers scholars many promising and hardly tilled fields.

Acknowledgement

The editor and publishers gratefully acknowledge the generous support given by the Nuffield Foundation towards the translation costs of several articles which appear in this title.

Notes

1. They are singled out with a progressive number between square brackets – e.g. Gerschenkron [1].
2. More details and narrative accounts of the growth can be found in IPSOA 1985 (which includes a reprint of Corbino 1931–35); Clough 1965; Romani 1976; Luzzatto 1963; Castronovo 1975; Toniolo 1980; De Rosa 1980; Federico and Chesi 1987; Toniolo 1988; Zamagni 1990a. On agriculture see Daneo 1979; on industry Fossati 1951; Caizzi 1965; Romeo 1965; Castronovo 1980; on economic policy see Zamagni 1981; La Francesca 1971, 1973; Cohen 1979; Bottiglieri 1991.

Further bibliographical references on the literature can be found in reviews by Mori 1959; Castronovo 1979; Avagliano 1988; De Rosa 1990; Fumi 1989–90; Bigazzi [13].

3. According to Eckhaus [21] in 1861 the income in the North was 15–20 per cent higher than in the South. Esposto (1990) estimates the per capita income in 1870, according to the current division into three large areas – North-West, with a per capita income of 353 1911 lire, the North-East and Centre (396) and the South (333), adding up to a national average of 361. Both estimates are flawed: the former is a simple guesstimate from a collection of different sources, the latter is based on official data of the agricultural output in 1870–74 which clearly overstates the southern output.
4. The literature on foreign trade is particularly abundant, possibly because statistics are easily accessible and fairly reliable (Tena 1989). It includes aggregate studies (Lanino 1916; Capanna and Messori 1940; Paradisi 1976) and case studies for groups of commodities – agricultural products (Somogyi 1966; Federico 1991b), cereals (Federico 1984), primary products (Federico 1979) and silk goods (Federico 1992a and 1994).
5. Most of these series date back to the original work by the Central Statistical Institute in the 1950s (ISTAT 1957). Subsequent revisions (Ercolani 1969; Maddison 1992; Rossi, Toniolo and Storgato 1993; Fuà and Gallegati 1993) have added some new ones and have changed deflation and weighting procedures, without altering the basic data.
6. In 1861, the Italian per capita income (if converted at the official exchange rate) would have been 94 per cent of the French and 95 per cent of the German one – and this conflicts with all the qualitative sources on the comparative level of development (Toniolo 1988). According to a new estimate (Rey 1992) the GDP in 1911 was 7.9 per cent higher than the ISTAT figure.
7. A high labour/land ratio could be a mixed blessing. It bars some patterns of development (such as a staple growth) but to some extent favours an early specialization in manufacturing.
8. While this is widely known since the Gerschenkron–Romeo debate as the Gramsci thesis, it is worth noting that Sereni's contribution went much further than Gramsci's idea of failed agrarian revolution. He turned an exclusively political intuition into a general interpretation of Italian economic history.
9. He argues that the Italian iron and steel and engineering industries were then too backward to supply rails and rolling stock. If the state had waited, it would have been possible to place many more orders with national firms, fostering their development, as had happened before in other European countries. For a general assessment of Gerschenkron's model see Federico and Toniolo [5].
10. The difference between Cafagna and Fenoaltea is largely a question of timing if the former's idea is rephrased in terms of rate of growth (that is supposing that each wave's leading industry had a higher than average rate of growth). Industries like textiles showed (relatively) slow rates of growth after 1861 because they had already had their period of boom during Cafagna's first wave of development. The aggregate cyclical pattern of engineering can be explained as the result of the different trends of its various components. In each wave there was some fast-growing new production which raised the overall rate of growth above the long-term rate of traditional (i.e. already established) ones.
11. Export growth would be an external cause if due to a shift of the demand curve (e.g. an increase of world income, a change of tastes), but not if caused by a technical progress in the production of exportables.
12. Focusing on the supply of credit, he leaves the demand side somewhat in the shade. In some passages he seems to accept Fenoaltea's 'political' hypothesis, in others to argue that firms would have used any sum the banking system was willing to give them.
13. One could expect that booms were accompanied – or perhaps anticipated – by an increase of net imports or by a decrease of net exports. According to the existing series of balance of payments (ISTAT 1957), the inflow of capital was massive during the 1880s, while during the Giolitti years Italy was a net exporter of capital, implausible as this may seem. Net imports would also have been large during the 1860s, a period of very slow growth. These data, unfortunately, are very shaky. Not only are they a part of a highly controversial set (see above), but the annual balance of interest payments is not consistent (at ongoing interest rates) with the cumulated foreign liabilities.

14. What follows is an abridged version of Federico 1992b, where it is possible to find more references. A representative example of the conventional wisdom is Daneo 1979. The most detailed analysis of Italian agriculture – mainly from the point of view of social history – is the massive *Storia dell'agricoltura italiana* (Bevilacqua (ed.) 1989–91).
15. Labour got only 45 per cent of agricultural value added on the eve of the First World War (Zamagni 1975; Serpieri 1910), leaving the rest to capital and land (including those supplied by the peasants). In the following years, the labour share was drastically increased by wartime inflation (Zamagni 1984b), but peasants used their higher incomes mainly to buy land (INEA 1938).
16. This evidence may be somewhat biased, because most of the descriptions were written by people with a clear political agenda of social reform.
17. In some mountain areas, relics of communal rights to grazing and wood cutting survived till the end of the nineteenth century. Their economic relevance was scarce, and they were eroded by a slow process of expropriation.
18. In some southern regions a higher level of crime could have hampered the entrepreneurial activity (Banti 1989a). A recent book (Gambetta 1992) explains the growth of the Mafia as a very costly substitute to a (nearly) absent state in offering businessmen enforcement and protection.
19. This argument, however, does not rule out the possibility that sharecropping had later become inefficient.
20. This last statement implies that any other tenancy system would have been suboptimal given the pattern of cultivation and that the costs of changing this latter would have been higher than the possible advantages of a different system.
21. Recent studies have questioned another tenet of the conventional wisdom, that is the contrast between the backward latifundium (the so-called 'bone' of southern agriculture) and the thriving and progressive coastal areas (the 'flesh'). On the contrary, they have stressed that the two agricultural systems were linked together through the labour and commodities markets (Lupo 1990b).
22. The study uses the sample of household budgets collected for the study on mercantilization (Federico [10]) for an econometric analysis of the peasants' choices from three options – mixed farming, specialization in one or a few crops and work outside the farm (Federico 1987). It shows that the lower was the land/labour ratio, the higher were the degree of specialization of crop mix (and consequently the lower the degree of self-sufficiency) and the share of outside work on total income.
23. Italy had had a clear technological leaderhip in one industry, silk reeling (to a lesser extent also in throwing), from the middle of the nineteenth century to the 1930s. The equipment was supplied by specialized mechanical firms and technical progress was fairly steady and quick (Federico 1994). Competitors (China, Japan) were, however, industrially even more backward than Italy.
24. The ensuing reduction of energy price caused the introduction of energy-intensive technologies in other industries (Giannetti 1985, 1986).
25. A larger plant size could even have been detrimental if the required workforce had been larger than the local supply of manpower, and therefore the firm had to incur larger outlays for recruiting workers from outside (higher wages, board and lodging expenses and so on).
26. Most of the research in this field has been done by social historians, and by trade union historians, who were searching for the economic basis of the birth and behaviour of these organizations. There are many industry-specific works, quoted later, some general works (Procacci 1961; Paci 1982; Barbadoro 1977; Merli 1976; De Clementi 1976; Lay and Pesante 1981) and area studies on Naples (Marmo 1978), Turin (Musso 1980) and Milan (Della Peruta 1987).
27. The national supply of these technicians was scarce and sometimes, especially in earlier times and/or for the use of more modern equipment, firms recruited them from abroad, usually with disappointing results. In the long run, the Italian education system improved and succeeded in training them (Zamagni 1973, 1993).
28. Women's main agricultural task in the North, a densely populated area, was the raising of silkworms in late spring. The conflict with industrial work was sometimes avoided by closing the factories during that period.
29. Opportunity costs (the agricultural productivity) were, though higher than those of female labour, nevertheless still rather low, especially for part-time jobs during the slack agricultural seasons.
30. The standard reference on emigration is Sori 1979; a case study of emigration from a northern

region (Veneto) is Lazzarini 1981. The population of northern cities grew more than the total Italian one thanks to immigration from the surrounding countryside (Mortara 1908; and for case studies De Maddalena 1961; Gribaudi 1987). Long-range internal migrations began in the interwar years (Treves 1976; Golini 1974), but the bulk of them happened later, in the 1950s and 1960s.

31. It is well-known (but sometimes neglected) that in traditional agriculture many essential tasks had to be performed in a short span of time. This feature left plenty of time in other periods of the year to search for outside employment. These part-time activities have only recently attracted some attention (Villani (ed.) 1989).
32. Many small rural villages were thus transformed into industrial towns in a short time (Sori 1973; Aliberti 1975; and, for fascist 'development poles' Petri 1990). In some cases, they became the centre of thriving industrial areas, in others they remained isolated spots in the countryside or, as they were later called 'cathedrals in the desert'. Many locations were chosen for economic reasons, such as the existence of raw materials or a low cost of electrical energy (due to the existence of falls, dams and so on), others because of the lobbying by powerful local politicians.
33. The wealth of fine ancient buildings in Italian cities is notorious. Less known but probably greater was the value of the work for land reclamation needed because of the hilly and marshy nature of most of the Italian landscape (Biagioli 1981; Bevilacqua 1989). Most of this work was done by peasants, and so it is not included in investment according to the (absurd) definition of national accounts.
34. The main type was an unredeemable bond (the 'rendita'), with a nominal rate of 5 per cent (3.5 per cent after 1905). Sometimes their nominal price was reduced by waves of mistrust in Italian government and the effective rate soared up to 9 per cent (Zamagni 1988). It is difficult to compare these rates with industrial profits, because data on these latter are very scarce (Zamagni 1978 for 1911; Romano 1992 for the cotton industry).
35. The only econometric test has been performed by Fenoaltea in his Ph.D thesis and briefly reported in Fenoaltea 1969. The banking variable did not result significant in explaining industrial growth.
36. The same means (account overdrafts, short-term loans) were used for providing both working capital (a normal banking practice) and funds for new fixed investments (a 'strategic' loan).
37. The German management of the Italian banks is suspected to have dictated the investment plans of electrical firms to foster sales of the German engineering equipment (Mori 1977; Webster 1974b).
38. As noted, some authors (Farina 1976, 1980; Zamagni 1978) argue that the mixed banks' intervention could even have been harmful to the national economy as a whole, biasing the allocation of capital towards capital-intensive industries and/or technologies. These authors do not explain why banks preferred to lend to certain industries and/or larger corporations: the most plausible explanations are lower perceived risks of default and lower screening costs.
39. If the appropriate technology needed a minimum size of the plant which was superior to the domestic consumption, it would either be used at a suboptimal productive capacity or it would be substituted by another, inferior one. In both cases, production costs would be higher. Without scale economies, the alleged shortage of demand is a truism, because potential aggregate consumption is unlimited.
40. At the beginning of the twentieth century, duties were reduced by trade treaties (Coppa 1970). In 1921 a new tariff was issued. It was on average higher than the previous one, and it filled some manifest gaps (e.g. chemicals). In subsequent years another wave of treaties lowered the rate of protection, which was raised again after 1927.
41. All these estimates are somewhat unsatisfactory either because of the time span or because of technical shortcomings. Liepmann's figures refer to 1913, 1927 and 1931 only, and they are weighted by a same set for all the European countries. Capie's ones are obtained as a ratio of total customs revenue to total imports, inclusive of non-dutiable items. Therefore they understate protection and are biased by composition effects. Finally, Tattara's article deals only with Italy in the interwar years (and in 1913). Figures for previous years are available for some products only – cereals (Federico 1984), chemicals (Zamagni 1990b) and engineering (Toniolo 1977).
42. They called 'natural' those industries which did not rely on imported inputs (the best example is silk weaving) or, less frequently, those which could balance the disadvantage of foreign raw material with the low cost of labour (like cotton).
43. Since 1903, exports of engineering products enjoyed a drawback on the duty on steel. Moreover

Italian exports of engineering were composed mainly of low valued added products like boilers, military ships and other weapons, which were the most damaged by the duty.

44. Fluctuations in railways expenditures before 1914 were distinctly pro-cyclical, but their contribution to cycles in building and engineering output was a minor one (Fenoaltea [15]). Their aggregate importance was *a fortiori* smaller.
45. This figure is obtained by weighting estimates of the share of public procurements on the total engineering output (one-third in both years, possibly historical peaks, see Zamagni 1978; Jacoboni 1949) by the percentage of engineering on total value added in 1911 (Fenoaltea 1992) and 1938 (Ercolani 1969) and adding some points so as to take into consideration orders to other industries.
46. It was pursued by clearing agreements (Tattara 1985), a monopoly of foreign exchange transactions, a system of licensing foreign trade and incentives to use the internal endowment of raw materials.
47. Exchange rates are assumed to be fixed (under the gold standard) and price elasticities to be very low throughout. Capital flows are implicitly treated as exogenous.
48. He implicitly assumes the internal supply of manufactures to be inelastic in the short and medium run, so that any increase of consumption would have been transferred to imports.
49. Fratianni and Spinelli attribute to the perceived country risk the wide differences between actual Italian prices and interest rates and their expected values (i.e. their PPP equivalents). Fenoaltea attributes the divergent paths of Italian and British interest rates to changes in risk assessment.
50. Before 1893, there were several banks of issue, which acted as commercial banks also. Many times they placed their own profit before their institutional role. The weakness of this system was made clear during the financial crisis at the end of the 1880s, which caused one of these banks to fail (this failure being instrumental in establishing the Banca d'Italia). The benefits of the new system were evident in 1907, when an efficient and skilfully managed central bank limited the effects of the international financial crisis to a decrease of the growth rate (Bonelli 1971).
51. Some years ago, Pettenati (1969) compared the performance of Keynesian and monetarist models in explaining the cycle. The former gives slightly better results, but the models are too simple (and the data too unreliable) to make this result conclusive.
52. Moreover, according to Masi (1989), it was instrumental to the monetization of Italian economy because it made the circulation of paper money compulsory. The significance of monetization *per se* – as distinct from mercantilization – is, however, dubious (Federico 1985b).
53. The difference was actually less clear-cut than implied in these highly stylized descriptions. Industries could probably be ordered in a continuum ranging from textiles (above all silk) on one side to iron and steel on the other.
54. These parameters are a weighted average of those of (allegedly) oligopolistic activities and of the rest of the economy. Either those of the former were extremely high, or market imperfections were diffused not only in heavy industries and utilities but also in other industries, agriculture and services (which is hardly plausible). Pushed to the extreme those results would deny the very existence of a dualism because the whole economy would have been oligopolistic. Besides, any change in parameters can be partially accounted for by composition effects and/or by other externalities (e.g. education).
55. Actually it included not only the large companies but also many smaller firms, the more widely known of which is Falck (Mori 1978; Bonelli 1978, 1982; Frumento 1952). During the 1920s and 1930s these latter succeeded in raising their market share and growing remarkably while the former experienced a serious crisis (Pozzobon 1982; Tattara 1980).
56. There are at least two possible shortcomings. The size of firms is proxied by their paid-up capital and not, as would be more appropriate, by sales or assets. The concentration is understated because financial or ownership ties between firms cannot be considered; this bias is, however, compensated by the omission from the sample of companies other than joint-stock.
57. They affirm that the government had destroyed southern industry by the free-trade policy (which destroyed the existing industries), had seized the capital (and used it for investments in the North) by taxation and by the sale of Church land and had forcibly thwarted the growth of the Banco di Napoli (the bank of issue of the southern state). These authors are almost alone in praising the Bourbonic economic policy.
58. Southern writers resented mainly two decisions: the adoption of the free-trade policy in 1861 and

the so-called 'perequazione fiscale' (fiscal equalizing). The former abruptly exposed to foreign competition industries which had been previously strongly protected – and hardly survived (Aliberti 1973). The latter raised taxes on land, previously much lower than in the North. According to Nitti (1900), the South paid the state more than it received, but his calculations were contested by Gini (1914).

59. Actually, a partial agrarian reform was implemented after the Second World War, and from the 1950s onwards, large resources have been poured into the South to finance public works and to subsidize industries. The results have been disappointing, but this does not completely rule out the possibility that earlier efforts could have been more successful.

References

Abramowitz, Moses (1989), 'Thinking about growth' in *Thinking about Growth*, Cambridge, MA: MIT Press.

Acquarone, A. (1965), 'La politica sindacale del fascismo', now in A. Acquarone and M. Vernassa (eds), *Il regime fascista*, Bologna: Il Mulino, 1974, pp. 233–57.

Aleotti, Alessandro (1990), *Borsa ed industria*, Milano: Ed. Comunità.

Aliberti, Giovanni (1973), 'Industria e società meridionale nell'età liberista', in *Ricerche di storia sociale e religiosa*, **3**, pp. 317–39.

Aliberti, Giovanni (1975), 'Sviluppo urbano e industrializzazione nell'Italia liberale: note su un modello di interdipendenza', in *Storia contemporanea*, **VI**, pp. 211–40 and 411–64.

Amatori, Franco (1980), 'Entrepreneurial typologies in the history of industrial Italy', *Business History Review*, **54**, pp. 359–86.

Angeli, Stefano (1989–90), 'Impresa e cultura degli interessi nell'Italia Giolittiana', *Annali di storia dell'impresa*, **5/6**, pp. 47–127.

Anselmi, Sergio (1990), 'Mezzadri e mezzadrie nell'Italia Centrale', in Bevilacqua (1989–91), Vol. II.

Arcari, Paola (1936), 'Le variazioni dei salari agricoli in Italia dalla fondazione del Regno al 1933, *Annali di statistica*, series VI, **36**, Roma: ISTAT.

Are, Giuseppe (1965), *Lo sviluppo industriale italiano nell'età della Destra*, Pisa: Nistri-Lischi.

Are, Giuseppe (1974), *Alle origini dell'Italia industriale*, Napoli: Guida.

Avagliano, Lucio (1988), *L'Italia industriale nelle sue regioni: bilancio storiografico*, Napoli: Edizioni Scientifiche Italiane.

Baglioni, Guido (1974), *L'ideologia della borghesia industriale nello stato liberale*, Torino: Einaudi.

Balloni, Valeriano (1969), 'L'andamento delle importazioni e delle esportazioni' in Fuà (1969), Vol. 2, pp. 309–404.

Banti, Alberto M. (1989a), 'Gli imprenditori meridionali: razionalità e contesto', *Meridiana*, no. 6, pp. 63–89.

Banti, Alberto M. (1989b), *Terra e danaro*, Padova: Marsilio.

Barbadoro, Idomeneo (1977), *Storia del sindacalismo italiano, vol. II la CGdL*, Firenze: La Nuova Italia.

Bardini, Carlo (1991), 'L'economia energetica italiana (1861–1913): una prospettiva inconsueta per lo studio del processo di industrializzazione', *Rivista di storia economica*, n.s., **8**, pp. 81–114.

Bardini, Carlo and Hertner, Peter (1992), 'Decollo elettrico e decollo industriale', in AA. VV., *Storia dell'industria elettrica in Italia vol. I Le origini (1882–1914)*, Bari: Laterza.

Barone, Giuseppe (1972), 'Sviluppo capitalistico e politica finanziaria in Italia nel decennio 1880–1890', in *Studi Storici*, a.13, pp. 568–99.

Bevilacqua, Piero (1985), *Uomini, terre, economie*, in *Storia d'Italia. Le regioni: la Calabria*, Torino: Einaudi.

Bevilacqua, Piero (ed.) (1989–91), *Storia dell'agricoltura italiana in età contemporanea*, Padova: Marsilio, 3 vols.

Bevilacqua, Piero (1989), 'Clima mercato e paesaggio agrario nel Mezzogiorno', in Bevilacqua (1989–91, Vol. I.

Bevilacqua, Piero (1993), *Breve storia dell'Italia meridionale*, Roma: Donzelli.

Biagioli, Giuliana (1981), 'I problemi dell'economia toscana e della mezzadria nella prima metà dell'Ottocento', in *Contadini e proprietari nella Toscana moderna*, Firenze: Olschki, Vol. II, pp. 85–172.

Biagioli, Giuliana (1987), 'The spread of mezzadria in central Italy: a model of demographic and economic development', in A. Fauve-Chamoux (ed.), *Evolution agraire et croissance démographique*, Liège: Ordina, pp. 139–54.

Biffoli, Cristina and Lungonelli, Michele (1985), 'Una classe operaia in formazione: i siderurgici di Portoferraio', *Studi storici*, a. 26, pp. 53–65.

Bigazzi, Duccio (1981), 'Grandi imprese e concentrazione finanziaria', in AA. VV., *Storia della società italiana*, Vol. XX, Milano: Teti.

Bigazzi, Duccio (1988), *Il Portello*, Milano: F. Angeli.

Bonelli, Franco (1968), 'Osservazioni e dati sul finanziamento dell'industria italiana nel secolo XIX', in *Annali della Fondazione L. Einaudi*, pp. 257–79.

Bonelli, Franco (1971), *La crisi del 1907*, Torino: Fondazione L. Einaudi.

Bonelli, Franco (1975), *Lo sviluppo di una grande impresa in Italia: la Terni dal 1884 al 1962*, Torino: Einaudi.

Bonelli, Franco (1978), 'La siderurgia italiana del 1900 al 1930', *Ricerche storiche*, **VIII**, pp. 95–103.

Bonelli, Franco (1982) (ed.), *Acciaio per l'industrializzazione*, Torino: Einaudi.

Bonelli, Franco (1991) (ed.), *La Banca d'Italia dal 1894 al 1913*, Bari: Laterza.

Bottiglieri, Bruno (1987), 'Alle origini di una grande impresa', in *I primi quindici anni della FIAT*, Milano: F. Angeli, Vol. 1, pp. 17–54.

Bottiglieri, Bruno (1991), 'La funzione dello stato', in AA. VV., *Storia dell'economia italiana*, Vol. III, Torino: Einaudi.

Brosio G. and Marchese C. (1987), *Il potere di spendere*, Bologna: Il Mulino.

Busino, Giovanni (1977), *W. Pareto e l'industria del ferro nel Valdarno*, Milano: Banca Commerciale Italiana.

Cafagna, Luciano (1961), 'La formazione di una "base industriale" in Italia fra il 1896 ed il 1914', *Studi Storici*, a.2, now in Cafagna (1989), pp. 223–59.

Cafagna, Luciano (1962), 'Industrialismo e politica economica dopo l'Unità d'Italia', *Annali Feltrinelli*, V, pp. 150–80, now in Cafagna (1989), pp. 223–61.

Cafagna, Luciano (1978), 'La politica economica e lo sviluppo industriale', in *Atti del XLIX Congresso di storia del Risorgimento italiano*, Roma: Istituto per la storia del Risorgimento, Vol. 1, pp. 141–57, now in Cafagna (1989), pp. 261–80.

Cafagna, Luciano (1983a), 'Protoindustria o transazione in bilico? (a proposito della prima onda dell'industrializzazione in Italia), *Quaderni storici*, **17**, pp. 971–84 now in Cafagna (1989), pp. 359–72.

Cafagna, Luciano (1983b), 'La formazione del sistema industriale: ricerche empiriche e modelli di crescita', *Quaderni della Fondazione G.G. Feltrinelli*, no. 23, pp. 27–38, now in Cafagna (1989), pp. 385–400.

Cafagna, Luciano (1988), 'Modernizzazione passiva', *Meridiana*, **2**, pp. 229–40.

Cafagna, Luciano (1989), *Dualismo e sviluppo nella storia d'Italia*, Padova: Marsilio.

Caizzi, Bruno (1965), *Storia dell'industria italiana dal XVIII secolo ai giorni nostri*, Torino: UTET.

Calderoni, Ugo (1961), *I cento anni della politica doganale italiana*, Padova: CEDAM.

Calzavarini, Mirella (1966), 'Il protezionismo industriale e la tariffa doganale del 1887', *Clio*, **2**, pp. 55–94.

Cantwell, John (1992), 'Historical trends in international patterns of technological innovations', in J. Foreman-Peck (ed.), *New Perspectives on the Late Victorian Economy*, Cambridge: Cambridge University Press.

Capacelatro, Edmondo M. and Carlo, Antonio (1972), *Contro la 'questione meridionale'*, Roma: Samonà e Savelli.

Capanna, Alberto and Messori, Ottavio (1940), *Gli scambi commerciali dell'Italia con l'estero*, Roma: Unione editoriale d'Italia.

Capie, Forrest (1983), 'Tariff protection and economic performance in the nineteenth century', in J. Black and A.L. Winters (eds), *Policy and performance in International Trade*, London: Macmillan, pp. 1–24.

Caracciolo, Alberto (1969a) (ed.), *La formazione dell'Italia industriale*, Bari: Laterza.
Caracciolo, Alberto (1969b), 'La crescita e la trasformazione della grande industria durante le prima guerra mondiale', in Fuà (1969), Vol. III, pp. 187–240.
Cardillo, Giuseppe (1978), 'Considerazioni sui caratteri dello sviluppo economico italiano', *Cahiers internationaux d'histoire économique et social*, no. 9, pp. 255–78.
Cardini, Antonio (1981), *Stato liberale e protezionismo in Italia (1820–1900)*, Bologna: Il Mulino.
Carparelli, Antonella (1982), *I perchè di una 'mezza siderurgia'. La società ILVA, l'industria della ghisa ed il ciclo integrale negli anni Venti*, in Bonelli (1982), pp. 5–158.
Carreras, Albert (1992), 'La produccion industrial en el muy largo plazo: una comparacion entre España e Italia', in V. Zamagni and L. Prados de la Escosura (eds), *El desarrollo económico de la Europa de Sur: España e Italia en perspectiva histórica*, Madrid: Alianza Editorial.
Castronovo, Valerio (1964), *L'industria laniera in Piemonte nel secolo XIX*, Torino: ILTE.
Castronovo, Valerio (1965), *L'industria cotoniera in Piemonte nel secolo XIX*, Torino: ILTE.
Castronovo, Valerio (1975), 'La storia economica', in *Storia d'Italia Einaudi*, Vol. IV: *Dall'Unità ad oggi*, Torino: Einaudi.
Castronovo, Valerio (1979), 'Lo sviluppo economico nell'Italia Unita', *Rivista storica italiana*, **XCI** (1), pp. 107–43.
Castronovo, Valerio (1980), *L'industria italiana dall'Ottocento ad oggi*, Milano: Mondadori.
Cianci, Ernesto (1977), *Nascita dello stato imprenditore in Italia*, Milano: Mursia.
Ciocca, Pierluigi (1976), 'L'economia italiana nel contesto internazionale', in Ciocca and Toniolo (1976).
Ciocca, Pierluigi and Toniolo, Gianni (1976) (eds), *L'economia italiana nel periodo fascista*, Bologna: Il Mulino.
Clough, Sheperd (1965), *Storia dell'economia italiana dal 1861 ad oggi*, Bologna: Cappelli.
Cohen, Jon S. (1967), 'Financing industrialization in Italy 1894–1914: the partial transformation of a late-comer', *Journal of Economic History*, **XXVII**, pp. 363–82.
Cohen, Jon S. (1973), 'La svalutazione della lira nel 1927: uno studio sulla politica estera fascista', in Toniolo (1973).
Cohen, Jon S. (1975), 'Italy 1861–1914', in R. Cameron (ed.), *Le banche e lo sviluppo del sistema industriale*, Bologna: Il Mulino, pp. 383–411.
Cohen, Jon (1977), *Finance and industrialization in Italy*, New York: Arno Press.
Cohen, Jon (1979), 'Fascism and agriculture in Italy: policies and consequences', *Economic History Review*, **XXXII**, pp. 70–97.
Confalonieri, Antonio (1974–76), *Banca ed industria in Italia 1894–1906*, Milano: Banca Commerciale Italiana, 3 vols.
Confalonieri, Antonio (1982), *Banca ed industria in Italia dalla crisi del 1907 all'agosto 1914*, Milano: Banca Commerciale Italiana, 2 vols.
Conti, G. (1993), 'Finanza di impresa e capitale di rischio in Italia (1870–1939)', in *Rivista di storia economica*, 10, pp. 307–32.
Coppa, Frank J. (1970), 'The Italian tariff and the conflict between agriculture and industry: the commercial policy of liberal Italy', *Journal of Economic History*, **XXX**, pp. 742–69.
Corbino, Epicarmo (1931–35), *Annali dell'economia italiana*, Città di Castello, (now republished as the first five volumes of IPSOA, 1985).
Corner, Paul (1984), 'Manodopera agricola e industria manifatturiera nella Lombardia post-unitaria', *Studi Storici*, a. 25, pp. 1019–27.
Corner, Paul (1990), *Il contadino-operaio dell'Italia padana*, in Bevilacqua (1989–91), Vol. II, pp. 751–83.
Corona, Gabriella and Massullo, Gino (1989), 'La terra e le tecniche: innovazioni produttivie e lavoro agricolo nei secoli XIX e XX', in Bevilacqua (1989–91), Vol. I, pp. 353–449.
Covino, Renato, Gallo, Giampaolo and Mantovani, Enrico (1976), 'L'industria dall'economia di guerra alla ricostruzione', in Ciocca and Toniolo (1976).
Daneo, Camillo (1979), *Breve storia dell'agricoltura italiana*, Milano: Mondadori.
D'Angiolini, Piero (1972), 'La svolta industriale italiana negli ultimi anni del secolo scorso e le reazioni dei contemporanei', in *Nuova rivista storica*, pp. 53–121.
Da Pozzo, Mario and Felloni, Giuseppe (1964), *La Borsa Valori di Genova nel secolo XIX*, Torino: ILTE.

Davis, John A. (1990), 'Technology and innovations in an industrial late-comer. Italy in the nineteenth century', in P. Mathias and J. Davis, *Innovations and Technology in Europe*, Oxford: Blackwell.
De Cecco, Marcello (1990), 'Introduzione', in M. De Cecco (ed.) *L'Italia ed il sistema finanziario internazionale 1861–1914*, Bari: Laterza.
De Clementi, Andreina (1976), 'Appunti sulla formazione della classe operaia in Italia', *Quaderni storici*, no. 32, pp. 684–728.
De Felice, Franco (1971), *L'agricoltura in Terra di Bari dal 1880 al 1914*, Milano: Banca Commerciale Italiana.
Dell'Orefice, Anna (1980), 'Una occasione mancata: la legge speciale per Napoli', *Cahiers internationaux d'histoire économique et social*, no. 18, pp. 159–266.
Della Peruta, Franco (1987), *Milano lavoro e fabbrica 1815–1914*, Milano: F. Angeli.
Del Monte, A. (1977), 'Profitti e sviluppo economico negli anni 1881–1961, con particolare riferimento al periodo fascista', *Rivista internazionale di scienze sociali*, **LXXV**, pp. 241–66.
Del Panta, Lorenzo (1984), *Evoluzione demografica e popolamento nell'Italia dell'Ottocento (1796–1914)*, Bologna: CLUEB.
Del Vecchio, Edoardo (1978), *La via italiana al protezionismo*, Roma: Camera dei Deputati.
De Maddalena, Aldo (1961), 'Rilievi sull'esperienza demografia ed economica milanese dal 1861 al 1915', in AA. VV., *L'economia italiana dal 1861 al 1961*, Milano: Giuffrè.
De Mattia, Renato (1990) (ed.), *Gli istituti di emissione in Italia*, Bari: Laterza.
De Rosa, Luigi (1969), 'Difesa militare e sviluppo economico in Italia (1861–1914)', in *Rassegna economica*, now in De Rosa (1980).
De Rosa, Luigi (1980), *La rivoluzione industriale in Italia*, Bari: Laterza.
De Rose, Luigi (1982–83), *Storia del Banco di Roma*, Roma: Banco di Roma, 2 vols.
De Rosa, Luigi (1982), 'Economics and nationalism in Italy', *Journal of European Economic History*, **XI**, pp. 537–74.
De Rosa, Luigi (1990), 'La storiografia economica italiana nell'età contemporanea', in L. De Rosa, *L'avventura della storia economica in Italia*, Bari: Laterza.
Dewerpe, Alain (1985a), *L'industrie aux champs*, Roma: Ecole française.
Dewerpe, Alain (1985b), 'Modi di organizzazione e retribuzione produttiva all'Ansaldo, 1900–1920', *Studi storici*, a. 26, pp. 29–52.
Dewerpe, Alain (1991), 'Verso l'Italia industriale', in *Storia dell'economia italiana*, Vol. III, Torino: Einaudi, pp. 5–58.
Di Nardi, Giovanni (1953), *Le banche di emissione nel secolo XIX*, Torino: UTET.
Donvito, Anna and Garbarini, Giovanni (1984), '"Senz'altra formalità che il reciproco preavviso": le officine di Savigliano 1904–1914', *Italia contemporanea*, no. 157, pp. 47–62.
Donvito, Anna and Garbarini, Giovanni (1985), 'Ottanta mestieri per trenta centesimi: officine di Savigliano stabilimento di Torino (1904–1914)', *Società e storia*, no. 29, pp. 595–625.
Donzelli, Carmine (1990), 'Mezzogiorno fra "questione" e purgatorio. Opinione comune, immagine scientifica, strategie di ricerca', *Meridiana*, no. 9, pp. 13–53.
Doria, Marco (1989), *Ansaldo*, Milano: Franco Angeli.
Ercolani, Paolo (1969), 'Documentazione statistica di base', in Fuà (1969), Vol. III, pp. 380–460.
Esposto, Alfred (1990), 'Institutions and regional disparities in the Italian economy 1861–1914', PhD thesis, Temple University.
Esposto, Alfred (1992), 'Italian industrialization and the Gerschenkronian "great spurt": a regional analysis', *Journal of Economic History*, VII, pp. 353–62.
Fano Damascelli, Ester (1971), 'La "Restaurazione antifascista liberista". Ristagno e sviluppo economico durante il fascismo', now in Acquarone and Vernassa (1974), pp. 281–305.
Farina, Francesco (1976), 'Modelli interpretativi e caratteri del capitalismo italiano', *Quaderni Storici*, no. 32, pp. 487–514.
Farina, Francesco (1980), 'Note sul ruolo della banca mista nello sviluppo italiano', *Società e Storia*, no. 19, pp. 919–27.
Favilli, Paolo (1974), *Capitalismo e classe operaia a Piombino 1861–1918*, Roma: Editori Riuniti.
Federico, Giovanni (1979), 'Per una analisi del ruolo dell'agricoltura nello sviluppo economico italiano: note sull'esportazione di prodotti primari (1863–1913)', *Società e Storia*, no. 5, pp. 379–441.

Federico, Giovanni (1982a), 'Per una valutazione critica delle statistiche della produzione agricola italiana dopo l'Unità (1860–1913)' *Società e Storai*, no. 15, pp. 87–130.
Federico, Giovanni (1982b), 'La domanda siderurgica negli anni Trenta', in Bonelli (1982), pp. 370–412.
Federico, Giovanni (1984), 'Commercio dei cereali e dazio sul grano in Italia (1963–1913). Una analisi quantitativa', *Nuova Rivista Storica*, **LXVIII**, pp. 46–108.
Federico, Giovanni (1985a), 'Sviluppo industriale, mobilità della popolazione e mercato della forza-lavoro in Italia. Una analisi macroeconomica', in Società italiana di Demografia Storica (S.I.DE.S.), *L'evoluzione demografica dell'Italia nel secolo XIX: continuità e mutamenti (1796–1914)*, Bologna: CLUEB, pp. 497–96.
Federico, Giovanni (1985b), 'Autoconsumo e mercantilizzazione: spunti per una discussione', *Società e Storia*, no. 27, pp. 197–212.
Federico, Giovanni (1987), 'Contadini e mercato: tattiche di sopravvivenza' *Società e storia*, no. 38, pp. 877–913.
Federico, Giovanni (1988), 'Commercio estero e "periferie". Il caso dei paesi mediterranei', *Meridiana*, no. 4, pp. 163–96.
Federico, Giovanni (1991a), 'Household budgets as a source for the study of rural economy: commercialization and peasants' behaviour (Italy 1860–1940', in T. Pierenkemper (ed.), *Zür ökonomik des privaten haushalt*, Dusseldorf: Campus Verlag, pp. 182–97.
Federico, Giovanni (1991b), 'Oltre frontiera: l'agricoltura italiana nel mercato internazionale', in Bevilacqua (1989–91), Vol. III, pp. 182–93.
Federico, Giovanni (1992a), 'La tessitura italiana ed il mercato mondiale', in I. Granata and A. Scalpelli (eds), *Setaioli e contadini. Movimento operaio e industrializzazione a Como dall'Unità al fascismo*, Milano: F. Angeli, pp. 27–62.
Federico, Giovanni (1992b), 'Agricoltura e sviluppo economico italiano: una visione di lungo periodo (1820–1950)', paper presented to the XXX Annual meeting of the Società degli economisti, Roma.
Federico, Giovanni (1994), *Il filo d'oro. Una storia economica dell'industria serica*, Padova: Marsilio.
Federico, Giovanni and Chesi, Marco (1987), 'Lo sviluppo economico italiano', in AA. VV., *Storia della società italiana, vol 17, Le strutture e la classi nell'Italia Unita*, Milano: Teti, pp. 13–70.
Fenoaltea, Stefano (1969), 'Decollo, ciclo e intervento dello stato', in Caracciolo (1969a).
Fenoaltea, Stefano (1973a), 'Riflessioni sull'esperienza industriale italiana dal Risorgimento alla prima Guerra Mondiale', in Toniolo (1973).
Fenoaltea, Stefano (1973b), 'Le ferrovie e lo sviluppo industriale italiano', in Toniolo (1973).
Fenoaltea, Stefano (1982), 'The growth of utilities industries in Italy', in *Journal of Economic History*, **XLII**, pp. 601–27.
Fenoaltea, Stefano (1987), 'Le costruzioni in Italia 1861–1913', *Rivista di storia economica*, n.s., **4**, pp. 1–34.
Fenoaltea, Stefano (1988a), 'The growth of Italy's silk industry 1861–1913: a statistical reconstruction', *Rivista di storia economica*, n.s., **V**, fasc. 3.
Fenoaltea, Stefano (1988b), 'The extractive industries in Italy 1861–1913: general methods and specific estimates', *Journal of European Economic History*, **17** (1), pp. 117–25.
Fenoaltea, Stefano (1992), 'Il valore aggiunto dell'industria', in Rey (1992).
Fenoaltea, Stefano (1993), 'Politica doganale, sviluppo industriale, emigrazione: verso una riconsiderazione del dazio sul grano', *Rivista di storia economica*, n.s., **10**, pp. 65–77.
Ferrari, Paolo (1986), 'La produzione di armamenti nell' età giolittiana', *Italia contemporanea*, no. 162, pp. 113–39.
Filosa, Renato, Rey, Guido M. and Sitzia, Bruno (1976), 'Uno schema di analisi quantitativa dell'economia italiana durante il fascismo', in Ciocca and Toniolo (1976), pp. 51–103.
Fisher, Douglas (1992), *The Industrial Revolution. A Macroeconomic Reinterpretation*, London: St Martin's Press.
Fossati, Antonio (1951), *Lavoro e produzione in Italia*, Torino: Giappichelli.
Fratianni, Michele and Spinelli, Franco (1984), 'Italy in the gold standard period', in M. Bordo and A.J. Schwartz, *A Retrospective on the Classical Gold Standard*, Chicago: University of Chicago Press, pp. 404–38.

Fratianni, Michele and Spinelli, Franco (1985), 'Currency competition, fiscal policy and the money supply process in Italy from the Unification to World War I', *Journal of European Economic History*, **XIV**, pp. 473–99.
Frumento, Armando (1952), *Imprese lombarde nella storia della siderugia italiana. Il contributo dei Falck*, Milano: AFL Falck.
Fuà, Giorgio (1969) (ed.), *Lo sviluppo economico in Italia*, Milano: Franco Angeli.
Fuà, Giorgio (1981), *Lo sviluppo economico in Italia*, Milano: Franco Angeli.
Fuà, G. and Gallegati, M. (1993), 'Un indice a catena annuale del prodotto "reale" dell'Italia, 1861–1989', *Rivista di storia economica*, n.s., **10**, pp. 281–306.
Fumi, Giovanni (1989–90), 'Per lo studio delle imprese agrarie: un itinerario attraverso la produzione storiografica', *Annali di storia dell'impresa*, **5/6**, pp. 412–511.
Galassi, Francesco (1986), 'Stasi e sviluppo nell'agricoltura toscana 1870–1914: primi risultati di uno studio aziendale', *Rivista di Storia economica*, n.s., **3**, pp. 304–37.
Galassi, Francesco (1992), 'Tuscans and their farms: the economics of share tenancy in fifteenth century Florence', *Rivista di storia economica*, n.s., **9**, pp. 76–94.
Galassi, Francesco and Cohen, Jon (1992), 'La agricultura italiana, 1860–1930: tendencias de la produccion y differencias en la productivitad regional', in V. Zamagni and L. Prados de la Escosura (eds), *El desarrollo económico de la Europa de Sur: España e Italia en perspectiva histórica*, Madrid: Alianza Editorial.
Gambetta, Diego (1992), *La mafia siciliana*, Torino: Einaudi.
Ganugi, Piero (1989), 'Financial deepening, risparmio forzato e accumulazione in Italia 1881–1936', *Rivista di storia economica*, n.s., **6**, pp. 321–56.
Giannetti, Renato (1985), *La conquista della forza*, Milano: Franco Angeli.
Gianetti, Renato (1986), 'Elettricità ed industrializzazione dall'età del decollo alla seconda guerra mondiale', *Società e storia*, no. 33, pp. 595–613.
Gianetti, Renato (1992), 'Cambiamenti non adattativi nell'organizzazione industriale: l'industria elettromeccanica italiana', *Annali di storia dell'impresa*, no. 7, pp. 130–205.
Gianetti, R. (1993), 'Mutamento tecnico e sviluppo economico italiano, *Rivista di storia economica*, **10**, pp. 177–208.
Giannetti, R., Federico, G., Toninelli, P.A. (forthcoming), 'Size and strategy of Italian industrial enterprises: empirical evidences and some conjectures', *Industrial and Corporate Change*.
Gigli Marchetti, Ada (1983), *I tre anelli: mutualità, resistenza, cooperazione dei tipografi milanesi 1860–1925*, Milano: Franco Angeli.
Gini, Corrado (1914), *L'ammontare e la composzione della ricchezza delle nazioni*, Torino: Bocca.
Glazier, I., Bandera, V.N. and Berner, R.B. (1975), 'Terms of trade between Italy and the United Kingdom, 1815–1913', *Journal of European Economic History*, **IV**, pp. 5–49.
Golini, Antonio (1974), 'Distribuzione della popolazione, migrazioni interne e urbanizzazione in Italia', Roma Istituto di demografia della facoltà di statistica, Pubbl. no. 23.
Golzio, Silvio (1942), *L'industria dei metalli in Italia*, Torino, Einaudi.
Gregor, James (1979), *Italian Fascism and Developmental Dictatorship*, Princeton: Princeton University Press.
Gribaudi, Maurizio (1987), *Mondo operaio e mito operaio*, Torino: Einaudi.
Grifone, Pietro (1971), *Il capitale finanziario in Italia*, Torino: Einaudi (1st edn 1945).
Gualerni, Gilberto (1982), *Lo stato industriale in Italia*, Milano: Etas Kompass.
Hertner, Peter (1978), 'La società "Tubi Mannesmann" a Dalmine: un esempio di investimento internazionale (1906–17)', *Ricerche storiche*, **VIII**, pp. 105–23.
Hertner, Peter (1981), 'Il capitale straniero in Italia (1883–1914)', *Studi storici*, a. 22, pp. 767–95.
Hertner, Peter (1982), 'Capitale tedesco e industria meccanica in Italia: la "Esslingen" a Saronno 1887–1913', *Società e storia*, no. 17, pp. 583–621.
Hertner, Peter (1983), *Il capitale tedesco in Italia dall'Unità alla prima guerra mondiale*, Bologna: Il Mulino.
Hertner, Peter (1987), 'Industria italiana degli armamenti e capitale straniero: il silurificio Schwartzkopff', *Venetica*, no. 8, pp. 65–93.

Hunecke, Volker (1977), 'Cultura liberale e industrialismo nell'Italia dell'800', *Studi Storici*, a. 18, pp. 23–32.

Hunecke, Volker (1982), *Classe operaia e rivoluzione industriale a Milano 1859–1982*, Bologna: Il Mulino.

IPSOA (1985), *Annali dell'economia italiana*, Milano: IPSOA.

Istituto Centrale di Statistica (ISTAT) (1957), *Indagine statistica sullo sviluppo del reddtio nazionale dell'Italia dal 1861 al 1959*, Annali di statistica serie VIII, Vol. 9.

Istituto Nazionale di Economia Agraria (INEA) (1938), *Inchiesta sulla piccola proprietà coltivatrice formatasi nel dopoguerra*, vol. XV (G. Lorenzoni) *Relazione finale*, Roma: INEA.

Izzo, Luigi (1965), *Storia delle relazioni commerciali fra Italia e Francia dal 1860 al 1875*, Napoli: Edizioni Scientifiche Italiane.

Jacoboni, Attilio (1949), *L'industria meccanica italiana*, Roma: Cemtro Studi e piani tecnico-economici.

Jannaccone, Pasquale (1936), 'Relazioni fra commercio internazionale, cambi esteri e circolazione monetaria in Italia nel quarantennio 1871–1913', in *Prezzi e mercati*, Torino: Einaudi, pp. 167–272.

Kaelble, Helmut (1989), 'Was Prometheus most unbound in Europe? The labour force in Europe during the late XIX and XX century', *Journal of European Economic History*, **18**, pp. 65–104.

Kuznets, Simon (1967), 'Quantitative aspects of the growth of nations X level and structure of foreign trade: long term trends', *Economic Development and Cultural Change*, **15**, pp. 1–140.

La Francesca, Salvatore (1971), *La politica economica italiana dal 1900 al 1913*, Roma: Ed. dell'Ateneo.

La Francesca, Salvatore (1973), *La politica economica del fascismo*, Bari: Laterza.

Lanaro, Silvio (1979), *Nazione e lavoro*, Padova: Marsilio.

Lanino, Pietro (1916), *La nuova Italia industriale*, Roma: L'Italiana, 4 vols.

Lay, Adriana and Pesante, Maria Luisa (1981), *Produttori senza democrazia*, Bologna: Il Mulino.

Lazzarini, Antonio (1981), *Campagne venete ed emigrazione di massa*, Vicenza: Istituto per le ricerche di storia sociale e religiosa.

Liepmann, Herbert (1938), *Tariff Levels and the Economic Unity of Europe*, London: George Allen & Unwin.

Lombardi, M. (1959), *La politica doganale italiana*, Napoli: ESI.

Lupo, Salvatore (1990a), *Il giardino degli aranci*, Padova: Marsilio.

Lupo, Salvatore (1990b), 'I proprietari terrieri nel Mezzogiorno', in Bevilacqua (1989–91), Vol. II, pp. 105–49.

Luzzatto, Gino (1963), *L'economia italiana dal 1961 al 1894*, Milano: Banca Commerciale (reprinted Torino: Einaudi 1968).

Maddison, Angus (1991), *Dynamic forces in capitalist development*, Oxford: Oxford University Press.

Maddison, Angus (1992), 'El crecimiento economico italiano 1861–1989: una revision', in L. Prados de la Escosura and V. Zamagni (eds), *El desarrollo économico en la Europa del Sur: Espana e Italia en perspective historica*, Madrid: Alianza edn.

Maizels, Alfred (1963), *Industrial Growth and World Trade*, Cambridge: NIESR.

Marconi, Diego (1982), *La politica monetaria del fascismo*, Bologna: Il Mulino.

Marianelli, Alessandro (1983), *Proletariato di fabbrica e organizzazione sindacale in Italia: il caso dei lavoratori del vetro*, Milano: F. Angeli.

Marmo, Marcella (1978), *Il proletariato industriale a Napoli in età liberale 1880–1914*, Napoli: Guida.

Masi, Paola (1989), 'L'influenza del debito pubblico sulla costituzione dei sistemi finanziari: il caso italiano 1860–1893', *Rivista di Storia Economica*, n.s., **6**, pp. 60–86.

Merger, Michele (1986), 'Un modello di sostituzione: la locomotiva italiana dal 1850 al 1914', *Rivista di storia economica*, n.s. **3** (1), pp. 66–108.

Merli, Stefano (1976), *Proletariato di fabbrica e capitalismo industriale*, Firenze: La Nuova Italia.

Morandi, Rodolfo (1931), *Storia della grande industria in Italia*, Torino: Einaudi.

Mori, Giorgio (1959), 'La storia dell'industria italiana contemporanea nei saggi, nelle ricerche e nelle publicazioni ginbiliari di questo dopoguerra', *Annali Feltrinelli*, **II**, pp. 264–346.

Mori, Giorgio (1977), 'Appunti e spunti per una riconsiderazione sulla storiografia economica sull'Italia post-unitaria', *Rassegna economica*, **XLI** (1), pp. 25–46.

Mori, Giorgio (1978), 'La siderurgia italiana dall'Unità alla fine del secolo XIX', *Ricerche storiche*, **VIII**, pp. 7–34.

Mori, Giorgio (1979), 'The process of industrialization in general and the process of industrialization in Italy', *Journal of European Economic History*, **VIII**, pp. 61–82.

Mori, Giorgio (1981), 'Introduzione alla seconda edizione', in G. Mori (ed.), *L'industrializzazione in Italia*, Bologna: Il Mulino.

Mori, Giorgio (1989), 'Le industrie senza industrializzazione: La penisola italiana dalla fine della dominazione francese all'Unità', *Studi storici*, **30** (3), pp. 603–34.

Mori, Giorgio (1992), 'L'economia italiana dagli anni Ottanta alla prima guerra mondiale', in AA. VV. *Storia dell'industria elettrica in Italia*, Vol. I, Bari: Laterza, pp. 1–106.

Mortara, Alberto (1908), *La popolazione delle grandi città italiane*, Torino: UTET.

Musso, Stefano (1980), *Gli operai di Torino 1900–1920*, Milano: Feltrinelli.

Negri, Gugliemo (1989) (ed.), *Giolitti e la nascita della Banca d'Italia*, Bari: Laterza.

Niccoli, Alberto (1969), 'Ricerche econometriche sugli investimenti', in Fuà (1969), Vol. II, pp. 337–68.

Nitti, Francesco S. (1900), 'Il bilancio dello stato dal 1862 al 1896–97', now in ID (1958), *Scritti sulla questione meridionale*, Vol. II, Bari: Laterza.

O'Brien, Patrick and Prados De La Escosura, Leandro (1992), 'Agricultural Productivity and European Industrialization', *Economic History Review*, **XLV**, pp. 514–36.

Orlando, Giuseppe (1969a), 'Progressi e difficoltà nell'agricoltura', in Fuà (1969), Vol. III, pp. 17–95.

Orlando, Giuseppe (1969b), 'La stima della produzione lorda vendibile e degli investimenti agricoli per zone', in Fuà (1969), Vol. III, pp. 538–52.

Orlando, Giuseppe (1984), *Storia della politica agraria in Italia dal 1848 ad oggi*, Bari: Laterza.

Paci, Massimo (1982), *La struttura sociale italiana. Costanti storiche e trasformazioni recenti*, Bologna: Il Mulino.

Pantaleoni, Maffeo (1895), *La caduta della Società Generale di Credito Mobiliare Italiano*, Milano: Giuffrè, 1977.

Paradisi, Mariangela (1976), 'Il commercio estero e la struttura indusriale', in Ciocca and Toniolo (1976).

Parravicini, Giannino (1958), *La politica fiscale e le entrate effettive del Regno d'Italia 1860–1890*, Torino: ILTE.

Pedone, Antonio (1969a), 'La politica del commercio con l'estero', in Fuà (1969), Vol. II, pp. 241–59.

Pedone, Antonio (1969b), 'Il bilancio dello Stato', in Fuà (1969), Vol. II, pp. 203–40.

Pegorari, Paolo (1989), *Il protezionismo imperfetto*, Venezia: Istituto vento di Scienze Lettere ed Arti.

Pescosolido, Guido (1977), 'Lo sviluppo industriale italiano nel dibattito dell'ultimo ventennio', *Clio*, **XIII**, pp. 186–237.

Pescosolido, Guido (1979), 'L'andamento della produzione agraria durante il primo ventennio post-unitario', *Nuova rivista storica*, **LXII**, pp. 33–114.

Petri, Rolf (1990), *La frontiera industriale*, Milano: F. Angeli.

Petrusewicz, Marta (1990), *Latifondo*, Padova: Marsilio.

Pettenati, Paolo (1969), 'Stabilità comparativa della velocità di circolazione e del moltiplicatore keynesiano nell'esperienza italiana', in Fuà (1969), Vol. II, pp. 297–313.

Pezzati, Mario (1990), 'I prodotti chimici per l'agricoltura in Italia nel primo trentennio del secolo', in F. Amatori and B. Bezza (eds), *Montecatini 1888–1966*, Bologna: Il Mulino.

Pezzino, Paolo (1987), 'Quale modernizzazione per il Mezzogiorno?', *Società e storia*, no. 37, pp. 649–74.

Piloni, Rita (1985), 'L'industria della bicicletta a Milano dalla fine dell'Ottocento al 1914', *Storia in Lombardia*, **IV**, pp. 81–99.

Pino Pongolino, Francesca (1991), 'Sui fiduciari della Comit nelle società per azioni (1898–1918)', *Rivista di storia economica*, n.s. **8**, pp. 115–48.

Piva, Francesco and Toniolo, Gianni (1987), 'Sulla disoccupazione in Italia negli anni Trenta', *Rivista di storia economica*, n.s. **4**, pp. 345–83.

Polsi, Alessandro (1993), *Alle origini del capitalismo italiano*, Torino: Einaudi.

Porisini, Giorgio (1971), *Produttività e agricoltura: i rendimenti del frumento dal 1815 al 1922*, Torino: ILTE.

Porisini, Giorgio (1978), *Bonifiche e agricoltura nella bassa Valpadana*, Milano: Banca Commerciale Italiana.

Pozzobon, Martino (1981), 'L'industria tessile nel Milanese 1900–1930', in Cristofoli, Maria Cristina and Pozzobon, Martino, *I tessili milanesi*, Milano: Franco Angeli, pp. 11–84.

Pozzobon, Martino (1982), 'L'industria padana dell'acciaio nel primo trentennio del Novecento', in Bonelli (1982), pp. 161–214.

Procacci, Giuliano (1961), 'La classe operaia italiana agli inizi del secolo XX', *Studi storici*, a. 2, now in G. Procacci, *La lotta di classe in Italia agli inizi del secolo XX*, Roma: Editori Riuniti, 1978, pp. 7–80.

Prodi, Romano (1965–66), 'Il protezionismo nella politica e nell'industria italiana dall'Unificazione al 1887', *Nuova rivista storica*, **XLIX**, pp. 597–626 and **L**, pp. 42–86.

Ramella, Franco (1984), *Terra e telai. Sistemi di parentela e manifattura nel Biellese dell'Ottocento*, Torino: Einaudi.

Rey, Guido M. (ed.) (1992), *I conti economici dell'Italia. 3 Una stima del valore aggiunto per rami di attività per il 1911*, Collana storica della Banca d'Italia. Serie Statistiche, Vol. I, tomo 2, Bari: Laterza.

Romani, Mario (1976), *Storia economica d'Italia nel secolo XIX*, Milano: Giuffrè.

Romano, Roberto (1978), 'Le basi sociali di una localizzazione industriale: l'industria cotoniera lombarda nell'Ottocento', *Storia Urbana*, no. 4, pp. 3–19.

Romano, Roberto (1992), *L'industria cotoniera lombarda dall'Unità al 1914*, Milano: Banca Commerciale Italiana.

Romeo, Rosario (1958), Problemi dello sviluppo capitalistico in Italia dal 1861 al 1887', *Nord e Sud*, also in *Risorgimento e Capitalismo*, Bari: Laterza, 1961.

Romeo, Rosario (1965), *Breve storia della grande industria in Italia 1861–1961*, Bologna: Cappelli.

Roselli, Alessandro (1992), 'Crisi bancarie ed intervento pubblico', *Rivista di storia economica*, n.s. **9**, pp. 175–207.

Rossi, Ernesto (1966), *Padroni del vapore e fascismo*, Bari: Laterza.

Rossi, Nocola, Sorgato, A. and Toniolo, Gianni (1993), 'I conti economici italiani: una ricostruzione statistica', *Rivista di storia economica*, **10**, pp. 2–47.

Russo, Saverio (1991), 'La storiografia sul Mezzogiorno nell'ultimo quarantennio', in C. Cassina (ed.), *La storiografia sull'Italia contemporanea*, Pisa: Giardini.

Salvemini, Biagio (1984), 'Note sul concetto di Ottocento meridionale', *Società e storia*, no. 26, pp. 917–45.

Sannucci, Valeria (1989), 'The establishment of a central bank: Italy in the 19th century', in M. De Cecco and A. Giovannini (eds), *A European Central Bank?*, Cambridge: Cambridge University Press.

Sapelli, G. (1991), 'Technical change, microeconomic evolution and growth: an introductory view of Italian industrial development', in G. Dosi, R. Giannetti and P. Toninelli (eds), *Technology and Enterprise in a Historical Perspective*, Oxford: Oxford University Press.

Schultz, Theodore (1964), *Transforming Traditional Agriculture*, New Haven: Yale University Press.

Sereni, Emilio (1947), *Il capitalismo nelle campagne (1860–1900)*, Torino: Einaudi (reprinted in 1972).

Sereni, Emilio (1958–59), 'Il nodo della politica granaria', *Politica ed economia*, now in Sereni (1966).

Sereni, Emilio (1966), *Capitalismo e mercato nazionale*, Roma: Editori Riuniti.

Serpieri, Arrigo (1910), *Il contratto agrario e le condizioni dei contadini dell'Alto Milanese*, Milano: Soc. Umanitaria.

Serpieri, Arrigo (1930), *La guerra e le classi rurali italiane*, Bari: Laterza.

Somogyi, Giovanni (1959), 'Cento anni di bilanci familiari in Italia, (1857–1956)', *Annali Feltrinelli*, **II**, pp. 121–257.

Somogyi, Giovanni (1966), *La bilancia alimentare dell'Italia*, Bologna: Il Mulino.

Sori, Ercole (1973), 'Assetto e redistribuzione della popolazione italiana 1861–1961', in Toniolo (1973), pp. 283–323.

Sori, Ercole (1979), *L'emigrazione italiana dall'Unità alla Seconda Guerra Mondiale*, Bologna: Il Mulino.

Spinelli, Franco (1988), 'Pasquale Jannaccone: a neglected originator of the monetary approach to balance of payments and exchange rates', *Journal of European Economic History*, **17** (3), pp. 665–97.

Spinelli, Franco and Fratianni, Michele (1990), *Storia monetaria d'Italia*, Milano: A. Mondadori.

Spinelli, Luciana (1985), 'Disciplina di fabbrica e lavoro femminile: le operaie della manifattura dei tabacchi (1900–1914)', *Società e storia*, pp. 319–72.

Supino, Camillo (1929), *Storia della circolazione cartacea in Italia dal 1860 al 1928*, Milano: Soc. ed. Libraria.

Sylos Labini, Paolo (1973), 'Aspetti dello sviluppo economico', in ID, *Problemi dello sviluppo economico*, Bari: Laterza, 1972, pp. 105–96.

Tattara, Giuseppe (1980), 'Protezione effettiva e sviluppo di alcuni settori dell'industria manifatturiera italiana dal 1921 al 1930', *Studi economici*, no. 11, pp. 82–151.

Tattara, Giuseppe (1985), 'An example of countertrade: the Anglo-Italian clearing', *Rivista di storia economica*, n.s., **2**, International issue, pp. 115–54.

Tattara, Giuseppe and Piva, Francesco (1983), *I primi operai di Marghera*, Padova: Marsilio.

Tattara, Giuseppe and Toniolo, Gianni (1976), 'L'industria manifatturiera: cicli, politiche e mutamenti di struttura (1921–1937)', in Ciocca and Toniolo (1976), pp. 103–70.

Tena, Antonio (1989), 'On the accuracy of foreign trade statistics', *Rivista di storia economica*, n.s., **6**, pp. 87–112.

Tena, Antonio (1992), 'Proteccion y competitividad en España u Italia 1890–1960', in V. Zamagni and L. Prados de la Escosura (eds), *El desarrollo económico de la Europa de Sur: España e Italia en perspectiva histórica*, Madrid: Alianza Editorial, pp. 321–55.

Tilly, Richard (1986), 'German banking 1850–1914: developmental assistance for the strong', *Journal of European Economic History*, **15**, pp. 113–52.

Toniolo, Gianni (1973) (ed.), *Lo sviluppo economico italiano 1861–1940*, Bari: Laterza.

Toniolo, Gianni (1977), 'Effective protection and industrial growth: the case of italian engineering', *Journal of European Economic History*, **VI**, pp. 659–73.

Toniolo, Gianni (1980), *L'economia dell'Italia fascista*, Bari: Laterza.

Toniolo, Gianni (1988), *Storia economica dell'Italia liberale*, Bologna: Il Mulino.

Toniolo, Gianni (1989) (ed.), *La Banca d'Italia e l'economia di guerra*, Bari: Laterza.

Tremelloni, Roberto (1937), *L'industria tessile italiana*, Torino: Einaudi.

Treves, Anna (1976), *Le migrazioni interne nell'Italia fascista*, Torino: Einaudi.

Vasta, Michelangelo (1990), 'Innovazioni e sviluppo economico: l'uso dei brevetti nell'analisi del settore elettrotecnico italiano nel periodo 1895–1914', *Rivista di storia economica*, n.s., **7**, pp. 47–74.

Villani, Pasquale (1989) (ed.), *La pluriattività negli spazi rurali*, monographic issue of Annali dell'Istituto G. Cervi.

Villari, Lucio (1966), 'Per la storia del protezionismo in Italia', *Studi Storici*, a. 7, pp. 483–500 e 651–63.

Vitale, Egidio (1972), *La riforma degli istituti di emissione e gli scandali bancari in Italia 1892–1896*, Roma: Camera dei Deputati.

Vivarelli, Roberto (1990), 'La questione contadina nell'Italia Unita', *Rivista storica italiana*, **CII**, pp. 87–165.

Warglien, Massimo (1985), 'Nota sull'investimento industriale in macchinari ed altre attrezzature meccaniche Italia 1881–1913', *Rivista di storia economica*, n.s., **2**, pp. 125–46.

Warglien, Massimo (1987), 'Investimenti industriali e instabilità finanziaria in Italia 1878–1913', *Rivista di storia economica*, n.s., **3**, pp. 384–439.

Webster, Richard A. (1974a), *L'imperialismo industriale italiano*, Torino: Einaudi.

Webster, Richard A. (1974b), 'The political and industrial strategies of a mixed investment bank: Italian industrial financing and the Banca Commerciale', in *Viertel jahrschrift fur sozial un wirtschaftgeschichte*, pp. 321–71.

Zamagni, Vera (1973), 'Istruzione e sviluppo economico in Italia, 1861–1913', in Toniolo (1973), pp. 187–240.

Zamagni, Vera (1975), 'Le radici agricole del dualismo italiano', *Nuova rivista storica*, **LIX**, pp. 55–99.

Zamagni, Vera (1976), 'La dinamica dei salari nel settore industriale', in Ciocca and Toniolo (1976).

Zamagni, Vera (1978), *Industrializzazione e squilibri regionali*, Bologna: Il Mulino.

Zamagni, Vera (1979–80), 'Distribuzione del reddito e classi sociali nell'Italia fra le due guerre', *Annali Feltrinelli*, **XX**, pp. 17–50.

Zamagni, Vera (1980), 'The rich in a late industrializer: the case of Italy 1800–1945', in W.D. Rubinstein (ed.), *Wealth and the Wealthy in the Modern World*, London: Croom Helm.
Zamagni, Vera (1981), *Lo stato italiano e l'economia*, Firenze: Le Monnier.
Zamagni, Vera (1983), 'Ferrovie e integrazione del mercato nazionale nell'Italia post-unitaria', in AA. VV., *Studi in onore di Gino Barbieri*, Verona: IPEM, Vol. 3, pp. 1635–49.
Zamagni, Vera (1984a), 'Sui salari industriali nell'età giolittiana', *Rivista di storia economica*, n.s., **I**, pp. 183–221.
Zamagni, Vera (1984b), 'Le alterazioni nella distribuzione del reddito in Italia nell'immediato dopoguerra, (1919–1922)', in AA. VV., *La transizione dall'economia di guerra all'economia di pace in Italia e in Germania dopo la prima guerra mondiale*, Bologna: Il Mulino, pp. 509–32.
Zamagni, Vera (1987), 'Cuestion meridional o cuestion nacional? Algunas consideraciones sobre el desequilibrio regional en Italia', *Revista de historia economica*, **V**, pp. 11–29.
Zamagni, Vera (1988), Il debito pubblico in Italia', in Ministero del tesoro, *Relazione del Direttore generale alla Commissione Parlamentare di vigilanza. Il debito pubblico in Italia 1861–1987*, Roma Poligrafico dello stato.
Zamagni, Vera (1990a), *Dalla periferia al centro*, Bologna: Il Mulino.
Zamagni, Vera (1990b), 'L'industria chimica in Italia', in F. Amatori and B. Bezza (eds), *Montecatini 1888–1966*, Bologna: Il Mulino.
Zamagni, Vera (ed.) (1991a), *Dall'ammoniaca ai nuovi materiali*, Bologna: Il Mulino.
Zamagni, Vera (1991b), 'Industrial wages and workers' protest in Italy during the "biennio rosso" (1919–1921)', *Journal of European Economic History*, **20**, pp. 137–53.
Zamagni, Vera (1992), 'Debito pubblico e creazione di un nuovo apparato fiscale nell'Italia unificata (1861–1876)', in AA. VV., *Il disavanzo pubblico in Italia: natura strutturale e politiche di rientro*, Vol. II, Bologna; Il Mulino, pp. 9–94.
Zamagni, Vera (1993), *L'offerta di istruzione in Italia 1861–1987: un fattore guida dello sviluppo o un ostacolo?*, mimeo.

[1]

Excerpt from Alexander Gerschenkron, *Economic Backwardness in Historical Perspective: A Book of Essays*, 72–89.

4

Notes on the Rate of Industrial Growth in Italy, 1881–1913

It is obvious that in the decades following its political unification Italy's economy remained very backward in relation not only to that of England, but also to the economies of industrially advancing countries on the continent of Europe. The same conclusion will result, whatever gauge one may choose for the purposes of comparison, be it qualitative descriptions of technological equipment, organizational efficiency, and labor skills in individual enterprises; or scattered quantitative data on relative productivity in certain branches of industry; or the numbers of persons employed in industry; or the density of the country's railroad network; or the standards of literacy of its population. It is true that there were very large differences in this respect among the individual regions of the Peninsula; but according to Pantaleoni's computations, which — subject to a considerable margin of error as they are — probably give a correct idea of the order of magnitudes involved, the private per-capita wealth of the richest and most advanced areas in northern Italy in the second half of the eighties was still very much below one half of the contemporaneous figure for France as a whole.[1]

At the same time, it is equally undeniable that by 1914 a great industrial transformation had taken place in Italy. Under these

[1] Maffeo Pantaleoni, "Delle regioni d'Italia in ordine alla loro ricchezza ed al loro carico tributario," *Scritti varii di economia*, 3rd ser. (Rome, 1910), pp. 242, 252.

circumstances, it seemed legitimate to inquire whether and to what extent the processes of industrialization, when at length launched in the country, betrayed the same characteristic features as those displayed by other relatively backward European countries of the nineteenth century. In other words, the present writer approached the Italian material with a series of historical questions or expectations in mind, some of which may be summarized as follows:

1. The process of modern industrialization in conditions of considerable economic backwardness was likely to assume at a fairly early stage the form of a big initial push, showing a relatively high rate of industrial growth. The beginning of such a period may have been aided by coinciding with the turning point at the bottom of an international cycle, but the push was specifically "long-term" in its nature and therefore not coterminous with short-run fluctuations: once begun, it was likely to make the country fairly immune to the next cyclical recession.

2. In the course of such an initial industrial upsurge, a backward country typically tended to favor output of producers' goods as against that of consumers' goods because in conditions of the period it happened to be in the field of the former that recent technological process had been most rapid. Heavy industries, therefore, offered far-reaching opportunities for utilizing as far as possible the advantages inherent in a late arrival upon the industrial stage.

3. Along with the productive structure of industry, its organizational structure was also likely to be affected in the direction of a considerable stress on concentration in various forms.

4. These basic features of delayed industrializations were likely to be reinforced by the use of specific institutional instruments, such as the investment policies of banks and various policies of the state. In cases of very great backwardness the role of the government was more prominent and the banks did not participate in the process until a certain degree of industrial progress had been achieved.

The following pages, then, purport to discuss the process of Italian industrialization before 1914 in terms of its conformity with, or deviation from, the pattern just described. Admittedly, this is a rather narrow approach and, in addition, only a few of the pertinent aspects of the problem can be touched upon here.

ECONOMIC BACKWARDNESS IN HISTORICAL PERSPECTIVE

I

The approach as sketched in the preceding section called first of all for some measurement of the rate of growth of Italian industry during the period under review. It necessitated, therefore, the construction of an index of Italian industrial output for the years 1881–1913, the choice of the initial year being essentially determined by statistical availability.

A detailed description of the index has been included in this volume (see Appendix I). The reader will find there, along with a complete statement on source materials and methods of computation (some of which unfortunately had to be rather involved), some critical evaluation of the deficiencies of that index as well as a comparison with some previous attempts in the same direction by French and Italian scholars. Let it therefore be mentioned briefly that the index comprises six main series which have been combined by using as weights the writer's estimates of value added pertaining to the years 1902–1903.[2]

There is no question that the paucity of the underlying data and the manifold uncertainties of the weighing process detract seriously from the value of the computations. Nevertheless, it seems that the index serves sufficiently the present purpose, which is to obtain a general view of the speed of the Italian industrialization in various periods and subperiods before 1914.

Table 1 shows the aggregate index for the whole period. The development of the six index industries over the period is presented in Table 2.

[2] The six series are:
(1) mining,
(2) metalmaking,
(3) engineering,
(4) textiles,
(5) chemicals,
(6) foodstuffs.

Also two alternative computations based on weights derived from data on employment and horsepower, respectively, have been prepared. The results as presented in the following are all in terms of an index based on value-added weights.

Table 1. Index of Italian industrial output, 1881–1913

1881	54	1891	67	1901	104	1911	174
1882	57	1892	64	1902	109	1912	182
1883	64	1893	70	1903	114	1913	184
1884	63	1894	72	1904	117		
1885	65	1895	73	1905	126		
1886	67	1896	75	1906	139		
1887	73	1897	78	1907	152		
1888	74	1898	86	1908	163		
1889	72	1899	92	1909	168		
1890	72	1900	100	1910	169		

Table 2. Index of output of six industries, 1881–1913
(1900 = 100)

Year	Mining	Metalmaking	Textiles	Engineering	Chemicals	Foodstuffs
1881	71	22	54	62	9	63
1882	79	18	53	76	11	65
1883	80	27	62	92	13	68
1884	77	25	58	90	15	70
1885	77	40	61	94	17	69
1886	72	55	65	98	20	68
1887	68	66	73	118	22	67
1888	70	91	73	115	24	67
1889	71	119	71	96	26	69
1890	72	91	80	79	28	71
1891	76	72	73	62	28	70
1892	82	56	72	53	27	68
1893	80	67	85	58	26	69
1894	79	65	93	59	31	65
1895	72	68	93	62	42	66
1896	79	70	94	62	49	67
1897	90	77	93	65	56	69
1898	92	95	101	72	61	80
1899	88	101	104	89	72	86
1900	100	100	100	100	100	100
1901	103	103	105	100	102	106
1902	100	99	114	98	110	111
1903	107	120	111	108	115	120
1904	106	127	119	121	121	112
1905	108	170	124	144	132	115
1906	103	212	136	171	159	119
1907	99	218	153	196	185	122
1908	98	283	142	247	228	127
1909	93	346	136	261	257	128
1910	95	374	122	276	281	130
1911	89	377	128	287	260	141
1912	96	392	142	280	276	146
1913	98	381	134	272	281	166

The choice of subperiods into which a fairly long stretch of growth should be divided is necessarily arbitrary. For the purposes of a presentation that aims at isolating the big upsurge, an inspection of the data seems to yield the following division:

1881–1888 Moderate growth
1888–1896 Stagnation
1896–1908 Very rapid growth
1908–1913 Reduced rate of growth

The rates of growth implied in the index for these subperiods are given in Table 3.

Table 3. Annual average rates of growth of Italian industrial output for 1881–1913 and subperiods

Period	Percentage change
1881–1888	4.6
1888–1896	.3
1896–1908	6.7
1908–1913	2.4
1881–1913	3.8

Note: computed on the assumption of a geometric rate of growth between the first and the last years of the specified periods.

Table 4 presents, for the same periods, the rates of growth implied in the indices of output of the six industrial groups.

Table 4. Annual average rates of growth of the six index industries for 1881–1913 and subperiods (percentage change)

Industry	1881–1888	1888–1896	1896–1908	1908–1913	1881–1913
Mining	0.0	1.3	1.8	0.0	1.0
Metalmaking	22.0	−3.2	12.4	6.1	9.3
Textiles	4.4	3.2	3.5	−1.2	2.5
Engineering	9.2	−7.4	12.2	2.0	4.7
Chemicals	15.1	9.4	13.7	1.8	11.3
Foodstuffs	.9	0.0	5.5	5.5	3.1

Note: see Table 3, note.

THE RATE OF INDUSTRIAL GROWTH IN ITALY

II

One point seems to emerge with sufficient clarity from the data contained in the preceding tabulations: Italy did have its period of a big industrial push. While there may be some questions concerning the exact choice of the initial and terminal years for the individual subperiods, it seems appropriate to locate the period of the great push between the years 1896 and 1908. Before 1896 lay the years of a laborious return from the low of 1892 to the level of 1888. After 1908, the rates of growth of all the index industries but one were greatly reduced.

Rather characteristic for such a period of "long-term" growth is the ease with which it rode horse and foot across the intervening depression of 1900. It may be instructive in this connection to take a glance at Wesley Mitchell's diagrammatic "Conspectus of Business Cycles in Various Countries" for the period concerned.[3] The United States and Canada remained untouched by the depression of 1900, but elsewhere its effects were grave, particularly on the continent of Europe. It broke the back of the long industrial push in Russia and it affected severely the countries in Central Europe which, as a result of the long tariff war with France, had become Italy's principal trading partners. There is little doubt that the capacity of these countries to absorb Italian exports was considerably diminished; at the same time, the competition of their industrial products with domestic goods in Italian markets was intensified. And yet the effect on Italian industrial development, although discernible, seemed almost negligible. Very similarly, a few years earlier Russia, then in the midst of her great industrial upsurge, felt no more than a light ripple of the wave of the severe international depression of the early nineties; her rate of industrial growth remained unaffected on the whole.[4]

At the same time, the period was characterized by a rapid increase in the share of producers' goods in total output, even though to some extent the change must reflect the workings of the accelerator. This is shown clearly in Tables 2 and 4. For the six index industries,

[3] Wesley Mitchell, *Business Cycles: The Problem and its Setting* (New York, 1927), p. 445.

[4] Alexander Gerschenkron, "The Rate of Industrial Growth in Russia since 1885," *The Tasks of Economic History*, Supplement VII (1947), 151.

that share was 28 percent of the index total (using value-added weights) in 1896. It had been at the same level in 1881, although 1888 showed a higher percentage. But by 1908 the share of producer goods, so computed, had jumped to 43 percent and was to reach 47 percent in 1913.

All this is quite in accordance with the expectations set forth in section one of this essay. This, no doubt, is comforting. But the disappointments are just around the corner.

It is implied in what has been said earlier that the rate of growth in a backward country during the early periods of its industrialization may be assumed to vary directly with the degree of the country's industrial backwardness. The more belated the big industrial upswing, the stronger it is likely to be when it comes. It seems that, considering the great delays in Italian industrialization on the one hand and similar periods in other countries on the other, the rate of industrial growth in Italy during 1896 and 1908 was lower than what might have been expected. It may be noted that Germany of the nineties was far beyond its period of initial growth and still its annual average rate of industrial growth for the years 1888–1896 amounted to almost 5.5 percent, which was indeed lower than the Italian rate in 1896–1908 but not very significantly so. When it comes to countries like Sweden, Russia, or Japan, the pertinent rates are a good deal higher than the Italian rate. Swedish industry grew at a pace of almost 12 percent a year between 1888 and 1896; Japan, between 1907 and 1913, showed an annual rate of growth of 8.5 percent; Russia of the nineties increased its industrial output at the rate of more than 8 percent a year.[5]

True, comparisons of this sort are precarious and too great a reliance on them is hardly warranted. But this is not the whole story. The method of computing rates of growth as used in the foregoing fastens attention on the initial and terminal years of each period and does not take into account the history of the intervening years. An inspection of the behavior of the index in the course of the period 1896–1908 suggests some differences as compared with cases of the

[5] The German and Swedish rates have been computed from data given in *Industrialization and Foreign Trade* (League of Nations, 1945). For the Russian and Japanese rates, see Gerschenkron, p. 156.

great spurt in other European countries: the industrial growth in Italy, while free from any severe setbacks, seems to have proceeded in a less uniform and more jerky fashion, denoting perhaps a more delicate state of public confidence and greater entrepreneurial uncertainties and hesitations. It may be useful to ponder a little some of the reasons that may have prevented Italy's big industrial push from displaying its full potential force.

III

It is not intended, of course, to supply here a comprehensive list of all the retarding forces that may have influenced the industrial development of Italy around the turn of the century. Anything beginning with the poor endowment of natural resources and ending with the mysteries of national or regional character might legitimately go on such a list. Such a broad discussion would overstep the limits set to this paper and probably not shed much additional light on its specific subject. The purpose of this section is rather to concentrate upon those factors that may be of some significance from the point of view of the general pattern of development as described earlier.

As mentioned before, the historical experience of European countries seems to warrant the generalization that in cases of very considerable backwardness the policies of the state tended to play a very important positive role during the years of the big upsurge of industrial development. In the classical case of Count Witte's Russia of the nineties, it would seem altogether meaningful to regard the policies of the government as the strategic factor, primarily responsible for the great spurt in industrialization of the period. Nothing comparable seems to have taken place in Italy. Not that the successive Italian governments showed no interest in the industrial future of the country. At one time or another, the government helped to launch some important industrial enterprises, the huge steelworks at Terni (1884) being perhaps the outstanding example. Government orders did play some role in the development of Italian industry. There was the policy of subsidies to shipbuilding and navigation which was initiated in 1885[6] and extended in a somewhat revised

[6] See "Legge concernante la marina mercantile," *Raccolta ufficiale delle leggi e dei decreti del Regno d'Italia*, LXXIX, no. 3547 (December 6, 1885).

form in 1896; there was the partial waiving of governmental royalties flowing from the iron-ore mines on Elba. State aid of this nature there certainly was; yet what strikes the observer of these policies is not only their desultory character, not only the fact that they were rather less than more in appearance during the period of the great push of 1896–1908, but primarily the onesided nature of the government's interest in industrial development — that is to say, its concentration on the least deserving branches of industrial activity.

The ineptness of governmental industrialization policies becomes quite obvious as one moves from the measures just mentioned to a consideration of the Italian tariff, which must be viewed as the real *pièce de résistance* of those policies. One might rightly wonder how much importance one should in general ascribe to tariff policies in the history of European industrializations. In some cases it was not the tariff, but its abandonment, or at least reduction, that opened the road to industrialization. In other cases, the tariff seemed subordinate to the great variety of more direct and more vigorous measures that were taken by the government. At any rate, it would seem difficult to attribute much positive influence to the tariff structure that existed in Italy during her big industrial upswing. In fact, it is more reasonable to regard that tariff as one of the obstacles in the road of the Italian industrialization.

The pillars of Italian protectionism were three: grain, cotton textiles, and iron and steel. In the case of grain the march of protection began in 1887 when the tariff on wheat was raised from a nominal level to 3 lire per quintal. The first step was taken gingerly. Uncandidly, the purpose of the increase was said to be a purely fiscal one.[7] The lawmakers' consciences were far from easy. The measure was unpopular and had to be adopted against the recommendations of the detailed report prepared by the special parliamentary committee on Agrarian Inquiry.[8] But thereby the dam was broken.

[7] See the speech by Minister of Finance Magliani, July 5, 1887, *Camera dei Senatori, Discussioni*, Sessione 1886–87 (Rome, 1887), p. 1461.

[8] "Atti della Giunta per la inchiesta agraria e sulle condizioni della classe agricola," *Relazione finale sui resultati dell'inchiesta redatta per incarico della Giunta dal Presidente, Conte Stefano Jacini* (Rome, 1884), XV, Fascicolo I; also, "Atti della Commissione d'Inchiesta per la revisione della tariffa doganale," *Relazione del Senatore Lampertico* (Rome, 1885), I. *Parte Agraria*, Fascicolo I, p. 184.

Further increases followed, and by 1895, with a duty of 7.50 lire per quintal, Italy's wheat production had become the most heavily protected among the major countries of the continent.[9] True, this policy was part and parcel of a widespread European response to changed conditions of wheat supply in the world markets. But two things must be remembered. On the one hand, Italy's agriculture had at its disposal methods of adjustment that were not available to an equal degree north of the Alpine wall; on the other hand, if Germany with its rapidly developing industry could afford (economically, not politically) the luxury of agrarian protectionism, Italy with its much less favorable conditions never should have dared subject the tender plant of its industrial growth to the rigors of a protectionist climate in agriculture.

But what about the industrial side of the tariff? It need not be gainsaid that, at least in principle, Italy's industrialization could have been aided by a rationally conceived and executed tariff. Such policies would have had to start from the basic fact that in a historical period in which coal exercised the main locational pull, a country deprived of the mineral, forced to obtain it (on an average) at a price twice as high as that in the coalmining countries, and thus laboring under the disadvantage of high cost in industry and transportation, should have concentrated on those branches of industrial endeavor in which the expenditure for coal was small in relation to other cost items. Furthermore, a backward country, so disabled, should have felt particularly keenly the need to promote output of new products and new industries. The vast and variegated area of engineering offered the greatest promise in this respect.

What happened in fact was the adoption in 1878 of a tariff chiefly devoted to the protection of cotton textiles and ferrous metalmaking. The former was an old industry with a moderate rate of modern technological progress and accordingly relatively limited possibilities in a backward country on the European continent; the

[9] Ghino Valenti, *Granaglie, produzione, commercio, regime doganale*, Comitato nazionale per le tariffe doganale e per i trattati di commercio (Rome, 1920), p. 97; and H. Liepmann, *Tariff Levels and the Economic Unity of Europe* (London, 1938), pp. 64, 68, 72, 81, 87. In 1913, the Italian wheat duty amounted to 41.5 percent ad valorem. The corresponding figures for France, Germany, and Austria were 34.5, 38, and 36 percent, respectively.

latter was a coal-consuming industry par excellence. While a variety of engineering products was included in the tariff, the rates imposed on those products as a rule were such as to provide the machinery industry at best with a partial compensation for the duties accorded to iron and steel.[10]

It is true that the rates on machinery were generally increased in 1887. The cases of protectionism in reverse were eliminated and a margin of genuine protection created. But that margin, if computed ad valorem, was almost negligible. Moreover, it should be noted that the important branches of textile and agricultural machinery came to be protected by duties hardly in excess of those on steel; that the rates on machine parts were very low, thus encouraging assembling of machines rather than their production within the country; that, finally, the rate on "nonspecified" machinery — the very area of innovations — was particularly low. None of this should cause surprise, since tariff makers everywhere as a rule protected the existing and vocal interests, while the promise of future innovations tended to lie beyond their range of vision.[11] As one follows the parliamentary debates on the tariff of 1887, one is struck by the fact that it was with respect to engineering alone that the speakers found it advisable to pay their respects to the liberal tradition inherited from Cavour. That tradition was quickly forgotten as soon as they turned to cotton textiles and iron and steel.[12] But this is not the end of the story. During the debates, Minister Magliani promised that the excesses of the Tariff Act would be mitigated in the course of the subsequent negotiations on commercial treaties.[13] Yet, if a generaliza-

[10] Thus, for example, the rate on steel was 10 lire per quintal while that on locomotives was 10, that on railroad freight cars 9, and on steam engines 8 lire per quintal. "Legge che approva la tariffa doganale d'importazione e d'esportazione," *Raccolta ufficiale delle leggi e dei decreti del Regno d'Italia*, LIII, no. 439 (May 30, 1878).

[11] "Legge che riforma la tariffa doganale," *Raccolta ufficiale delle leggi e dei decreti del Regno d'Italia*, Parte Principale, Series 3a, LXXXV, no. 4703 (July 14, 1887).

[12] A good example among many is the Report of the Committee on Tariff Inquiry, the industrial part of which was written by V. Ellena: "Atti della Commissione d'Inchiesta per la revisione della tariffa doganale," II. Parte Industriale, *Relazione del Deputato V. Ellena* (Rome, 1886), 242, 361, 420.

[13] Atti parlamentari, Camera dei Senatori, Sessione 1886–87, July 9, 1887 (Rome, 1887), p. 1621. Incidentally, a few weeks earlier, in order to allay the un-

tion is possible with regard to those treaties, it is this: the duties on cotton textiles and ferrous metals remained substantially unchanged or at best were slightly changed. The great field of tariff concessions was supplied precisely by the duties on machinery where the slim margins established in 1887 were reduced and sometimes eliminated.[14] The Italian machinery industry was largely left to its own devices.

When in addition it is noted that the equally promising field of the chemical industry, pregnant with many innovational possibilities and well suited to the conditions of the country, was quite ignored by the tariff makers of 1887, the conclusion seems justified that the main action of government policies in the field of Italian industrialization was likely to retard rather than promote its development. The Italian government's participation in, and contribution to, the big industrial push in the country certainly fell far short of what one might have expected on the basis of the industrial history of other backward countries such as Russia or Hungary.[15]

---

easiness of the Lower Chamber with regard to the lopsidedness of the tariff, it was promised that an opportunity for revising the rates on machinery would be provided when the House reconvened after the summer vacation. Such a revision never was undertaken. See Atti del Parlamento Italiano, Camera dei Deputati, Sessione 1886–87, June 23, 1887 (Rome, 1887), p. 3967.

[14] See, for example, in *Trattati e convenzioni fra il Regno d'Italia e gli altri stati:* treaty with Austria-Hungary, December 6, 1891, XII (Rome, 1892); treaty with Switzerland, April 19, 1892, XIV (Rome, 1895), and July 7, 1904, XVII (Rome, 1907); treaty with Germany, December 3, 1904, XVII (Rome, 1907); treaty with Austria-Hungary, February 11, 1906, XVIII (Rome, 1930).

[15] In his interesting article ("The North-South Differential in Italian Economic Development," *Journal of Economic History,* XXI, no. 3, 314), Richard Eckaus is reluctant to accept this negative appraisal of the Italian tariff because the rates of growth of output in cotton textiles and iron and steel were higher than the average rate of growth for the index-number industries as a whole. But obviously what is called for is a historical judgment rather than a mechanically arithmetical one. The trouble lay precisely in the fact that unsuitable industries were allowed to grow fast at the expense of others. A historian has to take into account not only the impasse in which the unduly swollen cotton industry found itself by the end of the index period, but also the fact that flooding the country with expensive domestic steel necessarily retarded the growth of those branches of industry whose potentialities were great indeed. Considering the magnitudes involved, it is very reasonable to assume that, given lower prices of raw materials and shifts in capital allocations in the proper direction, the rate of growth of the young industrial branches, particularly in engineering, would have been a multiple of the one actually achieved. [A. G., 1962]

Another weakness of the Italian industrialization of 1896–1908 may have derived from the fact that by that time the great period of Italian railroad building was largely a thing of the past. During the years of the great Russian industrialization, 1886–1900, the railroad network increased by more than 70 percent. There is little doubt that during that period the railroads were the fulcrum around which the industrial level of the country was being rapidly lifted. By contrast, the accretion to the Italian railroads during the years 1896–1908 amounted to less than 10 percent. Special circumstances in Italy tended to accentuate the difference. The law of 1885 by which the operation of state-owned railroads was entrusted to three private companies for a period of sixty years foreshadowed a possible discontinuation of the arrangement after only twenty years. The uncertainties created by this provision greately influenced the investment policies of the companies in the last eight or ten years before 1905, the year in which the agreements could, and in fact did, expire. Partly for this reason, the flow of capital into the special investment funds established under the Act of 1885 was hesitant and insufficient.[16] True, after 1905, when the operation of the railroad system had reverted to the state, ambitious plans were launched to modernize and to expand tracks and rolling stock. These plans, however, matured in the last years of the period 1896–1908 and came too late to change its general character.

One is free to argue that the early completion of the bulk of railroad building was likely to benefit the country's industrialization in subsequent years by releasing to industry capital that otherwise may have been attracted to railroads. But the argument does not carry much force. For the implicit assumption of a unified capital market in Italy seems to do violence to the actually existing conditions. Many a large-scale investor who stood ready to purchase railroad bonds issued or guaranteed by the government was most reluctant to engage his funds in industrial ventures. At the turn of the century, Giulio Einaudi found strong words to castigate this attitude

[16] As a result, a special provision of that act under the terms of which the railroads were compelled to afford an additional preference of five percent to domestic suppliers remained rather ineffective. "Legge per l'esercizio delle reti mediterranea, adriatica e sicula, e per la costruzione delle strade ferrate complementari," *Raccolta ufficiale,* Art. 21, LXXV, no. 3048 (April 27, 1885).

of "veneration of 4 percent." [17] The small saver who took his money to the branches of the Postal Savings System or to cooperative banks was even more security-minded; accordingly, his funds went into short-term commercial loans or into financing of public works by municipalities and provinces. It is significant in this connection that the period 1896–1908 was characterized by massive repatriation of Italian securities held abroad. The compartmentalization of the Italian capital market was great, and herein lay one of the specific functions of the big investment banks, whose role is touched upon in the concluding paragraphs of this essay.[18] Thus, absence of large railroad investments did not necessarily mean increased capital availabilities to industry, and the failure of the industrial "push" to coincide with a period of "railroad fever" with its specific stimulations to industrial activities may well have kept the rate of industrial growth below what it would have been, had the Russian situation reproduced itself in Italy.

Another factor, which tends to point in the same direction, deserves mention here. The political situation in Italy at the beginning of the period 1896–1908 was not propitious to quiet economic growth. The disastrous harvest of 1897, coupled with the government's prolonged hesitations to suspend or to reduce the wheat duties, led in the course of the *anno terribile* — 1898 — to unrest and disorders in several regions. These disturbances culminated in the Milan insurrection in May of that year and were followed by two years of repressive policies under the Pelloux governments. Then came the electoral shift of 1900 and the regicide of the same year. A new page in Italy's political history was opened. It was to be overshadowed by the genius of Giovanni Giolitti's conciliatory statesmanship. An integral part of his policy of pacification was the government's adherence to the principle of strict neutrality in wage conflicts. Consequently, the strike waves rose to quite unprecedented heights. Between 1901 and 1913 there was only one year when the number

[17] *Un principe mercante, Studio nell' espansione coloniale Italiana* (Turin, 1900), p. 160. A translation into English of this fascinating essay in entrepreneurial economic history by the former President of the Italian Republic would seem very desirable.

[18] See also, Epicarmo Corbino, *Annali dell'economia italiana*, V, 1901–1914 (Citta di Castello, 1938), 423f.

of days lost by strikes remained below the million mark; in some years of the period it exceeded three and was under four million.[19]

Few would begrudge the poverty-ridden Italian laborer the resulting very modest improvements in his economic position. But the difference in historical situations must be pointed out. While in other countries a period of very rapid industrial growth tended to be *followed by* a period of upward adjustments in the standard of living, in Italy the two processes tended to coincide. Had the industrial upsurge in Italy taken place one or two decades earlier, in all likelihood it would have been much less disturbed by industrial strife. Great delays in industrialization do tend to be compensated for by the rapidity of the ensuing development. Yet the two factors just discussed seem to suggest that the validity of this generalization does not transcend certain limits. Along with the advantages of being late, there are also many definite disadvantages to being very late — a point that may deserve special attention with regard to the underdeveloped countries of our time.

In speaking of the possible sources of the relative weakness of the Italian industrialization of 1896–1908, one final remark may be in order. In studying the periods of rapid initial industrialization of the major countries in Europe, one does not find it too difficult to discern some specific industrialization ideologies under the auspices of which the development proceeded: economic liberalism in England, Saint-Simonism in France, nationalism in Germany, Marxism in Russia of the nineties, all seem to have performed a function in the process and to have performed it well. What strikes the observer of the comparable Italian development is the absence of any strong ideological stimulus to industrialization. Cavour's *liberismo* belonged to an era that was gone. Italian protectionism was an instrument of vested interests and failed to develop into a strong intellectual movement. The nineties in Italy were indeed a period in which Marxism seemed to have captivated the imagination of large strata of the Italian intelligentsia.[20] Some aspects of this sudden ideological swing do

[19] See *Annuario Statistico*, 1905–1907, p. 840; 1911, pp. 234–36; and 1915, pp. 313–14.

[20] Benedetto Croce, *Storia d'Italia dal 1871 al 1915* (Bari, 1953), p. 157. Croce himself was, of course, a case in point.

evoke comparisons with contemporaneous events in Russia. But, unlike the Russians, the Italian Marxists showed, if at all, a very restrained interest in the problems of industrial evolution of the country, although, misguidedly and somewhat ashamedly, the leaders of the Italian labor movement did lend their support to the existing industrial-tariff structure. It is not at all clear that they, or the Italian public in general, had any desire to speed up the change that was afoot in the land.

The aggregate effect of these disabilities does not seem to be negligible. In particular, as one considers the ineptitudes of the Italian tariff structure, one cannot but marvel at what was actually achieved during those years within the engineering and chemical industries. The Italian entrepreneurs in those branches deserve praise indeed. But if one were to look for a single important factor that succeeded in offsetting at least some of the great obstacles to the country's industrialization, one could not fail to point to the role performed by the big Italian banks after 1895.

These banks were formed or reorganized after the disastrous banking crashes of the early nineties. The most important of them, the Banca Commerciale Italiana, was established in 1894 under German leadership and with German capital, including some Austrian and Swiss participation.[21]

In a sense, the moment was favorable. There were many industrial enterprises that the preceding storm had left stranded or drifting helplessly. They were content to accept the tutelage of the newcomers. Still the task of the latter was not light. The terrifying *vestigia* of the Credito Mobiliare and the Banca Generale — the two giant victims of the great catastrophe — remained unobliterated for a long time afterward. Burdened with these remembrances; surrounded by a distrustful public and an unfriendly scholarly opinion whose somewhat monotonous insistence on the need for prudence at times seemed to verge on folly; denounced as an instrument of foreign economic penetration; faced by the effects of tariff and subsidy policies which they could not ignore, the Italian banks enjoyed a much more limited

[21] These participations were part of an agreement among the founders designed to preclude institutions like the Austrian Credit-Anstalt from competing with the Banca Commerciale in the field of Italian investment.

freedom of action than their counterparts in Germany or Austria. To some extent their interest in cotton textiles and iron and steel was predetermined by governmental decisions, and it was these two industries that found themselves in difficulties after 1908. In the case of cotton it also may have been the German influence that, for some years at least, had guided the Italian banks into a line of activities in which the German banks at home traditionally showed much less interest. It is also true that the Italian banks may have shown more interest than they did in certain innovations such as automobiles. By and large, however, what took place in Italy was a deliberate application of techniques of investment banking as evolved in Germany in the course of attempts to overcome its own economic backwardness.

The Italian investment banks of the previous period, oriented as they were upon French patterns, had never been able to advance fully to the stage of "universal banks" and to become real "department stores" in the field of banking. This was rather dramatically shown by the futility of the attempt to transform the Credito Mobiliare into a commercial bank at a time when its operations were already fully obscured by the shadows of the approaching storm.[22] It is possible to surmise that the upsurge of 1896–1908 was largely made possible by the importation of the great economic innovation of German banking in its most developed and mature form. As in Germany, not only capital but a good deal of entrepreneurial guidance was channeled to the nascent and expanding industrial enterprises. As in Germany, the policy was to maintain an intimate connection with an industrial enterprise and to nurse it for a long time before introducing it to the capital market, which as often as not meant placing its stock among the banks' own clients.[23] As in Germany, the banks tried to influence and modernize the methods of interenterprise credit relations. As in Germany, they were ever eager to "discipline production" of industrial branches, which bland phrase meant reduction or abandonment of competition in favor of various monopolistic compacts.[24] On the

[22] Maffeo Pantaleoni, "La caduta del Credito Mobiliare Italiano," *Studi storici di economia* (Bologna, 1936), pp. 261ff.

[23] See, for example, Banca Commerciale Italiana, *Relazione del Consiglio d'Amministrazione* (Milan, 1905), p. 11.

[24] The literature on the activities of the Italian banks during the period under review is very scant. There is nothing even remotely comparable to Pantaleoni's great

other hand, it would be difficult to discover in Italy *serious* signs of a growing independence from the banks on the part of the industrial enterprises. Such tendencies became very strong in Germany after 1900. Their absence in pre-1914 Italy is not surprising and must be taken to reflect the belatedness of the country's industrialization effort. In these respects at least, the Italian case fits well into the general pattern of European industrialization in varying conditions of economic backwardness.

study of the Credito Mobiliare. The writer, however, had the privilege of access to at least a part of the archives of the Banca Commerciale.

[2]

Excerpt from Alexander Gerschenkron, *Continuity in History and Other Essays*, 98–127.

5

The Industrial Development of Italy: A Debate with Rosario Romeo

GERSCHENKRON: Needless to say, I greatly appreciate this opportunity to meet Rosario Romeo in person and to exchange ideas with him. The most fruitful way of starting the discussion would probably be for me to concentrate on those matters where certain disagreements exist between my views and his. For I could easily spend two or three hours talking about those aspects of his book with which I am in perfect agreement. By contrast, a quarter of an hour or so should suffice to circumscribe the area of my dissent. Thus I can be brief and leave Professor Romeo plenty of time for his rebuttal.

When I speak of disagreement or dissent, I have essentially two points in mind. First of all, there are concepts, or sets of concepts, which I find it difficult to accept. And proceeding from conceptual — or perhaps merely semantic — problems, I arrive at somewhat different evaluations of Italian industrial history. I should like therefore to say a word or two about our conceptual differences before discussing the substantive problems and the hard facts of industrial development.

The conceptual problems essentially relate to an old Marxian idea which of late has celebrated some well-deserved resuscitation in our literature. The reference is to the concept of original accumula-

Note. This debate, presented here in my translation from the Italian, was organized by Svimez and took place in Rome in July 1960. The book mentioned in the first paragraph is Romeo's *Risorgimento e capitalismo* (Bari, 1959); see also "Rosario Romeo and the Original Accumulation of Capital," in my *Economic Backwardness in Historical Perspective*, pp. 90–118.

tion of capital, also known as primitive or preliminary accumulation. Marx himself left the concept in a state of some confusion, as I have tried to point out elsewhere.[1] It was, however, an interesting idea and in fact an exciting historical intuition; it is regrettable that, after having presented a brief sketch, Marx abandoned the main line of approach and allowed himself to be deflected into a discussion of enclosures. This was a blind alley as far as the development of the concept was concerned, even though one can readily understand the political reasons that tempted and propelled Marx in that direction.

Naturally, everybody is his own master in forming his own concepts, and there are many possible ways to define the concept of original accumulation. I should like to present briefly three possible ways of looking at the phenomenon. First of all, we can define original accumulation in monetary terms, that is to say, as previously accumulated claims against current national income. "Previously" in this sense means not only that the accumulations result from past national income, but also that they antedate the period of industrialization. The accumulations must be in such a form that they can be readily converted into effective claims against current national income. When the time is ripe and "the hour of industrialization strikes," they can be quickly aroused from their prolonged sleep and put into active entrepreneurial hands to be used for the deflection of resources from production of consumers' goods to production of producers' goods. The function of original accumulation then is to change at a strategic moment the distribution of national income as between consumption and investment. What is implied in the concept is precisely the idea of the "hour that strikes," of the "strategic moment," that is to say, of the beginning of industrialization. Of course, there is something artificial in placing a dam of this sort across the continuous flow of history. In a way it is our own work. In speaking of "the beginning of industrialization," we assert that at this point certain definite changes have taken place, important enough for us to regard what lies beyond that point as a new historical period. It is in this sense, involving the plausibility of our historical judgment, that we speak of an original or previous accumulation.

1. *Economic Backwardness in Historical Perspective*, pp. 33–38.

But this is only one of the possible concepts. We can construct another one which has nothing to do with previously accumulated claims. The accumulation can derive from current income. If we persist in speaking of original accumulation, we do so because income to be devoted to the purpose of investment in industry comes from branches of the economy that are nonindustrial, we might say preindustrial. The originality or previousness of the accumulation then lies in its distinction from accumulation in a fully developed industrial economy, where industrial profits constitute the primary source of industrial investment. In this sense particularly there is something "previous" about savings derived from agriculture — the original branch of the economy — which are used to finance the new, nontraditional economic pursuits. This is still a monetary concept of accumulation, but it differs from the first *inter alia* because it does not involve any processes of forced savings. Depending on the circumstances, the concept may possess independent usefulness in clarifying historical sequences.

There is, finally, a third concept of original accumulation. Unlike the first two, it is not related to the sources but to the use made of the funds. If they are employed in sectors of the economy which in some sense can be regarded as specific preindustrial investments, that is to say, as a precondition or prerequisite to industrial development, then we may speak of previous accumulation — this time not in monetary terms, but in real terms and thus in a different and very specific sense. It seems to me that Romeo has ignored the first concept of original accumulation and has combined the second and third into a new unified concept, upon which he bestows the name of primitive accumulation of capital. So far so good. The procedure is perfectly sound and unexceptionable. As said before, any concept may do. The proof is in the eating, in the enlightenment that can be derived from the concept, and there is little doubt that Romeo has been able to make good use of his own conceptual creation.

Let me note in parentheses that Romeo's welding together of the two concepts of original accumulation has distinct advantages from the point of view of statistical measurement If we are faced with a situation where savings made in agriculture — be they voluntary or exacted through taxes — are channeled into other economic activities, it is very probable that, given appropriate statistics, we should be able to measure the quantitative importance of these processes with very little difficulty. But the first concept of original accumulation is much more refractory as far as empirical application is concerned. The concept involves forced savings in the specific sense of the term, and forced savings — whether a result of original accumulation or of credit creation by banks — entail changes in relative prices and, by the same token, require use of complicated and hazardous techniques of deflating current values. It is always precarious to estimate *ex ante* processes from *ex post* data. But the difficulties are not insuperable. And, at any rate, to say that a concept is difficult of application does not mean that it is in principle nonoperational. It can still be very illuminating even if it resists precise and comprehensive statistical measurement. We may still collect enough partial and approximate information to justify some meaningful conclusions and to enable us to say, for instance, that in England in a certain period a fair portion of financing of the nascent industrial enterprises was obtained by utilizing, in one form or another, previously accumulated wealth and by unleashing processes of forced savings with their specific effect on relative prices.

Returning now to Romeo's concept and to his application of it to the industrial history of Italy after the Unification, it seems to me that he is primarily interested in what nowadays is often described as "infrastructure." This is not a very elegant term. On the other hand, "social overhead capital," which may sound better, is rather misleading since it is never quite clear what actually is "social" and "overhead" about the stock of capital created in this fashion. And elegance apart, there is something all too suggestive or autosuggestive about the term "infrastructure." The moment you use it, things begin immediately to look impressively logical, in fact, much too logical to make for convincing history. There are things that are at the bottom and things that are on top, and naturally the former must come first. Who would think of starting a house with the roof? Clearly, you must start with the foundations. Similarly, development must begin with infrastructure to be followed by superstructure, that is, by constructing and equipping factories and hiring labor.

Before speaking of the empirical disabilities of this approach, let me say that Romeo's case is well defined. He shows clearly how in the 1860's and 1870's Italy succeeded in getting from agriculture, through voluntary contributions and taxes, funds that were used to finance railroad building. In this fashion, Romeo says, a prerequisite was created for the subsequent industrialization that took place in the eighties. The proof, then, of the whole argument is the spurt of the eighties.

The industrial expansion of the eighties has become somewhat controversial since the publication by Benedetto Barberi of his "Indagine statistica,"[2] according to which the decade of the eighties was marked, if anything, by a decline of output rather than by the considerable increase I believe to have ascertained through my own researches. But pending further research and the presentation of Barberi's computations, I see no reason to change my position and, accordingly, am quite willing to accept Romeo's view on the course of industrial events in the eighties. This then, as I see it, is Romeo's story of Italy's industrial development in the three decades after the Unification. I hope I have presented it fairly, and very fortunately he will be able here to correct any wrong impression of his views I may have given.

Now it seems to me that there are primarily two difficulties with Romeo's scheme, as I tried to point out in my earlier essay on the subject. First of all, there is the relative insignificance of the savings supplied by agriculture. I agree that agriculture did well in the first two decades after Unification and that there was a considerable expansion of agricultural output — this is out of dispute. What is dubious is the volume of savings made available; furthermore, neither the volume of public works nor that of investment in general was in any way remarkable during this period. In other words, the events that Romeo has described and their interrelationship are correctly observed, but their quantitative importance was much too small to have had any significant effect.

I should like to offer still another consideration, which I did not mention, but probably should have mentioned, in my essay. On the basis of my studies of industrial development and particularly of

2. "Indagine statistica sullo sviluppo del reddito nazionale dell'Italia dal 1861 al 1956," *Annali di statistica*, IX (Rome, 1957).

railroad construction, I have come to believe that the problem of capital supply for the railroads in European countries (France, Germany, Italy, and pre–1914 Russia) did not present extraordinary difficulties. I realize, of course, that railroad construction was an expensive business, and perhaps nowhere more so than in Italy. A few days ago I traveled once more by train from Bologna to Florence across the Apennines, and once more I could not help marveling at the tremendous achievement of burrowing those innumerable tunnels through the proud rock of the mountains. And yet, once the initial aversion to the innovation was overcome, funds to cover the stupendous cost were readily found. Not so in industry. While capital from foreign and domestic sources flowed into railroads, capital for industrial investment was timid and reluctant. This difference impressed me particularly in my observations of the Italian capital market as it operated around the turn of the century. The investors certainly had pronounced preferences for railroad securities over industrial paper. Hence the creation of the infrastructure was much less of a problem than is implied in Romeo's presentation.

I must return now to industrial development in the eighties, which plays such a crucial role in Romeo's scheme. In appraising that decade, much depends on the kind of spectacles through which one wishes to look at the events. If you favor rosy spectacles you might say: "After all, it was quite a spurt. True, the rate of growth was not very high but still, such as it was, it kept up for a fair number of years." On the other hand, using grey spectacles the picture you get is less encouraging. And there are good reasons for choosing the grey hue. There *is* such a thing as a great spurt of industrialization, which is not to be confused with normal cyclical fluctuations. A great spurt, a tidal wave, once it starts rolling, tends to pass through an international depression with almost no loss in speed and impetus. This at least is what we have learned from the industrial experience of Europe. Now what occurred in Italy in the eighties certainly was not a great spurt of the kind just described. The expansion went on for a while, then stopped and was followed by one of the most difficult decades in the economic history of the new state. Those years were marked by banking failures and a general lack of confidence in the economic future of the country. This situation led toward the end of the decade to widespread political unrest. Taking all this into consideration, it is difficult indeed, if not impossible, to describe the Italian experience of the eighties as a specific great spurt of industrial development. If, for example, Russian industrialization between 1885 and 1900 *was* a great spurt, then the Italian upswing of the eighties was a phenomenon of an altogether different order. Italy had to wait for another ten years, until 1895–96. Then the great spurt came, bringing along with it a radical structural transformation of Italian industry. The spurt did possess such great momentum that the Italian economy remained essentially undisturbed by the great European depression of 1900. To be sure, there was some unpleasantness — enforced shifts in foreign commerce, shrinking of export markets — but the spurt was great enough to carry the country through the depression without any significant reduction in the rate of growth.

I believe, therefore, that the historical problem presents itself as follows: Why was the upswing of the eighties so short-lived? In trying to answer the question, I think it useful to recall the first concept of original accumulation and to use it as background for discussing Romeo's second and third concepts. As I see it, the crux of the matter is that the upswing of the eighties began in conditions of very considerable relative backwardness. At the same time, the first concept of original accumulation, based as it is on previously amassed wealth, is peculiar to more advanced countries. Such countries were able to develop methods for channeling the previously accumulated funds into the proper hands, and to do it through special institutional arrangements or thanks to favorable general attitudes of relevant groups of the population. (Let me add here something I should have said earlier, namely, that one of the advantages of the way Romeo uses his concept is that he does not simply speak of savings and availabilities of funds, but tries to ascertain whether and how such funds actually found their way into investment projects. Hence his model is fully developed and ranges from the creation of surpluses to their use in railroad construction and public works).

But once we keep the first concept of original accumulation in mind, concepts two and three appear to be closely related to it. What I mean is that Romeo's two concepts can be regarded as *substitutes* for the first and more fundamental concept of original accumulation.

For those concepts should not be regarded as prerequisites of industrialization in the same sense that concept one can be. What took place in Italy, in a very important sense, was not creation of prerequisites but substitution for missing ones. Since "previous wealth" was inadequate or could not be attracted into industry, it was necessary to have recourse to savings produced by current national income in general, and agricultural income in particular. These processes of substitution are far from simple. In fact, as I have said, the greater the degree of a country's backwardness on the eve of its industrialization, the more complex are the patterns of substitution for what may be regarded as prerequisites in more advanced countries. Hence we find that, in a country like England, previously accumulated funds came forth and were made available to industrial entrepreneurs partly through the stock exchange, but even more so by family relations, friends, people interested in developing and utilizing certain inventions, and so on. In a backward country, such processes are much less in evidence, and accordingly recourse to various patterns of substitution becomes much more important. This is the point at which I find myself farthest away from Romeo. For I believe that the substitutions (which are implied in his concepts two and three) simply were not quantitatively strong enough to launch the Italian economy upon the road of the great spurt, upon the road, that is, of a high rate of growth sustained for a sufficiently long time to create major structural changes in the industrial economy.

Italy had to wait for ten long years. Why? I believe that what the country was waiting for — to put it teleologically — was the disappearance of the old banks and the creation of an atmosphere more propitious for the appearance of a new factor. Personally, I attribute very great importance to the arrival of German financial institutions in Italy in the middle of the nineties. The German banks came to Italy essentially for two reasons. The first is precisely because the old Italian banks, including the most significant of them, the Credito Mobiliare, had disappeared. These banks had been less interested in industrialization and much preferred to invest in city housing. Housing in itself is, of course, a respectable area of investment, and it is not up to me to express a political opinion here as to whether building up Rome at that particular time and at that speed was or was not a good thing. The emphasis on *edilizia* in Rome may have been "natural" in terms of the historical situation and as such, so to speak, "inevitable." But the effects of this policy are perfectly clear: concentration on housing prevented a generous and far-sighted industrial policy on the part of the old banks. Moreover, having their origins in French rather than German tradition, they never succeeded in becoming an efficient instrument of industrial financing, as did the German banks — those jacks of all trades, veritable department stores in the field of banking. When the old banks were swept away by the economic crisis, the great opportunity came for a new start. The German banks could both gather the flotsam of industrial enterprises that had been connected with the old banks and launch into new ventures, unimpeded by the competition of the defunct banks.

The second reason for the coming of the German banks is that a historical period was then drawing to its close in Germany. German industry, after a period of rapid growth, was less and less in need of aid and guidance from the banks. Industry was becoming self-reliant and independent. True, this evolution did not reduce the banks to the status of their English counterparts, for the German banks were always to remain *sui generis* by comparison. But by 1900 the period of the banks' ascendancy over German industry was over, and hence the banks had much reason and incentive to begin large-scale exports of their capital and of their rich experience in the field.

Perhaps I may be allowed to insert a few words on certain aspects of the functioning of the new banks in Italy. [The late] Gino Luzzatto made extensive excerpts from the archival material of the Banca Commerciale in Milan and very kindly allowed me to consult his papers. In examining them, I could not help being greatly impressed by the boundless energy with which the Banca plunged into the business of creating and financing important Italian enterprises. Since the Italian directors of this bank were accountable to headquarters in Germany, their correspondence is most revealing of their methods and intentions. At least two conclusions can be drawn. At times it is said that Italian economic development started slowly and belatedly because the Italian bourgeoisie was not permeated with the right spirit — because, as Einaudi would have said, there were no *principi mercanti*, no proud heroes of industrial adventure, but only small men, parochially limited and destitute of great ideas. This is clearly and emphatically not the impression I received from my study of those archives. From the very beginning, the German directors of the Banca Commerciale were fascinated by the availability in Italy of men possessing entrepreneurial vision and constructive ideas. What troubled them was something else — the fear lest such men allow their imagination to carry them beyond the boundaries of prudence and circumspection. In other words, one might say that Italian entrepreneurs were viewed by the Banca Commerciale as corresponding much more to the entrepreneurial image of Werner Sombart than to that of Max Weber. The bank's solution often consisted in letting an enterprise be led by an Italian entrepreneur, supported by a German manager or at least by a German chief accountant. In this way they felt the audacity of an innovating entrepreneur could be combined with, and held in check by, the accountant's rational calculus.

The second point that emerges from the correspondence is, if anything, even more surprising. As one scrutinizes the literature of the period, one finds it very hostile to the penetration of the German banks into Italy. Contemporaneous articles both in professional economic journals and in more popular periodicals, the daily press, public opinion in general, were unanimous in viewing German banking with great suspicion. In left and right circles alike, there was a general tendency to regard the newcomers as spearheads of German imperialism. It was therefore extremely curious to see how quickly the German directors in Italy assimilated the environment. The process of their "Italianization" was rapid indeed. Time and again one finds in the correspondence insistent orders from Germany to appoint a German director for this or that industrial enterprise. But the German representatives in Milan resisted such orders, pointing out that such an appointment would not be favorably received in Italy; moreover, it was entirely unnecessary to appoint foreigners to such posts since native Italian talent was abundantly available and the Italians were perfectly able to manage their own affairs. It seems that, relatively soon, the Germans in Milan began to grow more and more independent of German capital and were even anxious to establish contacts with France in order to use French capital as a counterpoise to the German influence.

At any rate, as one studies the story of the new banking in Italy after the mid-1890's, one can only admire the vigor, the perseverance, and the optimism with which these men went about their business. They proceeded exactly as they had in Germany, applying the lessons they had learned so well through the trials and errors of several decades. They took care of an industrial enterprise from its establishment on, supported it over a number of years, collected a number of similar enterprises, waiting patiently for the opportune moment when they could be welded together into a really significant entity; they opened generous lines of short-term credit to their fledglings, knowing full well that the short-term funds would be invested long, into fixed capital. But, at least in the early years, they had the assurance that their German principals would bail them out if something went wrong, and they assumed that in a very desperate situation they could count on aid from the Banca d'Italia. These expectations provided sufficient guarantees for them to engage in "unsound" operations and to conduct them in Italy with the same measure of success that they had had in Germany.

My main point is that these activities of the banks were a strategic factor. They were the real substitution for the missing prerequisites and must be held responsible, more than anything else, for the fact that Italy finally, after 1896, had its great spurt. For this reason, I believe that Romeo's concepts two or three, however interesting and original, do not really touch on the crucial factors at work in that period.

All this does not mean, of course, that I disagree with Romeo as far as the original motivation of his book is concerned. He started from a survey of Marxian historians in Italy after the last war and found them to stand under the strong influence of Antonio Gramsci. Romeo opposed the thesis according to which everything would have been just fine in Italy, if only an agrarian reform upon the French pattern had been carried out. Here I find myself in agreement. He has criticized effectively the inconsistency in operating with two "half problems": the industrial revolution in England and the political revolution in France. The two very different phenomena have been very confusingly merged into a hybrid construct of necessary prerequisites, intimating that economic development everywhere must conform to the model of English industrial history, while agrarian reform and the political transformation must follow the French pattern and "feudalism" must be destroyed exactly as it had been in France. I believe, and I am sure Romeo will agree, that feudalism in this sense is not an operational term and that the relation between the preindustrial institutional framework and industrialization is much more complex than is suggested by the bland use of simplicist formulas. Gramsci and the Italian historians who follow him have failed to notice that many retarding factors, those behind the slow economic development in postrevolutionary France, had their origin in the extent to which the small family farm had existed in France. It is altogether possible that the Jacobins bear some measure of guilt for the disabilities of French economic growth in the nineteenth century.

It may be in order for me to mention one more area of agreement with Romeo: the fundamental fact that there was an impressive industrial development in Italy between 1896 and 1914. What happened during those years must be neither belittled nor exaggerated. It must be viewed with a clear sense of proportion. On the one hand, nothing is more unfair than to speak of the "little Italy of the Risorgimento" or of the mediocrity of the Italian bourgeoisie, which allegedly proved unable to launch a substantial economic offensive. On the other hand, it may be true that the period failed to produce very great business leaders, even though some entrepreneurs did leave a permanent imprint upon the economic history of the country; at the same time, the rate of growth did not quite reach levels that might have been expected on the basis of the general condition of the country. Between the extremes there is much room for the view that, such as it was, the great spurt after 1896 did entail a magnificent transformation of the Italian economy. This much is certain. But, for the rest, it must also be recognized that we have not done much more than scratch the surface and that much deeper study of the relevant facts and problems is called for. To give just one example, there is still the previously mentioned unresolved divergence between Barberi and myself with regard to the behavior of the index of industrial output in the eighties. Who knows? Perhaps Barberi is right and there was no upswing at all during that decade. Clearly, further research is urgently needed. And thus one has every reason to welcome the fact that this area of study has aroused the interest of a man of Romeo's talents. I do hope that he will continue his research in the direction he has so felicitously inaugurated, and that we may expect from him further work as fruitful and stimulating as his previous studies.

Romeo: I wish to thank Alexander Gerschenkron for the attention he has devoted to my book — an attention which, I believe, should be attributed not so much to my conclusions as to my attempt to pose certain questions, upon which his own studies have cast much light. The questions under discussion certainly deserve a much more penetrating analysis than the one they have received so far. I should like, therefore, to thank Professor Gerschenkron not only in my own name, but also in the name of many Italian scholars who have so greatly appreciated his contribution to the study of problems that have been hardly touched upon by our research in Italian economic history.

It is precisely the complexity of the problems that Gerschenkron has raised here which makes it difficult for me to reply to all of his points; or, I should say, renders it difficult to give expression to all the trains of thought he has stimulated in my mind. Gerschenkron has here added important new elements to the problems treated in his last year's essay in the *Rivista storica italiana* and elsewhere. I shall confine myself, therefore, to a few aspects of the problem which seem to me to be most essential.

Gerschenkron has said that, of the three senses in which the concept of original accumulation can be understood, I have preferred to use the two last concepts, combining them into one. (Let me add in parentheses that I have never intended to use the concept of original accumulation in the strict Marxian sense, and I have said so explicitly.) On the other hand, Gerschenkron thinks that the proper key to the understanding of Italian industrial development can be found precisely in concept number one, which I have excluded. The concept refers to savings already existing in the Italian economy around the middle of the nineteenth century and their use for industrial investment, that is, their transformation into a factor of production, or capital in the real sense of the term.

THE INDUSTRIAL DEVELOPMENT OF ITALY

Indeed, I am not inclined to overestimate the volume of savings in Italy that antedated her capitalist development. Although it is true that money for railroad construction was found with relative ease, it is also true that at the beginning those large investments had been made possible only with the help of large financial institutions abroad or through government intervention. The latter either took the direct form of railroad construction, or proceeded through concessions equipped with profit guarantees and contributions to the cost of operations. In this way investments, which in terms of strict private accounting would have been neither sufficiently secure nor sufficiently promising, were rendered attractive and economically possible. Still, despite this reservation, Gerschenkron is certainly correct when he stresses the central importance of the moment when pre-existent savings, which had eschewed industrial employment in the past, begin to turn to it. This is the meaning of his emphasis on that phase in Italian economic history which is marked by a new type of banking investment in industry, and is closely connected with economic development during Giolitti's era. But to pose the question in this way immediately leads to the next question: What determined this change in the direction of investment?

In order to answer this question, it is necessary to clear the air of a misunderstanding that perhaps is the only one remaining between me and Gerschenkron. It refers to my evaluation of economic significance of the period 1881–1887 in Italian history.

In fact, I have never regarded the eighties as the time of radical industrial transformation of the Italian economy. As I have explicitly stated, my starting point has been the index of industrial output constructed by Gerschenkron. According to his findings, the critical period of Italian industrial development, our "industrial revolution," falls between 1896 and 1907. But the years 1881–1887, to my mind, show with particular intensity the process that characterized the whole flow of Italian economic history from 1860 till the beginning of the industrial revolution in 1896. I am referring to the modernization of the economic structure, to the replacement of old modes of production by new ones, to the appearance of new forms of marketing, to the creation of a network of infrastructures, and so on. To be sure, if we look at the growth of Italian national income in the years before

1896 (rather than before 1888), we are certainly struck, as is Gerschenkron, by the insignificance of the quantitative change in national income and, in particular, the industrial contribution thereto. But there is a real danger that, by riveting our eyes exclusively to the quantitative aspect of the matter, we fail to notice the transformation in the structure of productive processes. Let me give an example that, to my mind, appears especially convincing. As is generally known, production of ferrous metals in Italy was declining in the second half of the nineteenth century because the industry's charcoal-fed blast furnaces were unable to stand the competition of French and English iron and were being closed down one after the other. Output of Italian pig iron plummeted. But then there appeared a new demand for pig iron with the opening of new and modern blast furnaces in Terni. The total volume of iron output in the period is small, resulting as it does from the expansion of output of modern plants and from the decline of the old ones. However, the economic significance of the process should not be measured in aggregate terms. The total volume of output may have remained unchanged, but it makes all the difference in the world if a large part of that output is no longer produced by an antiquated and declining industry, but by modern and efficient plants.

Analogously, the economy went through a process of decline in the putting-out system. There is plentiful evidence that the processing of materials, particularly that done by peasants in their homes, gradually diminished. As the volume of their output fell from year to year, its place was taken by the volume of output produced by the new textile mills. Naturally, the output of the mills does not appear to rise very fast, because the aggregate figures also reflect the shrinking of the putting-out system. But, in reality, the rate of growth of output of modern plants is much higher than appears from data for the whole industry.

More important than quantitative increases in output, however, were the complex consequences of the application of new methods, which became evident quite a while before the advent of the industrial revolution. The latter cannot begin unless it is necessarily preceded by changes, or at least by initiation of changes, in a number of economic relationships. Previously dominant positions must be undermined. And this is precisely what took place, slowly but steadily, in the decades before 1896. Now, in causing these transformations, a central role was played not so much by pre-existing savings — which, as Gerschenkron reminds us, were still reluctant to move spontaneously into industry — but rather by incomes from current outputs. These incomes were either impounded by the state through taxation or else accumulated by landowners and agrarian entrepreneurs through pressure upon payments to agricultural producers before the advent of the agrarian crisis (which in Italy came around 1880). These funds then were used to finance public works in close collaboration with a number of important foreign firms. It was this capital whose job it was to demolish old economic structures, thereby rendering possible, that is to say, economically profitable, investment of private savings (both current and pre-existing) in industry, whether directly or through the medium of the big banks that came after 1894 and combined the normal functions of commercial banking with those of the *crédit mobilier*.

In fact, if we neglect these antecedents, the phenomenon of the industrial revolution itself becomes rather incomprehensible. There are, of course, various interpretations of Italian economic expansion in the second half of the nineties. We may neglect the alleged widening of peasant markets for industrial goods, which is said to have come after the agrarian strikes, for this development belongs to the period after 1900 and cannot be used to explain the original recovery. More convincing among these interpretations is the reference to the level of prices in world markets (which started rising precisely in 1896) and to the stimulating effect of price increases first upon exports and then upon the whole economic system. But there had been periods of rising prices before, for instance between 1849 and 1874, that is, before the Great Depression, which did not elicit any response on the part of the Italian economy. Why then was the effect so radically different after 1896? Obviously it was because, in the interval, things came into being that had not been in existence earlier. And, indeed, there had occurred a commercialization of the Italian economy, a general modernization of the organization and the modes of production, so that new economic structures had emerged which *were* able to respond to the stimulus of rising world prices.

In the earlier period, when our economy was largely insulated from international markets, the foreign impulses were not felt and the beneficial effects did not materialize.

Gerschenkron, on the other hand, assigns the role of strategic factor in the Italian great spurt to another factor, to wit, to the appearance of new banks of the mixed German type and to their activities within the Italian body economic. Everything he has said in this respect is of extraordinary interest in view of the decisive role played by these banks in our industrial system, not only before the First World War but also after it until the very beginning of the world depression in 1929. But even then we must ask ourselves whether the activity of the banks should not be seen in relation to the structural changes in the Italian economy of which I have spoken earlier. It would seem to me that the banks could not have performed in the same way within an economic framework that existed, say, in the seventies, when collecting deposits and passing them on to industry would have been a much more arduous task. Suffice it to see, for example, what institutions such as the Credito Mobiliare Italiano or the Banca Generale were doing prior to 1894. Of course, they were not banks of the German mixed type, and they were much less adapted to the job of industrial investment. But if we compare their activities with similar institutions abroad, say with the French Crédit Mobilier, we easily see that their investment policies were kept at a level below what could have been reached even within the then-existing banking structure. To be sure, both the Banca Generale and the Credito Mobiliare (for which we have better documentary evidence) had a certain importance in the industrial evolution of the country. But the effects on the whole were small. If we look at the most important sectors of Italian manufacturing at the time, for example, the textile industry, by far the most significant one, it is clear that it developed almost entirely independently of the banks. The old branches of manufacturing, such as silk, wool, linen, and foodstuffs — with the exception of the cotton industry — all continued to be more independent of the banks than the branches created later in the period dominated by the Banca Commerciale, the Credito Italiano, the Banco di Roma, and the Società Bancaria Italiana. Where we find a closer connection between investment of bank capital and industry after 1896 is always in the new sectors of the industrial economy, such as ferrous metals, machinery, chemicals, and electricity.

Hence if we concentrate our attention on the new factor, on the appearance of the mixed bank of the German type in 1894, the basic question still remains: Why did the new banks begin their activity at that point and not earlier? I do not believe that this question can be satisfactorily answered simply by reference to the new orientation of Italian foreign policy, that is to say, by reference to Crispi's asking the German government for assistance in establishing a new bank designed to defend Italian government securities against short-selling speculations on the stock exchange in Paris. I believe that in reality the innovation came when domestic conditions had matured to assure it of a durable success. This is shown by the fact that the first newcomer — the Banca Commerciale — was quickly followed by others which proved no less successful. This success expressed itself in a performance for whose historical significance in our economic development I must refer you to the lucid exposition by Professor Saraceno, which does not need much additional elaboration.

Thus, to my mind, the significance of the pre-1896 period in Italian economic history lies in the creation of preconditions for modern economic development. For some thirty years after 1896, this development pivoted on the powerful activities of banks. No more than the preconditions were created before 1896, because considerable increase in our national income, and especially in industry's contribution to it, came only after that date. What happened in the years 1881–1887 was the first appearance of large-scale enterprises in industry and, for the first time, a considerable quickening of the rhythm of industrial growth. Gerschenkron's index confirms the increases in output that occurred in the eighties, although the data of our Central Institute of Statistics show a different picture. As between the two indices I believe that Gerschenkron's is closer to the truth. I am not saying this for reasons of statistical techniques, since I should not deem myself qualified to decide on the relative merits of two highly competent technical studies. But I am saying this, as it were, for general historical reasons. For we have evidence on the industrial expansion in Italy between 1881 and 1887 from a large multiplicity of sources. It is attested to in economic literature and in political literature. We can infer it from the foundation dates of many enterprises and the opening of many plants. The fact of expansion is made clear to us from purely literary sources depicting the change in customs and social life in general, and particularly in the large cities of the North. It is true that from 1888 to 1895 the Italian economy went through a very grave crisis. But from a proper point of view, those years, characterized as they are by the abolition of old systems of banks of issue, by the reform of monetary circulation, and by the disappearance of the old banks of the *crédit mobilier* type, are in reality a period of transition from the phase of preconditions to that of the actual "industrial revolution." In these intervening years the old structures that had exhausted their usefulness were removed, and others, better adapted to the needs of the new epoch, were formed. In saying this I do not wish, of course, to indulge in hindsight justifications, and to deny the grave hardships and the retardation that the depression inflicted upon the economy of the country.

This is the essence of the fleeting thoughts that were occurring to me as I listened to Gerschenkron's exposition. And once more I wish to thank him in the name of all those in Italy who approach those problems not in the spirit of ideological schematism, but moved by the desire and will to understand how things really happened.

Gerschenkron: Let me first of all thank Professor Romeo for his kind words. For the rest, I shall try to be brief. I am not sure that I can readily accept Romeo's vision of a slow, and perhaps not easily perceptible, structural change which, he says, preceded the actual start of industrialization. In general, as far as concerns the industrial development of backward countries in Europe of the nineteenth century, I am rather suspicious of any attempt to find too much orderly sequence in that process. First, it is said, certain prerequisites are created; then certain structural changes take place; then there is a purge of things that do not belong in the new age, and so the putting-out system and other preindustrial formations are eliminated and the land is cleared for industrialization. Up to a point, all this is plausible and, in fact, appears extremely logical. I have said myself that the disappearance of the old banks was a step on the road of industrial progress. But when it comes to structural changes, in particular the elimination of small artisans and domestic industries, I am not at all sure that the industrialization of a backward country proceeds in this way. Something of the sort Romeo describes certainly did take place in England. There the industrial revolution ushered in the textile age, and the textile industry then looked back upon a long premodern history: single artisans, artisans united in craft guilds, merchant employers, and so on. In England, the modern factory had to compete against all these preindustrial formations before it could assert itself.

Now, one advantage of a backward country — and the great spurt in Italy came a century or so after England's — is precisely that it can channel its major industrial effort into sectors where preindustrial formations either are few or do not exist at all. In the machinery industry or the chemical industry, but particularly in the former, there are no preindustrial formations. The field is wide open. And if Italy, in fact, did witness a considerable upswing of her textile industries, this was a rather abnormal phenomenon and essentially the result of the protectionist policy of the Italian government, a policy altogether ill advised and misguided from the point of view of the country's economic development. Moreover, I believe that the same is true with regard to the production of iron and steel. Of course, there were political problems, political ambitions, ideas relating to the position of Italy as a great power. But if one may abstract from politics and confine oneself to economic factors, then we should ask in which way the rate of industrial growth in Italy could have been maximized. Then, I believe, the answer is clear. We cannot escape the conclusion that Italy had no economic interest in promoting the iron and steel industry, the huge consumer of coal that had to come from afar, doubling its price between Newcastle and Genoa. So Italy never should have tried to build up an iron and steel capacity of such dimensions. But the structure of the Italian tariff, particularly in the early years of protectionism, was clearly oriented to the protection of iron and steel at the expense of the most promising Italian industry — that is, the machinery industry, whose development therefore came later together with the chemical and automobile industries.

Incidentally, as far as the automobile industry is concerned, let me record another surprising — and this time negative — impression I received while studying the archives of the Banca Commerciale. The bank failed to appreciate the importance of the automobile industry for the economic development of the country. Apparently it considered the new vehicle as something primarily for the racing sports, at best a luxury item. The otherwise sharp-eyed bankers showed a blind spot when it came to discerning the immense potentialities of producing motor cars within the Italian socioeconomic environment.

But more surprising than what the banks did not do is what they did do. In a country like Italy, one could have reasonably expected the state to play — for some time — a considerable role in furthering industrial progress. I have the suspicion that Romeo and I do not quite see eye to eye on this point either. He finds merit with the industrial policy of the government, whereas my judgment of it is rather negative. And let me say that, as a matter of principle, I have no objections, no objections at all, to state intervention. The contrary is true. I do believe, however, that the policy of the Italian government in this area was quite inadequate. Given Italy's degree of backwardness, protection of grains was much too expensive and burdensome a policy. It was ill advised even in a country like Germany, but there at least the country was already sufficiently developed to be able to pay the price, and the grave damage was political rather than economic. In Italy, agrarian protection was folly, just as it was folly to subsidize industries that proved such a heavy drag on the country's development (and I have more in mind than the iron and steel industry). If the government was not ready to pursue a constructive, rational policy of protection, it would have done better to have crossed its arms and remained inactive. If the Italian government had pursued a reasonable policy in the beginning of the eighties, it is quite likely that the promising beginning would not have been nipped in the bud in the decade's second half. The process could have continued, and it would have continued if it had been supported by a sufficiently large demand for industrial goods on the part of the government and if, on the other hand, provision had been made for an adequate supply of capital both through credit institutions and through the state budget.

THE INDUSTRIAL DEVELOPMENT OF ITALY

What was needed was precisely substitution for the missing prerequisites. It was not made, and this was a serious failure. When the banks came, they played a decisive role, and on this we are in agreement. In a sense, though, the banks were but a second-best solution. If the banks had been properly supported by government policy, the great spurt after 1896 may well have become even greater in speed and scope. As I said before, Romeo sees a logical sequence of things: first the prerequisites, that is to say, the infrastructure; then changes in structure; then development. It is difficult for me to discern this straight line in the industrial evolution. I believe that we can explain why development in Italy did not follow that logical course. As long as the period of railroad construction was underway, it would have been relatively easy to provide the nascent industry with the external economies and the growing demand it needed. During the eighties, given appropriate government support, industry would have benefited from concomitant railroad building. But the opportunity was allowed to pass unutilized. When the great spurt came, the railroad network had been essentially completed. One could possibly argue that this was all to the good, since in this fashion capital was released for industrial investment. But such an argument would misconceive the nature of the Italian capital market, which was divided in water-tight compartments — hence, as Romeo says, it was easy to secure funds for the railroads and difficult to obtain them for industry. When railroad construction was completed, the funds that theoretically could have begun flowing into industry in actual fact shunned industrial employment: they either went into local savings banks to be used for municipal public works or else went abroad in exchange for foreign securities. This is a clear example of how complex are the processes of substitution in a backward country. Things that are *first* logically may be *last* historically. The "prerequisites" to a process and the process itself can be so completely interconnected and intertwined that it is impossible to disentangle the skein. And it is in this sense that Italy in the eighties, as it were, missed the bus. The industrial transformation that came a decade later was less impressive than it might have been otherwise — perhaps only a pale reflection of what the upswing of the eighties could have been, if it had been properly guided and supported.

Let me add that this aspect of the process is assuming more and more importance in my general cogitations about Europe's industrial development in the nineteenth century. At the same time, I am less inclined to adhere completely to my previous and perhaps too rigid view according to which growing relative backwardness is accompanied by *steadily* increasing advantages from the point of view of the country's subsequent industrialization. I used to think that, the more delayed the beginning of the great spurt, the easier it would be to profit from these accumulations of advantages. This is often the case. But I also believe now that greater attention should be devoted to what may be called the peaks, the optimal points in this process. The advantages of backwardness do indeed accumulate until they reach a certain high point; such a point was reached in Italy in the eighties. Once the point was passed and railroad construction was over, however, the advantages diminished and vested interests, such as iron and steel and probably also cotton textiles, became strong enough to influence the policy of the government in a less than perfectly desirable way. The favorable moment was lost. A period of depression came during which it was not the advantages but the disadvantages of backwardness that dominated the scene.

The rhythm of these ups and downs no doubt relates to a large variety of factors. A technological innovation of strategic importance (railroads, automobiles, electrical power) may be of crucial importance in determining the location of the optimal points. These fluctuations in advantages and disadvantages of backwardness deserve a good deal of study. Italian industrial history before 1914 can teach us many useful things in this respect. And it is quite likely that similar relations can be discovered during the same period in other European countries.

Romeo: If I have understood Gerschenkron rightly, he maintains that my presentation of processes of economic change in Italy suffers from too "orderly" a view of the various phases of that change. He thinks that the eighties gave the Italian government a unique, nonrecurring opportunity to upset this orderly succession of phases. Had the development started then, it could have concentrated on machinery as against textiles and thus would have upset the normal

English pattern of development; this is not advisable in a backward country arriving on the industrial scene at a time when the machinery industry is in a dominant position.

What separates me from Gerschenkron is possibly a difference in points of view, which in turn reflects differences in purpose and interest. He is primarily eager to gather data and observations for the construction of a general theoretical model of economic development. What matters to me is, above all, to understand the historical process as it occurred in Italy. It is this difference in interests that has caused a certain shift of ground in our discussion, away from the original problem. Gerschenkron's assertion that in the eighties there was given an opportunity for a development that could not be recaptured later, and that the Italian government failed to grasp that opportunity, raises a number of problems that deserve deeper probing. Thus, for instance, one could ask whether the conditions for industrial development were really present, as long as both the railroad network and the commercialization of the economy which the railroads stimulated were still so far from completion. It is a matter of debate whether capital liberated by the completion of the railroads went into local banks or savings banks, which notoriously invested their deposits in local ventures; or whether the capital — I am referring to private Italian capital — did not actually continue to move within the ambit of the financial market in close proximity to industrial investment. Above all, it is permissible to ask whether it is in order in a historical discussion to lament that the Italian state of the eighties did not pursue the policy advocated by Gerschenkron, a policy based upon activation of public demand and creation of more effective instruments within the framework of the budget as well as upon an intensified building of infrastructures. (In this connection, let me say in parentheses that in those years expenditure for public works reached the highest percentage of total expenditures ever experienced in the whole history of the Kingdom.) In particular, the tariff policy of the state would have had to be altogether different. It seems clear to me that many of the measures referred to by Gerschenkron would have required a conception of governmental policy that was as yet quite alien to the economic culture of the nineteenth century. Gerschenkron himself shows clearly in his writings how governments developed effective policies of substitution only in the most backward countries, such as Russia. In countries that were more advanced, such as Germany and Austria-Hungary (and partly France), the task of substituting for the free market, in the effort to catch up with England, fell to the banks. When everything is said and done, I do not believe there is much reason to be astonished that the government and the ruling economic class in Italy pursued policies similar to those followed in countries that were in so many respects much closer to Italy than to imperial Russia, where an entirely different political and institutional system was in existence. It is true, of course, that a better tariff policy could have been pursued; but even with regard to the tariffs I believe, as I have said elsewhere, that from the vantage point of the present it is difficult to doubt the legitimacy of Italy's iron and steel industry, despite the manifold strictures of it from free traders, radicals, socialists, and others.

Something else is more important, however. Even if we went so far as to assume the correctness of all the strictures made by Gerschenkron with regard to Italian economic policy of the period, we would be able to do no more than identify a number of accelerating factors that were *not* present in the economic system. But this would not take us a single step farther along the road of understanding those factors which promoted the development that actually took place in historical reality. If what we are looking for is not what might have been a more effective industrial evolution, but what was the actual historical development, we must ask a series of questions. What were the results that Italian economic policy, despite all its errors, succeeded in achieving? Was there a destruction of old productive structures and the formation of new ones, and, if so, how did it proceed? Was there actually a process of commercialization in the Italian economy? This is the stuff Italian economic history is made of, and the history we are investigating is the history of Italian industry, which was shaped by the tariff policy such as it was and not by a different tariff policy — by a *given* relationship between the economic policy of the state and industrial activity rather than by any other.

Gerschenkron is right in stating that in reality things do not proceed in an orderly way. By this, I assume, he intended to say that the ordinary course of events — in which machinery construction comes after textiles and modern enterprise comes after domestic industries — could have been changed by a different policy of the government. But the fact remains that Italian economic history did in fact follow a certain order. This, by the way, does not mean that the process was free of complexity. It is not true that the old forms had to disappear — both in production and in distribution — before the new ones could appear on the scene. In reality, both the appearance of the new and the disappearance of the old were so closely interrelated as to constitute one indissoluble process. It is difficult indeed to distinguish in that process what came first and what came afterwards. A certain order does exist in the historical process, but only in the sense that we can ascertain factors as being more important than others and that, after a certain time, we can see this order reversed.

To return to the principal point: Gerschenkron has maintained that the policy of the Italian state basically retarded rather than promoted the economic development of the country. He says that if the state had confined itself to mere police functions, if it had been just a night watchman's state, if it had left the economy of the country to its own devices, development would have been more rapid. Yet even for him who accepts this now *in toto,* the fact remains that there was in fact an economic development and that it occurred in given historical circumstances. If the policy of the state proved a retarding factor, then we should not look at the retarding factor, precisely because it cannot explain how development did come about. We must look at those factors responsible for the development that actually took place. In other words, if we want to understand historical reality, we must look not so much at factors that obstructed development but at those that brought the development into being. To be sure, not even then is it possible to separate neatly the accelerating and retarding factors, which are very closely intertwined. But in the logic of our approach the principal factors are those which created the historical reality. If we look only at the factors that impede industrial development, we should know all the reasons for which industrial development does not take place, but still would know nothing of the reasons for which it actually occurs, and the latter are precisely the things we have wanted to learn about.

I have nothing else to add. But I should like to repeat that it would be very pleasant to have another opportunity of discussing these problems with Professor Gerschenkron.

Postscript

At a conference of Italian and Soviet historians, held in Moscow in 1964, Professor Romeo returned to the subject matter of the foregoing discussion. Unfortunately, his references there to my views on Italian industrial development are likely to give a distorted impression of my position. Hence a few words of clarification should be in order. Romeo said in Moscow that I "have denied that there was an industrial development in Italy after 1880" and he asserted further that such a denial was inconsistent with my own index of Italian industrial output, which clearly showed the fact of industrial development.[3] In making these misleading utterances (different in both tone and substance from his statements in the foregoing debate), Romeo regrettably failed to make clear that the point at issue between us is not a "denial" on my part of the short-lived upswing of the eighties, and still less that there was *some* industrial development between 1861 and 1896, but the question whether that upswing can be reasonably regarded as a great spurt of industrialization, comparable to what occurred in the years following 1896. It is quite possible, however, that this failure on Romeo's part to do justice to an opponent's views is unintentional, and due to a limited understanding of the scope of the historical problem under discussion, as was evidenced by his second rejoinder in our debate. He is in error in believing that a given rate of growth in an economy is merely the result of the accelerating factors at work. It is the composite result of both the accelerating and the retarding factors. And the latter are just as much an integral part of any historical evolution as the former. It ill behooves a historian of Romeo's talents to retreat behind Ranke's

3. "Atti del primo convegno degli storici italiani e sovietici, Mosca, ottobre 1964," in *I Quaderni di rassegna sovietica*, I (1965), 125–127.

"wie ist es eigentlich gewesen," a phrase that was not too felicitous coming from the pen of a great historian and then became fully meaningless when repeated *ad nauseam* by countless mediocrities. For the problem I was trying — alas unsuccessfully — to make clear to Romeo was not "wie es uneigentlich hätte sein können"; it was not an attempt to state what might have happened. The problem rather was to appraise the actual rate of industrial growth in Italy; that is to say, to ask whether the actually achieved rate of growth was or was not in line with the fundamental conditions in Italy on the eve of its great spurt. And if, using appropriate comparative material, I have come to believe that the rate of growth was lower than might have been expected, this inevitably impels one to search for an explanation of the fact — an explanation that must be looked for in the historical reality of Italy of the time. To forgo raising such questions and to abstain from attempts to answer them would mean refusal on the part of the historian to appraise the significance of the phenomena he claims to analyze. When it comes, therefore, to the question why the Italian government pursued its ill-advised economic policy, the reason may lie either in the government's incompetence and inability to withstand the pressures of vested interests, as I believe, or in the restraints imposed by the Western Zeitgeist, as Romeo believes. But whatever the answer, the fact itself is most relevant and directly pertinent to the understanding of Italian industrial history *as it actually occurred.*

I do not believe, therefore, that Romeo is right in saying that our disagreements stem from my interest in a general theoretical model of industrial development while he confines himself to exploring the industrial history of Italy. It is true indeed that I think we can perceive the industrial evolution in Europe in the nineteenth century as an intelligibly diversified unity, although the set of simple generalizations with which I have operated hardly deserves to be called theory. But the main point Romeo has failed to see is that such value as these generalizations possess lies precisely in raising relevant questions which help us to understand and evaluate the processes of industrialization as they occurred within the confines of individual countries.

THE INDUSTRIAL DEVELOPMENT OF ITALY

Rosario Romeo has started a most deserving line of research. It would be very unfortunate if resistance to an imperfectly understood criticism should cause him to constrain his work within unduly narrow limits and make him shun important and exciting aspects of a subject to which he has made such a promising initial contribution.

[3]

Excerpt from Carlo M. Cipolla (ed.), *The Fontana Economic History of Europe: The Emergence of Industrial Societies, Part One*, 279–328.

5. The Industrial Revolution in Italy 1830-1914

Luciano Cafagna

TWO KINDS OF OUTSIDE IMPETUS FOR NORTHERN ITALY'S ECONOMY BEFORE POLITICAL UNIFICATION (*c.* 1830–1860)

The influence of the industrial revolution on the predominantly agricultural economy of Italy's various regions before unification, during the first half of the nineteenth century, made itself felt in two important ways. Neither of them could yet be defined as the introduction of forms of modern industrialisation but they can nevertheless be regarded as its forerunners. The first, direct and palpable, concerned the development of trade exchanges with the rest of the world. It involved considerable expansion in a traditional export of primary products from certain northern regions of Italy, the export of silk, both raw and spun, for the spinning and weaving mills of France, Great Britain, Germany and Switzerland. The second, a matter of information and mental attitudes, concerns the various means by which the country was influenced or compelled to imitate those nations that had already embarked on industrial development.

The production of silk, a product of silkworm rearing and cultivation of the mulberry tree, was concentrated chiefly in North Italy, especially Piedmont and Lombardy. The explosion of industrial textile consumption in Western Europe and North America in the first decades after the Restoration[1] caused an increase in the demand not only for cotton and wool but also, if to a lesser degree, for silk. North Italy benefited particularly from this increased demand. For although European demand already tended to turn towards the East (first to Bengal, then, after the opium war, to China, concentrating in the last decades of the

1. i.e. the Restoration of the *status quo* after the Congress of Vienna.

nineteenth century on Japan), nevertheless a good deal of this demand could be satisfied within Europe itself, if only in those few privileged areas (in particular, North Italy and the South of France) which climatic conditions made suitable for silk production. These areas had traditionally, ever since the sixteenth century, fostered the development of mulberry plantations and of activities connected with the first transformation of the product of the silkworm, in other words the process of producing from the cocoon the filament of raw silk yarn (reeling) and the subsequent preparation of the filament silk for weaving (throwing). Much less progress had been made in weaving. This final phase in the cycle of silk textile production had become established on a considerably larger scale in France and also in other countries of Western Europe which relied chiefly on Italy for their supplies of raw or spun silk. Up to the middle of the eighteenth century techniques relating to these initial stages of silk textile production were more advanced in Italy than in the rest of Europe, even giving rise to one of the first notorious cases of industrial espionage.[2] Subsequently they remained at a standstill and were overtaken by the advances made in the rest of Western Europe. But between 1830 and 1850 the inducement of rising demand led to some modernisation of techniques, especially in the less elementary branch from the industrial point of view, that of throwing.

By about the middle of the nineteenth century there were in Piedmont and Lombardy together about 700–800 silk-throwing mills, mostly worked by water. At that time silk reeling and throwing gave employment to some 150,000, mainly peasants working seasonally (reeling went on for only one month of the year) in small mills scattered over the countryside and equipped with very simple machinery. But it is no exaggeration to say that these mills provided the first training in industrial labour for workers who were later used in other forms of production. It was also in connection with the sale of silk that capital-owning landowners

2. W. H. Chaloner, 'Sir Thomas Lombe (1685-1739) and the British Silk Industry', in *History Today*, vol. III, no. 11, Nov. 1953, pp. 778-785.

and merchant bankers first became interested on a large scale in an economic activity that was not purely agricultural. Moreover trade interests in silk-importing countries resulted in the influx into North Italy of Swiss and German businessmen who were to play an important part in turning Italy's first industrial efforts towards other directions. The development of silk production therefore contributed in several ways towards forming the external economies for a further industrial development. In this sense silk can be regarded as the first 'leading sector' for Italian economic development in the nineteenth century. For some hundred years, from the Restoration to the First World War, silk led the field in Italian exports, more or less regularly representing about a third of their total value.

As has been said, the final stage of silk production, weaving, was for a long time, and indeed up to the end of the nineteenth century, of considerably less importance, viewed quantitatively. The reason for this can easily be understood. Italy's economy, at this early stage, could only provide a large-scale response to the demand for a product for which she had a natural oligopoly and need face no competitors, a product for which trade lay with the foreign productive sector, not with the market of final consumers, which was controlled by the foreign industry. At the same time the Italian home market for finished goods could obviously not afford sufficient demand for a quality product like woven silk. Even the intermediary process of throwing (which provided the actual yarn) had a restricted and difficult development, confined in the eighteenth and early nineteenth centuries almost entirely to Piedmont, in virtue of a commercial policy which forbade the export of silk in its raw state. It must be emphasised that this mercantilism in fact went only halfway, lacking the courage and strength to extend as well to woven goods. Even this 'halfway' mercantilism was, however, abandoned around 1830.

The other branches of textile production—cotton, linen, and wool—were quantitatively much less important during the first half of the nineteenth century, though they were rather more industrial in character. Geographically, the cotton industry was concentrated in Piedmont and Lombardy, the linen industry in Lombardy alone, while wool manufacture was more widespread (in Piedmont, the Veneto, and Tuscany). The South, for its part, had a small nucleus of cotton production (Salerno) and of wool, both highly protected by customs duties. Except for flax and some wool, the raw materials used were not of domestic production. Indeed the greater part of finished goods consumed on the home market were imported, despite the customs protection they enjoyed. Many of the earliest small factories developed side by side with an import business, and were probably also used as cover for the importation of contraband finished goods, especially in the cotton trade. From about 1830 onwards cotton emerged as the most attractive commodity, after silk, for traders and for a small circle among the nobility who were prepared to interest themselves in non-agricultural economic activities. Italy's cotton industry, too, then began to experience the impetus of quite a number of immigrant Swiss or German businessmen who came, in particular, to Lombardy. '*The Golden Book* of industry and trade in Lombardy', wrote Nitti, 'abounded in guttural sounds and harsh terminations.'[3]

The productive phase of the textile sector which first began to assume industrial characteristics (i.e. concentration in small factories, use of centralised motive power and mechanical equipment) was that of spinning. Reference has already been made to the throwing and spinning of silk. In the other branches the greatest advances were in cotton and flax rather than in wool: wool was technically the most difficult to deal with, and also the individual regional markets (except for Piedmont, where supplies for the army could be counted on) afforded too restricted a demand.[4] Weaving, on the other hand, continued to be

3. F. S. Nitti, *L'Italia all'alba del secolo XX*, Turin — Rome, 1901; reprinted in *Scritti sulla questione meridionale*, vol. I, Bari, 1958, pp. 147ff.

4. Quazza, in *L'industria laniera e cotoniera in Piemonte dal 1831 al 1861*, Turin, 1961, observes (pp. 98–9) that 'the expansive capacity of cotton, regarded throughout Europe as the industry of tomorrow, the most profitable and the most susceptible of expansion, was seen to be greater

mainly of the nature of a handicraft, carried on for the most part in the peasants' own dwellings even though much of it was under the control of merchant-entrepreneurs. Prior to 1848 there were about sixty cotton-spinning mills in Piedmont and Lombardy, together with about 200,000 spindles. Thus the average number of spindles per mill was about 3,000–3,500, whereas in England at the same period the average was already around 10,000. A few mills were beginning to work on a larger scale: the Piedmontese *Manifattura di Annecy e Pont* had as many as 34,000 spindles. Productivity was very low: in Piedmont (1840–1843) the average was 28 spindles per worker, in Lombardy (1845) 31, whereas in England in those years the average was around 80.

A considerable part of the production was concentrated in larger and technically more modern mills. These mills strove to follow the rapid technological changes of other countries, but succeeded only partially and with several years' delay. The first mule-jennys of the early years of the century were followed, with a time-lag of 15–20 years as compared with other countries, by throstles around 1840; and semi-automatic mule-jennys came into use in Italy only in the years just before the unification, whereas in England self-acting machines had already appeared, a development that did not reach Italy till after 1860, five or six years after the Paris Exhibition of 1855 which launched them.

Thus it will be seen that the overall picture in the Italian textile industry was very restricted as compared with other countries: less than a thousand small factories for silk, cotton, flax and wool and of those only some fifteen of respectable size—surrounded by home-handicraft workers and seasonal work at the preparatory stage of silk-reeling. Nevertheless this small beginning, because of its concentration in particular areas, was already giving a new aspect to

---

than that of wool . . . The younger industry has the pre-eminence, because in it greater technical vitality is combined with greater economic convenience.'

certain agricultural regions situated at the outlets of the Alpine valleys.

Three basic conditions (over and above the natural factors favourable to silk) made this development possible: first, the availability of motive power, suited to small-scale factories, which was provided by the numerous streams coming down from the Alpine valleys; secondly, a good supply of cheap manpower recruited in an area of poor agriculture; and lastly the customs protection afforded by the tariffs adopted by the various Italian states after the Restoration. These conditions enabled Italy to produce goods of a rather coarse quality, destined for a poorer market, and so to compensate for the much lower productivity of her factories as compared with those of other countries.

We come now to the other type of influence exercised by the industrial revolution—what we described earlier as the 'informational' influence. The technological aspects of the industrial revolution aroused the interest of certain progressive intellectual circles and some more enterprising businessmen who were beginning to travel and study technical experiments in other countries. Propaganda about these innovations and about the need for up-to-date technical training appeared in various periodicals such as the *Annali Universali di statistica*, founded by Francesco Lampato with the collaboration of G. D. Romagnosi and Melchiorre Gioia (1818–1859), or the *Politecnico* of Carlo Cattaneo (1839–1844), both published in Milan. A small coterie of Italian businessmen aware of the need for modern techniques was also beginning to emerge, in addition to those of non-Italian origin. Societies and institutes arose to promote such knowledge, and schools for the instruction of qualified workers were founded in Milan and Turin. But all this took place in backward environments: even the technological publications were mainly concerned with agricultural techniques. Industrial circles were restricted and in general preferred to exploit the easy conditions afforded by low labour costs and customs protection. Innovations arrived late, and market conditions provided little stimulus to introduce them. Consequently the groups of intellectuals urging technical advance inveighed against protectionism and the exploitation of female and child labour. When men from these circles became councillors or—as in the case of Camillo Cavour in Piedmont after 1848—entered the Government, they worked for a more liberalising policy in trade which, by compelling the entrepreneurs to face competition for survival, would encourage innovation in the industrial sphere. This trend, furthered by favourable international conditions and by a policy of increased public expenditure, achieved positive results in Piedmont between 1848 and 1859.

Propaganda and action for the railways was the most important watchword of the movement for the modernisation of Italy on the model of the north-west European countries. The years of these first industrial beginnings in North Italy, between 1830 and 1860, were in fact the railway years for north-western Europe, where development of railways was combined with considerable developments in iron and steel and in engineering. In Italy the first railways were built quite early—the Naples–Portici line in 1830, and the Milan–Monza in 1832. But these were very short lines of small economic significance (in both cases they connected the capital with the King's palace!) and were not followed up for a long time by any further network. Before the unification of 1860 there was a good deal of talk about the lines to be constructed, but in general, except in Cavour's Piedmont, little was done. Inaction was blamed on the political division of the territory, and this was one of the important reasons contributing to a spread of unitary national consciousness. Up to the war of 1859–60 which led to the birth of Italy as a unified State, only 1,798 km. of railways had been built, of which 819 km. were in Piedmont and 522 km. in Lombardy and the Veneto.

Throughout this period no great impulse arose towards the development of iron and steel or engineering industries. Railways, retarded as they were, provided no such impulse; nor did the production of iron steamships, whose first sporadic manifestation in Italy was in 1855 (the *Sicilia* of 120 tons, built in the Orlando shipyards in Genoa); nor did the construction of machinery for other industries, for the limited demand for machines was met through purchases from other countries more technically advanced; nor, lastly, did any such impulse arise from military requirements since these, given the political division of the country, were on only a small scale. Nevertheless production for the limited military needs of the small individual Italian states constituted, together with agricultural equipment production, the basis of the modest iron industry existing in those regions of Italy where there were iron mines: chiefly Lombardy, followed by Tuscany, Piedmont (Val d'Aosta), and Calabria. In the main industrial countries the *direct* process of production of iron from the mineral (the *stuckofen* furnace, known in Italy as *catalano*) had by then been abandoned and in the first decades of the nineteenth century the *indirect* process had been generally adopted, whereby first the intermediary product of pig-iron was obtained from the mineral by means of casting in blast-furnaces. In England and other West European countries, however, the transition from the direct to the indirect process had been accompanied by the revolutionary substitution of coal instead of charcoal (which would have been impossible under the direct method); and this had drastically reduced fuel costs and led to concentration of works. In Italy, on the other hand, the lack of coalfields compelled producers to continue to use charcoal, thus seriously restricting the use of the possibilities offered by the new techniques. Iron works were therefore still dispersed among small separate factories each with its own small production. Blast-furnaces still used the puddling system (the Bessemer converter was invented only in 1856 and there were none at all in Italy at the time of the unification).

Nevertheless in the regions where some start had been made with railway construction before the unification (mainly Piedmont, as has been seen, and to a lesser degree Lombardy and, less still, around Naples), the first small-scale indications of a new machine industry were coming into existence. Genoa, Turin, and Milan, the towns of the future 'industrial triangle', witnessed the first signs of an activity which in the decades to come was to characterise their whole physiognomy as major industrial centres. For the time being, however, these were confined to repair workshops or at most assembly-shops for imported railway stock, such as the locomotives that emerged from the Ansaldo workshops in Genoa in 1855. But in general the first locomotives were imported ready-made from abroad, and domestic production's share in the great 'railway adventure' was modestly confined to supplying some of the wagons. This situation was to continue for a long time.

'THE FIRST COAT OF PAINT'. SLOW INDUSTRIAL DEVELOPMENT UNDER THE FIRST FREE-TRADE GOVERNMENTS (1860–1878)

The two most important economic ideals inspiring the men of the Risorgimento were, as has been said, the extension throughout Italy of that fundamental symbol of progress, railways, and free trade, which English economic literature had led them to regard as the principal propulsive factor of trade. These were the main directives of the economic policy of Italy's first governments as a unified state after 1860. Neither of them, however, gave any great impetus to the country's industrial development. Railway construction was speeded up, and between 1861 and 1876 reached a yearly average of 376 km. of new lines, as compared with 176 km. a year in the preceding decade;[5] but this had very little linkage effect on industrial activities. The demand for rails, engines, carriages and trucks, and iron for bridges continued to be supplied, with few insignificant exceptions, from abroad. It was administered by foreign concessionaire companies which had links with non-Italian firms and had no interest in undertaking or encouraging the far from easy venture of rapidly creating an Italian engineering industry

5. Construction of new lines averaged 290 km. a year in 1877–85, and 302 km. in 1886–1905. The years 1876, 1885, and 1905 marked changes in Italy's railway policy.

—to say nothing of an iron and steel industry, which would have involved facing up to the handicap of lack of domestic pit-coal. The only fractions of the demand on domestic resources to arise from railway construction were those relating to the least complicated technical aspects: the making of sleepers (which caused extensive deforestation of the mountainsides, leading to serious ecological damage particularly in the South) and processes connected with the construction of the tracks. This type of demand led, for example, to the first establishment of the cement industry, in Lombardy.

The other pivot of the early governments' economic policy, free trade, was born of a desire to intensify trade contacts with the rest of the world, and principally with the more advanced countries of Europe. Since Italy was a predominantly agricultural country (in the first twenty years after unification agriculture accounted for 57 per cent of the gross private national product), intensification of trade meant chiefly increasing exports of agricultural produce and imports of industrial goods. A free-trade policy therefore found favour among landowners and farmers producing goods for export (silk, oil, cheese etc.), who were considerably more numerous, stronger, and better represented in Parliament than the few industrialists concerned with cotton, wool, or iron. Protectionist trends received little backing in the country as long as agrarian interests were not seriously threatened by foreign competition—which came about only in the second half of the '70s, with the influx of cheap cereals from America—and as long as the modest efforts of domestic industries had not yet reached the point where the industrialists could adduce the argument of manpower employment to exercise pressure on the political authorities.

Italian industry made only slow progress up to about 1880. It profited chiefly from the greater scope afforded by a domestic market enlarged by the unification and somewhat invigorated by the increased public expenditure accompanying the establishment of the unified State. This came about very gradually, favoured by some unforeseen circumstances. The first of these was the Government's adoption of the *corso forzoso* (inconvertibility of banknotes),[6] made necessary by the heavy expenditure of the war of 1866 against Austria. The *corso forzoso*, by altering the rate of exchange, in effect operated like a devaluation of the lira, favouring Italian as compared with foreign products. The second was the economic boom following the Franco-Prussian war of 1870, the chief effect of which for Italian industry was a temporary reduction in the competitive pressure of foreign products on the national market. An exceptional and short-term situation such as this was seen as an opportunity for a qualitative change by many economic circles in North Italy: the first small group of industrial joint-stock companies came into being; and, especially in the sphere of textiles, some of the landed nobility were attracted towards employing capital in industry in the form of shares, while some banks began to be interested in industrial investments. The subsequent crisis of 1873 created great difficulties for these joint-stock companies and banks. But in general, though many banks went bankrupt, the industries that had become concentrated and strengthened financially kept on their feet, so that all in all it could be said that a step forward had been taken in the modernisation of the industrial sphere: concentration was tried out, and a search was begun for new forms of outside financing for industries.

While quite substantial progress between 1860 and 1880 can be established with some degree of precision in the spheres of railways and public works, it is much more difficult to determine the extent of industrial development during that period. The study of certain significant figures will show, however, that some moderate development did occur. The most striking progress was in textiles. Silk spinning in particular, underwent a minor revolution: spurred on by a crisis in the domestic supply of the raw material (due to a silkworm disease), the industry began to import some raw silk from abroad and definitely moved over to the final phase of the spinning process (i.e. throw-

6. Declaring the paper money of the banks of issue to be no longer convertible into gold or silver.

ing). The proportion of fully spun silk within total silk exports rose from 17 per cent in 1855 to 80 per cent in 1865. Estimated annual consumption of raw cotton by Italian spinning mills increased from around 100 quintals in 1860 to nearly 200 quintals a year in 1871–1875. The number of spindles in the cotton industry, reckoned at 400,000–450,000 in 1860–1861, reached 745,000 in 1876 (but, by way of comparison, it should be remembered that in England there were 33 million spindles by 1860). The increase in silk-spinning during this period was mainly concentrated in Lombardy, while that in cotton-spinning was in Piedmont, where also lay the main nucleus of wool production, especially at Biella. (Later on, however, though Piedmont continued to be the chief centre for wool, that for cotton moved over to Lombardy, presumably as a result of the exhaustion of a series of Lombard investments in the silk branch.) Perhaps even more important than the increases in productive capacity and production were the changes arising in the attitude of the industrialists themselves. They showed a greater readiness to assimilate technological advances, greater attention to the quality of production (which was still crude), and greater aggressiveness on the political plane: all this was indicative of a significant advance, though it did not become fully apparent until the subsequent period.

There were even fewer significant changes in the other industrial sectors. In the iron industry, the uneconomic production of pig-iron by means of charcoal-firing remained a problem; but Italian foundries in their manufacture replaced the archaic domestically-produced pig-iron by using instead imported pig-iron or scrap (which was becoming increasingly available on international markets at this time owing to the large-scale replacement on the railways of iron rails by steel). Consequently iron production increased around threefold between 1860 and 1880; but it was mainly an incomplete cycle of production (lacking the link of pig-iron production), and much of it was makeshift and of inferior quality (typical of the re-use of scrap). The component *steel*, which in these years was becoming the dominant characteristic of Western European metallurgical industry was, completely absent. The growth of the engineering branch remained modest, still confined to workshops carrying out marginal work for the railways or military commissions. Only small attempts were made to provide machinery for other industries, for example for the textile industry.

Nevertheless the front on which this modest progress took place was gradually expanding. Development affected a number of other branches as well as those of textiles and iron and machinery. First attempts at industrialisation were being made in the food industry: the first unit of a future big sugar-manufacturing complex opened in 1873; Francesco Cirio founded, in 1875, the jam and food preserves industry that was to become famous; and progress was made in the field of distilleries. Paper production rose from 240,000 quintals in 1862 to 600,000 in 1876. In 1872 G. B. Pirelli founded an industry, that of rubber, which was to have a remarkable future. First experiments were made in the production of chemical fertilisers (1875) and other chemical manufactures.

During these first twenty years, in short, there was a slow advance but no revolutionary development in the industrial field. The country's economic picture remained predominantly agricultural, and the exercise of an industrial activity still seemed like what the social scientists would term 'deviant behaviour'. Two factors, however, tended to diminish the isolation of these first industrial initiatives from their social environment. First, this limited development remained strictly concentrated within the country's north-western regions (which enjoyed the advantages of a more advanced agriculture and of proximity to the already industrialised European countries), and consequently their percentage weight within that area was higher than the national average within the country as a whole. Secondly, the three capitals of these regions—Milan, Genoa, and Turin—were acquiring the aspect of modern urban centres possessing considerable trade contacts with industrial countries: they were thus in a position to act as points of reference and bases for the industrialisation of their respective areas, not only through their factories, but also through their secondary schools and colleges (both Turin and Milan started polytechnics and technical schools during these years), their technical information publications, and the development of a financial and commercial milieu which was more prepared to support industrial initiatives. In Milan, in particular, the principal European firms producing machinery formed a commercial bridge-head towards the potential market they saw developing as a result of Italian industrialisation.

The years 1860 to 1880 can therefore be regarded as a prolongation—with no substantial break in continuity such as might have been expected from the political change—of the progress begun around 1830: a half-century in which, in the economic sphere of Italy's north-western regions, a 'first coat of paint' was applied, later to be embellished by the colours in which the future picture of industrialisation would be portrayed. In the 'seventies unmistakable signs of the growing importance of this infant industry could already be seen: in 1871–1873 a first industrial inquiry was carried out; in 1876 the first statistics of factories and employment in the principal sectors were compiled; and in 1878 the onset of the social problem in industry caused a first inquiry into strikes. Industrial activities received some undeniable benefits from Italy's political unification. But since economic policy remained anchored to the free-trade assumption of an international division of labour in which Italy occupied an eminently agricultural place, those benefits were strictly limited.

PROTECTIONIST TRENDS AND 'STIFLED' EXPANSION IN THE 1880'S (1878–1889). CRISIS IN THE CENTURY'S LATTER YEARS (1889–1895).

Around 1880 however an important change occurred with the adoption of a different line in economic policy. Protectionist customs tariffs were introduced, at first, in 1878, on a small scale, and later, in 1887, more extensively. The

State intervened with direct support for the iron and engineering industries, instituting privilege quotas for Italian machinery in orders for railway supplies (the Baccarini law of 1882), giving assistance to national shipyards (law of 1885), and promoting the development of a full-cycle iron and steel works at Terni (1886) to supply the merchant marine. An impetus was given to building developments in the big cities. In those years, too, the first provisions for social legislation were launched. Moreover in those years one of the main handicaps for the development of Italian industry lost much of its earlier weight: the reduction in freight-charges brought down the price of imported coal, which fell from an annual average of 370 lire a ton in 1871–1880 to 260 lire in 1881–1890 (the maximum price was 500 lire in 1872–1873, the minimum 230 lire in 1886–1888). Coal imports therefore rose considerably: in 1877–1878 they were around 1,300,000 tons, but from then onwards they increased progressively to reach over 4 million tons at the end of the next decade.

At the same time a larger amount of private capital became available for non-agricultural investments. The international crisis and the ending of the *corso forzoso* combined to produce this situation. The agrarian crisis which developed around 1876 with the increased import of North American cereals made investment in land and farming less attractive. It also removed the hostility of agricultural circles towards tariff protection, thus leading to the formation of an industrial-agricultural bloc of interests in favour of higher tariffs. Lastly, it created greater availability of manpower and brought down food costs to a low level. The ending of the *corso forzoso* in 1880 produced, in turn, a new influx of foreign capital, especially from France.

These new conditions at first had only limited effects on manufacturing activities. This was firstly because the new capital available tended to go into urban investments (building and public services such as lighting, transport, etc.) rather than into the manufacturing industries; and the same was true of labour which, when it left the countryside, went mainly into building in the towns. Secondly, the measures to encourage and support national industry (protectionism, State commissions) came up against an extremely unfavourable economic situation just when they were beginning to bear fruit: the years between 1889 and 1896 were the darkest years of the great depression in the international sphere and bore especially heavily on the Italian economy. The Italian banking system was wellnigh shattered by the effects of a paralysing crisis in the building industry, in which it was deeply involved. Consequently the promising impetus which seemed to have been given to the manufacturing industries, both through the new economic policies and through urban development (which produced a derivative demand for industrial goods such as building materials, wood, iron, and machinery for public services), received a severe check in almost all branches of industry.

The greatest and least impeded beneficiary of the new impetuses given to industry was the branch that had already established itself to a certain extent, in other words textiles, and especially cotton. Unlike other branches, the cotton industry had a practically uninterrupted rate of development and experienced no noticeable effects from the crisis around 1890. The main factors in this development—apart from those traditional factors that had favoured the birth of the industry—were the effects of tariff protection, the existence of channels of finance independent of the central nucleus of the banking system, and the enterprise shown in foreign markets by its businessmen. Tariff protection finally guaranteed the home market for the cotton industry, and as a result of urbanisation this was an expanding market. Consequently in this already established branch of industry the tariff of 1878 had an immediate effect, whereas in other branches such as iron and steel it proved, in the short run, insufficient to make up an already sizeable gap. The existence of a source of autonomous financing arose from the fact that a network of smaller banks had gradually developed on a local basis, often in the form of co-operatives, in the textile areas. These banks, it is important to note, remained largely immune from the crisis which between 1888 and 1894 hit the bigger banks, which were deeply involved in building speculation. Exports developed especially to Latin America, in the wake of the vast wave of emigration from Italy which began in those years. It then became apparent that in the cotton industry in a particular area of North Italy the most substantial nucleus of medium-scale entrepreneurship in the country had been developing. Though still tentative and unstable, this nucleus had from the outset certain definite characteristics which persisted right down to our own times, extending gradually to other branches of medium-scale business. The chief characteristic was its enterprise in placing surplus products in marginal areas of distant markets; but at the same time those outlets often proved difficult to maintain and the tendency was then to replace them as new opportunities arose. There was a general propensity to attach more importance to the commercial aspects of a business than to the technological or organisational sides, and much individualism still persisted, coupled with unwillingness for businesses to merge. And where this type of entrepreneurship prevailed, concentration was resisted, the family firm stood out against the formation of joint-stock companies, and self-financing was preferred to recourse to the capital market.

Some statistics demonstrate this situation. In 1876 the cotton industry had 627 factories with 52,000 workers; in 1900 there were 727 factories with 135,000 workers (it must of course be taken into account that in those 25 years the factories had gradually absorbed the work of the isolated handicraftsmen, especially in weaving). Of these 727 concerns, only 18 were shareholding companies. Nevertheless the average size of factories grew larger. The 745,000 spindles of 1876 had become 2,100,000 in 1900. Looms, numbering 26,800 in 1876, had in 1900 reached 78,306 of which 60,722 were mechanical. The value of cotton manufactures, estimated at 51 million lire in 1876, rose, despite the intervening fall in prices, to 304 million. Productivity consequently showed a considerable increase, from a production value of 940 lire per worker to 2,250 lire. The share of Italian cotton in world cotton production also increased:

in 1880 Italy consumed 1–1·25 per cent of the world's cotton, whereas in 1900–1901 she consumed 3·51 per cent. Production, however, still consisted mainly of crude-quality manufactures.

The second beneficiary of the new climate was at this stage, strange to say, the engineering industry rather than iron and steel. Here, however, the impetus was due less to customs tariffs than to other factors: the first large railway commissions given to national industry, orders arising from the formation of urban and suburban tramway networks in the main cities of the North (Milan and Turin), and finally the acquisition of a share in the market for machinery for the developing textile industry (especially for boilers, which became essential when medium-scale concerns expanded and moved over to steam-driven machinery). Shipbuilding was unable for the time being to take advantage of the provisions in its favour. It should be emphasised that these developments in the machine industry in general concerned less complicated types of work (for example, supplying industry's demand for boilers or turbines rather than for machine tools) or the assemblage of imported parts. The greater importance we have attached here to developments in the engineering industry rather than in iron and steel refers, of course, to the qualitative more than the quantitative aspects.

A new phase in metallurgical production, however, was just beginning to open up, based on the final abandonment of the traditional method of production (using charcoal for pig-iron) or the intermediary method (using scrap) and on the beginnings of steel production. This started at Terni and at Genoa in 1887 and seemed to show such promising growth up to 1889 that hopes were entertained of reaching and surpassing in quantity the national production of iron and even the amount of steel imported. But this process was halted by the economic crisis. The high point of steel production of 1889 was not reached again until 1904.

THE MOST IMPORTANT YEARS OF INDUSTRIAL DEVELOPMENT

STATISTICAL DATA OF A 'SPURT'

Not until after the end of the great depression can Italian industrialisation be said to have made a real spurt—though it remains to be seen whether it was a large or a small-scale affair. We shall discuss this point in the conclusion. The years from 1897 to 1913 undoubtedly witnessed a much greater increase than ever before in industrial production. The quantitative estimates available in this connection differ. According to the official valuations of the Italian Statistical Institute (ISTAT), manufacturing production on the eve of the First World War was about double that of before the great depression (the average level of manufacturing production in 1886–1890 was the same as that of 1896)[7]; according to an estimate of Gerschenkron, on the other hand, production over that period increased two-and-a-half times (he, however, maintains that between 1886 and 1896 there was a slight increase in manufacturing production despite the depression). According to the ISTAT valuation, the annual rate of increase in industrial production between 1896 and 1913 was 4.3 per cent, whereas Gerschenkron puts it at 5.4 per cent. Both indices register a greater increase in 1896–1908 than in 1908–1913. According to ISTAT, the share of industrial activities in the national product of the private sector rose over the period from a fifth to about a fourth.

A comparison of the censuses of 1901 and 1911 for population over the age of ten brings out a number of facts which, when analysed, demonstrate the transformation that took place during the crucial first decade of the new century.[8] The male population employed in manufacturing

7. This doubling is confirmed in Giorgio Fuà's review of the ISTAT estimates (v. bibliography).

8. Population over the age of ten is taken as a basis because work by children of under 15 was quite widespread at that time. The industrial

increased by about 400,000, absorbing 54 per cent of the total increase in male population over ten years of age. Female population employed in industry and handicrafts showed no significant net increase; but a study of the changes occurring in the various sectors shows that while 98,000 fewer women were employed in textiles—demonstrating the decline in work done at home in this sector, another indication of the industrial development—165,000 more women were employed in other branches; this meant a higher proportionate rate of increase than in the case of men (25 per cent as against 20 per cent). The figures for increase in employment in the various individual sectors show that the biggest increases occurred in the sectors that can be described as industrial in a modern sense, and the distribution between the sectors tends to become less concentrated and more diffused. This is a sign of the development of a more widely industrial society.

According to ISTAT's estimates, capital formation as a whole (dwellings, public works, plant and equipment) in the first decade of the twentieth century was 60 per cent higher (at constant prices) than in 1881–1890. But if capital investment in plant and equipment (whether in industry or in other sectors) is taken separately, it will be seen that capital formation increased more rapidly, being 114 per cent higher in 1901–1910 than in 1881–1890. The share of plant and equipment in total gross fixed investments, which was 54 per cent in 1881–1890, rose to 72 per cent in 1901–1910. With regard to industrial investments, confirmation of this trend, if only partial and indicative, should be looked for in direct findings of the time concerning mechanisation of manufacturing production. Between 1903 and 1911—years in which surveys of industrial activity were carried out—motor-power installed in manufacturing industries doubled, rising from 580,000 to 1,170,000 HP. Installation of electric motors was on a particularly large scale; they were used in converting a considerable part of

census of 1911 gives 228,000 such child-workers out of a total of 1,814,000 workers in industry.

the hydraulic power hitherto used directly in many industries, especially the textile industry. There was also quite a considerable increase in gas-driven motors, used especially for cereal-grinding and in the metallurgical branch. The efforts for greater mechanisation brought a considerable increase during these years in the importation of machinery and industrial equipment. Coal imports also increased from 30,904,000 quintals a year in 1881–1890 to 56,340,000 quintals in 1901–1905 and 91,944,000 in 1906–1913. Total motor power consumption (coal, electricity, and hydrocarbides), expressed in calorific power,[9] rose from an annual average of 25,286 milliard calories in 1881–1890 to an annual average of 48,748 milliard in 1901–1905 and 83,116 milliard in 1906–1913. The overall value of both equipment imports and energy consumption increased threefold between 1888–1890 (the last years of the expansion of the 'eighties) and 1913, the eve of the First World War. These figures, it must be remembered, include uses both in industry and in transport. The latter is known to have absorbed about a quarter of total energy consumption just before the First World War, and its share was probably about the same in the preceding period. It may be concluded that the graph of these figures reflects pretty accurately the advance in the uses in the industrial sector, which strengthens the plausibility of Gerschenkron's figures for industrial production.

Thus during this period there was a breakdown of resistance to industrial development such as had not been possible when the movement towards expansion first began around 1880. It must be emphasised that the success of these efforts in the years now under consideration arose from the fact that, aided by the favourable international situation, the new trends in economic policy could at last take effect, and fuller scope could be given to that reserve of new attitudes and modernising tendencies which had been developing during the preceding period, and which till then had been partially paralysed by a serious recession. The reasons for the failure to succeed of the expansionist

9. Equivalent used: 1 kwh = 1 kg. coal = 7,000 calories.

movement in the 'eighties—unlike what happened in other countries such as Russia, in a similar situation of international economic depression—are largely to be attributed, as has been said, to the fact that non-agricultural investments during those years turned in the direction of urban development rather than industry (the building boom contained within itself an imminent prospect of crisis). The estimates of the formation of fixed capital in fact confirm that in the decade 1881–1890 the share allocated to housing and public works was equal to that for plant and equipment, whereas in the period 1897–1913 the proportion altered considerably, to a level of 1 : 3 in favour of plant and equipment.

INDUSTRIALISATION AGAINST A BACKGROUND OF BALANCED FOREIGN ACCOUNTS

Italian industrialisation in the years 1897–1913 did not—and this is a fact to be emphasised—involve any drastic change-over from consumption to investment in the use of resources. During this period per capita consumption increased considerably, though naturally at a lower rate than investment.

An effort towards industrialisation involves strong pressure on consumption when the use of productive factors (labour and capital) has to be diverted from the production of consumer goods (for instance food) to that of capital goods, or when a part of the consumer goods produced has to be diverted from the home market to be exported in exchange for imports of capital goods, or, again, when importation of the consumer goods needed to build up domestic stocks of some commodities is reduced to make way for importation of capital goods. In such cases the reduced availability of consumer goods on the home market causes their prices to rise more steeply than the increase in nominal wages, thus producing a fall in real wages, that is to say, a distribution of the income produced that is more unfavourable than before to incomes derived from labour. This picture, however, in no way corresponds to what happened in Italy between 1897 and 1913.

The average availability of foodstuffs per inhabitant, expressed in calories, underwent a sharp increase at the beginning of the period under consideration; it then remained constant for about ten years, to increase again in the last years (1911–1913). This was made possible, in the first place, because although part of the labour force moved over from agriculture into industry, agricultural and livestock production increased considerably during the period in question. The demand for some types of goods most in request (cereals, meat) increased at a greater rate than domestic supplies, and consequently foodstuff imports increased; but the export of certain other foodstuffs (cheese, citrus fruits, dried fruit) also increased considerably, and consequently the agriculture and foodstuffs section of the balance of trade (a section which had usually shown a credit balance in the past), managed to remain equalised for several years and only went into deficit towards the end of the period. And it was only in the last years of the period that the share of foodstuffs in total imports (a share which had fallen in the previous years, despite the absolute increase) went up considerably.

The increase in consumption was general, affecting other commodities as well as foodstuffs. The rate of expansion of consumption as a whole was only a little lower than that of the national income and was 2·5–3 times greater than the rate of expansion of the population. The greater part of non-foodstuff consumption was connected with the new way of life arising from increasing urbanisation, the main items being housing and clothing. The increase was unequally distributed, the main beneficiaries being no doubt the urban middle classes, whose importance was growing. But there were also considerable improvements in some of the richer agricultural regions of the North.

The pressure of rising demand soon made itself felt, and food prices went up, though without serious effects until the later years. For many years, indeed, the prices of foodstuffs most in popular demand (bread, *pasta*, rice, wine, sugar) actually fell, while prices, of the more luxury-type commodities (meat, butter, eggs) rose more steeply and continuously. But the workers, both in industry and in agriculture, showed a combative spirit and combined in strong organisations, thus managing to secure considerable increases in real wages, which in industry had risen by about 25 per cent by the eve of the First World War in comparison with the beginning of the expansion (at the end of the century). Naturally these wages still remained very low if compared with those of already industrialised countries; there were also significant differences between sector and sector, region and region, and big and small concerns as well as between men and women workers.

The fact that the increased demand for foodstuffs kept pace with the development of agriculture and the production of food helped to keep a favourable balance of payments during the expansion period and to ensure a significant expansion of consumption. But there were two other important factors. The development of export industries made it possible to contain within certain limits the unavoidable deficit caused by industrialisation which called for the supply of energy, raw and semi-finished materials and machinery. And invisible earnings—freights, tourism, and emigrants' remittances also sustained the balance of payments.

The principal exporting industry was that of textiles, silk, in particular, touching the highest levels in both production and export during this period. In 1907 the value of silk exports began to fall, and there was talk of a crisis in this branch, but just before the war its credit value within the balance of trade was nevertheless higher than in the years before the expansion period. The value of silk exports continued to represent between a third and a quarter of total exports, and this share fell only slightly when subtracting imports in the sector, which also increased owing to the fact that Milan had now taken the place of Lyons as the principal European market. Exports of the cotton industry also developed considerably, accounting in some years for a tenth of total exports. The balance of trade in cotton (which included both raw material imports and domestic consumption) was practically equalised. This meant that increased domestic consumption of cotton textiles was compensated in the balance of trade by exports. This estimate can also be applied to domestic consumption of textiles as a whole when we consider that the deficit in the balance for wool was in turn compensated by high net exports of those other traditional exports, hemp and flax.

But the marginal phenomenon (in an economic sense) which contributed decisively towards a favourable balance of trade at this time was migration. Italian emigration, especially overseas, assumed important dimensions during these years. It had begun to increase sharply towards the end of the 1880s. But in the decade 1901–1910 it reached an annual average of 600,000 persons. The majority of the emigrant workers sent part of their earnings home to their families or brought back savings if they returned home themselves. Calculations for the period 1901–1913 show that, against a commercial deficit of 10,230 million lire, invisible items showed a credit of 12,291 million, over a third of which came from tourism and over a half from emigrants' remittances. Emigrants' savings constituted a peculiarly Italian form of workers' contribution to industrialisation and gave rise to a phenomenon which Marx might have included among those forming the picture of 'primitive accumulation'.

These three advantageous circumstances—an expanding agricultural production, development of the export industries, and an increase in the invisible sector of the balance of trade, due largely to emigrants' remittances—enabled the effort towards industrialisation to go ahead in these years despite the meagre participation of foreign capital, and to be conducted against a background of balanced foreign accounts, without serious tensions in the prices system, and therefore, despite protectionism, with a balanced expansion of internal consumption. Some imbalances did occur in the course of this effort but they came from other sources.

A 'TWO-SIDED' INDUSTRIALISATION: ONE SIDE LOOKING TOWARDS THE PAST

Since the decisive impact of Italian industrialisation occurred after the end of the great depression, it follows that its development took place within the framework of the European Industrial Revolution's 'second wind'[10], in which the 'technological climacteric' of the great depression was overcome through the development of new forms of production.

The basic technological features of the 'second wind' were the large-scale use of new materials (steel and new chemical products), the introduction of new sources of energy, and a remarkable development in the machine industry. That development covered a great many different sides, the most important being expansion of the assemblage industries, multiplication of machine tools endowed with the new capabilities made possible by the use of steel, and the birth of the automobile industry.

Italy's industrialisation effort during this period presents a curious duality, for while it profited from the acquisitions of the first phase of the Industrial Revolution, it adopted only partially the new productions and technological assets brought by the revolution's 'second wind'. This two-sided character of Italian industrialisation at the beginning of the new century provides the reasons for the limitations of this 'spurt' and for many of the difficulties which impeded the development of the country's economy in the subsequent twenty years between the two world wars. For the market prospects of many traditional forms of production (such as textiles), on which industrial efforts had been concentrated during the years 1896–1913, began to decline, while the success of the new forms of production had not yet become fully established.

The textile industry was the chief representative of that

10. For the significance of this term see D. S. Landes, 'Technological Change and Development in Western Europe, 1750–1914', in *The Cambridge Economic History*, vol. VI, Cambridge, 1965.

aspect of Italian industrialisation which still aimed to profit from the results of the first wave of the Industrial Revolution. Italy's greatest industrial development at this time still lay in the textile branch, where the fundamental silk and cotton industries reached their full maturity. In fact the textile industry more than any other could rely on a considerable amount of means and equipment and of entrepreneurial skill. Its rate of increase appeared lower than that of other branches during the years of expansion, for the obvious reason that the point of departure was higher. But the importance of the textile industry can be clearly seen when we recall that it was the country's sole big exporting industry, accounting for some 40 per cent of the total value of the credit side of Italy's trade balance in the years preceding the First World War, and for nearly 60 per cent of its non-alimentary exports. It continued to be the main source of employment for workers in the manufacturing branch, accounting for about a third of such workers in the 1911 census. Even up to the eve of the war, in 1913, according to ISTAT estimates the added value of the textile industry represented 20 per cent of the total product of the manufacturing industries.

Textile progress in these years can be summarised in the following terms: complete conquest of the domestic market; accentuation of its character as an exporting industry; industrial development of weaving—which till then had been mainly organised under the 'putting-out' system—as well as of spinning; and mechanisation and electrification of both spinning and weaving.

Italy's export of silk, which since before the unification had represented about a third of the value of Italian exports, slightly reduced its percentage share during the period 1896–1915, but this slight fall occurred within an increased total value of exports. The quality of the silks exported improved considerably.

Cotton's trade balance, confined to manufactured goods, at the turn of the century moved from deficit to credit, and Italy became an exporting country for cotton goods. The cotton balance as a whole remained in deficit, however, taking into account the fact that net imports of raw material were used chiefly for production for the home market. Flax and hemp production for export also continued to increase. Less progress was made in wool exports; though their value went up, it remained below that of imports, although here too the export/import relationship improved.

The development of industrial weaving within the various branches of the textile industry had remained somewhat limited throughout the whole of the earlier phase, during which the main developments were, as has been seen, in spinning. In the silk branch, in 1876 there were only 250 mechanical looms and 12,000 hand-looms; in 1890 the figures were 2,500 and 12,000 and even in 1898 there were only 3,000 mechanical looms as compared with the 12,000 hand-looms. But by 1912 the proportion was reversed, with 15,000 mechanical looms to 5,000 hand looms. Exports of woven silk as a percentage of total silk exports moved from 6 per cent in 1885 to 17 per cent in 1913, at a time of exceptional expansion of silk exports as a whole. Particularly remarkable was the increase in exports of Italian silk textiles to England, where they had conquered positions held in the past by silks from Lyons. The radical change that had taken place in the industrial attitude of the silk-weavers is illustrated by the efforts made in investment: production by hand-loom involved virtually no capital investment, for a hand-loom cost only about 200 lire and was capable of a product worth some 3,000 lire a year. The average price of a mechanical loom, on the other hand, was 6,000 lire, and its annual production of woven silk was worth between 8,000 and 9,000 lire. The increase in investment in mechanisation of silk-weaving between 1898 and 1912 can therefore be estimated at 72 million lire of that period.

In the cotton industry there were 65,000 mechanical looms in 1896; by 1912 these had risen to 115,000, thus reaching an increase of 59,000 units. There were then still 30,000 hand-looms. The automatic Northrop machine was still practically unknown; it came into use only after the war. Cotton exports, unlike those of silk, had from the first consisted mainly of woven rather than spun goods, being for a different market: the Italian silk industry had in fact, as we have seen, come to birth as an industry supplying semi-finished goods for the industry of industrial countries, whereas the export side of the Italian cotton industry was originally based on supplying the consumer market of non-industrial or partly-industrial countries. Consequently the development in cotton exports was the reverse of that in silk: it was only *after* advances had been made in the export of woven cotton that considerable quantities of spun yarn also began to be exported to countries where cotton-weaving factories were beginning to develop, in some cases with Italian capital. In 1895 Italy exported woven cotton goods to a value of 21 million lire and spun yarn to a value of 2 million. In 1913 exports of woven goods had increased ten-fold, reaching a value of 210 million, while those of spun yarn had increased twenty-fold, reaching 39 million. The trend was rather different in the flax and hemp industry, which had started as an export industry in Italy with characteristics similar to those of silk, in other words as a supplier to foreign industry of semi-finished goods, based on local raw materials. This predominant characteristic was maintained, if to a lesser degree: in 1895 the value of exports of spun yarn was 13 million lire, of woven goods 4 million; in 1913 spun yarn reached a value of 23 million and woven goods 17 million.

Progress was more difficult in the wool branch, where the problem was to achieve a better quality product, which called for greater technical efficiency than in the other textile branches. Because of these greater technical difficulties, the trade balance for woollen manufactures, unlike cotton, had not yet as was said earlier, reached a credit position by the First World War, though it came near to doing so. Domestic production in 1913 covered 319,000 quintals, or 91 per cent, of the estimated 350,000 quintals of domestic consumption. (The percentage in value was lower, however, because dependence on imports concerned the more costly combing wools.) But the woollen industry remained weak on the export side: in 1913 woven and mixed woollen goods were exported to a value of 31 million lire, while the value of imports was 54 million. The inferior quality of most Italian woollen goods can be seen from the fact that the value per kg. of woven woollen exports was 10.80 lire, whereas that of imports was 18.15 lire. But the home market had been conquered for wool too, except for the finer combing wools. Developments in mechanical weaving, which had made this success possible, can be summed up in the transition from 6,507 mechanical looms in 1894 to an estimated 12,000 in 1915.

The development of weaving—which represents the greatest innovation in the story of Italy's textile industry in these years—came about on the basis of a striking expansion in the number of spinning-mills. Silk-spinning (reeling and throwing) was an exception in this respect, for its increase in production was effected mainly through a more intensive use of its existing productive capacity, involving no great investment and virtually no increase in manpower; but the organisation of labour and its distribution throughout the year improved, as also did its productivity.

Considerable investment occurred, on the other hand, in cotton-spinning. The 1,910,000 spindles of 1898 had risen by 1914 to 4,620,000. In the first years of the twentieth century Italy's rate of increase in the number of cotton-spindles was the highest in the world. Cotton-spinning benefited greatly from the new source of hydroelectric power. The ring spindle was much more widely used in Italy than the self-acting spindle: in 1913 there were 3.5 million ring spindles as compared with 1.1 million self-actings. The preference was typical of the newer cotton-producing countries such as the United States, Japan, and India, whereas the reverse was true of Great Britain.[11] The use of ring spindles, which gave a third higher production than the self-actings, made it possible to achieve a considerable

11. Cf. R. E. Tyson, 'The Cotton Industry', in D. H. Alcroft ed., *The Development of British Industry and Foreign Competition (1875–1914)*, London, 1968, pp. 121ff.

increase in production with a reduced labour-force (thereby reducing the loss that regulations on night work caused to entrepreneurs) and to speed up production in general.

The main technical effort of the woollen industry, aided by tariff protection, consisted at this time in promoting the production of the finer and more costly combing wools in preference to the traditional carding wools. This effort chiefly affected spinning, whereas weaving suffered from it in a sense because with customs duties the cost of combing wools went up; consequently the wool balance continued to be in deficit as far as the finer and more costly combing goods were concerned. However the number of combing-spindles rose more rapidly than that of carding-spindles, and combing-machines began to be used, the most frequent type being the French rectilinear machine, with a lower hourly productivity than the circulating type of machine used in England.

It is worth noting, as an instance of the two-sided character of Italian industrialisation during this period, that in the textile industry as a whole the stage of manufacture represented by dyeing remained backward. Dyeing was linked with advances in chemicals and was therefore more orientated towards the 'second wind' stage. Despite the advances made in this field, most of the raw silk exported by Italy was not dyed, and much of the silk that needed to be dyed had to be temporarily exported to France, Switzerland or Germany for treatment. There was a similar situation in the cotton industry with regard to both mercerisation and dyeing, which were largely done in Germany.

According to ISTAT's estimates, the textile industry, together with the foodstuffs industries and other agricultural-manufacturing industries, in 1913 still represented 60 per cent of the total added value of the manufacturing industries. About 60 per cent of the 1.5 million workers registered in the manufacturing industries (1911 census) were also employed in that group, which could be considered the traditional side of the Italian industrial edifice and was still the most important from the quantitative angle. The group developed considerably during this period, not only in the textile branch but also in the branches of timber and foodstuffs industries. This development was particularly marked in certain foodstuffs sectors such as sugar (which was favoured by protectionism), alcoholic drinks (beer, liquor distilleries), sweets (especially chocolate), food preserves, and macaroni, sectors which had big export trade, especially to reception countries for Italian emigrants. Modern mechanisation and concentration began to develop in other important—and hitherto dispersed—industries, such as cereal-milling and olive-crushing.

PARTICIPATION IN THE 'SECOND WIND' OF THE INDUSTRIAL REVOLUTION

The aspect of Italy's industrial development in 1896–1914 which was more definitely orientated towards the Industrial Revolution's 'second wind' was undoubtedly the birth of a hydroelectrical industry. A large part of the capital set free by the nationalisation of the railways in 1905 was directed towards this branch of investment. Nor was it fortuitous that the big commercial banks, formed through German initiative after the banking crisis of the 1890s, turned their interest in this direction. These big banks evolved a positive strategy of intervention in relation to this particular opportunity for investment, resting as it did on the solid foundation of a patrimony of natural resources to be exploited in the big Alpine river basins. This strategy, according to many contemporary commentators, combined Italian industrial development with the export interests of German industry, first for electrical machinery, then for machinery in general, and finally for all kinds of industrial products, and it therefore tended in a certain sense to give Italian industrialisation a 'complementary' character. But it was nevertheless a project to be actively pursued, a sort of planning operation in a milieu that was not particularly rich in capital and initiatives. It did not edge out other plans, for no such other plans existed, and it therefore represented a positive way of promoting industrialisation.

Between 1895 (the year in which a law favouring the transport of power from a distance came into force) and 1914, a vast amount of capital was invested in electrical constructions. The value of the installations reached 1,000–1,200 million lire, a figure equal to around 4 per cent of all fixed investments in plant and equipment during that period. By 1914 these generating plants were producing a power of 1,150,000 kw. (of which 850,000 kw. was hydroelectric), with an annual production of 2,575 million kwh. This tremendous development had a great psychological effect in Italian economic circles, giving a sense of release from the industrial impotence to which many still believed Italy was doomed because of her lack of energy resources. People made the satisfactory discovery that hydroelectrical production alone could replace around 2 million tons a year of coal imports, or about a fifth of all the coal imported. It was not much, but on the eve of the war there were a great many hydroelectrical resources still to be exploited.

It must also be emphasised that the major part of the new hydroelectrical production was destined for industry. The textile industry absorbed the highest proportion, followed by the machine industry. Iron and steel's consumption was not very high (though in those years it was more widely believed than was later to prove technically justified that electro-metallurgy would have a great future), whereas that of the chemical industry was by comparison quite large—this was, in fact, one of the chief potential fields for industrial consumption of electric energy. Taken as a whole, the industrial census of 1911 shows that at that date half the power of the motors installed in the manufacturing industry was electric.

The other great 'new' industry to be born in this period was that of steel. In 1895 Italy's production of steel accounted for about a quarter of her total iron-and-steel production, which still consisted chiefly of iron. But the level of production was low, little more than 200,000 tons;

and the steel industry itself was still virtually non-existent. By the eve of the First World War, however, Italy had achieved some steel production, though it was still comparatively modest: 933,000 tons in 1913 (and 427,00 tons of pig-iron). Iron production at that date was only 193,000 tons. Thus Italy's economy seemed to have entered—with the aid of tariff protection—on the age of steel, viewed at least from the point of view of production in her iron-and-steel industry. The reality was unfortunately less satisfactory. First and foremost, unlike what happened in the other 'new' industry, electricity, the price of the existence of the iron-and-steel industry was really paid by the user sectors that were not protected, and chiefly by part of the machine industry. It must be borne in mind that the steel age is the era not only of its production but also, and more particularly, of its utilisation. Italy's industrialisation effort could realise to a certain extent the first condition; it was less able to realise the second.

Moreover, the course embarked on by the Italian steel industry was not calculated to help it to recover from its original disadvantage of low productivity in a nascent industry. Such recovery would in any case have been difficult given Italy's great drawback, her lack of low-grade anthracite deposits. The basic technological choice was the decision to adopt the Martin furnace in preference to the Thomas convector. This was the same choice that had been made by the steel industry in England, while it differed from the methods adopted in France and Germany. Now, as is well known, the Thomas process permitted quicker and therefore more economical production, despite the higher cost of the plant; but at the same time the Thomas process, because of its greater speed, called for greater skill and technical care and in general gave a less homogeneous product, less adaptable (in particular, less suitable for use in sheet form) and leaving more slag. A characteristic of the Martin process, on the other hand, was that it afforded the possibility of using scrap, in the proportion of fifty-fifty with pig-iron, in the production of steel. Moreover the Martin process was more fungible. Lastly, it allowed for greater elasticity in production and was thus better suited to the uncertainties of the market in which Italian production operated.

The reasons for Italy's iron-and-steel industry's choice of the Martin process, thus differing from that of other continental countries, were various and complex. They were to some extent the same that had prompted that choice in England, where the importance of the shipbuilding industry, with its demand for iron and steel plates, had played a part; but the context in Italy was different: there the birth of the iron-and-steel industry was closely connected with commissions for the navy and with the protection accorded to the shipbuilding industry. Secondly, this choice was influenced by the preceding structure of the Italian metallurgical industry with its high consumption of scrap and its reluctance to embark on the continuous process of manufacture, including the whole cycle of working the mineral. In the early stages, in other words, there was a shortage of pig-iron production, which would have afforded the advantage of large-scale vertical economies deriving from the thermic unity of production: steel production consequently started with the use of scrap and imported pig-iron, and this conditioned its subsequent development. Thirdly, various centrifugal forces pushed in the direction of a production divided into several units, and this both limited the advantages of large-scale economies and also impeded capital-intensive investment (the Thomas plant called for an investment at least ten times higher, and for a minimum size five or six times greater, than the Martin plant). Italy's iron-and-steel works were scattered in various different places: some in Liguria, connected with the naval shipyards; others in Lombardy which derived from the old iron industry of the valleys and were developed by an environment that was the most industrially advanced part of Italy; in Umbria there was the isolated works at Terni, established through government initiative; the vicinity of iron ore in the isle of Elba led to the location of pig-iron production in Tuscany; and, lastly, the first laws of 1904 providing incentives to establish industries in the backward South resulted in the establishment of a new iron-and-steel works near Naples. The results of this dispersed development, coupled with the serious disadvantage of having to import the necessary coal, meant that the Italian iron-and-steel industry led a very difficult life right up to the time of the reorganisation following the Second World War. The Italian industrial structure was endowed with the component of steel, but it had it in the form of a weak joint, in constant need of care and assistance.

The truer protagonist of the steel age, the machine industry, had an even more difficult progress. It is, in fact, relatively easier to further the birth of a metallurgical industry—by means of tariff protection and assured outlets (commissions for railways and naval shipyards)—than of a machine industry. The machine industry has a great variety of production; in order to specialise it needs vast industrial markets; it often needs to be in a position to compete on international markets in order to achieve sufficient dimensions; and, lastly, it needs a large number of skilled workers, who are difficult to come by in the early stages of an effort towards industrialisation. Despite the protection accorded to the naval shipyards, not even this branch of heavy engineering production succeeded in dominating the home market. England continued to be the chief supplier of merchant vessels for the Italian shipowners, who still preferred to rely on the old and well-tried capability of British shipyards. In 1913, against a national production of 536,000 tons, 1,495,000 tons of shipping was still imported, 893,000 tons of which came from England. The position was even more unfavourable in relation to ships' engines: 45,000 HP of national production, as against 146,000 HP of foreign production, of which 92,000 HP was British. National industry did, on the other hand, succeed eventually in securing the monopoly for railway construction material, as a result of the nationalisation of the railways in 1905. Even in this case circumstances were not particularly favourable for the Italian industry; in the three years following the passage of the railways into State hands, some 38 per cent of the largest and most urgent commissions had to be given to foreign industry, because during the last period of private management urgent requirements of rolling stock had accumulated to such an extent that the national industry alone could not cover them. This was the last unhappy chapter of that history of lost opportunities that the railways represented in Italian industry.

Henceforth, however, neither shipbuilding nor railway construction constituted the sinews of modern engineering. The modern machine industry was *par excellence* an industry for creating 'new' goods, whether producer goods (such as electric motors, internal combustion engines, machine tools for mass production, agricultural machinery, office machines, sewing machines, etc.) or consumer goods destined to change the way of life, such as bicycles or motor-cars. On the whole Italian industry did not participate at this stage in the field of 'new' investment goods except for some occasional rare and promising initiative such as that of typewriters, production of which was started by Camillo Olivetti at Ivrea in 1911, or of typographical machines. A breach was opened up, however, in the field of 'new' consumer goods by the bicycle and motor-cycle industries, and above all by the automobile industry. This last was probably one of the most brilliant and effective examples of Italian industry's participation in the new international industrial movement of those years, and, more generally, it was of great importance in opening the way for the rise of a modern machine industry in Italy by stimulating inventions in this field, creating a skilled labour force, and promoting the rise of collateral types of production (among which must be mentioned the aluminium industry). In the years immediately before the First World War some 20,000 motor vehicles a year were registered in Italy, only 3–4,000 of which were imported; this meant that the domestic market was controlled by national production. Naturally it was still a very limited market, for the automobile was then a luxury in a society like that of Italy, still a long way from the mass consumption age. Production reflected this characteristic of the market: it consisted chiefly of large cars, built by methods that still savoured of handicrafts, very different from the methods that were already gaining ground in the United States, where mass production, with an extensive development of cast and stamped parts, had begun. Because of this characteristic of Italian automobile production, there were at first too many isolated initiatives in this field; it was not until after a crisis arose in 1907 that a process of concentration began.

To complete the picture of the share of Italy's industrialisation movement in the 'second wind' during the years before the First World War, something must be said about developments in the chemical industry. This was one of the 'new' sectors in which development followed more routine lines: here there was no outburst of enthusiasm such as accompanied the early hydroelectrical advances, no rapid growth such as protection and commissions encouraged in steel, not even daring ventures such as men like Agnelli or Olivetti were attempting in some particular branch of the machine industry. The Italian chemical industry took practically no part in the two fields which had been opened up in that sector by the discoveries of the second half of the nineteenth century—the production of alkalies (used in the textile, soap, and paper-making industries) according to the new (Soda Solvay) methods, and the synthesis of organic components, which found its widest applications in the field of colouring materials, explosives, pharmaceutics, and photography, opening up the way—with artificial silk—to man-made fibres. Italy's absence from the more advanced sectors of chemical developments was due partly to her shortage of experienced scientists and technicians in this field, partly to the lack of those carboniferous products which formed the basis for the second of those developments.

The Italian chemical industry at the beginning of the twentieth century was concerned chiefly with fertilisers for agriculture, especially superphosphates, whose productive increase is shown in terms of production of sulphuric acid.

This rose from 139,000 tons in 1898 to 645,000 tons in 1913. Italian production of superphosphates covered 95 per cent of domestic consumption.

From 1905 onwards nitrogenous fertilisers were also produced, especially through the related production of calcium carbide, calcium cyanide, and ammonium sulphate. Production of these nitrogenous fertilisers, however, was both small as compared with that of more advanced countries and quite insufficient for the growing demands of Italian agriculture, which had to procure much of its supplies from abroad: in 1913, domestic production accounted for 134,000 quintals of ammonium sulphate, while 217,000 quintals were imported. Potassium fertilisers were little used at that time, and were all imported.

THE AGENTS OF THE SPURT: THE STATE, ENTREPRENEURSHIP, THE COMMERCIAL BANK

It would be a mistake to underestimate the fact that the Italian industrial development of the years 1896–1913 occurred within a favourable international economic climate, in the upper trend of what Kondratieff calls a 'long wave'. This appears the more significant when we recall the important part played in its growth by the export trade, both in agricultural and in industrial goods (especially textiles), a result of the rising trend of international demand. It is more difficult to estimate the effect of the movement of international prices, bearing in mind the big increases in imports made necessary by the growing dynamism of Italian industrial production. The terms of trade showed a tendency to worsen. Clearly, however, protectionism counteracted (at the expense of the home market, which nevertheless continued to expand) many of the negative effects both of falling and of rising international prices. Industrial investments were able to benefit overall from the fall in prices of imported machinery. The substitution of internal sources of energy (electricity) for imported sources (coal) enabled many industries to escape the effects of the periodical increases in coal prices. But it must be added that in the years of greatest expansion (1902–1905) the price of imported coal remained low.

Such was the international framework. But the favourable international situation does not suffice to explain Italy's industrial expansion at the beginning of the century. As was mentioned in the previous chapter, a strongly protectionist tariff was in force in Italy from 1887 (only slightly mitigated by the trade treaties concluded in the following years with various countries), but the crisis of the 1890s had impeded the effects of this measure. Its effects, however, became apparent as soon as the international economy emerged from the depression and optimism returned to business circles. State action for the promotion of industrial development was not, moreover, confined to tariff protection. Domestic industry received other forms of aid, the most important being orders for the railways, which had been nationalised in 1905, navigation bounties, and building awards for ships produced in Italian shipyards. This legislation in favour of the shipbuilding industry also went back to the 1880s (1885) but it had had no immediate effect because of the depression (which in this field had shown itself in a heavy fall in freight rates). These measures of support for heavy engineering went some way towards compensating for the greater burdens which that sector had had to sustain through tariff protection for the metallurgical industry. All the rest of the engineering industry, however, derived no benefit from such compensation, and this caused disputes, the echo of which still reaches us today from many historians who speak of the damage caused to the engineering industry by a largely metallurgical protectionism. It must however be emphasised that the more technologically efficient parts of the engineering industry—those concerned with machine tools for the industries or for electro-engineering—suffered less from the high cost of materials than from the shortage of skilled labour and from the still limited size of the market for industrial capital goods. A tariff protection of the engineering industry which was working for the other industrial activities, on the other hand, would probably have damaged the other industries' possibilities of securing equipment more than it would have helped the engineering industry itself.

The protection assured by the State to many industrial activities—metallurgy and heavy engineering, the textile industry and the food industry—was a very important factor in the spurt of these years. The State, however, itself played no part in entrepreneurial or financing activities, and its furtherance of industrial development did not take those forms (as it was later to do, after the First World War). Private entrepreneurs and certain financial operators therefore played a very important part in the development of industry.

There were quite a number of such capable private entrepreneurs: this can be seen from the fact that industrialisation at this time was carried on in numerous smaller factories rather than in large-scale concerns. Except for the iron-and-steel industry and one or two other concerns, the majority of factories were of small or medium scale. This was true of the textile sector and also of the more difficult engineering sector, which was not yet widely established but which, as has been seen, embarked on some promising ventures (automobiles, typewriters, typographical machines). The same can be said of the chemical industry. All this limited the advantages of concentration, but at the same time such diffusion meant that there was a more widely spread readiness for economic ventures which is one of the most difficult factors in industrial development. It could probably not have been overcome but for the fact that in the more advanced regions of the 'triangle' there was a long-standing tradition of small concerns, especially in the textile field, many of which had been strengthened, as was said earlier, by the influx at various times of foreign entrepreneurs who had imparted their methods. The Italians' capacity for entrepreneurship may not seem to have amounted to much when compared with that of English or German businessmen, and when account is taken of the support given by protectionism and the low wages paid. Their chief defect lay in factory organisation, but they showed a certain initiative in foreign markets and afforded some examples of technical ingenuity. There were some early instances of Italian businessmen who proved capable of embarking on the process of concentration or merging in sectors where dispersion had hitherto been the general rule (e.g. the automobile and chemical industries).

The activities of private industrial entrepreneurs in certain sectors found special support, both financial and otherwise, in the commercial banks. After the banking crisis which, beginning in 1889, had led in 1893 to the failure of the principal Italian banks, the void thus created in the banking system had been promptly filled through the initiative of German bankers, who had promoted the establishment of two new credit institutes, the Banca Commerciale Italiana and the Credito Italiano. These institutes operated after the German model of deposit and investment banks, becoming deeply involved in financing the birth and development of industrial undertakings in Italy. These banks, grasping the great possibilities of the hydro-electrical industry and also profiting by the conditions created by protectionism in certain fields (especially iron and steel), did not confine themselves to direct financing but also helped the concerns to form shareholding companies and to concentrate and reach agreements among themselves when this seemed advantageous. They also intervened in the running of the enterprise and gave technical assistance. It is interesting to note, in confirmation of the entrepreneurial activity of these banks, that they operated principally in the *new* sectors of Italian industry, almost completely neglecting the more traditional sectors such as the textile industry.[12]

And it was chiefly in the new industries that concentration and the formation of shareholding companies developed. According to the industrial census of 1911, the sectors in which share companies were most widespread were production and distribution of energy, mining, metallurgy, and

12. This emerges clearly in a dissertation by Jon Sheldon Cohen, *Finance and Industrialisation in Italy 1894–1914* (University of California), which the author kindly allowed the present writer to see.

chemicals. Formation of shareholding companies was on only a limited scale in the textile sector, especially in the more traditional branches such as the silk industry. But on the whole the progress of industrial share capital was remarkable: between 1896 and 1914 it increased around ninefold.

The spurt made by Italian industry in the years 1896–1913 was thus the result of a *combination* of different factors, none of which can claim an exclusive or predominant role in it. Some of these factors were traditional (such as private entrepreneurship), others were of the kind that operated especially in historic cases of retarded industrialisation such as that of Germany (the mixed deposit and investment bank). Even the State's protectionist policy (which was the only outstanding manifestation of State support for the industrial development) is not a particular characteristic of *late-joiners* countries. It was adopted by virtually all the countries that became industrialised during the nineteenth century, with the exception of Great Britain, whose industrial revolution had begun in the eighteenth century, and who, in any case, had had protectionist precedents in the mercantilist era.

CONCLUSION

In the formation of industrial Italy it is difficult to pinpoint any real 'big spurt'. Even the chief supporter of this theory, Gerschenkron, appears somewhat embarrassed at mentioning that the growth rates of Italian industrial production, even in the years of greatest development, do not approach the much higher rates achieved by other countries at similar stages.[13]

This impression seems to be confirmed when a comparison is made between the absolute levels of Italian industrial production and those of other industrial countries before and

13. Gerschenkron, *Economic Backwardness in Historical Perspective*, Cambridge, Mass., 1962, p. 78, mentions the cases of Sweden (12% per annum in 1888–96), Japan (8.5% per annum in 1907–13), and Russia (8% per annum in the last decade of the nineteenth century).

after the period 1896–1913. For example, the ratio between Italian iron and steel production and that of other European countries (U.K., Germany, France, Belgium) in 1889 was 1: 11.7: 10: 4: 2.4. In 1913 the ratio was 1: 8: 17: 4.6: 2.5.[14] As can be seen, except in relation to the United Kingdom, the ratio had worsened to Italy's disadvantage, rather than improved. The same phenomenon is evident from a comparison of the respective 'apparent consumption' of basic metallurgical products. Italy's relative share of the world seems to improve, however, in the textile sector: cotton spindles and looms installed in Italy, which in 1895 were respectively 1–1.85 and 2.48 per cent, had risen by 1913 to 4.11 and 5.07 per cent.[15] This may be regarded as a further confirmation of what we have called the two-sided character of Italian industrialisation in these years.

The percentage of the total population which was employed in industry in Italy remained not only well below that of other already highly industrialised countries such as Great Britain and Germany, but also below that of industrialised countries with a large agricultural population, such as France.[16]

The reasons for the lack of 'violent' growth in Italy *in a single period* (seeming to suggest, rather, a development by successive spurts of limited duration, some of them before, some after the spurt of 1896–1913) are probably to be sought in two directions: on the one hand, in the *composite* character of the agents of development, none of which really operated with great force and which therefore did not cause a great concentration of effort in any one par-

14. I. Svennilson, *Growth and Stagnation in the European Economy*, Geneva, U.N. Economic Commission for Europe, 1954, p. 261.

15. R. Tremelloni, *L'industria tessile italiana*, Turin, 1937, p. 142.

16. On the basis of data given in I. Svennilson, *op. cit.*, pp. 47 and 236, the percentage of the population employed in mining and manufacturing industries in the various countries on the eve of the First World War was as follows: Great Britain 12.9% (1907/1910), Germany 10.1% (1907/1910), France 7.7% (1901/1900), Belgium 10.1% (1910/1910), Switzerland 12.0% (1910/1910), Italy 4.7% (1911/1911). The years in brackets indicate respectively the year of the datum relating to population and the year of the datum relating to workers in industry.

ticular period; and, on the other hand, in the territorially restricted area in which this development took place. This generated a growth characterised in the middle period by certain factors of equilibrium (in the foreign trade accounts, in the relation between investment and consumption), but with the prospect, on a more long-term view, of growing imbalances. These imbalances showed themselves clearly after the First World War. Some important assets in the foreign accounts were then drastically reduced (notably emigrants' remittances); the most traditional component of the Italian industrial structure, and its largest exporter, the textile industry, entered upon a climacteric period; and the technological and territorial limitations of the preceding development exploded to produce a serious excess of productive capacity in the heavy industries, which found themselves faced with a territorially restricted domestic market (owing to the lack of economic progress in the southern regions) and endowed with a still largely archaic industrial structure.

The extent of the territorial concentration of Italy's industrial development in one particular area can be clearly seen from the relevant statistics. In 1911, the date of the first serious industrial census, 58.06 per cent of workers in industrial concerns employing more than ten persons were located in the three north-western regions in which 21.6 per cent of the population lived (the percentage falls to the still very high figure of 49.16 if we take into account concerns employing less than ten persons, in other words mainly handicraft workshops). Those three regions accounted for 48.89 per cent of all mechanised horse-power. In effect, more than half of the country's real industrial potential (factories and workers) was concentrated in an area inhabited by 9,412,000 persons, an area in which the relation between population and industrial potential was therefore about twice as high as the national average in that respect. Unfortunately no regional breakdown of the industrial product of that date is available. But it is obvious that the productivity of the Italian industrial apparatus concentrated in the three north-western regions was very much higher than in the rest of the country. If it was possible, therefore, to compare the product, and not merely the number of factories and workers, the degree of territorial concentration would be seen to be much higher, as also would be the difference in relation to the national average.

If we consider in isolation the industrialisation indices of the 'little country' composed of the three north-western regions, the difference in relation to the level of industrialisation of Central and Western Europe appears much less than if such a comparison is made in regard to Italy as a whole. In those three regions taken alone, in 1911 the percentage of the population employed in secondary activities was 9.6 per cent, as against 3 per cent in the rest of Italy (the national average was 4.7 per cent). In the three regions of the 'triangle', in short, the proportion is not very different from that found in the smaller central-western European countries such as Belgium or Switzerland.

To a certain extent, the process of industrialisation of the three north-western regions of Italy was conducted like that of an autonomous small country. Italy's political unity at the beginning of the twentieth century was still a very recent fact, which had not fully impinged upon the great differences of economic and social structure, mentality and customs which had grown up in the past. It is important, therefore, to emphasise that Italian dualism was not formed during the period of industrialisation—that period did not *create* differentiation in a previously homogeneous economic fabric, but merely intensified a profound differentiation that already existed. As an Italian economist, Saraceno, has said, administrative unification was not accompanied by a process of economic unification: the two Italys in fact continued to proceed separately along their earlier paths and each to maintain on its own account its prevailing economic relations with the rest of the world. This was especially true of the northern regions, where foreign trade, financial relations, and the exchange of entrepreneurial and technical experience with other countries had a strong influence on all economic activities, whereas relations with the southern regions remained extremely limited. This coincides remarkably with Kuznets' view that 'foreign trade has a greater importance in the economic activity of small nations than of large ones'. If we take into account the fact that the one great economic operation to include the whole of the national territory in the first fifty years of United Italy's history—the railways—was, as was mentioned earlier, of little importance for industry, we find further support for insisting on the analogy with the 'small country'.

Nevertheless the fact that the small industrial northern area formed part of a country of wider dimensions was not without influence on its own possibilities of development. In the first place, the level of public expenditure capable of providing an impulse to industrial production, especially of a military nature, was certainly higher than would have been possible for a small country. In the second place, although the basic domestic market for manufactured consumer goods was situated in the wealthier regions, the urban centres, at least, in the rest of Italy undoubtedly provided an appreciable share of that market. These factors may perhaps not be considered decisive. But there is a third factor that must not be under-estimated: the balance of the foreign accounts, within the framework of which, as has been seen, the effort for industrialisation of the new country's early years developed, received a decisive contribution from emigrants' remittances, and the majority of those emigrants were poor peasants from the southern regions. Thus one of the characteristic features of Italian dualism—the extreme poverty of the South—played a part as an organic component in the structure of the development process that went on between 1896 and 1913.

BIBLIOGRAPHY

The most important data are to be found in Istituto Centrale Di Statistica (ISTAT), *Sommario di statistiche storiche italiane 1861-1955*, Rome, 1958. A later edition (*Sommario di statistiche storiche dell'Italia 1861–1965*, Rome 1958) summarises the data for the period 1861–1920 in ten-yearly averages, and is therefore less useful to the historian. An official reconstruction of the historical progress of the national income and its components is given in ISTAT, 'Indagine statistica sullo sviluppo del reddito nazionale dell'Italia dal 1861–1956', in *Annali di statistica*, 1957, series VIII, vol. 9. This reconstruction has been critically reviewed and subjected to rectification by G. Fuà, *Notes on Italian Ecomomic Growth 1861–1964*, Milan, Giuffrè, 1965, who summarises the results of a team inquiry conducted on behalf of the Social Science Research Council of New York with a contribution from the Ford Foundation. This inquiry is now in course of publication (*Lo sviluppo economico in Italia. Storia dell'economia italiana negli ultimi cento anni*, edited by G. Fuà, Milan, Franco Angeli). For the historical development of industrial production, see A. Gerschenkron, *Economic Backwardness in Historical Perspective*, Cambridge, Mass., 1962, which gives a critical consideration of earlier writings on the subject.

A full history of Italy's economy after the Unification was begun by a historian of great experience, Gino Luzzatto, but he died before being able to complete it. Only the first volume has been published, *L'Economia italiana dal 1861 al 1914* (vol. I—1861–1894), Milan, Banca Commerciale Italiana, 1963. A general history is Shepherd B. Clough's *The Economic History of Italy*, Columbia University Press, 1964. A still irreplaceable work is E. Corbino, *Annali della economia italiana (1861–1915)*, 5 vols., Città di Castello, 1931–1938, which gives a full history of economic events and, more especially, of economic policy.

There are several general histories of Italian industry. The latest is by B. Caizzi, *Storia dell'industria italiana dal*

XVIII secolo ai nostri giorni, Milan, UTET, 1965, especially useful for the period before the political unification of 1861.

A brief outline which can form the basis for further reading is R. Romeo's *Breve storia della grande industria in Italia*, Bologna, 1963 (2nd edition, enlarged). Still useful for its definition of the outstanding characteristics of the industrialisation process is the first attempt at a general history in this field, R. Morandi's *Storia della grande industria in Italia*, Bari, Laterza, 1931 (frequently republished in recent years by Einaudi, Turin). Full and detailed information about the individual industrial concerns is given in A. Fossati, *Lavoro e produzione in Italia dalla metà del secolo XVIII alla seconda guerra mondiale*, Turin, Giappichelli, 1951. Useful works are the two volumes edited by the Confederazione Generale Dell'Industria Italiana, *L'industria italiana*, Rome, 1929, and *L'industria italiana alla metà del secolo XX*, Rome, 1953, which contain much historical information about various branches of industry including the less important ones. A work that can be regarded as a prelude to these volumes is the full survey done by a scholar of industrial problems during the First World War, P. Lanino, *La nuova Italia industriale*, Rome, L'italiana, 1916–1917, 4 vols.

A. Caracciolo (ed.), *La formazione dell'Italia industriale*, Bari, Laterza, 1969 (new edition), brings together some of the most recent critical contributions on the history of economic development and the formation of modern industry in Italy (Spaventa, Gerschenkron, Romeo, Dal Pane, Fenoaltea, Cafagna, Eckaus, Tosi, Zangheri). For a fuller range of Italian discussion of these problems see also E. Serni, *Capitalismo e mercato nazionale in Italia*, Rome, Editori Riuniti, 1966; R. Romeg, *Risorgimento e capitalismo*, Bari, Laterza, 1959; P. Saraceno, *L'Italia verso la piena occupazione*, Milan, Feltrinelli, 1963; M. Komani, 'L'unificazione economica', in *La formazione dello stato unitario*, Milan, Vita e Pensiero, 1963; G. Are, *Il problema dello sviluppo industriale nella età della Destra*, Pisa, Nistri-Lischi, 1965. Important contributions by various authors on particular aspects are to be found in *L'economia italiana dal 1861 al 1961*, Milan, Giuffrè, 1961 (Biblioteca della rivista *Economia e Storia*).

There are not many historical studies on the individual branches of industry. The textile industry has been the most fully covered, in the following volumes: R. Tremelloni, *L'industria tessile italiana. Come e sorta e come è oggi*, Turin, Einaudi, 1937; G. Quazza, *Industria laniera e cotoniera in Piemonte, 1831–1861*, Turin, Museo Nazionale del Risorgimento, 1961; V. Castronovo, *L'industria laniera in Piemonte nel secolo XIX*, Turin, ILTE, 1964, and *L'industria cotoniera Piemonte nel secolo XIX*, Turin, ILTE, 1965. Both the last two works are published in the important *Archivio Economico dell'Unificazione Italiana*, under the auspices of the IRI (Istituto per la Ricostruzione Italiana) and directed by C. M. Cipolla, which collects together numerous studies on particular aspects (prices, wages, production, foreign trade) and which was the first to initiate quantitative investigation of the period before Italy's political unification. For the iron and steel industry, still to be consulted is G. Scagnetti, *La siderurgia in Italia*, Rome, 1923. Few works exist about the engineering industry; among them see especially the recent volume by L. De Rosa, *Iniziativa e capitale straniero nell' industria metalmeccanica del Mezzogiorno, 1840–1904*, Naples, Giannini, 1968. A good geographical and historical study on an important agricultural-industrial product, sugar, is L. Gambi, 'Geografia delle piante da zucchero in Italia', in *Memorie di geografia economica*, 1955, A.VII, vol. XII.

A full selected bibliography including minor publications is G. Mori, 'La storia dell'industria italiana contemporanea nei saggi, nelle ricerche e nelle pubblicazioni giubilari di questa dopoguerra', in Istituto G. G. Feltrinelli, *Annali* 1959, a.II.

[4]

Italian Capitalism: General Interpretative Guidelines

Franco Bonelli

Introduction

We are looking at a country in which whole regions had no experience of enclosures until half way through the 20th century, even at a time when industrialization had already become an established fact; the aim, moreover, was not to increase the productivity of the land, but to reserve it for building speculation without controls. In this land there was still a common risk of infection from malaria; even of dying from it. It was not unusual for bread riots to occur, just as recounted in Manzoni's great novel, while at the same time major firms were mobilizing resources in order to apply the most advanced forms of industrial technology. A mass exodus of the population had become the most original means of maintaining the balance of payments at a moment when the process of development was at risk of being strangled by the difficulties in financing imports. And at the same time this country managed, in less than a century, to eliminate the distance between itself and countries which had been industrialized much earlier, so that today it merits the same degree of attention wherever remedies are being sought for the malfunctioning of world capitalism. Italy is placed in the top ranks of the scale of industrialized countries in quantitative terms, and yet there is a persistent impression that the qualitative story is very different. A country which presents such connotations and lives with such contradictions (and others of a similar kind) must certainly have something to contribute to the theory and history of development, even though systematic treatment of its own industrial revolution is almost routinely ignored.

Understanding the mechanisms which have allowed Italy to achieve the position which it occupies today in the capitalist West must begin from that point in the 18th century at which the various parts of the peninsula found for the first time, each on its own account, that they had to face the consequences of what had been happening in the rest of Europe. The 18th-century economic situation in fact represents the first stage of a long process, the last effects of which we are experiencing today. In the course of that century the economic basis of the bourgeoisie, which was to be the protagonist of Italy's national revolution, was being laid. In the pages which follow, the most recent period nearest to us in which the model of capitalist development has taken shape and become established in various geographical areas will be described, and we shall follow its progress as it spreads to the various areas of the economy and to different levels of society.

1. Agrarian Accumulation in Pre-Unification Italy

Analysis of the manner, times and places of agrarian accumulation is usually considered an essential step in the understanding of the processes which set in motion capitalist development. The difficulties which arise when the Italian case is examined are largely due to the particular way in which the accumulation of resources arising from the primary sector acted as a premise and support for the process of industrialization. This took place at various times over a long period, from the 18th century until very recently in the 20th. In the initial phase, an analysis of agrarian accumulation mechanisms in effect takes us back to the relations established in the 18th century between the many agricultural sectors of Italy and the European area, which had already begun to move along the path of industrialization. These relations defined, at least for a certain period, the terms of Italian participation in that whole complex of transformations and events which are known collectively as the Industrial Revolution. The progressive development in the European countries of a modern apparatus of manufacturing production, and the simultaneous appearance in those countries of a new income structure, together with the first signs of new patterns of consumption, were all translated into a demand for products – raw materials, semi-manufactured goods and food products, as well as services to a limited degree – which the Italian economy managed, in one way or another, to satisfy.

The image of Italy as a supplier of agricultural produce and raw materials to manufacturing Europe began to take shape in the 18th century and in the first half of the 19th. It was confirmed along with the spread of international trade and the evolution of the policy of Italian states towards free trade. Immediately after unification, the Italian economy seemed to have found a niche which would ensure indefinite progress for the new country, guaranteed by a type of income deriving from a position within the context of the international division of labour. This is an image rooted so deeply that it has long outlived the circumstances which justified it. It continued even after the events of the 1880s, in the course of which the great era of externally-induced agricultural accumulation had shown the first faint but unmistakable signs of exhaustion. It lasted for a further period after the path to industrialization had been embarked upon with conviction. The image of Italy as an agrarian and free-trading country was to be revived again and again, not only in the name of the development possibilities of Italian agriculture, but also more generally in the name of its 'natural' industries (including the production of emigrants…).

Even if we set aside the theory that a genuine model of development can be arrived at in this way, and even without taking account of the fate awaiting any model of this kind, one fact remains clear and should be noted. Over a period of several decades, the Italian economy, involved despite itself in the movement to industrialize, was able to seize quite substantial opportunities for accumulation in the agrarian sector. Seen in the light of certain factors which are features of the Italian model of industrialization (the absence of a widespread process of evolution of agricultural structures in the capitalist direction and the protectionist measures of the 1880s), this brings us at once to a question which certainly provides the key for interpreting the Italian capitalist model: by what means was such a bizarre process of agrarian accumulation made to function in the construction of an industrial system? As well as being an analysis of the times and methods of the creation and 'monetarization' of agrarian surplus (and the times involved are not brief), any full reply should identify the beneficiaries of the surplus, the sectors which absorbed it, and the ways in which transmission between the various sectors was achieved. The following pages cannot pretend to be a complete response; they are intended merely to suggest a scheme which can serve to trace the lines which should be followed.

In the Italian context, the increase in external demand for agricultural produce was linked for a long time to the numerical increase in population. This was both because *per capita* consumption was stationary, or virtually so, and also because of the lack of any increase in demand on the part of manufacturing industry. (The two factors are obviously not independent of one another.) Under these conditions, the appearance of an additional demand emanating from abroad undoubtedly set in motion new and important processes within the confines of the agrarian sector, as indeed it did at the level of society as a whole. The possibility of realizing a growing proportion of agricultural produce in monetary terms through its increased market value proved an incentive to technical improvements and land investments, financed by proprietors and tenant-entrepreneurs, alongside the various widespread and well-tried forms of capitalization of the labour of land workers.

For centuries the simplest mode of accumulation in agriculture was the employment 'on capital account' (as we might put it in bookkeeping terms) of the work of sharecroppers: tilling the soil, planting vines and olives, digging ditches and trenches, opening paths and roads, terracing uneven surfaces, and so on. All this was done either *ad meliorandum* (i.e. as a service at the expense of the owner-cultivator) or as a service due as a result of contractual agreement. As an alternative there was land investment, actively pursued or at least planned by the owner (either nobleman, ecclesiast or bourgeois proprietor), and financed by him in one way or another, with revenues accruing from agriculture (sale of products by the owner of the estate), from products which were only indirectly agricultural in origin (feudal rents, for instance), or even by purely speculative and mercantile, bureaucratic or (sometimes) manufacturing means.

During the middle decades of the 18th century, the pressure of external demand and the opportunities which it offered for cash conversion of the agricultural surplus led to the formation of liquidity among potential investors. This lay at the roots of various internal and external processes in the agricultural sector. In the case of internal processes, this was because investment in land and land improvement is a variable which depends to a great extent (though not exclusively) on the level and progress of cash-converted income. In external terms, a whole interwoven series of effects derives from the distribution of agricultural produce, its various stages of marketing, and the intermediary and final uses of the revenues resulting from it (e.g. consumption, investment, taxes, etc.). These effects accumulated in the economic, social and political fields with the passage of time. Thus, during the course of the 18th century, the geography of the various distribution channels began to gain definition, as did the internal and external exit points for agricultural products. There was a revival in the life of some towns and villages which had lain dormant for centuries. Some of the ports of the peninsula underwent a visible reawakening, and shipbuilding enjoyed an unmistakable boom. The contribution of the various waves of sales of ecclesiastical property, together with the elimination of some institutions which had stood in the way of land trading (e.g. fideicommissions, mortmains and majorats), stimulated the market in landed property and, through this, internal interchange among the class of landed proprietors, making it possible to extend the boundaries of this class. New circuits of business in merchant banking and speculation were opened up (the silk trade is a good example). Finally, to sum up the whole effect of these processes, it could be said that the character and potential for development, as well as the guidelines for future expansion of certain forms of 'regional' capitalism, were defined.

The connections between these phenomena and the factors which lie at their origins are certainly very much more complicated than can be deduced from the role ascribed to agrarian accumulation brought about by external factors. In particular, this seems to relegate to second place the importance and operative influence of 'endogenous' factors – factors such as the actual increase in population previously mentioned, the presence in some areas of a manufacturing demand for raw materials and semi-manufactured goods of agricultural origin, as well as the persistence (odd though it may seem) of certain manufacturing activities in close harmony with those of agriculture and their 'decentralization' away from traditional places of manufacture. However, for the purposes of a general description of the long period under examination, the mechanism described above – that of accumulation in Italy as a sub-product of the transformations that were taking place in the north-western economies – still contains a good deal of explanational value, even though there must be some reservations. This appears even more justified if we look at the factors which characterize the two or three decades preceding unification, and seek to fathom out the way in which this mechanism operated in concrete terms.

Until the 1880s, the pressure of external demand raised the development potential of that part of Italian industry which had been showing a 'market vocation' since the previous century and which had obtained at least primary market facilities. This had not only happened in the rather restricted zones where a genuine capitalist productive system had already been established (especially the area of the Po Valley where the figure of the entrepreneur, whether owner or tenant, dominated the agricultural industry). It had also taken place in various other contexts, such as those dominated by the share-cropping economy (the pre-Alpine zones and the Appenine hill country), and even the 'peasant' economy of the South, as well as areas which were more isolated from the trade circuits. In the latter cases, demand provided the opportunity for the emergence of a new figure: the intermediary. Through various devious channels, such intermediaries appropriated to themselves substantial portions of the agrarian surplus. In any case, the areas which benefited most from the favourable economic situation were those where the demand for products of European manufacturing industries (such as silk and hemp) had been felt for the longest period. Likewise, the demand for food products, both essentials (cereals) and those of higher quality (wines, citrus fruits, ordinary fruit, etc.), played a major role. These products were destined for an increasing population, or for centres of more concentrated 'bourgeois consumption'. In overall terms, however, the territorial bases for accumulation in Italian agriculture were to remain quite restricted for a long time, at least until the construction of a railway network opened up more and more widespread areas to the market.

It is difficult, especially given the present state of our knowledge, to draw anything like a clear diagram of the pattern of the dynamics of accumulation as these developed over a period of several decades. Such a diagram should in fact be an amalgamation of a number of lines of development, characterized by substantial variations and sometimes lasting for periods of only two or three years. It would also be related to a variety of productive forms and to various different areas of the peninsula. Certainly it seems incorrect to concentrate exclusively, as has been done in the past, on the 20-year period which followed unification, and even more, to isolate that period from what had happened in previous decades. It seems more appropriate to examine a series of periods, even though some of them may be quite brief, scattered across the whole time-span under review, and to examine the total range of phenomena which from time to time provided greater or lesser opportunities for accumulation in individual products and specific areas. In more analytical terms, we should first proceed to define the integrated relationships of the various Italian states with the advanced areas of Europe, and subsequently consider the various factors (such as industrial and financial crises at an international level, the appearance of new competitors among countries supplying raw materials, etc.) which caused substantial variations, both in the demand directed towards a given production zone and in local supply (seasonal cycles, spread of plant diseases, etc.). These factors, combined with a price scale basically determined at the international level, shaped the rhythm of accumulation of the various agricultural sectors concerned.

In overall terms, one may say that the decade 1850–60 was on balance a negative one, because of frequent bad harvests and the appearance of diseases both in silkworms and in vines. In contrast, silk exports resumed an important role in the period immediately following. Furthermore, the assertion that the two or three decades before mid-century had been vitally important in the formation of liquid assets in the hands of the landowning bourgeoisie is borne out by the fact that it was possible, as we shall see, to mobilize a volume of liquid reserves for the purchase of public debt stock and land in order to pay exceptional and very high fiscal charges. The formation of this reserve is largely explicable by reference to the previous period.

The extremely heterogeneous character of the social classes, who were the main beneficiaries of the agricultural surplus, reflects the variety of ways in which the conversion of production into money took place. It also explains the directions in which the accumulation was channelled, and hence the outcomes to which it led. As a first assessment, it could be said that the recipients of the agrarian surplus were the following: (1) a limited core of owner-entrepreneurs of medium and large-scale undertakings in the Po Valley; (2) a less restricted, but still not very large, group of major tenant-entrepreneurs in the Po Valley and a few other limited areas of Italy; (3) a much more substantial group of bourgeois proprietors, who might or might not be town-dwellers or absentees, existing in all parts of the country (in the North, but above all in the Centre, the South and the Islands); (4) some major absentee aristocratic or bourgeois proprietors, especially in the South; (5) a certain number of small family enterprises working their own land, especially in the pre-Alpine zones and central Italy and finally, alongside all these groups, (6) the composite class of merchants and intermediaries, operating at the marketing stage of agricultural production.

As regards the directions in which the accumulation was channelled, it is certainly difficult (and probably not essential for our purposes) to try to identify the typical behaviour of the individual social figures concerned. In general terms, however, we know that in these decades accumulation played a substantial role in financing the purchase of land by both established and recent proprietors. This was especially true where, sometimes as a result of the reforms of the Napoleonic era, a land property market had already been established. Accumulation also served to form reserves of liquid capital in the form of allocations of gold and silver, both in coinage and otherwise; it supplied land investments, even though these were limited to the areas where they had already become concentrated (to the extent of a so-called 'saturation' of investment opportunity in the areas concerned). It was used in far smaller measure than in previous cases for investment in public debt and other securities, and finally it contributed to finance fiscal demands which, in fact, remained stationary in overall terms in the states of Italy prior to unification.

These first broad-based conclusions allow us to lay stress on some initial data concerning the development of capitalism in Italy. Agrarian accumulation brought about largely by the external economic situation produced effects that varied widely in different parts of the peninsula, and only on a very limited – too limited – scale spurred on processes of modernization of agricultural structures. In a country which was not yet showing any need of imports to assist industry to function or to satisfy demands for mass consumption, exports, along with the other elements in the balance of payments, succeeded in assuring a favourable balance of trade with other countries.

Under these conditions, then, Italy's international position was the reflection of an internal balance of the agrarian-mercantile kind which, although based in reality on non-development, would very soon be taken as the postulate for the free-trade model adopted by the bourgeoisie, which took the lead in the country's national revolution. In this sense the issue of agricultural accumulation is obviously interwoven with that of the formation of this bourgeoisie itself – its regional characteristics, its cultural identity and the role which it played in the constitution and direction of the unified state.

2. The Economic Effects of the Creation of the Unified State

The general conditions which had set off the processes described above remained operative for the period of roughly 20 years following the binding together of the various parts of the peninsula into a single state in the years 1859–61. However, the role played by agricultural accumulation in the formation of capital differed from that in the previous period. And because of this change, the context of the situations which could influence the final destination of the surplus itself also changed. In other words, relations between agricultural Italy and industrial Europe remained virtually unaltered, as did the internal situations in the peninsula which essentially determined the opportunities for accumulation. But the financial circuits through which agricultural surplus (converted into money) passed from the hands of beneficiaries into the sectors where it was utilized were substantially altered.

The formation of a unified state and its immediate entry onto the scene as a principal financial operator throughout the whole peninsula comprised the new factor which intervened to modify the preceding mechanisms of capital growth. To begin with, after the financial and administrative unification of the various regions of Italy, the new state which emerged from the diplomatic and military events of 1859–61 imposed on those Italian regions now attached to Piedmont-Savoy the payment of interest on shares in the common public debt. This debt was effectively the bequest of the Piedmontese state to the new kingdom of Italy. In this way an original method of financing the expenses sustained by the Piedmontese *a posteriore* in the name of national unity was devised. Moreover, these expenses were translated into economic effects with innovative bearing on matters within the new national boundaries.

Although this cannot have appeared so obvious then, part of the resources which had previously been accumulated in the overall economy of the pre-unification states, including the partial mortgage imposed on the resources still to be formed, thus began to follow a course which, probably inaugurated on that occasion, was soon to become the norm. This was in fact an operation which should be noted not so much for its direct relevance to the issue which we are studying, but rather because it was just the first of a series of 'non-recurrent' operations destined to be repeated regularly, though in various forms and for purposes which were more immediately and specifically 'industrial'.

In any case, the policy which made it possible to finance the expenses of the new state had a far more decisive, obvious and direct effect on the financial flows deriving from the agrarian sector. This policy gave rise to a new and complex operation of draining resources from one part of the peninsula to another, and from agriculture towards other sectors. While on the one hand it continued to make use of foreign capital on the lines laid down by Piedmont-Savoy (which had permitted the opening of diplomatic, political and financial credit behind the unification process), the government of the kingdom took possession of the reserves of liquidity available in the country, especially in the South, by means of the issue of internal government bonds. It thus mobilized a growing proportion of the savings built up in previous decades. The fiscal levy affected all areas of the social system, to the point that, from the leading landowner to the poorest peasant, all were called on to give their contribution to the financing of state expenses. The tax on land sales was flanked by that on flour; forced loans were matched by the sale of ecclesiastical property. With greater and greater originality and readiness, recourse was made to the instrument of monetary policy. This becomes evident from 1866 onwards, when the state was forced to give up the support of foreign capital and lay more stress on greater mobilization of internal resources through the mechanism of compulsory savings on the part of the middle and less wealthy classes. With inflation at a forced rate, it was the poorer sections of the populace who were mainly penalized, while the most obvious consequences on the income of the bourgeoisie, even in the long term, derived from the sale of ecclesiastical property. The middle-class proprietors who purchased the goods of the church's estate not only lavished their previously acquired capital on this operation, but also committed what they expected to gain in the future. The indebtedness of landowners thus increased noticeably, requiring a substantial part of agricultural income to be earmarked to interest and capital repayment for a number of years. In fact the state was able to exact a high price for the aspirations of the middle classes to consolidate and increase their landownership as well as their position of social and political power in the running of the state. (It is enough to remember that in the first 20 years of united Italy, the right to vote depended on the payment of a certain amount of property tax.)

With the means obtained in this fashion, the state provided itself with a primary administrative organization, promoting the creation of a railway network and the modernization of the country (ports, roads, civic buildings, etc.). It also endowed itself with operative capacity in the military field (an army, a navy, guns, ships, military installations), and covered the costs of its war with Austria in 1866.

The consequences of the spreading of state activity at the levels mentioned were of far more decisive and lasting importance than is usually recognized. On the one hand, the state engaged in a definitive operation of breaking down the obstacles that lay in the way of the transfer of internal wealth on a far greater scale – both geographical and sectoral – than could have been achieved in the pre-unification states. In particular, as we have already noted, through finding a market for shares in the public debt by boosting the tendency among the bourgeoisie to purchase land, and more simply by the drainage effected by fiscal drag, various openings were made for the channelling of the resources of the source sector, which remained agriculture, into the remaining sectors of the economy. On the other hand, at the same time as this massive operation of redistribution of wealth was proceeding, the state contributed to the break-up of that internal equilibrium which we have called 'agrarian-mercantile', and also to the abandonment of its *laissez-faire* relations with industrial Europe.

A first significant move on the path to industrialization was thus undertaken, not as a result of the 'natural' diffusion of those processes which had led other European countries to embark on the road of capitalist development, but through state action which was able to move the effects of agricultural accumulation in a new direction, towards new equilibria. For this reason, Italian capitalism appears immediately and precociously as state capitalism, even before it really deserves that title in terms of the role that the state was to assume through specific forms of presence in the economy, both then and later.

The construction of the unified state and the consequent beginning of the process of modernization of the country thus altered significantly and in a single blow the traditional model of allocation of resources. It introduced new elements into the overseas relations of Italy and modified its position in the international markets. The function of agricultural exports, at the very moment when these appeared as the expression of a model which had reached fulfilment, were revealed as manifestly insufficient in the face of the emergence of new needs. In contrast to what had happened in the previous period, the Italian economic system began to express new import requirements, as a result of endogenous factors which were certainly not all or completely explicable in terms of the direct and indirect consequences of state expenditure. Although these factors have not been sufficiently recognized up to now, they should be given full consideration for the purposes of explaining the way in which, in the period under study, processes which can be termed 'industrial development' in the full sense began to appear for the first time.

We have to take note of episodes, some more isolated than others, taking the form both of initiatives in new sectors and of processes of reorganization within traditional areas of manufacturing industry (workshop machinery for the repair of locomotives or yards for the building of steel-plated ships). Again there is the example of the development of the factory system in the more well-tried textile sectors. In all these cases it is possible to note that, in this new phase, external relations were not exclusively or even preponderantly sustained by the 'golden rain' which Italy had enjoyed in the previous period from the export of agricultural products. External relations instead became the vehicle for the spread of experience which already typified the Industrial Revolution. Later on we shall consider the problem raised by some of the essential requisities for defining the Italian model of industrialization. Here we are forced to leave aside the issue of the nature of the agents of development in order to register the phenomenon which reflects their presence and their action, i.e. the new need for imports. This need became manifest not so much by an explosion or immediate generalization of new individual consumption (such as smuggling exercised in the pre-unification states more interested in opposing the competition of foreign industries), but mainly through the consumption of new products for collective use, semi-manufactured and instrumental goods.

Italy was for the first time forced to include in the liabilities of its balance-of-trade statements major items such as fossil fuels, locomotives, machinery, cast iron, metals, semi-manufactured goods for the textile industry (especially cotton), and even timber. Thus in a few years Italy moved from a balance of payments which, at national level, was maintained in credit as a result of current items, to a situation in which the backing of foreign capital became essential.

Thus there seem to be two basic factors in the stage which began with the birth of the unified state: on the one hand we find a new large-scale financial operation which intercepted the flow of finances originating from the monetization of the agricultural surplus (at the moment in which they passed through the hands of those who were their natural destinees); it then redirected part of those resources into the remaining sectors, altering the traditional model of employment of resources for the first time. On the other hand, the inadequacy of the resources which the agricultural sector was able to provide, in various forms and by different ways, made recourse to foreign credit inevitable, both for the financing of the state's expenses and in order to cope with foreign exchange needs.

In the course of the historical economic situation which produced the complex of radical transformations which we usually term the Industrial Revolution, the developments in Italy belong, in a long-term perspective, first of all to a marginal process of acceleration of the rhythms of agrarian accumulation induced by external demand. Subsequently the national revolution and the construction of a national state put in motion an integrated process of modernization of the economy, partly thanks to the support offered by financial integration at the European level. However this process was almost immediately translated into an increased dependence on foreign trade. These first considerations lead us to some of the crucial problems which were subsequently and regularly to accompany Italian capitalism. In the 1860s, immediately after unification, this future did not depend exclusively on the internal agrarian situation nor on the external demand for Italian goods, but on the financial conduct of the principal capitalist operating in the peninsula – the Italian state itself. It also depended on external capitalists, and thus on international political alliances, on the world monetary situation and on various other factors which were connected in one way or another.

The route which had led Italy to become reattached to Europe by forming itself into a nation-state was from that moment an uphill one, the possibility of shortening the distance from the countries which had preceded it very much depending on the way in which the new state played its role in the process of accumulation. The beginnings of the answer to this can be discerned in the 1860s and 1870s; a more complete answer was observable in the 1880s.

3. Italy's First Experiences of Industrialism: The Origins of the Difference

The customs tariff law of 1887 is normally and frequently identified as the symbolic sanction of a model of industrialization. This view can only be considered justifiable if it means that it was then that Italy made the initial nucleus of choices which we consider today, on the basis of their subsequent developments, to have been strategic. It is only justified, moreover, if we mean that in the 1880s a matrix was constructed on a reduced and simplified scale, from which the overall model for the development of Italian capitalism would be derived by means of subsequent modifications. However, we are here faced with an obvious over-simplification. This is true above all because, as is clear from what we have already said, the model in question can be seen as the product of an historic process in train for over a century. In terms of economic objectives, it can also be termed the outcome of the social and political alliances which arose out of the crucible of the earliest events in the life of the national bourgeoisie after unification. Finally, it is presented as a further explanation of the first experiences of capitalism, as they emerged at different levels of Italian society in the course of the previous 20 years. The understanding of the choices which were made in the course of the 1880s thus requires constant reference to all the modernization processes which had been promoted or directly achieved by the public administration since the eve of unification.

Some of these processes have already been mentioned, such as railway-building and the provision of plant and equipment to make the railways functional and to run them; building the first naval ships (though with essential parts coming mainly from abroad); undertaking vast programmes of military and civil building (from the 'forts' which were supposed to form a defensive ring around Rome to the extension of several ports and the construction of public buildings, bridges and roads). They also included taking advantage of the opportunities for building speculation provided by the transfer of the capital from Florence to Rome; taking part in the supply of war material; devoting resources to the purchase, sale and placement of substantial quantities of shares in the public and semi-public debt (such as debentures in the railway companies), and entering all the commercial and financial circles created by the emergence of new importation needs and the new geographical dimensions of the internal market. All these possibilities and a whole host of others which form the first manifestations of a single national market came to enrich the 'map of business' to which the national bourgeoisie dedicated its energies on the eve and in the aftermath of unification. The way in which the processes were set in motion at national level remains to be studied, as do the lines of growth – if such a term is allowable – followed by the economies of the pre-unification states and their individual areas in the course of the 18th century and the first half of the 19th. In this way we would have some means of understanding how the experiences from which the coordinates of Italian development sprang are for the most part to be sought in the process by which regional models of development gave way to what was to become the national model.

If we take as a point of departure the way in which the new capitalist experiences, of which the unified state was the main vehicle, imposed themselves on those which had been stratified in some areas of the country as a result of the mechanisms which had operated previously, we become aware of at least two considerations which are needed for a better definition. In the first case, we have to re-examine the structures of the Italian states before unification, with the aim of understanding the logic which governed their development. Secondly, we need to discover by what routes the unification mechanism, which was destined to set the pattern for the future, managed to impose itself. Over and above the reasons explaining why certain regional models ultimately proved too weak to survive, it may perhaps be useful to take a few examples from among those which did not become the guiding models, or which were (at most) fused with the latter at the cost of certain important variations. Such examples can help to give us an idea of the diversity of contexts from which the general lines of a united history were to emerge in the end.

It is difficult, for instance, to think of the technical and industrial experience which had become established in the pre-Alpine zone, while ignoring the 18th-century precedents in terms of production and state policy of the Colbertian/mercantilist type. We must ask ourselves whether the reason that this Piedmontese-Savoyard model could not be transferred to the wider stage of the national economy does not lie in the fact that in order to yield its best results, it would have had to function from the beginning within national geographical and political boundaries. In the case of Lombardy, there has been an attempt to portray a kind of English-style development, but without explaining why such a precocious example of a functional relationship between agriculture and manufacturing proved unable to bear fruit. However, even here, the temptation to find an answer without reference to the national state seems quite unconvincing in light of the relationship which this part of Italy enjoyed with the rest of Europe. Then there is the extraordinary matter of Genoese capitalism, which rebuilt its fortune in a few decades, after the débâcle at the end of the 18th century, with mercantile, shipbuilding and even limited industrial activities; however, it did not manage to become 'entrepreneurial' and fell back on financial speculation. Later, Genoa put all its investment in sectors of the financial market which were certainly 'new' but also exclusively protected at the financial and customs levels. In the odd phenomenon of Tuscan – or strictly speaking, Livornese and Florentine – capitalism, we could see the reflection of an agrarian-mercantile, free-market world which, according to one's viewpoint, could be viewed either as *sui generis* or textbook. It was not devoid of some valid prospects in terms of manufactures, but in the end seemed capable only of embarking on the venture of railway investment, of investment in 'Florence as capital' and in the exportation of capital. It thus exhausted itself without leaving any kind of legacy at regional level in terms of industrial structures comparable to those which Liguria ultimately possessed.

It was into these complex and varied regional situations that state activity irrupted after unification, and in which unified mechanisms at national level began to operate.

The running of the railways, and in general businesses which grew up in the shadow of public expenditure, was very often the field in which the new experiences of capital management of large-scale enterprises were formed. (These included the first group organizations, techniques of accounting and administration, the organization of companies in a broad sense, and so on.) It could also be argued that one way of understanding the reasons for the prevalence of one of the many 'spirits' of Italian capitalism is precisely that of reviewing the history of small and large private 'businesses' which were in some way linked to the action of the state as financial operator and principal investor (we need only cite the example of Bastogi or of the Veneta – the two biggest joint-stock companies of the period – or of the last of those banking firms which operated on the public income).

Undoubtedly in overall terms, new occasions for growth were offered to the various forms of regional capitalism, in addition to the fairly restricted ones which they were able to utilize before the breakdown of the barriers which divided the territories of Italy. And in every case, not only the centres which had shown greatest dynamism (like Turin, Genoa, Milan and Florence), but also the lesser but more or less vital ones (such as Venice, Bologna, Rome and Naples) all had a share in the process which would lead them to seize or let slip the chances which presented themselves during the first years of unification. The testing-ground of the emerging capitalist forces after unification – where these would be called upon to show their spirit and potential – was to be the circuit of business 'induced' by public expenditure. The development or extinguishing of pre-existing potential would, in many cases, depend on attitudes held towards entering this circuit.

The new geographical arrangement and the greater diversity of businesses which took shape after 1860 were accompanied by the transplanting and gradual adaptation to the 'Italian' situation of institutions which were essentially part of the Western capitalist system. This included both institutions which were typical phenomena of that system (such as note-issuing banks, stock exchanges and joint-stock companies) and those which arose from some of its specific developments (such as land credit and property credit banks, deposit and loan institutes, and so on). Naturally, these were institutions which did not take root in very deep soil, unlike those which were able to spring up against the background of Britain's great mercantile accumulation. They existed mainly on the thin subsoil of private experience, and only in a few supporting areas where the soil was deeper, such as those backed by state financing. Thus the issuing banks, for instance, soon found themselves 'at the service' of public spending policies, even before they could be of support in launching major private enterprises in the building and industrial fields. The stock exchanges were likewise conditioned in their development by a financial market dominated by public values, well before they could make themselves available for the purely speculative ventures of a limited group of operators. Similarly, the property banks were called on to act as an instrument of the state's financial policies before they could become instruments for transforming the structure of agriculture. And this was the general picture.

But apart from these 'original' aspects of Italy's first experience of capitalism – the implications of which were not slow to make themselves felt – the most notable fact remains the basic one: that a whole system of financial institutions, 'imported' from an area of capitalism more advanced and developed than the new context, was forming and adapting to the Italian situation in which they found their whole *raison d'être* conditioned by state action.

In fact the first 20 years of Italy's united history enable us to identify a whole series of innovations at all levels of social organization. These are difficult to discern in the usual kinds of comparisons based exclusively on statistical data for the 1880s and the 'Giolittian' period (for instance, the rate of increase in the national income and in individual sectors). However difficult it may be to measure, the really novel fact which contains the key to a great deal of what happened in the immediate and more distant future is the quality of development during this 20-year period. The multiple elements of continuity which link the phase of Italian capitalistic development beginning in the 1880s with the previous era are a first important vindication of this assertion.

The drive towards development of new industrial activities derived from a wave of public spending, even in the 1880s. The sectors in which the most obvious effects were seen were once again those of public and private building and the speculative activities linked to them, such as railway engineering and the metal industries. All these were sectors towards which the attention of the government and the ambitions of private entrepreneurs had been directed for some time; even the great *affare siderurgico*, a phrase which had become symbolic of these emerging interests, originally came from the development of what had been initiated by the state's building and railway-construction expenditure (the Veneta Company of Vincenzo Stefano Breda). However, while it was state expenditure which provided the impetus for the business boom, it was nevertheless foreign capital which played a decisive role in the various stages of the cycle. In the initial stages it flowed in, then increased and later (after 1886) confirmed its potential as a destabilizing element. This revealed the political effects which accompanied it, reflected in the changes of foreign allies and the flow of German capital to support the state's credit. All this occurred under the auspices of the two major property lending institutions backed, especially after 1886, by the issuing banks.

The whole process, which began with the abolition of forced circulation in 1882 and ended with the bank disaster and the reorganization of the issuing banks in 1893–94, is studded with episodes which show the persisting tendency by important groups of the Italian bourgeoisie to direct their capital towards investment in state securities or purely speculative and financial investments, or towards industrial businesses which were at least guaranteed by the state. These tendencies had already been marked in the previous 20-year period and were all attributable to the functions of the state as a capitalist operator in the market. Just as in the previous period this kind of business was both the cradle and the grave of certain groups of financial-speculative interests (e.g. the whole 'Florence-as-capital' affair), now, on an even broader scale, the first real emergence of some of the major capitalist groups ended with disastrous results in the field of building speculation in Rome, Naples and elsewhere (we could also cite the Turin group and, once again, that of the Veneta Company).

Thus state action, which became established as a decisive factor in the economic development of the country, took place during the 1880s along lines which had already been laid down. But it did gain in decisiveness and articulation. Now the state not only played the role of pathfinder, creating the necessary conditions for the flow of foreign capital (by the attempt at monetary stabilization and the consequent abolition of forced circulation); it also offered the opportunity for new business (by expenditure on public works). Moreover, it protected the interests of existing industries, such as cotton manufacture, by the introduction of import tariffs; this also applied to emerging industries such as groups engaged in basic metal production. It introduced privileges and facilities of other kinds, such as provision for shipbuilding yards, and it actually granted capital advances for the initiation of new-productive elements, in this way ensuring the satisfactory results of private investment, for instance in the case of the Terni iron and steel industry. With the incentive of state action, as with private initiatives, there was almost immediate movement; resources were mobilized in a variety of ways by the same financial institutions which had first appeared 20 years earlier – the issuing banks, the property credit-banks and their real estate and speculative branches. With these protagonists and with the basic support of foreign credit, the cycle of the 1880s took place. It consisted of the initial convulsive stage of building speculation followed by the era of bail-outs, in which the issuing banks became involved in attempts to delay the moment of liquidation of businesses which had collapsed. This was accompanied by the intervention of German capital in state finances. Finally came the collapse of the banking organization, which had been the earliest protagonist of the boom, under the weight of its tied assets.

Throughout the whole process, then, and especially in the last phase, a crucial role was played by the Treasury, the issuing banks and the major property banks. We do not yet know to what degree the ultimate outcome can be put down to inexperience and errors in technical conduct, or to the relations which were being established at this time between the world of the most reckless business adventurism and speculation on the one hand and governmental, political, parliamentary and court circles on the other. In any case, at the moment when the chapter was closed, in 1893 to 1894, it was the state which took on itself the burden of creating the numerous indispensable preconditions for the subsequent recovery – from the reform of the functions of the issuing banks by a lasting improvement in the position of the Bank of Italy, to all the remaining undertakings aimed at opening the way for the intervention of German capital, as well as the financial policy measures which would allow the forces of capitalism which had escaped from the disasters of the crisis to re-start on a new basis.

In effect, the epilogue of the events of the 1890s, although they provided a hard lesson for those within the ruling class who had become the spokesmen and protagonists of the policy of industrialization, did not in the end call the objectives of this policy into question. It could even be said that it had the effect of increasing awareness of the difficulties involved. Certainly, at the turn of the century the machinery with which the Italian economy prepared to approach the new ascending phase of the cycle appeared to be quite adequate for the needs of a modern industrial country in general, and for those of Italian development in particular.

4. Agrarian Backwardness and Development

However strange it may seem, the 1880s did show unmistakable signs of change, above all in terms of new factors related to the agrarian sector. In many ways, these were even more traumatic than those which we have already noted in the industrial field. In the latter, it seems, even the episodes which show the greatest signs of innovations can be understood as a further development from premises deriving from the previous 20 years. In the agrarian sector, on the other hand, situations arose which were largely unforeseen, resulting almost exclusively from a change in the position of Italian agriculture in the international market. In the course of a few years, these conditions altered the role of the latter in the process of capital formation.

The immediate reasons for what happened are generally acknowledged; the competition of American grain, the barriers which the European countries raised to defend their own agricultural sectors, and the beginning of a new protectionist phase, along with external reprisals and even what is sometimes referred to as a 'trade war' with France. A direct consequence of this was a sharp fall in the levels of accumulation, for which a remedy was sought in the import tax on grain, sanctioned in the 1887 tariff. The working classes, however, were forced to find their own response to the crisis, and that was emigration. The results and costs of these remedies are also widely known: in the first case, the defence of agrarian revenue, paid by the Italian consumer, rewarded the absentee landlords of the South, without any appreciable offset, though it may actually have been of some use in the productive conversion of the agriculture of the Po Valley. In the second case, a financial flow – the remittances sent home by emigrants – substituted and supplemented agrarian exports.

It is more difficult to estimate the more profound and less immediate reasons which caused Italian agriculture to suffer so heavily in this crisis, revealing structural weaknesses of which there was only a dim awareness at that time. The capacity for recovery which it showed was very limited indeed, even when the economic crisis diminished or came to a close. To some extent the reasons for this did not escape contemporaries. They realized that

Italian agriculture had in fact been taken by surprise by the crisis, with an inadequate capital endowment (meaning the whole complex of structures, equipment, technical capacity, development potential, etc. which is normally related not only to its level of productivity, but also to its attitude towards change). It will also be remembered that there was capital which the state had been prepared to supply to agriculture – by the land tax and other fiscal measures, by the offer of shares in the public debt, and by the sale of ecclesiastical property. Nature itself must shoulder part of the blame: it can hardly be said to have endowed Italy with land particularly adapted to radical or even semi-radical transformation. Finally, a certain amount of the blame must be apportioned to the absenteeism of the landowners. The various diagnoses which have been made since that time, apart from the different emphases laid on the responsibility of one factor or another, make it possible to arrive at a few conclusions which can be usefully integrated into the overall view which guides our observations. They may also prove to be essential in terms of the conclusions to which they point. First, the long and fortunate era of agricultural accumulation was exhausted in Italy without having generated an adequate or general transformation of the use of land as a productive factor in a capitalist economy. Secondly, for the purposes of understanding the redefining of the role of Italian agriculture which took place as from the 1880s, it is not so much the fact of an 'agrarian crisis' in itself that proves instructive, as the explanation of its less immediate causes.

In this view of things, the issue which comes to the forefront is the territorial and social bases of the long-term process of agricultural accumulation. In particular, the question arises of how restricted these bases were, and how small a minority of those who benefited from the monetarization of the agricultural surplus were ready to make functional investments in the development of agriculture. It is not enough to point to the 'sacrifices' experienced by the agricultural sector in the period immediately after the birth of the unified state to understand the reasons which for such a long time had condemned a large part of Italian agriculture to a state of backwardness. The fate of this sector had probably been in the balance for some time, and subsequent events in any case wiped out what feeble possibility there was for recovery.

Probably the great opportunity for agricultural exports had come too late, and perhaps the outcome of a process determined mainly by external forces would never be equal to the development of an internal market and intersectoral relations between agriculture and industry, except under very special conditions.

However this may be, there is no doubt that at the beginning of the 1880s – and perhaps even earlier – any areas which could have been converted to capitalist farming were already restricted by the existing constraints. These constraints, as the events of subsequent decades were to show, would be difficult to extend or to force outwards. The 'agricultural development' of the period 1860–70 was essentially a matter of quantity; it did not give rise to transformations in structure nor to important changes in productive methods.

In the Italian countryside in the 20 or 30 years which preceded the crisis, development and increase in land revenue meant little more than producing and selling a greater quantity of silk and hemp than in the period 1820–50. In certain cases there was also a small increase in the exports of wine, oil and citrus fruit, mainly thanks to the system of share-cropping. There was even some success in exporting grain to Europe, but only because the American supply had not yet reached its destination. In other words, the only achievement was in taking advantage of the favourable economic situation in the context of a productive organization that was anything but modern. Agriculture was also losing the last possibility of renewal outside the few areas which were already in the process of long-term evolution. External demand, good harvests and high prices meant that the opportunities for accumulation were better than in the past (allowing the simultaneous pursuit by the state of its huge operation of draining rural resources) but such factors did not increase the flow of investments which would have created the circumstances for increased productivity. The vast majority of middle-class Italian landowners devoted a large part of their income which was not absorbed by taxes to the purchase of land, the payment of mortgages, the purchase of state securities, and the provision of small loans at rather high interest rates. The regions benefiting from the last beneficent wave of foreign demand remained more or less those of 30 years earlier. For that vast area of Italian agriculture bearing the burden of family self-sufficiency, the favourable economic situation had no effect, because in this case, too, the already modest possibilities for accumulation available in the market were offset by an accelerating population increase.

Thus the era in which Italian agriculture might have presented itself as an unchallenged provider of products for industrial Europe had passed, leaving behind a state endowed with an administrative organization, an army, a navy, a railway network – in other words, with some of the prerequisites of an industrial revolution. But it did not leave an 'agricultural revolution'. Indeed, some have gone further, claiming that the sector's favourable position in the international market actually caused a sort of uncertainty in Italian agriculture. This uncertainty was destined to be damaging because it increased the tendency to follow the logic of a 'plunder economy', or at least to move within the limited confines of the short term. This seems to be true whether we are speaking about subsistence agriculture (in which case it might even be logical), or whether it simply refers to taking advantage of the best moment for placing certain products on the external market.

The direct and indirect consequences of the agrarian crisis at once became a further serious factor complicating the outcome of the imposing programme of investments set in motion in the 1880s. This came about under the impetus of decisions made about public expenditure, the flow of foreign capital and expansionist credit policies. Reviewing the development and the epilogue of the first attempt at industrialization in fact confirmed the strategic role that agriculture had come to assume in the process of capital formation. At the same time it revealed various unknown elements which depended on the types of relations evolving between agriculture and industrial development. We must therefore devote some further discussion to the role which agriculture played as a source of finance for industry before and after the 1880s.

Before the Italian economic system was affected by the need for imports (induced by the incipient development of industrial activity, by state expenditure and by railway investment – i.e. from the mid-19th century onwards), the agrarian sector had succeeded almost completely in financing imports on its own. Subsequently, from 1860 to 1870, agriculture had been virtually the only *internal* source of finance for state expenditure, as mentioned above. At about the same time external sources of finance became more important. About half of this foreign capital was invested in government bonds, the rest in bank loans and in railways, public buildings, etc. This inflow of capital stimulated further development leading to a new demand for imports. Agricultural exports helped to restrict the trade deficit.

Thus the risks involved in relying on the movement of capital for the balance of payments were effectively reduced.

The agrarian crisis thus gave rise to two types of consequences. On the one hand, the reduction of income which resulted weakened the state's capacity to finance itself in the internal market – and this occurred just at the moment when it was committed to a huge programme of expenditure. On the other hand, the fall in agrarian exports was immediately translated into a considerable degree of destabilization, which came to be embodied in what could and did result from the withdrawal of foreign capital. The salient episodes and various stages of the series of events which occurred from the beginning of the 1880s to the bank crash of 1892–93 thus confirmed the 'strategic' role which agriculture had played for the purposes of overall development. At the time, however, the difficulties in which agriculture found itself at the moment of its first impact with foreign competition (and with the protectionist measures which began to benefit rival agricultures) clarified the limits within which it could continue to support the process of industrialization. It was not possible to predict what the remittances from emigrants and the tourist exchange would amount to at this stage. In fact, up to the time when customs protection and other circumstances allowed Italy to export manufactured goods (which only began to happen during the Giolittian era) or until other factors intervened, the possibilities and rhythms of development were bound to depend on the joint action of the backing of overseas capital and the flow of agricultural exports along with other primary products. This would continue to be the case for many years. A solution to this problem was not to emerge until the 1890s and the first years of this century.

5. The 'Italian Road' to Industrialization

A century and a half of agrarian accumulation had had an increasingly incisive effect on Italian society. But even so this had not been enough to create the conditions for a model of development to emerge which could somehow provide a basis for the essential mechanisms required for coordination between the agrarian and industrial sectors (in other words, a model like the one which experts in comparative analysis point to, rightly or wrongly, as having originated with Gramsci).

This is a basic fact within the Italian situation. To this must be added the external conditioning represented by the protectionist movement. Apart from the industrial aspirations which were very gradually beginning to make themselves felt, protectionism had progressed far enough to leave little real leeway for arguments inspired by a different vision of the country's agricultural and industrial future.

Naturally, abandoning or straying from the path laid down in the past could not fail to drive Italy to seek urgently for an alternative. In the light of what happened in subsequent decades, and particularly if we look at these events from a longer overall perspective, the 1880s appear to be the years when Italy deserted the path on which it had embarked in the 18th century and headed for another, whose final outcome may not be clear, but whose general direction was immediately evident – that of industrialization. However, the interpretations put forward based on the assumption that the key point of this change was the Customs tariff of 1887 and the political and parliamentary alliance between protectionist industrialists from the North and wheat-growing landowners from the South do not seem to do justice to the complexity of this stage of Italy's capitalist development.

Above all, the prevalence of protectionism in no way implied stability or durability in the social and political alliances that chose that policy. While it is true that the basic objectives of the policy decided on in 1887 – the development of heavy industry – were no longer called into question, even so there would always have been room for subsequent mediation in favour of the agrarian and mercantile and manufacturing interests which seemed at that specific moment to have been sacrificed. Furthermore, certain of the schemes put into operation by the 1887 alliance were to continue to function subsequently, even when this alliance had been replaced by other, different and more clearly defined convergences of interests. Finally, the choice of economic policy adopted at that time was not the expression of an organic and conscious vision of the need to create a coherent series of circumstances favouring the birth and growth of certain industries and not of others. It was rather the result of options favourable to specific demands, which would indeed have affected certain key points in a policy of industrialization, as could be confirmed over a long period. But there and then its greatest effect was to cement together an alliance between the most powerful interest groups.

Thus no complete and conscious system of objectives emerged from the events of the 1880s. Instead, what happened was the sanctioning of certain choices destined to condition the development of the industrial system far beyond the immediate motives which determined them. Customs protection and the favours bestowed on the cotton, sugar and metallurgical industries, together with those which favoured cereal crop-growing, were certainly not sufficient to provide a model, nor would they be in the future. But they would be able to condition the 'distortions' – as the free-traders were wont to call them – which would shape one of the sectors in the long term, and above all would serve to 'provide a lesson' for other emerging sectors in the future. Thus one of the meanings of the events of the 1880s and the symbolic episode of the 1887 tariff law is that the latter represented a top-level compromise which opened the road to what would later become a model of industrialization. This was based on the availability of a productive apparatus in the basic sectors and in engineering (respectively the metal industry and war goods, first and foremost), and was substantially imposed from above. Certainly the episode in question was not an after-the-event sanction of the already existing spread of capitalist structures at different levels of society and geographical zones. Nor did it arise from the fact that one or other of the regional models finally succeeded in prevailing. In short it was a 'model' in which it is pointless to seek consistency in terms of the rationality of state intervention, but one which did not, even so, come into existence by sheer chance. This is shown by our previous discussion of the 20 years which followed unification. In this model there was a place both for certain pre-existing experiences of the 'Manchester' pattern, and for industries which, based on intensive capital input, took the lead in the most recent phase of industrial and technological development; these were factors of military and diplomatic power rather than of economics. It seems likely that not a few of the problems which arise when one seeks to fit the case of Italian industrialization into the schemes proposed by economic theory and historiography are in fact derived from the difficulty of taking full account of this initial mixing, which brought together in the 1880s in Italy elements belonging to the 'long wave' of the British Industrial Revolution, and those present in the subsequent processes of industrialization in Continental Europe.

Before the 19th century ended, quite a few paths comprising the 'Italian route to industrialization' seemed already to have been mapped out. Some of the devices of the comprehensive mechanism for capital formation, and in particular those which were put into motion by the state, had already given proof of how they might function. A financial system had already appeared in outline, and the overall picture of industrial organization already formed the background upon which the structures and experiences of the future would be based.

This contention, supported at a distance of many years by the results of the legacy of the 19th century, is not meant to attribute a special quality of irreversibility to the (nevertheless important) goals which had been achieved. Their meaning, in the long term, would depend not only on the will and capacity of the governing classes, but also on a whole complex of circumstances – what in modern terms might be called 'chains of development' – on which the inventiveness of technicians and politicians would have its effect. Indeed, certain of the perculiarities of Italian capitalism emerge specifically during the course of events which made it possible to exploit that far-off premise of the 19th century to the full, and then to avoid turning back from the stages which had been reached, in order to move ahead in its endeavour to catch up with the more advanced countries.

We are talking here of a process which was to be protracted over a number of decades. Its terms were to vary with the changing world context, with respect to which Italian capitalism could coordinate its position and define its objectives – in other words, modernize the model which had originally been chosen.

6. The Financing of Development and the Balance of Payments

The first and crucial question which the legacy of the 19th century leaves open concerns the way in which provision might have been made for financing imports when the Italian economy was newly launched on the course, and at the pace, of the 1880s. The range of this question, amply demonstrated by all the case histories of industrialization which took place in conditions of an open market, seems all the greater when we think of the particular way in which Italy succeeded in launching itself on the road of development – by seizing all the advantages of the economic situation and of the context of international economic relations – without suffering to any appreciable degree the disadvantages which might have damaged a 'late-comer' country. The fact that this was possible depended, as we shall see shortly, on the way in which Italy succeeded in resolving the problem of its balance of payments.

The events of the 1880s had dramatically demonstrated the risks implicit in relying on movements of capital in order to deal with serious defects in the balance of trade. This had provided a first example of the degree to which the economic development of Italy would depend on the efficacy of solutions found to the problem of financing imports. In the first half of the 1890s, the solution derived from the recession, which in a short period created conditions for the automatic readjustment of the balance of payments. In this stage, apart from the drastic reduction in various debit items, the greatest factors in the readjustment included a certain recovery of export capacity by those manufacturing industries which now complemented more traditional artisan-style production. But as soon as the trend towards depression gave way to a revival of investment (which this time took place on a wider front than in the 1880s), it became clear that neither the revival of exports of primary products nor the manufactured goods which Italian industry was able to sell abroad would be sufficient to cover the demand for imports necessary, not only for the functioning of industry (raw materials and semi-manufactured goods), but even to satisfy the most essential food supply requirements of an expanding population.

Apart from the overall dynamic and the changes in structure of exports, the relative capacity to provide for the financing of imports by means of exports was to remain for more than 50 years, and far beyond all prediction, virtually nailed to initial levels. The periodic threat of the need to set aside the objectives of development, which in the meantime had become unavoidable, would therefore have an important bearing on the Italian economy for a long time.

Among the varied and crucial moments in which, thanks to the operation of special mechanisms or the carrying out of certain policies, some success in staving off these threats was achieved, none appears so significant as the whole period from around 1898 to 1914. This is not only because, in the history of our development, there has rarely been such a long period of substantial equilibrium in the foreign balance of payments (even when out of balance, it was in such a way as not to alter substantially the general conditions of development), but also – and above all – because of the context in which this took place.

During the first phase, which runs from 1898 to 1907, we encountered all the classic situations of an economy open to external trade nevertheless undertaking a vast programme of industrial investment without initially having the autonomous capacity to finance its necessary imports. Beginning with 1898, after an initial leap ahead in exports caused by an upward phase of the world cycle, the trade deficit first increased and then exploded, beginning in 1906 until it again touched the high levels of 1885–87. In the following years, in a substantially altered economic situation, the high trade deficit became established as a structural and immovable factor in the functioning of the Italian industrial system. And yet, at the same time as the trade imbalance augmented, we can also see a rapid and decisive improvement in the situation of Italy's assets in relation to foreign trade. Italian savings first found a way of repurchasing from the foreign market those shares in the public debt which had been placed there, and then of absorbing a certain, admittedly limited, quantity of foreign securities. Foreign capital, which had entered Italy in the mid-1890s under German auspices, had fulfilled its role of reorganizing the host country's capitalist and entrepreneurial forces. Now it began to flow back towards its place of origin. Moreover it was the rebalancing of national assets that made possible the adoption in 1907 of a monetary policy capable of allowing the Italian financial situation independently to withstand the impact of international monetary tension. This tension deprived it of foreign support and backing, but the new policy prevented damage to the industrial structures which had been formed in the meantime, or which were still in the process of formation. But what counts for more, and can in fact be termed 'extraordinary' in the most literal sense, is that all these processes and events followed each other or overlapped in a period of roughly 15 years, accompanied by substantial balancing of foreign trade and leaving behind almost no foreign debt. There were even quite substantial gold reserves. As we can see, it was a unique combination of circumstances. But what was really unique and extraordinary was the explanation of why this happened: an explanation to be sought first of all in what we might call the Italian choice of economic model – meaning, of course, not the outcome of an intentionally preordained plan, but what gradually emerged as a coherent pattern in an on-going process. Secondly, the explanation is also to be sought in the uniqueness of the opportunity which was offered to Italy to exploit in a very particular way all the advantages which could come from abroad, thanks to the *belle époque* of free circulation of manpower and capital.

The circumstances which enabled Italy to become a modern nation, and those which launched it immediately afterwards on the road to capitalist development, did not transform the great mass of the peasantry into small farmers, either totally or in part. Hence, they did not become potential consumers of domestic industrial products. We need not go into the age-old question of why this was so, or of the possible alternatives and lost opportunities. What matters is the fact that, from the mid-1890s, Italy was already a country which had decided to export its workforce *en masse*. In this way those who, in a different scenario, could have comprised a mass of internal producer-consumers, departed to work abroad. The fruits of this choice were soon evident, and they increased as the number of people who took the path of emigration grew larger. Since a considerable proportion of these emigrants came from the agricultural sector and were young, this obviously became another means by which agriculture, once again, was placed at the service of industrialization.

Along with remittances from emigrants, the gap which the excess of imports constantly left in the overseas balance of trade was also covered in this period by a new type of tourism which was developing, along with new patterns of consumption among visiting European middle classes and also increasingly those from America. The satisfaction of the 'needs' of holiday travel and visits for individual health cures or other reasons gave way to a growing demand for 'élite' tourist services, of which Italy rapidly became a supplier; this was a result of its geographical position, its climate and its artistic and historical heritage. Until 1914, in an atmosphere not notably troubled by wars or other disturbances, Italy was able to benefit from an inflow of strong currencies, of no small importance for its foreign exchange needs.

Naturally, the lucky series of circumstances which permitted Italy to stave off the danger of an unmanageable trade deficit for a considerable number of years cannot be explained simply by its capacity to export its workforce and to be the favoured mecca of foreign middle-class tourists. It also demands constant reference to the system of free circulation of men and capital which reigned unchallenged until the outbreak of the First World War, and which functioned in a highly positive way for Italy throughout this phase. I have already referred to the steadiness which the Italian industrial system showed on the occasion of the international financial crisis of 1907. This episode may be taken as symbolic proof of what has been said above, if we remember that it was from the country at the centre of the crisis – the US – that Italy received not only its traditional flow of remittances, but an exceptional revenue as well in the form of the transfer of savings accumulated there by Italian workers. It is also in this context of free circulation, mentioned above, that we must place the unique factor of the existence of a group of countries which both individually and collectively were able to absorb a very high quota of the Italian workforce (there would never again be such massive emigration in Italian history). It would also never again be so easy for emigrants to transform such a large part of their earnings into savings in the financial system of their home country.

The equilibria on which a country's overseas accounts are based at any given moment are expressed not only in the number and dynamic of the individual items which appear in the balance of payments, but also and above all, in the way in which the complex mechanisms of the system operate. This is even more the case in a developing country. Any account of the economic development and balance of payments, even an introductory one like the present, cannot be limited to examining the patterns of terms of trade between a country and the rest of the world, however indicative these may be; it must also describe those traits of the model of development which have the most direct and effective links with the problem under review.

In the case of Italy, it was not only that, by the exportation of several hundred thousand workers abroad every year, these enthusiastically remitted money home instead of becoming consumers in their place of origin. Another factor was that the rural population which remained also failed to rise above the level of subsistence to which it had been pinned down for decades, or at best only just managed to surpass it. Moreover, in the overall context of an economy still dominated by family consumption, even the wage-earning masses which, because of industrialization, were concentrating in a few key points of the system, remained substantially limited to satisfying needs which were little more than basic. Certainly, the consumption of wage-earners did not have a very dynamic effect from the standpoint of the creation of new demand. Nor did the propensity of middle-class consumers, though for numerical reasons rather than the stereotype which portrays them as proverbial and indefatigable savers. For these reasons too, the driving force of the Italian economy, once it had overcome the first challenge of the needs induced by the investment boom, functioned at a pace which certainly required substantial imports as a basis for it to work. This requirement exceeded the capacity to finance it by means of exports, but in any case, it was not such as to create the conditions for a real take-off in demand for foreign products. The other side of the balance of overseas trade is therefore represented by extremely modest changes in the overall structure of consumption, as well as by low dynamism. It could even be said that in this particular context, the overseas trade balance was once again a balance of non-development, while recognizing that such a statement only has meaning if we believe that any other course than the one chosen was possible. The argument could in fact be overturned, in the sense that in the final analysis, the lack of development of consumption was the only condition, in this context, capable of ensuring the successful outcome of the attempt at industrialization. Whatever view we may take on this, the fact remains that the balance built on these bases proved to be quite fragile, and was soon to be dramatically put to the test.

Soon after the outbreak of the war, Italy, deprived of the foreign exchange support of remittances from emigrants, and of the possibility of importing raw materials and semi-manufactured goods for her industries, was faced with the alternatives of a neutrality which would certainly have condemned her to a long period of recession, and participation in the conflict which, though costly, would at least allow her to avoid being cut off from the sphere of international affairs, and to obtain the materials necessary for her industries to function. The political and diplomatic response to this dilemma was given in 1914–15, as is well-known, and the consequences which arose from it on the economic front were immediate. On this occasion, too, the Italian economic system succeeded in one way or another in overcoming the difficult economic circumstances without its dependency on external trade becoming a factor contributing to backwardness or arrested development. In fact, the Italian industrial economy enjoyed a period of major expansion during the First World War, though not without considerable difficulty.

In reality, even from the point of view of external commercial and financial relations (and the political relations which these involved), 1914 was a moment of clean break with the past in several different respects. Basically, during the Giolittian period, in the context of greater openness to the outside world in commercial policy and financial relations, some success had been achieved in reaching one specific objective: that of managing without the foreign ally whose influence had been decisive in the economic developments of the previous decades from the time of Cavour to that of Sonnino. As a result of the war, however, with the change in the system of international relations and the balance of power within the capitalist arena, Italy found itself no longer having to deal with 'automatisms', but more and more with external partners or, rather, still having to cope with the former on paper while dealing with the latter in practice. Despite appearances that might lead us to think otherwise, this may be the key to understanding the alternating events which took place between and after both world wars.

In the early years of the First World War, the productive effort, destined to be largely transformed into industrial development, was financed by the forced savings caused by inflation and by credits from allied countries, in addition to the consumption of the reserves built up in the past. In the post-war years, the financial contributions of the allies ceased, and the balance of payments was entrusted to short-term and speculative foreign private investment. In the first instance it was also hoped that there would be a revival of the mechanisms of rebalancing which had operated at the beginning of the century (exports of primary goods, remittances from emigrants, tourism). This was an illusion due to the fact that by the mid-1920s it was impossible to deal with a serious trade imbalance, especially one that occurred right in the midst of a huge commitment of state investments. At that point, new stress was laid on the support of foreign capital; in particular (thanks to the policy of stabilization), an attempt was made to secure an alliance with a 'strong' country (i.e. the US) and also a political guarantee for long-term private investments for which foreign backing proved to be a pathfinder.

There then followed the rapid exhaustion of reserves, and subsequently the radical return to the notion of autarchy, with an administrative management of the exchange rate designed solely to ensure the functioning of essential industries, which at this stage meant above all those serving rearmament. So overwhelmingly was this the case that towards the end of the 1930s there was even a moment during which the objective of financing imports exclusively with exports could be said to have been achieved.

The foreign ally, however, was back on the scene in the period after the Second World War. This time it entered the economic circumstances of the period of reconstruction and the subsequent development stage with a variety of forms of aid and of direct presence. The power which intervened, the US, was the same one that in the mid-1920s had contributed to establishing a financial position for Italy in the world context. This time, however, the intervention, apart from the varied ways in which it was realized and which assigned a direct role to the government and industries of the US itself, also involved other European countries and took on a different political significance and a particular political weight linked to the consequences which it provoked. However much it may have been requested and motivated, it was no longer merely an intervention of foreign capital with effects limited to the 'higher' areas of the system (as had been the case with German aid in the 1890s and American capital in 1925–27), but of an alliance whose internal contractors were the very political forces which controlled the management of the state. For this reason it would have repercussions at various levels of the management of power and society, even more than on strictly economic affairs.

This last observation, far from confirming an element of discontinuity in the evolution of the relationship between internal economic development and international relations, as it might seem to do, is only intended to show the qualitative changes which, from the years of the First World War onwards, accompanied the progressive growth of Italian capitalism's political dependency on the outside world. By 'political dependency' I mean the need to submit to the conditions dictated by a foreign ally, and to make the consequences of this acceptable on the political and social planes. By 'the outside world', I mean what became during this time the heart of a monocentric system from which a single and worldwide mechanism of capitalist development took its lead – in other words, the United States.

The whole complex of events in the period which includes the years of the two wars and the years between shows very clearly the type of conditioning which, on various occasions, external affairs have had on the internal choices of economic policy. When the attempt to reactivate the mechanism used early in the century failed half way through the 1920s, both the recourse to external capital, with preliminary monetary stabilization, and the subsequent policy of isolationist autarchy involved a constant internal growth of limits on the use of resources. It meant that the means by which these resources were channelled towards the key industries became more stringent and totalitarian, and it meant more extensive use of old and new forms of exploitation of agriculture. With 'the Battle of the Grain', for instance, in addition to its exports and to remittances, even the structures of agriculture were placed at the disposal of industrial development. The exploitation of the land was to be driven to extraordinary lengths, even at the cost of degrading it and threatening its future capacity for improvement. But above all, it was the margin for manoeuvre in the policy of industrialization which was progressively narrowing from the second half of the 1920s onwards, just at the time when it was necessary, in order to keep pace with the development of technology and with new forms of monopoly organization, to take a qualitative leap in decisions about investment. We shall see later how the internal mechanisms of accumulation brought their function into line with this situation. But we can state here and now that this process was not enough to reduce the technological and technical distance which separated Italian industry from that of the rest of Europe; in many cases it had the opposite effect. It is also significant that, immediately after the Second World War, external support was seen by many parties as a way of subjecting Italy's industrial system to a widespread 'injection' of technology, after the isolation brought about by fascist autarchy during the second half of the 1930s and the war years.

In many ways, during the first half of the century, the degree of Italy's external dependence, far from lessening, actually increased progressively; the possibility of reducing the conditioning which arose from this dependency was mainly left to lucky chances of a 19th-century kind. We only have to consider some of the conditions which stimulated revival after the Second World War, or the mobilization of remittances from Italian emigrants by which, in 1944, the 'Kingdom of the South' was already in possession of a minimal operative capacity. We could mention the role which the export of agricultural produce and that of certain more traditional sectors of industry and craftsmanship played in an initial phase. Or even the new hope aroused (in similar fashion to those which succeeded – remittances and tourism) by the event of the 'Holy Year' of 1950. All these mechanisms did in fact work, to one degree or another.

In reality, until the beginning of the 1950s, nothing had happened to suggest that the economy was near to freeing itself from the chains which had conditioned its development up to that moment. The far from brilliant precedents of certain heavy industries, and the facts which were available for consideration at that stage, even more than doctrinaire convictions, ensured that the idea took root in a large part of the ruling class that the path to follow must be one combining a measure of free trade with certain kinds of traditional protectionism. In short: agrarian and light-manufacturing exports, intervention of foreign capital, remittances from emigrants, foreign exchange income from tourism, the agricultural sector at the service of industry, and so on – not very different from what had happened in the past. In fact, it was blatantly regressive, going backward in time through the early 'free-marketing' phase of fascism (1922–25), to Giolittian mediation at the beginning of the century and even earlier, to the tariff reform of 1887 and the subsequent arrangements in commercial treaties.

The unknown factor which still existed, hidden, at the beginning of the 1950s was in a way the same as that of half a century earlier. But this time there was also some reasonable doubt about the future international position of an economy which was entrusted to 19th-century mechanisms for gathering resources in the context of a completely transformed capitalist development.

7. The Formation of Industrial Capital: Methods and Procedures

As we have seen above, the extended initial phase of industrialization in Italy was characterized by the fact that the process of growth did not occur in those sections from which the resources used to supply the process of capital growth were derived. This explains to a great extent the significance assumed by the accumulative mechanism which was put into action from above in the formation of industrial capital. Alternatively, this process of capital formation might be achieved by a deliberate diversion of resources towards certain areas of the economy, obviously along with the classical mechanisms of business accumulation (this applies to capitalist companies or firms which were more or less artisan in character). The effect of this on the analysis of the overall process of development is that it provides an opportunity to take account of the wide range of instruments and procedures to which recourse was made from time to time in order to mobilize savings and, more generally, of all the measures which we normally list under the label of 'economic policy' and which were not necessarily translated directly into financial flow.

Once again we must first take account of the functions of the agricultural sector: i.e. of the sector which, even as the 20th century advanced, continued for a long time to be the 'net provider' of resources for the remaining areas of the economy. Agriculture, placed from the very beginning at the service of industrialization, remained there (despite appearances) until quite recent times. This is certainly true to a far greater degree than the habit of measuring its backing role in the formation of capital on the basis of quantitative financial data would lead us to believe. It was the primary sector which nurtured a large part of the army of emigrants until they reached working age, and for many decades it also directed the flow of overseas savings (in the various moments which we have already described). It provided almost the whole of the recruitment which supplied the labour market inside the country from the late 1950s onwards, and which allowed northern industry to achieve rates of profit which only extraordinarily low labour costs could make possible. Even in the years of autarchic policy, as I have already mentioned, when it was no longer a supplier of emigrants and remittances, agriculture was subjected to the needs of industry. This meant that its structures were burdened with the cost of containing the foreign deficit in foodstuffs, even at the price of degradation (the 'Battle for the Grain'). This was indispensable to free the resources needed for the importation of products for industry. The agrarian sector began to pay further costs, for reasons of internal exchange, when it became a market for the produce of domestic industry; this concerned matters such as the purchase of chemical fertilizers or producer goods on the internal market, or selling its own products abroad without enjoying the privilege of favourable exchange rates, as happened between the two wars and again after 1945 in the case of certain industrial products. A not insignificant part of the value of agricultural production was always expropriated, and increasingly so, by the sector of mercantile intermediation or by the parasitic bureaucratic organization appointed for the management of policies pre-designed for its own advantage.

Finally, up to the Second World War, the agricultural sector was the real and only protagonist of the balance of low consumption which, however we may judge its ultimate effects, made it possible for the 'model' to function. One aspect, that of the propensity of the rural population to save, was well-known to financiers; the men of the government in the Giolittian era were well aware of it too. It was also well-known to those who defended savings to finance rearmament between the wars, and to the protagonists of the Einaudi period of economic policy in the post-war years. Indeed it was a familiar phenomenon to all those who were aware of the provenance of those tiny flows of savings which for decades were regularly deposited in post offices, savings banks and popular banks.

But it would appear, on the contrary, that the only periods in which there were transfers of resources of a certain consistency from other sectors to agriculture were the war years. (It remains to be seen how true this is, however, given the extent of requisitions during those times.) More certainly, it is true for the periods immediately following the two wars. If we were able or willing to calculate the exchange of resources between agriculture and other sections of the economic system, we would certainly discover that at least until the end of the 1950s, the former would prove to be almost constantly a net supplier of the latter. Even if this conclusion did not completely undermine the opinion currently held about the importance which accumulation from 'industrial' sources was slowly beginning to have in the formation of capital, it could certainly serve other purposes: both to provide an idea of the degree to which the 19th-century mechanisms for the 'exploitation' of agriculture had extended in time, and to assess the long-term historical effect of the upsetting which would occur in subsequent years of the balances on which their functioning was based.

Within the Italian industrial system, numerous complex mechanisms of capital accumulation operated at the same time, each contributing its own effect. I will describe the most significant types of mechanisms concerned, beginning with those which were clearly shaped by the events of the last 30 years of the 19th century.

The first and perhaps most original formula with which we meet is the one which permitted the development of 'new' sectors of the economy, and which proves to have been based directly on bank debt, state orders and rescue operations backed up by customs protection and other facilities. The sectors in which this formula was applied from the 1880s were the metallurgical industries, shipbuilding and shipowning, military hardware and railways. Apart from the guarantees which they continued to need even after their 'infancy' stage, these industries could count on an internal accumulation of capital worthy of the name only during brief but intense economic phases determined by waves of public spending, rearmament and war. Recourse to the practice of accelerated debt repayment or working 'on commission' at favourable moments was never enough to free such undertakings from the weight of bank debt. It is known that the mixed banks, for their part, maintained special relations with these industries for the whole of their existence. But their willingness to do so may have been conditioned to some extent by an awareness of the attention that the government would in any case pay to guaranteeing the survival of the debtor.

The state and the banks were the two protagonists who worked sometimes in tandem and sometimes alternatively. The banks might take the lead in the phase of initial construction of the plant (as long as a state order had been obtained), whereas the state would take over in moments of crisis, thus assuring the functioning of the accumulative mechanism. The procedures which the state followed to achieve this aim were not only expressed in ordinances, but in original *ex post* lending operations. These involved a complex of previously agreed investments by private individuals, in the context of private business, with the support of the mixed banks – and with advantages for the latter as for the former. (Good examples are the rescue of the basic metallurgical industry in 1911 and of the firm Ansaldo in 1922; above all, the intervention to support the mixed banks themselves in 1931–33.) In effect, these are exactly the sectors in which the state prematurely and directly took on the role of promoter in the creation of a productive basis, and subsequently the role of provider of the costs needed to keep them in existence. In certain cases, it even accepted direct responsibility for running them: this is the origin of the system of state-owned firms in the 1930s. The solution which was adopted, with the organization of IRI acting as manager of many of the industries which we are discussing, ensured that the last wave of profits produced by the preparations for the Second World War would in fact remain in the public domain rather than finance private businesses, as had happened on previous occasions. A new stage in the mobilization of resources, and a broadening of the productive capacity of the basic metallurgical and mechanical sectors, would take place in the post-war years and would again be managed to a large extent by IRI. In the basic sectors which had always enjoyed public support, the most incisive innovations in procedure as far as the mechanism of accumulation is concerned were therefore adopted in the 1930s, while those which should have been directed at the objectives were only introduced in the 1950s. In any case, it could be said that this was the section of the Italian industrial system in which the function of accumulation was undertaken in the most continuous manner, even though under various forms, by the state.

It is true that not all the routes towards accumulation necessarily passed through the humiliating process of bail-outs, but it is equally certain that all of them were paved with debt, which varied only in size and in the length of time required for the process of capital recovery. Thus it is worth noting those sectors which required substantial mobilization of external resources in their initial or subsequent phases, or in their normal operations, though later on they made use of systematic and sometimes substantial degrees of self-financing. Concrete examples occur in the whole history of the electrical industry, and especially in its expansion stage in the 1920s. Other examples in the same decade include the new chemical industry and telephone services. These were industries in a stage of expanding their productive capacity and of applying new technology; their need for capital was so great that it conditioned the whole picture of the financial market and the policies which operated in it. In substance, we find ourselves faced with a mechanism of accumulation which is profoundly different from the one which operated in the cases we have noted above, a mechanism characterized by the alternation of phases in which firms translated the capital accumulated in the areas where self-financing functioned into productive capacity.

The resources which permitted the growth of a productive base and the functioning of the firms thus had origins which varied according to the sectors for which they were intended, or the particular economic circumstances involved – and they often followed very different paths. In the case of self-financing, this route was substantially defined by the criteria and models of business management and determined by market variables. It is a path which could be very interesting to trace, especially in the case of the electrical industry (we need only mention the reasons for and consequences of its symbiosis with electro-chemicals, as well as tariff policies and the state contribution). However, in an analysis aimed essentially at examining the phenomenon of accumulation and the involvement of savings, it is essential to pay greater attention to the other of the two courses indicated. In this context, the fact that the most notable commitments of investment could be brought to an end with the support of special 'public' procedures by firms which were 'ultra-private' takes on particular importance. The justification was that they were pursuing an expansion of their productive base for the purposes of public utility. The instrument which the major firms found to hand was the issue of fiscally privileged debentures, guaranteed by public financial bodies (ICIPU and CREDIOP). Use could be made of this instrument because of the adoption of a particular monetary policy (the stabilization of 1926–27) and the consequent possibility of access to foreign – and in particular American – capital. Apart from the context in which the above precedent took place, we could say that, in this case too, we are faced with industries which tended to have recourse to privileged channels of finance. Strong confirmation of this occurred in subsequent epochs (e.g. the chemical industry in the 1970s).

For a whole area of the Italian industrial system, in fact, self-financing was the primary factor on which the development of the productive base depended in the middle to long term (i.e. apart from the reasons which might require it as a rule, including those imposed by the financial market). Within these boundaries, a great variety of endeavours found a place. At one end there was the huge family of artisan activities, both those which continued to survive for a long time because of the lack of development of a national market (and the consequent persistence of production-consumption circuits which were limited to very restricted local areas) and those which, because of their vitality, succeeded in transforming themselves and maintaining an important position in the productive apparatus. At the other end of the scale were the great capitalist firms – still, however, controlled for the most part by single families – which appeared as a belated manifestation in Italy of the British Industrial Revolution (wool, cotton, hat-making and related industries). Finally, there were the firms which, from the late 19th century onwards, took advantage of the possibilities offered by the standardization of production and the progressive broadening of consumption (the car industry, light mechanical goods, the food industry, rubber and the other 'non-basic' manufacturing industries in the process of industrialization).

Almost until the eve of the 1970s, this composite mass of very different elements, in which the residue of the past was mingled with the imminent possibilities of modern industrial development, continued to have one important common feature: with a few possible exceptions, they were all excluded from any form of guarantee-provision which in other cases assured the survival and development of the productive basis which was in the process of formation. The 'right of bail-out', for example, was to remain, at least until recently, unknown to Italy's manufacturing sector which, we should note, is virtually the kind which free-marketers are accustomed to term 'natural'. In fact, the sector demanded little or nothing from banks or the state, while in turn making a substantial contribution to the financing of imports needed for the activity of the major basic sectors.

8. Financial Institutions and Support Policies

The unusual nature of the ways in which capital formation was financed reflects to a great extent the logic by which the system of financial institutions was developing a structure of its own. It also reflects the role which these institutions were called upon to play in the various stages of Italian industrialization. In this context the attempts at various moments to insert into the Italian situation institutions which had proven their worth elsewhere acquire special significance.

Setting aside for a moment all the consequences of the late 'discovery' of the institution of the joint-stock company as well as the outcome of the experiences of property banks, the most instructive example is provided by the attempt to encourage the development in Italy of the stock market and, in particular, shareholding. This attempt was pursued for the first time right at the beginning of the 20th century, and then again in the 1920s. The aim was to accumulate funds to be invested in the larger enterprises. On the other hand, it is also significant that the financial institutions which grew up on the model of those operating abroad succeeded in taking root in Italy on one condition: that there was a partial revision of the strategy which had originally inspired their policy of intervention. Here we can point to the experience of the so-called 'mixed banks', which began and developed in Italy under the stimulus of the major German banks, not without notable traces of previous French experience in property banking. These succeeded for more than 30 years in providing very substantial financial support for basic industries; this proved possible because they directed their most risky commitments towards the sectors which enjoyed customs and financial backing from the state, and also because they almost always managed to ensure coverage for themselves by appropriate monetary policies.

The fundamental need to compensate for the inefficiency of the financial market, and in some way to guarantee the functioning of the credit mechanism, made the invention of peculiarly Italian institutions and procedures more and more necessary. Thus the direct assumption of responsibility on the part of the state for accumulating capital in order to finance 'emerging' sectors was added first of all in the 1920s to the various forms of financial guarantee provisions and the use of 'bail-out operations' as a means of ensuring the functioning of the credit mechanism and avoiding destructurization. This was accompanied by the promotion of a semi-public and privileged debenture market (Icipu and Crediop) and then, in the subsequent decade, by the radical reorganization of the financial basis of industry and the management of basic sectors (bank reform and constitution of IRI).

Thus, the broad lines of an Italian formula which was designed to meet the needs for financial support which might arise from time to time in the course of industrial development emerged quite quickly. The formula assigned a front-rank role to bank intermediation, flanked by certain 'special' channels of financing. Both had the backing of monetary policy, and more generally the practice of dividing up resources; in one way or another such divisions always finally reflected the agreements, encounters, compensations and equilibria between the major centres of industrial and financial interest.

More recent history shows how this solution had a number of limits built into the logic which governed its application. However, for a long period it did render a sort of financial planning possible whose character was more global and totalitarian in inverse ratio to the limits of manoeuvre imposed by the external financial world. (As an example, we may take the use which was made of credit policy in the 1920s and 1930s.) This made it possible, without irreparable trauma, to overcome those crucial phases in which it was necessary to guarantee that the system would 'hold'. On the other hand, it was the origin of a more and more evident alteration of the way in which the competitive mechanism worked. This was true to such an extent that one could in fact call it a 'segmentation' of the financial market or of its shaping, in time and space, into watertight compartments. On the level of entrepreneurial and political action, this meant creating the premises for a practice which would have led the various sectors (public and private, into which the industrial system was dividing) to obtain a contractual and more or less exclusive guarantee of access to credit at the political level. Thus, besides the fact that the same policies which were being introduced to maintain the continuity of financial intermediation had to be translated into some form of guarantee for the depositors and thus assure the solvency of the banks, it also implicitly involved the pursuit of an objective which contradicted the logic of competition, and thus delegated the maintenance of efficiency to interventions of various kinds.

The way in which the structure of the financial system in Italy was developing and its implicit long-term effects show the importance assumed by the political and institutional situation. This relates both to the phase when the formal structure of financial management was being set up and in the more strictly operative phase during which orientations and practices differing substantially from original intentions often prevailed. (We have only to think of the development of special credits, or the way in which the functions of IMI or even IRI itself were understood, or again the policy which was to be followed in the application of bank reform decided on in 1936.) In fact the adoption of radical measures of institutional revision is the condition which made it possible in 1893–94 (reform of the issuing institutions) and from 1933 onwards (so-called bank recovery) to take in hand a sort of *ex-post* financing – obviously at the expense of the community – of all the complex of investment decisions previously adopted by private individuals. In this way the malfunctioning of the financial mechanisms formerly in operation was obviated, but at some cost.

By 'straightening-out' interventions in entire sectors – by the creation of special institutes, by bail-outs in individual cases or by policies devised to deal with particular situations – a complex superstructure was created. This would serve the area of Italian industry which would continue to reabsorb resources from the rest of the system for a long time to come.

This, then, was the mechanism by which the state operated directly in specific banking and financial spheres in order to promote the creation of a productive basis. It did so particularly in the descending phase of the cycle, during which the durability of the system was assured by the major operations of institutional readjustment mentioned above.

The other direct way in which the state was able to operate in the same sense (formation of a productive base) was to acquire goods and services from those sectors which took advantage of its credit policies. From this standpoint, in fact, we may see how unfounded, in many cases, are the accusations often hurled against the state of absorbing capital which would otherwise have flowed into private industry. It is clear that the resources which the state extracted from the capital market in various ways were more often than not recycled towards the major firms in the form of state orders.

9. The Equilibrium of Low Consumption

The accusation against the role of mediation, which was to remain entrusted to public expenditure throughout the whole period of industrialization in Italy, adds a certain new dimension to the discussion of the overall mechanisms operating at the level of the whole system. It introduces a new element into the formation of demand which remains, at a basic level, the main path to be followed for the purpose of understanding the process of accumulation. Here we should explain, in line with what we have said about its role throughout the whole of the 19th century, that agriculture (and all the other sectors which were self-supporting) ended by financing the development of the 'basic' sectors and those which were highly capital-intensive. However, the former did not, on their own, create the demand which could have provided a sufficient outlet for the produce of the latter.

The basic and characteristic feature of capitalist accumulation in Italy is actually represented by the fact that it was not essentially the outcome of the growth and spread of sectoral interdependence on the whole front of productive activity; rather it was the result of the creation of appropriate financial channels and specific instruments of economic policy through which replacement mechanisms were brought into being. With regard to the nature and functioning of these replacement mechanisms, we need only continue our analysis of the financial apparatus which underlay them. To do this, we should update the identity of the protagonists who were respectively the eventual beneficiaries and the net providers of resources. The list of the former is already complete: along with the metallurgical industry, which would long continue to be a bottomless pit, we should add, as time went on, electricity, chemicals and public services (electrification of the railways, creation of the telephone network, etc.). We have already referred to the providers of resources on at least two occasions, when speaking of the new forms of 'exploitation' of agriculture in the post-18th century phase and when describing the sectors in which the classic mechanism of self-financing operated.

However, it does not seem to be simply a matter of tracing a line of demarcation between geographical zones or sectors of activities: in fact, it was the whole 'physiology' of entire sections of the system which was placed at the service of the mechanism in order to mobilize resources. There are important parts of this physiology – for instance, the action of direct and indirect taxes – which operate differently according to the sectors and social classes affected. There are the effects, similarly differentiated, of customs protection; also the impact of particular economic situations, with all the consequences of redistribution and forced savings which they entail (the war economy, inflationary processes, etc.). There is the operation of internal terms of trade, the different level of efficiency of commercial intermediation, and the whole complex of circumstances which kept a considerable part of the Italian population tied down to levels and modes of consumption nearer to those of a pre-industrial economy than to a society of mass consumption. It could also be claimed that the two aspects of Italian economic development to which we have just referred (non-development of sectoral interdependence and the simultaneous operation of alternative mechanisms of financial accumulation) seem merely to be the two facets of that single equilibrium which finally prevailed in the long term and which we have previously termed 'the equilibrium of low consumption'. In fact, the limiting of demand – first within the boundaries of subsistence consumption or something near it, and then, even in the 1950s, only just at the threshold of mass consumption – allowed the financial mechanisms of support for basic industry to function, and above all permitted the financing of the state's purchasing power.

The original path taken by Italian capitalism, while it shortened the distance between Italy and the Western capitalist countries and allowed it to keep pace with them, nevertheless gave rise to a system which maintained – and in some senses even demanded – the retention of substantial elements of difference from the Western model. On the level of the structure of the industrial system, the persistence of archaic patterns of consumption, which in the market translated into limited dimensions and low quality, caused the excessive survival of pre-capitalist productive structures. Sometimes these patterns relegated the functions of the market to purely local contexts, mainly linked to the agrarian logic of family subsistence. In the period under consideration here, the processes of de-structuring went on extraordinarily slowly, when not actually being delayed or stopped altogether. This also explains some deterioration in the dualistic phenomenon within the sectors themselves. It became clearer and clearer that the formative process of Italy's industrial system was thus taking shape as the grafting of certain advanced technical and industrial experiences onto a more or less pre-capitalist structure. This grafting would only give rise at a later stage and under certain special conditions to a general adoption of modern business structures in the productive and financial senses: this would have to be on the basis of a more mature development of productive interdependence. Neither customs and financial protection in the first case, nor autarchy later, would succeed in taking the place of the multiplicity of effects which would arise from a development of demand 'from below' (whether internal or external). In both cases, there would be no lack of obvious consequences on the type of company organization, especially in the 'heavy' sectors, as can be seen from the examples of vertical and horizontal integration between the metallurgical departments, the mechanical and shipbuilding sectors and electro-chemicals. But this is a phenomenon which belongs more to the organizational and financial logic within large basic units, rather than to the growth of global demand – which alone is capable of effecting transformation into scale economies. Even in the aftermath of the Second World War, the Italian industrial apparatus was to appear extremely heterogeneous in its parts and disjointed in its structures.

10. Economic Conditions and Accumulation

When so many different and often contrasting elements coexist within an organism, and when the points of communication between them are so limited and dependent on chance, many cognitive and methodological problems arise for anyone who seeks merely to define –

not even to measure – the way in which the economic situation and its crises operate both on the complex mechanism of accumulation and on the process of modernization of the productive structure. (This is not only true of the spreading of the multiplicatory effects of demand, but also of matters affecting the 'physiological' channels of circulation of capital in the first place.) Any definition of this kind must take account first of all of the combined action of at least three orders of factors. The first is represented by the friction which arises because of the disjointed nature of the system in the stage when the demands arising from the cycle are transmitted. The second is the product of the different nature and provenance of the demand which sets in motion the functioning of the various sections of the productive apparatus. The last consists of the weight rapidly assumed by the intervention of support policies for the benefit of certain sectors and not others. The division into periods which might be made (and which has sometimes been made) on the basis of the current statistical apparatus, using data on the national revenue, savings and investments, for instance, does not serve to explain the extent or the quality of the changes which economic conditions effect on the various elements of the system. This tends to invalidate any judgement one might seek to make about the effects of economic cycles on the process of capital formation in the long term.

In fact, the only points at which the whole economic organism seemed unmistakably and generally to feel the effects of a particular economic situation are to be found respectively before and after the timespan which we are considering. Specifically, this means the great period of agrarian crisis in the 19th century, and the years beginning with the 1960s in the 20th. In the first case, this is because the various economies of the peninsula all obeyed the unitary logic of an agrarian economy, however diversely they may have done so; in the second, it is because the overall mechanism of an industrial economy finally prevailed in all areas of the peninsula, even in those in which there was no industry in the strict sense. In the intermediary situations, on the other hand, there were factors present which operated in different ways and degrees, according to the sector or economic area concerned. It is not possible to register any one-directional or general effects caused by these factors.

We may take as an example the way in which the stimuli of the world cycle acted on the phases which are usually considered 'ups' or 'downs' for Italy. Demands originating from abroad were present between 1898 and 1906, subsequently in the years 1922–25, and again in the course of the period of reconstruction after the Second World War. They operated mainly at the cost of agriculture and certain 'light' sections of industry. On the other hand, conditions of this kind cannot be found during the phase from 1934 to 1939.

Internally the growth of industrial investment in the first two phases mentioned was the result of a kind of 'privatization' in the use of resources, achieved by the deliberate redimensioning of the activity of the state in the financial markets. In the second half of the 1930s, on the other hand, industrial investments (which in this instance mainly affected the industries involved in rearmament), came about through the financial mediation of the state and by the direct action of public expenditure. The supportive action of the public structures would again have substantial weight in post-war reconstruction, though within the framework of a policy specifically aimed at the recovery of private investment and intended to follow 'market indications'.

Factors of an international kind still lie at the origin of the particular economic conditions found in Italy in 1907, in 1921–22, and on the occasion of the depression of the years 1930–

33. But it is precisely on these occasions that the weight of internal policies seemed most effective in their influence on the characteristics and outcome of the crises. This indicates above all the peripheral position which Italy had come to occupy in the world economy, and also the fact that only limited parts of the economic system were directly and decisively affected by the world cycle. In 1907, the possible developments of a brief but intense crisis on the stock exchange and the banks were neutralized successfully by the intervention of the monetary authorities. In 1921–22 the policy of state bail-out and guarantee, especially in the form of customs protection, had the effect of shortening the time needed for recovery. It also circumvented the devastating effects of the world crisis of reconversion, even though this had had more acute effects in Italy than elsewhere. In 1930–31, the repercussions of the international crisis were combated with economic policy measures of even greater range, first with the well-tried interventions of financial backing, and then with a financial and managerial reorganization of basic industry, in anticipation of the kind of New Deal, Italian-style, which the policy of rearmament was to bring about.

Measures of economic policy aimed at ensuring that the basic structures of the industrial system would survive were once again at the centre of the long depressive phase which preceded the First World War (1908–14). During this phase the stagnation of business in the context of a world economy which was in a stage of revival is an indication of the inadequacy of internal demand for the produce of the country's major firms, and also of the inability of Italian industry to extend its presence in foreign markets.

In at least one case, the responsibility for determining and managing an economic situation lay entirely with economic policy. This was the occasion of the crisis in monetary stabilization which began in 1926, and which started a depressive stage which would be linked, with only one short interval, to the subsequent cycle of the great crisis. Among other factors, this was the only moment in which it proved necessary to resort to a deflationary manoeuvre, with the aim of directing a further flow of resources towards the basic sectors. (The possibility of both internal and external capital accumulation was realized in this way.) A further intention was to provide adequate compensation for sectors of the great chemical industry so that it could pay its way (achieved by protectionism, by the authoritarian reduction of wages and by the legitimization of monopolistic practices).

In general, the outcome of all the ascending phases, whether they were fed by external circumstances or internal expansionist policies, was provided by the widening of the productive bases in the 'new' sectors of the economy. These sectors subsequently become beneficiaries of the policy of support and the measures of rationalization which intervened in various ways in order to sanction and guarantee the presence of new basic structures in the economic organism during the phases of stagnation or recession.

The mechanism which made it possible to direct the various economic circumstances towards the formation of a productive base in the 'emerging sectors' assigned a double role to agriculture and to the various sectors of traditional activity which live in close contact with it (artisans and small family firms), and to some light manufacturing activities of a modern type. This double role operated both in the ascending part of the cycle and in recessionary periods. In the former, this whole area of the economic system, with its export capacity, made a substantial contribution to the financing of the purchase abroad of raw materials and semi-manufactured goods for the major industries. In the descending phases it sustained to a great extent the costs of support policies, whether in terms of rationing credit, by the effect of the intersectoral terms of trade, or again in terms of fiscal drag. In particular, in both cases, the sectors not yet adjusted to the methods and forms of capitalist production performed a function as important shock-absorbers of the waves of economic pressure, and this was precisely because of their backwardness. They made it possible to contain the pressure of wages in the expanding phases by providing manpower; they offered the possibility of 're-entry' in moments of crisis and increase of unemployment; and they constituted 'reserves' of the supply of goods and services at low cost. Finally they did not enter into competition in the capital market.

In overall terms, because of the characteristics which the process of formation of an industrial base assumed in Italy, we can say that, at least until recently, the economic developments in the advanced sectors have had only a limited influence on the evolutionary dynamic of the more backward ones. The processes of reduction of the areas occupied by economic activities of an archaic type have been quite slow: in overall terms, such areas seem to have felt more keenly the impact of exterior circumstances (such as foreign demand for manpower at the beginning of the century, or the ban on emigration during the fascist era), rather than the growth of the 'capitalist' sector. This also explains why the inclusion of the backward zones in the unitary mechanism of accumulation rarely happened through processes of progressive diffusion of capitalist elements to pre-industrial structures, with their consequent transformation. Instead it occurred most often through the preliminary and total destruction of the pre-existing economic situation (this was to happen, in fact, on a large scale in the course of developments after the Second World War).

11. Myths and Realities of the Return to 'Economic Freedom'

Some of the mechanisms which we have seen at work from the initial moments of industrial development were to continue or to return and play a major role – in some cases an essential one – in the phases of reconstruction and primary development in the 1950s. But the most surprising circumstance, which virtually symbolizes the whole mortgage which the past had imposed on the future of economic development, is represented by the fact that this time these mechanisms operated simultaneously and in a coordinated fashion, even though less incisively than in the past. They include exportation of the workforce and remittances from emigrants, tourism and Holy Years (1950 was so designated), exports by 'light' and 'traditional' manufacturing industry, and even agricultural exports. There was even the same backing from external allies (though under different forms and conditions from those of the past). The front from which the resources for financing development came this time was even more extended than on previous occasions. These elements, and the whole chain of implications which derived from the persistence of some typical and traditional conditions of the Italian social and economic scene (especially low wages and the slow increase in mass consumption), virtually gave the 1950s the form of the final segment of the diagram which we have been describing. I call it the 'final segment' because, apart from the presence and role of traditional factors, the changes which had intervened in the meantime also had their effect; moreover, the period in question appears as the preliminary and strategic moment for what would be Italy's 'new path' in the industrial revolution.

The initial datum, and also the one most imbued with consequences for the future, is represented by the fact that Italy now belonged to a given 'area', specifically that of the capitalist West. From this membership, which immediately assumed the significance of 'taking sides', a large number of developments derived, both on the internal front and in overseas relations.

At home, the revival of 'economic freedom' was translated first of all into delegating to the market the power to define the 'best' allocation of resources. This was followed logically by the repudiation of the use of instruments of economic control, with the exception of those aimed at pursuing monetary stability. The latter objective assumed the sacred character of an indispensable requirement in relation to the commitment to international integration (convertibility and fixed rates). In practice, this was equivalent to handing over the function of controlling the economic cycle to monetary policy (and *exclusively* to this, given the enormous delays involved in activating instruments based on fiscal policy). In connection with the re-attribution of power to the market, this essentially meant that those who had the direction of economic policy limited themselves to taking note of the choices for investment which were being made by the forces in the field (and especially by the major industrial and financial groups), and predisposing the so-called market conditions so that they could be fulfilled.

In this context the innovative scope of what some people have called the 'free-market turn' appears quite limited. It is not much more than an updated edition of the formula already tried in the past, which had seen decisions of fundamental importance to development taken on the strength of the pressure which the major centres of economic power could exert in political quarters and only secondarily by the work of mediation of the political class itself.

Naturally, at the beginning of the 1950s the picture is much more elaborate and complex than it was, for instance, in the 1880s or even in the 1920s. This was not only due to the obvious reason that the productive front had acquired a wider scope for capitalist development, but also because of the new readiness of the political class to listen to requests for a much broader alignment of democratic and social forces. A further factor was the actual logic of democratic representation, and the widely differing cultural matrices of the managerial class in politics and economics. But all this was more relevant to the greater difficulty which politicians faced in their work of mediation, rather than to the substance of the means by which they continued to make decisive choices. Only if we begin with these considerations is it possible to understand either of the following: (1) the variety of concrete instances and doctrinaire notions which underlay the overall scheme and the individual decisions in economic policy during those years; or (2) the freedom of movement and space which the ruling class granted to this or that interest group, or to the individual exponents of the entrepreneurial and financial world. In fact the whole extension of the front along which the initiatives were spreading can only be understood in this way. Such initiatives were aimed at developing existing technico-industrial experiences or at attempting to find new ones.

This is also the explanation of why, from the beginning of reconstruction until the end of the 1950s, when the Italian economy had already embarked on a well-defined course, the path of development proved to be a complex and contradictory interweaving of ancient and modern myths, old and new realities, episodes which seemed to be casual but which in the end proved to be strategic. For instance, the myth of a nation peopled by artisans, small businessmen and private farmers, and in general by a hard-working and savings-conscious lower and middle bourgeoisie is contrasted with the reality of a country moving towards a predominance of wage- and salary-earners. Policies were aimed at reconstruction and development of the industrial productive apparatus in the North, together with declarations of principle in the South. There were proposals (which never became anything more) to direct and control the development of the economy in some way and, at the same time, the appearance of a mechanism which assigned to the state and to economic policy the task of meeting the demands expressed by private economic operators. There was the myth of agrarian reform initiated under the aegis of the ancient cry of 'land to the peasants', contrasted with the bleaker reality of environmental conditions, relations with foreign countries, and ways of putting such aspirations into practice which condemned them to failure right from the start. The exaltation of 'economic rationality' and 'the behaviour of private individuals conflicted with the simultaneous abandonment of a large part of the structure of public administration to a destiny of survival or degradation (this included the extremely delicate structures of education and the taxation system). There was the decision to maintain in existence certain pillars of public intervention in the economy (the case of IRI comes to mind), but the lack of any policy directing their use for specified objectives. The widespread image of an industrial future for Italy centred on the potential of the light manufacturing sectors was in sharp contrast to the decision at the same time to relaunch the basic iron and steel industry, to establish an oil policy and to support the first initiatives in the nuclear and electronic fields and various other areas of basic and applied scientific research (e.g. chemicals and pharmaceuticals). The emphasis with which the role of agriculture in the development of the country was spoken of conflicted with the total subordination of policy in the agricultural field either to the internal needs of industrial policy or the external need for international integration.

The lines along which the Italian industrial apparatus was reviving and converting itself were therefore taking shape against the background of openness to the outside world, and all the conditions which immediately arose from this. These included not only material and financial assistance, or the so-called 'technological leap', but also the actual possibility of reactivating old mechanisms of 're-balancing', such as the emigration of the workforce and the manufacturing and agricultural produce. In this process, all the connotations and contradictions listed above were present. Truth to tell, in spite of the absence of precise guidelines of industrial policy and more generally of an economic policy, and in spite of all the other political reasons frequently referred to, on the eve of the so-called 'economic miracle' Italy seemed potentially capable of becoming just about anything. This is the way we can interpret the eclecticism of the lines of policy which began to take shape at the end of the 1940s and the beginning of the 1950s: the uncertain outcome of the last chance which was offered to this country to modernize and rationalize the industrial matrix operating from the 'supply side', thus anticipating the building of structures to which the future would assign a strategic role. Something similar, in short, to what had been done in the past with the metallurgical industry, with electricity and chemicals, in different ways and contexts. I called it an 'uncertain outcome' because, as we know, there were also steps in the direction of a resumption of the tradition which had seen the state acting as a pathfinder for the formation and broadening of the productive basis in 'key' sectors of the economy, as illustrated by the events of the metallurgical revival and the oil policy. But apart from the origins of these decisions, which if not purely accidental were certainly due to the political weight of those who made them, it remains a fact that any policy which sought to remain 'faithful to the past' would have demanded the predisposition of measures aimed at controlling the chain reactions which might derive from an expansion of consumption, as well as appropriate channels for the mobilization and transfer of resources in favour of basic or new sectors. All this obviously required that the state should once again be at the centre of the process of accumulation, even if with very different weapons and a new degree of incisiveness.

For this reason, the refusal to strengthen and rationalize the instruments of public intervention in the economy seems to be essentially a failure of one of the special features of Italian capitalism (occurring at the very moment when countries enjoying much older capitalist traditions than Italy were heading in an opposite direction). If we also take account of the weight exercised in these circumstances by the context of international integration, a fact of this significance can only confirm the conditioning reflected in the decisions that a whole ruling class was taking in this period.

12. The Evolution of the Productive System Between the Backing of State Mediation and the Automatic Stimuli of Demand

A final response to the many unknowns which continued to persist over the future of Italian industry at the beginning of the 1950s seemed to be offered by the developments of the subsequent decade and those of the early 1970s. This was not only because new factors emerged which seemed at once to take on the full weight and character of irreversible data, but also and above all because of the failure of certain features which had periodically tended to reinforce the image of 'strangled development' to which Italians had in some ways grown reconciled.

They had become accustomed to discontinuous growth in certain basic sectors, and were thus familiar with the functioning of a whole range of institutions and policies aimed at increasing the productive basis in these sectors, or merely at guaranteeing their survival. The 30 years beginning with the period of post-war reconstruction present us with a very different picture. First comes a long period of development which lasted beyond all prediction (except for a few insignificant pauses and a minor but significant 'hitch' in 1962), carried along on the wave of the international growth cycle. After this, beginning with the 1970s, there was a sequence of brief cycles of resumption and moments of interruption of development, caused mainly by the action of internal factors but conditioned and basically dominated in the background and in general terms by profound changes taking place in the outside world affecting the whole framework of capitalist development. The logic of the entire previous phase of industrialization had often affected the patterns and modes of survival of traditional sectors only marginally and within narrow limits, a logic reinforced to some extent by their own backwardness. In the 30 years of the post-war period, not only the long stage of development but also the stage of subsequent 'crises' affected ever more extensive areas of the economy. In the acceleration stage, the impact on traditional sectors was violent, causing unexpected, rapid and widespread destruction, while for the same reason the capacity which these sectors had shown in the past to cushion the effects of the cycle disappeared. In fact, as a result of the prevalence of a single 'physiology', which exposed the whole geographical area and very varied social classes to the effects of the grave economic situation, it was actually the so-called 'marginal' areas which suffered most. This was not what had happened in the past, when the task of shaping the directions which development was to take had been entrusted to internal decisions, operating in a completely original fashion from the 'supply side'. Now this same task was entrusted to the action of external factors which acted primarily on the 'demand side', thus reducing the main role of internal economic policy to that of creating the conditions in which these factors could fully exercise their influence.

In the last instance, all those factors operating in Italy directly or indirectly through the openings of international integration were reduced to demand – i.e. to the basic lever which controls all the mechanisms of capitalist development. In the case of indirect influences, this was because the world economy orchestrated a huge revival in exported labour, which was translated in time into a stimulus-factor for many internal transformations. Concerning direct influences, not only did the outside world demand from Italy particular kinds of manufactured goods (i.e. those of a mass-consumption economy), and thus showed what direction the productive system should take, but it also paved the way, by the products it offered and its patterns of consumption, for an explosion of internal demand. The world economy and external demand thus constituted the *deus ex machina* which intervened and reversed the lines of development which had always dominated the functioning of the system.

The whole series of rapid transformations which immediately gave credence to the opinion that Italy had finally found its industrial vocation, its position in Western capitalism and its model of development, originated in the intensity and duration with which external demand operated from the 1950s onwards. This was later supplemented by internal demand and the progressive homogenization of the structures of both. As a result of the spread and generalization of scale economies, a network of basic relations came to be created between the various productive sectors, while connecting linkages of firms and activities also took shape. These progressively filled many of the gaps which still existed in the industrial structure. Italy had built an industrial organization on asymmetrical lines and with considerable difficulty in a matter of a few decades. This was dominated by the contrast between the abnormal development of the major basic sectors and the extension of the area occupied by the old manufacturing system, artisan and otherwise. Now, in one short decade, it found itself in possession of a productive apparatus with a new equilibrium between its component parts, constructed in the image and likeness of that of the most advanced industrial countries and thus in a position to compete in the conquest and defence of a share of the market.

The whole series of events which seemed to bring Italy out through the Pillars of Hercules into a state of development characterized by low consumption and a few 'industrial gems' can therefore be understood from two different angles. First, as part of a broader picture of events on the world stage and, second, as one of the most important opportunities for this country to attempt to approach the average levels of development of the capitalist area. In reality, if we look at things in the latter perspective, and in spite of appearances, the results of the growth achieved in the 1960s in terms of structure show certain limits; while these reflect the whole weight of conditioning imposed by the past on the future, they also reopen certain questions concerning the context within which the so-called 'policy of development' has been pursued.

First of all comes agriculture. The parabola which the forms and stages of the subordination of work on the land to the objectives of creating a modernizing industry had been tracing for many decades reached its lowest point as a result of the violent destruction caused by the development mechanism. This was further abetted by the substantial subservience of the policies supposedly adopted 'in its favour'. This subordination was shown above all in relation to the requirements of the politico-social balance, but was also reflected in the decision to sacrifice the needs of agriculture to those of industry in the field of international contracts. From this moment, in any case, agriculture began to account for a growing portion on the debit side of the scales of the balance of payments, causing a revision of the logic which had always seen it as a provider of resources for the advanced sectors.

The other area of weakness in the economic system which took shape in the 1960s can be seen in the marginal position to which certain fundamental 'new sectors' seem to have been relegated. Their importance goes far beyond the need for completeness in the industrial matrix; it applies more specifically to their role as 'factors of production'. I refer in particular to basic and applied scientific research, to old and new energy sources, to electronics and new forms of generalized education, to ecology and certain types of services – in other words, to all those sectors to which the overall efficiency of a modern industrial system is linked. From this point of view, in comparison with the economies of other industrial countries, Italy's productive apparatus seems to be devoid of certain substantial points of strength, measurable not only in terms of the extension of the industrial matrix to strategic sectors, but above all in terms of the availability to businesses of 'external economies'; of provision for advanced technology, of a degree of multinationalism in the character of its firms and of levels of production. To explain the reasons which have determined or aggravated this imbalance in the physiognomy of the industrial system, we need to refer not so much to the limits of past development, but rather to more recent times, and especially to that 'delegation to the market', in the name of which both the phase of reconstruction and the subsequent one of development were carried out. Many of the guidelines which inspired public intervention in the economy are traceable to these factors.

It would appear at least that the absence of state action from a whole sphere of activity, the development of which was destined to become strategic for the future of the economic system, seems a very significant index of the degree of awareness of the past and the present shown by the ruling class. This is true above all because, as the contemporary experience of other industrial countries shows, qualitative developments in capitalism on a world scale demand as a *sine qua non* the presence of vast investments, belonging by their very nature to the state. (The example of West Germany's experience is very indicative in this context.) Secondly, because of the position which Italy had occupied in the international economy, it was even more necessary to devise appropriate policies of preparation for its lasting entry into the advanced capitalist area, and thus to aim at enlarging and completing the heritage of experience and potential development in what had in the meantime become new sectors of the economy.

At first sight, then, we are faced with something of a paradox. The country in which the state had operated as a guarantor and stimulator of the process of accumulation in its basic sectors for the longest time now found itself incapable of reactivating or renewing the very instruments which it had possessed for assigning to public intervention the role of creator of the productive base and of pathfinder of development – both seemingly new discoveries of modern world capitalism. In fact this is no more than an aspect, though certainly an extremely important one, of the evolution which the instruments and procedures for directing the economy underwent from the 1950s onwards. It is, in addition, part of the significance which the category, 'state capitalism', assumes in the Italian case.

In the majority of Western countries the spread of the area of state intervention was essentially motivated by the need to control the economic cycle and to satisfy collective demands. It is only more recently that the need to promote certain basic sectors and services related to the private economy has come to the fore (for instance research, education, land usage, and so on). In the majority of cases, however, the increased power of workers' organizations and the political needs arising therefrom have for some time conditioned both the quality of the instruments of intervention and the nature of the policies put into practice to increase the overall efficiency of the system.

In the case of Italy, the state, prematurely called upon to undertake a role of supporting the productive basis in certain sectors, has had as the main testing-board for is activities the terrain of political mediation between groups with strong oligarchic tendencies. From around the end of the 1950s it has operated in a context in which the capacity of trade union and working-class political organizations to exert pressure has been fairly limited. The state's incapacity to continue the role played in the past – by updating and modifying its instruments in relation to the changed picture of social equilibria and the new quality of economic development – has conditioned public intervention in Italy. This has been increasingly seen, not in the form of a complex of organized structures, laws, measures of control and procedures, etc., coordinated with clear objects in view, but rather as a jumble of initiatives, concessions and policies reflecting the dynamic of the power relations of those forces which have long controlled the state. We could even say that a situation of 'state *capitalisms*' has been in the making, profoundly modifying the operative logic of a major part of the instruments of public action.

Thus the new relationships between politics and administration have steadily weakened the latter. Their capacity to provide services has diminished while they have been given the role of supporting demand by means of expenditure on wages and pensions. In the absence of any context of objectives in which to assert its activities, the public managerial organization of state participation has not been able to fulfil the task which it had fulfilled, at least to some extent in the past: that of piloting the development of 'key' sectors. Fiscal policy, impeded from the beginning by enormous delays in updating a system of taxation, has run up against rapid petrifaction (because too many categories of expenditure were considered necessary for the purposes of social control), and has seriously influenced the way monetary policy has been used. Monetary policy has ended up by becoming an instrument of political mediation by which, from time to time, a response is made to the need to cover the public deficit. It also serves to stabilize the quantity of money for the industrial system and the consequent level of activity in relation to the foreign exchange rate (which in turn is linked to the demands of international policy). The banking system, when it has not limited itself to collecting occasional and often uncoordinated impulses from the outside world, has been drawn back into the unproductive mechanism and has in many cases ended up by carving out a space for itself in the speculative interstices of this situation.

If we consider the 'development policy' of the 1960s in light of the whole experience of Italian capitalism from the time of unification to the Second World War, the evolution of the role of the state as described above seems to be most clearly characterized by the events of the first decades after the war – especially when we take account of the eventual outcome of this development. This is not only because many of the peculiarities and limits of Italian capitalist development have derived from the role which the state has played in the process of accumulation, but also because, once again, the character of public involvement in the economy is one of the central elements in the difference between Italy and other Western capitalist countries – though perhaps in an opposite sense to what had been the case previously. We have already discussed some of the reasons for this diversity. We may now add, in more general terms, that while the majority of advanced capitalist societies have seen a progressive increase in public power and control over the complex of economic variables, and also an augmented degree of sensitivity within the economy to state action, in the Italian case the growing rigidity of the instruments of intervention and the lack of coordination between the various sectors of public administration (another sense in which it is possible to speak in the plural, of 'state capitalisms') have not only prejudiced any efficient and coherent controls, but in many cases have caused public activity itself to give rise to contradictory stimuli from time to time, and sometimes even to elements of destabilization.

At first sight, it might seem that there was never so much talk concerning public intervention as in the 1960s. And public interventions then there certainly were, varying greatly in nature, quality and destination. But an exact measurement of their extent compared with the amount of private involvement in the economy and in society would probably make it pale into insignificance and lead to a change of view. In fact, with a few exceptions, such as some interventions in the South, public intervention had never been so relatively limited as at that juncture, nor had it ever had so little effect on the direction of development. Neither had it ever been so subordinated to pressures from the private sector (as witness the results of the attempt at forward planning). The state proved incapable of assimilating the experience which was transferred to it by the more advanced countries (even when this was appropriately adapted to Italian needs). Indeed, by then it had ceased to pursue the very objectives which had previously always guided its action.

This assertion, which seems at first glance to plough a deep furrow between the industrial experiences which preceded and followed the years of the Second World War, seems less incomprehensible when we seek to explain the nature of the links which connect the most recent events in the capitalist development of our country with those which have been shaping its background for at least a century – not, perhaps all that obviously, but certainly with a high degree of tenacity and constancy. In other words we would need to think again about the character of what we might call the 'social model of industrialization' followed in Italy, and about the type of political mediation and the institutional framework to which this has given rise. In particular, we would need to reinterpret the way in which the front of the national bourgeoisie was being shaped and modified; also the practices through which the demands of the groups that were gradually emerging found a place alongside interests which had been consolidated for many years. Above all, we would need to understand that all this happened in a context in which the needs of a substantial part of the protagonists of the productive process found no expression, while the maintenance of a low standard of consumption was the given fact from which all the remaining decisions about the division of resources received their stimulus.

It would appear that from the Second World War onwards, the work of political mediation by the state had resolved itself essentially into giving official aid or sanction to the compromises which had been agreed between the industrial and financial oligarchies. Furthermore the logic which had guided the state's interventions in the economy was for the most part that of a partner in the private groups which moved within the context of contractual policies aimed at certain particular objects, really not tied very closely to strictly social purposes (armaments and warfare could certainly not be described as social). All this was done in exchange for the interests of these private partners.

While all this ended, on the one hand, by assigning an unprecedented role and weight in the history of Western capitalism to the work of mediation of the top political management, the connotations which this assumed – simply because of the field in which it operated – resulted in a weakening of the drive towards a progressive emancipation of the political and state organization from the pressure of private and contingent interests. It was reflected in the actual capacity to define the objectives of development. Thus, for example, the lines of economic policy adopted from time to time have fluctuated between the need to meet the requirements of emerging groups and the need to safeguard the positions of power attained (e.g. Giolitti's policy of commercial treaties, or the ambiguities which characterized the 'free-market phase' of the early years of fascism). Most frequently these were set off by measures and attitudes produced by chance alliances between the main interests in the field, and not by the search for any coherent and effective response to prescribed objectives.

If this logic was able to live with and even coincide with the objectives of 'development', it not only had a profound influence on the quality of the processes of growth, but also heavily mortgaged the day when the needs of that same development (mass consumption society) would make it imperative to take account of a far wider and more heterogeneous area of interests. Moreover, the search for consensus with the middle and lower bourgeoisie had, in the days of fascism, already marked an important achievement in terms of the standards of mediation and the need for their updating; this could only be pursued *against* the interests of the working class and at the cost of political and civil liberty.

The advent of a democratic regime at the end of the Second World War therefore placed the Italian governing class in the position of having to face twofold needs. In the first case, it had to respond to a request for mediation on a larger scale than in the past (because *all social ranks* were potentially interested in it), and in a more complex political situation (because the old political oligarchies had made way for a large number of centres of representation). Secondly, it needed to shorten the time for that reform and the modernization of state structures which had been taking place elsewhere (to some degree) under the aegis of political dialectic and which, in Italy, to the extent that it existed at all, had only occurred under the banner of a clear separation between development objectives and aims of a social character.

Whether there has been an adequate response to this kind of need, and to what degree, is something which I think can be deduced from what has been said in these pages, especially in reference to the evolution of the instruments and range of public intervention in the economy. The lack of formation of core priorities and compatibilities to which the ends and the means of political mediation should conform has meant that the state was left with the task of responding in a haphazard fashion to pressures and expectations from all kinds of different sources. State action has been diluted in performing this task and, as an apparatus, the state itself has progressively lost its capacity for direction and control.

From this point of view it may be observed that the persistence in running the state by methods anchored in the past has been translated into growing difficulty in equalling past achievements in new social and political conditions. In other words, it has failed to thrust Italy into the most advanced front representing the economic and technical progress of those countries which, because of the choices they made in this area in the aftermath of the war, it was impossible not to take as a model.

The illusion of being inevitably and almost automatically included as an equal in the Western economy, the lack of awareness of the conditioning and the implications of the 'diversity' of Italy's past experience, the 'delegation to the market' taken on board to cover up a general and indiscriminate privatization of resources, all these factors could obviously not give rise to a dynamic and progressive equilibrium compatible with the package of economic integration, models of consumption and civil and political liberties which constituted the new phase in the country's life. In other words it could not produce an equilibrium which was capable of replacing the old model founded on low consumption and political and social authoritarianism. But all this refers, obviously, to conditions which cannot be identified with those within which our analysis has been conducted, and which concern the relations which arise between politics and economics, between subjectivity and historical objectivity. For that reason we have to acknowledge that what we are saying can only be of introductory value.

Excerpt from Richard Sylla and Gianni Toniolo (eds), *Patterns of European Industrialization: The Nineteenth Century*, 197–217.

Chapter 10

Italy

Giovanni Federico and Gianni Toniolo

'Clio is not a tidy housewife'

(A. Gerschenkron)

ALEXANDER GERSCHENKRON ON THE ECONOMIC DEVELOPMENT OF ITALY

Italy takes an important place, second only to that of Russia and possibly Austria, among the individual countries specifically investigated by Gerschenkron within the framework of his general approach to European industrialization during the nineteenth century. To the Italian case he devoted three important papers (Gerschenkron 1962: 52–89, 90–118, 1968: 98–127) and the effort of constructing an *ad hoc* index of industrial production (Gerschenkron 1962: 367–421).

To use his own words, Gerschenkron 'approached the Italian material with a series of historical questions or expectations in mind' (Gerschenkron 1962: 73) reflecting his own generalizations about the features of the industrialization process in a relatively backward European country. Typically, he expected to find a 'big push' of considerable intensity and length favouring the 'output of producers' goods as against that of consumers' goods' (Gerschenkron 1962: 73) and inducing various forms of industrial concentration. Moreover, he expected these 'basic features of delayed industrialization to be reinforced by the use of specific institutional instruments, such as the investment policies of banks and various policies of the state' (Gerschenkron 1962: 73).

In order to test the consistency of the Italian case with his general view of European industrialization during the nineteenth century, Gerschenkron set out to build his own index of industrial growth covering the period 1881 to 1914. This was, at the time (1955), a pioneering work and a very welcome addition to the paucity of quantification in Italian economic historiography. The results allowed Gerschenkron 'to locate the period of great push between the years 1896 and 1908' and to see that it was, as he expected, characterized by a rapid increase in the share of producers' goods in total output (Gerschenkron 1962: 77). At the same time, comparing Italy's performance with that of other countries during their own 'spurts', Gerschenkron found that 'the industrial growth in Italy, while free from any severe setbacks, seems to have proceeded in a less uniform and more jerky fashion, denoting perhaps a more delicate state of public confidence and greater entrepreneurial uncertainties and hesitations' (Gerschenkron 1962: 79). The reasons listed for Italy's relatively poor industrial performance are: (a) inept government policies, (b) a supposed time inconsistency between railroad building and the 'spurt' (c) a political situation around the turn of the century 'not propitious to quiet economic growth' (Gerschenkron 1962: 85), and (d) 'the absence of any strong ideological stimulus to industrialization' (Gerschenkron 1962: 86). On the other hand, 'if one were to look for a single important factor that succeeded in offsetting at least some of the great obstacles to the country's industrialization, one could not fail to point to the role performed by the big Italian banks after 1895' (Gerschenkron 1962: 87). Gerschenkron is therefore able to conclude that 'in this respect at least, the Italian case fits well into the general pattern of European industrialization in varying conditions of economic backwardness' (Gerschenkron 1962: 89).

This chapter discusses Gerschenkron's appraisal of Italian industrialization before the First World War in the light of the later literature. The first section deals with measures of Italy's backwardness relative to other European countries, and is followed by a section reviewing the existing indices of industrial production. The role of such 'agents of industrialization' as the German banks, the state and ideology are then discussed. The last part of the chapter is devoted to a summary of the main points and to some general conclusions.

THE BACKWARDNESS OF THE ITALIAN ECONOMY

When asked about the operational value of the concept of backwardness Gerschenkron replied that no precise answer was possible because one could define the degree of backwardness in several ways and, while granting that 'this might seem discouraging and clumsy', he added that 'it was true of 19th-century Europe at least that, whatever measures used, individual countries were fairly easy to arrange in order of backwardness' (Rostow 1963: 385).

Gerschenkron's well-known concern with index number problems made him reluctant to suggest per capita output as a fully operational measure of backwardness. He also suggested that, in any event, information deriving from output levels should be used together with other parameters – such as literacy or the prevailing ideology – that 'would involve asking to what degree a country at a certain moment had developed the preconditions for subsequent economic development' (Gerschenkron 1962: 43).

How backward was Italy, in Gerschenkron's eyes, around the middle of the nineteenth century? The most important suggestion comes from the following passage:

Few would disagree that Germany was more backward than France; that

> Austria was more backward than Germany, that Italy was more backward than Austria and that Russia was more backward than any of the countries just mentioned. Similarly, few would deny England the position of the most advanced country of the time.
>
> (Gerschenkron 1962: 44)

Does research carried out in the last quarter of a century confirm at least this ranking? Measures of economic backwardness explicitly related to Gerschenkron's hypotheses were first provided by Barsby (1969). Relying on Colin Clark's pioneering work, he sees Italy's GNP per capita around 1890 to be equal to that of Russia and less than one-fourth that of Britain.

Subsequent work has considerably revised Colin Clark's estimates. We may refer directly to Crafts (1983) since this article takes into account the most relevant previous contributions (particularly Bairoch 1976), producing the least unreliable estimates of nineteenth-century per capita product to date. They are reproduced in Table 10.1 for the countries mentioned by Gerschenkron and for Spain. As regards Italy in the third quarter of the nineteenth century, Gerschenkron's appraisal of Italy's relative position seems to be confirmed for 1910 but not for 1870, when Austria displays a per capita income approximately equal to that of Italy. What is striking, and somewhat puzzling, in Table 10.1 is the relatively high level of Italy's income at about the time of its political unification, as well as the stagnation in the subsequent thirty-odd years which resulted in its slide down the rankings.

These data rest on two assumptions: (a) that we accept Kravis's (1982) purchasing power parities and relative income levels for 1970, and (b) that we

Table 10.1 Crafts' estimates of per capita national product (US dollars of 1970)

	1870	*1890*	*1910*
Great Britain	904	1130	1302
Germany	579	729	958
France	567	668	883
Northwestern Italy			(810)
Italy	466 (513)	466 (513)	548 (603)
Austria	466	664	802
Spain	391	554	547
Southern Italy			(450)
Russia	252	276	398

Source: Crafts (1983: 389, 394).
Italian data in parenthesis derive from the recent official upward revision by 10% of current (1980s) GNP estimates and their backward extrapolation, according to Crafts' methodology.
Italian regional estimates from Zamagni (1978).
Northwestern Italy includes Lombardy, Piedmont and Liguria.
Southern Italy includes the former Kingdom of Naples plus Sardinia.

believe long-term growth rates implicit in the existing historical national accounts statistics.

The second of these assumptions, i.e. the reliability of historical national accounts statistics, may prove difficult to accept in the case of Italy. The existing estimates – ISTAT (1957) and Fua's (1969) revision thereof – date back at least twenty years. Their validity has always been questioned at least on the basis of the authors' parsimony in the disclosure of their sources and methods. Recent work by Fenoaltea on industrial production shows that this distrust is not misplaced. The existing figures underestimate both the level of industrial production in 1911 and the attendant long-term growth rates.[1] Should these upward revisions be confirmed in the case of other industries, our overall view of the time-pattern of Italy's development would be in need of thorough reconsideration. The relevance of this point for the issues addressed by this chapter, and indeed for the entire economic history of modern Italy, can hardly be overstated. Nevertheless, the ranking of Italy with the countries in Table 10.1 is not likely to be altered substantially.

In view of Italy's pronounced economic dualism, any appraisal of her backwardness is likely to be incomplete without some kind of regional breakdown. According to Zamagni (1978), in 1911 the GNP per head of Italy's richer region (the northwest) was slightly lower than that of the whole of France (and therefore much lower than that of the richest comparable French areas). In the same year, per capita income in the south turns out to be only 15 per cent above that of Russia. The gap between north and south is likely to have widened as a result of industrial growth which took place mainly in the former region but it surely existed at the time of unification and much before then. Adopting a strict Gerschenkronian logic, therefore, one could expect a smooth industrialization along French lines in the northwest – where the institutional and cultural winds from across the Alps blew strong – and a state-driven spurt in the south. It is indeed possible to find some traces of these potentially divergent patterns in the first half of the nineteenth century (a market-driven growth of the textile, particularly silk, industry in the northwest, neo-mercantilistic attempts to create industry from above by the Bourbons in the south).

Backwardness, according to Gerschenkron, could not be measured by GNP taken in isolation. Most experts on economic development would agree with this proposition. Indeed, the current literature on economic development offers a number of standard-of-living indicators other than GNP. Among those, we have selected the so-called physical quality of life index (PQLI) devised by Morris (1979). The PQLI recommends itself on two grounds: (a) it is based on data that, when available, are rather accurate for nineteenth-century Europe, (b) it embodies an indicator (literacy) that Gerschenkron considered particularly relevant and two others (infant mortality and life expectancy) that are taken into account by the most recent historical research on standards of living.

The PQLI is an unweighted average of: the literacy rate of the population aged 15 years and older, infant mortality in the first year of life and life expectancy at age one. 'For each indicator the performance of individual countries is placed on the scale of 0 to 100, where 0 represents an explicitly defined "worst" performance and 100 represent an explicit "best" performance' (Morris 1979: 41). The three indicators are equally weighted. Such weighting is no more arbitrary than any other, and tests with different weights show that the *ranking* of individual countries in a large 1970 sample does not change significantly with changing weights.

In adapting the PQLI to nineteenth-century Europe, we made as few changes as possible to the definition of variables and to the parameters used by Morris. Two adjustments, however, were unavoidable. The first concerns the definition of literacy which, in our cases, was measured as the percentage of the population aged 6 or over to which most of our sources referred. The second adjustment relates to the scale (or 0–100 range) employed to index infant mortality and life expectancy. In both cases we had to widen the range in order to avoid negative values.[2] Data for infant mortality were taken from Mitchell (1975); five-year moving averages were preferred, given the large swings in yearly data. Literacy comes from Flora (1983) and from various contemporary Italian sources. When data were not available, literacy was estimated from the percentage of people who signed wedding documents, through regression analysis. In most cases, life expectancy at year one had to be estimated from mortality tables and other demographic material from each individual country. Because of such data limitations, Table 10.2 covers a much more limited range of countries than Table 10.1.

Table 10.2 confirms that, in 1870, Italy was an unmistakably backward country. Backwardness was still very visible in 1910 when Italy lagged more than a generation behind the most advanced European countries in terms of standards of living. At the same time, the data in Table 10.2 allow us to appreciate the considerable progress made by Italy between 1870 and 1900, during a period in which existing historical statistics see practically no increase in per capita incomes. Comparisons with countries less developed than those in Table 10.2 show that

Table 10.2 PQLI: Selected European countries and three main Italian regions, 1870–1910

Year	*Country*				*Italian regions*		
	England & Wales	*France*	*Belgium*	*Italy*	*North-west*	*North-east*	*South & islands*
1870	62.9	62.2	na	26.9	40.5	27.1	17.6
1880	70.8	64.4	na	36.9	47.0	41.2	28.4
1890	71.3	67.7	65.5	na	na	na	na
1900	78.9	73.7	75.9	56.7	66.8	62.1	46.0
1910	na	84.0	82.4	62.0	70.5	68.9	49.4

Methods and sources: see text.

infant mortality in Germany and Austria was higher than in Italy throughout the period. Relative to the same countries, however, Italy had a lower percentage of enrolment in primary school for the population aged 5–14 years.

The regional breakdown in Table 10.2 is consistent with income estimates referred to above. By 1910, the northwest was lagging behind the most advanced countries in Europe by about fifteen years, and Italy as a whole lagged by forty. The south was thirty years behind the northwest, despite the rapid progress made after the unification, particularly in life expectancy. These data provide one of the few aggregate indicators of the time-pattern in the welfare *gap* between large Italian regions. Its magnitude and its persistence over time make it difficult to discuss Italy's backwardness meaningfully in aggregate terms. At the beginning of the century, the area of the so-called Milan–Turin–Genoa 'triangle' (the northwestern region in Table 10.2) was larger than Belgium and had a per capita income and, to a lesser extent, a basic standard of living not much lower than the French averages. The south was more similar to Russia than to the northwest in terms of both variables.

INDICES OF INDUSTRIAL PRODUCTION

Gerschenkron's interpretation of Italy's industrialization rests pretty much on his own index of industrial production covering the years 1881–1913. Over the whole of this period the index yields an average annual rate of growth for Italian industrial production of 3.8 per cent (using value-added weights) resulting from a rather good performance during 1881–7 (4.6 per cent per annum), which was followed by a serious crisis that caused virtual stagnation until 1895. Italy had its 'big spurt' in 1896–1908, characterized by a rate of growth of 6.7 per cent. The index shows that during the 'spurt' the production of investment goods grew more rapidly than that of consumers' goods, a pattern consistent with Gerschenkron's expectations derived from the historical experience of other backward European countries.

The construction of Gerschenkron's index in 1955 was certainly a major breakthrough in Italian economic history. Nonetheless its technical pitfalls are quite serious. This is not the place to review them in full: it is enough to point briefly to some of the index's weakest features. Gerschenkron uses twenty elementary series but five of them account for 85 per cent of the index behaviour. Some of them are rather poor proxies for the underlying industries.[3] The index is, therefore, very sensitive to changes in the basic series and in the sample of industries they are supposed to represent.[4] Besides, Gerschenkron derives his weights from a highly questionable source, a survey of 1903 which is a partial and unreliable revision of enquiries undertaken in the 1880s and 1890s (Missaggia 1988). The index is, therefore, based on start-period weights. A reconstruction of Gerschenkron's index using 1911 weights yields substantially higher growth rates for the years 1881–8 (5.6 per cent against 4.6) and 1896–1908 (8.0 per cent against 6.7). This result, incidentally, contradicts the so-called 'Gerschenkron effect' in index numbers. Finally, the index itself is a poor proxy for the omitted industries, which accounted for about one-third of total value-added in 1911. Most of them were slow-growing traditional ones (such as leather works and furniture), their exclusion is, therefore, likely to have raised the rate of growth.

Since 1955 three other indices of industrial production have been estimated: the first by the Italian Statistical Institute (ISTAT),[5] the second – still unpublished – by Carreras (1982) and the third by Fenoaltea (1983).[6]

The present wealth of indices makes interpretation of the overall pattern of industrialization more difficult rather than easier since they yield different results, while none of them is so clearly superior to the others from the point of view of data sources and of method as to recommend itself for acceptance.

According to ISTAT, industrial development was slow and fluctuations limited both in depth and length. Carreras sees an accelerating trend coupled with rather pronounced cyclical swings. Finally, the picture portrayed by Fenoaltea's index of 1983 is similar to Gerschenkron's: slow growth until 1878, rapid development in the 1880s, followed by a serious slump and by a long boom from the mid-1890s onward. Fenoaltea's cyclical swings are, however, much wider then those of Gerschenkron.

None of these patterns seem to fit well with Gerschenkron's interpretation of Italy's industrial development. The most compatible with it is possibly the picture designed by ISTAT which shows a discontinuity with an acceleration of growth rates at the end of the nineteenth-century. But, then, the rate of growth is so slow as to make one wonder whether one might talk of a 'big spurt'. In the index of Carreras, on the other hand, there are no points of discontinuity. Fenoaltea has both the highest rates of growth and the largest cyclical swings: a discontinuity could be found in 1879 rather than in 1896 (a timing much more akin to Romeo's model). This interpretation, however, would conflict with Fenoaltea's denial of the very existence of a big spurt and with his assertion that Italy's industrial growth was cyclical rather than marked by discontinuity (Fenoaltea 1973a, 1988c). His view seems closer to the one put forward by Cafagna (1965: 143) and shared by Bonelli (1978) and Federico and Chesi (1987).

The above-mentioned aggregate indices are actually the sum of three different

Table 10.3 Indices of industrial production, 1861–1913 (annual average rates of growth in real terms)

Period	*Gerschenkron*	*ISTAT*	*Fenoaltea*	*Carreras*
1861–1913	na	1.95	3.42	2.51
1881–1913	3.78	2.26	4.18	3.19
1896–1908	6.68	5.21	7.87	5.00

Sources: Gerschenkron (1962), ISTAT (1957), Fenoaltea (1983), Carreras (1982).

sectorial patterns. The production of investment goods (engineering, chemicals, iron- and steel-making) shows higher growth rates than that of consumers' goods during both the so-called 'Giolittian era' (1896–1913) and the 1880s. The 1888–92 slump was characterized by a much more rapid decline of the former than of the latter industries. In fact, the whole pattern depends to a certain extent on the huge cyclical swings of the engineering industry (Fenoaltea 1973a; Warglien 1985). Traditional industries such as textile and food-processing industries developed rather slowly with no major cyclical swings. Most 'new' products, such as electric power, rubber and some branches of the chemical industries, started late and showed a high growth afterwards.

THE ROLE OF BANKS IN PROMOTING INDUSTRIAL DEVELOPMENT

At the beginning of the 1890s, Italy experienced a serious banking crisis. It resulted in the failure of one of the six banks of issue (Banca Romana) and the collapse of the two deposit banks (Credito Mobiliare and Banca Generale) which had been established after unification on the model of the French Crédit Mobilier. The void was filled in 1894 and 1895 by two new banks (Banca Commerciale and Credito Italiano), established by German and Swiss capital with German management. Gerschenkron sees the crisis of 1893 almost as a *felix culpa* of the Italian economy – and policymakers, in as much as they were responsible for it – since it brought to an end the existing banking system tailored as it was by the French, and made possible the importation 'of the great economic innovation of German banking in its most developed and mature form' (Gerschenkron 1962: 88). The main feature of such innovation consisted in turning investment banks into real 'department stores' in the field of banking. Their virtue, in a situation of relative backwardness, was to provide – to use Gerschenkronian terminology – efficient substitutes for missing prerequisites of industrialization. In particular, German banks, unlike their French counterparts, are seen as supplying not only long-term credit but also a good deal of entrepreneurship, a factor of production supposedly even more scarce than capital.

Gerschenkron was by no means the first to attribute an important role to the large banks in the development of Italy.[7] Gerschenkron's original contribution to Italian economic history, was to see the role of German banking in a framework in which the industrial development of the country appeared as just one case in the pattern of European industrialization. In the 1950s this was a seminal idea that gave new stimuli to discussion and research. Opinions varied from Cohen's strict Gerschenkronian orthodoxy (Cohen 1967: 382, 1972: 89) to Webster's (1974: 325) and Hertner's (1984) more shaded judgements, and to the decisively negative opinion of Farina (1976, 1980). The latter blames the 'German' banks for having distorted resource allocation in favour of capital-intensive industries and techniques, thus increasing 'dualism' and contributing to the oligopolistic nature of Italian development.

The analysis of quantitative aggregate trends is not of much help in elucidating the role of the mixed banks. An assessment of the time-path of aggregate financial variables carried out along Goldsmith's lines puts Italy's financial intermediation ratio at 0.38 in 1881 and at 0.47 in 1914 (Biscaini and Ciocca 1979: 92–7). Financial deepening did occur but the gap between Italy and the most advanced European countries remained unchanged. During the same period, the share of financial liabilities held by banks grew from 0.19 to 0.29. This positive trend, however, did not exhaust its momentum in 1913. The fact that banks retained an overwhelming importance in financial intermediation at least up to the 1960s is a well-known peculiarity shared by the Italian economy with the Japanese. There is little in these aggregate trends that will confirm or invalidate Gerschenkron's hypothesis.

In fact, Gerschenkron's hypothesis is mainly based on the stimulus provided by the mixed banks to a limited number of 'strategic' firms or industries. Therefore, a proper test of the hypothesis may come from careful archival research on the actual behaviour of the banks. A real breakthrough in this field of research was made by the monumental work by Confalonieri (1974–6, 1982). His conclusions may be summarized as follows: (a) long-term industrial financing came mostly as a result of other banking operations, (b) it resulted from normal scrutiny of clients' demand and from a desire to monopolize the entire range of their banking operations rather than from an autonomous initiative of the banks, (c) the latter, therefore, did not possess much of an *industrial* strategy of their own which was, perhaps, more pronounced in their predecessors of the 'French type', (d) the main novelty of the 'new' banks consisted in underwriting as part of a *banking* strategy directed 'plus à des *affaires* qu'a des *entreprises*' (Confalonieri 1974–6: 469). The early long-term involvement of the banks in the electric power industry is singled out by Confalonieri as an exception in their operations. Moreover, the operations of the French-type banks do not seem to be so different from those of the later German-type banks. The former not only financed the construction of the railways of the 1870s but, what matters more in a Gerschenkronian framework, played a prominent role in the rapid industrial growth of the 1880s.

If reliable, these findings would contradict Gerschenkron's hypothesis. If German-type banks did not provide relevant supply-side stimulus to investment, if they were as a rule not particularly interested in managing industrial enterprises, if they did not hold in their portfolios for long periods of time large quantities of industrial equities, then it is not easy to grant them the role of sole or main 'agents of industrialization'.

A few years ago, Hertner (1984) attempted to redress the balance in favour of 'Gerschenkron's approach which remains a very fertile research hypotheses, even though it requires some revisions and qualifications' (Hertner 1984: 159). His qualifications regard primarily the role of German capital and men in the Banca Commerciale and Credito Italiano which he sees as 'the first example of successful foreign direct investment in Italy in the banking sector'. The early withdrawal of the original German capital was not followed by a repatriation of the banks' top management, which was a crucial factor in maintaining strong links with the international banking world and, thus, assured stability for the two institutions. In general, he sees the two banks as concentrating mostly on the Italian domestic market, thereby giving 'a decisive contribution to the country's industrialization' (Hertner 1984: 155). Ongoing and yet unpublished research carried on at The Historical Archives of Banca Commerciale seems to indicate that, by 1913, the latter had established strong personal links between its own management and that of the industrial firms to which it supplied credit. These results are likely to stimulate new debates and research on the role played by the two German-type banks during the industrial growth of the period 1896–1913.

ECONOMIC POLICIES AND INDUSTRIAL DEVELOPMENT

Inept government policies seem to be, according to Gerschenkron, the single most important cause of the 'disappointingly low' rate of industrial growth during Italy's big spurt (Gerschenkron 1962: 78). The tariff of 1887 'must be viewed as the real pièce de résistance of those policies' (Gerschenkron 1962: 80).

The 1887 tariff marked a real turning point after fifteen years of free trade and ten years of moderate protection to a limited number of industries (Prodi 1965–6; Sereni 1966; Del Vecchio 1978). Italy's tariff policy is criticized by Gerschenkron on three grounds: (a) for subjecting 'the tender plants of industrial growth to the rigors of a protectionist climate in agriculture' (Gerschenkron 1962: 81), (b) for the attention given to cotton textiles, 'an old industry with a moderate rate of modern technological progress and accordingly relatively limited possibilities in a backward country on the European continent' (Gerschenkron 1962: 81), and (c) for neglecting the most promising industries such as chemicals and engineering, the latter being put at a disadvantage also by protecting its main inputs, iron and steel.

This judgement implies the counterfactual hypothesis of a more rational tariff and, therefore, is a much welcome disentanglement from the typical nineteenth-century debate of free trade versus unqualified protection. And it is unfortunate that most Italian economic historians have been unable to follow Gerschenkron along the lines of an assessment of the impact of the tariff on growth in terms of effective protection. Despite the vast literature on the subject, therefore, there is a lack of serious quantitative research on the specific points raised by Gerschenkron. Even the average nominal rate of protection is not precisely known: the only aggregate figure – 18 per cent in 1888 declining to 7.5 per cent in 1913 (Capie 1983) – probably underestimates the actual level.

Federico (1984) has put the average rate of protection for Italian wheat at 52 per cent in 1895. Increasing world prices reduced it thereafter to 33 per cent in 1913. On average, these rates are higher than those computed by Gerschenkron. Looking at the rather fortunate period of free trade, 1915–25, one is inclined to agree with Gerschenkron that 'Italy's agriculture had at its disposal methods of adjustment that were not available to an equal degree north of the Alpine wall'

(Gerschenkron 1962: 81) and that its comparative advantage outside the Po Valley was not in wheat. However, one must pay attention to Italy's social conditions, which Gerschenkron sees as one of the weakening factors in its process of industrialization. The late 1880s and early 1890s, to be sure, witnessed unprecedented social unrest in the countryside that the abolition of the duty on wheat would no doubt have made even more serious.

The cotton industry had already undertaken a process of import substitution under the shield of the 1878 tariff. This process was boosted by the higher duties introduced in 1887. By the end of the century Italy was a net exporter of cotton goods. Fixed capital formation proceeded at such a high rate that by 1907 the sector was burdened by excess capacity and had to resort to *dumping* exports. During the years of the Gerschenkronian spurt, therefore, no 'infant industry' argument could be invoked to justify duties on textile products.

The subsequent development of the Italian manufacturing industry leaves no doubt as to the importance of the chemical and engineering sectors. The demands of the former for adequate protection were met only by the tariff of 1921 (Zamagni 1991). The dynamic effects of the earlier lower duty are difficult to assess given the lack of research in the field. It is likely, however, that chemical production could have benefited from 'infant industry' protection. As for engineering, Toniolo (1977) has shown that its effective protection was negligible, due to the high import duties imposed on its main inputs, iron and steel. At the same time Toniolo has estimated that the most favourable alternative policy (i.e. a subsidy to iron- and steel-making) would have resulted in a 7 per cent increase of value-added by manufacturing in the period 1906–8 (upper bound estimate). The rate of industrial growth during 1896–1908 would have been 7.0 per cent a year against Gerschenkron's 6.7, hardly a dramatic change in Italy's economic history.

Gerschenkron's criticism of the Italian tariff *structure* during the years of rapid industrialization is well taken and its validity has been confirmed by subsequent quantitative research. If the 1887 tariff succeeded in fostering the development of some industries (Zamagni 1984: 14) the price paid by the whole economy in terms of misallocation of resources was probably high. It is difficult, however, to judge how high that price was. And we still 'wonder how much importance one should in general ascribe to tariff policy in the history of European industrializations' (Gerschenkron 1962: 89).

According to Gerschenkron, 'another weakness of the Italian industrialization of 1896–1908 may have derived from the fact that by that time the great period of Italian railroad building was largely a thing of the past' (Gerschenkron 1962: 84). This point was debated with Romeo who held, on the contrary, that the building of railways was a prerequisite for rapid industrialization (Gerschenkron 1968: 98–127).

A general equilibrium model of investment in railways (Fenoaltea 1973b) yields rather discouraging results about the likely magnitude of domestic demand generated by investment in railways, even on the most favourable exchange-rate conditions. Direct estimates (Fenoaltea 1983) show that railway expenditures were a minor component of the demand for engineering goods, which depended to a much larger extent on the building trade, an industry that Gerschenkron did not consider. Moreover, the increasing trade deficit accumulated by the engineering sector during 1896–1908 is clear evidence that its problems consisted of supply rigidities (bottlenecks) rather than inadequate domestic demand. However, the wave of investment in railways which followed nationalization in 1905 took place at a time when, after the 1907 crisis, the rate of growth of domestic demand fell sharply and it therefore provided a timely anticyclical support.

Adding military expenditure to that for railways (Zamagni 1981), a likely guesstimate may be that the state provided about one-third of the total demand for products by the engineering industry during the years 1896–1908. According to recent estimates (Brosio and Marchese 1987) total public expenditure (including that by local authorities) oscillated between 15 and 20 per cent of GNP over the pre-1913 long run. These ratios are higher than those for most other European countries and indicate that, at least in the aggregate, state demand was a relatively more important factor in Italy then elsewhere.

Historians have discussed at length the likely overall effects of fiscal policy on Italian economic development. It has been suggested that deficit spending had a positive macro-economic effect (Barone 1972). Gerschenkron (1962: 82) hinted that state bonds crowded out private investment. Several scholars have stressed the unfavourable redistributive effects (among regions, industries and social classes) of the combination of regressive taxation and high state expenditure on defence and interest on state bonds. At any rate, during 1896–1907, monetary and fiscal policy favoured private investment (Toniolo 1990) so that, all things considered, it is difficult to accept an entirely unfavourable judgement on the role of economic policy during the years of the 'big spurt'.

Finally, Gerschenkron sees in the social situation of the 'Giolittian era' another reason for the weakness of the Italian 'spurt'. The coincidence in time of the 'spurt' with improvements in the workers' standard of living – so the argument runs – shifted resources from investment to consumption. Moreover, 'had the industrial upsurge in Italy taken place one or two decades earlier, in all likelihood it would have been much less disturbed by industrial strife' (Gerschenkron 1962: 86). Three remarks are possible on this subject: (1) While it is true that real wages improved during 1896–1908 (Zamagni 1984), it is likely that product per man in manufacturing grew faster so that the ratio of profits to value-added increased, as did that of gross investment over GNP. (2) The strike figures given by Gerschenkron, according to whom 'between 1901 and 1913 there was only one year when the number of days lost by strikes remained below the million mark' and the number exceeded three million in some years of the period, do not indicate any unbearable loss in production. They include strikes in agriculture and, therefore, should be seen in the context of a labour force totalling about 10 million members, with 2.5 million engaged in industrial production. Even assuming an average of two million days of work lost by strikes in industry alone, the loss in physical output would amount to less than one-third of one percentage point. (3) Contrary to what Gerschenkron thought, 'had the industrial upsurge in Italy taken place a decade earlier' it would have been met by a much larger and widespread working class unrest and discontent. In all likelihood 'Giolitti's conciliatory statemanship' (Geschenkron 1962: 85) was, on balance, a bonus for the economy itself.

THE IDEOLOGICAL STIMULUS

Gerschenkron's opinion on the absence of an ideological stimulus to industrialization is widely shared by Italian scholars. Baglioni (1974) describes a ruling political class coming either from the landed gentry or from the liberal professions. Most entrepreneurs were bound to traditional social and cultural values while, with few exceptions, they shied away from the political arena. The recent business-history literature seems to confirm that most entrepreneurs were bound to the traditional social and cultural values and that their political demands were confined to such issues as tariff protection, subsidies, fiscal policy and, more broadly, to the maintenance of law and order. Some authors (e.g. Hunecke 1982) go as far as saying that most industrialists were reluctant to move their factories from the country to the town for fear of upsetting the existing 'social order'. Generalization is always difficult in these matters. There is, however, a growing literature that seems to indicate that in the 1860s and 1870s Italian entrepreneurs could not prosper without at least the indirect support of local politicians and large landowners. In fact, a number of industrial activities originated directly from the latter. There was, therefore, nothing like a swift emerging of a 'new' entrepreneurial class with an entirely different set of values that enabled it to create and impose its own ideology of industrialization.

Moreover, the Church, which retained a powerful influence on the majority of the population, drastically opposed the new liberal state both for its agnostic stance on religion and, more deeply, for its occupation of the territory of the Papal States. In these circumstances, at least until the death of Pius IX, the Church fought against all attempts at 'modernization' that came from the most far-sighted among the members of the liberal ruling class. With the advent of Leo XIII, the Church took greater interest in social and economic matters, as witnessed by the encyclical *Rerum Novarum* and by the creation of *Opera dei congressi*, an organization that was aimed at spreading the 'social doctrine' of the Church and at promoting engagement by Catholics in such fields as cooperatives and workers' organizations. In principle, the Catholic ideology opposed both capitalism and socialism. In practice, bishops and priests were tolerant of capitalism but resisted rapid changes that would undermine traditional social and moral values. They were, therefore, particularly concerned with keeping their flocks in the countryside. The growth of towns, emigration and large enterprises were seen as major evils.

The Socialist Party, established in 1892, remained in practice hostile to the capitalist system (Satta 1986). The party's propaganda spread among workers the expectation of a new social and economic order and consequently opposition to the actual industrialization process.

There were, therefore, considerable weaknesses in the ideological foundations of Italy's industrialization. Nevertheless, the picture is not as clear-cut as Gerschenkron saw it. The split between the old agrarian ruling classes and the emerging industrial interests was not always very clear. Behind several success stories in industrial entrepreneurship one may detect the financial help of landowners and sometimes the support of local politicians (e.g. Castronovo 1977; Fiocca 1984). Moreover, in the late 1880s and in 1890s the picture began to change from the point of view of the 'ideological stimulus to industrialization' as well. In a most interesting book, Lanaro (1979) has examined the ideology emerging with the rank and file of entrepreneurs, far from the most prestigious academic and cultural circles. A careful examination of pamphlets, speeches and articles in local newspapers had led him to conclude that the protectionist drive was backed by a strong nationalist ideology based on the assumption that, without channelling major resources to industry, Italy could not reach the status of a European power. At the same time, nationalists maintained that given the backwardness of the country only the state had the allocative power needed to promote rapid industrialization. It had, therefore, to be made more efficient by a strong and uncompromising leadership. Nationalists formed an intellectual movement with fuzzy ideological boundaries and multifarious followers rather than a political party.

An industrial ideology was, then, actively present in Italy during the longest period of its pre-war industrial growth. It was based to a large extent on a modified version of German nationalism. It was certainly a minority movement – liberals, Catholics and socialists were contending in the same ideological arena – but, then, Saint Simonism was not the ideology of the French masses either. What matters is that, by the beginning of the twentieth century, a growing number of industrialists and engineers had broken away from traditional values and had developed their own *Weltanschaung* which looked with optimism and hope to the future of Italy as an industrial power. If confidence and moral justification were needed, nationalism was there to provide them.

CONCLUSIONS

As far as Italy is concerned, in the mid-1950s, Gerschenkron's contribution was ahead of its time. A surprisingly deep understanding of the crucial problems in Italian history coupled with sound economic analysis enabled him to produce an elegant interpretation of the industrialization process centred around a limited number of relevant variables.

Backwardness proved to be a much more powerful and operational explanatory variable than others then fashionable such as 'agrarian-industrial concert', 'financial capitalism', 'foreign dependence' and the like. Gerschenkron's index of industrial production has been somewhat improved upon only in recent years. In analysing the likely impact of tariff policy he broke away from the muddling debate on advantages and disadvantages of free trade and set an agenda of research on effective protection that is far from being fulfilled. His assessment of the role of the German banks – possibly the most controversial part of his construction – contains a number of important insights into the working of Italian financial intermediation which are still providing fruitful research hypotheses. There is, therefore, little doubt that Gerschenkron provided a highly seminal contribution to the understanding of the industrialization process in Italy.

Italian historians, with few important exceptions, have been unable to capitalize on this wealth of historical and economic intuitions. It was particularly unfortunate that Gerschenkron's early quantitative seeds did not fall on fertile ground. We still know surprisingly little about a crucial period in the development of one of today's important industrial economies. Some good research has, nonetheless, been done in the field over the past twenty years. In the previous pages we have reviewed the results that seem to be more relevant in discussing Gerschenkron's hypotheses. To sum-up, the following points have emerged. (1) Gerschenkron was not off the mark in his ranking of Italy's backwardness relative to the other major European countries. (2) He was again quite right about the time-path of industrialization, although he underrated the importance of his own quantitative evidence about the industrial development that took place in the 1880s and possibly underestimated the magnitude of the 'spurt' of 1896–1908. (3) On economic policy, Gerschenkron's point about the tariff structure is particularly well-taken and deserves further quantitative analysis. (4) Subsequent research has come to some conclusions that are different from those of Gerschenkron, particularly as far as ideology and banking are concerned. Stress has been placed on the importance of the nationalist movement in providing an ideological climate favourable to industrialization, at least from the beginning of the twentieth century onward. The role of mixed banks as 'agents of industrialization' has been challenged by an analysis of their behaviour that seems to indicate that they were more interested in short-term banking (and profits) than in long-term planning of industrial development. Moreover, it has been argued that the distinction between French and German banks does not stand close scrutiny in the Italian case. However, Italian banking history is developing and new outcomes, more in line with Gerschenkron's hypotheses, may not be ruled out.

In focusing his attention on 1896–1908, Gerschenkron was certainly selecting the most dynamic period in Italian economic history before the 1950s. However, his explanation of the 'spurt' suffered from a neglect of previous industrial growth as well as of some factors that, if taken into account, might contribute to a better understanding of the causes of the rapid growth in the years preceding the First World War.

Quantitative evidence on industrial growth during the 1860s and 1870s is far from satisfactory. According to the existing national accounts estimates, GNP grew in line with population (at the moderate annual rate of 0.7 per cent) leaving per capita income constant. Fenoaltea's (1983) and Carreras' (1982) indices feature a positive but low rate of growth in industrial production per head of population. The overall picture for the 1880s is better established: all the existing indices show that industrial output developed at a respectable pace. There is ample evidence of a wave of private investment, caused by the change in expectations produced by the industrial policy of the 'left', by the resumption of the gold standard in 1882, by substantial government orders to the steel-making and engineering industries, by urban-renewal programmes and by foreign investment (e.g. Toniolo 1990). The banking system played an important role in speeding-up the process of resource allocation to fixed capital formation in industry and building (Confalonieri 1974–6; Sannucci 1989). The lame duck was agriculture: production stagnated and incomes were affected by the fall in prices. During 1896–1908, in contrast, output and productivity grew rapidly in the agricultural sector.

A deep, long depression followed the upswing of the 1880s, characterized by a serious banking crisis. It is surprising that, after drawing so much from Hilferding, Gerschenkron never took into consideration the possibility of a depression transmitted from the financial to the real sector as a result of a combination of large industrial debts, generous lending to risky borrowers, and swift withdrawal of short-term capital (Warglien 1987). This is precisely the story of 1888–1893. In the event, the behaviour of French-type banks contributed to financial instability. But German-type banks were not likely to produce a less volatile financial environment, as witnessed by the inter-war crises in Central Europe. Overall financial conditions were much more stable during 1896–1913. External finance was not as large as it was in the 1880s, there was little foreign short-term capital around, and – last but not least – the embryo of a central bank had been established in 1893. The latter took upon itself the role of lender of last resort, thereby creating a more stable financial environment, as shown during the crisis of 1907 (Bonelli 1978).

Conditions in the world economy must be taken into account when discussing the industrial boom of the so-called 'Giolittian era'. International trade and factor mobility are likely to have affected the behaviour of a relatively small and fairly open economy such as Italy through an export-led growth, particularly of primary goods (Cafagna 1973; Bonelli 1978) and a supply-push by foreign finance (Fenoaltea 1988c). Moreover, emigrant remittances, and to a lesser extent tourism, allowed growth to be free from balance-of-payments constraints.

A thriving agriculture, a stable financial setting, and a favourable international environment are factors likely to have made the industrial upswing of 1896–1913 more rapid and resilient than that of 1879–88. Such factors do not rule out the possibility that German banks played a role of their own as more or less important 'agents of industrialization'. There is indeed much research still to be done on this period but, by now, we know enough to argue that, around 1900, the Italian economy was probably richer and more diversified than Gerschenkron supposed, so that several causes were at work in producing the 'spurt'. This picture is more complex – and therefore intellectually less exciting – than that deriving from Gerschenkron's elegant mono-causal explanation of growth: Clio, as he knew, is often a messy housewife.

ACKNOWLEDGEMENT

The authors are indebted to Giuseppe Gesano and Nicola Rossi for advice, to Stefano Fenoaltea and Richard Sylla for comments, to Pierantonio Dal Lago and Sonia Soncin for research assistance. Financial support from CNR is gratefully acknowledged.

NOTES

1 Fenoaltea's estimates of value-added by mining in 1911 are 46 per cent higher than those of ISTAT (Fenoaltea 1988b: 123); value-added by building and construction exceeds ISTAT's by 82 per cent (Fenoaltea 1988b). Average growth rates (1863–1913) are 2.8 per cent and 3.3 per cent respectively (against ISTAT 0.6 per cent and 1.9 per cent).

2 In fact, the worst European performance (infant mortality of 307 per thousand for Germany in 1870) was 'worse' than the 'worst' one in 1970 for the sample of developing countries used by Morris (Gabon with 229 per thousand).

3 For instance, the production of raw silk is taken to represent silk weaving and a sizeable part of wool production; wheat consumption is taken as a proxy for the entire food-processing industry.

4 For instance, simply by substituting Gerschenkron's estimates of silk production with Fenoaltea's (1988a) estimates of value-added by silk industry (which includes throwing, weaving and dyeing) the rate of growth of the entire textile industry would rise to 3.9 per cent and the overall rate to 4.2 per cent.

5 The index is a by-product of the first reconstruction of Italy's national accounts since 1861. Afterwards it has been incorporated without changes in the Fuà revision (Fuà 1969) and hence in all the international collections of historical statistics (Mitchell 1975).

6 Fenoaltea's index was actually prepared in the mid-1960s and incorporated in his Harvard PhD dissertation. The author is now engaged in a major research aimed at producing a much more reliable estimate of industrial output from 1861 to 1913; partial results have been published in Fenoaltea (1982, 1984, 1985, 1987, 1988a, 1988b).

7 The acrimonious attacks on the Banca Commerciale in 1914–15, for instance, leave no room for doubt that its economic and political power was fully understood at the time by friends and foes alike. Moreover, such contemporary Italian economists as Pantaleoni, Einaudi, Barone, Bresciani-Turroni and Sraffa, if anything overstated the importance of large investment banks.

REFERENCES

Amatori, F. (1980) 'Entrepreneurial typologies in the history of industrial Italy', *Business History Review* 54, 359–86.

Are, G. (1965) *Lo sviluppo industriale italiano nell'età della Destra*, Pisa: Nistri-Lischi.

—— (1974a) *Alle origini dell'Italia industriale*, Naples: Guida.

—— (1974b) *Economia e politica nell'Italia liberale (1890–1915)*, Bologna: Il Mulino.

Baglioni, G. (1974) *L'ideologia della borghesia industriale nello stato liberale*, Torino: Einaudi.

Bairoch, Paul (1976) 'Europe's gross national product: 1800–1975', *Journal of European Economic History*, V, 273–340.

Barone, G. (1972) 'Sviluppo capitalistico e politica finanziaria in Italia', *Studi Storici* a13, 568–99.

Barsby, Steven (1969) 'Economic backwardness and the characteristics of development', *Journal of Economic History*, 449–72.

Biscaini, A.M. and Ciocca, P.L. (1979) 'Le strutture finanziarie: aspetti quantitativi di lungo periodo (1870–1970)', in F. Vicarelli (ed.) *Capitale industriale e capitale finanziario: il caso italiano*, Bologna: Il Mulino.

Bonelli, F. (1968) 'Osservazioni e dati sul finanziamento dell'industria italiana nel secolo XIX', *Annali della Fondazione L. Einaudi* 257–279.

—— (1975) *La cirsi del 1907*, Torino: Fondazione L. Einaudi.

—— (1978) 'Il capitalismo italiano. Linee generali di interpretazione' in *Annali della Storia d'Italia Einaudi*, vol. I, pp. 1126–255, Torino: Einaudi.

Brosio, G. and Marchese, C. (1987) *Il potere di spendere*, Bologna: Il Mulino.

Cafagna, Luciano (1965) 'Intorno alle origini del dualismo economico in Italia', in A. Caracciolo (ed.) *Problemi storici dell'industrializzazione e dello sviluppo*, Urbino: Argalia, pp. 105–50, reissued in L. Cafagna (1989), pp. 187–213.

—— (1973) 'Italy 1830–1914', in *Fontana Economic History of Europe*, vol. IV, reissued in L. Cafagna (1989), pp. 281–319.

—— (1989) *Dualismo e sviluppo nella storia d'Italia*, Padova: Marsilio.

Capacelatro, E.M. and Carlo, A. (1972) *Contro la "questione meridionale"*, Roma: Samonà e Savelli.

Capie, F. (1983) 'Tariff protection and economic performance in the nineteenth century', in J. Black and A.L. Winters (eds) *Policy and Performance in International Trade*, pp. 1–24, London: Macmillan.

Caracciolo, A. (ed.) (1969) *La formazione dell'Italia industriale*, Bari: Laterza.

Carreras, A. (1982) 'La producciò industrial espanyola i italiana des de mitian segle XIX fins a l'actualitat', unpublished dissertation, University of Barcelona.

Castronovo, V. (1977) *Giovanni Agnelli*, Torino: Einaudi.

Cohen, J. (1967) 'Financing industrialization in Italy, 1894–1914: the partial transformation of a late-comer', *Journal of Economic History* 27, 363–82.

—— (1972) 'Italy 1861–1914', in R. Cameron (ed.) *Banking and Economic Development. Some Lessons of History*, New York: Oxford University Press, pp. 58–90.

Confalonieri, A. (1974–6) *Banca e industria in Italia, 1894–1906*, 3 vols, Milan: Banca Commerciale Italiana.

—— (1982) *Banca e industria in Italia dalla crisi del 1907 all'agosto 1914*, 2 vols, Milan: Banca Commerciale Italiana.

Coppa, F.J. (1970) 'The Italian tariff and the conflict between agriculture and industry: the commercial policy of liberal Italy', in *Journal of Economic History* 742–69.

Crafts, N.F.R. (1983) 'Gross national product in Europe 1870–1910, *Explorations in Economic History* XX, 387–401.

D'Angiolini, P. (1972) 'La svolta industriale italiana negli utlimi anni del secolo scorso e le reazioni dei contemporanei', *Nuova Rivista Storica*, 53–121.

De Rosa, L. (1969) 'Difesa militare e sviluppo economico in Italia (1861–1914), in *Rassegna economica*, now in ID (1980), *La rivoluzione industriale in Italia*, Bari: Laterza.

Del Vecchio, Edoardo (1978) *La via italiana al protezionismo*, Rome: Camera dei Deputati.
Ercolani, P. (1969) 'Documentazione statistica di base' in G. Fuà (ed.) *Lo sviluppo economico in Italia*, vol. III, Milan: Franco Angeli, pp. 380–460.
Farina, Francesco (1976) 'Modelli interpretativi e caratteri del capitalismo italiano', *Quaderni Storici*, 32, 487–514.
—— (1980) 'Note sul ruolo della banca mista nello sviluppo italiano', *Societa e Storia*, 19, 919–27.
Federico, G. (1982) 'Per una valutazione critica delle statistiche della produzione agricola italiana dopo l'Unità (1860–1913)', *Società e Storia* 15, 87–130.
—— (1984) 'Commercio dei cereali e dazio sul grano in Italia (1963–1913). Una analisi quantitativa', *Nuova Rivista Storica* LXVIII, 46–108.
Federico, Giovanni and Chesi, Marco (1987) 'Lo sviluppo economico italiano', *Storia della societa italiana, vol. 17 Le strutture e la classi nell'Italia Unita*, Milan: Teti.
Fenoaltea, S. (1969) 'Decollo, ciclo e intervento dello stato', in A. Caracciolo (ed.) *La formazione dell'Italia industriale*, Bari: Laterza.
—— (1973a) 'Riflessioni sull'esperienza industriale italiana dal Risorgimento alla prima Guerra Mondiale', in G. Toniolo (ed.) *Lo sviluppo economico italiano 1861–1940*, Bari: Laterza.
—— (1973b) 'Le ferrovie e lo sviluppo industriale italiano', in G. Toniolo (ed.) *Lo sviluppo economico italiano 1861–1940*, Bari: Laterza.
—— (1982) 'The growth of utilities industries in Italy', *Journal of Economic History* XLII, 601–27.
—— (1983) 'Railways and the development of the Italian economy to 1913', in P. O'Brien, *Railways and the Economic Growth of Western Europe*, London: Macmillan, pp. 49–120.
—— (1984) 'Le costruzioni ferroviarie in Italia', *Rivista di Storia Economica*, n.s. 1, 61–94.
—— (1985) 'Le opere pubbliche in Italia 1861–1913', *Rivista di Storia Economica*, n.s. 2, 335–69.
—— (1987) 'Le costruzioni in Italia 1861–1913', *Rivista di Storia Economica*, n.s. 4, 1–34.
—— (1988a) 'The growth of Italy's silk industry 1861–1913', *Rivista di Storia Economica*, n.s. 3.
—— (1988b) 'International resource flows and construction movements in the Atlantic economy: the Kuznets cycle in Italy 1861–1913', *Journal of Economic History*, XLVIII (3), 605–37.
—— (1988c) 'The extractive industries in Italy 1861–1913: general methods and specific estimates', *Journal of European Economic History*, 17 (1), 117–25.
Fiocca, G. (ed.) (1984) *Borghesi ed imprenditori a Milano*, Bari: Laterza.
Flora, P. (1983) *State, Economy and Society in Western Europe 1815–1975*, London: Macmillan.
Fratianni, M. and Spinelli, F. (1985) 'Currency competition, fiscal and the money supply process in Italy from the unification to World War I', *Journal of European Economic History* XIV, 473–99.
Fuà, G. (ed.) (1969) *Lo sviluppo economico in Italia*, Milan: Franco Angeli.
Gerschenkron, A. (1955) 'Notes on the rate of industrial growth in Italy 1861–1913', *Journal of Economic History* now in Gerschenkron (1984).
—— (1962) *Economic Backwardness in Historical Perspective. A Book of Essays*, Cambridge, Mass.: Belknap Press.
—— (1968) *Continuity in History and Other Essays*, Cambridge, Mass.: Belknap Press.

Hertner, P. (1984) *Il capitale tedesco in Italia dall'unità alla prima guerra mondiale. Banche miste e sviluppo economico italiano*, Bologna: Il Mulino.
Hunecke, V. (1982) *Classe operaia e rivoluzione industriale a Milano 1859–1982*, Bologna: Il Mulino.
Istituto Centrale di Statistica (1957) 'Indagine statistica sullo sviluppo del reddito nazionale dell'Italia dal 1861 al 1959', *Annali di Statistica*, Serie VIII, 9.
Kravis, I.B. *et al.* (1982) *World Product and Income*, Baltimore: Johns Hopkins.
Lanaro, S. (1979) *Nazione e lavoro*, Padova: Marsilio.
Merli, S. (1976) *Proletariato di fabbrica e capitalismo industriale*, Florence: La Nuova Italia.
Ministero Agricoltura, Industria e Commercio (1906) *Riassunto delle condizioni industriali del Regno*, Roma.
Ministero del Tesoro (1988) *Relazione del direttore generale alla Commissione parlamentare di vigilanza. Il debito pubblico in Italia 1861–1987*, Rome: Poligrafico dello Stato.
Missaggia, M.G. (1988) 'Nota sulle statistiche ufficiali per l'industria in Italia: 1885–1903', *Rivista di Storia Economica* 2, 234–54.
Mitchell, B.R. (1983) *European Historical Statistics*, London: Macmillan.
Mitchell, R.C.O. (1975) *European Historical Statistics*, London: Macmillan Press.
Morris D.M. (1979) *Measuring the Conditions of the World's Poor: the Physical Quality of Life*, New York: Pergamon.
Nitti, Francesco S. (1900) *Il bilancio dello Stato dal 1862 al 1896–97*, now in ID (1958) *Scritti sulla questione meridionale*, vol. II, Bari: Laterza.
Nitti Francesco S. (1905) 'La conquista della forza', reissued in F.S. Nitti (1966) *Scritti di economica e finanza*, vol. III.
Pedone, A. (1969) 'Il bilancio dello Stato', in G. Fuà (ed.) *Lo sviluppo economico in Italia*, vol. II, Milan: Franco Angeli, pp. 203–40.
Prodi, Romano (1965–6) 'Il protezionismo nella politica e nell'industria italiana dall'Unificazione al 1887', *nuova rivista storica*, 42–86 and 597–626.
Romano, R. (1977) *Introduzione* in ID, *Borghesia industriale in ascesa: gli imprenditori tessili nella inchiesta industriale del 1870–74*, Milano: F. Angeli.
—— (1980) *I Caprotti. L'avventura economica ed umana di una dinastia industriale della Brianza*, Milan: F. Angeli.
—— (1985) *I Crespi*, Milan: F. Angeli.
Romeo, R. (1958) 'Problemi dello sviluppo capitalistico in Italia dal 1861 al 1887', *Nord e Sud* July–August, reissued in R. Romeo (1961) *Risorgimento e Capitalismo*, Bari: Laterza, pp. 87–120.
—— (1965) *Breve storia della grande industria in Italia 1861–1961*, Bologna: Cappelli.
—— (1974) *Gli scambi degli stati sardi con l'estero nelle voci più importanti della bilancia commerciale*, Torino: Centro di Studi Piemontesi.
Romeo, R. and Gerschenkron, A. (1961) 'Consensi dissensi ipotesi', *Nord e Sud*, November, reissued in A. Caracciolo (1969), pp. 53–81.
Rostow, W. (1963) *The Economics of Take-Off into Sustained Growth*, New York: St Martinus.
Roverato, G. (1987) *Una casa industriale. I Marzotto*, Milan: F. Angeli.
Sannucci, V. (1989) 'The establishment of a central bank in Italy in the 19th century', in M. De Cecco and A. Giovanni (eds) *A European Central Bank?*, Cambridge: Cambridge University Press, pp. 247–81.
Satta, V. (1986) 'I socialisti ed i problemi dello sviluppo economico', in *Clio* XXII, 248–73.
Sereni, E. (1972) *Il capitalismo nelle campagne (1860–1900)*, Torino: Einaudi, (first edition 1947).

—— (1966) *Capitalismo e mercato nazionale*, Rome: Editori Riuniti.
Toniolo, G. (ed.) (1973) *Lo sviluppo economico italiano 1861–1940*, Bari: Laterza.
—— (1977) 'Effective protection and industrial growth: the case of Italian engineering', in *Journal of European Economic History* VI, 659–73.
—— (1990) *An Economic History of Liberal Italy*, London: Routledge.
Warglien, M. (1985) 'Nota sull'invetsimento industriale in macchinari ed altre attrezzature meccaniche Italia 1881–1913', *Rivista di Storia Economica*, n.s. 2, 125–46.
—— (1987) 'Investimenti industriali e instabilità finanziaria in Italia 1878–1913', *Rivista di Storia Economica*, n.s. 3, 384–439.
Webster, R. (1974) 'The political and industrial strategies of a mixed investment bank: Italian industrial financing and the Banca Commerciale Italiana', *VierteGarharchiv fur Sozial und Wirtschaftgeschichte* 61, 320–71.
Zamagni, V. (1978) *Industrializzazione e squilibri regionali*, Bologna: Il Mulino.
—— (1981) *Lo stato italiano e l'economia*, Florence: Le Monnier.
—— (1984) 'Sui salari industriali nell'età giolittiana', *Rivista di Storia Economica*, n.s. I, 183–221.
—— (1988) *Il debito pubblico in Italia dal 1861 al 1987*, Rome: Istituto Poligrafico dello Stato.
—— (1991) *L'industria chimica in Italia* (forthcoming).

[6]

Economic History Review, 2nd ser. XLI, 1(1988), pp. 95–113

Was Italian fascism a developmental dictatorship? Some evidence to the contrary[1]

By JON S. COHEN

Postwar interpretations of the economic policies of Italian fascism can be grouped under three headings; fascism as stagnation, fascism as capitalism, and, for want of a better title, fascism as fascism.[2] Although I am concerned in this article with the last of these, it is useful for purposes of comparison to describe briefly the other two. In the first, fascism is seen as a repressive, inherently reactionary political system in which politics dominated economics, rents dominated profits, and economic stagnation dominated growth. Policies favoured monopoly interests in industry and semi-feudal landowners in agriculture.[3]

In the second, fascist policies are viewed as reasonably progressive, primarily because they reflected the interests of a modern, growth-oriented capitalist class. There were limits, of course, set by international conditions and domestic constraints to what could be done but, within these, policies encouraged capitalist accumulation.[4] The growth of state involvement in the private sector occurred not, as it might appear, at the expense of private interests but in support of them. In fact, with only slight exaggeration, it can be argued that with this intervention the machinery of the state was put at the disposal of private capital.[5]

In contrast with the first two, where fascist policies are thought to reflect the priorities of interest groups within the economy, from the perspective of 'fascism as fascism', fascist policies represent the aspirations of the fascist movement itself and not particular partisan interests. According to James Gregor, the principal protagonist of this view, fascism was a mass mobilizing development dictatorship in which economic policies, based on a coherent, logically consistent theory of modernization, promoted swift economic growth through rapid capital accumulation funded by large profits which were, in

[1] I would like to thank Donald Moggridge for a number of very helpful suggestions and Francesco Galassi for able research assistance. An earlier version of this paper was presented at the 1986 meetings of the Southern Economics Association. I am grateful to Richard Roehl, John Gillingham, and William McNeil for their comments. Naturally, I assume full responsibility for remaining errors and for the opinions expressed in the paper.

[2] It is worth emphasizing that since my purpose is to clear up misconceptions about the nature and consequences of fascist *economic* policies in *Italy*, very little attention is paid to the vast literature on the general nature, origins and theory of fascism and on the fascist experience in other countries.

[3] Revelli, 'Fascismo III'.

[4] The principal exponents of this position include Ciocca, 'L'economia italiana'; Castronovo, 'La storia economica'; Fano Damascelli, 'Restaurazione antifascista liberista'; Grifone, *Il capitale finanziario*; Sarti, *Fascism and the industrial leadership*.

[5] Revelli, 'Fascismo III' p. 429.

turn, the product of suppressed wages and salaries.[6] To make sure it all happened without external interference domestic self-sufficiency was encouraged, and to prevent internal prevarication state control was fostered. In other words, the fascists had an overriding goal, economic modernization, and it was this objective, not the petty personal interests of capitalists or landowners, that dominated and gave substance to fascist economic policies. Capitalists were given free reign as long as their interests coincided with those of the state; when they diverged, as Gregor maintains they did after 1926, the state stepped in and assumed control of the process of accumulation, at the same time abridging private property rights and substituting fascist functionaries for the old captains of industry and commerce. Gregor argues that Italian fascism is one of the first examples of a developmental dictatorship (others include bolshevism, Maoism, Castroism, and Nasserism) where the state in an economically backward country is committed above all to economic development and is prepared to sacrifice personal freedom, private property, the market economy, and anything else to achieve it.[7]

I

Gregor's views appeal to the modern social scientist for two reasons. First, he constructs a general theory of the nature of fascism and, second, with the theory, he assigns to the fascist experience a contemporary relevance that most historical approaches lack. The problem is that his theory is, for the most part, incompatible with fascist reality. He attributes to Mussolini's policies a coherence and consistency that they did not have. Moreover, there is simply no support in the historical record for the argument that fascist economic policies were guided by the overriding objective of rapid economic growth at all costs. Finally, while it is beyond dispute that the fascists meddled in the economic affairs of the private sector more than previous regimes, it would be incorrect to view this as the end of capitalist control of the economy.

Mussolini and his fascist cronies were not opposed to development but it was not the dominant goal of the regime. Mussolini was not a reformer, even if some of the ideologues associated with the regime were, but a second-rate journalist turned ruthless but effective politician whose concerns were and remained his own political career—how to gain and maintain power. For the most part, his economic policies were determined by others (except where they encroached on what he perceived to be his political interests) and were dictated not by some long-run goal but by international and domestic conditions which, in most cases, gave policy makers little room to manoeuvre. The overwhelming impression one gets from studying the period is that Mussolini had a keen sense of what was good and bad politically but very little understanding of, or interest in, economics and the way the Italian economy worked. Most of his economic advisors and policy makers were not fascists in any important sense. That is, while they may have been

[6] Gregor, *Italian fascism*.

[7] National socialism is, of course, another example with the unfortunate feature for Gregor that it happened to appear in an economically advanced country.

members of the party (many were not), they were, for the most part, well-trained liberal economists and/or pragmatic businessmen whose policies reflected not fascist ideology but their training and background. I would argue that fascist economic policies, far from conforming to a well-conceived plan of how to achieve rapid economic growth, represented, for the most part, *ad hoc* responses to particular problems, shaped in equal measure by political pressures and reasonably good economic analysis. While it is true that Mussolini had less admiration for the free market than many of his advisors and often clashed with business leaders over economic policies, there is no evidence that he had any intention of substituting state for private control of allocation, distribution, or accumulation. While it would be incorrect to view fascist economic policies as reflecting nothing more than the interests of capitalists, as some who subscribe to the second interpretation would have us believe, it would be equally wrong to mistake government intervention for state control. The truth, naturally enough, lies somewhere between the two extremes.

In the remainder of this paper, I try to show, through a critique of Gregor, how and why particular policies were introduced during the interwar period. Since one of the major weaknesses of Gregor's analysis is its lack of attention to details, I limit my discussion to a close examination of two important pieces of economic legislation, the revaluation of the lira in 1927, the so-called *quota novanta*, and the creation of IRI (*Istituto di Ricostruzione Industriale*); what might be called the constitution of the entrepreneurial state. In neither case do the facts sustain his interpretation. Gregor interlaces his text with data that, on the whole, convey a relatively positive picture of the performance of the economy under fascist tutelage. In the final section of the paper, after the policies are analysed, a more complete statistical portrait of the period is presented, a rather sombre one that contrasts sharply with that sketched by Gregor. In fact, on the basis of numbers alone, one would be inclined to argue that fascism retarded instead of abetted growth.

II

In December 1927, Mussolini pegged the value of the lira at roughly 90 to the pound. The rate had an intrinsic appeal (it was the one in force when the fascists took power in 1922), but it also had the peculiar feature that Mussolini had to impose it against the advice of his minister of finance, many economists, and most of the business community who wanted a lower rate.[8] Gregor argues that the *quota novanta* (Q 90) marked the beginning of phase two of the fascist development programme. 'Using the occasion of the international deterioration of the value of the lire [sic] as a pretext, Mussolini was prepared to launch Italy on the second phase of Fascism's development program. That program was designed to enhance the defensive, aggressive, and self-sufficiency capabilities of the nation in anticipation of expansion against plutocratic and capitalist nations. What this would ultimately entail would be autarchic development of key industries of the peninsula.'[9] The

[8] See De Felice, *Mussolini il fascista*, pp. 222-96; Sarti, 'Mussolini'; Toniolo, *L'economia*, p. 117.
[9] Gregor, *Italian fascism*, p. 147.

'Battle for the Lira', Gregor maintains, provided Mussolini with the opportunity to extend fascist control over the economy. In other words, the Q 90 was consciously chosen to promote autarchy and facilitate government intervention. One must assume that it was also compatible with the goal of economic modernization. Before Gregor's argument is evaluated, the policy must be placed in its historical context.

After three years (1922-5) of rapid economic growth, negligible inflation, and relatively stable exchange rates, inflation accelerated, the balance of payments worsened, the international value of the lira dropped, and pressure mounted for the government to do something. The question was what? Without going into the reasons, it is safe to assume that Mussolini wanted to stop the inflation, peg the value of the lira, and reduce the country's balance of payments deficit. Internal and external balance were linked as the following schema indicates. The domestic inflation stemmed, by and large, from excess aggregate demand facilitated by excess liquidity (money and other liquid assets), and in the very short run from the increase in the price of tradables (exports, imports, and import substitutes) as a result of the fall in the value of the lira.[10] The balance of payments deficit was directly linked to excess aggregate demand since it was the latter that provoked the excess demand for tradables. This imbalance, in turn, created an excess supply of lire and led to the currency's depreciation. Since the root cause of the difficulties was inflated aggregate demand, the solution was relatively straightforward—domestic deflation. This would reduce demand for tradables, thus augmenting Italian exports and reducing imports, and if done correctly, would leave domestic employment unchanged. It should be noted that the depreciation of the lira by raising the domestic price of tradables had corrective features of its own. It reduced domestic demand for tradables in favour of non-tradables (mostly services and utilities) and encouraged a shift of productive resources from the latter to the former. However, such adjustments took time and, in the face of prevailing inflationary pressures, were inadequate to resolve the pressing balance of payments problem. Although it can be argued that flexible exchange rates, especially for inflation-prone countries, are more inflationary than fixed exchange rates, Italy could have achieved internal balance (stable prices and roughly full employment) and external balance (zero excess demand for tradables) without pegging the international value of the lira. Mussolini, his advisors, and most of the business community, however, were anxious to return to gold. The overriding question was at what rate?

Although Toniolo argues that in terms of purchasing power parity the Q 90 was just right, most industrialists, economists, and policy makers favoured a Q 120.[11] Since the exchange rate and domestic deflation were linked, it seems reasonable to argue that the business community and policy makers wanted the lower rate because it would have entailed less deflation and fewer trade restrictions. If we assume that, at least in the short run, the price of non-tradables was rigid downward, the Q 120 would also have provoked less

[10] See Corden, *Inflation*, ch. 1.
[11] Toniolo, *L'economica*, p. 123.

unemployment. There is ample evidence to indicate that Mussolini knew all this, which makes his decision to overrule his advisors all the more puzzling. To understand why he opted for the Q 90 it is useful to consider some consequences of an upward revaluation of the lira.

Italy was a small, open economy which meant, first, that the price of Italian tradables in foreign currency was fixed and, second, that at the going price Italians could buy or sell as much as they wanted on the world market. With no intervention on the part of the government and, beginning from a point of internal and external balance with the lira pegged at 120 to the pound, an appreciation in its value to 90 would cause the domestic price of tradables to fall, demand for them to rise and demand for non-tradables to decline. At the same time, resources would flow from tradables to non-tradables, thus reducing the supply of the former and exacerbating the incipient balance of payments deficit. In a fixed exchange rate regime, unless the authorities are prepared to devalue (and Mussolini most certainly was not), other steps must be taken to eliminate the demand for tradables. In Italy's case, in order to sustain the Q 90, deflationary policies were intensified, trade restrictions multiplied, and, to restore some semblance of internal balance, across the board wage cuts of 15 to 20 per cent were imposed.

It is often argued that the Q 90 rewarded those who relied heavily on imported raw materials, such as iron and steel producers, shipbuilders, and chemical manufacturers, while it punished those such as textile and automotive firms and producers of citrus fruits, wine, oil, and cheese, who, prior to the revaluation, sold a large share of their output abroad.[12] The argument, however, is flawed. The revaluation lowered the price of all tradables, which meant that import competing firms as well as exporters were adversely affected. The argument would, perhaps, be more compelling if the industries that used imported raw materials were the same as those engaged in the production of non-traded commodities, but this was obviously not the case. Moreover, the severe deflation required to sustain the overvalued lira favoured no one. It was, in any case, the tariffs and other trade restrictions, definitely not the Q 90, that bolstered the fortunes of import-competing firms.

Gregor argues that the Q 90, together with the deflation and trade restrictions, played a major role in Mussolini's scheme to promote self-sufficiency, develop key industries, and transfer control from private industry to the state. Is the argument correct?

Consider first self-sufficiency. By lowering the domestic price of traded commodities, the Q 90 tended to make Italy more, not less, dependent on imports. Domestic deflation and tariffs would to some extent offset this tendency but trade data do reveal that, following the recession of 1927, imports rose in 1928-9. Table 1 indicates that this was particularly true for industrial raw materials such as scrap iron and steel, coal and coke, petroleum products, and rubber. The overall level of imports dropped from its 1925 peak but so did the level of domestic economic activity. The data in table 2 show that imports as a percentage of GNP dropped after 1925 but from

[12] Sarti, 'Mussolini' and *idem*, *Fascism and the industrial leadership*.

1926 remained roughly constant. Since the presumption is that the relative price of tradables fell with the revaluation and that of non-tradables rose, it can be argued that this calculation undervalues the increase in imports as a result of the Q 90. These results hardly reflect greater self-sufficiency.

There is another aspect of the Q 90 that needs to be stressed. Stabilization of the lira opened the U.S. capital market to Italian borrowers, and borrow they did. Although a consistent series on capital inflows into Italy for the period is unavailable, most of the fragmentary evidence suggests that after 1927 they were substantial.[13] Thus, since both capital and commodity imports rose after the revaluation, it is difficult to see how one can argue that the Q 90 promoted self-sufficiency. As Maier quite accurately observes, while superficially related to autarchy, the Q 90, in fact, had nothing to do with increasing domestic self-sufficiency.[14]

Table 1. *Selected raw material imports, 1922–1929 ('000 quintals)*

	Coal and coke	*Petroleum*	*Pig iron*	*Scrap iron and steel*	*Rubber*
1922	88,344	2,911	1,364	3,059	83
1923	91,337	3,489	1,322	4,337	112
1924	111,704	3,764	2,027	5,420	120
1925	105,129	4,284	2,651	9,609	169
1926	122,580	4,661	1,767	7,660	178
1927	140,587	5,368	1,221	6,993	178
1928	126,981	6,067	1,389	8,620	206
1929	146,028	6,991	1,777	9,944	250

Source: Istituto Centrale de Statistica, *Sommario di statistiche storiche italiane* (Roma, 1958), table 86, pp. 159–60.

Table 2. *National income and imports, 1922–1929 (current values, millions of Lire)*

	National income	*Imports*	*Imports as a percentage of national income*
1922	96.7	18.4	19.0
1923	105.5	20.2	19.1
1924	109.3	23.0	21.0
1925	136.9	29.2	21.3
1926	145.5	28.9	19.9
1927	126.8	22.9	18.0
1928	127.5	24.6	19.3
1929	127.1	23.9	18.8

Source: Istituto Centrale di Statistica, *Sommario di statistiche storiche italiane* (Roma, 1958), table 110, p. 210.

The issue of state control is more problematic. Clearly, the Q 90 rendered domestic producers vulnerable without more protection, and the government,

[13] Grifone, *Il capitale finanziario*, pp. 65-7.
[14] Maier, *Recasting*, p. 577.

through its manipulation of duties, was able to favour some sectors over others.[15] The revaluation also damaged exporters. In these ways, the government did indeed affect the composition of domestic production and, indirectly, the pattern of allocation and distribution.[16] There is also strong evidence to suggest that along with the deflation and revaluation went increased concentration which favoured large over small producers and heavy over light industry. The question is, what did these policies have to do with fascism? Although Gregor argues that they were essential parts of the long-range plan of the fascists to develop the economy, exactly the same trend towards concentration and state intervention can be found in Weimar Germany and the France of Clemenceau and Poincaré, neither of which could be regarded as prototypes of mass mobilizing development dictatorships. These similarities suggest that faced with the same kinds of internal and external pressures as politicians in Germany and France, the fascists responded, for the most part, in a similar fashion. As Maier observes, 'the major themes of economic reorganization in the 1920s [were] the restriction of output in lieu of the expansion of markets, the need to cartelize industry at home or bind it into price associations or pools, and the corporate response to insecurity, as powerful industries and the state sought to shield themselves from market uncertainties.'[17] The Q 90 proved consistent with general trends both inside Italy and in the international economy. Deflation gave the government greater voice over national economic policy even while it granted control over industry to the most powerful firms and associations. In the international arena, the Q 90 was Italy's contribution to the overall deflationary thrust of the late twenties.[18] To argue that fascist policy was unique to the totalitarian regime is simply to misread the history of the period.

Finally, if the goal of the fascists was actually rapid economic expansion in conjunction with the success of key sectors, one can certainly imagine a more cost-effective way of going about it. A lower exchange rate would have required lower tariffs and thus less dead weight loss. If raw material importers needed help, they could have been given subsidies. As it was, 1927 was a particularly bad year for domestic industry and, while conditions improved in 1928-9, industrial growth rates were substantially below those achieved in the period 1922-5 and by European competitors during these years (see table 3).

According to some, the Q 90 does not bear sole responsibility for the slowdown. The earlier boom was driven at least in part by foreign demand for Italian exports; however by 1927 world trade was in decline so that Italian exports would have suffered no matter what the government's

[15] Guarneri reports that tariffs went up on a very large number of commodities after 1926. From tariff changes alone, it is not at all clear who was favoured and who was not. (Guarneri, *Battaglie economiche*, p. 134.)

[16] It is worth pointing out that the only clear-cut beneficiaries of the Q 90 were producers of non-tradables.

[17] Maier, *Recasting*, p. 517.

[18] Ibid., p. 576; Sarti, *Fascism and the industrial leadership*, p. 99.

Table 3. *Annual growth rates of output of manufacturing industries, selected European countries, 1922–1937*

	Italy	Luxembourg	Germany (without Saar)	Belgium	France	Austria	UK	Sweden
1922–5	7.6	10.5	3.3	6.2	7.1	7.0	3.9	7.5
1926–9	1.7	7.5	8.2	6.0	3.2	4.1	7.5	5.7
1930–7	2.5	1.0	5.6	1.6	−1.1	1.4	6.2	6.2

Source: Organization of European Economic Cooperation, *Industrial statistics, 1900–1959* (Paris, 1959), table 4, p. 11.

exchange rate policy.[19] This argument is not entirely compelling. It assumes, contrary to what we know and what economic theory would lead us to expect, that an upward revaluation of the lira would leave domestic demand for exportables unchanged.[20] Although only suggestive, the data in table 4 show that Italian exports to the Balkans, one of Italy's prime markets, fell relative to those from Germany after 1927. It is difficult to believe that the revalued lira had no impact on the flow of Italian exports to this market.

Table 4. *Comparison of German and Italian exports to the Balkans,[a] 1922–1928*

	Italy ('000,000 current lire)	Germany ('000,000 current Reich Marks)
1922	345.5	n.a.
1923	823.7	182.7[b]
1924	1107.1	204.1
1925	1431.1	271.5
1926	1161.4	287.1
1927	977.9	365.9
1928	851.4	386.1

Notes: [a] Countries included are Albania, Bulgaria, Greece, Yugoslavia and Romania. [b] Value in post-stabilization Reich Marks.
Sources: Istituto Centrale di Statistica, *Annuario statistico italiano* (Roma), 1922–1929. *Statistisches jahrbuch für das deutche Reich* (Berlin, Verlag für Politik und Wirtschaft), 1923–1929.

If it is incorrect to view the *quota novanta* as part of Mussolini's long-run plan to sponsor autarchic development under state control, how then can it be explained? Showing his usual political astuteness, Mussolini saw in the Q 90 a way to gain prestige for his regime at home and abroad and, at the same time, to impose his political will on big business, the one group that

[19] Ciocca, 'L'economia italiana' and Cohen, 'The 1927 revaluation' argue in favour of export-led growth between 1922 and 1925. See Filosa, Rey, and Sitzia, 'Uno schema' for a critique of this argument. Toniolo, *L'economia*, p. 123 and Tattara and Toniolo, 'L'industria manifatturiera', argue that Italian exports would have declined with or without the revaluation.

[20] See Corden, *Inflation*, chs. 1 and 2.

still retained some autonomy. His ability to stabilize the lira at a rate that most considered too high and to do so with a minimum of domestic fuss could only enhance his standing in the eyes of foreign politicians and journalists.[21] On the home front, he managed to convert, for domestic consumption, a relatively straightfoward issue into a mythic struggle to preserve the symbol of the nation. He said as much in his Pesaro address in 1927:

> The fascist regime is prepared to impose on all the necessary sacrifices, but our lira, which represents the symbol of the nation, the sign of our riches, the symbol of our hard work, of our efforts, of our sacrifices, of our tears, of our blood, is defended and will be defended.[22]

This is not the place to go into Mussolini's relationship with the business community.[23] Suffice it to say that distrust existed on both sides, with reason. The Q 90 provided Mussolini with an ideal opportunity to assert his authority and he took it. Industrialists were compensated at least in part for the problems created by the revaluation—the idea, after all, was not to destroy the domestic economy—but it was Il Duce, not the captains of industry, who had the last word. I agree that both the regime and business leaders wanted deflation and saw stabilization as a way to achieve it. It is also true that the Q 90 gave the state somewhat more influence over allocation and investment decisions in the private sector than it had in the past. But I would contend that had the business community wanted the Q 90, Mussolini would have pressed for the Q 80 or even the Q 75 to achieve his objective. I cannot test this counterfactual but it is useful to recall that Mussolini struck terror into the hearts of Giuseppe Volpi, his minister of finance, and Volpi's business associates when he informed them that a Q 75 was under consideration.[24]

III

The most dramatic and enduring economic innovations of the fascist period were those associated with the creation of public enterprises such as AGIP (Associazione Generale di Petroli), IMI (Istituto Mobiliare Italiana), and IRI (Istituto di Recostruzione Italiano). According to Romeo, through such institutions by 1936 the Italian government owned a greater share of domestic industry than any other European country, with the exception of the Soviet Union.[25] Why were the public enterprises set up and what, if anything, did they have to do with fascism? To put the question another way, was this intervention the result of a planned, calculated take-over of the private sector by the state or was it, instead, the consequence of ad hoc reactions to particular economic events? Gregor, naturally, subscribes to the

[21] Contrast Italy's revaluation with England's return to gold in 1925. See Moggridge, *The return to gold* for the English story. Foreign investors were also impressed, which facilitated Italy's ability to borrow abroad.

[22] Quoted in Cohen, 'The 1927 revaluation', pp. 651-2.

[23] Melograno, *Gli industriali* and Sarti, *Fascism and the industrial leadership*, provide excellent, detailed accounts of these relationships.

[24] Toniolo, *L'economia*, p. 117.

[25] Romeo, *Breve storia*, p. 171.

former view. The purpose of this section is to show that the latter more accurately captures what was going on.

Gregor's argument goes as follows. A major long-term goal of fascism was to develop the Italian economy so that Italy could break the economic and political dominance of the plutocratic nations and assume its place in the pantheon of great powers.[26] To achieve this end, a strong interventionist state was necessary to articulate and carry out national policy, to coordinate local initiatives and interests and bring them into line with the national goal of modernization. To put it more concretely, in a relatively backward country such as Italy which lacked natural resources and capital, the government had to help mobilize and allocate these inputs to bring about rapid economic growth.

A keystone of this overarching plan was self-sufficiency. As Gregor puts it,

> If Italy were to assume the responsibility of a great power, it must enjoy military and economic capability sufficiently insulated from interdiction to allow national leadership the freedom of action necessary to any major nation in crisis circumstances.[27]

That is, in order to remain free from political blackmail Italy had to be self-sufficient. The argument is similar but not identical to the notion that a firm may, under certain conditions, buy out a supplier to avoid the risk of being overcharged. The difference is that the firm acts to maximize profits while the government, to achieve autarchy, sacrifices the gains from trade. To summarize Gregor's contention, state intervention in the private sector was necessary to achieve rapid, self-sufficient economic expansion. In this section, the focus is on the connection between state intervention and autarchy. In the final section, the economic performance of the economy during the interwar period is considered.

With the creation of IRI, the state became a fully fledged participant in the private sector. In some cases, IRI was no more than a minority shareholder in what remained an essentially privately owned company; in others, it was the sole or majority participant. In all cases, IRI firms operated in the private sector, competed with private enterprises, and, for the most part, faced the same opportunities and constraints as its competitors. The Italian economy, in effect, became a prototype of the mixed economy. To explain the nature and timing of IRI's intervention, it is necessary to set the historical scene, beginning with a quick sketch of the connections between the banks and industry and industry and the government in the pre-fascist period.

Although Toniolo quite rightly points out that there was a massive increase in the amount of industrial paper (loans, advances, stocks, and bonds) held by the commercial banks after 1926, especially by the Banca Commerciale Italiana (Comit) and the Credito Italiano (CI), it would be incorrect to ignore the role played by these banks in financing industry in the prewar period.[28]

[26] It would seem that the fascists were less concerned with the existence of such a plutocracy, whatever it means, than its composition. They wanted Italy to be a member.

[27] Gregor, *Italian fascism*, p. 153.

[28] See Confalonieri, *Banca e industria*.

They were involved (if not necessarily instrumental) in setting up a modern iron and steel sector, electric power production, shipbuilding, shipping lines, and chemical firms.[29] These relations outlived the war so that the change Toniolo observes after 1926 is one of degree, not kind. Moreover, even in the period before the First World War, there were many who worried about the dangers associated with a financial system where the portfolios of major banks were heavily weighted by potentially illiquid industrial assets while liabilities were, for the most part, highly liquid.[30]

Government ties with industry go back at least to the creation in 1886 of the iron and steel complex at Terni, a venture sponsored jointly by the military, the banks, and a few industrialists.[31] Although the government did not finance or manage the company, it did guarantee a market for its output and orchestrated a rescue operation when the company, a few years after its birth, teetered on the edge of bankruptcy. On more than one occasion between 1896 and 1914 the government through the Bank of Italy organized salvage operations to rescue banks and/or industrial concerns which faced serious but what were considered transitory difficulties.[32] The first instance of direct government involvement in the private sector occurred during the war, when the three note-issuing banks (the Bank of Italy, the Bank of Naples, and the Bank of Sicily) set up a general fund to provide advances on shares to manufacturers of war-related products to help them expand capacity quickly. The arrangement was to be self-liquidating; the firms were to buy back their shares from the banks, retire the advances, and that would be the end of that. For better or worse, nothing of the sort happened.

In March 1922, before Mussolini muscled his way into the government, a special fund (the Sezione speciale autonoma del Consorzio sovvenzione) was established to carry out the liquidation of the Banca Italiana di Sconto, the financial right arm of the giant defence contracting firm Ansaldo and, if necessary, help in the restructuring of Ansaldo itself. The special fund was related to, but financially distinct from, the general one set up during the war. They existed side by side, they engaged in similar activities, and both drew on the resources of the note-issuing banks. Salvage operations by the special fund continued under the fascists. By 1926, when it was reorganized and renamed the Istituto di Liquidazioni, it held controlling interests in, among other concerns, iron mines at Cogne and Alfa Romeo. Although shares in these firms were acquired more by accident than design, they marked the first time that the government assumed direct control over what had been private concerns. It was not to be the last. Cianci's summary comment on this first phase of government intervention is interesting. 'The first realization of the entrepreneurial state was not therefore a political

[29] Bonelli, *Lo sviluppo*; Confalonieri, *Banca e industria*.

[30] There have been a number of attempts to explain the phenomenon of the so-called industrial credit banks, more characteristic of continental countries such as Belgium, Germany, Austria, and Italy than of Britain. None are entirely satisfactory but, if we assume that a country gets the institutions it deserves (or needs), then this particular form of financial intermediation must represent a response to imperfect or incomplete capital markets combined with scale economies in production.

[31] Bonelli, *Lo sviluppo, passim*; Romeo, *Breve storia*, pp. 51-2.

[32] Bonelli, *La crisi*; Romeo, *Breve storia*, pp. 107-11.

choice, but only the inevitable fruit of an inheritance from the world war that those in power intended to liquidate, without unfortunately possessing the strength and the courage to overcome opposing interests.'[33]

In 1926-7, share prices on domestic exchanges, in response to deflationary pressures, dropped sharply. In an attempt to check the decline and thus to sustain the value of stocks in their portfolios, the commercial banks, especially the Comit and the CI, bought even more securities. Between 1929 and 1930, the amount of industrial assets held by the banks, already in excess of what many considered prudent, jumped dramatically. At the same time, the prices of these shares plummeted. By 1932, the commercial banks had the dubious distinction of holding controlling interests in a large number of major industrial concerns whose street value was, for all practical purposes, zero.[34] To make matters worse, the Bank of Italy, by this time the only note-issuing bank in the country, was in no position to provide assistance. Toniolo estimates that by the end of 1932 the central bank had already advanced funds to the Istituto di Liquidazioni and to the commercial banks to the tune of 7,382 million lire, a sum equal to roughly 54 per cent of currency in circulation.[35] The bank could do no more. Aside from the risks involved for the central bank in a further increase in advances to the private sector, the bank had to restrict liquidity for reasons of external balance. The lira was still pegged to gold at the old rate, which, with the pound devalued, meant that it was now equivalent to a *quota sessanta* (Q 60).

The country was confronted with a crisis that threatened to topple much of the financial system and a large chunk of industry. The commercial banks did make a last-ditch effort to unload some of their industrial assets, but to no avail. The state had essentially two choices. It could sit by and watch as the system collapsed with the hope that the private sector would dig itself out of the rubble and rebuild. In the very long run, such restraint might have produced a robust and invigorated private sector. In spite of the strong interventionist tradition of the state, this option was considered quite seriously by policy makers. It was decided, however, that the short-run economic and political costs were too great and, after an unsuccessful attempt to use the Istituto di Liquidazioni for salvage purposes, first IMI then IRI was created to handle the biggest rescue operation in the country's history.

From all that has been said, it is quite clear that IRI was not the logical fulfilment of a long-term plan but was instead an emergency measure taken to avert an economic disaster. It was equivalent to calling the fire department to put out a fire. The fascists were not responsible for the fire nor for the lack of good building codes that did nothing to prevent its spread. It could be argued that the overvalued exchange rate added fuel to the fire, but it was hardly the cause. The point is simple. Unless Gregor is prepared to argue that Mussolini instigated the depression and masterminded the pathological relationship between the banks and industry, both absurd, the notion that IRI was part of fascism's grand design is without foundation.

[33] Cianci, *Nascita*, p. 62.
[34] Cianci, *Nascita*, pp. 105-6 and *passim*.
[35] Toniolo, *L'economia*, p. 246.

In fact, with only slight exaggeration, it can be argued that Mussolini and his fascist cohorts had no conception of the gravity of the crisis and virtually no idea of the importance of the banks in financing industry.

All this said, it is still possible to argue that the fascists exploited the situation for their own ends. That is, while IRI may have emerged in response to a crisis, the fascists conceived and shaped it to advance their own goals. The facts, however, do not support this interpretation. Alberto Beneduce, the principal force behind IRI, was not and had never been a fascist. He was, in fact, highly suspect for his background and his views by the fascist hierarchy. None of his close associates in IRI, such as Menichella, Giordani, or Saraceno, were fascists. IRI was their creation and, for the most part, they determined its policy. Beneduce reported directly to Mussolini and, judging from the documents available, Il Duce gave him a free hand, especially during the early years.[36]

It should be pointed out that in both conception and action, IRI remained completely independent of the national council of corporations, the administrative embodiment of that much proclaimed fascist innovation, the corporate state.[37] Although this is not the place to discuss the economic content and impact (if any) of corporatism, Alberto Aquarone, author of the classic work on the organization of the totalitarian state in Italy, is probably correct in his assessment that, on the whole, the corporate state was 'more smoke than fire' (*più fumo che arrosto*). Of direct relevance to the issue at hand, he notes that the national council of corporations was not involved in the creation of IRI but merely informed, after the fact, of its existence.[38] Whatever the reasons for this independence from fascist control, the practical consequence for the directors of IRI was freedom to formulate policies not in allegiance to some preconceived ideology but on the basis of what they considered to be good economic analysis.

IRI's immediate tasks, as Beneduce saw them, were to facilitate liquidation by the banks of their devalued industrial assets and, at the same time, to provide financial sustenance for a malnourished industrial system. The premise to the act that constituted IRI puts it succinctly. 'Recognizing the necessity and urgency of restructuring the supply of credit [in Italy] through the creation of a new public Institute, whose action is directed particularly to the reorganization in industrial activity of the country . . . IRI is constituted.'[39] IRI raised money primarily by issuing convertible debentures to the public, and with these funds it took over the industrial assets held by the banks and assumed their debts with the Bank of Italy.[40] By 1935, IRI had controlling interest in enterprises that represented 42 per cent of the joint stock capital in the country.[41]

IRI was conceived as a temporary institution. Once the crisis ended, it

[36] See Cianci, *Nascita*, pp. 241-7.

[37] Ibid., pp. 253-7.

[38] Aquarone, '*L'organizzazione*', p. 193.

[39] Giotti, 'La gestione', p. 181.

[40] Cianci, *Nascita*, pp. 271-5; Toniolo, 'Crisi economica', pp. 321-4 and *passim*.

[41] Toniolo, *L'economia*, p. 249. This is a peculiar calculation but the only one that can be made given the data. One would prefer to know what percentage of industrial output or real capital IRI's firms accounted for.

was to liquidate its industrial assets, pay off its bond holders, and disappear. Given the previous history of such self-liquidating schemes Beneduce and company were perhaps naïve (even wilfully so), but all available evidence suggests that the intention was real enough. Gregor argues that the fascists viewed IRI as permanent from the outset, but there is absolutely no support for this contention. Naturally, assets were not liquidated and IRI did not fade away; in 1937, it was made permanent.

Although the fascists had nothing to do with the conception and birth of IRI, it may be possible, nonetheless, for Gregor to salvage some of his analysis by arguing that they gained control of the institute in its infancy and raised it to serve the goal of self-sufficiency. This hypothesis can be tested in the following way. If it can be shown that firms under IRI's control pursued autarchic policies (where a choice existed) then the hypothesis cannot be rejected. If the opposite is true, then there is reason to question its validity. It is impossible to provide a conclusive assessment of the hypothesis here but it is possible to make a start.

The iron and steel industry provides a perfect case for this purpose. When IRI took over the industrial assets of the Comit, it acquired controlling interests in ILVA, Terni, Dalmine, and SIACC, which together accounted for well over half the value added in the sector. Moreover, because iron and steel figured prominently on Mussolini's list of key industries that had to be controlled and supported by the state, the bias is in Gregor's favour.[42] However, even in this case the facts provide cold comfort for Gregor.

The overriding issue among the IRI-owned iron and steel firms after 1936 was whether they should convert to a fully integrated production process or simply stick with existing capital and adjust, if necessary, through marginal changes. Fascist leadership, on the whole, favoured the integrated cycle for one reason—that it made domestic industry less dependent on imported raw materials and thus contributed to self-sufficiency. Since the IRI firms in 1938 opted for the integrated approach, it would seem reasonable to conclude that the decision was politically motivated. Such a conclusion, however, would be hasty. As Bonelli, Carparelli, and Pozzobon observe, 'The leaders of IRI used the device of official adherence to fascism to achieve designs of firm policy developed by the planning office of the firms that . . . had in fact little or nothing to do with the objectives of the regime.'[43] In other words, the planners in IRI pushed through a policy that superficially conformed to fascist doctrine but, in fact, was motivated by entirely different considerations.

To understand why this was the case, it is necessary to know what was at stake. First of all, while non-integrated plants had to import coke and scrap, integrated ones had to rely on foreign sources for coke and iron ore. The implications of the two processes for the balance of payments and autarchy depended on input/output ratios and the relative prices of scrap and ore. It was, on the whole, more complicated than the fascists realized.

[42] As an example of the attitude to the sector, when Thaon de Revel took over as minister of finance in 1935, one of his first acts was to block IRI's attempt to sell Terni to private investors. On this see Avagliano, 'Lo sviluppo'; Castronovo, 'L'industria siderurgica'.

[43] Bonelli, Carparelli, and Pozzobon, 'La riforma siderurgica', p. 329.

Secondly, an integrated production facility required an enormous investment in fixed capital and, in consequence, a relatively large output to achieve minimum efficient scale. In other words, if IRI went for the integrated cycle, some of the small, privately owned firms in the industry would, in all likelihood, be forced out of business. Although this conformed with fascism's quest to extend its control over the sector, private operators were not prepared to accept the change without a fight.

It was, in fact, IRI planners, Sinigaglia and Rocca in particular, who favoured the integrated cycle and persuaded the fascists and private firms to accept it. To pacify the latter, they guaranteed them a minimum share of the domestic market, equal to what they had, and to convince the former, they argued, suppressing subtleties, that the integrated cycle was more autarchic than its non-integrated counterpart. The question then is why did the planners want the integrated cycle? Their true objective was to cut production costs in Italy so that steel prices would be competitive internationally; they supposed, correctly, that integrated production was the only way to achieve it. They even entertained the notion that, given the output necessary to minimize unit costs, Italy might have to become an exporter of steel products. According to Bonelli, Carparelli, and Pozzobon, those in IRI who promoted integrated production did so not because they saw it as a way to increase autarchy but because, in a peaceful, interdependent world, it would pay off for Italian industry.[44] The final irony of the story is that the integrated production process, completed after the war, played a crucial role in Italy's trade-based economic miracle.

IV

Is it correct to argue that, given the state of the world, fascist economic policies fostered more rapid industrial expansion than would have been achieved with alternative policies? Although Gregor does not pose the question in this way, it can be inferred from his assessment of the economy's performance under the fascists that his response would be a qualified yes.[45] Among other things, Gregor maintains that in spite of the suppression of consumption, neglect of non-industrial portions of the peninsula, and subvention of non-economic enterprises, the long-term positive result of fascist policy was a modern industrial sector fully capable in the post-war period 'of effectively insinuating itself into the economic boom of the 'fifties and 'sixties.'[46] Relying on data from Maddison, he shows that output per man-hour in Italy was higher in 1938 than in any other European country except Norway, and that the growth in the volume of output compared favourably with that achieved in Germany and Britain and was far superior to that of France.[47]

[44] Ibid., *passim*.

[45] Gregor, *Italian fascism*, p. 160, does argue that the fascists developed the economic base of Italy to the fullest extent possible given resource constraints and maximum commitment to self-sufficiency. If interpreted literally, this assertion is without content. It merely says that Italy did as well economically as could be expected given fascist policies. However, taking his argument as a whole, he seems to be making the counterfactual contention that I attribute to him.

[46] Gregor, *Italian fascism*, p. 158.

[47] See Maddison, *Economic growth*, appendices A and H in particular.

On the other hand, many strictly fascist policies, such as the Q 90, compulsory cartelization, prohibitive agricultural tariffs, investment and import licensing, and restrictions on labour mobility, raised the costs of doing business, promoted price rigidities, and led to an inefficient allocation of labour and other inputs, none of which, one would think, favoured economic expansion. While it is impossible, in this paper, to answer the counterfactual question posed at the beginning of this section, even a cursory review of the statistical record indicates that these distortions probably did inhibit growth.

As table 3 indicates, if limited to manufacturing output, Italy's performance over the entire period surpassed that of only Austria and France. Roughly the same picture emerges when the data are broken down into sub-periods, with Italy's comparative performance being particularly unimpressive in 1926-9 (the Q 90 epoch) and only marginally better in the thirties.

In table 5, the performance during the fascist period is compared by sectors with that in 1896-1914 and 1950-60 both in Italy and with other European countries. Once again, aside from the period 1922-5, the performance is unimpressive. Part of this is due to international conditions, but the poor performance of the economy in the period 1926-9 can be attributed directly to fascist policy. Note that Italy's ranking relative to other countries in Europe is lowest during the fascist era.

Table 6 contrasts particular industrial sectors across countries during the interwar period. As we might expect, given fascist disdain for consumption, food processing was, comparatively speaking, a disaster. Metal products, however, should have done better given the centrality of these industries to the fascist overall plan. However, aside from France, Italy's performance was poor. Only in chemicals does Italy triumph, in large part reflecting the growth in chemical fertilizer production induced by the Battle for Wheat.

Productivity figures are very hard to come by and since Maddison does not reveal his sources, his calculations are impossible to verify. In table 7, productivity estimates are reported for three sectors over the period 1931-6. According to these data, the growth of productivity in building and construction was impressive, while in manufacturing and mining productivity moved inversely with the business cycle, much as we might expect. While hardly conclusive, the data suggest that Maddison (and Gregor) may have substantially overestimated labour productivity in Italy during the period.

To conclude, Gregor wants us to believe that fascism was among the first of a class of mass-mobilizing developmental dictatorships that in a consistent and coherent fashion promoted economic growth and modernization under the aegis of an interventionist state and a self-sufficient economy. As Sarti points out, this is certainly what the fascists maintained and it may very well be that Gregor accepted the propaganda without examining carefully the historical record.[48] The implications of Gregor's analysis are important. He seems to be saying that while a fascist-type dictatorship is not a necessary condition for rapid development of a backward economy, it is a sufficient condition; at least it was in Italy's case. In other words, there was

[48] Sarti, 'Review'.

Table 5. *Annual growth rates of industrial production, selected European countries 1900–1913, 1922–1937, 1950–1960*

	Italy	*France*	*Germany*	*UK*	*Norway*[b]	*Sweden*	*Belgium*[c]	*Austria*
1900–1913	4.6	3.5	4.6	1.8	10.2	3.4	4.6	3.9
1922–1937	4.0	1.9	3.6[a]	4.9	5.6	9.4	3.1	4.1
1950–1960	11.8	7.1	13.4[a]	3.2	21.1	4.0	3.4	9.3

Notes: [a] German data 1925–1927; German data 1950–60 refer to West Germany. [b] Norwegian data begin in 1909. [c] Belgian data begin in 1901.
Source: B. Mitchell, *European historical statistics, 1750–1970* (London, 1975), table E1, pp. 355–7.

Table 6. *Annual growth rates, 1922–1938, selected industries in selected European countries*

	Italy	*France*	*Germany*	*UK*	*Sweden*	*Denmark*	*Norway*	*Belgium*
Food processing:								
1922–38	0.7		2.6	2.0	5.9		1.6	1.6
Metal products[a]								
1928–38	3.0	−2.4	4.9	5.3	10.6	3.9	6.5	
Chemicals								
1922–38	13.5		6.1	3.2	10.9		8.8	

Note: [a] Data before 1928 unavailable.
Source: Organization of European Economic Cooperation, *Industrial statistics, 1900–1955* (Paris, 1956), tables 5, 7, 11; pp. 7, 9, 11 respectively.

Table 7. *Output per man year, selected Italian industries, 1931–1936 (1938 lire)*

	Mining and quarrying	*Manufacturing*	*Building and construction*
1931	9,252	18,397	5,711
1932	10,285	20,819	5,815
1933	10,925	21,984	5,996
1934	10,501	20,413	6,441
1935	8,948	19,449	6,684
1936	8,668	18,860	7,384

Sources: Output data from P. Ercolani, 'Documentazione statistica di base', in G. Fua, ed., *Lo sviluppo economico in Italia*, Vol. III (Milano, 1969), p. 402. Industrial employment from Banca d'Italia, *L'economia italiana nel sessenio 1931–1936*, Part I (Roma, 1938), pp. 98–9.

compensation in the form of economic modernization for the vicious destruction of democratic institutions, the degradation of labour, the brutal attacks on personal freedom, and the demeaning vulgarity that accompanied fascism. The point of the story might be that Italians could not expect to make an omelette without breaking the eggs.

I have argued that Gregor totally misconstrued the economics of fascism. Fascist economic policies were not based on a logically consistent theoretical framework, Mussolini had no overriding long-term goal, and, for the most part, economic achievements of the regime were quite modest, in all probability inferior to that which non-fascist governments would have achieved. Besides, as Sarti notes, Italy was not an economically backward country in 1922 when the fascists took power, and thus hardly needed the dose of dictatorship (and castor oil) that fascism provided.[49] In strict cost-benefit terms, Italy paid dearly for its fascist experience. The real point of the story, if there is one, is that Italians ended up with broken eggs and no omelette.

University of Toronto

Footnote references

Aquarone, A., *L'organizzazione dello stato totalitario* (Torino, 1965).

Avagliano, L., 'Lo sviluppo dei settori IRI e il rapporto stato-gruppi privati', *Rassagna Economica*, 40 (1976), pp. 1125-95.

Bonelli, F., *La crisi del 1907. Una tappa dello sviluppo industriale italiano* (Torino, 1971).

Bonelli, F., *Lo sviluppo di una grande impresa in Italia. La Terni dal 1884 al 1962* (Torino, 1975).

Bonelli, F., Carparelli, A., and Pozzobon, M., 'La riforma siderurgica IRI tra autarchia e mercato (1935-42)', in F. Bonelli, ed., *Acciaio per l'industrializzazione* (Torino, 1982), pp. 217-334.

Castronovo, V., 'La storia economica', in *Storia d'Italia. Dall' unita a oggi*, 4, tomo 1 (Torino, 1975), pp. 5-508.

Castronovo, V., 'L'industria siderurgica e il piano di coordinamento dell' IRI (1936-39)', *Richerche Storiche*, VII (1978), pp. 163-88.

Ciani, E., *Nascita dello stato imprenditore in Italia* (Milano, 1978).

Ciocca, P., 'L'economia italiana nel contesto internazionale', in Ciocca, P. and Toniolo, G., eds., *L'economia italiana nel periodo fascista* (Bologna, 1976), pp. 19-50.

Cohen, J. S., 'The 1927 revaluation of the lira: a study in political economy', *Economic History Review*, 2nd ser, XXV (1972), pp. 642-54.

Confalonieri, A., *Banca e industria in Italia 1894-1906. Il sistema bancario tra due crisi*, II (Milano, 1975).

Corden, W. M., *Inflation, exchange rates, and the world economy* (Oxford, 3rd ed., 1985).

De Felice, R., *Mussolini il fascista. L'organizzazione dello stato fascista 1925-1929*, II (Torino, 1968).

Fano Damascelli, E., ' "Restaurazione antifascista liberista". Ristagno e sviluppo economico durante il fascismo', in *Movimento di liberazione in Italia*, 104 (1971), reprinted in Aquarone, A., and Vernassa, M., eds., *Il regime fascista* (Bologna, 1974), pp. 281-306.

Filosa, R., Rey, G., and Sitzia, B., 'Uno schema di analisi quantitativa dell'economia italiana durante il fascismo', in Ciocca, P., and Toniolo, G., eds., *L'economia italiana nel periodo fascista* (Bologna, 1976), pp. 51-102.

Giotti, M., 'La gestione dell' IRI dalla costituzione alla vigilia della transformazione in ente permanente', in *Banca e industria fra le due querre*, II (Bologna, 1981), pp. 181-202.

Gregor, A. J., *Italian fascism and developmental dictatorship* (Princeton, 1979).

Grifone, P., *Il capitale finanziario in Italia* (Torino, 1971).

Guarneri, F., *Battaglie economiche tra le due grande guerre*, I (Milano, 1953).

Maddison, A., *Economic growth in the west* (New York, 1964).

Maier, C., *Recasting bourgeois Europe* (Princeton, 1975).

Melograno, P., *Gli industriali e Mussolini* (Milano, 1972).

Moggridge, D., *The return to gold* (Cambridge, 1969).

Revelli, M., 'Fascismo III. La politica economica', in Levi, F., Levra, U., and Tranfaglia, N., eds., *Storia d'Italia*, I (Firenze, 1978), pp. 418-35.

Romeo, R., *Breve storia della grande industria in Italia* (Rocca San Casciano, 2nd ed., 1963).

Sarti, R., 'Mussolini and the Italian industrial leadership in the battle of the lira', *Past and Present*, 46 (1970), pp. 97-112.

[49] Ibid.

Sarti, R., *Fascism and the industrial leadership in Italy* (Berkeley, 1971).

Sarti, R., 'Review of A. James Gregor, *Italian fascism and developmental dictatorship*', *American Historical Review*, 86 (1981), pp. 169-70.

Tattara, G., and Toniolo, G., 'L'industria manifatturiera: cicli, politiche e mutamenti di struttura (1921-37)', in Ciocca, P. and Toniolo, G., eds., *L'economia italiana nel periodo fascista* (Bologna, 1976), pp. 103-70.

Toniolo, G., 'Richerche recenti e problemi aperti sull' economia italiana durante la "grande crisi" ', in Toniolo, G., ed., *Industria e banca nella grande crisi, 1929-1934* (Milano, 1978), pp. 18-34.

Toniolo, G., *L'economia dell' Italia fascista* (Bari, 1980).

[7]

Economic History Review, XLV, 3(1992), pp. 537–563

Catching up or falling behind? Italy's economic growth, 1895-1947[1]

By NICOLA ROSSI and GIANNI TONIOLO

In 1913, neither Asquith nor Giolitti would have wagered a bottle of claret that their two countries would enjoy roughly the same level of prosperity (measured by income per caput) well before the end of the century. After the event, however, this outcome does not surprise many economic historians and growth economists. The former speak of 'catching up' by 'latecomers' on the basis of some evidence from the economic history of today's developed countries; the latter of 'growth rates convergence' by assuming decreasing returns to capital accumulation. However, neither quantitative historical evidence nor modern growth theory provides firm ground for assuming 'catching up' as a universal growth pattern. Rather, they seem to support Abramovitz's view that long run convergence 'is only a tendency which emerges in the average experience of a group of countries', while an individual country's 'capability to exploit emerging technology depends on a social history that is particular to itself'.[2] A glance at table 1 illustrates this point. Secular growth rates are only roughly consistent with *ex ante* expectations based on the ranking of GNP per caput in 1900. Overall, Italy's performance is only slightly better than that of the entire group. As the 'catching up' approach predicts, Italy is outperformed by a 'latecomer' (Japan). The prediction, however, is not fulfilled in the case of such 'early comers' as Canada, Germany, and France, all of which have growth rates that are not significantly different from Italy's.

Table 1 demonstrates Italy's economic performance to be quite respectable, relative both to that of other countries[3] and to Italy's own economic record in the previous three centuries.[4] At the same time, given Italy's relative backwardness around the turn of the century, a higher long-term growth rate might have been expected. Therefore, the question of the country's

[1] We would like to thank Massimo Baldini, Patrizia Battilani, and Giulio Righi for excellent assistance in assembling and organizing the data. Financial support from the Italian National Research Council (Grant no. 91.04064.CT10) is gratefully acknowledged.

[2] Abramovitz, *Thinking about growth*, p. 406. He adds that 'there are changes in the character of technological advance that make it more congruent with the resources and institutional outfits of some countries but less congruent with those of others'. His suggestion seems to have been taken up by recent developments in growth theory which highlight the role of positive externalities (e.g. from investment in physical or human capital), institutional variables (such as more or less adequate protection of property rights), social factors (such as fertility), and government policies (such as distortionary taxation and public expenditure) in endogenously generating growth. For a survey, see P. M. Romer, 'Increasing returns and new developments in the theory of growth', NBER Working Paper no. 3098 (1989).

[3] Italy's recently acquired 'membership' of the club of the largest world economies, the G7 (group of 7) makes it appropriate to compare its performance with that of the club's members, of which all but Japan enjoyed a higher per caput income than Italy around the turn of the century.

[4] A recent book on the Italian economy since the unification bears the telling subtitle, 'Italy's second economic renaissance' (Zamagni, *Dalla periferia al centro*).

Table 1. *Growth rates in real per caput GDP, G7 countries, 1900-1987 (per cent, per annum)*

	1900-89	*1900-13*	*1913-50*	*1950-73*	*1973-87*
Canada	2.32	3.23	1.51	2.92	2.21
France	2.06	1.47	1.14	4.43	1.25
Italy	2.23	2.16	0.73	4.80	2.02
Germany	2.17	1.57	0.74	4.94	1.96
Japan	3.16	1.24	0.92	7.84	2.81
UK	1.38	0.70	0.84	2.53	1.54
USA	1.81	2.01	1.56	2.17	1.52
G7 Countries	2.06	1.93	1.31	3.44	1.89

Source: Maddison, *World economy*.

capability of exploiting domestic and international growth opportunities and offsetting its own disadvantages may legitimately be raised: 'could Italy have grown faster?'. Looking at the four sub-periods in table 1, the years 1913-50 and 1950-73 stand out, the former for a very low and the latter for a very high Italian growth rate relative to the G7 average. During 1900-13 and 1973-87, on the other hand, Italy's performance comes fairly close to the group average. In fact, during the interwar years, Italy's 'catching up' was not only halted but actually reversed. Had its 1913-50 growth rate been equal to the G7 average for the same period, Italy's secular (1900-87) growth rate would have risen to 2.46 per cent per annum, enough to produce a full 'catching up' by the late 1980s.[5] As table 1 shows, the economic performance of all European countries during 1913-50 was relatively poor,[6] as also was Japan's. However, Italy's growth in the same period turns out to be particularly unsatisfactory and, since wars, depression, and other exogenous shocks were common to all the countries in table 1, part of the slowdown in Italian economic growth is likely to depend on country specific factors: structural weaknesses and misguided policies. Therefore, in analysing Italy's long-run economic performance, attention should be focused on the period 1913-50.

This paper provides fresh quantitative evidence about the first half century in Italy's 'modern economic growth': we offer a new analysis of the 'structural features' of the Italian economy and pose the question: 'What, if anything, went wrong in the period when the country's growth rate in per caput income was far below its secular trend?'.

Among the factors most frequently stressed as characterizing Italy's recent economic history, the sizeable market power enjoyed by the 'representative firm' stands out. Other elements specific to Italy frequently quoted as affecting its growth are the lack of raw materials (reflected in the dependence on imports), and a combination of a mix of industries and timing of industrialization leading to an important role for economies of scale. Besides

[5] By 1987, Italy's GNP per caput would have been equal to the average for the G7 group.

[6] In fact, Abramovitz has pointed out that the catching-up process was, if anything, much weaker before than after 1950; Abramovitz, *Thinking about growth*, pp. 190-5.

looking at technical progress, the variable most likely to be the prime candidate in explaining economic development, our analysis will focus on the above mentioned features of the Italian economy. For this purpose, we have constructed a comprehensive database, providing quantitative information hitherto unavailable (see appendix A), and an econometric model that is particularly well suited to account for short-run disequilibria, economies of scale, and market power.

We shall proceed as follows. Section I describes the model. Section II provides a brief outline of Italy's economic history between 1896 and 1946. Section III discusses the most important structural features of the Italian economy and assesses the impact of technical progress, economies of scale, and market imperfections on growth. The last section is devoted to pulling the threads together and to making some final remarks. Relevant technical details are left to the two appendices.

I

Reviewing Rostow's monumental essay on theories of economic growth,[7] Dorfman 'scolds' the author for 'neglecting the right people ... those who studied the statistical data to detect the sources of the increases in productivity in progressing countries'.[8] The omission is particularly bewildering given Rostow's standing in the economic history profession, in which the causes of productivity growth are an important area of research: significantly the volume in the *Cambridge economic history of Europe* dealing with the development of modern industrial enterprises opens with a well-known essay on the sources of growth by Solow and Temin.[9]

There is, in fact, a fairly large body of historical literature in which aggregate production functions are used to analyse the economic performance of given countries or industries. As is well known, the standard finding of such studies is that total factor input 'explains' only a fraction of total output growth, the rest being accounted for by increases in the efficiency of production over time, that is in measures of total factor productivity (TFP). While such analyses have made an enormous contribution to our knowledge of the process of economic development, standard measures of TFP rest on assumptions that are not easy to establish for empirical reality. Those relating to perfect competition and full flexibility of factor inputs are particularly difficult to accept.

Drawing on the recent work by Morrison,[10] among others, this section outlines a general theoretical framework for productivity growth measurement which enables us to relax the binding assumptions of the traditional measures. Such a framework provides the conceptual basis for the empirical

[7] Rostow, *Theorists of economic growth*.
[8] Dorfman, 'Review article: economic development', p. 587.
[9] Solow and Temin, 'Introduction: the inputs for growth'.
[10] Morrison, 'Quasi-fixed inputs'; *idem*, 'Markups in US and Japanese manufacturing: a short run econometric analysis', NBER Working Paper no. 2799 (1988); *idem*, 'Unravelling the productivity growth slowdown in the US, Canada and Japan: the effects of subequilibrium, scale economies and markups', NBER Working Paper no. 2993 (1989); *idem*, 'Market power, economic profitability and productivity growth measurement: an integrated structural approach', NBER Working Paper no. 3355 (1990).

computations on which we base the analysis of the performance of the Italian economy.

To start with, let the representative firm's technology be described by a production function ($y = y(x,t)$), or equivalently, by a cost function ($c = c(w,y,t)$), where y is output, c is total cost, x is a vector of I inputs with corresponding price vector w, and t is a variable (usually a time counter) summarizing the state of technology. In this simplified setting, TFP growth is traditionally represented by total output (cost) growth net of the contributions of factor inputs (factor prices and output), that is by the output elasticity with respect to the technology indicator ($\partial \ln y/\partial t = \epsilon_{yt}$) or by the cost elasticity with respect to the same variable ($\partial \ln c/\partial t = \epsilon_{ct}$), respectively. Following Solow,[11] it can be shown that these residuals isolate increasing efficiency in production (technical change) if perfect competition prevails in the output market and if short-run as well as long-run fixities (increasing returns to scale) are ruled out.

Under these conditions, non-parametric estimation of productivity growth is usually accomplished by focusing alternatively on the revenue (primal) or cost (dual) component of the profit definition. In the primal measure, potential growth in output (for given inputs) when technology changes is given by

$$\epsilon_{yt} = (\dot{y}/y) - \sum_i s_{yi}(\dot{x}_i/x_i) \tag{1}$$

where s_{yi} is the share of the i-th input in terms of the value of total output ($w_i x_i/py$). Alternatively, and equivalently, the dual measure focuses on the potential cost reduction induced by technology changes (for given output and factor prices),

$$\epsilon_{ct} = (\dot{c}/c) - (\dot{y}/y) - \sum_i s_{ci}(\dot{w}_i/w_i) \tag{2}$$

where s_{ci} is the share of the i-th input in terms of the value of total costs ($w_i x_i/c$).

Once the above assumptions are relaxed, however, their impact on the productivity residual must be explicitly recognized. Returns arising from market power (imperfect competition), from varying utilization of inputs (short-run fixities), and from technological characteristics (scale economies) have to be accounted for, and the traditional productivity growth measures amended correspondingly. Therefore, let the reference model be given by a profit maximizing factor demand model under unrestricted returns to scale and quasi-fixed inputs. Imperfect competition is assumed to prevail in the output market. In this context, the functional characterization of the technology of a representative firm in short-run equilibrium is given by the restricted profit function or also by the restricted cost function. The latter ($c_v = c_v(w,y,k,t)$, otherwise known as the variable cost function) defines the minimum cost the firm incurs for a given volume of output (y), for a given vector of variable factor prices (the $I \times 1$ vector w), a given state of technology

[11] Solow, 'Technical change'.

(t), and a given level of quasi-fixed factors (indicated by the $M \times 1$ vector $\boldsymbol{k}$). The restricted cost function allows us to distinguish neatly between variable factors of production (utilized in amounts corresponding to minimum variable costs) and quasi-fixed ones (utilized in amounts that do not necessarily correspond to minimum costs but are typically characterized by some sort of partial adjustment).

Applying Hotelling's lemma to the restricted cost function yields the demand system for variable factors:

$$x = \partial c_v(w,y,k,t)/\partial w \tag{3}$$

where x is the $I \times 1$ vector of the short-run cost minimizing input levels. Given the cost minimizing variable input demands, profit maximization (conditional on the quasi-fixed factors) is achieved, as usual, by setting marginal revenue equal to marginal cost or, equivalently,

$$p = -y(\partial d(y,.)/\partial y) + (\partial c_v(w,k,y,t)/\partial y) = [1/(1+\epsilon_{py})]c_m(w,k,y,t) \tag{4}$$

where $d(y,.)$ denotes the inverse demand function for the firm's output, $\epsilon_{py} = (\partial \ln d(y,.)/\partial \ln y)$ is the inverse price elasticity, and short-run marginal costs are indicated by $c_m(w,k,y,t) = (\partial c_v(w,k,y,t)/\partial y)$. The system of variable input demand equation (3) and the price equation (4) describe all the firm's decisions that are relevant in the present context.[12] However, the potential value of this approach, firmly based on neoclassical production theory, is not confined to the possibility of describing the productive structure in the short run. On the contrary, the main implication of a temporary equilibrium model lies in the calculation of the levels and determinants of factor utilization, profit margins, and returns to scale, and hence of adjusted TFP growth measures.

To highlight these issues, it is worth remarking that, for a given level of quasi-fixed factors, the variable cost function is simply the difference between the total short-term cost function ($c_t(w,r,y,k,t)$) and the cost of the quasi-fixed factors, i.e.:

$$c_t(w,r,y,k,t) = c_v(w,k,y,t) + r'k \tag{5}$$

where r denotes the $M \times 1$ vector of *ex ante* market prices of quasi-fixed factors. Obviously, given (5), the description of the firm's long run behaviour is provided by the long run cost function ($c(w,r,y,t)$) which can be derived by minimizing the total cost (5) with respect to quasi-fixed inputs for a given utilization of variable inputs and a given volume of output. The first order condition of the latter optimization problem is given by:

$$\partial c_t(w,r,y,k,t)/\partial k = \partial c_v(w,k,y,t)/\partial k + r = 0 \tag{6}$$

which establishes the equality between the market price (r) of a generic fixed factor and its shadow price (q), defined by the potential reduction in variable costs for a unit variation in the level of the fixed factor itself,

[12] The model could, in principle, also incorporate the firm's decisions about the path of the fixed inputs maximizing the present value of total net receipts. This would require deriving the relevant Euler first order condition. However, for the case at hand, equations (3) and (4) contain all relevant information.

$$q = -\partial c_v(w,k,y,t)/\partial k > 0 \quad (7)$$

Let $\bar{k}(w,r,y,t)$ be the solution to (6), i.e. the vector of optimal quantities of quasi-fixed factors. Substituting it for k in (7) we immediately obtain the long run cost function:

$$c_t(w,r,k,y,t) = c_v(w,k,y,t) + r'k = c_v(w,\bar{k}(w,r,y,t),y) + r'\bar{k}(w,r,y,t) \quad (8)$$
$$= c(w,r,y,t)$$

Clearly, if equation (6) prevailed at all points in time, the firm's short-term equilibrium position would coincide with the long-term one, for equality between market price and shadow price would eliminate the incentive to change the quantities of quasi-fixed factors.

The difference between market and shadow prices for the quasi-fixed factor is therefore an obvious indicator of the existence of short-run fixities. In fact, Morrison has shown that:

$$1 - \sum_j \epsilon_{ck_j} = 1 - \sum_j (\partial c_t(w,r,k,y,t)/\partial k_j) \quad (9)$$
$$= 1 - \sum_j (r_j - q_j)k_j/c_t(w,r,k,y,t)$$

is a dual (cost) indicator of capacity utilization where capacity output is defined as the level of output that corresponds to the tangency point between short- and long-run cost curves or, to put it differently, the level of production the firm could attain if its productive factors were used efficiently.[13] Note that if demand is high with respect to supply, the firm will tend to make more intensive use of its stock of capital. Overutilization will result in a lowering of the productivity of capital and an increase in unit costs, which the firm must remedy by augmenting its stock of fixed factors to restore the equality between their shadow and market prices.[14]

In this generalized framework, Morrison[15] has shown that, in order to recognize sub-equilibrium and scale economies, dual (cost based) measures of productivity growth should be adapted as follows:[16]

$$\tilde{\epsilon}_{ct} = \epsilon_{ct} - \sum_j \epsilon_{ck_j}(\dot{k}_j/k_j) - \left[\left(1 - \sum_j \epsilon_{ck_j}\right)\epsilon_{cy} - 1\right](\dot{y}/y) \quad (10)$$

where $(1-\sum_j \epsilon_{ck_j})$ is the mentioned index of factor utilization rate and ϵ_{cy}

[13] This concept of capacity output, originally due to Cassels ('Excess capacity') and Klein ('Some theoretical issues'), should be contrasted with the one implied by measures of capacity utilization commonly used, that is the maximum possible output, given the state of technology and the volume of fixed factors. The latter is a perfectly legitimate evaluation from the engineering standpoint but it has no economic substance, because it does not vary with respect to the economic context in which firms operate.

[14] Clearly, in this situation, the (economic) utilization rate may exceed one, something that is inconceivable when a merely 'mechanical' concept of potential output is adopted.

[15] C. J. Morrison, 'Unraveling the productivity growth slowdown in the US, Canada and Japan, the effects of subequilibrium, scale economies and markups'. NBER Working Paper no. 2993 (1989).

[16] Notice that dual measures, being cost based, are not influenced by demand side adjustment such as the market power adjustment.

denotes the long-run elasticity of costs with respect to output and is an obvious indicator of scale economies. The two indexes adjust the traditional dual measure for short-run fixities and for non-constant returns, respectively. The corresponding primal measure of productivity growth is given by

$$\tilde{\epsilon}_{yt} = -\tilde{\epsilon}_{ct} + \tilde{\epsilon}_{ct}\left\{1 - \left[(1+\epsilon_{py})/\left(\left(1-\sum_{j}\epsilon_{ck_j}\right)\epsilon_{cy}\right)\right]\right\} \quad (11)$$

where one plus the inverse demand elasticity facing the firm is a natural index of market power. Clearly, if all inputs are variable, $\epsilon_{ck_j} = 0 (\forall j)$. Furthermore, if returns to scale are absent and perfect competition prevails in the output market, $\epsilon_{cy} = (1+\epsilon_{py}) = 1$, and equations (10) and (11) reproduce the traditional primal and dual measures.

If reliable proxies were available for the indices measuring the deviations from Solow's assumptions, then computing adjusted productivity growth measures would be immediate. Unfortunately, this is not the case for most if not all historical data sets. It is therefore necessary to specify parametrically the representation of the firm's technology and to revert to econometric methods to obtain coherent estimates of the relevant magnitudes.

Appendices A and B report in detail the specification, estimation, and testing of the relevant econometric model as well as the underlying statistical information. It is worth noting that our database extends in a number of respects the available official sources recently reviewed in Rey.[17] In particular, a special effort was made to acquire a consistent estimate of labour input (total hours worked) and of the wage rate. Assuming two variable inputs (labour and imports) and a single quasi-fixed factor (capital), the parameters of the two equations system (3) have been estimated over the sample 1894-1947 (allowing for the shorter time span for which labour input information is available, that is 1907-39). Details of the estimation procedures as well as of the overall (economic and statistical) performance of the model are set out in appendix B. In both respects the model appears to perform remarkably well. In particular, it is worth noting that, thanks to the highly flexible specification of the technology, no structural break (in a statistical sense) shows up in the period under examination. Nevertheless, the estimated coefficients turn out to imply substantial variations in key magnitudes, such as own and cross price elasticities.

Finally, it should be noticed that, extending the previous theoretical analysis, the estimated models incorporate two crucial additional effects. First, internal adjustment costs (stemming from gross changes in the quasi-fixed factor) are incorporated in the variable cost function. Second, the model allows for a direct effect of the social overhead capital on the representative firm's cost structure.

II

Having briefly discussed the theoretical reference framework, we proceed now to provide an equally brief historical framework for the discussion of

[17] Rey, *I conti economici dell'Italia*.

Italy's economic performance between 1895 and 1947. Italy's political unification in 1861 did not produce sizeable economic effects. Fuà's[18] national accounting statistics show virtually no change in GNP per caput between 1861 and 1896. This picture is now considered too pessimistic: indirect evidence from living standards[19] and new estimates by Maddison[20] indicate that the Italian economy was characterized by slow growth rather than stagnation.[21] Nevertheless, during the 30-odd years after unification, instead of 'catching up', Italy lost ground with respect to the more advanced European countries. It was only after a severe crisis in the early 1890s that the new kingdom enjoyed a long spell of substantial growth and experienced its first period of 'catching up'.

A cyclical industrial upswing took place between 1879 and 1887. There followed a depression of investment demand and manufacturing output which precipitated bank failures on an unprecedented scale, and these in turn triggered a political crisis almost leading to a coup d'état. In 1893-5 a comprehensive reorganization of the banking sector took place with the creation of the Bank of Italy, which undertook to exercise the functions of an embryonic central bank, and the establishment of two large 'universal banks' of the German type. In 1896, the resignation of Prime Minister Crispi opened a new phase in Italian politics characterized by a shift in focus from foreign to domestic and economic issues. Social tension was eventually eased; labour relations improved, as did public finance.[22] In other words, an actual 'regime change' took place both in the political and in the economic sphere. This is seen by historians as creating the preconditions for Italy not only to join in the expansionary phase of the world economy, but also to begin a 'catching up' process relative to countries with more advanced economies (table 1).

In fact, the so-called 'Giolittian era'—roughly coinciding with the first period in table 1—saw the first long spell of rapid economic growth in the history of Italy since the seventeenth century. In 1895 industrial output began to recover from the depression of 1888-93, setting in motion an expansionary wave which lasted—with minor setbacks and a slowdown after 1907—until the spring of 1914. Industrial growth was particularly rapid during 1898-1908.[23] Agriculture grew at a hitherto unprecedented rate, while at the same time releasing low productivity labour to domestic industry and emigration. Fiscal and monetary policies were deliberately designed to assist economic development: the ratio of outstanding state debt to GNP was curtailed, thereby 'crowding in' private investment, and the newly created Bank of Italy helped to stabilize financial markets.[24] Expectations were also enhanced by exchange rate stability and falling domestic interest rates relative

[18] Fuà, *Lo sviluppo economico*, III.

[19] Federico and Toniolo, 'Italy'.

[20] A. Maddison, 'A revised estimate of Italian economic growth, 1861-1989', *Nota di Lavoro* 91.02 (Dipartimento di Scienze Economiche, Università di Venezia, 1991).

[21] Ibid. Estimates an annual growth rate in per caput income of 0.5 per cent between 1861 and 1890.

[22] See, among others, Toniolo, *An economic history of liberal Italy*; Zamagni, *Dalla periferia al centro*.

[23] Estimates of industrial growth for the period vary from 7.87 p.a. (Fenoaltea, 'Railways and the development') to 5.00 p.a. (Carreras, 'La producciò industrial espanyola i italiana').

[24] The Bank managed to avoid a banking crisis in 1907.

to those in Paris and London. A new political climate made it possible to improve industrial relations. Needless to say, during this spell of rapid growth, the Italian economy underwent substantial changes. They cannot be fully appreciated merely by observing that the share of agriculture in GNP declined from 42 per cent (1890) to 35 per cent (1913), while that of manufacturing rose from 17 to 21 per cent. Of equal if not greater importance is the fact that a peripheral rather closed economy became more open and established closer links with the most advanced countries of the time. The tariff wall created in 1887 was slowly but consistently reduced by the signing of commercial treaties with the main trading partners.[25] Imports climbed from 11 to 18 per cent of GNP. A substantial trade deficit was financed by 'invisible' earnings, particularly emigrant remittances, so that the lira, not formally on a 'gold standard', was often traded above its gold parity. Italy's international standing in this regard was confirmed in 1906 when foreign holders happily accepted the conversion of their Italian consols from 4.75 to 3.75 per cent.

Such promising economic growth and transformation, it is often argued, was cut short by the ill-advised decision to join the powers of the *Entente* in May 1915. The plant of social and economic 'modernization' was too tender to be exposed to the rigours of total warfare. Postwar turmoil ended in Fascism, which produced economic retardation through inept economic policies and, more generally, through the freezing of the country's social transformation which had had such promising beginnings in the 'Giolittian era'.[26] On the other hand, some historians maintain that the Italian economy displayed considerable dynamism under Fascism.[27] In particular they point to the development of such 'modern' industries as chemicals, artificial silk, aircraft building, and electric power, and to the emergence of large-scale plants and enterprises.

In actual fact, 1914-46 and even 1922-43 (the Fascist years) were far from being homogeneous periods: not only were there exogenous shocks of a hitherto unprecedented magnitude, but economic policies were anything but consistent over time.[28] In particular, the years from 1922 to 1925, when Mussolini still headed coalition governments, were characterized by *laissez faire* policies and rapid growth. In 1925, when Mussolini assumed full dictatorial powers, the finance minister was replaced, the 'corn laws' reintroduced, and a number of import duties increased. In 1926-7, the return to gold at a high parity required monetary and fiscal deflation, active intervention on labour markets, and forms of price control. *Laissez faire* was definitely abandoned. The most important industrial interests were compensated for the loss of exports with legislation in favour of mergers, agreements, and cartels. The economy had just begun to recover from the

[25] Most such treaties included the 'most favoured nation clause'.

[26] For this view of Fascism, see Foà, 'Le strutture economiche e la politica economica del regime fascista'; Sereni, 'La politica agraria'. This line of thinking is shared, with some qualifications by Grifone, *Il capitale finanziario in Italia*.

[27] See for instance Mori, 'Per una storia'.

[28] See Toniolo, *L'economia dell'Italia fascista*; Ciocca and Toniolo, eds., *L'economia italiana nel periodo fascista*.

effects of the revaluation of the lira when the great depression forced the government to confront the following choices: to go off gold, to introduce new deflationary policies, or to insulate the economy as much as possible. As prestige considerations ruled out the first option, a mix of the other two was followed. In 1935, fiscal expansion needed to prepare for the war in Abyssinia made it necessary to enforce stricter exchange rate controls. They remained in force until 1947, when they began to be eased after Italy joined the IMF and postwar inflation had definitely been checked.

III

It is in this historical context that the main empirical findings of this paper should be viewed. In the first place, our estimates[29] neatly underline some structural characteristics stubbornly prevailing in the Italian economy throughout 1895-1947. They may be summarized as follows:

(1) During the entire half century, revenues never fell short of covering costs of production, including appropriate returns to capital. Over the period, the product price exceeded average costs by 70 per cent on average, thereby giving rise to substantial economic profits.
(2) High profitability originated from profit-maximizing behaviour under monopolistic competition. The representative firm's market power (as given by the ratio between output price and marginal costs), while changing considerably over time, remained of sizeable magnitude during the whole period under investigation, averaging 1.8.
(3) On the cost side, the pre-Second World War Italian economy appears to have been characterized by substantial long-run returns to scale.[30]. The inverse long-run cost elasticity with respect to output averaged 1.5 in the period 1895-1947.
(4) Furthermore, in both 1895 and 1946 the Italian economy turned out to be heavily undercapitalized, the shadow price of capital substantially exceeding its market price on the margin. This condition dominates more than two-fifths of the sample time span.
(5) Finally, social overhead capital formation is shown to be a complement to rather than a substitute for private investment: by producing a sizeable reduction in the representative firm's variable costs, it provided additional incentives to private fixed capital accumulation.

These long-run features of the Italian economy are relevant both for methodological and for substantive reasons. From the point of view of method, they indicate that all the assumptions underlying the standard Solow residual are untenable, at least as far as the economy described by our data set is concerned. The approach chosen in this paper seems, therefore, particularly well suited to the analysis of the long-term performance of the

[29] See appendix B.

[30] The finding of non-constant returns to scale in the aggregate is of dubious interpretation and should not be taken to imply internal firm scale economies. An interesting possibility based on external economies has recently been put forward by the modern theory of economic growth. See, among others, Romer, 'Increasing returns'.

Italian economy. Turning to empirical issues, it is worth noting that the existence (and persistence) of market imperfections throughout the first half of the twentieth century is consistent with time honoured 'qualitative' interpretations of Italy's economic history.[31] Briefly stated, these interpretations hold that, characterized as it was by low levels of capital formation, tiny market size, and lack of raw materials, the Italian economy was bound to rely on the state playing an active role and on 'investment banks' for the creation both of social overhead capital and of modern factories requiring large fixed investments. The state and the so-called finance capital, therefore, were directly involved in promoting industrial enterprises, thereby introducing monopolistic conditions in a number of industries. Gerschenkron held a modified version of this view describing the German 'mixed banks' introduced into Italy at the end of the nineteenth century, as 'agents' of industrialization in conditions of moderate backwardness.[32] Other scholars do not see state intervention in the economy, and the attendant market distortions, as a necessary condition for growth in the case of a country which, in the second half of the nineteenth century, developed its export crops in agriculture and a thriving silk industry. Rather than directly promoting industrialization, they argue, the state should have increased its efforts in social overhead capital formation. In due time, the country's 'animal spirits' would have reacted, generating a process of industrialization based upon Italy's comparative advantages. An extreme version of this view argues that the country paid dearly for state subsidies to heavy industry and for the ill-advised tariff policy introduced in 1878 and reinforced 10 years later. By providing market power to large (and inefficient) firms as well as to the large grain producers the state created and sustained precisely those who were to be behind the government takeover by Mussolini in 1922.[33]

Focusing specifically on the Fascist period, most authors agree that the domestic policy response to the developments in international trade and finance resulted in a further shift from competitive conditions, especially after 1926.[34] In particular, the following policy measures are worth recalling:

(1) The reintroduction in 1925 of the import duty on corn which had been abolished 10 years earlier. Shortly afterwards, Fascism proclaimed its 'battle for wheat' which resulted in further insulation of the sector from international competition and produced widespread inefficiencies in agriculture.[35]

(2) After 1925, 'German-type' banks came to control an increasing number of large manufacturing concerns. In 1931-4, as a result of its operations as a lender of last resort, the state took over the ownership of most enterprises of this kind.[36] It is obvious that both the banks and the state tried to avoid competition between the enterprises under their control as much as possible.

[31] See, for instance, Grifone, *Il capitale finanziario in Italia*; Sereni, 'Capitalismo e mercato nazionale'.
[32] Gerschenkron, *Economic backwardness in historical perspective*.
[33] See Toniolo, *An economic history of liberal Italy*.
[34] See Toniolo, *L'economia dell'Italia fascista*.
[35] See Sereni, 'La politica agraria'; Tattara, 'La battaglia del grano'.
[36] Ciocca and Toniolo, 'Industry and finance in Italy'.

(3) From 1927, the government sought to regulate wage bargaining, at times ruling by decree.
(4) Import duties on some items were raised in 1927 and 1928 as compensation to some industries for the overvaluation of the lira, following the return to gold. When, after 1931, the lira became outrageously overvalued, a veritable flood of legislation on import duties came into being.[37]
(5) Official government committees were set up to promote agreements and cartels among Italian producers.[38]
(6) Exchange controls were introduced from 1934. At the same time, the stipulation of clearing agreements with a number of trading partners became the main policy tool in the field. After 1935, all the above measures were reinforced and state control over foreign trade as well as domestic production became pervasive.[39]

The long-term structural features of the Italian economy emerging from our estimates are consistent with the picture of a relatively underdeveloped economic system, where undercapitalization and market inefficiencies were the rule rather than the exception. While this finding is based upon new aggregate quantitative evidence, it will not surprise those economic historians who have framed their interpretation of Italy's growth in the context of the country's relative backwardness. Some surprise, on the other hand, may arise from the analysis of the behaviour over time of the mark-up and capacity utilization indicators, since it suggests a pattern in Italian economic history which defies standard historical interpretations. The capacity utilization index ($1-\epsilon_{ik}$) reveals whether or not the economy operates at the desired level of capital stock. Between 1895 and 1947, the index displays a U-shaped time profile (appendix B, table B3). In the mid 1890s, the actual capital level was about one-half of the desired (optimum) level: on the aggregate, the economy was heavily undercapitalized. The investment boom of the following years, however, resulted in capital stock becoming increasingly adequate to meet the economy's needs. From 1905 to 1925 the index was, by and large, never significantly different from one, meaning that the economy was developing with an optimum level of capital stock. After 1925, the indicator again takes positive values. Capital was slightly below the desired level until the early 1930s. Thereafter, undercapitalization was once more considerable.

A plausible interpretation for the U-shaped pattern of the utilization index runs as follows. Around 1895, the shadow price of capital (that is, the cost reduction following a unit increase in the quasi-fixed factor) exceeded its market price, thereby giving rise to a substantial undercapitalization of the Italian economy. The phenomenon can possibly be explained by the stagnation in investment which characterized the previous decade. Moreover, structural reasons, which are typical of a backward economy, might be

[37] Guarneri, *Battaglie economiche*, pp. 423-4.
[38] Ibid., pp. 424-9.
[39] Ibid. provides a first-hand account (although not an objective and detached one) of the policy of control over foreign trade and domestic production; Guarneri was the cabinet minister in charge of foreign trade regulation.

thought of as lying behind capital shortage at the end of the century: high adjustment costs due to inefficient markets and, possibly, a shortage of social overhead capital. When aggregate demand shifted forwards, it took 10 years of high rates of investment growth to produce an adequate (optimum) capital stock. Then, for two decades after 1905, actual and desired capital stock grew at roughly the same rate: disequilibria were short lived due to better functioning markets as well as to relative price stability, both accounting for low adjustment costs. After 1925 new rigidities began to creep into the economy, at first slowly, then faster and more pervasively. At the same time, major changes and fluctuations characterized relative price behaviour. It is no surprise that the depression years (1930-3) were characterized by capital shortage: part of the existing stock of capital had become obsolete due to changes (upward) in the relative price both of labour and of imports; more labour saving and raw material saving investments were postulated by the new situation. High adjustment costs are the possible explanation of capital shortage in the late 1930s and, notwithstanding increasing inflation, during the Second World War.

Support for the view that the market economy functioned better in 1905-25 than in the previous and subsequent periods comes from the behaviour of the market power ($1/(1+\epsilon_{py})$) index,[40] taken as a proxy for market imperfection and inefficiencies (appendix B, table B3). While the index remains significantly positive throughout the half-century under investigation, its profile is again U-shaped. Starting from a high, and roughly constant, level around the turn of the century, the mark-up steadily declines from 1905 to the mid to late 1920s and picks up again thereafter. Market organization and functioning, typically inefficient in an underdeveloped economy, improved as a result of growth itself and of increasing international competition. The process continued until the mid 1920s when, as we have already recalled, tariff and non-tariff barriers were introduced step-wise and government intervention on domestic markets became ever more binding.[41] Similarly, economies of scale (as depicted by the reciprocal of the long-run cost elasticity with respect to output changes, ϵ_{cy}) present a U-shaped pattern, with constant returns to scale prevailing, by and large, from 1908 to 1928 (appendix B, table B3). Instead, in the 1895-1907 period (1929-39), marginal cost decreasingly (increasingly) falls short of average total cost over time. In short, the behaviour of the two indices of capital utilization and market efficiency suggests a new periodization for our analysis of Italy's economic performance: (1) 1895-1905, (2) 1905-25, (3) 1925-39. On this basis, we now turn to an analysis of Italy's economic growth. Table 2 synthesizes the performance of the Italian economy in the sub-periods suggested above by comparing a traditional measure of Solow residual with the adjusted measure,

[40] In the present simplified setting, the index is nothing more than the ratio of output price to marginal cost and, as such, it is uniquely determined by the price elasticity of demand. However, it can be shown that, in a more general framework, the index would also incorporate a measure of oligopoly such as the Hirschman-Herfindahl index of firms concentration.

[41] Along with a trend, a counter-cyclical pattern shows up clearly in the behaviour of the mark-up over time, confirming that in booms marginal cost increases more rapidly than price with the expansion of production, while the reverse occurs in downturns.

which takes into account the existence of quasi-fixed factors, of economies of scale, and of market power.

Table 2. *Total factor productivity growth: 1895-1939 (per cent, per annum)*

	1895-1905	*1905-25*	*1925-39*	*1895-1939*
Solow residual				
cost based (dual, ϵ_{ct})	−0.8	−0.2	−1.8	−0.8
revenue based (primal, ϵ_{yt})	1.6	1.0	1.4	1.3
Adjusted residual				
cost based (dual, $\tilde{\epsilon}_{ct}$)	0.3	−0.2	0.0	−0.1
revenue based (primal, $\tilde{\epsilon}_{yt}$)	−0.1	0.2	0.0	0.1
Bias				
cost based (dual, $\tilde{\epsilon}_{ct}-\epsilon_{ct}$)	1.1	0.0	1.8	0.7
revenue based (primal, $\tilde{\epsilon}_{yt}-\epsilon_{yt}$)	−1.7	−0.8	−1.4	−1.2

The evolution of TFP, as reflected in the traditional measure of Solow residual (measured as potential cost reduction for given factor inputs; that is, by the dual measure) reaches a trough between the 1910s and 1920s (0.2 per cent on average between 1905 and 1925), before picking up in the Fascist years (1.8 per cent on average between 1925 and 1939). In other words, by that measure, output growth in the first and second sub-periods could be largely imputed to factor growth, while increased efficiency in production would have counterbalanced the large drop in factor growth experienced in the Fascist years. As it turns out, though, much of this pattern simply reflects returns to scale and adjustment costs (short-run fixities). Once adjusted, as in the second panel of table 2, the dual TFP growth measure is severely reduced, with the periods 1895-1905 and 1925-39 showing no 'true productivity' gains.[42] More generally, here we have a different picture of the productivity pattern from the one deriving from Solow residuals. In the decade around the turn of the century, the dual measure of productivity shows a negative trend which is reversed in the following period (1905-25) where gains are moderate but positive. During the last period in table 2 there are no 'true productivity' gains. The impact of this adjustment is most apparent from the bias corrections reported in the bottom panel of table 2. Throughout the half century, output growth appears to be largely determined by input growth and cost characteristics. In particular, during the first and third sub-periods, cost decreases (productivity increases) far from originating from technical change, turn out to be attributed entirely to the combination of scale economies and short-run adjustment costs.[43]

When seen in this light, the performance of the Italian economy between 1895 and 1939 calls for a reassessment. First, productivity increases appear

[42] More generally, as in Morrison, 'Unraveling the productivity slowdown' (see note 15 above), adjusted residuals provide strong evidence of smaller productivity growth than generally thought.

[43] A similar message (incorporating also the effects of market power) is contained in the ratio between the primal and the (negative of the) dual (adjusted) TFP measures which, as equation (11) shows, is nothing more than a function of the indices assessing the extent of all the deviations with respect to Solow's original assumptions.

to be minor determinants of overall output growth, the latter being dominated by factor inputs growth and scale economies. Second, productivity increases coincide rather neatly with the years of increasing international competition. Third, the downturn of the Italian economy in the Fascist years incorporates a productivity slowdown. The latter's determinants cannot be assessed in the framework of the present analysis. However, the policy environment of the mid 1920s and of the 1930s can be safely expected to have militated against productivity improvements: higher barriers to entry, a lower rate of exit of the inefficient firms, and more generally the encouragement of restrictive practices all played a significant role in accounting for Italy's productivity trends. However, over and above these elements which, to a certain extent, also characterized the 1895-1905 period, we consider that increased insulation of the Fascist economy from the outside world meant a sudden, large drop in the import of capital goods, thereby halting the ability of the economy to import technology.[44]

IV

The macroeconomic literature has recently begun to re-focus attention on the importance and implication of characteristics of production processes such as instantaneous adjustment of inputs, constant returns to scale, and perfect competition. This paper shows that, far from being confined to the analysis of cyclical behaviour, these developments turn out to be of crucial importance for economic historians engaged in the assessment of long-term growth trends, as shown by our analysis here of Italian economic performance.

This has provided firmer quantitative foundations for time-honoured interpretations of Italy's economic growth. In particular, state intervention in the economy, and possibly the role of German-type banking, turn out to be a mixed blessing to the economy's aggregate performance. On the one hand, insofar as government and banks were responsible for the creation of economies of scale, they made a considerable contribution to growth. Moreover, public expenditure on social overhead capital has been shown to provide a powerful incentive to private fixed capital formation. On the other hand, indirect evidence has emerged pointing to government regulation of the economy as one of the main factors behind the slow down of the 1930s.

Our findings about the functioning of the market economy in Italy are quite novel and certainly deserve further research. Contrary to what seems to be the case in the US, late nineteenth-century markets appear to be far from perfect, burdened as they were with monopolistic competition and high adjustment costs. The 'corn laws' distorted the price mechanism and resource allocation in agriculture, while both the tariff and state subsidies endowed a number of industrial firms with substantial market power. Adjustment costs were high due to imperfect and segmented capital markets, poor

[44] In principle, the productivity slowdown could also be imputed to relative factor price changes if technical progress is biased towards the use of particular commodities. Alternatively, the role of research and development expenditures could be emphasized. However, while the behaviour of relative factor prices would tend to cast serious doubts on the first explanation, the time behaviour of industrial patents over the half century does not provide obvious support to the second.

transport and communication facilities, and high transaction costs owing to an inefficient bureaucracy and far from adequate law enforcement. Finally, profit expectations were lowered by government expenditure biased to military needs undertaken to accommodate what came to be known as 'beggar's imperialism'.[45] It is not difficult to recognize in this picture some of the distinctive features of an underdeveloped economy. As noted above, the situation began to improve around the turn of the century. New outward looking policies, lower import duties, better functioning capital markets, and improved transport and communications all contributed to better competitive conditions and lower adjustment costs. Interestingly enough, the First World War and the turbulent post war period did not alter this situation in any significant way. The first three years of Mussolini's government were characterized by a return to law and order, balanced budgets, free trade in agriculture, and mobility of labour and capital. The first departure from these conditions came *before* the great depression, as a byproduct of the restoration of the gold standard in 1926-7.

What, then, went wrong with Italy's economic performance after 1925? Our data show that labour and import inputs declined while capital input growth remained high. Government policies should have been aimed at making the most efficient use of investment, at least by keeping 'true productivity' growth at the previous level and possibly by enhancing it. Moreover, and probably more importantly, an attempt to lower adjustment costs was necessary in the face of the magnitude of the exogenous shocks. In the event, as we have seen, the government took exactly the opposite course of action. Imports of capital goods, most likely the main vehicle of technical progress, were severely curtailed, while at the same time what amounted to a mercantilistic economic system came to characterize the Italian economy.

Pending further research on an international basis, the present paper cannot produce conclusive evidence on the performance of the Italian economy as a 'catcher up' or a 'faller behind' vis-à-vis the major western economies. However, while casting serious doubts on the traditional assessment of economic convergence, it pinpoints Fascist economic policies of the 1930s as the most likely candidate for the role of the villain of the long-run performance story. If anything, it was Fascism that went wrong with the growth of the Italian economy in the long run.

University of Modena
University of Venice

Appendix A: the data

This appendix contains a brief description of methods and sources underlying the construction of the database for the present paper.

To a large extent, figures are drawn from the existing national accounts estimates recently reviewed by Rey.[46] However, as far as labour input and wage rates are concerned, the present paper provides hitherto unavailable information.

[45] In Italian, 'Imperialismo straccione'.
[46] Rey, ed., *I conti economici dell'Italia*.

y: extended value added at 1938 prices defined as the sum of gross domestic product at factor costs and total imports. Source: Fuà, *Lo sviluppo economico in Italia*, III, table XII.4.1A

p: implicit price deflator of the extended value added (1938=1). Source: Fuà, *Lo sviluppo economico in Italia*, III, table XII.4.1B

x_l: total hours worked by fully employed male equivalents in the private sector.

(i) *fully employed male equivalents in agriculture*. Following the methodology outlined in O'Brien and Toniolo, 'The poverty of Italy', labour force figures at population census dates 1901, 1911, 1921, 1931, 1936, and 1951 (source: Vitali, *Aspetti dello sviluppo*), were initially transformed into fully employed male equivalent days of work and then linearly interpolated. To convert available workforces in agriculture into labour input, the following assumptions were made: (a) male farmers aged 15-65 (including owner-occupiers, tenants, and share-croppers) owned or rented sufficient land to keep themselves fully employed for 230 days a year; (b) landless male labourers (*braccianti*) worked 190 days a year; (c) females, children, and elderly males worked 104 days a year regardless of their status as family or landless labour; (d) finally, in converting the days of labour time supplied by females, children, and elderly males into male equivalents, allowance was made for productivity differentials. Figures for days worked were then transformed into hours worked with reference to the available information on the average length of the working day (source: Arcari, 'Le variazioni dei salari agricoli').

(ii) *fully employed male equivalents in mining and quarrying*. Employment figures at industrial census dates 1911, 1927, 1937-40, and 1951 (source: ISTAT, *Censimento industriale*), were interpolated by means of the following indicators: (a) blue-collar employment in mining (available for the years 1893-1901, 1906-29, and 1933-8; source: ISTAT, *Annuario statistico italiano*), (b) blue-collar employment in quarrying and furnaces (available for the years 1901, 1906-29, 1931, and 1933-8; source: ISTAT, *Annuario statistico italiano*). Figures for days worked were then transformed into hours worked making reference to the available information on the average length of the working day in industry (source: Zamagni, 'La dinamica dei salari').

(iii) *fully employed male equivalents in manufacturing and construction, electricity, gas, and water*. Employment figures at industrial census dates 1911, 1927, 1937-40, and 1951 (source: ISTAT, *Censimento industriale*), were interpolated by means of the following indicators: (a) blue-collar employment in metal fabrication and non-ferrous mineral products industries (available for the years 1910-29; source: ISTAT, *Annuario statistico italiano*), (b) blue-collar employment in factories subject to female and children protection legislation (available for the years 1906-16; source: ISTAT, *Annuario statistico italiano*), (c) blue-collar employment index in mining and quarrying, manufacturing, and construction (available for the years 1926-39; source: ISTAT, *Annuario statistico italiano*). Figures for days worked were then transformed into hours worked, with reference to the available information on the average length of the working day in industry (source: Zamagni, 'La dinamica dei salari').

(iv) *fully employed male equivalents in transport and communication*. Employment figures at industrial census dates 1927, 1937-40, and 1951, source: ISTAT, *Censimento industriale*, were interpolated by means of the following indicator: employment in railways (available for the years 1906-40; source: ISTAT, *Annuario statistico italiano*). Figures for days worked were then transformed into hours worked, with reference to the available information on the average length of the working day in industry (source: Zamagni, 'La dinamica dei salari').

(v) *fully employed male equivalents in trade, finance, insurance, and other miscellaneous services*. Employment figures at industrial census dates 1927, 1937-40, and 1951 (source: ISTAT, *Censimento industriale*), were interpolated by means of the following indicators: employment in savings banks (available for the years 1893-1936; source: private information from Banca d'Italia). Figures for days worked were then transformed into hours worked, with reference to the available information on the average length of the working day in industry (source: Zamagni, 'La dinamica dei salari').

w_l: hourly wage rate.

(i) *hourly wage in agriculture*. Source: Arcari, 'Le variazioni dei salari agricoli'; ISTAT, *Annuario statistico italiano*.

(ii) *hourly wage in industry and construction*. Source: Zamagni, 'La dinamica dei salari'; *idem*, 'The daily wages'; ISTAT, *Annuario statistico italiano*.

(iii) *hourly wage in services*. Proxied by wage rates of low ranking government employees. Source: ISTAT, *Sommario di statistiche storiche*.

x_m: total imports at 1938 prices. Source: Fuà, *Lo sviluppo economico in Italia*, III, table XII.4.1A

w_m: total imports implicit price deflator (1938=1). Source: Fuà, *Lo sviluppo economico in Italia*, III, table XII.4.1B

k: private fixed net capital stock at 1938 prices (beginning of period). Source: Fuà, *Lo sviluppo economico in Italia*, III, table XII.3.3

r: user cost of capital defined as $r = w_b(i-\pi+\delta)$ where w_b is the fixed gross private investment deflator (source: see below), δ is the depreciation rate (source: Fuà, *Lo sviluppo economico in Italia*, III, tables XII.3.3, XX.4.14A, XII.4.17) and $(i-\pi)$ is the expected real interest rate. The latter is defined as the expected value of the difference between the interest rate on consols i (source: Fratianni and Spinelli, *Storia monetaria*) and π, the expected rate of change of w_b. The expected real rate of interest has been computed as the one period ahead forecast of a second-order autoregressive rolling regression. It is worth noting that in estimating the above regression, negative values of the real interest rate were set to zero.

x: social overhead net capital stock at 1938 prices (beginning of period). Source: Fuà, *Lo sviluppo economico in Italia*, III, table XII.3.3

b: fixed gross private investment at 1938 prices. Source: Fuà, *Lo sviluppo economico in Italia*, III, table XII.4.14A

w_b: fixed gross private investment deflator (1938=1). Source: Fuà, *Lo sviluppo economico in Italia*, III, table XII.4.14B

Table A1. *Output, inputs, and relative prices, 1895-1939 (per cent growth, per annum)*

	1895-1905	*1905-25*	*1925-39*	*1895-1939*
Output	2.6	2.3	1.3	2.0
Labour input	0.9	1.3	−0.1	0.8
Import	4.5	3.3	−4.4	1.0
Capital input	1.3	2.2	2.8	2.2
Product price	0.2	10.2	−1.1	4.2
Wage rate	4.3	11.1	−0.2	5.6
Import price	0.8	10.1	−1.2	4.3
Rental price	−0.4	7.4	−0.5	3.0

Table A1 summarizes the trends in the main variables over our relevant sub-periods. In describing the evolution of the Italian economy, we draw attention to the fact that our findings do not always agree with those of the two previous attempts at measuring productivity growth over a secular time span.[47]

The following points are worth noticing:

(a) Output data differ in a number of ways from GNP in table 1 (taken from Maddison, *World economy*, for purposes of international comparison). In particular, our figures are defined as 'resource availability', are *not* in per caput terms and use a 1938 (rather than 1980) price deflator.

[47] Fuà, *Lo sviluppo economico in Italia*, I; Maddison, *Phases of capitalist development*.

(b) For the first two sub-periods (1895-1905 and 1905-25) our labour input growth rates are significantly higher than those computed by Fuà,[48] (0.9 and 1.3 per cent p.a. as against 0.3 and 0.5 per cent, respectively).[49] This is likely to be the consequence of our adjustment to agricultural employment figures which makes allowance for 'disguised unemployment'. In contrast, Fuà's definition of agricultural employment coincides with that of labour force. It is worth noting that our findings are consistent with the view[50] that, during this period, Italy's most important available resource consisted of a large supply of cheap, relatively well-educated labour and that this resource was efficiently exploited.

(c) The period 1925-39 shows a considerable slowdown in the rate of growth of labour inputs due both to higher unemployment rates and to a reduction in length of the working day. This latter effect is not taken into account by Fuà and, therefore, his labour input growth is higher than ours (0.4 per annum).[51]

Tables A2, A3, and A4 report the full data set.

Table A2. *Output and inputs (1938 lire, billions)*

Year	*Output*	*Labour*[a]	*Imports*	*Capital*
1894	68.9	39.5	7.0	135.1
1895	70.8	40.5	7.7	135.9
1896	71.8	40.5	7.6	137.0
1897	69.1	38.7	7.4	137.9
1898	74.0	40.2	8.3	139.1
1899	75.4	40.6	8.8	140.1
1900	81.0	42.3	9.8	142.0
1901	85.3	43.2	10.4	144.2
1902	84.4	42.1	10.6	146.7
1903	87.2	42.8	10.9	149.1
1904	87.5	42.7	11.1	151.9
1905	91.2	44.1	12.1	155.2
1906	95.0	45.7	14.3	159.6
1907	104.8	48.7	15.9	166.0
1908	104.8	53.4	16.1	173.7
1909	111.3	50.0	17.2	182.0
1910	106.8	50.0	17.3	190.1
1911	112.4	50.2	17.3	198.1
1912	115.7	50.1	18.4	205.4
1913	119.9	50.2	18.2	212.6
1914	115.8	50.6	14.8	219.3
1915	131.7	50.2	18.7	224.6
1916	148.1	53.8	23.2	224.9
1917	151.1	53.0	22.5	223.3
1918	150.4	54.7	20.3	221.7
1919	131.3	49.6	21.0	218.8
1920	128.8	49.6	26.5	219.7
1921	118.5	47.3	18.1	222.7
1922	123.0	48.7	17.1	223.6
1923	130.4	51.7	18.1	226.6

(*continued*)

[48] Fuà, *Lo sviluppo economico in Italia*, I, pp. 246 ff. Maddison, *Phases of capitalist development*, pp. 96 ff computes input growth rates for 1870-1913 which are not comparable with ours.

[49] Our entirely new estimates of labour input and our more precise definition of capital inputs are likely to account for such a large discrepancy between our growth rates and those by Fuà.

[50] Toniolo, *An economic history of liberal Italy*; Federico and Toniolo, 'Italy', pp. 211-3.

[51] The estimates in Maddison, *Phases of capitalist development*, pp. 210-1, on the other hand, are based on a rather implausible decline by 25 per cent in the annual hours worked per person and result in a yearly decline of 0.7 per cent (1913-38).

Table A2. *Continued*

Year	Output	Labour[a]	Imports	Capital
1924	134.1	54.0	20.2	231.3
1925	144.0	58.9	22.5	238.6
1926	144.1	61.5	21.4	249.2
1927	139.7	59.1	19.5	259.5
1928	151.1	56.6	22.5	267.9
1929	155.1	57.7	22.4	278.0
1930	145.4	55.7	19.2	289.3
1931	139.1	54.4	14.4	297.6
1932	139.6	51.0	11.2	302.4
1933	140.6	53.8	12.6	305.3
1934	139.6	53.7	11.1	307.4
1935	150.6	53.0	10.9	312.5
1936	147.8	52.1	7.9	321.6
1937	165.5	53.9	15.6	333.7
1938	163.3	54.3	12.3	343.8
1939	172.5	56.6	10.9	352.8
1940	173.6	56.3	10.9	363.0
1941	169.1	55.4	8.2	371.0
1942	166.5	55.8	7.9	377.9
1943	153.4	54.3	9.9	375.0
1944	122.6	49.2	5.8	362.4
1945	98.9	46.2	7.2	344.0
1946	130.2	52.4	10.3	329.5
1947	162.3	64.7	21.6	330.8

Note: [a]Labour inputs for the years 1894-1906 and 1940-7 are ex-post forecasts from the estimated econometric model.

Table A3. *Output and factor prices (1938=1)*

Year	*Output price*	*Wage rate*	*Import price*	*Rental rate*
1894	0.168	0.118	0.164	0.012
1895	0.169	0.089	0.164	0.014
1896	0.167	0.095	0.167	0.011
1897	0.169	0.097	0.171	0.013
1898	0.179	0.097	0.178	0.014
1899	0.177	0.097	0.180	0.011
1900	0.176	0.099	0.182	0.012
1901	0.171	0.101	0.173	0.010
1902	0.166	0.107	0.172	0.018
1903	0.175	0.110	0.176	0.015
1904	0.174	0.119	0.178	0.011
1905	0.173	0.136	0.177	0.014
1906	0.179	0.138	0.185	0.009
1907	0.186	0.151	0.189	0.014
1908	0.180	0.154	0.188	0.007
1909	0.184	0.154	0.189	0.017
1910	0.191	0.160	0.196	0.011
1911	0.199	0.168	0.204	0.020
1912	0.205	0.175	0.210	0.011
1913	0.204	0.182	0.211	0.012
1914	0.205	0.194	0.209	0.014
1915	0.229	0.217	0.242	0.021

(continued)

Table A3. *Continued*

Year	*Output price*	*Wage rate*	*Import price*	*Rental rate*
1916	0.300	0.258	0.351	0.013
1917	0.416	0.338	0.591	0.031
1918	0.546	0.456	0.743	0.044
1919	0.672	0.667	0.768	0.042
1920	0.958	0.863	1.038	0.110
1921	0.999	1.005	1.017	0.030
1922	1.002	1.025	0.997	0.081
1923	1.003	1.026	1.011	0.076
1924	1.023	1.039	1.040	0.095
1925	1.205	1.121	1.222	0.058
1926	1.262	1.175	1.294	0.062
1927	1.106	1.124	1.131	0.075
1928	1.037	1.027	1.047	0.170
1929	1.007	1.013	1.019	0.098
1930	0.942	0.988	0.974	0.057
1931	0.850	0.895	0.888	0.091
1932	0.802	0.860	0.813	0.071
1933	0.751	0.843	0.754	0.099
1934	0.753	0.817	0.762	0.064
1935	0.787	0.798	0.779	0.064
1936	0.852	0.851	0.844	0.058
1937	0.940	0.960	0.927	0.032
1938	1.000	1.000	0.999	0.038
1939	1.034	1.084	1.035	0.054
1940	1.211	1.320	1.252	0.100
1941	1.418	1.521	1.462	0.037
1942	1.804	1.701	1.796	0.078
1943	2.714	2.466	2.333	0.082
1944	6.318	4.498	9.302	0.149
1945	14.409	11.682	20.642	0.475
1946	25.077	21.627	26.117	0.933
1947	42.216	46.440	46.389	1.527

Table A4. *Miscellaneous variables (1938 lire, billions)*

Year	*Depreciation rate*	*Gross investment*	*Social overhead capital*
1894	0.026	4.3	47.0
1895	0.026	4.6	47.8
1896	0.026	4.6	48.4
1897	0.027	4.8	48.7
1898	0.027	4.8	48.7
1899	0.027	5.6	48.7
1900	0.028	6.3	48.6
1901	0.028	6.5	48.6
1902	0.028	6.5	48.6
1903	0.028	6.9	48.7
1904	0.028	7.5	48.9
1905	0.029	9.0	49.0
1906	0.029	10.9	49.2
1907	0.029	12.5	49.2
1908	0.029	13.3	49.3

(continued)

Table A4. *Continued*

Year	*Depreciation rate*	*Gross investment*	*Social overhead capital*
1909	0.029	13.4	49.6
1910	0.029	13.6	50.0
1911	0.030	13.2	50.7
1912	0.030	13.3	51.4
1913	0.030	12.9	52.2
1914	0.030	12.2	53.1
1915	0.031	7.5	54.1
1916	0.031	5.2	55.0
1917	0.032	5.6	55.2
1918	0.033	4.5	55.0
1919	0.034	8.3	54.6
1920	0.035	10.6	55.0
1921	0.035	8.9	55.6
1922	0.036	10.6	56.5
1923	0.037	12.8	57.9
1924	0.038	16.5	59.5
1925	0.039	20.1	60.4
1926	0.039	20.1	60.8
1927	0.039	18.7	61.6
1928	0.040	20.7	62.6
1929	0.040	21.8	63.6
1930	0.040	20.5	64.7
1931	0.041	17.1	66.3
1932	0.042	15.0	67.9
1933	0.042	15.4	69.5
1934	0.043	17.7	71.8
1935	0.044	23.1	74.0
1936	0.044	25.8	75.8
1937	0.045	25.6	77.2
1938	0.045	24.2	78.3
1939	0.046	26.6	79.1
1940	0.047	25.5	80.5
1941	0.048	24.1	82.4
1942	0.048	20.6	84.0
1943	0.049	15.9	84.4
1944	0.050	9.6	83.3
1945	0.051	8.0	81.2
1946	0.051	18.5	80.2
1947	0.051	24.4	82.7

Appendix B: the model

The empirical implementation of the theoretical model outlined in section I requires specification of the unknown restricted cost function $c_v = c_v(w,y,k,t)$.[52]

The description of short-run firm behaviour is based on a flexible functional form known as Generalized Leontief (GL) due to Diewert, modified where necessary to account for the existence of fixed factors. Assuming two variable inputs (labour and imports, denoted by the subscripts l and m, respectively) and a single fixed factor (capital, k), we let:

[52] A thorough analysis of the determinants of firm's market power goes beyond the aim of this paper. Therefore the inverse demand function for the firm's output (equation 4) has not been specified and estimated.

$$c_v(w,y,k,t,b,x) = y\Bigg[\sum_i\sum_j \alpha_{ij}(w_iw_j)^{0.5} + \sum_i \beta_{it}w_it^{0.5} + \sum_j \beta_{ib}w_ib^{0.5} + \sum_i \beta_{ix}w_ix^{0.5} \tag{B1}$$

$$+ \sum_i \beta_{iy}w_iy^{0.5} + \sum_i w_i(\gamma_{yy}y + \gamma_{tt}t + \gamma_{bb}b + \gamma_{xx}x + \gamma_{yt}(yt)^{0.5} + \gamma_{yb}(yb)^{0.5}$$

$$+ \gamma_{yx}(yx)^{0.5} + \gamma_{tb}(tb)^{0.5} + \gamma_{tx}(tx)^{0.5} + \gamma_{bx}(bx)^{0.5})\Bigg]$$

$$+ y^{0.5}\Bigg[\sum_i \beta_{ik}w_ik^{0.5} + \sum_i w_i(\gamma_{yk}(yk)^{0.5} + \gamma_{tk}(tk)^{0.5}$$

$$+ \gamma_{bk}(bk)^{0.5} + \gamma_{xk}(xk)^{0.5})\Bigg] + \sum_i w_i\gamma_{kk}k$$

$$(i,j = l,m)$$

where the αs, βs and γs are technological parameters, and where the variable cost function has been extended so as to capture internal adjustment costs (stemming from investment in the quasi-fixed input, denoted by b) as well as an additional exogenous argument (x) representing the stock of public works.

Application of equation (3) yields the system of variable input demands:

$$x_i/y = (\partial c_v(w,k,y,t)/\partial w_i)(1/y) = \sum_j \alpha_{ij}(w_j/w_i)^{0.5} + \beta_{iy}y^{0.5} + \beta_{it}t^{0.5} + \beta_{ib}b^{0.5} + \beta_{ix}x^{0.5} \tag{B2}$$

$$+ \gamma_{yy}y + \gamma_{tt}t + \gamma_{bb}b + \gamma_{xx}x + \gamma_{yt}(yt)^{0.5} + \gamma_{yb}(yb)^{0.5}$$

$$+ \gamma_{yx}(yx)^{0.5} + \gamma_{tb}(tb)^{0.5} + \gamma_{tx}(tx)^{0.5} + \gamma_{bx}(bx)^{0.5} + \beta_{ik}(k/y)^{0.5} + \gamma_{yk}k^{0.5}$$

$$+ \gamma_{tk}(tk/y)^{0.5} + \gamma_{bk}(bk/y)^{0.5} + \gamma_{xk}(xk/y)^{0.5} + \gamma_{kk}(k/y)$$

Notice that, from the system of equations (B2), all the parameters characterizing the firm's short-run technology can be uniquely recovered, thereby allowing the computation of the market power and (short- and long-run) fixities referred to in the text.

The simultaneous system of equations (B2) has been estimated with maximum likelihood estimation methods over the sample period 1894-1947.[53] Table B1 reports some tests of specification and misspecification designed to shed some light on the overall performance of the model as well as on the admissibility of selected hypotheses of theoretical interest.

The first thing to notice is that some of the technological parameters turned out to be poorly determined and were therefore set to zero. The first line of table B1 provides a

Table B1. *Specification and misspecification tests*

Specification tests	*LR*[a]	$\chi^2_{0.05}(dof)$
zero restrictions	3.9	$\chi^2_{0.05}(7)$:14.1
constant returns to scale	18.1	$\chi^2_{0.05}(5)$:11.1
Misspecification tests		
dynamic specification	0.2	$\chi^2_{0.05}(4)$:9.5
structural stability: 1915-8	5.9	$\chi^2_{0.05}(6)$:12.6
structural stability: 1929-33	0.9	$\chi^2_{0.05}(10)$:18.3
structural stability: 1939-45	0.9	$\chi^2_{0.05}(12)$:21.0

Note: [a]*LR* denotes the likelihood ratio test, distributed as a $\chi^2(dof)$ where *dof* indicates the degrees of freedom.

[53] Actually, the estimation method takes into account the fact that the labour input ratio is only observed over the sub-sample 1907-39.

likelihood ratio test of the joint hypothesis $H_0{:}\alpha_{lm} = \gamma_{kk} = \gamma_{yy} = \gamma_{bx} = \gamma_{by} = \gamma_{tt} = \gamma_{tb} = 0$. As is apparent from table B1, the hypothesis has not been rejected at customary levels of significance.[54] Given the above zero restrictions, the second line of table A1 tests the hypothesis of constant returns to scale (H_0: $\gamma_{ty} = \gamma_{xy} = \gamma_{yk} = \beta_{ty} = \beta_{\mu} = 0$) which is soundly rejected by the data.

The hypotheses of no short-run fixities ($\epsilon_{ck} = 0$) and perfect competition ($\mu = 1$) cannot, however, be expressed in purely parametric terms and can therefore only be tested with reference to a specific period. As it turns out, the Italian economy appears to have been significantly undercapitalized in the sub-periods 1894-1901 and 1934-47 (with t-statistics testing the hypothesis H_0: $\epsilon_{ck} = 0$ ranging from 2.1 to 5.5), while significant overcapitalization shows up in 1911, 1915, and 1918-23 (with t-statistics ranging from 2.1 to 4.1). In the remaining years the available capital stock is not significantly different from its optimal level. As far as market power is concerned, the hypothesis H_0: $\mu - 1 = 0$ is not to be rejected only in the periods 1911, 1915, 1918-23.

The lower panel of table B1 assesses the overall performance of the estimated model. The results seem to suggest that there is no apparent sign of dynamic misspecification and that, moreover, the model seems to work quite well for forecasting purposes. Structural stability tests over the more troubled sub-periods (that is the First and Second World Wars and the Great Depression) confirm the latter statement.

Table B2 instead presents parameter estimates (with their asymptotic standard errors, adjusted for heteroscedasticity). On the basis of these estimates, attention should be drawn to the finding that, for a given capital stock, input-output coefficients could well be generated by a Leontief technology, their evolution being driven by changes in capital stock, output, and the technical progress, rather than by relative factor prices. Furthermore, in the short run, the stock of capital tends to displace both variable inputs in the whole sample period. In the long run, on the other hand, substitution effects characterize the relationship between capital and labour, and capital and imports. Labour and imports, instead, tend to be complements. In general, long-run cross and own price elasticity tend to be large as well as to fluctuate substantially in the sample period.

Table B2. *Parameter estimates (sample period 1895-1947)*

α_{ll}	−2.5244 (1.0484)[a]	γ_{yk}	−0.0634 (0.0189)
β_{lt}	−0.4706 (0.0645)	γ_{tk}	0.4568 (0.0828)
β_{lb}	0.1927 (0.0332)	γ_{bk}	−0.0929 (0.0269)
β_{ly}	0.5170 (0.0900)	γ_{xk}	−0.9108 (0.1408)
β_{lx}	−0.6366 (0.2907)	α_{mm}	−2.7376 (1.1356)
γ_{bb}	0.0069 (0.0037)	β_{mt}	−0.4327 (0.0622)
γ_{xx}	0.2142 (0.0474)	β_{mb}	0.1803 (0.0366)
γ_{yt}	−0.0455 (0.0124)	β_{μ}	0.5602 (0.0850)
γ_{yx}	−0.0920 (0.0173)	β_{mx}	−0.7136 (0.2938)
γ_{tx}	−0.0835 (0.0291)	β_{mk}	5.4533 (0.8129)
β_{lk}	5.5396 (0.8021)		
Log-likelihood: 249.058			

Note: [a] in parentheses, asymptotic standard errors adjusted for heteroscedasticity

Table B3 reports the evolution of the main indicators derived from the estimates: (i) profitability ($py/c_t(w,r,y,k,t)$), (ii) market power ($p/c_m(w,y,k,t)$), (iii) returns to scale ($1/\epsilon_{cy}$), (iv) short-run returns to scale ($(1-\epsilon_{ck})\epsilon_{cy}$), and (v) capacity utilization ($1-\epsilon_{ck}$).

Finally, it should be noted that the estimates presented here are part of a wider project on the structure and the evolution of the Italian economy in the twentieth century. In particular, it is envisaged that future research will provide improved estimates by (i) completing the model adding an Euler equation for investment, (ii) allowing for a fully specified demand equation, (iii) isolating the role of energy products in factor demand.

[54] 95 per cent critical values are reported in the fourth column of the table.

Table B3. *Main indicators*

Year	Profitability	Market power	Returns to scale	Short-run returns to scale	Capacity utilization
1894	1.575	1.462	2.149	1.077	2.315
1895	1.758	1.794	2.127	0.980	2.083
1896	1.797	1.812	2.106	0.991	2.088
1897	1.715	1.942	2.089	0.883	1.845
1898	1.807	2.180	2.047	0.829	1.697
1899	1.880	2.217	1.952	0.848	1.655
1900	1.862	2.243	1.827	0.830	1.517
1901	1.890	2.277	1.726	0.830	1.433
1902	1.565	2.370	1.685	0.660	1.113
1903	1.738	2.464	1.572	0.705	1.108
1904	1.736	2.397	1.505	0.724	1.090
1905	1.535	2.104	1.384	0.729	1.009
1906	1.688	1.963	1.265	0.860	1.088
1907	1.529	1.711	1.124	0.894	1.005
1908	1.601	1.678	1.078	0.954	1.028
1909	1.420	1.660	1.009	0.855	0.863
1910	1.536	1.827	1.021	0.841	0.858
1911	1.387	1.800	1.004	0.771	0.773
1912	1.562	1.781	0.999	0.877	0.876
1913	1.537	1.741	1.006	0.883	0.888
1914	1.463	1.943	1.098	0.753	0.827
1915	1.488	2.014	1.033	0.739	0.763
1916	1.902	1.890	0.896	1.006	0.901
1917	1.645	1.530	0.760	1.075	0.817
1918	1.648	1.676	0.626	0.983	0.615
1919	1.458	1.759	0.678	0.829	0.562
1920	1.336	1.772	0.675	0.754	0.509
1921	1.577	2.362	0.716	0.668	0.478
1922	1.385	2.027	0.760	0.683	0.520
1923	1.432	1.689	0.839	0.848	0.712
1924	1.390	1.488	0.945	0.934	0.883
1925	1.634	1.324	0.933	1.234	1.151
1926	1.630	1.362	0.932	1.197	1.115
1927	1.491	1.474	1.010	1.011	1.022
1928	1.212	1.324	1.008	0.916	0.923
1929	1.420	1.288	1.050	1.102	1.158
1930	1.569	1.478	1.194	1.062	1.268
1931	1.380	1.773	1.419	0.778	1.105
1932	1.473	1.923	1.606	0.766	1.231
1933	1.283	1.841	1.734	0.697	1.208
1934	1.526	1.713	1.868	0.891	1.664
1935	1.651	1.448	1.818	1.140	2.073
1936	1.804	1.432	1.937	1.260	2.440
1937	2.015	1.325	1.938	1.521	2.947
1938	2.067	1.400	2.052	1.477	3.030
1939	1.921	1.297	2.027	1.480	3.000
1940	1.688	1.287	2.149	1.311	2.817
1941	2.149	1.337	2.322	1.607	3.732
1942	2.128	1.519	2.477	1.401	3.469
1943	2.256	1.870	2.665	1.206	3.215
1944	2.328	2.226	3.003	1.046	3.140
1945	1.681	3.444	3.743	0.488	1.827
1946	1.904	1.843	1.995	1.033	2.061
1947	1.520	1.096	1.784	1.387	2.474

Footnote references

Official publications

ISTAT, *Annuario statistico italiano* (Rome, various years).
ISTAT, *Censimento industriale e commerciale* (Rome, various years).
ISTAT, *Sommario di statistiche storiche italiane, 1861-1955* (Rome, 1958).

Secondary sources

Abramowitz, M., *Thinking about growth and other essays on economic growth and welfare* (Cambridge, 1989).

Arcari, P. M., 'Le variazioni dei salari agricoli in Italia dalla fondazione del Regno al 1933', in ISTAT, *Annali di Statistica*, serie VI, XXXVI (1936), pp. 1-754.

Cassels, J. M., 'Excess capacity and monopolistic competition', *Qu. J. Econ.*, 51 (1937), pp. 426-43.

Carreras, A., 'La producció industrial espanyola i italiana des mitian segle XIX fins a l'actualitat' (unpub. Ph.D. thesis, Univ. of Barcelona, 1982).

Ciocca, P. and Toniolo, G., eds., *L'economia italiana nel periodo fascista* (Bologna, 1976).

Ciocca, P. and Toniolo, G., 'Industry and finance in Italy: 1918-1940', *J. Eur. Econ. Hist.*, XIII (1984), pp. 113-36.

Dorfman, R., 'Review article: economic development from the beginning to Rostow', *J. Econ. Lit.*, XXIX (1991), pp. 573-91.

Fenoaltea, S., 'Railways and the development of the Italian economy to 1913', in P. K. O'Brien, ed., *Railways and the economic growth of western Europe* (London, 1988), pp. 49-120.

Federico, G. and Toniolo, G., 'Italy', in R. Sylla and G. Toniolo, eds., *Patterns of European industrialization: the nineteenth century* (London, 1991), pp. 197-217.

Foa, V., 'Le strutture economiche e la politica economica del regime fascista', in VVAA, *Fascismo e antifascismo, 1918-36* (Milan, 1962), pp. 127-49.

Fratianni, M. and Spinelli, A., *Storia monetaria d'Italia* (Milan, 1991).

Fuà, G., *Lo sviluppo economico in Italia* (Milan, 1981), I-III.

Gerschenkron, A., *Economic backwardness in historical perspective* (Cambridge, Mass., 1962).

Grifone, P., *Il capitale finanziario in Italia* (Turin, 1945).

Guarneri, F., *Battaglie economiche fra le due guerre* (Milan, 1953).

Klein, L., 'Some theoretical issues in the measurement of capacity', *Econometrica*, 28 (1960), pp. 272-86.

Maddison, A., *Phases of capitalist development* (Oxford, 1982).

Maddison, A., *The world economy in the twentieth century* (Paris, 1989).

Mori, G., 'Per una storia dell'industria italiana durante il fascismo', *Studi Storici*, XII (1971), pp. 3-35.

Morrison, C. J., 'Quasi-fixed inputs in U.S. and Japanese manufacturing: a generalized Leontief restricted cost function approach', *Rev. Econ. Stat.*, 70 (1988), pp. 275-87.

O'Brien, P. K. and Toniolo, G., 'The poverty of Italy and the backwardness of its agriculture before 1914', in B. M. S. Campbell and M. Overton, *Land, labour and livestock: historical studies in European agricultural productivity* (Manchester, 1991), pp. 385-409.

Paradisi, M., 'Il commercio estero e la struttura industriale', in P. Ciocca and G. Toniolo, eds., *L'economia italiana nel periodo fascista* (Bologna, 1976), pp. 271-329.

Rey, G. M., ed., *I conti economici dell'Italia* (Rome, 1991).

Romer, P. M., 'Increasing returns and long-run growth', *J. Pol. Econ.*, 94 (1986), pp. 1002-37.

Rostow, W. W., *Theorists of economic growth from David Hume to the present: with a perspective on the next century* (New York, 1990).

Sereni, E., 'La politica agraria del regime fascista' in VVAA, *Fascismo e antifascismo, 1918-36* (Milan, 1962), pp. 266-86.

Sereni, E., *Capitalismo e mercato nazionale in Italia* (Rome, 1966).

Solow, R. M., 'Technical change and the aggregate production function', *Rev. of Econ. Stat.*, 39 (1958), pp. 312-20.

Solow, R. M. and Temin, P., 'Introduction: the inputs for growth', in P. Mathias and M. M. Postan, eds., *The Cambridge economic history of Europe*, VII, pt. I (Cambridge, 1978), pp. 1-27.

Tattara, G., 'La battaglia del grano', in G. Toniolo, ed., *L'economia italiana, 1861-1940* (Bari, 1978), pp. 337-80.

Toniolo, G., *L'economia dell'Italia fascista* (Bari, 1980).

Toniolo, G., *An economic history of liberal Italy* (London, 1990).

Vitali, O., *Aspetti dello sviluppo economico italiano alla luce della ricostruzione della popolazione attiva* (Rome, 1970).

Zamagni, V., 'The daily wages of Italian industrial workers in the Giolittian period, 1898-1913', *Rivista di Storia Economica*, International Issue I (1984), pp. 59-93.

Zamagni, V., 'La dinamica dei salari nel settore industriale', in P. Ciocca and G. Toniolo, eds., *L'economia italiana nel periodo fascista* (Bologna, 1976), pp. 329-52.

Zamagni, V., *Dalla periferia al centro: la seconda rinascita economica dell'Italia, 1861-1981* (Bologna, 1990).

[8]

A CENTURY OF CHANGE: TRENDS IN THE COMPOSITION OF THE ITALIAN LABOUR FORCE, 1881-1981

VERA ZAMAGNI (*)(1)

Abstract: Population and industrial censuses in Italy suffer from remarkable shortcomings when a diacronic view is superimposed upon them, because on the one hand they are not divided to respond to requirements of comparability through time and on the other hand the changes they depict are sometimes so radical to frustrate efforts aiming at an homogenization of data. The purpose of this paper is 1) to discuss the most important causes of discrepancy among the various censuses and to formulate ways of adjusting data to eliminate such causes and 2) to gain and comment important insights which can help to interprete the results.

Monthly surveys on employment and unemployment started in Italy only at the beginning of the 1950s, (2) while some partial data of this type are also available for the 1920s and 1930s with reference to the industrial sector.(3) A long view of the trend of sectoral employment in Italy, therefore, must inevitably rely on <u>population</u> and <u>industrial censuses.</u> Prior to any use of censuses is, however, a discussion of the concept of "labour force" employed by them. There is no doubt that, until very recently, the question asked by Italian <u>population</u> censuses was: "what is your profession?", the answer disregarding whether or not that profession was actually exercised, which implies that population censuses "labour force" included unemployed people. <u>Industrial</u> censuses, instead, required firms to assess their actual employment in the day the census was taken, which, as a matter of principle, excluded unemployed people. This is one reason why I consider both types of census in their own right useful to construct a long run view of sectoral (and regional) employment in Italy (other reasons will be mentioned later on).

Inevitably, censuses suffer from remarkable shortcomings when a diacronic view is superimposed upon them, because on the one hand they are not devided to respond to requirements of comparability through time and in the other hand the changes they depict are sometimes so radical to frustrate efforts aiming at an homogenization of data.

The purpose of this paper is first of all to discuss the most important causes of discrepancy among the various censuses administered in Italy and to formulate ways of adjusting data to eliminate such causes, whenever possible. In the process of so doing, important insights are gained which can help to interpret the results, the most relevant of which will be selectively commented upon in the last section of the paper.

(*) Address all communications to: Vera Zamagni, Universita Degli Studi di Bologna, Dipartimento di Scienze Economiche, Via Boldrini, 6, I-40126 Bologna, Italy.

I. Population Censuses

A good ground-work on Italian population censuses covering the period 1881-1961(4) was done some years ago by the statistician Ornello Vitali. Two earlier censuses of unified Italy (1861 and 1871) were not taken into account by him because they did not lend themselves to the kind of elaborations proposed. Although I think that something could be done at least with the 1871 census to link it with later ones, I have not considered it important to try it for this paper, so that I have bound myself in connecting the two most recent censuses (1971 and 1981) to Vitali's work and in discussing some unresolved questions.

The most crucial issue to be faced when one wants to compare censuses is the ceaseless alteration in the classification of occupations, mainly due to the different role - and perception of such a role - that certain occupations assume within society at different points in time. There are many examples. In the case of the foodstuffs and beverages industry, the allocation of manpower between production and retail trade activities has often lacked precision; sugar, as well as tobacco, have long been included in the chemical industries; repair shops of bicycles, motorcycles and cars were included in the engineering industry up to the last census, when they were moved to a category of their own; the production of plastic goods was placed originally in "other manufacturing" and only recently was moved to the chemical industry; the public sector, too, shows many incoherences together with the private personal services, as education and health have moved increasingly from the latter to the former.

One way of dealing with these issues is to assume one of the many classifications as the reference and to re-conduct the others, to the best of one's judgement, to that one. The choice should fall on an intermediate classification, to ease the problems of homogenization of data. In the case of Italy, I consider 1951 as the best choice (and this is in fact the date selected to reclassify industrial censuses in the next section). However, Vitali decided to take 1961 as the reference classification for population censuses and I have not tried to alter his data, given the almost coinciding nature of the 1951 and 1961 classification.

Other specific issues addressed by Vitali concerned a variety of causes of discrepancy: i) change in boundaries (particularly troublesome for the pre-1921 censuses, because of the need to use Austrian sources); ii) inclusion of working children aged less than 10 in the 1881 and 1901 censuses (to be eliminated); iii) incoherent treatment of military recruits; iv) imprecisions incurred in the 1921 census in certain regions; v) reintroduction in the 1936 census of the soldiers temporarily missing from the country as a result of the Ethiopian war.

Two major questions however, remain untouched by such manipulations of the data: the coherent evaluation of female labour in the countryside and of female labour in the domestic production of textiles (spinning and weaving) for the family. The first question had been addressed by the same statistician already mentioned in an earlier work of Vitali (5), where he was able not only to assess the existence of a substantial underevaluation of the female labour force in agriculture up to the recent censuses, especially in the sharecropping area, but also to propose estimates of it, that have increased the female and total activity rates. (6) Such estimates are embodied in Vitali's later work that has been used here. (7)

The second question, already raised in an earlier essay of mine (8) has instead remained untouched up to now. (9) The earlier Italian population censuses considered female domestic production of textiles for the family a form of "industrial" occupation, inflating as a result the figures referring to the "industrial" labour force. While many other forms of domestic industry were also included in population censuses, this particular one biases the data seriously because it was an activity aimed at self-consumption and not to the market. Moreover, as production of textiles was a fundamental industrial activity that in the XIX century witnessed great technological improvements, ambiguous data like the ones of Italian population censuses do not allow a correct interpretation of trends. It suffices to mention that, according to the original data, the textiles labour force declined from 1.337.108 units in 1881 to 783.253 units in 1901, to reach 673.968 units in 1911 (at the boundaries of the time, that did not change in this period). This in presence of a sizeable boom in the cotton and wool industries in the two decades after the introduction of the protective tariff in 1887, boom that is portrayed in table 1. Between 1876 and 1911, cotton spindles increased more than 5 times and cotton looms than 10 times; between 1876 and 1907, wool spindles almost doubled and wool looms increased by 50%. It is true that between 1876 and 1904, silk spindles halved and silk basins decreased by 25% – which are clear signs of the exhaustion of the silk wave in spite of the doubling of silk looms – but this could not cause by itself the enormous fall in the textile labour force revealed by population censuses.

The same data assembled in table 1 shows quite clearly, already in 1876, the geographical polarization of the textile industry: silk was concentrated in Lombardia, cotton in Lombardia-Piemonte and wool in Piemonte-Veneto. Almost no machinery existed in the South, with the exception of Campania.

To propose an adjustment of population censuses data referring to the textile industry, I have explored the relation between population and industrial censuses over a long period of time. The results are assembled in table 2. It can be seen that from the 1930s onwards there is a stable relationship of the type: industrial census/population census ≈ 90%, while in the period before the 1st World War the relationship did not exist. It must be mentioned that the two industrial surveys before 1911 were not censuses, but they were quite accurate in terms of including truly "industrial" units and their results agree with all the qualitative literature available on the development of the textile industry at the time. I have therefore decided to produce an estimate of the "industrial" labour force in textiles for 1881,1901 (10) and 1911 on the basis of the following procedure applied by regions: I have taken 110% of the industrial census figure, to allow for some "physiological" discrepancy, whenever this did not exceed the population census figure (in which case, the latter has been retained).

Some of the steps of this estimating procedure have been reported in table 3, together with a few elaborations of the results. It can first of all be noticed that the adjusted textile labour force rises from 346.912 units in 1881 to 441.018 units in 1901 and 535.592 units in 1911. The adjusted share of the labour force in manufacturing by regions (col. 10 and 12 of table 3) appears more in line with what is expected. Let me make an extreme example: Calabria was (and is) the poorest of all the Italian regions, with some tradition in the production of raw silk that in the second half of the XIX century was, however, dying away. (11) Notwithstanding, the population census of 1881 registered 224.002 employees in textiles, of which 99% were women. This raised the share of employment in manufacturing on total to an incredible 36.8%, much more than the 25.6% of Lombardia, and the activity rates to 62.9% (against an Italian average of 52.1%)! The adjusted figures bring the "industrial" employment in textiles down to only 3.519 units (at the boundaries of the time), which deflates the share of employment in manufacturing to 12.7% and the activity rate to 45.6%. We cannot conclude, however, that the procedure used in table 3 yields an implicit estimate of regional domestic employment in textiles, because it is very likely the case that different areas of the countries gave different answers to the questions of the population survey, as it is strongly suggested by an inspection of coll. 3 and 4 of table 3, and more women might have been spinning and weaving at home in Lombardia than the population census in fact revealed.

Particularly remarkable is that the adjusted figures cancel the previously inexplicable fall in industrial activity between the 1881 and 1901 censuses, a fall that was practically completely due to the behaviour of textiles and, being concentrated in the south, had induced some writers to talk of "deindustrialization" of the South. It is now possible to say that it was not a process of "deindustrialization" that took place but a gradual disappearance of domestic industry supplanted by foreign textiles at first and then by the textiles of northern industry. (12)

TABLE 1: DATA ON THE MACHINERY EMPLOYED IN THE ITALIAN TEXTILE INDUSTRY, 1876-1911

SILK

	1876 basins (1)	1876 number of spindles (2)	1876 looms (3)	1904 basins[d] (4)	1904 number of spindles (5)	1904 looms (6)
Piemonte/Val d'Aosta	17.427	357.038	828	7.533	154.822	947
Liguria	390	12.660	34	64	1.170	-
Lombardia	38.881	1.637.961	6.549	37.746	786.190	14.697
Veneto	14.729	54.067	74	11.048	10.880	105
Emilia-Romagna	1.717	3.422	53	912	-	-
Marche	2.776	6.264	-	2.426[a]	-	20[a]
Toscana	2.414	2.460	73	1.606	-	48
Umbria	368	-	-	...	-	-
Lazio	85	12	65	-	-	-
Campania	341	8.293	271			
Abruzzi Molise	56	-	-			
Puglia	-	-	-	1.474	1.250	345
Basilicata	-	-	-			
Calabria	3.071	150	16			
Sicilia	781	841	96	342	-	-
Sardegna	-	-	-	...	-	-
ITALIA	83.036	2.083.168	8.059	63.151	954.312	16.162

COTTON

	1876 number of spindles (7)	1876 looms (8)	1911 number of spindles (9)	1911 looms (10)
Piemonte/Val d'Aosta	310.174	3.790	1.253.400	30.400
Liguria	130.500	2.048	193.800	6.100
Lombardia	208.434	4.125	2.206.400	93.100
Veneto	37.040	513	551.600	6.350
Emilia-Romagna	350	170	23.300	1.000
Marche	-	-	28.600[a]	300[a]
Toscana	350	86	49.100	4.100
Umbria	...	-	...	...
Lazio	-	2	-	50
Campania	85.556	1.514		
Abruzzi Molise	-	-		
Puglia	-	40	26.300	4.150
Basilicata	-	-		
Calabria	-	-		
Sicilia	-	160	15.500	200
Sardegna	-	-	-	-
ITALIA	715.304	12.478	4.582.000	145.780

NOTES:
(a) including Umbria
(b) all these regions together had 17.355 spindles, or 3.5% of the total
(c) all these regions together had 1.602 looms, or 12.8% of the total
(d) 1913

Continued overleaf

TABLE 1: DATA ON THE MACHINERY EMPLOYED IN THE ITALIAN TEXTILES INDUSTRY, 1876-1911 (CONTIN.)

	WOOL					
	1876 number of		1907 number of		domestic looms in	
	spindles (11)	looms (12)	spindles (13)	looms (14)	1876 (15)	1903 (16)
Piemonte/Val d'Aosta	132.081	3.611	281.720	4.911	4.247	12.440
Liguria	11.084	123	(b)	(c)	4.468	2.471
Lombardia	7.239	551	62.602	1.474	19.690	19.974
Veneto	68.569	1.945	83.684	2.608	7.341	12.865
Emilia-Romagna	4.660	91	(b)	(c)	35.541	32.441
Marche	240	95	(b)	(c)	36.832	36.946
Toscana	26.460	836	44.435	1.872	12.629	25.184
Umbria	4.108	147	(b)	(c)	835	12.482
Lazio	4.458	141	(b)	(c)	2.378	3.063
Campania	24.890	786	(b)	(c)	16.937	14.864
Abruzzi Molise	240	8	(b)	(c)	6.454	31.864
Puglia	-	-	(b)	(c)	15.475	14.930
Basilicata	-	-	(b)	(c)	2.276	2.935
Calabria	420	10	(b)	(c)	11.353	16.446
Sicilia	-	-	(b)	(c)	39.173	36.952
Sardegna	-	9	(b)	(c)	13.909	19.366
ITALIA	284.449	8.353	489.796	12.467	229.538	295.223

NOTES:
(a) including Umbria
(b) all these regions together had 17.355 spindles, or 3.5% of the total
(c) all these regions together had 1.602 looms, or 12.8% of the total
(d) 1913

SOURCES: O. Vitali, op.cit.; V. Zamagni, Industrializzazione e squilibri regionali in Italia, Bologna, Il Mulino, 1978; M. Romani, Storia economica d'Italia nel secolo XIX, v. II, Milano, Giuffre, 1976; V. Ellena, "La statistica di alcune industrie italiane", in: Annali di Statistica, 2nd series, v. 13, Rome, 1880.

Table 2: DATA ON THE TEXTILE INDUSTRY 1876-1981 (at the boundaries of the time)

	Industrial Census (1)	Population Census (2)	(1)/(2) x 100 (3)
1876/1881	295.700	1.337.108	22
1903/1901	408.404	783.253	52
1911	508.076	673.968	75
1927/1931	645.358	704.674	92
1937-39/1936	604.556	662.440	91
1951	650.866	726.475	90
1961	598.565	665.075	90
1971	541.030	631.373	86
1981	493.470	561.268	88

SOURCE: Industrial and population censuses; for 1876, V. Ellena, op.cit; for 1903 MAIC, Riassunto delle notizie sulle condizioni industriali del Regno, Roma, 1906, part III.

Tables A.1 – A.6 of the Appendix report sectoral figures embodying all the described adjustments at the national level for the 10 population censuses between 1881 and 1981 (in 1891 no census was taken) and at the regional level for the 1881, 1911, 1936, 1961 and 1981 censuses. Out of the 10 sectors considered, perhaps the last two, named respectively "personal services" and "public administration" are the least coherent. The rationale of the grouping "public administration" should be that of including all the publicly supplied personal services. However, as the coverage of public services changed over time, the dilemma faced by anybody who tries to homogenize census figures is either to stick to the definition and include in PA entire sectors previously listed under personal services whenever they fall under public control or to assume the definition of PA existing at the reference census (in this case 1961) and keep in PA only those sectors that were public at such date. (13)

TABLE 3: ESTIMATION OF THE TEXTILES LABOUR FORCE IN 1881 AND 1911 AND AJUSTMENT OF POPULATION CENSUSES DATA.

	Industrial Employment in textiles		% Industrial Employment on population census employment		Textiles labour force at present boundaries (Vitalis Data)	
	1876	1911	1876/1881	1911/1911	1881	1911
	(1)	(2)	(3)	(4)	(5)	(6)
Piemonte	58.924	107.026	84.8	93.4	70.698	114.996
Liguria	6.421	11.765	32.7	67.8	20.107	17.763
Lombardia	152.205	268.282	70.0	99.0	222.448	270.981
Trentino	-	-	-	-	4.698	3.575
Veneto	27.421	51.646	67.6	90.1	35.381	43.526
Friuli	-	-	-	-	12.777	17.528
Emilia Romagna	6.285	8.905	11.9	47.1	58.875	20.071
Marche	6.323	8.846	19.0	68.1	34.583	13.023
Toscana	13.802	20.359	33.1	64.0	44.093	31.505
Umbria	1.731	2.207	33.3	35.9	4.792	5.920
Lazio	1.780	1.236	28.5	21.8	22.290	8.351
Campania	12.926	17.435	7.5	44.5	164.532	37.440
Abruzzi-Molise	302	966	0.4	9.7	80.633	9.331
Puglia	478	1.376	0.4	8.0	135.105	17.554
Basilicata	-	114	-	5.0	37.068	2.262
Calabria	3.199	2.814	1.4	5.6	222.240	50.475
Sicilia	3.848	2.807	2.0	16.8	194.510	16.775
Sardegna	55	22	0.8	1.0	7.605	2.312
ITALIA	295.700	505.806	22.1	75.0	1.372.435	683.388

SOURCES: (1) V. Ellena, op.cit.
(2) 1911 Industrial Census
All other data from O. Vitali, op.cit; for the procedure to estimate (7) and (8), see text.

42

TABLE 3: ESTIMATION OF THE TEXTILES LABOUR FORCE IN 1881 AND 1911 AND AJUSTMENT OF POPULATION CENSUSES DATA (CONTINUE).

	Estimated textiles labour force at present boundaries		% Labour force in manufacturing on total labour force			
	1881	1911	1881		1911	
			original	adjusted	original	adjusted
	(7)	(8)	(9)	(10)	(11)	(12)
Piemonte	65.961	114.996	16.6	16.3	21.7	21.7
Liguria	7.239	13.252	19.7	17.5	25.8	25.2
Lombardia	171.285	270.981	25.6	23.8	30.2	30.2
Trentino	3.758	3.218	12.2	11.9	11.1	11.0
Veneto	26.288	43.526	16.4	15.8	16.4	16.4
Friuli	10.222	15.775	17.7	17.2	20.1	19.8
Emilia Romagna	7.713	10.397	17.6	14.1	16.6	16.0
Marche	7.228	9.754	17.0	12.8	14.5	14.0
Toscana	16.050	22.180	20.2	18.3	22.6	22.1
Umbria	1.754	2.338	10.6	9.6	12.4	11.5
Lazio	6.999	2.004	14.9	13.0	15.0	14.3
Campania	13.656	18.308	25.8	17.1	19.3	18.2
Abruzzi-Molise	323	989	19.6	9.8	9.8	8.8
Puglia	540	1.545	26.1	12.6	15.0	13.6
Basilicata	-	124	21.0	10.0	9.3	8.5
Calabria	3.556	3.079	36.8	12.7	17.0	11.2
Sicilia	4.279	3.103	26.5	15.4	14.9	14.1
Sardegna	61	23	11.7	9.4	12.2	11.5
ITALIA	346.912	535.592	21.3	16.0	19.2	18.6

SOURCES: (1) V. Ellena, op.cit.
(2) 1911 Industrial Census
All other data from O. Vitali, op.cit; for the procedure to estimate (7) and (8), see text.

In the former case, we would have a coherent definition of PA, and personal services would become "private personal services", but rates of growth of the aggregates overtime would be greatly disturbed. In the latter case, both groupings would become hybrids whenever major changes in the degree of "publicness" of personal services would take place. Now, in the 10 censuses here considered, changes in the coverage of PA were minor up to the 1981 census, which should include in the PA of the health services passed under public control as a result of the creation of the National Health Service in 1978. According to the fixed framework of reclassification adopted in this work, such a change has not been recorded and health services are still embodied under the heading "personal services". A solution to these difficulties would of course be to combine the two groupings into one.

TABLE 3: ESTIMATION OF THE TEXTILES LABOUR FORCE IN 1881 AND 1911 AND AJUSTMENT OF POPULATION CENSUSES DATA (CONTINUE).

	Activity Rates			
	1881		1911	
	original	adjusted	original	adjusted
	(13)	(14)	(15)	(16)
Piemonte	57.6	57.5	58.6	58.6
Liguria	53.0	51.5	49.8	49.4
Lombardia	59.0	57.6	54.4	54.4
Trentino	57.6	57.4	54.7	54.7
Veneto	52.2	51.8	49.4	49.4
Friuli	56.7	56.3	48.6	48.5
Emilia Romagna	56.1	53.8	53.8	53.5
Marche	60.9	57.9	54.8	54.5
Toscana	55.8	54.5	54.3	54.0
Umbria	57.9	56.4	55.1	54.5
Lazio	55.4	54.2	48.2	47.8
Campania	54.3	58.6	48.1	47.4
Abruzzi-Molise	58.0	51.7	52.8	52.2
Puglia	53.9	45.5	44.1	43.4
Basilicata	57.8	50.8	51.9	51.5
Calabria	62.9	45.6	51.2	47.9
Sicilia	49.7	43.2	38.9	38.5
Sardegna	42.9	41.8	38.6	38.3
ITALIA	55.6	52.1	50.4	50.0

SOURCES: (1) V. Ellena, op.cit.
(2) 1911 Industrial Census
All other data from O. Vitali, op.cit; for the procedure to estimate (7) and (8), see text.

II. Industrial Censuses

Industrial censuses started in Italy in 1911, although, as we have seen in the previous paragraph, earlier surveys of industrial employment and horse power installed in certain branches of industry do exist. A close scrutiny of the 1911 census that I conducted some years ago (14) revealed quite clearly that much work had to be done before a diacronic use of industrial censuses could be made. This work of homogenization of data has been now accomplished by the writer (15) with the only exclusion of change in boundaries (both at the national and at the regional level)(16). It has, however, been possible to estimate that, at the national level, the areas added to Italy after the 1st World War accounted in 1927 (17) for 3.8% of total employment and the areas subtracted from Italy after the 2nd World War accounted in 1951 (18) for 1.7% of total employment. A rough adjustment of the nationally aggregate figures to present boundaries would therefore entail the addition of 2.1% employment to the 1911 figures and the subtraction of 1.7% employment from the two interwar censuses, 1927 and 1937-39. But sectoral and regional (19) adjustments are obviously much more complex.

44

Inter-censorial changes in classification of professions have been eliminated along the lines of what has been done for population censuses, the 1951 classification being taken as the reference with minor adjustments as already mentioned. A problem has arisen with the 1911 census, because of its requirement of surveying only units with two or more people active in it. This requirement, evidently introduced to avoid the inclusion of domestic work, was not retained in the subsequent censuses, which causes some degree of incomparability. An effort to deal with this problem has been made only at the national level, adding an estimate, produced on the basis of later censuses, of sectoral employment in units with only one worker (see table A.7, 1911 (b)).
As anticipated in the introduction, industrial censuses surveyed the actual labour force employed at the date of the survey (20) in industry and crafts, disregarding unemployment and all domestic employment even when production was not for self-consumption, but for clients, shops or firms. They give, therefore, a much coherent picture of the evolution of -"industrial"- employment proper than population censuses do - in spite of the adjustments that we have introduced in the preceding paragraph - at least up to 1981.
To better illustrate this statement and to gain some further insights on the nature of the population censuses (PCs) and of the industrial censuses (ICs), I propose some comparisons between the two. It must be mentioned in this connection that there are two cases in which ICs and PCs were not taken at the same time and both happen to be in the interwar years. Moreover, the second of the interwar ICs was streched over three years - 1937-39 - although most sectors were surveyed in 1938, (21) and aimed at recording employment at the date in which it was seasonally highest. The PC/IC comparability for the interwar-years is, therefore, imperfect, particularly for certain sectors, as we shall see later.
The first comparison proposed has been worked out in table 4. It can be seen that the coverage of PCs and ICs with relation to the manufacturing sector steadily converges, with only one case out of trend, namely the 1937-39 IC that, as expected, is therefore confirmed to have been a more inclusive census. It is also possible to show that the sectors responsible for most of the discrepancy between PCs and ICs are precisely those where domestic labour and underemployment were more widespread. This can be seen in table 5, where textiles, metallurgy (with the exception of 1911), engineering, chemicals, bricks-glass-cement production show a high degree of coincidence between PCs and ICs, while clothing, leather and furniture show a very low initial degree, though steadily increasing over time up to the 1981 census, when they converge towards a common pattern. (22) A special case is represented by construction, where the discrepancy between PC and IC was enormous in 1911, but remained very high also later. Beside the usual factors of "domestic" labour (here represented by single workers doing mainly apartments repairs) and of temporary

TABLE 4: SHARE OF ACTIVE POPULATION IN MANUFACTURING ACCORDING TO PC AND IC

	IC (1)	PC (2)	(IC/PC) x 100 (3)
1911	12.7	18.6	68
1927/1931	14.2	19.2	74
1937-39/1936	16.7	19.5	86
1951	17.3	22.3	78
1961	22.5	26.8	84
1971	28.1	32.2	87
1981	29.8	30.7	97

SOURCES: TABLES A.1 and A.7, with boundaries made compatible whenever needed.

45

TABLE 5: SELECTED SECTORIAL COMPARISONS BETWEEN ICs AND PCs (IC/PC x 100 at SELECTED DATES)

	1911	1937-39/1936	1951	1961	1981
Textiles	75	91	90	90	88
Metallurgy	52	77	81	83	97
Engineering	85	100	76	82	93
Chemicals	117 (a)	98	90	95 (a)	93 (a)
Bricks, glass, etc.	82	84	85	109 (a)	108 (a)
Clothing	29	50	55	62	96 (a)
Leather	46	60	65	77	101 (a)
Furniture	56	63	63	72	92
Construction	19	54	36	38	66

SOURCES: My elaborations from O. Vitali, Aspetti etc., cit., Table A.7 and the 1981 Population Census.

NOTE: (a) These incoherent figures are due to imprecisions in the inclusion of workers in the comparable categories.

employment, other causes of discrepancy could be a widespread "black economy" , both in the form of illegal subcontracting that permits firms to not declare part of their workers and in the form of small artisan units not declaring helpers.

As it was done for population censuses, I have collected in a table of the Appendix (table A.7) the results of all the elaborations performed on the seven industrial censuses of unified Italy at the national level, while four additional tables (A.8-A.11) report regional breakdowns for the 1911,1937/39, 1961 and 1981 censuses. The rigidity of the 1951 reference classification does not appear to have produced much dislocation in the sectoral aggregates except for one case. The production of plastic goods was placed in 1951 into "other manufacturing", being a small branch of uncertain affiliation. It then became firmly connected with the chemical industry and it increased substantially, up to becoming in 1981 about 2% of total employment in manufacturing. Its inclusion in other manufacturing inflates unduly this aggregate, while it restricts the chemical industry's share of employment.

III. A Century of Change: The Unbalanced Pattern of Modernization of Italy

The century elapsed between 1881 and 1981 did not witness a large increase in the Italian labour force (at constant boundaries), only 1/3 larger at the end of the period, with practically all the increase taking place in the first 50 years. This is due to a not too fast increase in population (it less than doubled), coupled with a decline in activity rates, slow at the beginning, rapid between 1936 and 1971, with some slight sign of inversion of the trend in 1981 (due to a higher women participation rate) (see table A.1).

The sectoral breakdown of this labour force, instead, changed dramatically, although much of this change appears concentrated in the second half of the period. Certainly the most impressive factor of the change has been the shrinking of the labour force in agriculture from 62-63% of the active population to 11%. This, accompanied by a greatly increased output of the sector, gives an impressive measure not only of the technological improvement, but of the great amount of underemployment that has always existed in Italian agriculture up to recent times. The downward trend of agricultural employment proceeded initially by two steps, one between 1901 and 1911, corresponding to the boom in manufacturing of the "Giolittian era", and the second between 1921 and 1931, implying an expansion in practically all other sectors (with the exception of manufacturing, that had to recover from a temporary regression in 1921). It later continued without interruptions at much faster rates than before 1931.

The expansion of manufacturing is not so easily depicted. According to population censuses, after the boom of the first decade of the XXth century and the regression in 1921, there appears to be another jump forward between 1936 and 1951, followed by an uninterrupted increase up to 1971 and then by a fall from 32.2% to 30.7% of the labour force. Industrial censuses, however (table A.7), tell that the increase in industrial employment proper has been continuous from around 13% of the active population in 1911 to 30% in 1981, indicating that the factors responsible for disturbing such a steadily upward trend in the population censuses are to be identified in domestic labour, unemployment and underemployment rather than in more structural causes. The rate of expansion of manufacturing employment, in any case, appears to have been faster between 1951 and 1971 also in the industrial censuses.
Sticking to the industrial censuses to analyse the composition of manufacturing employment, we can first of all observe that textiles remained the most important branch of industry only up to the 1929 crisis, while engineering, the second branch up to then, reached 25% of manufacturing employment already in 1938 and then continued to grow up to as much as 40% in 1981. If we add the share of employment in metallurgy, that more than doubled from 1.9% to 4.3% we have in 1981 almost half of the manufacturing labour force engaged in metal and machinery making. The other branch of modern industry that we expect to have grown during this period, namely chemicals, did in fact grow, but starting from a very low level of 2.6%. As I have already mentioned, it is not correct to conclude that its growth stopped in 1961, given the inclusion of plastic goods in other manufacturing, but certainly its most rapid period of growth is to be located between 1927 and 1961, when its share in manufacturing employment more than doubled. The wellknown weakness of the branch in Italy compared with the other industrial activities is revealed also by these generally low employment figures. On the other hand, the share of employment in traditional industries has declined, in a particularly drastic way in the food and beverages branch (from 14% to 6.5%). It might be noticed, however, that the decline in clothing has not been very large, because of the conversion of such sector in the last two decades to high quality production for the internal and foreign markets.
Coming back to population censuses and disregarding mining, never important in Italy, we can see that public utilities increased steadily, while construction shows a fall between 1881 and 1901, due to a serious crisis of the sector that produced much dislocation in the banking sector, then started growing, at a particularly fast rate between 1936 and 1961, to end up with a fall in the last decade. Here again if one would use the figures of the industrial census, the picture would be slightly different: a substantial increase in the sector is located in the ICs between 1927 and 1937/39 and then in the 1950s, which makes more sense, while no fall is revealed in the 1970s. It might be mentioned in this connection that in the last decade there was actually a fall in construction activity, which certainly caused a fall in the total labour force available, but not in that part of the labour force belonging to the more established and larger firms reckoned in industrial censuses, that on the contrary rose 27% (23).

Some comments, finally, on the service sector. Taken as a whole, the service sector's share of the labour force remained practically steady around 17–18% up to 1921, increasing at a rather slow pace up to 24.7% in 1951 and then at a steadily faster pace up to 47.4% – almost half of the labour force – 1981. Breaking the sector down in subsectors, one can see that, while transportation and banking employment shows a rather continuous growth throughout the century considered here, (24) the rise of the employment share of commerce–tourism and public administration is largely confined to the post-World War II period, which is marked by an explosion of private consumption previously very compressed, and by the growth of the government sector due to the diffusion of education (which is largely public in Italy), the multiplication of civil servants (not beyond European levels, however) and the enlargement of the welfare services. The rather peculiar behaviour of the remaining subsector of services, namely personal services, fluctuating around 6-7% up to 1971 and then increasing rapidly, is not easily explained at this level of aggregation of the data, because the nature of personal services has profoundly changed and old services, like those offered by servants, have been substituted by other kinds of services - laundry, hairdressing, beauty shops - up to the recent boom in leisure services coupled with the rise of new services to firms (software, engineering projects, modelling, advertising, and the like) (25).

The previous broad overview of the changes in the composition of the Italian labour force over the span of the last 100 years would suggest that very little modernization took place before the 1930s. This conclusion, however, has to be considered too hasty for a country like Italy, where the geographical polarization of industry in certain areas has been a longstanding feature of economic growth. We must turn, therefore, to a regional analysis of PCs and ICs. 1881 is a good starting year to observe changes in the structure of employment at the regional level too (see table A.2). In fact, the regional differentiation existing at that date is still embryonic: Lombardia stands out already as having more industrial labour force than the average, Liguria more employment in commerce and transport, Lazio more civil servants (Rome), while the little mining that there existed is confined to Sicilia (sulphur), Sardegna (zinc, lead) and Toscana (marble, some iron ore in Elba island). Agricultural employment is prevailing everywhere: certain regions show as much as 3/4 of the labour force in agriculture (Umbria, Abruzzi-Molise, Basilicata)!

The picture in 1911 (table A.3) reveals quite clearly what has happened meanwhile: the North-West area of the country (see chart) has already become the "industrial triangle". Another region, namely Toscana, appears to have at that date a higher than average share of employment in industry, but half of it was in domestic industry (especially straw processing for hats), while only 1/4 of the employment in manufacturing of the industrial triangle is not recorded in the IC (see table A.8), and can therefore be considered domestic (or precarious).

The regional breakdown of the 1936 population census (table A.4), together with the regional breakdown of the 1937-39 industrial census (table A.9) confirm that no regional change took place in the interwar years, with the industrial triangle firmly entrenched in its leading position and the rest of the country lagging behind, although certain regions reveal better capabilities than other regions in diversifying from agriculture.

It is only with the 1961 census (see table A.5 and A.10) that something new can be registered. While the industrial triangle appears strengthened, with Liguria becoming more and more specialized in commerce-tourism and transport, the industrial take-off of a large part of the North-East-Centre area (namely Friuli, Veneto, Emilia-Romagna, Toscana) is an accomplished fact. No industrial spurt is revealed in the South where, with the exception of Campania, the only region in the South that has traditionally maintained some industry (cfr. also the preceding censuses), the share of manufacturing labour force remains very low. However, some diversification of the southern regions from agriculture can be observed.

Some interesting remarks are finally called forth by the 1981 censuses (cfr. tables A.6 and A.11). Industry has become stronger in the North-East-Centre area, not only in the regions already industrialized by 1961, but also in Marche and Umbria. The only exceptions remain Trentino, where, however, there has been a boom of tourism, and Lazio, where the predominance of services (especially commerce and tourism, personal services and public administration) is overwhelming. The phenomenon of the industrialization of the North-East-Centre area has by 1981 already produced a vast amount of studies where the traditional North-South contrast has been modified into a more complex picture of "three Italies". (26) The first - the industrial triangle - of long-standing industrialization based on heavy industry and textiles, with a predominantly tayloristc organization of the labour force; the second - the North-East-Centre - of more recent industrialization, based on light industry and machine-tool, with a decentralized and flexible organization of labour (27); and the third - the South - still non-industrial, in spite of the large public efforts to improve its lot.

The 1981 censuses have, however, made necessary a qualification of these conclusions with reference to the South. Out of the seven southern regions, two - Abruzzi and Puglia - show, in fact, clear signs of having progressed remarkably towards industrialization. There has been recently much interest in this "Adriatic way" to industrialization (28) contrasted with the stagnation of the southern regions bordering on the Tirrenian sea and much of it has been explained with the absence along the Adriatic coast of illegal organizations such as the Mafia. (29) It is in any case an established fact that the Italian South is no longer a compactly backward area: the combined effects of emigration, government intervention, expansion of tourism, industrial growth and the uneven presence of illegal organizations have definitely broken the "southern question" into several differently shaped "questions".
Leaving aside for lack of space the more detailed analysis that can be made of the regional structure on the basis of tables A.8-A.11, some general conclusions can now be offered. As we have seen, the first wave of industrialization was experienced by Italy already before World War I in the industrial triangle, but it involved such a limited area of the country that national figures were hardly affected.Only in the 1930s the effects of such an industrialization started spreading to some other areas of the country, where pre-conditions were developed for an industrial spurt that actually took place after World War II, when markets - domestic and foreign - became more absorptive. The industrialization of the North-East-Centre in the 1950s and 1960s has to be accounted, therefore, as the second wave of industrialization in Italy. But it was only by then that Italy became an "industrial" country, because only by then a substantial area of the country was included in the industrial base and national figures were clearly affected. Can we also talk of a third wave of industrialization now under way in the South? It is too early to come to this conclusion, but movements in such a direction have become apparent at least in certain areas of the south.

What is certainly true is that the process of modernization of Italy has proceeded by successive waves over such a long stretch of time that the century considered in this work does not encompass it all. To embody new areas into the modern-industrial complex has not been an easy task, but neither has it been an impossible one. Regional mobility has proved to be possible, although certain regions, even after a century, do not yet show good preconditions to make such a mobility an actuality. If one would enquire about the main causes for this profoundly regional pattern of industrial growth in Italy, it would be necessary to resort to the medieval experience of communs and the subsequent great diversification of civilizations in the different areas of the country to identify the substratum responsible for the highly decentralized and unbalanced pattern of growth observed.

NOTES

(1) A preliminary version of this paper was presented at the workshop on the "History of the sectoral employment in 20th century Europe", Berlin, Freie Universität, 12-13 May, 1986. I thank all the participants, and particularly Prof. Kaelble, for their useful comments. The computing assistance by Federico Furlani and Marco Dazzi is gratefully acknowledged.

49

(2) For sources and comments, see V. Valli, L'economia e la politica economica Italiana dal 1945 ad oggi, Etas Libri, Milano, 1982.

(3) Cfr. Bollettino del Lavoro e della previdenza sociale for the 1920s and Bollettino di notizie economiche, 1928–1939.

(4) O. Vitali, Aspetti dello sviluppo economico italiano alla luce della ricostruzione della popolazione, Roma, Tip. Failli, 1970. Demographers have not generally been greatly interested in the employment aspect; see e.g. M. Livi Bacci, "I fattori demografici dello sviluppo economico", in G. Fua (ed.), Lo sviluppo economico in Italia, v. II, Milano, Franco Angeli, 1969.

(5) O. Vitali, La popolazione attiva in agricoltura attraverso i censimenti italiani, Roma, Tip. Failli, 1968.

(6) Because the number of "housewives" belonging to the non-active population has been reduced correspondingly.

(7) No adjustment of female labour in agriculture has been done for the 1971 and 1981 censuses, because the inaccuracy of the data had disappeared by then.

(8) V. Zamagni, "Istruzione e sviluppo economico. Il caso italiano 1861–1913", in G. Toniolo (ed.), L'economia italiana 1861–1940, Bari, Laterza, 1978. In this essay I proposed to disregard all female employment in textiles, which was obviously a very rough adjustment, lacking a better way of removing the distortion.

(9) O. Vitali refused to consider the question relevant, probably because his interests were narrowly demographical.

(10) The results for 1901 have only been reported in this essay at the national level.

(11) A sign of this tradition might be seen also in the high share of domestic looms registered in Calabria in both the 1876 and 1903 surveys (see coll. 15 and 16 of table 1).

(12) As I have argued in my article "Cuestión meridional o cuestión nacional? Algunas consideraciones sobre el desequilibrio regional en Italia con especial referencia a los anos 1861–1950", in Revista de Historia Economica, 1987, n.1, p. 20.

(13) This is actually the solution adopted here for coherence with the rest of the work. Public administration included, in 1961, beside central and local civil service, army and police, public education and public bodies for workers insurance, sports and leisure activities.

(14) See V. Zamagni, Industrializzazione etc., cit.

(15) With the help of a collaborator, who has recently published some of the results of the work: cfr. R. Chiaventi, " I censimenti industriali italiani 1911–1951: procedimenti di standardizzazione", in Rivista di storia economica, 1987, no.1.

(16) The exclusion is regrettably due to shortage of funds.

(17) First industrial census after World War I.

(18) First industrial census after World War II.

50

(19) Regional changes were substantial for Lazio and Campania, and of some importance for Emilia-Romagna, Toscana, Umbria and Abruzzi-Molise between 1921 and 1931 and for Veneto after World War II, because it surrendered the province of Udine to Friuli-Venezia Giulia, that in turn lost much of its territory to Yugoslavia as a result of war evénts. National changes (after 1881) took place once as a result of World War I (acquisition of Trentino-Alto Adige and Friuli-Venezia Giulia) and a second time after World War II (loss of part of Friuli-Venezia Giulia, as already mentioned).

(20) An accurate study has been made on the possible factors of distortion due to the changing dates of the censuses, but it has been concluded that the seasonal choice made was always quite wise and produced only a marginal impact on the quality of the data collected. The only exception is in the 1937/39 census.

(21) This rather peculiar choice was justified with the decision of devoting great care to the survey operations in presence of a scarcity of means on the part of the statistical office of the time. In fact, this is the first Italian industrial census that collected data not only on employment and horse power, but on production, value added and wages as well, and was very accurate in recording small businesses (domestic employment was, however, still excluded).

(22) The foodstuffs and beverages sector could not be compared because of the special treatment reserved by Vitali to such a sector, that he slimmed down considerably, transporting much of its employment into retail trade. It can, however, be noticed, observing the sequence of employment in industrial censuses alone, that the procedure used in the 1937-39 census revealed much more seasonal employment than usual, including at least some 130.000 extra workers.

(23) More accurate fiscal controls might also have increased the number of building firms compelled to legalize their status and therefore to declare their "true" employment levels.

(24) This steady growth accompanies the growth in manufacturing and construction.

(25) The appearance of these new types of services to firms makes the heading "personal services" not altogether correct.

(26) This has become a common expression since the publication of the book by A. Bagnasco, Tre Italie. La problematica territoriale dello sviluppo italiano, Bologna, Il Mulino, 1977.

(27) For an interesting description and interpretation of the growth of the "second" Italy, see G. Fuà and C. Zacchia (eds.), Industrializzazione senza fratture, Bologna, Il Mulino, 1987.

(28) See among the many publications, G. Lizzeri (ed.), Mezzogiorno possibile. Dati per un altro sviluppo, Milan, F. Angeli, 1983; E. Pontarollo, Tendenze della nuova imprenditoria nel Mezzogiorno degli anni '70, Milan, F. Angeli, 1981; M. D'Antonio, , Il Mezzogiorno degli anni '80: dallo sviluppo imitativo allo sviluppo autocentrato, Milan, F. Angeli, 1985. It is noticeable that Abruzzi and Puglia have overcome in terms of share of manufacturing employment the traditionally more industrial Campania.

(29) On the negative impact upon the local economy of the presence of mafia, see P. Arlachi, La mafia imprenditrice. L'etica mafiosa e lo spirito del capitalismo, Bologna, Il Mulino, 1983.

51

APPENDIX

The tables appearing in this appendix are my elaborations based on the following sources:

R. **CHIAVENTI** (1987). "I censimenti industriali italiani: 1911 – 1951: procedimenti di standardizzazione", Rivista di storia economica, n.1.
O. **VITALI** (1970), Aspetti dello sviluppo economico italiano alla luce della ricostruzione della popolazione attiva, Roma, Tip. Failli.
11 Censimento generale della popolazione, 24 ottobre 1971, Roma, 1977.
12 Censimento generale della popolazione, 25 ottobre 1981, Roma, 1985.
Censimento degli opifici e delle imprese industriali al 10 giugno 1911, Roma 1913-1914.
Censimento degli esercizi industriali e commerciali al 15 ottobre 1927, Roma 1932.
Censimento industriale e commerciale 1937-40, Roma 1932.
Censimento generale dell'industria e del commercio, 15 nov. 1951 Roma.
Censimento generale dell'industria e del commercio, 16 ottobre 1961, Roma 1965.
Censimento generale dell'industria e del commercio, 25 ottobre 1971, Roma 1975.
Censimento generale dell'industria, del commercio, dei servizi e dell'artigianato, 26 ottobre 1981, Roma 1985.

CONVERSION TABLE FOR POPULATION CENSUSES

The tables of conversion relative to the 1881-1951 censuses appear in O. Viteli, Aspetti etc., cit., pp. 221-235.

1971 Census

1961 classification	1971 classification
1	1
2	2
3	3 + 9.05.05 + 6.04.05
4	4
5	5 + 7.01.08
6	6 + 9.02.05 – (6.02.43, 6.04.05, 6.05.03, 6.05.04)
7	7 + 6.05.03 + 6.05.04 – 7.01.08
8	8
9	9 + 6.02.43 – (9.02.05, 9.04.01, 9.04.03, 9.05.05)
10	10 + 9.04.01 + 9.04.03

1981 Census

1961 classification	1981 classification
1	0 + 841
2	11 + 13 + 21 + 23
3	3 + 4 + 140.1 + 140.2 + 12 + 22 + 24 + 25 + 26 + 6b + 773.2 + 837.2 + 983.1 – 348.1
4	5 + 348.1
5	140.3 + 150 + 16 + 17 + 724
6	6 + 773.1 + 979.1 + 8.42 + 8.43 + 8.46 + 8.47 – (666, 643, 6b)

52

7	7 + 666 + 838.2 + 844 + 845 − (773.1, 773.2, 724)
8	8 − (833, 834, 835, 836, 837.1, 837.2, 838.1, 838.2, 839, 841, 842, 843, 844, 845, 846, 847)
9	643 + 833 + 834 + 835 + 836 + 837.1 + 838.1 + 839.9 − (938.1, 979.1 and the content of category 10)
10	963.1 + 967 + 961.1 + 962.1 + 940.1 + 990 + 977.1 + 932.1 + 932.1 + 932.2 + 932.3 + 933.1 + 934.1 + 91

CONVERSION TABLE FOR INDUSTRIAL CENSUSES

<u>1911 census</u>

1951 classification	1911 classification
3.01	3.3 + 3.4 + 3.5 + 3.001 + 3.002 + 3.003 + 7.12 + 7.14 + 7.15 + 7.16 + 7.17 − 3.31
3.02	7.112
3.03 + 3.05.07 + 3.05.08 + 3.05.09 + 3.05.10	3.6 − (3.61, 3.68, 3.69)
3.04	3.61 + 00.41 + 6 − (6.71, 6.85, 6.9, 6.00.2)
3.05 − (3.05.07, 3.05.08, 3.05.09, 3.05.10)	3.68 + 3.8 + 6.85 + 6.9 + 6.002 + 00.42 − (3.81, 3.82, 3.84, 3.85, 3.86, 3.87)
3.06	3.1 + 3.2 + 00.31 − 3.18
3.07	3.7
3.08 + 3.09	8.1 + 00.6 − 00.62
3.10	4.1 + 4.2
3.11 + 3.15.01 + 3.15.02	4 − (4.1, 4.2, 4.56)
3.12	5.1
3.13	6.71 + 7 + 00.5 − (7.12, 7.14, 7.15, 7.16, 7.17, 7.111, 7.112)
3.14	7.111
3.15 − (3.15.01, 3.15.02)	3.18 + 3.69 + 3.81 + 3.82 +ü 3.84 + 3.85 + 3.86 + 3.87 + 4.56
2	2 + 00.1 + 00.2
4	5 + 00.7 − 5.1
5	8.2 + 00.62

<u>1924 census</u>

1951 classification	1927 classification
.	V + XVI.15 − (V.1, V.26)
.	V.26
idem	VI + XIV.5 + XIV.6 − (VI.5, VI.6, VI.8, VI.9, VI.10, VI.11, VI.12, VI.13, VI.14, VI.15)
.	XIII + VI.5 + VI.6
.	XIV + VI.10 − (XIV.5, XIV.6, XIV.15)
.	IV − IV.8
.	VII
.	VIII + XXXVI

53

.	IX – (IX.4, IX.5, IX.7, IX.8)
.	X + IX.4 + IX.5 + IX.7 + IX.8 + XVII.4 – (X.12, X.33)
idem	XI
.	XVI – (XVI.15, XVI.23)
.	XVI.23
.	XIX + IV.8 + VI.8 + VI.9 + VI.11 + VI.12 + VI.13 + VI.14 + VI.15 + X.12 + X.33
.	III
.	XII
.	XVII – XVII.4

<u>1937 – 39 census</u>

1951 classification	1937 – 39 classification
.	IV + IX.175 – (IV.31, IV.32, IV.33)
.	XVI.273 + 273 bis
.	XII
.	XIII + XIV.255 + XVI.262 – XIII.223
.	XIV – (XIV.252, XIV.255)
idem	III
.	X
.	XI + XV + XVIII.284 + XVIII.285 + XVIII.286
.	V – V.76
.	VI + V.76 + XVI.265 + XVI.274
.	VII
.	IX + XIII.223 – IX.175
.	XVI.266 + XVI.269
.	XVI – (XVI.262, XVI.265, XVI.266, XVI.269, XVI.273, XVI.273 bis, XVI.274)
.	II
.	VIII
.	XVII

<u>1961 census</u>

1951 classification	1961 classification
.	3.01
.	3.02
.	3.07 + 3.08 + 3.06.07
.	3.03 + 3.04 + 3.05
.	3.06 + 3.06.07
idem	3.09 + 3.10
.	3.22
.	3.23 + 3.24
.	3.11
.	3.12 + 3.13 + 3.14 + 3.15 + 3.16 + 3.26.01 + 3.26.02
.	3.17
.	3.18 + 3.19 + 3.21
.	3.20
.	3.25 + 3.26 – (3.26.01, 3.26.02)

	54
.	2
.	4
.	5

<u>1971 census</u>

1951 classification	1971 classification
.	3.01 + 3.13.11 + 6.04.05 – 3.01.26
.	3.02
.	3.05 + 3.06 + 3.04.10 + 3.12.13
.	3.03
.	3.04 – 3.04.10
.	3.07 + 3.08
idem	3.16
.	3.17 + 3.18 + 9.05.05
.	3.09
.	3.10 + 3.11 + 3.20.04 – 3.10.46
.	3.12 – 3.12.13
.	3.13 + 3.15 – (3.13.11, 3.13.26)
.	3.14
.	3.19 + 3.20 + 3.13.26 + 3.10.46 – 3.20.04
.	2 + 3.01.26
.	4
.	5

<u>1981 census</u>

1951 classification	1981 classification
.	41 + 42 + 773.2 – (428.1, 429)
.	429
.	44 + 451 + 452 + 672 + 244
.	43
.	45 + 467.3 – (451, 452)
.	46 – 467.3
idem	471 + 472
.	473 + 474 + 493 + 345.2 + 983.1 + 837.2
.	22 + 312
.	3 + 491.1 + 6b – (312, 345.2, 348, 373.1, 672, 673)
.	24 + 491.2 – 244
.	12 + 14 + 25 + 26 – 140.3
.	481 + 482
.	483 + 49 + 373.1 – (491, 493)
.	11 + 13 + 21 + 23 + 428.1 – (234, 235, 236, 237, 238)
.	5 + 348.1 + 348.2
.	1b + 140.3 + 150

55

CHART OF THE ITALIAN REGIONS

1-2-3	Industrial Triangle - North West
1-2-3-4-5-6-7	North
4-5-6-7	North-East
8-9-10-11	Centre
12-13-14-15-16-17-18	South

1.	Piemonte - Val d'Aosta	10.	Umbria
2.	Liguria	11.	Lazio
3.	Lombardia	12.	Campania
4.	Trentino - Alto Adige	13.	Abruzzi-Molise
5.	Veneto	14.	Puglia
6.	Friuli - Venezia Guilia	15.	Basilicata
7.	Emilia-Romagna	16.	Calabria
8.	Marche	17.	Sicilia
9.	Toscana	18.	Sardegna

56

TABLE A.1: POPULATION CENSUSES 1881-1981 (AT PRESENT BOUNDARIES, 1961 CLASSIFICATION)

I. ABSOLUTE FIGURES

	1881	1901	1911	1921	1931
1. Agriculture	9.432.597	10.680.863	10.538.313	11.243.639	10.449.374
2. Mining	66.566	112.987	124.294	104.868	117.155
3. Manufacturing	2.443.470(a)	2.665.214(a)	3.309.253(a)	3.258.852	3.730.804
4. Construction	613.257	557.640	729.201	887.645	1.025.827
5. Electricity, gaz, water	1.483	25.041	36.470	43.474	66.297
6. Commerce and tourism	899.749	966.459	993.838	1.121.878	1.334.996
7. Transports, Communications	383.161	496.668	600.580	730.156	743.859
8. Credit, Insurance	22.599	30.219	55.524	71.580	109.149
9. Personal Services	1.088.306	1.062.986	1.085.186	1.102.559	1.221.309
10. Public Administration	289.144	333.237	366.292	472.337	626.018
11. Total active Population	15.240.332(a)	16.951.314(a)	17.838.951(a)	19.026.961	19.424.788
12. % Total Population	52.1(a)	50.8(a)	50.0(a)	50.9	47.8

	1936	1951	1961	1971	1981
1. Agriculture	10.502.913	8.980.583	6.008.808	3.234.710	2.241.318
2. Mining	126.552	179.508	145.062	83.248	81.684
3. Manufacturing	3.926.449	4.529.549	5.354.505	6.057.161	6.222.334
4. Construction	1.042.646	1.472.749	2.345.468	2.063.314	1.913.305
5. Electricity, gaz, water	70.270	96.789	118.420	155.453	190.660
6. Commerce and tourism	1.622.783	1.658.638	2.022.528	2.497.257	3.071.774
7. Transports, Communications	708.012	789.578	966.630	1.004.148	1.250.079
8. Credit, Insurance	97.904	176.247	218.351	283.678	430.720
9. Personal Services	1.421.514	1.200.825	1.483.874	1.651.067	2.219.073
10. Public Administration	688.858	1.194.314	1.352.033	1.802.884	2.630.290
11. Total active Population	20.207.901	20.278.780	20.015.679	18.832.920	20.251.237
12. % Total Population	47.8	42.7	39.5	35.5	36.0

(a) adjusted (see text)

TABLE A.1: POPULATION CENSUSES 1881-1981 (AT PRESENT BOUNDARIES, 1961 CLASSIFICATION)

II. PERCENTAGE COMPOSITION

	1881	1901	1911	1921	1931
1. Agriculture	61.8	63.0	59.1	59.1	53.8
2. Mining	0.4	0.7	0.7	0.6	0.6
3. Manufacturing	16.0	15.7	18.6	17.1	19.2
4. Construction	4.0	3.4	4.1	4.6	5.3
5. Electricity, Gaz, Water	0.1	0.1	0.2	0.2	0.3
6. Commerce and Tourism	5.9	5.7	5.6	5.9	6.9
7. Transports, Communications	2.5	2.9	3.4	3.8	3.8
8. Credit, Insurance	0.2	0.2	0.3	0.4	0.6
9. Personal Services	7.2	6.3	6.0	5.8	6.3
10. Public Administration	1.9	2.0	2.0	2.5	3.2
11. Total active population	100.0	100.0	100.0	100.0	100.0

	1936	1951	1961	1971	1981
1. Agriculture	52.0	44.3	30.0	17.2	11.1
2. Mining	0.6	0.9	0.7	0.4	0.4
3. Manufacturing	19.5	22.3	26.8	32.2	30.7
4. Construction	5.2	7.3	11.7	11.0	9.5
5. Electricity, Gaz, Water	0.3	0.5	0.6	0.8	0.9
6. Commerce and Tourism	8.0	8.2	10.1	13.3	15.2
7. Transports, Communications	3.5	3.9	4.8	5.3	6.2
8. Credit, Insurance	0.5	0.9	1.1	1.5	2.1
9. Personal Services	7.0	5.9	7.4	8.8	10.9
10. Public Administration	3.4	5.8	6.8	9.6	13.0
11. Total active population	100.0	100.0	100.0	100.0	100.0

TABLE A.2: 1881 POPULATION CENSUS BY REGIONS (AT PRESENT BOUNDARIES, 1961 CLASSIFICATION).

I. ABSOLUTE FIGURES

	Agricul-ture (1)	Mining (2)	Manufac-turing (a) (3)	Construc-tion (4)	Electricity Gaz, Water (5)	Commerce and Tou-rism (6)	Transports Communications (7)
1. Piemonte-Val d'Aosta	1.156.204	614	287.479	57.182	343	98.082	26.196
2. Liguria	241.361	989	80.928	20.605	75	39.234	26.030
3. Lombardia	1.181.989	2.491	503.687	80.809	203	141.862	36.300
4. Trentino Alto Adige	220.334	399	37.775	11.565	0	15.095	4.044
5. Veneto	762.722	1.822	189.918	28.945	128	82.621	28.326
6. Friuli Venezia Giulia	254.982	699	74.112	20.564	2	25.872	10.542
7. Emilia-Romagna	772.501	1.742	170.280	54.797	84	65.376	24.659
8. Marche	379.866	1.111	69.838	20.391	15	19.602	8.949
9. Toscana	693.004	9.157	215.192	47.708	60	72.006	33.272
10. Umbria	205.709	35	26.543	8.912	3	7.346	3.442
11. Lazio	422.922	848	90.002	27.456	178	41.503	20.150
12. Campania	688.697	2.441	219.298	64.306	114	109.785	49.047
13. Abruzzi-Molise	500.623	124	64.093	28.231	17	16.861	6.926
14. Puglia	477.985	4.169	92.422	31.171	18	38.180	26.453
15. Basilicata	204.293	99	26.734	5.769	1	7.397	4.622
16. Calabria	383.953	750	72.840	28.638	8	20.632	18.121
17. Sicilia	709.903	30.309	195.456	57.396	222	85.906	48.419
18. Sardegna	175.539	8.767	26.873	18.812	12	12.449	7.663

(a) adjusted see text

TABLE A.2: 1881 POPULATION CENSUS BY REGIONS (AT PRESENT BOUNDARIES, 1961 CLASSIFICATION).

I. ABSOLUTE FIGURES

	Credit Insurance (8)	Personal Services (9)	Public administration (10)	Total labour force (a) (11)	Total Population (12)
1. Piemonte-Val D'Aosta	2.470	102.207	29.470	1.760.247	3.062.239
2. Liguria	1.133	41.222	11.781	463.358	898.887
3. Lombardia	4.005	127.424	33.664	2.112.434	3.665.806
4. Trentino Alto Adige	44	20.807	6.503	316.576	551.452
5. Veneto	1.492	84.239	21.207	1.201.420	2.318.444
6. Friuli Venezia Giulia	714	34.425	8.102	430.014	763.123
7. Emilia-Romagna	1.680	91.894	22.319	1.205.332	2.223.976
8. Marche	419	35.460	9.015	544.666	940.023
9. Toscana	1.996	81.890	20.684	1.174.969	2.156.635
10. Umbria	199	19.055	4.254	275.498	488.204
11. Lazio	1.581	63.773	21.513	689.926	1.272.151
12. Campania	3.224	113.199	31.612	1.281.723	2.637.469
13. Abruzzi-Molise	195	30.864	9.279	657.213	1.272.295
14. Puglia	611	49.720	13.648	734.377	1.612.826
15. Basilicata	81	14.721	3.258	266.975	525.908
16. Calabria	228	39.439	9.618	574.227	1.260.294
17. Sicilia	2.204	108.896	27.265	1.265.916	2.929.970
18. Sardegna	323	29.071	5.952	285.461	682.929

(a) adjusted (see text)

TABLE A.2: 1881 POPULATION CENSUS BY REGIONS (AT PRESENT BOUNDARIES, 1961 CLASSIFICATION).

II. PERCENTAGE COMPOSITION

	Agriculture (1)	Mining (2)	Manufacturing (a) (3)	Construction (4)	Electricity Gaz, Water (5)	Commerce, Tourism (6)	Transports, Communications (7)
1. Piemonte-Val D'Aosta	65.8	...	16.3	3.2	...	5.6	1.5
2. Liguria	52.2	0.2	17.5	4.4	...	8.5	5.6
3. Lombardia	56.0	0.1	23.8	3.8	...	6.7	1.7
4. Trentino Alto Adige	69.6	0.1	11.9	3.7	...	4.8	1.3
5. Veneto	63.5	0.2	15.8	2.4	...	6.9	2.4
6. Friuli Venezia Giulia	59.3	0.2	17.2	4.8	...	6.0	2.5
7. Emilia-Romagna	64.2	0.1	14.2	4.5	...	5.4	2.0
8. Marche	69.8	0.2	12.8	3.7	...	3.6	1.6
9. Toscana	59.0	0.8	18.2	4.1	...	6.1	2.8
10. Umbria	74.7	...	9.6	3.2	...	2.8	1.2
11. Lazio	61.3	0.1	13.0	4.1	...	6.1	2.9
12. Campania	53.7	0.2	17.1	5.0	...	8.6	3.8
13. Abruzzi-Molise	76.2	...	9.8	4.3	...	2.6	1.0
14. Puglia	65.1	0.6	12.6	4.2	...	5.2	3.6
15. Basilicata	76.6	...	10.0	2.2	...	2.8	1.7
16. Calabria	66.9	0.1	12.7	5.0	...	3.6	3.2
17. Sicilia	56.1	2.4	15.4	4.5	...	6.8	3.8
18. Sardegna	61.5	3.1	9.4	6.6	...	4.4	2.7

(a) adjusted (see text)

TABLE A.2: 1881 POPULATION CENSUS BY REGIONS (AT PRESENT BOUNDARIES, 1961 CLASSIFICATION).

I. PERCENTAGE COMPOSITION

	Credit Insurance (8)	Personal Services (9)	Public administration (10)	Total labour force (a) (11)
1. Piemonte-Val D'Aosta	0.1	5.8	1.7	100
2. Liguria	0.2	8.9	2.5	100
3. Lombardia	0.2	6.0	1.6	100
4. Trentino Alto Adige	...	6.6	2.0	100
5. Veneto	0.1	7.0	1.7	100
6. Friuli Venezia Giulia	0.2	8.0	1.8	100
7. Emilia-Romagna	0.1	7.6	1.9	100
8. Marche	0.1	6.5	1.7	100
9. Toscana	0.2	7.0	1.8	100
10. Umbria	0.1	6.9	1.6	100
11. Lazio	0.2	9.2	3.1	100
12. Campania	0.3	8.8	2.5	100
13. Abruzzi-Molise	...	4.7	1.4	100
14. Puglia	0.1	6.8	1.8	100
15. Basilicata	...	5.5	1.2	100
16. Calabria	...	6.9	1.6	100
17. Sicilia	0.2	8.6	2.2	100
18. Sardegna	0.1	10.2	2.0	100

(a) adjusted (see text)

TABLE A.3: 1911 POPULATION CENSUS BY REGIONS (AT PRESENT BOUNDARIES, 1961 CLASSIFICATION).

I. ABSOLUTE FIGURES

	Agriculture (1)	Mining (2)	Manufacturing (a) (3)	Construction (4)	Electricity Gaz, Water (5)	Commerce and Tourism (6)	Transports Communications (7)
1. Piemonte-Val d'Aosta	1.167.370	9.563	434.516	79.549	4.718	105.295	52.642
2. Liguria	231.904	2.722	149.247	32.255	2.693	53.640	43.854
3. Lombardia	1.228.710	7.411	783.708	123.621	10.172	168.796	67.246
4. Trentino Alto Adige	228.218	1.033	37.881	12.921	453	23.654	8.145
5. Veneto	920.050	3.030	234.824	47.876	2.214	84.414	38.648
6. Friuli Venezia Giulia	255.375	2.380	97.210	22.704	1.432	37.468	20.266
7. Emilia-Romagna	937.916	2.539	235.845	74.814	2.275	72.875	38.949
8. Marche	426.528	1.385	83.752	16.121	835	17.409	13.812
9. Toscana	808.381	21.312	313.500	51.243	2.975	68.463	48.197
10. Umbria	240.637	1.323	37.053	9.264	291	8.482	5.824
11. Lazio	463.769	2.272	118.040	38.410	1.409	46.775	37.361
12. Campania	784.930	4.290	259.989	55.558	2.585	99.363	63.565
13. Abruzzi-Molise	579.077	1.168	63.540	13.422	544	17.902	11.840
14. Puglia	608.950	5.655	126.914	40.798	1.403	43.902	37.933
15. Basilicata	193.219	668	20.940	6.117	88	6.818	4.672
16. Calabria	495.774	1.033	75.370	19.707	342	19.443	19.381
17. Sicilia	768.823	40.412	199.266	72.194	1.717	106.124	77.526
18. Sardegna	198.682	16.092	37.658	12.627	324	13.015	10.719

(a) adjusted (see text)

TABLE A.3: 1911 POPULATION CENSUS BY REGIONS (AT PRESENT BOUNDARIES, 1961 CLASSIFICATION)

I. ABSOLUTE FIGURES

	Credit Insurance (8)	Personal Services (9)	Public administration (10)	Total labour force (a) (11)	Total Population (12)
1. Piemonte-Val D'Aosta	4.371	102.606	37.746	1.998.376	3.411.745
2. Liguria	3.860	51.984	19.278	591.437	1.196.237
3. Lombardia	8.145	161.356	39.738	2.598.803	4.781.202
4. Trentino Alto Adige	580	20.909	9.251	343.045	627.282
5. Veneto	3.664	73.479	24.727	1.432.926	2.902.017
6. Friuli Venezia Giulia	3.683	36.283	14.966	491.767	1.014.617
7. Emilia-Romagna	3.125	76.733	25.832	1.470.903	2.750.117
8. Marche	1.167	24.969	10.416	596.394	1.093.940
9. Toscana	4.518	78.258	24.392	1.421.245	2.634.249
10. Umbria	753	14.332	5.561	323.520	594.125
11. Lazio	4.144	76.151	34.700	823.031	1.721.396
12. Campania	6.503	116.833	36.852	1.430.468	3.016.101
13. Abruzzi-Molise	981	23.424	9.599	721.497	1.381.335
14. Puglia	2.119	49.162	17.783	934.619	2.154.460
15. Basilicata	233	9.389	2.945	245.089	476.109
16. Calabria	1.020	30.309	10.302	672.681	1.405.396
17. Sicilia	5.919	110.888	34.077	1.416.946	3.679.450
18. Sardegna	839	28.121	8.127	326.204	851.952

(a) adjusted (see text)

TABLE A.3: 1911 POPULATION CENSUS BY REGIONS (AT PRESENT BOUNDARIES, 1961 CLASSIFICATION)

II. PERCENTAGE COMPOSITION

	Agricul-ture (1)	Mining (2)	Manufac-turing (a) (3)	Construc-tion (4)	Electricity Gaz, Water (5)	Commerce, Tourism (6)	Transports, Communica-tions (7)
1. Piemonte-Val D'Aosta	58.4	0.5	21.7	4.0	0.2	5.3	2.6
2. Liguria	39.2	0.5	25.2	5.5	0.5	9.1	7.4
3. Lombardia	47.3	0.3	30.2	4.7	0.4	6.5	2.6
4. Trentino Alto Adige	66.5	0.3	11.4	3.7	0.1	6.8	2.4
5. Veneto	64.2	0.2	16.4	3.3	0.2	5.9	2.7
6. Friuli Venezia Giulia	51.9	0.5	19.8	4.6	0.3	7.6	4.2
7. Emilia-Romagna	63.8	0.2	16.0	5.1	0.1	5.0	2.6
8. Marche	71.6	0.2	14.0	2.7	0.1	2.9	2.3
9. Toscana	56.9	1.5	22.1	3.6	0.2	4.8	3.4
10. Umbria	74.3	0.4	11.5	2.9	0.1	2.6	1.8
11. Lazio	56.3	0.3	14.3	4.7	0.2	5.7	4.5
12. Campania	54.9	0.3	18.2	3.9	0.2	6.9	4.4
13. Abruzzi-Molise	80.3	0.2	8.8	1.9	0.1	2.5	1.6
14. Puglia	65.2	0.6	13.6	4.4	0.1	4.7	4.0
15. Basilicata	78.8	0.3	8.6	2.5	...	2.8	1.9
16. Calabria	73.7	0.2	11.2	2.9	...	2.9	2.9
17. Sicilia	54.3	2.8	14.1	5.1	0.1	7.5	5.5
18. Sardegna	60.9	4.9	11.5	3.9	...	4.0	3.3

(a) adjusted (see text)

TABLE A.3: 1911 POPULATION CENSUS BY REGIONS (AT PRESENT BOUNDARIES, 1961 CLASSIFICATION)

II. PERCENTAGE COMPOSITION

	Credit Insurance (8)	Personal Services (9)	Public administration (10)	Total labour force (a) (11)
1. Piemonte-Val D'Aosta	0.2	5.2	1.9	100
2. Liguria	0.7	8.8	3.1	100
3. Lombardia	0.3	6.2	1.5	100
4. Trentino Alto Adige	0.2	6.0	2.6	100
5. Veneto	0.3	5.1	1.7	100
6. Friuli Venezia Giulia	0.7	7.4	3.0	100
7. Emilia-Romagna	0.2	5.2	1.8	100
8. Marche	0.2	4.2	1.8	100
9. Toscana	0.3	5.5	1.7	100
10. Umbria	0.2	4.4	1.8	100
11. Lazio	0.5	9.3	4.2	100
12. Campania	0.4	8.2	2.6	100
13. Abruzzi-Molise	0.1	3.2	1.3	100
14. Puglia	0.2	5.3	1.9	100
15. Basilicata	0.1	3.8	1.2	100
16. Calabria	0.2	4.5	1.5	100
17. Sicilia	0.4	7.8	2.4	100
18. Sardegna	0.3	8.6	2.6	100

(a) adjusted (see text)

TABLE A.4: 1936 POPULATION CENSUS BY REGIONS (AT PRESENT BOUNDARIES, 1961 CLASSIFICATION).

I. ABSOLUTE FIGURES

	Agricul- ture (1)	Mining (2)	Manufac- turing (3)	Construc- tion (4)	Electricity Gaz, Water (5)	Commerce and Tou- rism (6)	Transports Communica- tions (7)
1. Piemonte-Val d'Aosta	974.513	9.926	543.755	90.743	8.722	174.781	55.422
2. Liguria	209.252	3.759	188.065	46.491	4.397	93.247	60.198
3. Lombardia	1.023.051	9.989	1.085.925	169.720	13.221	299.124	81.070
4. Trentino Alto Adige	213.565	2.055	45.004	25.617	1.390	34.930	9.994
5. Veneto	973.584	7.496	290.600	85.197	4.501	132.774	48.309
6. Friuli Venezia Giulia	269.731	2.753	104.914	49.527	2.159	53.584	26.163
7. Emilia-Romagna	1.121.246	3.920	248.503	78.415	4.628	121.693	48.493
8. Marche	466.565	3.699	83.054	22.986	1.378	29.853	13.751
9. Toscana	804.369	25.152	291.514	63.620	4.422	115.654	53.857
10. Umbria	269.140	1.707	50.902	12.026	1.049	15.497	7.682
11. Lazio	579.631	4.673	166.089	86.061	5.424	107.591	56.107
12. Campania	780.635	5.279	260.384	71.761	6.343	139.426	73.888
13. Abruzzi-Molise	582.684	1.375	61.839	21.277	1.948	30.224	13.078
14. Puglia	557.366	10.157	182.139	60.097	3.620	73.893	41.591
15. Basilicata	200.287	239	20.829	9.445	488	8.780	4.529
16. Calabria	520.800	1.226	75.860	33.822	1.379	35.804	23.359
17. Sicilia	731.511	21.387	186.874	90.717	4.056	130.694	74.803
18. Sardegna	224.983	12.002	40.299	25.324	1.146	25.234	15.758

TABLE A.4: 1936 POPULATION CENSUS BY REGIONS (AT PRESENT BOUNDARIES, 1961 CLASSIFICATION)

I. ABSOLUTE FIGURES

	Credit Insurance (8)	Personal Services (9)	Public administration (10)	Total labour force (11)	Total Population (12)
1. Piemonte-Val D'Aosta	9.487	133.197	57.013	2.057.559	3.525.546
2. Liguria	6.265	75.201	31.633	718.266	1.482.866
3. Lombardia	22.529	247.725	79.505	3.031.759	5.805.008
4. Trentino Alto Adige	1.598	29.466	15.697	379.316	693.478
5. Veneto	6.749	104.689	45.755	1.699.654	3.546.462
6. Friuli Venezia Giulia	3.998	44.739	25.383	582.951	1.124.752
7. Emilia-Romagna	7.334	101.275	48.027	1.783.534	3.326.736
8. Marche	3.152	30.954	17.960	672.352	1.262.166
9. Toscana	7.128	98.710	46.499	1.510.725	2.965.520
10. Umbria	945	18.674	9.812	387.433	720.771
11. Lazio	12.103	147.444	95.840	1.260.963	2.683.544
12. Campania	5.894	118.030	59.146	1.520.786	3.679.060
13. Abruzzi-Molise	1.436	27.015	18.874	759.750	1.554.880
14. Puglia	2.641	60.837	35.435	1.027.736	2.643.560
15. Basilicata	358	8.502	6.226	259.683	538.141
16. Calabria	1.304	36.169	19.589	749.312	1.741.551
17. Sicilia	5.011	107.230	58.200	1.410.483	3.970.988
18. Sardegna	972	31.657	18.264	395.639	1.036.170

TABLE A.4: 1936 POPULATION CENSUS BY REGIONS (AT PRESENT BOUNDARIES, 1961 CLASSIFICATION)

II. PERCENTAGE COMPOSITION

	Agricul-ture (1)	Mining (2)	Manufac-turing (3)	Construc-tion (4)	Electricity Gaz, Water (5)	Commerce, Tourism (6)	Transports, Communica-tions (7)
1. Piemonte-Val D'Aosta	47.4	0.5	26.4	4.4	0.4	8.5	2.7
2. Liguria	29.1	0.5	26.2	6.5	0.6	13.0	8.4
3. Lombardia	33.7	0.3	35.8	5.6	0.4	9.9	2.7
4. Trentino Alto Adige	56.3	0.5	11.9	6.8	0.4	9.2	2.6
5. Veneto	57.3	0.4	17.1	5.0	0.3	7.8	2.8
6. Friuli Venezia Giulia	46.3	0.5	18.0	8.5	0.4	9.2	4.5
7. Emilia-Romagna	62.9	0.2	13.9	4.4	0.3	6.8	2.7
8. Marche	69.4	0.6	12.4	3.4	0.2	4.4	2.0
9. Toscana	53.2	1.7	19.3	4.2	0.3	7.7	3.6
10. Umbria	69.5	0.4	13.1	3.1	0.3	4.0	2.0
11. Lazio	46.0	0.4	13.2	6.8	0.4	8.5	4.4
12. Campania	51.3	0.3	17.1	4.7	0.4	9.2	4.9
13. Abruzzi-Molise	76.7	0.2	8.1	2.8	0.3	4.0	1.7
14. Puglia	54.2	1.0	17.7	5.8	0.4	7.2	4.0
15. Basilicata	77.1	0.1	8.0	3.6	0.2	3.4	1.7
16. Calabria	69.5	0.2	10.1	4.5	0.2	4.8	3.1
17. Sicilia	51.9	1.5	13.2	6.4	0.3	9.3	5.3
18. Sardegna	56.9	3.0	10.2	6.4	0.3	6.4	4.0

69

TABLE A.4: 1936 POPULATION CENSUS BY REGIONS (AT PRESENT BOUNDARIES, 1961 CLASSIFICATION)

II. PERCENATGE COMPOSITION

	Credit Insurance (8)	Personal Services (9)	Public administration (10)	Total labour force (11)
1. Piemonte-Val D'Aosta	0.5	6.5	2.7	100
2. Liguria	0.9	10.5	4.3	100
3. Lombardia	0.7	8.3	2.6	100
4. Trentino Alto Adige	0.4	7.8	4.1	100
5. Veneto	0.4	6.2	2.7	100
6. Friuli Venezia Giulia	0.7	7.6	4.3	100
7. Emilia-Romagna	0.4	5.7	2.7	100
8. Marche	0.3	4.6	2.7	100
9. Toscana	0.5	6.4	3.1	100
10. Umbria	0.2	4.8	2.6	100
11. Lazio	1.0	11.7	7.6	100
12. Campania	0.4	7.8	3.9	100
13. Abruzzi-Molise	0.2	3.6	2.4	100
14. Puglia	0.3	5.9	3.5	100
15. Basilicata	0.1	3.3	2.5	100
16. Calabria	0.2	4.8	2.6	100
17. Sicilia	0.4	7.6	4.1	100
18. Sardegna	0.2	8.0	4.6	100

70

TABLE A.5: 1961 POPULATION CENSUS BY REGIONS (1961 CLASSIFICATION).

I. ABSOLUTE FIGURES

	Agricul-ture (1)	Mining (2)	Manufac-turing (3)	Construc-tion (4)	Electricity Gaz, Water (5)	Commerce and Tou-rism (6)	Transports Communica-tions (7)
1. Piemonte-Val d'Aosta	442.883	8.137	752.871	143.878	14.044	188.632	73.634
2. Liguria	81.922	3.039	190.791	74.574	5.578	101.392	78.526
3. Lombardia	428.013	12.903	1.525.318	308.451	24.769	378.219	126.119
4. Trentino Alto Adige	101.929	3.384	66.172	35.669	3.320	49.805	13.041
5. Veneto	446.178	9.083	459.533	181.055	9.235	175.270	68.236
6. Friuli Venezia Giulia	96.197	3.557	136.673	77.076	3.309	63.656	31.669
7. Emilia-Romagna	584.180	5.987	415.814	162.333	7.925	185.747	73.848
8. Marche	264.788	3.578	113.424	59.070	2.178	44.376	21.747
9. Toscana	350.909	23.092	415.860	128.862	6.928	151.251	69.830
10. Umbria	146.240	1.950	65.983	37.749	1.431	23.949	13.062
11. Lazio	275.597	7.109	243.790	204.291	10.889	168.737	96.639
12. Campania	584.875	6.145	318.279	227.698	9.074	151.837	96.700
13. Abruzzi-Molise	285.159	3.942	78.360	98.118	2.296	40.864	21.107
14. Puglia	663.419	12.283	222.555	121.506	4.708	88.615	49.692
15. Basilicata	151.850	573	24.401	44.582	827	10.935	6.637
16. Calabria	328.176	2.780	76.449	149.568	2.129	42.220	29.184
17. Sicilia	610.333	18.480	199.426	222.889	7.710	119.640	74.361
18. Sardegna	166.160	19.040	49.106	68.099	2.610	37.383	22.598

TABLE A.5: 1961 POPULATION CENSUS BY REGIONS (1961 CLASSIFICATION)

I. ABSOLUTE FIGURES

	Credit Insurance (8)	Personal Services (9)	Public administration (10)	Total labour force (11)	Total Population (12)
1. Piemonte-Val D'Aosta	20.697	124.080	82.516	1.851.354	4.015.209
2. Liguria	11.062	64.587	52.476	663.947	1.735.349
3. Lombardia	49.555	268.776	136.121	3.258.244	7.406.152
4. Trentino Alto Adige	3.311	30.898	26.718	334.247	785.967
5. Veneto	13.654	117.991	86.124	1.566.359	3.846.562
6. Friuli Venezia Giulia	5.615	40.152	46.902	504.506	1.204.298
7. Emilia-Romagna	16.576	111.354	93.891	1.657.655	3.666.680
8. Marche	4.450	36.764	33.811	584.186	1.347.489
9. Toscana	15.366	94.354	89.403	1.345.855	3.286.160
10. Umbria	2.161	21.258	19.535	333.318	794.745
11. Lazio	29.281	183.159	217.002	1.436.494	3.958.957
12. Campania	14.217	118.735	123.809	1.651.369	4.760.759
13. Abruzzi-Molise	3.213	30.259	39.608	602.926	1.564.318
14. Puglia	7.173	65.721	81.757	1.317.429	3.421.217
15. Basilicata	943	10.412	12.795	263.955	644.297
16. Calabria	3.645	35.374	44.575	714.100	2.045.047
17. Sicilia	14.599	96.712	123.092	1.486.702	4.721.001
18. Sardegna	2.851	33.288	41.898	443.033	1.419.362

72

TABLE A.5: 1961 POPULATION CENSUS BY REGIONS (1961 CLASSIFICATION)

II. PERCENTAGE COMPOSITION

	Agriculture (1)	Mining (2)	Manufacturing (3)	Construction (4)	Electricity Gaz, Water (5)	Commerce, Tourism (6)	Transports, Communications (7)
1. Piemonte-Val D'Aosta	23.9	0.4	40.7	7.8	0.8	10.2	4.0
2. Liguria	12.3	0.5	28.8	11.2	0.8	15.3	11.8
3. Lombardia	31.1	0.4	46.8	9.5	0.8	11.6	3.9
4. Trentino Alto Adige	30.5	1.0	19.8	10.7	1.0	14.9	3.9
5. Veneto	28.5	0.6	29.3	11.5	0.6	11.2	4.4
6. Friuli Venezia Giulia	19.1	0.7	27.0	15.3	0.6	12.6	6.3
7. Emilia-Romagna	35.2	0.4	25.1	9.8	0.5	11.2	4.5
8. Marche	45.3	0.6	19.4	10.1	0.4	7.6	3.7
9. Toscana	26.1	1.7	30.9	9.6	0.5	11.2	5.2
10. Umbria	43.9	0.6	19.8	11.3	0.4	7.2	3.9
11. Lazio	19.2	0.5	17.0	14.2	0.8	11.7	6.7
12. Campania	35.4	0.4	19.3	13.8	0.5	9.2	5.9
13. Abruzzi-Molise	47.3	0.7	13.0	16.3	0.4	6.8	3.5
14. Puglia	50.4	0.9	16.9	9.2	0.4	6.7	3.8
15. Basilicata	57.5	0.2	9.3	16.9	0.3	4.2	2.5
16. Calabria	46.0	0.4	10.7	20.9	0.3	5.9	4.1
17. Sicilia	41.1	1.2	13.4	15.0	0.5	8.0	5.0
18. Sardegna	37.5	4.3	11.1	15.3	0.6	8.4	5.1

TABLE A.5: 1961 POPULATION CENSUSBY REGIONS (1961 CLASSIFICATION)

II. PERCENTAGE COMPOSITION

	Credit Insurance (8)	Personal Services (9)	Public administra-tion (10)	Total labour force (11)
1. Piemonte-Val D'Aosta	1.1	6.7	4.4	100
2. Liguria	1.7	9.7	7.9	100
3. Lombardia	1.5	8.2	4.2	100
4. Trentino Alto Adige	1.0	9.2	8.0	100
5. Veneto	0.9	7.5	5.5	100
6. Friuli Venezia Giulia	1.1	8.0	9.3	100
7. Emilia-Romagna	1.0	6.7	5.6	100
8. Marche	0.8	6.3	5.8	100
9. Toscana	1.1	7.0	6.7	100
10. Umbria	0.6	6.4	5.9	100
11. Lazio	2.0	12.8	15.1	100
12. Campania	0.9	7.1	7.5	100
13. Abruzzi-Molise	0.5	5.0	6.5	100
14. Puglia	0.5	5.0	6.2	100
15. Basilicata	0.4	4.0	4.8	100
16. Calabria	0.5	5.0	6.2	100
17. Sicilia	1.0	6.5	8.3	100
18. Sardegna	0.6	7.5	9.6	100

74

TABLE A.6: 1981 POPULATION CENSUS BY REGIONS (1961 CLASSIFICATION).

I. ABSOLUTE FIGURES

	Agricul-ture (1)	Mining (2)	Manufac-turing (3)	Construc-tion (4)	Electricity Gaz, Water (5)	Commerce and Tou-rism (6)	Transports Communica-tions (7)
1. Piemonte-Val d'Aosta	150.433	5.862	788.186	131.019	19.410	273.821	99.841
2. Liguria	32.687	1.983	149.727	52.087	8.164	130.700	73.721
3. Lombardia	140.700	11.320	1.635.636	278.290	33.542	574.174	180.174
4. Trentino Alto Adige	37.202	1.977	76.147	36.102	3.422	79.299	17.779
5. Veneto	144.266	4.629	640.388	151.738	15.345	280.889	92.677
6. Friuli Venezia Giulia	27.347	1.437	142.959	47.858	4.338	84.893	33.824
7. Emilia-Romagna	215.032	4.455	574.148	140.609	12.710	278.459	92.923
8. Marche	65.115	1.778	207.226	51.235	4.068	78.080	28.448
9. Toscana	94.040	8.528	518.173	104.357	3.045	233.204	84.953
10. Umbria	32.138	1.018	98.139	31.107	12.308	40.758	17.361
11. Lazio	106.941	7.118	326.248	148.007	20.050	263.140	150.074
12. Campania	266.733	5.023	329.541	148.675	13.507	189.314	114.870
13. Abruzzi-Molise	88.479	2.705	117.840	70.203	4.596	71.278	26.603
14. Puglia	310.405	5.956	236.211	125.062	9.337	147.416	67.831
15. Basilicata	56.018	613	26.765	37.427	2.132	18.798	8.053
16. Calabria	144.222	1.798	67.651	103.202	5.054	64.951	40.269
17. Sicilia	267.415	8.723	207.505	186.893	13.281	187.111	89.159
18. Sardegna	62.145	6.761	79.844	69.434	6.351	75.489	31.519

TABLE A.6: 1981 POPULATION CENSUS BY REGIONS (1961 CLASSIFICATION)

I. ABSOLUTE FIGURES

	Credit Insurance (8)	Personal Services (9)	Public administration (10)	Total labour force (11)	Total Population (12)
1. Piemonte-Val D'Aosta	40.534	195.807	169.614	1.874.527	4.591.384
2. Liguria	16.937	83.999	87.772	637.777	1.807.893
3. Lombardia	102.188	432.099	297.282	3.685.405	8.891.652
4. Trentino Alto Adige	7.274	41.801	45.033	346.036	873.413
5. Veneto	29.101	173.769	163.358	1.696.160	4.345.047
6. Friuli Venezia Giulia	10.727	55.982	66.465	475.830	1.233.984
7. Emilia-Romagna	37.181	188.369	169.384	1.713.270	3.957.513
8. Marche	9.576	52.848	66.109	564.483	1.412.404
9. Toscana	31.294	145.399	175.975	1.408.231	3.581.051
10. Umbria	5.101	33.340	42.430	304.437	807.552
11. Lazio	61.868	253.910	358.671	1.696.027	5.001.684
12. Campania	20.979	157.420	262.561	1.508.623	5.463.134
13. Abruzzi-Molise	6.427	46.871	80.403	515.405	1.546.162
14. Puglia	13.840	110.160	183.137	1.209.355	3.871.617
15. Basilicata	1.865	13.281	34.905	199.857	610.186
16. Calabria	6.613	47.159	115.367	596.286	2.061.182
17. Sicilia	22.560	133.730	224.754	1.341.131	4.906.878
18. Sardegna	6.655	53.129	87.070	478.397	1.594.175

TABLE A.6: 1981 POPULATION CENSUS BY REGIONS (1961 CLASSIFICATION)

II. PERCENTAGE COMPOSITION

	Agricul-ture (1)	Mining (2)	Manufac-turing (3)	Construc-tion (4)	Electricity Gaz, Water (5)	Commerce, Tourism (6)	Transports, Communica-tions (7)
1. Piemonte-Val D'Aosta	8.0	0.3	42.0	7.0	1.0	14.6	5.3
2. Liguria	5.1	0.3	23.5	8.2	1.3	20.5	11.6
3. Lombardia	3.8	0.3	44.4	7.6	0.9	15.6	4.9
4. Trentino Alto Adige	10.7	0.6	22.0	10.4	1.0	22.9	5.1
5. Veneto	8.5	0.3	37.8	8.9	0.9	16.6	5.5
6. Friuli Venezia Giulia	5.7	0.3	30.0	10.1	0.9	17.8	7.1
7. Emilia-Romagna	12.6	0.3	33.5	8.2	0.7	16.2	5.4
8. Marche	11.5	0.3	36.7	9.1	0.7	13.8	5.0
9. Toscana	6.7	0.6	36.8	7.4	0.9	16.6	6.0
10. Umbria	10.6	0.3	32.2	10.2	1.0	13.4	5.7
11. Lazio	6.3	0.4	19.2	8.7	1.2	15.5	8.8
12. Campania	17.7	0.3	21.8	9.9	0.9	12.5	7.6
13. Abruzzi-Molise	17.2	0.5	22.9	13.6	0.9	13.8	5.2
14. Puglia	25.7	0.5	19.5	10.3	0.8	12.2	5.6
15. Basilicata	28.0	0.3	13.4	18.7	1.1	9.4	4.0
16. Calabria	24.2	0.3	11.3	17.3	0.8	10.9	6.7
17. Sicilia	19.9	0.6	15.5	13.9	1.0	13.9	6.6
18. Sardegna	13.0	1.4	16.7	14.5	1.3	15.8	6.6

TABLE A.6: 1981 POPULATION CENSUS BY REGIONS (1961 CLASSIFICATION)

II. PERCENTAGE COMPOSITION

	Credit Insurance (8)	Personal Services (9)	Public administration (10)	Total labour force (11)
1. Piemonte-Val D'Aosta	2.2	10.5	9.0	100
2. Liguria	2.7	13.2	13.8	100
3. Lombardia	2.8	11.7	8.1	100
4. Trentino Alto Adige	2.1	12.1	13.0	100
5. Veneto	1.7	10.2	9.6	100
6. Friuli Venezia Giulia	2.2	11.8	14.0	100
7. Emilia-Romagna	2.2	11.0	9.9	100
8. Marche	1.7	9.4	11.7	100
9. Toscana	2.2	10.3	12.5	100
10. Umbria	1.7	10.9	13.9	100
11. Lazio	3.7	15.0	21.1	100
12. Campania	1.4	10.4	17.4	100
13. Abruzzi-Molise	1.2	9.1	15.6	100
14. Puglia	1.1	9.1	15.1	100
15. Basilicata	0.9	6.6	17.5	100
16. Calabria	1.1	7.9	19.4	100
17. Sicilia	1.7	10.0	16.8	100
18. Sardegna	1.4	11.1	18.2	100

78

TABLE A.7: INDUSTRIAL CENSUSES 1911-1981 (1951 CLASSIFICATION, AT THE BOUNDARIES OF THE TIME)

I. ABSOLUTE FIGURES

	1911 (a)	1911 (b)	1927	1937-39
1. Food and beverages	284.232	307.151	317.922	480.859
2. Tobacco	20.336	20.341	25.512	48.745
3. Leather, Shoes	120.282	168.356	209.108	215.528
4. Textiles	505.806	508.076	645.358	604.556
5. Clothing	167.669	198.147	304.306	284.689
6. Furniture	220.673	264.332	282.950	283.576
7. Paper	36.102	36.432	45.749	56.127
8. Printing, Photographing	47.328	48.124	65.225	80.521
9. Metallurgy	42.663	42.706	89.158	103.175
10. Engineering	345.791	369.844	503.676	854.798
11. Bricks, Glass, Tyles	182.701	187.171	171.922	206.762
12. Chemicals	57.071	57.649	83.573	153.042
13. Rubber	2.720	2.731	15.251	26.064
14. Other	10.297	11.271	41.478	33.306
15. Manufacturing	2.043.671	2.222.371	2.801.188	3.431.748
16. Mining	98.362	99.362	98.778	137.404
17. Construction	128.182	134.279	331.386	558.544
18. Electricity, Gaz water	34.187	35.128	58.502	42.221
19. Industry, Total	2.304.402	2.491.140	3.289.854	4.169.917

(a) excluding units with 1 worker
(b) including units with 1 worker

TABLE A.7: INDUSTRIAL CENSUSES 1911-1981 (1951 CLASSIFICATION, AT THE BOUNDARIES OF THE TIME)

I. ABSOLUTE FIGURES

	1951	1961	1971	1981
1. Food and beverages	360.058	396.947	374.307	395.072
2. Tobacco	52.496	26.561	21.133	19.039
3. Leather, Shoes	200.203	227.388	232.881	299.249
4. Textiles	650.866	598.565	541.030	493.470
5. Clothing	249.901	335.899	414.025	467.580
6. Furniture	293.570	381.251	396.594	446.128
7. Paper	63.449	84.208	94.256	98.800
8. Printing, Photographing	85.550	131.822	166.579	216.555
9. Metallurgy	145.071	191.794	245.648	256.797
10. Engineering	909.261	1.399.902	1.937.812	2.408.364
11. Bricks, Glass, Tyles	206.668	318.730	328.891	338.098
12. Chemicals	199.811	270.900	317.346	322.590
13. Rubber	40.127	53.759	84.568	85.909
14. Other	41.189	77.798	144.616	186.621
15. Manufacturing	3.498.220	4.495.584	5.299.686	6.034.272
16. Mining	118.662	104.150	78.788	67.245
17. Construction	532.055	894.407	997.534	1.264.609
18. Electricity, Gaz water	92.964	116.046	155.156	177.124
19. Industry, Total	4.241.901	5.610.187	6.531.164	7.543.250

TABLE A.7: INDUSTRIAL CENSUSES 1911-1981 (1951 CLASSIFICATION, AT THE BOUNDARIES OF THE TIME)

II. PERCENTAGE FIGURES

	1911 (a)	1911 (b)	1927	1937-39
1. Food and beverages	13.9	13.8	11.4	14.0
2. Tobacco	1.0	0.9	0.9	1.4
3. Leather, Shoes	5.9	7.6	7.5	6.3
4. Textiles	24.8	22.9	23.0	17.6
5. Clothing	8.2	8.9	10.9	8.3
6. Furniture	10.8	11.9	10.1	8.3
7. Paper	1.8	1.6	1.6	1.6
8. Printing, Photographing	2.3	2.1	2.3	2.4
9. Metallurgy	2.1	1.9	3.2	3.0
10. Engineering	16.9	16.7	18.0	24.9
11. Bricks, Glass, Tyles	8.9	8.5	6.1	6.0
12. Chemicals	2.8	2.6	3.0	4.5
13. Rubber	0.1	0.1	0.5	0.7
14. Other	0.5	0.5	1.5	1.0
Total Manufacturing	100.0	100.0	100.0	100.0
15. Manufacturing	88.7	89.2	85.2	82.3
16. Mining	4.3	4.0	3.0	3.3
17. Construction	5.5	5.4	10.0	13.4
18. Electricity, Gaz, Water	1.5	1.4	1.8	1.0
19. Industry, Total	100.0	100.0	100.0	100.0
15. as a% of active population	---	12.7(c)	14.2(c)	16.7(c)
19. as a% of active population	---	14.3(c)	16.6(c)	20.3(c)

(a) excluding units with 1 worker
(b) including units with 1 worker
(c) the adjustment suggested in the text has been made to eliminate the effects of change in boundaries; these percentages, therefore, are reffered to present boundaries.

TABLE A.7: INDUSTRIAL CENSUSES 1911-1981 (1951 CLASSIFICATION, AT THE BOUNDARIES OF THE TIME)

II. PERCENTAGE FIGURES

	1951	1961	1971	1981
1. Food and beverages	10.3	8.8	7.1	6.5
2. Tobacco	1.5	0.6	0.4	0.3
3. Leather, Shoes	5.7	5.7	4.4	5.0
4. Textiles	18.6	13.1	10.2	8.2
5. Clothing	7.1	7.5	7.8	7.6
6. Furniture	8.4	8.5	7.5	7.4
7. Paper	1.8	1.9	1.8	1.6
8. Printing, Photographing	2.4	2.9	3.1	3.6
9. Metallurgy	4.2	4.3	4.6	4.3
10. Engineering	26.0	31.1	36.6	40.0
11. Bricks, Glass, Tyles	5.9	7.1	6.2	5.6
12. Chemicals	5.7	6.0	6.0	5.3
13. Rubber	1.1	1.2	1.6	1.5
14. Other	1.8	1.7	2.7	3.1
Total Manufacturing	100.0	100.0	100.0	100.0
15. Manufacturing	82.5	80.1	81.1	80.0
16. Mining	2.8	1.9	1.2	0.9
17. Construction	12.5	15.9	15.3	16.8
18. Electricity, Gaz water	2.2	2.1	2.4	2.3
19. Industry, Total	100.0	100.0	100.0	100.0
15. as a% of active population	17.3	22.5	28.1	29.8
19. as a% of active population	20.9	28.0	34.7	37.3

TABLE A.8: 1911 INDUSTRIAL CENSUS BY REGIONS (1951 CLASSIFICATION, AT THE BOUNDARIES OF THE TIME)

I. ABSOLUTE FIGURES

	Food, beverages	Tobacco	Leather, shoes	Textiles	Clothing	Furniture	Paper	Printing, photography	Metal	Engineering
1. Piemonte-Val d'Aosta	25.491	1.517	12.392	107.026	27.064	27.688	7.479	5.657	4.948	53.478
2. Liguria	13.763	1.332	5.630	11.765	10.047	11.573	1.228	2.479	8.591	40.423
3. Lombardia	44.100	2.619	19.903	268.282	41.941	43.094	10.646	13.451	10.562	92.231
4. Trentino Alto Adige										
5. Veneto	23.400	1.079	7.176	51.646	13.508	24.409	3.762	3.108	1.178	27.049
6. Friuli Venezia Giulia										
7. Emilia-Romagna	28.714	1.883	7.168	8.905	13.471	18.814	1.534	3.047	620	23.830
8. Marche	6.198	1.212	3.956	7.409	4.302	5.308	1.910	812	238	5.335
9. Toscana	18.907	3.878	9.816	20.359	11.073	21.838	3.134	4.773	5.949	24.801
10. Umbria	5.348	49	2.553	3.646	1.750	2.103	204	792	4.119	3.817
11. Lazio	9.458	769	4.979	1.238	8.339	8.109	2.095	5.888	355	10.001
12. Campania	27.543	2.298	13.369	17.437	12.767	17.364	3.439	3.247	4.603	31.140
13. Abruzzi-Molise	8.812	0	4.454	966	3.378	4.226	119	482	302	3.910
14. Puglia	27.548	1.556	6.610	1.378	5.695	11.799	123	1.274	465	11.578
15. Basilicata	3.185	0	1.505	114	964	1.315	2	92	0	1.164
16. Calabria	11.518	0	5.667	2.814	4.260	5.283	131	282	12	3.003
17. Sicilia	24.938	1.456	12.539	2.807	8.096	14.505	245	1.641	590	11.366
18. Sardegna	5.309	688	2.545	14	1.014	3.245	51	303	131	2.665

82

TABLE A.8: 1911 INDUSTRIAL CENSUS BY REGIONS (1951 CLASSIFICATION, AT THE BOUNDARIES OF THE TIME)

I. ABSOLUTE FIGURES

	Bricks, glass, tyles	Chemi-cals	Rubber	Other	TOTAL MANUFAC-TURING	Mining	Construc-tion	Public Utilities	TOTAL
1. Piemonte-Val d'Aosta	26.958	7.527	1.497	1.288	310.010	8.398	19.227	4.781	342.416
2. Liguria	6.575	3.544	52	258	117.260	2.236	10.836	2.271	132.603
3. Lombardia	39.125	11.444	850	4.541	602.789	7.299	36.657	11.098	657.483
4. Trentino Alto Adige									
5. Veneto	23.211	5.117	11	662	185.316	3.084	7.687	2.572	198.659
6. Friuli Venezia Giulia									
7. Emilia-Romagna	18.350	3.447	25	595	130.403	2.348	11.861	1.734	146.301
8. Marche	6.713	1.254	0	299	44.946	1.292	2.010	1.257	49.505
9. Toscana	26.272	5.183	244	605	156.832	21.592	6.915	2.706	188.045
10. Umbria	2.745	2.159	0	193	29.474	1.225	1.259	269	32.231
11. Lazio	5.496	1.345	16	246	58.334	2.066	10.778	1.179	72.357
12. Campania	7.132	5.724	22	710	146.795	3.011	5.938	2.375	158.119
13. Abruzzi-Molise	5.085	840	0	143	32.717	963	2.735	551	36.966
14. Puglia	3.077	2.502	0	301	73.906	2.393	5.092	1.289	82.680
15. Basilicata	576	89	0	0	9.006	111	2.379	66	11.562
16. Calabria	3.380	1.308	0	81	37.739	703	1.657	259	40.358
17. Sicilia	6.843	5.348	3	313	90.690	26.130	2.458	1.463	120.741
18. Sardegna	1.163	240	0	62	17.450	15.511	738	317	34.016

TABLE A.8: 1911 INDUSTRIAL CENSUS BY REGIONS (1951 CLASSIFICATION, AT THE BOUNDARIES OF THE TIME)

II. PERCENTAGE COMPOSITION

	Food, beverages	Tobacco	Leather, shoes	Textiles	Clothing	Furniture	Paper	Printing, photography	Metal	Engineering
1. Piemonte-Val D'Aosta	7.44	0.44	3.62	31.26	7.90	8.09	2.18	1.65	1.45	15.62
2. Liguria	10.38	1.00	4.25	8.87	7.58	8.73	0.93	1.87	6.48	30.48
3. Lombardia	6.70	0.40	3.03	40.78	6.38	6.55	1.62	2.04	1.61	14.02
4. Trentino Alto Adige										
5. Veneto	11.78	0.54	3.61	26.00	6.80	12.29	1.89	1.56	0.59	13.62
6. Friuli Venezia Giulia										
7. Emilia-Romagna	19.63	1.29	4.90	6.09	9.21	12.86	1.05	2.08	0.42	16.29
8. Marche	12.52	2.45	7.99	14.97	8.69	10.72	3.86	1.64	0.48	10.78
9. Toscana	10.05	2.06	5.22	10.83	5.89	11.61	1.67	2.54	3.16	13.19
10. Umbria	16.59	0.15	7.92	11.31	5.43	6.52	0.63	2.46	12.78	11.84
11. Lazio	13.07	1.06	6.88	1.71	11.52	11.21	2.90	8.14	0.49	13.82
12. Campania	17.42	1.45	8.46	11.03	8.07	10.98	2.17	2.05	2.91	19.69
13. Abruzzi-Molise	23.84	0.00	12.05	2.61	9.14	11.43	0.32	1.30	0.82	10.58
14. Puglia	33.32	1.88	7.99	1.67	6.89	14.27	0.15	1.54	0.56	14.00
15. Basilicata	27.55	0.00	13.02	0.99	8.34	11.37	0.02	0.80	0.00	10.07
16. Calabria	28.54	0.00	14.04	6.97	10.56	13.09	0.32	0.70	0.03	7.44
17. Sicilia	20.65	1.21	10.39	2.32	6.71	12.01	0.20	1.36	0.49	9.41
18. Sardegna	15.61	2.02	7.54	0.04	2.98	9.54	0.15	0.89	0.39	7.83
19. Italia	12.4	0.9	5.2	22.0	7.2	9.6	1.6	2.0	1.9	15.0

TABLE A.8: 1911 INDUSTRIAL CENSUS BY REGIONS (1951 CLASSIFICATION, AT THE BOUNDARIES OF THE TIME)

II. PERCENTAGE COMPOSITION

	Bricks, glass, tyles	Chemi-cals	Rubber	Other	TOTAL MANUFAC-TURING	Mining	Construc-tion	Public Utilities	TOTAL
1. Piemonte-Val d'Aosta	7.87	2.20	0.44	0.38	90.54	2.45	5.62	1.40	100.00
2. Liguria	4.96	2.67	0.04	0.19	88.43	1.69	8.17	1.71	100.00
3. Lombardia	5.95	1.74	0.13	0.69	91.63	1.11	5.57	1.69	100.00
4. Trentino Alto Adige									
5. Veneto	11.68	2.58	0.01	0.33	93.28	1.55	3.87	1.29	100.00
6. Friuli Venezia Giulia									
7. Emilia-Romagna	12.54	2.36	0.02	0.41	89.13	1.60	8.08	1.19	100.00
8. Marche	13.56	2.53	0.00	0.60	90.79	2.61	4.06	2.54	100.00
9. Toscana	13.97	2.76	0.13	0.32	83.40	11.48	3.68	1.44	100.00
10. Umbria	8.52	6.70	0.00	0.60	91.46	3.80	3.91	0.83	100.00
11. Lazio	7.60	1.86	0.02	0.34	80.62	2.86	14.90	1.63	100.00
12. Campania	4.51	3.62	0.01	0.45	92.84	1.90	3.76	1.50	100.00
13. Abruzzi-Molise	13.76	2.27	0.00	0.39	88.51	2.61	7.40	1.49	100.00
14. Puglia	3.72	3.03	0.00	0.36	89.39	2.89	6.16	1.56	100.00
15. Basilicata	4.98	0.77	0.00	0.00	77.89	0.96	20.58	0.57	100.00
16. Calabria	8.38	3.24	0.00	0.20	93.51	1.74	4.11	0.64	100.00
17. Sicilia	5.67	4.43	0.00	0.26	75.11	21.64	2.04	1.21	100.00
18. Sardegna	3.42	0.71	0.00	0.18	51.30	45.60	2.17	0.93	100.00
19. Italia	7.9	2.5	0.1	0.4	88.7	4.3	5.5	1.5	100.00

TABLE A.9: 1937-39 INDUSTRIAL CENSUS BY REGIONS (1951 CLASSIFICATION, AT THE BOUNDARIES OF THE TIME)

I. ABSOLUTE FIGURES

	Food, beverages	Tobacco	Leather, shoes	Textiles	Clothing	Furniture	Paper	Printing, photography	Metal	Engineering
1. Piemonte-Val d'Aosta	42.697	1.802	22.235	134.234	37.127	27.321	9.807	9.446	21.824	145.328
2. Liguria	18.180	0	5.849	11.240	9.910	8.879	1.462	3.200	14.272	74.843
3. Lombardia	68.689	2.090	48.299	282.886	69.959	60.968	19.304	23.120	31.438	297.092
4. Trentino Alto Adige	5.071	1.001	2.927	3.212	3.709	7.847	1.113	849	1.818	5.792
5. Veneto	50.614	1.485	16.522	75.597	21.705	29.059	6.668	5.251	5.204	46.121
6. Friuli Venezia Giulia	11.017	2.761	2.989	4.745	7.370	7.302	1.032	1.490	1.537	34.100
7. Emilia-Romagna	62.030	3.796	14.229	12.951	24.953	17.790	3.324	4.562	387	54.231
8. Marche	10.098	1.595	6.872	7.955	8.979	7.071	1.421	962	50	10.605
9. Toscana	29.105	4.690	16.515	36.686	23.158	25.632	3.902	5.732	12.739	47.883
10. Umbria	7.818	1.180	3.147	4.341	3.069	4.512	430	1.419	4.717	14.305
11. Lazio	19.729	1.507	7.739	2.184	13.007	11.144	5.780	14.556	358	34.634
12. Campania	42.378	7.099	18.520	15.956	18.036	20.841	1.401	3.882	6.313	38.286
13. Abruzzi-Molise	12.689	1.677	6.059	2.862	6.636	5.969	131	819	0	5.321
14. Puglia	32.259	15.903	10.898	3.476	12.097	12.213	157	1.606	430	19.818
15. Basilicata	3.509	5	3.159	501	2.017	3.256	0	133	0	1.666
16. Calabria	13.917	17	6.684	1.719	6.403	10.268	18	435	419	3.835
17. Sicilia	40.441	1.410	19.163	3.044	12.590	16.578	134	2.544	4	16.358
18. Sardegna	10.618	727	3.722	967	3.964	6.926	43	515	1.665	4.598

TABLE A.9: 1937-39 INDUSTRIAL CENSUS BY REGIONS (1951 CLASSIFICATION, AT THE BOUNDARIES OF THE TIME)

I. ABSOLUTE FIGURES

	Bricks, glass, tyles	Chemi- cals	Rubber	Other	TOTAL MANUFAC- TURING	Mining	Construc- tion	Public Utilities	TOTAL
1. Piemonte-Val d'Aosta	24.260	24.583	6.713	3.609	510.986	10.364	57.479	4.380	583.209
2. Liguria	8.515	12.258	260	1.299	170.167	3.859	29.415	3.500	206.941
3. Lombardia	39.309	41.532	16.479	11.379	1.012.544	9.480	119.941	8.764	1.150.729
4. Trentino Alto Adige	1.844	1.210	19	226	36.638	2.973	12.268	849	52.728
5. Veneto	21.693	12.936	142	3.589	296.586	6.733	50.942	3.660	357.921
6. Friuli Venezia Giulia	3.840	3.887	45	156	82.271	13.199	10.853	1.234	107.557
7. Emilia-Romagna	17.657	9.567	898	4.410	230.785	3.381	45.506	2.376	282.048
8. Marche	5.778	2.070	60	3.498	67.014	4.074	13.476	542	85.106
9. Toscana	34.303	13.291	340	1.112	255.088	24.889	32.451	2.305	314.733
10. Umbria	4.102	4.225	18	12	53.295	2.404	6.208	249	62.156
11. Lazio	10.112	7.948	737	1.577	131.012	4.284	70.629	4.041	209.966
12. Campania	9.972	7.252	260	2.129	192.307	3.226	22.028	5.085	222.646
13. Abruzzi-Molise	4.307	2.875	16	43	49.404	1.994	15.869	590	67.857
14. Puglia	5.308	1.792	35	55	116.047	4.540	16.538	245	137.370
15. Basilicata	802	44	0	0	15.092	427	4.437	110	20.066
16. Calabria	3.656	2.593	7	6	49.977	1.612	11.417	584	63.590
17. Sicilia	8.828	4.468	28	167	125.757	17.565	25.263	3.192	171.777
18. Sardegna	2.476	511	7	39	36.778	22.400	13.824	515	73.517

TABLE A.9: 1937-39 INDUSTRIAL CENSUS BY REGIONS (1951 CLASSIFICATION, AT THE BOUNDARIES OF THE TIME)

II. PERCENTAGE COMPOSITION

	Food, beverages	Tobacco	Leather, shoes	Textiles	Clothing	Furniture	Paper	Printing, photography	Metal	Engineering
1. Piemonte-Val D'Aosta	7.32	0.31	3.81	23.02	6.37	4.68	1.68	1.62	3.74	24.92
2. Liguria	8.79	0.00	2.83	5.43	4.79	4.29	0.71	1.55	6.90	36.17
3. Lombardia	5.97	0.18	4.20	24.58	6.08	5.30	1.68	2.01	2.73	25.82
4. Trentino Alto Adige	9.62	1.90	5.55	6.09	7.03	14.88	2.11	1.61	3.45	10.98
5. Veneto	14.14	0.41	4.62	21.12	6.06	8.12	1.86	1.47	1.45	12.89
6. Friuli Venezia Giulia	10.24	2.57	2.78	4.41	6.85	6.79	0.96	1.39	1.43	31.70
7. Emilia-Romagna	21.99	1.35	5.04	4.59	8.85	6.31	1.18	1.62	0.14	19.23
8. Marche	11.87	1.87	8.07	9.35	10.55	8.31	1.67	1.13	0.06	12.46
9. Toscana	9.25	1.49	5.25	11.66	7.36	8.14	1.24	1.82	4.05	15.21
10. Umbria	12.58	1.90	5.06	6.98	4.94	7.26	0.69	2.28	7.59	23.01
11. Lazio	9.40	0.72	3.69	1.04	6.19	5.31	2.75	6.93	0.17	16.50
12. Campania	19.03	3.19	8.32	7.17	8.10	9.36	0.63	1.74	2.84	17.19
13. Abruzzi-Molise	18.70	2.47	8.93	4.22	9.78	8.80	0.19	1.21	0.00	7.84
14. Puglia	23.48	11.58	7.93	2.53	8.81	8.89	0.11	1.17	0.31	14.43
15. Basilicata	17.49	0.02	15.74	2.50	10.05	16.23	0.00	0.66	0.00	8.30
16. Calabria	21.89	0.03	10.51	2.70	10.07	16.15	0.03	0.68	0.66	6.03
17. Sicilia	23.54	0.82	11.16	1.77	7.33	9.65	0.08	1.48	0.00	9.52
18. Sardegna	14.44	0.99	5.06	1.32	5.39	9.42	0.06	0.70	2.26	6.25

TABLE A.9: 1937-39 INDUSTRIAL CENSUS BY REGIONS (1951 CLASSIFICATION, AT HE BOUNDARIES OF THE TIME)

II. PERCENTAGE COMPOSITION

	Bricks, glass, tyles	Chemi-cals	Rubber	Other	TOTAL MANUFAC-TURING	Mining	Construc-tion	Public Utilities	TOTAL
1. Piemonte-Val d'Aosta	4.16	4.22	1.15	0.62	87.62	1.78	9.86	0.75	100.00
2. Liguria	4.11	5.92	0.13	0.63	82.23	1.86	14.21	1.69	100.00
3. Lombardia	3.42	3.61	1.43	0.99	87.99	0.82	10.42	0.76	100.00
4. Trentino Alto Adige	3.50	2.29	0.04	0.43	69.48	5.64	23.27	1.61	100.00
5. Veneto	6.06	3.61	0.04	1.00	82.86	1.88	14.23	1.02	100.00
6. Friuli Venezia Giulia	3.57	3.61	0.04	0.15	76.49	12.27	10.09	1.15	100.00
7. Emilia-Romagna	6.26	3.39	0.32	1.56	81.82	1.20	16.13	0.84	100.00
8. Marche	6.79	2.43	0.07	4.11	78.74	4.79	15.83	0.64	100.00
9. Toscana	10.90	4.22	0.11	0.35	81.05	7.91	10.31	0.73	100.00
10. Umbria	6.60	6.80	0.03	0.02	85.74	3.87	9.99	0.40	100.00
11. Lazio	4.82	3.79	0.35	0.75	62.40	2.04	33.64	1.92	100.00
12. Campania	4.48	3.26	0.12	0.96	86.37	1.45	9.89	2.28	100.00
13. Abruzzi-Molise	6.35	4.24	0.02	0.06	72.81	2.94	23.39	0.87	100.00
14. Puglia	3.86	1.30	0.03	0.04	84.48	3.30	12.04	0.18	100.00
15. Basilicata	4.00	0.22	0.00	0.00	75.21	2.13	22.11	0.55	100.00
16. Calabria	5.75	4.08	0.01	0.01	78.59	2.53	17.95	0.92	100.00
17. Sicilia	5.14	2.60	0.02	0.10	73.21	10.23	14.71	1.86	100.00
18. Sardegna	3.37	0.70	0.01	0.05	50.03	30.47	18.80	0.70	100.00

TABLE A.10: 1961 INDUSTRIAL CENSUS BY REGIONS (1951 CLASSIFICATION, AT THE BOUNDARIES OF THE TIME)

I. ABSOLUTE FIGURES

	Food, beverages	Tobacco	Leather, shoes	Textiles	Clothing	Furniture	Paper	Printing, photography	Metal	Engineering
1. Piemonte-Val d'Aosta	35.860	890	18.910	132.305	37.331	33.844	14.335	14.559	41.169	290.492
2. Liguria	12.222	456	4.060	6.311	8.021	9.238	2.159	3.779	20.446	65.484
3. Lombardia	69.674	1.132	55.171	262.886	80.156	87.668	27.965	43.952	76.967	508.850
4. Trentino Alto Adige	4.693	1.041	1.446	2.560	4.003	11.590	1.170	1.382	5.553	13.928
5. Veneto	32.776	3.793	26.386	51.793	30.088	40.632	8.684	8.921	9.345	98.629
6. Friuli Venezia Giulia	8.835	797	4.392	13.020	7.011	15.032	3.015	2.510	3.837	37.067
7. Emilia-Romagna	52.255	2.239	17.976	24.490	31.088	34.817	4.988	8.254	2.014	115.751
8. Marche	7.352	973	13.802	4.365	8.603	12.674	2.088	1.332	296	18.686
9. Toscana	21.259	3.452	29.926	62.342	34.869	34.660	6.406	7.440	12.102	76.050
10. Umbria	6.475	657	2.201	4.662	3.352	4.317	407	1.929	4.211	9.402
11. Lazio	18.256	1.951	6.210	5.868	15.839	17.359	6.817	23.562	1.294	45.910
12. Campania	43.113	4.624	19.637	10.913	20.057	21.756	1.850	4.775	10.398	44.891
13. Abruzzi-Molise	10.192	312	3.128	2.888	9.230	7.400	1.438	974	297	9.331
14. Puglia	26.194	2.818	6.855	5.834	17.096	14.214	1.539	2.600	2.000	20.792
15. Basilicata	3.108	110	1.488	722	2.667	2.296	40	219	23	2.323
16. Calabria	12.327	18	3.188	2.543	7.009	8.738	325	873	651	5.581
17. Sicilia	25.340	886	10.069	3.702	15.299	18.427	806	3.894	494	29.875
18. Sardegna	7.016	412	2.543	1.361	4.180	6.589	176	927	697	6.488

TABLE A.10: 1961 INDUSTRIAL CENSUS BY REGIONS (1951 CLASSIFICATION, AT THE BOUNDARIES OF THE TIME)

I. ABSOLUTE FIGURES

	Bricks, glass, tyles	Chemi-cals	Rubber	Other	TOTAL MANUFAC-TURING	Mining	Construc-tion	Public Utilities	TOTAL
1. Piemonte-Val d'Aosta	29.568	32.686	13.939	10.404	706.292	7.509	95.995	14.110	823.906
2. Liguria	10.234	16.288	581	1.411	161.054	2.181	50.109	5.078	218.422
3. Lombardia	57.071	110.150	26.297	37.252	1.445.199	10.253	187.541	25.984	1.668.977
4. Trentino Alto Adige	3.113	1.802	133	745	53.159	2.994	21.572	3.717	81.442
5. Veneto	37.519	19.971	1.218	8.203	377.958	5.865	80.580	9.440	473.843
6. Friuli Venezia Giulia	6.183	3.587	1.442	618	107.346	1.954	28.487	2.245	140.032
7. Emilia-Romagna	35.525	19.347	3.507	4.967	355.218	4.416	90.226	8.001	457.861
8. Marche	8.328	2.348	350	6.527	87.724	1.533	22.900	2.107	114.264
9. Toscana	46.104	17.287	1.808	2.572	356.277	20.728	63.390	5.762	446.157
10. Umbria	5.817	6.143	149	120	49.842	1.397	11.612	1.624	64.475
11. Lazio	17.443	16.387	2.048	1.192	180.136	5.322	62.660	8.817	256.935
12. Campania	18.001	9.729	808	2.278	212.830	3.527	43.180	7.900	267.437
13. Abruzzi-Molise	8.077	1.196	208	211	54.882	2.038	20.161	2.164	79.245
14. Puglia	10.679	2.233	392	464	113.710	5.911	29.905	5.000	154.526
15. Basilicata	1.159	160	28	7	14.350	558	10.957	1.019	26.884
16. Calabria	5.200	1.718	231	270	48.672	1.515	19.346	2.180	71.713
17. Sicilia	15.629	9.292	482	371	134.566	13.179	38.311	7.983	194.039
18. Sardegna	5.080	576	138	186	36.369	13.270	17.475	2.915	70.029

92

TABLE A.10: 1961 INDUSTRIAL CENSUS BY REGIONS (1951 CLASSIFICATION, AT THE BOUNDARIES OF THE TIME)

II. PERCENTAGE COMPOSITION

	Food, beverages	Tobacco	Leather, shoes	Textiles	Clothing	Furniture	Paper	Printing, photography	Metal	Engineering
1. Piemonte-Val D'Aosta	4.35	0.11	2.30	16.06	4.53	4.11	1.74	1.77	5.00	35.26
2. Liguria	5.60	0.21	1.86	2.89	3.67	4.23	0.99	1.73	9.36	30.15
3. Lombardia	4.17	0.07	3.31	15.75	4.80	5.25	1.68	2.63	4.61	30.49
4. Trentino Alto Adige	5.76	1.28	1.78	3.14	4.92	14.23	1.44	1.70	6.82	17.10
5. Veneto	6.92	0.80	5.57	10.93	6.35	8.57	1.83	1.88	1.97	20.81
6. Friuli Venezia Giulia	6.31	0.57	3.14	9.30	5.01	10.73	2.15	1.79	2.74	26.47
7. Emilia-Romagna	11.41	0.49	3.93	5.35	6.79	7.60	1.09	1.80	0.44	25.28
8. Marche	6.43	0.85	12.08	3.82	7.53	11.09	1.83	1.17	0.26	16.35
9. Toscana	4.76	0.77	6.71	13.97	7.82	7.77	1.44	1.67	2.71	17.05
10. Umbria	10.04	1.02	3.41	7.23	5.20	6.70	0.63	2.99	6.53	14.58
11. Lazio	7.11	0.76	2.42	2.28	6.16	6.76	2.65	9.17	0.50	17.87
12. Campania	16.12	1.73	7.34	4.08	7.50	8.14	0.69	1.79	3.89	16.79
13. Abruzzi-Molise	12.86	0.39	3.95	3.64	11.65	9.34	1.81	1.23	0.37	11.77
14. Puglia	16.95	1.82	4.44	3.78	11.06	9.20	1.00	1.68	1.29	13.46
15. Basilicata	11.56	0.41	5.53	2.69	9.92	8.54	0.15	0.81	0.09	8.64
16. Calabria	17.19	0.03	4.45	3.55	9.77	12.18	0.45	1.22	0.91	7.78
17. Sicilia	13.06	0.46	5.19	1.91	7.88	9.50	0.42	2.01	0.25	15.40
18. Sardegna	10.02	0.59	3.63	1.94	5.97	9.41	0.25	1.32	1.00	9.26

TABLE A.10: 1961 INDUSTRIAL CENSUS BY REGIONS (1951 CLASSIFICATION, AT HE BOUNDARIES OF THE TIME)

II. PERCENTAGE COMPOSITION

	Bricks, glass, tyles	Chemicals	Rubber	Other	TOTAL MANUFACTURING	Mining	Construction	Public Utilities	TOTAL
1. Piemonte-Val d'Aosta	3.59	3.97	1.69	1.26	85.72	0.91	11.65	1.71	100.00
2. Liguria	4.69	7.46	0.27	0.65	73.74	1.00	22.94	2.32	100.00
3. Lombardia	3.42	6.60	1.58	2.23	86.59	0.61	11.24	1.56	100.00
4. Trentino Alto Adige	3.82	2.21	0.16	0.91	65.27	3.68	26.49	4.56	100.00
5. Veneto	7.92	4.21	0.26	1.73	79.76	1.24	17.01	1.99	100.00
6. Friuli Venezia Giulia	4.42	2.56	1.03	0.44	76.66	1.40	20.34	1.60	100.00
7. Emilia-Romagna	7.32	4.23	0.77	1.08	77.58	0.96	19.71	1.75	100.00
8. Marche	7.29	2.05	0.31	5.71	76.77	1.34	20.04	1.84	100.00
9. Toscana	10.33	3.87	0.41	0.58	79.85	4.65	14.21	1.29	100.00
10. Umbria	9.02	9.53	0.23	0.19	77.30	2.17	18.01	2.52	100.00
11. Lazio	6.79	6.38	0.80	0.46	70.11	2.07	24.39	3.43	100.00
12. Campania	6.73	3.64	0.30	0.85	79.58	1.32	16.15	2.95	100.00
13. Abruzzi-Molise	10.19	1.51	0.26	0.27	69.26	2.57	25.44	2.73	100.00
14. Puglia	4.91	1.45	0.25	0.30	73.53	3.83	19.35	3.24	100.00
15. Basilicata	4.31	0.60	0.10	0.03	53.38	2.08	40.76	3.79	100.00
16. Calabria	7.25	2.40	0.32	0.38	67.87	2.11	26.98	3.04	100.00
17. Sicilia	8.05	4.79	0.25	0.19	69.35	6.79	19.74	4.11	100.00
18. Sardegna	7.25	0.82	0.20	0.27	51.93	18.95	24.95	4.16	100,00

94

TABLE A.11: 1981 INDUSTRIAL CENSUS BY REGIONS (1951 CLASSIFICATION, AT THE BOUNDARIES OF THE TIME)

I. ABSOLUTE FIGURES

	Food, beverages	Tobacco	Leather, shoes	Textiles	Clothing	Furniture	Paper	Printing, photography	Metal	Engineering
1. Piemonte-Val d'Aosta	42.482	392	10.678	72.956	38.907	27.882	13.409	21.475	46.158	413.974
2. Liguria	9.430	0	1.744	2.521	5.120	6.299	1.433	4.615	16.772	73.699
3. Lombardia	73.571	596	44.421	172.890	102.097	90.138	28.546	76.408	78.891	710.492
4. Trentino Alto Adige	5.499	609	862	2.933	3.568	13.149	2.126	2.620	5.121	29.046
5. Veneto	35.076	885	50.113	54.017	72.604	72.526	10.301	18.231	13.155	215.843
6. Friuli Venezia Giulia	8.011	352	3.442	6.979	4.322	30.380	3.990	3.587	6.324	63.893
7. Emilia-Romagna	50.977	1.529	20.552	39.602	47.352	36.758	6.319	16.840	7.832	250.231
8. Marche	9.959	757	52.283	7.908	23.669	27.377	3.433	2.771	2.081	47.192
9. Toscana	20.368	1.334	64.615	83.520	53.414	40.855	9.451	10.672	19.181	129.711
10. Umbria	9.650	432	2.455	8.907	13.695	6.692	1.805	2.155	8.685	22.640
11. Lazio	23.721	1.676	4.532	7.907	17.670	19.672	7.269	32.289	3.623	115.298
12. Campania	33.107	5.540	23.853	8.410	24.594	19.070	2.921	7.893	13.765	125.796
13. Abruzzi-Molise	12.793	547	5.271	4.106	18.987	8.824	2.395	1.964	2:007	38.446
14. Puglia	21.880	3.199	8.506	10.773	23.483	16.082	2.230	5.185	25.261	67.282
15. Basilicata	3.228	119	389	936	2.083	1.724	50	502	426	8.103
16. Calabria	9.397	132	981	2.227	2.855	5.999	339	1.543	1.048	14.153
17. Sicilia	17.476	670	3.787	3.891	11.167	15.312	1.802	5.888	1.860	64.203
18. Sardegna	8.447	270	765	2.987	1.993	7.389	981	1.917	4.607	18.416

TABLE A.11: 1981 INDUSTRIAL CENSUS BY REGIONS (1951 CLASSIFICATION, AT THE BOUNDARIES OF THE TIME)

I. ABSOLUTE FIGURES

	Bricks, glass, tyles	Chemi-cals	Rubber	Other	TOTAL MANUFAC-TURING	Mining	Construc-tions	Public Utilities	TOTAL
1. Piemonte-Val d'Aosta	20.100	25.250	24.951	24.563	783.177	4.733	105.135	19.589	912.634
2. Liguria	7.100	12.753	806	3.508	145.800	1.291	39.008	7.462	193.561
3. Lombardia	45.908	116.998	24.095	64.041	1.629.092	10.187	223.991	30.446	1.893.716
4. Trentino Alto Adige	3.333	2.602	623	3.265	75.356	2.970	33.571	3.504	115.401
5. Veneto	39.354	25.548	6.267	23.616	637.536	3.754	125.701	14.596	781.587
6. Friuli Venezia Giulia	7.104	3.904	673	2.312	145.219	1.793	49.177	3.948	200.137
7. Emilia-Romagna	62.426	20.677	4.028	18.389	583.512	4.066	126.850	12.231	726.659
8. Marche	7.999	3.477	2.762	11.081	202.749	1.519	45.338	3.845	253.451
9. Toscana	37.986	19.581	2.466	11.752	504.906	8.668	86.958	11.570	612.102
10. Umbria	8.755	5.849	368	1.707	93.795	1.183	23.240	2.833	121.051
11. Lazio	19.410	24.936	7.038	5.193	290.234	5.501	76.796	16.820	389.351
12. Campania	18.564	12.687	2.134	7.009	305.343	2.211	66.158	12.408	386.120
13. Abruzzi-Molise	13.179	3.183	1.428	2.750	115.880	1.544	43.427	4.321	165.172
14. Puglia	14.336	7.821	4.031	2.829	212.898	3.869	64.486	7.935	289.188
15. Basilicata	2.394	4.046	227	546	24.773	773	20.290	2.172	48.008
16. Calabria	6.340	3.533	675	488	49.710	575	32.856	4.697	87.838
17. Sicilia	16.532	18.310	2.687	2.746	166.331	6.361	64.875	12.866	250.433
18. Sardegna	7.278	11.435	650	826	67.961	6.247	36.752	5.881	166.841

TABLE A.11: 1981 INDUSTRIAL CENSUS BY REGIONS (1951 CLASSIFICATION, AT THE BOUNDARIES OF THE TIME)

II. PERCENTAGE COMPOSITION

	Food, beverages	Tobacco	Leather, shoes	Textiles	Clothing	Furniture	Paper	Printing, photography	Metal	Engineering
1. Piemonte-Val D'Aosta	4.65	0.04	1.17	7.99	4.26	3.06	1.47	2.35	5.06	45.36
2. Liguria	4.87	0.00	0.90	1.30	2.65	3.25	0.74	2.38	8.66	38.08
3. Lombardia	3.89	0.03	2.35	9.13	5.39	4.76	1.51	4.03	4.17	37.52
4. Trentino Alto Adige	4.77	0.53	0.75	2.54	3.09	11.39	1.84	2.27	4.44	25.17
5. Veneto	4.49	0.11	6.41	6.91	9.29	9.28	1.32	2.33	1.68	27.62
6. Friuli Venezia Giulia	4.00	0.18	1.72	3.49	2.16	15.18	1.99	1.79	3.16	31.90
7. Emilia-Romagna	7.02	0.21	2.83	5.45	6.52	5.06	0.87	2.32	1.08	34.44
8. Marche	3.93	0.30	20.63	3.12	9.34	10.80	1.35	1.09	0.82	18.62
9. Toscana	3.33	0.22	10.56	13.64	8.73	6.67	1.54	1.74	3.13	21.19
10. Umbria	7.97	0.36	2.03	7.36	11.31	5.53	1.49	1.78	7.17	18.70
11. Lazio	6.09	0.43	1.16	2.03	4.54	5.05	1.87	8.29	0.93	29.61
12. Campania	8.57	1.43	6.18	2.18	6.37	4.94	0.76	2.04	3.56	32.58
13. Abruzzi-Molise	7.75	0.33	3.19	2.49	11.50	5.34	1.45	1.19	1.22	23.28
14. Puglia	7.57	1.11	2.94	3.73	8.12	5.56	0.77	1.79	8.74	23.27
15. Basilicata	6.72	0.25	0.81	1.95	4.34	3.59	0.10	1.05	0.89	16.88
16. Calabria	10.70	0.15	1.12	2.54	3.25	6.83	0.39	1.76	1.19	16.11
17. Sicilia	6.98	0.27	1.51	1.55	4.46	6.11	0.72	2.35	0.74	25.64
18. Sardegna	7.23	0.23	0.65	2.56	1.17	6.32	0.84	1.64	3.94	15.76

TABLE A.11: 1981 INDUSTRIAL CENSUS BY REGIONS (1951 CLASSIFICATION, AT THE BOUNDARIES OF THE TIME)

II. PERCENTAGE COMPOSITION

	Bricks, glass, tyles	Chemi- cals	Rubber	Other	TOTAL MANUFAC- TURING	Mining	Construc- tion	Public Utilities	TOTAL
1. Piemonte-Val d'Aosta	2.20	2.77	2.73	2.69	85.82	0.52	11.52	2.15	100.00
2. Liguria	3.67	6.59	0.42	1.81	75.33	0.67	20.15	3.86	100.00
3. Lombardia	2.42	6.18	1.27	3.38	86.03	0.54	11.83	1.61	100.00
4. Trentino Alto Adige	2.89	2.25	0.54	2.83	65.30	2.57	29.09	3.04	100.00
5. Veneto	5.04	3.27	0.80	3.02	81.57	0.48	16.08	1.87	100.00
6. Friuli Venezia Giulia	3.55	1.95	0.34	1.16	72.56	0.90	24.57	1.97	100.00
7. Emilia-Romagna	8.59	2.85	0.55	2.53	80.30	0.56	17.46	1.68	100.00
8. Marche	3.16	1.37	1.09	4.37	80.00	0.60	17.89	1.52	100.00
9. Toscana	6.21	3.20	0.40	1.92	82.49	1.42	14.21	1.89	100.00
10. Umbria	7.23	4.83	0.30	1.41	77.48	0.98	19.20	2.34	100.00
11. Lazio	4.99	6.40	1.81	1.33	74.54	1.41	19.72	4.32	100.00
12. Campania	4.81	3.29	0.55	1.82	79.08	0.57	17.13	3.21	100.00
13. Abruzzi-Molise	7.98	1.93	0.86	1.66	70.16	0.93	26.29	2.62	100.00
14. Puglia	4.96	2.70	1.39	0.98	73.62	1.34	22.30	2.74	100.00
15. Basilicata	4.99	8.43	0.47	1.14	51.60	1.61	42.26	4.52	100.00
16. Calabria	7.22	4.02	0.77	0.56	56.59	0.65	37.41	5.35	100.00
17. Sicilia	6.60	7.31	1.07	1.10	66.42	2.54	25.91	5.14	100.00
18. Sardegna	6.23	9.79	0.56	0.71	58.17	5.35	31.45	5.03	100.00

[9]

International Resource Flows and Construction Movements in the Atlantic Economy: The Kuznets Cycle in Italy, 1861–1913

STEFANO FENOALTEA

Nineteenth-century Italy experienced the long swings in migration, capital flows, and construction characteristic of the international Kuznets cycle, but in an unusual combination: its external migration swing may have resembled Britain's, but its capital flows and construction swing resembled America's. Construction in Italy was finance-sensitive rather than population-sensitive, and reacted primarily to exogenous shifts in the supply of foreign capital. The Italian experience suggests that changes in perceived risk altered the relative supply of capital in Britain and abroad and thereby induced the opposite swings in construction and the swing in migration.

The "Atlantic economy" of the later nineteenth century was characterized by long swings in international resource flows, accompanied by largely opposite swings in construction activity in Britain on the one hand and in its overseas counterparts on the other. The transoceanic movement of European migrants and capital displayed long-swing peaks in the early 1870s, the late 1880s, and again on the eve of the First World War, with intervening troughs in the late 1870s and near the turn of the century. In the New World, including Canada, Argentina, and Australia as well as the United States, construction displayed this very same long swing; in Britain, the dominant exporter of capital as well as a major source of migrants, construction displayed

The Journal of Economic History, Vol. XLVIII, No. 3 (Sept. 1988). ISSN 0022–0507.

The author is affiliated with the School of Social Science, The Institute for Advanced Study, Princeton, NJ 08540.

For their helpful comments on earlier versions of this paper he wishes to thank Moses Abramowitz, Lee Alston, Arthur Bloomfield, Charles Calomiris, Michael Edelstein, Robert Gallman, Stephen Golub, David Gordon, Knick Harley, Robinson Hollister, Peter Lindert, Ellen Magenheim, Joel Mokyr, Hugh Rockoff, Richard Sylla, and Jeffrey Williamson; the participants at the 1985 Cliometrics Conference, the Conference on "Bilancia dei pagamenti e svíluppo economico nel caso italiano dall'Unità a oggi" (Cortona, 1987), and the Conference on "El desarrollo económico en la Europa del Sur: Italia-España, 1860–1986" (Alcalá de Henares, 1987); and the participants at seminars at Cambridge, Columbia, Harvard, Illinois-Chicago, Indiana, North Carolina State, Oxford, Rutgers, the Triangle Economic History Workshop, and the Banca d'Italia. He is also grateful to the National Science Foundation for supporting his research on Italian industrial production (Grant No. SES-7913427), to the Exxon Research and Engineering Company for supporting his tenure at the Institute for Advanced Study, and to the Banca d'Italia and the Istituto centrale di statistica for the use of their research facilities. He alone, of course, is responsible for the views expressed here.

its mirror image, peaking when transoceanic resource flows and New World construction were weakest and vice versa.[1]

The literature on these long swings or Kuznets cycles offers the usual variety of interpretations. H. J. Habakkuk, P. J. O'Leary and W. Arthur Lewis, and S. B. Saul, for example, dismiss the entire pattern as mere happenstance.[2] But theirs is a minority view; the authoritative tradition represented by Moses Abramowitz, Alec Cairncross, Allen Kelley, Brinley Thomas, Jeffrey Williamson, and Simon Kuznets himself sees a systematic relationship between the inverse construction movements and the transoceanic resource flows, even if it doubts that the long swing was a true self-perpetuating cycle. Migration is here the key element, causing opposite variations in the demand for construction—"population-sensitive capital formation," in Kuznets's telling phrase—in the source and destination areas; the parallel capital flows are similarly derivative, as they are themselves induced by (and of course facilitate the continuation of) the divergent rates of infrastructure investment.[3]

Newly available evidence obtained as part of an ongoing recalculation of Italian industrial production indicates that construction in Italy also followed the characteristic Kuznets cycle—with the peaks and troughs typical of the New World *recipients* of international migration. As is well known, Italy was also heavily involved in the international flows of labor and capital; and while the available time series are hardly what one would hope for, the evidence strongly suggests that the construction

[1] See, for example, Brinley Thomas, *Migration and Urban Development: A Reappraisal of British and American Long Cycles* (London, 1972), p. 4.

[2] H. J. Habakkuk, "Fluctuations in House-Building in Britain and the United States in the Nineteenth Century," this JOURNAL, 22 (June 1962), pp. 213, 227; P. J. O'Leary and W. Arthur Lewis, "Secular Swings in Production and Trade, 1870–1913," *The Manchester School of Economic and Social Studies*, 23 (May 1955), p. 127; S. B. Saul, "House Building in England, 1890–1914," *Economic History Review*, 2nd ser., 15 (Aug. 1962), p. 136.

[3] Moses Abramowitz, "The Nature and Significance of Kuznets Cycles," *Economic Development and Cultural Change*, 9 (Apr. 1961), p. 248, and "The Passing of the Kuznets Cycle," *Economica*, n. s., no. 140 (Nov. 1968), p. 366; Alec Cairncross, *Home and Foreign Investment, 1870–1913: Studies in Capital Accumulation* (Cambridge, 1953), pp. 195, 209, and "Economic Growth and Stagnation in the United Kingdom before the First World War," in Mark Gersovitz et al., eds., *The Theory and Experience of Economic Development: Essays in Honor of Sir W. Arthur Lewis* (London, 1982), p. 293; Allen C. Kelley, "Demographic Change and Economic Growth: Australia, 1861–1911," *Explorations in Entrepreneurial History*, 2nd ser., 5 (Spring/Summer 1968), pp. 207–77; Brinley Thomas, *Migration and Economic Growth: A Study of Great Britain and the Atlantic Economy* (Cambridge, 1954), pp. 174–75, and *Migration and Urban Development*, pp. 24–41; Jeffrey G. Williamson, *American Growth and the Balance of Payments, 1820–1913: A Study of the Long Swing* (Chapel Hill, 1964), p. 11; Simon S. Kuznets, *Capital in the American Economy: Its Formation and Financing* (Princeton, 1961), p. 327ff. See also J. Parry Lewis, "Growth and Inverse Cycles: A Two-Country Model," *Economic Journal*, 74 (Mar. 1964), pp. 109–18. Some authors stress the role of primary product prices and the terms of trade in determining the long swing in migration; see the early analysis in Cairncross, *Home and Foreign Investment*, pp. 189–195, the evidence in W. Arthur Lewis, *Growth and Fluctuations, 1870–1913* (London, 1978), p. 59, and especially C. Knick Harley, "Transportation, the World Wheat Trade, and the Kuznets Cycle, 1850–1913," *Explorations in Economic History*, 17 (July 1980), pp. 218–50.

cycle in Italy was related not to demographic developments but to financial ones.

Specifically, the long swings in Italian construction seem tied to changes in the supply of foreign capital, and thus to changes in British foreign investment—themselves attributable, it would appear, less to variations in domestic British investment opportunities than to changes in investors' perception of the relative safety of investment in Britain and abroad. An examination of the Kuznets cycle in Italy thus suggests that the forces generating the inverse long swings of the Atlantic economy were primarily financial rather than demographic, and that the fundamental distinction was between the exporters and importers of capital rather than between the exporters and importers of labor.

THE LONG SWING IN CONSTRUCTION

The new series documenting the long swing in construction in Italy are presented in Table 1 and illustrated in Figure 1.[4]

Column 1 is an index of urban construction, obtained by chaining the geometric average of year-to-year growth rates in a sample of cities (five at the very beginning, quickly rising to fifteen to twenty; most are in the North, the rest in the Center). These city-specific growth rates are calculated from data on the consumption of binders (plaster, lime, cement) subject to consumption tax; that tax was levied as the goods crossed the urban consumption-tax perimeter, which normally coincided with the city walls. Since binders are bulky and not easily smuggled, the data are intrinsically of relatively high quality.

This index displays a clear long swing, with peaks in 1862–65, 1873, 1887, and 1912, and intervening troughs in 1868, 1877–79, and 1895 (Figure 1, line 5). That long swing is apparent in the basic series, and does not need to be teased out by taking long moving averages or otherwise manipulating the data in a way that risks creating the phenomenon one is investigating; it is also diffused through the sample, and not the result of a few outliers.[5]

Columns 2 through 5 are estimates of actual new construction at 1911 prices. Column 2 refers to railway construction. These estimates are obtained as weighted sums of quantity series tracing the length of new rail and tramway lines entering service (distributed over the relevant construction period) on the one hand, and rail consumption in excess of that absorbed by network extensions (to represent improvements and

[4] These series are derived in Stefano Fenoaltea, "Public Works Construction in Italy, 1861–1913," *Rivista di storia economica*, 3 (International issue, 1986), pp. 1–33, and "Construction in Italy, 1861–1913," *Rivista di storia economica*, 4 (International issue, 1987), pp. 21–53; see also "Railway Construction in Italy, 1861–1913," *Rivista di storia economica*, 1 (International issue, 1984), pp. 27–58.

[5] While the spectrum of growth rates across cities is always very wide, the entire spectrum moves as the index does; see Fenoaltea, "Construction in Italy," table 1.

TABLE 1
CONSTRUCTION: NEW SERIES

Year	Index of Urban Construction (1911 = 100) (1)	New Construction (million lire at 1911 prices)			
		Social Overhead Capital			
		Railways (2)	Other (3)	Private Buildings (4)	Total[a] (5)
1861	30.6	188	109	100	396
1862	40.3	210	114	158	482
1863	35.9	214	143	134	492
1864	38.5	191	145	153	490
1865	37.9	182	179	128	490
1866	31.8	157	132	98	387
1867	33.3	113	114	110	337
1868	30.4	111	127	89	327
1869	32.4	96	116	107	320
1870	32.4	106	140	95	341
1871	34.2	114	128	122	364
1872	36.4	122	153	126	401
1873	38.3	136	167	174	476
1874	38.1	141	149	212	502
1875	36.4	111	140	152	404
1876	35.6	97	140	139	376
1877	34.2	83	166	137	387
1878	34.2	89	172	127	388
1879	34.2	123	156	120	399
1880	36.8	147	167	126	440
1881	37.5	168	154	147	469
1882	39.0	211	171	178	559
1883	42.3	236	196	175	607
1884	46.6	231	219	183	632
1885	48.9	234	218	207	659
1886	55.4	223	238	209	671
1887	56.4	198	277	160	635
1888	56.7	205	298	116	619
1889	52.0	176	286	124	585
1890	45.9	175	247	164	586
1891	42.7	181	210	181	572
1892	38.6	179	182	163	524
1893	38.9	151	166	186	503
1894	36.1	165	151	183	498
1895	35.7	73	143	177	393
1896	36.4	43	142	177	361
1897	36.0	46	141	176	363
1898	40.9	36	143	176	356
1899	44.1	34	154	177	365
1900	42.3	43	165	183	391
1901	44.3	51	173	204	428
1902	47.6	60	191	239	490
1903	49.9	58	202	274	533
1904	54.7	70	198	306	573

TABLE 1—continued

Year	Index of Urban Construction (1911 = 100) (1)	New Construction (million lire at 1911 prices)			
		Social Overhead Capital		Private Buildings (4)	Total[a] (5)
		Railways (2)	Other (3)		
1905	56.9	73	226	335	635
1906	70.8	83	278	329	690
1907	72.1	91	302	349	742
1908	78.6	95	337	373	805
1909	84.6	116	413	444	973
1910	89.3	141	477	519	1,137
1911	100.0	150	495	555	1,201
1912	100.9	155	506	564	1,225
1913	91.6	151	501	547	1,199

[a] Numbers need not add, due to rounding.
Sources: Columns 1, 4, and 5 from Stefano Fenoaltea, "Construction in Italy, 1861–1913," *Rivista di storia economica*, 4 (International issue, 1987), pp. 21–53. Columns 2 and 3 from Stefano Fenoaltea, "Public Works Construction in Italy, 1861–1913," *Rivista di storia economica*, 3 (International issue, 1986), pp. 1–33.

the like) on the other; the weights are the corresponding unit values at 1911 prices.

Column 3 refers to other social overhead capital formation. Its smaller component is a sum of quantity series tracing the additions to privately financed gas, power, water, and irrigation works, again weighted by the corresponding unit values at 1911 prices; its larger one traces the deflated expenditure on public buildings and on other non-railway projects (including those financed from private sources).

Column 4 refers to private building construction. The larger component of this series refers to taxable (basically, non-farm) buildings. From the early 1870s, it is calculated by deflating the reported or estimated increments in buildings-tax assessments attributable to new construction, allowing for public buildings, and then scaling the result to convert deflated assessments into actual construction values. This series is then extrapolated back to 1861 with the aid of the urban construction index in column 1, allowing for public works. The complementary estimates for exempt (farm) buildings are extrapolated from the preceding series, allowing primarily for the relative intercensal movements of the relevant populations (including those induced by demolitions) and secondarily for the discrepancies between urban and non-farm construction.

Column 5 is the estimate of aggregate construction, obtained as the sum of columns 2 through 4. It too displays a clear long swing in the raw series, with peaks in 1862–65, 1874, 1886, and 1912, and intervening troughs in 1869, 1876, and 1898; and as can be seen in Figure 1, this

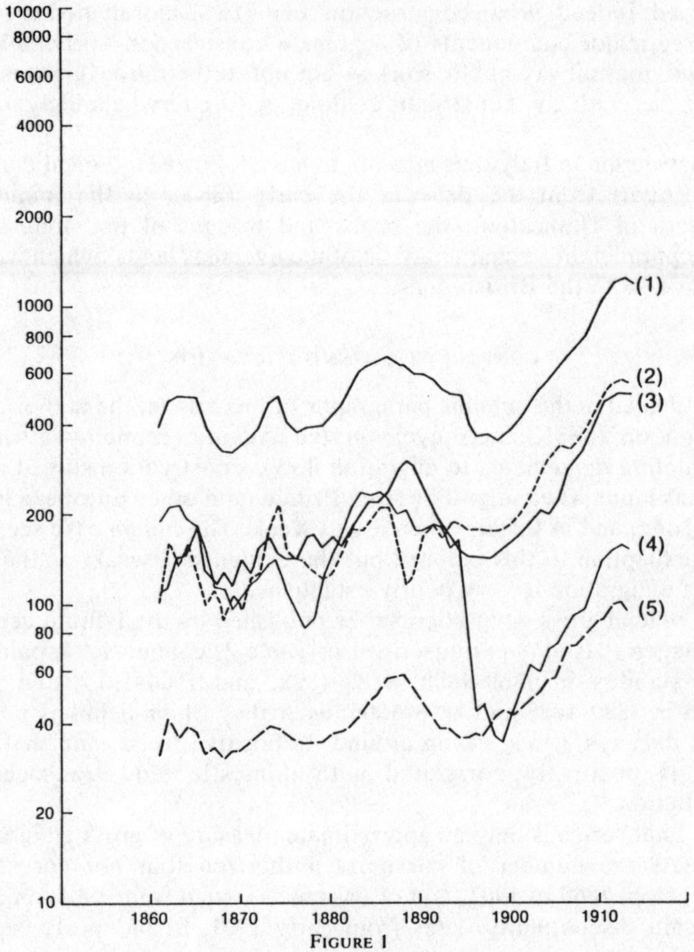

FIGURE 1

CONSTRUCTION

(1) Aggregate value of new construction (Table 1, column 5: million lire at 1911 prices).
(2) Value of new construction: private buildings (Table 1, column 4: million lire at 1911 prices).
(3) Value of new construction: non-railway social overhead capital (Table 1, column 3: million lire at 1911 prices).
(4) Value of new construction: railways (Table 1, column 2: million lire at 1911 prices).
(5) Index of urban construction (Table 1, column 1: 1911 equals 100).

pattern was largely common to all three major components of the aggregate.

The direct estimates of aggregate construction and the index of urban construction thus display much the same cyclical pattern. There are differences between them, of course, most noticeably in the last full cycle between the late 1870s and the late 1890s; but these too are readily explained. Indeed, urban construction seems to be closely tied to two of the three major components of aggregate construction—private buildings and non-railway public works—but not to the third; this stands to reason, as railway construction alone was overwhelmingly extra-urban.[6]

Construction in Italy thus appears to have followed a typical Kuznets cycle. Apart from the peak in the early 1860s, in the immediate aftermath of Unification, the peaks and troughs of that long swing largely parallel those characteristic of the overseas lands, which were in turn inverse to the British ones.

CONSTRUCTION AND MIGRATION

As recalled in the opening paragraphs of this article, the authoritative tradition on the Kuznets cycle in the Atlantic economy attributes construction movements to migration flows: construction surged in the overseas lands when migration from Britain (and other European lands) was strong, and in Britain when it was weak. The Italian case seems to be an exception to this pattern; but the evidence is weak, as the time path of emigration is very poorly established.

The official gross emigration series published by the Istituto centrale di statistica ("Istat") is transcribed in Table 2, column 1.[7] It points to rough stability in 1869–1880, 1888–1898, and 1906–1913, and rapid growth in 1880–1888 and 1898–1906; as Arthur Bloomfield has pointed out, it displays a long swing around its positive trend, and that long swing is positively correlated with domestic (and transoceanic) construction.[8]

The Istat series is only an approximate measure of gross emigration: it reflects the number of passports authorized (but not necessarily issued) from 1869 to 1903, and of passports issued from 1904.[9] A more significant discontinuity dates from early 1901, as passports became

[6] Ibid., pp. 26–27 and fn. 14.

[7] Istituto centrale di statistica, *Sommario di statistiche storiche italiane, 1861–1955* [henceforth *Sommario*] (Rome, 1957), p. 65.

[8] Arthur I. Bloomfield, *Patterns of Fluctuation in International Investment Before 1914* (Princeton, 1968), p. 32 fn., asserts that "Italian emigration shows clear long-swing movements that tended to have a positive relation to the swings in the domestic variables but to be even more closely related to and influenced by the Kuznets cycle in the United States." The domestic variables are railway track added and industrial production, as measured in my own early work, while emigration is measured by the series at hand (pp. 32, 49). In a similar vein, Francesco Lauricella, "Emigrazione italiana di massa in Argentina e in Brasile e ciclo agricolo (1876–1896)," in Franca Assante, ed., *Il movimento migratorio italiano dall'Unità nazionale ai giorni nostri* (Geneva, 1978), vol. 2, p. 372, plots an 11-year moving average of the absolute changes in gross overseas migration; his series displays a long swing with high levels in the 1880s and 1896–1909, with an intervening trough in the early 1890s (and another very sharp one after 1910, as the war years get averaged in). His interpretation stresses the push of declining grain prices in the 1880s, and the pull of overseas labor markets in the later surge (pp. 379, 382–383).

[9] *Sommario*, p. 5.

TABLE 2
DEMOGRAPHIC VARIABLES: EXISTING SERIES

Year	Gross Emigration (000s) (1)	Net Emigration (000s) (2)	Number of Marriages (000s) (3)	Marriage Rate (per 1000) (4)
1861			211	
1862		30	213	16.4
1863		25	214	16.4
1864		20	210	16.0
1865		15	241	18.2
1866		10	149	11.2
1867		3	180	13.4
1868		4	195	14.4
1869	135	5	218	16.0
1870	107	5	200	14.6
1871	122	6	204	14.8
1872	146	32	208	15.0
1873	152	33	221	15.8
1874	108	29	213	15.2
1875	103	31	237	16.8
1876	109	33	233	16.4
1877	99	31	223	15.6
1878	96	32	207	14.4
1879	120	43	220	15.2
1880	120	47	204	14.0
1881	136	51	237	16.2
1882	162	55	230	15.6
1883	169	60	241	16.2
1884	147	66	248	16.6
1885	157	71	241	16.0
1886	168	76	240	15.8
1887	216	82	245	16.0
1888	291	111	243	15.8
1889	218	96	239	15.4
1890	216	103	228	14.6
1891	294	123	236	15.0
1892	224	118	237	15.0
1893	247	126	236	14.8
1894	225	119	237	14.8
1895	293	143	236	14.6
1896	307	147	231	14.2
1897	300	162	235	14.4
1898	284	172	227	13.8
1899	308	183	242	14.6
1900	353	178	240	14.4
1901	533	117	241	14.4
1902	532	118	246	14.6
1903	508	120	243	14.4
1904	471	106	256	15.0

Continued overleaf

TABLE 2—continued

Year	Gross Emigration (000s) (1)	Net Emigration (000s) (2)	Number of Marriages (000s) (3)	Marriage Rate (per 1000) (4)
1905	726	131	263	15.4
1906	788	138	268	15.6
1907	705	130	270	15.6
1908	487	109	293	16.8
1909	626	124	275	15.6
1910	651	124	277	15.6
1911	534	124	269	15.0
1912	711	298	275	15.2
1913	873	449	272	15.0

Sources: Column 1 from Istituto centrale di statistica, *Sommario di statistiche storiche italiane, 1861–1955* (Rome, 1957); column 2 from Franco Giusti, "Bilanci demografici della popolazione italiana dal 1861 al 1961," in Istituto centrale di statistica, *Sviluppo della popolazione italiana dal 1861 al 1961* (Rome, 1965); columns 3 and 4 from Stefano Somogyi, "Nuzialità," in *Sviluppo della popolazione italiana dal 1861 al 1961*.

free, so that an increased proportion may have been issued to people who did not in fact depart; on the other hand, their validity was extended to three years, so that seasonal migrants could well exit Italy a number of times without being counted more than once.[10] Moreover, significant numbers of individuals departed without any passport, especially to or through other European countries. Transoceanic immigration figures thus exceed the corresponding Italian data by about one quarter between 1879 and 1900; after 1901, when passports became compulsory for transoceanic migrants, the discrepancy is much reduced (Argentina) or changes sign (Brazil, United States).[11]

In any case the conceptually relevant variable is not gross emigration but net emigration; and the former is a poor guide to the latter, as the return flow was high, variable, and documented only in part (the transoceanic component, based on ships' passenger lists, from 1902).[12] On the other hand, net emigration is reasonably well established between successive censuses as the difference between the natural increase and the actual increase. The relevant census dates are December 31, 1861, 1871, and 1881; February 10, 1901; and June 10, 1911. No

[10] Francesco Coletti, "Dell'emigrazione italiana," in R. Accademia dei Lincei, *Cinquanta anni di storia italiana* (Milan, 1911), vol. 3, pp. 10–11.

[11] J. D. Gould, "European Inter-Continental Emigration. The Road Home: Return Migration from the USA," *Journal of European Economic History*, 9 (Spring 1980), pp. 88–90; see also Ercole Sori, *L'emigrazione italiana dall'Unità alla seconda guerra mondiale* (Bologna, 1979), p. 55.

[12] Gould, "European Inter-Continental Emigration," pp. 79, 84–85; *Sommario*, pp. 65, 67. The transatlantic return flow figures, compiled by the Commissariato dell'emigrazione, are not comparable to the outflow data; see Coletti, "Dell'emigrazione," pp. 14–15, 38, 74.

census was taken in 1891; for present purposes, this omission is a critical deficiency.

The intercensal changes yield annual net emigration rates rising from 0.1 per thousand in the 1860s to 1.3 in the 1870s, 3.8 in the 1880s and 1890s together, and 4.7 in the 1900s.[13] Taken at face value, these suggest at a minimum that construction and emigration peaked together after the turn of the century; but a case can fairly be made that the June date of the 1911 census tends to overstate net migration, as the different seasonal pattern of departures and returns led to a disproportionately greater counting of the former.[14]

Annual estimates of net migration on a consistent calendar-year basis have been compiled by Franco Giusti (Table 2, column 2).[15] These were calculated by taking the year-end population in the census years (as reported or estimated ad hoc), and then distributing the intercensal totals over the intervening years with an eye to the path of gross migration. Giusti's figures yield annual rates of net migration equal to 1.3 per thousand in 1872–1881 (as above), 2.8 in 1882–1891, 4.6 in 1892–1901 (3.8 for the two decades together), and 3.6 in 1902–1911—suggesting, against the crude figures obtained directly from the censuses, that the peak in net emigration coincided not with the peak but with the trough in domestic construction.[16]

This conclusion seems questionable, on two separate grounds. In the first place, Giusti's estimate of the population at the end of 1911 seems too high, as it implies an implausibly high level of net immigration in the months after the census; he thus seems to have underestimated net emigration in 1911 and therefore in the 1902–1911 decade as a whole. In the second place, his allocation of the total net migration between 1882 and 1901 seems to allow too little to the 1880s and too much to the 1890s, as it implies an implausible variation in the repatriant ratio from decade to decade. As detailed in the Appendix, prudent corrections would increase Giusti's net migration figures for 1902–1911 (and reduce his end-1911 population figure) by some 100,000 souls, and reallocate some 257,000 of the net migrants between 1882 and 1901 from 1892–1901 to 1882–1891.

These revisions imply that the annual net migration rate per thousand rose from 1.3 in 1872–1881 to 3.7 in 1882–1891, 3.8 in 1892–1901, and 3.9

[13] Massimo Livi Bacci, "I fattori demografici dello sviluppo economico," in Giorgio Fuà, ed., *Lo sviluppo economico in Italia* (2nd edn, Milan, 1975), vol. 2, p. 21.

[14] Gould, "European Inter-Continental Emigration," p. 82.

[15] Franco Giusti, "Bilanci demografici della popolazione italiana dal 1861 al 1961," in Istituto centrale di statistica, *Sviluppo della popolazione italiana dal 1861 al 1961. Annali di statistica*, series 8, vol. 17 (Rome, 1965), p. 116.

[16] Gould, "European Inter-Continental Emigration," pp. 79–87, investigates and explains the differences between the Livi Bacci and Giusti figures. While not unaware of the weaknesses of the latter, particularly as an annual series, he accepts Giusti's implication that "the Italian *net* population loss through emigration peaked in the 1890s" (p. 87).

TABLE 3
CONSTRUCTION AND DEMOGRAPHIC VARIABLES: DECADAL VALUES

	1862–1871	1872–1881	1882–1891	1892–1901	1902–1911
1. Total construction[a]	4.030	4.242	6.125	4.182	7.779
2. Rate of net emigration[b]	0.01	0.13	0.37	0.38	0.39
3. Population growth rate[b]	0.69	0.60	0.69	0.70	0.71
4. Population increment[c]	1.784	1.659	2.011	2.192	2.383
5. Ratio of row 1 to row 4	2.3	2.6	3.0	1.9	3.3
6. Marriages[c]	2.031	2.147	2.316	2.293	2.578
7. Ratio of row 1 to row 6	2.0	2.0	2.6	1.8	3.0

[a] Billion 1911 lire.
[b] Percent per year.
[c] Millions.
Sources: Row 1 from Table 1, column 5; rows 2, 3, 4, and 6 from the text.

in 1902–1911. The differences in the net migration rates across these last three decades, in short, appear to be insignificant. On a decadal basis, therefore, the Italian case does not fit the pattern of the "Atlantic economy," in which surges in construction are associated with higher immigration or lower emigration. In Italy the rise in construction from the 1870s to the 1880s is associated with a rise in net emigration; the subsequent decline in construction in the 1890s, and its recovery in the 1900s, are not associated with opposite movements in net emigration (Table 3, rows 1 and 2).

One would of course prefer to examine the correlation of construction and net migration with more numerous data points; but pending a revision of Giusti's annual figures the Italian evidence cannot be taken to reveal net migration over periods shorter than a decade. On the other hand, the shorter-term movements of net migration from Italy presumably paralleled those of aggregate migration to the New World (not least because of the unifying impact of the business cycle in the receiving areas); and the latter was closely correlated with local construction, which as noted was closely correlated with construction in Italy.[17] Presumably, therefore, the generally positive association of construction in Italy and net migration from Italy revealed by the decadal figures would appear even stronger with more fine-grained data.

CONSTRUCTION AND POPULATION GROWTH

In a sense, of course, the relation between migration and construction is a secondary issue. The Kuznetsian description of construction is after all not "migration-sensitive" but "population-sensitive" capital formation; migration matters to the extent that it alters the growth rate of

[17] As indicated in the Appendix, the impact of conditions in the receiving areas on Italy's net emigration is clearly apparent in the available figures for transoceanic repatriation after the turn of the century.

population in general and household formation in particular. The Italian experience could thus still fit the Kuznetsian view, whatever the path of net migration, if the long swing in construction was positively related to domestic demographic variables.

Once again, however, this does not appear to be the case. At decade intervals, the year-end population within the borders of 1871 to 1913 equaled 25.017 million in 1861 (census figure), 26.801 in 1871 (census figure), 28.460 in 1881 (census figure), 30.471 in 1891 (my figure, from the Appendix), 32.663 in 1901 (Giusti's figure), and 35.046 in 1911 (my figure, from the Appendix). These yield the population growth rates and absolute increments transcribed in Table 3, rows 3 and 4, which can be compared with the corresponding cumulations of total construction in row 1. Except for the dip in the 1870s, the decadal population growth rate is virtually constant; clearly, the long swing is not in population growth but in construction per additional person (row 5).[18]

Comparisons based on particularly significant subsections of the population are unfortunately possible only for intercensal periods, and thus fail to separate the 1880s from the 1890s. The number of men aged 25 to 65, which may be a fair proxy for the number of households, increased by 49,900 per year in the 1860s, 33,700 in the 1870s, 19,100 in the 1880s and 1890s, and 24,000 in the 1900s.[19] Comparing these intercensal changes to the construction recorded in the corresponding decades, one obtains a construction-per-additional-man equal to 8.1 constant lire in the 1860s, 12.6 in the 1870s, 27.0 in the 1880s and 1890s together, and 32.4 in the 1900s. The strong trend is apparent; the long swing, if any, is lost within the intercensal periods.

A limited but telling comparison is that between the population living in dispersed rural housing and the population engaged in agriculture. From 1861 to 1901, the censuses suggest that both these populations grew relatively smoothly, the dispersed population increasing by 2.9 million as the agricultural population increased by 3.8 million. From 1901 to 1911, on the other hand, the dispersed population grew by a further 0.7 million while the agricultural population declined by 0.3 million.[20] In this last decade whatever construction accompanied the movement of the agricultural population was clearly independent of its ostensible demographic base: new farmhouses were built not because

[18] A long swing similarly appears in the real per capita stock of private buildings. That stock is indexed, with a short lag, by the estimates of the corresponding maintenance at 1911 prices; the maintenance figures for the six population benchmark years yield successive decadal increases in the per capita stock equal to −0.4, 1.4, 2.1, 0.8, and 5.1 percent. See Fenoaltea, "Construction in Italy," table 4 and pp. 34, 37–39.

[19] Stefano Somogyi, "Evoluzione della popolazione attraverso il tempo," in Istituto centrale di statistica, *Sviluppo della popolazione italiana*, p. 55.

[20] The dispersed rural population grew from 6.3 million in 1861 to 9.2 million in 1901 and 9.9 million in 1911; the agricultural population, from 13.5 million in 1861 to 17.3 million in 1901, declining to 17.0 million in 1911. See Fenoaltea, "Construction in Italy," table 3.

there was a growing pool of farmers, but because the farmers in the existing, shrinking pool were improving their location patterns and style of life.

Annual series are available for the number of marriages and the marriage rate (Table 2, columns 3 and 4, and Figure 2, lines 7 and 8).[21] From January 1, 1866, the State recognized only the marriages performed by the civil authorities. This caused a surge of (religious) weddings in advance of that deadline, and a consequent drop-off in its aftermath. In addition, from 1866 until about 1872 religious marriages exceed those recorded here by about 20,000 per year, while in 1874–1876 there is a difference of about 10,000 per year in the opposite direction—apparently as marriages contracted earlier before the religious authorities alone were regularized before the civil authorities.[22] From the late 1870s these jurisdictional differences appear to have been resolved; the marriage rate then displays a mild long swing, averaging 7.84 in 1882–1891, 7.24 in 1892–1901, and 7.65 in 1902–1911, and the number of marriages correlates well with the level of construction (+0.775, from 1878 to 1913).[23]

The marriage swing is so mild, however, that the swing in construction appears again as a swing in construction per unit: this is made clear by Table 3, rows 6 and 7, which transcribe total marriages over the usual decades (including the corrections suggested by the reported differences between religious and civil ceremonies) and compare them to total construction. From 1901 to 1911, in particular, construction nearly trebled, both in toto and in the component devoted to private buildings; the parallel increase in the number of marriages was just 12 percent (29 percent from the trough in 1898 to the peak in 1908).[24]

It is accordingly difficult to interpret the correlation between marriages and construction as evidence that the movements of the former account for the larger part of the movements of the latter, for the implied elasticity is implausibly high. The more reasonable views are that the

[21] Stefano Somogyi, "Nuzialità," in Istituto centrale di statistica, *Sviluppo della popolazione italiana*, p. 375. The geographic basis of the early figures is not clear: contrast Somogyi, "Nuzialità," p. 320, and *Sommario*, pp. 4, 43. The rate figures are based on the population estimates which are challenged above; but for these purposes the errors should be minor.

[22] Somogyi, "Nuzialità," pp. 322–24.

[23] The correlation between the reported number of marriages (table 2, column 3) and the level of construction (table 1, column 5) falls to +0.724 if it is calculated over the full period from 1861 to 1913, that is, without shedding the defective marriage figures for the early period.

[24] The relation between marriages and household formation *in Italy* is in any case moot, as it was common practice to marry before emigrating, leaving the bride at home; see Gould, "European Inter-Continental Emigration," p. 71. The emigration-related marriages would not result in the formation of a new household in Italy unless and until the migrant returned home to stay; they could nonetheless be correlated with domestic construction because the latter was itself correlated with overseas construction and transoceanic migration. Marriages were also related to return migration, and the 1908 marriage peak is attributed precisely to the large number of repatriants from the New World in that year; see Sori, *L'emigrazione italiana*, pp. 189, 195.

small swing in marriages accounts for a small part of the much larger swing in construction, leaving most of the latter to be explained by other influences; that the small swing in marriages was itself the result of the larger swing in construction, with a plausibly low elasticity of the one to the other; or of course that marriages and construction both reacted, with different elasticities, to some common external influence.

The conclusion remains that the construction swing in Italy does not appear traceable to demographic factors, whether migration, population growth, or household formation. In contrast to the pattern of the Atlantic economy, construction in Italy does not appear to be particularly population-sensitive: the long swing in construction appears as a long swing in amenities per capita against a background demographic trend, rather than in the demographic variables against a background trend in amenities per capita.

CONSTRUCTION AND CAPITAL FLOWS

The Atlantic economy displayed a long swing in international capital flows, mainly from Britain, parallel to that in European migration: British capital exports rose as construction rose in the New World and fell in Britain, and fell as construction fell in the New World and rose in Britain (Table 4, column 1, and Figure 2, line 1).[25] As noted above, the Kuznets cycle in Italy paralleled that of the overseas lands; and the parallel here extends to the association of the long swing in construction with a long swing in capital imports.[26]

Once again the Italian data are weaker than one might wish. The official estimate of the balance of merchandise trade is transcribed in Table 4, column 2.[27] This series is relatively reliable, as it was obtained from the product of recorded quantities and the corresponding average values established annually, ex post, by a committee of experts; the only correction of note concerns the transformation of import values from c.i.f. to f.o.b. The time path of this series closely matches that of the construction cycle: it displays major peaks in 1864–1865, 1874, 1887, and 1912, and intervening major troughs in 1871, 1878, and 1899 (Figure 2, line 2).

The official estimate of capital imports is transcribed in Table 4,

[25] See Williamson, *American Growth*, p. 11; Thomas, *Migration and Urban Development*, pp. 77 ff., 124; Michael Edelstein, *Overseas Investment in the Age of High Imperialism: The United Kingdom, 1850–1914* (New York, 1982). Williamson sees the long swing in capital flows as induced by, and in turn permitting, that in infrastructure growth; Thomas, in this second book, suggests that the actions of the Bank of England generated the long swing in capital flows and thereby the common construction cycle in the recipients of British capital and European migrants. The British capital export series in table 4, column 1 is from Edelstein, *Overseas Investment*, pp. 313–14.

[26] This association also is noted in Bloomfield, *Patterns of Fluctuation*, p. 32.

[27] Istituto centrale di statistica, *Indagine statistica sullo sviluppo del reddito nazionale dell'Italia dal 1861 al 1956. Annali di statistica*, series 8, vol. 9 [henceforth *Reddito nazionale*] (Rome, 1957), p. 253.

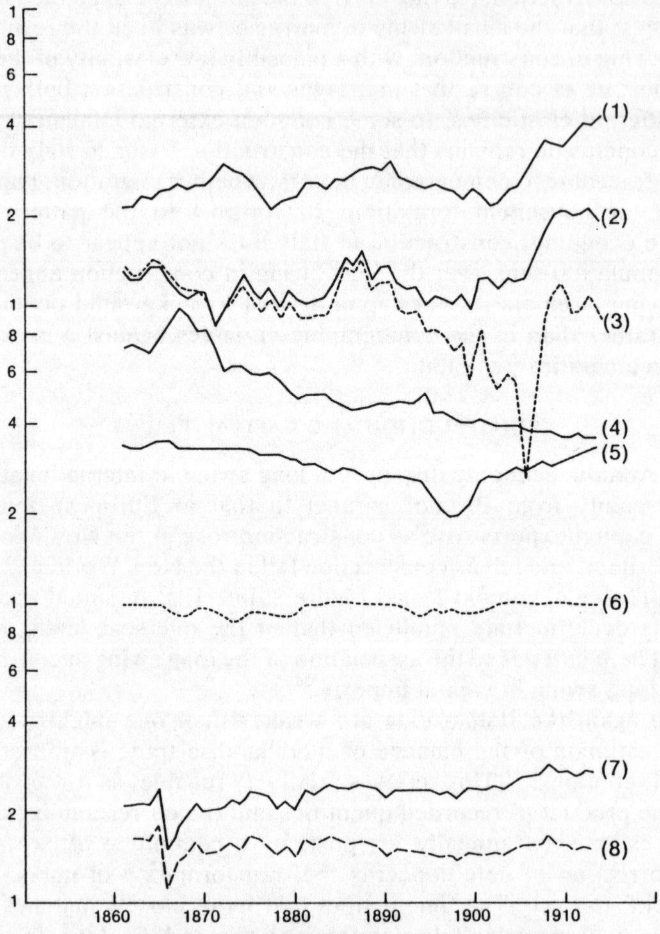

FIGURE 2

FINANCIAL AND DEMOGRAPHIC VARIABLES

(1) British capital exports (Table 4, column 1), augmented by 200 million pounds to limit vertical variation (near 200 million pounds).

(2) Italian trade deficit (Table 4, column 2), augmented by 1,000 million lire to limit vertical variation (near 1,000 million lire).

(3) Italian capital imports (Table 4, column 3), augmented by 1,000 million lire to limit vertical variation (near 1,000 million lire).

(4) Italian consol yield (Table 4, column 5; between 1 and 10 percent per year).

(5) British consol yield (Table 4, column 6; between 1 and 10 percent per year).

(6) Italian exchange rate (Table 4, column 4; near 1.00).

(7) Number of marriages (Table 2, column 3; near 200,000).

(8) Marriage rate (Table 2, column 4; near 10 per 1,000).

TABLE 4
FINANCIAL VARIABLES: EXISTING SERIES

Year	British Capital Exports (million pounds) (1)	Italian Trade Deficit[a] (million lire) (2)	Italian Capital Imports (million lire) (3)	Italian Exchange Rate (gold lire per paper lira) (4)	Italian Consol Yield (percent per year) (5)	British Consol Yield (percent per year) (6)	Italian Yield Premium[b] (7)
1861	L.12	L.313	L.325	1.000	7.17%	3.32%	.537
1862	14	223	244	1.000	7.39	3.27	.558
1863	31	231	255	1.000	7.22	3.28	.546
1864	28	367	410	1.000	7.08	3.37	.524
1865	41	367	392	1.000	8.00	3.39	.576
1866	46	219	262	.943	8.91	3.45	.613
1867	52	109	158	.932	9.90	3.27	.670
1868	42	71	116	.913	9.54	3.24	.660
1869	51	101	113	.964	8.32	3.27	.607
1870	55	101	95	.958	8.35	3.28	.607
1871	76	−152	−144	.953	7.34	3.27	.554
1872	97	−35	−44	.923	6.07	3.28	.460
1873	86	96	37	.867	6.35	3.28	.483
1874	78	264	182	.902	6.35	3.28	.483
1875	57	132	20	.934	5.96	3.24	.456
1876	31	62	−58	.933	5.93	3.16	.467
1877	10	171	72	.919	5.97	3.14	.474
1878	23	−6	−101	.918	5.68	3.15	.445
1879	31	121	31	.907	5.22	3.08	.410
1880	33	35	−88	.929	4.92	3.05	.380
1881	60	27	−88	.990	4.97	2.90	.416
1882	61	36	−68	.984	5.03	2.94	.416
1883	49	51	−72	1.003	5.05	2.83	.440
1884	70	204	77	1.007	4.67	2.72	.418
1885	62	452	358	1.001	4.61	2.85	.382
1886	78	373	293	1.007	4.46	2.81	.370
1887	88	524	452	.994	4.51	2.72	.397

Continued overleaf

TABLE 4 (continued)

1888	91	220	132	.996	4.57	2.62	.427
1889	83	363	195	.999	4.64	2.63	.433
1890	107	362	203	.990	4.65	2.67	.426
1891	72	194	−26	.988	4.77	2.68	.438
1892	63	161	−58	.977	4.71	2.65	.437
1893	57	172	−39	.931	4.69	2.60	.466
1894	50	9	−202	.915	5.05	2.55	.495
1895	55	84	−168	.960	4.39	2.29	.478
1896	50	68	−209	.940	4.39	2.06	.531
1897	41	18	−292	.960	4.21	1.96	.534
1898	29	101	−259	.931	4.11	2.00	.513
1899	47	−29	−429	.938	4.06	2.18	.463
1900	34	244	−192	.946	4.09	2.53	.381
1901	19	246	−393	.968	4.03	2.67	.337
1902	24	166	−467	.997	3.94	2.66	.325
1903	43	240	−414	1.009	3.97	2.75	.307
1904	52	214	−442	1.009	3.96	2.84	.283
1905	88	234	−742	1.013	3.88	2.78	.284
1906	121	494	−550	1.003	3.80	2.83	.255
1907	162	813	−129	1.001	3.73	2.97	.204
1908	150	1,059	103	1.013	3.69	2.91	.211
1909	142	1,098	217	1.009	3.66	2.98	.186
1910	174	1,028	−31	1.001	3.66	3.09	.156
1911	204	1,035	−22	.999	3.71	3.15	.151
1912	203	1,155	106	.994	3.64	3.28	.099
1913	234	991	−95	.986	3.62	3.40	.061

[a] Merchandise only.
[b] Column 5 minus column 6, divided by column 5.
Sources: Column 1 from Michael Edelstein, *Overseas Investment in the Age of High Imperialism: The United Kingdom, 1850–1914* (New York, 1982); columns 2 and 3 from Istituto centrale di statistica, *Indagine statistica sullo sviluppo del reddito nazionale dell'Italia dal 1861 al 1956. Annali di statistica*, series 8, vol. 9 (Rome, 1957); column 4 from Istituto centrale di statistica, *Sommario di statistiche storiche italiane, 1861–1955* (Rome, 1957); column 5 (1862–1913) from Bruno Bianchi, "Appendice statistica: il rendimento del consolidato dal 1862 al 1946," in Fausto Vicarelli, ed., *Capitale industriale e capitale finanziario* (Bologna, 1979), (1861) extrapolated using Mario Da Pozzo and Giuseppe Felloni, *La borsa valori di Genova nel secolo XIX* (Turin, 1964), p. 469; column 6 (1873–1913) from C. Knick Harley, "The Interest Rate and Prices in Britain, 1873–1913: A Study of the Gibson Paradox," *Explorations in Economic History*, 14 (Jan. 1977), pp. 69–89, (1861–1872) extrapolated using Sidney Homer, *A History of Interest Rates* (New Brunswick, 1963), p. 196.

column 3; it was obtained by adding to the balance of merchandise trade the corresponding estimates of the balance on services, labor and capital income, and unilateral transfers.[28] Through the 1880s the level and movements of these capital imports are quite close to those of the trade balance; they then diverge, opening up a gap that reaches about one billion lire per year in 1905–1913. This gap implies that Italy's capital imports declined almost steadily from the peak in 1887 to a trough in 1905 (at which time capital exports were supposedly nearly twice capital imports at the previous peak), only to rise dramatically to a new (positive) peak in 1909 (Figure 2, line 3); it further implies that Italy was a net long-term capital exporter—rather impausibly, in view of Italy's labor abundance and relatively low income levels, not to mention the evidence of substantial direct and portfolio foreign investment in Italy that does not seem counterbalanced by Italian investment abroad.

In fact, all the major components of the balance of payments series other than the balance of merchandise trade are extremely weak and tentative, and neither the level nor the time path of the capital import series (from the 1890s on) inspires confidence. For example, almost nothing is known about the tourist trade, which is estimated to have yielded net exports rising from under 100 million lire per year at the start of the period at hand to some 600 million at the end. Private, and therefore total, interest and dividends are similarly unknown. They are estimated to have yielded a net outflow rising quickly from 57 million lire in 1861 to about 100 to 150 million lire per year, with a peak in excess of 200 in the late 1880s and early 1890s, and a terminal (1913) value of 140 million lire; given the long-term decline in interest rates, this increase from 1861 to 1913 is hardly compatible with net capital exports.

Perhaps the most questionable estimates are those concerning the remittances of Italy's emigrants. These rise relatively smoothly from under 15 million lire per year in the early 1860s to about 440 in 1900, jumping to about 660 in 1901 and again beyond 900 in 1905; about 90 percent are attributed to temporary migrants and counted as the earnings of current labor services, with the residual attributed to permanent migrants and counted as unilateral transfers.

One notes, first of all, that the terminal level of these figures seems to be much too high: well-informed contemporary experts writing in 1911 estimated current remittances—including the cash brought back by returning migrants—at something over 500 million lire per year.[29]

[28] Ibid., pp. 159–177, 253–59, whence the following discussion is drawn.

[29] Bonaldo Stringher, "Gli scambi con l'estero e la bilancia dei pagamenti italiana," in R. Accademia dei Lincei, *Cinquanta anni di storia italiana*, vol. 3, pp. 120–22. Stringher was then head of the Banca d'Italia. His estimate of earnings from tourists is under 500 million lire per year (ibid., pp. 122–25), again below the figure entering the balance of payments series. An estimate of remittances similar to Stringher's is provided in Coletti, "Dell'emigrazione," pp. 238–44.

Second, the jumps in 1901 and 1905 are suspect, to say the least. The source of these jumps, it seems, is the jump in gross emigration in those years, as the time path of remittances was estimated with an eye to the migration figures.[30] This estimating procedure would make perfect sense if all migrants were seasonal, as the stock of Italians abroad remitting funds would then coincide with the annual flow; but if all migrants were permanent, then the stock of Italians abroad would coincide with the *cumulation* of the annual flow (minus some depreciation, as individuals die or lose their emotional connections to their country of origin), and after decades of substantial emigration the annual flow of remittances would have only a tenuous relation to the annual flow of new emigrants. Reality, of course, was between these polar cases; but even if most migrants were temporary, the bulk of remittances seems to have come from the United States, where even temporary migrants remained, on average, a good number of years.[31] In 1909, in particular, the flow of annual emigrants, as reported, was close to 600 thousand; the stock of Italians abroad was estimated at 5.5 million, up from 0.5 million in 1871, 1.0 in 1881, 2.0 in 1891, and 3.3 in 1901.[32] The actual flow of remittances thus almost certainly exhibited a much smoother time path than the official estimates would have us believe.

In sum, the balance of merchandise trade is reasonably well established; but the aggregate gap between that balance on the one hand and capital imports on the other appears to have grown more smoothly, and to a considerably smaller total, than the existing series would indicate. The level and cyclical path of actual capital imports were thus presumably altogether closer to the level and cyclical path of the merchandise deficit than the existing series allows: confirming that in Italy, as in the United States, the long swing in construction was accompanied by a long swing in the deficit on current account and in capital imports.

[30] *Reddito nazionale*, p. 175. Francesco Balletta, "Emigrazione italiana, cicli economici e rimesse (1876–1976)," in Gianfausto Rosoli, ed., *Un secolo di emigrazione italiana, 1876–1976* (Rome, 1978), p. 81, provides a graph illustrating annual gross emigration and deflated remittances (as per the official balance of payments series; p. 66). Until 1940 these move very much together, confirming the indication in the *Reddito nazionale*. In later years, when the series were obtained independently, their movements appear uncorrelated.

[31] Coletti, "Dell'emigrazione," pp. 240–42; Stringher, "Gli scambi," p. 121; Gould, "European Inter-Continental Emigration," pp. 55–56. These considerations further suggest that the balance of payments series' allocation of total remittances between temporary and permanent migrants is grossly biased toward the former, particularly if "temporary" is identified with "seasonal."

[32] Coletti, "Dell'emigrazione," p. 80. These figures include those temporarily abroad as well as long-term migrants, and presumably include migrants' children even if born abroad. One notes the deceleration in the growth of this stock in the 1890s, and its acceleration in the 1900s; but these totals are not precisely dated, as they are collations from a variety of non-contemporaneous sources. See also Direzione generale della statistica, *Annuario statistico italiano*, 1912, pp. 31–32.

CAPITAL FLOWS: DEMAND PULL VERSUS SUPPLY PUSH

Williamson's pioneering analysis of the American experience argues that the swings in the deficit on current account were caused by those in capital imports, which were themselves caused by those in domestic construction.[33] The path of the exchange rate of the lira indicates that the swings in capital imports caused those in the deficit on current account, and not vice versa, in the Italian experience as well; but the path of interest rates and related evidence on crowding out suggest that the swings in Italy's capital imports were also the cause, and not the effect, of the swings in domestic construction.[34]

The lira was defined by its metallic content (equivalent to that of the French franc), but convertibility was readily and repeatedly suspended; in practice, therefore, Italy found itself with a semi-pegged exchange rate, free to float below par, but with an upper limit at the gold-import point.[35] Given a floating currency, capital flows induced by the balance on current account will be inversely related to the exchange rate: an increase in domestic activity attributable to an autonomous surge in export demand, for example, will be associated with an appreciating exchange rate but reduced capital imports (a lower trade deficit); an increase in the demand for imports attributable to an autonomous surge in domestic activity will be associated with increased capital imports (a higher trade deficit) but a depreciating exchange rate. Capital flows and the exchange rate will instead move together if the capital flows are causally prior to the balance of trade: as in the recent American experience, capital imports induced by financial disequilibrium will themselves induce an appreciation of the currency and a rise in the deficit on current account.[36]

The exchange of the paper lira is transcribed in Table 4, column 4.[37] Except for a brief episode in the very early 1870s, the lira was strong when the trade deficit and capital imports were high, and weak when they were low (Figure 2, line 6).[38] The correlation of the exchange rate and the trade deficit is +0.517 (Table 5); and it would have been considerably higher, judging from the relevant price movements, had

[33] Williamson, *American Growth*.

[34] In the absence of evidence sufficient fully to identify the relevant demand and supply curves, the analysis here seeks to identify only the dominant autonomous shifts. For example, an increase in price and quantity together establishes that demand increased; supply may have moved in either direction, but if it increased at all its shift was less than that in demand.

[35] Michele Fratianni and Franco Spinelli, "Currency Competition, Fiscal Policy and the Money Supply Process in Italy from Unification to World War I," *Journal of European Economic History*, 14 (Winter 1985), pp. 473–99.

[36] Robert A. Mundell, *International Economics* (New York, 1968), chap. 18.

[37] This series appears in the *Sommario*, p. 166.

[38] For the reasons given above, the path of capital imports (up to a trend correction) seems best represented by that of the merchandise deficit; for simplicity, the present discussion ignores the differences between them.

TABLE 5

CONSTRUCTION AND FINANCIAL VARIABLES: CORRELATION COEFFICIENTS

	Italian Construction (1)	British Capital Exports (2)	Italian Trade Deficit (3)	Italian Exchange Rate (4)	Italian Consol Yield (5)	British Consol Yield (6)	Italian Yield Premium (7)	Year (8)
1.	1.000							
2.	.890	1.000						
3.	.898	.817	1.000					
4.	.529	.334	.517	1.000				
5.	−.534	−.432	−.411	−.361	1.000			
6.	.158	.165	.212	−.047	.591	1.000		
7.	−.854	−.755	−.769	−.468	.797	.039	1.000	
8.	.635	.600	.562	.349	−.879	−.513	−.827	1.000

Sources: Variable 1: Table 1, column 5; variables 2, 3: Table 4, columns 1, 2; variables 4 through 7: Table 4, columns 4 through 7.

the upward variation of the exchange not been limited by the currency's par value.[39]

With the exception noted, therefore, the trade deficits were clearly the effect, and not the cause, of the capital imports.[40] As in the American case analyzed by Williamson, the swings in capital imports cannot be attributed to the swings in construction through induced swings in domestic activity and the trade deficit; the swings in construction and in capital imports were linked (if at all) through the international market for financial assets rather than for goods.

What remains to be seen is whether the swings in construction induced those in capital imports (as Williamson argues occurred in the United States), or the swings in capital imports induced those in construction. The relevant evidence here concerns the interest rate and crowding out. An autonomous surge in domestic construction increases the supply of domestic bonds, and puts upward pressure on domestic interest rates; this pressure leads to capital imports and (unless these are sufficient actually to prevent an upward movement in interest rates) the crowding out of other domestic borrowing and investment. An autonomous surge in capital imports increases the demand for domestic bonds, and puts downward pressure on domestic interest rates; this increase in the supply of capital induces parallel increases in construction and in other domestic borrowing and investment.[41]

The path of the nominal yield on Italian consols is transcribed in Table 4, column 5 (Figure 2, line 4).[42] It is negatively correlated with construction and capital imports (Table 5): rising construction and capital imports are clearly associated with falling interest rates, and falling construction and capital imports are (somewhat less clearly) associated with stagnant or rising interest rates. Consol yields were thus

[39] With the nominal exchange at par, the equilibrating variations in the real exchange rate occur through changes in the price level; and since the prices of tradable goods are constrained by their international values, the variations will be concentrated in the prices of nontradable goods and services. The evidence on the latter provided by the wage and rent series in Fenoaltea, "Public Works Construction," table 4, "Construction in Italy," table 2, points to a strong swing in step with that in construction and the trade deficit; the rent swing would presumably have been even stronger but for the small parallel swing in the real per-capita stock of buildings noted in fn. 18.

[40] While capital imports and the exchange rate were both higher in the mid-1870s than in the neighboring years, the trough in capital imports in 1871 was also associated with a temporarily high exchange rate. That appears to be the one clear case in which the exchange and capital flows were dominated by the market for goods rather than by that for financial assets, as exports surged in response to the Franco-Prussian war; see Stringher, "Gli scambi," p. 16.

[41] This discussion assumes that capital is rationed by the interest rate. A more complete view would recognize that access to capital is rationed directly as well as by price; the evidence on crowding out thus provides information additional to that provided by the interest rate.

[42] Italian consol rates are reported in Bruno Bianchi, "Appendice statistica: il rendimento del consolidato dal 1862 al 1946," in Fausto Vicarelli, ed., *Capitale industriale e capitale finanziario* (Bologna, 1979), pp. 156–58; they are here extended to 1861 with the aid of the comparable series in Mario Da Pozzo and Giuseppe Felloni, *La borsa valori di Genova nel secolo XIX* (Turin, 1964), p. 469.

near 7 percent in the early 1860s, with high construction and capital imports, and rose to nearly 10 percent in the later 1860s, as construction and capital imports declined. From the late 1860s to the early 1870s, as construction and capital imports recovered, yields declined by a third, to about 6 percent.[43] Yields remained near that level for half a decade, as construction and capital imports again declined; yields then fell by a quarter, to 4.5 percent, as construction and capital imports surged in the decade to 1886–87. The subsequent decline in construction and capital imports was accompanied by a slight rise in yields, to a peak of 5 percent in 1894; and the final long boom in construction and capital imports occurred in the context of steadily declining yields, which fell to some 3.6 percent by 1913. In this last period, in particular, the likely drift from deflationary to inflationary price expectations suggests that the real interest rate was cut approximately in half.[44] The path of interest rates thus suggests that the periodic capital flows were not pulled into Italy by episodes of domestic scarcity; rather, capital appears to have been periodically pushed into Italy by episodes of foreign abundance.

The evidence on crowding out, or rather the lack of it, quite supports this interpretation. Within construction, as noted, investment in railways, other social overhead capital, and private buildings all tended to move together. A partial exception might be found in the collapse of investment in private buildings in 1887–88, as public works reached their peak; but that collapse appears to be due to the bursting of a speculative building bubble fueled—tellingly—by bank credit, and not to crowding out, as other privately financed construction (minor railways, other public works) moved with (publicly financed) public works.[45] Nor did construction as a whole crowd out other sectors. Industrial investment in plant and equipment also surged from the late 1870s to the late 1880s, fell back to the mid-1890s, and then surged again until the eve of the Great War; indeed, in Rosario Romeo's seminal interpretation of Italy's industrialization those periods of strong industrial growth are attributed precisely to the loosening of a capital-supply constraint.[46] Finally, government borrowing and spending, on defense

[43] This discussion ignores the war-induced blip in capital flows in 1871; see fn. 40.

[44] The change in price expectations is plausible not only because prices stopped falling and started rising, but because that change could be associated with the gold discoveries at the end of the nineteenth century. Price expectations during the inflation of the early 1870s are more difficult to pin down, as the price level may then have been expected to revert to its "natural" level; but some evidence that the real interest rate moved inversely to capital imports and construction before the turn of the century as well as after it is provided by the Genoa stock price index calculated in Da Pozzo and Felloni, *La borsa valori*, pp. 499–508. That index, equal to 34 in 1861, exhibits peaks in 1863 (46), 1873 (93), and 1887 (98), and troughs in 1867 (33), 1877 (72), and 1896 (44, the terminal value of the series).

[45] See Fratianni and Spinelli, "Currency Competition," pp. 490–91; Fenoaltea, "Railway Construction," table 2, "Public Works Construction," table 3.

[46] See Stefano Fenoaltea, "Decollo, ciclo, e intervento dello Stato," in Alberto Caracciolo, ed., *La formazione dell'Italia industriale* (Bari, 1969), pp. 95–114, and "Riflessioni sull'esperienza

in particular, also followed a long swing similar to that of construction, with peaks in the 1860s, 1880s, and 1910s.[47]

The time paths of the various components of construction, other capital formation, and public borrowing and spending were thus largely parallel; they accompanied similar movements in stock prices, and opposite movements in the interest rate.[48] All this strongly suggests that swings in the supply of capital were causally prior to those in construction, and incidentally confirms that the latter were not generated by demographic change.[49] Since capital imports were *positively* correlated with domestic capital formation, moreover, the dominant swings in the supply of capital were clearly imported rather than domestic.[50] In short, only an autonomous increase in the supply of foreign capital seems capable of accounting for the association of rising trade deficits and capital imports with rising public and private construction, rising other investment and other public borrowing, appreciating exchange rates, and falling interest rates. Construction in Italy followed a typical Kuznets cycle, but on the basis of the evidence reviewed here construction should be labeled finance-sensitive, rather than population-sensitive, capital formation.

THE LONG SWING IN THE SUPPLY OF FOREIGN CAPITAL

The Kuznets cycle in Italy thus appears attributable *in primis* to a long swing in the supply of foreign capital. Britain's capital exports were much the largest single component of aggregate international lending at this time, and the only ones to display a clear long swing.[51] It is

industriale italiana dal Risorgimento alla prima guerra mondiale," in Gianni Toniolo, ed., *Lo sviluppo economico italiano 1861–1940* (Bari, 1973), pp. 121–56; Massimo Warglien, "Nota sull'investimento industriale in macchinari e altre attrezzature meccaniche: Italia, 1881–1913," *Rivista di storia economica*, n.s., 2 (Feb. 1985), pp. 125–46; Rosario Romeo, *Risorgimento e capitalismo* (Bari, 1959), and *Breve storia della grande industria in Italia* (Bologna, 1961). Romeo thought that investment was constrained by domestic saving, and oddly attributed the industrial expansion from the 1880s to a putative decline in infrastructure investment. For a brief presentation and evaluation of the Romeo hypothesis, see Stefano Fenoaltea, "Italy," in Patrick K. O'Brien, ed., *Railways and the Economic Development of Western Europe* (London, 1983), pp. 54–60.

[47] Antonio Pedone, "Il bilancio dello Stato e lo sviluppo economico italiano: 1861–1963," *Rassegna economica*, 31 (Mar.-Apr. 1967), pp. 285–341.

[48] On stock price movements see fn. 44.

[49] Had the swings in construction been set in motion by population growth or household formation, they would have put upward pressure on interest rates and crowded out other domestic borrowing and capital formation. As noted in fn. 34, the evidence reviewed here reveals only the dominant shifts in the underlying schedules; it thus supports the exact range of hypotheses advanced in the penultimate paragraph of the section on construction and population growth.

[50] An autonomous increase in the domestic demand for bonds (supply of capital) would similarly put downward pressure on domestic interest rates and lead to increased domestic borrowing and investment across the board; but it would lead as well to capital exports or reduced imports, and thus to a *negative* correlation of capital imports with domestic capital formation.

[51] Bloomfield, *Patterns of Fluctuation*, pp. 8, 47; Albert Fishlow, "Lessons from the Past:

accordingly reasonable to look to Britain as the source of the Kuznets cycle in Italy, even though foreign investment in Italy was primarily French, Belgian, and German rather than British: because continental capital competed with British capital at local margins throughout the world, more foreign capital from *all* sources would flow into Italy when Britain pushed more capital out into the world.

Sample regression equations exploring the correlations between construction in Italy and sundry financial variables are reported in Table 6. Interestingly, a relative abundance of capital in Italy seems tied not only to abundant capital flows out of Britain and into Italy, but to a relative scarcity of capital within Britain: the long swing in capital flows was apparently due less to changes in relative investment opportunities and returns than to changes in the relative premium required by investors to set those flows in motion.

Equation 1 regresses construction in Italy on measures of capital flows, Italy's exchange rate and consol rate, and a time trend. Both British capital exports and the Italian trade deficit appear highly significant, despite their strong intercorrelation (Table 5), presumably because they are both close but imperfect indices of Italy's actual capital imports. The Italian consol rate is also significant, with the expected negative sign; not unreasonably, given the gestation period of construction projects, it seems to do somewhat better if introduced with a lag. All three of these variables are of course measures of the abundance of capital in the Italian market; their simultaneous significance may be taken to indicate that capital was rationed by quantity as well as by price, or, as before, that the available series are all imperfect proxies for more directly relevant variables.[52]

Equation 2 includes the British consol yield (Table 4, column 6, and Figure 2, line 5), also with a one-year lag.[53] Like British capital exports, the British consol yield is statistically significant despite the presence of the corresponding Italian variable; unlike British capital exports, however, the British consol yield does not appear to act primarily as a duplicate of the corresponding Italian variable. Its regression coefficient is positive rather than negative, as indeed is its simple correlation to construction (0.158, against −0.534 for the Italian yield, ignoring lags: Table 5); and while its impact on the regression coefficients of the other

Capital Markets during the 19th Century and the Interwar Period." *International Organization*, 39 (Summer 1985), pp. 388–89, 393–95.

[52] Since the capital-flow variables do not perform better if lagged, one may surmise that the interest rate affected the decision to build, while quantitative restrictions influenced construction as the project proceeded. The nominal consol rate is of course a proxy both for other nominal (mortgage) rates, and for the relevant real rates.

[53] The British consol yield is taken as reported in C. Knick Harley, "The Interest Rate and Prices in Britain, 1873–1913: A Study of the Gibson Paradox," *Explorations in Economic History*, 14 (Jan. 1977), p. 87, for 1873 ff., and extended to 1861 in proportion to the comparable series in Sidney Homer, *A History of Interest Rates* (New Brunswick, 1963), p. 196.

TABLE 6
CONSTRUCTION AND FINANCIAL VARIABLES: REGRESSION RESULTS

Equation	Constant (1)	British Capital Exports (2)	Italian Trade Deficit (3)	Italian Exchange Rate (4)	Italian Consol Yield[a] (5)	British Consol Yield[a] (6)	Italian Yield Premium[a] (7)	Year (8)	MA(1)[b] (9)	AR(1)[c] (10)	$\bar{R}^2$ (11)	Durbin-Watson Statistic (12)
1863–1913												
1.	4,909	2.26	.243	655	−40.7			−2.65	.479	.294	.940	1.96
	(1.4)	(6.1)	(4.3)	(2.0)	(−2.9)			(−1.5)	(1.9)	(1.4)		
2.	−8,787	1.36	.157	−21.6	−37.7	173		4.72	.401	.599	.954	1.96
	(−1.8)	(3.2)	(2.9)	(−0.1)	(−2.3)	(3.0)		(1.8)	(1.9)	(4.2)		
3.	4,113	1.63	.168	561			−787	−2.09	.522	.282	.955	1.96
	(1.9)	(5.1)	(3.3)	(2.0)			(−4.9)	(−1.9)	(2.1)	(1.5)		
1863–1887												
4.	−151	1.29	.155	925	−39.0			−.059	.716	−.426	.859	1.92
	(−0.0)	(4.3)	(2.7)	(5.1)	(−4.9)			(−0.0)	(0.8)	(−0.5)		
5.	19,053	1.36	.134	343	−44.0	−370		−9.36	.589	−.544	.893	1.91
	(2.9)	(5.6)	(3.0)	(1.3)	(−6.5)	(−3.1)		(−2.9)	(0.1)	(−0.1)		
6.	−2,133	1.14	.162	883			−581	1.04	.295	.089	.838	1.88
	(−0.4)	(2.4)	(1.8)	(3.1)			(−2.7)	(0.4)	(0.4)	(0.1)		
1888–1913												
7.	−8,328	1.64	.331	73.7	−30.2			4.60	1.03	.228	.960	1.75
	(−0.8)	(2.7)	(3.1)	(0.1)	(−0.3)			(0.9)	(3.1)	(1.1)		
8.	5,248	1.62	.202	−952	−122	283		−2.18	.783	.084	.954	1.94
	(0.5)	(2.6)	(1.9)	(−1.4)	(−1.3)	(3.4)		(−0.4)	(1.9)	(0.2)		
9.	11,609	1.50	.192	−1,028			−1,217	−5.13	.739	.047	.954	1.94
	(1.7)	(2.4)	(1.8)	(−1.5)			(−3.6)	(−1.5)	(1.8)	(0.1)		

[a] Lagged one period.
[b] Parameter of the first-order moving-average component of the error process.
[c] Parameter of the first-order autoregressive component of the error process.
Notes: The dependent variable is construction in Italy (Table 1, column 5); the independent variables (2–8) are the same as in Table 5; the estimation procedure is non-linear least squares with ARMA(1,1) error process; the figures in parentheses are *t*-statistics.

variables is clearly perceptible, the variable least affected is precisely the Italian yield. The positive relation of Italian construction to the British consol yield thus seems to be real enough—primarily, one presumes, because both display a sharp fall and subsequent recovery over the mid and later 1890s.

This rules out the simple attribution of the periodic abundance of capital (and high construction activity) in Italy to a corresponding abundance of capital in Britain; for if this were so the differences in the time paths of the British and Italian interest rates would be comparatively insignificant, and British capital exports, Italian capital imports, and Italian construction would all vary inversely to the British interest rate as well as to the Italian interest rate.[54] The apparently meaningful difference in the signs of the coefficients of the British and Italian yields in equation 2 suggests, rather, that Italian construction was sensitive not only to the domestic interest rate but to the relation between the Italian and the British yields.

Since investors could readily switch between Italian and British consols, the Italian yield premium (Table 4, column 7) was presumably required to equilibrate ex ante risk-discounted yields. An equilibrium yield premium is of course at one and the same time a measure of the inducement to hold the higher-yielding bond, and of investors' reluctance to hold it.[55] Since Italy's capital imports varied inversely with the yield premium (Table 5), they were governed by changes in foreign investors' reluctance to hold Italian bonds at given levels of inducement more than by changes in the inducements at given levels of reluctance.[56]

Construction in Italy may have been sensitive to that premium for at least two reasons. The first, again, is the fact that capital is not rationed by price alone: a falling yield premium indicates a greater willingness of investors to hold Italian assets, and therefore, plausibly, a loosening of quantitative restrictions on credit in Italy. The second is that construc-

[54] Edelstein, *Overseas Investment*, argues that the swing in British capital exports resulted from the interaction of a relatively steady rate of accumulation by British savers and an autonomous long swing in domestic investment opportunities (tied to internal demographic and productivity movements) in Britain (p. 232). If British capital exports were thus essentially a residual, they should be high when low domestic investment made for low interest rates; but that seems to be the opposite of what actually occurred, at least from the 1880s. The correlation of British capital exports and the British consol yield from 1880 to 1913 is +0.680, and the cyclical paths of the real and nominal rates seem to have been quite similar (Harley, "The Interest Rate," p. 85). See also H. W. Richardson, "British Emigration and Overseas Investment, 1870–1914," *Economic History Review*, 2nd ser., 25 (Feb. 1972), pp. 102, 106.

[55] If the British yield is risk-free, and the only risk attached to the Italian yield is a probability p of permanent default, then the British yield will equal $(1 - p)$ times the Italian yield, and the relative yield premium calculated here is exactly the perceived probability of default p. In actuality, of course, the perceived risks include those of currency depreciation and changes in tax treatment as well as of the simple suspension of interest payments.

[56] In light of this, Fratianni and Spinelli's claim that "net capital inflows . . . were responding to a high interest-rate differential" ("Currency Competition," p. 483) and their contempt for contemporary economists' stress on investors' attitudes (ibid.) both seem unwarranted.

tion was sensitive to the (unobserved) real interest rate rather than to the nominal rate; and since national real rates plausibly varied more than their international average, a rising yield premium was plausibly associated with a rise in the real interest rate in Italy.

In fact, construction was far more closely correlated with the consol yield premium than with the Italian or British yields (Table 5). The lagged yield premium is used in lieu of the separate yields in equation 3; the increase in the sum of squared residuals is small enough to suggest that the substitution need not be considered inappropriate.[57]

Equations 4 through 9 repeat equations 1 through 3 over the two halves of the period in question. The coefficients of the capital flow variables are gratifyingly stable across specifications and time periods. The coefficients of the national interest rates are instead relatively unstable; but this is hardly surprising, as the nominal British yield in the earlier period and the nominal Italian yield in the later period both lack strong cycles, even though these may have been present in the corresponding real rates.[58] More significantly, the yield premium performs relatively similarly in both subperiods (equations 6 and 9), and in this specification at least there is no strong evidence of structural change from one quarter-century to the other.[59]

The upshot of all this is that the primary cause of the long swing in the supply of capital and therefore construction activity in Italy appears to be the variation in the relative premium required to attract foreign investment. In the 1860s, when Italy's construction movements were out of phase with British foreign investment and construction overseas, the variations in the yield premium and in capital imports appear to reflect changes in the perceived risk of investing specifically in Italy when that country faced war and massive public deficits.[60] Over the last three decades to the World War, when the swing in Italian construction closely paralleled that in British foreign investment and construction

[57] The corresponding F statistic equals just 0.58.

[58] Harley, "The Interest Rate," p. 85, suggests that the real consol rate in Britain rose from the mid-1870s to the late 1880s, in opposition to the movement of the nominal rate; the negative coefficient on the British yield in equation 5 is thus not particularly troublesome. In the Italian case, deflationary price expectations in the 1890s may have temporarily raised the real rate above the nominal rate.

[59] The value of the F statistic comparing the sum of squared residuals in equations 6 and 9 together to that in equation 3 is just 0.25. To return to an earlier topic, the regressions in equations 1 through 9 were repeated with the addition of the number of marriages (Table 2, column 3). Whether introduced contemporaneously or with a one-year lag, this variable never comes close to having a significantly positive impact on construction; even in the later subperiod, when the marriage data seem generally accurate, its t statistic varies from -0.1 to -1.6.

[60] The sharp blip in the yield of the *consolidato* in 1894 similarly seems tied to the nervousness caused by major bank failures in Italy. Italy's exchange rate may also be a measure of country risk, considered lower when the exchange was at par than when it was floating below par; since the first suspension of convertibility was no doubt that of greatest symbolic significance, it stands to reason that the exchange rate seems to matter more in the earlier decades.

overseas, the inverse swing in the yield premium appears instead to reflect a much more general variation in attitudes toward investment in the capital-importing periphery: the temporary surge in the yield premium in the later 1890s appears to be common to the non-British world, as in the wake of the Baring crisis nominal rates declined across the board on British securities but remained high on foreign ones.[61]

Over the half-century at hand, indeed, the inverse association between the yield premium and construction in Italy seems to break down only in the later 1870s, when the former fails to display a cyclical peak in connection with the trough in the latter (and in British capital exports). This may mean that a (supply-induced) scarcity of capital in Italy at that time was temporarily tied to a parallel (demand-induced) scarcity of capital in Britain; but it may mean only that the effective yield premium is poorly measured in those years, as the temporary elimination of the budget deficit over the later 1870s may have kept the Italian consol rate from peaking along with the rates faced by private borrowers.[62]

SUMMARY AND EXTENSIONS

Construction in Italy displayed clear cyclical movements. Apart from a short-lived boom in the early 1860s, in the immediate aftermath of Unification, Italian construction followed the characteristic long swing of the international Kuznets cycle; but the Italian swing paralleled that of the overseas lands, rather than the opposite British one.

Construction movements in Italy are in no way attributable to the ebb and flow of international migration. On a decadal basis, construction and *e*migration rose together to a peak in the 1880s; emigration rates then remained roughly constant through the decline of construction in the 1890s and its surge in the 1900s. The Italian data do not reveal net migration over shorter periods; but if it can be inferred from the swing in overseas immigration, construction in Italy was higher, in general, when *more* people were leaving Italy.

To the extent that domestic construction can be associated with internal migration, it would seem that internal and external migration moved together, producing a strong cycle in departures from the rural

[61] Edelstein, *Overseas Investment*, unpublished appendix 7. I am grateful to the author for making this material available to me. "The extreme discredit which overtook foreign investment after the . . . crises of the early nineties" is noted, for example, by H. J. Habakkuk, "Fluctuations in House-Building," p. 226. The distinction between changes in attitudes and changes in objective conditions at that time is stressed by Lewis, *Growth and Fluctuations*, p. 180: "There was a large bandwagon effect in foreign lending . . . . With lending to the USA, Australia and Argentina out of fashion, all other countries would find themselves deprived of loans beyond any point that objective economic analysis of their own economic solutions could justify."

[62] See Pedone, "Il bilancio dello Stato," p. 333, and fn. 44. Perhaps not coincidentally, the decline in construction over the later 1870s was concentrated in railways and private buildings.

sector. In Britain, in contrast, the rural sector seems to have lost emigrants at a relatively constant rate, and the strong cycle was in the alternation between internal and external destinations.[63] In the overseas lands, external migration was of course an inward movement rather than an outward one; but there too internal and external migration seem to have moved together as they did in Italy.[64]

The association of the long swing in transoceanic migration with the opposite swings in transoceanic and British construction has led to the view that construction was specifically population-sensitive. The Italian experience would still fit that view, had there been a cycle in the natural rate of reproduction sufficient to yield a positive association between population growth and construction despite the impact of migration. But that does not seem to be the case: whether one looks at the total population or at specific components of it, the long swing in construction shows up primarily as a swing in capital formation per unit.

Construction in Italy seems not population-sensitive but finance-sensitive; and the specific cause of its long swing appears to be a cycle in the supply of *foreign* capital, as construction, other borrowing and investment, stock prices, capital imports, and the exchange rate all moved together and in opposition to the interest rate. The long swing in the supply of foreign capital, in turn, seems related to the long swing in British capital exports; but these were clearly not a mere vent for savings surplus to domestic British investment needs, as British capital exports did not move inversely to the interest rate in Britain. Over most of the period at hand, the critical swing seems to have been in the attitude of investors: as they were increasingly disenchanted with non-British investment, for example, the wedge between British and foreign rates increased, and capital became more abundant in Britain and less abundant abroad. In Britain itself, construction appears to have been as finance-sensitive as it was in Italy: there too, unprecedentedly low interest rates led to unprecedentedly high levels of capital formation, in a cycle far too sharp to be attributed to demographic change.[65]

The Italian experience is thus not merely an exception to, and therefore destructive of, the unified interpretation of the Atlantic economy which attributes construction to migration, and capital flows to construction. It suggests an alternative and equally unified interpretation, in which capital flows caused construction, and construction—that employer of the unskilled par excellence—caused migration. In this alternative view the critical distinction is no longer that between old

[63] Thomas, *Migration and Urban Development*, pp. 20–58.

[64] Richard A. Easterlin, *Population, Labor Force, and Long Swings in Economic Growth: The American Experience* (New York, 1968), p. 31.

[65] Charles H. Feinstein, *National Income, Expenditure and Output of the United Kingdom, 1855–1965*, Studies in the National Income and Expenditure of the United Kingdom, vol. 6 (Cambridge, 1972), pp. 192, T88–89.

lands and new, but that between capital exporters (Britain) and importers (Italy and the New World). When non-British investment was out of favor, capital was relatively abundant in Britain and relatively scarce abroad, construction boomed in England and collapsed abroad, Britons migrated within Britain and non-Britons postponed migration to better days; when investors favored non-British investment, capital was relatively scarce in Britain and relatively abundant abroad, construction collapsed in Britain and boomed abroad, Britons migrated abroad and non-Britons migrated—within the old lands, within the new, and of course within the broader non-British world from the old to the new. Should further investigation of the international Kuznets cycle bear out this hypothesis, the Italian case will appear not as the exception to the rule, but as its first clear expression: the first case to have been examined, that is to say, in which demographic and financial variables are sufficiently uncorrelated to allow the identification of the causes of the long swing in construction.

Appendix

THE ESTIMATES OF NET MIGRATION

Giusti's annual estimates of net migration and year-end population seem to overstate the numbers present at the end of 1911, and correspondingly to understate net migration in that year.[66]

The 1911 census counted 34.671 million people on June 10; Giusti allows 35.146 at year-end, for an increase of 0.475 million. The natural increase equaled 0.351 million for the whole year, and thus perhaps 0.196 million for the 204 days after June 10; Giusti therefore implies a net *im*migration over the last 204 days of 1911 equal to 0.279 million. This figure seems much too high. Of the 0.534 million recorded departures in 1911, no more than some 60 percent (0.320 million) are likely to have occurred in the first 161 days of the year, leaving a balance of 0.214 million for the last 204 days.[67] The number of returnees in those same 204 days is in turn unlikely to reach 80 percent of the year's sum of recorded departures for Old World destinations (0.271 million, on the extreme assumption that all were temporary migrants) and overseas returnees (0.217 million, from ships' passenger lists), or 0.390 million; deducting the estimated 0.214 million departures, the net immigration in those 204 days is unlikely to have reached 0.176 million. A prudent correction would thus reduce Giusti's end-1911 population figure by some 0.100 million, to 35.046 million, and correspondingly increase the decade's net emigration to 1.324 million, for an annual rate of 3.9 per thousand (instead of 3.6, as implied by Giusti, or 4.7, as computed from the raw census data).

A separate question concerns the allocation of the net migration in 1882–1901 over the two decades concerned. In the absence of more immediate constraints that can be imposed a priori, that allocation is here approached by focusing on the repatriant ratio (and its complement, the ratio of permanent to total emigrants). Assume, for simplicity, that all migrations within the Old World were temporary, and consider overseas migration alone. The recorded overseas departures totaled 0.286 million in 1872–1881,

[66] Giusti, "Bilanci demografici," p. 116.

[67] The seasonal pattern of departures is documented in Coletti, "Dell'emigrazione," p. 70.

1.097 million in 1882–1891, 1.639 million in 1892–1901, and 3.498 million in 1902–1911.[68] As noted above, the bias in these figures varies over the decades; correcting them as suggested by the overseas countries' data, "true" overseas departures are here estimated at 0.372 million in 1872–1881, 1.371 in 1882–1891, 2.049 in 1892–1901, and 3.218 in 1902–1911.[69] The corresponding net migration figures equal 0.362 million in 1872–81 (calculated directly from the census data and the natural increase), 2.308 million in 1882–1901 (taking Giusti's year-end figure for 1901), and 1.324 million, as corrected, in 1902–1911; the ratio of permanent to total overseas emigrants thus works out to 0.97 in 1872–1881, 0.67 in 1882–1901, and 0.41 in 1902–1911, confirming the secular rise in the share of temporary migrants in overseas migration.[70]

The trend in the mix of temporary and permanent overseas migrants was due primarily to technical change and the concomitant decline in the real cost of an ocean passage; it was thus presumably relatively uniform, and one would expect the separate ratios for the 1880s and 1890s to interpolate those for the 1870s and 1900s. In any group of years, to be sure, cyclical factors could loom large, as the repatriant ratio rose sharply in years of crisis in the receiving countries.[71] But from this perspective also there do not appear to be more crisis years in the receiving countries in 1882–1891 than in 1892–1901; so the presumption that the decadal repatriant ratio rose relatively smoothly can be allowed to stand.

Against this, Giusti's figures for net migration over 1882–1901 would imply that the ratio of permanent to total overseas migrants declined from 0.97 in 1872–1881 to 0.62 in 1882–1891, only to rise to 0.71 in 1892–1901 before declining sharply to 0.42 (0.38 using his figures for 1911) in 1902–1911. This suggests that he underestimated net migration in 1882–1891 and overestimated it in 1892–1901. A more reasonable allocation of the 2.308 million net emigrants in 1882–1901 would attribute say 1.100 million (rather than 0.843 million) to 1882–1891, and 1.208 million (rather than 1.465 million) to 1892–1901; with these estimates, the ratio of permanent to total overseas migrants drops smoothly over the four decades from 0.97 to 0.80 to 0.59 to 0.41.[72]

These revised estimates imply that year-end population grew from the census figure of 28.460 million in 1881 to Giusti's figure of 32.663 million in 1901 through 30.471 million, rather than 30.728 million, in 1891.[73] The corresponding annual rates of net migration equal 3.7 per thousand in 1882–1891 and 3.8 in 1892–1901.

Giusti's year-to-year figures appear to be even less reliable than his decadal totals. Their path is one of near-monotonic growth from the late 1870s to 1900, followed by a sudden drop to a plateau maintained in 1901–1911, and by a very sharp rise in 1912–13 (Table 2, column 2); one suspects that his technique for distributing the total net migration between census years overemphasized continuity between census years, at

[68] *Sommario*, p. 65.

[69] The correction factors are 1.30 in 1872–81 (somewhat higher than in later years, as suggested by Sori, *L'emigrazione italiana*, p. 54), 1.25 in 1882–1901 (as suggested by Gould's figures cited in the text; the discrepancy includes people leaving without passports, and people leaving for Old World destinations but then moving overseas), and 0.92 in 1902–1911 (again from Gould's figures; the discrepancy reflects people obtaining passports but not departing).

[70] Sori, *L'emigrazione italiana*, p. 337ff.

[71] See, for example, the spectacular rise in return migration from the United States in 1908, *Sommario*, p. 67; and Argentina in 1890, Sori, *L'emigrazione italiana*, p. 56.

[72] Gould, "European Inter-Continental Emigration." p. 87, asserts that the repatriant ratio was "probably higher in the '80s than in the '90s." Since he gives no reason as to why this should be expected a priori, the most likely basis for his claim is simply the pattern thrown up by Giusti's estimates.

[73] The present calculations accept Giusti's estimate of the year-end population in 1901, even though it is no more reliable than his corresponding figure for 1911; given the lack of data on repatriants, and the discontinuity in the gross emigration series, its bias is not easy to evaluate.

the cost of severe and implausible discontinuities in the census years themselves (the fact that the break is between 1900 and 1901 suggests that the February 10, 1901 census figure was used initially to calculate the population at the end of 1900, rather than 1901). The transoceanic repatriant figures available from 1902, which Giusti does not appear to have used, suggest much greater variations from year to year, with sharp outflow peaks in 1905–06 and 1909–10 (as well as 1912–13), and significant net *im*migration in 1908.[74] The influence of the cycle in the receiving areas is readily apparent.

[74] *Sommario*, p. 65; Coletti, "Dell'emigrazione," p. 74.

[10]

Commercialization and Economic Development in Italy (1860–1940)

G. Federico

1. Introduction

This paper presents the results of research into the commercialization of Italian agriculture during a crucial period of its development, between the end of the 19th century and the first half of the 20th.[1] Scholars following diverse approaches to the problem of contemporary society[2] seem to unanimously agree on the relevance of the process of commercialization as both an index to and a consequence of subsequent economic development. On the one hand, socio-anthropologists define the predominance of the cultivation of produce for farmers' personal consumption as one of the particular characteristics of a peasant economy, thus implying that the disappearance of that society was caused by the spread (spontaneous or forced) of trade.[3] On the other hand, economic analysts adopt a concept of development that, by definition, involves an increase of intersectoral exchange. In fact, development is often defined as a change in the sectoral distribution of occupations, involving a transfer of labour from agriculture to industry and to the services sector. The primary sector must supply the foodstuffs and the raw materials needed by industry and must also absorb the manufactured articles (the so-called roles of 'product' and 'market' according to Kuznets).[4] This is made possible only by an increase – absolute and proportional – in the quantity of agricultural produce sold on the market. Raising the productivity of the agricultural sector can be achieved by greater specialization and better division of labour. It is for this reason that commercialization has been defined in a recent study as 'one of the chief dynamic elements in the development of Europe'.[5] The differences between these two approaches mainly concern assumptions about the reasons for agricultural workers' behaviour and therefore the underlying causes of the process of commercialization – a theme which cannot be discussed here.[6]

A word of caution is needed about the risks involved in the uncritical use of the percentage of production sold as an index of the level of commercialization of the economy. First, absolute percentages depend on how the macroeconomic aggregates are defined.[7] In fact, if, as would be theoretically more correct, all the domestic services supplied by the family (cooking, cleaning, etc.) were valued at the market price and included in the national income, the share of output not marketed would be high even in advanced economies. Moreover, the level of self-sufficiency of the household-firm can be determined, in each case, by a number of technical-productive and socioeconomic characteristics, such as the size of farms, the available techniques in use and the crop mix, the manner and the extent of requisition by landowners and/or the state.[8] Finally, the choice to consume the farm's output instead of selling it is not necessarily motivated by an *a priori* rejection of the market; therefore a reduction in market participation does not necessarily reflect a change in farmers' attitudes to trade.[9]

An extensive and theoretically correct analysis would require the use of more detailed information on the workings of the market and on the behaviour of peasants (for example, the elasticity of their supply).[10] In the case of Italy, the available sources do not allow sophisticated analysis; indeed, apart from vague statements, it is difficult even to assess the importance of consumption of home produce. Not without reason, the topic has been relatively neglected in historical debates where more attention has been paid to the integration of the economies of the 'pre-unity' states.[11] The development of a market economy has almost always been touched upon in a casual way (for example, describing the economic features of a specific area). Scholars in any case tend to stress the existence of market imperfections, the isolation of farmers and the predominance of production for home consumption.[12]

Till now the issue has been seriously tackled only by E. Sereni. He considered commercialization of agriculture as an essential component in the process of formation of a national market, suggesting that it happened in the 20 years from the unity of Italy (1861) to the 1880s, for several reasons: the construction of the railways, free-trade policy and the agrarian crisis.[13] Unfortunately it seems very difficult to verify his hypothesis since the first quantitative estimates refer to much more recent years (1936–38). The Italian economy was already predominantly commercialized: with home consumption accounting for one-third of total food consumption.[14] For previous years, one can quote an ingenious but debatable official valuation for wheat[15] and single statements which contradict each other. According to G. Valenti, in the pre-war years, consumption of home produce absorbed two-fifths of production while, according to A. Serpieri, this total was less than one-third.[16] The difficulties of estimations are serious even now, with C. Barberis being forced to present his estimates for 1980 (equal to 8.7 per cent of production) as only a 'preliminary evaluation for an inquiry still to be carried out'.[17]

In order to overcome the impasse, this research uses a microeconomic source, following pioneering work by G. Somogyi[18] – the so-called 'household budgets'. These consist of records of income and expenditure of households in a certain year. After some elaboration, it is possible to obtain an estimate of the monetary value of home consumption and to calculate its ratios to production and consumption. The definition of home consumption is a strictly microeconomic one: it includes only those goods produced by the farm or received as payment in kind and consumed by the family. Therefore the procedure of estimation differs both from direct macroeconomic ones (based, for example, on the amount of transported products[19]) and from indirect microeconomic estimates which are based on a comparison between production and (estimated) consumption requirements.[20] The latter do not measure home consumption in a strict sense, but the potential (not necessarily exploited) for food self-sufficiency provided by the farm.

2

After necessary information about sources and a brief illustration of the methods of elaboration used, results will be presented into two parts. The first part (section 4) will focus on household-firms, that is to say, those managed either by their owners or by tenant farmers. The analysis will discuss the home consumption/output and home consumption/total consumption ratios for foodstuffs, examining not only variations in time, but also structural differences between regions and types of tenancy. In the second part (section 5) these microeconomic figures will be used to estimate a macroeconomic home consumption/total consumption ratio for the whole Italian economy in the second half of the 1870s and in the 1930s.

The overall results neither meet the expectations nor confirm the conventional wisdom of a slow diffusion of market transactions during Italian economic development. In fact, the farms of the sample sold on average two-thirds of their production and the households bought one-third of the foodstuffs they needed, shares which seem to have remained stable over time. The aggregate percentages turn out to be between 20 and 25 per cent in both benchmarks (in the 1930s, less than Barberi's estimate). These figures are definitely low, if compared not only to the ideal type of peasant economy (or to the description of the 'backward sector' in dualistic models of development), but also to other countries. The home consumption/consumption ratio is in fact similar to that of advanced European countries like Switzerland and France[21] and is decidedly higher than that of the former Yugoslavia[22] and Russia.[23] It even seems to be only slightly higher than that of the US in 1910.[24] In the last section some hypotheses are suggested to frame these results in the general context of Italian economic development.

2. Concept and Methods

The household budgets used are taken from the 'monographies de famille', prepared according to a method developed and applied for the first time by the French economist and sociologist, F. Le Play,[25] in the middle of the last century. As opposed to large surveys relying on families themselves[26] to fill in standard forms, the 'monographie' focused on one household only. The budget had to be preceded by substantial description of the way of life, habits, history and mentality of the household. The 'monographie' therefore required vast reams of information which were collected by a scholar interviewing the members of the household. Such a time-consuming method could therefore be applied only to a small number of cases: the validity of any general inference is thus questionable.

Some of the budgets examined in this study were published in a collection of surveys by the International Society of Social Economy founded by Le Play[27] and therefore follow his method faithfully. Others were compiled by individual scholars, particularly at the beginning of this century. However, the majority are taken from two official surveys, one in the 1870s and the other in the early 1930s.[28] Roughly a quarter refer to families of wage earners. Some were full-time employees, receiving a predetermined quantity of goods and sometimes also small plots of land to cultivate with their families. Others were day labourers whose wages in kind consisted only of meals on working days. The consumption of these wages in kind therefore differs in principle from home consumption in the strict sense, inasmuch as it assumes, by definition, the presence of a market transaction (not using money by choice of the parties).[29] It can nevertheless be included in a wider definition of 'natural economy'.

The household budgets are made up of a double list of the monetary values of goods and services, one for income (the farm's products and other earnings) and the other for expenditure (the household's consumption and production costs). Theoretically, the consumption side should include finished goods only (for example, bread), and the income side should include the value added of domestic processing of farm products (e.g. milling and baking). Most budgets neglect both such entries, reporting on each side only the value of raw agricultural commodities.

The quantitative estimate of the consumption of home produce is immediate and leaves no room for doubt in the household budgets compiled by the Le Play method,[30] which calls for a breakdown for payments in kind. Therefore it is easy to separate re-uses (the use of part of the production as input), payments in kind to third parties (purchase of goods and services off the farm) and real consumption of home produce. Unfortunately, only 93 of the 255 household budgets of the sample[31] indicate such distinctions, while the others do not state how much of the output was used by the household and how much was sold. Home consumption (or re-use) is assumed to consist of those goods which appear on both sides of the budget under exactly the same heading. That is to say, it is assumed that farmers preferred to consume their own products directly rather than sell them and buy the same goods again later.[32] A different pattern of behaviour could have been imposed on them by usurious credit. Peasants could have been forced to sell their produce just after harvest to meet accumulated debts, only to buy the same goods in the following months on credit (from money lenders or from the landowner). In this case, the methodology used would tend to over-value the level of home consumption: however, it is not possible to correct this, as all the household budgets of the sample were compiled on a yearly basis. It must also be pointed out that in many cases the budgets tend to under-value the Gross Saleable Production (GSP) of cattle-raising, as the figures of 'profits from livestock' (from the sale of bred animals) are usually on a net basis.[33] In these cases the home consumption/GSP is consequently over-valued by the reduction of the denominator. Finally, the entries are usually very generic and do not state the exact quality of the goods (e.g. corn): if the farmer sold his own products and bought goods of inferior quality,[34] home consumption would have been over-valued.

In order to obtain a degree of uniformity in the classification and presentation of the data, the numerous goods which appear in the household budgets have been grouped together[35] according to their commodity features, separating foodstuffs from other products. The former have been divided as follows:[36]

1. cereals
2. other seed products for food use (potatoes, pulses etc.)
3. livestock products (meat, eggs, milk, etc.)
4. arboricultural products (wine, oil, fruit, etc.)

Other goods (wood, textile fibres, cocoons, etc.) have been grouped together under 'miscellaneous and industrial cultures'. Expenditures have been divided into the four entries for foodstuffs already mentioned, 'other foodstuffs' (not produced by the farmer such as salt, dried cod, colonial goods, etc.), clothes,[37] lodging (rent,[38] heat, light) and other outlays (health, pleasure, charity, etc.). Home consumption has been estimated for the four groups of foodstuffs and for the 'other goods' (always wood and sometimes textile fibres).

The calculation of the home consumption/total consumption ratio is straightforward. As milling involved a payment to third parties,[39] the ratio for cereals should, strictly speaking, always be less than 100. On the contrary, the ratio of home consumption to output can vary according to three possible definitions of agricultural income:

- total gross production (the total of all goods and services produced);
- gross saleable production (GSP), equal to the previous one[40] net of re-uses;[41]
- the net product, equal to GSP minus depreciation.

Households were not actually interested in any of these calculations (all of them being accounting measures). Instead they were concerned with the sum (here defined as 'net income') which they could get from the farm's crops to use for consumption or savings. This is equal to the net product of the land minus outlays for wages, rent (if existent) and property taxes.[42] It thus represented the (net) remuneration of inputs supplied by household-labour, capital[43] and possibly land (in the case of ownership). The sum of this 'net income' and of other incomes (jobs undertaken outside the farm and/or other sources – gifts, annuities, etc.) makes up the household's 'disposable income'. Combining these definitions of income and of income in kind, it is possible to derive a number of measures, including the following:

1. the ratio of home consumption of the family to the net product;
2. the ratio of home consumption to GSP;
3. the ratio of the sum of home consumption and of production costs in kind to GSP;
4. the ratio of the sum of home consumption, production costs in kind and re-uses to total gross product.

The last index is the most general one, inasmuch as it includes all the forms of 'uses in kind' of farm production;[44] the third one is nearest to the concept of 'natural economy',[45] while the first two are more directly comparable to macroeconomic data of agricultural production (respectively to value added and to GSP).[46] It is also possible to calculate the surplus available for sale (or 'marketable surplus'), as the difference between GSP and home consumption. This includes, by definition, all those goods traded outside the farm, either in kind or for money, on the market or privately.[47] Finally, the sum of the marketable surplus and of income obtained outside the farm (presumably in cash, unless otherwise stated) makes up the monetary income.

In order to work out the budgets of wage-earners, it was necessary to adopt a less refined breakdown by commodities, because fairly frequently such budgets report only indivisible, general items (like 'meals'). Incomes have been divided into wages in kind – further split into foodstuffs and others services (board and lodgings, wood, etc.) – wages in cash and other incomes (subsidies, proceeds from proto-industry and others). Correspondingly, home consumption is estimated for foodstuffs and for other goods. It must be noted that the share of incomes in kind depended largely on how many members of the family had a yearly contract, which usually implied substantial wages in kind. In most cases only the head of the family (and/or a son) had such a contract, while other members worked as daily labourers.

It is possible to calculate national ratios weighting the microeconomic percentages with an index of the ratio of the peasant economy to the total Italian economy.[48] Output includes the rent in kind paid by sharecroppers[49] and above all the production of capitalistic farms.[50] Consumption includes that of non-agricultural households.

3. The Sources

This study takes into account 255 household budgets[51] which can be grouped together in four 'samples' according to their source and period[52] (Table 1). The households pooling incomes from farming and outside work are classified among farms. This choice follows the census criteria[53] and is justified by the need to avoid making an arbitrary division between farmers with an outside income and day-labourers with a small plot of land to cultivate.[54]

Table 1 Composition of the sample

	Farms	Yearly contract workers	Day labourers	Total
Notizie	53	21	21	95
Mantovani	26	–	–	26
Others	32	3	12	47
INEA	70	13	4	87
Total	181	37	37	255

Sources: See pp. 6–7.

Before examining the characteristics and evaluating the reliability of the household budgets, it is worth stressing that they are an indirect source of information. The data were collected by 'experts' from outside the family circle whose task was not easy because of the difficulty in measuring both the output and consumption of certain goods (mainly marginal ones like fruits, vegetables, eggs, etc.).[55] Many budgets (especially in the oldest sample) are therefore not precise. Besides, one could suspect the existence of deliberate distortions by both parties. On one hand the 'experts' may have wanted to provide an optimistic picture of the farmers' condition, for example to minimize the reasons for their protests or to exalt certain forms of management like sharecropping;[56] on the other hand, farmers were notoriously reluctant to reveal their real earnings to outsiders (or to the landowners who drew up some of the family budgets). The first of these (possible) biases would imply an overvaluation of the incomes and consumption of the families, and the second an under-valuation.

The first sample is the result of a survey carried out by the Ministry of Agriculture, Industry and Commerce at the end of the 1870s.[57] The method used in this investigation is not clearly stated[58] and the results are somewhat uncertain. Some of the budgets are clearly incomplete (non-food consumption is reported in some 20 cases only); in most of these, items are only vaguely specified, and their measurement is very imprecise.[59] It is possible to calculate GSP with some approximation[60] in only 27 cases (only six of these also allow the calculation of gross production), while in the other 26 the absence of indication of production costs leads one to interpret the 'earnings' as being equal to net income.[61] In the following analysis, the two groups of budgets have been kept separate, labelling those with GSP 'sample A' and those with net income 'sample B'. Moreover, nine budgets report only quantities: values have been estimated by multiplying quantities by prices taken from other examples in the same geographical area. Finally, no less than 33 farms are concentrated in the provinces of Sondrio (11), Cosenza (8), and Grosseto and Foggia (7 each).[62] This fact raises some additional doubts, even though pooling together[63] budgets from these provinces does not substantially change the results.[64]

The Mantovani 'sample' (from the name of the author) consists of households of sharecroppers in the province of Treviso[65] in the years 1893–95.[66] Although more accurate and complete in the definitions of items, these budgets are nevertheless far from ideal. Income and expenditure are expressed only in monetary terms (which makes it impossible to estimate home consumption on the basis of physical quantity) and all cereals are combined in one unique entry. This has been divided into components (wheat, maize, oats, etc.) on the basis of information provided by Mantovani on the rotation of crops and on yields.[67]

The third sample consists of family budgets from various sources from 1859 to 1914.[68] Some 20 of them were compiled in the first years of this century: in the following pages they will be called 'other cases'. The majority of these budgets appears to be fairly accurate, probably having been collected by better trained scholars. The best ones are the five originally published in the 'Ouvriers des deux mondes', whereas the budgets of the two Lombardy households are full of gaps, probably because the authors were more interested in nutrition than in the economic conditions of the households.[69]

Finally, the most consistent sample was collected between the end of the 1920s and the beginning of the 1930s, by local branches of the National Institute of Agrarian Economy.[70] These budgets apparently do not contain defects: earnings in cash and in kind are clearly divided; items are precisely specified and their listing is complete.[71] The lay-out shows the existence of a well-conceived survey plan, implemented by really skilful surveyors.[72] However, one could suspect the presence of 'political' biases even though it seems unlikely that they seriously affected the budgets, exactly half of which are in the red. In fact, the introductions to the volumes frequently stress the hardships of the economic situation and the sacrifices sustained by the farmers, even with regard to the recent past. However, one cannot exclude the possibility that political considerations influenced the selection of case studies, for example by choosing some which were better off or more ideologically 'aligned'.[73] This problem of 'micro-representativeness' could also apply to the budgets of other 'samples'.

4. A Statistical Analysis of Commercialization

The Statistical Appendix below reports the averages for each sample.[74] These tend, in part, to hide the large variances in means, which, however, appear clearly from the high levels of standard deviations in three out of the four samples (Notizie, other cases and INEA).[75] The exception is Mantovani's sample, which refers to a homogeneous group of household-firms and is also characterized by decidedly higher percentages of home consumption. The figures for the other three samples are all very similar. In the whole period, almost a century long, there does not appear to have been any tendency towards a reduction of home consumption, with the ratios actually higher in the most recent sample, that of INEA. Moreover, considerable differences appear in the composition of GSP and of consumption. In the pre-war samples, cereals accounted for approximately 40 per cent of output (the figure is distinctly higher than the national one),[76] while products from breeding and arboriculture did not exceed 20 per cent (less than the Italian total). In the INEA sample, cereals accounted for a lower share of total GSP than livestock products, though the mix of output was substantially the same as the national one. Consumption changed in a similar way (the share of cereals and of livestock products increased), probably as a consequence of the increase in per capita income.[77]

The essential features of involvement in the market are more or less common to all three 'samples'. Home consumption accounted for roughly 40 per cent of GSP, leaving the rest (theoretically) available for sale or for payments in kind. These last can be reckoned only for a small group of budgets (those from the INEA sample budgets and a few others). On average these payments did not exceed 4 per cent of GSP, with a maximum of 15–20 per cent if rent was paid in kind. Levels of commercialization were higher for livestock output (particularly for the Notizie sample) and, to a lesser extent, for wine, oil and fruits than for cereals and other seed products. Items of the last two groups were mainly consumed by households. In the two first samples the home consumption/GSP ratio is remarkably higher for wheat (a 'quality' product for the market and as rent) than for corn (used by farmers' families). This difference disappeared in the 1930s, probably as a result of changes in eating habits, due to increases in income. A considerable part of the monetary income was used for the payment of taxes, of rent and of production costs (also including, in many cases, the employment of labourers) and for non-food expenditure. All the families resorted to the market either to augment insufficient production (mainly of cereals) or to buy goods they did not produce. Home consumption satisfied on average little more than half of the food needs of households in the 'Other cases' sample, while it accounted for less than two-thirds of the needs of the other two samples. Percentages by groups of product usually do not differ between samples: the exception is the low figure for livestock products in the Notizie region. Finally, home consumption of non-food items (mainly firewood and, in a few cases, textile fibres), did not exceed 10–15 per cent.[78] Overall, these households bought (or perhaps exchanged in kind) over half of the goods they consumed.

In order to assess whether the ratios remained stable over time (that is the absence of commercialization), one can resort to an analysis of the variance of the averages.[79] More precisely, an F-test can be used to verify the null hypothesis that the averages are different from each other as against the alternative that they are equal; if the former is accepted, the different average or averages are identified with a Scheffè test, at a conventional 5 per cent probability level. In the second column, crosses mark the distributions which prove to be heteroschedastic according to a Bartlett–Box test (the analysis of the variance assumes the distribution to be homoschedastic).[80] Both the global averages and those for groups of food products are analysed.[81] The Mantovani 'sample'[82] is excluded because it is not representative; the Notizie sub-sample A is also dropped from the analysis of consumption/output ratios, because data on GSP are not available.

The results are summarized in Table 2. They appear reasonable from a statistical point of view: the averages which are significantly different are either homoschedastic or pass the F-test at 1 per cent. The results do not confirm the conventional wisdom about commercialization. With only one exception (the home consumption/consumption ratio for wine, oil, fruits, etc.), the averages are either equal or significantly higher in the 1930s than before. Also the ratios for other goods ('various') come out to be higher for the INEA sample than for the 'Other cases'.[83] Generally speaking, the differences are smaller for aggregate ratios than for single groups of products, probably because of the different composition of GSP and of consumption. In fact changes in composition, *ceteris paribus*, would have reduced the share of home consumption, thus balancing the movement of single components.[84]

Table 2 Change in home consumption ratios

	1	2	3
in GSP:			
cereals	**	+	I>A I>A
other seed products	–	–	–
livestock	**	–	I>N
arboriculture	–	–	–
Total foodstuffs	*	–	–
in consumption:			
cereals	*	–	I>N
other seed products	**	+	I>N I>A
livestock	**	+	I>N I>A
arboriculture	*	–	N>A
Total foodstuffs	–	–	–

Column 1: F-tests (differences significant at ** = 1 per cent, * = 5 per cent); column 2: Bartlett-Box test for heteroschedasticity (+ if the average is heteroschedastic); column 3: significantly different averages (N = Notizie sample; A = Other cases; I = INEA)
Source: Statistical Appendix below, Table II.

These aggregate averages could obscure a process of commercialization in some areas and/or for some types of tenancies. To explore this possibility, households are divided first between owners, sharecropper and tenants[85] and then according to location (North, Centre, South). As Table VI of the Statistical Appendix clearly shows, in the majority of cases the level of home consumption does not show significant differences; either this or the test is invalidated by heteroschedasticity. However the few valid cases which exist confirm the higher percentages of the INEA sample, with two or three exceptions.

These results seem to show that the level of home consumption remained substantially stable in the long run, though possibly fluctuating in the short run. Such fluctuations might explain the higher percentages of the 1930s.[86] Most scholars believe[87] that the crisis of that decade had widened the scope of subsistence agriculture, which would have absorbed unemployed people from manufacturing and services (assuming they had not broken their

Table 3 Global analysis of home consumption ratios

	variables			l.s.	two-way			three-	
	C	A	R		C/A	C/R	A/R	way	%
On GSP									
cereals	–	**	*	**	–	–	–	–	36
other seed products	–	**	–	–	–	–	–	*	25
livestock	**	–	**	–	–	–	–	*	41
arboriculture	–	–	–	**	*	*	–	–	31
Total foodstuffs	–	–	–	–	–	–	–	–	27
On consumption									
cereals	**	–	**	**	–	*	–	–	30
other seed products	**	**	–	**	*	**	**	–	41
livestock	*	**	*	*	–	*	–	–	39
arboriculture	–	**	–	*	–	**	–	–	30
Total foodstuffs	–	–	*	*	–	–	–	–	26

Variables significant at * = 5 per cent ** = 1 per cent; l.s. = degree of significance of the interactions; two-way = interaction between pairs of variables; three-way = interactions among the three variables; % = explained percentage of total variance
Sources: Statistical Appendix, Tables II, III, IV.

links with the rural family of origin). It is also possible that changes in terms of trade against agriculture and changes of relative prices within agriculture (an increase in prices of cereals), besides modifying the composition of aggregate GSP,[88] had caused home consumption to increase.[89]

Differences of area and tenancy might have influenced the level of commercialization. One would expect a higher level in more developed areas (the North) and for tenants who had to pay rent to landowners.[90] In fact, many differences turned out to be significant (especially for home consumption/output ratios), while the high levels of F-tests downplayed the risks of heteroschedasticity.[91] The hypothesis that the level of commercialization (aggregate and for cereals only) for tenants was higher than for sharecroppers or owners is confirmed. Contrary to the hypothesis, the ratios are lower for Southern households than for those of other areas of the country. It must be noted, however, that the two results are strictly linked, because three-quarters of Southern households were tenancies. The levels of commercialization on the consumption side were also high in the South. The percentages are lower than those of the other regions for all groups of goods, save cereals. Since these farms specialized in cereal production, the scope for home consumption of other foodstuffs was correspondingly reduced. On the other hand, the more advanced agricultural areas of the North (the Po Valley) are excluded from the analysis, because the farms there were large capitalistic estates.[92]

In conclusion, it is possible to take jointly into consideration the effects of the three explanatory variables (C sample, A area and T tenancy) and of interactions between them in order to avoid any possible biases due to the composition of the samples. As expected, the results (reported in Table 3) show that in the previous analysis the relevance of any explanatory variable could have been over-valued if considered on its own. The sample (that is the change in time) is significant in only four cases – all concerning single groups of goods – instead of six as shown in Table 2. This result confirms the absence of a process of commercialization.

5. A Tentative Macroeconomic estimate

It is possible to estimate the aggregate share of the home consumption of foodstuffs by weighting the microeconomic ratios either on the consumption or on the output side. The results should in principle be very similar. The numerator (home consumption) is identical, while the differences in denominators (consumption or agricultural GSP) should not be particularly large. Consumption is in fact equal to the sum of GSP, the net trade balance (with the opposite sign) and the value added of food processing. In the budgets, this last element is often left out of the estimates of consumption,[93] while the trade balance is not only small in absolute terms in both periods[94] but, being positive, also tends to reduce the difference. It is preferable to calculate the percentage on the side of consumption for three reasons: it is possible to use the whole Notizie[95] sample, the results are more directly comparable with Barberi's data[96] and relatively less 'daring' assumptions are required in order to make estimates.[97]

It is necessary to use the share of total population (taken from the censuses) as a proxy for the otherwise unknown percentage of consumption of peasant households. The two figures would be equal if the per capita average consumption of foodstuffs by farmers were equal to that of the rest of the population. If, as is probable, it was higher (and/or characterized by a higher proportion of 'poor' goods, like cereals and pulses), the aggregate percentages obtained (as shown in Table 4) would be underestimated. The bias however should not be substantial.[98]

The census of 1931,[99] which is considered fairly reliable, classified families on the basis of the profession of the head of the family (owners, sharecroppers, tenants, contract workers and day labourers) as well as on the number of family members.[100] This census classified as peasants all households which farmed on their own account, no matter how small their holdings: therefore it probably tends to over-estimate the number of peasants.[101] As already indicated, this research adopts the same criteria.[102] Actually in the INEA 'sample', smaller farms (including day labourers' micro-allotments) are most decidedly under-represented.[103] However it is difficult to evaluate the remaining bias: there are no theoretical reasons for establishing a positive correlation between the size of farms and home consumption ratios. Finally, in the census all the wage-earners are grouped under the general heading of 'workers', while a considerable number of householders are classified as 'other employees in agriculture' (not otherwise specified). These two categories are summed together. The percentage of day labourers in the total is assumed to be equal to that reported for men only.[104]

The use of the 1881 census involves more difficult questions[105] since it breaks down the agriculturally active population by sex and profession into farmers (owners, sharecroppers, tenants), contract workers and day labourers.[106] The survey is undoubtedly more accurate in terms of the male population[107] which therefore is used to calculate the weights. This introduces two further assumptions (in addition to those already applied to the 1931 census): that the proportional distribution of households by category was equal to that of active males, and that all households (peasant and others) had the same composition.[108]

On the whole, these weights assume that the Italian agricultural population could be divided into three categories: farmers, who could consume their own production, wage-earners, who could consume goods received as wages in kind, and urban households (or, more precisely, households not engaged in agriculture) which supposedly had no access to home consumption. This assumption could bias the results to some extent, for it ignores incomes in kind derived from the cultivation of kitchen gardens[109] and/or received as gifts (for instance the 'onoranze' to landowners from their tenants). The entity of this 'urban' home consumption is difficult to evaluate however.

A further weighting of peasant households is needed because of sampling problems, as shown by some X^2 tests.[110] They compare the distribution of samples with the distribution of the universe (the total population), if disaggregated according to location and type of tenancy.[111] Only the Notizie sample turns out to be representative, and for tenancy only. In all the samples Northern families are under-represented, while two samples out of three (the Notizie and 'Other cases') over-represent Southern families. The exception is the INEA sample, which over-represents families from the Centre. Both the INEA 'sample' and 'Other cases' contain too many sharecropping households and too few owners.[112]

The number of available budgets is too small to cross-classify the whole sample according to both criteria at the same time.[113] Only one of them can be used: that which maximizes the difference between the averages has been chosen.[114] The aggregate and cereal consumption ratios are weighted according to tenancy arrangements, the other three according to geographical location.

The results are shown in Table 4, where they are compared with Barberi's estimates[115] (averaging the years 1936 and 1938). The apparent growth in the total percentage of home consumption for farms is caused by a composition effect; that is, by an increase in the percentage of owners at the expense of tenants.[116] If the composition of the population had remained the same, the percentage for the 1930s (12.12 per cent) would have been very similar to that of the 1880s.[117] Even including wages in kind, the overall share of home consumption turns out to be very low. This is a result of the (relatively) high ratio of day labourers and non-agricultural households to the total Italian population. In fact, even if farmers and contract workers met all their food requirements with home consumption or wages in kind (an obviously extreme hypothesis), home consumption would have slightly exceeded 35 per cent in both periods.[118] The change in the composition of population by categories (the fall of the percentage of contract workers and the increase of peasant-owners) has increased the percentage of home consumption from 60 per cent to 95 per cent of the total 'non-monetary economy' (home consumption plus wages in kind).

It is difficult to identify the causes of the differences between this estimate and Barberi's, mainly because he does not state his method of calculation.[119] He reports extremely detailed estimates, suggesting figures for all goods of any importance. Most of these are nicely rounded off, which presumably implies simple guesstimates.[120]

Table 4 Aggregate home consumption/consumption ratio

	Notizie	INEA	Barberi
Cereals	15.93	18.50	46.32
(wheat)	14.26	19.58	45.88
(corn)	17.86	18.97	
Other seed products	15.14	28.52	16.92
Livestock	8.63	20.22	22.75
arboriculture	14.40	19.48	43.49
(wine)	16.75	22.14	
(oil)	7.40	4.32	
Total (farms)	13.42	19.61	
Year worker	7.88	0.60	
Day labourers	1.82	2.00	
Total	23.12	20.22	33.72

Sources: Statistical Table II and text.

Wheat is the exception to this rule: the percentage is calculated by subtracting the flour used in industrial processing (in the production of 'pasta' and bread)[121] from the total available flour. In other words, Barberi assumes that all the residual flour (including that used in making bread for third parties, which is considered separately in the industrial census) was used for home consumption. This procedure is tantamount to including in home consumption all goods which are subject to some degree of home processing, even if ingredients, for instance, are bought on the market (e.g., bread made at home with purchased flour).

6. Conclusions

The analysis of household budgets outlined above has shown that the percentage of home consumption has been stable over the time period under consideration and also lower than expected. These conclusions could be questioned because of the recognized complexity of Italian peasant society and the paucity of case studies, which are not always entirely representative or reliable. As a general rule, any source is better than none; moreover, the results can be confirmed by macroeconomic analysis of the supply and demand for foodstuffs.

Demand came mainly from non-agricultural households; among agricultural ones, demand came from day labourers: together, these two categories represented about two-thirds of the total population. Neither offered much scope for consumption of home produce, though this was not necessarily nil.[122] Many peasant households (perhaps the majority) were forced to buy part of their requirements on the market because the production of their own farms was insufficient. This was the case of 'specialized' farms, producing only a small bundle of goods (sometimes even only one), which were not always consumed in significant amounts by the household.[123] Examples ranged from temporary cereal-growing (often unstable) in the Southern latifundia[124] to intensive flower and vegetable cultivation in the Ligurean Riviera. Even if these specialized farms sold, *ceteris paribus*, a relatively larger share of their output than others, sales were substantial from all types of farms. Exceptions were characterized by a combination of insufficient output (for lack of resources) or substantial monetary incomes from outside sources (for example, emigration): these cases seem fairly frequent in the mountain areas, especially the Alpine ones. Naturally, peasants' farms were not the only – and perhaps not the main – suppliers of foodstuffs to the market. Supply also came from large capitalistic estates (especially in the Po Valley) and from rents which were almost entirely sold,[125] either by the landowner if paid in kind or by the tenant himself if paid in cash.[126]

A low and stable home consumption/output ratio since the 1870s implies that the commercialization of agriculture preceded economic development. It is difficult to put forward any hypothesis about its timing: one cannot even rule out the possibility that commercialization took place around the middle of the last century or immediately thereafter, as Sereni contends. However, it is more likely that the process goes back several centuries, perhaps even to the Lower Middle Ages, the first period of urban growth in Italy.[127] The sharecropping of Central Italy is a good example. According to agrarian economists of the 19th century, this system was distinguished by isolation from the market and by the absolute predominance of home consumption (it is quite true that these farms enjoy the highest home consumption ratios). However, the sharecropping farms not only produced consistent saleable surpluses (at least the landowners' share, equal to about one-half of production), but the system itself expanded during the Lower Middle Ages to supply the cities with foodstuffs.[128]

Therefore it seems that industrialization merely increased an already existent demand, without any radical change, at least until the 'economic miracle' of the 1950s and 1960s, which precipitated an exodus from the countryside. Previously, the rate of growth of the urban population had been fairly low,[129] partly because of the relatively high initial level of urbanization, but above all because many factories were scattered in the countryside, at least during the first stages of development (the 'textile wave', in Cafagna's words).[130] Many industrial workers were thus still sustained by the agricultural output of other members of the family (enacting a sort of intersectoral exchange within the household).[131] On the other hand, rents and the proceeds of sales of the output from the capitalistic estates tended to be concentrated in only a few hands, thus shrinking the potential demand for mass-produced manufactures and the 'market' role of the agricultural sector. This explains the insufficient market size which, according to Bonelli,[132] has caused the continuing imbalance in Italian industrialization.

Appendix A List of the Household Budgets

A U. Peruzzi (1931), 'Monografia di una famiglia di mezzadri nei dintorni di Firenze (year 1857)', in INEA, *Monografie di famiglie agricole*, Vol. I, Rome, pp. 106–31.

B P. Cuppari (1860), 'Spese e proventi di una famiglia colonica', *Giornale agrario toscano*, n.s., **VII**, pp. 298–304.

C A. Rabbeno (1931–39), 'Monografia di una famiglia di mezzadri nel comune di Reggio Emilia (1893)', in INEA, *Monografie*, Vol. VI, pp. 69–74.

D E. Sella, A. Preziotti and G.O. Priore (1906), 'Le condizioni economiche dei contadini dell'Umbria', *Riforma Sociale*, **XIII**, pp. 582–647.

E L. Camboni (1906), 'Monografie di famiglie agricole del comune di Mores (Sassari)', *Giornale degli economisti*, May, pp. 469–89 and June, pp. 553–73 (3 cases).

F O. Sciassi (1905), 'Il colono dell'Altipiano Milanese e le sue condizioni di vita', *Riforma Sociale*, **XII**, pp. 787–820.

G F. Chessa (1906), Le condizioni economiche e sociali dei contadini dell'agro di Sassari, *ibid.*, **XIII**, pp. 38–63 and 266–98.

H E. Gruner (1906), 'Studi sulle condizioni del contadino in Lombardia. Osservazioni fatte in una azienda del comune di Parabiago', *Annali dell'istituzione agraria dott. A. Ponti*, **VI**, pp. 4–25.

I E. Gruner (1907), Studi sulle condizioni del contadino in Lombardia. Comuni di Brugherio e Cologno Monzese, *ibid.*, **VII**, pp. 7–33.

L *Inchiesta parlamentare sulle condizioni dei contadini nelle province meridionali e nella Sicilia*, Vol. V: *Basilicata e Calabria*, Tome I, Rome 1909, pp. 278–307.

M *Ibid.*, Vol. VI: *Sicilia*, Tome I, Rome 1910, pp. 244–51.

N G. Curato (1910), 'Monografie di famiglie borghesi del comune di Troja', *Riforma Sociale*, **XVII**, pp. 736–79 (third, fourth and fifth cases).

O *Inchiesta parlamentare*, Vol. IV: *Campania*, Tome I, Rome 1909, from p. 407 (3 cases).

P A. Brizi (1931–39), 'Una monografia di mezzadri nella pianura di Assisi (1909)', in INEA, *Monografie*, Vol. II, pp. 130–41.

Q E. Gramignani (1931–39), 'Una famiglia di mezzadri della collina della tenuta di Casalina', in INEA, *Monografie*, Vol. II, pp. 142–55.

R G. Tassinari (1914), 'Una famiglia di mezzadri nel comune di Castellina in Chianti', *Atti della R. Accademia dei Georgofili*, Series V, **XI**, pp. 283–310.

S S. Dolfin (1912), 'Una famiglia di mezzadri in provincia di Parma', *Giornale degli economisti*, July–August, pp. 81–130.

T I. Canavari (1913), 'Una famiglia colonica della regione subappenninica umbro-marchigiana', *Atti della R. Accademia dei Georgofili*, Series V, **X**, pp. 310–51.

U Società Umanitaria, Ufficio del Lavoro (1904), *L'industria dei mobili in Brianza e le condizioni dei lavoratori*, Milan, pp. 27–8.

V G. Curato, 'Appendice', in Ufficio del Lavoro (1909), *Materiali per lo studio delle condizioni dei lavoratori della terra nel Mezzogiorno*, Part I: *Capitanata e Puglia*, Pubblicazioni dell'Ufficio del Lavoro, Series B, No. 24, Rome, pp. 668–74.

Z *Ouvriers des deux mondes*, Paris (2nd series):

1. No. 63: U. Guerin (1890), *Vigneron precariste et metayer de Valmontone.*
2. No. 68: I. Santangelo-Spoto (1891), *Paysan agriculteur de Torremaggiore (Fg).*
3. No. 85: J. P. Assirelli (1896), *Paysan metayer de la commune de Roccasancasciano (Romagne Toscane)* (the family budget refers to 1878–79).
4. No. 108: D.A. Lojodice (1908), *Paysan cultivateur de Ruvo de Puglia (Ba).*

Statistical Appendix Household Budget Data[133]

Table I Averages (per cent) and Standard Deviations

A. *Crop mix*

	Cereals	Other seed products	Livestock products	Wine, oil fruits	Others
1. Notizie					
Sample A					
aver.	40.08	6.26	27.17	23.95	2.54
SD	23.21	6.86	20.47	24.86	2.55
Sample B					
aver.	45.81	12.44	18.13	19.05	4.58
SD	19.49	10.59	14.63	19.91	6.55
2. Treviso sharecroppers					
aver.	32.19	4.98	35.91	10.01	16.92
SD	6.62	1.98	7.12	5.93	5.36
3. Other cases (1903–13)					
aver.	42.67	10.22	18.67	19.95	8.50
SD	28.68	17.08	17.89	26.87	13.35
4. INEA					
aver.	24.79	13.18	32.36	17.21	12.46
SD	19.05	18.33	18.87	14.62	19.94

B. *Composition of the marketable surplus*

	Cereals	Other seed products	Livestock products	Wine, oil fruits	Others
1. Notizie					
Sample A					
aver.	19.67	4.56	44.64	26.08	5.05
SD	29.12	10.04	33.49	34.52	5.15
Sample B					
aver.	32.93	11.18	27.77	20.88	7.25
SD	25.83	13.16	23.97	25.51	10.43
2. Treviso sharecroppers					
aver.	34.72	0.08	32.07	8.12	25.01
SD	9.77	0.36	11.27	7.81	13.68
3. Other cases (1903–13)					
aver.	34.16	6.02	27.30	21.70	10.82
SD	35.84	17.12	29.11	32.36	20.30
4. INEA					
aver.	13.95	13.76	41.05	18.31	12.93
SD	20.01	22.84	28.23	21.04	24.20

C. *Composition of foodstuff consumption*

	Cereals	Other seed products	Livestock products	Wine, oil fruits	Others
1. Notizie					
aver.	51.99	9.96	15.09	17.74	5.22
SD	14.07	8.85	13.24	10.58	3.05

2. Treviso sharecroppers					
aver.	36.94	9.21	37.67	12.58	3.60
SD	6.83	2.72	5.64	5.44	0.97
3. Other cases (1903–13)					
aver.	51.22	10.47	14.81	16.78	6.72
SD	16.12	6.82	8.82	11.38	9.57
4. INEA					
aver.	41.35	8.59	25.19	17.10	7.77
SD	12.20	3.60	10.14	6.89	4.20

Table II Home Consumption Ratios by Samples

A. On GSP

	Cereals	Other seed products	Livestock products	Wine, oil fruits	All foods	Total output
1. Notizie						
Sample A						
n.	26	23	24	21	26	26
aver.	78.13	71.79	20.09	53.03	48.05	46.84
SD	28.50	35.11	27.30	32.05	18.06	17.75
Sample B						
n.	27	26	22	20	27	27
aver.	57.40	52.92	20.75	38.57	40.47	39.00
SD	23.72	32.84	23.60	26.36	14.12	14.33
2. Treviso sharecroppers						
n.	26	26	26	25	26	26
aver.	54.48	99.52	61.72	69.08	61.02	57.15
SD	5.43	2.45	10.50	19.32	7.80	4.39
3. Other cases (1903–13)						
n.	24	22	16	14	26	24
aver.	54.03	59.29	40.26	41.09	38.70	35.64
SD	33.75	39.50	33.73	30.44	21.01	18.66
4. INEA						
n.	63	70	69	63	70	70
aver.	77.61	64.58	39.38	51.61	47.74	43.56
SD	23.13	33.67	25.31	32.46	18.51	17.91

B. On consumption

	Cereals	Other seed products	Livestock products	Wine, oil fruits	All foods	Total output
1. Notizie						
n.	53	53	45	51	53	13
aver.	75.86	68.09	38.13	63.95	64.23	48.04
SD	24.73	33.60	38.53	38.99	17.79	17.44
2. Treviso sharecroppers						
n.	26	26	26	26	26	26
aver.	76.32	79.76	87.69	75.00	78.07	63.24
SD	21.78	8.06	6.49	25.08	11.92	10.32
3. Other cases (1903–13)						
n.	26	24	26	24	26	24
aver.	62.48	60.02	44.58	36.54	52.90	38.18
SD	32.64	37.18	43.49	40.91	24.30	20.63

4. INEA						
n.	70	70	70	70	70	70
aver.	62.05	84.36	64.59	57.01	61.66	48.41
SD	32.52	21.83	26.08	30.64	18.85	14.78

Table III Home Consumption Ratios by Type of Tenancy

A. On GSP

	Cereals	Other seed products	Livestock products	Wine, oil fruits	All foods	Total output
1. Owners						
n.	52	54	50	44	57	57
aver.	73.39	62.80	40.38	45.54	44.88	41.46
SD	29.45	35.11	34.22	32.36	19.55	18.46
2. Sharecroppers						
n.	99	98	97	89	100	100
aver.	68.96	74.31	34.31	56.31	51.67	49.56
SD	22.02	32.04	23.79	27.73	14.41	13.25
3. Tenants						
n.	22	23	17	17	24	24
aver.	44.30	50.67	38.43	34.90	32.87	28.04
SD	30.75	41.00	28.36	36.71	20.54	16.57

B. On consumption

	Cereals	Other seed products	Livestock products	Wine, oil fruits	All foods	Total output
1. Owners						
n.	57	56	55	56	57	36
aver.	60.19	70.49	48.41	53.56	56.31	40.27
SD	31.10	32.03	38.70	36.32	20.52	15.91
2. Sharecroppers						
n.	100	100	97	98	100	84
aver.	74.46	80.00	60.64	64.85	69.41	55.79
SD	24.43	23.67	31.54	32.08	15.05	13.03
3. Tenants						
n.	24	23	21	23	24	20
aver.	63.37	66.49	60.90	47.39	57.66	39.70
SD	38.89	36.90	41.99	45.95	25.87	21.25

C. Statistical analysis of the differences among means

HC/GSP	1	2	3	HC/C 1	2	3
Cereals	**	+	O>F,S>T	*	+	–
Other seed products	–	–	–	–	–	–
Livestock	**	+	O>S	–	–	–
Wine, oil, fruits	–	–	–	–	–	–
Total foodstuffs	**	+	O>F,S>T	**	+	O>F,S>T

1: F-test (differences significant at: * = 5 per cent, ** = 1 per cent); 2: heteroschedasticity (marked by +); 3: different averages (O = owners, S = sharecroppers, T = tenants)

Table IV Home Consumption Ratios by Area

A. On GSP

	Cereals	Other seed products	Livestock products	Wine, oil fruits	All foods	Total output
1. North						
n.	60	62	61	55	63	63
aver.	66.31	88.69	45.67	58.07	54.13	48.08
SD	24.50	23.86	24.87	28.12	17.21	17.48
2. Centre						
n.	60	61	61	58	61	61
aver.	80.46	60.38	26.81	54.08	48.93	49.22
SD	20.18	34.01	18.46	28.71	13.24	13.08
3. South						
n.	53	52	42	37	57	57
aver.	53.05	51.10	37.59	34.53	37.18	34.40
SD	29.36	35.73	37.42	33.10	19.40	16.47

B. On consumption

	Cereals	Other seed products	Livestock products	Wine, oil fruits	All foods	Total output
1. North						
n.	63	63	63	59	63	49
aver.	68.14	81.67	68.70	72.12	68.74	53.72
SD	30.30	22.18	31.50	28.37	19.86	17.96
2. Centre						
n.	61	61	61	61	61	48
aver.	68.04	82.23	57.75	64.53	65.13	51.74
SD	26.26	24.38	31.46	29.09	15.19	11.92
3. South						
n.	57	55	49	57	57	43
aver.	69.37	60.26	40.28	39.58	56.67	42.18
SD	32.13	34.17	39.27	41.38	21.46	18.43

C. Statistical analysis of the differences among means

HC/GSP	1	2	3	HC/C 1	2	3
Cereals	**	+	C>N,C>S	–	–	–
Other seed products	**	–	N>S	**	+	N>S,C>S
Livestock	–	–	–	*	–	C>S
Wine, oil, fruits	*	–	C>S	**	+	N>S,C>S
Total foodstuffs	**	+	C>S	–	–	–

1: F-test (differences significant at: * = 5 per cent, ** = 1 per cent); 2: heteroschedasticity (marked by +); 3: different averages (N = North, C = Centre, S = South)

Table V Home Consumption Ratios for Selected Commodities

A. On GSP

	Wheat	Corn	Wine	Olive oil
1. Notizie				
Sample A				
n.	21	21	21	8
aver.	73.72	91.16	48.81	56.69
SD	29.94	21.25	35.33	40.87
Sample B				
n.	23	11	15	10
aver.	42.33	78.82	47.32	32.05
SD	41.02	30.12	37.31	24.05
2. Treviso sharecroppers				
n.	0	26	26	0.00
aver.	0.0	94.14	66.47	0.00
SD	0.0	9.72	22.29	0.00
3. Other cases (1903–13)				
n.	23	26	11	5
aver.	48.77	73.07	45.71	25.61
SD	39.65	31.93	35.75	34.21
4. INEA				
n.	62	41	43	16
aver.	80.96	82.20	60.91	83.31
SD	24.53	29.19	35.01	27.82

B. On consumption

	Wheat	Corn	Wine	Olive oil
1. Notizie				
n.	41	44	43	35
aver.	84.70	67.03	76.74	48.15
SD	29.08	34.96	41.49	50.04
2. Treviso sharecroppers				
n.	0	26	26	0
aver.	0.00	83.03	91.85	0.00
SD	0.00	24.39	26.09	0.00
3. Other cases (1903–13)				
n.	26	16	21	17
aver.	61.93	72.77	37.65	17.65
SD	43.11	38.32	49.22	39.30
4. INEA				
n.	70	48	70	68
aver.	62.47	65.59	53.22	17.89
SD	33.55	40.52	46.70	37.16

Table VI A Diacronic Analysis of Commercialization

A. By tenancy

	Owner			Sharecroppers			Tenants		
HC/GSP	1	2	3	1	2	3	1	2	3
Cereals	–	–	–	–	–	–	–	–	–
Other seed products	–	–	–	–	–	–	–	–	–
Livestock	*	–	O>N	**	+	I>N	–	–	–
Wine, oil, fruits	–	–	–	–	–	–	*	+	I>N
Total foodstuffs	–	–	–	–	–	–	–	–	–
HC/C									
Cereals	**	–	O>N	–	–	–	*	–	–
Other seed products	–	–	–	**	+	I>A,I>N	–	–	–
Livestock	**	+	I>A,I>N	**	+	I>N	*	+	I>A
Wine, oil, fruits	–	–	–	–	–	–	*	–	N>A
Total foodstuffs	*	–	I>A,N>A	–	–	–	–	–	–

B. By area

	North			Centre			South		
HC/GSP	1	2	3	1	2	3	1	2	3
Cereals	–	–	–	*	–	–	–	–	–
Other seed products	–	–	–	–	–	–	–	–	–
Livestock	–	–	–	*	+	I>N,I>A	*	–	I>N
Wine, oil, fruits	–	–	–	–	–	–	–	–	–
Total foodstuffs	–	–	–	–	–	–	–	–	–
HC/C									
Cereals	–	–	–	*	–	–	–	–	–
Other seed products	–	–	–	*	+	I>N	*	–	I>A
Livestock	–	–	–	**	+	I>N	*	–	I>A
Wine, oil, fruits	–	–	–	–	–	–	–	–	–
Total foodstuffs	–	–	–	–	–	–	*	–	–

1: F-test (differences significant at: * = 5 per cent, ** = 1 per cent); 2: heteroschedasticity (marked by +); 3: different averages (N = Notizie sample; O = Other cases sample; I = INEA sample)

Table VII Sample Representativeness: X^2 Tests

1. Notizie					
	1881 census	Sample		1881 census	Sample
North	50	34	Owners	48	53
Centre	24	25	Sharecroppers	38	30
South	26	42	Tenants	16	17
X^2 7.64			X^2 1.14*		
2. Other cases (1909–13)					
	1911 census	Sample		1911 census	Sample
North	50	22	Owners	40	19
Centre	24	25	Sharecroppers	40	59
South	26	53	Tenants	19	22
X^2 14.13			X^2 6.33		
3. INEA					
	1931 census	Sample		1931 census	Sample
North	45	17	Owners	60	33
Centre	17	57	Sharecroppers	23	59
South	38	26	Tenants	17	9
X^2 81.21			X^2 50.03		

The figures are the percentages of each class compared to the total (of households for the 1911 census and of male workers for the other two – see above pp. 11–12); the asterisk means that the null hypothesis of equal share can be accepted at 5 per cent.

Notes

1. The theoretical problems of the anaysis of commercialization have been dealt with by G. Federico (1984), 'Azienda contadina e autoconsumo fra antropologia ed economia: considerazioni metodologiche', *Rivista di storia economica*, n.s., **1** (2), pp. 222–68; some preliminary results appeared in G. Federico (1986), 'Una prima stima dell'autoconsumo sulla base dei bilanci familiari (1850–1914)', in *Mercati e Consumi; Atti del primo congresso nazionale di storia del commercio*, Bologna: Analisi, pp. 751–69.
2. For a definition see the bibliography in Federico, 'Azienda', *op. cit.* For example, T. Shanin, 'The Nature and Logic of Peasant Economy', *Journal of Peasant Studies*, October 1973 and January 1974; also D. Grigg (1981), *The Dynamics of Agricultural Change,* London, pp. 91ff. For the formulation of quantitative criteria of identification of 'peasant society', see D. Thorner, 'Peasant Economy as a Category in Economic History', in T. Shanin (ed.) (1975), *Peasants and Peasant Societies*, Harmondsworth, pp. 202–15.
3. As an example of global analysis of a process of commercialization (dealing also with social and psychological consequences), see the recent volume by R. Price (1983), *The Modernization of Rural France*, London.
4. See S. Kuznets (1969), *Sviluppo economico e struttura*, Milan, pp. 191–315; in spite of being more than 20 years old, this synthesis still seems valid if judged by the standards of more recent works as, for example, S. Ghatak and K. Ingersent (1984), *Agriculture and Economic Development*, Brighton, pp. 26–69.
5. E. Hoffmann and J. Mokyr, 'Peasants, Potatoes and Poverty: Transaction Costs in Pre-Famine Ireland', in P. Uselding (ed.) (1984), *Research in Economic History*, 3rd Supplement, Greenwich, p. 128.
6. See Federico, 'Azienda', pp. 223–4.
7. For estimation methods in today's less developed countries, see D.W. Blades (1975), *Non-Monetary (Subsistence) Activities in the National Accounts of Developing Countries*, Develop-

ment Centre of the OECD, Paris. The method is the same (based on samples and surveys), but the problem is different. In the historical analysis (at least for Italy), 'subsistence' activities have to be deducted from the total, while in LDCs they have to be added to market transactions.

8. These points are covered in more detail in G. Federico (1985), 'Autoconsumo e mercantilizzazione: spunti per una discussione', *Società e Storia*, no. 27, pp. 210–12; for instance, the level of commercialization in Italy was changed by the increase of peasant ownership after the First World War (see below, p. 12).
9. See Federico, 'Azienda', pp. 240–41.
10. See *ibid.*, pp. 245–7. As an example of a more articulated analysis, based on much richer sources, see W. Rothemberg (1983), 'The Market and Massachusetts Farmers, 1750–1855', *Journal of Economic History*, **XLI**, June, pp. 283–314.
11. See Federico, 'Autoconsumo', pp. 197–8.
12. A comprehensive bibliography would be too long and probably of little use; for an overall judgment which seems to sum up conventional wisdom well, see B. Caizzi (1975), *Il commercio*, Turin, pp. 35–6.
13. See E. Sereni, 'La formazione del mercato nazionale (1860–1900)', now in his (1981), *Capitalismo e mercato nazionale*, Rome, pp. 77ff. (he refers mainly to the diffusion of industrial products, not to traditional homemade rural ones).
14. B. Barberi (1942), 'Il valore monetario dei consumi alimentari ed il reddito della popolazione italiana', *Economia*, **xxix** (5–6), pp. 145–57: on an aggregate level, the percentages of consumption and production are much the same (see p. 12 for discussion on this point).
15. Ministry of Agriculture, Industry and Commerce (MAIC) (1914), *Il frumento in Italia, Produzione, consumo, prezzi*, Rome, pp. 39–46. Home consumption seems to have accounted for 50.6 per cent of production: the methodology used is dubious in as much as it assumes, *a priori*, that the rural population consumed only wheat produced on the farms.
16. See G. Valenti (1911), '*L'Italia agricola dal 1861 al 1911*', in *Cinquant'anni di storia italiana*, Milan, Vol. III, p. 99 and A. Serpieri (1930), *La guerra e le classi rurali italiane*, Bari, p. 105.
17. See C. Barberis (1983), 'L'autoconsumo in Italia', in *Storia d'Italia Einaudi. Annali, 6: Economia naturale ed economia monetaria*, Turin, p. 760; nowadays, the percentage of consumption should be lower because of the heavy trade deficit in foodstuffs and the substantial value added in food processing (higher than in the 19th century).
18. See G. Somogyi (1959), 'Cento anni di bilanci familiari in Italia (1861–1957)', *Annali Feltrinelli*, no. 2, pp. 151–257.
19. See P.R. Gregory, 'Grain Marketings and Peasant Consumption, Russia 1885–1913', in *Explorations in Economic History*, Vol. 17, 1980, pp. 135–64 and *Russian National Income (1885–1913)*, Cambridge, 1982, pp. 222–3. He quotes household budgets among the possible sources, but does not use them: the problems arising from this method are discussed in Federico, 'Autoconsumo', pp. 204–5.
20. See L.K. Ford (1985), 'Self-Sufficiency, Cotton and Economic Development in the South Carolina Upcountry, 1800–1860', *Journal of Economic History*, **XLV** (2), June, pp. 261–7. He applies to single farms the macroeconomic procedure suggested by R.E. Gallman in 1970 ('Self-Sufficiency in the Cotton Economy of the Antebellum South', *Agricultural History*, **XLIV** (1), June, pp. 5ff.). The same idea is implicit in C.H. Danhof's definition of the 'commercialized farm' ('The Farm Enterprise: The Northern United States', in P. Uselding (ed.) (1979), Research in Economic History, Vol. IV, Greenwich, p. 130) as one in which output was greater than the minimum requirements of the average family.
21. According to A. De Cambiaire (1952) in *L'autoconsommation agricole en France*, Paris, pp. 179 and 196, the home consumption/GSP ratio in Switzerland was 28 per cent in 1901–05, 22 per cent in 1906–19, 17–18 per cent in 1931–46 and 24 per cent in 1938 in France.
22. In 1938 home consumption would have accounted for 42 per cent of output (see R. Bicanic (1944), 'The Effects of War on Rural Jugoslavia', *Geographical Journal*, pp. 31–2).
23. According to Gregory (*Russian*, Appendix E), in 1913 the percentage was 65 per cent for total Russian agricultural production and 75 per cent for cereal production. The latter percentage (calculated with the method described in Note 19 above) had remained stable since 1885.

24. According to figures published by Barberis ('L'autoconsumo', p. 756, quoting as his source the US Department of Agriculture), the home consumption/output ratio in the US would have fallen from 17 per cent in 1910 (an already high level of commercialization) to 7 per cent in 1950 and to 1 per cent in 1979.
25. For Le Play's ideology (the issue cannot be dealt with here), see G. Orsini (1984), *Il lavoro operaio nella ricerca sociologica di P. F. G. Le Play*, Milan (with extensive bibliography) and L. Assier-Andrieu (1984), 'Le Play et la famille-souche des Pyrenees', *Annales*, **39** (3), May–June pp. 495–512.
26. In the 1880s the Prussian statistician Engel proposed a different method. The task of gathering information was entrusted to peasants themselves, who either filled *ex-post* forms or kept daily accounts ledgers. See the discussion between Engel and Le Play's students in 'Compte rendu de la troisième session de l'Institut international de statistique (Vienna 28ix–3x 1891)', in *Bulletin de l'Institut international de statistique*, Tome VI, Vol. 1, pp. 163–4. This method, a more modern one, allowed for larger samples to be taken into consideration and therefore proved to be much more useful from the point of view of historical surveys. Unfortunately, it was only later applied in Italy and not to rural households (which were in the overwhelming majority illiterate and therefore unable to fill in forms or to keep diaries). For a review of the state of research in this field immediately after the First World War, see International Labour Office (1926), *Methods of Conducting Family Budget Enquiries*, Series N (Statistics), no. 9, Geneva.
27. See L. Einaudi (1936), 'Il peccato originale e la teoria della classe eletta in F. Le Play', in *Rivista di storia economica*, pp. 112–18.
28. MAIC, Direzione generale dell'agricoltura, *Notizie intorno alle condizioni dell'agricoltura negli anni 1878–79*, Rome 1881–82, Vol. III, pp. 585–759 (hereafter named Notizie) and Istituto nazionale di economia agraria (INEA), *Monografie di famiglie agricole*, 17 vols, Rome, 1931–39. For a more detailed analysis of these sources, see infra, paragraph 3.
29. See 'Azienda', pp. 248–9.
30. For an exposition of methodology see F. Le Play (1879), *Ouvriers des deux mondes*, Tome 1: *La méthode d'observation*, Tours, pp. 210–378; G. Cheysson (1896), 'La monographie de famille', in *La reforme sociale*, pp. 605–19 and U. Guerin (1888), 'De la méthode des monographies de famille', in *Bulletin de l'Institut international de statistique*, Tome III, Vol. 1, pp. 141–76.
31. That is, all the monographies by INEA, the five in the *Ouvriers*, and that labelled S.
32. While this assumption (also used by Hoffmann and Mokyr, 'Peasants'), is compatible with whatever the reason for the choice of production may have been, it implies that the external 'usage costs' were always greater than the "internal' ones (see Federico, 'Azienda', p. 240).
33. These 'profits' would in fact be equal to the GSP only if the animals were born on the farm and raised on feed produced there; if on the contrary they were purchased from outside and/or raised on purchased feed, the 'profits' are, by definition lower than the GSP. With regard to this, it must also be noted that the 'profits' could have remained on paper as simple variations of the accounting value of animals left in the cattle-sheds (the accounting treatment of such cases was widely discussed by agrarian accounting experts; cf., for example, INEA, 'Risultati economici di aziende agrarie nell'anno 1931–32', *Studi e monografie*, no. 19, Rome, pp. 99–110).
34. This behaviour is attested in some of the large Tuscany estates within the so-called 'conti colonici' (farm accounts between sharecroppers and the landowner). The peasants handed over high-quality wheat as their share of payment of their debts after the harvest, while during the year the landowner lent them wheat of an inferior quality, purchased on the market.
35. Estimates of the home consumption of main crops (wheat, corn, oil and wine) are reported in the Statistical Appendix below, Table V.
36. This aggregation differs from that used in macroeconomic estimates of GSP (cf. Istat (1958), 'Indagine statistica sullo sviluppo del reddito nazionale in Italia dal 1861 al 1956', in *Annali di statistica*, Series VIII, Vol. 9, from p. 54). Foodstuffs are disaggregated because of their

relevance, but the whole production of firewood is included (whereas in national accounts the latter is divided between agriculture and forestry).

37. Also included here is the cost of household linen, not only because it is not reported as a separate entry in most budgets, but also because in doing so it is possible to obtain an overall estimate of the consumption of textile products.
38. Rent is taken into account only if paid in cash. Few budgets include the same sum on both sides as opportunity cost and as income of the house owned by the family or given free as part of the tenancy agreement. These entries do not appear in the majority of budgets, and therefore have been dropped altogether for the sake of consistency.
39. Most budgets omit milling costs (therefore allowing the home consumption/consumption ratio to reach 100). In some cases, these could have been taken into account by including the wheat left to the miller as payment in kind for his work in the overall consumption of cereals of the household.
40. The GSP of sharecropping farms is the sum of the peasants' share of farm output and the proceeds of some activities traditionally performed by the household for its own exclusive profit (poultry, kitchen garden, etc.). It is therefore inferior to the actual GSP of the farms, which includes the landowner's share of output as well.
41. In theory, technical choices could have determined the extent of re-uses (for example the use of machines instead of animals could have reduced the number of cattle, thus freeing for sale a portion of their feed). Therefore, *ceteris paribus*, they could have influenced the composition of GSP (which is here used as an index of productive choices). The bias should not be large, however, as all the farms adopted similar techniques.
42. Strictly speaking, land taxes should have been deducted from the farm's income, while income taxes should have been deducted from total household income. For simplicity, however, all taxes have been pooled and deducted.
43. Some budgets include the family's capital gains, if any, on the income side (generally calculated at a fixed rate) and a similar sum as an opportunity cost among expenditures. These flows were excluded from the estimates for reasons of consistency (cf. Note 38 above) and because of the impossibility of distinguishing depreciation from profit.
44. For reasons in favour of this index, see Blades, *Non-Monetary*, pp. 56ff.
45. See Federico, 'Autoconsumo', pp. 198–200.
46. It must again be remembered that the ratios could be perfectly homogeneous only adding the landowner's share of sharecropping output to the denominator.
47. They include the goods handed over to landowners as rents in kind or as repayments of previous advances. In principle, they should be classified under the heading 'other payments in kind', but this is only possible in a few budgets.
48. These averages were calculated by excluding the cases in which the denominator (consumption or GSP) is nil (no goods in the group in question were consumed or produced), but including those with a nil numerator (home consumption).
49. Some budgets (particularly, those of sharecroppers of the Mantovani sample) also state total GSP (including rent in kind) and allow estimates of the 'real' home consumption/GSP ratio, which of course turns out to be lower.
50. For the national weighting of percentages on consumption, see pp. 11–13 below.
51. For various reasons, it was not possible to use two fairly consistent groups of budgets. Those of the labourers in Puglia gathered by MAIC, Ufficio del lavoro (1909), *Materiali per lo studio delle condizioni dei lavoratori della terra nel Mezzogiorno*, Part I, *Capitanata e Puglia*, Pubbl. Series B, no. 24, Roma, do not take into account home consumption (as explained *ibid.*, p. xvii), while those of Piedmontese wages-earners (*Atti della giunta per l'inchiesta agraria e sulle condizioni della classe agricola*, Vol. VIII, Tome I, relazione di G. Meardi, Rome 1883, pp. 587–617) do not state the composition of the families surveyed.
52. For the sources, see below, pp. 6–7. The term 'samples' has to be used with caution because they are not randomly selected.
53. See below, p. 11 for a discussion of the 1931 Census (used for weighting to estimate an aggregate ratio), but also, for example, MAIC, Direzione generale della statistica (1904),

Censimento della popolazione del regno d'Italia al 10.II.1901, Vol. V: *Relazione*, Rome, p. LXXIV.

54. For a tentative definition of a quantitative distinction between the various categories, see A. Serpieri, *La struttura sociale dell'agricoltura italiana*, Rome, pp. 25ff.
55. Sometimes various goods are grouped together under a general heading ('other products', etc.) or it is stated explicitly that incomes are from certain activities (for example the raising of courtyard animals) and similarly for the corresponding relative consumption.
56. For a cultural–political interpretation of some of these budgets (which seems to rule out their use as sources) see L. Musella (1984), *Proprietà e politica agraria in Italia (1861–1914)*, Naples, pp. 112ff.
57. Notizie.
58. The Introduction (*ibid.*, p. 585) vaguely mentions a questionnaire which was distributed to the households, allowing them to make modifications if necessary. The source reports the name of the author of each budget (generally landowners or directors of agrarian institutions), but it says nothing about the number of experts consulted or the criteria for their selection.
59. However, the budgets of Apulian peasants are fairly favourably reviewed in a report by G.A. Angeloni (1884), in *Atti della giunta*, Vol. XII, Part 1, Rome, p. 459.
60. Twenty-one budgets report on the income-side general entries (e.g. 'other incomes') though on the expenditure-side, costs of seed or feed are missing. If these costs were covered by re-uses, the income would be equal to the GSP.
61. Some budgets explicitly state that incomes were net. In others it is simply a cautious assumption; in effect production costs of the farm could have been negligible or nil.
62. Also budgets of wage-earners' households are to some extent geographically concentrated: four provinces (Cremona, Foggia, Bari and Cosenza) have four cases each of yearly contracts, while for day labourers, only Foggia stands out, with five cases out of 21.
63. The stratified averages are computed giving the budgets in the relevant provinces a weight equal to $1/n$ (where n is the number of cases involved).
64. This table compares home consumption/GSP and home consumption/consumption ratios of the stratified and full sample (the stratification is extended to the INEA sample, which includes 29 cases from Tuscany, 17 of which are from Pistoia):

	Total 'samples'	Stratified
HC/GSP	46.89 (18.14)	43.67 (19.00)
HC/C	63.72 (19.72)	60.77 (20.96)

Obviously the differences are not significant.

65. F. Mantovani (1890), 'Bilanci di trenta famiglie di contadini in provincia di Treviso', *Riforma Sociale*, **V**, pp. 45–56, 134–56 and 421–31.
66. Strangely enough, there are yearly figures for consumption, but only one (in all probability a three-year average) for output. If annual figures were reported for production as well, it would have been possible to analyse the effects of fluctuations of harvests on consumption.
67. A five-year crop rotation was used, with two years of corn, one of pasture, one of oats and one of wheat: on the basis of data on yields and prices it is possible to reckon that wheat accounted for 29.70 per cent of the cereals' GSP, corn for 56.75 per cent and oats for 13.55 per cent.
68. See the list in Appendix A.
69. The household budgets in question are H and I. They do not state prices for many of the products, which have been proxied by prices taken from budgets F and U.
70. INEA, *Monografie*.
71. The method is described by A. Serpieri (1929), *Guida alle ricerche di economia agraria*, INEA, Studi e monografie, No. 1, Rome, pp. 123–32. Only a few cases differ from the standard lay-out: for example two budgets of Umbrian sharecroppers do not separate in-kind and cash transactions.
72. See P. Magnarelli (1977), 'L'INEA, una istituzione del fascismo', *Quaderni storici*, No. 12, pp. 888–98 and P. Bertolini (1983), 'A. Serpieri e l'attività di ricerca dell'INEA durante il ventennio

fascista', in *Agricoltura e forze sociali in Lombardia nella crisi degli anni Trenta*, Milan, pp. 421–33.

73. The desire of the Fascist regime to show an enthusiastic peasantry is manifest in the introduction to some budgets (politically the most tricky part of the monographs); many others, however, stress the peasants' indifference to political problems.
74. See Statistical Appendix, Tables I and II and (for single commodities) V.
75. The coefficients of variations of the aggregate ratios are:

	GSP	Consumption
Notizie	34.90	27.70
Other cases	54.29	45.94
INEA	38.75	30.57

76. According to the two available estimates (Istat, *Indagine*, from p. 54 and P. Ercolani, 'Documentazione statistica di base' in G. Fuà (ed.) (1968), *Lo sviluppo economico in Italia*, Vol. III, Milan, p. 410), the composition of Italian GSP remained more or less stable over this whole period. Cereals accounted for one-quarter (or a little more according to Istat) of the total, livestock production and arboriculture one-third each. See Statistical Appendix, Table IA.
77. See Statistical Appendix, Table IC. The per capita income of farmers (at 1913 prices, deflated with the coefficients provided by Istat (1961), *Il valore della lira nei primi cento anni dopo l'Unità,* Rome) was 220 lire in the Notizie sample, 226 lire in Mantovani, 222 lire in 'Other cases' and 273 lire in INEA.
78. This statement is based solely on the samples of INEA and 'Other cases', as the averages for Notizie were based on too few budgets to be representative.
79. The statistical procedures used are described by H. Scheffè (1959), *The Analysis of Variance*, New York.
80. In fact, heteroschedasticity implies a risk of type I error; that is to say, finding significant differences between means which are actually the same. For heteroschedastic samples, a nominal 1 per cent probability test is equivalent to a true 3–4 per cent test.
81. Only foodstuffs have been taken into consideration because the estimates of the home consumption of other products are unreliable or missing in too many budgets of both the Notizie and 'Other cases' samples.
82. The variance of this sample is markedly less than to that of the other three so that its inclusion would, by definition, violate the assumption of homoschedasticity.
83. These differences are statistically significant at 5 per cent; also the aggregate home consumption/output and home consumption/consumption ratios turn out to be lower in the 1930s, although the difference for the former is significant only at 10 per cent.
84. See above p. 12; if the composition of consumption and of GSP had remained the same, the percentages of home consumption would have been equal to 60 per cent and 63 per cent respectively.
85. All the households who supplemented their estate by renting out or by shareholding some additional land have been classified as owners. The results would have remained the same even if these households had been classified as tenants.
86. This growth of self-sufficiency at a microeconomic level is different from aggregate growth due to the changing composition of the rural population (discussed below on p. 12). The effect of the latter was probably manifest in the 1920s, but unfortunately budgets are not available for those years.
87. See E. Fano, 'Problemi e vicende dell'agricoltura italiana fra le due guerre', and A. Cadeddu, S. Lepre and E. Socrate, 'Ristagno e sviluppo nel settore agricolo italiano', both in *Quaderni storici*, (1975), nos 29–30, respectively pp. 490 and 514; also C. Daneo (1980), *Breve storia dell'agricoltura italiana*, Milan, p. 136; according to G. Della Valentina ('Agricoltura e sviluppo economico in Lombardia fra le due guerre', in *Agricoltura e forze sociali*, pp. 41ff.), it was the result of a deliberate political–economic strategy aimed at deepening a dualism which accorded with the interests of big business.

88. See G. Tattara, 'Cerealicoltura e politica agraria durante il fascismo', in G. Toniolo (ed.) (1980), *Lo sviluppo economico italiano dal 1861 al 1940*, Bari, pp. 147–55.
89. An increase in home consumption (described as certain by the authors cited in Note 87) could be determined either by a fall of the opportunity cost of home-consumed goods (in terms of industrial products) or by the growth of costs of market transactions; cf. Federico, 'Azienda', p. 240.
90. On the basis of the methodology applied, the two alternatives are equal (see below p. 12). The actual home consumption/GSP ratio should be lower than for owners for sharecroppers as well. However, total GSP of sharecropping farms is not known (see above p. 6) and the ratios are computed using the GSP pertaining to households as a denominator.
91. See Statistical Appendix, Tables III and IV.
92. See below p. 6.
93. See above p. 4 for the differences between the value of goods produced and consumed due to value added in processing.
94. The net balance of trade in foodstuffs accounted for 1.42 per cent of consumption in 1881–85 and 1.00 per cent in 1931–35 (trade data from G. Somogyi (1965), *La bilancia alimentare italiana*, Bologna, p. 57; consumption from Istat, *Indagine*, p.260).
95. See above p. 7.
96. See above pp. 12–13.
97. In fact, a weighting of ratio on GSP would need data on the share of production of peasant farms in the total Italian GSP. Such data do not exist and it does not seem possible to find an appropriate proxy.
98. For example supposing, with an evidently exaggerated hypothesis, that consumption by rural families was 50 per cent higher than the average; the aggregate percentage would be 30.94 per cent in the 1870s and 32.02 per cent in the 1930s.
99. Istat (1936), *VII Censimento della popolazione*, Vol. IV, Rome, Part II, pp. 22ff.
100. The average size of households changed according to status: 4.93 members for owners, 5.68 for tenants, 6.55 for sharecroppers and 4.19 for workers.
101. According to E. Sereni (*La questione agraria nella rinascita nazionale*, Turin 1975, pp. 100–101), this criterion (also applied in the agricultural census) was inspired by the desire to hide the social polarization of the countryside, exalting instead the efficiency of the fascist agrarian policy aimed at the reduction of the number of day labourers ('*sbracciantizzazione*'). According to Della Valentina (*Agricoltura*, pp. 42–3), however, the idea was to take a census of all those families with possibilities for home consumption.
102. See above, p . 6.
103. This emerges from an X^2 test for the distribution of farms by size in the 'sample' and in the whole of Italian agriculture (see Istat (1936), *Censimento generale dell'agricoltura*, Vol. II, Rome). It appears that the INEA sample includes too many farms larger than five hectares and too few small ones (less than one hectare).
104. See Istat, *Censimento*; the same method was used to break down the (few) 'other workers' which appear in the 1881 Census.
105. MAIC, Direzione generale della statistica (1884), *Censimento della popolazione del Regno d'Italia al 31 XII 1881*, Rome, Vol. III.
106. As opposed to that of 1931, the 1881 Census did not state the criterion used to allocate households with different sources of income to particular classes. Therefore one cannot exclude the possibility that some farmers were classified as day labourers.
107. See O. Vitali (1968), *La popolazione attiva in agricoltura attraverso i censimenti italiani*, Rome, pp. 25–6.
108. This assumption implies two further conditions:
(a) that the average number of active males per farming household (of any status) was equal to that of non-farming families.
(b) that the average number of inactive males and females was equal for all households.
109. According to C. Barberis ('L'autoconsumo in Italia', from p. 756), these activities, which he calls 'home consumption of the rich', are a characteristic of more advanced societies.

110. This test also allows the evaluation of the representativeness of the samples used in the analysis of commercialization. For this reason it was also applied to the 'Other cases' sample.
111. See above, p. 10.
112. See Statistical Appendix, Table VII.
113. In a total of 18 'entries', eight (five of the Notizie 'sample' and three of INEA) would have less than five cases.
114. See above, p. 12. This choice implicitly means that differences according to the other criterion were nil.
115. See Barberi, *Il valore*, pp. 150–51.
116. The increase in smallholdings was the subject of a famous survey (INEA, *Inchiesta sulla piccola proprietà coltivatrice formatasi nel secondo dopo-guerra*, 15 vols., Roma 1931–38, especially Vol. XV: *Relazione finale*, a cura di G. Lorenzoni). This is not the place to discuss the political use made by fascist propaganda of the growth in smallholdings. The percentages of the various classes according to the Census (see later p. 12):

	1881	1931
Owners	10.23	18.67
Sharecroppers	7.58	5.93
Tenants	3.25	9.48
Contract workers	14.09	1.40
Day labourers	20.26	13.00

117. This figure is obtained by weighting the percentages of the INEA sample with the proportions of the households (according to the type of tenancy) drawn from the 1881 Census.
118. The numbers of farmers and workers with a yearly contract accounted for 34.91 per cent in 1881 and of 35.48 per cent in 1931 of the total population. See also Note 98.
119. To be precise, the percentages for groups of products in Table 4, referring to farms only, are not perfectly comparable to Barbieri's figures, which include all home consumption.
120. The home consumption/consumption ratios are assumed to be 60 per cent for corn and potatoes, 50 per cent for wine and milk, 40 per cent for vegetables, pulses, fruit, poultry, eggs, olive oil and salumi, and 15 per cent for butter and cheese; home consumption of beef, colonial goods, dried fish and groceries is considered nil.
121. See Istat (1940), *Censimento industriale e commerciale del 1937–1940*, Vol. I: *Industrie alimentari*, Part I, Table B, Rome. See also B. Barbieri (1940), 'Le disponibilità alimentari della popolazione italiana', in *Bollettino mensile di statistica*, Supplement to the *Gazzetta Ufficiale* of 22 April, No. 95.
122. See above pp. 3–4.
123. It is difficult to assess if and how this specialization influenced the pattern of consumption (possibly even with the same per capita income and household composition), because the opportunity cost of goods was lower if produced on the farm than if purchased.
124. The samples include some Sicilian farms and some in Puglia: they sold more than four-fifths of their output (wheat, pulses) and employed many day labourers. The home consumption/consumption ratio approached 50 per cent, because of the very high share of cereals in household consumption, higher than that in families with a comparable per capita income.
125. A substantial share of rents in kind were used to feed the landowners' household (including everyone living under the same roof). The extent of this consumption may have decreased with the decline in the number of servants from the middle of the 16th century (see M. Barbagli (1985), *Sotto lo stesso tetto*, Bologna, pp. 229ff).
126. Rents could have been paid with cash earned from other activities, keeping the produce of the farm for household consumption. However, the ratios of households with large outside incomes were not higher than the average.
127. See (particularly for wheat) U. Tucci's synthesis (1983), 'Prezzi e autoconsumo nel Medioevo italiano', in *Storia d'Italia Einaudi. Annali, 6: Economia naturale ed economia monetaria*, pp. 290ff.

128. See G. Biagioli, 'La diffusion de la metairie dans l'Italia centrale: un modèle de developpement demographique et economique', in A. Fauve-Chamoux (ed.) (1987), *Evolution agraire et croissance démographique*, Liège, pp.139–54.
129. See L. Del Panta (1984), *Evoluzione demografica e popolamento dell'Italia dell'Ottocento*, Bologna, pp. 110ff. and also the quantitative analysis by C. Carozzi (1975), *Il processo di urbanizzazione e modernizzazione*, Bologna, pp. 321–47.
130. See L. Cafagna (1983), 'Protoindustria o transizione in bilico?', *Quaderni storici*, **XVIII**, pp. 971–84 and G. Federico (1985), 'Sviluppo industriale, mobilità della popolazione e mercato della forza-lavoro: una analisi macroeconomica', in *La popolazione italiana nell'Ottocento*, Bologna, pp. 447–95. See also G. Aliberti (1975), 'Sviluppo urbano e industrializzazione nell'Italia liberale: note su un modello di interdipendenza', *Storia contemporanea*, **VI**, pp. 211–40 and 411–64.
131. In a sample of 102 families, studied by Serpieri in 1910 (*Il contratto agrario e le condizioni dei contadini nell'Alto Milanese*, Milan, pp. 249ff) 508 agricultural workers 'kept' 234 industrial workers.
132. See F. Bonelli (1979), 'Il capitalismo italiano. Linee generali d'interpretazione', in *Storia d'Italia Einaudi. Annali, 1: Dal feudalismo al capitalismo*, Turin, pp. 1195–255; who resumes a thesis put forward by Sereni (*Capitalismo*) in a slightly different context.
133. GSP = Gross saleable production
HC = Home consumption
C = Consumption

[11]

Economic History Review, 2nd ser., XLIII, 4(1990), pp. 646–656

Sharecropping and productivity: 'feudal residues' in Italian agriculture, 1911[1]

By JON S. COHEN and FRANCESCO L. GALASSI

There exists a wide consensus among Italian scholars that the prevalence of share tenancy contracts in central Italy in the period before 1914 contributed to the backwardness of farming practices in that area compared with those in the northern regions of the Po valley. Sereni's observation captures the essence of this consensus:

> The concentration of feudal residue [sharecropping] in the property relations on the land . . . takes on, in a large part of central and southern Italy, a sufficient importance so as to seriously inhibit the free development of productive forces.[2]

One way to interpret this observation, and the one we use in this paper, is that the differences in agricultural techniques and productivity that existed between the advanced regions of the north and the less advanced regions of the centre in 1911 were due to different tenurial arrangements in the two areas.[3] We call this, for want of a better term, the institutionalist position, and in this paper we report the results of our attempt to assess its validity.

The institutionalist argument needs to be enriched if it is to be tested. It is possible to extract from the literature three reasons why sharecropping had a negative impact on agricultural productivity.[4] First, sharecropping, because it denied to the landowner the full return on capital expenditures in agriculture, discouraged investment. Second, as a corollary to the first, sharecropping promoted an excessive use of labour: in effect, a substitution of labour for capital because the marginal cost of labour to the landowner

[1] The research for this paper was funded by a grant from the Social Sciences and Humanities Research Council of Canada. We would like to thank Albert Berry, Loren Brandt, James Irwin, Joel Mokyr, Michael Huberman, and Vera Zamagni for comments on one version or another of this article. We are especially grateful to Stefano Fenoaltea for his suggestions; they have greatly improved the paper. Errors are, of course, the responsibility of the authors.

[2] Sereni, *La questione agraria*, p. 83. The argument is not limited to Italian scholars nor to modern times. Arthur Young considered the sharecropping practised in central Italy '. . . [the] most contemptible of all modes of letting land . . .' (quoted in Mill, *Principles*, pp. 375-6), while John Bowring, in his 1839 report to the British parliament, held it responsible for Tuscany's 'stagnant and backward civilization' (Bowring, 'Report on the statistics of Tuscany', p. 40). Milward and Saul maintain that sharecropping blocked innovation (Milward and Saul, *The development of the economies of continental Europe*, p. 235). Trebilcock also identifies tenure as one of the elements contributing to Italy's dual economy (Trebilcock, *The industrialization of the continental powers*, p. 315).

[3] Another way of putting it, very much in the spirit of the quotation, is that semi-feudal property relations held back the development of capitalist productive forces. This argument is not unique to the Italian case. See, for example, Robertson, *The dynamics of productive relationships*.

[4] See Sereni, *Il capitalismo* and *idem*, *La questione agraria*; Giorgetti, *Contadini e proprietari*; and Pazzagli, *L'agricoltura in Toscana*.

was only a fraction of its marginal product.[5] Third, share tenancy arrangements, because croppers retained a considerable degree of autonomy and were thus able to influence what was grown, led to an excessive production of wheat. The former two arguments imply that inputs were combined inefficiently (capital/labour and land/labour ratios were suboptimal), while the third implies that the crop mix was not the profit maximizing one (too much wheat was grown).

It is useful to make explicit the conceptual framework on which the institutionalist argument rests. Sharecropping is viewed as an exploitative system which, in spite of efficiency losses, appealed to the landowning class because it obtained a relatively large share of a small pie. Although the pie would have been larger under a less exploitative system of tenure, the slice going to landowners might have ended up substantially smaller, thus making them worse, not better, off.

There is, of course, an alternative view of share tenancy, in which it is argued that sharecropping represents a perfectly reasonable response to incomplete or imperfect markets. Share contracts, that is, exist not because of their distributional implications but because they constitute the best way to organize farm operations in a less than perfect world. Sharecropping is seen not as a source of inefficiencies, but as a consequence of non-removable constraints. Some attribute these constraints to poorly developed markets for managerial and supervisory skills, others to imperfections in labour markets, while still others point to inadequate credit markets.[6] Although the inefficiency implications vary with the constraint or constraints that give rise to share tenancy in the first place, there is a general consensus that with multiple constraints Pareto-optimality cannot be achieved.[7] According to the

[5] The argument that sharecropping promoted excessive use of labour implies that landlords were able to force sharecroppers to supply more labour than the latter would have done if left to their own devices, which in turn enabled landlords to economize on their own inputs. Put more formally, labour would be used until its marginal product equals zero. In fact, the landlord's net income (y) may be expressed as:

$$y = s\, q(l,h) - rh,$$

where s = rental share ($0<s<1$); $q()$ = production function;
l = labour; h = land; r = opportunity cost of land.

Maximizing y with respect to l:

$$s\, q'_l = 0,$$

which, for positive values of s, can only be true if $q'_l = 0$. Another implication of this is that land will be undersupplied, because maximizing y with respect to h yields

$$s\, q'_h = r,$$

which means that land will be supplied only up to the point where a share (s) of its marginal product equals its opportunity cost. If this argument is correct, that is, if landlords were powerful and tenants powerless, we would expect to observe high land productivity and low labour productivity in sharecropping areas. Data in tab. 2, however, are at odds with this position.

[6] For those who favour supervisory and managerial constraints, see Reid, 'White land, black labor', *idem*, 'The theory of sharecropping', and Eswaran and Kotwal, 'A theory of contractual share'; for labour imperfections, see Stiglitz, 'Incentives and risksharing'; Newbery, 'Risksharing, sharecropping'; and Mazumdar, 'The theory of sharecropping'. For capital market problems see, among others, Wright, *Old South, new South*. For a concise clear statement of the relationship between imperfect or incomplete markets and sharecropping see Bardhan, *Land*, ch. 12.

[7] Binswanger and Rosenzweig, 'Contractual arrangements'.

institutionalists, efficiency is, essentially, a non-issue: sharecropping and the excessive use of labour are synonymous.[8]

In the remainder of this paper, we attempt to discover if the institutionalist position is supported by the evidence.[9] We first discuss our data, then use them to answer two questions. First, did significant differences exist in factor intensities and input/output ratios between the predominantly sharecropped provinces of central Italy and the non-sharecropped provinces of the north, and second, can these differences be attributed to the differences in tenure systems?

In brief, we find the institutionalist position wanting on both counts. In answer to the first question, we conclude that while differences did exist, they do not conform with those predicted by the institutionalists. The second question is more straightforward: the differences in tenure systems were unrelated to contractual arrangements. In conformity with the views of the non-institutionalists, we consider that differences in tenure and farming practices in the centre and the south resulted from non-removable constraints that limited scope for innovation in these areas. In a nutshell, tenure was a response to these constraints, and the apparent backwardness of these areas is to be understood in relation to the same forces that determined tenure choice.

I

Although Sereni's critique of sharecropping lacks precision, it can be argued that if share tenancy did, as he supposed, have a negative impact on the 'free development of productive forces', the result must have been (1) lower capital/labour ratios, (2) lower land/labour ratios, (3) excessive production of wheat, (4) higher output per hectare, and (5) lower output per worker, than would have been the case had a more 'progressive' tenure system (fixed rent or owner operated) existed. Since it is impossible to test the assumptions embodied in this counterfactual directly, that is, it is impossible to make direct estimates of what would have been and compare them with what was, a second best approach (and one perfectly consistent with the institutionalist argument) is to compare productivity estimates in those areas with a high proportion of sharecropped farms with those regions in the north (Piedmont, Lombardy, Venetia, and parts of Emilia-Romagna[10])

[8] There exists another approach in which it is also argued that share contracts are necessarily inefficient, although the inefficiency is the exact opposite of that identified by the institutionalists. In this analysis, usually called the 'Marshallian approach', the rental share is viewed as a 'tax equivalent' disincentive leading tenants to under-supply labour and over-use land. This framework is ignored in this paper for two reasons: first, because as Cheung (*The theory*) and others have argued, it is relatively easy to remove the inefficiency; and, second, because no scholar, as far as we know, has ever maintained that land was over-used and labour under-worked in Italian sharecropping.

[9] We are unable to present and test in this paper a full alternative model of Italian sharecropping. This is a task reserved for a subsequent work. We restrict ourselves instead to the simpler but no less important job of dealing with the institutionalist argument.

[10] Emilia-Romagna constitutes a borderline case. This region covers the south-eastern end of the Po Valley, stretching from the Po river in the north to the Apennines in the south. In parts of the region, the area properly called Emilia (the provinces of Modena, Reggio nell'Emilia, Parma, Ferrara, and Piacenza), share tenure was seldom used. Towards the eastern end, along the Adriatic coast, and specifically in the provinces of Forli, Ravenna, and Bologna, sharecropping was the predominant tenure system. The latter is the area called Romagna. Therefore, while Romagna is geographically part of

which were the most agriculturally advanced in Italy at the time and where sharecropping was virtually unknown. The advantage of this approach is that it establishes a clear cut benchmark against which to compare productivity performance in sharecropped areas and tends, as well, to bias results in favour of the institutionalists.[11] The problem, of course, is that such an approach rests on the implicit (and clearly unwarranted) assumption that the only feature which distinguished the northern provinces from those in the centre was the form of tenure.[12] It can, however, be argued that although they are perhaps insufficient as a proof that sharecropping mattered, regional factor and productivity disparities are at the very least necessary to make the issue a compelling one. That is, if we were to find that sharecropped areas had lower yields per hectare and higher capital/labour ratios and yields per worker than those in the north, then it would be difficult to make a case that sharecropping promoted backwardness.

This brings us to a discussion of the data. We require, first of all, information on the geographical distribution of tenure systems in the north and the centre. Since our objective is to compare the impact of tenure differences on farming practices in the two areas, we would ideally like to know the number of farms and the amount of land in each province (a province in Italy is the rough equivalent of a county in the US or a shire in England) worked under different contractual arrangements. Our data, instead, drawn from the 1911 population census (the only source of reasonably consistent information on tenure systems), are broken down by individuals.[13] Census takers asked all persons ten years of age or older engaged in agriculture to indicate which of four categories, owner operator, fixed rent tenant, sharecropper, or wage worker, best described their situation.[14] We are compelled to assume that individuals represent an acceptable proxy for farm land so that, for example, two provinces with the same percentage of the active population working under share contracts are assumed to have roughly the same percentage of land worked by share croppers. We have no way of estimating the bias created by this assumption, but we do make some attempt to see how sensitive our results are to alternative definitions of sharecropped provinces.

northern Italy, its contract structure is closer to that of central Italy. In carrying out our comparisons between sharecropping and non-sharecropping areas, we have calculated productivity and factor intensity both including and excluding Emilia-Romagna (tab. 2).

[11] The bias arises because, by taking this approach, we implicitly accept that the only feature which distinguished the northern provinces from those in the centre was the form of tenure. We are, in effect, attributing the full productivity gap to incentive structures set up by tenure forms, while in reality some, if not most, of this gap must have been caused by the lower quality of land in the centre.

[12] As it happens, this is precisely the nature of the institutionalist position. See, for example, Pazzagli, *L'agricoltura*, pp. 108-10, and *idem*, *Per la storia*, ch. 3.

[13] See MAIC, *Censimento generale della popolazione*.

[14] Each of these categories comprised a number of similar, but not identical, tenure groups, distinguished on the basis of length of contract, accessory clauses, and other minor legal distinctions of no practical importance for present purposes. There were a few additional categories of agricultural labourers, such as forestry workers, truffle and mushroom pickers, and so on, amounting to between 2 and 3 per cent of the total agricultural labour force. These workers were, for the most part, independent and thus not classified under any contract system. They are, therefore, excluded from our calculations. The raw labour force data have been transformed into standardized man-years by means of the coefficients reported in Serpieri, *Guida*, p. 20.

The data raise another problem which, fortunately, is easier to resolve. The general types of contracts reported by the population census fail to capture the actual variety of contractual arrangements found in Italy in 1911. The difficulty is that the generic term *mezzadria* (sharecropping) encompasses a multitude of contracts, some of which conform more or less to the conventional notion of share tenancy while others more closely resemble fixed rent contracts at one extreme and wage labour agreements at the other. In other words, unlike Gertrude Stein's rose, a sharecropper was not always a sharecropper. Regional monographs on agricultural practices during the period, however, indicate that while differences between the north and the centre were often substantial,[15] variations within the centre were relatively minor. A share tenant from Florence and one from Ancona, for the most part, fit the same basic type. In table 2, we report factor intensity and productivity differentials between all sharecropped and all non-sharecropped provinces.[16] To bias the comparison in favour of the institutionalist argument, we exclude from the sample of northern provinces all those located in the mountains.[17] In this way, sharecropping areas are compared with the parts of the country that were supposedly the most productive. The provinces used in our sample are detailed in table 1.

The region of Emilia-Romagna, clearly part of the north today, fell, at the time, between the two zones: in the provinces of Bologna, Forli, and Ravenna (Romagna), a substantial fraction of the farm population worked as share tenants, while in other provinces, such as Reggio Emilia, Parma, and Piacenza (Emilia), a relatively small percentage was engaged in sharecropping. Share contracts in Romagna also differed from those further south. The *boario*, as the cropper was called in this region, often supplied all the capital for farm operations, unlike the *mezzadro* of the centre who in most cases shared such expenses with the landowner. We try to control for the special features of this region by working with two sets of sharecropping provinces, one which includes Bologna, Forli, and Ravenna, the other which excludes them. In a similar manner, we create two sets of non-sharecropping provinces, one with the provinces of Ferrara, Modena, Parma, Piacenza, and Reggio, the other without them. The results are included in table 2.

The institutionalist argument runs as follows. Productivity (output per worker) was lower on sharecropped farms in central Italy than on non-sharecropped farms in the north because landowners in the former system invested in less than the optimum amount of capital per worker and per unit of land and because more than the optimum amount of wheat was grown. As a consequence (if the argument is sound), the capital/labour and

[15] See the description of Tuscany's share tenure system in Pazzagli, *L'agricoltura*, as opposed to the sharecropping practised in the provinces of Romagna, discussed in Poni, *Fossi e cavedagne*.

[16] We define a province as sharecropped if at least 35 per cent of its agricultural labour force in 1911 was reported in the census as *mezzadri* or *coloni parziari*. The difference between these two categories is minor (for example, *mezzadri* resided on the farm, while *coloni parziari* did not) and carries no practical importance for our analysis.

[17] A mountainous province for us is one in which 50 per cent or more of wheat land is in the mountains. The measure is crude but it does single out those provinces that by most other measures would also be identified as mountainous. Land data were derived from MAIC, *Notizie periodiche*. Topographical information was taken from MAIC, *Annuario*.

Table 1. *Breakdown by tenure contract of agricultural labour in sample provinces in Italy, 1911 (percentages)*

Provinces with over 35% of agricultural labour force in sharecropping

	O	F	S	W
Northern Italy				
Bologna	5	6	45	41
Forli	9	1	64	23
Ravenna	4	6	51	35
Central Italy				
Arezzo	8	3	60	23
Florence	6	2	67	21
Lucca	23	5	37	31
Pisa	8	3	59	26
Siena	5	—	69	21
Ancona	10	1	64	23
Ascoli	14	1	57	25
Macerata	13	1	52	30
Pesaro	12	1	60	23
Perugia	13	1	47	33

Provinces with under 35% of agricultural labour force in sharecropping

	O	F	S	W
Northern Italy				
Alessandria	48	5	7	38
Cuneo	44	9	7	37
Novara	26	10	3	58
Turin	50	9	2	36
Brescia	23	14	11	46
Cremona	7	12	3	72
Mantova	10	17	7	61
Pavia	17	8	3	70
Padova	8	38	3	47
Rovigo	7	8	4	75
Treviso	17	29	25	28
Udine	40	7	16	35
Venice	5	30	16	41
Verona	19	12	3	59
Vicenza	33	19	5	40
Ferrara	4	8	7	73
Reggio Emilia	19	18	22	39
Parma	23	9	18	47
Piacenza	34	12	17	35
Modena	13	10	17	53

Notes:
— = less than 1%;
O = Owner operators; F = Fixed rent tenants; S = Sharecroppers; W = Wage labourers (both daily workers and permanent employees.)
See note 14 for an explanation of why the percentages in each province do not sum to 100.
Source: see appendix.

the land/labour ratios were lower in sharecropped than in non-sharecropped provinces, and wheat production was excessive as measured both by the amount of land devoted to wheat and by wheat production as a percentage of total output. Excessive is a slippery concept and certainly does not mean the same as suboptimal.[18] It is, however, the best we can do. The argument is simple. The land and climate are much less suited to cereal production in central Italy than in the north. If we find that a greater percentage of land in the centre was devoted to wheat production and that wheat accounted for a greater percentage of total farm output than in the north, we have *prima facie* evidence that farmers in central Italy were inefficiently fond of wheat growing. The next step is to look at the data and see if they conform with the institutionalist argument.

[18] To clarify, if farmers prefer a safety-first strategy, and if wheat is desirable as a form of insurance because it guarantees subsistence, in a risky environment the amount of wheat grown may be 'excessive' (when compared with a risk-neutral choice), but not necessarily 'suboptimal', in that farmers optimize by choosing more wheat than risk-neutral agents would have.

Table 2. *Productivity, factor proportions, and wheat cultivation, in sharecropping and non-sharecropping provinces in Italy, 1911*

	Non-sharecropping provinces		*Sharecropping provinces*	
Productivity (current lire)				
Output/worker	697.4	(645.4)	705.3	(632.1)
Output/hectare (incl. pasture)	312.5	(314.5)	218.9	(209.6)
Output/hectare (excl. pasture)	479.0	(500.8)	256.6	(242.8)
Factor proportions				
Steam engines/worker	0.0028	(0.0024)	0.002	(0.002)
Mechanical H.P./worker	0.044	(0.04)	0.02	(0.018)
Horses/worker	0.18	(0.19)	0.175	(0.16)
Cattle/worker	1.28	(1.18)	0.85	(0.7)
Hectares/worker (incl. pasture)	2.34	(2.2)	3.3	(3.14)
Hectares/worker (excl. pasture)	1.64	(1.5)	2.8	(2.7)
Wheat cultivation (current lire where relevant)				
Value of wheat output as % of value of total output	27	(25)	34	(33)
Wheat land as % of total crop land	31	(29)	29	(29)
Value of wheat output as % of value of total crop output	37	(34)	41	(39)
Wheat output/hectare (in lire)	407.7	(410.1)	305.1	(269.3)

Notes: 'crop land' refers to agricultural land excluding pasture: 'crop output' refers to agricultural output excluding all animal products.
Figures in brackets refer to sharecropped and non-sharecropped provinces excluding those in Emilia and Romagna (see pp. 650, 654).
Source: see appendix.

The data on inputs contained in table 2 provide cold comfort for the institutionalists. Average output per hectare is higher in non-sharecropping provinces than in sharecropping ones, and average output per worker is virtually the same. Similarly, while the average capital/labour ratio is higher in the non-sharecropping than in the sharecropping provinces (as measured by steam engines, mechanical horsepower, and cattle, per worker), or virtually the same (horses per worker), the land/labour ratio is lower. The first and most clear-cut conclusion one can draw from these results is that sharecroppers were as productive as their non-sharecropping compatriots. This contradicts the institutionalist position, because if sharecropping indeed led to an excessive use of labour resources, average labour productivity should be lower in sharecropping than in non-sharecropping areas.[19] Second,

[19] We would, in principle, like to compare marginal (not average) products. While our data compel us to work with averages, it is possible to infer something about the marginal product from our results. If farms in the two areas were on the same production function, identical average products would necessarily mean identical marginal products. If, on the other hand, sharecropping farms were on a

while sharecroppers in the centre may have had less capital to work with than farmers in the north, they had more land. Moreover, if it is assumed first that the opportunity wage of farm workers in sharecropping provinces was no higher than that in non-sharecropping ones (a reasonable assumption given that most industry was located in the north), and, second, that technology was roughly comparable across the two areas, then the results indicate that the northern worker was probably squeezed harder than the sharecropper. That is, it was farm hands in the north rather than share tenants in the centre who, at least in relative terms, were being exploited. This second result is not surprising since a sharecropper maintained some control over his or her labour time while the wage worker did not.[20]

The data on wheat production appear to be only marginally more supportive of the institutionalist argument than are the input and productivity data. The average value of wheat output as a percentage of total output was higher in sharecropping than in non-sharecropping provinces. But the proportion of crop land allocated to wheat in the former was marginally lower than in the latter, contrary to the predictions derived from the institutionalist model. Yet, since wheat yields per hectare were substantially higher in the non-sharecropping north than in the centre, this would seem to be compelling evidence that sharecroppers were inordinately (and inefficiently) fond of growing wheat. While it may be justified to argue that share tenants grew too much wheat, the very fact that they did so raises difficulties for the institutionalists.

A keystone of the institutionalist argument is that landowners in central Italy (and in the Romagna area of the north) opted for sharecropping because it allowed them to exploit the labour resources of their tenants and to avoid committing large amounts of (labour-saving) capital to their farms. Sharecroppers would have been better off under a different tenure system and, presumably, would have preferred one, but it was the landowners, not the tenants, who had the power to dictate contracts. It is, however, difficult to reconcile this notion with the argument that sharecroppers were able to impose an inefficient crop mix on landowners. If landowners were able to rig the tenure system in their favour, they must have had the clout to determine what was grown. Either landowners were less powerful than the institutionalists maintain, or the crop mix was, at least from the viewpoint of the landowners, efficient. In either case the institutionalist view is called into question.

In any event, there does exist a rationale for the heavy emphasis on wheat production in sharecropping areas. Wheat was the basic food grain in the

lower production function throughout the relevant range, then an identical average product would imply that labour had a higher marginal product on sharecropped than on non-sharecropped farms. The institutionalists maintain that the marginal product of sharecroppers was lower than that of labourers working under the tenure contracts common in the north. Their argument is inconsistent with the data.

[20] A word of warning is in order here. Although the results reported in table 2 are superficially consistent with an under-supply of labour and an over-use of land, that is, with the kinds of distortions associated with a 'Marshallian' approach, it would be incorrect to infer from them that 'Marshallian' inefficiency prevailed in Italian sharecropping. Resource endowments (climate, land quality) in the north and centre were not the same and therefore farmers in the two areas were unlikely to have been operating on the same production functions.

Mediterranean, and had been so for millennia. Preliminary data we have gathered suggest that access to credit was significantly more restricted for farmers in central Italy than for their colleagues in the north.[21] Under such circumstances, considering also that crop insurance was non-existent in the centre, diversification was to be preferred to specialization, and subsistence was the first order of business. It is thus easy to understand why the cropper favoured a high proportion of wheat mixed in with the olives and grapes. But what of the landowner? He was, presumably, less dependent on the land for subsistence, and more prepared to reap the rewards of specialization. He was, however, also the main source of credit and insurance for his sharecroppers. Although we can only speculate at this point, lack of credit and alternative forms of insurance may have made wheat growing the cheapest form of insurance from the landowner's perspective as well.

In an attempt to see if our results are sensitive to the way in which sharecropping and non-sharecropping provinces are defined, we report in table 2 the results of our calculations excluding the provinces of Emilia and Romagna. The differences in the two sets of results are relatively minor, and thus provide no greater comfort for the institutionalists. It is worth noting that wheat is still more important in the sharecropping provinces than elsewhere, and, in fact, the disparity in yields grows as a result of the sample change. This suggests (but of course does not prove), that in the centre farmers may have been willing to forgo the more profitable grapes and olives in favour of the less profitable, but safer, wheat because of inadequate alternative sources of insurance.

II

The data on input ratios, on productivity, and on crop mix, all fail to sustain the institutionalist position. There is no compelling evidence that sharecroppers were exploited. On the other hand, it is reasonable to argue that sharecropping areas were unusually fond of wheat. This does not mean that sharecroppers were able to impose a suboptimal crop mix on their landlords: rather, it probably represents a 'safety-first' response in areas where credit and insurance were difficult to obtain.[22]

Although the conclusions reached in this paper are, for the most part, negative, they constitute an essential first step towards establishing a more convincing explanation of the gap in technology and productivity between different areas of Italian agriculture. As any good sharecropper knows, it is usually necessary to clear the land before planting the crop.

University of Toronto; Nipissing University College

[21] On credit to Italian agriculture in this period, see Muzzioli, *Banche*, pp. 157-85.

[22] It should be obvious that there is, in fact, an illogicality in the view that landlords had the power to force an over-use of labour but were unable to regulate the crop mix. If they could manage one, surely they could handle the other. The same contradiction exists with regard to the notion that sharecropping created a disincentive to invest. If landlords were able to force tenants to supply more labour than the latter considered optimal, then it makes no sense to argue that landlords had no power to reap the full benefit of their investments. If, on the other hand, they could not modify the distributive parameters of the contract, then it seems unreasonable to argue that they had the power to impose on tenants a greater exertion than allowed for by labour's opportunity wage.

APPENDIX

The data used in compiling tables 1 and 2 are far from perfect: absolute accuracy and completeness cannot be claimed for either the Central Statistical Institute (ISTAT) or the Ministry of Agriculture (MAIC) series. Yet there is no reason to believe that errors and omissions in either series are in any way related to provincial boundaries. In other words, it is not necessary for our argument that the absolute value of our results be beyond question: what counts is whether the relative standings of different provinces are correct. Unless it can be shown that accuracy and completeness in data gathering varied consistently between sharecropping and non-sharecropping provinces, errors or omissions in the data may be considered random, and do not invalidate our results.

Data in table 2 were compiled as described below. All data were gathered on the basis of the 1911 provincial boundaries, to which the 1911 population census refers.

Output: data derived from MAIC, *Notizie periodiche*. They include average output for the years 1910-2 of wheat, corn, rice, olive oil, wine, potatoes, and beets. Wholesale prices (national averages) included in ISTAT, *Sommario di statistiche storiche* were used to value the quantity data. An attempt was also made to estimate the value of meat and dairy production for 1911. The stock of animals was taken from ISTAT, *Osservazioni sulla consistenza del patrimonio zootecnico*. The stock was converted into a flow of slaughtered animals based on ratios derived from ISTAT, *Sommario di statistiche storiche*, tables 52, 58. The 1908 livestock census data were used to estimate the stock; slaughter ratios from 1905-10 were used to calculate the flow. Provincial boundaries changed between 1908 and 1930. The 1930 publication recorded all data according to 1930 provincial boundaries. We adjusted these to reflect the boundaries of provinces in 1908 (the same as those in 1911), so as to conform with our other 1911 series. In a similar fashion, milk output was derived from an estimate of the stock of cows present in Italy in 1908 taken from ISTAT, *Osservazioni sulla consistenza del patrimonio zootecnico*, and an estimate of annual milk yield per cow based on data in ISTAT, *Sommario di statistiche storiche*. Wool output was derived from these same sources using a comparable technique.

Prices: all output figures were converted to value estimates using wholesale prices (national mean) included in ISTAT, *Sommario di statistiche storiche*. National (instead of regional or provincial) prices were used in order to ensure that productivity data would be comparable across provinces (that is, to prevent local price variations from showing up as productivity differences).

Land: estimates of land used for any given crop and for pasture land were taken from MAIC, *Notizie periodiche*.

Labour: labour force data were taken from MAIC, *Censimento generale della popolazione*, and transformed into standardized man-years using the ratios included in Serpieri, *Guida*, p. 20.

Capital: estimates of capital stock in agriculture proved the most difficult to obtain (and the least reliable). There appears to be no information concerning capital embodied in buildings, earthworks, canals, and the like. We had to use four different capital stock measures:

(1) Steam engines used in agriculture, derived from MAIC, *Statistica delle forze motrici*, table V.

(2) Horsepower produced by steam engines in agricultural use from the same source as (1).

(3) Number of horses, derived from ISTAT, *Osservazioni sulla consistenza del patrimonio zootecnico*.

(4) Number of work oxen, from the same source as (3).

Footnote references

Official publications

Bowring, J., 'Report on the statistics of Tuscany, Lucca, the Pontifical and the Lombardo-Venetian states' (P.P. 1839, XVI).

Istituto Centrale di Statistica (ISTAT), *Censimenti agricoli, B., Studi sui censimenti, vol. I, parte 3, Osservazioni sulla consistenza del patrimonio zootecnico al marzo 1930-VIII: Confronti tra i censimenti 1908 e 1930* (Rome, 1934).

ISTAT, *Sommario di statistiche storiche dell'Italia, 1861-1975* (Rome, 1976).

Ministero di Agricoltura, Industria, e Commercio (MAIC), *Annuario statistico italiano, 1912* (Rome, 1913).

MAIC, Direzione Generale della Statistica, Ufficio del Censimento, *Censimento generale della popolazione del regno d'Italia al 31 marzo 1911* (Rome, 1913).

MAIC, Direzione Generale di Statistica e del Lavoro, Ufficio di Statistica Agraria, *Notizie periodiche di statistica agraria, anni 1911-2, 1912-3* (Rome, 1912, 1913).

MAIC, Ispettorato Generale dell'Industria e del Commercio, *Statistica delle forze motrici impiegate al 1 gennaio 1904 nell'agricoltura e nelle industrie del Regno* (Rome, 1906).

Secondary sources

Bardhan, P.K., *Land, labour, and rural poverty* (Delhi, 1984).

Binswanger, H.P. and Rosenzweig, M.A., 'Contractual arrangements, employment, and wages in rural labour markets: a critical review', in *idem*, eds., *Contractual arrangements, employment, and wages in rural labor markets in Asia* (New Haven, 1984).

Cheung, S.N., *The theory of share tenancy* (Chicago, 1969).

Eswaran, M. and Kotwal, A., 'A theory of contractual share in agriculture', *Amer. Econ. Rev.*, 75 (1985), pp. 162-77.

Giorgetti, G., *Contadini e proprietari nell'eta moderna* (Turin, 1977).

Mazumdar, D., 'The theory of sharecropping with labour market dualism', *Economica*, 42 (1975), pp. 261-71.

Mill, J.S., *Principles of political economy*, 1 (1871).

Milward, A.S. and Saul, S.B., *The development of the economies of continental Europe, 1850-1914* (1977).

Muzzioli, G., *Banche e agricoltura* (Bologna, 1983).

Newbery, D.M.G., 'Risksharing, sharecropping, and uncertain labour markets', *Rev. Econ. Stud.*, 44 (1977), pp. 585-94.

Pazzagli, C., *L'agricoltura in Toscana nella prima meta dell'800* (Florence, 1973).

Pazzagli, C., *Per la storia dell'agricoltura toscana nei secoli XIX e XX. Dal catasto particellare Lorenese al catasto agrario del 1929* (Turin, 1979).

Poni, C., *Fossi e cavedagne benedicon le campagne* (Bologna, 1982).

Reid, J.D., 'The theory of sharecropping revisited—again', *J. Pol. Econ.*, 85 (1977), pp. 403-8.

Reid, J.D., 'White land, black labour, and agricultural stagnation', *Exp. Econ. Hist.*, 16 (1979), pp. 31-55.

Robertson, A.F., *The dynamics of productive relationships* (Cambridge, 1987).

Sereni, E., *Il capitalismo nelle campagne, 1860-1900* (Turin, 1947).

Sereni, E., *La questione agraria nella rinascita nazionale italiana* (Turin, 1975).

Serpieri, A., *Guida alle ricerche economico-agrarie* (Rome, 1929).

Stiglitz, J.E., 'Incentives and risk-sharing in sharecropping', *Rev. Econ. Stud.*, 61 (1974), pp. 219-56.

Trebilcock, C., *The industrialization of the continental powers, 1780-1914* (1981).

Wright, G., *Old South, new South* (New York, 1986).

[12]

Excerpt from Bruce M.S. Campbell and Mark Overton (eds), *Land, Labour and Livestock: Historical Studies in European Agricultural Productivity*, 385–409.

15 *Patrick K. O'Brien and Gianni Toniolo*

The poverty of Italy and the backwardness of its agriculture before 1914

Italy's agriculture had at its disposal methods of adjustment that were not available to an equal degree north of the Alpine wall.

A. Gerschenkron, 1962.[1]

I On the backwardness of Italian agriculture

Labour productivity in Italian agriculture may have been the highest anywhere in western Europe during the renaissance. Thereafter, although the population of the Peninsula never suffered severely from Malthusian crises and famines, food supplies probably kept just in step with population growth. The ratio of agricultural to non-agricultural population remained high, particularly in relation to its neighbours in western Europe, especially Holland and France, but above all England.[2]

Between 1780 and 1914, while the workforce available to British agriculture remained stable, agricultural output in Britain rose by 240 per cent.[3] Compared with this remarkable achievement, historians of Italy convey the impression that during the long period of European industrialisation labour productivity in Italian agriculture remained roughly constant.[4] This implies that the gap in real incomes between the rural populations of England and Italy probably widened right

Financial support from CNR (grant number 870122510) is gratefully acknowledged.

1 A. Gerschenkron, *Economic backwardness in historical perspective*, Cambridge, Mass., 1962.

2 E. A. Wrigley, 'Urban growth and agricultural change: England and the Continent in the early modern period', *Journal of Interdisciplinary History*, XV, 1985, pp. 683–728.

3 P. K. O'Brien and C. Keyder, *Economic growth in Britain and France 1780–1914: two paths to the twentieth century*, London, 1978, pp. 92–4.

4 G. Federico, 'Mercantilizzazione e sviluppo economico in Italia (1860–1940)', *Rivista di Storia Economica*, III, 1986, pp. 149–86.

down to the closing decade of the nineteenth century. Only towards the end of the century, during the 'Giolittian' upswing (1896–1913), is there evidence of convergence, when Italy began to 'catch up' with the rest of western Europe.[5]

Italian agriculture has often been held responsible for the country's economic retardation. Its low, and for long periods deteriorating, levels of labour productivity imply that the primary sector could not supply investible funds or provide rural markets required to support more rapid industrialisation and urbanisation.

Well-argued critiques of Italian agriculture can be traced back at least to the Enlightenment: it is well known that reformers maintained that political and economic freedom was a prerequisite for economic progress.[6] Thus, in 1789, upon crossing from France into northern Italy, the fertile and irrigated areas of Lombardy impressed Arthur Young. But as he travelled eastward towards the Veneto, he discovered poverty in the countryside which he found became deeper and more widespread as he moved south into Tuscany. In Young's view – and his perception remained common to almost all English classical economists commenting upon Mediterranean societies – rural poverty and poor agriculture could be connected directly to small holding and to sharecropping. Both institutions operated to restrain investment in animals, soil amelioration, tools and implements.[7]

Several decades later, in 1860, Carlo Cattaneo recommended the farming he found in lower Lombardy as a model for most of northern and central Italy. For Cattaneo, good irrigation, a special feature of the Po Valley, appeared to be a less important source of high yields than Lombardy's emulation of north European crop rotations, a good balance between arable and animal husbandry, and well-functioning markets.[8]

According to the final report of a Parliamentary Committee of Enquiry chaired by S. Jacini, around mid-century and compared with most of Europe, Italian agriculture could not be represented as backward, but it had fallen behind other economies during the Risorgimento when resources and human energies were diverted to political ends. Retardation had, moreover, been exacerbated by other

5 G. Toniolo, *An economic history of liberal Italy 1850–1918*, London, 1990.
6 G. M. Galanti, *Nuova descrizione storica e geografica delle Sicilie*, Naples, 1786, pp. vii ff.
7 A. Young, *Travels during the years 1787, 1788, and 1789*, II, *Italy*, Bury St Edmunds, 1792.
8 C. Cattaneo, 'Dell'agricoltura inglese paragonata alla nostra', pp. 269–300 in *idem*, *Memorie di economia pubblica dal 1833 al 1860*, I, Milan, 1860.

and essentially temporary problems, such as phylloxera and other plant diseases which had seriously afflicted the production of grapes, silk cocoons and oranges. Agriculture was also depressed by social unrest in the south, by the return to the gold standard which restrained agricultural exports, and by the heavy tax burdens.[9] But when it focused upon the structural problems of farming *per se*, the report contradicted its otherwise optimistic general view about the potential efficiency of Italy's agriculture and observed that most of the sector remained 'simple in that it basically involved fertile soil and human labour'. Only about 20 per cent of all land was cultivated as a 'rural industry' requiring capital and entrepreneurial skills.[10]

With the passing of the Tariff Act of 1887, discussion on agricultural efficiency shifted into a debate between protectionists and free-traders. The liberal argument rested not merely on the losses from the misallocation of resources but also from the baneful effects of propping up southern latifundia – a form of tenure and organisation regarded as inimical not only to industrial but also to agrarian development itself. Marxist historians later joined with liberals in condemning the tariff of 1887, but more for its dynamic than for its short-run allocative effects. Thus for R. Zangheri – for whom 'agricultural backwardness is the key to understanding many of the distinctive characteristics of the Italian economic development' – the duty on cereals meant a renunciation of agricultural progress based on the north European model 'Italian agriculture remained a deadweight on economic expansion.'[11]

A. Gramsci's explanation of Italian backwardness is both political and institutional in form, since 'the unification of Italy occurred without changes in economic and social conditions that are typical of a bourgeois revolution'.[12] For Gramsci the absence of French-style agrarian reform is at the root of the backwardness of Italian agriculture, especially in the south, a region dominated by an unprogressive *blocco agrario*.[13] According to Gramscian interpretations, the survival of inefficient institutions accounts both for the slow pace of agricultural

9 S. Jacini, *I risultati dell'inchiesta agraria (1884)*, Turin, 1976, pp. 30–9.

10 Jacini, *I risultati*, pp. 84–5.

11 R. Zangheri, 'The historical relationship between agricultural and economical development', pp. 23–41 in E. L. Jones and S. J. Woolf, eds., *Agrarian change and economic development*, London, 1969, p. 25.

12 A. Soboul, 'Risorgimento e rivoluzione borghese: schema di una direttiva di ricerca', pp. 801–16 in Istituto Gramsci, *Problemi dell'Unità d'Italia*, Rome, 1962, p. 81.

13 A. Gramsci, *Il Risorgimento*, Turin, 1950; E. Sereni, *Il capitalismo nelle campagne (1860–1900)*, Turin, 1974.

growth and lack of original accumulation which underlies the mediocre performance of Italian industry for some three to four decades after unification.[14]

R. Romeo was one of the few historians who argued that Italy's tenurial institutions did not restrain growth and capital accumulation in the 1860s and 1870s, particularly in the north and centre of the Peninsula. For Romeo the major constraint on agricultural growth came basically from the 'corn laws' of 1887.[15]

More recently, G. Orlando agreed that more appropriate agrarian policies were required but asserted that neither the *laissez-faire* of the Right, before 1876, nor the more interventionist policies pursued thereafter, created favourable conditions for agricultural development. In his view, liberals, especially after Cavour's death, proved incapable of fostering state investment in social-overhead capital, technical education, and agricultural credit. While the governments of Depretis, Crispi, and Giolitti merely provided farmers with limited subsidies and protection, only towards the end of the century did early experiments in co-operation begin to produce some favourable results before being swept away by Fascism.[16]

To sum up: contemporary observers and most historians present Italian agriculture as backward without, however, providing a systematic definition or any estimates of backwardness. Three main explanations for the poor performance of Italian agriculture have been advanced. Firstly, institutional deficiencies, which include the lack of political and civil liberties, persisting until late into the nineteenth century, as well as inefficient tenurial systems – share-cropping in the north-east and centre of Italy and the maldistribution of landownership with absentee proprietors in the south. Secondly, ill-designed economic policies, particularly the protection of cereal cultivation as well as the state's failure to provide an adequate infrastructure of credit institutions and agrarian education. Thirdly, natural resource deficiencies in the south and the centre of Italy.

This essay confronts Italian historiography with an exercise in productivity comparison across two frontiers. Comparative economic history at macro, sectoral, or micro levels seeks to expose what may be general, particular, or deficient in a country's economic development.

14 E. Sereni, *Capitalismo e mercato nazionale*, Rome, 1966; and Zangheri, 'The historical relationship'.

15 R. Romeo, *Risorgimento e capitalismo*, Bari, 1955.

16 G. Orlando, *Storia della politica agraria in Italia dal 1848 ad oggi*, Rome–Bari, 1984.

In this case it is to be expected that the placing of Italian agriculture on a scale for comparison with the most advanced agriculture in Europe should both expose the 'degree' to which the sector was inefficient and help historians to specify the nature and sources of Italian economic backwardness before 1914.

Methodologically, this attempt to analyse the relative efficiency of Italian agriculture in value terms differs from most other exercises in quantification contained in this volume, which are conducted in terms of physical yields and productivities. Values combine volume with price data and explicitly include national consumers' preferences as bounds on the choices faced by producers of food and raw materials. Essentially, the exercise has been designed to ascertain how far and why the value of all the agricultural output produced by Italian farmers (constrained as they were by national patterns of demand, ecology, and institutions, as well as by the inputs of land, labour and capital available to them) fell short of the standards set by farmers operating within a different set of environmental and economic constraints in the United Kingdom.

Economic historians generally use physical indicators (such as kilograms per hectare or per worker) to compare productivity changes through time or across regions. These ratios are clearly useful as measures of how technical possibilities for the cultivation of crops and rearing of farm animals varied over the centuries. They may be used under *ceteris paribus* assumptions about natural conditions to represent institutional or entrepreneurial successes or failures to deploy best-practice techniques. Nevertheless, such ostensibly revealing numbers do not measure differentials in economic efficiency. For example, even an acceptable demonstration that environmental conditions were similar in Lincolnshire and Lombardy and that crop yields (bushels per sown acre) in the English county were way above the levels obtained in northern Italy, has only limited economic meaning. To measure economic efficiency, further information is required on the prices of crops sold and consumed, and on rents, interest, and wages, imputable as costs to the inputs of land, capital, and labour utilised to produce output. Economic efficiency is measured by the ratio between *values* of inputs used to produce a given output (or mix of commodities) and the market *value* of that output.

In this essay relative productivities are estimated and compared as far as possible in economic terms. Ideally, *all* factors should be combined into a weighted index and expressed as a ratio of aggregate output in order to estimate total factor productivities for the two agricultures. Unfortunately, there is no hard information on capital deployed by

Italian or by British farmers, and only partial productivity indicators can be estimated for labour and land. Finally, available figures refer to a rather short span of years immediately preceding the Great War when agricultural censuses happened to be taken. How far the relative productivity of the labour and land used in Italian agriculture *c.*1910 can be used to make inferences about more long-term and persistent facets of Italian backwardness will emerge in the conclusions to this chapter. Meanwhile, methods will be used which have been extensively discussed in modern economics literature to homogenise first outputs and then the inputs of labour and land in order to compare productivities between the most advanced and one of the more backward sectors of European agriculture.[17]

II Outputs in Italian and United Kingdom agricultures valued in pounds and lire, *c.*1910

Theoretically, the problems involved in comparing the values of outputs supplied by United Kingdom and Italian farmers are analogous to more familiar index-number problems implicit in comparing real values of different mixes of outputs separated by time. For example, how much produce a medieval peasant obtained from a 50-hectare plot of land compared with his modern successor cultivating the same plot is a question that can only be tackled by valuing the mix of crops harvested at prices prevailing in medieval and modern times. Similarly, the question of how much output Italian farmers supplied compared with their English counterparts can only be answered by valuing the agricultural outputs produced in the two countries in two sets of national prices.

Equally valid comparisons can then be made in sterling or lire. Differences reflect British and Italian preferences which in turn reflect needs, tastes, income levels and income distribution, productive efficiency and, to go round the circle, the structure of relative prices in the two economies. The conversion of Italian output into sterling equivalents conceptualises Italian agriculture from a British standpoint. The totals purport to measure what Italian farm output might have

17 For example, D. Paige and G. Bombach, *A comparison of national outputs and productivity*, Paris, 1959; I. Kravis, 'A survey of international comparisons of productivity' *Economic Journal*, LXXXVI, 1976, pp. 1–41; I. Kravis, Z. Kenessy, A. Heston and R. Summers, *International comparison of real product and purchasing power*, Baltimore, 1975; I. Kravis, A. Heston and R. Summers, *World product and income*, Baltimore, 1978.

been worth 'if' sold on British markets at British prices. Similar estimates of what British farm output might have commanded in lire on Italian markets conceptualises British agriculture from an Italian standpoint.[18]

In Table 15.1, the quantities of various crops and livestock products produced in the two countries are valued, first in British and then in Italian prices. Several problems emerged including: the quality of the basic price and quantity data; numerous difficulties involved in matching British and Italian outputs product by product; the estimation of shadow prices in sterling for 'unique' crops such as wine, rice and olive oil (not grown in the United Kingdom) and similar prices in lire for hops (uncultivated in Italy).

Essentially, accurate estimates were required of the quantities produced and the prices obtained or potentially obtainable (farm-gate prices) for comprehensive lists of agricultural outputs produced upon farms throughout Italy and the United Kingdom. As always the data turned out to be neither accurate nor comprehensive. For example, no figures were found for rabbits, wild birds or soft fruit produced by Italy's farmers. Some vegetables and horticultural products and timber are missing for both countries.

For United Kingdom quantities and prices, the results of E. Ojala's research were the main source used.[19] His quantities relate to 1904–10 and are from official sources, and his estimates were cross-checked against agricultural censuses for Britain and Ireland.[20] The British census was based upon a survey covering all farm holdings of an acre and above. In a later study, J. Bellerby accepted Ojala's figures but preferred to work with a somewhat lower estimate for meat production based upon different techniques of estimation.[21] United Kingdom farm-gate prices are from the same sources and Ojala's farm-gate prices for 1910–14 are based upon information collected in the census of agricultural production for 1925 and extrapolated backwards using wholesale price indices.[22]

On comparing Ojala's figures with the Agricultural Census, it

18 D. Usher, *The measurement of economic growth*, Oxford, 1980.
19 E. M. Ojala, *Agriculture and economic progress*, London, 1952, pp. 192–217.
20 Department of Agricultural and Technical Instruction for Ireland, *The agricultural output of Ireland 1908 (in connection with the Census of Production Act, 1906)*, Dublin, 1912, pp. 4–27.
21 J. R. Bellerby, 'The distribution of farm income in the United Kingdom 1867–1938', *Journal of Proceedings of the Agricultural Economics Society*, X, 1953, reprinted as pp. 259–80 in W. E. Minchinton, ed., *Essays in agrarian history*, II, Newton Abbot, 1968.
22 *Census of agricultural production 1925*, *BPP*, XXV, Cmd.2815, London, 1927, p. 291.

became clear that the data available for fruit and vegetables, poultry and eggs are likely to be underestimated because such commodities tended to be produced on small holdings where fairly high proportions were consumed by farmers and their families.[23] Despite these and other minor shortcomings, the censuses and other official sources available to Ojala and Bellerby can be accepted with a fair degree of confidence.[24]

Italian data for both quantities and prices are less satisfactory largely because no complete agricultural census was taken in Italy at the time. The source underlying most available data for quantities of crops produced is the *Monthly Bulletin of the Statistical Office of the Ministry of Agriculture, Trade and Industry*, 1911–13. After 1909 (when the results of the '*Catasto Agrario*' were made available) the scope and quality of these sample surveys improved. In the 1950s the Central Statistical Office (ISTAT) produced a volume of historical statistics which included data on quantities and prices for Italy's main agricultural crops and products from 1861 to 1955.[25] These post-war figures suggested a sharp upward revision for outputs of fruit and vegetables compared with the original estimates of the Ministry of Agriculture. ISTAT's figures have been reviewed and amended recently by V. Zamagni who made a computation of the amount of total output that was recycled within the agricultural sector.[26] In constructing Table 15.1 ISTAT and Zamagni were heavily relied upon for 'net' quantities of crops cultivated from 1909 to 1913.[27]

The quantities of meat, poultry, eggs, and dairy produce published by ISTAT can be depended upon with less confidence because neither that publication nor *Annali Statistica* provide information on how estimates for animal produce were compiled, and attempts to trace the figures back through original sources failed. Censuses for the 'stock' of animals go back to 1891 and a census was taken for 1908. But how flows of dead meat were derived from stock figures is not yet clear because no slaughterhouse data appear to have been published before 1939.[28] With reluctance, the estimates published by ISTAT as amended recently by Zamagni were simply accepted. Italian prices are wholesale

23 Department of Agricultural and Technical Instruction for Ireland, *The agricultural output*, pp. 5–9.

24 Ojala, *Agriculture*, pp. 58–60; Ministry of Agriculture and Fisheries and Food, *A century of agricultural statistics*, London, 1968, chapters IV, V, IX.

25 ISTAT, *Sommario di statistiche storiche*, Rome, 1958.

26 V. Zamagni, 'Le radici agricole del dualismo italiano', *Nuova Rivista Storica*, LIX, 1975, pp. 55–99.

27 ISTAT, *Sommario*; Zamagni, 'Le radici agricole'.

28 Gazzetta Ufficiale, *Supplemento straordinario al n. 49*, Rome, 1939.

prices reported by chambers of commerce and other official bodies for major towns. They are summarised into annual averages in ISTAT. No sources were found for farm-gate prices or estimates of differentials between farm and wholesale prices. Price variations from town to town in Italy were probably greater than for comparable regional price variations in the United Kingdom. Mark-ups for transport and distribution are unlikely to be high but the use of unadjusted market prices biases the comparison in favour of Italy. For both countries the quantities quoted in Table 15.1 are expressed net of the volume of gross output 'recycled' as inputs (*reimpieghi*) within agriculture as seed, animal feed, and fertilisers.[29]

Matching Italian and United Kingdom outputs commodity by commodity proved to be feasible in the majority of cases, and it was assumed that most crops under comparison (wheat, potatoes, peas, wool, and so on) were similar in quality. In so far as the quintals of a crop presented in the sources under a particular head contain farm produce of widely different qualities, then variations in average prices and output values simply reflect differences in the mix of crops listed under that given category. For 'other vegetables', 'fruit and nuts', 'meat', 'butter and cheese' and 'poultry and eggs', these 'composite categories' were broken down as far as possible into their constituent subcomponents and the quantities of each crop and animal product priced by its own price in sterling and lire. But the sources do not provide the refined breakdowns required for higher accuracy and estimates of the variegated and high-value Italian output presented under these labels are likely to represent lower-bound figures.

Six Italian crops were encountered not cultivated in the United Kingdom: maize, rice, tobacco, silk cocoons, wines and olive oil. Various procedures have been adopted by other investigators to estimate the 'other country's' prices for such 'unique commodities'.[30] The solution preferred here was to begin with United Kingdom imports of these commodities from Italy expressed in (c.i.f.) unit values.[31] The values were then adjusted to exclude the costs of shipping commodities from Italian to British ports and further reduced by 20 per cent to allow for charges for moving goods from Italian farms to Italian ports.[32]

29 Ojala, *Agriculture*, pp. 190–298; Bellerby, 'Distribution of farm income'; Zamagni, 'Le radici agricole', p. 8.
30 Kravis, Kenessy, Heston and Summers, *International Comparison*.
31 *BPP, Accounts and papers*, London, 1909–14.
32 L. Isserlis, 'Tramp shipping cargoes and freight', *Journal of the Royal Statistics Society*, CI, 1938, pp. 73–86.

Table 15.1 *Agricultural outputs of United Kingdom and Italy, c.1909–14 valued in sterling and lire*

	Quantity		*Prices*		*Value of production*			
	(quintals)		*(per quintal)*		*(thousands of pounds)*		*(millions of lire)*	
	UK	*Italy*	*£*	*Lire*	*UK*	*Italy*	*UK*	*Italy*
Cereals								
Wheat	12,547	46,809	0.693	29.2	8.695	32.439	366	1,367
Barley	13,772	312	0.639	20.9	8.800	0.199	288	7
Oats	8,163	1,023	0.615	21.4	5.020	0.629	175	22
Rye	43	675	0.482	21.7	0.021	0.325	1	15
Maize	0	13,100	0.426	19.4	0.000	5.581	0	254
Rice	0	5,300	0.720	25.5	0.000	3.816	0	135
Vegetables								
Potatoes	46,032	19,068	0.189	12.3	8.700	3.604	566	235
Beans, peas	2061	7,756	0.689	27.1	1.420	5.344	56	210
Other veg.	12,155	30,374	0.348	12.0	4.230	10.570	146	364
Raw materials								
Flax, hemp	75	886	4.920	100.0	0.369	4.359	8	89
Beetroot	0	16,721	0.106	2.7	0.000	1.772	0	45
Wool	1,092	155	3.214	188.0	3.510	0.498	205	29
Tobacco	0	70	0.233	96.0	0.000	0.016	0	7
Hops	187	0	9.679	0.0	1.810	0.000	46	0
Fodder	36,610	12,300	0.770	8.5	28.190	9.471	311	105
Equine					2.400	0.817	60	20
Silk cocoons	0	463	11.400	285.0	0.000	5.278	0	132
Fruit & nuts	18,270	37,090	0.277	19.4	5.061	10.274	354	720
Wine (hl.)	0	50,515	1.260	39.3	0.000	63.649	0	1985
Olive oil (hl.)	0	1,659	2.780	90.0	0.000	4.612	0	149
Meat and dairy products								
Meat	14,804	5,670	5.840	199.1	86.455	33.113	2,947	1,129
Milk (hl.)	52,550	12,260	0.730	20.0	38.362	8.950	1,051	245
Butter, cheese	1,170	2,260	6.580	218.0	7.699	14.871	255	493
Poultry, eggs	1,680	2,890	6.930	185.8	11.642	20.028	312	537
Total					222.384	240.215	7,147	8,294

Notes

All quantities are net of products 'recycled' as agricultural inputs. Aggregate prices are weighted averages of individual components. Wholesale prices in lire for Italy; farm-gate prices in pounds for the UK.

Source

General sources are described in the text. A detailed description of sources and methods are contained in an unpublished appendix, available on request.

These steps provide a proxy for a farm-gate price in Italy for commodities delivered by Italian farmers to United Kingdom consumers. In most cases, and particularly for wines, they in fact sold only the very best qualities to Britain. Thus, United Kingdom prices of, for instance, wine and olive oil exported had to be adjusted downwards to approximate to sterling prices for modal qualities produced and consumed within Italy. The procedure followed was, either, to estimate price ratios of modal to high quality farm produce within Italy (by using Italian prices for diverse qualities) and apply these ratios to the sterling prices of Italian exports as calculated above, or, alternatively, to search for equivalent United Kingdom import prices, adjusted and converted at current rates of exchange. For sound theoretical reasons, utilising the commercial rate of exchange was avoided, but such compromises are less objectionable when modal qualities of the commodity in question (e.g. silk cocoons) were exported from Italy to the United Kingdom.

In textbook theory the British prices used here to represent sterling values for wine, silk cocoons, olive oil, maize, tobacco and rice represent proxies for the marginal utilities to British consumers of these uniquely Italian products. They are not, however, equal to the marginal costs of producing British substitutes for such goods. But given the quantities involved, the choice of any 'plausible' set of prices for unique commodities other than wine would be of no statistical significance for the purpose of this particular exercise, which is to estimate partial productivity indicators for Italian and United Kingdom agriculture.

For wine – a large component of Italian agricultural output – any British price adopted definitely affects the valuation of Italian agricultural output in pounds sterling. For example, it would make a huge difference to the value of Italian farm output priced in sterling if the price selected represented the cost of producing substitute wines in Britain and Ireland in 1910. It is, however, important to realise that there can be no single theoretically correct answer to the question: what is the value of wine consumed in Italy in British prices? First, there is no *ex ante* way of measuring utility which is inferred from expenditures. Why purchases occurred or did not occur historically is a complex matter to explain which would take this argument off towards the study of cultural anthropology, distribution networks, advertising, and traditions. The preferred approach was to find a price that British consumers might have been prepared to pay for modal Italian wine if they had been a nation of wine drinkers, which clearly they were not.

Information is available on the price differentials within Italy between standard and quality wines and the price that some segments of the British population were prepared to pay for quality imported Italian wines. It was assumed that this particular sub-group were likely to have had similar perceptions of quality differences to Italian consumers. Thus, the price that English people might have been prepared to pay for standard Italian wine was estimated by applying the differential in price between modal and quality wine on the Italian market to the prices of Italian wines sold on British markets adjusted for mark-ups for transport and distribution costs.

Alternative and equally plausible solutions to the problem were also tried. They included comparisons of the price British consumers might have been prepared to pay for beverages with comparable alcoholic content. The alcoholic content of a modal litre of English beer and the alcoholic content of a litre of standard Italian wine are known. That differential was applied to the price of beer in order to proxy a hypothetical evaluation by British consumers of Italian wine. Another approach was to price wine in terms of the differential between beer and wine prices in countries (such as Germany and Austria) where both beverages were in mass consumption. Both methods generated higher sterling values than the preferred solution, which then emerged as a lower-bound numerical solution to the problem of how to price unique and significant Italian products such as wine in sterling.

Table 15.1 presents a breakdown of the aggregated values produced by Italian and United Kingdom farmers weighted by the prices that their crops, raw materials, meat, dairy produce, fruit, and vegetables commanded on their respective home markets or might have commanded on the domestic market of the other country. Italian output in sterling thus measures the total value of agricultural output produced in Italy and hypothetically sold to British consumers, and vice versa.

III Inputs of labour

In order to estimate equivalents for hours of labour-time employed in producing United Kingdom and Italian agricultural outputs, information was required on:

(a) numbers of males, females, and children enumerated in censuses as available for work in agriculture;

(b) numbers of days per year and hours per day worked by fully-employed agricultural workers;

(c) the degree to which the days and hours worked by different categories of people classified as agricultural workers fell below full employment levels;
(d) differences in output per hour of labour input between prime male adult workers on the one hand and females, children, and elderly males on the other.[33]

Italian workers were not employed on Sundays (except at harvest times), on holidays of obligation, or, obviously, on days lost through inclement weather and ill health. Italian farm workers were potentially available for employment for up to 265 days a year. Although farm workers in the United Kingdom enjoyed less time off for religious festivals they almost certainly lost more days through bad weather. Hours worked per day varied in both economies from 14 or 15 at harvest to around five in mid-winter. No reliable figures have been published on the average length of the working day for British or Italian agricultural workers, but their hours can be expected to be comparable.[34]

Converting available workforces into labour inputs can only be a matter of guesswork. The hypothesis that in both economies a fully-employed agricultural worker could have been engaged for 265 days a year for comparable hours each day provides a beginning. Although a majority of male adult workers in the United Kingdom probably remained fully employed throughout the year, that assumption cannot be applied either to female and child labour engaged on farms in the United Kingdom or to the Italian workforce as a whole. Before 1914 the massive and endemic under-employment which afflicted most men, women, and children employed in Italian agriculture varied region by region and was probably related to the terms upon which families obtained access to land. Involuntary unemployment was certainly more severe among landless labourers (*braccianti*) and their dependents than among farmers and their families who owned or hired land, regardless of the form of tenure.[35] In an attempt to formulate plausible estimates for the numbers of days worked per year by males, females, and children employed as family or as wage labour, official and private investigations

33 J. T. Dunlop and V. T. Diatchenko, *Labour productivity*, New York, 1964; E. Dennison, *Why growth rates differ?*, Washington, 1967.

34 R. C. O. Matthews, C. H. Feinstein and J. Odling-Smee, *British economic growth 1856–1973*, Oxford, 1982, pp. 563–6; A. Maddison, *Economic growth in the west*, New York, 1964; *idem*, *Phases of capitalist development*, Oxford, 1982.

35 A. Serpieri, *Il contratto agrario e le condizioni di vita dei contadini nell'alto milanese*, Milan, 1910; G. Medici and G. Orlando, *Agricoltura e disoccupazione. I braccianti nella bassa padana*, Rome, 1951; INEA, *Monografie di famiglie agricole*, Rome, 1933.

Table 15.2 *The labour force and labour inputs utilised in Italian agriculture in 1911*

Categories of farm labour	*Labour force (000s)* [a]	*Estimated days of labour supplied per head for 1911*	*Productivity conversion coefficients*	*Labour input converted to fully-employed male-equivalents (000s)*
Male Farmers aged 15 to 65	2,235	265	1.0	2,235
Landless male labourers (*braccianti*) aged 15–65	2,608	220	1.0	2,165
Males aged 10–15	675	120	0.5	153
Males over 65	607	120	0.6	165
Females aged 15–65	3,410	120	0.6	926
Females aged 10–15	341	120	0.5	77
Totals (upper-bound)	9,876			5,721

Note
[*a*] O. Vitali, *La popolazione attiva in agricoltura attraverso i censimenti italiani*, Rome, 1973, pp. 10–21.

Source See text.

into under-employment in Italian agriculture were surveyed. On this evidence the following assumptions were made which provide the basis for the estimates set out below:

(a) male farmers aged 15–65 (including owner-occupiers, tenants and share-croppers) owned or rented sufficient land to keep themselves fully employed for 265 days a year;
(b) *braccianti* (landless male labourers) worked 220 days a year;
(c) females, children, and elderly males worked 120 days a year regardless of their status as family or landless labour.

The figures for days worked during the year presented in column two of Table 15.2 are definitely too high. More defensible estimates have been published for particular regions and categories of workers. For current purposes it was appropriate to select published figures which represented upper-bound figures of the days actually worked by farmers, labourers, and their families in agriculture for 1911 in order to bias the calculation against Italy.

Table 15.3 *The labour force and labour inputs utilised in United Kingdom agriculture in 1908*

Categories of farm labour	*Labour force (000s)*	*Estimated days of labour supplied per head in 1908*	*Productivity conversion coefficients*	*Labour input converted to fully-employed male-equivalents (000s)*
Male farmers and labourers aged 15+	2,080	265	1.0	2,080
Female family labour aged 15+	235	133	0.6	71
Female workers aged 15+	145	265	0.6	87
Male and female workers under 15	109	133	0.5	27
Total	2,569			2,265

Source
See text. Fuller details on data and assumptions are contained in an unpublished appendix, available on request.

Finally, in converting the days of labour time supplied by females, children and elderly men into 'male equivalents', conversion coefficients were utilised. Procedures of this kind rest upon the premise that females, children and elderly men were on average less skilled, were weaker in terms of physical capacities for hard work, and diverted more of their potential working time to leisure, to household tasks and to manufacturing activities inside and outside the home.

Estimates for the agricultural workforce and labour input for the United Kingdom in Table 15.3 above were constructed from data in the British and Irish agricultural censuses.[36] Working assumptions were:

(a) all males aged 15 and above (and non-family female workers), regardless of occupational status, were fully employed throughout a working year of 265 days;
(b) female family workers aged 15 and above worked half of the year producing farm output;

36 Department of Agricultural and Technical Instruction for Ireland, *The agricultural output*, pp. 17–19, 18, 25.

(c) workers classified by the agricultural censuses as 'person temporarily employed' worked half the working year on the production of farm output;
(d) young workers (under 15 years of age and regardless of their occupational status) worked half the working year on the production of farm output;
(e) the same productivity-conversion coefficients were employed as those applied to the Italian work force.

No doubt, other assumptions could be made to convert workforces classified as 'available for employment' in agriculture into labour inputs. There is certainly a wide gap between the Italian agricultural workforce – listed in the population census to include nearly 10 million men, women and children – and the labour input, estimated as 5.7 million man-years, 'required' to produce total farm output for 1911. The difference reflects the extent of under-employment in the Italian countryside which was described in numerous secondary sources as well as in major official reports on conditions of employment among the rural population for 1911, 1933 and the early 1950s.[37]

That particular gap was far narrower in the United Kingdom, where male and female adults are presumed to have been fully employed. The United Kingdom economy offered many more jobs outside farming, and by 1911 agricultural workers formed less than a tenth of the total workforce, compared with over half in the Italian case.

IV Land

To define and to measure the input of land utilised for agricultural production is far from simple, largely because of the uncertainties which surround the areas of rough and mountain pasture used to support farm animals (as well as the considerable variations in the quality of the soil used for both arable and animal husbandry). In Table 15.4 the total amount of land utilised for agricultural purposes is classified under comparable categories. Ideally, all land inputs should be transformed into equivalent units of arable land. Unfortunately, the existing data do not allow a procedure to be followed which is similar to that used above to estimate labour inputs. Simple and arbitrary

37 *Inchiesta Parlamentare*, 1909; Serpieri, *Capitalismo*; INEA, *Monografie*; *Inchiesta Parlamentare*, 1953–4; G. Toniolo and F. Piva, 'Unemployment in the 1930s: the case of Italy', pp. 221–45 in B. Eichengreen and T. Hatton, eds., *Interwar employment in international perspective*, London, 1988.

Table 15.4 *Hectares of land utilised for agricultural production in the United Kingdom and Italy, c.1907–09*

	Italy (000s)	*GB (000s)*	*Ireland (000s)*	*UK (cols. 2+3) (000s)*
1. Arable land	13,233	5,988	1,895	7,883
2. Permanent pasture	6,080	7,048	4,091	11,139
3. Tree crops (vines, fruit trees, olive trees, etc.)	1,486			
4. Total land inputs (1+2+3)	20,799	13,036	5,986	19,022
5. Rough grazing		5,181		5,181
6. Mountain grazing			999	999
7. *Incolto produttivo* (marginal land)	1,035			
8. Woodlands	4,564	1,126	122	1,248
Total agricultural land (4+5+6+7+8)	26,398	19,343	7,107	26,450

Source See text.

solutions are usually adopted by economists. For example, E. Dennison converts permanent pasture into arable land at a ratio of three to one and omits rough grazing from his productivity estimates.[38] J. Hayami and V. Ruttan utilise an 'unweighted aggregation of arable and pasture'.[39] Both these methods tend to underestimate land inputs used by the agricultural sector of the United Kingdom, because 'rough-grazing' land certainly supported considerable numbers of sheep and other livestock.[40] For purposes of calculating yields per hectare, total land inputs as given in Table 15.4 represent 'agricultural land'.

V Productivity: Italy compared with the United Kingdom

It is now possible to present estimates of agricultural product per unit of labour and per unit of land in the two countries. As Table 15.5

38 Dennison, *Why growth rates differ?*, pp. 183–4.
39 J. Hayami and V. Ruttan, *Agricultural development, an International Perspective*, Baltimore, 1975, pp. 312–13.
40 Ministry of Agriculture, *Agricultural statistics*, pp. 5–15.

Table 15.5 *Gross output per unit of labour and land in United Kingdom and Italian agriculture, 1909–14*

	Output per worker (fully employed male-equivalent units)		*Output per hectare of cultivated land*	
	At British prices (£)	*At Italian prices (lire)*	*At British prices (£)*	*At Italian prices (lire)*
United Kingdom	98	3,156	11.7	376
Italy	42	1,449	11.5	399
Ratio Italy/UK	42.8%	45.9%	98.2 %	106.1%

Source Tables 15.1–15.4.

shows, a fully-employed British agricultural worker produced more than twice as much as his Italian counterpart, and this gap turns out to be slightly wider when measured in English prices. A unit of land yielded in the United Kingdom a mix of agricultural produce roughly comparable in value to that yielded by a unit of Italian land. Since labour inputs for Italy are overestimated, the ratios represent upper-bound estimates of the gap in product per man that existed between Italy and the United Kingdom on the eve of World War I.

By excluding rough grazing, land inputs will underestimate the land actually used to produce animal and raw-material outputs in the United Kingdom and will therefore bias the comparison of gross output per hectare against Italy.

In order to estimate value added (net output) per worker and per hectare, the value of inputs purchased outside the agricultural sector should be subtracted from the gross-output values set out in Table 15.1. Unfortunately, no estimates exist for the quantities and prices of such inputs commodity by commodity. Plausible but macro guesstimates must rely entirely upon the work of Ojala and Zamagni who put the aggregate value of industrial inputs at 37 per cent and 11 per cent of the value of gross agricultural output in the two economies respectively.[41] Accepting their percentages, estimates of value added per worker and per unit of land can then be compared in the two countries (Table 15.6).

The numerical results in Table 15.5 are sensitive to the methods

41 Ojala, *Agriculture*, Zamagni, 'Le radici agricole'.

Table 15.6 *Value added per unit input of labour and land into United Kingdom and Italian agriculture, 1904–14*

	Net output per worker (fully employed male-equivalent units)		Net output per hectare of cultivated land	
	At British prices (£)	At Italian prices (lire)	At British prices (£)	At Italian prices (lire)
United Kingdom	62	1,988	7.4	237
Italy	37	1,290	10.2	355
Ratio Italy/UK	59.7%	64.9%	137.8%	149.8%

Source Tables 15.1–15.5.

employed to convert people 'available for work in the countryside' into fully-employed male equivalents. If gross outputs are divided instead by agricultural workforces, as listed in censuses of population, output per worker in Italian agriculture declines to about one-third of British levels. This ratio does not approximate to a productivity but rather to a welfare differential between farmers and their dependents in the two societies. It is this index that captures the poverty of the Italian rural population which so struck travellers from England in the late nineteenth century. But they mistakenly equated rural poverty with backward agriculture. That is why it is important to emphasise the current price estimates of gross and net output per hectare of cultivated land. These yield ratios capture the radically different soil conditions, terrain, hydrology, and climate found within the borders of the Peninsula compared to the United Kingdom. They also encapsulate differences in the mix of crops produced, techniques of cultivation, variable farm sizes, contrasting tenurial institutions, government policies, and agrarian social-overhead capital.

Partial productivity indicators are perhaps even more difficult to interpret than they are to measure. But comparisons between Italy and the most advanced agricultural sector in Europe are consistent with the presumption that Italian farmers made an efficient use of the resources available to them. At the very least, these numbers shift the *onus of proof* on to those who maintain that an unhealthy, illiterate peasantry, deficient tenurial institutions, and defective policies seriously constrained Italian agriculture from operating close to its production-possibility frontier.

Agrarian historians are aware of the varieties of agriculture and farming regions encompassed within the Peninsula and to some degree within the United Kingdom. There are few countries in Europe where soil, irrigation and climate vary as they do in Italy. From the Alps to Sicily, the traveller finds the well-irrigated and developed Po Valley, the rough Appennines, the vines and olives of Tuscany and Umbria, the intensive vegetable farming of Latium and Campania, the poor pastures of Abruzzo, the rich Tavoliere, and the wheat and citrus groves of Sicily.

Not long before the period under discussion, the whole of southern Italy (Mezzogiorno) was a large independent kingdom with its own traditions, culture and legal system. A large body of Italian historiography perceives the Mezzogiorno as a major drag on the overall development of Italy. Lombardy, on the other hand, has long been praised for an agriculture held to be the equal of the most advanced farming systems found in England, Holland and northern France. It is therefore illuminating to compare gross agricultural output per unit of labour input across three regions of Italy against the standard set for labour productivity found in the agriculture of the United Kingdom.

First, a word about data. According to the 1911 census figures (revised by O. Vitali), one-third of the Italian labour force resided in provinces previously territory of the Kingdom of Naples and in Sardinia (hereafter the 'South'), a region where 61 per cent of the labour force was employed in agriculture. For Italy as a whole, the ratio of the labour force in agriculture to the total labour force was about 57 per cent, and for Lombardy alone, 41 per cent. Following procedures adopted above, it can be estimated that 2.189 million fully-employed male-equivalent units approximated to the labour input into southern agriculture. The methods used to derive gross output for the South are less accurate than those for the Peninsula as a whole. Total gross output of the South can be estimated at £77.7 million or at Lire 2,932 million. No attempt was made to provide value-added estimates because no reliable figures for inputs purchased from outside agriculture exist on a regional basis. Assuming that such inputs would be higher in the north than in the South, the 'gap' between the two areas measured in value-added rather than in gross-output terms would then be narrower than the estimates suggested in Table 15.7.

Table 15.7 suggests that on this index the backwardness of Italian agriculture cannot be attributed, except in an entirely marginal sense, to the weight of a 'retarded' South. The productivity of labour – and presumably of land – seems to have been roughly on a par with the rest of Italy, despite the supposed deficiencies of its *latifundia*.

Table 15.7 *Output per unit of labour in three main Italian regions, c.1911*

	Output per man (lire)	*Index (UK = 100)*
Lombardy	1,593.7	51.4
North and Central Italy	1,518.6	49.0
South	1,341.4	43.3

Source See text.

VI The backwardness of Italian agriculture in a comparative perspective

Between the French Revolution and the last decades of the nineteenth century, output per worker and the contingent standard of living among Italy's rural population deteriorated (perhaps markedly) compared with the United Kingdom where the labour force available for work in agriculture remained roughly constant while output went up by a multiple of around 2.4. Unfortunately, the data do not allow for the measurement of output or productivity change in Italy until the boom of 1897–1913, when labour productivity seems to have increased at the remarkable rate of 2 to 3 per cent per annum.[42] Before that upswing (which also witnessed the massive migration of landless labourers to the Americas) it is likely that the agricultural production barely kept pace with a rural population and workforce growing at around 0.7 per cent per annum.

Thus, over the very long run British agriculture had released (or expelled) redundant labour from work on the land, while Italian agriculture absorbed more labour than it could employ. The differentials in rural incomes and consumption standards widened. To English travellers who visited Italy at the end of the nineteenth century, not only did the peasantry suffer from a poverty more widespread and dire than anything observed in the United Kingdom, but these observers suggested that the country's tenurial institutions, its illiterate and unskilled farmers, indifferent landowners, and misplaced governmental policies could be held responsible for conditions in the countryside. The poverty and relative deprivation they observed becomes evident on the basis of an index constructed by dividing agricultural incomes by the agricultural population as listed in the Population Census for

42 G. Fuà, ed., *Lo sviluppo economico in Italia*, III, Milan, 1968; Toniolo, *An economic history*.

1911: the level of rural income per capita was £24 a year in Italy compared with £85 in the United Kingdom. But this gap does not mean that Italian agriculture can be indicted for widespread failures to adapt best-practice techniques of cultivation or for a serious misallocation of resources. Historians have blamed successive governments for not undertaking reforms to property rights and institutions required to expel far more redundant labour from the countryside. Tampering with property rights was not, however, on the political agenda of most parts of western Europe for more than a century after the French Revolution had run its course. More realistic critiques focused upon the lack of courage displayed by successive Italian governments from 1878 to 1914 in not resisting demands for protection against imports of American grain. But it is unlikely that a more open trading regime in agriculture would have prompted more rapid emigration from the countryside to the towns and the Americas.

Apart from the imposition of tariffs, Italian statesmen preferred to leave rural populations to do the best they could with the supplies of land, capital and skills at their disposal. These endowments seem meagre by British and French standards. For example, by 1911 the land to labour ratio in Italy amounted to 2.1 cultivable hectares per agricultural worker, compared with 5.4 hectares in France and nearly 9 hectares in the United Kingdom.[43] British farmers also utilised far greater quantities of machinery, energy, chemicals, and other industrial inputs purchased from outside agriculture (see Section V).

Despite the small supplies of land and capital at their disposal, Italian farmers emerge from these exercises in productivity measurement with a creditable record. When placed on a scale which allows for limited but nevertheless revealing comparisons with farmers in the most advanced economy in Europe, they appear to have performed well enough to undermine suggestions that widespread failures of an institutional, market, policy, or entrepreneurial kind had depressed Italian agricultural output well below some optimal and attainable level. Just before the Great War, value added per unit of labour input stood at 60 per cent of the standard achieved by farmers in the United Kingdom. And even in that poorly-endowed and much maligned agrarian economy of the Mezzogiorno, labour productivity was not far below the average for Italy as a whole.

Operating with an abundance of labour, Italian farmers had obviously intensified their efforts to maximise yields from the land

43 O'Brien and Keyder, *Economic growth*, p. 105.

they cultivated. Their 'success' is gauged in Tables 15.5 and 15.6 which show gross output per hectare cropped (measured in pounds or lire) to be around United Kingdom levels. In terms of net value added per hectare, they performed better than their more educated, capitalised, and industrialised counterparts in Britain and Ireland. While releasing labour, United Kingdom farmers still obtained relatively high yields per hectare by utilising greater quantities of machinery, energy, and chemicals, while Italians relied above all on highly-priced crops cultivated with ample supplies of cheap labour to raise the aggregate value of agricultural output. That strategy maintained people on the land (at tolerable levels of subsistence), minimised outlays on intermediate goods, economised on capital, and depressed output per worker.

In Mediterranean agriculture, intensifying labour inputs could not raise the physical yields per hectare for major field crops such as grains, potatoes and pulses to the standards set by England, Holland and northern France. The environmental constraints (soils, precipitation, elevations) were simply too strong to be overcome by human toil. Unfortunately, that bundle of knowledge and techniques which successfully raised yields for grain and fodder crops in north-western Europe could not be diffused over large areas of the Italian peninsula. New fodder and root crops inserted into rotations in England, northern France and the Low Countries supported higher animal populations and generated increased supplies of organic manure and draught power. These new crops required a certain minimal amount of rainfall during their short growing season and particularly over the summer months when they lose moisture through transpiration. And during the Italian wet season the hours of sunshine were usually too few for the new crops to survive. Furthermore, the higher-yielding varieties of wheat seeds which had proved successful in north-western Europe could not survive Mediterranean drought. To retain moisture in summer and arrest soil erosion during the months of heavy rainfall in winter, Italian farmers planted three crops (olives, vines and fruit) around and across their fields – a response to nature which, together with a hilly terrain, made deeper ploughing difficult – except on the irrigated plains of the Po Valley.[44]

This 'inter-cropping' not only made ecological sense, it provided Italian farmers with a mix of high-value produce to compensate for their lower grain yields and small populations of farm animals. Through

44 F. Galassi, 'Stasi e sviluppo dell'agricoltura toscana 1870–1914', *Rivista di Storia Economica*, new series, III, 1986, pp. 304–37.

a process of trial and error they had (like managers of the land in Britain and Ireland) adapted cropping patterns and techniques of cultivation to local variations in soil climate and terrain in order to optimise yields. The Peninsula contained land and environmental conditions naturally suited to the cultivation of such high-value and labour-intensive crops as vines, tobacco, flax, silk cocoons, olives, vegetables and fruit. Through their long involvement in networks of trade with towns and with international commerce, Italian farmers were responsive to demand. Indeed, by the late nineteenth century something like 70 per cent of agricultural output was traded on markets, and foodstuffs and agricultural raw materials dominated the nation's exports.[45]

Given the relatively high levels of gross- and net-value-added achieved per hectare of land cultivated in Italy, and recognising the real constraints imposed by soil, climate and terrain on the diffusion of north European agronomic techniques, there are grounds for believing that the value of Italian agricultural output may not have fallen far short of the optimal obtainable.

What, then, can be concluded about the undeniable poverty experienced by Italian peasants before the Great War? The answer to this question should be sought primarily in the demographic history of the Peninsula over the previous three centuries. By 1911 the total labour force available for work in agriculture amounted to nearly 10 million men, women and children, working on average well below full employment levels (see Table 15.2). Despite the mass emigration witnessed over the previous three decades, and the accelerated growth of production experienced after 1896, the classical problem of excess population in the countryside remained visible and serious right down to the war.

Italian agriculture had adapted to this situation by concentrating upon a mix of crops that maximised the utilisation of labour. From an area of land comparable to that cultivated in Britain and Ireland, Italian farmers wrested an agricultural net output that was in value terms about 40 per cent higher than the agricultural product of the United Kingdom. But that income had to be shared through institutional arrangements, such as the extended family, among an agricultural population three to four times larger than the population sustained on the land of their more fortunate European neighbours to the north in the United Kingdom.

45 Federico, 'Mercantilizzazione'.

Some historians continue to blame Italian agriculture for the retardation of the economy and the slow pace of structural change. In the light of this exercise in comparative economic history an alternative hypothesis appears more plausible, namely that the agriculture was caught in what M. Elvin refers to as a 'high level equilibrium trap'.[46] The poverty of the rural population before 1914 may be more realistically attributed to the fact that Italy's industrial and urban economy (and the international economy as a whole) had not developed rapidly enough to pull under-employed labour from the countryside of Mediterranean Europe.

46 M. Elvin, *The pattern of the Chinese past*, London, 1973.

[13]

Business History in Italy: A Provisional Review and Research Prospects

Duccio Bigazzi

1. Business History in Italy Today

The belated and in many ways difficult progress of business history in Italy appears surprising in light of those characteristics known to underlie our country's industrial development: the early emergence of an oligopolistic structure leading, in contradictory ways, to an economic system in which a limited number of groups undertake domestic financial, industrial and distributive functions; the longevity, or at least the notable capacity for reincarnation, of the large enterprises which continue to dominate the economic scene today; the parallel presence – at the level of individuals – of a true aristocracy of capital, perpetuating the role of the major entrepreneurial dynasties and clearly contradicting the commonplace of a 'third generation crisis'. This picture of the 'dominance' of large-scale private enterprise and great dynasties is naturally complicated by the sudden emergence and (at least until now) equally rapid reabsorption of the numerous 'financial outsiders'[1] who have studded the entire course of Italian industrialization. But, above all, a counterpoint is provided by the exceptional weight assumed by public enterprise[2] as the result of a now secular process involving, in the first place, repeated state intervention in key sectors of the economy, while thereafter specifically created bodies have had to reassemble the fragments of industry accumulated in the portfolios of the big banks.

The picture can certainly be made more complete – though not contradicted – by the attention presently being given to 'industrial districts', in the sense that 'the enterprise no longer appears as an island of coordination in a sea of uncoordinated relations (the market), but as a semi-impermeable cell of the market'; therefore, 'the exact borders of the single enterprise become extremely debatable'.[3] At the same time, one can agree with those identifying the specificity of the Italian case in recent years in the 'simultaneous presence of … two sets of forces of economic development: large-scale, macro-impulses institutionalized in the consolidated nationalization of part of our economy, on the one hand; micro-impulses of small and medium scale, institutionalized by pervasive subcultures of "municipal government", on the other'.[4] Despite the stimulating contributions produced by the economists and sociologists who have developed these themes, it is my conviction that a renewal of economic history must still come essentially through an understanding of, firstly, the internal dynamics marking the evolution of the large private enterprise and, secondly, of the government action which has radically modified the economic structure, leading to the formation of the public sector.

Such a rethinking of industrial development in the light of the role played by the business system should certainly not undervalue those provisional contributions made since Rodolfo Morandi's essay (1931), undoubtedly the first example of a reflection on the characteristics of the Italian case in which the major enterprises receive significant consideration.[5] But it should also be said that the ideas contained in Morandi's work have only recently been taken up and developed. In fact, in the period between the 1930s and the 1960s, Fossati's *Lavoro e produzione in Italia*, which appeared in 1951, constitutes a wholly isolated example. In it, moreover, as Luciano Cafagna observed immediately following the publication of this voluminous work, the radical shift of attention towards 'enterprises, entrepreneurs and collaborators ... evoked by name' coincided with a 'firm's eye view' which downplayed or ignored altogether the economic policy choices and wider social reality which were conditioning Italian industrialization.[6]

On a very different level, it should not be forgotten that the syntheses of varying chronological scope attempted by Romeo, Luzzatto, Caizzi and Castronovo, among others, deal to some extent with the men and firms who acted as the actual protagonists of growth.[7] But it is only in Castronovo's work that the task of giving such protagonists the predominant role they deserve is taken up seriously – to the extent that the fundamental limitation of *Industria italiana dall'Ottocento ad oggi* appears to be the lack of primary studies capable of adequately supporting such an effort of synthesis. In contrast, the works of the other three influential masters of Italian economic history appear tied to a formulation viewing the individual case as either an exemplification of general tendencies or, conversely, as a significant exception to the general picture, drawn on the basis of basic economic policy choices and described by recourse to the main macroeconomic variables. Luzzatto, while he stressed the necessity of studying the 'most typical individual enterprises', reduced the contribution which could thus be derived to the integration and enrichment of the data furnished by the industrial censuses. In short, the 'particular' alongside the general in order to present 'a vivid and lively picture of the life and state of development of industry'.[8] Romeo, on the other hand, clearly manifested his intention of avoiding the risk of getting bogged down in a multiplicity of repetitive events irreducible to a unitary design: '[It is necessary] to keep in mind throughout that a history of "industry" is not, and should not be, the sum of the histories of individual "industries" [read "enterprises", but the term used is already revealing, DB], and that its specific object is, above all, industrial development as a whole and within the framework of the economic life of the country'.[9]

This is an observation with which one must certainly agree, although it has led in practice to the neglect of such central aspects of the firm's existence as methods of financing, technological choices, market orientation, organizational forms, juridical forms etc. Consequently, the role played by the major enterprises in determining in concrete terms the actual course of the industrial development and economic life of the country has inevitably ended up being underestimated. It is not so much a question of counterposing a microeconomic to a macroeconomic approach, a 'view from below' with a 'view from above' or, worse, an empirical versus a theoretical approach, as of realizing that – as Joseph Schumpeter has forcefully maintained – 'the mechanisms of economic change in capitalist society pivot on entrepreneurial activity' and any picture of industrial development which ignores the daily problems raised at that specific level inevitably loses verisimilitude and credibility.[10]

2. From the Era of Celebration to the First 'Models'

The rapid review of Italian business history which will be conducted in the following pages does not pretend to provide an exhaustive survey.[11] Rather it aims to present an interpretation of the state of development of the field of study with which we are concerned, the necessary premise for an 'agenda' for the immediate future.

It is beyond doubt, first of all, that the initial traces of an Italian business historiography are to be found in the celebratory and illustrative publications which, having already begun to appear in the course of the 19th century, became ever more frequent from the 1930s.[12] Giorgio Mori, in a well-known contribution on the subject, has tellingly underlined the common features which characterize this approach:

> The certainty in the great destiny of the firm ..., the exaltation of the courage, audacity and initiative of the founders and the foresight and superior productive, economic and political capabilities of their successors; their paternal concern for the workers they employed (allusions to their conditions of life, to the origins of the trade unions, to strikes and agitations are rare); the tendency to play down the conflicts and difficulties which manifested themselves time and again during the life of a given enterprise, whether due to unfortunate productive decisions, financial setbacks or bad forward planning; the absence of any evaluation of the weight which, individually and collectively, the great entrepreneurs must surely have represented in determining certain lines of state economic (and not only economic) policy in decisive moments of national life.[13]

Apparently, this strongly ideological vision is deeply rooted in the genre, often leading the description of what takes place in the firm to levels totally incongruent with real events. In fact, the implicit conviction that the processes of economic development are dominated by the 'invisible hand' of the market is combined – in a way which has its own coherence – with a demiurgic image of entrepreneurship. If the nature of these publications is thus such that very often they furnish evidence useful only for studying the image which enterprises have of themselves (or at least exhibit to the outside world), it is on the other hand a recognized fact that not a few celebratory publications provide a contribution of prime importance for the detailed reconstruction of technical processes and production choices.[14] Besides obvious deprecation of the missed encounter between economic history and the world of industry (deserving, however, of careful analysis), it would certainly be interesting to reconstruct the ways in which groups of intellectuals of a scientific background – generally working in the universities but also not uncommonly involved directly in the companies' research departments – contributed to these publications or in some cases produced them in their entirety.

In any case, the fact is that in Italy business history themes were brought into focus only at the beginning of the 1960s, with the publication of an article and a book, by Giorgio Mori and Angelo Pagani respectively, analysing the theoretical insights and the activities of the

Research Center in Entrepreneurial History of Harvard University (founded in 1948 and wound up in 1958).[15] It should immediately be said that these are two exemplary accounts, both for their breadth of bibliographical information on the state of the debate as well as the clarity of exposition with which it is presented to the Italian reader.

The diversity of ideological approach and cultural background of the authors naturally led to different judgments concerning the value of the work done by the North American school. Mori – strongly critical of the '*intrinsically* "apologetic" attitude'[16] towards entrepreneurship adopted by Cole, Redlich, Cochran and other scholars attached to the Center – identified the basic limitation of their approach as the loss of a more general vision of the process of social and economic development. The progressive orientation towards 'setting the whole problem in psycho-sociological terms' appeared functional to what Mori singled out as the characteristic tendency of dominant economic theory: the distancing of the figure of the entrepreneur 'from the process of production as a whole [and from] the relations of production which could be evoked by association with profit'. At this point, however, the value of the Center's contribution for Mori was reduced to its strong encouragement of 'the careful study of the life of a particular enterprise [...] or a notable protagonist'.[17] Too little, certainly, given the intellectual stimulus provided by the Center's animators and, above all, the scientific results which were shortly to be obtained by the young scholars who had completed their apprenticeship there: just think of David Landes and Alfred Chandler, to mention only the most famous names.[18]

Pagani, for his part, discussed the merits of the attempts to revise Schumpeterian theory put forward in the course of the Center's activities, initially inspired by the conception proposed by the Austrian economist of the entrepreneur as innovator. Vindicating the coherence of the Schumpeterian definition – even against the undoubtedly valid criticisms of A.P. Usher regarding the impossibility of distinguishing rigorously between invention and innovation – Pagani denied that the diminution of the figure of entrepreneur into that of *decision-maker* could resolve the problem of the distinctive character of entrepreneurship. Doubts were then expressed as to whether it was opportune to utilize, at a high level of abstraction, concepts such as *role* and *deviance*. He considered that, at the level of historical investigation, the really promising lines of research were instead on origins, motivations and the degree of social approval. It was precisely to the contribution of a sociologist such as Pagani, and to the first historical works on the origins of Italian entrepreneurship (among them the article in which Giuseppe Are drew attention to the documentary importance of the 1870–74 industrial inquiry), that the group of young scholars, who in 1965 founded the Centro di storia imprenditoriale [Centre for Entrepreneurial History] at the Institute of Economic History of the University of Pavia, turned. Created on an initiative, and with resources, external to the University, the Centre nevertheless pursued considerable seminar work organized on an interdisciplinary basis. The slight interest shown by the academic world in the subject of entrepreneurship, the difficulties of access to sources and the social climate of the period itself, privileging as it did the field of criticism over that of empirical research, rendered the life of the Centre difficult. And, indeed, it closed in 1969 when Pagani left Pavia for the University of Milan.[19]

To find a real point of departure for business history research, it is therefore necessary to proceed to an even more recent date, with the publication in 1971 of Valerio Castronovo's biography of Giovanni Agnelli. A biography certainly, but clearly in the first instance a case study of an enterprise, given the pre-eminent identification of the protagonist with his industrial creation, and even more the author's interest in locating FIAT in the social context of Turin and in examining the relationship between the enterprise and the state economic apparatuses before and during fascism. It should be pointed out that the almost total absence of a FIAT historical archive at the time contributed in no small measure to this approach, impeding exhaustive analysis of the company's management, organizational structure, productivity trends, etc. This problem was in part side-stepped by notable inductive ability and partly resolved (as mentioned) by the examination of FIAT's social and political relations with the outside world. An objective weakness in the available evidence thus stimulated an investigation which, for the first time, demonstrated the contribution that a case study could furnish to the understanding of more general processes of economic and social development.[20]

The starting point for what can today be considered the other fundamental 'pillar' of business history in our country, Franco Bonelli's study of the evolution of Terni (which appeared in the same period), was exactly the reverse. Here at last the researcher investigated a considerable part of the firm's records, deposited in the local state archive thanks to the far-sightedness of a public manager.[21] Despite inadequacies in the documentation, and its dispersed and disorganized state, it was possible to reconstruct with sufficient precision the internal workings of the management groups whose succession marked the various stages of the company's existence: the ambitious steel programme pursued by its founder, Vincenzo Stefano Breda; the conjunction of military-steel production and shipbuilding in the years of the Odero–Orlando administration; the transformation into a multisectoral group based upon electricity distribution and electro-chemicals in the Bocciardo period. The possibility of analysing in depth technological, productive and financial decisions through reasonably complete statistical series constituted an element of particular novelty. While the analysis of the firm's economic development, and that of the constellation of enterprises associated and intertwined with it, was more than exhaustive, the reconstruction of one of the most significant relationships between primary industry and the state, illuminating the social dimension in this case, turned out to be almost wholly absent. A deliberate and explicitly declared omission, convincing from the point of view of the tasks which the author set himself, and yet such as to require further research for a fuller understanding of the 'steelwork phenomenon' in the factory town of Terni.[22]

Antonio Confalonieri who, while starting from interests related to the origins of the banking system, can without exaggeration be considered one of the 'founding fathers' of business history in Italy, had recourse to the substantial company archives of the Banca commerciale italiana (now opened to public consultation). As well as describing analytically the history of the great Milanese bank from its foundation until 1914 (and also in part that of its twin, the Credito Italiano), the five volumes of his monumental work fully illustrated the financial policies adopted by the major Italian enterprises. These included recourse to indebtedness, and the complex 'chinese box' mechanisms favoured by the steel trust led by ILVA; the not entirely transparent stock-market operations which accompanied the impetuous growth of FIAT; the role of German and Swiss capital in the creation of a large number of electrical enterprises; the exemplary self-financing strategies adopted by Pirelli, Falck and Edison, right down to the variously tormented stories of many minor firms. In this varied panorama the propulsive role played by the mixed banks, and by the Banca commerciale italiana (Comit) in particular, emerged in a new perspective in the sense that the principal, or at least the ideal, 'model of intervention' for the bank of Piazza della Scala lay in the subordination of 'industrial business' (the setting up of businesses, the issuing and buying of shares, medium-term credit) to the necessity of assuring the possibility of carrying on 'normal' banking activity. In fact, with differing interpretative emphases, the basic conclusions of Confalonieri's research have been largely accepted by scholars who have since concerned themselves with the subject, while his ability to adapt modern techniques of accounting analysis to the still primitive bookkeeping methods used by industrial enterprises in the period certainly remains unequalled.[23]

3. Recent Developments

The three works whose historiographical importance has just been briefly underlined have undoubtedly attracted followers, although the intellectual stimulus provided by other scholars (Mori and Cafagna, in particular) and other research, mostly of a sectorial character, has been of prime importance.[24] On the other hand, the recent growth of business history in Italy clearly cannot be traced to some kind of spontaneous generation, derived purely from the publication of important 'chapters' dedicated to FIAT, Terni and the Comit F. Their reception has undoubtedly been enhanced by social changes attracting scholars from quite different backgrounds to the field. From this point of view the Italian situation presents a close affinity with that outlined for France in a recent article by Jean-Pierre Daviet.[25]

The unheard-of interest in history displayed by business institutions themselves certainly represents a point of departure. The image crisis which hit Italian enterprises between 1968 and the early 1970s discouraged to a certain extent the tendency to reduce historical investigation to mere celebration. In the presence of evident signs of decline, or at least of conjunctural difficulties linked to social crisis and ongoing technological restructuring, self-celebration appeared inappropriate or even counterproductive. Meanwhile, the critical reassessment of recent experience by new proprietorial regimes or management groups opened the way to less strictly apologetic considerations of the histories of companies. An analogous phenomenon, moreover, was also associated with the widespread revival of interest in the pioneer generation, however much this was cloaked in nostalgia. The pressure of scholars and archive administrators who turned to account the early, pilot experiences of opening businessmen's records and company archives for consultation acted on this terrain, which certainly proved more fertile than in the past.[26]

On the other hand, this pressure (stubborn and insistent, it may justly be said, and not without personal experience) reinforced demands maturing in another arena of the Italian industrial crisis of the period, reflecting in a certain way a 'social demand' for knowledge and investigation. If the cultural climate which had characterized the University revolt was certainly not favourable to research on business – as the experience of the Centre promoted by Pagani at Pavia showed – in the years immediately following there was a much more general revival of interest in at least certain aspects of the subject which it appeared possible to confront without cutting unacceptably across the social grain.

The years of conflict between 1968 and 1973 had revolved around issues linked to overcoming rigid, Fordist organizational models and had raised questions concerning the nature of work skills, the work ethic, etc. A non-ideological consideration of these problems at the historical level demanded closer examination of relatively little-known aspects of the factory: entrepreneurial choices in the field of technology; the activity of the 'organizers of production'; the internal composition of the proletariat and the nature of industrial relations, from health and working conditions to forms of bargaining. The explanatory key capable of clarifying this whole issue appeared to many that of reconsidering the stages by which Taylorist methods were introduced into Italian factories. From that to new attention to the history of the firm was a short and, without doubt, necessary, step. In 1976, in an article which had a notable influence on the direction of research in this field, Giulio Sapelli wrote:

> The elaboration of the statistical material on the importation and production of machines, on fixed capital investment or amortization (to list the most commonly used sources, in descending order of importance) cannot constitute the main element for a study of the problem [of mechanization and the diffusion of mass production] other than by conducting a discussion which explicitly declares its status as a general indicator, useful for comparison with more specific tendencies verifiable at the level of the firm. In fact, if Italian industrial development is dualistic, it is not only so territorially, but also between monopolistic and non-monopolistic sectors, dynamic and non-dynamic, between different commodity sectors and divisions. The study of the firm thus appears the privileged ground for our analysis because, when based on the necessary documentary sources, it provides the clearest evidence of processes which cannot otherwise be reconstructed, at least insofar as regards their phase of application.[27]

Local communities, in particular the company towns and the working-class suburbs of big cities, raised other questions: the process of deindustrialization, beginning to leave huge and disquietingly ruinous monuments to work in its wake, aroused the aesthetic fascination and the civic activism of a variegated band of 'industrial archaeologists'. At the same time, the progressive extension of areas of desolation and abandonment amongst squalid housing estates and anachronistic industrial villages attracted the attention of town-planners and geographers who were not content merely to quantify the 'urban vacuum'.[28]

A similar ferment was created in the historical field by the diffusion of oral history methodologies[29] and by that complex of subject choices, research techniques and style of exposition which, for reasons of convenience, may be defined as 'social history'. From whence developed investigations on the formation of the industrial proletariat, and its separation from the peasant environment, the working-class family and its life cycle, mobility inside and outside the factory, etc. From whence, necessarily, the micro-analytical scale of much of the work on these topics.[30]

Much of the research sharing the characteristics and motivations outlined above can only indirectly be included in business history, that is to say insofar as it is concerned with the factory, or rather with individual factories and with circumscribed geographical contexts. Yet it is significant that many of the authors referred to, having conducted their early research on industrial relations, and more particularly on the introduction of 'scientific management', turned to business history.[31] Moreover, it is one of the many paradoxes of the 'success' of *business history* in Italy that such a quantitatively significant contribution has been furnished by research carried out within the ambit of trade union organizations, institutes for the history of the Resistance, foundations for the history of the labour movement and local associations and bodies, all working independently of, and occasionally in overt opposition to, the business world. All the more so since a number of these institutions now seem oriented to promoting research in which the entrepreneurial element is even more decisively situated at the centre of investigation.[32]

As is natural, however, the growing interest manifested in the firm since the mid-1970s has more directly influenced scholars coming from the field of economic history. If 'the entrepreneurial' formerly appeared as an element to which it was necessary to give specific attention within sectoral or regional studies,[33] monographic research on individual firms is now firmly established and no longer constitutes an exception, dependent on the chance discovery of archive material of particular importance.[34]

Supporting these tendencies, and partly a product thereof, it is necessary to mention the creation of organizations putting the promotion of the study of the firm at the centre of their activity. In order of appearance, the first which needs to be considered is the Centro di ricerche sull'economia delle imprese pubbliche e di pubblico interesse [Centre for Research on the Economy of Public and Public-Interest Companies], better known as CIRIEC. This centre, created in the now-distant 1956 and responsible for studies of considerable importance on state intervention in the economy, has in recent years taken on with increasing zeal the task of investigating the historical path leading to the present structure of the Italian public sector. In the historical field its work has until now been directed predominantly towards the figures of the great managers, a series of biographies of 'protagonists of public intervention' appearing in the journal *Economia pubblica* from 1974 (collected in a single volume edited by Alberto Mortara in 1984), although the commencement of a series of historical case studies of particular firms dates from 1987.[35]

Founded in 1982 and equally active in its own particular field, the Centro per la documentazione storica ed economica dell'impresa [Centre for the Historical and Economic Documentation of the Firm] evolved out of an analogous centre whose interests were restricted to public enterprise. Arising from the necessity of ordering and rendering fruitful company archives, the centre (stimulated by Valerio Castronovo) has commenced and in many cases completed this task for such enterprises and business organizations as Breda, Confindustria, Dalmine, Enea, Enel, Ilva, Italtel, Setemer-Ericsson and Sip. Simultaneously with the reorganization of archives, the centre has carried out research on the documentary sources for industrial history, promoted conferences and published a series of volumes.[36] This activity, particularly efficacious in the field of public enterprises, has developed alongside the numerous projects begun by companies, business organizations, local government and archival authorities,[37] so that one can now say that the exceptional backwardness which characterized the state of sources of Italian industrial history until only a few years ago is on the way to being overcome.

Finally, the Associazione di Storia e Studi sull'Impresa (ASSI) [Association for the History and Study of the Firm] is distinguished by its marked 'tendency' character (created in 1983, it has been a Foundation since 1986). Promoted at the outset by a group of scholars with predominantly historical backgrounds, the ASSI set as its particular objectives, on one hand, the integration of the historical contribution with that of the other social sciences and, on the other, the confrontation of scientific research with the issues raised in the actual strategic and operative practice of the firm. The need for such an approach was already noted in the document which constituted the preparatory platform for the new organization in 1981:

> In Italy today the industrial enterprise appears to be one of the most important subjects of investigation for economic history. … On the other hand, the researcher who today confronts industrial history – with all the difficulties which typically face the explorer given, in addition, the often chaotic state of the sources – not infrequently finds himself under the necessity of resolving serious conceptual problems. Having abandoned a merely narrative style or the crutches of ideology, appropriate interpretative frameworks are lacking, while at times an insufficient familiarity with important foreign developments is evident. … It is therefore opportune to foster contacts with scholars from other disciplines: the historian of economic thought, the economist interested in the theory of the firm, the industrial sociologist, the organization theorist, the psychologist, the political scientist working on decision-making, the legal theorist. But not only with the above; there are also the protagonists – entrepreneurs, managers, trade unionists – who can be asked to contribute and to whom, moreover, we may offer for our part some stimuli to reflection on present problems.[38]

To what extent has this programme been put into practice? Firstly, the seven volumes of the *Annali di storia dell'impresa* (launched in 1985 and edited by F. Amatori) appearing to date have certainly contained a range of different approaches and methodologies which makes them a novel experience in the Italian scientific debate. While the series of 'Studies' published by Franco Angeli and Il Mulino presents titles more directly concerned with the field of historical research,[39] the interdisciplinary effort has been concentrated around the biennial conferences held in Terni and in Milan: topics under discussion have included big and small enterprise (1985); enterprise and technology (1987); finance and enterprise (1989); organization and strategy (1991).[40] This latter series of initiatives, in which scholars of international prominence have participated, undoubtedly testifies to a promising interest in theoretical reflections on the part of a new generation of historians, engaged in a broadening of their conceptual horizons and area of inquiry. However, important obstacles to a full acceptance of the contribution of history on the part of economists and sociologists certainly remain: the underlining of the necessity of an historical perspective on the part of some schools of economists, in fact, does not yet seem to have exceeded the domain of methodology, so that even now the domain of economic theory proper remains privileged. The problem is not new: as Arthur H. Cole had occasion to point out, 'there has long been a notion prevalent in academic circles that a theoretical hypothesis, however shaky its bases, is somehow superior in intellectual quality to a historical finding, however broad and well supported by evidence; and the deduction has followed that historians should study theory, but theorists may be excused from immersing themselves in facts'.[41]

Many years have since passed, and the recognition has become ever more widespread that, as Louis Galambos observed, 'a joint effort would help history and theory: both hypotheses and evidence are essential to both crafts, but at this point the economists have a monopoly on the former and the business historians have a surplus of the latter'.[42]

Actually putting this sort of exchange of surpluses into effect, however, requires a radical modification of attitude which is not easily achieved. As far as the historiographical side (the object of the present discussion) is concerned, it is undeniable that a 'poor relative' mentality is still present, as fearful of engagement on its own ground as it is prone to lament its own supposed victimization. Despite these problems, it must be acknowledged that the ASSI's ambitious project has laid the bases for a dialogue with international historiographical circles which is not limited to the mere translation to the Italian context of themes proposed by schools, however prestigious, such as that of Chandler. Discussions have included reference to theories of the firm – like the 'evolutionist' proposal of Richard Nelson and Sidney Winter – which go beyond the maximizing assumptions of orthodox models; an appeal to Nathan Rosenberg's research on the relationship between technical progress and economic development; attention to the sociological theory of complex organization – all of which can provide equally vital and penetrating analytical tools and stimuli for historical research.[43]

What Giulio Sapelli has defined as 'the new and second phase of business history in Italy' has emerged against this contradictory, but undoubtedly lively, background.[44] As noted at the outset, I leave it to others to examine in detail the cognitive results obtained in these years, limiting myself instead to proposing three examples of different approaches to the study of the firm.

The first is *Energia e sviluppo*, a collective volume on the history of Edison resulting from research sponsored by the Progetto cultura Montedison and coordinated by the Fondazione ASSI.[45] The authors (G. Sapelli, C. Pavese, L. Segreto, P. Hertner, B. Bezza and R. Giannetti) focus on the strategies adopted by the top management, analysing from this perspective the Milanese enterprise's relations with its financial partners, foreign electrical producers and other Italian firms operating in the sector.

The articles contained in the book rest on the solid foundations of Confalonieri's already-mentioned work on the Comit, on the research of Hertner on foreign capital in Italy and that of Giannetti on technological choices in the electrical sector.[46] But the results of the research certainly go beyond the mere repetition or refinement of themes developed elsewhere. Edison's success escapes simple, anachronistic rationalization, as demonstrated particularly in the article by Pavese; both the basic difficulties which the company had to face and the strategies adopted to overcome them are considered. These include mobilizing entrepreneurial resources from among the engineers of an intellectually advanced environment, like the Politecnico of Milan; the definition – first imposed and then conscious – of a business strategy founded on 'indirect expansion', and the dynamic utilization of a revenue position achieved thanks to its own precocious development; the centrality of the technological dimension, with the exploitation of the possibilities offered by the Italian electrical engineering and electrical industries, and a sort of pragmatic compromise with foreign technology; the development of a model of finance which, whilst it created a privileged alliance with the Comit, retained that autonomy which would constitute the premise for becoming 'its own boss' immediately following the First World War. If other issues still need to be tackled and, above all, if the role of Edison in the Fascist and post-Second World War years still largely remains to be examined, each of the above areas opens doors to comparative lines of research which appear extremely promising.

In the second work which will be referred to, Giorgio Roverato's history of Marzotto,[47] the fundamental effort is directed to the conjoint interpretation of the company's development and the decisions taken by the entrepreneurial dynasty which directed it through successive generations. The personality and psychological character of the Marzotto family (in particular Vittorio Emanuele and his son, Gaetano) are elucidated with considerable penetration, while the mechanisms of growth of the company are analytically explored from the financial, technological and commercial points of view.

However much Roverato distances himself from a tendency to 'total analysis', emphasizing his concentration on the behaviour of the 'principal actors' (the Marzotto, that is), it nevertheless seems to me that one of the most outstanding achievements of Roverato's work is to be found in the identification of the specific nature of the links between the company and the social environment of Valdagno. The arrival and untroubled growth of the large-scale, centralized factory in a traditional context are certainly explained by the 'given' socioeconomic characteristics of the Agno Valley, but they appear more than anything else the result of an entrepreneurial vision of surprising coherence. The 'paternalism' of the Marzotto does not appear, in fact, a mere mask for the exigencies of social control, but rather an organic ideology which acted as a 'surrogate' for the political and administrative authorities: the 'social town' is founded on a new authority, having its roots in the firm itself and in its role as a productive entity. In Roverato's analysis, the history of the company – or at least of this type of company – is interwoven with that of its environment, an environment which, in the long term, is decisively shaped by it.

As far as the third approach proposed here is concerned, I trust the reader will realize that reference to a work by the author of the present essay has the sole function of indicating tendencies, and leaves out of consideration any critical evaluation of the adequacy of the results with respect to its intentions. In the case of the history of Alfa Romeo from its foundation until its passage into public hands,[48] the intention was to interpret conjointly the 'worlds' of the different participants: the entrepreneurial groups who succeeded one another in running it and the variegated whole of the 'producers' who collaborated with or confronted them. Firm and factory are together, therefore, in a reconstruction which deals with themes which can be traced to business history proper, the history of the trade union movement, political parties, etc.

This approach was undoubtedly imposed by the urban context in which Alfa Romeo found itself operating and by the conflict which characterized its history in the period examined; but it also corresponds to the propensity of the author to consider workers, foremen and white-collar workers as conditioning, and not only conditioned, actors in the company's history. The economic unit is here seen also as a 'cell' of society, in which different forms of behaviour and cultures are in constant interaction.

These considerations, while they should justify the point of view adopted in this study, are not intended to introduce surreptitiously a criterion relating to the greater or lesser inclusivity of the terrain of investigation chosen. The three examples presented here as representative of diverse approaches to research come from different traditions of study and can be equally appropriate in relation to the characteristics of the case being examined. They confirm clearly, in any event, the breadth of Italian business history's current interests, which are undoubtedly not enclosed within the confines of specialism. The use of analytical tools from other disciplines to focus on the subject does not seem to have ruptured continuity with the most stimulating lines of economic and social history.

4. The Dilemma of 'Company History'

In 1979, in his detailed survey of 'economic development in Italy since Unification', Valerio Castronovo called for monographs to be written on the major industrial and banking firms and on the leading private and public entrepreneurs. At the time, the historiography had little enough to offer: regarding industrial enterprises, for example, Castronovo could cite only the works on 'Falck, Olivetti, Terni, on Agnelli, and on the first employers' confederations'.[49] Since then, as we have attempted to show, much progress has been made and, although lacunae still remain, a range of situations and personalities about which little or nothing was known has now received attention.

From this point of view, the increasingly widespread appeals to the necessity of pulling together the threads of this micro-analytic work may be considered a sign of maturity, or at least that the infancy stage has been left behind. Silvio Lanaro, for example, recommended recently that 'an inventory … an atlas of industrial Italy'[50] should be compiled on the basis of company histories and entrepreneurial biographies. On the other hand, criticism of the empiricism which would appear intrinsic to monographic research on individual enterprises and entrepreneurs is becoming increasingly general – 'anecdotes without an intelligible plot' in the graphic definition given by Gianni Toniolo.[51] It may not perhaps be a great satisfaction, but here we can finally boast of motives for reproval shared with countries where business history has a much longer tradition.

This problem has in fact been on the agenda for some time in the United States and Great Britain, to take only the two 'leading nations': already between the end of the 1950s and the early 1960s the North American school considered that a turning point had been reached beyond which research produced diminishing returns.[52] The proliferation of case studies has not halted, however, and the problem of stemming the tide continues to provoke discussion and polemic. Florid epithets and exhortations to change direction seem to no avail. Roy Church declared in 1976 that 'there is no field of contemporary history so formidably dull as business history';[53] a decade on, Donald Coleman was compelled to recapitulate in rather brutal terms the abuses most frequently revealed by critics: 'anecdotal, soap-opera history; unreadable academic company histories which are all narrative and without analysis of issues; a mere public relations purpose in commissioning company histories; and all unread histories'.[54]

Is this really the case in Italy? There is no doubt that, yes, it is, if one looks at or reads – a more arduous task one has to admit – many of the monographs listed in this bibliography. From this point of view, business history suffers from limitations common to much of Italian contemporary historiography: the restriction of vision to the national, if not local, level; acritical treatment of sources, whether documentary or archival; a propensity to chronological reconstruction which tends to slip into mere chronicle, and so on. But it is also true that these limitations are aggravated by certain peculiarities of the field in question. These are linked in particular to the importance assumed by research 'on commission', which, even when inspired by properly scientific intentions, carries with it not a few risks.[55] First of all, the not easily avoided tendency to self-censorship which can result, by omission and selection, in effects not dissimilar in the last analysis from those produced by the explicit encomium of the celebratory publications. A second risk is the pressure generally exerted on scholars by the need to meet tight deadlines tied to the 'institutional' requirements of the commission, in conflict with the necessarily lengthy time required by research. Thirdly, the loss of scientific quality which generally results from the, however laudable, pressure or desire for an easily readable product. Even where these distorting mechanisms are not in operation, or at least not all simultaneously, the problem nevertheless remains that the research is oriented to themes originating from outside, not necessarily the most relevant or the most urgent for the development of the discipline. These problems demand serious reflection, all the more so in the presence of a revival, in a more up-to-date form certainly, of the celebratory literature which just a few years ago seemed exhausted[56] and to which more or less well-intentioned neophytes and scholars in search of a shop-window lend themselves.[57]

In this sense, the use of the term 'caso' [case] to define a monograph often brings to mind the common-sense meaning (an 'accidental' development irreducible to a general process), rather than the Anglo-Saxon connotation of a 'precedent', relevant and revealing for the comprehension of the past, but also for locating historical fact in the context of the present.[58]

In spite of all this, one cannot skate over the fact that, in the Italian context, the danger of saturation is very far from manifesting itself as a real one, such and so numerous are the (at times basic) gaps in our knowledge. Analogous considerations have been raised in the French context by Jean-Pierre Daviet in the article cited earlier. On a more significant, methodological level, moreover, it seems senseless to counterpose company history to economic history in the manner suggested, in an implicitly self-critical way, by Roberto Romano, to whom indeed we owe an excellent book on the Caprotti cotton dynasty, truly to be considered a 'case study' in the best sense of the term.[59]

The dilemma, or pseudo-dilemma, inherent in such a counterposition has been appositely compared by Donald Coleman to the not unconvincing paradox on which Joseph Heller's novel, *Catch-22*, is based:

> It will be recalled that Joseph Heller's novel was set in an American Air Force bomber unit operating in Italy during the Second World War. If pilots went on flying more and more bombing raids (or 'combat missions' in USAF terminology) they were crazy and could be grounded. But if they applied to be grounded they were not crazy but sane, and therefore could be required to go on flying more missions. That was Catch-22. Or, as the OED puts it, 'a dilemma in which the victim always loses'. Business history's very own Catch-22 works like this. Business history, by definition, must use the records of business companies. The only way that business historians can normally get access to those records, however, is to be commissioned to write company histories. But if they go on writing company histories, they are failing to write business history in the wider sense. So they are stuck with their 'single cases' and 'inveterate empiricism'.[60]

With necessary modifications, particularly regarding what would seem to be a relatively fortunate position *vis-à-vis* archival access, the dilemma takes an analogous form in the Italian context: the need is felt for a business history 'in the wider sense', but at present the empirical ground for such a history is slippery and perilous; the case studies upon which to base an effectual comparison remain too few; above all, those which exist present only limited points of contact due to both archival inadequacies and the different approaches adopted by researchers.[61] Business history, and its 'pilots', would thus seem caught in a vicious circle.

In reality, a good many general reasons exist, not a few of them reinforced by the particular character of Italian industrial development, for believing that such a dilemma can be avoided, or at least that the risk of research becoming bogged down can be attenuated. Precisely in relation to the subjects of industry and business, Giorgio Mori underlined the dangers of a polarized historiography in which supporters of a 'history from below' oppose advocates of a 'history from above'; nevertheless (with this basic warning), he reaffirmed that investigation at the 'micro level' constitutes 'an experimental platform of an efficacy perhaps unsuspected'.[62] This potential efficacy, I would suggest, lies precisely in the alternation – to the point of convergence – of these two points of view; the 'depth of field' to be adopted being that which (to continue the metaphor borrowed from photography) guarantees the maximum 'definition' of the object against its natural background. The most significant contribution which company history can make is exactly that of rendering *visible* basic tendencies and characteristics which would otherwise remain indeterminate and unfocused.

Here I will proceed by hints, without any pretension to a systematic treatment. The first point to be dealt with is that of stages of development, a subject which has seen ever more frequent questioning of the Gerschenkronian periodization. To it has been explicitly contrasted, even if in problematic terms, a 'gradualist model' whose paternity should be attributed in the first instance to Franco Bonelli and Luciano Cafagna.[63] In this perspective, the discontinuities induced by the economic cycle or, more broadly, by major political decisions (the formation of an industrial base in the early years of the century, the 'mobilization' of the First World War, the war economy of the second half of the 1930s) are seen as contradictory; thus the role attributed to them by other scholars as epochal turning points, either singly or jointly, is removed. Such a model, structured on an evolution in successive waves up to the 'great transformation' of the years 1952–63, does not at all reduce the importance which the leading enterprises – stimulated and supported by the mixed banks and the state – have had in Italian economic development. On the contrary, it postulates a more detailed analysis of the long-term conditions which permitted their success.

To clarify, if a 'big spurt' model suggests the literal explosion, in the space of just a few years, of a nucleus of large enterprises in leading sectors, the gradualist model demands an understanding of what was at the basis of the emergence of such systems, as were promoted by the 'industrial house' of Marzotto or by Giovanni Agnelli, taking two examples considered earlier. Roverato's response is based, as was seen, on the ability of the Marzotto to integrate modernity and backwardness, developing the centralized factory on the basis of a 'soft' transition lasting a number of decades.[64] Castronovo, for his part, highlights the way in which the progressive affirmation of the Turin enterprise proceeds apace with the industrial apprenticeship of Giovanni Agnelli, symbolically coming from a sector as traditional as that of silk.[65] The, by now widespread, acceptance of the 'gradualist' perspective presupposes, in short, a reconsideration of the role of the entrepreneur in a relatively backward country – one which permits the emergence from wider social strata than historical research had supposed, which highlights the marriage within these strata of traditionalism and cultural modernity, and which singles out the concrete ways in which accumulation and the locating of resources are carried out. The specification, more than the reduction, of the role of external agents (the banks and the state) therefore allows a more positive evaluation of the endogenous energies, undoubtedly underestimated in the Gerschenkron-inspired literature,[66] animating the process of industrialization. This is all the more important since the application of the latter perspective to the Italian case has been grafted on to a liberal economic tradition of historiography which itself succeeded in finding very few 'heroes' to personify the type of entrepreneur whom it was hoped would appear.[67]

The 'eclectic' approach of Cafagna–Bonelli, precisely in that it grasps the dual character of an industrialization which contains indissolubly mixed Manchesterian and Gerschronkronian characteristics,[68] permits, on the other hand, a social figure with a determining role in the Italian context to be fully taken into account. I am referring to that category – the 'assisted' entrepreneur – in which such men as Vincenzo Stefano Breda, the Perrone brothers, Max Bondi and many, many others can be included. The rapid rise and, generally speaking, even more sudden fall of these protagonists cannot be considered simply as epiphenomena produced by the action of the banks and the state. The problem has been put with the greatest clarity by Cafagna himself:

> The conviction that the rise of enterprises was largely *assisted* does not justify disinterest in the specificity of the entrepreneurial component. In the first place this is because an *assisted* enterprise is not for that without an entrepreneurial component, with its own margins of initiative, of choice, of capacity to exploit the occasion. In the second place because it is necessary not to confuse forms of intervention which create, almost *ex novo*, the space for the initiative (e.g. steel) and those arising from the direct demand of constituted industrial interests which, for just that reason, are therefore already in some way in existence (and the demands themselves can also be considered as entrepreneurial acts *sui generis*).[69]

The names cited above already demonstrate the breadth of the category of the 'assisted' entrepreneur. Certainly Volpi differs from, let us say, Bondi, not only in the more favourable fate of the initiatives undertaken by the former, but also for a far more dynamic vision in finding capital, in alliances between groups, and in what was to be asked of the state. It is equally undeniable, however, that the line of demarcation which separates Volpi from Motta, Donegani or the more celebrated champions of private enterprise is a fairly fine one.

In this respect it seems to me that one must agree with Silvio Lanaro, who has recalled the decisive importance that political decisions have had on the actual structure of the Italian economy: from current legislation which, for example, has consistently favoured the diffusion of private road transport, to the great turning points such as the nationalization of electricity, permitting the survival of Edison and laying the bases for the creation of an anomalous colossus like Montedison. To be surprised by all this today seems rather ingenuous. Only the persistence of the commonplace of 'a productive apparatus expanding by itself … under the spontaneous impulse of a civil society which miraculously succeeds in freeing its energies from the fetters of the state'[70] can explain the clamour raised, for example, by the recent work of Alan Friedman[71] (the fundamental objection to which, incidentally, should be aimed at the image of absolute exceptionality attributed to the Italian case). The remarks made by Federico Caffè some years ago on this subject remain entirely appropriate:

> It does not appear to me, referring to the big private enterprises of the Italian economic system, that their salient characteristics are captured when the emphasis is placed on the connections, collusions and compromises with political power; nor when their influence in directing economic planning decisions along the lines most advantageous to their sectoral interests is underlined; nor in noting the flexibility with which they insert themselves into 'new models of development', where that shows itself fruitful for the consolidation of their hegemonic position – with the acquisition of large public contracts, for example. … At a general level, it seems incongruous to find motives for the condemnation of large-scale Italian enterprise as a whole in forms of behaviour typical of the oligopolistic structures which mark the present phase of capitalism. Its persistence – not without imperfections and contradictions, obviously, but still vigorous and creative – is due precisely to the adaptability and manoeuvrability of the great oligopolistic groups, an integral part of which is constituted by political pressure and collusion.[72]

This raises a second point: precisely, that is, the early and accentuated oligopolistic features of our country's economic development. One is dealing with a well-established fact, extensively discussed in the historiography[73] which has exhaustively illustrated the case of the steel sector and confirmed, at least in general terms, the image of a 'super-capitalism' – dominant since the 1930s – drawn by observers such as Alberto de' Stefani and Ettore Conti.[74] Nevertheless, even here it appears that much work still needs to be taken further or even begun.

Almost 30 years after the publication of Chandler's *Strategy and Structure* (a veritable lesson in method) and all the more since the grand synthesis provided by *The Visible Hand*, one cannot doubt the fertility of an historiographical approach aimed at understanding the large-scale enterprise, nor its capacity to clarify the alterations brought about by such enterprise in the structure of the principal economic sectors and the economy more generally.[75] According to Chandler, the theoretical 'suspicion' with which big business was viewed, at least until the 1930s, by the majority of economists – convinced that 'the modern, multi-unit enterprise, by its very act of administrative coordination, brings imperfect competition and misallocation of resources' – was accompanied by an even more prolonged lack of interest on the part of historians in the 'new institution' which the modern corporation represented.[76] On the basis of the firm opinion that such organisms represented nothing more than an aberration, investigating their *raison d'être* and intrinsic logic became superfluous. If their bulky presence on the scene could hardly be passed over in silence, successes and failures were imputed to the psychological character of the 'tycoons' deemed responsible for them. In any case, the corporations emerged as awkward elements in a picture where the real forces of development were traced to the subterranean action of a myriad of anonymous economic operators.

All of this is true in an even more accentuated fashion for the Italian case. Economic history, profoundly influenced by economic liberalism (even in practitioners with an entirely different ideological orientation), has traditionally condemned attempts at vertical integration and horizontal combination actuated by enterprises operating in primary sectors, and in particular in steel, chemicals and energy. The attention given to the clamorous failures of ILVA and Ansaldo, added to the predominantly journalistic evaluations of the braking role played by such enterprises as Montecatini and Edison, have not until very recently been accompanied by any serious examination of the decisions taken by these enterprises. The same is also true of cases which are generally indicated as examples of 'balanced', as opposed to distorted, growth – FIAT and Pirelli in particular.

The work which began with the important article of Ernesto Galli della Loggia (1970) and has since been undertaken on the case of Ansaldo indicates that, in reality, the Perrones' initiative – while undoubtedly out of proportion to the resources of the Genovese enterprise and the post-war Italian context – was the product of a situation created by the industrial backwardness of the country. Besides, the choice of an integrated and multi-sectoral advance had in an earlier phase been the key to the rise and fortunes of the Perrone.[77] Similarly, the new attention with which the steel industry has been examined in recent years has put in doubt the inevitability of the failure of Max Bondi's project, which in and of itself did not imply any industrial irrationality.[78]

The picture of large-scale Italian enterprise which emerges from these works – with the most provocative examples in relation to the historical common sense of just a few years ago having deliberately been chosen – permits a better understanding of the weight and importance of the growth strategies pursued by the successful enterprises. With respect to the international context, the technological adequacy of the leading experiments in many key sectors of the Italian economy in the period of the second industrial revolution is now beyond doubt; these include military and railway engineering, the automobile industry, electricity and rubber. But this is also true of a number of branches (or phases) of production even in those sectors where disequilibria and contradictions are more evident (steel, chemicals, artificial fibres, etc.). Nor does the situation of large-scale Italian enterprise appear so backward, with regard to management or the organization of production, at least in the European context. These conclusions have been made possible by studies placing the company at the centre of the field of observation, and which have thus succeeded in ranging across the various branches of production in which it was involved. The efficiency, manifest or potential, of the enterprise is often in danger of being overlooked by purely mono-sectoral research, just as the strict national perspective of many studies misses the activity of companies whose strategy for overcoming the restrictions of the internal market anticipated (even in the years before the First World War in some cases) a significant multinational engagement.[79] If all this is true of the big industrial complexes, it should be underlined that companies of a smaller dimension also operate, as Arthur Cole has noted, in 'interconnected, mutually supporting congeries of business units'. In contrast with the respresentation provided by economists who limit themselves to 'aligning' enterprises into branches of industry, the business historian must take into account the links and overlaps between the object of his/her analysis and the complex business system in which the single unit operates.[80] Whatever its limitations, such a viewpoint is extraordinarily sensitive to phenomena much less easy to observe from other angles. By adopting it, conflicts with rival enterprises in the national and international fields, with allied or hostile financial bodies and with the various branches of the state can be clearly highlighted, all of which implies a closer examination of the historical alternatives which existed and their possible outcomes.

All of this undoubtedly facilitates going beyond the assumptions lingering around an interpretation of Italian capitalism as being conditioned by 'original sins' and 'distortions'.[81] As should be taken for granted, the nature and significance of the imbalances inherent in the evolution of the industrial structure of our country are beyond doubt. What it is vital to reject, however, is the idea that the 'distortions' in Italian development are the inevitable result of deviation from a 'normal' model, assumed to be perfect or perfectible, in which everyone should (to quote Hirschman) 'perform at his peak form',[82] with the stragglers inevitably dropping out to be replaced by more adapted competitors. The history of the major productive units active in the Italian context – including those whose development appears, retrospectively, the most linear and optimizing – demonstrates that many of the crucial decisions taken by them were probably risky and certainly founded on a limited knowledge of the market; yet they were capable of recognizing and gathering 'resources and abilities that are hidden, scattered or badly utilized'.[83] The apparent simplicity of the productive combinations developed by pioneers such as Cantoni, Pirelli, Tosi, Breda, Agnelli and so on, should not hide the fact that their initiatives represented the rupturing and forcing of a situation which did not automatically lead in the direction of growth. On the contrary, the real functioning of the mechanism has operated, and continues to operate, through its being founded on a 'chain of disequilibria';[84] it is precisely within this chain, in more or less efficient and appropriate forms, that the spur to action on the part of businesses or public economic bodies is generated. The approach advocated tenaciously, but not without self-critical spirit, by Hirschman contains, moreover, an implicit invitation to the historical case study: 'To look at unbalanced growth means, in other words, to look at the dynamics of the development process *in the small*. But perhaps it is high time that we did just that.'[85]

In this logic the backwardness of sectors of the economy or industry is sought in the actual action of the most active cells of the system whilst, on the other hand, the utilization or failure to utilize available resources is not only the result of the greater or lesser congruence with an ideal model, but arises from the play of the conflicting forces in the field. Insofar as one of its fundamental aims is to verify the causes and forms of what Schumpeter defined as 'an indefinite state of warfare between firms',[86] from this point of view business history can also contribute to a new understanding of the historically given process of economic development in our country.

5. 'Agenda' for Business History in Italy

These are at least some of the reasons for which it appears not only opportune but particularly advantageous, for understanding the course of Italian industrial development, to continue research into company history. But it is necessary to reaffirm decisively that business history cannot limit itself to case studies, but must at the same time, and increasingly, set itself the task of comparison and generalization. Here, little more than a list of subjects on the agenda can be presented; while in some cases the work has already begun, in others it is a question of opening up paths into virtually unexplored territory.

Until now the distinction between enterprise and entrepreneurs has been avoided, not only for simplicity of exposition, but also in the conviction that it is impossible 'to write business history without writing the history of entrepreneurs and vice versa';[87] for that reason the definition of the boundary between the two fields was unnecessary for a preliminary treatment. That does not at all mean, evidently, that it is not necessary to give overt attention to the social figure of the entrepreneur and his three 'faces': personal, managerial and, more specifically, entrepreneurial.[88] It is precisely this subject which must be touched upon first. The background, behaviour and culture of entrepreneurs certainly do not comprise an area in which the Italian historiography under examination here is most deficient. On the contrary, it could be said that the empirical approach and narrative propensity largely dominating the relevant case studies have lavished attention on the human and social figure of the entrepreneur: to such an extent that many of them, including some of the best, are in the form of biographies. Nevertheless, we are a long way from possessing sufficient basic material to justify the realization of a 'biographical dictionary' of Italian businessmen comparable to those already produced in Great Britain and the US.[89] Even were such an initiative able to find the economic resources necessary, it is unlikely that it could be completed in the relatively short space of time which saw the publication of the five-volume dictionary promoted by the Business History Unit.[90] At the present stage of development of research in Italy, an effort of these proportions would, on the contrary, risk absorbing the intellectual energies of too many scholars for too long and might thus retard rather than further the advancement of research along broader lines.

This state of affairs is sufficient explanation for the inadequacy of the only attempt made until now to develop a picture of the historical development of Italian entrepreneurship as a whole: the volume of Martinelli, Chiesi and Dalla Chiesa which, particularly in the chapter dedicated by Chiesi to the 'origins of the economic ruling class', analyses a sample of 190 biographies.[91] The more than legitimate stress on the deficiencies of the empirical data available[92] only in part absolves Chiesi's study from the numerous factual errors and arbitrariness with which the material collected and its elaboration are strewn. The patent unrepresentativeness of the sample, on the other hand, renders highly dubious the statistical analysis conducted upon it, independently of the objections which could be advanced on the variables chosen and the use to which they are put.[93]

As far as a general synthesis of the characteristics of Italian entrepreneurship is concerned, prospects seem conditioned by the continuation of the basic work of producing biographies of men and 'dynasties', whether in the guise of essays of more or less ample scope and analytical depth, or in the less ambitious – but often extraordinarily penetrating – form of biographical essays.[94]

An indirect but essential contribution to this entrepreneurial 'census', moreover, will undoubtedly be furnished by the analyses of the formation and specific character of regional and 'local' economic systems, which (as is well known) represent one of the principal lines of development of recent economic history. If the 'success' of the regional dimension is fostered by vast editorial projects, it nonetheless has solid foundations. In the first place there is dissatisfaction with (or at least suspicion of) general interpretations of Italian history in which the enormous richness and complexity of local experience, without doubt deserving of attention, can only with difficulty be included. This is true for the relationship between development and underdevelopment in the far from immobile South, described by Bevilacqua, Barone and an array of young scholars; for the dual vocation, both industrial and financial, of the Veneto, for whom the role of 'third industrial region' is claimed in the analyses of Roverato, Lanaro and others; and for the indigenous entrepreneurial energy found in areas of diffuse industrialization in Tuscany or the Marches.[95]

In this way, a variety of issues have become the object of study in recent research: the network of interpersonal relationships – of kinship and acquaintance – at the basis of the often difficult task of finding the necessary financial means to begin an industrial enterprise; the economic hinterland and inter-regional exchanges; the greater or lesser degree of interpenetration with foreign capital; attempts at integration in the local and national administrative and political classes; the evolution of the particular culture or subcultures of the different actors, etc.[96]

The observations – in my view realistic – made so far on the backwardness of more general research on entrepreneurship and the necessity of postponing a synthesis do not by any means exclude the opportuneness of developing broad themes which go beyond a local or regional level. The classic question of the relationship between property and control, and the delayed emergence of the manager, represent a crucially important area. Here we have at our disposal the studies by Rugafiori and Bezza respectively, on the formation of the managing group of the publicly-owned steel industry and of Montecatini, the leading firm in the chemicals sector,[97] while the same problem is dealt with in other works on petroleum, communications and, above all, the financial sector.[98] It would certainly be interesting to complete the analysis of 'public' management, examining recruitment channels, careers, relations with political power, networks of friendship or common orientation, but it also seems necessary to verify the extent of the above-mentioned delays within the various sectors of private industry. It appears evident, in fact, that in the most technically advanced areas of production (such as electricity, chemicals and numerous branches of engineering), the emergence of a group of managers at various levels of the company hierarchy is a phenomenon which can be dated at least to the inter-war years and goes well beyond the emblematic case of Vittorio Valletta.[99]

The other pole of the problem of the manager is naturally that of the industrial dynasties. The maintenance of family control of firms transformed for decades into limited companies has led to the linearity of the genealogies on which its structure is founded, even to this day being identified as one of the typical characteristics of Italian capitalism. To borrow the well-known metaphor of Schumpeter, in the *Hotel Italia* – 'always full of people' – the guests who occupy the various rooms, and especially the best suites, always seem much the same.[100] Certainly many families have declined or even left the scene altogether, above all in the 1970s and early 1980s, as clearly demonstrated by a simple comparison of the list of the top hundred companies of today with that of 20 years ago.[101] But the important families have survived (it is sufficient to cite the names of Agnelli, Falck, Marzotto, Orlando, Pirelli, Pesenti) and with them a considerable number of those on the intermediate and lower rungs of the business ladder (one is assured that there are more than 400 cases of firms having reached the third generation).[102] This fact is widely celebrated in economic journalism, intent it seems on constructing around these great, contemporary industrial families that aura of social leadership which the founders lacked and, above all, were not inclined to assume – occupied as they were by the full development of their Marshallian 'nervous strength'.[103] Beyond these considerations, however, which might more profitably be investigated by scholars of the 'modern-day myth', the timeliness of extending a vein of research which until now has seen various single studies but no sectoral or regional works is evident.[104] The utilization of the techniques of family reconstruction developed in historical demography and, above all, the rich sociological literature on kinship will clearly be decisive here. On this basis it will be possible to deal with a series of questions extending well beyond the 'Buddenbrook syndrome' (or, to use the more common expression, the crisis of the third generation) which seems to have tormented out of all proportion not only superficial popularizers but also theorists of notable intelligence.[105]

The organizational forms and structure of enterprises present an analogous problem of formulating typologies at present largely non-existent, other than in the limited form for the years 1950–70 studied by Pavan.[106] Here one may note that Chandler's work has met with greater difficulties of diffusion in Italy than in other countries – such as Great Britain, Germany and Japan – and even today more often receives generic references of esteem rather than real attention to the indications for research which it can provide.[107] The centrality for the American historian of the development of an organization's structure from a functional to a multidivisional basis has probably led to a belief in the paradigm's inapplicability to a context such as the Italian one in which this passage has only become general since the 1960s and amidst not a little uncertainty and back-pedalling. Looking closely, this is not Chandler's central point, however, which on the contrary is founded on the nexus established between strategy and structure, between the modality of an enterprise's expansion and the organizational forms adequate (or, exactly the point, inadequate) to it.[108] The problem then becomes one of verifying the changes in the methods and substance of organization in Italy in the decades in which the company 'boss', whether owner-entrepreneur or salaried manager, prevailed. Are we sure, that is, that the 'delegation of power' was so irrelevant in the running of firms which were certainly expanding into forms of notable complexity at the level of integration, diversification and the penetration of new markets?[109] And even were this true, what were the causes of the failure to adapt structurally, and what the consequences? Moreover, how is it possible to fit into the evolutionary scheme of business organization the holding company, which in Italy assumed and in part continues to have characteristics completely different from those which this form has presented in the North American economy? Lastly, which types of bureaucratic organization were nevertheless developed within the predominantly functional structure?[110]

Remaining on the ground of comparative analysis and the 'forms' assumed by enterprise, the evolution of the juridical form of the company seems to be a field of research completely overlooked. A sort of rediscovery of the share-holding partnership, for example, seems to be underway at this moment, with the evident intention – despite its partisans' assertions to the contrary[111] – of maintaining secure family control over enterprises which have assumed a large share-holding participation. A significant theme of research might be represented precisely by the verification of the radically different role played by the partnership in the early stages of industrial development when, whilst it constituted a guarantee for the owners of capital *vis-à-vis* the entrepreneurial partner, also permitted the latter an agile and dynamic running of the firm. Along the same lines, one might undertake a detailed analysis of the crucial years of the all but general passage from the (usually simple) partnership to the limited company, while it would be necessary to conduct a systematic investigation of the influence exercised by the differences between Italian company law and that of such other countries as Great Britain, France and Germany.[112] Moreover one might study the application of company law within the dominant form of the public company itself. Undoubtedly business historians must begin to pick up the numerous suggestions for research furnished by legal historians, and in particular by the important volume of Paolo Ungari.[113]

Coming more particularly to the theme of the internal functions of the enterprise, we must once again return to Chandler, who has affirmed the necessity of not limiting oneself to the examination of the enterprise as 'essentially a unit of production', but to consider it as a complex institution in which decision-making processes and organizational forms closely interact.[114] In effect, for the reasons which we have sought to clarify, research in Italy has decidely favoured the productive function, placing at the centre of investigation product choices, plant and technological solutions and, to a certain extent, the methods of work organization. The latter subject – generally examined, as in the case of personnel functions, through its relationships with the trade unions – has been dealt with above all by historians of the labour movement who in recent years have approached the study of the firm.

Such an approach has brought significant rewards and is in part undoubtedly the result of a conscious choice aimed at avoiding the separation of business history from that of society more generally. In this sense the attention given to the productive process and the relations of production was a positive characteristic of the emergence of the discipline from a tradition which has refused to renounce its basic premises. But it is also true that this emphasis has resulted in the neglect of questions whose importance not only merits greater attention, but which appears essential to the understanding of the actual operation of the firm. This is precisely the case of the role which, according to Chandler, is played by the creation of distributive and service networks in the evolution of organizational forms.

If, for example, relationships with the banks have been thoroughly investigated (also because their papers can be integrated or substituted for lost company records), one cannot therefore affirm that financial functions have been studied sufficiently. The subject of business finance has generally been examined from the point of view of the banks, and by banking historians. Budgets, ledgers and other accounting instruments, even where they have survived destruction, have obtained scant attention from historians not always equipped for their interpretation. Thus, even now accounting methods and their evolution remain all but buried in obscurity.[115]

The other functions of the company remain equally obscure. Leaving aside research and development, which suffers in great measure from the backwardness of the technological history of the contemporary period,[116] this refers to the commercial sector as a whole. With a few exceptions, related to cases in which distribution played a preeminent role,[117] the creation of a commercial network, technical assistance and sales financing are generally mentioned only in passing in the text or relegated to footnotes. This is true even for enterprises such as automobile firms for whom the mass commercialization of the product constituted one of its decisive challenges.[118] If little or nothing is known, therefore, of marketing in general, neither can much weight be placed on the early studies of publicity and company image, focusing as they do on the aesthetic and communicative dimension.[119]

This long, and yet far from exhaustive, list of tasks and fields of investigation as yet unresearched would undoubtedly be such as to discourage rather than stimulate the scholar's work if it were not recognized that, as Schumpeter indicated, the fate of research seems to be to raise more problems than it has been able to resolve.[120] It should be added that in such a perspective – only apparently frustrating – historians have a place in the front line. Thus it will not be the task of an historian to underline the contribution which knowledge of the past can furnish to the various participants in the business system for their present activity. This should be taken for granted, on the condition that one shrinks from proposing once more the idea – ingenuous when not openly 'promotional' – that business history as a discipline can provide immediately applicable solutions for problems currently under discussion.

> The historian – has written Alfred D. Chandler – feels he has a different and more modest task. He merely hopes to re-create, or partially re-create, some small part of man's activities in the past. He is skeptical of predictions, particularly those based on past experience; he has seen so many of these go wrong. He is more concerned, I believe, with the real alternatives facing men, and why men took the alternatives that they did.[121]

Such a reminder of the limits of historical knowledge is all the more significant in that it was formulated within an historiography which has particularly insisted on the need to create models of the problems confronting, and choices made by, enterprises in the course of time. It is also significant in that the reminder of the primary and distinctive necessity to reconstruct human activity comes from an historian who certainly cannot be accused of descriptivism or empiricism. But the reader may have recognized an echo of Weber's observation, to which moreover Chandler explicitly refers: that which should be investigated is not the event, but the 'social action' of men, directed in view of the behaviour of other men. In other words, the event takes place in a given social context, follows reasons to be individualized, and presents regularities or irregularities which lend themselves to comparison:

Not every type of contact of human beings has a social character; this is rather confined to cases where the actor's behaviour is meaningfully oriented to that of others. For example, a mere collision of two cyclists may be compared to a natural event. On the other hand, their attempt to avoid hitting each other, or whatever insults, blows, or friendly discussion might follow the collision, would constitute 'social action'.[122]

Notes

1. This definition was proposed in A.D. Chandler Jr. and H. Daems, 'Introduction. The rise of managerial capitalism and its impact on investment strategy in the Western world and Japan', in H. Daems and H. van der Wee (eds) (1974), *The Rise of Managerial Capitalism*, Louvain–The Hague: Leuven University Press–M. Nijhoff, p. 28. According to the authors three types of decision-makers can be identified: entrepreneurs properly speaking, managers, and the 'financial outsiders', the last comprising 'the financial intermediaries such as banks and holding companies but also the Japanese Zaibatsu combines and the financial entrepreneurs represented by such famous names as J.P. Morgan and the Rothschilds'. The Italian equivalents of these institutions and protagonists seem obvious: besides the bankers who guided industrialization during the Giolittian period, there are the outstanding losers of the past (Bondi, the Perrone, Gualino, etc.), while the future of some of those involved in the clamorous events of recent times is open to question.
2. For a defence of the 'cognitive and classificatory' value of the concept of public enterprise against the 'sceptical thesis' which views it as 'a private enterprise run by the public administration', cf. S. Cassese (1985), 'L'impresa pubblica: storia di un concetto', *Economia pubblica*, pp. 3–6; now in S. Cassese (1987), *E' ancora attuale la legge bancaria del 1936? Stato banche e imprese pubbliche dagli anni '30 agli anni '80*, Roma: La Nuova Italia Scientifica, pp. 199–207.
3. G. Becattini and G. Bianchi, 'I distretti industriali nel dibattito sull'economia italiana', in G. Becattini (ed.) (1987), *Mercato e forze locali: il distretto industriale*, Bologna: Il Mulino, pp. 172–3.
4. G. Sapelli (1989), *L'Italia inafferrabile. Conflitto, sviluppo, dissociazione dagli anni cinquanta ad oggi*, Venezia: Marsilio, p. 48.
5. R. Morandi (1966), *Storia della grande industria in Italia*, Torino: Einaudi. Published originally in 1931 in Laterza's *Biblioteca di cultura moderna*, it was republished in 1959 by Einaudi in the *Opere di Rodolfo Morandi*. One cannot, however, fail to mention, among works on a regional scale, at least the classic study of G. Luzzatto (1923), 'L'evoluzione economica della Lombardia dal 1860 al 1922', in *La Cassa di risparmio delle provincie lombarde nella evoluzione economica della regione, 1823–1923*, Milano: Tip. Alfieri e Lacroix, pp. 447–526.
6. A. Fossati (1951), *Lavoro e produzione in Italia dalla metà del secolo XVIII alla Seconda guerra mondiale*, Torino: Giappichelli. For the judgment and quotations cited, see Cafagna's review in *Movimento operaio*, 1952, n. 3, pp. 527–30; but also the concordant remarks of G. Mori, 'La storia dell'industria italiana contemporanea nei saggi, nelle ricerche e nelle pubblicazioni giubilari', now in G. Mori (1967), *Studi di storia dell'industria*, Roma: Editori Riuniti, 2nd ed., pp. 275–80, where the accent, moreover, is placed on the precious documentary material collected in the pages of Fossati, to which it is necessary to refer even today more often than might be wished.
7. R. Romeo (1988), *Breve storia della grande industria in Italia 1861–1961*, Milano: Il Saggiatore (1st ed., reprinted and updated several times: Bologna: Cappelli, 1961); G. Luzzatto (1968), *L'economia italiana dal 1861 al 1894*, Torino: Einaudi, (1st ed.: Milano: Banca Commerciale Italiana, 1963); B. Caizzi (1965), *Storia dell'industria italiana dal XVIII secolo ai giorni nostri*, Torino: Utet; V. Castronovo (1980), *L'industria italiana dall'Ottocento ad oggi*, Milano: Mondadori.

8. G. Luzzatto (1957), *Per una storia economica d'Italia. Progressi e lacune*, Bari: Laterza, p. 24.
9. Romeo, *Breve storia* cit., p. 3. A not dissimilar warning appeared in the introduction to Roberto Tremelloni's (1947), *Storia dell'industria italiana contemporanea. Dalla fine del Settecento all'Unità italiana*, Torino: Einaudi, pp. xvii–xviii: 'The detailed history of single industries, each having its own particular story, has been omitted for the time being, since the size of the work would have been greatly increased, often at the expense of the unity of the narrative'.
10. For the 'above'–'below' contrast, cf. G. Mori (1983), 'Storiografia dell'impresa in Italia', *Studi storici*, no.1, pp. 132–3. For the quote from Schumpeter, cf. 'The Creative Response in Economic History', *Journal of Economic History*, **7** (2), November 1947, p. 150; translated in A. Pagani (ed.) (1967), *Il nuovo imprenditore*, Milano: Angeli.
11. The only two surveys specifically dedicated to business history in Italy appeared in the American *Business History Review*: cf. A.M. Romani (1966), 'Recent Developments of Business History in Italy', **XL**, pp. 108–17 and F. Amatori (1980), 'Entrepreneurial Typologies in the History of Industrial Italy (1880–1960): A Review Article', **LIV**, pp. 359–86.
12. For a remarkably complete survey, see G. Mori, 'La storia dell'industria' cit., pp. 251–381. To the bibliographic information on around 420 jubilee publications appended to that article must be added a further 50 titles noted in Mori (1970), 'Orientamento sulle fonti per la storia dell'industria e dell'imprenditorialità italiana nell'Ottocento', in *L'imprenditorialità italiana dopo l'Unità. L'inchiesta industriale del 1870–1874*, Milano: Etas Kompass. Mori's research would certainly merit expanding and updating, but such a task is obstructed, as indeed was confirmed during the preparation of the present bibliography, by the fact that commemorative publications in public and private libraries are often missing. For examples of such bibliographies, cf. H. Corsten (1937), *Hundert Jahre Deutscher Wirtschaft*, in *Fest- und Denkschriften, Eine Bibliographie*, Köln (more than 4,000 titles on German companies); *Verzeichnis der Fest- und Denkschriften von Unternehmungen und Organisationen der Wirtschaft im Hamburgischen Welt-Wirtschafts-Archiv*, 1961 (photostat, about 4,000 titles on companies throughout the world); Committee on the memorial project of the 10th anniversary of the foundation of Business History Society of Japan (comp.) (1979), *Union Catalog on Enterprise Histories and Biographies of Businessmen in the World outside of Japan*, Tokyo: Yushodo Booksellers Ltd. (about 6,000 from throughout the world possessed by Japanese and Soviet libraries).
13. Mori, 'La storia dell'industria' cit., p. 353.
14. At least the following should be cited: *Nel cinquantenario della Società Edison 1884–1934* (edited by Giorgio Mortara), Milano: Edison (tip. Bertieri), 1934, 4 vols; *La Società Montecatini ed il suo gruppo industriale nel venticinquesimo anno di amministrazione dell' onor. ing. Guido Donegani. Milano anno 1935/XIV E.F.*, Milano: Montecatini (tip. Bertieri), 1936; *ILVA. Alti forni ed acciaierie d'Italia 1897–1947*, Bergamo: Ist. it. d'arti grafiche, 1948; *Società di Monteponi. Centenario. 1850–1950*, Torino: Tip. Bona, 1950; A. Frumento, *Imprese lombarde nella storia della siderurgia italiana. Il contributo dei Falck. Vol. I: 1883–1913*, Milano: tip. Allegretti, 1952; E. Gazzo, *I cento anni dell'Ansaldo 1853–1953*, Genova: Ansaldo (tip. Sigla), 1953; *Franco Tosi Società per Azioni 1876–1956*, Legnano: F. Tosi (Milano: Unione tipografica), 1956; C. Ucelli, *La Riva in cento anni di lavoro 1861–1961*, Milano: Riva (Alfieri & Lacroix), 1961.
15. G. Mori, 'Premesse e implicazioni di una recente specializzazione storiografica americana: la Entrepreneurial History', in *Studi di storia* cit., pp. 43–79 (originally published in *Studi storici*, 1959–60, pp. 775–92); A. Pagani (1967), *La formazione dell'imprenditorialità*, Milano: Etas Kompass (1st ed.: Milano: Comunità, 1964).
16. L. Cafagna (1973), 'L'avventura industriale di Giovanni Agnelli e la storia imprenditoriale italiana', *Quaderni storici*, no. 22, p. 150. This and other essays cited have finally been collected in Cafagna (1989), *Dualismo e sviluppo nella storia d'Italia*, Venezia: Marsilio.
17. Mori, 'Premesse e implicazioni' cit., pp. 55, 62 and 78.
18. For the Center's role in Chandler's formation, see T.K. McCraw, 'The Intellectual Odyssey

of Alfred D. Chandler, Jr.' in McCraw (ed.) (1988), *The Essential Alfred Chandler. Essays Toward a Historical Theory of Big Business*, Boston MA: Harvard Business School Press, pp. 6ff.; for a careful study of the Center's history, see S.A. Sass (1986), *Entrepreneurial Historians and History. Leadership and Rationality in American Economic Historiography 1940–1960*, New York and London: Garland.

19. Information on the Pavia Centre's activities was given to me by Mathias Deichmann, who, with Giancarlo Origgi, was among its founders. As far as the historiographical results of the Centre's work are concerned, one can mention the volume *L'imprenditorialità italiana dopo l'Unità cit.*, containing contributions by M. Abrate, G. Are, M. Deichmann, F. Indovina, G. Mori, G. Origgi and A. Pagani. The article by Are referred to is 'Una fonte per lo studio della fondazione industriale in Italia: l'inchiesta del 1870–74', *Studi storici*, 1963, no. 2, pp. 241–91 and no. 3, pp. 479–520, reprinted in Are (1974), *Alle origini dell'Italia industriale*, Napoli: Guida, pp. 5–112. As was inevitable given his background, Pagani's proposal for historical verification was more favourably received in sociological circles. Among the most significant incursions into the historical field by sociologists, note G. Baglioni's (1974) study, *L'ideologia della borghesia industriale nell'Italia liberale*, Torino: Einaudi, and the articles by other scholars of the Institute of Sociology of the Università Cattolica di Milano such as Agopik Manoukian, Giancarlo Provasi and Guido Romagnoli. Whilst Baglioni's attempt to create a typology of entrepreneurial ideology does not appear particularly revealing for historians, important results should be recognized in the examination of orientations towards social dynamics and class conflict. The dearth of historical literature available at the time, on the other hand, forced Baglioni to eschew a systematic treatment and fall back on the examination of specific industrial situations and personalities; among these, the chapter dedicated to the social conservatism of the Milanese industrial bourgeoisie is without doubt particularly illuminating and well supported by original research.

20. V. Castronovo (1971), *Giovanni Agnelli*, Torino: Utet (reprinted in 1977 with the title *Giovanni Agnelli. La Fiat dal 1899 al 1945*, Torino: Einaudi). In the debate which followed its publication, the intervention by Cafagna, 'L'avventura industriale' cit., which will be referred to often in the following pages, stands out for the range of issues raised. In a recent examination of historical work on Piedmontese industry, Giulio Sapelli identifies the 'conducting thread' of Agnelli's biography in the analysis of the 'government of the enterprise and in the relationships enterprise-technology, enterprise-market' ('Storia dell'industria e storia dell'impresa del Piemonte dal 1861 ad oggi. Un contributo alla discussione' in L. Avagliano (ed.) (1988), *L'Italia industriale nelle sue regioni: bilancio storiografico*, Napoli: Esi, p. 70). I agree more with Sapelli on the major historiographical importance of Castronovo's 'diptych', *L'industria laniera in Piemonte nel secolo XIX*, Torino: Ilte, 1964 and *L'industria cotoniera in Piemonte nel secolo XIX*, Torino: Ilte, 1965. If the work on Agnelli has been favoured here, it is solely due to its 'paradigmatic' importance for business history.

21. F. Bonelli (1975), *Lo sviluppo di una grande impresa in Italia. La Terni dal 1884 al 1962*, Torino: Einaudi. The research begun with the work on Terni laid the foundations for a further study by Bonelli and a group of researchers coordinated by him, on the controversial introduction of the integrated cycle in the Italian steel industry; cf. Bonelli (ed.) (1982), *Acciaio per l'industrializzazione. Contributi allo studio del problema siderurgico italiano*, Torino: Einaudi. The manager referred to concerning the deposit of Terni's records was Gian Lupo Osti, then managing director of the firm. I may note in passing his ironic remark on the excessive caution with which the majority of enterprises have in the past confronted (and in part continue to confront) the issue of opening company archives to scholars: basically, he suggested, 'a pirate ancestor is not a problem in the genealogy of the best families'; in 'Tavola rotonda sugli archivi delle imprese industriali', *Rassegna degli Archivi di Stato*, gennaio-aprile 1973, p. 54.

22. See Bonelli, *Lo sviluppo di una grande impresa* cit. pp. x–xi; among recent studies on Terni and the history of the working class, see especially G. Gallo (1983), *Ill.mo Signor Direttore ... Grande industria e società a Terni fra Otto e Novecento*, Foligno: Editoriale Umbra, and

A. Portelli (1985), *Biografia di una città. Storia e racconto: Terni 1830–1985*, Torino: Einaudi.

23. Cf. A. Confalonieri (1974–76), *Banca e industria in Italia 1894–1906*, Milano: Banca Commerciale Italiana, 3 vols (reprinted in paperback edition: Bologna: Il Mulino, 1979–80); Confalonieri (1982), *Banca e industria in Italia dalla crisi del 1907 all'agosto 1914*, Milano: Banca Commerciale Italiana, 2 vols. For the expressions quoted, cf. *Banca e industria* cit., vol. III, pp. 251 and 461. A contribution of particular importance for contextualizing the Italian situation in the wider European banking system is provided by Peter Hertner's article, 'Banche e formazione di capitali nell'età giolittiana', in Hertner (1984), *Il capitale tedesco in Italia dall'Unità alla prima guerra mondiale. Banche miste e sviluppo economico italiano*, Bologna: Il Mulino, pp. 161–274.
24. Among the most stimulating work appearing during the years of developing interest in entrepreneurship see, besides those already noted: G. Mori (1966), *L'industria del ferro in Toscana dalla Restaurazione alla fine del Granducato (1815–1859)*, Torino: Ilte; M. Abrate (1967), *La lotta sindacale nella industrializzazione in Italia 1906–1926*, Milano: Angeli; S. Zaninelli (1967), *L'industria del cotone in Lombardia dalla fine del Settecento all'unificazione del paese*, Torino: Ilte; L. de Rosa (1968), *Iniziativa e capitale straniero nell'industria metalmeccanica del Mezzogiorno, 1840–1904*, Napoli: Giannini; V. Castronovo (1969), *Economia e società in Piemonte dall'Unità al 1914*, Milano: Banca Commerciale Italiana; G. Doria (1969 and 1973), *Investimenti e sviluppo economico a Genova alla vigilia della prima guerra mondiale*, Milano: Giuffrè, 2 vols; F. Bonelli (1971), *La crisi del 1907. Una tappa dello sviluppo industriale in Italia*, Torino: Fondazione L. Einaudi; B. Caizzi (1972), *L'economia lombarda durante la Restaurazione (1814–1859)*, Milano: Banca Commerciale Italiana; R. Webster (1974), *L'imperialismo industriale italiano 1908–1915. Saggio sul prefascismo*, Torino: Einaudi; as well as the collection of essays by G. Are, *Alle origini dell'Italia industriale*, cit. and G. Mori (1977), *Il capitalismo industriale in Italia*, Roma: Editori Riuniti. Among the monographs: S. Spreafico (1968), *Un'industria, una città. Cinquant'anni alle Officine 'Reggiane'*, Bologna: Il Mulino; B. Caizzi (1969), *Camillo e Adriano Olivetti*, Torino: Utet; L. Avagliano (1970), *Alessandro Rossi e le origini dell'Italia industriale*, Napoli: Libreria Scientifica Editrice. For less summary references, see the detailed review by V. Castronovo (1979), 'Lo sviluppo economico nella storia dell'Italia unita', *Rivista Storica Italiana*, no.1, pp. 107–43.
25. J.P. Daviet (1987), 'Existe-t-il une Business History française?', *Annali di storia dell'impresa*, no. 3, pp. 428–84.
26. On the development and present situation of company archives, see especially the monographic number of *Rassegna degli Archivi di Stato*, 1984, no. 2–3, edited by P. Carucci; L. Borghi and G. Fabbrici (eds) (1986), *Archivi d'impresa e archivistica industriale. L'archivio storico dell'Azienda Consorziale Trasporti di Reggio Emilia*, Bologna: Analisi; and the journal *Archivi e Imprese*, edited by Fondazione Assi beginning in 1990.
27. Sapelli (1976), 'Appunti per una storia dell'organizzazione scientifica del lavoro in Italia', *Quaderni di Sociologia*, no. 2–3, p. 155 (now collected in Sapelli (1990), *L'impresa come soggetto storico*, Milano: Il Saggiatore). The research suggestions made in this article have been developed by Sapelli himself in the essays, *Organizzazione, lavoro e innovazione industriale nell'Italia tra le due guerre*, Torino: Rosenberg & Sellier, 1978, and 'Gli "organizzatori della produzione" tra struttura d'impresa e modelli culturali', *Storia d'Italia. Annali*, Vol. 4, Torino: Einaudi, 1981, pp. 655–71, and also in a number of articles contained in Vol. XX (1979–80) of the *Annali della Fondazione Gian Giacomo Feltrinelli* on 'La classe operaia durante il fascismo'. For a survey of the debate in the 1970s, see A. Pescarolo (1979), 'Storia della classe operaia e "operaismo" in Italia. Alcuni problemi interpretativi', *Movimento operaio e socialista*, no. 1, pp. 104–28. Among the most important volumes to appear in the period covered by the bibliography, see the articles contained in Vol. I (1980) of the *Annali dell'Istituto Veneto per la Storia della Resistenza* on 'Impresa e manodopera nell'industria tessile'; G. Berta (1978), 'Dalla manifattura al sistema di fabbrica: razionalizzazione e conflitti di lavoro', *Storia d'Italia. Annali*, Vol. I, Torino: Einaudi, pp.

1081–129; A. Camarda and S. Peli (1980), *L'altro esercito. La classe operaia durante la prima guerra mondiale*, Milano: Feltrinelli; M.S. Rollandi (1981), *Miniere e minatori in Sardegna. Dalla crisi del primo dopoguerra alla nascita di Carbonia (1919–1939)*, Cagliari: Della Torre; P. Rugafiori (1981), *Uomini, macchine, capitali. L'Ansaldo durante il fascismo 1922–1945*, Milano: Feltrinelli; G. Procacci (ed.) (1983), *Stato e classe operaia in Italia durante la prima guerra mondiale*, Milano: Angeli; B. Bezza (1986), *Salario e cannoni. Tra la fabbrica e il fronte durante la grande guerra*, Roma: Ediesse; S. Musso (1987), *La gestione della forza lavoro sotto il fascismo. Razionalizzazione e contrattazione collettiva nell'industria metallurgica torinese (1910–1940)*, Milano: Angeli.

28. An 'historical-thematic bibliography' of industrial archaeology research (edited by L. Bisi, O. Selvafolta and D. Volontè) appeared in A. Castellano (1982), *La macchina arrugginita. Materiali per un'archeologia dell'industria*, Milano: Feltrinelli; for an update, see the informational note (unfortunately rendered abundantly cryptic by editorial carelessness) by L. Palmucci Quaglino (1988?), 'Le fonti bibliografiche', in *Archeologia e storia industriale nel biellese. Archivi e fonti. Atti del Convegno, 23–24 ottobre 1987*, Biella: Comitato per l'archeologia industriale, s.d., pp. 147–151. At least the following exhibition catalogues, edited with scientific rigour, can be noted: *Arte e industria a Firenze. La Fonderia del Pignone 1842–1954*, Milano: Electa, 1983; C. Binel (ed.) (1985), *Dall'Ansaldo alla Cogne. Un esempio di siderurgia integrale 1917–1945*, Milano: Electa; M. Dezzi Bardeschi and F. Foggi (eds) (1985), *Le Officine Galileo, La filigrana, i frammenti, l'oblio*, Firenze: Alinea; F. Foggi (ed.) (1985), *Nel segno di Saturno. Origini e sviluppo dell'attività conciaria a Santa Croce sull'Arno*, Santa Croce sull'Arno: Museo della zona del cuoio and Centro di documentazione e informazione sull'archeologia industriale; *Immagini e spazi urbani. Sestri Ponente 1860–1960*, Milano: Electa, 1986.
29. Among the most significant and methodologically aware studies, note L. Passerini (1984), *Torino operaia e fascismo. Una storia orale*, Roma and Bari: Laterza; G. Contini (1985), *Memoria e storia. Le officine della Galileo nel racconto degli operai, dei tecnici, dei manager 1944–1959*, Milano: Angeli; A. Portelli, *Biografia di una città* cit.; L. Ganapini (ed.) (1986), *...anche l'uomo doveva essere di ferro. Classe e movimento operaio a Trieste nel secondo dopoguerra*, Milano: Angeli.
30. Particularly worthy of note in this context, for the solidity of formulation, are F. Piva and G. Tattara (eds) (1983), *I primi operai di Marghera. Mercato, reclutamento, occupazione 1917–1940*, Venezia: Marsilio, and F. Ramella (1984), *Terra e telai. Sistemi di parentela e manifattura nel Biellese dell'Ottocento*, Torino: Einaudi. Also to be noted is a precursory study of Olivetti by G. Maggia, 'Sviluppo economico e condizione operaia in un'area in via di industrializzazione: il Canavese tra le due guerre. Documentazione statistica di base', in E. Passerin et al. (1978), *Movimento operaio e sviluppo economico in Piemonte negli ultimi cinquant'anni*, Torino: Cassa di risparmio di Torino, pp. 263–452. For more detailed references, see also M. Lungonelli (1990), 'Una fonte per un mutamento di prospettiva: la classe operaia italiana nei libri matricola', *Archivi e Imprese*, no. 1, pp. 20–26.
31. Among the very diverse studies produced by authors coming from the field mentioned, see G. Berta (1980), *Le idee al potere. Adriano Olivetti tra la fabbrica e la comunità*, Milano: Comunità; also the contributions of M. Pozzobon in M.C. Cristofoli and M. Pozzobon (1981), *I tessili milanesi. Le fabbriche, gli industriali, i lavoratori, il sindacato dall'Ottocento agli anni '30*, Milano: Angeli, and in *Acciaio per l'industrializzazione* cit.; F. Levi (1984), *L'idea del buon padre. Il lento declino di un'industria familiare*, Torino: Rosenberg & Sellier; B. Bezza (ed.) (1986), *Energia e sviluppo. L'industria elettrica italiana e la Società Edison*, Torino: Einaudi; the contributions of Paletta and Bottiglieri in V. Castronovo, G. Paletta, R. Giannetti and B. Bottiglieri (1987), *Dalla luce all'energia. Storia dell'Italgas*, Roma and Bari, Laterza; B. Bottiglieri (1988), *Stet. Strategie e struttura delle telecomunicazioni*, Milano: Angeli; D. Bigazzi (1988), *Il Portello. Operai tecnici e imprenditori all'Alfa Romeo (1906–1926)*, Milano: Angeli; F. Amatori (1989), *Proprietà e direzione. La Rinascente 1917–1969*, Milano: Angeli; B. Bottiglieri (1990), *Sip. Impresa, tecnologia e Stato nelle telecomunicazioni italiane*, Milano: Angeli.

32. Cf. for example, in relation to Lombardy, M.C. Cristofoli and M. Pozzobon, *I tessili milanesi* cit., a volume realized on the initiative of the Filtea-Cgil di Milano; the two volumes promoted by the Ires-Cgil Lombardia (1985), *Pirelli 1914–1980. Strategia aziendale e relazioni industriali nella storia di una multinazionale*, Milano: Angeli; the two studies of P. Macchione, sponsored respectively by the Fiom-Cgil of Varese and the district of Busto Arsizio-Legnano: *L'Aeronautica Macchi. Dalla leggenda alla storia*, Milano: Angeli, 1985, and *L'oro e il ferro. Storia della Franco Tosi*, Milano: Angeli, 1987; and also G. Cortella (1989), *I Badoni e l'industria del ferro nell'800 lecchese*, Milano: Angeli, published in the series edited by the Consorzio degli archivi e dei centri di documentazione Cgil Lombardia.
33. Among studies of industrial sectors or local areas published since the works of Castronovo, Bonelli and Confalonieri referred to in the text, one can mention: the monographic issue of *Ricerche Storiche*, 1978, no.1, on 'La siderurgia italiana dall'Unità ad oggi'; V. Zamagni (1978), *Industrializzazione e squilibri regionali in Italia. Bilancio dell'età giolittiana*, Bologna: Il Mulino; a number of articles contained in G. Toniolo (ed.) (1978), *Industria e banca nella grande crisi 1929–1934*, Milano: Etas Libri; J. Davis (1979), *Società e imprenditori nel regno borbonico 1815–1860*, Bari: Laterza; M. Pizzigallo (1981), *Alle origini della politica petrolifera italiana (1920–1925)*, Milano: Giuffrè; S. Angeli (1982), *Proprietari, commercianti e filandieri a Milano nel primo Ottocento. Il mercato delle sete*, Milano: Angeli; Bonelli (ed.), *Acciaio per l'industrializzazione* cit.; L. Mio (1983), *Industria e società a Pordenone dall'Unità al fascismo*, Brescia: Paideia; G. Fiocca (ed.) (1984), *Borghesi e imprenditori a Milano dall'Unità alla prima guerra mondiale*, Roma and Bari: Laterza; R. Giannetti (1985), *La conquista della forza. Risorse, tecnologia ed economia nell'industria elettrica italiana (1883–1940)*, Milano: Angeli; S. Zaninelli (ed.) (1988–91), *Storia dell'industria lombarda*, Milano: Il Polifilo (3 vols); G. Barone and C. Torrisi (eds) (1989), *Economia e società nell'area dello zolfo (secoli xix–xx)*, Caltanissetta: Sciascia; R. Romano (1990), *La modernizzazione periferica. L'Alto Milanese e la formazione di una società industriale 1750–1914*, Milano: Angeli; R. Petri (1990), *La frontiera industriale. Territorio, grande industria e leggi speciali prima della Cassa per il Mezzogiorno*, Milano: Angeli; A. De Benedetti (1990), *La Campania industriale. Intervento pubblico e organizzazione produttiva tra età giolittiana e fascismo*, Napoli: Athena; R. Romano (1992), *L'industria cotoniera lombarda dall'Unità al 1914*, Milano: Banca commerciale italiana.
34. On case studies of firms or entrepreneurs, adopting the same criteria as in the preceding notes, see: G. Busino (1977), *Vilfredo Pareto e l'industria del ferro nel Valdarno*, Milano: Banca Commerciale Italiana; R. Romano (1980), *I. Caprotti. L'avventura economica e umana di una dinastia industriale della Brianza*, Milano: Angeli; M. Pizzigallo (1984), *L'AGIP degli anni ruggenti (1926–1932)*, Milano: Giuffrè; R. Romano (1985), *I Crespi. Origini, fortuna e tramonto di una dinastia lombarda*, Milano: Angeli; G. Conti (1985), *La politica aziendale di un istituto di credito immobiliare: il Monte dei Paschi di Siena dal 1815 al 1872*, Firenze: Olschki; G.L. Fontana (ed.) (1985–86), *Schio e Alessandro Rossi. Imprenditorialità, politica, cultura e paesaggi sociali del secondo Ottocento*, Roma: Ed. di Storia e Letteratura (2 vols); G. Roverato (1986), *Una casa industriale. I Marzotto*, Milano: Angeli; S. Candela (1986), *I Florio*, Palermo: Sellerio; Castronovo, Paletta, Giannetti and Bottiglieri, *Dalla luce all'energia* cit.; A. Casali and M. Cattaruzza (1990), *Sotto i mari del mondo. La Whitehead 1875–1990*, Bari: Laterza; G. Doria (1990), *Debiti e navi. La compagnia di Rubattino 1839–1881*, Genova: Marietti; A.M. Falchero (1990), *La Banca italiana di Sconto 1914–1921*, Milano: Angeli; C. Fumian (1990), *La città del lavoro. Un'utopia agroindustriale nel Veneto contemporaneo*, Venezia: Marsilio; A. Giuntini (1990), *Dalla Lyonnaise alla Fiorentinagas 1839–1989*, Bari: Laterza; *I Duchi di Galliera. Alta finanza, arte e filantropia tra Genova e l'Europa nell'Ottocento*, Genova: Marietti, 1991 (2 vols); P. Rugafiori (1992), *Ferdinando Maria Perrone da Casa Savoia all'Ansaldo*, Torino: Utet.
35. The results of the CIRIECs work may be judged by glancing at the list of titles published from 1956 in the series 'Studi e documenti sul settore pubblico dell'economia', 'Studi e ricerche CIRIEC' and 'Studi e monografie' (the latter published privately); the review 'Economia pubblica' has been published since May 1971 in continuation of the 'Bollettino dell'economia

pubblica' and 'CIRIEC. Notizie ai soci'. The volumes specifically referred to in the text are: A. Mortara (ed.) (1984), *I protagonisti dell'intervento pubblico in Italia*, Milano: Angeli; Bottiglieri, *Stet* cit.; G. Are and M. Costa (1989), *Carbosarda. Attese e delusioni di una fonte energetica nazionale*, Milano: Angeli; M. Doria (1989), *Ansaldo. L'impresa e lo Stato*, Milano: Angeli; B. Bottiglieri (1990), *Sip* cit.; L. Segreto (1991), *Monte Amiata. Il mercurio italiano: strategie internazionali e vincoli extraeconomici*, Milano: Angeli; A. Marchi and R. Marchionatti (1992), *Montedison 1966–1989*, Milano: Angeli; A. Mantegazza and C. Pavese (1992), *L'ATM di Milano*, Milano: Angeli.

36. *La Breda. Dalla Società italiana Ernesto Breda alla Finanziaria Ernesto Breda 1886–1986*, Milano: Pizzi; *La nazionalizzazione dell'energia elettrica. L'esperienza italiana e di altri paesi europei*, Bari: Laterza, 1989; *Confindustria, Guida all'Archivio storico della Confindustria 1910–1990*, Roma: Sipi, 1990; *Dalmine, Archivio storico,* Dalmine, 1991; G. Mori (ed.) (1992), *Storia dell'industria elettrica in Italia. 1. Le origini 1882–1914*, Bari: Laterza (first of a series of five volumes).
37. Besides the conferences promoted in 1982 by Ansaldo ('Beni culturali ricerca storica e impresa') and the Azienda Municipale dei Trasporti of Genova ('Salvaguardia e valorizzazione degli archivi d'impresa'), in 1984 by FIAT ('La memoria dell'industria'), note the volumes produced by the CNR and the Sovrintendenza archivistica per la Toscana (1982), *Archivi di imprese industriali in Toscana*, Firenze: All'Insegna del Giglio; by the Soprintendenza archivistica per il Lazio (1987), *Guida degli archivi economici a Roma e nel Lazio*, edited by M. Guercio, Roma: Ministero per i beni culturali e ambientali; by the Sovrintendenza archivistica per il Veneto (1987), *Archivi delle Aziende municipalizzate*, edited by G. Bonfiglio Dosio, Venezia: Giunta Regionale del Veneto; and by the Regione Lombardia (1990), *Gli archivi d'impresa nell'area milanese. Censimento descrittivo*, edited by D. Bigazzi, Milano: Bibliografica. As far as business organizations are concerned, the projects underway on the part of chambers of commerce were presented at a conference held in Perugia in November 1988, promoted by the Fondazione ASSI, the Fondazione A. Olivetti, the Istituto per la storia dell'Umbria contemporanea (Isuc) and the Sovrintendenza archivistica per l'Umbria: *Gli archivi delle camere di commercio*, edited by Giampaolo Gallo, Perugia: Editoriale Umbra, 1989.
38. 'Per la costituzione di un gruppo di studio permanente sui problemi di storia dell'impresa' (report of a meeting held at the Gramsci Institute of Turin on 19 May 1981).
39. Besides Giannetti, *La conquista della forza* cit. and Roverato, *Una casa industriale* cit., the following have appeared in the series: F. Marcoaldi, *Vent'anni di economia e politica. Le carte De' Stefani (1922–1941)*, 1986; Fondazione Assi-Isuc (ed.), *Piccola e grande impresa: un problema storico*, 1987; D. Bigazzi (ed.), *La storia d'impresa in Italia. Saggio bibliografico: 1980–1987*, 1989 (all published by Angeli of Milan); F. Amatori and B. Bezza (eds), *Montecatini 1888–1966. Capitoli di storia di una grande impresa*, 1990; P.A. Toninelli, *La Edison. Contabilità e bilanci di una grande impresa elettrica* (1884–1916), 1990; M. Balconi, *La siderurgia italiana (1945–1990). Tra controllo pubblico e incentivi del mercato*, 1991; R. Giannetti and P.A. Toninelli (eds), *Innovazione, impresa e sviluppo economico*, 1991; M. Lungonelli, *La Magona d'Italia. Impresa, lavoro e tecnologie in un secolo di siderurgia toscana (1865–1975)*, 1991; M. Magatti, *Mercato e forze sociali. Due distretti tessili: Lancashire e Ticino Olona 1950–1980*, 1991; G. Roverato, *Nuovo Pignone. Le sfide della maturità*, 1991; G. Sapelli and S. Zan, *Costruire l'impresa. La Cooperativa Muratori e Cementisti di Ravenna dal 1945 al 1972*, 1991; P.P. Saviotti, L. Simonin and V. Zamagni, *Dall'ammoniaca ai nuovi materiali. Storia dell'Istituto di ricerche chimiche Guido Donegani di Novara*, 1991 (all published by Il Mulino of Bologna). Other publications arising from the scientific activity of the ASSI include: G. Gallo (ed.) (1987), *Archivi d'impresa: un problema aperto. Atti del seminario di Perugia, 27 marzo 1987*, Foligno, Editoriale Umbra (also in collaboration with the Istituto per la Storia dell'Umbria contemporanea) and Bezza (ed.), *Energia e sviluppo* cit.
40. While the proceedings of the conference on 'large and small enterprise' were published by Angeli (see preceding note), those from the conference 'enterprise and technology' were

published by Il Mulino (see preceding note) and by Clarendon Press: G. Dosi, R. Giannetti and P.A. Toninelli (eds) (1991), *Technology and Enterprise in an Historical Perspective*.

41. *Business Enterprise in its Social Setting*, Cambridge MA: Harvard University Press, 1959, p. xi (cited in L. Galambos, *Business History and the Theory of the Growth of the Firm*, 'Explorations in Entrepreneurial History', 2nd series, 1966, n.1, p. 16).
42. Ibid.
43. F. Amatori, 'Introduzione' to A.D. Chandler Jr. (1981), *La mano visibile: la rivoluzione manageriale in America*, Milano: Angeli, pp. 11–36; C. Ciborra (1985), 'Scambio, potere e coordinamento: il dibattito recente sullo sviluppo dell'impresa', *Annali di storia dell'impresa*, no. 1, pp. 13–53; P.A. Toninelli (1987), 'Il progresso tecnico e la storia: ovvero come rendere virtuoso il paradigma economico', ibid., no. 3, pp. 11–28; R. Giannetti, 'Clio e la scatola nera: l'analisi del progresso tecnico tra storia e teoria economica', ibid., pp. 29–43; C. Antonelli, 'L'impresa rete: cambiamento tecnologico, internalizzazione e appropriazione di quasi rendite', ibid., pp. 79–115; G. Sapelli (1987), 'Gruppi d'impresa e trasformazione della sovranità popolare', *Stato e mercato*, no. 21, pp. 345–73.
44. G. Sapelli (1987), 'Il professor Roverato e il professor Bairati: ovvero dell'utilità e del danno della "storia d'impresa" in Italia', *Società e Storia*, no. 38, p. 949 (now collected in G. Sapelli, *L'impresa come soggetto storico* cit.).
45. Bezza, *Energia e sviluppo* cit.
46. Cf. Confalonieri, *Banca e industria* cit.; Hertner, *il capitale tedesco* cit.; Giannetti, *La conquista della forza* cit.
47. Roverato, *Una casa industriale* cit.
48. Bigazzi, *Il Portello* cit.
49. Castronovo, *Lo sviluppo economico* cit., pp. 121–2; the volumes to which Castronovo was referring were: Frumento, *Imprese lombarde* cit.; B. Caizzi, *Camillo e Adriano Olivetti* cit.; Bonelli, *Lo sviluppo di una grande impresa* cit.; Castronovo, *Giovanni Agnelli* cit.; Abrate, *La lotta sindacale* cit.
50. S. Lanaro (1988), *L'Italia nuova. Identità e sviluppo 1861–1988*, Torino: Einaudi, p. 19.
51. G. Toniolo (1988), *Storia economica dell'Italia liberale 1850–1918*, Bologna: Il Mulino, p. 236. But Luciano Cafagna already indicated many years ago the necessity of going beyond the 'simple description, or vital statistics of company histories' (*L'avventura intellettuale* cit., p.151n). Dissatisfaction with case-study analyses in management studies is, however, also widespread among industrial economists; cf., for example, M. Rispoli (1985), 'Per un approccio storico allo studio dell'impresa', *Economia e politica industriale*, no. 46, pp. 8–9.
52. Cf. P.L. Payne (1962), 'The Uses of Business History: a Contribution to a Discussion', *Business History*, no. 1, p. 15 and D. Coleman (1987), 'The Uses and Abuses of Business History', ibid., no. 2, p. 145, both referring to the debate in *Business History Review*, 1959 and 1962. For an account of the debate, presented as a proposal for going beyond the dead end of a purely methodological debate, see Galambos, *Business History* cit., pp. 3–4.
53. R. Church (1976), 'Business History in Britain', *Journal of European Economic History*, p. 215.
54. Coleman, *The Uses and Abuses* cit., p. 154 (taking up again the recurrent self-criticisms voiced within the Business History Unit between 1979 and 1983; cf. ibid., p. 141).
55. As examples of work done on commission in which prestigious historians certainly did not express the best of themselves, it is enough to cite L. de Rosa (1982–83), *Storia del Banco di Roma*, Vols I–II, Roma: Banco di Roma (Corograf); G. De Rosa (1984), *Storia del Banco di Roma*, Vol. III, Roma: Banco di Roma (Corograf); V. Castronovo (1983), *Storia di una banca. La Banca Nazionale del Lavoro e lo sviluppo economico italiano 1913–1983*, Torino: Einaudi; V. Castronovo (1985), *Gilardini 1905–1985. Storia di un gruppo industriale*, Torino: Gilardini (Ages Arti Grafiche).
56. Leaving aside actual commemorative publications, documented (if with a necessarily limited 'coverage') in the bibliography, I will mention only those works which, while presenting themselves as by 'independent' biographers, nevertheless assume those irritatingly celebratory characteristics which constitute the worst aspects of company publications: P. Bairati

(1983), *Vittorio Valletta*, Torino: Utet; L. Offeddu (1984), *La sfida dell'acciaio. Vita di Agostino Rocca*, Venezia: Marsilio; P. Bairati (1986), *Sul filo di lana. Cinque generazioni di imprenditori: i Marzotto*, Bologna: Il Mulino; C. Barberis (1987), *Corrado Merloni. Storia di un uomo e di un'industria in montagna*, Bologna: Il Mulino.

57. This explains the tone, unusual in Italian historical discussion, used in Sapelli, *Il professor Roverato* cit., pp. 949–75.
58. For a reminder of the peculiar recourse to precedent (case) in Anglo-Saxon law, see the penetrating remarks of Marc Bloch in the introduction to an essay by Norman S.B. Gras, translated for the French public in the now distant 1931: 'Culture historique et action économique: à propos de l'exemple américain', *Annales d'histoire économique et sociale*, 1931, pp. 2–3. Bloch expressed well-founded doubt concerning the possibility of directly utilizing historical knowledge; if the past furnishes, in more or less restricted or broad fields, numerous examples of 'phenomena almost alike', the accent should in the first place be put on the 'almost', the most important contribution the historian can make is therefore in understanding change rather than continuity and similarity; many years ago Giorgio Mori reminded readers of these few golden pages (*Premesse e implicazioni* cit., p. 50).
59. Cf. R. Romano (1984), 'Storia dell'industria e storia delle imprese. A proposito di un convegno torinese', *Società e Storia*, no. 26, pp. 947–50.
60. *The Uses and Abuses* cit., pp. 141–2.
61. Roverato, *Una casa industriale* cit., p. 10, emphasizes this point.
62. Mori, *Storiografia dell'industria* cit., pp. 132–4.
63. This definition was proposed by L. Cafagna (1983), 'La formazione del sistema industriale: ricerche empiriche e modelli di crescita', in Fondazione Giangiacomo Feltrinelli, *Quaderni*, no. 25, pp. 34–5, referring to F. Bonelli (1978), 'Il capitalismo italiano. Linee generali di interpretazione', *Storia d'Italia Annali*, Vol. 1, Torino: Einaudi, pp. 1193–255; L. Cafagna, 'Italy 1830–1914', in C.M. Cipolla (ed.) (1973), *The Fontana Economic History of Europe*, Vol. IV, London: Collins, pp. 279–328; G. Federico (1980), 'Di un nuovo modello dell'industrializzazione italiana', *Società e Storia*, no. 8, pp. 433–56. A stimulating suggestion for periodizing development by successive 'waves' is to found in L. Cafagna (1983), 'Protoindustria o transizione in bilico? (A proposito della prima onda della industrializzazione italiana)', *Quaderni storici*, no. 54, pp. 971–84.
64. For the expression cited, cf. Roverato, *Una casa industriale* cit., p. 69; see also the remarks of Sapelli, *Il professor Roverato* cit., pp. 954–5.
65. Cafagna, in *L'avventura industriale* cit., pp. 157–9, also insists on this.
66. Cf. ibid., pp. 152–3 and Castronovo, *Lo sviluppo economico* cit., pp. 121–2.
67. Apart from the classic case of Enrico Dell'Acqua, the subject of Luigi Einaudi's (1900) *Un principe mercante. Studio sulla espansione coloniale italiana*, Torino: Bocca. In 1986, Einaudi proposed, according to the very appropriate synthesis of Riccardo Faucci, 'the definition of an economic "ideal type": an average entrepreneur who risks capital prevalently his own, is diffident of the limited company, does without intermediaries and produces goods for final consumption' (*Luigi Einaudi*, Torino: UTET, 1986, p. 20); but see also G. Are (1974), *Economia e politica nell'Italia liberale (1890–1915)*, Bologna: Il Mulino, p. 135.
68. Cf. Bonelli, *Il capitalismo italiano* cit., p. 1219; Cafagna, *La formazione del sistema industriale* cit., p. 34. The 'eclecticism' of this model (in the sense that 'suggestions taken from other authors' are utilized, 'conferring upon them a pregnancy and meaning very often different from that of the original') is stressed by Federico, *Di un nuovo modello dell'industrializzazione* cit., pp. 438–47.
69. Cafagna, *L'avventura industriale* cit., p. 154.
70. Lanaro, *L'Italia nuova*, pp. 100–106 (quote on p. 100).
71. Friedman (1988), *Tutto in famiglia*, Milano: Longanesi.
72. F. Caffè, 'Aspetti strutturali ed evolutivi del sistema imprenditoriale italiano', in Caffè (1976), *Un'economia in ritardo*, Torino: Boringhieri, pp. 85–6.
73. Cf. in particular F. Farina (1976), 'Modelli interpretativi e caratteri del capitalismo italiano', *Quaderni storici*, no. 32, pp. 499–502, and Zamagni, *Industrializzazione e squilibri* cit., pp.

213–16. For a quantitative confirmation of the degree of industrial concentration, see the data presented in J.S. Bain (1966), *International Differences in Industrial Structure. Eight Nations in the 1950s*, New Haven and London: Yale University Press, especially pp. 96–102.

74. This refers to the document sent by de' Stefani to Mussolini on 24 November 1933 and the diary entry (15 September 1939) of Ettore Conti, cited in, among others, R. Romeo (1970), 'Aspetti storici dello sviluppo della grande impresa in Italia', *Storia contemporanea*, no. 1, pp. 19–21.
75. Cf. A.D. Chandler Jr. (1962), *Strategy and Structure: Chapters in the History of the American Industrial Enterprise*, Cambridge MA: MIT Press, and Chandler (1977), *The Visible Hand. The Managerial Revolution in American Business*, Cambridge MA: Belknap Press.
76. Ibid., pp. 4–5.
77. Cf. E. Galli della Loggia (1970), 'Problemi di sviluppo industriale e nuovi equilibri politici alla vigilia della prima guerra mondiale: la fondazione della Banca Italiana di Sconto', *Rivista storica italiana*', no. 4, esp. pp. 827–8 and 875; R.W. Webster (1978), 'La tecnocrazia italiana e i sistemi industriali verticali: il caso dell'Ansaldo (1914–1921)', *Storia contemporanea*, no. 2, pp. 205–39; M. Doria, *Ansaldo* cit; A.M. Falchero, *La Banca italiana di Sconto* cit.; P. Rugafiori, *Uomini macchine capitali* cit.; Rugafiori, *Ferdinando Maria Perrone* cit.
78. Cf. A. Carparelli (1978), 'La siderurgia italiana nella prima guerra mondiale: il caso dell'llva', *Ricerche storiche*, no. 1, in particular pp. 160–61 and Carparelli, 'I perché di una "mezza siderurgia". La società llva, l'industria della ghisa e il ciclo integrale negli anni Venti', in Bonelli (ed.), *Acciaio per l'industrializzazione* cit., esp. pp. 27–35.
79. In this regard it is necessary to underline the stimulus provided by the research directed by Peter Hertner at the Istituto Universitario Europeo di Firenze. Besides the more general work of Hertner himself, see the articles by S. Licini (Ercole Marelli) and A. Mantegazza (Caproni) in P. Hertner (ed.) (1987), 'Per la storia dell'impresa multinazionale in Europa', *Quaderni della Fondazione Feltrinelli*, no. 33; B. Bezza (1987), 'L'attività multinazionale della Pirelli (1883–1914)', *Società e storia*, no. 35, pp. 53–80; L. Segreto (1989), *Una joint-venture fallimentare. La Vickers, la Terni e l'industria italiana degli armamenti (1905–1933)*, Ancona: Ersu; D. Bigazzi (1991), 'Esportazione e investimenti esteri: la Fiat sul mercato mondiale fino al 1940', in *Fiat 1899–1930. Storia e documenti*, Milano: Fabbri, pp. 77–168.
80. A.H. Cole (1962), 'What is Business History?', *Business History Review*, p. 100.
81. The most effective contribution to overcoming a line of research based on the verification of Italian development's deviation from a 'normal' model has, in my view, been furnished by Luciano Cafagna; cf. in particular, 'La formazione di una "base industriale" fra il 1896 e il 1914', in A. Caracciolo (ed.) (1969), *La formazione dell'Italia industriale*, Bari: Laterza, pp. 158–61 (originally published in *Studi storici*, 1961, nos 3–4); 'Intorno alle origini del dualismo economico italiano', in A. Caracciolo (ed.) (1965), *Problemi storici della industrializzazione e dello sviluppo*, Urbino: Argalia, pp. 147–8.
82. A.O. Hirschman (1970), *Exit, Voice and Loyalty: Responses to Decline in Firms, Organizations and States*, Cambridge MA: Harvard University Press, p. 21.
83. A.O. Hirschman (1958), *The Strategy of Economic Development*, New Haven: Yale University Press, p. 5.
84. Ibid., p. 65.
85. Ibid., p. ix.
86. J.A. Schumpeter (1947), *Capitalism, Socialism and Democracy*, New York and London: Harper (2nd ed.), p. 79.
87. Sapelli, *Il professor Roverato* cit., p. 950. It is worth recording the suggestion made by Louis Galambos during the already-mentioned debate among American business historians: 'As the first step toward a synthesis, business historians might do well to decide whether they are going to focus primarily upon the businessman or upon the business organization. The failure to make this decision has caused a considerable amount of confusion. This is so, in part, because the problems of abstraction and generalization for the two subjects are different. ... At the present time the best way to make some progress toward synthesis is to

designate historical periods and to formulate an analytical framework which stress the evolution of the business unit. This does not mean that the individual would be ignored; it merely proposes that monographic research and in particular biographical studies should address themselves to a coherent body of questions about business organizations.' (*Business History* cit., pp. 4–5). If this approach has indeed led to extremely worthwhile results, it must also be admitted that it has not always succeeded in taking fully into account the social figure of the entrepreneur and the 'real' relations between the various groups involved in the enterprise.

88. For the distinction between these kinds of firms, Alfred Chandler and Herman Daems have affirmed: 'Before 1850, most owners managed their enterprises. The firms were still small enough and their level of activities low enough for individual partners to make day-to-day operating and long-term investment decisions. Such enterprises can be termed personals. As the size of enterprises increased and the range and volume of their activities grew, full-time managers had to be hired. While such personnel took over many of the day-to-day operating decisions, the entrepreneur who created the enterprise, his family, and one or two close associates continued to make major policy decisions, particularly those involving long-term investment. Such enterprises can be designated as entrepreneurial. As the enterprise grew still larger and as its capital stock came to be held by hundreds and often thousands of individuals, full-time salaried managers began to make long-term investment decisions as well as short-term operating ones. No longer did an entrepreneur, or family, or few individuals have a controlling share of the stock. Such enterprises can be called managerial.' ('Introduction', *The Rise of Managerial Capitalism* cit., pp. 5–6.)
89. Cf. D.J. Jeremy (ed.) (1984–86), *Dictionary of Business Biography. A Biographical Dictionary of Business Leaders Active in Britain in the period 1860–1980*, London: Butterworths, 5 vols; A. Slaven and S. Checkland (eds) (1986–87), *Dictionary of Scottish Business Biography 1860–1960*, Aberdeen: Aberdeen University Press, 2 vols; J.N. Ingham (1983), *Biographical Dictionary of American Business Leaders*, Westport (Conn.): Greenwood Press.
90. Cf. L. Segreto (1984), 'I magnifici mille. Biografie di imprenditori inglesi', *Passato e presente*, no. 6, pp. 165–74.
91. Cf. A. Martinelli, A.M. Chiesi and N. Dalla Chiesa (1981), *I grandi imprenditori italiani. Profilo sociale della classe dirigente economica*, Milano: Feltrinelli, pp. 23–62.
92. Ibid., pp. 53–6.
93. To give only a few examples, the sample lacks such well-known figures as Abegg, Amman, Barilla, Bassetti, Binda, Brioschi, Candiani, Cenzato, Cini, Costa, Esterle, Feltrinelli, Florio, Luzzatto, Maraini, Mazzonis, A. Pirelli, Puricelli, Riva, Rocca, Silvestri (these are, however, only the first to come to mind and for whom the collection of essential biographical information would have been easiest); on the other hand, many of those included do not seem to fit the required criteria, in particular insofar as representatives of the banking world are concerned. The most surprising thing, however, is the peremptory manner in which assertions made on the basis of so manifestly unreliable sources are presented: for example, regarding the socioeconomic origins of entrepreneurs, processes of mobility, political behaviour, etc.
94. Besides those studies mentioned in note 34, the biographical essays collected by Mortara, *I protagonisti dell'intervento pubblico* cit., and others since appearing in *Economia pubblica*, it should be noted that about 160 entries on entrepreneurs and managers, public and private, have been published to date in the *Dizionario biografico degli italiani*, now comprising 40 volumes. For an example of research on a regional scale, see F. Amatori (1987), 'Per un dizionario biografico degli imprenditori marchigiani', in S. Anselmi, *Le Marche*, Torino: Einaudi, pp. 591–627.
95. The reference is in the first instance to the volumes of Einaudi's *Storia d'Italia. Le regioni dall'Unità ad oggi* and in particular: S. Lanaro (ed.), *Il Veneto* (1984); G. Mori (ed.), *La Toscana* (1986); M. Aymard and G. Giarrizzo (eds), *La Sicilia* (1987); S. Anselmi (ed.), *Le Marche* (1987); R. Covino and G. Gallo (eds), *L'Umbria* (1989?); P. Macry and P. Villani (eds), *La Campania* (1990).
96. In addition to the articles contained in the volumes cited in the preceding note, see G. Barone

(1986), *Mezzogiorno e modernizzazione. Elettricità, irrigazione e bonifica nell'Italia contemporanea*, Torino: Einaudi, and S. Lupo (1990), *Il giardino degli aranci. Il mondo degli agrumi nella storia del Mezzogiorno*, Venezia: Marsilio (on the Mezzogiorno and Sicily in particular); G. Fiocca (a cura di), *Borghesi e imprenditori a Milano* cit.; C.G. Lacaita (1984), *Sviluppo e cultura. Alle origini dell'Italia industriale*, Milano: Angeli; A.M. Banti (1989), *Terra e denaro. Una borghesia padana dell'Ottocento*, Venezia: Marsilio; A. Millo (1990), *Le élites del potere a Trieste 1891–1938. Una biografia collettiva*, Milano: Angeli; G. Sapelli (1990), *Trieste italiana. Mito e destino economico*, Milano: Angeli (for Northern Italy); R.P. Coppini (1983), 'L'aristocrazia fondiario-finanziaria nella Toscana dell'Ottocento. Note per una ricerca', *Bollettino storico pisano*, a. LII, pp. 43–90; A. Polsi (1984), 'Possidenti e nuovi ceti urbani: l'élite politica di Pisa nel ventennio post-unitario', *Quaderni storici*, no. 56, pp. 493–516 (for Tuscany).

97. Cf. P. Rugafiori, 'I gruppi dirigenti della siderurgia "pubblica" tra gli anni Trenta e gli anni Sessanta', in Bonelli, *Acciaio per l'industrializzazione* cit., pp. 335–68; B. Bezza, 'I dirigenti della Montecatini: carriere, profili e organizzazione interna (1920–1940)', in F. Amatori and B. Bezza (a cura di), *Montecatini 1888–1966* cit., pp. 205–71.
98. See Pizzigallo, *Alle origini della politica petrolifera* cit.; Pizzigallo, *L'Agip* cit.; B. Bottiglieri, *Sip*, cit.; Bottiglieri, *Stet*, cit.; V. Castronovo (1983), *Storia di una banca. La Banca Nazionale del Lavoro e lo sviluppo economico italiano 1913–1983*, Torino: Einaudi; G. Rodano (1983), *Il credito all'economia. Raffaele Mattioli alla Banca Commerciale Italiana*, Milano-Napoli: Ricciardi; *Alberto Beneduce e i problemi dell'economia italiana del suo tempo. Atti della giornata di studio per la celebrazione del 50 anniversario dell'istituzione dell'Iri*, Roma: Edindustria, 1985; Donato Menichella (1986), *Testimonianze e studi raccolti dalla Banca d'Italia*, Bari: Laterza.
99. Lanaro, *L'Italia nuova* cit., pp. 35–7, disagrees.
100. J.A. Schumpeter (1949), *The Theory of Economic Development*, Cambridge MA: Harvard University Press (3rd ed.), p. 156.
101. Cf. M. Borsa (1988), 'Rinascimento post '68', *Il Mondo*, 7 November, pp. 84–9. The continuity of the preceding period emerges from the study of R.J. Pavan (1973), *Strutture e strategie delle imprese italiane*, Bologna: Il Mulino. Between 1950 and 1970 the number of family-controlled companies included in the 100 most important enterprises fell by only 10 per cent, from 48 to 44 (p. 98).
102. Cf. P. Bairati, 'Le dinastie imprenditoriali', in P. Melograni (ed.) (1988), *La famiglia italiana dall' Ottocento a oggi*, Roma and Bari: Laterza, p. 154.
103. A. Marshall (1961), *Principles of Economics*, London: Macmillan, in particular pp. 194 and 204.
104. The brief sketch by Bairati, *Le dinastie imprenditoriali* cit., is not sufficient to fill this gap.
105. For the principal references in international historiography, see the article by D. Henri (1988), 'Capitalisme familial et gestion industrielle au XIXe siècle', *Revue française de gestion,* no. 70, pp. 141–50. As is well known, the problem of the third generation is present in A. Marshall, *Principles of Economics*, cit. pp. 299–301 and Schumpeter, *The Theory of Economic Development* cit., p. 156.
106. Pavan, *Strategie e strutture* cit.
107. The Italian translation of *Strategy and Structure*, with an introduction by A. Martinelli, was available only in 1976, 14 years after the original edition; only four years, on the other hand, separated the appearance of the *Visible Hand* from the Italian edition, introduced, as already mentioned, by F. Amatori. In France, moreover, if the first of these works appeared in 1972, the second is only now due to be published. For the international diffusion of Chandler's work, see McCraw, *The Essential Alfred Chandler* cit., in particular pp. 14–15 and the complete bibliography pp. 505 ff.
108. *Strategy and Structure* cit.
109. This is the thesis of R. Romano (1986), 'La delega del potere: la struttura direttiva delle imprese cotoniere lombarde (1859–1914)', *Storia in Lombardia*, no. 2, pp. 49–68, which still examines interesting empirical material.

110. For an historical definition of the management models operating in Italian firms, cf. Sapelli, *Organizzazione lavoro* cit., pp. 179–207 (a subject he returned to in Gli *organizzatori della produzione* cit. and in 'L' impresa italiana tra economia e politica: il management. Riflessioni su una superabile inconciliabilità', *Quaderni di industria e sindacato*, no.12 (1984), pp. 88–122). Also stimulating, L. Gallino (1987), 'Tre tipi di alti dirigenti', in Id., *Della ingovernabilità. La società italiana tra premoderno e neo-industriale*, Milano: Comunità, pp. 154–80.
111. Cf. for example, the arguments put forward by the lawyer Franzo Grande Stevens – consultant to the Agnelli family, among others – reported in an interview by M. Panara, 'L'anello forte del capitale', *La Repubblica*, 26 febbraio 1988.
112. Hints in this direction occur in B. Supple (1977), 'The Nature of Enterprise', in *The Cambridge Economic History of Europe*, Cambridge: Cambridge University Press, Vol. V, pp. 436–47 and in P.L. Payne (1978), 'Industrial Entrepreneurship and Management in Great Britain', ibidem, Vol. VII, 1, pp. 194–6.
113. Cf. P. Ungari (1974), *Profilo storico del diritto delle anonime in Italia (Lezioni)*, Roma: Bulzoni.
114. Chandler, *The Visible Hand* cit., p. 5. For a discussion on the theory of the firm and criticisms directed at the neoclassical approach, see the following surveys, sufficiently exhaustive, if not up-to-date on most recent developments: R.M. Cyert and C.L. Hedrick (1972), 'Theory of the Firm: Past, Present and Future: an Interpretation', *Journal of Economic Literature*, pp. 398–40 (esp. pp. 398–9) and R. Marris and D.C. Mueller, 'The Corporation, Competition and the Invisible Hand', ibid., pp. 32–63.
115. The growth of studies in accounting history (which have a long tradition in Italy, but are limited to the mediaeval and modern periods) in the Anglo-Saxon countries should be underlined; see, in particular, *The Accounting Historians Journal*, appearing since 1971, and the bibliographical note in B. Colasse (1988), 'Les trois âges de la comptabilité', *Revue Française de Gestion*, no. 70, pp. 83–7 and 209–11. See, however, P.A. Toninelli, *La Edison* cit., while an analogous study by C. Pavese on the period 1917–39 is forthcoming.
116. With the remarkable exception of the work of Renato Giannetti and of P. Saviotti, L. Simonin and V. Zamagni, *Dall'ammoniaca ai nuovi materiali*, cit.
117. See the studies by F. Amatori, *Proprietà e direzione* cit.; *Benjamin Ingham nella Sicilia dell'Ottocento*, Marsala: Associazione marsalese per la storia patria, 1987; G. Barberis (1989), *Omaggio al cappello. La Borsalino di Teresio Usuelli*, Milano: Scheiwiller; P. Cirio (1990), *Carlo and Camillo Gancia, Strategie industriali 1850–1935*, Cuneo: Gribaudo.
118. This is the case in *Giovanni Agnelli* cit. by Castronovo and the work of the author of the present article, *Il Portello* cit.; but neither does G. Volpato's 1986 study, 'L'evoluzione delle strategie di marketing nell'industria automobilistica internazionale', *Annali di storia dell'impresa*, no. 2, pp. 119–208 make a decisive contribution to our knowledge concerning the Italian case.
119. See, for example, V. Fagone and G. Siribaldi Luso (1980), *Campari, la costanza dell'immagine. Iconologia della pubblicità di un'azienda italiana dal 1900 al 1980*, Milano: Campari; *Design Process Olivetti 1908–1983*, Ivrea: Olivetti, 1983; *L'immagine Ansaldo: architettura, grafica e pubblicità*, Milano: Electa, 1986; *1872–1972. Cento anni di comunicazione visiva Pirelli*, Milano: Scheiwiller, 1990; *Manifesti dall'Archivio Fiat 1900–1940*, Milano: Fabbri, 1991.
120. Schumpeter, *Capitalism, Socialism and Democracy* cit., p. 162.
121. A.D. Chandler, Jr., 'Comment to Alfred H. Conrad', in R.L. Andreano (ed.) (1970), *The New Economic History: Recent Papers on Methodology*, New York: Wiley, p. 145. It is in this sense that Chandler's teaching method foresees case study; cf. A.D. Chandler Jr. and R.S. Tedlow (1985), *The Coming of Managerial Capitalism. A Casebook on the History of American Economic Institutions*, Homewood (Ill.): Irwin. Norman Gras and Henrietta Larson, introducing an analogous collection of case studies in 1939 (*Casebook in American History*, New York: F.S. Crofts), used terms not dissimilar to those of Chandler: 'Its purpose [of the volume] is to facilitate understanding of the various possible choices of action and the

implications thereof. The training along this line lies in thinking of alternatives of action and in seeing the results of that action. History is of value in the study of business because it presents a background for the present, provides a rich variation of settings for action, leads to the formation of a perspective, and often provides a more nearly complete and objective presentation than is possible in current cases' (p. V). It is rather the conclusion drawn which differs, the lesson of Marc Bloch (cf. note 58) appearing to have been lost sight of: 'The old problems arise again and again in business' (ibid.).

122. M. Weber (1964), *The Theory of Economic and Social Organisation* (trans. A.M. Henderson and T. Parsons; ed. and intro. T. Parsons), New York: Free Press (original edition Oxford University Press, 1947), p. 113.

[14]

Excerpt from Peter Scholliers (ed.), *Real Wages in 19th and 20th Century Europe: Historical and Comparative Perspectives*, 107–39.

V. ZAMAGNI

5. An International Comparison of Real Industrial Wages, 1890–1913: Methodological Issues and Results

After many years of intermittent work on the wages of various categories of workers in Italy,[1] I tried in my last essay[2] to set up an international comparison. This attempt raised innumerable methodological problems. I then became interested in finding out whether it would be possible to improve upon such comparisons, and in examining the interpretative relevance such comparisons might have especially in terms of illustrating the development path of the European economies in the nineteenth century. I therefore extended my research mainly along methodological lines, around the following three questions which are the subject of this paper:

I. The construction of wage series by country
II. The measurement of industrial workers' living standards
III. Wages and productivity

The issues involved are many and complex; most of the conclusions reached can only be provisional. This is due partly to theoretically unresolved controversies and partly to wild empirical discrepancies. As far as both of these problems are concerned, I am absolutely convinced that, if we are going to make a real leap forward, the only truly viable solution is an international research project that would fill in existing gaps using common methods. The remarks offered in the following pages could form the basis for the agenda of such an international project. Some of them, however, are generally relevant for inter-country comparisons of per capita income and welfare estimates.

1. 'La dinamica dei salari nel settore industriale', in P. Ciocca and G. Toniolo (eds), *L'economia italiana nel periodo fascista*, Bologna, 1976; 'Distribuzione del reddito e classi sociali fra le due guerre', *Annali*, Feltrinelli, XX, 1980; 'Le alterazioni nella distribuzione del reddito in Italia nell'immediato dopoguerra (1919–1922)', in P. Hertner and G. Mori (eds), *La transizione dall'economia di guerra all'economia di pace in Italia ed in Germania dopo la prima guerra mondiale*, Bologna, 1983.
2. 'The Daily Wages of Italian Industrial Workers in the Giolittian Period (1898–1913)', *Rivista di storia economica*, 1984, I, International Issue.

Industrial Wages and Cost of Living Series

There are at present two available sources offering industrial wage series for more than one country: the fundamental work by Phelps Brown,[3] which gives series of real and money wages for France, Germany, the UK, Sweden and the USA for the period 1869–1960; and the statistical collection published by Mitchell,[4] which supplies money wage series and cost of living indices for a number of European countries, including (for the period under consideration here) Belgium, France, Germany, Italy, Sweden and the UK.

A collection of data from these two sources, along with some from other sources when available, is presented in Tables 5.9–5.14 of appendix 5.1. From these, the following remarks can be derived:

1. *France*. The four wage series available differ only marginally as far as their trend is concerned; they are all based on very piecemeal data of hourly or daily rates. The only good source of cost of living data is the work by Singer-Kérel, but that only processes Paris data. Of the three indices she offered, I consider the '213 items' one the most appropriate; in any case, they all show 'la fameuse crise de vie chère, génératrice de troubles importants'[5] of the years 1911–12, which severely cut down the rising trend of real wages. Phelps Brown's wage series has been retained, recalling that it has fixed 1905 employment weights.

2. *Germany*. In the case of Germany, too, four money wage series are available, but two are the basic series (Kuczynski and Desai), of which the other two (Bry and Hoffmann, respectively) are slight variations. Desai's series grows considerably more over the period (about 20 per cent more) and appears to be constructed with great care. It is an annual wage series derived from excellent sources. The four price series are all very similar up to 1910. Kuczynski then reports a burst of inflation similar to the French one, while the other series give a much less pronounced inflation. Hoffmann's implicit deflator of private consumption (corresponding to the French, '214 items' index) cannot be used to deflate wage data. Desai and Orsagh's cost of living series are very similar. In conclusion, Desai's wage

3. E. H. Phelps Brown with M. H. Browne, *A Century of Pay*, London, 1968.
4. B. R. Mitchell, *European Historical Statistics, 1750–1970*, London, 1968. The quality of the Belgian series is so poor that it has not been taken into consideration here.
5. 'Les classes populaires urbaines', in F. Braudel and E. Labrousse (eds), *Histoire économique et sociale de la France*, Paris, 1979, IV, vol. I, 493. Other works on French wages do not add new data. See J. Lhomme, 'Les enseignements théoriques à retirer d'une étude sur les salaires dans la longue période', *Revue économique*, 1965; J. Rougerie, 'Remarques sur l'histoire des salaires à Paris au XIX siècle', *Mouvement social*, 1968.

series and Orsagh's cost of living series appear to be the best choice.

3. *Italy*. The *Cassa Infortuni*'s series used by Mitchell and by many other statistical collections were criticised in my last essay, while the implicit deflator of private consumption cannot substitute ISTAT's time-honoured cost of living series,[6] which is therefore retained here. In my last essay I gave daily wages in several industries with moving employment weights.

4. *Sweden*. The wage series is an average of annual wages in several industries, with fixed 1913 employment weights; the cost of living series is constructed with weights taken from national consumption 1881–90.

5. *UK*. The Wood-Bowley series have won wide acceptance, as the recent contribution by Gourvish recognised[7]; we retain them in Phelps Brown's more accurate version. The money wage series is built on weekly wages, with variable employment weights. The cost of living series has variable weights as well.

6. *USA*. The two annual money wage series do not differ much, while the cost of living series show wide discrepancies; Rees's series, employed by Phelps Brown, appear more solid.

The selected money wage and cost of living series, and the resulting real-wage series, have been reported in Figures 5.1–5.6 to allow a visual appreciation of their behaviour. Some overall remarks are now in order.

Money wages. It is possible to identify three pairs of countries behaving somewhat similarly. France and UK form the first pair, with slowly growing wages and a very similar trend. USA and Germany form the second pair, with a very similar growth of wages after 1900, but a dissimilar performance in the preceding decade. Considering the whole span 1890–1913, the German behaviour would actually be more comparable to that of the third pair of countries, namely Italy and Sweden. This last pair

6. Since I wrote my essay, I had the possibility of seeing a work on wages that I had not examined (M. Berra and M. Revelli, 'Salari', in *La Storia d'Italia, Il mondo contemporaneo*, La Nuova Italia, 1978, vol. I, 3), but the authors quote the usual wage series employed by everybody, though they advance some interpretative reservations. Of the three new articles published, two provide a confirmation of my results: C. Biffoli and M. Lungonelli, 'Una classe operaia in formazione: i Siderurgici di Portoferraio, 1901–1905', *Studi storici*, 1985, n. 1; and G. Barberis, 'Torchi e meccanica. Appunti per una storia della Negro', *Rassegna economica della provincia di Alessandria*, 1985, n. 4. The third one (A. Dewerpe, 'Modi di retribuzione e organizzazione produttiva all'Ansaldo (1900–1920)', *Studi storici*, 1985, n. 1) analyses wages by categories and the use of new forms of remuneration, but does not offer quantitative elaborations that could be used.
7. In his essay, T. R. Gourvish, 'The Standard of Living 1890–1914', in A. O'Day (ed.), *The Edwardian Age: Conflict and Stability 1900–1914*, London, 1979, reports a few additional regional wage series confirming the stationary trend of the national series. Interesting are the 'qualitative' observations offered.

Figure 5.1 Wage Indices for France, Germany and Italy

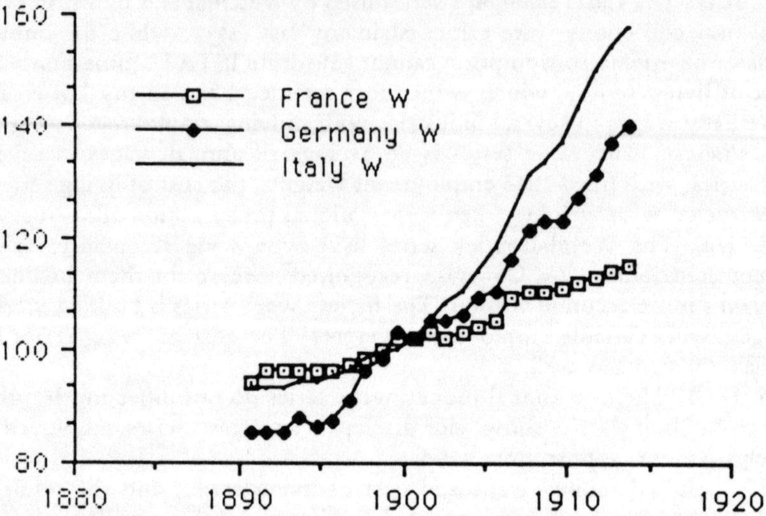

Figure 5.2 Wage Indices for Sweden, the UK and the USA

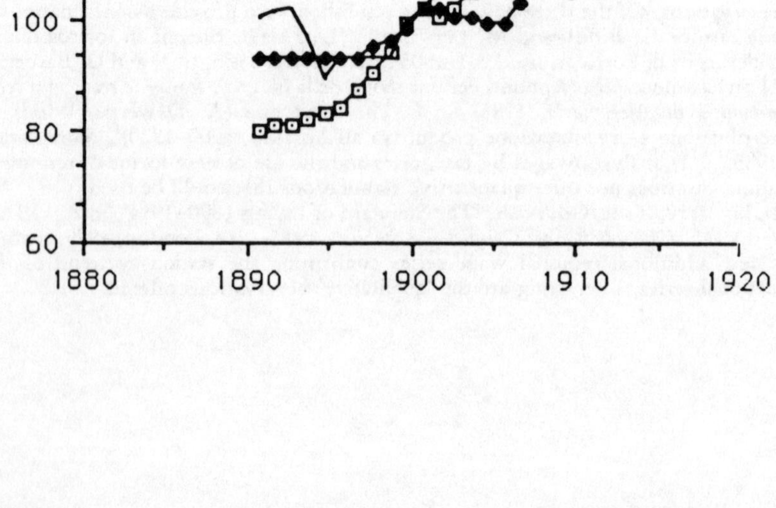

Figure 5.3 Cost of Living Indices for France, Germany and Italy

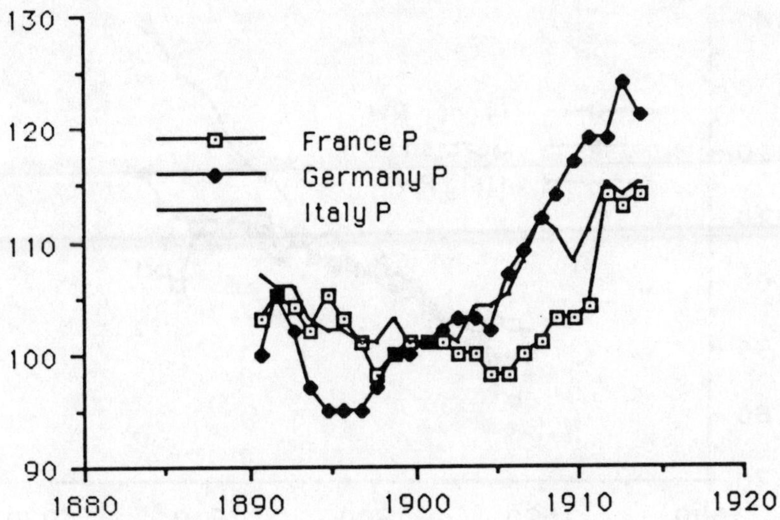

Figure 5.4 Cost of Living Indices for Sweden, the UK and the USA

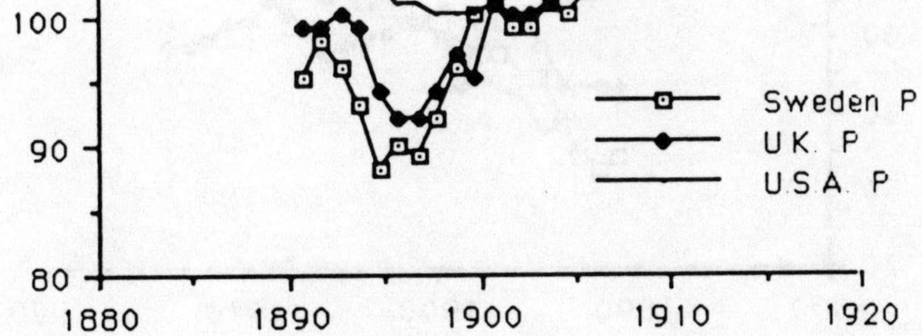

Figure 5.5 Real Wage Indices for France, Germany and Italy.

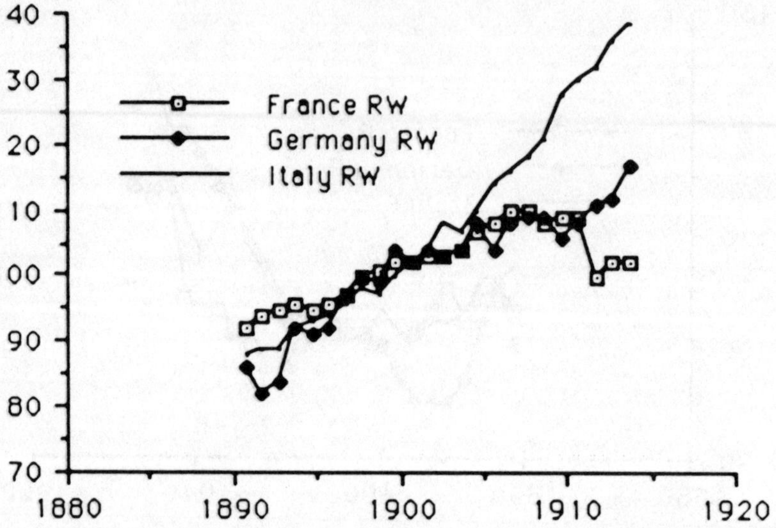

Figure 5.6 Real Wage Indices for Sweden, the UK and the USA.

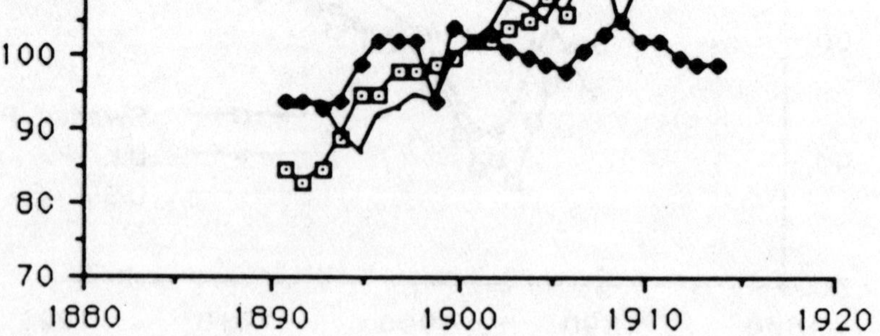

shows a very dynamic wage trend, slightly more so in Sweden than in Italy over the whole period (78 per cent increase against 71 per cent), but with a different growth path, more rapid in Sweden in the 1890s and in Italy after the 1907 crisis. Concerning the effects of the 1907 crisis, they can clearly be noticed in the USA and UK, less so in Sweden and Germany; Italian and French wages do not seem to have suffered appreciably.

Cost of Living. While in Figure 5.1 I had to stick to the same pairs identified for the comparison of money wages, the performance of the six cost of living series is everywhere broadly similar: a fall in the 1890s followed by a rise to the 1907 crisis, a second short-lived fall (with the exception of Germany) and a final rise. However, the amplitude of the cycles and the timing of the turning points differ.

Real Wages. The grouping of countries in three pairs has retained some meaning: the ranking of real-wage performance is the same as for money wages but for the two fast-growing countries: Italy has outstripped Sweden, as a result of the stronger Swedish inflation in the period. More detailed comments are in order, however. UK wages show some increase in the first half of the 1890s followed by cyclical stagnation; French real wages, on the other hand, show a continuous rising trend up to 1906, followed by four years of near stagnation and then by an abrupt fall. Both American and German real wages are highly cyclical on a clearly upward trend, more marked in the German case. The effects of the 1907 crisis on the American real wages appear quite devastating.

Finally, Swedish real wages are more dynamic than the Italian ones in the 1890s (and similar to the German wages), but show years of standstill (and even reversal) after 1900. An inflationary outburst similar to that of the French is responsible for Swedish real wages losing touch with the Italian trend in the very final years of the period.

On average, the yearly growth rate of real wages between 1890 and 1913 is the following: UK 0.2 per cent; France 0.5 per cent; USA 1.0 per cent; Germany 1.4 per cent; Sweden 1.6 per cent; Italy 2 per cent.

The conclusions reached are open to revisions on a number of accounts, the most important of which are now briefly mentioned:

i) Annual wages are often the result of elaborations based on the daily (or weekly) rates mutliplied by a fixed coefficient. This is, for example, the case with UK (weekly wages multiplied by 49 weeks), France (daily wages multiplied by a factor of 5.4 to get weekly wages and then by 49 weeks) and Italy (daily wages multiplied by a factor of 6 and then by 49 weeks). It would be possible to be more precise on the length of the working week,[8] but not on that of the working year for those countries

8. Information on hours of work per week can be found in Phelps Brown (pp. 55–6,

not having direct figures for annual wages.

ii) Wage series by industries are sometimes combined into on overall average by means of fixed employment weights; this has been so with France and Sweden. In this case, the effects of structural change are not captured and the growth rates of wages are usually understated;

iii) Short-time and overtime, as well as piece-rates and other forms of remuneration, are generally not taken into account. Only data coming from single firms' bookkeeping can provide such detailed information. Unemployment and underemployment also become an issue when wages are used to construct wage bills, annual wage rates usually referring to a 'normal' full year of work.

iv) Price series are usually of the cost of living type, but their coverage, the weight of the items included as well as the type of index-number formula used are unknown, more often than not. Their importance for a correct evaluation of real-wage rates cannot be overemphasised.[9]

The International Comparison of Industrial Workers' Living Standards

The basis on which to build an international comparison of the standard of living of industrial workers might be considered easily defined: the average workers' remuneration in the national currency, with reference to some agreed-upon span of time (day/week/year). But here again things are ambiguous. First of all, *average* wages should (although for empirical limitation they do not always) include all sectors — skilled as well as unskilled workers, women, apprentices and youth, large as well as small firms. My experience suggests that small firms, apprentices and youth, and more traditional sectors with very high and very low wages are usually under-represented. (I comment upon this in the case of Italy in my last essay, see especially footnotes 20, 21, 26.) This tends in general to overstate average wages.

Secondly, it must be remembered that average wages rise or fall not only as a result of rising or falling basic rates, but also as a result of more weight acquired by high-wage sectors, by skilled versus unskilled workers, by high-wage regions. Wage data that do not mirror this structural change

---

207), in the Board of Trade *Reports* (quoted in my essay on p. 92) and in various other works quoted here; they have never been systematically studied. See also Table 5.1 in the text.

9. An example of the strategic importance of a different cost of living index is given in the recent essay by P. Scholliers, 'A Methodological Note on Real Wages During the Interwar Years', *Historical Social Research*, January 1987, n. 41.

usually tend to show lower growth rates, as has already been mentioned. However, if one wants to evaluate the progress in welfare of single categories of workers, wages by profession should be used. In international comparisons, too, it might be of interest to compare the earnings of workers in the same industry, as Scholliers has done.[10] An example of what could be done in this direction is provided in Table 5.1, where I have gathered weekly wage rates in three industries (building, engineering and printing) for six countries in 1905. All wage figures come from the British Board of Trade (BOT) reports,[11] with the exception of the Italian figures, derived from the sources quoted in my last essay.

In Table 5.1 it is possible to detect a ranking of each country in comparison with Britain. If Britain = 100, USA ranks more than 200, Germany around 80, France around 70, Belgium around 60 and Italy around 45, but differentials differ by industry and by country. The ratio of unskilled to skilled workers' wages ranges from 0.59 to 0.72 (with the exception of American labourers/bricklayers, which is 0.50). It appears highest in Germany and lowest in the USA.

Using the figures for engineering wages quoted in Scholliers[12] and the corresponding figures of Table 5.1, one can draw the picture of the trend in relative wages 1850–1905, appearing in Table 5.2. The gap with Great Britain was progressively closing, very rapidly for Germany (which started from a low level).

Having analysed average wages in the first section of this papers an international comparison of average wages will now be my main concern. It will be done with reference to the same year — 1905 — already used in Table 5.1, because of the availability of cost of living data from BOT. In Table 5.3 I have gathered annual earnings for seven countries: Germany, Sweden, GB and USA come from Phelps Brown; France comes from Phelps Brown as well, but the figure has been put up 11 per cent to correct what I consider to be an inconsistency in Phelps Brown's estimation procedure.[13] The Italian estimate derives from daily rates multiplied by

10. P. Scholliers, *Industrial Wage Differentials in 19th Century Belgium*, mimeo, August 1986.
11. Besides the Board of Trade *Reports* quoted in my essay on p. 92, I have also used *Report of an Inquiry by the Board of Trade into Working Class Rents, Housing and Retail Prices, together with the Rates of Wages in Certain Occupations in the Principal Industrial Towns of Belgium*, London, 1910.
12. P. Scholliers, *Industrial Wage Differentials*, table 4 and table 7.
13. The French weekly rate estimated by him on the basis of daily rates results from the use of 54 hours of work per week, while all sources (and, strangely enough, Phelps Brown himself) agree that the French working week was still of 60 hours before the First World War. There are other reasons suggesting that Phelps Brown's estimate, even after the present adjustment, might still be too low. In

Table 5.1 Wages and Hours of Work in Certain Industries and Occupations in 1905 (shillings per week, hours per week)

	Wage Rates												Hours of Work					
	Great Britain	index GB = 100	Germany	index GB = 100	France	index GB = 100	Belgium[a]	index GB = 100	Italy	index GB = 100	USA[b]	index GB = 100	GB	Germany	France	Belgium	Italy	USA
	(1)	(2)	(3)	(4)	(5)	(6)	(7)	(8)	(9)	(10)	(11)	(12)	(13)	(14)	(15)	(16)	(17)	(18)
Building													53	59	$64\frac{1}{2}$	$67\frac{1}{2}$	60	47
bricklayers	39	100	29	74	25	64	22	56	14	36	117[c]	300						
labourers	26	100	21	81	18	69	16	62	9	35	59	227						
Engineering													53	59	$60\frac{1}{2}$	$60\frac{1}{2}$	60	56
fitters	34	100	29	85	26	76	21	62	17	50	68	200						
labourers	20	100	20	100	17	85	14	70	12	60	40	200						
Printing													$52\frac{1}{2}$	54	$59\frac{1}{2}$	$59\frac{3}{4}$	54	49
compositors	30	100	25	83	24	80	21	70	19	63	75	250						

(a) Data refer to June 1908; a footnote in the BOT report for Belgium (p. xxxiv) warns, however, that rates in the industries considered had not changed since 1905.
(b) Data refer to February 1909. From table A.6 US money wages appear at this date to be at a level not substantially different from that reached in 1905, after two years of rise and a sharp fall in 1908, following the 1907 crisis.
(c) The BOT Report comments upon the very high comparative level of US bricklayers' wages.
Sources: BOT Reports for all countries, except Italy; my own sources for Italy.

Table 5.2 Relative Wages in Engineering (Great Britain = 100)

	1850	1896	1905*
Great Britain	100	100	100
France	42	61	78
Belgium	36	52	64
Germany	28	59	89

*Fitters 2/3; labourers 1/3

6×49, which is probably too 'full' a working year for Italian industrial workers; the Belgian estimate is an extrapolation to 1905 of a 1913 estimate in Baudhuin (see description of procedure in Table 5.3). The ranking of Belgium and France with reference to Great Britain is very similar to that already established above for engineering wages alone, while the German average index is 14 percentage points lower, signalling that the wage of the industries selected by BOT (see column 5 of Table 5.3) was comparatively higher in Germany. A similar comment applies to the USA where, as has been commented in a footnote in Table 5.1, bricklayers' wages were abnormally high. It can therefore be seen that the comparison of average wages offers a comprehensive view that is not adequately conveyed by wage comparisons for single industries.

However, a simple conversion of wage rates (expressed in national currencies) into one common monetary standard through official exchange rates does not give a reliable picture of the relative purchasing power of wages (as well as that of income). I refer the reader to the relevant technical literature for the debate on the causes of this.[14] It is clear that, while the use of official exchange rates in a period of exchange-rate stability (like the one under consideration in this paper) at least does not produce the same

the essay by L. A. Vincent, 'Les comptes nationaux', in A. Sauvy, *Histoire économique de la France entre les deux guerres*, vol. 3, Paris, 1972, p. 332, a 'salaire par tête et par an', for the industrial sector is reported for 1913. It is equal to F. F. 1620, i.e. 44 per cent higher than the yearly wage that can be arrived at applying the index of Phelps Brown's monetary wages to the corrected value in Table 5.1. It must be noted that Vincent's estimates include white-collar workers and foremen; but even so, it seems to imply a higher average wage. Also, Phelps Brown has used, with one exception only, non-Paris rates, which are reported in all sources to have been much lower (sometimes as much as half) than Paris rates, perhaps ending up with playing down too much the weight of Paris workers in the aggregate.

14. See especially I. B. Kravis and R. E. Lipsey, 'Toward an Explanation of National Price Levels', *Princeton Studies in International Finance*, Nov. 1983, n. 52, and I. B. Kravis, 'Comparative Studies of National Incomes and Prices', *Journal of Economic Literature*, XXII, March 1984.

Table 5.3 Average Industrial Wages in 1905

	Yearly wages in national currencies (1)	Exchange rate of the £ (2)	Yearly wages in £ (3)	Index of (3) GB = 100 (4)	BOT index GB = 100 (5)
Belgium	907 B.Fr.	25.40 B.Fr.	35 14s	64	63
France	1021 F.Fr.	25.15 F.Fr.	40 12s	72	75
Germany	856 M.	20.45 M.	41 17s	75	83
Italy	623 lire	25.15 lire	24 15s*	44*	–
Sweden	851 Kr.	18.16 Kr.	46 17s	84	–
GB	56 £	–	56 2s	100	100
USA	487 $	4.86 $.	100 4s	179	232

*A slight imprecision in the original version has been corrected

Sources: Col. 1 Germany, Sweden, GB and USA are from Phelps Brown; France also comes from Phelps Brown, but using a working week of 60 hours; Italy comes from my own computations. Belgium's estimate has been derived as follows: from F. Baudhuin, *Histoire économique de la Belgique 1914–1939*, vol. 1, Bruxelles, 1946, p. 409, I have taken the yearly wage for 1913 (1125 B. Fr.), which has been reported to 1905 using Mitchell's money wage index.

volatility of results as in times of fluctuating exchange rates, nevertheless the purchasing-power parity issue has to be tackled.

The Purchasing Power Parity (PPP) Approach

A working class budget, calculated first using the prices of one country and then the prices of a second country, can provide a ratio, through which it is possible to determine an exchange rate that allows a bilateral comparison of wages based on PPP. Given that such a procedure can be applied taking both countries' budgets in turn, two estimates of such PPP exist. While I refer the reader to Appendix 2 of my last essay for the steps and the sources needed for the application of this procedure, I have reported the results,[15] with the addition of Belgium, in Table 5.4. It can be seen that 'real' average wages in 1905 would appear to be very close in Belgium, France and Germany, substantially higher in Sweden, substantially lower in Italy. Great Britain would still be firmly ahead of all the European countries, but not ahead of the USA.

15. In Appendix B of my last essay, I had used, to estimate the Italian diet, quantities that were the average quantities consumed in the nation. I can now substitute quantities derived from the enquiry made by Pugliese in July 1913 on fifty-one Milanese working-class families with 210 members, which yields the results gathered in Table 5.5.

Table 5.4 Comparison of Industrial Wages in 1905 and 1913 Based on Purchasing Power Parities

	Yearly wages in 1905 at the official exchange rate in £ (1)	Index of (1) GB = 100 (2)	Cost of living index[a] GB = 100 (3)	Index of real wages in 1905 GB = 100 (4)	Index of real wages in 1913[b] GB = 100 (5)
Belgium	35 14s	64	91–95	67–70	65–68
France	40 12s	72	104–112	64–69	60–64
Germany	41 17s	75	107–117	64–70	68–75
Italy	24 15s	44	108–117[c]	38–41	45–49
Sweden	46 17s	84	103–115	73–81	82–92
GB	56 2s	100	100	100	100
USA	100 4s	179	143–153[d]	117–125	126–134

(a) only foodstuffs and rents, excluding coal
(b) applying the indices from Tables 5.9–5.14
(c) corrected through the use of working-class budgets (see footnote 15)
(d) the cost of living comparison GB/USA refers to 1909, but the change in prices in the two countries between 1905 and 1909 was similar and therefore the comparison can be considered valid for 1905 as well.
Sources: Table 5.1, my calculations, Board of Trade report for cost of living in Belgium (rents have been combined with cost of foodstuffs with a weight of 16.7 per cent).

A refinement of this approach could be obtained by applying the devices suggested by UN researchers.[16] These devices have found wide acceptance,[17] although there is a less than general consensus on the meaning of the 'international dollar' built to value the GNP of each country, and other methods have been suggested.[18] After a deep inspection of the UN method it has seemed to me that the extensive computations necessary to apply it to

16. I. B. Kravis, A. Heston, R. Summers, *World Product and Income. International Comparisons of Real Gross Product*, Washington, D.C., 1982.
17. R. Marris, 'Comparing the Incomes of Nations: a Critique of the International Comparison Project', *Journal of Economic Literature*, XXII, March 1984, states that the 'work by Kravis, Heston and Summers . . . represents one of the great contributions to applied economics' (p. 40). N. F. R. Crafts, 'Gross National Product in Europe 1870–1910: Some New Estimates', *Explorations in Economic History*, 1983, n. 4 bases on it a set of backward extrapolations to revise Bairoch's estimates of income per capita in the European countries before the First World War.
18. P. Pashardes, *True Purchasing Power Parities and Real Consumption Comparisons with an Application to EEC Countries*, Birkbeck College paper, London, 1984 suggests a method that explicitly embodies at least part of the substitution effects, while A. Maddison, 'A Comparison of Levels of GDP per Capita in Developed and Developing Countries, 1700–1980', *Journal of Economic History*, March 1983 declares himself in favour of quantity estimates (rather than value estimates) à la Usher.

Table 5.5 Average Food Consumption of Milanese Working-class Families in 1913

	Unit prices in lire			British Budget			Italian Budget	
	GB	Italy	Kg. or l. consumed	Cost at British prices (lire)	Cost at Italian prices (lire)	Kg. or l. consumed	Cost at British prices (lire)	Cost at Italian prices (lire)
	(1)	(2)	(3)	(4)	(5)	(6)	(7)	(8)
Bread	.29	.36	9.98	2.89	3.59	9.20	2.67	3.31
Flour	.30	.38	4.54	1.36	1.73	.47	.14	.18
Potatoes	.10	.12	7.71	.77	.93	2.39	.24	.29
Beef	1.56	1.90	2.04	3.18	3.88	1.80	2.81	3.42
Pork	1.85	1.68	.23	.43	.39	.60	1.11	1.00
Lamb	1.48	1.37	.68	1.01	.93	.20	.30	.27
Butter	3.06	2.80	.91	2.78	2.55	.35	1.07	.98
Milk	.32	.24	5.65	1.81	1.36	5.50	1.76	1.32
Cheese	1.62	1.30	.34	.55	.44	.49	.79	.64
Sugar	.46	1.49	2.42	1.11	3.61	.74	.34	1.10
Bacon	1.85	1.60	.68	1.26	1.09	.53	.98	.85
Totals				17.15	20.50		12.21	13.36

The ratio of the total of column (8) to the total of column (7) yields 109, rather than 111 as stated in my last essay.

Sources: (1)–(5) from Table B.1 in my last essay.
(6) from A. Pugliese, 'L'alimentazione della famiglia operaia milanese durante la guerra', in P. Albertoni and A. Pugliese, *Studi sull'alimentazione*, Naples, 1937, p. 455.

my inter-country wage comparisons could not yield any new insight. The whole exercise, in fact, basically amounts to an averaging out of the prices prevailing in the countries considered for each of the items included in the budget, with country-weights decided *a priori*. This would allow a multilateral rather than a bilateral comparison of real wages based on PPP. It would only be worth reconsidering the issue if wages from many more countries would be available for comparison, and if the quality of the data could be improved and standardised. In addition, we must not forget the theoretical shortcomings of this approach stemming from the use of the time-honoured consumer's theory which has recently been very seriously criticised.[19] These considerations have pushed me to take into consideration the heuristic validity of other approaches.

The 'Basic Needs' Approach

This approach in its 'recommended food allowances' version still appears relevant in a context of widespread poverty like the one prevailing in early twentieth-century Europe, although it would be much less acceptable in present-day Europe (in fact, today it is used mainly in the analysis of LDCs). The main difficulties in its use lie in the quantitative determination of a subsistence diet, which varies at least according to age, sex, body, size, climate, type and intensity of work,[20] and also according to the various biological theories in use.[21] For the period under consideration here, a relevant study can be cited. It was produced for the *Commission scientifique interalliée du ravitaillement* (CSIR), an organisation formed in Paris in 1917 to assist governments of the Allied countries in the adoption of correct measures to provide enough food for their populations.[22] The study was

19. My theoretical referee is here, (as in my section on the 'capabilities' approach in this paper), A. Sen. In particular, A. Sen, 'The Welfare Basis of Real Income Comparisons: a Survey', *Journal of Economic Literature*, XVII, March 1979.
20. In an article by C. Gini, 'Sui confronti internazionali dei salari reali', *Rivista di politica economica*, Jan. 1927, the author, after having reviewed the issue, concluded that 'the adoption of the calories approach gives . . . more troubles than advantages in comparison to the budget approach' (p. 12, my translation).
21. Daily recommended allowances in terms of calories appear to have been revised substantially downwards over time, while their requirements of vitamins and other nutrients have been more explicitly stressed.
22. The works of CSIR took place in six sessions between March 1918 and April 1919. The CSIR calculated the food requirements of the human and animal population of the Allies, the energetic content of national production and the ensuing import needs. CSIR suggestions were obviously consultative; Italy, for example, is said never to have been able to guarantee the recommended food imports, although the diet of the Italian population did not deteriorate appreciably during the war.

presented by the well-known Italian statistician, Corrado Gini, at the fifth session of the CSIR (December, 1918).[23] It aimed at the quantitative assessment of the differences, if any, in the recommended allowances for each of the three countries considered (France, Great Britain and Italy).

Starting with the assumption of 3,300 gross calories (3,000 net) as the daily recommended allowances for an average adult male, Gini develops a set of convincing arguments,[24] leading to the conclusion that Italy and Great Britain needed 2,650 calories per capita and France needed 2,740. We could easily extend his argument to the Belgian and German populations, but the more rigid climate and some types of very heavy forest work might indicate a need to raise the average for Sweden.

At this point, the problem becomes one of availability of historical material useful for this line of research. For Italy, there are plenty of works allowing us to go further in this direction. There is, for instance, a very accurate work by L. Spina calculating the overall calories available to the Italian population in 1910–14.[25] The main results of such work have been arranged in Table 5.6, together with a similar analysis developed by Pugliese on a sample of fifty-one Milanese working-class families. The following can be noted:

a) On average, the Italian population in 1910–14 barely reached the daily recommended allowances, if we accept the above cited estimation by Gini, or was just under it, if we adopt the estimate by Spina (Table 5.6, Column 3). In any case, the weight of proteins derived from vegetable-food was higher, and that of proteins derived from animal-food much lower, than the recommended weight;

b) The diet of the Milanese working-class family offered substantially

23. C. Gini, 'Sull'influenza di alcuni fattori sopra il fabbisogno Alimentare del uomo medio', *Problemi sociologici della guerra*, Bologna, 1921.
24. The daily recommended allowances were so specified by Gini by age, sex and type of work:

Children 0–5 years		Calories	1,500
Boys/Girls 5–15 years		"	2,400
Employed in agriculture	males	"	3,500
	females	"	3,250
Employed in heavy jobs	males	"	3,900
Employed in less heavy jobs	males	"	3,250
	females	"	3,000
Employed in sedentary jobs and non-working	males	"	2,450
	females	"	2,300

25. The computation of calories and nutrients in the average Italian diet has been subsequently extended to all the years from 1861, with a variable degree of reliability due to the different quality of the basic data. Cf. ISTAT, *Sommario di statistiche storiche dell'Italia*, Rome, 1958.

Table 5.6 The Italian Daily Food Allowances in the Prewar Years

		Recommended allowances per adult male (1)	Actual allowances of the Italian population 1910–14 per capita (2)	Actual allowances of the Italian population 1910–14 per adult male (3)	Actual allowances of 51 Milanese families 1913, per adult male (4)
Calories		3300	2696	3220[a]	2853[b]
Proteins	Vegetable (g.)	58	61.42	73.38	45.18
	Animal (g.)	42	20.00	23.81	39.39
Fats (g.)		75	53.03	63.34	70.92
Carbohydrates (g.)		540	412.39	492.70	411.12
Average cost (lire)		–	.64[c]	.76[c]	1.07[d]

(a) of which 273 calories are from wine
(b) of which 240 calories are from wine
(c) bread and pasta have been included at the cost of flour
(d) the cost has been calculated by me using average prices reported in L. Spina, op. cit.: for bread and pasta prices come from *Idea cooperativa*, Milan, 30 July 1911, n. 233. The difference between the cost of the diet of the Milanese working-class families and the cost of the average Italian diet is large because in the former more animal proteins appear (which are dearer than vegetable proteins), and because bread and pasta are bought ready-made (and are therefore more costly than their flour content).

Sources: (1)–(3) L. Spina, 'I consumi alimentari della popolazione italiana nell'anteguerra (1910–14) e negli ultimi anni (1926–30)', *Metron*, 1932, n. 1–2.
(4) A. Pugliese, 'Il bilancio alimentare di 51 famiglie operaie milanesi' and 'L'alimentazione della famiglia operaia milanese durante la guerra', in P. Albertoni and A. Pugliese, *Studi sull'alimentazione*.

fewer calories than recommended, though animal proteins were present in a higher amount compared to the average for Italy.[26] It must be underlined that the families surveyed by Pugliese were admittedly selected from among the least poor of the Milanese proletariat!

Data referring to the cost of the average Italian diet (Table 5.6, columns 2 and 3) and of the Milanese working class diet (Table 5.6, column 4) are also interesting. Though the former is in agreement with other estimates given at the time, it does not represent the minimal cost of a diet offering the same amount of calories and nutrients. (Such a minimal cost diet could be easily computed and compared with the actual one.) The extra cost of the

26. Milan was known to be the Italian town where more meat per capita was consumed (157 gr. per day before the First World War), 30 per cent more than Turin and Genoa, 40 per cent more than Rome, double the consumption in Naples and three times the consumption in Bari and Catania.

working-class diet exemplifies this problem even further, showing how the purchase of ready-made bread and pasta rather than flour — plus an extra amount of more costly animal proteins and sugar — can make a lower calories diet 41 per cent dearer.

How does the cost of such diets compare with average wages? A simple (though not completely exact) answer could be given by comparing the cost of an adult male diet with the going average male wage.[27] This can be done by drawing upon one of my students' work[28] which gives an estimate for female wages of 1.50 lire[29] per day in 1911. Given that the overall average wage was 2.67 lire for the same year and the percentage of female workers in the total was 32.74 per cent, it follows that an average male wage was 3.25 lire per day. Reduced by a factor of 0.805 (294 days of work out of 365) or, more realistically, 0.712 (260 days of work out of 365), the daily wage rate becomes the daily disposable income (2.62 lire or 2.31 lire) of an Italian male industrial worker in 1911 (no direct taxation existed on wages at the time). Using Gini's recommended allowances (footnote 24), a male worker (1) with a housewife (0.9) and two children 5–15 years of age (0.7 each) would spend 2.51 lire each day in food, using the lower-cost diet (and 3.53 lire using the higher cost one!). Everyone can see that one male wage was not enough to support even a modest family. Two or more wages[30] or no children[31] was necessary to cross the threshold of dire misery. Once again, family incomes and dependency ratios appear crucial. This last remark paves the way to a brief discussion of a third approach.

27. The inexactness is given by the presence in the average male wages of the wages of youth less than 15 years old, which, in 1911, formed 10 per cent of the male labour force. An appropriate adjustment could be to put up the male adult wage to 3.40–3.50 lire.
28. M. Giovanna Incerti Dal Monte, *Il lavoro femminile in età giolittiana*, thesis defended in 1984, University of Florence, a brief summary of which has been published in *Rivista di storia economica*, 1985, II, 3.
29. It can be noted in passing that female wages were 46 per cent of male wages in Italy in 1911, while they were 44.4 per cent in Great Britain (see R. C. O. Matthews, C. H. Feinstein, J. C. Odling Smee, *British Economic Growth 1856–1973*, Oxford, 1982, p. 630).
30. The existence or non-existence of residual ties with the land, as well as the diffusion of female employment, become relevant issues in this context. For example, the widespread female employment in textiles, coupled with the presence of engineering and metal sectors, made the industrial working class in Lombardy definitely more prosperous (than in, say, Liguria, where textiles were unimportant), as a result of higher *family* incomes.
31. A. Pugliese, 'Il bilancio alimentare', p. 380, notes that fourteen out of his fifty-one families were without children and fourteen had only one. He comments, 'The idea that it is convenient to limit the number of children born has already . . . penetrated the Milanese working class' (my translation).

The 'Capabilities' Approach

The limitations shown by the PPP and basic needs approaches have led me to the study of the theory developed by A. Sen in the last ten years.[32] He has underlined first the necessity of using income distribution to evaluate correctly income per capita figures — the *entitlement* approach[33] — and then, through a sweeping critique of utility theory, he has moved his emphasis from measurement of commodity bundles to the illustration of functionings — *capabilities* — as better suited to measure and compare, objectively, levels of welfare reached. In referring the reader to Sen's writings for a demonstration of this approach, I have to say that I find the implications of it — the use of non-market indicators — very interesting.

Indicators such as life expectancy, infant mortality, child death rates, adult literacy, schooling, malnutrition and the like were already used in the past, either under the generic heading of the 'quality' of life or, instrumentally, to help fill the gaps of income statistics.[34] They could be used more extensively and systematically today, if some sort of ranking and/or a well-specified connection with the welfare of a society could be identified.

Wages and Productivity

One of the interesting exercises that are possible with industrial wage rates is a comparison with productivity in industry (Y_I/L_I), something already tried by Phelps Brown and various other authors.[35] The trouble is that, if the assessment of wage rates is difficult, an estimate of productivity in industry is not easier. I have gathered the most recent estimates of overall productivity (GNP/L) around 1913 in Table 5.7, and I have tried in Table 5.8 to derive Y_I/L_I. Here is a brief commentary on the results, by country:

32. A. Sen, *On Economic Inequality*, Oxford, 1973; idem; *Poverty and Famines, An Essay on Entitlement and Deprivation*, Oxford, 1982; idem, *Resources, Values and Development*, Oxford, 1984; idem, *Commodities and Capabilities*, Amsterdam, 1985.
33. An application of the distributive emphasis suggested by Sen to the wage field would be the analysis of wages by categories, age, skill, male, female, regions, etc.
34. See, for example, S. L. Barsby, 'Economic Backwardness and the Characteristics of Development', *Journal of Economic History*, XXIX, 1969 and N. F. R. Crafts, op. cit.. The Chenery-Syrquin approach (H. B. Chenery and M. Syrquin, *Patterns of Development*, Oxford, 1975) adopted by N. F. R. Crafts, 'Patterns of Development in Nineteenth Century Europe', *Oxford Economic Papers*, XXXVI, 1984, is a more skilful (but not substantially different) variation along the same lines.
35. Among them, P. O'Brien and C. Keyder, *Economic Growth in Britain and France 1780–1914. Two Paths to the Twentieth Century*, London, 1978, and N. F. R. Crafts, 'Economic Growth in France and Britain, 1830–1910: A Review of the Evidence', *Journal of Economic History*, March 1984.

Table 5.7 Estimates of Output per Worker around 1910–13

	Crafts 1910					Maddison 1913					Bairoch 1913				
	GNP/P 1970 $	Index of (1) GB = 100	% active population	GNP/L 1970 $	index of (4) GB = 100	GNP/P 1970 $	index of (6) GB = 100	% active population	GNP/L 1970 $	Index of (9)[b] GB = 100	GNP/P 1960 $	Index of (11) GB = 100	% active population	GNP/L 1960 $	index of (14) GB = 100
	(1)	(2)	(3)	(4)	(5)	(6)	(7)	(8)	(9)	(10)	(11)	(12)	(13)	(14)	(15)
USA	–	–	–	–	–	1810	116	43	4150	117	–	–	–	–	–
France	883	68	52	1698	59	1177	76	50	2331	66	695	70	52	1337	60
Germany	958	74	44	2177	75	1073	69	43	2466	70	781	78	44	1775	80
Italy	548	42	45	1218	42	836	54	46	1829	52	441	44	45	980	44
Sweden	763	59	40	1907	66	994	64	46	2147	61	680	68	40	1770	77
GB	1302	100	45[a]	2893	100	1555	100	44	3533	100	996	100	45	2213	100

(a) from R. C. O. Matthews, C. H. Feinstein, J. C. Odling Smee, pp. 222–3.
(b) the index of GDP per man hours calculated by Maddison, p. 98 practically coincides.

Sources: (1) N. F. R. Crafts, 'Gross National Product'.
(3), (13) from Mitchell.
(6), (8) from A. Maddison, *Phases of Capitalist Development*, Oxford, 1982 Appendices A, B, C.
(11) from P. Bairoch, 'Europe's Gross National Product: 1800–1975', *Journal of European Economic History*, 1976, n. 2.

Table 5.8 Estimates of Output per Worker in Industry around 1910–13

	L_I/L 100	Y_I/Y 100	Y_I/L_I Crafts 1910 1970 $	Maddison 1913 1970 $	Bairoch 1913 1960 $	PB 1913 current $	ppp $	Index of Y_I/L_I GB = 100 (3)	(4)	(5)	(6)	(7)	Index of Real Industrial Wages in 1913 GB = 100
	(1)	(2)	(3)	(4)	(5)	(6)	(7)	(8)	(9)	(10)	(11)	(12)	(13)
USA	29	27	–	3864	–	944	638	–	120	–	195	132	126–134
France	29(32)	36(41)	2108(2176)	2896(2988)	1660(1714)	–	–	80(83)	90(93)	83(85)	–	–	60–64
Germany	41	43	2283	2588	1863	442	395	87	81	93	91	81	68–75
Italy	24	24	1218	1829	980	–	–	46	57	49	–	–	45–49
Sweden	26	31	2278	2559	2026	504	462	87	80	101	104	95	82–92
GB	44	40	2630	3212	2012	485	485	100	100	100	100	100	100

Sources: (1)–(2) data come from Mitchell, with the exception of: figures in parenthesis for France, which are revisions suggested by F. Caron, *An Economic History of Modern France*, London, 1979; figures for Italy, which come from P. Ercolani, 'Documentazione statistica di base', in G. Fuà (ed.), *Lo sviluppo economico in Italia* Milan, 1969, vol. III; figures for Great Britain, which are taken from R. C. O. Matthews, C. H. Feinstein, J. C. Odling Smee, op.cit.; and figures for USA, which come from A. Maddison 'Growth and Slowdown in Advanced Capitalist Economies: Techniques of Quantitative Assessment', *Journal of Economic Literature*, June 1987.
(3)–(5) my elaborations on the basis of (1), (2) and data in Table 5.6
(6) from Phelps Brown
(7) (6) made comparable at PPP price through the index of Column (3), Table 5.4
(13) from Table 5.4

USA: The two estimates of Y_I/L_I available rank the USA at the same level with respect to Britain as real wages.

France: The estimates of French industrial productivity range from 83 per cent to 93 per cent of the British level, while real wages stand at 60 to 64 per cent. The gap seems to me very wide indeed, and I consider this one further piece of evidence that French wages are undervalued.

Germany: In this case we have four estimates of industrial productivity ranging between 81 and 93 per cent of the British level, again in presence of wages distinctly lower in comparative terms, although not so distant as in the French case. As there is no reason to doubt the quality of German wage data, we might be inclined to advance the hypothesis of a real competitive advantage in the cost of labour on the part of German industry.

Italy: The ranking of industrial productivity and wage rates broadly agree.

Sweden: Industrial productivity estimates range between 80 and 101 per cent. With the exception of Bairoch's estimate, which is distinctly higher, they are in line with the ranking of wages.

A better quality of industrial productivity data and their availability at more than one date would allow a comparison between rates of growth of productivity and rates of growth of wages (as I have done in the case of Italy 1898–1913 in my last essay). Also, the trend in strikes and profits could be compared with that of wages, when such data are available.

Appendix 5.1: Money Wages and Cost of Living Series 1890–1913

All figures reported in the tables are indices 1900=100.

Appendix 5.2: Construction of the Money Wages Series for Italy, 1890–7

The construction of the average money wage rates series for Italy 1890–7 has followed a two-stage approach. First, the series for individual industries have been built extrapolating the 1898–1913 series (already available in my earlier essay) on the basis of the trend in wages in various firms available in ASI 1895, 1900, 1905/7, and in A. Geisser and E. Magrini, 'Contribuzione alla storia e statistica dei salari industriali in Italia nella seconda metà del secolo XIX', *La riforma sociale,* 1904. Next, a weighting system has been devised that assigns more weight to textiles (and to silk in particular) in 1890, less weight to mining and chemicals, less to building (which had a deep crisis at the beginning of the 1890s) and a cyclical performance to metal-engineering. Quarrying has been embodied into mining; bricks and tiles, gas (very small before 1898) and tobacco have been combined into chemicals for lack of direct information. The details of the computation are collected in Table 5.15.

Table 5.9 Money Wages and Cost of Living — France 1890–1913

	Money Wages				Cost of Living				Real Wages (3):(6) × 100
	Singer-Kérel				Singer-Kérel				
	All France (1)	Paris (2)	Phelps Brown (3)	Kuczyn-ski (4)	Ouvrier A (5)	213 items (6)	214 items (7)	Kuczyn-ski (8)	(9)
1890	94	96	92	92	108	102	102	105	90
1891	94	96	94	92	110	104	102	107	92
1892	94	96	94	93	111	103	101	101	93
1893	94	96	94	93	104	101	100	99	94
1894	95	98	94	93	106	104	101	102	93
1895	95	98	94	93	105	102	100	101	94
1896	96	100	95	94	103	100	100	100	95
1897	96	100	96	95	104	97	98	100	98
1898	97	100	98	97	106	99	99	101	99
1899	98	100	100	100	103	100	99	99	100
1900	100	100	100	100	100	100	100	100	100
1901	101	100	101	99	101	100	100	94	101
1902	101	100	100	97	101	99	100	92	101

1903	102	100	101	99	103	99	99	100	102
1904	103	100	102	99	101	97	99	98	105
1905	105	100	103	99	103	97	99	94	106
1906	109	101	107	104	104	99	100	93	108
1907	111	103	108	105	104	100	101	98	108
1908	112	103	108	108	103	102	102	100	106
1909	113	106	109	109	106	102	102	99	107
1910	106	107	110	111	110	103	103	103	107
1911	106	110	111	113	114	113	108	112	98
1912	107	111	112	114	119	112	108	116	100
1913	108	113	113	115	118	113	108	113	100

The consumer price series in A. Maddison, op. cit., table E 2, is the one reported here in 6. It must be noted, however, that Maddison must have reported his series from p. 105 of the book by Singer-Kérel where, as a result of a quite apparent printing mistake, the figure for 1910 has been interchanged with the figure for 1911.

Sources: Phelps Brown: Wages are an estimate from various sources, detailed at p. 363; Prices: index for ouvrier A constructed by J. Singer-Kérel, *Le coût de la vie à Paris 1840–1954*, Paris, 1961. Mitchell: Wages from unspecified source (not reported here because incomplete); Prices: same sources as Phelps Brown, but it is the index 'coût de la vie 214 articles' (column 7) including wages of servants and using 'bourgeois' weights. Kuczynski: J. Kuczynski, *Die Geschichte der Lage der Arbeiter unter dem Kapitalismus*, vol. 33, *Darstellung der Lage der Arbeiter in Frankreich seit 1848*, Berlin, 1967. The author comments at p. 170 on the discrepancies between his indices and those calculated by Singer-Kérel.

Table 5.10 Money Wages and Cost of Living — Germany 1890–1913

	Money Wages				Cost of Living				Real Wages
	Kuczynski (1)	Bry (2)	Desai (3)	Hoffmann (4)	Kuczynski (5)	Orsagh (6)	Desai (7)	Hoffmann (8)	(3):(6) (9)
1890	91	87	83	84	97	99	96	98	84
1891	91	87	83	86	100	104	100	99	80
1892	91	87	83	85	99	101	99	93	82
1893	91	87	86	86	97	96	95	92	90
1894	91	87	84	86	96	94	94	91	89
1895	91	87	85	88	95	94	94	93	90
1896	92	91	89	89	94	94	94	95	95
1897	93	91	94	92	96	96	96	95	98
1898	96	95	96	95	99	99	98	95	97
1899	99	97	101	97	99	99	96	97	102
1900	100	100	100	100	100	100	100	100	100
1901	100	99	103	100	101	101	101	100	102
1902	100	99	103	101	101	102	102	100	101
1903	101	100	104	104	101	102	102	100	102

1904	104	103	107	107	103	101	103	101	106
1905	107	107	108	110	106	106	106	104	102
1906	112	112	114	115	113	108	109	110	106
1907	116	119	119	121	114	111	112	109	107
1908	116	117	121	121	114	113	114	108	107
1909	117	119	121	122	117	116	116	112	104
1910	120	121	125	125	119	118	117	117	106
1911	122	124	129	130	123	118	118	116	109
1912	126	128	135	134	130	123	124	118	110
1913	132	133	138	137	130	120	122	118	115

Phelps Brown uses Desai's series; Mitchell uses Kuczynski's; A. Maddison (op. cit., table E 2) uses Hoffmann's. Three recent works of interest have appeared: R. Gömmel, *Realeinkommen in Deutschland. Ein internationaler Vergleich 1810–1910*, Nürnberg, 1979, where Desai's series are used; the more comprehensive and detailed E. Wiegand, 'Zur historischen Entwicklung der Löhne und Lebenshaltungskosten in Deutschland', in E. Wiegand and W. Zapf (eds), *Wandel der Lebensbedingungen in Deutschland*, Frankfurt–New York, 1982, where a full discussion of all series available is provided; and T. Pierenkemper, 'The Standard of Living and Employment in Germany, 1850–1980: An Overview', *Journal of European Economic History*, Spring 1987, where Wiegand's elaborations are reported without further comment.

Sources: A. V. Desai, *Real Wages in Germany 1871–1913*, Oxford, 1968; G. Bry, *Wages in Germany 1871–1945*, Princeton, 1960 (slightly revised version of Kuczynski's series); J. Kuczynski, *Die Geschichte der Lage der Arbeiter in Deutschland von 1789 bis in die Gegenwart*, Berlin, 1954; W. G. Hoffmann, *Das Wachstum der deutschen Wirtschaft seit der Mitte des 19. Jahrhunderts*, Berlin, 1965 (the cost of living series is the implicit deflator of private consumption); T. J. Orsagh, 'Löhne in Deutschland 1871–1913. Neuere Literatur und weitere Ergebnisse', *Zeitschrift für die gesamte Staatswissenschaften*, 125, 1969, p. 481.

Table 5.11 Money Wages and Cost of Living—Italy 1890–1913

	Money Wages Cassa Infortuni	ZM	Cost of living ISTAT	Implicit deflator of private consumption	Real Wages (2):(3) ×100
	(1)	(2)	(3)	(4)	(5)
1890	–	91	106	102	86
1891	–	91	105	102	87
1892	–	91	105	97	87
1893	–	92	102	96	90
1894	–	92	101	95	91
1895	–	93	101	99	92
1896	–	94	100	95	94
1897	–	96	100	96	96
1898	100	97	102	102	95
1899	100	98	100	99	98
1900	100	100	100	100	100
1901	100	103	101	96	102
1902	103	106	100	94	106
1903	104	108	103	101	105
1904	104	112	103	98	108
1905	102	116	104	99	112
1906	106	122	107	104	114
1907	119	129	111	104	116
1908	119	131	110	103	119
1909	134	135	107	106	126
1910	131	141	110	113	128
1911	133	148	114	115	130
1912	137	152	113	119	134
1913	143	156	114	120	137

Sources: For wages, see all references in my last essay. For the years 1890–7, see Table 5.15; Mitchell uses the *Cassa Infortuni* series; ISTAT's cost of living series has never been challenged by any other estimate; the implicit deflator of private consumption reported in column 4 comes from P. Ercolani, op. cit., table XII.4.4 and is used by A. Maddison, op. cit., table E2. I do not think its use is correct in this context, as it has been argued already in the case of France and Germany.

Table 5.12 Money Wages and Cost of Living—Sweden 1890–1913

	Money Wages		Cost of Living	Real Wages (1):(3) ×100
	Phelps Brown (1)	Mitchell (2)	(3)	(4)
1890	78	74	94	83
1891	79	75	97	81
1892	79	76	95	83
1893	80	78	92	87
1894	81	79	87	93
1895	82	80	89	93
1896	85	83	88	96
1897	88	87	91	96
1898	92	92	95	97
1899	97	96	99	98
1900	100	100	100	100
1901	98	100	98	100
1902	100	102	98	102
1903	103	103	100	103
1904	105	107	99	106
1905	105	110	101	104
1906	114	116	104	110
1907	121	122	108	112
1908	121	125	110	111
1909	121	129	109	111
1910	129	135	109	118
1911	132	137	107	123
1912	136	142	115	118
1913	139	144	115	121

It appears that at p. 441, column 1 of Phelps Brown there is a printing mistake (891 rather than 981), which I have corrected.

Sources: Both Phelps Brown and Mitchell have used G. Bagge, E. Lundberg, I. Svennilson, *Wages in Sweden*, London, 1933. Cost of living universally used comes from G. Myrdal and S. Bouvin, *The Cost of Living in Sweden 1860–1930*, London, 1933.

Table 5.13 Money Wages and Cost of Living—United Kingdom 1890–1913

	Money Wages		Cost of Living		Real Wages
	Phelps Brown (1)	Mitchell (2)	Phelps Brown (3)	Mitchell (4)	(1):(3) ×100 (5)
1890	91	91	98	–	92
1891	91	92	98	–	92
1892	91	90	99	103	91
1893	91	91	98	99	92
1894	91	90	93	94	97
1895	91	89	91	92	100
1896	91	90	91	91	100
1897	93	91	93	96	100
1898	94	93	96	99	92
1899	96	96	94	94	102
1900	100	100	100	100	100
1901	100	99	99	100	101
1902	98	98	99	101	99
1903	98	97	100	102	98
1904	97	97	101	102	97
1905	97	97	101	102	96
1906	101	99	102	101	99
1907	106	102	105	104	101
1908	105	102	102	107	103
1909	103	100	103	107	100
1910	105	101	105	109	100
1911	105	101	107	109	98
1912	107	104	110	114	97
1913	109	107	112	114	97

Sources: The money wages series come from G. H. Wood, 'Real Wages and the Standard of Comfort since 1850', *Journal of the Royal Statistical Society*, March 1909 and A. L. Bowley, *Wages and Income in the United Kingdom since 1860*, Cambridge 1937. Mitchell appears not to have excluded agricultural workers. The Phelps Brown cost of living series is from Bowley, op. cit.; the Mitchell cost of living series is from the eighteenth *Abstract of Labour Statistics*.

Table 5.14 Money Wages and Cost of Living—United States 1890–1913

	Money Wages		Cost of Living		Real Wages
	Phelps Brown	Abstract	Phelps Brown	Douglas	(1):(3) (1):(3) ×100
	(1)	(2)	(3)	(4)	(5)
1890	98	101	108	98	91
1891	99	102	108	95	91
1892	100	103	108	96	92
1893	95	97	107	94	88
1894	87	89	102	92	85
1895	91	96	100	92	90
1896	91	93	100	93	91
1897	91	94	99	94	93
1898	91	95	99	94	92
1899	97	98	99	96	98
1900	100	100	100	100	100
1901	103	105	101	102	102
1902	110	109	102	105	106
1903	111	112	105	109	105
1904	109	110	106	108	103
1905	113	114	105	108	107
1906	122	116	107	112	114
1907	125	120	112	119	111
1908	112	109	109	114	102
1909	119	119	108	114	109
1910	125	128	113	121	110
1911	126	123	113	125	111
1912	131	126	115	125	113
1913	135	133	118	129	115

Sources: Phelps Brown's annual money wage series in manufacturing comes from A. Rees, *Real Wages in Manufacturing 1890–1914*, Princeton, 1961. The other series comes from the US Department of Commerce, *Historical Statistics of the United States*, Washington, 1961, series D 605 (from P. H. Douglas, *Real Wages in the United States 1890–1926*, Boston, 1930).

Phelps Brown's cost of living series comes from Rees and is more reliable than Douglas's series reported in the US Department volume, which is too heavily built with wholesale prices.

Table 5.15 Daily Wage Rates in Italian Industry 1890–1897 (lire)

	Metal-Engineering		Chemicals, Etc.		Wool		Cotton		Silk		Textiles Average		Paper	
	rates (1)	weight (2)	rates (3)	weight (4)	rates (5)	weight in textiles (6)	rates (7)	weight in textiles (8)	rates (9)	weight in textiles (10)	rates (11)	weight (12)	rates (13)	weight (14)
1890	2.85	15	2.0	10	1.75	5	1.40	20	1.00	75	1.12	50	1.25	2
1891	2.80	14	2.0	11	1.75	5	1.45	20	1.00	75	1.12	50	1.28	2
1892	2.75	14	2.0	11	1.78	6	1.45	20	1.00	74	1.14	49	1.28	2
1893	2.80	14	2.0	12	1.80	6	1.48	21	1.00	73	1.15	48	1.30	2
1894	2.85	13.5	2.0	12	1.80	7	1.50	23	1.00	70	1.17	48	1.30	2
1895	2.90	13.5	2.0	12	1.80	7	1.52	25	1.00	68	1.19	47	1.30	2
1896	2.90	13.5	2.0	12	1.82	8	1.55	25	1.00	67	1.20	46	1.30	2
1897	2.90	13.5	2.0	13	1.82	8	1.58	26	1.00	66	1.22	45	1.32	2

	Printing		Leather		Mining, Etc.		Building		Average Money Wage	Cost of Living Index 1913=1	Average Real Wages 1913/lire	Index 1900 = 100 of (23)	Index 1900 = 100 of (25)
	rates (15)	weight (16)	rates (17)	weight (18)	rates (19)	weight (20)	rates (21)	weight (22)	(23)	(24)	(25)	(26)	(27)
1890	3.00	2.5	1.90	2.5	1.80	8	1.80	10	1.66	1.0730	1.78	91.2	86.4
1891	3.20	2.5	1.90	2.5	1.90	8	1.80	10	1.66	1.0764	1.79	91.2	86.9
1892	3.20	2.5	1.90	2.5	1.95	8	1.70	11	1.66	1.0858	1.80	91.2	87.4
1893	3.20	2.5	1.90	2.5	1.90	8	1.70	11	1.67	1.1099	1.85	91.8	89.8
1894	3.20	2.5	1.90	2.5	1.80	8.5	1.70	11	1.68	1.1148	1.87	92.3	90.8
1895	3.20	2.5	1.90	2.5	1.70	9	1.70	12	1.69	1.1211	1.89	92.9	91.7
1896	3.20	2.5	1.90	2.5	1.90	9	1.70	12	1.71	1.1261	1.93	94.0	93.7
1897	3.20	2.5	2.00	2.5	1.95	9	1.70	12.5	1.75	1.1287	1.98	96.2	96.1

(24) from ISTAT, *Il valore della lira dal 1861 al 1956*, Rome, 1966.

[15]

Excerpt from Patrick O'Brien (ed.), *Railways and the Economic Development of Western Europe, 1830–1914*, 49–120.

3 Italy

STEFANO FENOALTEA

1. INTRODUCTION

This survey examines the contribution of the railway to the modernisation of the nineteenth-century Italian economy, with particular attention to industrial growth.

The growth of Italy's railways was heavily influenced by political events. Only the first regional networks, notably in Tuscany and Piedmont, were built in the 1840s and 1850s. The achievement of political unity in 1861 led to a first railway boom, mainly in the construction of national trunk lines. The transfer of parliamentary power from the Right to the Left led to a sharp increase in public spending and a second railway boom, mainly in the construction of secondary lines, in the 1880s and early 1890s. A third railway boom, mainly in reconstruction and improvement, followed the railways' nationalisation in 1905.

Industrial production, in turn, appears to have grown slowly in the 1860s and 1870s, and relatively rapidly in the 1880s. The 1890s were marked by recession and recovery, and the early 1900s by a second decade of rapid growth. That experience has been interpreted as a sequence of stages of growth induced by the loosening of supply-side constraints on industrial production; but the evidence suggests that the supply side was generally permissive, as resources flowed readily into and out of Italy, and that the primary source of the fluctuations in industrial production was a cycle in the demand for durables.

An examination of the railways' consumption of industrial products suggests that the market for modern industry created by the mature railway system was altogether more significant than that created by railway expansion. One reason is the shift in the composition of railway investment: initial construction was mostly a matter of traditional pick-and-shovel work, while rails and rolling stock absorbed a far greater share of the subsequent expenditure for reconstruction and improvement. The other reason is the growth of railway maintenance, especially of rolling stock. On a value-added basis, the maintenance of these vehicles was as important as their initial fabrication; and, unlike the latter, it was quite immune from foreign competition.

The direct impact of railway investment on the composition of production thus appears to have been small, and to industry's advantage only from about 1900. The indirect impact may have been more significant, since railway investment could induce international resource flows and thus alter even the level of aggregate production. Preliminary explorations with a very simple model suggest that railway investment may have somewhat amplified the cycle in industrial production; more significantly, it may have induced the tariffs on semi-finished metal that locked the domestic engineering industry into the small and fluctuating domestic market. These induced effects cannot be established empirically, however, without far more information than is currently available.

As a provider of transportation, the railway appears to have improved the Upper Po Valley's access to the sea, but to have done relatively little to unify the domestic market. This limited impact seems due not only to the relatively high operating costs induced primarily by the rugged terrain, but also to implicit taxes that kept railway rates well above marginal costs. The state thus discouraged the utilisation of the railway network even as it encouraged its extension; while this policy was certainly curious, the constraints on public revenues, the military value of the railways, and the electoral advantages of public works projects all suggest that it may not have been as irrational as it seems.

The net benefits provided by the railways may be assessed by comparing the capital costs incurred by their construction to the producers' and consumers' surplus generated by their use. Sample estimates for the entire network suggest that the benefits of the entire system were at most just equal to its costs. Disaggregated estimates suggest that the major Po Valley lines yielded significant net benefits, while the other major lines incurred significant net costs. The large system of minor lines also incurred net costs, but on a much reduced scale, as a majority at least of these lines appear to have paid for themselves. The large-scale construction of minor lines undertaken by the Left in the 1880s and 1890s thus appears altogether less wasteful, and that of peninsular trunk lines undertaken by the Right in the 1860s and 1870s altogether less useful, than is commonly thought. The most useful lines were those in northern Italy, largely built before the achievement of national unity; and since internal waterways were available from the Lombard lakes to the Adriatic, the most conspicuous net beneficiaries from the construction of those lines were no doubt Piedmont and the neighbouring Ligurian ports.

2. THE GROWTH OF THE RAILWAYS

Italy's railways experienced four main periods of development before the First World War (1). The first period, from the opening of the first rail line on Italian soil (Naples-Portici) in 1839 up to the creation of the Kingdom of Italy in 1861, saw the establishment of the first local systems. A mere 500 kilometres were built in the 1840s, including the early lines around Naples (some 50 kilometres linking royal residences and military camps), the major Tuscan valley lines (some 200 kilometres linking Leghorn, Pisa, Siena and Florence), a good part of the line from Milan to Venice (some 200 kilometres along the northern edge of the Po Valley), and the first Piedmontese line (some 50 kilometres from Turin to Asti). A further 1500 kilometres, most of them in northern Italy, were added through 1860. The Piedmontese network quickly became the largest in Italy, with 800 kilometres in a grid linking the major centres of the Upper Po Valley to each other and to the sea at Genoa. The line from Milan to Venice was completed in 1857, and subsequently extended to reach Piedmont in the west, Tyrol in the north and Illyria in the east, for a total of approximately 600 kilometres. The Neapolitan and Tuscan systems were extended to some 100 and 300 kilometres, respectively; and in the late 1850s the first railways appeared in Latium (some 100 kilometres, most of them from Rome to the sea at Civitavecchia) and in Emilia-Romagna (some 100 kilometres along the southern edge of the Po Valley from Piedmont through Parma to Bologna). By the end of 1860, then, Italy possessed some 2000 kilometres of rail lines. This was a relatively paltry figure on the Western European scale, placing Italy well behind Great Britain, France and Germany, and roughly on a par with Spain (Table 3.1, cols 1-3); but even this limited mileage was enough to link Italy's major inland cities, and the future 'industrial triangle', to the sea.

The second period, from 1861 to 1880, saw the establishment of a national network. The strategic value of peninsular trunk lines to the new national state produced a sharp acceleration in the pace of construction: 4000 kilometres of line were added in the 1860s, trebling the existing network, and a further 2500 kilometres were added in the 1870s. The railhead at Bologna shot forward to and along the Adriatic coast, on relatively easy ground entirely within the Kingdom; Ancona was reached in 1861 and Lecce, at the tip of the boot's heel, in 1866. The further extension of this line along the Ionian coast was altogether slower, and the entire route to Reggio Calabria, at the tip of the boot's toe, was not completed

Table 3.1: *Railway development in Western Europe, 1860 and 1913*

	(1)	(2)	(3)	(4)	(5)
		1860		*1913*	
	Area (a) (000 sq km)	*Population (a) (000,000)*	*Railways (a) (000 km)*	*Population (000,000)*	*Railways (000 km)*
Italy	287	25	2	35	18
Great Britain	228	23	15	42	33
France	536	35	9	39	41
Germany	541	37	12	68	64
Spain	504	16	2	20	15

(a) within the borders of 1913.

Source: See the Appendix to this chapter.

until 1875. The central valley route that provided the initial links between the existing local systems was also quickly established: Rome and Naples were joined in 1863, Bologna and Florence in 1864, and Florence and Rome in 1866. The west coast line branched out of the Tuscan network, growing south to reach Civitavecchia and Rome in 1867, and north, through the more difficult Riviera, to reach Genoa and the French border in 1874. With the further addition of the first Sicilian and Sardinian lines (from the early 1860s and early 1870s, respectively), and of a succession of transpeninsular routes (from Rome to the Adriatic in 1866, from Naples to the Adriatic in 1870, from Naples to the Ionian in 1880), the Italian trunk system was, by 1880, virtually complete.

The third period, from 1881 to 1895, saw a renewal of very rapid growth: 6500 kilometres were added in fifteen years, increasing the total network by over 75 per cent. This expansion was part of the vast programme of public spending introduced by the Left shortly after it came to power in 1876; while it included the southern extension of the west coast trunk route along the poor and rugged coast from Naples to Reggio Calabria, its principal focus was the construction of a large number of minor lines, of essentially local interest.

In the fourth period, from 1896 to 1913, the growth of the railway network reverted to the slow pace of its early years: only 2500 kilometres were added in nearly twenty years, for a total system, on the eve of the First World War, of about 17500 kilometres. On the Western European scale, this total left Italy much where it had been fifty years earlier: still well behind Great Britain, France and Germany, and roughly on a par with Spain (Table 3.1, cols 1, 4-5).

Administratively, Italy's early railways were built and operated by a relatively large number of concessionaires. Numerous minor lines were to survive as independent entities; but the main network underwent three major reorganisations. In 1865, it was entrusted to five regional groups: the Alta Italia, operating north of Pisa-Florence-Bologna; the Romane, operating the west coast and valley routes between Florence and Naples; the Meridionali, operating the Adriatic coast line south of Bologna and across Southern Italy to Naples; the Calabro-Sicule (taken over by the Meridionali in 1873) operating in the lower South; and the Sarde, operating in Sardinia. In 1885, the operation of the main network, by then largely in public ownership, was entrusted to four companies, including two major systems on the continent (the Rete Mediterranea in the west and the Rete Adriatica in the east) and two minor systems on the islands (the Sicule and the Sarde). In 1905, finally, the operations of the main network was taken over by the Ferrovie dello Stato. The latter inherited a system that had been badly run down in the expectation of that takeover; as they rebuilt and replaced their track and rolling stock, they gave rise to a reconstruction boom comparable in intensity to the construction booms of the 1860s and 1880s. Italy thus experienced three major waves of railway investment: two in new construction, induced by political change (the achievement of national unity, the parliamentary triumph of the Left); and one in reconstruction, induced by administrative change (the shift from private to public operation).

3. THE GROWTH OF INDUSTRY

In general, it would appear, Italy's industry grew slowly in the 1860s and 1870s, and rather faster in the 1880s; it fell back and then recovered in the 1890s, grew rapidly in the first decade of the present century, and slowed again in the last few years before the war. The limits and intensities of the growth spurts differ from index to index (Table 3.2): Gerschenkron's 1955 index (col 1) indicates growth at 5 per cent per annum from 1881 (its initial year) to 1887, and 7 per cent per annum from 1896 to 1907; Istat's 1957 index (col 2) indicates growth at 3 per cent per annum from 1880 to 1887, and 6 per cent per annum from 1898 to 1908; and my own 1967 revision and extension of the Gerschenkron index (col 3) indicates growth at 8 per cent per annum from 1879 to 1887, and 11 per cent per annum from 1902 to 1908. The specific differences between the Istat index and the others are hard to trace, since the description of the calculations underlying that index are very sketchy; the differences between the Gerschenkron index and my own are traceable in part to a revision of the underlying series (which tends to raise the growth rate in the 1880s, and reduce it around the turn of the century), and in part to a different weighting scheme (which increases, perhaps to excess, the volatility of my index). But these differences in dates and growth rates are ultimately a matter of detail, of little import given the crude nature and limited scope of all three of these indices. In the large, the three series agree on the existence of an earlier, weaker growth spurt in the 1880s, and a later, stronger one in the early 1900s (2).

This rough consensus on the facts of Italy's industrial growth has been accompanied by thorough disagreement as to their interpretation. In the late 1950s and early 1960s, the most vigorous polemic was that between Gerschenkron and Romeo (3). They shared a certain amount of common ground: both understood Italy's early industrial development as a sequence of stages, with an 'industrial revolution' or 'big push' early in this century; and both attributed the acceleration in trend growth rates to an increase in the supply of industrial capital.

Table 3.2: *Indices of industrial production (1900=100)*

	(1) Gerschenkron (1955)	(2) Istat (1957)	(3) Fenoaltea (1967)
1861		57	37
1862		57	37
1863		57	37
1864		57	37
1865		62	36
1866		62	37
1867		59	39
1868		59	39
1869		65	40
1870		68	42
1871		62	42
1872		65	43
1873		70	45
1874		73	46
1875		73	47
1876		73	47
1877		73	48
1878		70	48
1879		70	48
1880		68	53
1881	54	76	57
1882	57	73	61
1883	64	76	65
1884	63	78	67
1885	65	81	72
1886	67	78	76
1887	73	84	88
1888	74	81	88
1889	72	81	86
1890	72	81	82
1891	67	76	73
1892	64	76	69
1893	70	76	72
1894	72	81	76
1895	73	84	78
1896	75	81	79
1897	78	84	82
1898	86	84	88

Continued

Table 3.2 - *Continued*

	(1) *Gerschenkron* (1955)	(2) *Istat* (1957)	(3) *Fenoaltea* (1967)
1899	92	89	97
1900	100	100	100
1901	104	97	101
1902	109	105	104
1903	114	108	113
1904	117	111	119
1905	126	116	133
1906	139	127	152
1907	152	141	172
1908	163	149	196
1909	168	149	203
1910	169	149	211
1911	174	151	218
1912	182	162	222
1913	184	159	220

Source: See the Appendix to this chapter.

Beyond that, however, their approaches and conclusions were very different. Romeo's interpretation, rooted in a sophisticated critique of the Gramsci thesis, portrayed Italy's development as a relatively ordered process favoured by public policy and largely conditioned by railway construction; Gerschenkron's interpretation, rooted in his model of prerequisite substitution, portrayed Italy's initial industrial growth as a false start, public policy as a brake on development, and railway construction as a missed opportunity.

The so-called Gramsci thesis is the view that Italy's capitalist development was stunted by the failure of the Risorgimento to encompass an agrarian revolution creating peasant properties out of large estates (on the French model, and not of course on the largely opposite English one) (4). To Romeo's mind, a Gramscian land reform would have sharply reduced the supply of savings, and thus the rate of accumulation, by dissipating the agricultural surplus as peasant consumption. As it was, the peasants were forced to save; and the governments of the 1860s and 1870s created the infrastructure necessary for economic growth by taxing the surplus collected by the landlords. From the 1880s, the nation's scarce savings could be, and were, invested in industry, which was then aided by government orders and tariff protection; the industrial spurt of that decade was the lineal antecedent of the subsequent more general one. In this interpretation, industrialisation followed railway construction, causally as well as chronologically: because industry required the cheap transportation the national railway network would provide; and because industry was starved of scarce capital while the national railway network was being built. The direct contribution of railway orders for industrial equipment in the 1880s and early 1900s is also recognised, but considered altogether secondary.

The Gerschenkron model of prerequisite substitution links the institutional matrix of accumulation to the relative backwardness of the economy when rapid industrialisation begins (5). In advanced areas (e.g. England), private factories take the lead; in moderately backward areas (e.g. Germany), industrial banks substitute for scarce individual capital and enterprise; and in very backward areas (e.g. Russia), the state substitutes even for the banks. In Italy, the intensive railway construction of the 1880s provided a fine opportunity for a 'big push' in conditions of considerable backwardness; but the government did not rise to the occasion. Tariff policy was particularly inept, as it protected metal-making a (low value-added industry) rather than engineering (a high value-added industry). The growth of those years thus led nowhere; and the 'big push' was delayed fifteen years, until the German-style industrial banks entered Italy (1895) and began to play the entrepreneurial, capital-accumulating role that neither individuals (because of Italy's general backwardness) nor the government (because of public ineptness) had been able to play. When the 'big push' did occur, moreover, it was slowed by the inappropriate tariff structure and the fact that railway construction was, by then, largely an accomplished fact (though a minor positive role may be attributed to railway reconstruction after 1905). In this interpretation, the railway as provider of cheap transportation is almost invisible; it is dismissed also as an absorber of scarce savings (on the grounds that the Italian capital market was not unified, so that railways and industry did not compete), and survives only as a purchaser of industrial equipment, in a role that could have been major (in the 1880s), but was in fact minor.

By the late 1960s, stages-of-growth models were clearly falling from favour; and my own early work questioned their applicability to the Italian experience as well (6). Italy's major industries, it seems, fall into three basic groups. The first consists of old consumers' goods industries such as milling and textiles; these grew at a relatively steady pace throughout the relevant period, either in step with the domestic market (milling) or with a steadily improving position in the international market (textiles, where decreasing imports gave way to increasing exports). The second group consists of new industries such as electric power generation and sugar extraction. Power generation appeared in Italy in 1883, just months after the world's first plant opened in the United States, and grew lustily ever after; sugar extraction took off with the successful introduction of the sugar beet in the Lower Po Valley in the late 1890s, and conquered the domestic market in the space of a few years. The third group consists of durable goods industries such as engineering and metal-making. Their production movements account for the fluctuations of the aggregate index; and those movements appear to result from an elastic adjustment to the fluctuations in domestic demand, both when it boomed in the 1880s and 1900s and when it collapsed in the 1890s. Metalmaking also achieved some import-substituting growth, thanks largely to increases in tariff protection in 1878 and 1887; but that same tariff increased the materials costs of the engineering industry, and apparently prevented it from breaking out of the small and fluctuating domestic market into sustained export-led growth.

In the circumstances, there are a number of reasons *not* to interpret the acceleration of growth from the 1880s to the 1900s as progress from an inferior stage of growth to a superior one. The first is simply that the acceleration in the aggregate index stems primarily from the secularly declining weight of slow-growing traditional industries, and not from any broadly-based acceleration within individual sectors. The second is of course the essential similarity of the earlier and later growth periods, as both were led largely by the demand for durables. The first upswing was thus inherently as mature as the second; and, since the demand for durables is inherently cyclical, the second was inherently as fragile as the first (7). The third and strongest reason is that there was no apparent change in industry's patterns of behaviour. This is clearly true of the cyclical industries, since their production rose and fell in step with their market opportunities; and it is also true of the new industries, since their appearance is traceable to novel opportunities (created by agricultural and technological development) rather than to improved response to existing opportunities (8).

In particular, there is no evidence of a discontinuous improvement in response traceable either to the completion of the infrastructure or to the importation of German-style industrial banks. On the former point, the essential difficulty with Romeo's interpretation is that the infrastructure was not an indivisible investment that absorbed funds in the 1860s and 1870s, and provided transportation from the 1880s. Rather, it was a highly divisible investment that yielded transportation improvements incrementally, with a relatively short average lag; and the level of investment in railways and other public works was conspicuously higher in the 1880s and 1900s, when industry was growing most rapidly, than in the 1860s and 1870s. The virtual completion of the railway trunk system around 1880 was thus in no way a watershed. On the benefits side, the supply of transportation expanded continuously as those lines were built, and any acceleration after 1880 would owe more to current investments than to long past ones; on the cost side, the absorption of capital by the infrastructure displays not a sharp decrease around 1880 but an increase (9).

On the latter point, the essential difficulty with Gerschenkron's interpretation is a straightforward econometric result: the growth of the German-style banks is simply not correlated with a growth in the ability of domestic industry to capture existing markets. This result is perfectly compatible with the fact that these banks were heavily involved with industry, and even with the presumption that they improved its absolute performance (10). It does mean, however, that there is no evidence that they improved its *relative* performance; no evidence, that is to say, that they represented the solution to a problem (the accumulation of capital in industry) that was more severe in Italy than in more developed countries; no evidence, in sum, that they were in any way more important to Italy's industrial development than any other innovation that was widely adopted, in banking or anywhere else.

In general, then, Italy's early industrial growth appears to have been characterised not by a sequence of stages but by a business cycle; not by supply-side bottlenecks and breakthroughs but by the interaction of a fluctuating demand side and a permissive supply side. This apparent ease with which domestic industry could attract the resources needed for expansion seems explainable, in turn, by two sorts of considerations. One is simply that domestic industry was a relatively small part of the domestic economy; in the presence of functioning resource markets, industry was accordingly without much influence on resource prices. The second and more significant argument, which overcomes the limitations of the first, is that the entire Italian economy was a similarly small part of a larger international economy, with similarly functioning resource markets: domestic industry was accordingly without much influence on the price even of specialised industrial resources (and these are, of course, the ones that matter). The lack of supply-side bottlenecks and breakthroughs thus seems attributable, in the first instance, to the readiness with which not only goods but labour, capital, entrepreneurs, technology and institutions could flow into and out of Italy. One recalls, in particular, the familiar international flows of labour, so large that nearly six million Italians were living abroad in 1911, so easy that over one million of these were temporary migrants (11). One recalls also the capital flows that not only covered the widening trade deficits during the investment booms of the 1880s and 1900s, but allowed the lira to appreciate in the process - strongly suggesting that the capital flows were induced directly by the domestic demand for funds, and were thus rather the cause of, than caused by, the deficits in the balance of trade (12).

Two more general points deserve perhaps to be made explicit. The first is that the reliance on foreign capital to finance such major investment programmes as railway construction does not indicate that shortages of domestic capital prevented development, or that domestic suppliers of capital failed to react rationally to investment opportunities. Rather, such capital imports indicate only that international supply curves are more elastic than domestic supply curves (which is only to be expected, since a single country's new investment needs are a far smaller part of current world investment than of its own current investment), and that domestic consumption can be stabilised by borrowing from outside (just as when an individual borrows to buy a house). Analytically, such capital imports are entirely compatible with ordinary market behaviour, and do not imply any sort of market failure; empirically, they were as significant in the United States as in 'backward' Italy or Spain. The second point is that economists customarily assume that factors of production are perfectly mobile within 'nations', and perfectly immobile between them. From this perspective, the substantive point at issue here concerns the relation between economic 'nations' and historically defined political units; there is obviously no reason to assimilate them to each other a priori (13).

4. THE RAILWAYS' CONSUMPTION OF INDUSTRIAL PRODUCTS

The railways' consumption of the products of the construction, engineering and metalmaking industries is illustrated by the estimates in Tables 3.3-3.6 (14). The construction series (Table 3.3, cols 1-4) and the rail consumption series (Table 3.6, col 2) clearly reflect the major waves of construction activity beginning in 1861, 1881 and 1906, as well as the progressive shift from first construction to improvement. The rolling-stock consumption series (Table 3.4, col 2) is also markedly cyclical, but with a strong trend reminiscent of that in construction for improvements (and

Table 3.3: *Construction value added in the construction and maintenance of rail- and tramway lines (million lire per annum at 1911 prices)*

	(1)	(2)	(3)	(4)	(5)	(6)	(7)	(8)	(9)
	First construction			*Railway improvements*	*Maintenance*			*Rail- and tramway total*	*Construction industry total*
	Railways	*Tramways*	*Total*		*Railways*	*Tramways*	*Total*		
1861-65	112		112		3		3	115	400
1866-70	66		66		5		5	71	350
1871-75	67		67	4	8		8	79	400
1876-80	48	5	53	11	11		11	75	400
1881-85	94	8	102	23	14	1	15	140	500
1886-90	88	4	92	21	19	1	20	133	550
1891-95	76	3	79	2	20	2	22	103	500
1896-00	13	9	22	5	23	2	25	52	400
1901-05	23	5	28	11	28	3	31	70	450
1906-10	25	6	31	35	35	3	38	104	600
1911-13	47	15	62	39	41	4	45	146	750

Source: See the Appendix to this chapter.

Table 3.4: *Engineering value added in the manufacture and maintenance of rail- and tramway rolling stock: aggregate estimates (million lire per annum at 1911 prices)*

	(1)	(2)	(3)	(4)	(5)	(6)	(7)	(8)	(9)	(10)	(11)	(12)
	Rail- and tramway rolling stock					*Track acces-sories (c)*	*All machinery (a)*			*Fabricated metal and machinery (a)*		
	Domestic produc-tion	*Production plus imports*	*Main-tenance*	*Domestic total*	*Overall total (b)*		*Produc-tion*	*Main-tenance*	*Total*	*Produc-tion*	*Main-tenance*	*Total*
1861–65	2.2	6.2	3.1	5.3	9.3	0.7	21	16	37	49	273	322
1866–70	2.0	5.2	5.1	7.1	10.3	0.6	22	21	43	50	283	333
1871–75	3.1	8.5	8.2	11.3	16.7	1.0	26	27	53	59	294	353
1876–80	1.7	3.7	10.7	12.4	14.4	1.4	31	33	64	70	305	375
1881–85	9.0	13.5	15.6	24.6	29.1	3.0	55	43	98	123	321	444
1886–90	15.4	23.2	20.5	35.9	43.7	2.7	79	53	132	174	336	510
1891–95	4.6	4.7	22.7	27.3	27.4	1.1	52	62	114	113	351	464
1896–1900	11.8	14.1	27.1	38.9	41.2	0.9	65	74	139	139	369	508
1901–05	19.8	26.0	34.6	54.4	60.6	1.3	83	93	176	176	394	570
1906–10	45.8	66.8	44.4	90.2	111.2	3.1	166	114	280	347	422	769
1911–13	53.5	56.6	54.6	108.1	111.2	4.0	200	135	335	412	446	858

(a) excludes shipbuilding and the production of wood road vehicles.
(b) domestic total plus imports.
(c) production plus imports.

Source: See the Appendix to this chapter.

Table 3.5: *Engineering value added in the manufacture and maintenance of railway rolling stock: composition (million lire per annum at 1911 prices)*

	(1)	(2)	(3)	(4)	(5)	(6)	(7)	(8)	(9)
	Domestic production			*Production plus imports*			*Maintenance*		
	Locomo-tives (a)	*Passenger cars (b)*	*Freight cars (c)*	*Locomo-tives (a)*	*Passenger cars (b)*	*Freight cars (c)*	*Locomo-tives (a)*	*Passenger cars (b)*	*Freight cars (c)*
1861-65	0.1	0.6	1.5	1.6	1.3	3.3	1.4	0.7	1.0
1866-70	0.2	0.5	1.3	1.3	0.9	3.0	2.3	1.1	1.7
1871-75	0.4	0.5	2.2	2.3	0.9	5.3	3.4	1.8	3.0
1876-80	0.1	0.5	1.1	1.2	0.7	1.8	4.4	2.3	4.0
1881-85	0.7	2.0	6.3	3.9	2.4	7.2	6.8	3.3	5.5
1886-90	1.8	3.3	10.3	4.9	3.9	14.4	9.3	4.3	6.9
1891-95	1.1	1.2	2.3	1.2	1.2	2.3	10.4	4.9	7.4
1896-1900	3.7	2.0	6.1	3.4 (d)	1.9 (d)	8.8	13.1	5.4	8.6
1901-05	5.4	3.9	10.5	6.2	5.4	14.4	17.8	6.5	10.3
1906-10	10.8	5.1	29.9	17.8	9.5	39.5	23.3	8.9	12.2
1911-13	12.5	7.1	33.9	14.4	7.7	34.5	28.6	11.5	14.5

(a) includes rail-cars.
(b) includes mail and cell cars.
(c) includes baggage cars and tenders.
(d) production minus exports.

Source: See the Appendix to this chapter.

Table 3.6: *Metalmaking value added in the manufacture of rail, accessories and metal for railway rolling stock (million lire per annum at 1911 prices)*

	(1)	(2)	(3)	(4)	(5)	(6)	(7)	(8)
	Rails (a)			Rolling stock metal (a)			Total market for railway metal (a)	
	Domestic production	Production plus imports	Accessories: production plus imports (a)	Maintenance consumption (b)	Total consumption (b)	Potential consumption (c)	Actual	Potential
1861–65		1.2	0.2	0.1	0.3	0.6	1.7	2.0
1866–70		1.0	0.2	0.3	0.5	0.8	1.7	2.0
1871–75		1.7	0.3	0.4	0.8	1.5	2.8	3.5
1876–80		2.4	0.4	0.6	0.8	1.0	3.6	3.8
1881–85		5.3	1.0	0.9	2.0	2.5	8.3	8.8
1886–90	3.0	4.7	0.8	1.2	3.0	4.0	8.5	9.5
1891–95	1.6	2.0	0.4	1.3	1.8	1.8	4.2	4.2
1896–1900	0.8	1.5	0.3	1.5	2.9	3.3	4.7	5.1
1901–05	1.4	2.2	0.4	2.0	4.3	5.0	6.9	7.6
1906–10	4.4	5.5	1.0	2.5	8.2	10.6	14.7	17.1
1911–13	6.9	7.0	1.3	3.1	9.6	10.0	17.9	18.3

Continued

Table 3.6 - *Continued*

	(9)	(10)	(11)	(12)
	Total domestic value added			
	Semi-finished ferrous metal	*All ferrous metal*	*All metal*	*Semi-finished ferrous metal: ratio of output to consumption*
1861-65	3.8	4.1	6.1	0.49
1866-70	3.3	3.6	5.9	0.42
1871-75	4.4	4.7	6.9	0.44
1876-80	6.8	7.0	9.7	0.54
1881-85	13.0	13.3	17.5	0.57
1886-90	24.4	24.5	31.6	0.64
1891-95	18.4	18.5	26.8	0.75
1896-1900	24.3	24.5	35.0	0.81
1901-05	30.0	32.2	45.4	0.79
1906-10	64.9	67.1	85.2	0.78
1911-13	86.5	90.9	112.7	0.83

(a) value added in the manufacture from pig or scrap; manufacture from iron ore would raise the rail figures by 30 per cent, the other metal figures by 20 per cent.
(b) value added in metal actually produced or imported as such.
(c) includes the metalmaking value-added content of imported rolling stock.

Source: See the Appendix to this chapter.

indeed related to it, since both are induced by growing traffic). In addition, the high plateau in railway construction in 1881-95 appears here as a sharp peak in 1886-90. One reason for this is that it takes much longer to build the right of way than the rolling stock, so that the upsurge in railway construction naturally preceded that in the production of complementary rolling stock; another is the business depression of the early 1890s, which allowed the rolling stock needs of new lines to be met, at that time, largely by transferring otherwise underutilised vehicles from the existing network. A third reason would appear to be the reorganisation of the railway system, which had much the same effect in 1885 as in 1905: since the rolling stock was the responsibility of the operating companies, purchases would tend to decline as reorganisation drew closer, and surge in its immediate aftermath (15).

A comparison of these time series to each other sheds light on the internal composition of railway investment demand. As it turns out, railway construction involved a great deal of traditional construction activity to prepare the right of way (especially in the difficult terrain that characterises much of Italy); even allowing for track accessories and rolling stock metal (Table 3.4, col 6, Table 3.6, col 3 and the difference between cols 6 and 4), the consumption of metal and machines was comparatively quite minor. In fact, such goods account for a far more significant share of investment for replacement and improvement than of investment for expansion: paradoxically, perhaps, a mature railway system buys relatively more from heavy industry than a growing one.

To illustrate this point, the present time series may be reduced to two sets of averages: one for 1861-95, when the network was largely being established; and one for 1896-1913, when the network, though still growing, was substantially mature. Allowing for the other materials consumed by construction, engineering and metalmaking, one obtains an average annual investment close to 180 million lire per annum (at 1911 prices) in both these periods. In 1861-95, however, construction alone accounted for approximately 50 per cent of that figure, and the quarrying and processing of construction materials accounted for another 25 per cent (60 per cent of it in quarrying); engineering and metalmaking accounted for 8 per cent between them (75 per cent of it in engineering), and the balance was taken up by mining and natural resources (including some 2 per cent for land, up to 3 per cent for scrap iron, and 12-15 per cent for coal and iron ore). In 1896-1913, the share of construction was reduced to 33 per cent, and that of the quarrying and processing of construction materials to 10 per cent;

engineering and metalmaking took 30 per cent between them (80 per cent of it in engineering), and the balance was again taken up by mining and natural resources (including some 2 per cent for land, up to 10 per cent for scrap iron, and 15-25 per cent for coal and iron ore) (16).

These patterns are reinforced if we consider the proportion of railway investment accruing to the domestic economy rather than to imports. Construction, construction materials and quarrying are all essentially shielded from foreign competition; on the other hand, Italy imported a substantial share of its rails and rolling stock, particularly before the tariff increases of the late 1870s and especially the late 1880s. Thus, in 1861-95, the domestic engineering and metalmaking industries accounted for only 3-5 per cent of railway investment (including 3-4 per cent in engineering and 0-1 per cent in metalmaking), or approximately half of the 8 per cent for domestic production and imports together; in 1896-1913, the share of those domestic industries rose to 21-25 per cent (including 19-20 per cent in engineering and 2-5 per cent in metalmaking), or approximately three-fourths of the 30 per cent for domestic production and imports together (17).

An established railway network appears even more important than its original construction, as far as the consumption of industrial products is concerned, if its maintenance needs are considered along with its investment needs. Maintenance demand, though initially much smaller than investment demand, grew over time to quite significant levels; and it was always relatively strongly orientated towards engineering, and almost entirely reserved to domestic industry. As a result, it represented about half of domestic industrial value added to railway order even at the peak of the post-nationalisation re-equipment boom; and in the early decades, when most railway investment was for expansion and rails and rolling stock were largely imported, it represented much the larger part of it. The establishment of repair shops clearly emerges as the early railways' most significant direct contribution to domestic industry (18).

The estimate of railway maintenance demand for construction, engineering and metalmaking are presented in Tables 3.3 (cols 5-7), 3.4 (col 3), and 3.6 (col 4). For these three industries combined, maintenance demand averaged 25 million lire (of value added at 1911 prices) per annum in 1861-95, and nearly thrice that in 1896-1913; by way of comparison, investment demand averaged 111 million lire per annum in 1861-95, and 104 million lire per annum in 1896-1913. In the case of metalmaking, maintenance demand (the consumption of metal in the maintenance of rolling stock; Table 3.6, col 4) was relatively minor: an average value added of just 0.7 million lire (of which perhaps half was lost to imports) per annum in 1861-95, and still only 2.2 million lire (of which perhaps one fifth lost to imports) per annum in 1896-1913. But even these paltry figures represented a significant share of the railway's relatively small consumption of metal (cols 7 or 8): around 15 per cent in 1861-95, and 20 per cent in 1896-1913 (19). Maintenance demand for construction (Table 3.3, col 7) was altogether greater: an average value added of 12 million lire per annum in 1861-95, and 34 million lire per annum in 1896-1913. In relative terms, these equalled 12 per cent of total railway demand for construction (col 8) in 1861-95, and 37 per cent in 1896-1913. The maintenance demand for engineering (Table 3.4, col 3), in turn, was marginally greater than that for construction: an average value added of 12 million lire per annum in 1861-95, and 39 million lire per annum in 1896-1913. In relative terms, however, maintenance demand equalled 57 per cent of the railway's total demand for machinery (col 5) in 1861-95, and 50 per cent of it in 1896-1913 (20). Allowing for the importation of new rolling stock, which was particularly significant in the early decades, one finds that the share of maintenance in the total domestic rolling stock industry equalled a dominating 69 per cent in 1861-95, and 55 per cent in 1896-1913. Moreover, the disaggregated estimates of engineering production (Table 3.5) indicate that maintenance was concentrated in the technologically most demanding type of vehicle (locomotives) whereas purchases and production were concentrated in the technologically least demanding type (freight cars). From the standpoint of industrial skills ('human capital'), even more than from that of engineering value added in general, the railways' maintenance needs appear to overshadow their demand for new production.

The importance of railway demand for the construction, engineering and metalmaking industries can be assessed, within broad limits, by comparing the railway-specific production and consumption figures discussed above to the typically much rougher industry totals presented within those same Tables 3.3-3.6.

In the case of construction, first of all, railway demand (Table 3.3, col 8) averaged some 23 per cent of the industry total (col 10) in 1861-95, and 16 per cent in 1896-1913; this reduction is the result of a 15 per cent decline in average railway construction, and a 19 per cent increase in average total construction. Finer comparisons are difficult, pending the calculation of less imprecise figures for the industry as a whole; for what the present estimates may be worth, a comparison of the change in railway construction (col 8) to the corresponding change in total construction (col 9) suggests that the former represented about 90 per cent of the industry's (minor) decline from 1861-5 to 1866-70, about 40 per cent of its increase from 1876-80 to 1886-90, about 55 per cent of the subsequent decline to 1896-1900, and about 25 per cent of the subsequent increase to 1911-13. A comparison of the change in railway construction to the corresponding initial level of total construction suggests that railway construction by itself represented a 15 per cent increase in total construction from 1876-80 to 1886-90, and a 24 per cent increase in it from 1896-1900 to 1911-13; both of these are equivalent to an average growth rate of approximately 1.5 per cent per annum (21).

In the case of engineering, secondly, the possible comparisons are multiplied by the presence of imports on the one hand, and of a variety of possible 'industry totals' on the other (22). The selection of the level of aggregation is particularly critical, since the relative shares of machinery and fabricated metal were very different in railway-related activity on the one hand and in aggregate activity on the other; railway demand thus appears altogether more significant next to the machinery industry by itself than next to engineering as a whole. Some relevant estimates are collected in Table 3.7. From the first group of comparisons, one sees that railway-related production and maintenance activities accounted for roughly one quarter to one third of the machinery industry (col 3), but only one twentieth to one tenth of the entire engineering industry (col 7); and that these figures are not much increased if one adds imports to domestic production (cols 4 and 8). If one neglects maintenance and considers new production only, one obtains somewhat lower ratios to the machinery industry (especially in the early years), but somewhat higher ones to engineering as a whole (cols 1-2, 5-6) (23). From the second group of comparisons, one sees that the change in railway-related activity represented roughly one third to two fifths of the machinery industry's growth from 1876-80 to 1886-90, and again from 1891-5 to 1911-13, but closer to one fifth of the entire industry's growth at those times; the hypothetical inclusion of imports again results in only relatively small increases in these ratios, while the neglect of maintenance (which grew relatively rapidly in the case of rolling stock) would here reduce those ratios across the board (cols 1-8). From the third group of comparisons, one sees that over those two major periods of growth the growth of railway-related activity represented an annual growth of about 3-4 per cent per annum for the machinery industry (whether maintenance is included or not), but only 1-2 per cent per annum for the engineering industry as a whole. A peak rate of nearly 5 per cent per annum, for machinery production alone, is achieved if imports are added to domestic manufacture: far from negligible, to be sure, but still quite small compared to the 20 per cent per annum and more characteristic of leading sectors.

In the case of metalmaking, thirdly, a variety of distinctions again multiply the possible comparisons; a broad sample of these is collected in Table 3.8. The distinction between industry totals here has only a relatively minor impact: since the manufacture of semi-finished ferrous metal typically accounted for close to two thirds of all metalmaking, the shares of railway-related production in the latter are generally a comparable proportion of its share in the former (compare cols 1-2 and 3-4, 5-6 and 7-8) (24). The distinctions between rails and other railway metal on the one hand, and between output and imports on the other, are more significant. From the first group of comparisons, one sees that rail production was actually only a minor part of the total: about one twentieth of semi-finished ferrous metals production, against one sixth for all railway metal (cols 1 and 5). The addition of imports to domestic production would have had a major impact in the early decades, trebling the share of rails and doubling that of all railway metal together (cols 2 and 6). From the second group of comparisons, one sees that the growth of railway metal represented about a quarter of the growth of semi-finished ferrous metalmaking from 1876-80 to 1886-90, and one fifth of it from 1891-5 to 1911-13; rails were the larger contributor to the earlier growth, and other railway metal to the later one (cols 1 and 5). In this case, the addition of imports to domestic production affects the figures only slightly (cols 2 and 6: the contribution of rails is reduced because the proportion of imports declined over the relevant periods, while that of all railway metal is increased because the growing imports of rolling stock resulted in an overall rise in railway metal imports). From the third group of comparisons, finally, one sees that the growth of railway metal production represented an annual growth of about 6 per cent per annum in semi-finished ferrous metalmaking from 1876-80 to 1886-90, and 3 per cent per annum from 1891-5 to 1911-13 (col 5). Once again, rail production dominates the earlier contribution, and other metal the later one (col 1); since much of the early growth in rail production was import substituting, its contribution would be sharply reduced by

Table 3.7: *Comparisons of railway-related and total production in engineering*

	(1)	(2)	(3)	(4)	(5)	(6)	(7)	(8)
	Machinery only				*All engineering*			
	Production		*Total (a)*		*Production*		*Total (a)*	
	Actual	*Potential (b)*	*Actual*	*Potential (b)*	*Actual (c)*	*Potential (b)*	*Actual (c)*	*Potential (b)*
1. Level to level								
1861-95	0.13	0.21	0.23	0.27	0.08	0.11	0.05	0.06
1896-13	0.25	0.30	0.31	0.34	0.13	0.16	0.11	0.11
2. Change to change								
1876-80 to 1886-90	0.29	0.36	0.35	0.40	0.14	0.19	0.18	0.22
1886-90 to 1891-95	0.40	0.53	0.47	0.63	0.20	0.29	0.22	0.33
1891-95 to 1911-13	0.33	0.34	0.37	0.37	0.17	0.18	0.20	0.22
3. Change to initial level, converted to annual percentage rates								
1876-80 to 1886-90	3.7	4.8	3.2	3.7	2.0	2.6	0.6	0.8
1886-90 to 1891-95	-2.9	-4.7	-1.3	-2.4	-1.9	-2.3	-0.4	-0.7
1891-95 to 1911-13	3.6	3.7	2.9	2.9	2.0	2.1	0.9	0.9

(a) production plus maintenance.
(b) calculated by adding rolling stock imports to domestic production.
(c) counts all track accessories as domestic production.

Source: See the Appendix to this chapter.

the addition of imports to domestic production (col 6).

In summary, the growth in railway-related production seems to have represented significant growth for the machinery and metalmaking industries, but relatively unimpressive growth for the entire metalworking group, both in the 1880s and the 1900s; and this conclusion is substantially unaffected by the hypothetical addition of imports to domestic production. In the 1880s, the heyday of railway construction, the railway's consumption of industrial goods was too restricted to have represented an opportunity for a 'big push', even with a totally protected engineering industry; in the 1900s, the railway's consumption of industrial goods was significantly higher than it had been twenty years earlier precisely because it represented the industry-oriented maintenance and replacement demand of a mature system, and not the construction-oriented demand of a rapidly growing one. In this sense at least, the fact that Italy's railway network was largely completed by the turn of the century can be taken to have strengthened, and not weakened, the industrial growth of the early 1900s.

5. THE IMPACT OF RAILWAY INVESTMENT

The railway's direct purchases of domestic industrial products are of course only one element of the overall impact of current railway investment on domestic industrial production. A more comprehensive evaluation must gauge the net impact of that investment both on the composition of final demand, and on its level; the latter also matters here, in view of the access to international resource markets, and the resulting flexibility of resource employment levels, that apparently characterised the nineteenth-century Italian economy. The empirical difficulty is that these overall effects of railway investment can only be traced through a general equilibrium model of the entire relevant economic system, and the results one obtains are accordingly very sensitive to the identity, as well as to the structure, of the relationships one chooses to contemplate.

Some illustrative estimates, and an indication of at least some of the critical variables and relationships, have been obtained with the aid of a very simple (static, linear, six-equation) model adapted from Mundell's analysis of capital movements and stabilisation policy under fixed and flexible exchange rates (25). On the one hand, that model is extended to include railway investment and industrial production as explicit variables; on the other, it is simplified by assuming that Italy is too small a part of the international

Table 3.8: *Comparisons of railway-related and total production in metalmaking*

	(1)	(2)	(3)	(4)	(5)	(6)	(7)	(8)
	Rails only compared to:				*All rail-related metal compared to:*			
	Semi-finished ferrous metal		*All metal*		*Semi-finished ferrous metal*		*All metal*	
	Actual	*Potential (a)*	*Actual*	*Potential (a)*	*Actual (b)*	*Potential (c)*	*Actual (b)*	*Potential (c)*
1. Level to level								
1861-95	0.06	0.21	0.04	0.15	0.16	0.35	0.12	0.27
1896-13	0.06	0.08	0.05	0.06	0.17	0.23	0.13	0.17
2. Change to change								
1876-80 to 1886-90	0.17	0.14	0.14	0.11	0.27	0.31	0.22	0.25
1886-90 to 1891-95	0.23	0.37	0.29	0.44	0.36	0.58	0.45	0.67
1891-95 to 1911-13	0.08	0.07	0.06	0.06	0.19	0.20	0.15	0.16
3. Change to initial level, converted to annual percentage rates								
1876-80 to 1886-90	3.7	2.3	2.7	1.8	5.5	4.6	4.1	3.7
1886-90 to 1891-95	-1.2	-2.2	-0.9	-1.7	-2.5	-4.0	-1.4	-3.2
1891-95 to 1911-13	1.3	1.2	1.0	0.9	2.8	2.9	2.1	2.2

(a) calculated by adding rail imports to domestic production.
(b) assumes that railway metal other than rail was produced and imported in the same ratio as all semi-finished ferrous metal.
(c) calculated by adding rail imports and estimated other railway metal imports to domestic production.

Source: See the Appendix to this chapter.

economy to affect international interest rates. The alternative characterisations of the exchange rate are instead retained, since Italy went off the gold standard in 1866, and the lira traded below par through the 1870s and again in the 1890s. The essential relationships contemplated by the adapted model may be summarised under the following three headings. First, value added in industrial production is related directly to the value of railway investment, other investment and other income (expenditure); the parameters of these equations reflect the share of domestic manufactured goods in these various types of expenditure. Second, aggregate expenditure (income) is defined as the sum of consumption, investment and the balance of trade (exports minus imports). Consumption, non-railway investment and imports themselves depend on aggregate expenditure; exports and imports also depend on the exchange rate. Third, money demand is assumed to vary with aggregate expenditure, and set equal to money supply.

With the lira at par, and the exchange thus pegged at the gold-import point, the model behaves in a straightforward Keynesian fashion. Railway investment has the usual multiplier effects on aggregate income, and therefore a markedly positive indirect effect on industrial production (which varies with the induced income, and even more strongly with the induced investment); the money supply varies passively, through specie flows, to adapt to money demand. In this context, the results depend critically on the assumptions concerning induced investment, since the resulting multiplier (and therefore the measured effect of the exogenous impulse) can grow without limit. Railway investment can thus be made as important as one wants (in terms of the measured proportion of income and industrial production which is attributed to it), without for all that ever becoming more important than a similar amount of exogenous spending for anything else (since the same high multiplier would apply there too) (26). With the lira below par, and the exchange free to vary, the model behaves altogether differently. The money supply is exogenously given, and money-market equilibrium determines aggregate income. Railway investment does not affect the level of aggregate demand: it is offset by the deterioration in the balance of trade, as the exchange rate appreciates in response to the capital flows induced by the pressure of investment demand on the domestic interest rate. Its effects on industrial production are exhausted by its effects on the composition of demand, and therefore depend in the first instance on the difference between the domestic industrial content of railway investment expenditure on the one hand and the displaced (i.e. 'all other') expenditure on the other. The critical assumption, of course, is here the constancy of the income velocity; but it is worth noting that its essential result is to undercut the expansionary real effects that are otherwise obtained by allowing international factor movements. In a word, the flexible-exchange-rate model mimics, through its restrictions on demand, the behaviour of a classical fixed-resource, full-employment model restricted on the supply side. In both cases, aggregate production is fixed, and the only impact of railway investment is on its composition (27). As noted above, moreover, the domestic (and also total) industrial content of railway investment was relatively high in the case of replacement and improvement, but relatively low in the case of original construction. Railway investment thus plausibly altered the composition of production to industry's advantage from the turn of the century or thereabouts, but to industry's *dis*advantage in the preceding decades.

With plausible parameters, the demand-expansion effect on industry is considerably larger than the demand-composition effect (the former is essentially a product of railway investment, a Keynesian multiplier, and the share of industry in ordinary expenditure, while the latter is essentially the product of unmultiplied railway investment and the *difference* between the share of industry in railway investment and in ordinary expenditure). The measured effect on industrial production of railway investment, considered as a pure addition to exogenous spending, thus varies primarily with the presence or absence of the demand-expansion effect, i.e. with the state of the exchange. In 1866-80 and 1891-1900, with a floating exchange rate, the measured effect is the demand-composition effect alone; it is thus small and plausibly negative (of the order of minus 1 per cent, with illustrative parameter values). In 1861-5, 1881-90 and 1901-13, with a pegged exchange, the measured impact is dominated by the demand-expansion effect; it is thus positive and not insignificant (of the order of plus 5 per cent with illustrative parameter values, and this despite a negative composition effect in the 1860s and 1880s). The measured effects of railway investment thus follow a cycle that is roughly coincident with, but much stronger than, the cycle in railway investment itself; but the cycle in the effects is attributable to the changes in the exchange rate (and thus the impact of a unit of exogenous spending) rather than to the changes in the volume of railway investment.

If the model is expanded to include a public budget constraint, railway investment is plausibly assumed to have been financed not by borrowing alone but by a combination of borrowing, money creation, tax increases and reductions in other public investment (28). With the addition of this relationship, the state of the exchange becomes far less significant: the expansion of demand with fixed exchange rates is sharply limited by the offsetting increase in taxes and reduction in other public investment; and the increase in the money supply now allows demand to expand even with flexible exchange rates. The plausible impact of railway investment on industrial production thus becomes small but positive even with flexible exchange rates (of the order of plus 1 per cent, with illustrative parameter values), and not much larger with fixed exchange rates (of the order of plus 2 or 3 per cent). With this expanded model, the cycle in the measured effect of railway investment is attributable, in roughly comparable proportions, to the changes in the exchange rate on the one hand and in the level and composition of railway investment on the other.

In general, then, it would seem likely that the cycle in railway investment somewhat amplified the largely synchronous cycle in industrial production; but the size of its effect can only be conjectured. Moreover, as one recalls, that cycle in industrial production seems attributable not only to the fluctuations in domestic demand for investment goods, but to the failure of the domestic producers of those goods to break out of the small and fluctuating domestic market into sustained export-led growth. The cause of that failure appears to be the tariff on iron and steel, which raised the costs of the Italian engineering industry to internationally uncompetitive levels; and one wonders to what extent the tariff on iron and steel was not itself due to the lure of the market for rails and other metal created by railway investment. It is altogether possible that railway investment influenced Italy's industrial growth primarily, and deleteriously, by altering the balance of political power between the free-traders and the protectionists. The actual effect of railway investment on Italian industry cannot be measured, in sum, until more is known about the mechanisms that determined private and public spending, international resource flows, the exchange rate, money supply and demand, and tariff policy; and even this list is only partial and preliminary (29).

6. THE IMPACT OF RAILWAY TRANSPORTATION

In a closed economy, cheaper transportation increases the productivity of domestic resources: as it unifies the market, it induces a reallocation of resources to exploit relative advantages and economies of scale. In an open economy, cheaper internal transportation further increases the productivity of domestic resources, and normally increases their density as well: as it breaks down the barriers between the interior and world markets, it eliminates domestic resource and demand constraints, and attracts those internationally mobile brokering and processing activities that characterise the commercial capitals and workshops of the world (30). In Italy, the rail links from the Upper Po Valley to the sea may thus have permitted the development of the 'industrial triangle' between Turin, Milan and Genoa; but railway transportation appears to have done little to unify the domestic market and undermine the traditional patterns of production that prevailed through most of the peninsula.

In 1911, for example, the railways loaded some 40 million tons of goods. About 11 million tons were loaded at various seaports (45 per cent of them in Genoa alone, and another 25 per cent in nearby Savona and in Venice); another 2 million were imported by rail (all of them, of course, into northern Italy); and only 27 million tons were loaded in the country's interior (31). In that same year, ships unloaded some 22 million tons of goods, including 17 million tons arriving from foreign ports and 5 million tons from domestic ones (32). With imports by rail offsetting the likely share of domestic goods in railway seaport loadings, the volume of imports loaded by the railways may be estimated at 11 million tons, or about 55 per cent of total imports and 28 per cent of total railway shipments. Domestic commodities accounted for the other 72 per cent of railway shipments, or 29 million tons; and the latter figure implies that average shipments by modern overland means, per ton of domestic commodity production, were then just one fifth of the level achieved with the cheap transportation of our own day (33). Of the residual four-fifths, a large part was no doubt moved by traditional means; and another large part was no doubt not moved at all, as resources consumed in direct production were substituted for relatively expensive transportation.

An essentially similar picture emerges from the disaggregated evidence in Table 3.9. Column 1 presents the tonnages of the principal commodity groups shipped by the state railways in 1911. Since such rankings are heavily influenced by relative degrees of disaggregation, and the table covers only 60 per cent of total shipments, the present sample may seriously underrepresent some significant groups of commodities; but it is clear (and not at all surprising) that fuels, construction materials and agricultural outputs and inputs by themselves accounted for over half of total shipments by rail. Cols 2-4 provide a comparison to imports, exports and domestic production. The railways seem heavily involved in the distribution of bulk imports: thus coal, most spectacularly, but also cereal (1.3 million tons of which were loaded at the seaports) phosphates and Thomas slag, raw cotton and probably lumber (34). The collection of bulk exports is also discernible, clearly in the case of sulphur, and more ambiguously in that of building stone (marble) or citrus fruit. The volume of internal shipments, in contrast, seems relatively limited. Of the goods produced in large quantities, only high-grade construction materials (lime and cement) and chemical fertiliser travelled extensively by rail; significantly, these are industrial products that are both relatively valuable (compared to other bulk industrial goods) and sold to widely dispersed consumers (construction,agriculture). Low-grade construction materials, agricultural products and semi-finished industrial products (metal) appear instead to have used the railways only a small percentage of the time (particularly since the railway-shipment categories often group commodities across successive stages of production, while the present production figures refer to only one such stage) (35). The limited shipments of semi-finished industrial products no doubt reflect the spatial concentration of industrial production in the 'industrial triangle', and perhaps a relatively high degree of vertical integration; but since industrial structures and location are themselves influenced by transport costs, the observed configuration of industry may well be, at least in part, an endogenous response to expensive transportation. The limited shipments of agricultural and other bulk commodities point instead to a low volume of interregional trade, and correspondingly, to the large-scale survival of the traditional local economies based on an exchange between the towns and their immediate surroundings. The influence of expensive transportation was here no doubt compounded by that of emigration, as the emigrants' remittances allowed the South to pay for imported manufactures without exporting more of its limited food supply. But emigration too reflects in part the incidence of high transport costs: the barriers between the interior and world markets helped make the South a relatively high-cost location, with a tendency to export labour services directly rather than as value added to commodity exports. For similar reasons, the major cities of the South were nearly all located on the seacoast; but the relatively high cost of overland transport meant that coastal locations were more cheaply reached - and, in the absence of tariff barriers, often more cheaply supplied - from northern Europe by sea than from northern Italy by rail (36).

The Italian railways' ability to unify the domestic market thus seems to have been limited by the high price of their services, and not, as the international comparisons of network lengths in Table 3.1 might have suggested, by the

Table 3.9: *Principal railway shipments, international trade and comparable domestic production in 1911 (million tons)*

	(1) Shipments (a)	(2) Imports	(3) Exports	(4) Comparable production
1. lime and cement	1.7	0.0	0.0	2.6
2. lumber	1.7	1.5	0.0	1.1
3. building stone	1.3	0.0	0.4	13.9
4. bricks and tiles	1.2	0.1	0.1	7.8
5. sand	0.6	?	?	1.4
6. asphalt	0.1	0.0	0.0	0.2 (rock only)
Subtotal	6.8			
7. cereal and flour: wheat	1.8	1.5	0.1	5.1 (cereal only)
8. cereal and flour: other	1.8	0.6	0.1	4.0 (cereal only)
9. wine	0.9	0.0	0.1	4.8
10. animal feed, straw, etc.	0.5	?	?	23.4 (forage crops only)
11. sugar beet	0.5	?	?	1.6
12. animals	0.4	0.1	0.0	0.9 (slaughtered live weight only)
13. grapes and must	0.3	0.0	0.0	7.7 (grapes only)
14. citrus fruit	0.3	0.0	0.4	1.0
15. sugar, coffee, etc.	0.3	0.1	0.0	0.2 (crude sugar only)
Subtotal	6.7			

Continued

Table 3.9: *Continued*

	(1) Shipments (a)	(2) Imports	(3) Exports	(4) Comparable production
16. coal, lignite, charcoal	6.0	9.8	0.1	0.7 (mine products only)
17. firewood	0.3	0.1	0.0	2.5
Subtotal	6.3			
18. chemical fertiliser	0.7	0.0	0.0	1.0
19. phosphates, Thomas slag	0.4	0.6	0.0	0.0
20. natural fertiliser	0.4	0.0	0.0	?
Subtotal	1.5			
21. pig and scrap iron	0.4	0.6	0.0	0.7
22. ingot and semi-finished metal	0.3	0.2	0.0	1.1 (semi-finished metal only)
Subtotal	0.7			
23. yarn and cloth	0.2	0.0	0.1	0.3 (yarn only)
24. raw cotton	0.2	0.2	0.0	0.0
25. other textile fibres	0.1	0.1	0.1	0.1
Subtotal	0.5			

Continued

Table 3.9: *Continued*

	(1) Shipments (a)	(2) Imports	(3) Exports	(4) Comparable production
26. other chemicals	0.4	0.3	0.1	0.4 (final products only)
27. sulphur	0.4	0.0	0.4	0.4 (fused sulphur only)
28. mineral and vegetable oils	0.3	0.3	0.1	0.2 (petroleum and olive oil only)
29. paper	0.2	0.0	0.0	0.2
Total	23.8			

(a) on the state railways

Source: See the Appendix to this chapter.

comparatively small size of their network. This is clearly brought out by the turn-of-the-century figures on the intensity of network use on the major Italian, French and German systems: even allowing for the relative incidence of multiple tracking, the Italian rail lines were relatively lightly used (Table 3.10, rows 2-4). This restricted use of the railway network, in turn, seems only partly justified by inescapably high operating costs; much of it seems due to a public policy that kept prices well above marginal costs.

Wages in Italy were rather lower than elsewhere; but this advantage was more than offset by high energy prices, an unfavourable terrain, diseconomies of small scale, and probably unbalanced traffic flows as well. The high price of imported coal made for expensive fuel, and also, though less so, for expensive energy-intensive materials and activities (metal parts, repairs and the like). The high incidence of curves and gradients made for high fuel consumption, slow speeds, light or often double-headed trains, and rapid deterioration of the right of way. The low utilisation of rail lines meant that administrative, surveillance and station personnel costs were distributed over a small volume of output; that frequencies could only be maintained by accepting light average loads; and that the rail lines were rationally equipped to relatively low standards, thus constraining engine weights and power and effectively compounding the limitations imposed by the terrain (37). Chronological or directional imbalances in demand may have been relatively severe, in view of the importance of bulk imports and agricultural perishables in the Italian systems' traffic (Table 3.9); and such imbalances would make for high capacity costs per unit of output, whether load factors were allowed to drop or kept high by pruning off-peak capacity (38).

The comparative figures in Table 3.10 provide some evidence of the impact of these various handicaps. Overall, current costs per unit of output (row 21) were about two thirds higher on the Italian systems than on the major French and German ones. Load factors in both passenger and freight operations (rows 6-7) were close to the averages of those prevailing elsewhere (and not relatively high, as they presumably would have been if the relatively high cost of hauling empty cars had not been compounded by relatively difficult demand conditions). Since freight load factors were everywhere much higher than passenger load factors, however, the low share of freight traffic on the Italian systems made for low overall load factors (rows 5 and 8); and the latter imply that the Italian systems' costs appear somewhat less high per unit of capacity (row 22) than per unit of output.

Table 3.10: *Comparative statistics for the principal Italian, French and German railway systems in 1898*

	(1) RM (a)	(2) RA (b)	(3) Nord (c)	(4) PLM (d)	(5) VPH (e)
1. Kilometres of line track	6909	6277	6236	13178	41948
Traffic per kilometre of line track:					
2. thousand passenger kilometres	168	146	321	226	294
3. thousand freight ton-kilometres	178	173	496	406	531
4. thousand total traffic units (f)	346	319	817	631	826
5. Share of freight in total traffic	0.514	0.542	0.607	0.643	0.643
6. Load factor: in passenger operations	0.215	0.221	0.202	0.219	0.249
7. in freight operations	0.383	0.375	0.344	0.419	0.404
8. in all operations	0.278	0.284	0.270	0.316	0.331
9. Average loads: passengers per passenger train	57	49	63	59	93
10. freight tons per freight train	113	135	125	171	145
11. payload units (g) per train	79	75	92	105	121
12. payload units (g) per locomotive	57	52	75	83	?
Employment per million traffic units (f):					
13. in administration	0.8	1.0	0.3 (h)	0.4 (h)	0.5
14. in track surveillance and maintenance	6.6	8.3	2.0	2.2	2.7
15. in other activities (i)	12.9	10.8	6.2	6.4	6.8
16. total	20.3	20.1	8.5	9.0	10.0

Continued

Table 3.10: *Continued*

	(1) RM (a)	(2) RA (b)	(3) Nord (c)	(4) PLM (d)	(5) VPH (e)
17. Labour costs per employee (thousand lire)	1.32	1.23	1.59 (j)	1.59	1.50
Current costs actually incurred:					
lire per thousand traffic units (f):					
18. for labour	26.9	24.7	13.5 (k)	14.3	15.0
19. for fuel	5.8	5.1	1.6	2.6	3.1 (1)
20. other	8.9	9.8	6.8	6.8	8.1 (1)
21. total	41.6	39.6	21.9	23.7	26.2
22. lire per thousand capacity units (m)	11.6	11.3	5.9	7.5	8.7
23. lire per thousand actual weight units (n)	23.3	21.6	10.7	12.6	14.0
Current costs, calculated with Italian wages and material costs:					
24. lire per thousand traffic units (f)	41.6	39.6	28.4	28.6	32.1
25. lire per thousand capacity units (m)	11.6	11.3	7.7	9.1	10.6
26. lire per thousand actual weight units (n)	23.3	21.6	13.9	15.2	17.1
Operating revenues:					
27. lire per thousand passenger kilometres	45.7	45.4	33.9	42.4	33.6
28. lire per thousand freight ton-kilometres	68.2	69.2	47.9	54.4	46.2
29. Ratio of operating revenues to current costs	1.38	1.47	1.94	2.11	1.59

Continued

Notes:

(a) Rete Mediterranea
(b) Rete Adriatica

Table 3.10: *Continued*

Notes: Continued

(c) Chemins de Fer du Nord
(d) Chemins de Fer de Paris à Lyon et à la Méditerranée
(e) Vereinigte Preussische und Hessische Staatseisenbahnen
(f) traffic units are unweighted sums of passenger kilometres and freight ton-kilometres
(g) payload units are unweighted sums of passengers and freight tons
(h) estimated on the basis of expenditure
(i) sales, operations and rolling stock maintenance
(j) assumed equal to that on the PLM
(k) based on estimated labour costs per employee
(l) assumes the same distribution of non-labour costs as on the PLM
(m) capacity units are unweighted sums of seat-kilometres and capacity ton-kilometres
(n) actual weight units are ton-kilometres computed with the actual weight of the passenger and freight cars and payloads

Source: See the Appendix to this chapter.

On the other hand, if one also allows for relative vehicle and payload weights, a unit of freight traffic represented a much higher gross weight actually hauled than a unit of passenger traffic; so the low share of freight on the Italian systems also means that their relative costs per unit of output understate their relative costs per ton-kilometre of gross weight actually hauled (row 23).

Most of the Italian systems' relative disadvantage seems traceable to unusually low labour productivities. Fuel costs (row 19), though often stressed in the literature, seem relatively unimportant: even if high coal prices and high fuel consumption made for fuel costs some three times higher than in France or Germany, the share of fuel in total costs was so low that its overall impact was clearly very minor (39). The prices and consumption levels of other non-labour items (row 20) may also have been relatively high in Italy, and their share of total costs was significantly larger than that of fuel; since their prices reflected Italy's relatively low wages as well as its high coal prices, however, the Italian systems' cost disadvantage in these items cannot have been more than a fraction of their disadvantage in fuel alone. Estimates of the French and German systems' costs on the basis of Italian-level fuel costs (calculated per ton-kilometre of gross weight actually hauled), other non-labour costs (calculated with a generous two-thirds increase over their actual levels), and labour costs per employee thus leave more than half of the actual cost differences still to be explained (rows 24-6) (40). This large residual points to Italian staffing levels significantly higher, and correspondingly to labour productivities significantly lower, than can be accounted for by the relatively low ratio of wages to materials prices. The Italian systems' high employment levels and labour costs were thus not just the indirect result of high non-labour costs, but largely the direct result of a poor operating environment. The rugged terrain made for high maintenance needs, low (and unbalanced) traffic made for underutilised administrative, surveillance and station personnel, and both together made for light average loads per train and especially per locomotive; as a result, the output productivities of Italian railway workers were relatively low right across the board (rows 9-16).

The optimal utilisation of the railway network is in principle that which results from prices equal to marginal costs. Italy's unfavourable topography and natural resource endowment no doubt meant that marginal costs at any given level of utilisation were relatively high, and optimum utilisation rates relatively low. The utilisation rates that actually prevailed appear to have been well below the optimum, however, since public policy kept prices well above marginal costs. The state was both generically responsible for railway fares (which were subject to public control), and specifically responsible for claiming a 28 per cent share of the operating revenues of the Rete Mediterranea and the Rete Adriatica (with no corresponding contribution to their costs). This revenue-sharing arrangement was equivalent to an excise tax on railway fares at the rate of 39 per cent (the ratio of 28 per cent to the residual 72 per cent); and it imposed a twofold constraint. In the first place, since the companies had to be induced to stay in business, the general fare level had to be high enough to allow expected total revenues gross of tax to exceed expected total costs by at least 39 per cent, or not much less than the average actually observed (row 29); and since the diseconomies of small scale meant that marginal costs were below average costs, the average railway fare had to exceed marginal costs by a correspondingly even greater percentage (41). In the second place, since the companies had to be induced to pursue sales at every relevant margin, *every* railway rate and marginal revenue gross of tax had to exceed the corresponding marginal cost by at least 39 per cent. The rates faced by marginal traffic would be constrained by average cost plus tax if the configuration of market demands or legally imposed price ceilings prevented significant price discrimination; they would instead be constrained by marginal cost plus tax if inframarginal costs could be recovered by above-average inframarginal rates, and marginal traffic pursued by below-average marginal rates. A priori, all one can say is that the revenue-sharing arrangement would make all railway rates at least 39 per cent too high, with an even greater excess in some or most (42).

The state seems constantly to have kept railway rates high enough to yield, and let it capture, a significant operating surplus. Its arrangements with the early regional groups had made for operating revenues 60 per cent above current costs in 1875; the state's share of marginal revenue was then typically 50 per cent, implying railway rates and marginal revenues equal to at least 200 per cent of marginal costs (43). In 1911, the state railways' operating revenues were still 20 per cent above current costs; and most of the decline from the roughly 40 per cent of 1898 seems attributable not to fare reductions but to a sharp increase in costs following the railways' nationalisation (44). At the same time, the state constantly stimulated the construction of railways, either by building them directly or by guaranteeing the builders a subsidy per kilometre of line, and its annualised subsidy and construction costs generously exceeded its annual income from railway operations (45). On the face of it, this policy of simultaneously encouraging the construction of railways and discouraging their use was self-contradictory and absurd; but a number of considerations warrant a more cautious judgement.

The taxation of railway traffic no doubt meant that the network was inefficiently used, and therefore, in principle, that total income was lower than it would otherwise have been. In practice, however, the state surely faced a financial constraint, and railway income was no doubt far more easily taxed than the even greater income that would have accrued to railway users had prices been set closer to marginal costs. The inefficient use of the railway network cannot therefore be condemned as wasteful without an appreciation of the possibly greater inefficiencies that would have been produced by increasing other public revenues or curtailing public spending. Nor is it at all certain that the damage done by the tax could have been reduced, at constant yield, by altering its form. As noted above, a tax built into an operating contract in a context of economically or politically constrained price discrimination would limit utilisation through its effect on *average* cost, and its form was to that extent a matter of indifference. In the case of concessions, where the tax on revenue was in fact a progressive reduction of the construction subsidy, the alternative of a fixed net subsidy and lower railway rates would apparently have resulted in an improvement in utilisation with no deterioration in the net financial position of either the State or the concessionaire. But the appeal of these lump-sum transfers that do not distort choices at the margin need not survive as the analysis moves from a static context to a dynamic one. Railway construction was a very long-term, risky investment; a fixed net transfer would have put all of the risk on the concessionaire, while the actual sliding scale transferred much of it back to the state. The premium necessary to compensate the concessionaire for a much increased risk would have taken the form of a higher subsidy (and therefore higher taxes elsewhere) or a higher net operating income (and therefore higher railway rates): a priori, one cannot say that the distortions produced by the risk-sharing marginal tax rates would not have been exceeded by the distortions produced by the risk-concentrating fixed payments (46).

In the second place, railways have a military and strategic significance as well as a commercial one; it may thus be entirely rational for the state to build them even if they are not to see much peacetime use, and reduce current net income rather than increase it. These military-strategic considerations seem always to have been important in Italy, and never more so than in the first wave of railway construction after 1861: the Franco-Piedmontese victories over the Austrians that paved the way for national unification had been due precisely to the use of railways to achieve a rapid concentration of forces, and the early national governments faced the need to consolidate their hold on a South that was still often hostile (47). In the third place, of course, even wasteful railway construction may be politically rational as a pork-barrel project with which to favour one's constituents. The Left's spendthrift ways, its ear for business interests, and its reputation for dubious financial practices all suggest that such considerations may have been particularly significant during the second wave of railway construction, after 1880, when public funds were poured into projects often of purely local interest (48). But here too one cannot be sure that sordid motives produced social waste; at a minimum, as we shall see, the local lines built after 1880 were altogether more useful than the trunk lines built in the preceding twenty years.

7. THE IMPACT OF THE RAILWAY: AN ASSESSMENT

A comprehensive assessment of the overall impact of the railway would of course evaluate the effects of railway transportation together with those of railway construction. The unsurmounted empirical difficulties discussed above in connection with the effects of construction are equally relevant to the effects of transportation; and where the former have received at least an exploratory quantification, not even that much can be claimed for the latter (49). Nor is it possible, in the context of international factor mobility, to provide even a summary 'social saving' measure of the increase in national income attributable to the reduction in transport costs. On the one hand, the resources saved by transport improvements may simply emigrate, so that the income gain accrues to the broader international economy rather than to the small part of it in which we happen to be interested. On the other hand, as noted above, the reduction in transportation costs will typically induce resource *im*migration, as the area now more cheaply served is correspondingly more attractive to internationally mobile activities; the income gain of the domestic economy then includes both the 'social saving' and the income lost by the rest of the world. In either case, the domestic gain from transport improvements cannot be measured without evidence on the transportation-elasticity of the domestic resource base (50).

For the present, all that can be hazarded is an overall assessment of the extent to which the cost of building the railways was actually warranted by the resulting reduction in current transportation costs (51). The sample calculations in Table 3.11 (rows 1-4) suggest that the internal rate of return, including both the state's and the companies' net income from operations, equalled just 3 per cent per annum in the mid 1870s, and declined to roughly 2 per cent per annum in the early years of the present century (col 4). The global rate of return, which includes the surplus accruing to the consumers, is of course very difficult to pin down; but some plausible upper-bound estimates can be obtained on the assumption that demand curves were linear, and that prices were so set as to maximise total revenue (52).

Prices that maximise revenue are lower than those which maximise profits (and therefore allow a larger consumers' surplus); such prices were plausibly imposed by a state whose own direct income from railway operations was, before nationalisation, a given fraction of total revenue. After nationalisation, the state's direct income is the operating profit, so that nationalisation would if anything lead to higher prices rather than lower ones; but there is no evidence of a broadly-based rate increase before 1910 (53). To be sure, the state might impose lower fares, not least because it was able, in principle, to capture consumers' surplus as well as producers' surplus; as seen above, however, the fact that it taxed railway revenue at all suggests that its ability to capture consumers' surplus was in fact severely limited. Moreover, prices would have to exceed the revenue-maximising level wherever demand was relatively elastic even at the lowest price that would cover marginal costs. The assumption that prices maximised revenue may therefore somewhat overstate the price level and understate consumers' surplus; but not, presumably, by very much. In any case, any downward bias on this score is plausibly more than offset by the likely overstatement of consumers' surplus that results from the assumption that demand curves were linear. Whatever the shape of the demand curves for transportation in general, the demand curves for railway transportation in particular are likely to be convex from below, as possible substitutes for the railway become attractive at higher railway rates. In practice, then, the assumption that consumers' surplus equalled half of total revenue (which is what the present combination of assumptions amounts to) seems a more than generous one, and the global rates of return calculated on that basis are more likely to be too high than too low (54). The actual global rate of return thus seems to have averaged under 6 per cent per annum (col 5): no more, and perhaps less, than the internal rate earned by capital invested elsewhere at comparable risk

Table 3.11: *Sample rates of return on the investment in railways*

	(1) Total investment (end of year) (b)	(2) Total operating revenues (b)	(3) Total operating costs (b)	(4) Internal rate of return (a)	(5) Global rate of return (a)	(6)	(7) Total length of lines (d)
					Upper bound (c)	Best estimate	
1. Total network: in 1875	2 296	155.2	90.1	2.8	6.2		
2. in 1890	4 139	271.8	173.4	2.4	5.7		
3. in 1901	5 604	347.3	247.2	1.8	4.9		
4. in 1910	6 962	604.0	452.4	2.2	6.5		
Components of the network in 1910:							
5. major Po Valley lines	1 822	226.8	142.0	4.7	10.9	9.0	2 483
6. other major lines	2 107	191.2	164.3	1.3	5.8	3.1	4 114
7. minor lines	3 032	186.0	146.1	1.3	4.4	4.4	11 328
Minor lines earning per kilometre, in 1910:							
8. less than 10 000 lire	833	32.3	30.2	0.3	2.2	2.2	4 866
9. more than 10 000 lire	2 199	153.7	115.9	1.7	5.2	5.2	6 462

(a) per cent per annum
(b) million lire
(c) calculated by adding half of total revenue to the operating surplus
(d) kilometres

Source: See the Appendix to this chapter.

levels (55). The capital invested in Italy's railways seems to have yielded barely enough to cover its own cost, if that.

Two glosses may here be in order. In the first place, of course, the marginal social profitability of railway investment implies a negligible 'social saving'; but this does not quite imply a negligible impact on the size of the domestic resource base. While the railways did not reduce the social cost of transportation, they did transfer much of that cost from user charges to public debt-service costs; the latter were covered by taxes, and could therefore be imposed, unlike user charges, without regard to benefits received. If these costs were imposed on internationally immobile resources ('land'), mobile resources might be attracted into Italy by the lower user charges alone; in the opposite case, of course, the net losers would be the mobile resources, and these would accordingly tend to emigrate. The resulting resource movements (in either direction) are perhaps unlikely to have been significant; but they cannot be excluded a priori. In the second place, the present calculations of the railways' benefits do not take their strategic or political value into account. As noted above, these benefits may warrant railway construction even if the 'social saving' is negative; or, to put the same point in different terms, a 'social saving' measure that included the saving of alternative spending on defence and pork-barrel projects would presumably be positive. To the extent that these benefits represent no more than the increased military and electoral security of a ruling estate, however, they do not appear as benefits to the internationally mobile resources; the size of the domestic resource base is thus more likely to respond to the narrower 'social saving' considered above (with all the indicated caveats) than to the broader one considered here.

The social profitability of the successive waves of expansion of the Italian railway network cannot be gauged from the changes in cumulative investment and in total surplus, since the former also reflects the improvement of older lines, and the latter also reflects system-wide changes in operating conditions; but a rough surrogate is provided by a measure of the rate of return earned on different parts of the network near the end of the period at hand. The tentative estimates in Table 3.11 (rows 5-7) disaggregate the network into three parts: the major lines of the Po Valley, with their principal links to the sea and to foreign rail lines; the major lines in the peninsula and the islands; and the minor lines. These correlate, somewhat loosely, with the lines originally built before 1861; the lines built in 1861-80; and the lines built after 1880 (and, mostly, by 1895) (56).

The first striking result of these calculations is that the

internal rate of return of the investment in minor lines was no lower than that of the major lines outside the Po Valley, as their relatively low gross earnings per kilometre were accompanied by low current costs per kilometre and especially by low capital costs per kilometre (rows 6-7, cols 1-4 and 7). The traditional evaluations that consider only relative gross earnings per kilometre, and attribute relatively high capital costs to the minor lines, seem correspondingly wide of the mark (57). Those major lines admittedly outperform the minor lines if one adds half of gross revenue to the operating surplus (rows 6-7, col 5); but there is here a strong presumption that the comparison is vitiated by the figures' differential bias. The minor lines were overwhelmingly inland routes, typically with no competition beyond that provided by relatively inefficient horse-drawn road vehicles. Since interlocal price discrimination was surely subject to political and administrative constraints, this limited intermodal competition also increases the likelihood that prices were below the level that would have maximised revenues on those particular routes; as a result, the nominal upper bound is here actually a relatively conservative best estimate. The major lines outside the Po Valley were instead overwhelmingly coastal or transpeninsular routes, and thus typically subject to efficient waterborne competition. There is no doubt that that competition bit deeply into the demand for railway transportation: while the railway's superior speed and comfort gave it a margin of superiority over the coasting trade in carrying passengers and express freight, it found it extremely difficult to win over other freight traffic without the aid of special discounts (58). A best estimate might allow these lines a consumers' surplus equal to 20 (rather than 50) per cent of gross revenue; the result is a global rate of return that is quite low both with respect to that earned by the minor lines (rows 6-7, col 6) and with respect to the likely cost of capital.

The major drain on the global profitability of the Italian rail system thus appears to have been the trunk system in the peninsula and the islands, and not, as is widely thought, the large mileage of minor lines. No doubt, the latter included a conspicuous wasteful fringe, as the approximately 5000 kilometres earning less than 10 000 lire per annum appear to have yielded a global rate of return below even that of the peninsular trunk lines (rows 6 and 8, cols 4-6). But the loss on these fringe lines was only about half that incurred on the major lines outside the Po Valley, and the other 6500 kilometres of minor lines seem to have come close to covering their costs (row 9, col 6) (59). A breakeven return may also have been earned on the cheaper portions of the peninsular trunks, for instance along the Adriatic coast; and even apparently unprofitable lines may actually have paid for themselves by enhancing traffic and surplus on the rest of the system. But with all due allowance for the weakness of the present measures, the locus of socially costly construction seems to have been the trunk system much more than the local lines. This result, though at odds with the prevailing evaluations of the Italian railways, should come as no surprise. A cheaply built rail line may represent a major improvement in the accessibility of a land-locked site; but there is no commercial advantage to drilling through a mountain if one can sail around it (60).

This re-evaluation of the peninsular trunks and minor lines points naturally to a re-evaluation of the railway-construction policies of the Right and of the Left. The trunk lines built by the Right in the immediate aftermath of national unification seem to have done little to lower transport costs; to the extent that one can judge from their rate of return many years later, their cost had to be justified at least as much by military and strategic benefits as by commercial ones. The early flurry of railway construction thus appears not as the progressive fulfilment of a precondition for economic growth but as a drag on development, no different, in this light, from 'investment' in a large standing army. The Left was responsible for that final and most wasteful link in the peninsular trunk system, along the western coast of southern Italy; but a majority at least of the local lines built in the 1880s and 1890s seem to have been warranted by their commercial benefits alone. The reduction in transport costs per unit of railway investment thus plausibly increased, rather than decreased, around 1880; and whatever limited modernisation was induced in the peninsula by the fall in transport costs before the diffusion of the internal combustion engine seems better attributed to the later minor lines than to the earlier trunks. Again, perhaps, not surprisingly, the railways resulting from the Right's high-minded pursuit of what it took to be the national interest seem to have done altogether less to improve the material conditions of the population than the railways resulting from the Left's rather corrupt pliancy to the wishes of its constituents (61).

The major Po Valley routes, largely laid out before 1861 (and substantially extended and improved, of course, in later decades), were clearly the most valuable parts of the Italian railway system. Their internal rate of return equalled nearly 5 per cent per annum, or over three times the average earned on the rest of the system (rows 5-7, col 4). The upper-bound estimate of their global rate of return is in the neighbourhood of 11 per cent per annum; and the present best estimate, at 9 per cent per annum, is handsomely above both the return to the rest of the network and the likely cost of capital. This best estimate is based on a ratio of consumers' surplus to revenue equal to 35 per cent, midway between the 50 per cent allowed the minor lines and the 20 per cent allowed the other major lines, to reflect the availability of natural and artificial navigable waterways from the Lombard lakes to the Venetian lagoon. These remained in use, providing some competition for the railways, despite near-total public neglect; and they had apparently allowed the first development even of the Piedmontese textile industry, in the area adjoining the Lombard lakes, before the coming of the railway (62).

The existence and possible development of this water-based alternative suggests that the railway made its greatest contribution to the upper reaches of the Po Valley and to the Ligurian ports. In the Upper Po Valley, navigable waterways were not available, and water resources were probably too limited to allow for navigation without sacrificing irrigated agriculture (63). Limits on the local water supply, and the difficulty of the terrain, similarly seem to have ruled out canal links across the Ligurian Apennines from Genoa and Savona to the Po; While these were planned in the early nineteenth century, they were never built, and these ports remained largely without a hinterland until the coming of the railway (64). Lower in the Po Valley and along its Adriatic shore, the increased availability of waterways limited the gain from the railway, and the trade created by the development of the upper valley was balanced, wholly or in part, by the diversion of trade to the Ligurian ports. Had transport improvements been pursued by improving navigation rather than by building railways, the focus of Italy's industrial growth would no doubt have been located rather lower in the valley than it actually was, and served through Venice rather than through Genoa. The limits to this counterfactual industrial development depend, of course, on the long-run supply curve of internal navigation. If the latter could have been cheaply and abundantly expanded, the net effect of choosing railways over waterways would be little more than a westward shift in the location of industry and a redirection of trade; if the waterways' potential was instead extremely limited, a large portion, as well as the location, of Italy's industrial growth may be attributed to the railway. In either case, however, the industrial development of the Upper Po Valley, and its primary orientation to the western Mediterranean, remain the work of the railway.

The infrastructure that most mattered to Italian industrial growth as it actually took place was thus the regional network in northwest Italy, largely laid out in the 1850s. From a national point of view, the extension of the railway network throughout the peninsula after 1861 may have been of doubtful value; from a regional point of view, the gain from the railway construction launched by the pre-unification Piedmontese state was undoubtedly large.

NOTES AND REFERENCES

I wish to thank the Ente per gli studi monetari, bancari, e finanziari 'Luigi Einaudi' and the National Science Foundation (grant no. SES79-13427) for their financial support, and V. Ceriani, P. Ciocca, K. Kimbrough, J. Pincus, the members of the 1979 Renfe seminar and the Triangle Economic History Workshop, and the editor of this volume for their helpful comments and suggestions. Responsibility for the views expressed here is of course mine alone.

1. There is a vast and varied literature on Italy's railways. The histories by A. Crispo, *Le ferrovie italiane* (Milan, 1940) and F. Tajani, *Storia delle ferrovie italiane* (Milan, 1939) are old but still useful; so too the detailed account in I. Sachs, *L'Italie: ses finances et son développement économique* (Paris, 1885). The present chronology of railway construction is derived initially from R. Ispettorato generale delle strade ferrate, *Relazione sull'esercizio delle strade ferrate italiane* (henceforth *Relazione SFI)*, e.g. 1899 pp. 60-90, and subsequently from Direzione generale della statistica, *Annuario statistico italiano* (henceforth *Annuario)*, e.g. 1913 p. 231.
2. The rapid growth of the Istat index in the late 1860s and early 1870s was not confirmed by my subsequent index. The indices are described in A. Gerschenkron, *Economic Backwardness in Historical Perspective* (Cambridge, Mass., 1962) pp. 367-421; Istituto centrale di statistica (Istat), *Annali di statistica*, series 8, vol. 9: *Indagine statistica sullo sviluppo del reddito nazionale dell'Italia dal 1861 al 1956* (Rome, 1957; henceforth *Reddito nazionale)* pp. 98-9; S. Fenoaltea, 'Public Policy and Italian Industrial Development, 1861-1913', unpublished PhD dissertation, Harvard University (Cambridge, Mass., 1967) chs. 1-3. See also S. Fenoaltea 'Decollo, ciclo, e intervento dello Stato', in A. Caracciolo (ed), *La formazione dell'Italia industriale*

2. *Continued*

(Bari, 1969) pp. 96-9, and S. Fenoaltea, 'Railroads and Italian Industrial Growth, 1861-1913', *Explorations in Economic History*, IX (1972) 349. My own effort to extend and improve the available information base is currently under way: see S. Fenoaltea, *Italian Industrial Production, 1861-1913: A Statistical Reconstruction* (incomplete typescript, 1980; forthcoming, Cambridge University Press).

3. Gerschenkron, *Economic Backwardness;* A. Gerschenkron, *Continuity in History and Other Essays* (Cambridge, Mass., 1968); R. Romeo, *Risorgimento e capitalismo* (Bari, 1959); R. Romeo, *Breve storia della grande industria in Italia* (Bologna, 1961).
4. Romeo, *Risorgimento e capitalismo*, pp. 17-18.
5. Gerschenkron, *Economic Backwardness*, pp. 5-30, 353-64.
6. Fenoaltea, 'Public Policy and Italian Industrial Development'; Fenoaltea, 'Decollo'; S. Fenoaltea, 'Riflessioni sull'esperienza industriale italiana dal Risorgimento alla prima guerra mondiale', in G. Toniolo (ed), *Lo sviluppo economico italiano 1861-1940* (Bari, 1973). The popularity of stages-of-growth models peaked with W. W. Rostow, *The Stages of Economic Growth* (Cambridge, Mass., 1960), as much of the work inspired by that dramatic essay failed to find empirical support for its generalisations.
7. On the familiar accelerator principle, the demand for durables depends not on the desired level of capacity but on the change in that level; an increase in the desired level of capacity leads to a *temporary* increase in the demand for durables. The domestic demand for metal goods had in fact begun to fall by 1913; but its likely continued decline was turned into a sharp increase by the outbreak of war (which had the advantage, from the point of view of the metalworking industries, of turning their products into current consumables).
8. In the case of the new industries, one should strictly speaking say 'not untrue' rather than 'true', since there is no proof that the response to new opportunities would have been equally prompt in earlier years. There is also some question as to whether the introduction of the sugar beet induced the increased protection against imported sugar, or vice versa; but this issue is here immaterial.
9. On the time path of public works construction, see Fenoaltea, *Italian Industrial Production*. The benefits of railway transportation are discussed in sections 6

9. *Continued*

and 7 below.

10. It has recently been pointed out that the growth of German-style banks came largely at the expense of other financial instruments, so that even their absolute contribution to capital accumulation in industry would be limited to their superiority over existing institutions - a superiority which is typically taken for granted, but the extent and institutional basis of which have yet to be established. See A. M. Biscaini Cotula and P. Ciocca, 'Le strutture finanziarie: aspetti quantitativi di lungo periodo (1870-1970)'. in F. Vicarelli (ed), *Capitale industriale e capitale finanziario: il caso italiano* (Bologna, 1979).
11. *Annuario*, 1913 p. 46. See also J. D. Gould, 'European Inter-Continental Emigration. The Road Home: Return Migration from the USA', *Journal of European Economic History*, IX (1980) 41-112.
12. Istituto centrale di statistica (Istat), *Sommario di statistiche storiche italiane, 1861-1955* (Roma, 1958; henceforth *Sommario*) pp. 152, 172.
13. Over the last few decades, for example, the German and Swiss economies have notoriously been characterised by a flexible resource base, as the number of 'guest workers' responded elastically to domestic demand; these economies therefore combined low unemployment figures (even when employment had been falling) with the lack of resource constraints commonly attributed to underemployed economies. See J. C. Lambelet and K. Schiltknecht, *On the Importance of an Elastic Supply of Labor and Capital: Simulation Results for the Swiss Economy* (Zurich, 1973).
14. These tables cover tramways as well as railways, since much of the basic evidence (on employment, production and international trade) does not distinguish between them.
15. The similar effect one would have expected around 1865 may have been masked by the more rapid relative growth of the entire railway network.
16. These figures are obtained as follows. Value added in construction, from Table 3.3, cols 3-4. Value of construction, value added divided by 0.55. Land value, 3 per cent of value in construction. Value of rails, value added (Table 3.6, col 2) divided by 0.29; value of accessories, engineering value added (Table 3.4, col 6) divided by 0.50. The rest of the value of construction is distributed as follows: 30 per cent, value added in processing construction materials; 45 per cent, value added in quarrying; 25 per cent, value of fuel. Value

16. *Continued*

added in engineering, from Table 3.4, cols 2 and 6. Value of engineering, value added in freight cars (Table 3.5, col 6) divided by 0.66, and other value added divided by 0.50. Value of metal consumed in engineering, value added (Table 3.6, col 3 plus col 6 minus col 4) divided by 0.32. The rest of the value of engineering is attributed, for simplicity, to fuel and natural resources. Value added in metalmaking, from Table 3.6, col 8 minus col 4. Value of metalmaking, value of rails plus value of metal consumed in engineering, as above. Value of metalmaking raw materials: 80 per cent scrap and 20 per cent fuel, or 40 per cent ore and 60 per cent fuel. Total value, value of construction plus value of engineering. See also the appendix to this chapter summarising the derivation of the estimates in the tables, and Fenoaltea, *Italian Industrial Production*. Strictly speaking, of course, scrap metal was not a 'natural' resource, and coal costs, in Italy, consisted largely of international transportation.

17. The lower figures are based on certain domestic production (Table 3.4, col 1 and Table 3.6, col 1), while the higher ones include possible domestic production, i.e. the consumption that cannot be allocated between domestic production and imports (Table 3.4, col 6 and Table 3.6, col 3 plus col 5 minus col 4); the metal content of imported rolling stock (Table 3.6, col 6 minus col 5) is assumed to have been imported.
18. In the early years, in fact, the repair shops appear to have accounted for a significant proportion of the domestic production of vehicles as well as for their maintenance.
19. The actual estimates are 14 per cent and 19 per cent if the metal content of imported rolling stock is included in total consumption (col 8), and 16 per cent and 21 per cent if it is not (col 7).
20. The corresponding shares of the total railway demand for engineering (fabricated metal and machinery: cols 5 plus 6) are 53 per cent in 1861-95 and 48 per cent in 1896-1913.
21. These ratios are based on a simple comparison of the changes in railway production (Table 3.3, col 8) to the changes in, or initial levels of, total production (col 9); they thus entirely ignore possible indirect effects. The latter are returned to below.
22. In the present case, the industry totals are all defined to exclude shipbuilding and the production of wood road

22. *Continued*

vehicles.

23. The distinction between new production and maintenance is admittedly arbitrary; in the present case, the maintenance of fabricated metal is the largest single component of the engineering industry because it is taken to include the entire large blacksmithing sector, the size of which appears related to the stock, rather than to the flow, of fabricated metal. Any transfer of engineering value added from maintenance to new production would of course reduce the size of railway demand relative to current new production.
24. The comparisons to all metalmaking would be even closer to the comparisons to semi-finished ferrous metalmaking if railway metal were assumed to have been manufactured from ore rather than from scrap; see Table 3.6, note (a).
25. See R. A. Mundell, *International Economics* (London, 1968), ch. 18 and Fenoaltea, 'Railroads and Italian Industrial Growth', to which the reader is referred for a more complete discussion.
26. To an extent, this problem stems from the static nature of the model, which forces the full effect of any cause into a single time period; more generally, it is the usual result of joint causation, no more paradoxical than the hanging of twelve men for a single murder.
27. With realistically finite elasticities, the displaced production would not be quite the same in the two cases: in a demand-limited context, it would probably include a more than proportionate share of other investment; in a supply-limited context, it would probably include a more than proportionate share of other construction (and of other activities using unskilled labour). But the essential point remains.
28. This assumes that interest rates varied across risk classes, and that government bonds became riskier as public debt increased. The government thus faced a rising cost-of-borrowing curve even though it did not affect 'the' interest rate (i.e. the interest rate within each risk class).
29. Three sources of dissatisfaction with the model in Fenoaltea, 'Railroads and Italian Industrial Growth' may be pointed out, beyond the obvious ones implicit in its static nature and small size. The first one, which addresses the entire model, is the fact that the parameters are very crudely guessed, and not directly measured. The second one is the neglect of construction materials, which are also industrial products, in the

29. *Continued*

composition of railway investment. The third and most troubling one is the lack of an explicit formulation of the determinants of domestic prices, real wages and international labour movements. These were neglected on the understanding that the flexibility in labour employment levels stemmed from significant domestic unemployment; I am now sceptical of the latter (since the one million industrial workers counted by the 1911 demographic census but missed by the simultaneous industrial census seem to have been not so much unemployed as self-employed in artisanal operations: Fenoaltea, 'Railroads and Italian Industrial Growth', 328n), and incline to stress international mobility instead. See also note 49 below.

30. Venice, the Netherlands and England are obvious cases in point. For an analysis of a negative example, where the possible density of resources was limited by poor transportation, see D. R. Ringrose, 'Transportation and Economic Stagnation in Eighteenth-Century Castile', *Journal of Economic History*, XXVIII (1968) 51-79.

31. The state railways' total shipments (39 million tons), seaport loadings (11 million tons, disaggregated by port), and rail imports (2 million tons) are reported in Direzione generale delle ferrovie dello Stato, *Relazione dell'amministrazione delle ferrovie esercitate dallo Stato* (henceforth *Relazione FS)*, 1911-12 pp. 293-9. An estimate of the other railways' total shipments (6 million tons) is based on the preceding year's figure in Ufficio speciale delle ferrovie e tramvie e degli automobili, *Relazione sull'esercizio delle strade ferrate concesse all'industria privata* (henceforth *Relazione SFC)*, 1910 p. 319; since these railways were very largely confined to the country's interior, their direct seaport loadings and rail imports are here considered negligible. The combined shipments of the state and other railways (45 million tons) are reduced by 5 million tons to allow for double-counting; this figure includes some 3 million tons transshipped from the state to the other railways, and some 2 million tons transshipped in the opposite direction. The former transshipments are estimated as 1.3 times the latter, from the evidence on the directional imbalance at the domestic rail transshipment points in Direzione generale delle ferrovie dello Stato, *Statistica dell'esercizio* (henceforth *Statistica FS)*, 1911 part 2 pp. 439-43; the latter transshipments are instead obtained as the difference between the state

31. *Continued*

railways' loadings from all other rail systems on the one hand, and from foreign rail systems only on the other (*Relazione FS*, 1911-12 pp. 292, 299). Loadings in the interior are obtained by deducting seaport loadings and rail imports from estimated total shipments.

32. *Sommario*, pp. 144, 146.
33. In 1973, overland shipments by modern means totalled 1168 million tons (89 per cent of them by road, 6 per cent by pipeline, and 5 per cent by rail: Ministero dei trasporti, *Compendio di statistiche sui trasporti*, 1977 pp. 59, 62, 94, 102). Imports totalled 217 million tons (*Annuario*, 1976 p. 271); domestic shipments by modern overland means thus equalled (at least) 951 million tons, or about 33 times the comparable level in 1911. Total commodity production, in turn, increased in value from some 14.1 thousand million lire to some 40.8 million million lire; these estimates are obtained as domestic value added in commodity production plus half the value of imports (*Sommario*, pp. 152, 213; *Annuario*, 1976 pp. 271, 413), on the assumption that the other half of imports were consumed directly or in the production of services. Since the wholesale price index increased from 1.00 in 1911 to 429 in 1973 (*Annuario*, 1971 p. 307, 1975 p. 313), physical commodity output in 1973 was only about 6.7 times the comparable level in 1911. Shipments per ton of commodity output grew as the ratio of the growth in total shipments to the growth in physical commodity output (33/6.7), or approximately five-fold from 1911 to 1973.
34. Seaport loadings for cereal and various other major items, but not lumber, are reported in the *Relazione FS*, 1911-12 p. 306. However, the international trade statistics suggest that roughly half of Italy's lumber imports arrived directly by rail from Austria-Hungary and Switzerland. See Direzione generale delle gabelle, *Movimento commerciale del Regno d'Italia* (henceforth *Movimento commerciale*), 1900 pp. 196-7, 1911 part 1 p. 168.
35. Sand is here a partial exception, in that the proportion of output moved by rail seems unusually high for a good whose value per ton was under half that of bricks and tiles, and perhaps one tenth that of lime and cement. A likely explanation is the availability of a special low rate, as suggested (with all due allowance for possible variations in the average haul) by railway revenues of about 2 lire per ton of sand, against a typical range of 4 to 10 lire per ton (*Relazione FS*, 1911-12 p. 312).

36. See e.g. Comitato d'inchiesta industriale, *Atti* (10 vols, Florence and Rome, 1873-4), *Deposizioni orali* category 8 sub 1 - 2 - 3 instalments I pp. 2, 8, instalment III pp. 2, 9, instalment VI p. 3; R. Corpo delle miniere, *Rivista del servizio minerario* (henceforth *Rivista mineraria)*, 1898 p. 238. Coal freight rates suggest that the cost of sea transport from England to Italy was typically equivalent to the cost of rail transport over 300 to 600 kilometres, while the distance from Turin to Naples is nearly 1000 kilometres. See E. A. V. Angier, *Fifty Years' Freights* (London, 1920); R. Commissione per lo studio di proposte intorno all'ordinamento delle strade ferrate, *Atti* (10 vols, Rome, 1903-6; henceforth *Atti CSO)*, vol. 5 parts 1-2 p. 100. The South's relatively inefficient industry, built up behind the prohibitive tariff walls of the Kingdom of Naples, was thus largely destroyed by foreign competition when the low Piedmontese tariff was extended to the entire peninsula in 1860; what survived does not appear to have been affected by the completion of the first all-rail route to the North in 1866. See G. Luzzatto, *L'economia italiana dal 1861 al 1914*, vol. 1 (Milan, 1963) pp. 27-35; also E. Sereni, *Capitalismo e mercato nazionale in Italia*, 2nd edn (Rome, 1974) pp. 71, 93. Sereni's view that the railways were the means by which Italy's ruling bourgeoisie welded the local markets into a national one is undermined both by the evidence of limited inter-regional transportation presented in Table 3.9 and, more directly, by the evidence that the peninsular trunk lines did little or nothing to reduce interregional transport user charges; see Sereni, *Capitalismo*, pp. 69-76 and note 58 below.
37. See for instance G. Baglioni, *Per la riforma ferroviaria* (Milan, 1910); M. Diegoli, 'La trazione a vapore', *Ingegneria ferroviaria*, XVI (1961) 671-80; M. Maroni, 'L'armamento del binario', *Ingegneria ferroviaria*, XVI (1961) 595-600. In fact, the incidence of curves and gradients reflects a trade-off between capital and current costs, and therefore expected utilisation levels, just as much as the equipment standard for the existing lines; the only difference is that the construction of the basic right of way involves a relatively longer time horizon. In either case, improvements allow for marginal costs inclusive of additional capital costs lower than marginal costs with the existing track and equipment.
38. The pruning of off-peak capacity to raise load factors tends to raise costs per unit of capacity, since the variable costs saved by such adjustments are a relatively small part of total costs; the labour force, in particular,

38. *Continued*

remains relatively constant, and is simply underutilised at off-peak times. The superior solution is, of course, the systematic use of discriminatory pricing to offset the fluctuations in demand and 'flatten the load curve'; but this seems to be a relatively recent development. See J. R. Nelson (ed), *Marginal Cost Pricing in Practice* (Englewood Cliffs, NJ, 1964).

39. Relative fuel costs are probably best compared on the basis of ton-kilometres of gross weight actually hauled (within rounding error, row 19 times row 23 divided by row 21), since these seem least affected by extraneous factors (input substitution, traffic composition and so on). The possible impact of relative fuel costs is better gauged by scaling fuel costs up on the foreign systems than by scaling them down on the Italian systems: in the presence of input substitution, the former estimate provides an upper bound, the latter a lower one. Relative fuel costs are stressed e.g. in *Atti CSO*, vol. 5 parts 1-2 pp. 119-20; see also *Relazione FS*, 1906-7 p. 12 and Baglioni, *Per la riforma ferroviaria*, p.14.

40. Unlike fuel costs, other non-labour costs are scaled up by an ad hoc allowance because they seem so highly subject to input substitution that none of the available comparisons can reveal the influence of relative prices and terrain-related consumption levels alone. The estimated cost levels of the French and German systems are in principle upper bounds, since they neglect the savings that could have resulted from substitution among inputs.

41. Marginal cost is difficult to evaluate directly, since the time-series evidence is here more than usually ambiguous. Traffic rose relatively constantly from 1898 to 1913; but measured productivity (train-kilometres per employee) rose from 1898 to 1905, then fell sharply to 1907, and then recovered. The main influence here was the reduced hiring by the private companies in the last few years of their contracts, the 28 per cent increase in staff in the two years after nationalisation, and the subsequent virtual freeze on hiring. Service also deteriorated to notoriously poor levels early in this century, and apparently did not recover until the state railways had digested their new personnel, and improved their equipment, after a few years of operation. See *Relazione FS*, 1910-11 pp. 8-15; also e.g. Baglioni, *Per la riforma ferroviaria*, p. 42 and Tajani, *Storia delle ferrovie italiane*, pp. 115-23. The international comparisons in row 29 indicate that the ratio of operating

41. *Continued*

revenues to current costs was even higher on the major French and German systems than on the Italian ones. However, their lower average revenues suggest lower prices (rows 26-7; see also the sample rates in *Atti CSO*, vol. 5 parts 1-2 pp. 99-117), and their high utilisation levels (row 4) suggest that marginal costs may have exceeded average costs. On the Nord and the Preussische-Hessische, especially, one cannot say from the evidence at hand that prices were obviously too high.

42. The 28 per cent-72 per cent revenue split discussed here applied to the main lines of the Rete Mediterranea and Rete Adriatica, on which they earned some 95 per cent of their revenue. On the minor lines, they received a small fixed subsidy per kilometre of line, and operating revenues were shared with the state on a 50-50 basis (equivalent to a 100 per cent excise tax). See *Atti CSO*, vol. 4 part 2 pp. 8-10; *Relazione SFI*, 1898 cols 933, 944-5; Sachs, *L'Italie*, pp. 1061-4. The state could waive its share of revenue to allow special low rates, but this was very rarely done. See R. Ispettorato generale delle strade ferrate, *Relazione intorno all'esercizio delle strade ferrate delle reti Mediterranea, Adriatica, e Sicula dal 1º luglio 1885 al 1900* (4 parts in 6 vols, Rome, 1901), part 3 pp. 209-29; also *Atti CSO*, vol. 3 p. 556. In addition to thus sharing revenue, the state levied explicit excise taxes at the rate of 13 per cent on passenger and 'grande velocità' freight, and 2 per cent on 'piccola velocità' freight; e.g. *Annuario*, 1904 p. 494.

43. These arrangements were relatively complex, since they covered construction as well as operation. Taxes on revenue were imposed as a reduction in the construction subsidy, normally on a sliding scale; a 50 per cent marginal rate, equivalent to a 100 per cent excise, seems to have applied to the Romane, the Meridionali and the recent lines of the Alta Italia. The old Piedmontese state lines were instead sold to the Alta Italia, so that the state could immediately obtain the capitalised operating surplus allowed by the fares specified in the act of sale; these fares were in any case the same as those applicable on the lines subject to tax. The railway reorganisation of 1885 was accompanied by a significant reduction in railway rates, apparently on the companies' initiative; since cost levels changed relatively little, the reduction in fares is plausibly attributed to the lower marginal tax rates introduced by the new conventions.

43. *Continued*

The fiscally optimal fare level was also probably reduced by the elimination of the state's former interest in the maximisation of expected net revenue on the lines it sold to the Alta Italia, and the consequent generalisation of its interest in the maximisation of the railways' gross revenues. See *Annuario*, 1878 part 1 p. 140, 1905-7 p. 669; E. Corbino, *Annali dell'economia italiana*, vol. 3 (Città di Castello, 1933) p. 305; *Raccolta ufficiale delle leggi e dei decreti del Regno d'Italia*, XI (1865) pp. 696, 765, 768, 819, 855; Sachs, *L'Italie*, pp. 966-7.

44. *Annuario*, 1913 p. 242; *Relazione FS*, 1910-11 pp. 10-11.
45. See e.g. *Relazione SFI*, 1898 pp. 8-9 and *Relazione FS*, 1910-11 pp. 23-4.
46. A similar argument applies to the possibility of a lump-sum tax in operating contracts. In fact, the decline of the state's typical share of revenue from 50 per cent to 28 per cent suggests that growing experience reduced uncertainty and allowed the companies to shoulder a greater portion of the remaining risk. Taxes on profits were also possible in principle; in practice, however, they were difficult to administer, and would blunt the incentive to control costs about as much as they would redistribute risk. Public operation would let the state bear the risk directly, but would encounter similar cost-control problems; moreover, though practised as a last resort, it was politically infeasible as a permanent solution in the 1880s, and then legally infeasible until the expiration of the twenty-year conventions signed in 1885. The likelihood that the prevailing system was the result of rational choice is strengthened by the evidence that the state was aware of the traffic-reducing incentives associated with high marginal revenue tax rates, and knowingly accepted them. See e.g. Commissione d'inchiesta sull'esercizio delle ferrovie italiane, *Atti* (3 parts in 7 vols, Rome, 1879-84; henceforth *Atti CIE)* part 2 vol. 2 pp. 559-63; Corbino, *Annali dell'economia italiana*, vol. 3, pp. 288-96.
47. See e.g. Luzzatto, *L'economia italiana*, pp. 24-6; Tajani, *Storia delle ferrovie italiane*, p. 62; S. J. Woolf, 'La storia politica e sociale', in R. Romano and C. Vivante (eds), *Storia d'Italia*, vol. 3 (Turin, 1973) p. 508. The railway requirements of the military were considered in *Atti CIE*, part 2 vol. 3 pp. 1237-96 and *Atti CSO*, vol. 3 pp. 9-38, 63-143.
48. E.g. Baglioni, *Per la riforma ferroviaria*, pp. 90-2; Corbino, *Annali dell'economia italiana*, vol. 3, pp. 218, 268, 309,

48. *Continued*

313, 320-4, 342-3; A. Plebano, *Storia della finanza italiana*, vol. 2 (Turin, 1900) pp. 162-70.

49. A calculation of the effect of the post-1861 extensions of the railway network was admittedly presented in Fenoaltea, 'Railroads and Italian Industrial Growth', but the results of that tentative effort are of little value. On the one hand, in light of the evidence in Table 3.9, the metal import-substitution there attributed to railway transportation seems vastly overestimated. On the other, there is no attempt to measure what was surely the most immediate effect of the provision of railway transportation: namely, the reduction in the transportation provided by, and therefore in investment in, alternative transport modes. While the railways' apparent lack of superiority over these alternatives warranted neglecting the income effect, as it were, the substitution effect was plausibly significant.

50. A familiar analogy is provided by the impact of technical progress on a particular industry. If the elasticity of demand for its output is low, the decline in costs will lead to a decline in the volume of resources employed in the industry; at the limit, output remains constant, and all the resources saved by technical change migrate to other industries. An industry facing a highly elastic demand will instead recruit additional resources and expand its production by far more than the productivity gain alone would allow.

51. The railways' construction costs would not need to be deducted from their gross benefits to the Italian economy if Italy had had the wit to export those costs, as some did, by importing the needed capital and then defaulting on the debt.

52. A linear demand curve is elastic above its midpoint, and inelastic below it; the midpoint accordingly defines the price that maximises total revenue. With always positive marginal costs, the price that maximises profits falls necessarily in the elastic portion of the curve, i.e. above the price that that maximises total revenue. The operative demand curve is here the one that allows for induced resource movements; the total surplus defined by this demand curve and the railway transportation supply curve accordingly measures the world's gain from Italy's railways, and not Italy's own gain (which includes the transfer price of immigrant resources, or excludes that of emigrant resources).

53. E.g. *Relazione FS*, 1909-10 pp. 59-67. A general rate

53. *Continued*

increase was sanctioned by the law n. 310 of 13 April 1911 (arts. 14-15); but this seems to have been a response to increasing costs rather than a switch to profit maximisation.

54. The essential point is that intermodal competition would tend to reduce the ratio of consumers' surplus to railway revenue; a convex demand curve, and a linear demand curve that is highly elastic even at the lowest acceptable price, are essentially alternative manifestations of the same phenomenon. Price discrimination, which transformed into railway revenue what would otherwise have been consumers' surplus, would here have an equivalent effect. Since railway rates were set for long periods, the assumption that prices continuously maximised revenues produces a cyclical variation in the bias of the present year-specific estimates; by the same token, however, the present rate-of-return figures may be considered partly sheltered from cyclical disturbances.
55. That rate appears to have been close to 6 per cent per annum until the mid-1880s; it then declined to about 5 per cent per annum by the mid-1890s, and remained near that level up to the eve of the First World War (Biscaini Cotula and Ciocca, 'Le strutture finanziarie', pp. 122-6). The global rate of return to railway investment is properly compared to the internal rate of return to alternative investment if the capital invested in railways was imported or withdrawn from marginal projects with negligible surplus.
56. The network length figures in Table 3.11, col 7, refer to the 'operated network', which double-counts those segments common to more than one line; the figure in Table 3.1, col 5, refers instead to the unduplicated 'installed network'. The two measures are reconciled e.g. in *Relazione SFC,* 1910 p. 65, *Statistica FS,* 1910 pp. 58-60.
57. E.g. Baglioni, *Per la riforma ferroviaria,* pp. 90-2; *Relazione FS,* 1906-7 pp. 12-13. The latter erroneously measured the capital costs of the minor lines from the secular growth in average investment per kilometre, neglecting the improvement of older lines.
58. See e.g. *Atti CIE,* part 1 vol. 2 pp. 83 and 99, vol. 3 p. 306. Particularly significant is the railways' 1886 petition, which was denied, for special rates with which to attract traffic from traditional sailing coasters. See R. Ispettorato generale delle strade ferrate, *Annali del consiglio delle tariffe delle strade ferrate,* 1886 pp. 56-7.

59. If the cost of capital is estimated as 6 per cent per annum, the capital loss incurred by the major lines in row 6 is 2107 million lire times (6.0 - 3.1)/6.0, or roughly 1000 million lire; that incurred by the minor lines in row 7 is 3032 million lire times (6.0 - 4.4)/6.0, or roughly 800 million lire, of which over 500 million from the low-yield lines in row 8. However, the minor lines were generally built later than the major lines, and thus benefited from lower interest rates (above, note 55); a conservative 5.5 per cent per annum would reduce the loss on the minor lines in row 7 to 600 million lire, of which all but 100 million are traceable to the low-yield lines in row 8.
60. In a similar vein, the varying availability of water-based competition meant that American railroads were attributed a greater 'social saving' in short-haul transportation than in long-haul transportation. See R. W. Fogel, *Railroads and American Economic Growth: Essays in Econometric History* (Baltimore, 1964) pp. 208-19.
61. It is tempting to view the measured losses incurred by the construction of minor lines in disadvantaged areas as a socially desirable transfer of resources to deserving groups; but one would need to show that these redistribution benefits were not nullified by the regressivity of the taxes imposed to pay for them.
62. See *Atti CSO,* vol. 5 parts 1-2 pp. 477, 480, 499, 526; Commissione per la navigazione interna, *Atti del comitato tecnico-esecutivo. Relazione riassuntiva* (Rome, 1908) pp. 76-89; *Enciclopedia italiana,* vol. 27 p. 182.
63. *Atti CSO,* vol. 5 parts 1-2 pp. 477, 521.
64. *Atti CSO,* vol. 5 parts 1-2 pp. 482-9.

APPENDIX

In Table 3.1, the area figures (col 1) are adapted from *Encyclopedia Britannica,* 11th edn, vol. 10 p. 775, vol. 11 p. 808, vol. 15 p. 527, vol. 25 p. 527, and vol. 27 p.599. The population and railway-mileage data (cols 2-5) are adapted from B. R. Mitchell, *European Historical Statistics 1750-1970* (London, 1975) pp. 20-4, 581-4, with the exception of the Italian railway-mileage figure for 1913, which is taken from *Annuario,* 1913 p. 231 (Mitchell's higher figure is equal to that in *Sommario,* p. 137, for the network within the borders of 1924).

In Table 3.2, the Gerschenkron index (col 1) is that first published in A. Gerschenkron, 'Notes on the Rate of Industrial Growth in Italy, 1881-1913', *Journal of Economic History,* XV

(1955) 362 and reprinted in Gerschenkron, *Economic Backwardness*, p. 75. The Istat index (col 2) is that which appeared in *Reddito nazionale*, p. 218, and again in G. Fuà (ed), *Lo sviluppo economico in Italia*, vol.3 (Milan, 1969) p. 40. The Fenoaltea index (col 3) is from Fenoaltea, 'Public Policy and Italian Industrial Development'.

Tables 3.3-3.6 are based on preliminary calculations for Fenoaltea, *Italian Industrial Production*. In Table 3.3, value added in first construction (cols 1-2) is the sum of separate estimates for the (future) state railways, other railways, extra-urban tramways, electric urban tramways and horse-drawn urban tramways. Value added per completed kilometre is estimated at about 55 per cent of the corresponding value (excluding the value of improvements from that of the state railways) and distributed over five years (state railways), three years (other railways), or two years (tramways). Value added in improvements (col 3) is obtained by distributing 55 per cent of the estimated cumulative value of improvements (to the state railways) in proportion to rail consumption in excess of the amount needed for first construction. Value added in maintenance (cols 5-6) is estimated directly from expenditure data for each major type of system in 1909-11, and then extrapolated in proportion to system-specific indices of track use (total vehicle-kilometres or axle-kilometres). Value added in the construction industry as a whole (col 9) is obtained as the sum of separate estimates for railway construction, other public works and private construction; the present figures are very rough and preliminary.

In Table 3.4, the rolling stock figures (cols 1-5) are the sums of the disaggregated estimates in Table 3.5. Track accessories (col 6) are such fabricated metal as spikes, fishplates, turntables and the like; only total consumption can be estimated here, in the absence of data on either output or imports. Value added is here estimated as 57 per cent of the value added in rail production plus imports (Table 3.6, col 2); this coefficient allows accessories and rails 25 per cent and 75 per cent, respectively, of their combined cost, and a ratio of value added to value equal to 29 per cent in the case of rails and 50 per cent (for fabrication only) in accessories. The industry-wide estimates (cols 7-12) are again very rough figures, obtained by interpolating direct estimates for 1862 and 1911. Value added in the production both of machinery (col 6) and of fabricated metal and machinery together (col 9) is indexed by the consumption of semi-finished ferrous metal other than rails. The estimates of value added in maintenance (cols 7 and 9) instead assume constant geometric growth in the maintenance of clocks and watches (from 6 million lire per annum in 1861-5 to 12 million in 1911-13), of other non-railway machinery (from 7 million lire per annum in 1861-5 to 68 million in 1911-13), and of fabricated metal (from 257 million lire per annum in 1861-5 to 311 million in 1911-13), and add the resulting figures to those for railway rolling stock (col 3).

In Table 3.5, the production and acquisitions figures (cols 1-6) are obtained as the product of vehicle-specific estimates of tons produced or purchased on the one hand, and value added per ton at 1911 prices (50 per cent of value for locomotives and passenger cars, 66 per cent for freight cars) on the other hand. Tons purchased are estimated from current evidence on numbers purchased by each major type of system, and unit weights specific to each year and type of system; tons produced are estimated initially as a percentage of those purchased (in the 1860s and 1870s, when year-specific import figures are not available) and later by deducting reported imports from estimated purchases. Value added in maintenance (cols 3-9) is estimated initially for the state railways in 1906, from particularly abundant information on employment in the railway's own repair shops, the share of subcontracted maintenance, and relative expenditure for each type of vehicle; these estimates are then extrapolated to other systems and to other years on the basis of type-specific vehicle- or axle-kilometres.

In Table 3.6, the rail figures are obtained as the product of tons produced (col 1), or tons produced plus imports (col 2), and value added per ton at 1911 prices (about 29 per cent of value). Value added in the manufacture of (domestic or imported) track accessories (col 3) is estimated as 18 per cent of value added in rail production; this coefficient is analogous to that underlying the figures in Table 3.4, col 6, allowing a ratio of value added to value in accessories of 16 per cent (for metalmaking) instead of 50 per cent (for fabrication). Value added in rolling stock metal is estimated as value added per ton (about 32 per cent of a value figure itself 58 per cent higher than the value of rails) times the estimated tonnage of metal consumed in the maintenance (col 4) and domestic manufacture (col 5 minus col 4) of railway rolling stock, or in the manufacture of imported rolling stock as well (col 6 minus col 5). Tons of metal consumed per ton of rolling stock manufactured are assumed to equal 1.2 for locomotives; 0.14 for passenger cars in 1861-5, growing linearly to 0.44 in 1876-80 and 0.50 in 1881 ff; and 0.43 in freight cars in 1861-5, growing to 0.63 in 1866-70 and 0.75 in 1871 ff. Metal consumption for maintenance is estimated from value added in rolling stock maintenance (Table 3.5, cols 7-9), and ratios of metalmaking value added to engineering value added equal to half those obtained for new construction. The total-market figure in col 7 is the sum of cols 2, 3 and 5;

that in col 8 is the sum of cols 2, 3 and 6. The estimates for the entire industry in col 9 cover the manufacture of rails and other semi-finished metal, including castings, from pig or scrap; col 10 further covers the manufacture of pig iron from ore; and col 11 further covers the manufacture of other ingot metal from ore and other semi-finished metal from ingot.

Tables 3.7 and 3.8 are based on Tables 3.4 and 3.6. In both of these, the first set of estimates compares the average level of railway-related value added to the average level of total value added: e.g. Table 3.7, col 1 (0.13 in 1861-95) is the ratio of Table 3.4, col 1 (an average of 5.4 million lire per annum in 1861-95) to Table 3.4, col 7 (an average of 40.9 million lire per annum in 1861-95). The second set of estimates compares the period-to-period changes in railway-related value added to the changes in total value added: e.g. Table 3.7, col 1 (0.29 from 1876-80 to 1886-90) is the ratio of the change in Table 3.4, col 1 (13.7 million lire per annum from 1876-80 to 1886-90) to the change in Table 3.4, col 7 (48 million lire per annum from 1876-80 to 1886-90). The third set of estimates compares that same period-to-period change in railway-related value added to the total value added in the initial period, and reduces the result to an annual rate: e.g. Table 3.7, col 1 (0.04 per annum, obtained as the equivalent of 0.44 in 10 years, from 1876-80 to 1886-90) is obtained from the ratio of the change in Table 3.4, col 1 (13.7 million lire per annum from 1876-80 to 1886-90) to the level of Table 3.4, col 7 in the initial period (31 million lire per annum in 1876-80).

In Table 3.7, as indicated, col 1 is derived from Table 3.4, cols 1 and 7. Col 2 is derived from Table 3.4, col 2 on the one hand and col 7 plus the difference between cols 2 and 1 on the other. Col 3 is derived from Table 3.4, cols 4 and 9. Col 4 is derived from Table 3.4, col 5 on the one hand and col 9 plus the difference between cols 5 and 4 (or 2 and 1) on the other. Col 5 is derived from Table 3.4, col 1 plus col 6 on the one hand, and col 10 on the other. Col 6 is derived from Table 3.4, col 2 plus col 6 on the one hand, and col 10 plus the difference between cols 2 and 1 on the other. Col 7 is derived from Table 3.4, col 4 plus col 6 on the one hand, and col 12 on the other. Col 8 is derived from Table 3.4, col 5 plus col 6 on the one hand, and col 12 plus the difference between cols 5 and 4 (or 2 and 1) on the other.

In Table 3.8, col 1 is derived from Table 3.6, cols 1 and 9. Col 2 is derived from Table 3.6, col 2 on the one hand and col 9 plus the difference between cols 2 and 1 on the other. Cols 3 and 4 are analogous to cols 1 and 2, substituting Table 3.6, col 11 for col 9. Col 5 is obtained from Table 3.6, col 1 plus the product of col 12 and the sum of cols 3 and 5 on the one hand, and col 9 on the other. Col 6 is obtained from Table 3.6, col 2 plus col 3 plus col 6 on the one hand, and col 9 plus the difference between col 2 plus col 3 plus col 6 and col 1 plus the product of col 12 and the sum of cols 3 and 5 (i.e. 9 + ((2 + 3 + 6) - (1 + 12 (3 + 5)), where these figures are the column numbers) on the other. Cols 7 and 8 are analogous to cols 5 and 6, with the substitution of Table 3.6, col 11 for col 9.

In Table 3.9, the railway-shipment figures (col 1) are obtained as the average of the 1910/11 and 1911/12 figures in *Relazione FS*, 1910-11 pp. 305-6, 1911-12 pp. 311-12, with the animal head count converted to weight (row 12) at the rate of 0.15 tons per head (from the stock proportions and unit live weights in *Annuario*, 1913 p. 144, 1977 p. 153). The import and export figures (cols 2 and 3) are from *Movimento commerciale*, 1911 part 1 pp. 23-58. The domestic production figures (col 4) are typically extremely rough estimates, obtained from a variety of sources. Rows 1, 16, 18-19, 22 and 26 are from Fenoaltea, *Italian Industrial Production*. Row 21 is based on that same source, allowing 1.1 tons per ton of rails and 1.2 tons per ton of other semi-finished ferrous metal, and deducting imports. Rows 2 and 17 are from *Sommario*, p. 118, multiplying the 1911 figures by the ratio of the 1932 figures to the 1931 figures (to convert potential to actual yields) and by specific gravities equal to 0.65 and 0.35, respectively. Rows 3-5 are estimated as 1.67 times the 1901 figures reported in *Rivista mineraria*, 1901 pp. CI, CVIII. Rows 6-9, 11-15, and 27-9 are from *Sommario*, pp. 106, 108, 110, 113-14, 124, 126, 134. Row 10 is from *Annuario*, 1913 p. 132. Row 23 is estimated as 90 per cent of fibre consumption; net imports are obtained analogously to cols 2 and 3, and domestic production (rows 24 and 25) from *Annuario*, 1913 p. 132 and *Sommario*, p. 115.

In Table 3.10, the line track figures in row 1 are calculated from the track-length figures in *Atti CSO*, vol. 6 cols 10-14; single-track lines are counted once, double-track lines twice, and so on, and service track is excluded. The traffic per kilometre figures in rows 2 and 3 are obtained from row 1 and traffic figures obtained as follows. For the Italian systems, the source is *Relazione SFI*, 1898; aggregate passenger-kilometres are transcribed from col 622, and aggregate freight ton-kilometres are estimated as 10 per cent of col 705, plus 40 per cent of col 717, plus col 770, plus 20 per cent of col 780, plus 200 per cent of col 783, plus col 822. For the French systems, the source is Direction des chemins de fer, *Statistique des chemins de fer français*, 1898 part 1 (henceforth *Statistique CFF)*; aggregate passenger-kilometres are transcribed from p. 170 col 3, and aggregate freight ton-kilometres are estimated by scaling up the 'petite vitesse' figures in p. 183 col 13 in proportion to the ratio of total freight capacity to 'petite vitesse' capacity alone (see below). For the German system, passenger-kilometres and freight ton-kilometres are transcribed from *Atti CSO*, vol. 6 cols 150 and 160. The total traffic per kilometre figures in row 4 are obtained from row 1 and the sum of passenger-kilometres and freight ton-kilometres; within rounding error, they equal the sum of the partial figures in rows 2 and 3. The shares of freight in total traffic in row 5 are the ratios of row 3 to row 4. The passenger load factors in row 6 are the ratios of passenger-kilometres (as above) to seat-kilometres; the freight load factors in row 7 are the ratios of freight ton-kilometres (as above) to freight capacity ton-kilometres. The Italian systems' capacity figures are obtained from *Relazione SFI*, 1898; passenger capacity is the sum of cols 378 and 381, and freight capacity is the sum of cols 384, 387 and 390. The French systems' capacity figures are calculated from *Statistique CFF*. Passenger capacity is estimated as the product of average seats per car and passenger car-kilometres; the former are calculated from the distributions in p. 152 cols 3-14, and the latter are reported in p. 200 col 12. Total freight capacity is obtained as the sum of separate figures for 'grande' and 'petite vitesse', each of which is estimated as the product of average freight capacity per car (p. 152 cols 18 and 21) and car-kilometres (p. 200 cols 13-14). The German system's capacity figures are from *Atti CSO*, vol. 6; passenger capacity is the product of cols 113 and 134, and freight capacity the product of cols 123 and 136. The overall load factors in row 8 are the ratio of the sum of passenger-kilometres and freight ton-kilometres to the sum of seat-kilometres and freight capacity ton-kilometres. The average loads per passenger train in row 9 are the ratio of passenger-kilometres to passenger-train kilometres. The latter are reported in *Relazione SFI*, 1898 col 264 for the Italian systems, *Statistique CFF*, p.189 col 14 for the French systems, and *Atti CSO*, vol. 6 col 128 for the German system; the Italian and French figures include, but the German one excludes, the mileage of mixed trains. The average loads per freight train in row 10 are the ratio of freight ton-kilometres to freight train-kilometres. For the Italian systems, these ratios relate total freight ton-kilometres (as above) less those at 'grande velocità' (*Relazione SFI*, 1898, 10 per cent of col 705 plus 40 per cent of col 717) to freight train-kilometres (exclusive of mixed trains' mileage) (*Relazione SFI*, 1898 col 268). For the French systems, these ratios relate 'petite vitesse' freight-kilometres to 'petite vitesse' freight train-kilometres (*Statistique CFF*, p. 183 col 13, p. 188 col 18). For the German system, these ratios relate total freight ton-kilometres to total freight and mixed train-kilometres (*Atti CSO*, vol. 6 cols 129, 160). Because of this different treatment of mixed trains, the German figures in rows 9 and 10 are not strictly comparable to the others: that in row 9 is rather too high, and that in row 10 rather too low. The average loads per train in row 11 are the ratios of total traffic units (the sum of total passenger-kilometres and total freight-ton kilometres, as above) to total train-kilometres (for the Italian systems, *Relazione SFI*, 1898 col 269; for the French systems, *Statistique CFF*, p.189 cols 14 plus 18; for the German system, *Atti CSO*, vol. 6 cols 128 plus 129). The average loads per locomotive in row 12 are the ratios of those same total traffic units to total locomotive-kilometres; the latter are reported in *Relazione SFI*, 1898 col 172 for the Italian systems, and in *Statistique CFF*, p. 195 col 9 for the French systems. The employment figures in rows 13-15 are normally those reported in *Atti CSO*, vol. 6 cols 228 (row 13), 232 (row 14), and 236 plus 240 (row 15), divided by total traffic units. Exceptionally, the very low French figures in col 228 are re-estimated as follows: administrative labour costs are estimated as 55 per cent of the total expenditure for administration (col 188), and divided by unit labour costs in administration (the ratio of col 229 to col 228). The employment totals in row 16 are the sum of rows 13-15. The labour costs per employee in row 17 are normally the ratio of total labour costs to total employment (*Atti CSO*, vol. 6 cols 246 and 248). Exceptionally, the administrative employment and labour costs of the Paris-Lyon-Méditerranée are re-estimated as above, and the figure for the Nord simply repeats that obtained for the Paris-Lyon-Méditerranée. This is preferred to the much lower figure (1200 lire per employee) obtained as the ratio of labour costs to employment (re-estimated as for the Paris-Lyon-Méditerranée), since major elements of the labour cost figures on the Nord seem peculiarly low (possibly because of subcontracted maintenance and the like; the employment figures seem less affected, either because indirectly employed workers were included in total employment, or because of an offsetting bias from part-time employment). The current costs per traffic unit in rows 18-21 are obtained by dividing total traffic units into total current cost figures obtained as follows. Total labour costs (for row 18) are taken as reported (*Atti CSO*, vol. 6 col 248) for the Italian and German systems, as re-estimated above for the Paris-Lyon-Méditerranée, and as the product of estimated total employment and estimated labour costs per employee (as above) on the Nord. Total fuel costs (for row 19) are taken as reported in

Relazione SFI, 1898 col 1039 for the Italian systems, and in *Statistique CFF*, p. 236 col 5, for the French systems; the figure for the German system assumes the same percentage distribution of non-labour costs as on the Paris-Lyon-Méditerranée. Other current costs (for row 20) are simply the difference between total current costs and labour plus fuel costs; total current costs (for row 21) are themselves taken as reported *(Atti CSO*, vol. 6 col 200). The total current costs per capacity unit in row 22 are those same total current costs, divided by the sum of seat-kilometres and freight capacity ton-kilometres. The total current costs per actual weight unit are those same total current costs, divided by estimates of the total ton-kilometres of gross weight actually hauled. These estimates are obtained by assuming tare weights of 0.21 tons per passenger seat and 0.56 tons per freight capacity ton (from the figures for the major French systems together, *Statistique CFF*, p. 152 cols 3-21), and payload weights of 0.10 tons per passenger and (obviously) 1.00 tons per freight tons. Total weight units in passenger operations are obtained as total passenger-kilometres times actual weight units per passenger-kilometre; the latter equal to the payload weight (0.1 tons) plus the tare weight (0.21 tons per seat divided by the load factor). Total weight units in freight operations are estimated in the same way, and the sum of the passenger and freight figures yields the desired totals. In rows 24-6, total costs per traffic, capacity and actual weight unit are re-estimated on the basis of Italian wages and materials costs. The figures for the Italian systems (cols 1-2) simply repeat those in rows 21-3; the others are obtained as follows. Foreign labour costs per employee are scaled down to the average Italian level (1280 lire), and foreign fuel costs per thousand actual weight units are scaled up to the average Italian level (3025 lire); since the latter were probably little affected by input substitution, they can be taken to reflect the influence of fuel prices and terrain features (fuel consumption) alone. Other foreign costs are simply increased by two thirds; a suitably direct indicator of relative prices and consumption levels does not seem to be available, since consumption levels may have been heavily influenced by input substitution. The revenues per passenger-kilometre in row 27 are the ratio of passenger revenues to total passenger-kilometres; the revenues per freight ton-kilometre in row 28 are, analogously, the ratio of freight revenues to total freight ton-kilometres. The revenue figures are obtained, for the Italian systems, from *Relazione SFI*, 1898 (passengers, col 895; freight, cols 898 plus 901 plus 904); for the French systems, from *Statistique CFF* (passengers, p. 212 col 3; freight, p. 210 col 10 plus p. 224 col 3);

for the German system, from *Atti CSO*, vol. 6 (passengers, col 170; freight, col 179). The ratio of operating revenues to current costs is the ratio of passenger and freight revenues together to current costs (all as above).

In Table 3.11, the total investment figures in col 1 correspond in principle to cumulative, undepreciated expenditure on capital account. The total operating revenues in col 2 include the excise taxes imposed by the laws n. 1945 of 14 June 1874 and n. 101 of 22 March 1900. The internal rate of return in col 4 is the difference between these total revenues and the corresponding total costs in col 3, divided by col 1; it is thus a ratio of surplus to total investment with both numerator and denominator gross of depreciation allowances, as if the investment were perpetual. The upper-bound estimates of the global rate of return in col 5 are based on the surplus obtained by deducting col 3 from 1.50 times col 2. The corresponding best estimates in col 6 are based on the surplus obtained by deducting col 3 from, respectively, 1.35 (row 5), 1.20 (row 6), and 1.50 (rows 7-9) times col 2. The length of the lines reported in col 7 refers to 'operated length', and double-counts segments common to more than one line. The figures in cols 4-6 are thus obtained from the other entries in the table; cols 1-3 and 7 are instead obtained as follows. In rows 1-3, cols 1-3 are obtained directly from aggregate data. Col 1 is transcribed from *Annuario*, 1878 part 1 p. 133, 1904 p. 498. Row 1, cols 2 and 3 are obtained from *Relazione SFI*, 1875 p. 329, the one as 1.13 times cols 14, 15 and 17, plus 1.02 times col 16, the other as 0.621 times col 19. Row 2, cols 2 and 3 are obtained from *Relazione SFI*, 1888-1889-1890 vol. 1 part 3 pp. 210-12 (1.13 times cols 183 and 186, plus 1.02 times cols 189 and 192, plus the reimbursements reported on p. 212) and 224 (col 239). Row 3, cols 2 and 3 are obtained from *Relazione SFI*, 1901 pp. 320-7 (1.13 times cols 980 and 983, plus 1.02 times cols 986 and 989, plus col 1006, plus the surcharges on the Rete Mediterranea, Rete Adriatica and Rete Sicula equal to 0.03 times cols 980 and 983 and 0.01 times cols 986 and 989) and 383 (col 1122). Row 4 is obtained as the sum of separate figures for the state railways and for other railways. The state railways' total investment is estimated as the average of the mid-1910 and mid-1911 figures in *Relazione FS*, 1909-10 p. 25, 1910-11 p. 24. These figures probably exclude the equipment no longer in the railways' inventory, but include the value of current stocks of raw materials; the resulting net bias appears to be very slight (compare also the increment between rows 3 and 4 to the 1911-price gross investment implied by Tables 3.3 and 3.4, allowing for the roughly 35 per cent increase in unit construction costs from 1901 to 1910; Fenoaltea, *Italian Industrial Production*). Their total revenues and costs are estimated from *Statistica FS*, 1910 part 1 pp. 308-9 (1.13 times cols 5, 8 and 9, plus 1.02 times cols 10 and 11, plus cols 12, 20 and 24) and 369 (col 53). The other railways' investment, revenue and cost figures are obtained from *Relazione SFC*, 1910 pp. 108 (col 203), 326-7 (1.13 times cols 980 and 983, plus 1.02 times cols 986 and 989), and 359 (col 1088). Rows 5-7 are a disaggregation of row 4, obtained as follows. The major Po Valley lines are those identified in *Statistica FS*, e.g. 1910 part 1 pp. 152-289, by the numbers 1-2, 17-18, D.18, 21, 27-8, 34-5, 41-2, 44, 47-8, 61-3, 70, 72-4, 84, 90-2, 94, 96-7, 97.I-II, D.97-8, 103, 108 and 128; they cover the Modane-Turin-Novara-Milan-Venice-Udine-Pontebba line, with the spurs from Novara to Luino and from Milan to Domodossola and to Chiasso; the Turin-Savona, Milan-Genoa, Milan-Piacenza-Bologna-Ancona, Parma-Spezia and Venice-Bologna lines; and the lines radiating from Alessandria to Novara, Turin, Savona, Genoa (via Acqui and via Novi Ligure), and Piacenza. The other major lines are those identified by the numbers 100-2, 104-5, 109-11, 116, 118-20, 129-30, 134, 141-4, 150, 159-64, 166-9, 193-4, 198 and 201; these cover the entire west coast line from the French border to Reggio Calabria, the east coast line from Ancona to Lecce, the Ionian coast line from Brindisi to Taranto and Reggio Calabria, the Sicilian coast lines from Messina to Palermo and Catania, the transpeninsular routes from Rome to the Adriatic, Naples to the Adriatic, and Naples to the Ionian, and the inland routes from Florence to Bologna, Pisa (via Pistoia and via Empoli), and Rome. The minor lines are the residual. The lengths of the corresponding operated networks (col 7) are obtained as follows. The figures in rows 5-6 are obtained directly by cumulating the line-specific data in *Statistica FS*, 1910 part 1 pp. 152-289 col 5; that in row 7 is the reported total of those state railways figures (14 329 kilometres), less those of the major lines (6597 kilometres, for a balance of 7732 kilometres), plus the reported total for the private railways (3596 kilometres: *Relazione SFC*, 1910 p. 65 col 17). Capital costs (col 1) are distributed by allowing the private railways their reported total, equivalent to 159 000 lire per operated kilometre, and the minor state railways twice that average, or 318 000 lire per operated kilometre; the resulting estimate leaves the major railways a total of 3930 million lire (row 4 minus row 7), for an average 596 000 lire per operated kilometre. This pattern of average capital costs is broadly confirmed by the cost data in *Relazione SFI*, 1903 pp. 123-9, which yield an average capital cost of over 400 000 lire per kilometre for the most significant 8817 kilometres (summing over groups Al.1.Aa, Al.1.AbI, Al.1.B, Al.1.Da, Al.2.Aa, Al.2.AbI, Al.2.Ba, and Al.3.Aa), and under 230 000 lire per kilometre for the residual 6895 kilometres; one notes that the more expensive group includes some 2200 kilometres of what are here considered minor lines, and that both rolling stock and subsequent improvement expenditures were presumably concentrated on the major lines (e.g. Baglioni, *Per la riforma ferroviaria*, p. 42). The major lines' estimated capital cost is here distributed between rows 5 and 6 in proportion to the two groups' total axle-kilometres (respectively 1142 million for the major Po Valley lines and 1321 million for the other major lines, against 3283 million in all; *Statistica FS*, 1910 part 1 pp. 152-289 col 61) rather than to their operated lengths; while this procedure allows for the likely relative incidence of double-tracking and other improvements, it probably tends to overestimate the cost of the Po Valley lines and underestimate that of the others. Total operating revenues (col 2) are distributed as follows. For simplicity, the major Po Valley lines (row 5) and the other major lines (row 6) are attributed the same share of the estimated total revenues of the state railways (564.1 million lire, entering row 4) as of reported revenue net of tax (respectively 40.2 per cent and 33.9 per cent of 535.7 million lire: *Statistica FS*, 1910 part 1 pp. 312-57 col 17); row 7 is obtained as row 4 minus rows 5 and 6. Total operating costs (col 3) are distributed as follows. The private lines are allowed their reported total (30.5 million lire, as in row 4), equivalent to some 0.141 lire per axle-kilometre (allowing 108.3 million vehicle-kilometres, *Relazione SFC*, 1910 p. 123 col 264, and 2 axles per vehicle); the other minor lines are allowed that same unit figure for each of their 820 million axle-kilometres (the reported total less the major lines' figures, as above), or another 115.6 million lire. The major lines are thus allowed a total of 306.3 million lire (row 4 minus row 7), equivalent to 0.124 lire per axle-kilometre; these costs are also distributed between rows 5 and 6 in proportion to the axle-kilometres reported above. Since traffic density (axle-kilometres per kilometre was over 50 per cent higher on the state railways' minor lines than on the other minor lines, and over 50 per cent higher on the major Po Valley lines than on the other major lines, the results of the present procedure plausibly overestimate the operating costs of the minor lines and underestimate those of the major lines outside the Po Valley, while the figure for the major Po Valley lines is subject to opposite biases. Rows 8-9, finally, are a disaggregation of row 7, obtained as follows. Row 8 refers to those minor lines earning less than 10 000 lire per kilometre, net of tax, in 1910; these are the lines identified in *Statistica FS,* 1910 by the numbers 3, 11-13, 15-16, 20, 24, 49, 75, 79, 123, 125, 135-37, 140, 145, 147, 152, 154-8, 171-3, 179-81, 183-4, 186, 188-92, 196, and 206 (pp. 312-57, col 18) and in *Relazione SFC,* 1910 by the numbers 6-9, 16-17, 21-4, 26-30, 33-6, 39, 41-2, 44-55, 59-63, and 67 (pp. 329-31, col 1010). The figures in row 8, cols 1-3 and 7 are accordingly obtained by summing over separate estimates for the appropriate groups of state and private lines. The private lines totalled 2492 kilometres in operation, 358 million lire of capital costs (equivalent to 144 000 lire per kilometre), 13.9 million lire of revenues net of tax (36.6 per cent of the reported total 38.0 million lire), and 14.0 million lire of operating costs *(Relazione SFC,* 1910 pp. 101-8 col 203, 324-31 cols 17 and 1009, 356-9 col 1088). For simplicity, their total operating revenues are estimated as 36.6 per cent of the 39.9 million lire entering row 4, col 2 for all the private lines together, or 14.6 million lire. The state group totalled 2374 kilometres in operation, 16.8 million lire of revenues net of tax (3.14 per cent of the reported total 535.7 million lire), and 115.1 million axle-kilometres *(Statistica FS,* 1910 part 1 pp. 152-289 cols 5 and 61, 312-57 col 17). For simplicity, their total operating revenues are here estimated as 3.14 per cent of the 564.1 million lire entering row 4, col 2 for all the state railways, or 17.7 million lire; their total operating costs are estimated, as above, on the basis of 0.141 lire per axle-kilometre, for a total of 16.2 million lire; and their capital costs are estimated on the basis of 200 000 lire per kilometre, for a total of 475 million lire. The figures in row 9, cols 1-3 and 7 are the difference between those in row 7 and those in row 8.

[16]

Italian Financial Structures: Long-Term Quantitative Aspects (1870–1970)

Pierluigi Ciocca and A.M. Biscaini Cotula

1. Introduction

A great deal is known about the Italian financial system today and its post-war development, fields in which it is not so much a question of improving the available data as of deepening the analysis. By contrast, research on the 19th century often has to contend with a lack of essential stylized facts which, even if statistically uncertain, would help identify a set of problems, thus forming the basis for a preliminary interpretation. This contradictory situation is yet another sign of the unsystematic, unprofessional approach in Italy, both to the study of contemporary economic history and to long-run structural questions.

We felt that a long-term statistical framework, particularly for the period from the 1870s to the Italian banking legislation of 1936, would be useful, not least to supplement investigation of the highly complex and inherently qualitative issues of the relationships in Italy's history between 'banking' and 'commerce', between 'real' and 'financial' capital, and between money and development. We opted for an inductive approach, albeit one that is more descriptive than analytical, at least in an initial phase. A factor in this decision was the often uncertain quality of the results of earlier theoretical treatments of these problems.[1]

Although this paper is predominantly statistical, we chose to omit an exhaustive discussion of the sources used, the problems left unresolved and the methods of calculation employed. During our preparatory work we turned up a wealth of previously unknown quantitative and qualitative information, not all of which we actually used. Considerable scope therefore remains for more systematic research – leading, even if not to a picture of financial assets as accurate as that available for the last 25 years,[2] at least to more efficient use of the information that is available by applying the current techniques of financial analysis. 'Perfect' data do not exist, of course, but this does not preclude the discovery of source materials that are interesting and solid enough to warrant further refinement in order to make them less imperfect. We think such materials can be found for extensive periods of Italian financial history; whether or not they are then used will obviously depend on the nature of the problem studied.

On the other hand, even a highly empirical study must be guided by a logical framework, however broadly conceived. Ours can be summarized in three propositions:

1. The focus of interest is Italy's *financial superstructure* in the past hundred years, that is (a) the volume and composition of the financial instruments in use, and (b) the methods of operation of the financial markets and, above all, of the financial intermediaries. Accordingly, the complex relationship between finance and development, which still largely awaits theoretical clarification, was split into two as a first approximation and attention centred mainly on the first of the two terms of this dialectical nexus.
2. The analysis of point (a) is based on the interpretative-accounting framework developed by Goldsmith, particularly as published in *Financial Structure and Development*: '… a framework which will reduce to a manageable number of determinants the most important characteristics of a country's financial structure at a point of time – the ratio of new issues of financial instruments to national product, the ratio of financial assets to national wealth, the role of direct as compared to indirect financing, the relative importance of the different types of financial institutions and financial instruments, a framework that thus will identify the determinants of the changes in structure between two points, i.e. of financial development'.[3]
3. The analysis of point (b) is based on microeconomic concepts that define the forms of market and, in particular, the degree of their perfection.[4] Historical research has shown the relevance of such concepts to financial structures, particularly in the case of the US,[5] and has verified that economic development has been accompanied by a progressive 'perfection' of financial markets in the broad sense (including, that is, both bank and non-bank intermediation and the capital markets proper). This is so even though concentration among financial intermediaries has probably tended to increase, partly owing to economies of scale.[6]

We shall present a number of statistical and institutional facts relating to financial structures. The presentation is divided into two sections, corresponding to the two interpretative keys already mentioned, and consists of a list of these facts, together with a concise statement of the reasons why they held the greatest interest for us. Broadly speaking, the reasons we cite are that the indications can be inferred from the facts themselves; also, they either contrast sharply with previous descriptions and interpretations or, on the contrary, accord closely with them.

Note, lastly, that the reconstruction and presentation of the statistical data reflect our focus on trends observable in the long term (20–30 years), and sometimes in the very long term. Pending further research to validate the information used, reference was made to cyclical movements of financial variables only in rare cases where the data permitted and the problem demanded it.

2. The Stock of Financial Instruments and their Composition

Table 1 shows the stock of financial instruments in Italy in six years between 1861 and 1971, together with figures for the national wealth in the same six years, as estimated by

R.W. Goldsmith, in collaboration with S. Zecchini of the Research Department of the Bank of Italy.[7]

Uncertainties remain as to the reliability not only of the estimates of wealth, but also of several components of the financial aggregate – notably the liabilities of (i) firms *vis-à-vis* operators other than financial intermediaries, (ii) local authorities and autonomous government agencies, and (iii) the foreign sector. Accordingly, we decided to consider the fewest number of years that would permit the identification of significant sub-periods of the Italian economy's development following national unification.

Estimates were also made with reference to other dates, primarily to control the trends found for each sub-period. We chose not to publish them here for the sake of clarity and so as not to convey the impression that the data so laboriously reconstructed constitute real 'series' having a constant degree of reliability. The only exception we considered appropriate concerns the historical series of annual data on the liabilities of (both bank and non-bank) financial intermediaries, which is based on large integrations, some modifications and a further check on the reliability of similar series published by De Mattia up to 1936 and by the Bank of Italy subsequently.

The data we present on the composition of the financial instruments reflect two different conceptual approaches. One distinguishes by holder, i.e. the liabilities of issuers other than domestic intermediaries (namely firms, the public sector, households and the foreign sector) held by domestic intermediaries are distinguished from those placed directly with 'investors'; the other distinguishes among the liabilities issued according to the different categories of intermediary.

The statistical and methodological principles on which the reconstruction of the data is based broadly reflect those indicated by Goldsmith in the second chapter of his book. In particular, we also sought to consider only unconsolidated accounts for each category of operator. Departures from these principles due to statistical constraints are mentioned in the detailed notes to the tables.

2.1 *Financial Instruments and National Wealth*

The best summary indicator of the development of the financial superstructure compared with that of the real resources available in the economy is FIR, the ratio of the total stock of financial instruments outstanding to wealth at current prices.

In the past hundred years or so, real income (total and per capita) and FIR have both tended to grow. Between 1881 and 1971, FIR increased from 0.4 to 1 (Table 2). This further confirms Goldsmith's general hypothesis of the existence of a relationship, albeit not a close one, between economic growth and the development of the financial superstructure, at least in quantitative terms. Goldsmith's hypothesis implies, moreover, that FIR is likely to continue to grow in Italy (albeit at a slower pace), as the value in 1971 was still below his 'asymptopic' value of 1.5.

Goldsmith breaks down FIR into a series of elements, or 'determinants'. The one that most directly reflects the financial decisions of operators is ANIR, the ratio of the total flow of liabilities – issued by firms, households, the public sector, intermediaries and the foreign sector – to the national income. Other conditions being equal, the growth of ANIR tends to raise FIR and, from the strictly quantitative viewpoint adopted in this section, can itself be taken as a sign of 'financial development'.[8]

In the case of Italy, ANIR, like FIR, increases almost continuously (Table 2). The pattern is similar in the five developed countries with which we compared Italy (France, Germany, the UK, the US and Japan; see Table 3).

In the early 1960s – when comparison with a larger number of countries is possible, using homogeneous data constructed by Goldsmith – Italy's FIR (0.8) was much larger (though still less than those of the UK and especially Japan) than the theoretical value based on the hypothesis of a linear relation between FIR and real per capita income, with the latter proxying for the degree of economic development (Figure 1).

Additional indications are derived by examining the three major sub-periods: 1881–1914, encompassing Italy's industrial 'takeoff'; 1914–38, years of great instability; and 1938–71, marked by rapid and sustained growth recorded after the war. In particular, we reach the following conclusions:

(a) The growth of FIR, also in comparison with that of other countries, is highest in the second sub-period and lowest in the first. This confirms the 'loose' nature of the relationship between economic growth and the development of the financial superstructure, as already underscored by Goldsmith. In point of fact, the rate of growth of real income (total and per capita) is highest in the third sub-period and lowest in the second. Moreover, until 1963 the narrowing of the gap between Italy's FIR and the average of the most developed countries is largely independent of reductions in the disparities in the level of economic development (Table 4). On the other hand, the behaviour of FIR in the three sub-periods does not lend quantitative support to the proposition that the overall role of finance, irrespective of changes in its composition, was more important during Italy's first industrial takeoff, in view of the 'forced' nature of the process, than in other periods. The ratio of the liabilities issued by non-financial operators to the national income is also very low during the 'Giolittian era' compared both with the other sub-periods (Table 5) and with the other developed countries (Table 3). The ratio of such issues to investment provides similar indications. In particular, Table 4 shows that the external financing of investment was lowest (42 per cent) precisely in the period 1881–1914. It is worth emphasizing that the results do not appear to be very sensitive to further subdivision of the three sub-periods (effected on the basis of provisional estimates that are not published here). In particular, the financial characteristics of the Giolittian era do not change if the reference period is restricted to 1895–1914, the core years of Italy's industrial takeoff. On the other hand, as was to be expected on the basis of the more abundant and systematic studies and data available for the last 20 years,[9] the values and growth rates of the indicators of financial development shown in the tables are highest in 1963–71.

(b) The growth of the financial superstructure between the two World Wars is particularly surprising and raises interesting questions. One possible explanation is that the role of the state grew appreciably, first in the period 1915–19 and then again in the 1930s, while the tendency of the economy to stagnate impeded an increase in the incidence of taxation. Account must also be taken of the fact that public spending in relation to the national income diminished sharply between the early 1920s and the early 1930s.[10] In fact, the shares of total financial liabilities attributable to the public sector, firms and intermediaries are similar (around 30 per cent) and remain unchanged between 1914 and 1938 (Table 1). A further line of interpretation is thus that there was a generalized *financial deepening*, i.e. an increase both in the propensity of households to hold financial assets (primarily currency and bank deposits) as a result of high real interest rates and in that of firms, as well as the government, to issue debt instruments, even if at high cost, in order to finance restructuring investment and avoid bankruptcy in conditions of stagnation and crisis. Between 1914 and 1938 the new issues of firms and the public sector reach very high values in relation to gross investment (Table 4). This interpretation is consistent with the hypothesis that during periods of stagnation and/or recession, entrepreneurs are willing to pay 'any' interest rate demanded by rentiers (intermediaries and savers) to keep their firms running and hence to avoid a curtailment of their social role, which for them is even more important than the profit rate itself. Accordingly, such periods may result in a strengthening of rentiers' position in the economy.[11]

2.2 *The Respective Roles of Financial Intermediaries and the Capital Market*

The key aspect of the composition of financial instruments concerns the amount of liabilities final users of funds place respectively with intermediaries and the capital market, i.e. directly with other operators.

The indicator used for this purpose is the ratio of the assets of intermediaries to the combined liabilities of the public sector, firms, households and the foreign sector. This indicator, which we shall designate as FIN, can be calculated on either stocks or flows.

Confirming another of the statistical regularities reported by Goldsmith, in Italy the ratio of intermediation calculated on both flows and stocks has increased almost without interruption (Table 5).

FIN calculated on stocks shows a very high annual rate of increase (2.5 per cent) in the sub-period 1881–1914. The rate drops appreciably in the subsequent sub-period (0.9 per cent) and then recovers in the final sub-period, reaching a peak value of 5.9 per cent in 1963–71. FIN calculated on flows is consistent with these movements, with notably high values in the Giolittian era, when almost 60 per cent of the new issues of firms, the public sector, households and the foreign sector were placed with financial intermediaries. The ratio is slightly lower for the interwar years, but it rises to very high values in the third sub-period, and most markedly in 1963–71.

Comparison with the other countries for the years 1949–63 shows that Italian FIN, as calculated on flows by Goldsmith, is appreciably higher than the average for the five developed countries (Table 3). In 1963–71 the ratio we calculated for Italy (Table 5) is higher than the average values of between 0.75 and 0.85 for all the countries with which comparison could be made (that is to say, including countries with 'backward' capital markets).[12] Issues of intermediaries corresponding to interbank transactions, estimated as accounting for between one-quarter and one-sixth of the total, were subtracted from the original figures, as Goldsmith did for the other countries. Such issues inflate the ratio and do not reflect intermediaries' acquisitions of liabilities issued by other operators. The fact that for Italy and other countries FIN tends to remain greater than one even after this adjustment

'... points to the possibility of an underestimation of the nonfinancial domestic or the foreign issue ratios ... or, what is less likely, to an overestimation of the financial institutions' new issue ratio'.[13]

International comparison likewise shows that FIN based on flows was already higher in Italy than in the other five developed countries in 1881–1914 (Table 3).

Taken together, these general indications confirm that the Italian case fits the banking-oriented model of financing rather than that based on capital markets.[14] This is particularly true of the last decade and is beyond question at the present. However, Italy's financial structures were already decisively oriented towards intermediaries in the Giolittian era, at least in the sense that the institutionalization of credit activity, through the growing role played by financial intermediaries, developed faster and earlier in Italy than in other countries at a comparable level of development.

The rapid increase in FIN in 1881–1914 and particularly in 1895–1914 is, as noted, accompanied by relatively modest growth in FIR. Apart from a scaling down of the overall quantitative role of finance in Italy's industrial takeoff, this suggests that the credit provided by intermediaries, and particularly by 'mixed banks', replaced rather than supplemented other credit in this period. This contrasts with what is implicit in some versions of the mainstream interpretation of the takeoff, at least insofar as the latter merely emphasize the rapid growth of the activity of the mixed banks,[15] without specifying exactly which qualitative features of that activity were particularly suited to assisting industrial development, albeit in an overall context in which external financing remained relatively low compared with investment (Table 4). Such an approach is either lacking altogether or restricted to highly schematic references in the main surveys of industrialization in the Giolittian period.[16] It is incorporated for the first time in the recent studies by Confalonieri,[17] whose treatment of the operational and institutional aspects of the mixed banks may pave the way for more rigorous statistical and other tests of the main interpretative hypotheses.

2.3 *The Composition of the Activity of the Financial Intermediaries*

Our statistical analysis of the composition of financial intermediation is based on the shares of the aggregate balance sheet of the financial system attributable to each category of intermediary. The historical series of the intermediaries' annual balance sheet data is given in Table 6.

As a first approximation, again following Goldsmith for the sake of comparability, the entire system of intermediaries can be divided into five functional categories: (a) central banks, (b) commercial banks, (c) savings institutions, (d) insurance institutions, and (e) other intermediaries ('special' institutions). The classification refers to certain features of the assets and, still more, of the liabilities of each category of intermediary. Central banks and commercial banks issue liabilities – respectively, banknotes and readily transferable deposits – that performed the functions of 'money' in Italy as elsewhere in the period under review. Central banks, or at least the most important ones, have also played a growing and increasingly deliberate role in implementing economic policy. For the Bank of Italy this is true especially after 1900,[18] even if until 1936 central banking in Italy was not separated from routine commercial banking activity with private non-bank customers.[19] Savings institutions – savings banks, postal savings banks, cooperative banks and pledge banks – differ from commercial banks primarily in having a lower rate of deposit turnover, attributable to the technical form and maturity of their deposits and the characteristics of their deposit-holders; their assets are mainly loans and securities with a correspondingly longer maturity. The insurance institutions that accumulate large reserves (in respect of life insurance and social insurance) invest these funds not only in real assets but also in primarily long-term financial assets, and thus engage in intermediation that is complementary to their basic and in many respects specialized institutional activity. Though a residual, in Italy the fifth category comprises the credit institutions specialized in long-term lending and/or lending to specific economic sectors, such as agriculture and building and, subsequently, industry.

Comparison with the average structures of financial intermediation in other countries that were developed in 1880 is useful to integrate the institutional and quantitative descriptions of the Italian credit system immediately after national unification – most notably the very accurate work of Tullio Martello and Augusto Montanari.[20] Moreover, the comparison can be extended to cover the years through 1967 (Table 7). At the outset (1880), the Italian credit system was dominated by the banks of issue (27 per cent of total intermediation, compared with 13 per cent in the other countries) which still dealt mainly with private, non-bank customers, and by the savings institutions (50 per cent, as against 16 per cent elsewhere). In an economy that evidently was still only partly 'monetized', the commercial banks were relatively underdeveloped (16 per cent, as against 46 per cent), as were the intermediaries specialized in long-term lending and equity investment (6 per cent, compared with 18 per cent). Intermediation by the insurance institutions was practically nil (0.5 per cent, as against 7 per cent).

Ninety years later (1973) the share of the banks of issue (from 1926 that of the single bank of issue) had fallen by more than half (from 27 to 10 per cent), as had that of the savings institutions (from 50 to 24 per cent). These falls were matched by increases in the shares of the insurance institutions (from 0.5 to 4 per cent) and, above all, the commercial banks (from 16 to 39 per cent) and the 'special' credit institutions (from 6 to 23 per cent).

The following points stand out with regard to Italy in comparison with the other countries for the period from 1880 to 1967: (a) the fall in the share of the banks of issue was considerably larger owing to its higher initial level; (b) elsewhere the share of the savings institutions did not fall, but in Italy they nonetheless still accounted for a much larger share in 1967 (28 per cent, compared with 19 per cent); (c) the increase recorded by the insurance institutions was not enough to make up for their relative lag; (d) by contrast, the expansion of Italy's special credit institutions was extremely rapid, particularly after the Second World War. The outstanding point to note, however, is that the increase in the share of Italy's commercial banks is in marked contrast to the strong opposite trend in the other countries; it should be added, however, that after the Second World War the rate of increase in Italy fell to levels similar to those prevailing elsewhere.

A mechanical extrapolation of the trends and comparisons described above would imply growth in the relative importance of the insurance institutions and other institutional investors to the detriment of the savings institutions.

2.4 The Structure of the Banking System

The banking system – central banks, commercial banks and savings institutions – was predominant in Italian financial intermediation from the beginning and has remained so. In 1880 banks' assets made up more than 90 per cent of the total balance sheet of financial intermediaries; in 1973 their share was still above 70 per cent (Table 7). This justifies an examination of the composition of the balance sheet of the banking system (Tables 6 and 8).

The analysis shows that the shares of the different categories of bank were generally stable when account is taken of the change in the status of Banco di Napoli and Banco di Sicilia from banks of issue to public-law banks. The only notable exception is the large loss of share suffered by the postal savings banks to the benefit of the public-law banks beginning in the second half of the 1930s. A second noteworthy characteristic is the relatively large fluctuations around the trend lines. On the one hand the banks of issue saw their share increase considerably in wartime (1866, 1914–18, 1939–45); on the other hand, deposits shifted from the postal banks to the savings banks during banking crises (particularly around 1870, 1890 and 1930).

The structure of interest rates (Tables 12 and 14) is broadly consistent with the values of market shares. In particular, at the outset of the period considered (1870–80) the lending rates of the banks of issue are the lowest, and the differential between the lending and deposit rates smallest for the savings banks; the structurally low deposit rates offered for postal savings (in view of the zero risk for the depositor) explain the large shares claimed by the banks of issue, savings banks and postal savings system.

The patchy information available on the structure of interest rates from around 1890 to the Second World War does not appear to indicate any significant changes, in line with the relative stability of market shares. By contrast, the disintermediation of the postal savings system after the war was certainly due to the fact that the rates on postal savings deposits were the lowest in the system, having ceased to keep sufficiently in step with the market. The overall impression is that of a banking system in which price competition plays a relatively small role.

A final aspect worth noting concerns the activity of the so-called mixed banks and relates to our previous observation regarding the slow growth of FIR and rapid growth of FIN during the Giolittian era. The assets of the four leading mixed banks for the years 1895–1925 are shown in Table 9. Their share of the total assets of the banking system and of all financial intermediaries rose almost uninterruptedly between 1895 and the crisis of Banca italiana di sconto in 1920, increasing from 2 to around 30 per cent. The increase was particularly rapid from 1895 to 1913 and indicates that the contribution of the mixed banks to the growth of FIN was considerable in that period. The scale of these banks' activity – coupled with their specific 'qualitative' vocation, which awaits further study – undoubtedly contributed to Italy's industrial and economic development in the Giolittian era, even if within the context of relatively modest growth of the country's overall financial superstructure.

3. Operational Characteristics of the Intermediaries and the Financial Markets

In this section the general hypothesis that the quantitative growth of the financial superstructure was accompanied by a gradual perfection of the capital markets, in the broad sense, will be subjected to a number of initial tests, each focusing on one of the components of the concept of perfect markets. The focus is more on the activity of the financial intermediaries than on the capital market in the narrow sense of the market (that allows *direct* financing transactions between units in surplus and units in deficit). This reflects both the prevalent and growing importance of intermediation in Italy and the lack of long-term information on the *modus operandi* of Italy's stock exchanges.[21]

The perfection of the markets for the financial instruments of intermediaries has to be evaluated primarily on the basis of the latter's operational efficiency and stability and the prevailing degree of competition. With reference to the capital market in both the narrow and the broad sense, the concept of perfection is certainly identified 'with the truism of economic theory that there can be only one price for identical goods in a perfect market'.[22] According to a part of the literature, this implies a type of market 'in which every price fully reflects all the available information so that any new relevant information is reflected in prices extremely rapidly (and cannot be used to make abnormal returns)'.[23]

Our analysis will centre on the period preceding the banking legislation of 1936, which introduced a comprehensive supervisory system for Italy's financial structures. Since 1936, and more particularly since the war, the credit system has at least potentially been conditioned by the structural policy orientations of the supervisory authorities. Only a much deeper analysis could distinguish the respective roles of credit policy and the market in determining the financial arrangements that have prevailed in the last 30 years. The importance of structural interventions was presumably smaller, though obviously not nil, in the years preceding 1936.

3.1 Bank Concentration

The first significant fact is the absence in the Italian banking system – the banks of issue, commercial banks and savings institutions – of the tendency towards concentration found in some countries,[24] a tendency implicit in the economies of scale achievable in the sector[25] and consistent with the existence of supervisory systems designed, *inter alia*, to prevent banking monopoly.[26] On the contrary, in Italy all the indices of concentration, both for the system as a whole and by type of intermediary, show a very-long-term trend towards the reduction of concentration.

The limitations of the data to which the indices in Table 10 refer need to be underscored.[27] It was only possible to consider the entire population for savings banks. For commercial and cooperative banks the sample is neither random nor stratified, nor is its representativeness constant. The inclusion of the banks of issue in the category of commercial banks is also debatable. Finally, the other categories of credit institution were omitted altogether.

Nonetheless, in the case of the savings banks the tendency for concentration to decline after national Unification is clear-cut and irrefutable. The only period in which the trend of the H index halted and reversed is the 1930s, when policies were adopted with the express aim of reducing the number of institutions. Developments in the other two categories of banks are less clear-cut up to the years immediately following the First World War: a phase in which concentration diminished (1870–86) is followed, with particular reference to the H index, by a sizable increase in concentration in 1910–20, for which there is no parallel among the savings banks and which may be due to a break in the series (see the notes to Table 10). On the other hand, the birth and growth of mixed banks (included with commercial banks) and the developments affecting cooperative banks do not allow us to exclude the possibility of there actually having been an increase in concentration, as indicated by the data, between the 1890s and the early 1920s. By contrast, from 1921 onwards for the banks of issue and commercial banks and from 1936 for the cooperative banks, there is a clear and uninterrupted tendency for concentration to decline. The index for the system (i.e. for the aggregate of the banks of the three categories that it was possible to consider) reflects that decline, attenuated by the continuing deceleration of concentration among savings banks. The system-wide trend towards a continuous diminution of concentration begins in 1921, despite the fall in the total number of banks from 4,600 in 1926 to 1,000 at present (Table 11).

Evaluating the *levels* of bank concentration is more difficult. With reference to the H index, the most significant one, values above 0.10–0.20 can be considered 'high' in that, owing to a well-known property of the index, they are consistent with a structure consisting of respectively 10 and 5 units of equal size. The values of the H index in Italy until 1920 are not unlike those calculated for the 1970s in a number of developing countries, which are considered high. By contrast, the current levels of concentration in Italy are similar to those in Switzerland (0.06) and Japan (0.04), and distinctly lower than in Canada (0.17) and Denmark (0.14), the only developed countries with which uniform comparison is possible.[28] The resulting impression is that the Italian banking system went from an initial situation of 'high' concentration' to one of 'low' concentration, and that the latter pattern was already established in the years following the Second World War.

Against the background of a decline in concentration towards 'low' values, it is particularly interesting to note that, with a single exception, all the other indices relating to the competitiveness and efficiency of the banking system contradict the idea that competition and efficiency are stimulated by a low degree of concentration.

3.2 *The Operating Costs of the Banking System*

The exception we refer to is that of the average unit intermediation costs of the banking system. If economies of scale exist – an assumption justified by the empirical studies that have been made of contemporary banking systems – unit costs should tend to increase as concentration diminishes, other things being equal. This is particularly true where the diminution of concentration is accompanied by an increase in the average number of branches per bank, as in Italy from 1912 onwards (Table 11). Financial statement data show that the ratio of ordinary credit banks' and cooperative banks' expenses to total assets more than doubled between the 1880s and the 1950s, rising from less than 2 to more than 4 per cent. The expenses of savings banks grew by around 40 per cent between the 1920s and the 1950s.[29] The increase in the average size of the banks (Table 11) evidently failed to compensate for the higher costs stemming from lower concentration, the expansion of the branch network and other possible factors (wage rates in banking, the structure of balance sheet assets and liabilities), on which, however, the available information does not permit an accurate calculation of the related costs.

Table 11 does nonetheless provide some general indications as to the trends of productivity both per employee within the credit sector as a whole and per bank branch. Taking account of the fact that the exceptional productivity gains recorded in the 1950s were partly due to postwar recovery, the most striking development is probably the far-reaching reorganization of the financial system in general and of the banking system in particular in the years between 1926 and 1936. The figures on the number of banks, branches, towns and cities served by banks, as well as the number of employees, point to two clearly distinct phases in the structural evolution of the banking industry between 1912 and 1936: explosive and, according to many observers,[30] inefficient growth from 1912 to 1926, followed by evident restructuring in the ten years from 1926 to 1936. In the latter period the number of banks fell by 56 per cent and that of bank branches by 33 per cent, while the number of towns and cities served by banks declined by 22 per cent and the entire credit sector's workforce shrank by 26 per cent. The smaller decline in the number of banking centres compared with bank branches indicates that the functional efficiency of the branch network probably increased. The figures on concentration examined earlier (Table 10) also provide evidence of a rationalization of the banking system.

The enhancement of the system's efficiency, unaccompanied, as will be seen, by a narrowing of the spreads between lending and deposit rates, can be ascribed both to a deliberate policy of the monetary authorities and to the pressures of the economic crisis.[31] The relative importance of these two factors still has to be determined. A policy undeniably did exist and is a further element contradicting the proposition that the changes in the banking system prior to the legislation of 1936 were mainly or exclusively determined by market forces. The 1926 provisions on the protection of savings required the formation of new credit institutions and the geographical expansion of existing ones to be authorized by the Ministry of Finance. Concentrations were also controlled and in fact encouraged. This is obvious in the case of savings banks and pledge banks: the law of 1927 made it compulsory for institutions located in the same province or region with deposits of less than 5 million lire to merge, and empowered the Minister for the National Economy to order mergers between institutions with deposits of between 5 and 10 million lire where this was considered appropriate. The same law also made it compulsory for the savings banks and pledge banks of a province to group together in confederations, and envisaged a similar requirement for those of adjacent provinces. The purpose of these confederations included delimiting their members' geographical area of operations and coordinating their action. Government regulation of the savings banks and pledge banks went so far as to empower the Minister for the National Economy to order the closing of branches of different institutions located in the same municipality.

3.3 The Differences between Bank Lending and Deposit Rates

As noted, the statistics on costs are largely incomplete. In particular, the absence of data on the savings banks for the years from 1920 to 1950 and for the ordinary credit banks and cooperative banks for the longer period from 1880 to 1950 does not allow the identification of trends.

Further information on the efficiency and degree of competition of Italian banks can nonetheless be drawn from the historical series of lending and deposit rates, and hence of the interest rate spread, which we reconstructed on the basis of data referring to the entire population of savings banks and a sample of ordinary credit banks and cooperative banks (Table 12).

Examining the longer and more complete series for the savings banks, it is possible to distinguish a first phase, lasting to the years 1910–20, when the difference between lending and deposit rates was relatively stable, from a second phase, lasting to 1940, when a general tendency of the spread to widen may have been accompanied by a rise in unit costs.

The figures for the other two categories of banks, limited to 1871–86, confirm the absence of clear trends in that period.

3.4 *Bank Profits*

A long-term analysis of bank profits (1906–38) is only possible for banks formed as joint-stock companies. A comparison with industrial and commercial companies provides two indications, taking the balance sheet figures at face value or in any case assuming that the reliability of the balance sheets of banks and other companies is roughly equivalent.

On the one hand, the profit rate of the banks was structurally higher between 1906 and 1935. Assuming that a comparison of levels is statistically justified, there may have been more than one reason for the difference (e.g. greater riskiness, a higher degree of monopoly and greater efficiency in the banking sector). On the other hand, both the rate and the volume of bank profits, though also reduced during the economic stagnation of 1927–33, showed smaller fluctuations. In particular, during the recessions of 1921 and 1930–31 the other companies recorded losses, whereas the banks continued to make profits (Figure 2).

This last observation confirms that, during phases of economic crisis, the relationships between banking and industry can be dialectical and even sharply conflicting.[32]

3.5 *The Level of Banking Risk*

A structural determinant of banks' level of risk and stability is the ratio of their own funds to deposits.[33] This is particularly true for the Italian banking system up to 1936, given the absence both of a deposit-insurance scheme and of comprehensive prudential supervision. In addition, the role of the banks of issue as lenders of last resort only developed in the wake of episodic banking crises, while the imperfections of the money markets, particularly that for interbank funds, prevented banks from having recourse to liability management.

Figure 3 shows that the ratio of own funds to deposits fell in Italy after 1900, especially during and after the First World War. Subsequently, own funds did not increase enough to offset the effects of the major reduction caused by wartime inflation.

Limiting the analysis of risk to the capital/deposits ratio would be unduly restrictive, even in the case of the Italian banking system up to 1936. Reference needs to be made to the balance sheet assets and liabilities of individual banks (or, in our case, of the entire banking system). Accordingly, Figure 3 plots other balance sheet ratios, where rises indicate increased risk. The criterion followed considers the riskiest earning assets at one extreme, and liquidity and equity capital at the other. The picture that emerges is necessarily summary and unclear. One possible interpretation, however, is explored in the following points:

(a) Until 1900 the proportion of risky earning assets fell with respect to the high values recorded in 1870, the ratio of capital to deposits remained unchanged at high levels (around 50 per cent), and liquidity ratios diminished appreciably. The third trend may have compensated or reflected the first to some extent, but it may also have been due to the progressive, albeit certainly imperfect, integration of the country's money and financial markets. On the whole, it would appear that the riskiness of banking remained unchanged or tended to diminish in this period. The high values of the risk indicators at the start of the period are not in contrast with the occurrence of the banking crisis of 1873–74, but their low and declining values in the last 15 years of the century do not seem to anticipate or reflect the bank collapses of 1893–94, at the end of the economic crisis that had begun in 1887.[34] It should be noted, however, that the repercussions of this last crisis on banking were primarily due to its impact on the construction sector, whose close relationship with the banking system does not emerge from the data on which the indices of risk were based.

(b) At the turn of the century a phase of growing risk began, with a steady deterioration in the ratio of capital to deposits, followed by an outbreak of wildcat banking immediately after the First World War. This is confirmed by all the risk indicators considered and by the structural data presented in Table 11.

(c) From the mid-1920s until 1936 the prevailing tendency was towards the containment of risk, coinciding with the consolidation of the sector through bankruptcies and concentration.

3.6 Interest Rate Variability

As noted earlier, an indicator of the perfection of financial markets is the degree of uniformity of interest rates on financial liabilities that are comparable in terms of technical form, type of lender and borrower, and economic context. Practical verification of the conditions of *ceteris paribus* is always difficult and, to be rigorous, should involve a complete explanation of the variability of interest rates based on cross-section data. Gaps in information on the Italian economy until the late 1930s make the task formidable. In this section we shall therefore provide only two indications based on bank interest rates (pertaining particularly to the savings banks): the variability of rates between banks and between different geographical areas.

The dispersion of interest rates among banks of the same category, measured by the coefficient of variation, was largest in 1880–90 for the ordinary credit banks, intermediate for the cooperative banks and smallest for the savings banks (probably because they were most exposed to competition from the postal savings system, at least as regards deposits). For the savings banks it was possible to construct a continuous series of the coefficients of variation from 1861 to 1940 for deposit rates, from 1876 to 1940 for lending rates and from 1906 to 1940 for the rates on their bill portfolios. The figures show no tendency to diminish; if anything, they tend to increase. The banking markets thus do not approach perfection (in the sense of 'the same price for the same product') and, indeed, preserve characteristics of monopolistic competition. Alternatively, the data could be interpreted as reflecting the increased, or at least the undiminished, disparity of Italy's economic structures and, hence, the segmentation of bank customers in the first eight decades after unification.

Similar indications regarding the segmentation of the banking markets are provided by a geographical (regional) analysis of the variance of the savings banks' lending rates for the four years 1876, 1890, 1910 and 1930. The results, presented in Table 13, show that the location of the savings banks is correlated with the level of lending rates. The relationship is statistically very significant in the first three years considered; its significance diminishes considerably in 1930, probably because the restructuring of the savings banks in 1920–30 tended to even out the degree of monopoly they enjoyed in their respective local markets.

3.7 The 'Imperfections' of the Share and Bond Markets

The persistent and perhaps increasing imperfections that we observed in the Italian banking market would appear to have had parallels in the capital markets proper.

Mention has already been made of the 'intermediary-based' orientation that characterized the Italian financial system as early as the Giolittian era. The stock market crash of 1907[35] seems to have been a watershed, a point after which the capital markets ceased growing in relative terms and remained fragile, incomplete and imperfect. This is confirmed both by the pattern of FIN and by the changes in the proportion of company liabilities consisting of shares and bonds (Table 1): after standing at around 50 per cent in 1861, it fell to about 30 per cent in 1881 and subsequently fluctuated around this very low level until 1971.

The ability of share prices, adjusted for inflation, to reflect the 'real' performance of the economy in the medium term appears to have been greater in 1861–96 than in 1918–38.[36] Figure 4 shows that real GNP growth was mirrored by a comparable rise in share prices, deflated with the cost-of-living index, until around 1890. By contrast, after the First World War only the fluctuations of the two variables continued to be correlated, while rising output was accompanied by broadly stagnant 'real' share prices. This appears to provide further confirmation of the Italian stock exchange's low functional efficiency (after, one is tempted to say, the probable watershed of the 1907 crisis).

3.8 The Trend of Interest Rates

The indicators examined thus far in this section appear to reveal that, until 1936, Italy's banking system and financial markets functioned in ways that were relatively distant from the models of perfection and showed no clear tendency to approximate them.

This situation generated forces that impeded a fall in the interest rate, i.e. a downward movement of the entire structure of rates on financial instruments.

To establish the quantitative significance of these forces compared with that of the other long-term real and monetary determinants of the interest rate is plainly a very complex problem, given the persisting uncertainty of theory as to the nature of such determinants.[37]

The series of bank interest rates we constructed and that on the public debt produced by Bruno Bianchi nevertheless provide some general indications (see Tables 12 and 14). Up to the First World War, nominal rates showed a fairly clear downward trend, apart from the spike recorded for the yield on public debt at the time of the war of 1866, which severely strained the finances of the Kingdom of Italy. The period 1914–38 is very different, with interest rates high or rising. Referring to Figure 5, it can be seen that the behaviour of interest rates was not appreciably affected by that of prices in the first period; in the second period, however, the large variations in prices – rising from 1914 to 1925, falling from 1926 to 1934 and rising again from 1935 to 1938 – may have influenced inflationary or deflationary expectations, causing nominal rates to shift with respect to real rates, with which we are primarily concerned.

For the long period extending from 1870 to 1913, it can therefore be concluded that other forces probably played a more important role in determining a decline in real interest rates than the persistence of the foregoing functional inefficiencies. This conclusion is also supported by the fact that, despite such inefficiencies, a domestic capital market was born in Italy in the years immediately after unification and necessarily established growing ties with the international financial market, as is confirmed by the convergence of Italian long-term rates towards the European average (Figure 5).

By contrast, for the subsequent period, extending to the end of the 1930s, the lack of econometric analysis of the link between nominal rates and inflation expectations makes it impossible to reject the hypothesis that real rates rose, or ceased to fall, along with nominal rates. This would appear a reasonable assumption in the light of the persistence and, in some cases, worsening of the imperfections of Italy's credit system during that period.

4. Conclusions

The indications provided by the statistical material collected here can be summed up in three propositions:

(a) The tendency of the Italian financial superstructure to grow rapidly in relation to national wealth, at rates exceeding those recorded for most of the countries for which data are available, can be traced far back in Italian economic history.
(b) Similarly, the pattern of financing oriented towards financial intermediaries rather than capital markets proper has prevailed in Italy for several decades.
(c) At least until 1936, there is no evidence of a trend towards greater efficiency and competition in the banking system, nor towards increasing functionality of the capital markets proper.

These conclusions, drawn from an initial examination of the data, raise important and complex questions concerning the causes and consequences of the trends described and the possible need to modify these structural tendencies.

It is our impression that the answers are to be sought, first and foremost, by clarifying whether, and for what historical reasons, resource mobilization in Italy made less recourse than elsewhere to forms other than of a 'financial' nature, sharing the common feature of being aimed at reducing the separation between savers and investors.[38] Accordingly, analysis needs to focus primarily on Italy's institutional structures in the various phases of the country's history, and on the connections between variations in the distribution of income and wealth on the one hand and the propensity to invest, acquire financial assets and issue financial liabilities on the other, with a more detailed breakdown of the broad categories of operators considered in this study.

At the same time the interconnections between points (a), (b) and (c) require further investigation, to verify which of two possible approaches is more correct on the theoretical plane and which best fits the facts of the Italian case.

The first of these two approaches posits that the rapid growth of the financial superstructure (point a) was imposed by features of the process of economic and social development that could not be modified. In view of its rapidity, this process could only unfold through growing recourse to financial intermediaries (point b), resulting in an appreciable shortening of the phase of security capitalism[39] in Italy, to the detriment of the 'perfecting' of Italy's credit structures in general and its money and financial markets in particular (point c).

According to the other approach, the above-mentioned process of perfection was slowed down by obstacles – associated with markets? of an institutional nature? deriving from equilibria between groups, and particularly from the short-sightedness of intermediaries, entrenched in the defence of oligopolistic positions? – that were internal to the financial structures. This necessarily led the system to be oriented largely towards financial intermediation, implying in turn a rapid growth of FIR (for example, by way of sizable interbank dealings, or 'double intermediation').

Study of the nature and origins of the imperfections in question, which have never been analysed in sufficient historical breadth or depth in Italy, is indispensable as a guide to choosing between the two alternative interpretations outlined above.

What especially needs to be tested is the ability of a deliberate economic policy to foster the perfection of credit structures.

Such an examination is particularly important for the period following 1936, the year beyond which we decided not to extend our analysis in several cases, inasmuch as it marked the establishment of a comprehensive apparatus for the control and supervision of the financial system, radically changing the entire institutional framework. If, on the other hand, both of the foregoing interpretations were to be rejected in favour of another, we believe the more modest endeavour of a further check of the validity of the statistical 'facts' indicated in this paper and a more systematic testing of the possible explanations for each of them would nonetheless yield significant results.

Turning to today's operating realities, the creation of a genuine share market is a key problem. A more developed share market would favour greater recourse to external financing in conditions of equilibrium, both directly and through the higher levels of maximum leverage available to firms as a result of the greater scope for issuing equity, enabling them to maintain their actual leverage at the desired 'maximum'. In addition, the indifference of shareholders between dividends and capital appreciation would increase the elasticity of the payout ratio. The benefits that could be obtained are evident from the qualitative standpoint and primarily concern the volume of private investment and the financial stability of firms. The historical and comparative analyses set forth or referred to in this paper should help to define the quantitative limits of these benefits, particularly with regard to the large share of investment that firms could finance by resorting to sources other than internally generated funds. In any case, the specific nature of the imperfections of the Italian share market, which impede its development primarily on the side of demand, has been known for some time, as have the possible institutional, fiscal and organizational remedies.

The problem, therefore, is one of 'political' will to overcome the resistance of the interests that would suffer if an efficient share market existed. At the same time, it is necessary to dispel the technically and historically mistaken notion that a share market would develop naturally and in a stable manner once firms' profitability was restored (to what level?); that is, that it would develop, at least transiently, precisely when least needed, as was the case in the 1950s.

More generally, the conditions have to be created in Italy for the formation of channels of financing and refinancing that are alternative to the banking system. Only by making it possible for higher-risk and less profitable assets to be transferred to deep and stable capital markets can the problem of the 'mixed bank' be prevented from arising again in new forms at times of economic crisis – a problem that the Italian Banking Law of 1936 in itself cannot resolve in the absence of such markets. It goes without saying that correction of this outstanding shortcoming would not entirely resolve the problems of efficiency and functionality of the Italian financial system,[40] which also persist within the banking sector.

Notes

1. See F. Vicarelli (1979), 'Introduzione', in F. Vicarelli (ed.), *Capitale industriale e capitale finanziario: il caso italiano*, Bologna: Il Mulino, pp. 15–57.
2. See, in particular, M. Caron and F. Cotula (1971), 'I conti finanziari dell'Italia', Banca d'Italia, *Bollettino*, November–December, pp. 839–919.
3. R.W. Goldsmith (1969), *Financial Structure and Development*, New Haven: Yale University Press, pp. 51–2; for an approach that is similar in many respects, see J.G. Gurley and E.S. Shaw (1957), 'The Growth of Debt and Money in the United States, 1800–1950: A Suggested Interpretation', *Review of Economics and Statistics*, pp. 250–62.
4. The relevant literature is extensive and the subject remains at the centre of intense and far-reaching discussions among economists belonging to the various schools. The following are useful references: A. Koutsoyiannis (1975), *Modern Microeconomics*, New York: Wiley, for an updated and even-handed review at the institutional level; M.H. Dobb (1969), *Welfare Economics and the Economics of Socialism*, Cambridge: Cambridge University Press, for a vigorous but not preconceived Marxist critique of the traditional 'welfare economy'; H. Leibenstein (1976), *Beyond Economic Man: A New Foundation for Microeconomics*, Cambridge, MA: Harvard University Press, for an original approach based on a rejection of the axiom that firms minimize costs.
5. See L.E. Davis (1965), 'The Investment Market, 1870–1914: The Evolution of a National Market', *Journal of Economic History*, pp. 355–99; G.J. Stigler (1967), 'Imperfections in the Capital Market', *Journal of Political Economy*, pp. 287–92; R. Sylla (1969), 'Federal Policy, Banking Market Structure, and Capital Mobilization in the United States, 1863–1913', *Journal of Economic History*, pp. 657–86; L.E. Davis (1971), 'Capital Mobility and American Growth', in R.W. Fogel and S.L. Engerman (eds), *The Reinterpretation of American Economic History*, New York: Harper & Row; G. Smiley (1975), 'Interest Rate Movement in the United States, 1888–1913', *Journal of Economic History*, pp. 591–620; J.G. Williamson (1974), *Late Nineteenth-Century American Development: A General Equilibrium History*, Cambridge: Cambridge University Press; J.A. James (1976), 'Banking Market Structure, Risk, and the Pattern of Local Interest Rates in the United States, 1893–1911', *Review of Economics and Statistics*, pp. 453–62; H.T. Rockoff (1977), 'Regional Interest Rates and Bank Failures, 1870–1914', *Explorations in Economic History*, pp. 90–95. For the application of several of the above-mentioned microeconomic concepts to the policy of credit structures in the US, see *Studies*

in Banking Competition and the Banking Structure, Washington: US Treasury Department, 1966.

6. See R.W. Goldsmith (1975), 'Some Reflections on the Past, Present and Future of Financial Institutions', in P. Frantzen (ed.), *Current Problems of Financial Intermediaries*, Rotterdam: Rotterdam University Press.
7. All tables and figures appear at the end of the text.
8. Conversely, quantification of the relative contribution of the growth of FIR to that of ANIR would imply adopting not only Goldsmith's accounting framework, but also the assumptions underpinning the application of the formulas of FIR he developed. These assumptions appear questionable, at least with reference to several phases of Italian economic development. See, in particular, *Financial Structure and Development*, pp. 80–91. Goldsmith applied the formula of 'calculated' (theoretical) FIR to his own estimates of the Italian data for 1881–1913. Using the values of ν (0.05) and τ (0.54) provided by Goldsmith, the estimates we give in Table 1 for ANIR (0.078), the ratio of 1881 financial liabilities to 1914 wealth (0.18), the value of α (43.1) deducible from the Istat series and, lastly, the value of β^{-1} (0.18) based on the estimates of the ratio of capital to output calculated by A. Graziani ('Il rapporto capitale/prodotto nell'economia italiana', *Rassegna Economica*, 1958, Table 1, p. 696), Goldsmith's formula provides a 'calculated' value of FIR $[(0.078 \times 1.05 \times 43.1 \times 0.18 \times 0.54) + 0.18 = 0.52]$ around 10 per cent higher than the value we observed in 1914 (0.47).
9. G. Della Torre, 'L'interrelazione tra accumulazione reale e aggregati finanziari' (forthcoming), analyses the Italian data from 1948 to 1975 adopting Goldsmith's methodology, with some interesting modifications. Della Torre's results confirm and synthesize those obtained by others, particularly with reference to the years after 1963 (his paper provides an extensive bibliography). The inferences that Della Torre draws from the very useful data relating to the preceding period nonetheless seem to be somewhat conditioned by the fact that in the initial years considered (1948, 1951), all the indicators of the financial superstructure are greatly reduced and in any case made less significant by the war and, above all, by wartime and postwar inflation.
10. See P. Ciocca (1975), 'L'Italia nell'economia mondiale', *Quaderni Storici*, Table 2, p. 363.
11. On this subject see L. Harris (1976), 'On Interest, Credit and Capital', *Economy and Society*, **5** (2), pp. 145–76.
12. See R.W. Goldsmith, *Financial Structure and Development*, p. 318, and 'Some Reflections', p. 79.
13. R.W. Goldsmith, *Financial Structure and Development*, p. 318.
14. See T.M. Rybczynski (1974), 'Business Finance in the EEC, USA and Japan', *Three Banks Review*, pp. 58–72. In 1977 the growth in the banking system's assets almost completely matched that in the volume of total domestic credit. See Banca d'Italia, *Relazione annuale per il 1977* (Rome, 1978).
15. See, for example, J.S. Cohen (1972), 'Italy, 1861–1914', in R. Cameron (ed.), *Banking and Economic Development*, New York: Oxford University Press.
16. Even Gerschenkron's observations about the role of mixed banks in Italy seem to reflect a mechanical transposition to Italy of German banking experience ('As in Germany, the banks ...'); see A. Gerschenkron (1962), 'Notes on the Rate of Industrial Growth in Italy, 1881–1913', in *Economic Backwardness in Historical Perspective*, Cambridge, MA: Harvard University Press, pp. 87–9. On the abundant work that remains to be done to verify the Harvard historian's seminal hypothesis with scientific methods, see R. Sylla, 'Financial Intermediaries in Economic History', in R.E. Gallman (ed.) (1977), *Recent Developments in the Study of Business and Economic History*, Greenwich: J.A.I. Press.

    Rosario Romeo follows Gerschenkron's position on the subject, adding some descriptive elements and the remark that 'in a country afflicted by a radical shortage of capital ... resort on a large scale to domestic savings was an essential condition for development'; see R. Romeo (1972), *Breve storia della grande industria in Italia*, 4th ed., Bologna: Cappelli, p. 71. If Romeo's statement implies a particularly intense recourse to external financing by firms and the government, it is not supported by the data in Table 4 on the ratio of issues to investment.

Luciano Cafagna, in turn, underscores the qualitative element represented by the fact that the mixed banks, as shown by Cohen, concentrated their activity in the 'new' sectors of Italian industry; however, he does not investigate the causal connection between the development of these sectors and their financial relations with the mixed banks; see L. Cafagna (1971), 'The Industrial Revolution in Italy, 1830–1914', in *The Fontana Economic History of Europe*, Vol. IV, London: Fontana, extract, p. 46.

17. A. Confalonieri, *Banca e industria in Italia, 1894–1906*, 3 vols., Milan, 1974–76, Bologna: Il Mulino, 1979–80.
18. See P. Ciocca, 'Note sulla politica monetaria italiana, 1900–1913', now in G. Toniolo (ed.) (1978), *L'Economia italiana, 1861–1940*, Bari: Laterza.
19. See Ministero per la Costituente, Commissione Economica, *Credito e assicurazione. Relazione* (Rome, 1946).
20. T. Martello and A. Montanari (1874), *Stato attuale del credito in Italia e notizie sulle istituzioni di credito stranieri,* Padua: Fratelli Salmin.
21. For a recent study of these problems, referring to the current Italian financial markets and based on advanced methodology, see G. Cristini (1978), 'I rendimenti delle azioni e l'efficienza della borsa', *Contributi alla Ricerca Economica del Servizio Studi della Banca d'Italia*, **8**, December.
22. R. Sylla, 'Financial Intermediaries in Economic History', p. 56.
23. I. Friend (1977), 'Recent Developments in Finance', *Journal of Banking and Finance*, p. 113. Friend raises many criticisms of the use of this concept in empirical research and in capital market regulation.
24. See R.W. Goldsmith, 'Some Reflections'.
25. See P. Ciocca, C.A. Giussani and G. Lanciotti (1974), *Sportelli, dimensioni e costi: uno studio sulla struttura del sistema bancario italiano*, Rome: Enti Einaudi, and the literature cited therein.
26. See H.G. Johnson (1968), 'Problems of Efficiency in Monetary Management', *Journal of Political Economy*, pp. 971–90.
27. For the properties of the indices used and a comparison with other possible measures of concentration, see, among others, D.R. Kamerschen and N. Lam (1975), 'A Survey of Measures of Market Power', *Rivista internazionale di Scienze Economiche e Commerciali*, pp. 1133–56.
28. See B.K. Short (1977), 'An International Comparison of Bank Concentration and Performance', International Monetary Fund, typescript, 20 July, DM/77 (65).
29. For the ordinary credit banks and cooperative banks, the data are taken from Ministero di Agricoltura, Industria e Commercio, *Bollettino bimestrale delle situazioni dei conti delle banche popolari, delle società di credito ordinario, delle società e istituti di credito agrario, degli istituti di credito fondiario*, for the 1880s, and from Banca d'Italia, Servizio Studi, *Bollettino*, various years, for the 1950s. For the savings banks, the data are taken from Ministero di Agricoltura, Industria e Commercio, *Bollettino semestrale delle Casse di risparmio ordinarie*, for the 1920s and from Banca d'Italia, Servizio Studi, *Bollettino*, various years, for the 1950s.
30. See the *Relazione* of the Governor of the Bank of Italy, Bonaldo Stringher, to the General Meetings of Shareholders for 1929 (especially pp. 53 and 56) and 1930 (especially p. 46).
31. See Banca d'Italia, *Struttura funzionale e territoriale del sistema bancario italiano, 1936–1974* (Rome, 1977), 'Introduzione', pp. XXIII–XXV.
32. Concerning the likelihood of this occurring, due note has been taken of the similarity of the position of two economists as different from each other as Marx ('The rate of interest reaches its peak during crises when money is borrowed at any cost to meet payments') and Robertson ('if activity is allowed to develop into a crisis … only money will serve … thus we may get sharply falling prices of goods associated with a sharply rising rate of interest'). See L. Harris, *op. cit.*, p. 154.
33. This is a matter of much debate. Most recently, see E.P.M. Gardener (1977), 'A Note on the

Philosophy of Bank Capital Adequacy and Prudential Bank Regulation', Bangor: Institute of European Finance, whose opinions we share.

34. For information on these crises, see G. Luzzatto (1968), *L'Economia italiana dal 1861 al 1894*, Turin: Einaudi, pp. 80–81.
35. For a detailed description, see F. Bonelli (1971), *La crisii del 1907*, Turin: Fondazione Einaudi.
36. For a treatment that is similar in several respects, see E.H. Solomon (1955), 'Economic Growth and Common Stock Values', *Journal of Business*, pp. 213–21.
37. Despite this uncertainty, highly simplified theoretical frameworks have been applied in econometric studies. One such framework is proposed by T.J. Sargent (1969), 'Commodity Price Expectations and the Interest Rate', *Quarterly Journal of Economics*, pp. 127–40. For another, applied to the UK rather than to the US, see D. Demery and N.W. Duck (1978), 'The Behaviour of Nominal Interest Rates in the U.K., 1961–1973', *Economica*, pp. 23–37.
38. See P. Ciocca (1982), 'Intermediari finanziari e sviluppo nella teoria e nella storiografia economica', in *Interesse e profitto. Saggi sul sistema creditizio*, Bologna: Il Mulino, pp. 75–104, and the literature referred to therein.
39. See R.W. Goldsmith, 'Some Reflections'.
40. In the UK, for example, the Bank of England attributed the lack of shareholders' 'active concern in the commercial performance of the companies whose shares they held' to the fact that institutional investors 'regard the sale of shares through the market as the only appropriate course when an investment looked like deteriorating. ... The very breadth of the securities markets, and the specialization of function between one set of institutions and another, seemed partly responsible for this apparent defect.' See Bank of England, 'Savings and Investment: Recent Developments in Financing Arrangements', *Quarterly Bulletin*, 1977, p. 316.

Tables

Table 1 Financial liabilities and national wealth in Italy (billions of current lire to 1938; subsequently, trillions of lire)

	1861	1881	1914	1938	1963	1971
I. Financial intermediaries	0.8	4.7	19.3	189.6	43.6	134.3
II. Other domestic operators	8.3	22.9	45.6	370.1	61.4	122.6
1. Public sector:	2.6	14.1	21.6	177.4	16.2	33.8
a) Central government	2.4	13.2	19.6	162.9	11.2	17.6
b) Local authorities	0.2	0.9	2.0	14.5	3.0	10.5
c) Autonomous government agencies	—	—	—	..	2.0	5.7
2. Non-financial firms:	4.0	6.2	20.0	180.7	41.5	80.6
a) Bonds	0.9	1.0	1.3	5.9	2.1	5.9
b) Debts to financial intermediaries	0.4	1.9	7.0	68.2	17.3	42.4
c) Trade debts	1.7	2.5	6.8	59.0	7.0	14.0
d) Shares	1.0	0.8	4.9	47.6	15.1	18.3
3. Individuals: Mortgage debts	1.7	2.6	4.0	12.0	1.6	2.4
4. Households	..	..	..	..	2.1	5.8
III. Foreign sector (net)	–0.3	–2.2	1.3	..	0.8	7.9
Total financial liabilities (I+II+III)	8.8	25.4	66.2	559.7	105.8	264.8
National wealth	..	66.2	140.5	820.0	130.7	266.8

In this and all other tables, the symbol '—' indicates that the phenomenon in question does not occur, and the symbol '..' that reliable data are not available.

Sources:

I: For 1881–1971, see 'Total liabilities of the financial intermediaries', Table 6 below, and the sources cited there. The figure for 1861 was estimated on the basis of the information found in R. De Mattia (ed.) (1967), *I bilanci degli Istituti di emissione italiani (1845–1936)*, Rome: Banca d'Italia, subsequently referred to as R. De Mattia, *I bilanci*, with regard to the balance sheet items of the banks of issue (Table 2, 'Total' net of memorandum accounts), ordinary credit banks (Table 22, items relating to capital and fund-raising) and ordinary savings banks (Table 22, figures for endowment funds and deposits for 1863).

II 1(a): For 1861–1963, Istat, *Annuario statistico italiano*, various issues, tables on 'Patrimonio dello Stato: riassunto delle attività e passività finanziarie'. For 1971, see Banca d'Italia, *Relazione annuale per il 1972* (Rome, 1973), Appendix, Table a103, pp. 124–5 (excluding the liabilities of the Deposits and Loans Fund, which are taken from the series referred to under point I above.

II 1(b): For 1961, see R.W. Goldsmith and S. Zecchini, 'National Balance Sheet of Italy' (Banca d'Italia, typescript, 20 June 1975), Table III, the item 'Enti territoriali'. The essay by Goldsmith and

Zecchini is also the source of the schema of Table 1. For 1881–1938, the figures are the sum of the municipal and provincial debts derived from Istat, *Annuario statistico italiano*, various issues (the figure for 1881 was obtained by averaging those for 1880 and 1882). The figure for 1914 is the sum of municipal borrowings for 1911 and provincial borrowings for 1915. The figure for 1938 was assumed to be equal to that for 1934. For 1963, see M. Caron and F. Cotula, *op. cit.*, Table 1, pp. 864–5. For 1971, see Banca d'Italia, *op. cit.*

II 1(c): For 1963, see M. Caron and F. Cotula, *op. cit.* For 1971, see Banca d'Italia, *op. cit.*

II 2(a): For 1861–1914, see Associazione fra le Società italiane per Azioni, *Notizie statistiche sulle società italiane per azioni* (Rome, 1928), pp. 193–9 (the values were estimated on the basis of the data for bond issues, assuming straight-line amortization of the principal). For 1938, see Associazione fra le Società italiane per Azioni, *Notizie statistiche sulle società italiane per azioni* (Rome, 1934 and 1940), tables summarizing the balance sheet values of non-financial firms. For 1963, see M. Caron and F. Cotula, *op. cit.*, Table 1, pp. 910–11. For 1971, see Banca d'Italia, *op. cit.*

II 2(b): For 1861–1938, see R. De Mattia, *I bilanci*, sum of asset item 2 of Table 2 and asset item 2 (excluding sub-item d) of Table 23. For 1861, the 1864 figures for savings banks and 1870 figures for other banks were used. For 1938, the figure was estimated by assuming that the share of loans to the public, not in the form of securities, in relation to the total balance sheet assets of non-bank intermediaries was equal to that of the banks as at 1936. For 1963, see M. Caron and F. Cotula, *op. cit.*, Table 1, pp. 864–5 (sum of the items 'Crediti a breve termine' and 'Crediti a lungo termine' under 'Passività delle Imprese'). For 1971, see Banca d'Italia, *op. cit., loc. cit.* (sum of the items 'Crediti a breve termine' and 'Crediti a lungo termine' under 'Passività delle Imprese').

II 2(c): See R.W. Goldsmith and S. Zecchini, *op. cit.,* the item 'Crediti commerciali'.

II 2(d): For 1861, see R.W. Goldsmith and Zecchini, *op. cit.*, the item 'Azioni'. For 1881–1914, see Associazione fra le Società italiane per Azioni, *op. cit.* (Rome, 1932), pp. 137–9. For 1938, see Associazione fra le Società italiane per Azioni, *Le società italiane per azioni al 31 dicembre 1938, 1945, 1951*, Table VII, pp. 34–5. For 1963, see M. Caron and F. Cotula, *op. cit.*, Table 1, pp. 910–11. For 1971, see Banca d'Italia, *op. cit.*

II 3: See R.W. Goldsmith and S. Zecchini, *op. cit.*, the item 'Debiti ipotecari di privati'.

II 4: For 1963, see M. Caron and F. Cotula, *op. cit.*, Table 1, pp. 864–5. For 1971, see Banca d'Italia, *op. cit.*

III: For 1861–1914, see Istat, *Sommario di statistiche storiche italiane 1861–1955* (Rome, 1958), Table 113, pp. 214–15 (sum of the balances on current account of the balance of payments). For 1963, see M. Caron and F. Cotula, *op. cit.*, Table 1, pp. 864–5. For 1871, see Banca d'Italia, *op. cit.*

National wealth: see R.W. Goldsmith and S. Zecchini, *op. cit.*, Table 1, modified to take account of some differences in the valuation of item III.

Table 2 Indicators of the 'financial superstructure'

	FIR[1]			ANIR[2]	
Year	Value	Annual % Change			Value
1881	0.38	1914/1881	+0.7	1861–1881	0.08
1914	0.47	1938/1914	+1.9	1881–1914	0.09
				1914–1938	0.19
1938	0.68	1963/1938	+0.8	1938–1963	0.38
1963	0.81	1971/1963	+2.8	1963–1971	0.42
1971	0.99	1971/1938	+1.1	1938–1971	0.41

[1]Ratio of the stock of financial assets to national wealth.
[2]Average ratio of the change in financial liabilities to GNP for each year within the1963 period.

Sources: Table 1; Istat, *Sommario di statistiche storiche italiane, 1861–1955*, Table 110, p. 210; Istat, *Sommario di statistiche storiche dell'Italia, 1861–1975* (Rome, 1976), Table 132, p. 176.

Table 3 *Indicators of the financial superstructure: Italy (I) compared with five developed countries (DC)**

	FIR		ANIR	Issues of financial intermediaries / National income (1)	Issues of firms, gen. govt., households, foreign sector / National income (2)	Ratio of intermediation (3=1:2)
1881		1861–1881				
I	= 0.38	I	= 0.08	0.02	0.06	0.31
DC	= 0.65	DC	= 0.14	0.04	0.10	0.37
I/DC	= 0.58	I/DC	= 0.59	0.51	0.61	
1914		1881–1914				
I	= 0.47	I	= 0.09	0.03	0.06	0.56
DC	= 0.85	DC	= 0.15	0.05	0.10	0.46
I/DC	= 0.55	I/DC	= 0.59	0.67	0.55	
1938		1914–1938				
I	= 0.68	I	= 0.19	0.07	0.12	0.54
DC	= 1.10	DC	= 0.17	0.07	0.10	0.66
I/DC	= 0.62	I/DC	= 1.11	0.97	1.20	
1963		1949–1963				
I	= 0.81	I	= 0.33	0.19	0.14	1.36
DC	= 1.21	DC	= 0.30	0.14	0.15	0.94
I/DC	= 0.67	I/DC	= 1.17	1.32	0.91	

* UK, US, France, Japan and Germany (arithmetic means).

Sources:

FIR: For Italy, Table 2; for the other countries, see R.W. Goldsmith, *Financial Structure and Development* (for 1881 and 1913, p. 314; for 1963, Table 7.8, p. 322; for 1938, estimate based on Graph 9.2, p. 377, assuming the value of 1 for France).

ANIR: For Italy, from 1861 to 1938, Tables 2 and 5; for the other countries and for Italy, 1949–63, see R.W. Goldsmith, *op. cit.*, (for the period 1861–81, Table 3.3, p. 119, Table 3.20, p. 175, and Table 4.7, p. 191; for the period 1881–1914, Table 7.9, p. 338; for the period 1914–38, Table 3.3, values relating to the 1920s for the UK, Japan and the US and simple mean of the values for the periods 1901–13 and 1949–63 for France and Germany, Tables 3.20 and 4.7; for the period 1949–63, Table 7.1, p. 313).

*Table 4 Indicators of the financial superstructure: Italy (I) compared with five developed countries (DC)**

	Ratio of Italian FIR and average FIR of DCs	Ratio of real per capita income in Italy to average of DCs	Difference in percentage points
	(1)	(2)	[3=(1–2)×100]
1881	0.58	0.66	–8
1914	0.55	0.55	0
1938	0.62	0.43	+19
1963	0.67	0.54	+13

	Issues of firms, general government and households / National income		Investment / National income		Issues / Investment	
	(4)		(5)		(6=4:5)	
	I	DC	I	DC	I	DC
1881–1914	0.06	0.10	0.12	0.16	0.52	0.65
1914–1938	0.12	0.10	0.14	0.14	0.89	0.74
1949–1963	0.14	0.15	0.20	0.22	0.70	0.70

*UK, US, France, Japan and Germany (arithmetic means).

Sources:
Column (1): See Table 3.
Column (2): A. Maddison (1977), 'Phases of Capitalist Development', *Banca Nazionale del Lavoro Quarterly Review*, pp. 103–37 (the average includes Italy).
Column (4): See Table 3.
Column (5): For Italy, the two previously cited summaries of historical statistics published by Istat; for the other countries, R.W. Goldsmith, *Financial Structure*, Table 3.7, p. 132.

Table 5 Composition of financial liabilities

	Liabilities of financial intermediaries / National wealth	Liabilities of firms gen. govt., households, foreign sector, / National wealth	Ratio of intermediation		
	(1)	(2)	(3=1:2)		
			Level	% annual change	
1881	0.07	0.31	0.23	1914/1881	2.5
1914	0.14	0.33	0.41	1938/1914	0.9
1938	0.23	0.45	0.51	1963/1938	1.5
1963	0.33	0.48	0.70	1971/1963	5.9
1971	0.50	0.49	1.03	1971/1938	3.1

	Change in liabilities of financial intermediaries / National income	Change in liabilities of firms, gen. govt., households, foreign sector / National income	Ratio of intermediation
	(4)	(5)	(6=4:5)
1861–1881	0.02	0.06	0.31
1881–1914	0.03	0.06	0.56
1914–1938	0.07	0.12	0.54
1938–1963	0.16	0.22	0.71
1963–1971	0.24	0.18	1.33
1938–1971	0.21	0.20	1.03

Sources: Table 1 and Istat.

Table 6 Liabilities of the financial intermediaries in Italy (millions of lire to 1938; subsequently, billions of lire)

	Banking system							
		Commercial banks				Savings institutions		
	(1) Banks of issue	(2) Ordinary credit banks	(3) Banking firms	(4) Public-law banks	(5) Banks of national interest	(6) Savings banks	(7) Deposits and Loans Fund	(8) Pledge banks
1870	1,466.8	237.6	..	—	—	398.3	..	..
1871	1,674.6	356.3	..	—	—	447.5	..	..
1872	1,904.8	864.4	..	—	—	496.6	..	..
1873	1,992.4	943.4	..	—	—	497.9	..	..
1874	1,153.7	831.7	..	—	—	522.1	..	..
1875	1,137.4	805.5	..	—	—	586.8	..	..
1876	1,202.1	694.2	..	—	—	646.3	1,293.0	..
1877	1,220.8	692.0	..	—	—	682.6	1,360.3	..
1878	1,294.0	727.8	..	—	—	707.7	1,417.5	..
1879	1,341.6	750.9	..	—	—	776.9	1,511.5	..
1880	1,404.5	795.7	..	—	—	816.5	1,504.4	..
1881	1,578.0	869.5	..	—	—	858.7	770.4	..
1882	1,399.9	934.2	..	—	—	897.2	396.8	..
1883	1,389.5	944.9	..	—	—	963.0	594.9	..
1884	1,503.1	1,006.6	..	—	—	1,038.5	793.0	..
1885	1,645.8	1,248.5	..	—	—	1,112.8	812.7	..
1886	1,774.4	1,512.1	..	—	—	1,212.7	896.7	..
1887	1,931.4	1,652.3	..	—	—	1,263.6	938.8	..
1888	1,981.3	1,642.0	..	—	—	1,312.0	1,083.6	..
1889	2,080.0	1,583.8	..	—	—	1,391.6	1,259.4	..
1890	2,154.1	1,376.7	..	—	—	1,428.1	1,372.0	..
1891	2,189.1	1,253.8	..	—	—	1,451.2	1,490.6	..
1892	2,179.1	1,196.3	..	—	—	1,505.5	1,747.0	..
1893	2,318.2	1,102.7	..	—	—	1,553.7	1,852.5	..
1894	2,233.3	975.7	..	—	—	1,613.0	1,597.1	..
1895	2,226.3	984.5	..	—	—	1,657.8	1,715.3	..
1896	2,178.9	863.5	..	—	—	1,623.7	1,733.0	169.4
1897	2,162.4	935.4	..	—	—	1,693.9	1,905.5	..
1898	2,221.3	974.9	..	—	—	1,728.9	1,965.5	..
1899	2,088.2	1,061.3	..	—	—	1,786.6	1,987.8	148.5
1900	2,096.9	1,195.9	..	—	—	1,827.6	2,062.4	145.8
1901	2,125.9	1,335.9	..	—	—	1,909.0	2,133.3	154.9
1902	2,084.3	1,356.6	..	—	—	1,982.0	2,240.9	168.8
1903	2,253.7	1,573.0	..	—	—	2,069.1	2,400.8	176.8
1904	2,327.4	1,820.8	..	—	—	2,174.7	2,555.8	187.1
1905	2,536.0	2,228.8	..	—	—	2,307.8	2,674.1	198.0
1906	2,687.6	2,275.7	..	—	—	2,392.5	2,852.2	204.1
1907	2,971.0	2,204.7	..	—	—	2,571.8	3,060.0	218.5
1908	2,946.2	2,405.9	..	—	—	2,709.8	3,265.0	221.9
1909	3,061.8	2,537.5	..	—	—	2,906.3	3,323.0	242.6
1910	3,234.5	2,670.7	..	—	—	3,054.2	3,587.2	258.1

Banking system			Special credit institutions					
Savings institutions		(11)	(12)	(13)	(14)	(15)	(16)	Total
(9) Cooper-ative banks	(10) Rural and artisans' banks	Total	Agri-cultural	Real estate	Industrial	Total	Insurance institu-tions	financial inter-mediaries (17=11+15+16)
51.2	—	2,153.9	0.6	36.9	—	37.5	11.0	2,202.4
100.2	—	2,578.6	8.1	52.2	—	60.3	11.2	2,650.1
118.7	—	3,384.5	32.2	73.4	—	105.6	11.5	3,501.6
127.7	—	3,561.4	28.9	104.0	—	132.9	12.0	3,706.3
158.0	—	2,665.5	30.3	122.6	—	152.9	12.0	2,830.4
175.9	—	2,705.6	31.8	138.1	—	169.9	12.2	2,887.7
187.6	—	4,023.2	38.0	159.6	—	197.6	14.5	4,235.3
210.2	—	4,165.9	36.6	181.5	—	218.1	17.0	4,401.0
235.0	—	4,382.0	41.9	205.0	—	246.9	20.0	4,648.9
244.8	—	4,625.7	46.6	234.8	—	281.4	22.0	4,929.1
260.2	—	4,781.3	52.2	264.7	—	316.9	24.0	5,122.2
278.6	—	4,355.2	54.5	289.3	—	343.8	26.0	4,725.0
304.0	—	3,932.1	54.1	311.8	—	365.9	29.0	4,327.0
354.4	..	4,246.7	49.0	330.9	—	379.9	31.0	4,657.6
398.0	..	4,739.2	50.2	343.8	—	394.0	34.0	5,167.2
455.6	..	5,275.4	54.7	361.2	—	415.9	35.9	5,727.2
555.8	..	5,951.7	50.5	457.4	—	507.9	44.0	6,503.6
611.8	..	6,397.9	55.0	582.9	—	637.9	53.0	7,088.8
629.0	..	6,647.9	60.2	723.1	—	783.3	62.0	7,493.2
624.7	..	6,939.5	57.2	792.7	—	849.9	70.0	7,859.4
625.4	..	6,956.3	54.5	883.2	—	937.7	80.0	7,974.0
588.7	..	6,973.4	55.7	976.4	—	1,032.1	88.0	8,093.5
606.6	..	7,234.5	50.8	982.2	—	1,033.0	97.0	8,364.5
583.3	..	7,410.4	30.0	994.5	—	1,024.5	106.0	8,540.9
552.3	..	6,971.4	27.8	1,003.8	—	1,031.6	115.0	8,118.0
571.9	..	7,155.8	28.0	1,001.0	—	1,029.0	123.4	8,308.2
564.9	..	7,133.4	28.0	1,011.0	—	1,039.0	142.0	8,314.4
562.1	..	7,259.3	28.0	941.4	—	969.4	160.0	8,388.7
606.1	..	7,496.7	30.3	931.2	—	961.5	179.0	8,637.2
641.9	..	7,714.3	25.5	920.4	—	945.9	198.0	8,858.2
677.5	..	8,006.1	22.7	900.8	—	923.5	216.0	9,145.6
725.8	..	8,384.8	19.3	881.1	—	900.4	235.0	9,520.2
779.5	..	8,612.1	16.5	879.9	—	896.4	253.0	9,761.5
849.9	..	9,323.3	15.8	861.5	—	877.3	271.0	10,471.6
915.0	..	9,980.8	17.8	849.5	—	867.3	290.0	11,138.1
1,000.7	47.8	10,993.2	17.0	838.3	—	855.3	307.9	12,156.4
1,065.7	..	11,477.8	20.0	834.0	—	854.0	335.0	12,666.8
1,220.2	..	12,246.2	20.0	827.8	—	847.8	363.0	13,457.0
1,356.2	57.1	12,962.7	14.3	836.8	—	851.1	391.0	14,204.8
1,544.7	64.2	13,680.1	18.8	847.6	—	866.4	420.0	14,966.5
1,674.9	99.4	14,579.0	26.1	875.0	—	901.1	448.0	15,928.1

Table 6 continued

	Banking system							
		Commercial banks				Savings institutions		
	(1) Banks of issue	(2) Ordinary credit banks	(3) Banking firms	(4) Public-law banks	(5) Banks of national interest	(6) Savings banks	(7) Deposits and Loans Fund	(8) Pledge banks
1911	3,364.9	2,816.3	..	—	—	3,179.8	3,726.0	287.1
1912	3,333.4	3,023.0	..	—	—	3,254.1	3,869.3	294.9
1913	3,313.7	3,473.6	..	—	—	3,403.9	3,990.0	312.3
1914	4,506.2	3,302.1	..	—	—	3,433.7	4,140.7	321.5
1915	5,932.7	3,576.2	..	—	—	3,537.9	4,384.4	342.1
1916	7,114.2	5,251.1	..	—	—	3,932.6	4,512.7	366.2
1917	14,364.6	7,245.7	..	—	—	4,556.4	5,222.4	414.3
1918	15,838.2	10,590.9	..	—	—	5,690.6	6,362.0	490.0
1919	21,281.9	17,537.0	..	—	—	7,110.6	8,413.8	580.0
1920	24,926.7	23,315.3	..	—	—	8,426.4	11,251.3	656.4
1921	25,612.5	29,144.1	..	—	—	10,386.1	12,951.2	791.0
1922	24,032.1	29,435.6	..	—	—	11,804.2	13,702.6	978.8
1923	25,634.8	31,496.1	..	—	—	12,781.1	14,295.8	1,104.8
1924	26,734.6	35,645.6	..	—	—	15,123.6	14,987.7	1,379.8
1925	28,787.0	41,106.1	..	—	—	16,429.9	16,098.9	1,485.3
1926	27,057.5	41,198.2	2,127.2	4,601.9	—	16,958.2	16,926.7	1,316.5
1927	23,730.9	42,066.6	2,172.7	4,705.0	—	18,252.3	17,234.8	1,475.0
1928	22,083.5	44,218.0	2,328.8	5,265.3	—	20,171.1	18,266.9	1,510.9
1929	22,275.3	45,982.4	2,244.9	5,597.6	—	21,271.7	19,364.4	1,477.1
1930	21,657.6	44,768.9	1,898.8	5,805.1	—	22,542.5	21,649.6	1,525.8
1931	20,369.4	41,409.4	1,569.3	6,015.6	—	23,360.0	23,569.2	1,828.6
1932	20,077.4	37,794.9	1,340.6	6,215.7	—	24,469.9	25,560.2	1,966.9
1933	18,101.1	35,366.6	1,336.3	7,846.4	—	25,152.5	29,442.7	1,055.7
1934	18,353.7	33,286.7	1,260.6	7,989.1	—	25,038.3	32,725.1	1,074.7
1935	19,374.9	31,559.3	1,074.1	8,426.0	—	24,678.8	31,785.3	1,090.0
1936	20,424.4	30,796.3	1,059.2	12,682.9	—	23,430.0	32,814.1	1,073.0
1937	21,452.0	10,569.2	1,035.0	14,539.2	20,245.8	19,631.2	36,755.3	..
1938	23,598.2	12,202.0	1,162.1	16,518.4	22,992.9	22,328.9	40,350.1	..
1939	29.6	14.4	..	17.8	24.1	24.9	43.9	..
1940	39.2	16.6	..	23.7	27.8	25.9	51.3	..
1941	58.3	22.1	..	30.8	35.6	30.8	62.4	..
1942	94.4	31.8	..	39.5	41.9	37.8	77.7	..
1943	209.3	35.7	..	44.5	55.5	43.5	80.9	..
1944	399.7	60.2	..	80.3	97.4	60.5	84.9	..
1945	506.6	111.2	..	120.7	142.4	103.3	113.6	..
1946	705.4	217.7	..	214.9	296.5	181.8	196.8	..
1947	965.9	332.0	..	440.9	421.5	285.6	304.7	..
1948	1,299.0	476.4	..	600.6	665.7	413.6	515.3	..
1949	1,644.3	562.8	..	733.9	670.6	511.9	779.1	..
1950	1,656.5	657.6	..	879.5	825.7	601.4	1,022.5	..
1951	1,859.9	789.9	..	1,099.5	1,027.8	687.1	1,211.3	..
1952	1,954.4	976.6	..	1,286.2	1,191.7	841.7	1,533.7	..

Banking system			Special credit institutions					
Savings institutions		(11)	(12)	(13)	(14)	(15)	(16) Insurance institutions	Total financial intermediaries (17=11+15+16)
(9) Cooperative banks	(10) Rural and artisans' banks	Total	Agricultural	Real estate	Industrial	Total		
1,726.1	95.4	15,195.6	27.0	918.5	—	945.5	475.0	16,616.1
1,787.9	102.6	15,665.2	36.2	963.2	—	999.4	635.1	17,299.7
1,574.3	100.6	16,168.4	44.0	997.1	—	1,041.1	738.7	17,948.2
1,589.7	100.6	17,394.5	46.8	1,028.6	—	1,075.4	865.7	19,335.6
1,631.8	100.0	19,505.1	51.2	1,045.2	60.1	1,156.5	1,214.5	21,876.1
1,914.7	142.1	23,233.6	57.5	752.2	73.9	883.6	1,279.6	25,396.8
2,019.6	150.9	33,973.9	67.1	739.1	82.9	889.1	1,367.5	36,230.5
3,496.2	193.4	42,661.3	84.0	712.9	91.4	888.3	1,642.5	45,192.1
5,017.0	282.0	60,221.5	103.8	705.6	123.0	932.4	1,541.6	62,695.5
5,664.2	360.1	74,600.4	150.2	693.1	456.0	1,299.3	2,001.3	77,901.0
5,287.0	452.8	84,624.7	175.8	727.8	812.1	1,715.7	2,497.9	88,838.3
6,115.5	512.3	86,581.1	175.3	829.6	1,109.3	2,114.2	3,052.7	91,748.0
7,424.2	796.9	93,533.7	260.0	906.1	1,008.3	2,174.4	3,642.3	99,350.4
9,485.2	956.5	104,313.0	292.9	1,197.1	1,277.6	2,767.6	4,403.2	111,483.8
10,070.4	1,116.1	115,093.7	421.9	1,414.8	1,539.1	3,375.8	5,493.6	123,963.1
9,069.5	1,444.8	120,700.5	587.3	1,715.4	2,088.2	4,390.9	6,349.5	131,440.9
9,395.7	1,397.0	120,430.0	721.0	2,142.1	2,889.3	5,752.4	7,307.7	133,490.1
9,880.4	1,410.2	125,135.1	1,349.4	2,889.4	3,394.0	7,632.8	8,583.1	141,351.0
9,906.7	1,506.8	129,626.9	1,580.3	3,730.1	3,594.9	8,905.3	9,967.1	148,499.3
8,785.0	1,452.6	130,085.9	1,659.6	4,597.2	3,700.7	9,957.5	11,229.8	151,273.2
8,102.0	1,365.9	127,589.4	2,007.0	5,356.2	4,380.0	11,743.2	12,318.5	151,651.1
7,279.8	1,254.6	125,960.0	2,340.6	5,771.2	5,477.2	13,589.0	13,061.0	152,610.0
6,732.9	1,126.5	126,160.7	2,877.0	6,018.7	9,267.4	18,163.1	13,561.6	157,885.4
6,098.3	1,089.1	126,915.6	2,121.0	6,158.5	9,597.5	17,877.0	14,656.7	159,449.3
5,817.6	929.3	124,735.3	2,073.4	6,158.4	9,448.1	17,679.9	15,795.8	158,211.0
6,470.9	898.5	129,649.3	2,641.2	6,087.8	9,498.1	18,227.1	17,934.8	165,811.2
5,898.5	751.1	130,877.3	3,275.0	6,318.4	10,512.4	20,105.8	19,317.5	170,300.6
6,640.6	1,162.1	146,955.3	4,063.0	6,549.0	12,055.0	22,667.0	19,928.7	189,551.0
8.2	..	162.9	4.5	6.6	13.0	24.0	23.9	210.8
9.8	..	194.2	4.4	6.7	13.4	24.4	28.7	247.4
13.6	..	253.6	6.0	6.6	16.8	29.3	34.4	317.4
17.3	..	340.5	7.6	6.6	34.6	48.8	41.3	430.6
21.2	..	490.6	8.0	6.5	59.6	74.1	49.6	614.3
36.1	..	819.2	14.2	6.4	61.8	82.5	59.5	961.2
59.7	4.0	1,161.4	15.4	6.1	69.1	90.7	71.4	1,323.5
107.2	6.9	1,927.2	29.3	7.8	53.5	90.6	79.5	2,097.2
167.3	9.2	2,927.1	35.0	11.6	65.1	111.7	100.9	3,139.6
235.0	15.1	4,220.8	60.5	17.4	184.5	262.4	127.9	4,611.1
279.1	18.2	5,200.0	60.6	32.2	245.2	338.1	151.3	5,689.2
318.0	20.4	5,981.6	62.3	62.1	362.1	486.6	184.2	6,652.4
374.3	23.0	7,072.9	91.1	85.0	447.5	623.5	222.9	7,919.3
451.5	27.4	8,263.2	114.6	116.6	570.0	801.1	260.4	9,324.7

Table 6 continued

	Banking system							
		Commercial banks				Savings institutions		
	(1) Banks of issue	(2) Ordinary credit banks	(3) Banking firms	(4) Public-law banks	(5) Banks of national interest	(6) Savings banks	(7) Deposits and Loans Fund	(8) Pledge banks
1953	2,031.9	1,148.7	..	1,460.5	1,391.1	991.5	1,824.4	..
1954	2,229.7	1,309.7	..	1,689.1	1,554.9	1,181.6	1,964.6	..
1955	2,437.3	1,513.1	..	1,898.9	1,747.1	1,422.1	2,052.4	..
1956	2,597.9	1,731.5	..	2,076.9	1,903.6	1,648.5	2,252.3	..
1957	2,801.0	1,927.0	..	2,292.1	2,050.3	1,912.8	2,382.6	..
1958	3,257.0	2,331.6	..	2,615.2	2,382.0	2,321.3	2,707.1	..
1959	3,513.4	2,726.9	..	2,967.7	2,743.4	2,712.3	2,904.6	..
1960	3,609.3	3,088.4	..	3,535.3	3,177.8	3,125.3	3,166.9	..
1961	4,190.9	3,607.1	..	4,140.8	3,713.7	3,687.0	3,580.4	..
1962	4,970.0	4,315.6	..	5,046.0	4,579.9	4,342.5	4,054.6	..
1963	5,523.8	4,838.4	..	5,625.9	5,092.0	5,031.4	4,856.2	..
1964	6,076.1	5,147.1	..	6,278.1	5,392.8	5,600.4	5,515.5	..
1965	6,570.9	6,096.6	..	7,143.9	6,247.4	6,691.0	6,322.6	..
1966	7,166.6	7,161.2	..	8,203.1	7,217.8	8,028.9	6,625.4	..
1967	8,148.6	8,429.8	..	9,351.1	8,115.3	9,333.2	6,982.1	..
1968	8,902.8	9,675.8	..	10,831.9	9,577.9	10,603.3	7,657.8	..
1969	10,413.4	11,018.7	..	12,368.6	11,497.4	11,998.6	8,674.3	..
1970	11,586.7	13,055.1	..	14,601.5	13,910.8	13,897.4	8,880.2	..
1971	13,596.0	16,085.2	..	17,008.7	16,548.9	16,560.9	9,924.9	..
1972	16,553.6	20,835.8	..	22,308.8	23,324.2	20,282.2	12,321.7	..
1973	21,775.5	26,499.5	..	27,078.8	30,003.1	24,191.7	14,675.1	..

Sources:
For 1870–1938, R. De Mattia, *I bilanci*, Table 2 (total net of memorandum accounts) for banks of issue; Table 22 for ordinary credit banks, banking firms, public-law banks, savings banks, pledge banks, cooperative banks, rural and artisans' banks and real estate credit institutions.

For 1937, Banca d'Italia, *Relazione annuale per il 1938*, pp. 174–5, for ordinary credit banks, banking firms, public-law banks, banks of national interest, savings banks and pledge banks (together), cooperative banks and rural and artisans' banks. For 1938, the figures were estimated by (a) assuming that the shares of the individual categories (except for rural and artisans' banks) in relation to the total for all intermediaries were unchanged from 1937, and (b) applying these ratios to banks' total liabilities as given in Banca d'Italia Servizio Studi, *Bollettino*, January–April 1949, no. 1–4 (Table XVI). The liabilities of the rural and artisans' banks were determined as the difference between total liabilities and the sum of the estimates for the individual categories.

The figures for 1939–41 relating to public-law banks, banks of national interest, ordinary credit banks and banking firms (together) and cooperative banks and savings banks (together) are from Banca d'Italia Servizio Studi, *Bollettino*, January–April 1949, no. 1–4, Tables XVII, XVIII and XIX. The corresponding figures for 1942–45 are from Banca d'Italia Servizio Studi, *Bollettino*, June–August 1946, no. 6–8, Tables XV, XVI, XVII and XVIII. For the above categories and for rural and artisans' banks, liabilities for 1946–73 are from Banca d'Italia Servizio Studi, *Bollettino*, various years, tables of the principal assets and liabilities of banks *in operation* at 31 December.

Banking system			Special credit institutions					
Savings institutions		(11)	(12)	(13)	(14)	(15)	(16)	Total
(9) Cooper-ative banks	(10) Rural and artisans' banks	Total	Agri-cultural	Real estate	Industrial	Total	Insurance institu-tions	financial inter-mediaries (17=11+15+16)
535.1	31.8	9,414.9	139.8	167.3	729.3	1,036.3	354.0	10,805.3
623.0	38.0	10,590.7	175.6	228.9	870.5	1,274.9	455.5	12,321.0
721.5	46.3	11,838.7	237.0	300.2	1,183.3	1,720.5	568.2	14,127.4
840.3	54.9	13,105.9	278.0	366.4	1,338.2	1,982.6	706.8	15,795.3
954.9	66.8	14,387.5	316.2	447.2	1,497.1	2,260.5	863.9	17,511.9
1,152.2	81.7	16,848.1	430.0	539.3	1,744.8	2,714.2	1,031.2	20,593.4
1,350.7	99.6	19,018.5	473.4	643.0	2,190.4	3,306.7	1,222.2	23,547.4
1,537.9	123.3	21,364.2	499.1	801.7	2,683.5	3,984.4	1,377.4	26,726.0
1,797.5	154.8	24,872.1	539.1	1,083.7	3,362.1	4,984.9	1,600.6	31,457.6
2,181.5	196.8	29,686.9	597.1	1,433.8	4,345.3	6,376.2	1,857.5	37,920.6
2,456.3	241.4	33,665.4	665.7	1,793.1	5,330.6	7,789.4	2,163.3	43,618.0
2,652.4	275.8	36,938.3	757.0	2,115.2	6,247.6	9,119.9	2,501.6	48,559.7
3,040.6	339.5	42,452.4	824.3	2,475.6	7,377.5	10,677.5	3,004.0	56,133.8
3,492.9	417.8	48,313.7	835.8	2,950.0	9,324.3	13,110.1	3,465.0	64,888.8
3,981.7	497.4	54,839.1	968.6	3,499.9	10,899.1	15,367.6	3,966.0	74,172.7
4,483.2	586.2	62,319.0	1,120.3	4,243.6	12,780.2	18,144.1	4,480.0	84,943.1
5,063.0	675.7	71,709.7	1,231.4	4,979.0	15,270.8	21,481.2	5,015.0	98,205.9
5,815.8	792.1	82,539.6	1,335.6	5,863.5	17,883.4	25,082.5	5,552.0	113,174.1
6,938.7	990.0	97,653.2	1,488.8	6,876.7	21,940.7	30,306.2	6,336.0	134,295.4
8,640.5	1,287.1	125,553.9	1,590.8	7,886.6	27,710.9	37,188.3	7,102.0	169,844.2
10,698.1	1,645.2	156,567.0	1,692.8	9,628.1	38,348.9	49,669.8	7,743.0	213,979.8

The figures for the following categories of intermediaries were derived from the sources or with the methods set out below.

Banks of issue: For 1937–68, 'Situazioni della Banca d'Italia (1936–1968)', edited by F. Masera (Banca d'Italia, internal document; total net of memorandum accounts); for 1969–73, Banca d'Italia, *Relazione annuale*, balance sheet (total net of memorandum accounts).

Ordinary credit banks: The figures for 1917–20 were estimated by assuming that the share of the four major banks – those covered by R. De Mattia – did not change during the years in question with respect to the share calculated for 1916 on the basis of the figures published in R. De Mattia, *I bilanci*, and U. Bava, *I quattro maggiori istituti italiani di credito* (Genoa: Valugani, 1926). From 1939 onwards, the figures for ordinary credit banks include those relating to banking firms.

Deposits and Loans fund: For 1863–76, R. De Mattia, *I bilanci* (Table 22); for 1877–1973, 'Cassa Depositi e Prestiti. Rendiconti consuntivi', published by Ministero del Tesoro and, for 1935–38, Ministero delle Finanze (balance sheet total net of related operations except for the part regarding relationships between such operations and the Deposits and Loans Fund, as shown in the item 'Contabilità speciali'). The figures for 1883, 1933 and 1938 were estimated by linear interpolation.

Pledge banks: Total liabilities for 1896 were assumed to be equal to the sum of the liabilities given in R. De Mattia, *I bilanci* (Table 22). From 1937 onwards the liabilities of this category are grouped with those of savings banks.

Cooperative banks: The figures for 1918–23 were estimated by assuming percentage changes for total liabilities equal to those for the liabilities given in De Mattia, *I bilanci* (Table 22).

Rural and artisans' banks: Where total assets and total liabilities differed, liabilities were assumed to be equal to the higher figure.

Agricultural credit institutions: For 1870–1905, R. De Mattia, *I bilanci* (Table 22); the figures for 1893–1905 were estimated by assuming percentage changes for total liabilities equal to those for the liabilities given in De Mattia. For 1906–37, Istat, *Annuario statistico*, various years (1907, estimated). For 1938–46, Banca d'Italia Servizio Studi, *Bollettino*, no. 3–6, March–June 1950, Table LXI (total assets decreased by the share of stockpiling bills rediscounted with the Bank of Italy, which was assumed to be equal to the ratio of stockpiling bills rediscounted by the special credit institutions to the Bank of Italy's portfolio in 1947; see Banca d'Italia Servizio Studi, *Bollettino*, January–February 1961, no. 1, Tables 2 and 34). For 1947–60, ibid., Table 34. For 1961–73, Banca d'Italia Servizio Studi, *Bollettino*, various issues (tables on the balance sheet situation of the agricultural credit institutions).

Real estate credit institutions: For 1870–1936, R. De Mattia, *I bilanci* (Table 22). For 1936–46, Banca d'Italia Servizio Studi, *Bollettino*, January–April 1949, no. 1, Table XLVIII. For 1947–55, Banca d'Italia, *Bollettino*, January–February 1961, no. 1, Table 31. For 1956–73, Banca d'Italia, *Bollettino*, various issues (tables on the balance sheet situation of the real estate and building credit institutions). The figure for 1937 was estimated by linear interpolation. From 1947, building credit institutions are included.

Industrial credit institutions: For 1915–37, the figures were obtained by summing the balance sheet totals of the following institutions: Consorzio sovvenzioni su valori industriali, Istituto di credito alle opere pubbliche, Istituto di credito per le opere di pubblica utilità and Istituto mobiliare italiano. For 1938–46, Banca d'Italia Servizio Studi, *Bollettino*, March–June 1950, no. 3–6, Table LIII (total net of the portfolio rediscounted by Consorzio sovvenzioni su valori industriali with the Bank of Italy as shown in ibid., Table IX). For 1947–60, Banca d'Italia, *Bollettino*, January–February 1961, no. 1, Table 29. For 1961–73, Banca d'Italia, *Bollettino*, various issues (tables on the balance sheet situation of the industrial and public-works credit institutions).

Insurance institutions: For 1870–1911, estimates obtained by graphical interpolation on the basis of the ten-year averages published in Istat, *Sommario di statistiche storiche dell'Italia 1861–1975*, Table 124. The figure for 1912 was obtained by increasing that for 1911 by 20 per cent. For 1913–51, the values are the sum of the mathematical reserves constituted by: (1) private insurance companies, for 1915–38 from Associazione fra le Società Italiane per Azioni, *Notizie statistiche sulle società italiane per azioni* (Rome) 1925, p. 152; 1922, p. CX; 1937, pp. 194 and 251; and for 1946–51 from Istat, *Annuario statistico*, various years; (2) Istituto Nazionale delle Assicurazioni, for 1913–29 from *Piccolo annuario statistico* (1925 and 1930) and for 1930–51 from Istat, *Annuario statistico*, various years; (3) Istituto Nazionale della Previdenza Sociale, for 1913–52 from Istat, *Annuario statistico*, various years (up to 1937 total liabilities were used instead of mathematical reserves). The figures for 1939–45 were estimated by assuming an annual increase of 20 per cent. The figures for 1953–64 were obtained by adding to that for 1952 the changes in the non-state sector's claims on the insurance institutions, reproduced in M. Caron and F. Cotula, 'I conti finanziari dell'Italia', Banca d'Italia, *Bollettino*, November–December 1971, Table 3, pp. 914–15. For 1965–70, M. Caron and F. Cotula, *op. cit.*, Tables 3–8 (mathematical reserves of the insurance and social security institutions). For 1971, Banca d'Italia, *Relazione annuale per il 1972* (Rome, 1973), Appendix, Table a103, pp. 124–5 (mathematical reserves of the insurance and social security institutions).

Table 7 Balance sheet assets by category of financial intermediary: percentage shares of the total for all intermediaries in Italy (I) and the developed countries (DC)

	1		2		3		4		5	
	Central banks		Commercial banks		Savings institutions		Insurance institutions		Other	
	I	DC	I	DC	I	DC	I	DC	I	DC
1880	27	13	16	46	50	16	1	7	6	18
1900	23	9	13	42	52	20	2	11	10	19
1913	18	7	19	43	52	19	4	14	6	18
1929	15	9	36	40	36	20	7	16	6	16
1938	12	11	28	30	37	20	11	22	12	17
1948	28	19	38	35	26	18	3	19	6	10
1957	16	13	36	32	30	19	5	24	13	13
1967	11	9	35	33	28	19	5	23	21	16
1973	10	..	39	..	24	..	4	..	23	..

Sources: For Italy, Table 6; for the developed countries, R. W. Goldsmith, 'Some Reflections on the Past, Present and Future of Financial Institutions', Table 3, p. 90.

Table 8 Balance sheet assets of the various categories of bank: percentage shares of the total for the banking system

	Banks of issue	Ordinary credit banks	Banking firms	Public-law banks	Banks of national interest	Savings banks	Deposits and Loans Fund	Pledge banks	Cooper-ative banks	Rural and artisans' banks
1870	68.1	11.0	..	—	—	18.5	..	..	2.4	—
1880	29.4	16.6	..	—	—	17.1	31.5	..	5.4	—
1890	31.0	19.8	..	—	—	20.5	19.7	..	9.0	..
1900	26.2	14.9	..	—	—	22.8	25.8	1.8	8.5	..
1910	22.2	18.3	..	—	—	20.9	24.6	1.8	11.5	0.7
1920	33.4	31.3	..	—	—	11.3	15.1	0.9	7.6	0.4
1930	16.6	34.4	1.5	4.5	—	17.3	16.6	1.2	6.8	1.1
1936	15.8	23.8	0.8	9.8	—	18.1	25.3	0.8	5.0	0.6
1938	16.1	8.3	0.8	11.2	15.6	15.2	27.5	..	4.5	0.8
1950	27.7	11.0	..	14.7	13.8	10.1	17.1	..	5.3	0.3
1960	16.9	14.5	..	16.5	14.9	14.6	14.8	..	7.2	0.6
1970	14.0	15.8	..	17.7	16.9	16.8	10.8	..	7.0	1.0

Source: Table 6.

Table 9 Balance sheet assets of the 'mixed banks' (millions of lire and percentages)

	Banca commerciale italiana	Credito italiano	Banca italiana di sconto	Banco di Roma	Total of the 4 banks	% share of total assets of financial inter-mediaries	% share of total assets of the banking system
1895	78.7	49.8	2.6	3.7	134.8	1.6	1.9
1896	81.9	48.6	3.1	4.5	138.2	1.7	1.9
1897	141.8	59.4	3.4	5.2	209.9	2.5	2.9
1898	175.2	83.4	4.3	10.7	273.6	3.2	3.6
1899	204.8	108.6	22.4	27.0	362.8	4.1	4.7
1900	261.3	124.8	26.8	27.3	440.1	4.8	5.5
1901	315.1	150.2	29.7	34.8	529.8	5.6	6.3
1902	306.2	142.8	34.4	47.5	538.8	5.5	6.3
1903	431.3	202.7	47.1	55.6	736.8	7.0	7.9
1904	498.3	251.1	85.0	72.4	906.8	8.1	9.1
1905	599.6	267.8	140.1	133.9	1,141.4	9.4	10.4
1906	668.0	329.6	204.6	153.6	1,355.8	10.7	11.8
1907	727.9	396.0	189.1	157.1	1,470.1	10.9	12.0
1908	753.6	435.9	168.7	185.2	1,543.4	10.9	11.9
1909	776.2	470.2	201.9	266.3	1,714.6	11.5	12.5
1910	812.6	509.2	221.4	357.4	1,900.6	11.9	13.0
1911	921.9	561.9	264.3	497.7	2,245.8	13.5	14.8
1912	1,092.7	601.0	322.7	532.7	2,549.1	14.7	16.3
1913	1,186.7	667.5	373.6	535.8	2,763.6	15.4	17.1
1914	1,101.9	633.7	368.2	413.1	2,516.9	13.0	14.5
1915	1,136.5	813.8	468.5	327.7	2,746.5	12.6	14.1
1916	1,672.0	1,310.9	868.9	378.8	4,230.4	16.7	18.2
1917	2,515.8	1,937.2	1,469.5	598.5	6,520.9	18.0	19.2
1918	3,346.0	2,682.2	2,578.8	924.8	9,531.8	21.1	22.3
1919	5,030.6	4,026.5	4,315.5	2,410.6	15,786.3	25.2	26.2
1920	6,847.6	5,070.6	5,842.7	3,248.7	21,009.6	27.0	28.2
1921	7,383.2	5,288.7	..	4,067.2	16,739.2	18.8	19.8
1922	7,118.2	4,811.8	..	3,963.2	15,893.1	17.3	18.4
1923	7,676.5	5,082.5	643.4	2,279.0	15,681.4	15.8	16.8
1924	8,650.6	6,085.1	..	2,586.4	17,322.1	15.5	16.6
1925	9,582.3	6,374.7	2,157.6	2,444.6	20,559.2	16.6	17.9

Sources: For the four banks, U. Bava, *I quattro maggiori istituti italiani di credito*, annexes, balance sheets, sum of the assets. The shares refer to the figures in Table 6, columns 11 and 17 respectively.

Table 10 Indicators of banking concentration

	Savings banks		Banks of issue and commercial banks		Cooperative banks		Banking system		
	H	G	H	G	H	G	H	G	T
	(1)	(2)	(3)	(4)	(5)	(6)	(7)	(8)	(9)
1840	0.24	—	—	—	—	—	—	—	—
1850	0.23	—	—	—	—	—	—	—	—
1860	0.33	—	—	—	—	—	—	—	—
1870	0.33	0.88	0.21	0.86	0.11	0.73	0.16	0.90	—
1880	0.21	0.87	0.15	0.86	0.09	0.79	0.08	0.89	—
1886	0.21	0.89	0.11	0.86	0.04	0.80	0.06	0.86	—
1900	0.17	—	—	—	—	—	—	—	—
1910	0.12	0.86	0.24	0.83	0.08	0.56	0.10	0.88	—
1913	—	—	—	—	—	—	—	—	—
1919	—	—	—	—	—	—	—	—	—
1921	0.07	0.84	0.20	0.89	0.11	0.56	0.13	0.89	—
1925	0.07	—	—	—	—	—	—	—	—
1930	0.08	0.74	0.16	0.90	0.18	0.67	0.09	0.86	—
1936	0.09	0.74	0.10	0.85	0.27	0.72	0.05	0.81	—
1940	0.09	—	—	—	—	—	—	—	—
1951	0.07	0.67	0.08	0.87	0.20	0.84	0.04	0.86	—
1957	0.07	0.67	0.07	0.85	0.18	0.82	0.03	0.85	—
1958	—	—	—	—	—	—	—	—	1.69
1962	0.06	0.65	0.06	0.83	0.14	0.78	0.03	0.81	—
1967	0.06	0.64	0.06	0.83	0.10	0.74	0.03	0.81	—
1968	—	—	—	—	—	—	—	—	1.51
1971	0.05	0.63	0.06	0.82	0.09	0.71	0.03	0.82	—
1972	—	—	—	—	—	—	—	—	1.40

H = Herfindahl index
G = Gini index
T = Theil index

Methodology and Sources:
Savings banks: The H and G indices refer to the entire population of savings banks. For 1840–1900 the indices are calculated from the sum of the loans and capital and reserves of every bank, taken from Ministero di Agricoltura, Industria e Commercio (1906), *Le casse di risparmio ordinarie in Italia dal 1822 al 1904*, Rome: Bertero. Subsequently, the indices are calculated from total assets, taken from Ministero di Agricoltura, Industria e Commercio, *Bollettino semestrale delle casse di risparmio* for 1910–30 and from Ispettorato per la difesa del risparmio e l'esercizio del credito, *Bollettino delle casse di risparmio ordinarie e dei monti di pegno di I^{a} categoria* for 1936 and 1940. Finally, the indices for the years from 1951 onwards are based on the sum of deposits (of customers

and special credit institutions), funds managed for government bodies, and capital and reserves, taken from financial statements (averages of quarterly data).

Banks of issue and commercial banks: The H and G indices refer to the banks of issue – included until 1930 – and only those ordinary credit banks for which figures on the volume of business could be found. The representativeness of the latter sample in relation to the total category in Table 7 ranges from between 80 per cent (1910) to nearly 100 per cent (1880), with reference to the measure of the volume of business used to calculate the indices. This consists of the total of balance sheet assets to 1936 and subsequently of the sum of deposits of customers and special credit institutions, funds managed for government bodies and capital and reserves. The figures for the banks of issue are from R. De Mattia, *op. cit.*, Table 2, 'Totale generale al netto dei conti d'ordine'. The figures for the ordinary credit banks were derived from the following: for 1870, from Ministero di Agricoltura, Industria e Commercio, *Bollettino delle situazioni mensili dei conti*; for 1880, from *Id., Bollettino bimestrale della situazione dei conti delle banche popolari, delle società di credito ordinario, delle società e istituti di credito agrario, degli istituti di credito fondiario;* for 1886, from *Id., Bollettino semestrale del credito cooperativo, ordinario, agrario e fondiario;* for 1910–30, from Credito italiano (subsequently, Associazione fra le Società italiane per Azioni), *Notizie statistiche sulle società italiane per azioni,* various volumes; for 1936, from Ispettorato per la difesa del risparmio e l'esercizio del credito, *Supplemento bimestrale al bollettino. Situazioni al 31.12.1936*; for subsequent years, from financial statements. The present public-law banks are included among the ordinary credit banks from 1930 onwards; the pertinent figures were taken from Associazione fra le Società italiane per Azioni, *op. cit.*, up to 1936 and thereafter from financial statements.

Cooperative banks: The H and G indices only refer to banks for which data on the volume of business could be found. The items considered and sources are the same as those used for the ordinary credit banks. The representativeness of the sample in respect of the total category in Table 7 ranges from 45 per cent in 1910 to nearly 100 per cent in 1880.

Banking system: The H and G indices refer to the aggregate consisting of savings banks, banks of issue, commercial banks and cooperative banks indicated above. The representativeness of the aggregate ranges from 80 per cent (1910) to nearly 100 per cent (1880) in relation to the total assets of those categories of bank as shown in Table 7, and from 60 per cent (1910) to 90 per cent (1871) in relation to the assets of the entire banking system as shown in Table 7. The values of these ratios are of course affected by the sometimes imperfect fit between the items that make up the aggregate of the denominator and those included in the numerator. The Theil indices refer to the broader aggregate consisting of the banks surveyed by the Bank of Italy and are taken from P. Ciocca, C.A. Giussani and G. Lanciotti, *op. cit.*, Table 2, p. 17.

Table 11 The structure of the financial intermediaries in Italy

	1912	1920	1926	1936	1951	1961	1971
1. Banks	3,408	3,601	4,657	2,042	1,230	1,257	1,152
2. Branches	4,227	6,012	11,444	7,656	7,814	9,252	10,892
3. Towns and cities served by banks	..	..	5,000	3,920	4,083	4,655	5,320
4. Staff	47,095	64,139	92,919	68,418	108,778	142,332	190,786
5. Branches per bank (5=2:1)	1.2	1.7	2.5	3.7	6.3	7.4	9.5

Average annual % changes	1920/1912	1926/1920	1936/1926	1951/1936	1961/1951	1971/1961
6. Total intermediation (a) per employee	–5.3	1.6	16.4	–3.7	22.6	13.9
7. Bank intermediation (a) per bank	–2.5	2.9	30.0	2.0	26.9	22.1
8. Bank intermediation (b) per branch	–5.2	–3.2	15.9	–1.7	22.4	15.0

(a) As in Table 6, column 17, in 1913 lire (Istat series of wholesale prices).
(b) As in Table 6, column 11, in 1913 lire (Istat series of wholesale prices).

Sources:
Banks: For 1912 and 1920, the data were obtained by integrating the number of banks given in R. De Mattia, *I bilanci,* Table 22, with the number of banking firms derived from Associazione Bancaria Italiana, *Annuario di banche e banchieri,* (Rome, 1921–22); the figure for 1926 was also taken from R. De Mattia, *I bilanci.* The figures for 1936 onwards are from Banca d'Italia (1977), *Struttura funzionale e territoriale del sistema bancario italiano (1936–1974)*, Rome, Table 1.

Branches: For 1912 and 1920 the figures were obtained as follows: (1) *Ordinary credit banks*: the number of branches of the four major Italian banks, from R. Bachi (1920–22), *L'Italia economica per gli anni 1919–1920–1921*, Città di Castello: Lapi, increased by the number of branches of the other ordinary credit banks given in Credito Italiano, *Notizie statistiche sulle società italiane per azioni* for 1912 and 1920 and by the number of banks not included therein, which were assumed to be unit banks; (2) *Banking firms:* Associazione Bancaria Italiana, *op. cit.,* which gives the date when banks were established but not the date of branch openings. It was assumed that all branches in operation in 1920 existed in 1912. The resulting overestimation is partly offset by not considering banks that went out of business between 1912 and 1920; in any case, its effect on the total number of branches is marginal; (3) *Cooperative banks*: A. Marchesini (1957), *Considerazioni sulla distribuzione degli sportelli bancari in Italia con particolare riguardo alle banche popolari*, Luino: Cerutti & Pozzi. The figures for the first two years indicated in the table refer respectively to 1908 and 1921; (4) *Savings banks:* the number of savings banks increased by the number of branches of Cassa di Risparmio delle Provincie Lombarde, Casse di Risparmio Vittorio Emanuele delle Provincie Siciliane, Cassa di Risparmio di Verona, Vicenza e Belluno and Cassa di Risparmio della Provincia di Macerata taken, respectively, from *La Cassa di Risparmio delle Provincie Lombarde nella evoluzione economica della regione, 1823–1923* (Milan: Alfieri e Lacroix, 1923), Casse di Risparmio Vittorio Emanuele per le Provincie Siciliane, *La Cassa Centrale di Risparmio Vittorio Emanuele per le Provincie Siciliane, 1861–1971* (Palermo, 1973), Cassa di Risparmio di Verona, Vicenza, Belluno, *La Cassa di Risparmio di Verona, Vicenza, Belluno nella prima metà del XX secolo* (Verona, 1956), and Cassa di Risparmio della Provincia di Macerata, *La Cassa di Risparmio della Provincia di Macerata nel CXXV anniversario della sua fondazione, 1844–1969* (Macerata, 1970); (5) *Other categories*: the number of pledge banks and rural banks in R. De Mattia, *I bilanci.* The figure for 1926 was obtained by increasing the number of branches shown in Associazione Bancaria Italiana, *op. cit.*, by the number of banks not considered therein. For 1951–71 the data are from Banca d'Italia, *op. cit.*, Table 4.

Towns and cities served by banks: The figure for 1926 was assumed to be equal to that estimated for 1927 by M. Mazzantini in the monograph, 'Alcune indagini statistiche sull'organizzazione bancaria italiana', published in 1946 as an annex in Ministero per la Costituente, *Rapporto della Commissione Economica* (Rome: Istituto Poligrafico dello Stato). The figures from 1936 onwards are from Banca d'Italia, *op. cit.*, Table 4.

Staff: The figures for 1912–61 are from O. Vitali, *Aspetti dello sviluppo economico italiano alla luce della ricostruzione della popolazione attiva* (Rome, 1970), Table 1. The figure for 1971 is from Istat, *V Censimento generale dell'industria e del Commercio 25.10.1971,* Vol. VI, *Credito, assicurazione, imprese finanziarie di controllo e gestioni esattoriali* (Rome, 1976), Table 2, p. 3.

Table 12 Bank rates and their percentage coefficients of variation

	Savings banks						Difference between loan and deposit rates	Difference between bill portfolio and deposit rates	Lending rate
	Deposits		Bill portfolio		Loans				
	Rate	Coefficient	Rate	Coefficient	Rate	Coefficient			
1861	3.77	9.9	..	..	..	..	..	..	..
1862	3.77	9.8	..	..	..	..	..	..	..
1863	3.77	9.8	..	..	..	..	..	..	..
1864	4.07	4.9	..	..	..	..	..	..	..
1865	4.12	6.9	..	..	..	..	..	..	..
1866	4.13	7.0	..	..	..	..	..	..	..
1867	4.15	7.5	..	..	..	..	..	..	..
1868	4.15	7.1	..	..	..	..	..	..	..
1869	4.15	7.3	..	..	..	..	..	..	..
1870	4.14	7.2	..	..	..	..	..	..	..
1871	4.18	8.3	..	..	..	..	..	..	..
1872	3.95	12.7	..	..	..	..	..	..	..
1873	3.97	13.2	..	..	..	..	..	..	..
1874	3.97	13.0	..	..	..	..	..	..	..
1875	3.91	11.4	..	..	..	..	..	..	..
1876	3.85	10.5	..	..	5.22	8.8	1.37	..	..
1877	3.82	10.4	..	..	5.23	9.5	1.41	..	..
1878	3.83	10.6	..	..	5.29	9.7	1.45	..	..
1879	3.83	10.9	..	..	5.32	9.6	1.48	..	..
1880	3.58	16.5	..	..	5.27	9.3	1.69	..	..
1881	3.58	16.0	..	..	5.25	10.5	1.66	..	..
1882	3.57	15.8	..	..	5.27	10.9	1.69	..	..
1883	3.76	10.2	..	..	5.32	11.9	1.55	..	..
1884	3.74	10.0	..	..	5.16	10.9	1.42	..	..

1885	3.70	9.2	..	..	5.13	10.5	1.43	..	..
1886	3.61	12.0	..	..	5.06	10.3	1.44	..	..
1887	3.56	10.9	..	..	5.04	10.0	1.48	..	..
1888	3.56	10.9	..	..	5.05	10.0	1.48	..	..
1889	3.55	10.7	..	..	5.05	10.0	1.49	..	..
1890	3.56	10.7	..	..	5.04	10.1	1.48	..	..
1891	3.53	10.4	..	..	5.01	9.5	1.48	..	..
1892	3.52	10.3	..	..	4.99	8.9	1.46	..	..
1893	3.51	10.2	..	..	4.98	8.8	1.46	..	..
1894	3.40	12.8	..	..	4.99	8.9	1.59	..	..
1895	3.31	11.6	..	..	4.95	8.1	1.63	..	..
1896	3.28	12.2	..	..	4.88	8.5	1.60	..	..
1897	3.25	10.7	..	..	4.82	8.9	1.57	..	..
1898	3.20	11.1	..	..	4.65	10.4	1.45	..	..
1899	3.04	13.1	..	..	4.56	10.8	1.52	..	..
1900	3.03	13.2	..	..	4.55	10.6	1.52	..	..
1901	3.03	13.0	..	..	4.51	10.3	1.48	..	..
1902	3.01	12.8	..	..	4.55	9.6	1.53	..	..
1903	2.97	12.7	..	..	4.51	9.0	1.54	..	..
1904	2.93	11.2	..	..	4.45	8.7	1.52	..	..
1905	2.90	10.3	..	..	4.44	8.3	1.54	..	..
1906	2.87	9.4	5.03	13.5	4.41	7.9	1.53	2.15	..
1907	2.86	8.3	4.92	12.1	4.40	7.1	1.54	2.05	..
1908	2.86	8.1	4.77	12.9	4.39	7.1	1.53	1.91	..
1909	2.86	8.1	4.67	14.9	4.37	7.1	1.50	1.81	..
1910	2.87	8.4	4.69	14.6	4.37	7.1	1.49	2.01	..
1911	2.89	8.5	5.05	15.6	4.48	7.0	1.59	2.16	..
1912	2.95	10.5	5.52	12.6	4.47	7.5	1.51	2.57	..
1913	2.94	10.0	5.51	11.3	4.55	8.0	1.60	2.56	..
1914	2.94	9.9	5.77	11.9	4.62	9.7	1.68	2.82	..
1915	2.97	10.4	5.73	15.2	4.67	10.1	1.70	2.75	..
1916	2.97	10.0	5.49	13.9	4.69	9.9	1.72	2.52	..

Table 12 *continued*

	Savings banks						Difference between loan and deposit rates	Difference between bill portfolio and deposit rates	Lending rate
	Deposits		Bill portfolio		Loans				
	Rate	Coefficient	Rate	Coefficient	Rate	Coefficient			
1917	2.96	10.1	5.64	11.4	4.73	9.1	1.77	2.67	..
1918	2.96	9.5	5.64	10.9	4.72	10.6	1.76	2.68	..
1919	3.28	11.8	5.67	9.1	4.77	10.6	1.49	2.38	5.00
1920	3.10	11.8	6.60	8.1	5.00	12.0	1.90	3.50	6.06
1921	3.02	12.6	6.91	7.7	5.32	14.6	2.29	3.88	6.29
1922	3.02	13.2	6.78	8.2	5.41	16.4	2.38	3.75	5.71
1923	3.05	13.6	6.79	8.9	5.60	13.8	2.54	3.74	5.30
1924	3.04	13.5	6.73	8.7	5.63	13.9	2.58	3.68	5.15
1925	3.20	13.9	7.59	7.2	5.98	13.4	2.77	4.39	8.29
1926	3.27	14.5	8.00	9.5	6.26	13.6	2.98	4.72	8.00
1927	3.35	14.0	7.50	10.0	5.70	13.0	2.35	4.15	7.49
1928	3.35	13.0	7.00	11.0	5.20	12.0	1.85	3.65	5.48
1929	3.50	12.0	8.00	12.0	6.40	11.0	2.90	4.50	6.64
1930	3.20	11.2	7.25	14.3	6.60	10.5	3.40	4.04	5.82
1931	3.17	9.4	7.48	8.3	6.66	9.8	3.49	4.31	5.67
1932	2.89	8.3	6.79	19.6	6.37	11.6	3.48	3.90	5.53
1933	2.66	9.1	6.40	17.1	6.03	11.0	3.37	3.73	4.08
1934	2.45	9.0	6.37	14.0	5.85	10.0	3.40	3.92	3.34
1935	2.39	9.2	6.34	11.3	5.78	8.8	3.39	3.95	4.25
1936	2.33	6.8	6.45	12.0	5.81	9.4	3.47	4.12	4.75
1937	2.32	6.5	6.55	10.2	5.80	9.8	3.47	4.23	5.25
1938	2.32	6.9	6.55	10.2	5.88	9.1	3.56	4.23	5.25
1939	2.31	6.3	6.51	10.9	5.83	9.5	3.52	4.20	..
1940	2.33	6.6	6.69	8.7	5.85	9.9	3.51	4.35	..

Table 12 *continued*

	Ordinary credit banks				Difference between lending and deposit rates	Cooperative banks				Difference between lending and deposit rates
	Deposits		Bill portfolio			Deposits		Bill portfolio		
	Rate	Coefficient	Rate	Coefficient		Rate	Coefficient	Rate	Coefficient	
1871	3.41	15.6	5.87	12.1	2.46	3.91	12.4	5.98	9.8	2.07
1872	3.35	12.6	6.02	7.2	2.67	3.76	13.9	5.79	8.1	2.03
1873	3.50	15.2	6.86	13.7	3.36	3.96	13.0	6.47	13.3	2.51
1874	3.42	18.4	6.30	12.0	2.88	3.78	11.7	5.99	9.4	2.21
1875	3.32	19.3	6.24	10.5	2.92	3.54	17.6	5.92	9.2	2.38
1876	3.04	27.5	6.10	9.7	3.06	3.57	16.6	5.73	11.3	2.16
1877	3.21	29.6	6.06	9.1	2.85	3.72	13.3	5.76	11.8	2.04
1878	3.26	27.5	5.99	10.9	2.73	3.64	12.5	5.59	14.5	1.95
1879	3.39	30.8	5.85	13.1	2.46	3.55	16.7	5.62	14.1	2.07
1880	3.32	25.0	5.80	14.3	2.48	3.38	17.7	5.63	13.9	2.25
1881	3.54	22.6	5.85	12.1	2.31	3.47	14.9	5.69	14.1	2.22
1882	3.62	13.1	6.11	9.2	2.49	3.61	13.3	5.93	11.3	2.32
1883	3.38	15.2	6.15	10.3	2.77	3.65	11.1	5.97	12.3	2.32
1884	3.18	18.7	5.82	10.8	2.64	3.54	12.6	5.95	12.9	2.41
1885	3.27	15.9	5.86	10.4	2.59	3.59	13.8	5.96	13.7	2.37
1886	3.18	14.8	5.99	9.9	2.81	3.47	15.0	6.01	14.5	2.54

Methodology and sources:

The *deposit rates* and short-term *lending rates* (bill portfolio) of the cooperative banks, ordinary credit banks and savings banks and long-term lending rates (loans) of the savings banks are averages of the rates applied by the individual banks weighted by the values of the corresponding balance sheet items (respectively deposits, bill portfolio and loans) at the end of each year, with the exception of the deposit rates of the savings banks to 1904, for which the amount of deposits was held constant during each ten-year period at the level recorded at the end of that period. Where a bank changed its rates during the year, an average annual rate weighted by the number of months was calculated.

For *ordinary credit banks* and *cooperative banks,* the figures are from Ministero di Agricoltura, Industria e Commercio, *Bollettino delle situazioni mensili dei conti* (from 1875, *Bollettino bimestrale delle situazioni dei conti delle banche popolari, delle società di credito ordinario, delle società e istituti di credito agrario, degli istituti di credito fondiario;* from 1883, *Bollettino semestrale del credito cooperativo, ordinario, agrario e fondiario).*

For *savings banks,* the figures for 1861–1905 are from Ministero di Agricoltura, Industria e Commercio, *Le Casse di Risparmio, op.* cit.; for 1906–35, from Ministero di Agricoltura, Industria e Commercio, *Bollettino semestrale delle Casse di Risparmio ordinario;* for 1936–40, from Ispettorato per la difesa del risparmio e per l'esercizio del credito, *Bollettino delle Casse di risparmio ordinarie e dei Monti di pegno di l^a cargoria.*

The *lending rate* is an average annual of the monthly rates published for the years 1919–29 in Comitato per gli indici del movimento economico italiano, *L'economia italiana dal 1919 al 1929,* Table III, no. 13, and for 1929–35 in Istat, *Bollettino mensile.* For 1936–38 the rate is an average of the minimum and maximum rates applied for discounting commercial paper in Milan, taken from Consiglio provinciale delle Corporazioni di Milano, *Compendio statistico per la provincia di Milano,* 1938, Table XVI, p. 112.

The coefficient of variation is the percentage ratio between the mean square deviation and the average interest rates of the various branches in each year.

Table 13 Regional variance of savings bank lending rates

1876

Variance { a) within regions = 0.295; b) between regions = 1.682 }

$n_1 = 12; n_2 = 67$

$$F = \frac{1.682}{0.295} = 5.7; \quad F_{.05} = 1.9; \quad F_{.01} = 2.5$$

1890

Variance { a) within regions = 0.360; b) between regions = 3.628 }

$n_1 = 14; n_2 = 105$

$$F = \frac{3.682}{0.360} = 10.1; \quad F_{.05} = 1.8; \quad F_{.01} = 2.2$$

1910

Variance { a) within regions = 0.402; b) between regions = 3.441 }

$n_1 = 13; n_2 = 132$

$$F = \frac{3.441}{0.402} = 8.6; \quad F_{.05} = 1.8; \quad F_{.01} = 2.3$$

1930

Variance { a) within regions = 0.842; b) between regions = 1.244 }

$n_1 = 13; n_2 = 74$

$$F = \frac{1.244}{0.842} = 1.5; \quad F_{.05} = 1.8; \quad F_{.01} = 2.4$$

Methodology and sources: For the notation and methodology used, see D.B. Suits (1963), *Statistics: An Introduction to Quantitative Economic Research*, Chicago: Rand McNally, ch. VI. The data are from the same sources as cited in the notes to Table 12.

Table 14 Money market rates

	Official discount rate	Rate on postal deposits		Official discount rate	Rate on postal deposits
1861	5.35	..	1900	4.92	2.88
1862	5.08	..	1901	4.83	2.82
1863	5.71	..	1902	4.77	2.76
1864	7.87	..	1903	4.56	2.76
1865	5.42	..	1904	4.45	2.76
1866	6.08	..	1905	4.45	2.76
1867	5.29	..	1906	4.62	2.64
1868	5.00	..	1907	4.95	2.64
1869	5.00	..	1908	4.50	2.64
1870	5.08	..	1909	4.34	2.64
1871	5.00	..	1910	4.62	2.64
1872	5.00	..	1911	4.94	2.64
1873	5.00	..	1912	5.47	2.64
1874	5.00	..	1913	5.47	2.64
1875	5.00	..	1914	5.42	2.64
1876	5.00	3.00	1915	5.35	2.64
1877	5.00	3.00	1916	5.02	2.64
1878	4.92	3.00	1917	4.86	2.64
1879	4.50	3.50	1918	5.04	2.70
1880	4.50	3.50	1919	4.97	2.64
1881	4.58	3.50	1920	5.69	2.64
1882	5.00	3.50	1921	5.83	2.64
1883	5.00	3.50	1922	5.55	2.64
1884	4.46	3.50	1923	4.95	2.64
1885	5.08	3.50	1924	5.29	2.64
1886	4.75	3.50	1925	6.44	2.64
1887	5.50	3.25	1926	6.83	2.64
1888	5.50	3.25	1927	6.78	2.64
1889	5.25	3.25	1928	5.59	3.00
1890	6.00	3.25	1929	6.55	3.00
1891	5.83	3.25	1930	5.91	3.00
1892	5.21	3.25	1931	5.73	3.00
1893	5.25	3.25	1932	5.33	3.00
1894	5.71	3.25	1933	3.87	2.76
1895	5.00	3.12	1934	3.10	..
1896	4.65	3.00	1935	4.16	..
1897	4.42	3.00	1936	4.69	..
1898	4.20	2.88	1937	4.50	..
1899	4.42	2.88	1938	4.50	4.16

Table 14 continued

	Official discount rate	Rate on postal deposits		Official discount rate	Rate on postal deposits
1939	4.50	4.22	1956	4.00	3.20
1940	4.50	4.25	1957	4.00	3.19
1941	4.50	4.26	1958	3.72	3.15
1942	4.50	4.14	1959	3.50	3.21
1943	4.50	3.97	1960	3.50	3.21
1944	4.40	4.19	1961	3.50	3.21
1945	4.00	4.09	1962	3.50	3.20
1946	4.00	4.04	1963	3.50	3.00
1947	4.40	4.07	1964	3.50	3.03
1948	5.50	4.18	1965	3.50	2.93
1949	4.77	3.84	1966	3.50	3.09
1950	4.15	3.84	1967	3.50	3.13
1951	4.00	3.82	1968	3.50	3.13
1952	4.00	3.82	1969	4.34	3.05
1953	4.00	3.67	1970	6.57	3.64
1954	4.00	3.26	1971	6.40	3.96
1955	4.00	3.24	1972	4.63	4.11

Sources:
Official discount rate: For 1861–96, annual averages of the average of monthly minimum and maximum rates, from R. De Mattia, *op. cit.,* Table 10; for 1897–1936, see Banca d'Italia, *Relazione annuale*, various years, averages of the various rates applied during the year, weighted by the amount of discounts granted; for 1938–72, average of the rates in effect during the year weighted by the months in which they were in effect, from Banca d'Italia, *Bollettino*, November–December 1958, no. 6, Table 13 up to 1958 and, subsequently, Banca d'Italia, *Bollettino,* January–February 1974, no. 1, Table 59.

Rate on postal deposits: For 1876–1905, see Ministero di Agricoltura, Industria e Commercio, *Le Casse di Risparmio in Italia dal 1822 al 1904, op. cit.*; for 1906–33, simple averages of the rates applied on the various categories of postal deposit and published in the *Gazzetta Ufficiale* of the Kingdom of Italy; for 1938–72, averages of the rates applied on the various categories of postal deposit, weighted by the relative size of each category of deposit; see Banca d'Italia, *Bollettino,* November–December 1958, no. 6, Table 13, and January–February 1974, no. 1, Table 59, for the rates, and Banca d'Italia, *Bollettino,* various issues (tables on deposits with banks and the postal administration) for the weights (in particular, the series from 1938 onwards is given in *Bollettino,* 1958, no. 1, Table 15).

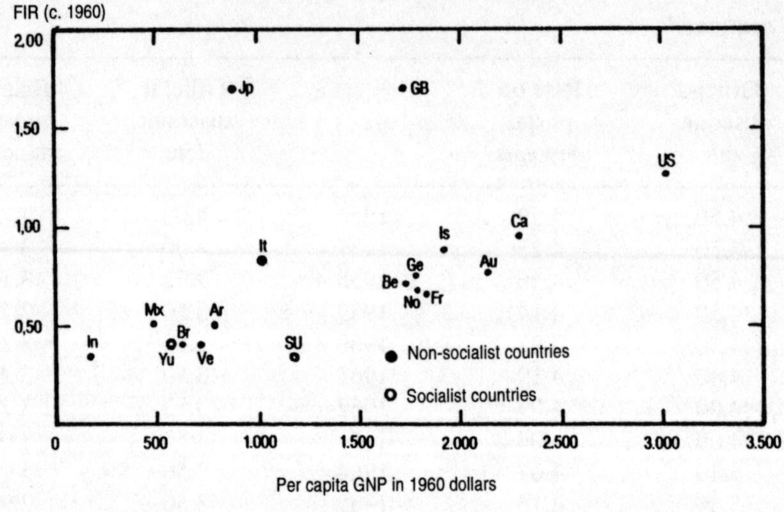

Source: R.W. Goldsmith, *Financial Structure and Development*, p. 374. The figure of FIR for Italy (0.81) is from our Table 2 and is consideraly lower than that originally estimated by Goldsmith (1.06).

Figure 1 FIR and the level of development in 18 countries (1963)

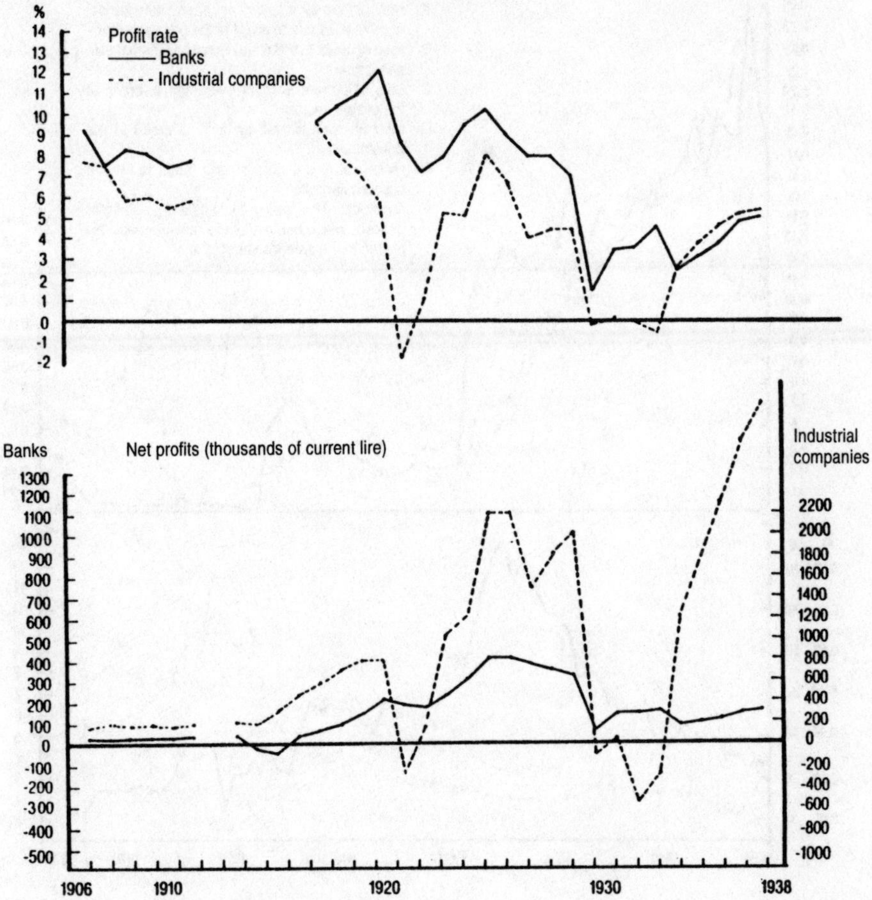

Source: Credito Italiano (subsequently Associazione fra le Società Italiane per Azioni), *op. cit.*

Figure 2 Bank and industrial profits

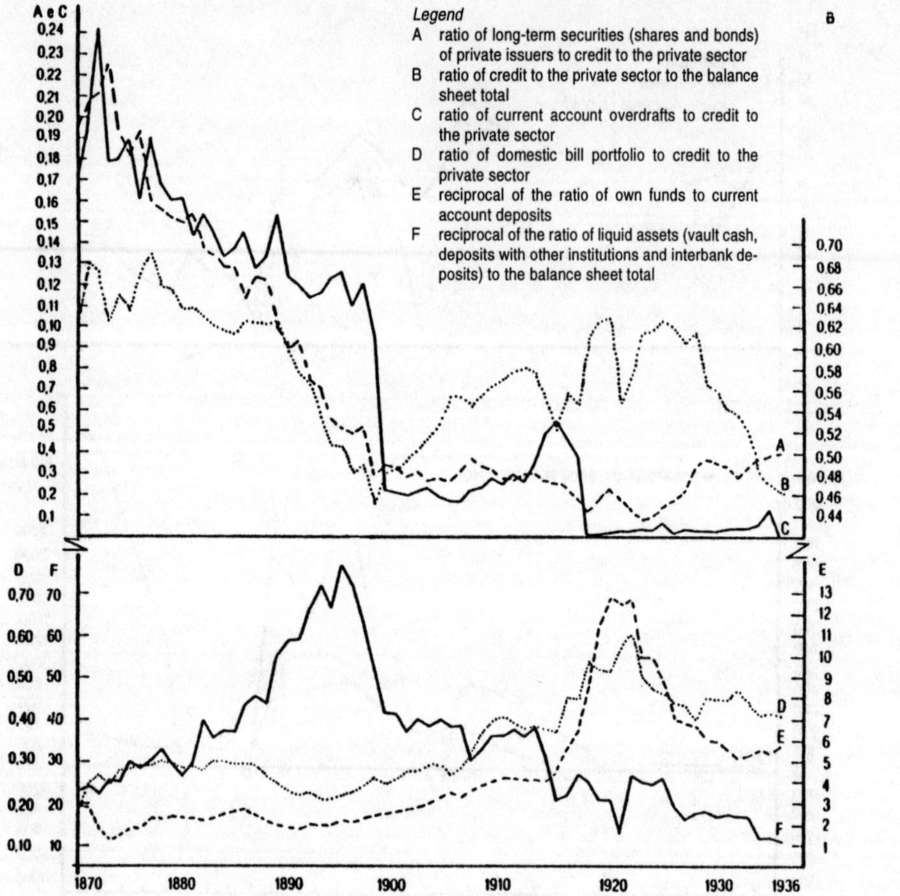

Source: R. De Mattia (ed.), *I bilanci degli istituti di emissione italiani, 1845–1936*, Tables 22 and 23.

Figure 3 Indicators of risk in the Italian banking system (excluding banks of issue)

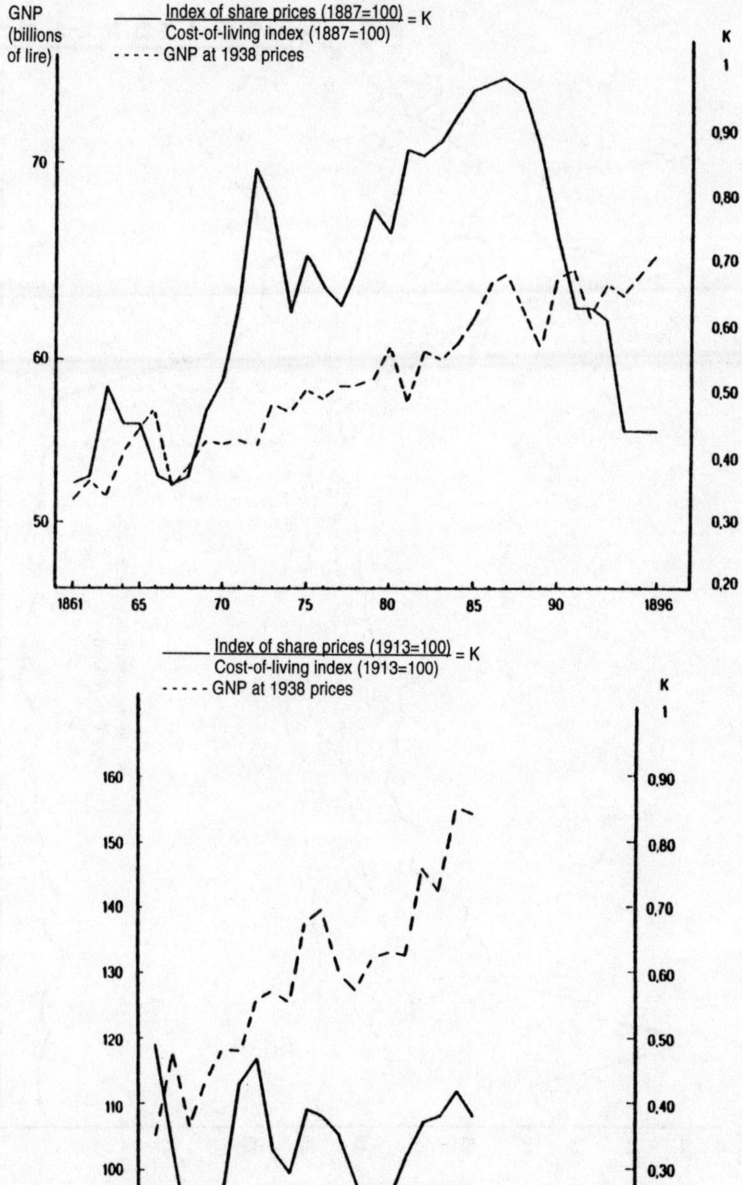

Sources: Share prices 1861–96, M. Da Pozzo and G. Felloni (1964), *La borsa valori di Genova nel secolo XIX*, Turin: ILTE, Table LXVI; share prices 1913–38, L. Rosania (1954), 'Indice del corso secco e rendimento dei titoli quotati in borsa', *Bollettino della Banca d'Italia*, November–December, Table 1, pp. 26–7; cost-of-living index and GNP, Istat.

Figure 4 Share prices and economic development in Italy

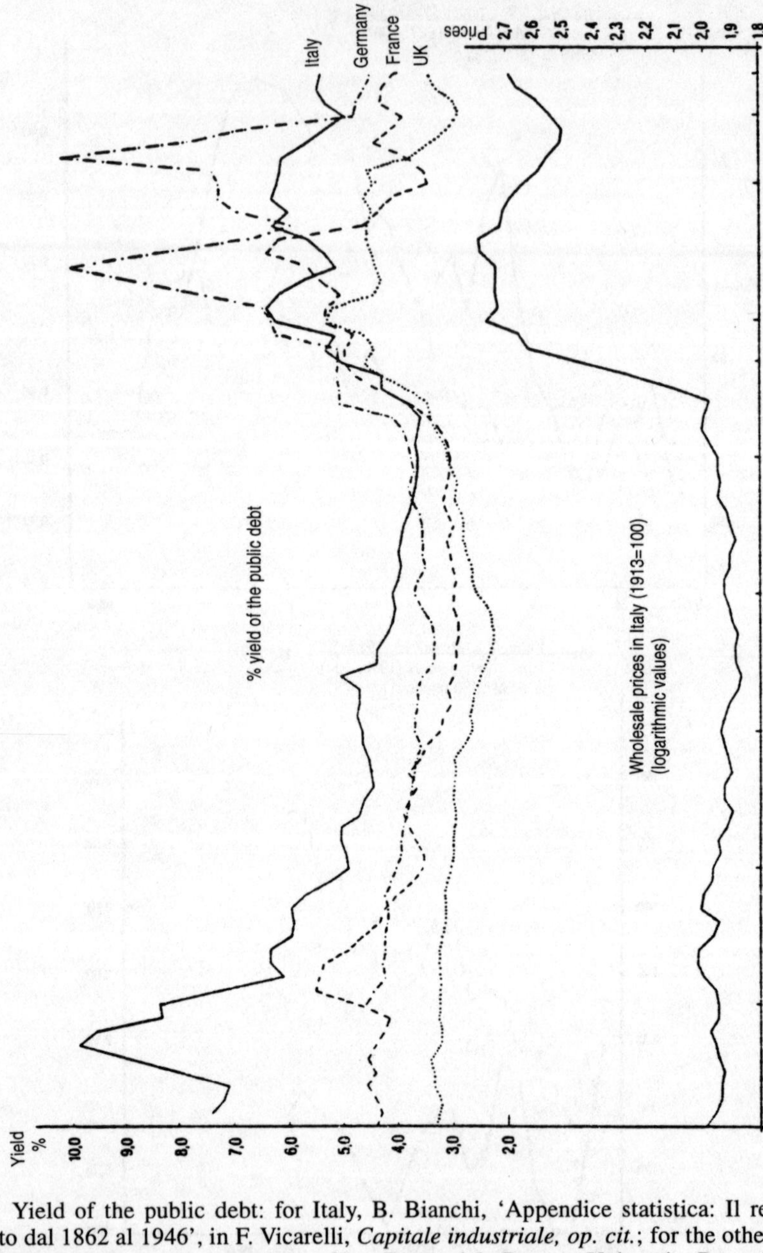

Sources: Yield of the public debt: for Italy, B. Bianchi, 'Appendice statistica: Il rendimento del consolidato dal 1862 al 1946', in F. Vicarelli, *Capitale industriale, op. cit.*; for the other countries, S. Homer (1963), *A History of Interest Rates*, New Brunswick: Rutgers University Press; UK, Table 19, p. 196 and Table 57, pp. 409–10; France, Table 25, p. 223 and Table 60, pp. 426–7; Germany, Table 32, pp. 260–61 and Table 66, p. 461. For Italian wholesale prices, Istat.

Figure 5 Yield of the public debt in Italy and other countries and level of wholesale prices in Italy

[17]

Industry and Finance in Italy, 1918-1940

Pierluigi Ciocca - Gianni Toniolo
Bank of Italy - University of Venice

The aim of the present paper is to show how the developments of the early Twenties affected subsequent events by determining new financial patterns and new relations between Finance and Industry as well as a more straightforward policy of state intervention; how, in turn, economic policies influenced industrial financing as well as the behaviour of the banking system and of the public in the various phases of the cycle; how a new organization of the financial system was created and consolidated to the point of lasting, with minor adjustments, to the present day.

Contrary to the prevailing opinion, the twenties rather than the first decade of the century seem to be the moment when the so-called "mixed banks" came to control a substantial portion of Italy's large industrial firms. The process had two phases. The first one (1922-25) was characterized by conditions particularly favourable to the "mixed banks" both in the real and in the financial markets. In the second phase (1926-29) the increase in the portfolio of industrial equities and in long-term lending was determined by the need both to avoid too rapid a fall in the market price of equities and to support industry at a time of weaker demand.

The watershed between the two phases can be identified in the deflationary demand and income policies followed to restore the gold standard at a parity of 90 lire to the pound (the so called *quota 90*).

During the Great Depression of the thirties, the objective of keeping the lira on the gold standard maintained priority. Nonetheless, increasing recourse was made to exchange control, and, on the all, monetary and fiscal variables moved in an anticyclical way. The banking system underwent significant structural changes, but succeeded in escaping a generalized liquidity and solvency crisis. This was limited to the big "mixed banks" albeit involving the central bank itself. The State had to step in on a large scale, through interventions — the creation of I.R.I. in 1933 and the new banking law in 1936 — which reshaped the relationship between Industry and Finance.

Pierluigi Ciocca - Gianni Toniolo

1. *The Main Trends of the Period*

The rate of growth of Italy's real GNP between 1921 and 1938 averaged 2.2 per cent a year. This figure is in line with the secular trend (1861-1967) but below the records of the periods of "catching-up" of this latecomer to European industrialization in the twenty odd years preceding the first World War and in those following 1945.[1] The overall performance of the Italian economy in the inter-war years was, needless to say, the result of pronounced cyclical movements; at the same time, it resulted in important changes in the composition of the real economic aggregates.

Italy's business cycles in the period 1919-1940 can be roughly described in the following way.[2] After the end of the conflict there was, as in most other European countries, a boom followed by a severe slump. Recovery began in the first months of 1922. For the following four years, to the spring of 1926, the rate of growth of Italian manufacturing production was probably the second highest in Europe; agriculture too developed quite rapidly. This short-lived but hectic boom in the first part of the twenties was followed by a slump — the severity rather than the timing of which seems to be connected with the policies pursued in order to return to the gold standard — and a slow recovery beginning early in 1928. The onset of the great depression can be dated at the end of the Summer of 1929, as in most other European countries. The slump was very serious for the industrial sector and lasted longer than elsewhere. Real recovery only began early in 1935 with rearmament for the war in Abyssinia, which produced three years of rapid growth concentrated in the heavy and import-substituting industries. A rapid sequence of slump and recovery preceded the fatal August of 1940.

Trends in production can be summarized by pointing to two phases of rapid growth (1922-26 and 1935-37) framing a decade of stagnation. The latter was, however, characterized by substantial structural changes — with increasing shares of the industrial and services sectors in GNP and of the engineering and chemical industries in manufacturing production — that were partly induced by huge movements in relative prices.

[1] The national accounts and production statistics referred to in the present paper are those produced by Giorgio Fuà's team and presented in P. ERCOLANI, "Documentazione statistica di base", in G. FUÀ (ed.), *Lo sviluppo economico italiano*, Angeli, Milano, 1969, pp. 380-460.

[2] For a description of the methods employed in assessing the turning points and for a detailed analysis of the characteristics of the individual cycles from the point of view of both "real" and financial variables, see G. TONIOLO, *L'economia dell'Italia fascista*, Laterza, Roma-Bari, 1980.

Table 1. % SHARES OF THE TOTAL BALANCE SHEET ASSETS OF THE SYSTEM OF FINANCIAL INTERMEDIARIES OF EACH CATEGORY OF INTERMEDIARY, IN ITALY (I) AND IN THE DEVELOPED COUNTRIES (DCs)

	1 Central banks		2 Commercial banks		3 Thrift institutions		4 Insurance institutions		5 Other intermediaries	
	I	DCs	I	DCs	I	DCs	I	DCs	I	DCs
1913	18	7	19	43	52	19	4	14	6	18
1929	15	9	36	40	36	20	7	16	6	16
1938	12	11	28	30	37	20	11	22	12	17
1957	16	13	36	32	30	19	5	24	13	13

% SHARES OF THE BANKING SYSTEM'S TOTAL BALANCE SHEET ASSETS OF EACH CATEGORY OF BANK

Year	Bank of issue	Ordinary credit banks	Banking houses	Public law banks	Banks of national interest	Savings banks	Post office savings banks	Pledge banks	Cooperative banks	Rural and artisans' banks
1910	22.2	18.3	..	—	—	20.9	24.6	1.8	11.5	0.7
1920	33.4	31.3	..	—	—	11.3	15.1	0.9	7.6	0.4
1930	16.6	34.4	1.5	4.5	—	17.3	16.6	1.2	6.8	1.1
1938	16.1	8.3	0.8	11.2	15.6	15.2	27.5	..	4.5	0.8
1960	16.9	14.5	..	16.5	14.9	14.6	14.8	..	7.2	0.6

Source: A.M. Biscaini Cotula - P. Ciocca, "Le strutture finanziarie: aspetti quantitativi di lungo periodo (1870-1970)", in F. Vicarelli (ed.), *Capitale industriale e capitale finanziario: il caso italiano*, Il Mulino, Bologna, 1979, tables 7 and 8, pp. 112-113.

In a secular perspective, the financial side of the Italian economy between the wars was characterized by the following main features; a) financial deepening; b) a smaller weight of intermediation, c) an important reorganization of the banking sector and of the entire system of financial intermediation. Let us briefly examine each of these points.[3]

The ratio of the stock of financial instruments to national wealth — Goldsmith's FIR — shows, as in other countries, a rising long-term trend from 0.4 in 1881 to 1 in 1971. Between 1914 and 1938 the ratio rose extremely fast (at nearly 2 per cent per year on average) even though the rate of increase in total and per capita real income in the same years was rather low. Between 1881 and 1914 and between 1938 and 1971 the average annual increase in Italy's FIR was smaller (respectively 0.7 and 1.1 per cent). Between 1914 and 1938 it was greater than the average of the major industrial countries, despite the widening of the gap between Italy's per capita income and that of the other countries.

The ratio of the intermediaries' assets to total financial assets (FIN), which also shows an upward long-term trend, rose particularly slowly in the period 1914-1938. International comparisons of flow data show, analogously, that the ratio of the intermediaries' issues to total issues was lower in Italy than in the other major countries, contrary to previous and subsequent periods.

Within the total activity of the financial intermediaries, there was a marked decline in the share of the banks of issue; a very large increase, partly offset by a sharp fall after 1928, in that of the commercial banks; a decline, during the twenties, in the weight of the thrift institutions; and an increase in the shares of the insurance institution and other non-bank intermediaries. Table 1 shows, furthermore, that the changes were more pronounced in Italy than in the other developed countries.

The aggregate changes just outlined took place mostly in the thirties as an adjustment to changes induced by the depression. However, it should be pointed out that the period 1921-25 was one of hectic banking activity (even of "wildcat" banking to some extent) characterized by a) an increasing weight of *banking* intermediation, b) a rising share of the "mixed banks", c) a very lively stock exchange market for industrial securities (one of the few such moments recorded in Italian economic history to the present day). The deflationary policies implemented to stabilize the currency and the Great Depression put an

[3] For statistics on the development of the Italian credit system in the interwar period set within the framework of longer term trends, see A.M. Biscaini Cotula and P. Ciocca, "Le strutture finanziarie: aspetti quantitativi di lungo periodo (1870-1970)", in F. Vicarelli (ed.), *Capitale industriale e capitale finanziario: il caso italiano*, Il Mulino, Bologna, 1979.

abrupt end to the wild activity of banks and, after 1930, resulted in serious liquidity problems for the most prominent of them which required resort on a large scale to central bank lending. This, in turn, opened the way to policies that brought about a major and permanent change in the structure and style both of financial intermediation and of the relations between state, banks and industry. This change considerably favoured a shift toward non-banking intermediation.

2. *The Structure of Financial Intermediation around 1920*

The role played by financial intermediaries is one of the main issues in the debate about the pattern of Italy's industrialization in the fifty odd years preceding the first world war. In Gerschenkron's view the "agents" of industrialization in Italy, given the relative backwardness of the country within Europe, can be identified in the "German" or "mixed" banks.[4] He found that it was only after the establishment of Banca Commerciale Italiana (1894) and of Credito Italiano (1895) that Italy experienced its "big spurt" of growth in manufacturing. The role of these "new" financial intermediaries seems to be crucial — according to Gerschenkron — because, following the practice of their forebearers, they were able to concentrate the scarse supply of loanable funds into key industrial sectors and firms. Furthermore, they could make the best use of entrepreneurial talents that were even scarcer than financial capital. To do this, so the story goes, they had to take a permanent stake and interest in manufacturing companies which they provided with a steady flow of funds and of which they held, in various ways, large amounts of shares.

The debate about the patterns of Italy's industrialization from 1860 to 1914 is still open and does not need to concern us here except, perhaps, for a few remarks about the financial side of the question. One could note, for instance, that the practice of "industrial banking" was very well known in Italy before the crisis of the early nineties. Banca Generale and Credito Mobiliare were "mixed banks" of the French blend of the Peréire brothers and probably quite essential in determining both the spurt in railway construction that followed the unification and the industrial "boom" of the eighties that, as Fenoaltea has rightly pointed out,[5] cannot be easily dismissed as an unimportant episode in the industrialization of the country. More relevant to the present paper, however,

[4] A. Gerschenkron, *Economic Backwardness in Historical Perspective*, Beknap Harvard, Cambridge Mass., 1962.

[5] S. Fenoaltea, "Riflessioni sull'esperienza industriale italiana dal Risorgimento alla prima guerra mondiale", in G. Toniolo (ed.), *L'economia italiana 1861-1940*, Laterza, Roma-Bari, 1978.

is the careful research of Confalonieri on the actual behaviour of the "German banks" and, particularly, of the most prominent of them, the Banca Commerciale Italiana (Comit), before world war one.[6] According to this author the role of Comit as an autonomous promoter of new industrial ventures was not a crucial one and only in the case of the electric power industry can we see a clear strategy for a deliberate intervention by the bank in a sector that promised to yield large profits. Otherwise, long-term financing of a given project was seen by the management of the Banca Commerciale as a way of establishing a permanent connection with a group of businessmen and, thus, acquiring a permanent flow of "normal" commercial operations for the bank. The latter usually underwrote new issues of industrial bonds only to sell them, at a profit, to its own clients.

In any event, while the overall importance of financial intermediation in the process of Italian industrialization before the first world war remains an open and difficult question, there seems to be little doubt that the magnitude of the industrial portfolio of the "mixed banks" throughout that period was never particularly large, probably not exceeding 10 per cent of the outstanding industrial shares. Earlier research by Bonelli[7] on the crisis of 1907 confirms this finding. This point raises the question, crucial to the present paper, of the timing of and the reasons for the acquisition of the industrial bonds that we find in such large amounts in the portfolios of the "mixed banks" in the early thirties.

Italian banking history is not well documented over the period 1915-18. It is therefore difficult to see what changes in the structure and behaviour of the banking system were induced by war finance. On purely quantitative grounds one may note that the relative importance of the "mixed banks" in total bank lending to the private sector increased from 42 to 73 per cent over the period 1914-18.[8] From a more qualitative point of view the important novelty of these years is the emergence of Banca Italiana di Sconto, the off-spring of a steelmaking and engineering concern of Genoa (Ansaldo). The novelty of this case lies in the fact that the bank was established and operated as the financial branch of an industrial enterprise.

After the war, the "mixed banks" participated intensively in the lending boom of the inflationary months that followed the armistice and they were

[6] A. Confalonieri, *Banca e industria in Italia 1894-1906*, Banca Commerciale Italiana, Milano, 3 Voll., 1974, 1975, 1976.

[7] F. Bonelli, *La crisi del 1907*, Fondazione L. Einaudi, Torino, 1971.

[8] As a proxy for the "mixed banks" we take the statistics for the Società ordinaria di credito collected and reconstructed in R. De Mattia (ed.), *I bilanci degli istituti di emissione italiani 1845-1936*, Banca d'Italia, Roma, 1967, Vol. I, Tome II, pp. 917 ff.

subsequently hit by the industrial slump of 1920-21. Again, we have to say that the monetary and financial history of the post-war cycle is not well known despite its interest as probably a typical case of debt deflation *à la* Fisher. Two banks were caught in heavy liquidity problems: the above-mentioned Banca Italiana di Sconto and the Banco di Roma. The lender of last resort had to step in but the solutions for the two cases were rather different. The Banco di Roma was given enough liquid funds to continue its operations as one of the leading "mixed banks" of the country, while the Banca Italiana di Sconto was allowed to fail. In the latter case, however, a state agency took over the parent industrial concern (Ansaldo). We have here, as Saraceno[9] has repeatedly pointed out, the first case of direct management by the state of an important Italian manufacturing firm. This development was not so important in overall quantitative terms (even if Ansaldo emerged from the war as one of the giants of Italian industry) as it was for the creation of a new institutional arrangement that was to be highly developed in the early thirties.

As a result of the crisis of 1920-21, the position of the Banca Commerciale and Credito Italiano (needles to say entirely in Italian hands by then) was strengthened by the disappearance of their most dangerous competitor. The other important "mixed banks" around 1922 were the Banco di Roma and the Banca Nazionale di Credito.

On the whole, the structure of the Italian banking system after the adjustments that took place in the postwar boom and slump can be described as follows.

In the early 1920s, compared with an average of now developed countries, the Italian system of financial intermediaries was sufficiently endowed with deposit-taking institutions but was lacking in specialized non-bank institutions (Table 1).

There were about 3,600 banks, mostly unit banks since the ratio of branches to banks was no higher than 1.7 (Table 2). The deposit-taking institutions were divided into: banks of issue, commercial banks (mainly in the form of joint-stock companies) and four categories of thrift institutions (ordinary and postal savings banks, cooperative banks and rural banks). The share of the banking system's assets held by the three banks of issue (Banca d'Italia, Banco di Napoli and Banco di Sicilia), which still carried out operations with private non-bank customers, was about one third, or more than twice that of other countries. The four major "mixed banks" — on whose lending the (long payback and high risk)

[9] P. Saraceno, *L'IRI, origine, ordinamenti e attività*, Studies edited by the Ministry of Industry, Vol. III, UTET, Torino, 1956, and more recently his paper at the Banco di Roma Conference, "Banca e industria fra le due guerre", Il Mulino, Bologna, 1981.

Table 2. STRUCTURAL DATA ON FINANCIAL INTERMEDIARIES IN ITALY

Number of:	1912	1920	1926	1936	1951
1. Banks	3,408	3,601	4,657	2,042	1,230
2. Bank branches	4,227	6,012	11,444	7,656	7,814
3. Localities served	..	..	5,000	3,920	4,083
4. Employees in the financial system	47,095	64,139	92,919	68,418	108,778
5. Branches per bank (2:1)	1.2	1.7	2.5	3.7	6.3

Source: A.M. Biscaini Cotula - P. Ciocca, *op. cit.*, Table 11, p. 120.

investment of the leading industrial firms depended — accounted for only a slightly smaller share. The remaining third of bank intermediation was carried out by the thrift institutions — especially the savings banks, which specialized in taking small deposits and lending to central and local governments — and the myriad very small banks.

Non-bank intermediaries accounted for only 4 per cent of total intermediation — a fraction equal to no more than 1/5 of that of the other countries — and consisted almost exclusively of real estate, agrarian and insurance institutions. There was only one industrial credit institution, which had been set up during the war by the government to help firms in difficulty and was strengthened when its services were required in connection with the above mentioned take-over of Ansaldo by the State.

3. *The Banking Boom 1922-25*

The general economic conditions of the early twenties — low wages, economic recovery in Europe, the displacement of German exports and the depreciation of the lira — were very favourable to a substantial, albeit short-lived, boom of Italian manufacturing.

The rapid growth of the real sector was permitted by a very high elasticity of supply of financial capital to the private sector deriving from: a) an unusually high savings ratio, b) a very rapid decrease of public spending, c) the behaviour of banks as very active financial intermediaries.

Opportunities for banking activities were very large. Between 1922 and 1925 demand and time deposits grew at an average annual rate of 14.4 per cent (2.5 times the growth of national income at current prices). Total bank lending to the private sector increased at an average annual rate of 23.7 per cent while bank lending to the public sector grew at the much more modest rate of 9.9 per cent.

The number of banks rose substantially (by some 1,000 units) between 1920 and 1926 and so did the number of their branches and that of the employees in the sector (Table 2), an interesting case of the tendency for the banking sector to speculate and overtrade under conditions allowing easy entry into the sector.[10]

The evidence we have about interest rates shows that lending rates were either stable or slightly increasing between 1921 and 1925 (with a sharp jump in short term rates in the latter year for reasons that will be discussed below); there was an increase in the spread between borrowing and lending rates, which, in the case of the savings banks (for which more detailed figures are available), rose from 3.5 to 4.7 percentage points.[11]

Since labour costs per unit of intermediation do not seem to have increased, profits per unit of intermediation are likely to have shown a rise. The figures available for a large sample of joint-stock banks show that between 1922 and 1925 net profits doubled in absolute terms and rose from around 7 to about 10 per cent of own funds.[12]

The surviving balance sheets of the various types of banks, on the other hand, do not permit an assessment of their involvement in the long-term financing of industrial enterprises or an estimate of the holdings of industrial shares in their portfolios. The events of 1930-34, however, indicate that the weight of such securities was very large indeed. A comparison with the previous industrial banking boom of the early 1900s shows (Bonelli, Confalonieri) that during that period the industrial securities in the portfolio of the major banks amounted to some 10-15 per cent of their total assets, a figure much lower than the one emerging from the study of the balance sheets of the major banks during the 1930-34 crisis.

The problem of industrial management by these banks remains open. This is one of those clear instances where only individual case studies can shed light on the essential question, which can be summarized as follows: did banks generally take a strictly financial approach to their industrial interests or did they mainly (or also) adopt the industrialist's approach, which is more concerned with a) the survival of the firm, b) its size and c) long-term rather than

[10] For a general analysis of this tendency, see C. Barclay, "Competition and Financial Crises: Past and Present", in *Competition and Regulation of Banks*, University of Wales Press, Bangor, 1978.

[11] Cfr. A.M. Biscaini Cotula and P. Ciocca, *op. cit.*, Table 12, p. 125.

[12] *Ibid*, Figure 2, p. 133.

short-run profit maximization? What scattered evidence we have does not allow any form of generalization. The Credito Italiano, for instance, was dominated to a certain extent by the interests of the electric power industry and it seems *prima facie* that at least some of the bank's financial operations were subordinated to the strategy of that industrial group. The Banca Commerciale on the contrary was in the hands of men of finance: some of its involvements in industrial ventures were purely financial operations aimed either at reaping huge profits in the stock market or, on the contrary, at saving previous investments endangered by the financial or other difficulties of the industrial firms concerned. We have one instance of long-term management of an industrial manufacturing enterprise by Comit, the steel concern ILVA, which does not seem to have been managed too badly — given the poor standards of the time — if compared, for instance, with the already state owned Ansaldo.[13]

The early Twenties were among the very few years in Italy's economic history characterized by buoyant activity on the stock exchange. In the four-year period 1922-25 the share price index rose by 160 per cent. When deflated by the increase in the cost of living, this is a rise that had no precedent on the Italian stock exchange.[14] At any rate the flow of money into industrial securities and the issue of new industrial shares promoted heavy trading; a sharp rise of their price index took place. The major banks were very active in this market: so much so that it seems very likely that many of the industrial securities found in their portfolio after 1930-31 did not derive from deliberate long-term industrial investment but from short-term ("speculative") investments made before 1925 that could not be liquidated owing to the dramatic fall in prices after the spring of that year. The risky forward trading of commercial banks grew from 1922 to 1924 at an annual average rate of 70 per cent.

To sum up, the early twenties were years of high growth of industrial production, and high rates of investment and saving. On the financial side the supply of funds to the private sector was highly elastic, in part because of decreasing government pressure on the financial market.[15] This situation

[13] Cfr. G. Toniolo, "Crisi economica e smobilizzo pubblico delle banche miste", in G. Toniolo (ed.), *Industria e banca nella grande crisi 1929-34*, Etas Libri, Milano, 1978, pp. 286-90.

[14] Cfr. A.M. Biscaini Cotula and P. Ciocca, *op. cit.*, Figure 4, p. 135, and the sources cited there.

[15] Total lending of the banking system:

Banks of issue:	to the public sector	58%	38%
	to the private sector	42%	62%
Other banks:	to the public sector	27%	3%
	to the private sector	73%	97%

Source: R. De Mattia, *op. cit.*

offered tremendous profit opportunities to the banking system as a whole and to the more enterprising "mixed banks" in particular, so that their involvement in industrial lending reached a point never previously attained. It is quite safe to assume that a large proportion of the industrial positions in the banks' portfolios at the time of the great crisis originated from operations undertaken in the years 1922 to 1924.

4. *From the Return to the Gold Standard to the Onset of the Great Depression*

Early in 1925 the government was worried both by the excess of money creation through the banking system and by the rapid rise in the values of equities on the Milan stock exchange, which seemed to be almost entirely financed by borrowing. Measures were taken to make forward contracts more expensive. These measures were probably introduced at the wrong moment, when the stock exchange was already slowing down. Whatever the cause — which does not need to concern us here — the general index of the Milan stock exchange began to fall in the spring of 1925.[16]

This reversal of the price trend for industrial equities was the first important factor to affect the behaviour of the "mixed banks". Their intervention in the stock market, previously motivated by the huge profit opportunities for their clients and themselves, was in the following months the result of their willingness to limit the fall in prices of those shares that they held in large quantities and, ultimately, to limit their losses. In this way their holdings of industrial securities were further augmented.

In March 1926 the situation was so gloomy that the four main "mixed banks" formed a "consortium", which received heavy financial support from the Bank of Italy itself, aimed at buying securities in order to support their market price. By the end of the year the Consortium (Società Italiana Finanziamento Titoli) had bought and kept in its portfolio industrial securities for 600 million lire without being able to stop the fall of their prices and had to ask the Bank of Italy for a delay in paying back its debt.

What happened in the stock market implied, incidentally, that after 1925 industrial enterprises had to rely more than before on credit from banks to meet their financial needs.

The second crucial element in changing the behaviour of the commercial banks and particularly of the "mixed banks" is to be found in two closely related

[16] Between February and December 1925 the general index of share prices fell by 28 per cent. For more details about these operations see G. Toniolo, *L'economia dell'Italia fascista*, Laterza, Roma-Bari, 1980, pp. 77-78.

Pierluigi Ciocca - Gianni Toniolo

Figure 1. INTEREST RATES, MONEY, AND MONEY-INCOME RATIOS IN ITALY

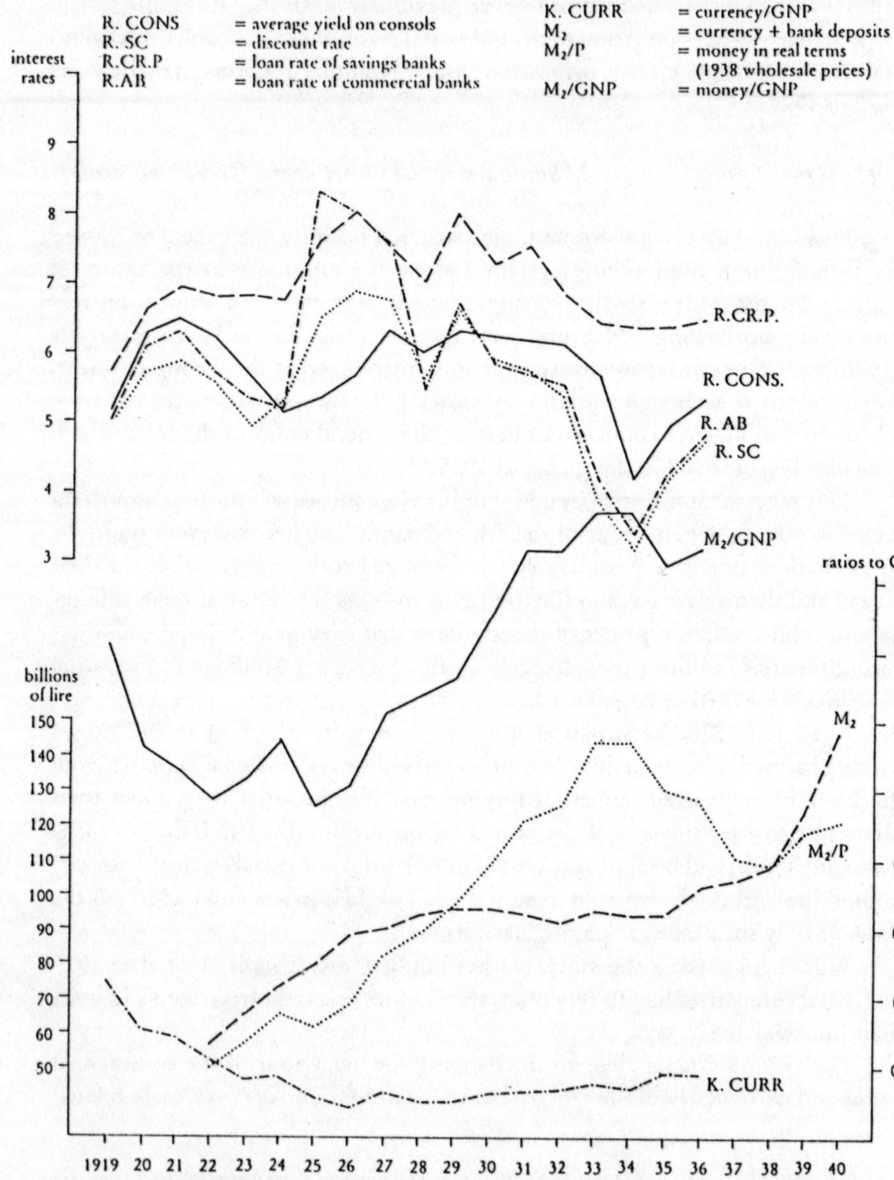

Source: A.M. Biscaini Cotula - P. Ciocca, *op. cit.*; R. De Mattia (ed.), *I bilanci degli istituti di emissione italiani 1845-1936*, Banca d'Italia, 1967; ISTAT.

factors: the slowing down of economic growth and the economic policies enacted to bring the lira back to the gold standard and to maintain the new high parity (the so-called *quota 90* or 90 lire to the pound).

The turning point of the cycle (the end of the boom of the early twenties) can be placed in the spring of 1926. At the end of the summer a series of monetary and fiscal measures were taken to implement the so-called stabilization policy that would eventually bring the lira back to the gold standard. As far as we are concerned here, it is worth noting that these policies were of a markedly pro-cyclical nature. They consisted of deflationary measures that relied not only on traditional fiscal and monetary instruments but called upon a political mobilization of the Fascist party to impose generalized wage and price cuts. In this way, much to the astonishment of foreign observers and central bankers,[17] the Italian Government was able to impose a high rate of exchange against the pound and the dollar (30 per cent higher than that chosen by Poincaré in France) and to hold it in the years that followed without much apparent effort. The cost, however, was high unemployment, a slower rate of growth in manufacturing and — as we shall see — a strain on the "industrial banks".

A restrictive fiscal and monetary stance had already been adopted in 1925 in the face of a 12 per cent increase in wholesale prices, a current account deficit that had risen to 1 per cent of GNP, and capital outflows reflecting the improbability that the gold parity would be re-established at the pre-war level. Public expenditure fell from 35 to 13 per cent of GNP between 1922 and 1926 and in the same years the budget swung from a deficit of 18.9 billion to a surplus of 0.1 billion current lire (Table 3).

Monetary conditions also became more restrictive. In 1925 and in 1926 the whole structure of interest rates rose. Specifically, the average discount rate of the three banks of issue and the lending rates of the commercial and savings banks rose to the highest level of the whole inter-war period in 1926 (Figure 1). In the same two-year period the ratio of both currency in circulation and the money supply (M_2) to GNP fell to new lows. In 1925 it was realized that the curb on domestic demand and the depreciation of the exchange rate were not enough to restore domestic equilibrium and, by reducing the current account deficit, external balance.

[17] Cfr. for instance the *memorandum* prepared by R. Warren for Harrison in R.H. MEYER, *Bankers' Diplomacy*, Columbia University Press, New York, 1970, pp. 47-48, but also, more generally, the view expressed by E. MOREAU (*Souvenirs d'un Gouverneur de la Banque de France*, Librairie de Medicis, Paris, 1954) and by Keynes himself (*Tract on Monetary Reform*, McMillan, London, 1923).

[18] Other European countries were similarly affected. Cfr. R. NURKSE, *International Currency Experience*, League of Nations, Geneva, 1944.

Table 3. FISCAL POLICY IN ITALY
1922-1940

	Public expenditure (in % of GNP)	Deficit of the public sector (in billions of lire)	Deficit of the public sector (in % of GNP)
1922	35	− 18.2	− 18.9
1923	19	− 4.3	− 4.0
1924	17	− 2.0	− 1.8
1925	17	− 1.6	− 1.3
1926	13	+ 0.1	+ 0.1
1927	14	− 2.4	− 1.5
1928	15	− 2.1	− 1.5
1929	16	− 1.5	− 1.1
1930	16	− 1.9	− 1.4
1931	19	− 2.5	− 2.1
1932	23	− 6.0	− 5.4
1933	22	− 5.6	− 5.2
1934	27	− 8.5	− 8.6
1935	25	− 6.0	− 6.1
1936	31	− 15.0	− 13.3
1937	37	− 19.0	− 16.0
1938	29	− 13.0	− 9.2
1939	28	− 14.0	− 9.3
1940	37	− 29.0	− 17.3

Source: G. Fuà (ed.), *Lo sviluppo economico in Italia*, vol. III, Milano, F. Angeli, 1969, Tav. XII.4.8, p. 433.

Hourly wages in industry had already fallen in real terms by 20 per cent between 1921 and 1926, primarily as a result of the increases in the cost of living.[19] To have continued to erode wages by devaluing the external value of the lira would have involved the risk of an accelerating inflation and a consequent undermining of the consensus upon which the fascist regime was based. Thus there gradually emerged the policy of financing the external disequilibria in an initial phase with foreign loans, attracted by the prospect of a revaluation of the lira, and of subsequently defending, if not actually increasing, competitiveness by imposing proportional reductions in nominal wages and prices. The implementation of the first phase was marked by the November 1925 Volpi-Mellon agreement on war debts, the more than 200 million dollars lent by the United States to the Italian government and enterprises during 1926, Mussolini's

[19] Cfr. V. Zamagni, "La dinamica dei salari nel settore industriale", in P. Ciocca and G. Toniolo (eds.), *L'economia italiana nel periodo fascista*, Il Mulino, Bologna, 1976.

speech at Pesaro of August 1926 calling on the country "to fight for the lira", the intervention on the foreign exchange market made possible by foreign loans, and the appreciation of the lira from 153 lire to the pound in July 1926 to 110 at the end of October. In 1927 large cuts were made in wages and prices (further wage cuts were to be agreed upon in 1930 and again in 1934). In May 1927 Mussolini indicated *quota 90* as the lira/pound exchange rate corresponding to the new gold parity, which was established at the end of the year.

The curbs imposed on domestic demand in 1926, the fall in foreign demand caused by the loss of competitiveness produced by the delay in cutting nominal wages after the revaluation of the lira to a level at which it was considerably overvalued, and the high and rising *ex post* real interest rates stemming from a largely unexpected deflation all combined to make conditions extremely difficult for enterprises, and especially for those in the industrial sector that were export-oriented and highly indebted. 1927 was a recession year, especially in the industrial sector: GNP fell 2.4 per cent in real terms, while industrial production declined 3.7 per cent. The relaxation of the fiscal and monetary restrictions and, above all, the fact that the cuts in wages in 1927 were larger than those in prices produced a slight recovery in 1928. This was short-lived, however, since it was interrupted by the crisis of 1929. The subsequent cuts in wages up to 1934 were strictly in line with those in prices,[20] so that real wages in industry settled at a sort of rigid floor. The deflationary climate continued to depress entrepreneurial expectations and thus strengthened the tendency for the economy to stagnate. If the decision to stabilize and to go back to gold was perhaps forced by circumstances, the choice of *quota 90* undoubtedly gave the Italian economy, and especially the sectors producing tradable goods, a recessionary bias.[21]

The major "mixed banks" and particularly the Banca Commerciale were in fact strongly opposed to the high value placed upon the lira. Rather they favoured a return to the gold standard at a parity of about 120-110 lire to the pound. This shows their concern for the performance of the industrial sector and of the economy as a whole since in purely financial terms, given the structure of their foreign liabilities they actually stood to gain from an overvaluation of the lira. But, as it turned out, a slower rate of growth meant lower margins on domestic lending to industrial enterprises and a much lower rate of

[20] *Loc. cit.*

[21] Estimates currently being made by P. Ciocca and A. Ulizzi on the real exchange rate of the lira (*vis-à-vis* its 6 main trading partners) show a loss of price competitiveness of 8 per cent in 1926 and of 11 per cent in 1927. The wage cuts produced a slight recovery of the index in the following two years.

increase of bank deposits (these grew at an average annual rate of 16.6 per cent between 1922 and 1926 and of only 3.7 per cent from 1926 to 1929).

All in all, this situation probably meant a higher demand for credit from industry and the necessity for banks to shift to sources of finance other than deposits. Encouraged by the government, in fact, the main Italian banks borrowed heavily abroad, mostly on a short-term basis, from 1927 to 1929. They also had greater recourse to advances from the central bank.

5. *The Great Depression, Monetary Policy and the Banking World*

Between 1930 and 1932 production in the manufacturing sector declined by from 15 to 25 per cent (according to the various available estimates), unemployment rose to 15 per cent of the industrial workforce, gross investment fell by 27 per cent and wholesale prices by about the same amount. This was the most severe phase of the depression. 1933 marked an improvement in all these indicators but 1934 was again a year of substantial stagnation and high unemployment. It was only with the beginning of 1935 and the policy of heavy deficit spending in preparation for the Abyssinian war that the Italian economy found its way out of the Depression.

In this situation the monetary and fiscal policy followed by the Government was certainly dominated by the objective of keeping the lira on the gold standard. After September 1931 the overvaluation of the Italian currency was extremely high[22] and could not be supported without some measure of exchange control. It must be said, however, that, given the situation, the Government and the Bank of Italy pursued a monetary policy that was — at least as far as its sign is concerned — of the appropriate (anti-cyclical) kind. There are no clear indications that this was the result of a deliberate action rather than of the lucky mix of several elements: at all events, during the recession the stock of money remained practically stable in nominal terms and rose substantially in real terms, the ratio of money supply to GNP increased quite sharply and short and long-term interest rates were allowed to decline in nominal terms until 1934 (see Figure 1).

Between 1929 and 1933-34 the implicit price deflator of GDP declined every year, on average by about 5 per cent. The question — raised in the United States by the "monetarist" critics of P. Temin[23] — as to whether real *ex ante*

[22] The real exchange rate of the lira (see footnote 21) appreciated by 9 per cent in 1932 over 1931.
[23] Cfr. K. Brunner (ed.), *The Great Depression Revisited*, M. Nijhoff, Boston, 1981.

Figure 2. NOMINAL (A) AND REAL (B)*
LONG TERM INTEREST RATES

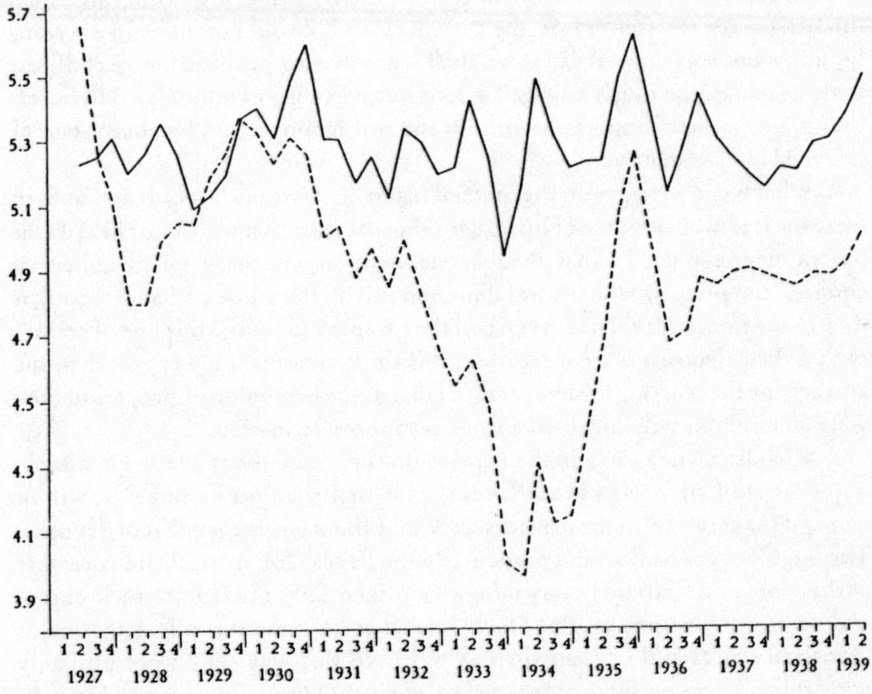

* The estimate of the real rate is based on the following equation:

$$r_n(t) = \underset{(154)}{5.3} + \sum_{i=0}^{34} a_i\, p_{t-i} \qquad \sum_{i=0}^{34} a_i = .11$$

$R^2C = .85$ DW = 1.2 SER = .14 Mean lag: 16 quarters

Source: C. Nanni, *Il tasso 'reale' d'interesse in Italia secondo lo schema di I. Fisher: la crisi degli anni '30 e le tendenze di lungo periodo*, forthcoming.

interest rates did not actually rise instead of falling therefore applies also in the case of Italy. Estimates of Fisher's equation using the yield on consols (*Rendita Italiana 5 per cento*) nonetheless show that this did in fact decline in real terms between end-1929 and end-1933, though much less than in nominal terms (Figure 2). Therefore an explanation *à la* Friedman of the Italian depression does not find any empirical support, whatever its merits in explaining the American cycle.

The banking system taken as an aggregate witnessed an increase in the ratios of both deposits and total lending to GNP, with the former increasing more than the latter. As a matter of fact, the system as a whole did not undergo a serious liquidity and solvency crisis: as we shall see, solvency problems were confined to those banks previously engaged in long-term lending to industry. However, they were crucially important both for the real economy and for the system of financial intermediation.

What went wrong with the "mixed banks"? One must recall: a) that they were the traditional source of finance for those sectors that were most heavily hit by the depression, b) that their assets were largely made up of industrial equities, the price of which was falling rapidly on the stock exchange[24] so that they could not be liquidated, even had they wanted to follow this line of action, c) that their deposits were increasing, this time, at a much lower rate than the average for the banking system, and d) that at the beginning of the period they were all rather heavily indebted abroad on a short-term basis.

What happened early in the depression (i.e. throughout 1930) was a rapid withdrawal of all foreign funds from the major Italian banks and a growth of demand for credit from the private sector four times larger than that of deposits. The huge "mixed banks" and particularly the Banca Commerciale Italiana were at the same time extremely unwilling to cut their lines of credit to their clients and to stop operating on the Stock Exchange to limit the fall of the major industrial shares and of their own as well. In this way they were probably performing a very useful counter-cyclical action but inevitably ran rather quickly into serious liquidity problems.

Apart from those that affected the large "mixed banks", profound changes took place in the banking system as a whole in the longer period 1926-1936. The number of banks fell by 56 per cent, that of branches by 33 per cent and the localities served by 22 per cent. The average size of banks increased considerably in terms of their balance sheets at both current and, *a fortiori*, constant prices. At the same time the long-term downward trend of the degree of

[24] Bachi's general index of share prices fell by 63 per cent between June 1930 and June 1932, the Rosania index fell by 59 per cent over the same period.

concentration of the Italian banking system — as measured by the indices of Herfindahl, Gini and Theil[25] — slowed or, in the case of the savings and cooperative banks, reversed. The number of employees fell by 27 per cent with a consequent sharp increase in productivity. Economies of scale probably made an important contribution to the small decline in bank profits compared with those in industry.[26]

All the different categories of banks recorded a reduction in number. The public authorities took deliberate measures in this direction, which reinforced market pressures for financial concentration. More specifically, a law passed in 1927, the effects of which were particularly felt in 1928-29, required that the smallest savings and pledge banks should be concentrated at the provincial or regional level. In the case of the ordinary credit and cooperative banks the process was most pronounced in the years 1931-33. The difficulties created by the crisis meant that bankruptcies were about five times as frequent as take-overs.[27]

6. *Changes in Bank-Industry-State Relations as a Result of the Great Depression*

It is impossible to enter here into the rather complicated technical details of the operations which, between 1931 and 1934, completely reshaped the Italian system of financial intermediation giving it a form that, with minor adjustments, has continued to the present day. We have reconstructed and described these details elsewhere and they need not be repeated here.[28] However, a brief description of the main events and of their significance cannot be dispensed with.

After the summer of 1930 it became clear to the monetary authorities that most of the "mixed banks" were running into serious liquidity problems. After the withdrawal of foreign lines of credit, the banks could only meet their liquidity requirements through advances from the Bank of Italy, which was rather quick to respond as lender of last resort. By 1932 outstanding advances to the three major "mixed banks" — advances that were formally on a very short-term basis, but which had to be renewed indefinitely since the banks could not pay them back — were equivalent to 57 per cent of the currency in circulation.

[25] Cfr. A.M. Biscaini Cotula and P. Ciocca, *op. cit.*, Table 10, pp. 116-117.

[26] *Ibid.*, Figure 2, p. 133.

[27] Cfr. Banca d'Italia, *Struttura funzionale e territoriale del sistema bancario italiano, 1936-1974*, Roma, 1977, pp. XXI-XXVI.

[28] Cfr. G. Toniolo, *Crisi economica e smobilizzo pubblico*, cit.

By the end of 1930 it was already clear that the government and the central bank were facing the alternative of letting quite a few of the medium-sized and even of the big banks go bankrupt with unforeseeable consequences for the entire financial system, or of stepping in on a large scale to avoid this, though at a cost that was considered to be very high. There was no question of not choosing the second alternative but the authorities decided to act in such a way as to recreate an acceptable level of liquidity for the entire system (and to avoid any chance of a hidden immobilization of the central bank itself) and lay the foundation of a reform of the entire system aimed at preventing similar liquidity problems in the future.

The existence of an established dictatorship made it possible to undertake all the necessary steps with great rapidity and secrecy. The result of this action was the signing of two agreements between Credito Italiano (February 1931) and Banca Commerciale (October 1931) on the one hand, and the Ministry of Finance and the Bank of Italy, on the other. These agreements contained the following provisions:

a) the two banks had to sell all their industrial and similar securities to two separate *holding* companies — Sofindit and Sfi — previously created by the banks themselves but to be *de facto* controlled thereafter by the Ministry of Finance and the Bank of Italy;
b) the latter would make sufficient advances to these *holding* companies to cover the first instalment of the sum to be paid by Sofindit and Sfi to the banks as the price of their industrial portfolio;
c) this sum was calculated not on the basis of a market price of the securities but with the aim of restoring an acceptable degree of liquidity for the banks;
d) under these agreements the latter formally committed themselves never to undertake any long-term credit operation in the future nor to hold substantial amounts of industrial securities in their portfolio: this meant the disappearence of the "mixed banks" from the Italian financial scene.

The above measures taken in the depression solved the liquidity problem of the major banks and avoided the suspensions of payments, bank holidays, panics and similar phenomena that characterized the financial crises in Central Europe and the United States. Indeed it was probably the most effective anti-cyclical action undertaken in Italy at the time.

But two other problems remained at the end of 1931 that could not be swept under the carpet. The first was the rather awkard position of the central bank, with over 50 per cent of the outstanding circulation tied up in advances to banks with a large quantity of industrial equities in their portfolios. It became immediately apparent that the shares could not be sold in the market at prices that would allow the holding companies to pay their debts to the Bank of Italy.

It was not the first time in Italian history that the lender of last resort had to shoulder the weight of illiquid and rather dubious assets deriving from the "rescue" of credit houses but this time their amount was dangerously large.

The second problem was created by the "rescue" operation itself: the major industrial firms of the country found themselves cut off almost overnight from their traditional lines of long-term credit at a time when these were desperately needed. The creation in 1931 of a public institution for long-term industrial finance, the Istituto Mobiliare Italiano (IMI), failed to produce, in the short run, any meaningful result owing to the limited amount of resources at its disposal and to the very conservative financial outlook of its first managers.

The solution of both problems was found early in 1933 with the creation of the Istituto per la Ricostruzione Industriale (IRI), a state owned holding company which received from the two holding companies (Sofindit and Sfi) all the industrial equities "inherited" from the "mixed banks". The financial innovation consisted in the fact that IRI was allowed to issue long-term bonds bearing an attractive fixed interest and characterized by being basically equivalent to state bonds (they were guaranteed by the state and enjoyed fiscal privileges similar to those of state bonds).

These characteristics made IRI bonds particularly attractive to the typical Italian saver and in fact their subsequent issues were all well received by the market. In this way, IRI was able to set up a plan for the repayment of the full amount of the Bank of Italy's advances to the "mixed banks" and for the provision of fresh cash to the industrial firms under its control.

This innovation involved a major change in the organization and management of Italian industry and created a basic prerequisite for the reshaping of financial intermediation. The state took over from the banks whatever entrepreneurial role they had previously performed and became actively involved in the management of a large share of Italy's manufacturing, shipping, electric power and communications industries.

The device created on that occasion had little to do with nationalization: for all practical purposes these companies were treated by Italian law as private ones and could act accordingly. The difference was that their majority shareholder was quite often the state, through IRI. And the state could act in the industrial sector through the normal means provided by law to any majority shareholder of any Italian company.

Both the setting up of IRI in January 1933 and its main interventions in the spring and summer of the same year came some months after the upturn in the cycle sometime in the second half of 1932.

The cyclical turnround cannot, therefore, be attributed to the reforms that were started with the creation of IRI. They nonetheless played an important role in the subsequent phase of recovery and expansion, which, amidst delays and contradictions, got under way in 1933. IRI's intervention involved its crediting the rehabilitated banks with 12 billion lire: half in connection with the holdings it took over and half simply to cover their losses. The total amount was close to 10 per cent of GNP and considerably more than that resulting from previous "rescue" intervention by state financial agencies — such as those in 1922-24 and 1931-32, neither of which had amounted to 4 per cent of GNP. Moreover, between 1934 and 1937 (when it was put on a permanent footing) IRI advanced a further 2.7 billion to the same banks. These funds were obtained through bond issues and asset sales, rather than from the central bank with a corresponding creation of monetary base.

The scope and scale of IRI's operations were exceptional; not only did they prevent a chain of bankruptcies among large firms and banks but they also had strong expansionary effects at the macro-economic level. Speculative demand for liquid assets declined — together with the financial risk borne by the private sector — more than their supply contracted as a result of IRI's repayment of the central bank with funds raised through the issue of securities.

7. The Banking Law and the Permanent Features of the New System

In 1934 three "conventions" were signed between the state, IRI and the three main former "mixed banks" — Banca Commerciale, Credito Italiano and Banco di Roma — by virtue of which IRI became the majority shareholder of the banks (thus strengthening the overall position of the state at the centre of the Italian system of financial intermediation). The banks again formally agreed not to grant long-term credit and were reorganized as deposit-taking institutions engaged only in short-term lending.

In 1936 a new law reorganized and officially reshaped the Italian banking system. The Banca d'Italia was given a legal status as a public institution with wide powers of supervision over all the banks in the system and with better instruments to act as a modern central bank for the management of monetary policy. This was a timely decision: in October 1936 Italy went off the gold standard, for good, thus making correct currency management both more complicated and more crucial than before. Credit was declared to be a function of public interest. This was not in the sense of replacing an essentially entrepreneurial function by a public utility, but in that of designing a regulatory framework that would enable both publicly and privately owned financial intermediaries to operate in conditions of stability, minimum costs and prices, and allocative efficiency. Apart from paying lip service to the rhetoric of fascist "planning", the new law did not intend to create, through state control of the major banks, new tools of economic policy for the allocation of resources to specific uses decided by the state. The fundamental aim was to avoid any risk of the big banks being taken over by industrial firms and to prevent excessive concentration in the financial sector: ultimately, to foster competition and to preserve a dialectical relationship between Industry and Finance.

As a necessary condition for the attainment of these goals, the banks have to maximize an objective function in which profit is the main argument and a basic constraint is represented by indifference, or "neutrality", towards the firms and investment projects to be financed, apart from the return and the risk of the loan. Industry and Finance should be separated and they have to follow different behaviourial criteria: the specific role of Finance is not to select investment projects, but to choose, on the basis of purely financial considerations, the firms best equipped to realize them.

The existence of two independent judgements on what to produce, and how to produce it, is assumed to improve the allocation of resources. Competition, structural controls and prudential regulation were seen as complementary ways to pursue stability and efficiency. In the same vein, the 1936 banking law provided for a formal distinction between short-term credit (which was called "ordinary credit"), to which all the various deposit-taking banks had to confine themselves, on the one hand, and long-term operations, on the other. The latter had to be performed only by *ad hoc* non-bank financial intermediaries — most, but not all, of which were created and controlled by the state.

As for IRI, it was originally — but never very convincingly — conceived as a temporary institution. The idea was that the state should provide both new finance and new management to "ailing" (it was the word most used at the time) industries, putting them in better shape and waiting for the end of the depression and the recovery of the stock market. This position ignored the fact that in Italy some sectors — such as iron and steel — were traditionally the offspring of close cooperation between banks and the state and that, by eliminating the mixed-banks, they were almost bound to have to be taken over by the state. The idea of selling IRI's industrial equities back to private investors was also inconsistent with the fact that the very creation of IRI had relegated, at least in the short run, the skock market to a role of secondary importance very unlikely to be able to cope with a wave of selling offers without major shocks. Finally, the way Italy climbed out of the depression, through import substitution and military expenditure, made the idea of IRI as a temporary institution conflict with the aims of the economic policy being pursued. In fact, it was not until 1935, when Mussolini gave his orders to prepare to attack Abyssinia, that Italy's industrial production recovered from the depression. A large deficit spending policy concentrating on heavy industry and, quite soon, a strengthening of all the measures to promote import-substituting industries (the so-called "autarky" program) were the engine of recovery. But at this stage it became clear that the factories crucial for a war effort (such as steelmaking, armaments, shipbuilding, etc.) were controlled by IRI. Far from being requested to get rid of these sectors, the state industrial holding company had to undertake programmes to improve their organization and efficiency.

In 1937 IRI was declared a permanent institution and, to the present day, has been a characteristic feature of the particular blend of Italy's "mixed economy".

As is often the case, more deeply rooted reasons and forces — together with contingent factors — played a role in shaping the new institutional setting. Private capital was simply not prepared to enter most of the productive sectors in which IRI had a majority stake. The risk was too high because of the need to concentrate scarce investible funds into a few projects with long pay-back periods.

It can be argued, on more general grounds, that, at least within a sort of "capitalism without capitalists", the architects of the 1933-37 reforms were quite farsighted.

Publicly controlled firms can be used to achieve economic policy aims; beyond their use for specific and changing purposes, they can guarantee a regular supply of goods and services that private firms are not prepared to produce. In sectors where private firms also operate they can, if managed in accordance with economic criteria, provide valuable competition. A necessary condition for the success of such a system was, and still is, to avoid any confusion between the two aspects: the Italian economy needed new rules for the longer term and, in particular, a public entrepreneurial ability that would be independent of political influence and which, by pursuing efficiency, would supplement and stimulate the private sector. The effective planning of a mixed economy presupposes the setting up of a system of separate resource allocation mechanisms and requires the use of instruments designed to have an indirect influence on the composition of supply.[29]

The aim in 1933-37 was to put the publicly controlled firms and the capital market on a footing that would enable them to operate efficiently independently of the contingent course of economic policy. At the same time, their proper working was intended to make the whole economy more responsive to the fiscal, legislative and administrative tools that the authorities use to influence both private and public economic agents while respecting their "objective functions".

[29] P. Ciocca, "Disproportionalities, Allocative Mechanisms, and Stagflation", forthcoming in the *Journal of Postkeynesian Economics*.

[18]

Excerpt from Michael D. Bordo and Anna J. Schwartz (eds), *A Retrospective on the Classical Gold Standard, 1821–1931*, 405–41.

9 Italy in the Gold Standard Period, 1861–1914

Michele Fratianni and Franco Spinelli

9.1 Introduction

Little is generally known about Italian experience under the gold standard, especially during the gold standard period before World War I, since Italy adhered to the standard only intermittently. The Italian-language literature on the subject is mainly qualitative in nature, while the English-language literature is virtually nonexistent. For a long time the inadequacy or outright lack of data impeded progress. But relevant statistics are now available and we intend to exploit them to remedy, at least in part, this void.

Our strategy is to study the 1861–1914 period in light of what the literature today considers to be the important issues; these are discussed in the following section. Section 9.3 gives the reader a brief history of the period—a background essential for a deeper appreciation of the quantitative evidence presented in section 9.4. The salient findings of the paper are summarized in section 9.5. Some data not easily accessible are appended to the paper.

9.2 Theoretical Issues

9.2.1 Hume versus the Monetary Approach to the Balance of Payments (MAPA or Perfect Arbitrage)

Kreinin and Officer (1978, p. 10), in their survey of the monetary approach to the balance of payments, remark that

Michele Fratianni is professor of economics at Indiana University, Bloomington, Indiana. He was serving as senior staff economist at the Council of Economic Advisers when the paper was prepared.

Franco Spinelli is an economist with the International Monetary Fund.

it is often suggested that the new monetary approach is the intellectual grandchild of the price-specie-flow mechanism developed by David Hume in the eighteenth century. Monetary flows are central to both theories, and both regard external imbalances as self-correcting. However, in the price-specie-flow mechanism, monetary flows rectify external disequilibria through their effect on relative commodity prices. In contrast, the monetary approach views a stable demand for money as the core of the mechanism, and relative commodity prices play no role in the adjustment process. Price elasticities are therefore considered irrelevant. In fact, some monetarists hypothesize that perfect international arbitrage ensures that one price will prevail internationally on all commodity and capital markets, so that no changes in relative commodity prices are even possible—let alone necessary—for international adjustment.

This distinction is fundamental and deserves close scrutiny. The world of Hume is traditionally analyzed in a two-country setting. Assume that an exogenous increase in the monetary gold stock takes place in country A, the effect of which is to raise, with a lag, the price level in A relative to country B. The changing terms of trade cause A to run a trade-account deficit matched by a surplus in country B. The deficit is financed by gold moving from A to B. On the assumption that the authorities do not sterilize gold flows, the trade imbalance produces a redistribution of the world monetary gold stock with the subsequent effect, again with a lag, of bringing the price level in A in line with the price level in B. At that point, equilibrium is restored in the external accounts as well as in the money markets. The world price level would be higher if the gold increase in A represented an increase in the world supply of gold.

The original formulation places the entire stress of the adjustment mechanism on the trade account. When capital is allowed to move, there is less stress on the trade account: the outflow of capital brought about by the monetary shock reduces the adjustment in the trade account that would have been required in the absence of capital movements. Several testable implications of this theory emerge: (1) money-supply changes affect the price level with a lag; (2) gold flows are a significant, if not dominant, cause of variation of the domestic money supply; (3) the domestic price level or its rate of change is inversely correlated with the foreign price level or its rate of change; (4) there is a real exchange rate that is serially correlated for relatively long periods of time; (5) a real depreciation of the home currency improves the trade account, which in turn reduces the real depreciation.

The version of the monetary approach that assumes perfect international arbitrage (MAPA)—of which McCloskey and Zecher (1976) are ardent proponents—departs from the Humean theory in a fundamental way. Gold flows do not serve to realign country A's price level with the price level prevailing in country B but to restore equilibrium in the money market. Prices of (traded) commodities and assets are determined in the world market. Each country is too small to have a lasting influence on its own price level or interest rates. The law of one price in goods and asset markets prevails. Gold flows are only one of the means to enforce the law of one price; other commodities move from one region to another but gold flows may be quantitatively more relevant because transport costs are smaller relative to bulkier and lower priced goods. The testable implications of MAPA are: (1) purchasing-power parity and interest-rate parity hold in the short run as well as in the long run; (2) the trade account does not respond to changes in relative commodity prices, partly because the law of one price prevents the emergence of such changes and more fundamentally because spending decisions are influenced by changes in money demand and supply only; (3) gold flows are a small source of variation of the money stock, implying that changes in the domestic component of the monetary base dominate gold flows.

9.2.2 The Demand for and Supply of Money

In both Hume and MAPA a stable demand for money, influenced by a few variables and in a manner independent of the forces determining money supply, plays an important role. In MAPA an increase in the supply of money relative to demand generates an excess of spending over income which leads in turn to an outflow of money through a deficit in the balance of payments. The end result is that the monetary shock alters not the total stock of money but its composition between domestic and foreign source components. In Hume the same monetary shock instead affects the total money stock, its composition, and the domestic price level.

The two approaches diverge in five respects in their treatment of the supply of money. First, Hume assigns a large role to gold in the money stock process, while for MAPA the role of gold is small. More to the point, a fractional gold-bullion standard gives the monetary authorities the ability to create monetary-base liabilities against the acquisition of domestic assets, be those claims on government or the private sector. Second, for MAPA, foreign exchange is a significant component of international reserves. For Hume this is not a basic consideration. Third, for MAPA, neither authorities nor the so-called rules of the game play a role, for gold flows as well as changes in foreign exchange are automatically offset by opposite changes in the domestic source components. If a presumptive case for sterilization by monetary authorities can be made, can one discriminate changes in domestic source components of base money that cause opposite movements in foreign source components from sterilization behavior? Fourth, the two approaches differ on the link between monetary policy in Italy and monetary policy in the other member-states of the Latin Monetary Union. Finally, the two approaches assign different roles to the public and banks in the money-supply process.

These issues are explored in some detail in the next two sections. We first assess the evidence qualitatively as we guide the reader through the relevant historical account, and subsequently more formally.

9.3 Historical Account

For brief periods in Italy, paper money was convertible at the official price in either gold or silver.[1] For the most part, fractional reserves of gold and silver bullion were held against paper money (i.e., the monetary base) created by banks of issue and the government. Italy did not develop a single monetary authority until 1926. Up to that time several banks, legally permitted to issue notes, held metallic reserves.

Despite the fact that Italy adopted the gold standard intermittently and for brief periods of time, her experience on the whole was not different from what it would have been had she adhered to the standard throughout, particularly from 1900 to 1913. The reason was that Italy's decision makers were aware of the limits of operating on a paper standard. Either they operated responsibly without gold or pulled back from the brink when acting irresponsibly. Briefly put, Italy was guided by the norm of the gold standard.

9.3.1 Competition versus Monopoly of Issue

Upon becoming a unified nation in 1861, Italy inherited the financial structures of the constituent states. Some of these states had banks that possessed characteristics of a central bank; others did not. In brief, there were three banks whose currencies (coins and paper money) were legal tender: the Banca Nazionale (BN) operating in Piedmont and Genoa, the Banca Romana operating in Rome, and the Banca Nazionale Toscana, operating in Tuscany; and six banks whose currency was fiduciary in the strict sense of the word and thus not legal tender (i.e., its acceptance depended on the trust of economic agents): the Banco di Napoli and the Banco di Sicilia, both operating in the Kingdom of the two Sicilies, the Banca Toscana di Credito per le Industrie ed i Commerci d'Italia operating in Tuscany, the Banca degli Stati Parmensi operating in Parma, the Stabilimento Mercantile di Venezia operating in Venice, and the Banca Pontificia per le Quattro Legazioni operating in Bologna.

Two intellectual and political groups competed in Italy to give shape to the country's monetary system. One supported more competition in banking and, in particular, complete freedom of currency issue; the other believed that the political and economic integration of Italy would be enhanced by a strong single monetary authority whose liabilities would be legal tender. The intellectual leaders of the liberal camp (in the English tradition) were the economists Francesco Ferrara (1868), who became minister of finance in 1867, and Antonio Garelli (1879); the leader of the monopoly faction was the powerful Prime Minister Camillo Benzo di Cavour.[2] In Parliament the procompetition group usually was stronger than the monopoly-of-issue group.

The tug of war between the two opposing camps undoubtedly explains some of the haphazard, if not chaotic, development of banking. For example, in the early 1860s, the senate approved a bill that would have merged BN with the Banca Nazionale Toscana in a single bank of issue, but the lower house of Parliament defeated it. Numerous bills introduced in Parliament would have enlarged the number of banks of issue.

In addition to the nine banks noted above, a number of firms and individuals printed their own money. However, Parliament put a stop to this practice in 1874 for fear that the bankruptcy of one of them would endanger the entire banking system. In 1893 the Banca Romana failed. BN and the two Tuscan banks merged to form the Banca d'Italia (Bank of Italy). A law of 1894 prescribed that only the Bank of Italy, Banco di Napoli, and Banco di Sicilia had the right to issue currency. This situation lasted until 1926 when the Bank of Italy finally emerged as the institution with a monopoly of issue.

In short, though there was intellectual and political opposition to the creation of a single central bank, the belief that a competitive industry would overissue and the failure of a large bank finally prevailed over the opposition to a more centralized and legalistic structure.

9.3.2 The Bimetallic Standard and the Latin Monetary Union

In 1862, the newly elected Parliament of Italy approved a currency reform closely resembling that of France. Three options were open to the lawmakers: a gold standard, a silver standard, and a bimetallic standard. Policymakers preferred the gold standard; so did BN which had operated on that principle for several years. However, silver was the dominant money in the South, Lombardy, and Venice. The split between North and South was further complicated by the fact that France, the closest and most important trading partner of Italy, was de jure on a bimetallic standard. We stress de jure because de facto silver had disappeared from circulation in 1848 following the gold discoveries in Australia, California, and Russia.[3] At the official rate of exchange between silver and gold set at a ratio of 15.5 to 1, silver was undervalued relative to market conditions. Therefore, as predicted by Gresham's law, gold drove silver out of circulation.

Confronted with the three possibilities, Parliament chose a formal bimetallic standard where silver nominally could be exchanged for gold at the ratio of 15.5 to 1, but in fact, by diminishing the silver content of silver coins of denominations smaller than five lire,[4] established the ratio of 14.38 to 1—a ratio that was in line with prevailing market conditions. As to silver coins of larger denominations used in international trade, the 1862 law provided for their issue only upon request; since the official parity undervalued silver relative to the market, the provision served to eliminate large-denomination silver coins. In this manner, Italian policy-makers found a compromise between form and the realities of the market.

The 1862 law also granted legal tender to the coins of Belgium, France, and Switzerland. In 1865 Italy joined these countries to form the Latin Monetary Union; their coins circulated freely in the union.[5] In effect, the union decreed one common money without setting up a common monetary policy.

Less than a year after the birth of the union, Italy in 1866 suspended convertibility (see Martello 1881). Italian paper money depreciated relative to gold which was exported to the rest of the Latin Monetary Union. The world demand for gold, however, increased. In 1871 Germany adopted a gold standard; the Scandinavian countries, Holland, and the United States subsequently followed the German example. Concomitantly, the world demand for silver fell, while its supply rose due to new discoveries in Nevada (De Cecco 1984). The market-exchange ratio of silver for gold rose to 18 to 1 in 1876. The Latin Monetary Union, which overvalued silver, was flooded with the metal and by 1878 suspended the free coinage of silver. Although the union had manifestly failed in retaining a bimetallic standard, it was formally kept alive for a few more years.

9.3.3 The First Inconvertibility Period, 1866–84

The state of public finances in Italy in the period from 1861 to 1865 quickly deteriorated (see Fratianni and Spinelli 1982, and figure 9.1). Budget deficits, financed by an increase in public debt, rose over the five years to about 6 percent of average national income. The external accounts over the same period did not fare any better: the cumulative trade account represented about 4.5 percent of average national income. At the start of 1866 the government announced another large budget deficit, while another war against Austria was imminent. The market perceived Italy to be a decided risk. Bond prices fell dramatically, more so abroad than at home. Foreign-capital inflows dwindled, while domestic capital moved massively abroad, in particular to Paris, to exploit the large profit opportunities from arbitraging differences in bond prices (Majorana 1893). The outflow of gold was so large that some banks were on the verge of bankruptcy. Even the dominant BN had to reduce its portfolio of earning assets to a minimum to cope with the liquidity drain. On 1 May 1866, the authorities decreed *corso forzoso*—the inconvertibility (into gold) of paper money.

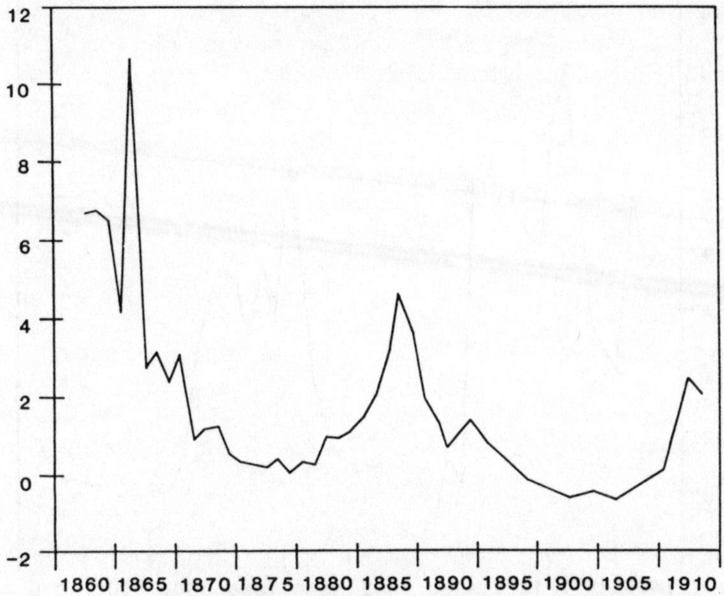

Fig. 9.1 Budget-deficit-to-GNP ratio, Italy, 1862–1913. Budget deficit is the difference between government expenditures and revenues as reconstructed in Pedone 1967, table A.1. *Source*: GNP at current prices: ISTAT 1957, table 35.

The exchange rate between the lira and the French franc, and the annual rate of change of the money stock, shown respectively in figures 9.2 and 9.3, capture the essence of the aforementioned events. The money stock exploded in 1866; so did the exchange rate. The fact that these two developments accompanied inconvertibility should not be a surprise. Inconvertibility was brought about partly by the injudicious fiscal policy of the government and partly by the war against Austria. Inconvertibility benefited the government by enabling it to monetize the deficit through direct borrowing from the banks of issue. The government's action was backed by the export sector which perceived the devaluation of the lira would stimulate the demand for their products.

The 1866 law granted the right to issue inconvertible notes not only to BN and the two Tuscan banks, but also to the Bank of Naples, the Bank of Sicily, and eventually (in 1870) the Roman Bank.[6] The major beneficiary of the new law was BN, since its paper money became legal tender throughout the nation. As a result of this provision, BN notes sold at a premium with respect to the paper money of the other five banks of issue. To limit the issue, all six banks had to keep a gold and silver cover of one-third against their note liabilities.

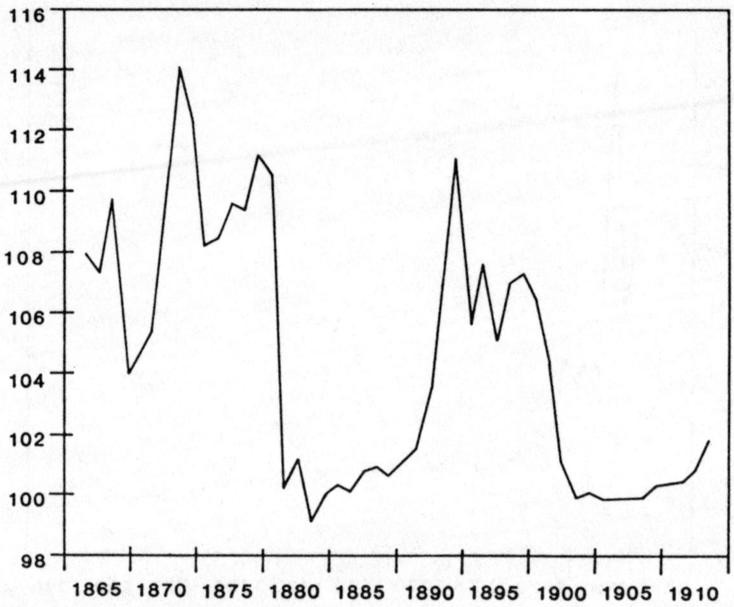

Fig. 9.2 Lira-franc nominal exchange rate, 1866–1913. *Source*: Number of lire per French franc (ELF, table 9.A.1, col. 11), from Borgatta 1933.

No sooner was inconvertibility in effect than Parliament contemplated a return to convertibility, creating a commission to study its feasibility (Commissione Parlamentare di Inchiesta 1868–69). Parliament was so eager to act on this matter that a law was passed in 1868—before the commission even produced its report—setting the maximum issue of BN notes at 750 million lire—approximately the amount then in circulation. The growth rate of the monetary base came to a halt in 1868 (see figure 9.3).

Monetary discipline lasted less than two years. Budget deficits then rose again. The government desired to finance the deficits by printing money,[7] so BN made loans directly to the Treasury. In return, BN was authorized to print additional currency, ignoring the existing gold-cover requirement. The consequence of these events may be gleaned from figures 9.1 through 9.4. The growth rate of the monetary base took an upward leap, as did the money stock. The lira depreciated drastically against the French franc, reaching its highest level of the sample period. The rate of inflation measured by the annual percentage change of the consumer price index which rose in 1871 reached an all-time peak in 1872 (see figure 9.4).

The 1866 law, as noted, gave a competitive advantage to BN, to the

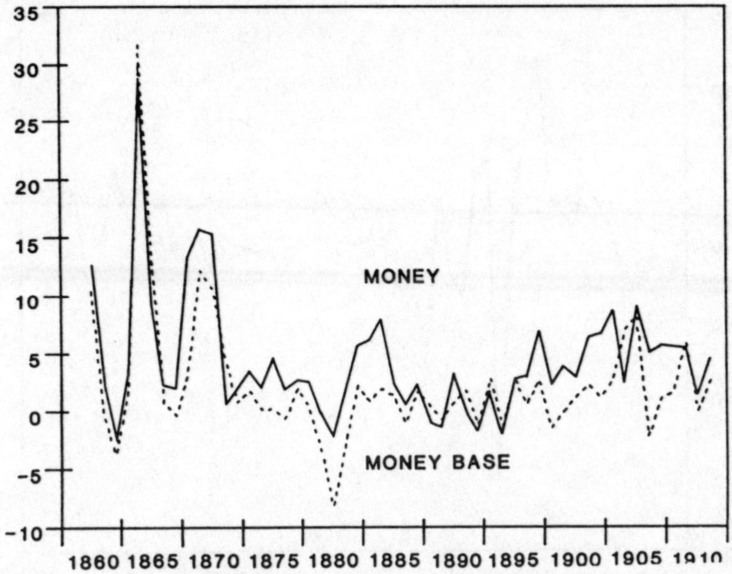

Fig. 9.3 Money and money base, annual percent change, 1862–1913. The money base is equal to *C*. *Sources*: *C* = total currency outstanding from De Mattia 1969, tables 5, 6, 7, and 14; *D* = total bank deposits from De Mattia 1969, tables 2, 2a, 2b, and 23.

distress of the procompetitive contingent in Parliament. Thanks to their efforts, in 1874 a law was passed designed to eliminate that advantage. The legislation included the following provisions. First, the six banks of issue were asked to repay the outstanding government indebtedness to BN. The repayment changed the ownership of claims on the government. The economic meaning of the transaction is that BN sold its claims on the government to the other banks against an equivalent reduction of BN notes in circulation and an equivalent increase of notes issued by the other five banks. Therefore, while the aggregate amount of notes in circulation did not change, the composition changed against BN notes and in favor of the notes of the other five banks. Second, legal-tender status was granted to the notes of all six banks. Third, the ceiling on currency issue was set at three times each bank's net worth as of the end of 1873.[8] Finally, the issue of notes by other institutions was made unlawful. Apparently, the procompetition faction had to concede this point in return for a more equitable market-share arrangement among the six banks of issue.[9]

By 1874 the government managed to balance its budget (see figure 9.1). The return to fiscal discipline was reflected immediately in low growth of the monetary base. The lira appreciated vis-à-vis the franc by

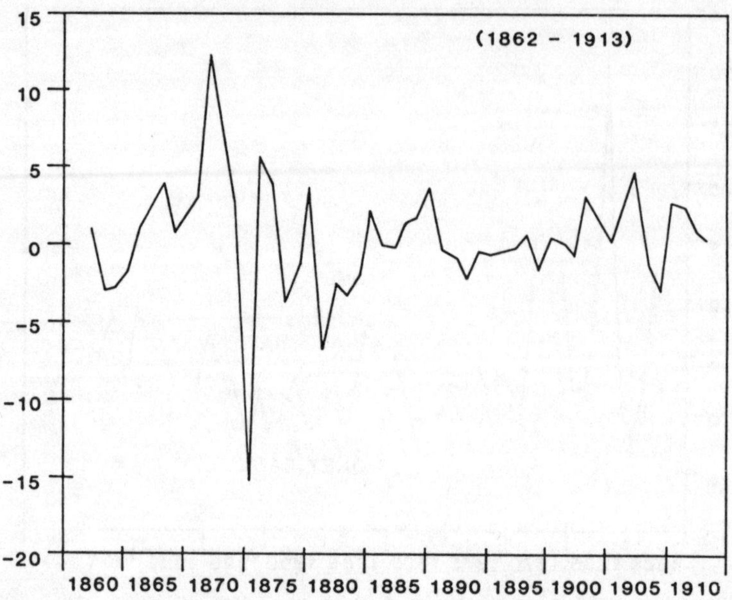

Fig. 9.4 Consumer price index, annual percent change, 1862–1913. *Source*: Consumer price index (table 9.A.1, col. 8) from De Mattia 1977, table 7.

5.5 percent in two years. The rate of change in the price level fell from +6 percent in 1873 to −16 percent in 1875, in response partly to domestic deflation and partly to the precipitous decline in world prices in 1874 (see figure 9.4).

The fall in Italian prices paved the way for serious policy discussions about a return to metallic convertibility. A bill was introduced in Parliament in 1880 to allow the government to borrow abroad up to 644 million lire to repay its indebtedness to the six banks of issue. The repayment would enable the banks to keep reserves only in the form of precious metals and would restore convertibility at a fixed price between paper money and gold and/or silver.

Disinflationary expectations were thus promoted. Individuals shifted from goods and real assets to money to capitalize on the anticipated increase of purchasing power.[10] Domestic prices fell sharply in 1881 (see figure 9.4). The appreciation of the lira was so pronounced that parity with the franc was restored (cf. figure 9.2).

Parliament approved the bill on 1 April 1881. The ensuing sale of government bonds was well received by the market. Since the bulk of the sale was to foreigners, Italy enjoyed a sizable capital flow. The proceeds of the bond sale were used to repay the loans extended by the six banks to the government. Currency was taken out of circulation and the monetary base fell by 8 percent (cf. year 1888 in figure 9.3).

9.3.4 Return to Converbitility in 1884

On 1 March 1883, the government announced that convertibility would be restored on 12 April 1884. Banks were given the option to convert paper money into either gold or silver. Since the official exchange rate between silver and gold had remained fixed at a ratio of 14.38 to 1 and the market exchange rate had risen above 18.5 to 1, convertibility took place only in silver. Again, Gresham's law dictated that cheap money would displace dear money. In addition, Gresham's law—in the context of a world that was operating on a gold standard—implied that gold would be exported and silver imported. In fact, from 1883 to 1885 the outflow of gold coins from Italy rose from 9.2 to 101.3 million lire while imports of silver coins increased from 50.7 to 103.7 million lire (De Mattia 1969, table 10).

The course of public finances deteriorated again in the middle of the 1880s (see figure 9.1). The yield on Italian government bonds "Rendita Italiana," quoted in Paris, was higher than its yield at home, reflecting country risk as a factor affecting the market's valuation of Italian bonds. From 1883 to 1888 the lira depreciated marginally but continuously with respect to the French franc. Banks of issue raised the cost of exchanging silver for paper money (Supino 1929, p. 107), while overissuing notes—the Roman Bank was the main culprit—in relation to what was permitted by law. In 1891 the government decided to legalize the currency in circulation in contravention of the law. The aggregate ceiling for the entire system was raised from 755 million to 1064 million lire, which implied a reduction of the gold-silver cover from one-third to one-quarter.

In 1892 the revelation of the illegal practices of the Roman Bank precipitated a run on the bank that led to its failure. Widespread distrust of the banking system ensued, reflected in a sharp depreciation of the lira on the exchange markets. Banca Nazionale (BN) merged with the two Tuscan banks to strengthen its liquidity position and acquired the name of Banca d'Italia(BI). In the wake of the merger, Parliament passed a law in 1893 which entrusted BI with the task of absorbing the liabilities of the defunct Roman Bank, providing for the substitution of BI notes for Roman Bank notes. The law also made it unlawful for BI, Bank of Naples, and Bank of Sicily to issue notes without direct supervision of the state. "Excessive" circulation was to be reduced over several years, while the reserve requirement in bullion was to be raised to 40 percent.[11] Finally, the law called for full convertibility.

The economic essence of the 1893 law was that monetary discipline was postponed to the future (Majorana 1893). The call for convertibility was assessed by the market to be wishful thinking. The continuous depreciation of the lira in the exchange markets tells the story very eloquently. The government acknowledged what the market already knew in 1894 when Italy was back to *corso forzoso* (forced legal tender of the paper currency).

9.3.5 The Second Inconvertibility Period, 1894–1913

This period was the most stable and prosperous of the entire sample period. Budget deficits were first reduced and later converted into surpluses (cf. figure 9.1). Monetary policy was consistently tight. The monetary base grew at a rate below the rate of growth of output. Concomitant with a world boom in economic activity, Italy's real output grew dramatically—at an average annual rate of 2.4 percent from 1897 to 1913, compared to 0.86 percent for the period 1861 to 1896 (cf. figure 9.5). Not surprisingly the lira started to appreciate vis-à-vis the franc in the mid-1890s. By 1903 its rate of exchange fell within the gold points and remained there until 1911. The period ended with World War I.

In sum, the historical account permits us to draw a few conclusions.

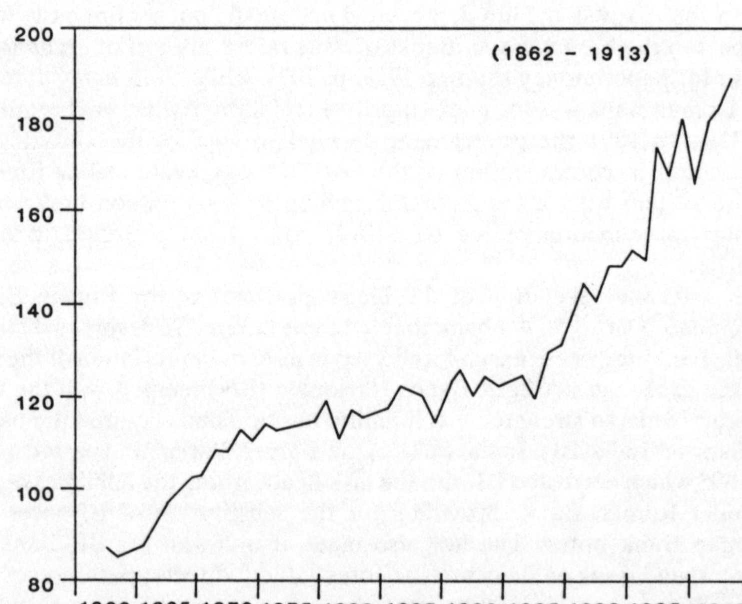

Fig. 9.5 Real GNP, 1862–1913 (millions of 1913 lire). *Sources*: Real GNP = *RYI* (table 9.A.1, col. 7), computed as GNP at current prices divided by the GNP price deflator, *PYI*: De Mattia 1977, table 7.

First, the government budget appeared to be responsible for the vicissitudes of the lira and Italy's alternate experiences with the gold standard. Budget deficits caused the abandonment of the gold standard in 1866, the monetary explosion of 1866–67 and 1870–72, and the return to inconvertibility in 1894. As the budget returned to equilibrium, Italy regained monetary and exchange-rate stability—aided by exceptional real growth. Second, the banks of issue tended to overissue. The government induced, tolerated, and legitimized excessive circulation, and possibly was responsible for unlawful note creation that ultimately led to the failure of the Banca Romana. That banks preferred inconvertibility to convertibility and more than once tested the government to see how much they could get away with is supported by some evidence (Supino 1925, p. viii). Third, gold played an explicit role in the period up to 1866; afterwards the system can be best described as a gold-silver-bullion standard. Fourth, the historical account suggests that the monetary base is exogenous relative to prices and income, in light of the tight link between budget deficits and money creation. Finally, the gold standard was not a sufficient condition for stability. Politicians had no difficulties in throwing off the straightjacket of the gold standard when it stood in the way of financing large budget deficits. On the other hand, the proper conduct of fiscal and monetary affairs was sufficient to guarantee stability, whether or not the country was on the gold standard. Indeed, the record indicates that the formal adoption of a standard was not very important. Politicians knew the limits of the paper standard and were willing to return to judicious policies after periods of laxity. It is clear, for example, that little would have changed had Italy returned to a formal gold standard in the first thirteen years of the twentieth century.[12] This assessment of the record permits us to treat statistically the periods of inconvertibility as qualitatively similar to the periods of convertibility.

9.4 Evidence

Having outlined the principal theoretical issues in section 9.2 and the broad historical facts in section 9.3, we are now ready to submit more formal evidence concerning the process of money creation, the demand for money, the interaction between the exchange rate and the difference between the domestic and external price level, and more generally the relative explanatory power of the two hypotheses of Hume and MAPA about the balance-of-payments adjustment mechanism.

9.4.1 Data and Sources

The foresight of the Instituto Centrale di Statistica (ISTAT) and the Banca d'Italia made possible the quantitative aspect of this study. Some time ago, these two institutions began a painstaking reconstruction of historical time series of the real and monetary sectors of the economy. Three volumes are of particular importance: one by ISTAT (1957) deals for the most part with real-sector data and two by De Mattia (1969, 1977) with monetary statistics. The work of De Mattia is of very fine quality, certainly comparable to the reconstruction of monetary data made for approximately the same period for the United States by Milton Friedman and Anna Schwartz (1963).

Many of the time series we used—in particular those we think foreign researchers may have difficulty finding—are shown in appendix A, which also lists definitions and sources.

A few words are in order about the definition of the monetary base. While currency holdings of the banking system (i.e., banks other than banks of issue) are known, deposits of the system with banks of issue are not. There is no way to assess the size of this measurement omission, but qualitative accounts suggest it is small. It follows that our definition of the monetary base is equal to the outstanding stock of currency, and that the reserve-deposit ratio is measured by currency holdings of the banking system divided by all private-bank deposits.

9.4.2 The Money-Supply Process

We define the money stock M at time t as

$$M_t = m_t \cdot MB_t, \tag{1}$$

where MB denotes the monetary base and m the multiplier which depends inversely on the currency-deposit ratio (c), and the reserve-deposit ratio (r) (cf. Brunner and Meltzer 1961; Friedman and Schwartz 1963; Cagan 1965):

$$m_t = \frac{1 + c_t}{c_t + r_t}. \tag{2}$$

The relative contribution of m and MB to the growth of the money stock is obtained directly from (1):

$$1 = \frac{\dot{m}_t}{\dot{M}_t} + \frac{\dot{MB}_t}{\dot{M}_t}, \tag{3}$$

where a dot above the variable indicates the first difference of its natural logarithm. The first difference of the money multiplier, in turn, can be decomposed as follows:

$$\dot{m}_t = \left[\ln m_t - \ln \frac{(1 + c_{t-1})}{(c_{t-1} + r_t)}\right] + \left[\frac{\ln(1 + c_{t-1})}{(c_{t-1} + r_t)} - \ln m_{t-1}\right], \tag{4}$$

where the terms inside the two bracketed parentheses capture, respectively, the contribution to $\dot{m}$ of the currency-deposit ratio and the reserve-deposit ratio. Next, the growth rate of the monetary base depends on the weighted average of the growth rates of the domestic- (*BD*) and foreign- (*IR*) asset components of the consolidated balance sheet of the banks of issue:

$$(5) \qquad \frac{\Delta MB_t}{MB_{t-1}} = \left(\frac{BD}{MB}\right)_{t-1} \frac{\Delta BD_t}{BD_{t-1}} + \frac{(IR)}{(MB)_{t-1}} \frac{\Delta IR_t}{IR_{t-1}}.$$

Finally, the growth rate of the foreign component reflects the growth rate of metallic reserves (*IRA*) and foreign-exchange reserves (*IRFE*), weighted by their initial relative shares:

$$(6) \qquad \frac{\Delta IR_t}{IR_{t-1}} = \left(\frac{IRA}{IR}\right)_{t-1} \frac{\Delta IRA_t}{IR_{t-1}} + \frac{(IRFE)}{(IR)_{t-1}} \frac{\Delta IRFE_t}{IRFE_{t-1}}.$$

Table 9.1 shows the basic facts of the process of money-supply creation during the sample period. The first three rows relate to equation (3): column (2) gives the yearly sample means of $\dot{M}$, $\dot{m}$ and $\dot{MB}$; column (3), the long-run relative contributions of $\dot{m}$ and $\dot{MB}$ to $\dot{M}$; and column (4), the short-run relative contributions. In the long run both $\dot{m}$ and $\dot{MB}$ turn out to be of roughly equal importance with a slight tendency for the monetary base to dominate. In the short run—and this result is hardly surprising—the multiplier rises in importance relative to *MB* (lines 1–3). Changes in the currency-deposit ratio, in turn, dominate the short- as well as the long-run behavior of the multiplier (lines 4–5).

The domestic component of the monetary base is at least as important for the long-run growth of *MB* as the foreign component. In the short run, however, matters change dramatically: changes in *BD* affect *MB* negatively, while changes in *IR* influence *MB* positively (lines 6–8). A more detailed breakdown of the data is provided in table 9.2 which pairs yearly changes in *BD* and *IR*—the sort of evidence Nurkse (League of Nations 1944) and later Bloomfield (1959) considered to determine whether monetary authorities followed the so-called rules of the game. In the words of Nurkse:

> Whenever gold flowed in, the central bank was expected to increase the national currency supply not only through the purchase of that gold but also through the acquisition of additional domestic assets; and, similarly, when gold flowed out, the central bank was supposed to contract its domestic assets also. (P. 66).

Table 9.1 The Money-Supply Process, 1862–1914

Variables (1)	Mean Yearly Value (2)	Relative Long-Run Contributions of Mean Yearly Values to Growth Rate of M (3)	Relative Short-Run Contributions of Mean Yearly Values to Growth Rate of M (4)
1. $\dot{M}$	4.50	—	—
2. $\dot{m}$	1.96	43.6	59.1
3. $\dot{MB}$	2.54	56.4	40.9
Relation of currency ratio and reserve ratio to the multiplier			
4. $1n\ m_t - 1n\left(\frac{1+c_{t-1}}{c_{t-1}+r_t}\right)$	1.96	100.0	91.0
5. $1n\left(\frac{1+c_{t-1}}{c_{t-1}+r_t}\right) - 1n\ m_{t-1}$	0.00	0.00	9.0
Relation of domestic and foreign components to monetary base			
6. $\Delta MB/MB_{-1}$	2.77	—	—
7. $(\Delta BD/BD_{-1})\ (BD/MB)_{-1}$	1.56	56.3	−813.1
8. $(\Delta IR/IR_{-1})\ (IR/MB)_{-1}$	1.21	43.7	913.1
Relation of gold and foreign-exchange reserves to foreign component of monetary base			
9. $(\Delta IR/IR_{-1})$	6.57	—	—
10. $(\Delta IRA/IRA_{-1})\ (IRA/IR)_{-1}$	6.04	91.93	6.65
11. $(\Delta IRFE/IRFE_{-1})\ (IRFE/IR)_{-1}$	0.53	8.07	92.88

Source: Table 9.A.1.

Notes: Lines 4–5, 7–8, 10–11 sum to 100.00 in cols. (3) and (4) except for rounding errors. M = money stock; m = money multiplier; MB = monetary base; c = currency ratio ($(C–CB)/D$); r = reserve ratio (CB/D); BD = domestic-asset component of the base ($MB–IR$); IR = foreign-asset component of the base ($IRA + IRFE$); IRA = metallic reserves; $IRFE$ = foreign-exchange reserves; dot above a variable = first difference of its natural logarithm.

Table 9.2 **Yearly Changes in Domestic and Foreign Component of the Monetary Base, 1862–1914 (millions of lire)**

	BD	*IR*	Comove-ment		*BD*	*IR*	Comove-ment
1862	101.6	12.4	+	1891	−49.5	33.0	−
1863	−26.7	24.9	−	1892	15.1	4.5	+
1864	−31.8	−10.7	+	1893	44.8	−0.6	−
1865	12.5	3.9	+	1894	−118.1	90.0	−
1866	447.1	−26.9	−	1895	−63.4	−6.3	+
1867	198.7	15.5	+	1896	−58.0	28.6	−
1868	−81.3	91.4	−	1897	64.6	1.1	+
1869	−6.0	−0.2	+	1898	7.3	7.0	+
1870	39.3	20.1	+	1899	73.0	−5.1	−
				1900	−52.0	17.6	−
1871	260.9	−24.5	−				
1872	247.5	−16.8	−	1901	−26.4	26.6	−
1873	103.8	4.0	+	1902	−8.0	37.2	−
1874	27.5	−8.0	−	1903	−138.7	196.1	−
1875	103.8	−58.6	−	1904	7.1	23.0	+
1876	−1.0	5.6	−	1905	−123.1	190.6	−
1877	4.6	0.3	+	1906	43.3	144.8	+
1878	−15.6	1.5	−	1907	30.6	206.9	+
1879	53.1	−3.1	−	1908	−117.3	51.1	−
1880	−19.8	29.8	−	1909	17.3	17.2	+
				1910	33.0	14.7	+
1881	−42.7	−40.2	+				
1882	−211.6	20.9	−	1911	119.7	66.5	+
1883	−222.6	163.6	−	1912	−35.3	35.4	−
1884	1.3	48.5	+	1913	22.8	61.8	+
1885	52.8	−32.5	−	1914	639.0	79.6	+
1886	37.3	6.9	+				
1887	−2.3	33.6	−				
1888	−79.1	56.3	−				
1889	40.7	3.3	+				
1890	40.7	−29.1	−				

Source: Table 9.1.

Notes: *BD* = domestic-asset component of the monetary base; *IR* = foreign-asset component of the monetary base.

There are twenty-four instances in which ΔBD and ΔIR move in the same direction, and twenty-nine where they move in the opposite direction. Abstracting from lags, this evidence would indicate, according to Nurkse and Bloomfield, that the five banks of issue on the whole contravened the rules of the game through a policy of sterilizing foreign-exchange flows. However, these twenty-nine observations are also consistent with the monetary theory of the balance of payments (both Hume and MAPA) which predicts that autonomous increases (decreases) in *BD* cause outflows (inflows) of *IR*. And indeed there are several historical episodes that we can identify in support of the monetary hypothesis. Take, for example, 1866, 1871, and 1872 when the government ran large budget deficits that were monetized by the banks of issue. The increases in *BD* were clearly autonomous in the sense that they were not induced by balance-of-payments considerations; yet they produced an outflow of foreign reserves. These outflows are consistent with a condition of excess supply in the domestic money market that finds its way abroad. As another instance, consider 1882 and 1883 when the government deliberately financed its deficits by borrowing abroad. The reduction in *BD* cannot be interpreted as a violation of the rules of the game, but as a way to restore equilibrium in the domestic money market, while at the same time raising the ratio of foreign reserves to total base money. The key point is that the occurrence of a negative correlation between the two source components of the monetary base cannot be interpreted *tout court* as evidence in favor of the reserve-sterilization hypothesis. The Nurkse-Bloomfield test ignores the compensatory response of *IR* to changes in *BD*. On the other hand, we do not pretend to shed light on the issue of how much of the observed negative correlation between ΔIR and ΔBD is attributable to "offset" behavior as opposed to sterilization practices. For that we would require the specification and estimation of the reaction function of the banks of issue (as well as of the underlying macro model), a task we are not ready to tackle.[13]

Returning to table 9.1, we note that gold flows were the main long-run driving force of the growth of international reserves; as a matter of fact, it was not until 1893 that banks were allowed to count foreign exchange as part of international reserves. But in the short run, once again, the findings are quite different, with gold movements accounting for less than 7 percent of changes in *IR* (lines 9–11).

In sum, the long-run growth of the money stock can be explained by the fall in the currency-deposit ratio (with a relative contribution of 45 percent), the expansion of domestic credit (30 percent), and net inflows of gold (22 percent). The ratio *c* falls from a value of 7.8 in 1861 to 0.35 in 1913, a steady decline interrupted by a sharp upswing in 1866–67 when convertibility was suspended and in 1873 when metal coins appreciated relative to paper money and deposits. The secular decline of *c* reflects the corresponding secular fall in the cost of maintaining deposit balances relative to currency. The contribution of *BD* to the growth of *M* is not surprising in light of section 9.3. Table 9.3 presents, as summary, parameter estimates of money-supply functions for the entire period and the subperiod 1895–1914. These results corroborate our earlier findings, namely, that changes in the multiplier are influenced predominantly by changes in *c* and that the elasticity of *M* with respect to *MB* is unitary. The estimates also suggest that the reserve-deposit ratio plays a more signifi-

Table 9.3 Money-Supply Equations (*t*-statistics in parentheses)

Dependent Variable and Sample Period	Constant	$\dot{c}$	$\dot{r}$	$\dot{MB}$	ρ^a	D.W.	R^2
$\dot{m}$	.004	−.292	−.022		.348	1.65	.73
1863–1914	(1.015)	(−11.039)	(−1.556)		(2.650)		
	−.001	−.644	−.046		.06	1.08	.99
1895–1914	(−1.679)	(−55.468)	(−5.042)		(.260)		
$\dot{M}$	.008	−.270	−.018	.913	.326	1.60	.89
1863–1914	(1.727)	(−9.370)	(−1.333)	(18.347)	(2.460)		
	−.001	−.618	−.039	.950	.226	1.47	.99
1895–1914	(.598)	(−37.604)	(−4.600)	(40.208)	(1.001)		

Source: See table 9.1.
Notes: m = money multiplier; M = money stock; c = currency ratio; r = reserve ratio; MB = monetary base; dot above a variable = first difference of its natural logarithm.
[a]First-order autocorrelation parameter (Cochrane-Orcutt estimation technique).

cant role in the money-supply process from 1895 to 1914 than in the earlier period.

9.4.3 The Demand for Money

One of us (Spinelli) has demonstrated that there was a well-defined demand-for-money function in Italy during the period under consideration. However, in light of an inadvertent error in the money-stock series that was used and the availability of an expanded data set, we reestimated the demand-for-money function. The model, the statistical procedure, and findings are discussed in appendix B. On the whole, the results do not change appreciably. Money was a "luxury" good over the sample period, a finding that is similar to Friedman and Schwartz's (1963) for the United States (see figure 9.6). As Sylla points out in his comments on this paper, the "secular fall in velocity in Italy, as elsewhere, was in part—perhaps in great part—the result of more and more economic units and activities becoming specialized, commercialized, and monetized."[14]

9.4.4 Deviations from Purchasing-Power Parity

A cursory look at the lira–French franc exchange rate (E_N) confirms that for long periods of time this rate was not contained within the gold points (figure 9.2). In fact, E_N was above the upper gold point from 1866 to 1881 and from 1891 to 1901.[15] The question posed by this observation is whether the evolution of E_N reflects differences in the two countries' price levels; namely, does purchasing-power parity (PPP) hold?

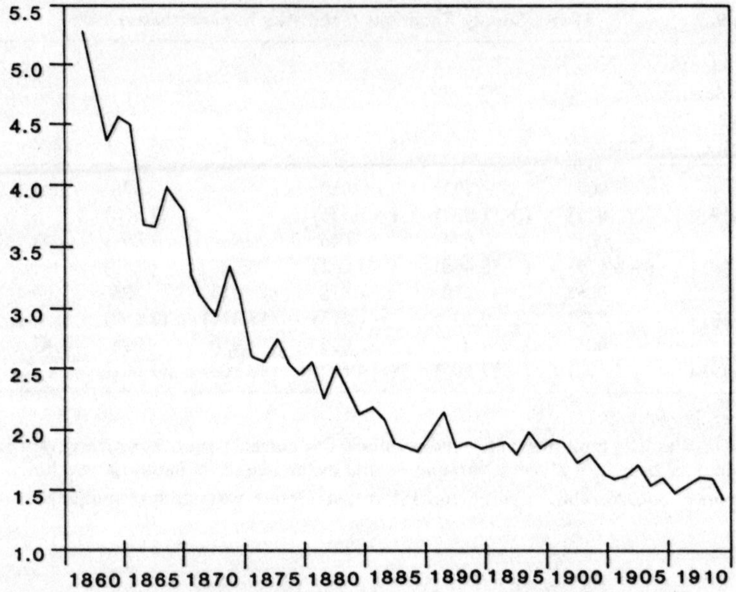

Fig. 9.6 Velocity of circulation, 1862–1913. Velocity is calculated as GNP at current prices divided by *M*.

A short answer to this question is provided by examining the behavior of the real exchange rate:

$$E_R = \frac{E_N \cdot P_F}{P_I} \tag{7}$$

where

E_R = the real exchange rate;

P_F = the wholesale price index in France 1913 = 100;

P_I = the wholesale price index in Italy 1913 = 100.

E_R is plotted in figure 9.7. PPP holds if E_R stays close to the parity line of 100. Upward sizable deviations from 100 imply a real depreciation of the lira; downward deviations, a real appreciation. By assumption, the 1913 exchange rate is at PPP. The figure tells a lucid story. On the whole, PPP did not hold. For a period of about twenty years, 1866–83, the lira was systematically undervalued relative to PPP. Yet the path of the inflation differential between Italy and France was very erratic (figure 9.8). The lira again became undervalued from 1892 to 1894 in the wake of the failure of the Roman Bank and of generalized mistrust of the banking system. Only the 1900s can be characterized as approximating long-run PPP.

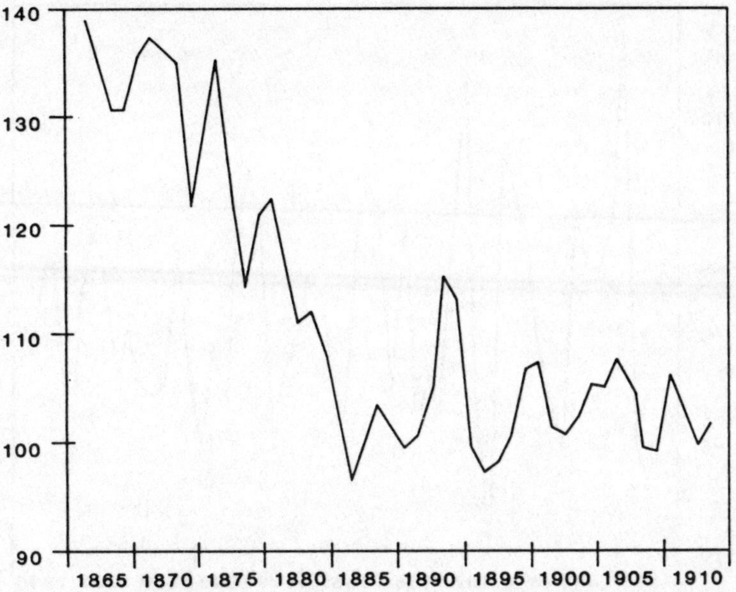

Fig. 9.7 Lira-franc real exchange rate, 1866–1913. *Sources*: Nominal exchange rate (*ELF*) times French wholesale price index from Mitchell 1978, divided by Italian wholesale price index: De Mattia 1977, table 7.

This assessment does not change when we regress changes in the log of E_N on changes in the log of P_F and P_I (see table 9.4). Both the explanatory power of the hypothesis (R^2) and the parameter estimates of the price variables (which a priori should be equal to unity) provide grounds for rejection. We performed modifications of the reported regressions—constrained estimation on the two inflation variables as well as introducing distributed lags—which however yielded no appreciable change in the statistical results.

If PPP cannot explain the movement in the exchange rate, what can? We considered the following model (see Meese and Rogoff 1981):

$$\dot{E}_N = b_0 + b_1\ (\dot{M}_I - \dot{M}_F) + b_2\ (\dot{Y}_I - \dot{Y}_F) + b_3\ (\Delta i_{s,I} - \Delta i_{s,F}) + b_4\ (\Delta i_{1,I} - \Delta i_{1,F}) + b_5\ CA_I + b_6\ CA_F + \epsilon \qquad (8)$$

where

E_N = number of lire per French franc;
i_s = short-term interest rate;
i_1 = long-term interest rate (a proxy for the anticipated inflation rate);
Y = real GNP;

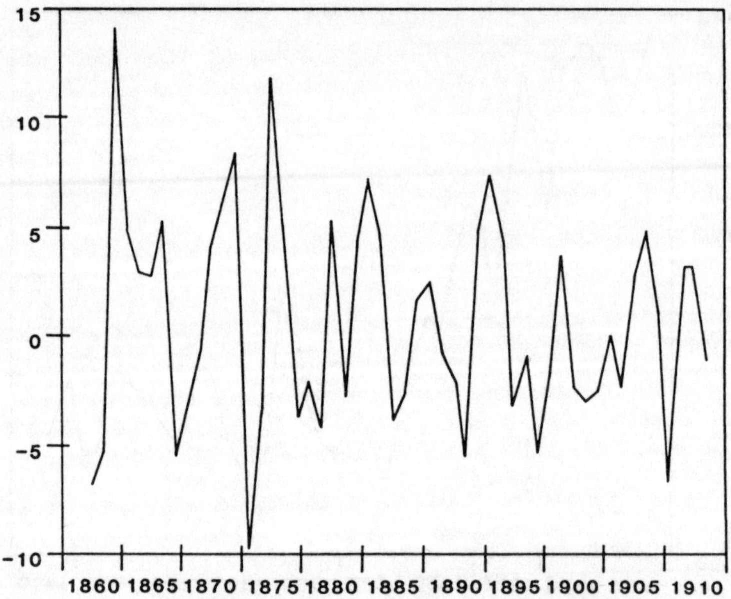

Fig. 9.8 Italy-France inflation differential, 1863–1913. Percentage change in the Italian wholesale price index (table 9.A.1, col. 9) minus percentage change in the French wholesale price index.

CA = current-account balance;
dot above a variable = first difference of its natural logarithm;
subscripts I and F = Italy, France.

Equation (8) is a testable implication of a rather eclectic asset view of the exchange rate, which incorporates the pure monetary model ($b_4 = b_5 = b_6 = 0$) with short-run deviations from PPP ($b_5 = b_6 = 0$) and possibly long-run deviations from PPP. The interested reader may refer to Meese and Rogoff and the literature cited therein for a deeper discussion of the theoretical and empirical issues underlying equation (8).

We fitted equation (8) for both the lira–French franc and the lira-pound exchange rates for the period 1882–1913. The results were disappointing: the parameter estimates were either inconsistent with theory or statistically insignificant and often both. A possible difficulty with equation (8) is that the sample period under consideration cannot be characterized as a regime of flexible exchange rates. Often changes in international reserves bore the brunt of the adjustment process. In light of this consideration, we replaced E_N with the composite variable, measuring exchange market pressure,

Table 9.4 Tests of the PPP Hypothesis (*t*-statistics in parentheses)

Exchange-Rate Changes for Italy vis-à-vis	Sample Period	Constant	Inflation: Domestic	Inflation: Foreign	R^2	D.W.
France	1867–1913	−.002	.173	−.053	.10	2.04
		(−.522)	(2.192)	(−.539)		
United Kingdom	1882–1913[1]	.001	−.063	.026	.01	2.12
		(.166)	(−.666)	(.170)		

Sources: Lira-franc exchange rate: table 9.A.1, col. (11); lira-pound exchange rate: table 9.A.1, col. (12); wholesale price indexes: Italy, table 9.A.1, col. (9); France, Mitchell 1978; GNP deflator: Italy, table 9.A.1, col. (10); United Kingdom, Lewis 1978.
[1]Sample period was restricted by data limitations.

$$\frac{\Delta IR}{MB_{-1}} + \frac{\Delta \dfrac{1}{E_N}}{\left(\dfrac{1}{E_{N_{-1}}}\right)},$$

used by Girton and Roper (1977) in their study of post–World War II Canada. The outcome was that the coefficient of the Italian-money variable (in this case $\Delta BD/MB_{-1}$) turned out to be significant and of the correct sign; for the other parameters, however, there was no improvement. In sum, we can explain (marginally) more of the evolution of the composite variable of E_N, but the power of the explanation is far from satisfactory.

Again, we pose the question: What drives the exchange rate? Are nominal and real-exchange-rate changes largely unpredictable, or is there a common force underlying the large and persistent deviations from PPP? Our answer is that there is a common factor underlying the movements of the real exchange rate and that this factor can be labelled for short "country risk." More specifically, whenever financial markets perceived that the Italian government was not following prudent fiscal and monetary policies, the markets rated Italian debt instruments as less than risk-free assets. Potential owners of Italian debt instruments demanded a premium for the nonzero probability of a complete or partial default. Consider a model of interest-rate parity (IRP) between debt instruments of wide circulation:

$$D_t = \ln(1 + i_{I,t}) - \ln(1 + i_{F,t}) + \ln E^t_{t+1} - \ln E_t \tag{9}$$

where

$i_{I,t}$ = yield on Italian bonds at time t (table 9.A.1, col. 13);

$i_{F,t}$ = yield on French bonds at time t (table 9.A.1, col. 14);

E^{e}_{t+1} = the rate of exchange for $t + 1$ expected at t;

E_t = the rate of exchange at t (table 9.A.1, col. 11);

D measures deviations from IRP (when $D = 0$, IRP holds perfectly).

What is of interest here is not so much the absolute value of D, which can be influenced by transaction costs and differences in tax arrangements, but how it changes over time. We interpret these changes as changes in risk premia.

Equation (9) was computed using the yield on the Rendita Italiana (table 9.A.1, col. 13), a long-term government bond that was traded both at home and abroad, especially in Paris; the yield on a comparable French government bond (table 9.A.1, col. 14); and assuming perfect foresight in the exchange market, i.e., $ln\ E^{e}_{t+1} = ln\ E_{t+1}$.[16] Four periods are of interest: 1867 to 1884 when the lira was consistently undervalued relative to PPP; 1885 to 1892 when the nominal exchange rate was within the gold points and the real exchange rate oscillated around parity; 1893 to 1901 when deviations from PPP again became pronounced; and finally 1902 to 1912 when the nominal exchange rate remained within the gold points and the real exchange rate oscillated around parity. The yearly average values for D for these four periods were 2.37 percentage points, 0.02, 1.95, and 0.58.

Clearly, large and persistent deviations from PPP were associated with Italian financial assets carrying a higher yield, inclusive of exchange-rate appreciation, than French financial assets. These differences in D are too large and their timing too coincident with the underlying real-exchange-rate series to be explained by changes in transaction costs, exchange control, or tax treatment. The underlying force—we posit—is the changing perception by domestic and foreign markets of Italian country risk.[17]

Additional episodic evidence can be marshalled in favor of the hypothesis. In 1866 the lira depreciated by eight percentage points vis-à-vis the French franc, yet the Italian price level was below the French one.

As noted in section 9.3, two important events took place in 1866: a large budget deficit (figure 9.1) and the decision to make the lira inconvertible. In 1881 the nominal exchange rate appreciated suddenly (figure 9.2)—too suddenly to reflect changes in underlying competitiveness. However, that was the year the Italian government decided to return eventually to the gold standard. The anticipation that fiscal and monetary discipline would be restored had an immediate impact on the exchange markets. From 1891 to 1894 the lira depreciated dramatically; during this period uncertainties about presumed banking malpractices culminated with the failure of the Roman Bank. All these historical episodes confirm the more general evidence presented above: Italy was perceived for long periods of time to be a substantial risk. That risk, in turn, was based on investors' assessment of Italian economic policy as imprudent enough to justify a positive probability of default on its debt instruments.

An alternative explanation for the persistence of deviations from PPP could be positive transaction costs that would inhibit arbitrage in both goods and securities markets. A variable risk premium that causes variations in the real exchange rate does not signify foregone opportunities to arbitrage across goods or between assets and goods. The aim of our tests is to uncover a variable risk premium. They are silent concerning the average transaction cost borne by a purchaser of Italian goods who intends to resell them in France for profit. We have no facts about transaction costs, but the downward trend in the real depreciation of the lira from 1866 to 1883 is consistent with falling transaction costs. The building of railroads, roads, and canals, the development of a merchant marine, and the ongoing process of commercialization that took pace in this period favor an explanation of declining transaction costs. In short, our risk-premium hypothesis does not necessarily imply irrationality in the goods market.

9.4.5 Causality Tests

So far we have identified the determinants of the money market and the exchange rate. In particular, we have demonstrated that PPP did not hold over the sample period, a fact that is more consistent with the Humean view of the adjustment mechanism than with MAPA's. We now want to marshal additional evidence to discriminate more effectively between the two hypotheses.

Table 9.5 contains summary information derived by applying Granger-Sims causality tests to variables of interest. The symbol $\tilde{x}$——>$\tilde{z}$

Table 9.5 Causal Relationships

A.	$\widetilde{MB}_t \xrightarrow{\quad + \quad} \begin{cases} \tilde{Y}_{t+1} \\ \tilde{P}_{t+1}, (\tilde{P}_{t+2}) \\ \tilde{E}_{N_{t+1}} \end{cases}$
	$\tilde{P}_{t+1}, \tilde{P}_{t+2} \xrightarrow{\quad - \quad} \widetilde{IRA}_{t+3}$
B.	$\tilde{P}^*_t \xleftrightarrow{\quad + \quad} \tilde{P}_t$
C.	$\tilde{P}^*_t \xrightarrow{\quad + \quad} \begin{cases} \widetilde{IRA}_{t+2} \\ \tilde{Y}_{t+2} \end{cases}$

Notes: P = wholesale price index used in B; GNP price deflator used in A and C; Y = real GNP; E_N = lira-French franc exchange rate; P^* = Sauerbeck price index for Great Britain (proxy for world prices); $\tilde{}$ = indicates that the variable has been appropriately prefiltered. The reported relationships are statistically significant at least at the 5 percent level.

should be read as follows: prewhitened x, denoted $\tilde{x}$, causes prewhitened z, denoted $\tilde{z}$, in the sense that past values of $\tilde{x}$ explain current values of $\tilde{z}$; better than would ignoring past values of $\tilde{x}$. Causality in this sense is a matter of timing relationships. The sign $\leftrightarrow$ indicates bidirectional causality; + or − refer to the sign of the significant cross-correlation coefficient. Finally, the time subscripts denote the "causality lag." For example, changes in the monetary base "cause" changes in the price level with a lag of up to two years.

Several observations about the table are in order. First, the monetary base is unresponsive to changes in output, prices, and exchange rates while the converse does not hold. This evidence suggests that the supply of money is independent of the forces that influence the demand for money. Second, changes in domestic and foreign prices take up to two years to affect gold and silver flows—the external imbalance (table 9.5, part A). This evidence is consistent with the Humean adjustment process. Finally, there is bidirectional causality between foreign and domestic prices, a finding that is consistent with the Humean world but not with MAPA.

In the end the crucial difference between Hume and MAPA is that while the latter emphasizes changes in the money stock as the variable for restoring equilibrium in the balance of payments, the former recognizes also the importance of relative commodity prices. This difference can be tested by considering the following equation:

$$EDG = b_0 + b_1\, ESM + b_2\, E_R + b_3\, \bar{g} + b_4\, \bar{\tau} + \epsilon, \tag{10}$$

where

EDG = excess demand for goods;

ESM = excess supply of money;

$\bar{g}$ = deviations from trend of real government expenditures;

$\bar{\tau}$ = deviations from trend of tax rate;

ϵ = error term.

Assume that both Hume and MAPA share the common vision that $\bar{g}$ and $\bar{\tau}$ have a role to play in the excess demand for goods with $b_3 > 0$ and $b_4 < 0$. The dispute concerns b_2 which is zero for MAPA and positive for Hume. Note that the dispute is independent of the prevailing-exchange-rate regime. At issue is the existence of a real as opposed to a nominal exchange rate and its effect on the goods market. Hume posits that deviations from PPP are part of the engine that drives the adjustment mechanism. MAPA, instead, rules out such a mechanism and goes even further by postulating that PPP holds beyond the "momentary" run. The coefficient b_1 is positive. An increase in the domestic component of the monetary base creates excess supply in the money market which spills over into the goods market by raising spending relative to income, which in turn causes a deficit in the trade account. For unchanged values of E_R, $\bar{g}$, and $\bar{\tau}$, equilibrium in the balance of payments is restored when the outflow of reserves restores equilibrium in the money market and in the goods market.

We tested equation (10), using annual data for the period 1867–1914. *EDG* was proxied by the log of real income minus the log of its trend value; *ESM* by the residuals of the demand money (cf. table 9.A.2); E_R by the log of the real exchange rate shown in figure 9.1; $\bar{g}$ by the log of real government expenditures minus the log of its trend value; and $\bar{\tau}$ by the log of the ratio of total taxes to nominal GNP minus the log of its trend value. Both $\bar{g}$ and $\bar{\tau}$ were lagged one period. The parameter estimates (absolute *t*-values in parentheses) and other statistics of equation (10) are:

$$\underset{(.86)}{\hat{b}_0 = -.007}, \quad \underset{(2.14)}{\hat{b}_1 = .38}, \quad \underset{(3.7)}{\hat{b}_2 = .22}, \quad \underset{(.33)}{\hat{b}_3 = -.002}, \quad \underset{(6.13)}{\hat{b}_4 = -.33},$$

$$R^2 = .63, \text{ D.W.} = 1.77,$$

which suggests that the data are more consistent with the Humean view of the adjustment mechanism than MAPA's. Not only is arbitrage activity insufficient to equalize the lira price of Italian and French commodity indexes, but changes in these indexes play an important role in reequilibrating the external accounts.

9.5 Summary and Findings

Italy was not on the gold standard except for brief periods of time, and for the most part the lira was inconvertible in either gold or silver, yet fiscal and monetary policies in the latter part of the sample period, especially in the 1900s, achieved stability of nominal magnitudes. Indeed, Italian experience did not differ on the whole from what it would have been had the country adhered formally to the standard throughout.

The lira–French franc exchange rate, representative of other exchange ratios, floated more often than not and moved above the upper gold point in twenty-five out of forty-eight years, returning within the gold points during the 1900s when the lira was inconvertible. Deviations from PPP were sizable and long lasting. That persistence cannot be explained by either an Italian inflation rate systematically higher than the world inflation rate or by an expanded-asset theory of exchange-rate determination. Change in the valuation of the lira relative to PPP is best reconciled with the existence of changing perceptions of country risk. Investors demanded a risk premium for holding Italian debt instruments as compensation for a nonzero probability of complete or partial default. That risk, in turn, emerged whenever the market perceived that Italy was engaging in imprudent fiscal and monetary policies; it disappeared when policies reverted to normal. Our evidence in favor of a risk-premium hypothesis does not necessarily imply irrationality in the goods market. Transaction costs on Italian goods, while probably falling from 1866 to 1883, could have been larger than implied by risk-premium calculations.

Deviations from PPP were found to have a considerable impact on the goods market and hence on the trade account. The fact that changes in the terms of trade could affect trade flows, and for that matter the very existence of these changes, differentiates the Humean view of the adjustment mechanism from the perfect-international-arbitrage version of the monetary theory of the balance of payments. The Italian evidence supports the former more than the latter. In favor of Hume, one may also note the one- and two-year lag of changes in the Italian price level over changes in the Italian monetary base and the two-year lag of changes in gold flows over changes in the domestic and foreign price levels. On the other hand, the strong form of Hume implies that gold flows are a significant, if not dominant, cause of variations in the domestic money supply. In fact, 45 percent of the long-run growth of the Italian money stock from 1862 to 1914 can be traced to a fall in the currency-deposit-ratio, 30 percent to expansion of the domestic component of the monetary base, and only 22 percent to net inflows of gold. Over the short run, the foreign component, being more volatile than the domestic component, exerted a larger impact on the growth of the money stock.

Italy did not have a monopoly bank of issue until 1926. Throughout the period under study several banks were authorized by the government to issue notes. Such an arrangement, however, did not prevent the government from monetizing its deficits. Fiscal and monetary policies were closely intertwined.

Yearly changes in the domestic component of the monetary base were in the majority of the cases compensated by oposite changes in the foreign component of the base. Nurkse and Bloomfield would consider these observations as evidence that the authorities did not play according to the rules of the game. Our interpretation is that this negative correlation is often more consistent with causality running from ΔBD to ΔIR, as implied by the monetary approach to the balance of payments, rather than as the reaction of the authorities to ΔIR.

The Latin Monetary Union which Italy joined in 1865 was never an effective constraint on Italian economic policy. Absence of policy coordination doomed the union to failure.

Money was as much a luxury good in Italy as it was in the United States during the same period. The demand for real-cash balances responded to changes in real permanent income with an elasticity of about 1.5. The impact on desired real-cash holdings of changes in the opportunity cost of holding such balances is statistically less clear.

Appendix A

Table 9.A.1 Basic Annual Data

	Money Stock (*M*) (1) (2) − (3) + (4)	Currency (*C*) (2)	Bank-held Currency (*CB*) (3)	Bank Deposits (*D*) (4)	Metallic Reserves (*IRA*) (5)
	(millions of lire)				
1861	1179.0	1044.4	n.a.	134.6	118.0
1862	1337.9	1159.3	n.a.	178.6	130.4
1863	1371.5	1157.5	n.a.	214.0	155.3
1864	1336.0	1115.0	7.4	228.4	144.6
1865	1386.8	1131.4	9.0	264.4	148.5
1866	1859.5	1551.9	9.5	317.1	121.6
1867	2041.0	1766.1	15.9	290.8	137.1
1868	2089.7	1776.2	11.3	324.8	228.5
1869	2131.5	1770.0	12.5	374.0	228.3
1870	2432.7	1829.4	31.1	634.4	248.4
1871	2845.2	2065.8	38.6	818.0	223.9
1872	3317.0	2296.5	66.7	1087.2	207.1
1873	3339.6	2405.0	61.7	996.3	211.8
1874	3412.7	2423.7	62.4	1051.4	203.0
1875	3536.7	2468.9	55.5	1123.3	144.4
1876	3613.7	2473.5	57.7	1197.9	150.0
1877	3781.3	2478.4	57.6	1360.5	150.3
1878	3855.5	2464.3	55.3	1446.5	151.8
1879	3960.0	2514.3	67.6	1513.3	148.7
1880	4066.5	2524.2	81.8	1624.1	178.5
1881	4055.2	2441.3	80.4	1694.3	138.3
1882	3968.4	2250.6	61.8	1779.6	159.2
1883	4057.7	2191.2	74.1	1940.6	322.8
1884	4292.5	2241.0	76.7	2128.2	371.3
1885	4561.6	2261.3	85.5	2385.8	338.8
1886	4943.4	2305.5	87.4	2725.3	345.7
1887	5071.2	2336.8	95.4	2829.8	379.3
1888	5107.0	2314.0	106.4	2899.4	435.6
1889	5226.1	2358.0	83.5	2951.6	438.9
1890	5178.2	2369.6	78.2	2886.8	409.8
1891	5110.8	2353.1	80.4	2838.1	442.8
1892	5275.7	2372.7	71.0	2974.0	447.3
1893	5270.6	2416.9	64.9	2918.6	446.7
1894	5186.0	2388.8	67.9	2865.1	514.2
1895	5269.8	2319.1	60.8	3011.5	506.2
1896	5173.2	2289.3	65.0	2948.9	516.5
1897	5317.0	2355.0	73.3	3035.3	465.5
1898	5478.1	2369.3	74.5	3183.3	477.8
1899	5871.4	2437.2	83.8	3518.0	469.5
1900	6009.4	2402.8	78.0	3684.6	468.4
1901	6247.8	2403.0	81.6	3926.4	494.7
1902	6431.2	2432.1	87.6	4086.7	528.4
1903	6850.5	2489.5	97.5	4458.5	721.6

Table 9.A.1 (continued)

	Money Stock (*M*) (1) (2) − (3) + (4)	Currency (*C*) (2)	Bank-held Currency (*CB*) (3)	Bank Deposits (*D*) (4)	Metallic Reserves (*IRA*) (5)
	(millions of lire)				
1904	7327.6	2520.1	102.9	4910.4	728.0
1905	7985.9	2587.6	129.6	5527.9	919.9
1906	8179.8	2775.7	134.8	5538.9	1068.6
1907	8960.3	3013.2	178.1	6125.2	1270.4
1908	9428.2	2947.0	189.4	6670.6	1314.7
1909	9984.5	2981.5	198.9	7201.9	1331.7
1910	10564.7	3029.2	198.7	7734.2	1344.6
1911	11160.7	3215.4	204.1	8149.4	1397.0
1912	11329.9	3215.5	231.9	8346.3	1433.9
1913	11849.3	3300.1	229.7	8778.9	1495.7
1914	12797.7	4018.7	276.1	9055.1	1532.3

	Foreign-Exchange Reserves (*IRFE*) (millions of lire (6)	Real GNP (*RYI*) (millions of 1913 lire) (7)	Consumer Price Index (*CPI*) (1913 = 100) (8)	Wholesale Price Index (*WPI*) (1913 = 100) (9)	GNP Deflator (*PYI*) (1913 = 100) (10)
1861		84.1358	82.0	97.58	73.94
1862		87.1822	82.5	91.19	74.74
1863		85.3033	80.1	87.17	70.22
1864		86.4842	77.9	87.17	70.51
1865		87.9622	76.6	85.80	70.86
1866		91.8083	77.4	89.73	74.71
1867		97.4362	79.3	90.18	76.84
1868		99.9044	82.5	95.75	83.68
1869		103.0410	83.0	89.27	78.93
1870		103.4800	84.2	88.54	78.16
1871		108.5480	86.8	91.28	80.14
1872		108.3870	98.1	99.14	90.02
1873		113.1790	104.0	105.08	98.64
1874		110.8970	106.5	104.89	95.90
1875		114.4030	91.2	92.91	80.68
1876		113.0780	96.5	90.04	81.97
1877		113.7130	100.4	102.11	91.59
1878		114.8740	96.7	98.85	85.99
1879		115.0260	95.5	92.82	89.12
1880		119.4100	99.0	93.30	87.12
1881		111.2060	92.6	87.26	82.99
1882		117.5900	90.4	89.56	85.16
1883		115.8470	87.5	83.91	80.90
1884		116.4960	85.8	80.36	78.99
1885		117.9630	87.7	84.67	84.73
1886		122.2680	87.6	85.15	85.28

Table 9.A.1 (continued)

	Foreign-Exchange Reserves (*IRFE*) (millions of lire (6)	Real GNP (*RYI*) (millions of 1913 lire) (7)	Consumer Price Index (*CPI*) (1913=100) (8)	Wholesale Price Index (*WPI*) (1913=100) (9)	GNP Deflator (*PYI*) (1913=100) (10)
1887		121.1680	87.4	79.41	79.27
1888		120.2110	88.5	80.75	78.77
1889		114.5710	90.0	85.44	83.66
1890		123.0170	93.2	87.64	85.33
1891		126.2310	92.9	85.25	87.34
1892		120.3140	92.1	81.03	82.06
1893		124.5200	90.1	75.96	80.67
1894	22.5	122.5690	89.7	73.75	78.56
1895	24.2	123.3080	89.2	77.59	80.40
1896	42.5	124.9400	88.8	78.16	79.07
1897	94.6	119.8550	88.6	76.63	80.03
1898	89.3	129.8240	89.2	78.74	83.96
1899	92.5	131.2540	87.8	80.75	83.03
1900	111.2	137.2890	88.2	84.50	84.10
1901	111.5	144.9760	88.3	84.10	81.31
1902	115.0	140.8630	87.7	81.30	79.46
1903	117.9	148.4830	90.3	80.60	83.08
1904	134.9	148.2080	91.4	77.00	82.29
1905	133.6	151.6760	91.5	80.30	82.63
1906	129.7	149.7520	93.2	83.30	88.60
1907	134.8	173.6640	97.6	89.80	88.32
1908	141.6	167.6950	96.6	87.40	86.86
1909	141.8	179.7000	93.9	88.10	88.67
1910	143.6	165.6680	96.5	88.20	94.17
1911	157.7	179.2430	98.9	95.30	96.69
1912	156.2	182.6290	99.8	102.60	99.42
1913	156.2	188.8500	100.0	100.00	100.00
1914	199.2	184.5260	100.0	95.80	98.94

	No. of Lire per French Franc (*ELF*) (11)	No. of Lire per British Pound (*ELUK*) (12)	Yield on Long-term Government Bonds (percent per year): Italy (*RII*) (13)	France (*RIF*) (14)
1861	n.a.	n.a.	6.97	4.38
1862	n.a.	n.a.	7.26	4.28
1863	n.a.	n.a.	7.09	4.39
1864	n.a.	n.a.	7.55	4.54
1865	n.a.	n.a.	7.83	4.42
1866	107.99	n.a.	9.23	4.55
1867	107.37	n.a.	9.66	4.41

Table 9.A.1 (continued)

	No. of Lire per French Franc (*ELF*) (11)	No. of Lire per British Pound (*ELUK*) (12)	Yield on Long-term Government Bonds (percent per year) Italy (*RII*) (13)	France (*RIF*) (14)
1868	109.82	n.a.	9.32	4.27
1869	103.94	n.a.	8.95	4.17
1870	104.50	n.a.	9.00	4.76
1871	105.35	n.a.	7.20	5.51
1872	108.66	n.a.	5.98	5.47
1873	114.20	n.a.	6.25	5.34
1874	112.25	n.a.	6.25	4.90
1875	108.27	n.a.	5.88	4.66
1876	108.47	n.a.	5.84	4.35
1877	109.63	n.a.	5.88	4.27
1878	109.42	n.a.	5.60	4.06
1879	111.19	n.a.	5.15	3.73
1880	110.53	n.a.	4.88	3.56
1881	100.28	25.40	4.87	3.54
1882	101.26	25.55	4.97	3.67
1883	99.15	25.03	4.97	3.83
1884	100.00	25.23	4.61	3.88
1885	100.38	25.38	4.56	3.79
1886	100.19	25.31	4.14	3.66
1887	100.82	25.54	4.46	3.78
1888	100.98	25.57	4.52	3.63
1889	100.67	25.42	4.58	3.51
1890	101.15	25.54	4.60	3.26
1891	101.55	25.65	4.71	3.18
1892	103.55	26.06	4.66	3.07
1893	107.97	27.19	4.63	3.10
1894	111.08	27.94	4.59	2.98
1895	105.57	26.58	4.37	2.96
1896	107.63	27.11	4.35	2.94
1897	105.14	26.45	4.18	2.90
1898	106.97	27.05	4.06	2.92
1899	107.32	27.07	4.01	2.98
1900	106.44	26.77	4.02	2.98
1901	104.30	26.25	3.97	2.96
1902	101.21	25.46	3.91	2.99
1903	99.95	25.15	3.91	3.06
1904	100.12	25.20	3.90	3.11
1905	99.94	25.14	3.82	3.03
1906	99.94	25.15	3.87	3.08
1907	99.97	25.18	3.69	3.16
1908	100.00	25.13	3.63	3.13
1909	100.42	25.29	3.61	3.07
1910	100.51	25.35	3.60	3.06

Table 9.A.1 (continued)

	No. of Lire per French Franc (*ELF*) (11)	No. of Lire per British Pound (*ELUK*) (12)	Yield on Long-term Government Bonds (percent per year): Italy (*RII*) (13)	France (*RIF*) (14)
1911	100.52	25.39	3.67	3.14
1912	100.93	25.47	3.60	3.27
1913	101.77	25.68	3.58	3.44
1914	n.a.	26.24	3.75	3.78

Sources: Col. (2), Del Mattia 1969, tables 5–7, 14; col. (3), ibid., table 22; col. (4), ibid., tables 2, 2a, 2b, 23; col. (5), ibid., tables 11–15, 19, 23, 26, 28; col. (6), ibid., table 19; cols. (7)–(10), De Mattia 1977, table 7; cols. (11)–(12), Borgatta 1933; col. (13), De Mattia 1969; col. (14), De Mattia 1977, table 81.

Appendix B *New Estimates of the Demand for Money Function*

Despite the research already done by one of us (Spinelli 1980) on the demand for money in Italy for the period 1867–1965, three reasons were persuasive for reestimating the function. First, our money-stock series excludes currency held by banks whereas Spinelli included it by oversight. Second, Spinelli used the official discount rate as a measure of the opportunity cost of holding money. We have uncovered a long-term rate of interest that is in principle superior to the discount rate. Third, we wanted to ascertain the sensitivity of the demand-for-money function to a change in the sample period.

The model employed is that used by Spinelli (1980). It postulates that the demand for money depends upon permanent income and the opportunity cost of holding money. Actual real-money balances adjust slowly to the difference between actual and desired real balances; permanent income is a weighted average of past actual values of income. Such a partial-adjustment–adaptive-expectations model can be represented by the following equations:

(A1) $$M_t^* = a + bY_t^* + ci_t;\ a,\ b > 0,\ c < 0;$$

(A2) $$M_t - M_{t-1} = \alpha(M_t^* - M_{t-1}) + u_t;\ 0 < \alpha \leqslant 1;$$

(A3) $$Y_t^* - Y_{t-1}^* = \beta(Y_t - Y_{t-1}^*);\ 0 < \beta \leqslant 1,$$

where M^* is the desired stock of real-money balances, M is the actual stock, Y^* and Y permanent and actual real income and i the proxy for the

Table 9.A.2 Money Demand (*t*-statistics in parentheses)

a	*b*	*c*	*t*	α	β	R^2	D.W.
−.925	.868	−.138	.016	.968	.278	.99	2.106
(−1.700)	(2.320)	(−1.160)	(5.938)	(5.309)	(2.562)		

Sources: Real income is GNP at constant prices (*RYI*, table 9.A.1, col. 7). Real permanent income is solved out by the model. The rate of interest is the yield on the long-term government bonds *Rendita Italiana* (*RII*, table 9.A.1, col. 13).

opportunity cost of holding money. The model is estimated for the period 1867–1914. Money data were centered at midyear and deflated by the consumer price index. All relevant variables were deflated by population. A time trend was added as a regressor; its coefficient is denoted by *t*. The functional specification is logarithmic, except for the time variable. We employed a nonlinear OLS estimation procedure which is subject to the well-known single-equation bias. However, we believe this bias is quantitatively small and not worth pursuing here (cf. Laidler 1977a). Calliari, Spinelli, and Verga (1981) show that simultaneous-equations estimates for Italy are about the same as single-equation ones.

The parameter estimates are given in table 9.A.2. The permanent-income coefficient, *b*, is not significantly different from unity. To correctly evaluate the inflationary impact of monetary growth, however, we cannot overlook the role of the time variable which is strongly significant and has an elasticity of about 0.5.

The relative interest insensitivity of the demand for money confirms the earlier results of Spinelli (1980). The reader is cautioned not to draw the conclusion that velocity is unresponsive to interest rates. Changes in transitory income may be regarded as a proxy for interest-rate changes. To the extent that the demand for money responds to permanent income, the estimates are compatible with a positive relationship existing between velocity and interest rates (cf. Laidler 1977b).

The adjustment between actual and desired money balances is completed within a year; learning takes longer.

Notes

1. The U.S. Commission of Gold and Silver Inquiry (U.S. Congress 1925, pp. 347–52) has a compact but useful history of this period.

2. The economist R. Busacca (1870) also supported the monopoly thesis.

3. In addition to the increase in gold supply, the increase in the market price of silver relative to gold possibly resulted from the shift of the source of European cotton imports from the Civil War–ravaged United States to Far Eastern countries with silver standards (De Mattia 1959).

4. Gold lire and gold francs had equivalent gold content. Silver lire of denominations of five and above and silver francs also had equivalent silver content.

5. There was a condition: Within two years after its secession from the union, a member-state pledged to repurchase, with gold or foreign exchange, small-denomination coins circulating outside its territory.

6. The five minor banks of issue received BN notes for an amount equal to their metal holdings. Since this transaction did not alter the aggregate amount of currency in circulation, the law can be explained as a governmental scheme to raise the market share of BN, thus paving the way for BN as the only bank of issue.

7. The then–Minister of Finance Sella stated several times that so long as the prices of bonds were low, it was preferable to monetize the deficits.

8. The net worth of each bank was as follows (in million lire): BN 450, Banca Nazionale Toscana 63, Banca Toscana di Credito 15, Banca Romana 45, Banco di Napoli 146.25, and Banco di Sicilia 36.

9. The intended effects of the legislation were not fully realized. The national branch network of BN and the regional character of the other five banks of issue preserved the premium of BN notes over their notes.

10. The immediate impact of a change in regime on the exchange rate is not limited to the Italian experience. British economic history offers similar evidence.

11. Paper money in circulation was to be reduced from 1097 to 864 million lire. As to the reserve requirement, the law prescribed that gold had to account for 33 percent and silver for 7 percent of note liabilities. There was no reserve requirement against deposit liabilities.

12. This point is often stressed by Triffin (1964).

13. See Herring and Marston 1977 for an approach of this sort applied to Germany of the 1960s.

14. Velocity of circulation fell by 131 percent from 1861 to 1913 (figure 9.6).

15. The observation for 1865, which we could not discover, is presumed to be 100. In the empirical work this observation is omitted.

16. An obvious criticism is that a careful application of equation (9) requires one-year rather than long-term bonds. Unfortunately, we had no alternative to our procedure.

17. Lindert's evidence (1969) of asymmetries between the interest differentials required to attract funds to major money-market centers may be in agreement with our hypothesis; e.g., the interest differential required to attract funds from small countries to London was greater than that required to attract funds to Paris. Our evidence suggests that if Lindert's asymmetries incorporate differences in country risks, they are far from being constant over time. It may well be that France was preferred to Italy at all times—an inference consistent with the data reported above—but this difference was not time independent. In sum, the variability of Lindert's asymmetries is explained by a variable risk premium against the lira.

References

Bloomfield, Arthur I. 1959. *Monetary policy under the international gold standard, 1880–1914*. New York: Federal Reserve Bank of New York.

Borgatta, Gino. 1933. *Bilancia dei pagamenti*. Milano: Giuffre.

Brunner, Karl, and Allan H. Meltzer. 1966. A credit-market theory of the money supply and an explanation of two puzzles in U.S. monetary policy. In *Essays in honor of Marco Fanno: Investigations in economic theory and methodology*, ed. Tullio Bagiotti. Padova: Cedam.

Busacca, R. 1870. *Studio sul corso forzoso dei biglietti di banca in Italia*. Firenze: Tipografia della Gazzetta d'Italia.

Cagan, Phillip. 1965. *Determinants and effects of changes in the stock of money, 1875–1960*. New York: Columbia University Press.

Calliari, Sergio, Franco Spinelli, and Giovanni Verga. 1984. The demand for money in the Italian economy: A survey of the literature and new estimates. *Manchester School of Economics and Social Studies* 54 (forthcoming).

Commissione Parlamentare di Inchiesta. 1868–69. *Relazione della Commissione sul corso forzoso dei biglietti di banca*. Firenze.

De Cecco, Marcello. 1984. *International gold standard: Money and the empire*. New York: St. Martin's Press.

De Mattia, Renato. 1959. *L'unificazione monetaria italiana*. Torino: I.L.T.E.

———. 1969. *I bilanci degli istituti di emissione italiani 1865–1936*. Roma: Banca d'Italia.

———. 1977. *Storia del capitale della Banca d'Italia e degli istituti predecessori*. Roma: Banca d'Italia.

Ferrara, Francesco. 1868. *Del corso forzato e della maniera per abolirlo*. Firenze: Nuova Antologia.

Fratianni, Michele, and Franco Spinelli. 1982. The growth of government in Italy: Evidence from 1861 to 1979. *Public Choice* 39 (no. 2): 221–43.

Friedman, Milton, and Anna J. Schwartz. 1963. *A monetary history of the United States, 1867–1960*. Princeton: Princeton University Press.

———. 1982. *Monetary trends in the United States and the United Kingdom: Their relation to income, prices, and interest rates, 1867–1975*. Chicago: University of Chicago Press.

Garelli, Antonio. 1879. *Le banche*. Biblioteca dell'Economista. Serie 3, vol. 6. Torino: UTET.

Girton, Lance, and Don Roper. 1977. A monetary model of exchange market pressure applied to the postwar Canadian experience. *American Economic Review* 67 (Sept.): 537–48.

Haugh, L. D. 1976. Checking the independence of two covariance stationary time series: A univariate residual cross-correlated approach. *Journal of the American Statistical Association* 71 (June): 378–85.

Herring, Richard J., and Richard C. Marston. 1977. *National monetary policies and international financial markets*. Amsterdam: North-Holland Publishing Co.

ISTAT. 1957. *Indagine statistica sullo sviluppo del reddito nazionale dell' Italia dal 1861 al 1956*. Annali di Statistica Serie 8, vol. 9. Roma.

———. 1976. *Sommario di statistiche storiche dell'Italia 1861–1975*. Roma: Istituto Poligrafico di Stato.

Kreinin, Mordechai E., and Lawrence H. Officer. 1978. *The monetary approach to the balance of payments: A survey*. Princeton Studies in International Finance, no. 43. Princeton: Princeton University Press.

Laidler, David. 1977a. *The demand for money: Theories and evidence*. New York: Dun Donnelley.

———. 1977b. Demand management in Britain from a monetarist viewpoint. Paper presented at the Conference on Demand Management, London.

Lewis, W. A. 1978. *Growth and fluctuations, 1870–1913*. London: Allen and Unwin.

Lindert, Peter H. 1969. *Key currencies and gold, 1900–1913*. Princeton Studies in International Finance, no. 24. Princeton: Princeton University Press.

Majorana, Giuseppe. 1893. *I dati statistici nella questione bancaria*. Roma: Loescher.

Martello, Tullio. 1881. *L'abolizione del corso forzoso*. Venezia: Visentini.

McCloskey, Donald N., and J. Richard Zecher. 1976. How the gold standard worked, 1880–1913. In *The monetary approach to the balance of payments*, ed. J. Frenkel and H. G. Johnson. Toronto: University of Toronto Press.

Meese, Richard, and Kenneth Rogoff. 1981. Empirical exchange rate models of the seventies: Are any fit to survive? International Finance Discussion Paper no. 184. Washington, D.C.: Board of Governors of the Federal Reserve System.

Mitchell, B. R. 1962. *Abstract of British historical statistics*. Cambridge: Cambridge University Press.

———. 1978. *European historical statistics, 1750–1970*. New York: Columbia University Press.

Nurkse, Ragnar. 1944. *International currency experience: Lessons of the inter-war experience*. Princeton: League of Nations.

Pedone, Antonio. 1967. Il bilancio dello stato e lo sviluppo economico Italiano: 1861–1963. *Rassegna Economica* 67 (Mar.–Apr.): 285–341.

Pierce, D. A., and L. D. Haugh. 1977. Causality in temporal systems: Characterizations and survey. *Journal of Econometrics* 5 (Aug.): 265–93.

Spinelli, Franco. 1980. The demand for money in the Italian economy, 1867–1965. *Journal of Monetary Economics* 6 (Jan.): 83–104.

Supino, Camillo. 1929. *Storia della circolazione cartacea in Italia dal 1860 al 1928*. Milano: Societa Editoriale Libraria.

Triffin, Robert. 1964. *The evolution of the international monetary system: Historical reappraisal and future perspectives*. Princeton Studies in International Finance, no. 12. Princeton: Princeton University Press.

U.S. Congress. Commission of Gold and Silver Inquiry. 1925. *European currency and finance*. Report prepared by John Parke Young. 67th Cong., 4th sess. Washington, D.C.: Government Printing Office.

[19]

The State and the Economy in the Industrialization of Italy from its Origins to the Welfare State

Franco Bonelli

Beginning with the 1880s, the process of capital formation began to be put decisively into effect by a state-inspired process which drained resources away from the agrarian and mercantile sectors, and directed them elsewhere. In later periods also, though in different forms and by different methods, Italian agriculture, both in its more developed components and in the more backward areas, together with the more traditional sectors in general, remained at the service of a cumulative mechanism which continued to show its best results in the 'modern' sectors, i.e. industry and services. This took place largely through processes of transfer of resources in which the state played the leading role, in many different ways, and with a constant process of updating.

From the beginning of the process of industrialization in Italy, the state operated as a customer, carried out bail-outs, guaranteed the basis of the credit mechanism and provided the means for the financial markets to operate. It undertook constant supportive action for the benefit of businesses. At the same time, the permanence of low levels of internal consumption – in many areas remaining at a subsistence level for long periods – operated in a dual sense: on the one hand as a factor contributing to limiting the possibilities of self-financing in the 'new' sectors, and on the other hand as an element which prevented the problem of the balance of payments from exploding and becoming unsolvable as a result of the trade deficit.

If we look at Italian economic development with an eye to the long term, we are strongly tempted to explain the constituent and functional elements of the model of industrialization in this or some similar way. It was a system which functioned for the whole period when Italy was working to provide itself with a productive apparatus of the kind which was already well-established and structured in other parts of the West. The period of time during which this took place was prolonged, and there was a certain amount of doubt about the outcome (we need only recall the hesitations in the development of iron and steel policy) right up to the 1950s. The results, measured in terms of industrial structures, could be said to be consistent with the premise: i.e. with the functioning and procedural conditions belonging to the model described in the opening paragraph.

The persistence of archaic models of consumption determined the survival of pre-capitalistic productive structures for a long time. Such models find their outlets in restricted and qualitatively limited dimensions in the market, or relegate their functions to purely local environments mainly tied to the logic of the agricultural economy and family consumption. When we take an overall view, the progress of destructuring in the 'traditional' economy has been very slow, alternating between acceleration and sudden stops. Above all it has left whole geographical areas and large productive sectors untouched. (This explains, among other things, some of the more extreme forms of dualism to be found within various sectors.)

The other area in which the effects of this relationship between low consumption and economic structure are registered is that of the 'new' sectors of the economy. By this I mean the productive sectors dominated by the presence of large modern firms whose development in Italy was vigorously backed by the state and the big 'mixed' banks. Whatever the causal direction of this nexus – in other words whether it passed from demand to structure or vice-versa – it is certain that limits in demand and low self-financing capacity among the firms on the one hand, and the role of the mixed banks and governmental policy on the other, are two sides of the same coin – i.e. of a particular version of the cumulative mechanism. In this mechanism the so-called 'basic' sectors, instead of developing as a result of pressure from below (demand for intermediary goods on the part of manufacturing industries), found the impetus for their growth in surrogate procedures of structuring the productive apparatus, based on the mobilization and transfer of resources by intermediary financial agents and by the state. These may act separately – especially in the descending phase of the cycle – or jointly. On the other hand, manufacturing industries, organized on a more or less capitalistic basis and more or less protected at import tariff level, were forced (given the premise) to have recourse to every kind of expedient in order to survive on the limited internal market. These limitations were caused by the weighty presence of the traditional sectors on the one hand, and on the other by the lack of multiplier effects on the level of wages from investment in the basic sectors. (There was much complaint about the effect of this on the credit market.)

In fact, the formative process of the Italian industrial system has come to be seen as the insertion of certain advanced technico-industrial experiences within the context of a pre-capitalist structure in the process of slow modernization (or rather of modernization zone by zone). It was only after some decades and under certain specific conditions that this insertion gave rise to a general adoption of modern business structures, both in productive and financial terms, on the basis of a more 'refined' structure of interdependence in the productive sector. Neither tariff and financial protection nor, subsequently, extreme solutions such as those tried by the fascist regime with the adoption of the autarchic model, succeeded in taking the place of the multiplier effects which could set in motion new surges of demand from below (internal or external). These decisions certainly produced obvious consequences for company organization, especially in the context of the 'heavy' sectors; this is shown clearly by the examples of vertical and horizontal integration between the different parts of the iron and steel, mechanical, construction and electro-chemical industries. But this was a question of phenomena appertaining more to the organizational and financial logic of large basic units than to the growth in global demand – the only factor which can truly be translated into scale economies. Again, on the eve of the Second World War, the Italian industrial apparatus seemed to be very variegated in its make-up and disjointed in its structure. This was typical of the coexistence of various levels of development between which there was only limited and occasional communication.

It we wish to draw these observations together and sum up the essence of the more than 80-year period that preceded the 1950s, we might say that the 'Italian way' to industrialization has been characterized by the intermingling, amalgamating and superimposing of innovations derived from the spread of the first industrial revolution in Europe and elsewhere. It also involves other innovations, promoted or fostered 'from above' through measures of forced development. Although such methods made it possible to narrow the gap between Italy and other Western capitalist countries, they nevertheless gave rise to a system which maintains, and to some extent demands, substantial elements of diversity from the Western model.

The phase which seems crucial and decisive is that of reconstruction and initial development in the 1950s. During this period, while the functional conditions which we have pointed out as typical of the cumulative mechanism in Italy continued to operate, some events which were highly charged with consequences in the medium to long term intervened to change the existing picture. Along with the reestablishment of political and trade union liberty, a model of social development was sanctioned in the Constitution whose essential ingredients were the broadening of the social basis of the democratic regime, access to levels of individual prosperity, and the advent of what, in current parlance, was to become the 'welfare state'; also the liberalization of trade and financial integration at the international level. The decade beginning in 1950 can be seen as both the 'final segment' of the longstanding diagram whose progress we are studying, and also the incubation stage of what was to happen in the near future: a genuine glimpse of what can justly be described as the second Italian industrial revolution.

The implications of the 'internal' choices of model and the changes which took place in the external picture during the course of the 1960s were to render useless the mechanisms of the model derived from the 19th century. The factors which proved most disruptive – leaving aside here the details of temporal and sectoral confusions – were to be found in the intensity, duration and quality of the internal and external demand for industrial manufactures, i.e. in the failure of that kind of 'Malthusian' balance of low consumption which up to that time had marked the complex course of Italian industrial development. The motive force operating this basic lever of capitalist development (constituted by demand) was full adherence to the 'Western' model and international integration. The first because, as the political conditions were found right, trade union liberties were put into effect and the premise for profound changes was created in the labour market; the second, because the picture of relations between the Italian and international economies radically and finally changed. From this moment onwards, in fact, Italy was not only confronted by a demand for overseas products on a scale not seen before (and in a way which influenced the development of its productive system), but external demand also served to prepare the road for the explosion of internal demand with the kind of products it offered and the model of consumption it advocated. In this way a process of homogenizing internal and external demand structures was put in motion which finally overturned the whole logic which had for so long prevailed in the way the system functioned.

As a result of the spread and general adoption of scale economies, a network of functional relationships was gradually built up between the various productive sectors, as well as connecting linkages between firms and activities. This began progressively to fill quite a large number of the gaps still present in the industrial edifice. After barely succeeding over many decades in building up an industrial structure along asymmetrical lines, dominated by the contrast between the abnormal development of the large basic sectors and the extended area occupied by the old manufacturing system (both artisan and otherwise), Italy suddenly found itself having available, in the course of one single decade, a productive apparatus whose character was not dissimilar to that of the most advanced industrial countries and capable of competing with them on the productive front.

Alongside the evolution of the general conditions of Italian economic development, we can observe a progressive alteration in the role which the state exercised in the traditional model. This change took place in various stages and as a result of various converging circumstances. First of all, in conjunction with the successes of the long favourable phase of the cycle, no care was taken to improve, update or correct the mode and objectives of state intervention in the economy. For the most part, faith was placed in the allocative functions delegated to the market, while there was heavy privatization of the economy. The result was a substantial lessening of the possibilities of control and direction of the economic system, not only immediately but (more importantly) for the future. The managerial structure of the state which originated in the 19th century, abandoned to its own devices, came up against an irreversible process of decline, even in the most traditional sectors of public intervention. As a result of the notable delays with which measures of fiscal policy were put into effect, the function of control of the cycle was assigned exclusively, or almost so, to monetary policy.

As the expectations of the welfare state came rapidly and irresistibly to the fore, the state machine proved completely inadequate to function as a provider of services, remaining confined to the role of a powerful agent for transferring resources. Moreover, as an owner of companies and as an entrepreneur itself, the state suffered the same counterblows as afflicted private businesses in the descending phase of the world economic cycle. In this way it transpired that Italy, which had acted for the longest period as a guarantor and stimulator of the process of accumulation, now found itself incapable of harnessing the necessary means to reactivate or modernize basic productive structures and output as currently demanded by world capitalism. On the reasons for this incapacity on the part of the state to measure up to the requirements of the new stage of internal and international development, we need to dwell in more detail for a moment.

We have already established that the state in Italy somewhat precociously fulfilled a role as promoter of industrial development. And, we might add, it did this first and foremost in a politico-institutional setting which left space for political and trade union liberties and for the development of forms of economic democracy (for instance, the economic and social policies of the local councils, and the cooperative movement up to the eve of the first World War). During the 20 years of fascism, that liberty and development were sacrificed. It has also been said that the specific and peculiar action of the state in support of the productive basis from time to time affected the 'new' sectors of the economy or, rather, the so-called 'key sectors'. However, in doing this, the state generally took account only of the demands of the industrial and financial groups which were slowly emerging (for example, the railways in the first period and then, in order, iron and steel, electricity, chemicals and others), almost always ignoring the needs of the other sizable part of the productive process, i.e. the working class. Even the interventions undertaken in the name of the defence of employment were most often motivated by reasons linked to internal balances among the main capitalistic groups. The work of political mediation by the state was thus carried out for a long time by favouring and sanctioning at institutional level the necessary compromises between the various industrial and financial oligarchies. By behaving as a partner of private groups, the state always operated in the context of negotiations which aimed, in exchange for the interest of these groups, at backing up a series of objectives which were very little affected by binding social factors.

Already during the fascist period, with its search both for consensus from the lower and middle bourgeoisie and for a policy which sought to compete with the welfare systems of democratic states, the need was felt to broaden the social basis of the recipients of state aid. This was done by making use of planning instruments (which, however, were usually not the ones which the regime claimed in its propaganda). However, given the ideological and political preoccupations of the regime, any modernization of the process of state intervention could only be entrusted to interventions from above – of an authoritarian character. These blocked the progress of experiments in reform and participation which had been made in previous decades. Also there was no hesitation in annulling political, trade union and civil liberties in the name of objectives which in the long run, and even more so than in the past, were pursued *against* the interests of the working class.

After the Second World War, as mentioned, with the advent of a democratic regime, Italy's governing class was faced with the need for more comprehensive mediation than in the past (because *all* social classes were potentially affected). It was also politically more complex because the old political hierarchies had yielded to a multiplicity of representative centres. But it proved necessary to wait for the 1960s before traces of welfare policies similar to those instituted in other Western countries could be found in Italy.

The first sorties of the democratic state in Italy into the field of social welfare developed under the impetus of the claims of the workers' movement, which had both continuity and substantial political content. They produced evident effects, in rapid fashion and in a period limited to a few years – coinciding with a genuine explosion of mass consumption. This was no mere chance: it marked the point when (as we have seen), together with the end of the Malthusian condition of low consumption, it became clear that the state was incapable not only of becoming (as demanded) a supplier of a huge range of services for the community at large, but also of maintaining and updating the functions it had always carried out in pursuit of the objectives of accumulation and productive growth.

The traditional modes and objectives of state intervention on the one hand, and the time that it took to introduce the welfare state on the other, are often cited as reasons to explain why there was no takeoff of the state as supplier of social services and promoter of the new policy of development.

In most Western countries, the extension of state intervention was essentially motivated by the need to control the cycle and satisfy primary collective needs. Only more recently did it become necessary to promote the development of basic sectors and services directly dependent on the private economy (research, education, land resources, energy, etc.). In any case, the presence of more or less strong workers' organizations, the controls they exercised, and the needs of a political kind which derive from them, have for some time conditioned the *quality* of the means of state intervention. The result has been a general advance in the capacity for intervention, with relative development of the procedures for planning and coordination, on a fairly wide front. This circumstance has certainly borne fruit when engaging the public administration in policies aimed at increasing the overall efficiency of the system by the provision of new services, or devising new means of planning and control in various sections of the economy.

However, in the Italian case, the state, called on prematurely to play a supporting and creative role in the productive basis of the economy, has had to make use of *ad hoc* instruments. It has frequently shown great flexibility and innovative capacity. But the direct administration, the so-called public service, generally given little attention by the ruling class, was very rapidly condemned to a role distressingly subordinate to the needs of industrial development (we could cite the cases of inefficiency which are directly related to the 'freedom' of the private sector, or of certain managements whose activities were directed towards the private interests of some of the 'parallel' public bodies). Given these premises, the administrative structures of the 19th-century state, built up in the aftermath of the national revolution, found that their functions were gradually undermined and distorted. In any case, even when efforts were made at modernization and adaption to the new demand for social services, these structures became involved in a process of more and more diffused mediation. They progressively lost their 19th-century character as a coordinated body of structures, laws, measures of control and procedure aimed at the pursuit of well-defined objectives, and took on more and more the aspect of an incoherent accumulation of institutions, easily beholden to particular interests.

For this reason, although in the past the Italian state proved capable of directing development towards 'major projects', carried out bail-outs, mobilized capital for the financing of whole industries and reorganized strategically important sectors on a new basis, it proved completely inadequate to the tasks required of it by the new phase. These included providing a very broad range of social services and of operating, so to speak, as a computer-brain for development, intervening in crucial sectors such as education, research, transport, energy and health, territorial organization and so on. From this point of view even the successes obtained by some of the efficient 'parallel' bodies hardly count: these are seen merely as substitutes which in the long run could not serve to resolve the problems which the state had to face in its unified function of supplier of services and policies.

We must also take account of the fate which state activities met with from the 1950s onwards – above all because of the effects which derived directly or indirectly from activities aimed at structuring both the industrial system and relationships between the state and business enterprises. We have said that the decade which bridged the 1950s and 1960s can be pointed to as the crucial phase. Alongside the traditional mechanisms by which the Italian economy functioned, others began to emerge at this time which were destined to change the actual premises of the initial model and to give a direct impetus to the efforts by which Italy had been seeking for decades to narrow the gap between itself and other Western industrialized countries. Too often, however, there is a tendency to ignore the limitations of this stage, which only occurred some years after the last echoes of the 'Italian economic miracle' had died away. To start with, we should point out that the facts into which the so-called 'swing towards free trade' of 1947–48 was converted are rather more prosaic than might have been expected on the basis of dogmatic assumptions, or at least of principle, from the label attributed to the economic policy of these years. In many ways it is nothing more than an updating of an experiment already tried in the first years of the 1920s, in a different institutional context and in the presence of international collaboration and a progressive liberalization of trade. As happened then, the key element of the return to economic liberalism was essentially the ample freedom of movement left to the enterprises already in the field – to those which were the expression of consolidated industrial and financial interests as well as emerging ones. It is no coincidence that an analysis of the lines of direction by which the Italian industrial apparatus was being rebuilt and converted in these years will inevitably demonstrate their essential eclecticism. In fact, there were a number of significant moves towards a return to the tradition which saw the state as the forerunner in forming productive bases in the 'key' sectors of the economy, as shown by the events of the iron and steel revival, by the increase in the productive apparatus of the electrical and chemical industries, and by the development of oil policy. But in reconstructing the background to these initiatives, we have the impression that we are faced with something different from the interventions of the Giolittian age, or even of the 1930s – something in which the weight of politics and the entrepreneurial importance of those responsible for these choices count for a great deal. The last opportunity presented to our country to follow a policy of completing the industrial matrix by operating from the side of supply (i.e. anticipating the establishment of structures to which the future seemed to assign a strategic role) thus concluded with an uncertain outcome. From this standpoint, i.e. from the point of view of the processes of modernization and updating of the industrial matrix at the hands of the state, the definitive reply to the unknown elements which had remained unresolved was to come later, in the course of the 1960s and 1970s.

What strikes one most about the economic development of Italy in those two decades is not so much the handing over of the economy to the allocatory processes of the market, which in any case was already implicit in the ideological and political premises of reconstruction, but the passivity with which the consequences were accepted on the economic and social planes. (This was also true at the urban development level, in the use of land and the defence of the environment.) The marginal nature of the corrective measures adopted by the state, which was constantly proving to be weaker and less and less efficient, is also a notable factor. In fact, what may seem to some intractable free-marketeers even now like the intrusive presence of the state was nothing more than a less and less coordinated ensemble of public interventions (the use of the plural is essential to convey the effect of the disruption of the state structure) aimed for the most part at satisfying demands imposed by the market itself. Italian industrial policy showed evidence of a shorter and shorter range, and more and more limited horizons. The process of formation of the Italian system thus began to lack a mechanism for investment decisions designed to pursue long-term objectives, a sort of 'large-scale projects section' for state enterprise, aimed at producing a firm basis for economic development.

One early but telling confirmation of this interpretation comes from the observation of certain of the macroscopic legacies of that stage of Italian economic development. Apart from being the cause of many dysfunctions from which the system is suffering, these cast worrying shadows over its future potential. There are two areas in which the system seems to show the greatest signs of weakness: in the first case, the agricultural sector, where the results can be seen of a policy which deceived itself into believing that it could quite easily perpetuate the role of agriculture as being 'at the service' of accumulation in other sectors. This policy and the logic behind it failed, progressively transforming agriculture from a primary to a 'subsidiary' sector which depletes resources from the system and increases the trade deficit. The other reason for weakness in the system specifically concerns the structure of the industrial apparatus and the marginal position to which certain basic 'new' sectors are relegated. I refer to sectors whose importance goes far beyond the fact of conferring completeness on the contemporary industrial matrix; this affects the availability of a series of goods and services which today fulfil the function of genuine productive factors.

I refer in particular to all the sectors of basic and applied scientific research, to old and new energy sources, to electronics and its application, to new forms of generalized education, to ecology and all those sectors linked to the overall efficiency of a modern industrial system. In the light of even a summary comparison with other countries of the Western industrialized world, it is clear that in the Italian economic system there is almost a total lack of those technological transformations and innovations which are spearheading a second industrial revolution on a world scale. Little or nothing has been done to develop the key sector *par excellence* today – the information technology field, understood not only as the availability of technical structures but also as an organizational culture. From this standpoint, it is natural to make a comparison with what was achieved at other times, specifically thanks to state intervention, in the fields of iron and steel and electricity. We cannot avoid the question of what destiny would have overtaken Italy if, at the end of the 19th century and the beginning of the present one, the attention of the ruling classes had remained concentrated on the traditional sectors which had led the way in the first English Industrial Revolution, instead of paying attention to the emerging ones, more or less 'heavy' and more or less capital-intensive, even when it seemed that the costs of providing them were enormously high for a restricted market and an essentially agricultural country, as Italy appeared to be at that time.

It would be out of place here to credit the observations made so far as a well-defined and definitive scheme of interpretation. Such a scheme, apart from describing the essential traits of the process of industrialization in Italy, would also need to point to a remedy capable of removing the difficulties which condition its development today. But the diagnosis formulated concerning the continuing incompatibility between the advent of the welfare state, the spread of mass consumption and international integration on the one hand, and accumulation and structuring of the industrial system on the other – even if it only partly corresponds to reality – unmistakably shows the following: that the necessary condition for overcoming that incompatibility lies in the role of the state, and that the only viable route to the recovery of that role lies in the reform of the administrative machine.

[20]

Discussion of the Origins of Italian Economic Dualism

L. Cafagna

1. The Dualism Existing Before Political Unification

Even in the years before the Second World War, it was possible for an authoritative economic historian to maintain that there were no organic differences between North and South (or, more precisely, between the Lombardy–Piedmont economy and that of the Neapolitan area) at the moment of Italian Unification.[1] Statements tending to minimize or reduce the extent of the differences can also be found in a large number of works which appeared after the war.[2]

The basis for this opinion, evidently influenced by the strongly controversial tone of conservative southern literature – which aimed at underlining the responsibilities of the Unitary government's political conduct – was given by the observation of what we could call economic 'macromorphology': the fact that both economies could be defined as substantially agricultural, with few beginnings of industrial activity. Evidently, this summary identification of evolutionary 'stages' seemed sufficient proof of equality in economic development. This point of view was supported by an external and descriptive type of comparison limited to listing the 'sectors' of industry already present in the two respective nuclei (i.e. those sectors which were, according to a simple classification, present in both the North and the South) and by the identification in both areas of a predominance of primary product exports, though the type of exports and the implications of linkages were not examined.

However, in the last few years some contemporary historians have, rather energetically, called attention to the need to look at the agricultural reality of the South in a less abstract way; also to evaluate fully the importance of a comparison between the structural aspects and the social and economic nature on the eve of Unification of agriculture of the northern regions, at least in Lombardy and Piedmont, and in the South. For example, accepting (even if it is still not confirmed) the opinion that there was no great disparity of industrial level between North and South in 1860, one of these scholars, Villani, felt it necessary to observe 'that the aspects of the socioeconomic development cannot be examined separately without the danger of being misunderstood'.[3] It seems to me that this is a rather important observation, in the sense that one must not make too much of a broad comparison of the 'stages' ('predominantly agricultural' is a formula which covers a vast number of rather different situations, especially with regard to dynamic potential). The true weakness of the South, adds Villani, was in the backwardness of the rural areas – the same sector where reserves of manpower would, at a more favourable time, assure the rapid evolution of Lombardy.

An American scholar, Eckaus,[4] was clearer than any other in expressing the idea that the relative backwardness of Southern Italy goes back before Unification, and that this (rather than government policy) was the reason for the difference in the development of the two areas, at least in the first period following Unity. In his research, Eckaus went beyond the agricultural sector to try to define the different levels reached by the two areas in manufacturing activities.

He attempted to do this by using the very first statistics produced after Unity and retropolating whenever possible. In fact, in terms of figures, he did not reach any conclusions which can be considered 'secure' at a macroeconomic level. Nevertheless, one point seems to emerge very clearly: the further one moves away from the figures or from the global or general indications and considers the importance of single items, the more readily relative differences become apparent. It is enough, in terms of agriculture, to look at the ratio between the cattle stock in the North, which is 46 per cent of the national total, while that of the South represents only 19 per cent! Concerning silk production, the value of the North's share is 88 per cent and that of the South only 3 per cent. The distribution of the production of the wool industry is 62 per cent in the North and 25 per cent in the South. Also of interest is the relevant difference per head in the development of the road network in the North and South, as well as the literacy rate which was 45.8 per cent in the North and 25.9 per cent in the South. All this in a context which shows the absolute levels of population in 1861 as being very close: 44.5 per cent in the North and 39.1 per cent in the South.[5]

There are many reasons for considering even these limited data as indicative of a situation of deep inequality, especially considering the importance of cattle stock for the agricultural economy of the time, of silk production in the general formation of surplus, and of the wool industry in the fairly limited industrial picture of the era. It would have been much more informative to provide data, not for the wool industry, but for cotton which was considerably more important. Unfortunately, census-type statistics are not available for this branch of industry for the years nearest to Unification. If anything, there were some indications that statistics could be misleading as, in the South, there were some cotton manufacturing concerns which were fairly significant by national standards. It was probably this unreliability which induced scholars like Milone to express doubts as to whether the industrial development in the North was really the more relevant.

Many estimates, attempted in different years for single regions, lead to the belief that of the 400,000 to 450,000 spindles of the cotton industry, which was the capacity of this sector after 1860, at least three-quarters were located in the North. There is, however, another aspect of importance which differentiates the cotton-mill of the North from that of the South at the time of Unification. The southern mills were, for that period, fairly large in size but few in number, while those of Lombardy–Piedmont were typically small- and medium-sized. That is to say, in the South the industrial concerns could be counted on the fingers of one or two hands, whereas in the North there were already hundreds of concerns which made up an industrial area for cotton which spread from the River Sesia to the River Serio.

2. The Mutual Independence of the Two Economies

Therefore, the idea that inequality between the two parts of Italy had its origins after Unification and was in some way the effect of policies followed by the government must clearly be discarded. Furthermore, it is wrong to suggest – on the basis of a difference not of productive structures (which however substantially existed) but of *costs* – that a competitive mechanism was in operation whereby the economy with lower costs overpowered that with higher costs, and that the former immediately took advantage of the share of the internal market taken away from the latter.[6]

But there is more; it is more suitable to look for the regionally (and obviously *relatively*) autonomous character of the pattern of development in the two parts of Italy. Then one would see that many opinions relating to the inter-relationship between the extremes of progress and poverty are part of a political controversy which does not itself help to explain either the historical development, the character of the responsibilities or the effective extent of the opportunities available. The knowledge of different pre-existing levels of initial development between the two parts of Italy at the moment of Unity is essential to a better understanding of the character of the persistent and intensified dualism which followed. If one ignores or minimizes this, one runs the risk of not understanding anything.

However, a simple 'weighing' of the two sectional economies in 1860 is not enough. Two problems remain to be clarified. In the first place, why, specifically in the South, did Unity bring about, not just confirmation of a relative backwardness, but also no positive dynamic effect? In the second place, what foundation is there for the opinion that Unity created the premise for the subordination of the southern economy to the development needs of the North, subordination which would be more or less decisive and without substantial compensation?

With regard to the first of these problems, if one accepts the principle of industrialization as an indispensable element in modern economic development (something not implicit in the way the problem was presented by the free traders of the late 1800s and the early 1900s), it can be broadly accepted that different levels of initial development of areas which join together in a single market end up by influencing, more or less decisively, their respective future developments. This is barring, of course, massive corrective interventions. It is legitimate, however, to doubt that the political unity of two areas with different initial levels must automatically affect only the more developed area, leaving the other in a state of either inactivity or very slow movement.

In order to see this problem clearly, one must not forget the limits within which each of the two regions participated in the dynamic development of the European economy of the 19th century, both at any given moment and in perspective. Nor should one ignore the extent of possible internal relations between the two regions in the context of that participation (again, both at any given moment and in perspective).

Two words are necessary on the issue of perspective. The approach one should start from is the following: the development of the Italian economy, in the pre-industrial phase, depended essentially on external impulses (foreign demand for primary goods) and therefore had a subordinate character. That is to say, it did not reproduce or imitate the development of those countries from which the impulse came. In order for the Italian economy to become industrialized, to acquire the same characteristics of development as those importing countries, an internal impulse or a system of internal impulses was necessary, created by the supply of secondary products and based on the possibility of *dominating* the market. The difficulty of achieving a position of dominance of this type through competitive capacity offered an option between renouncing or adopting protectionism. The second alternative was the one which, after a certain period – through the development of decisive political action – seemed to be preferred. Within the protected area, the rules of competition (which, simplified, can be considered as the function of accumulated capital and of external economies) prevailed. However, one must ask, in relation to the protected area, and on the basis of the internal impetus put into motion by protection, what was it that hindered an integrating mechanism similar to that on which pre-industrial development was based in relations between Italy and the rest of the world.

The second of the problems mentioned above – why Unity did not stimulate the South to make a significant contribution to the development proceeding in the North – can be considered as an offshoot of the first. The possibility of the southern regions contributing positively to the development of the northern ones would have meant the existence of a system of links between the two parts, even if this were more advantageous to one than the other. The achievement of political unity certainly widened the range of opportunities for links compared to that which was available between two separate countries. However, it also initiated a mechanism of non-advantageous relations to the less-developed part – a depressing integrating link for the latter. This is what is normally alluded to when talking of colonial or semi-colonial links. Expressions often used indiscriminately and loosely include for instance, a deformation of the productive structure of the colonial area, a worsening of the terms of trade more or less connected to factors of dominance, the use of the local workforce with special conditions of inferiority, etc. In every case, for such situations to arise, conditions of integration between the two economies must exist.

Now, the thesis underlying this paper is that the basic historical premise for Italian economic dualism can be summed up as the lack of original integrating links, actual or potential, between the two main sections of the country which had achieved political unity.

The main consequence of this thesis, once the fact is acknowledged and is thought worthy of consideration, is to cast doubts on the validity of all those statements which establish a more or less precise connection between the positive phenomenon of the historical development of the northern regions of Italy and the negative phenomenon of the persistent backwardness of the South. As is well known, statements of this sort, more or less crudely expressed, have frequently come up in the southern literature and have also moved into the field of historiography. Thus, we have had the controversial claim of the sacrificial contribution made by the South in the construction of industrial Italy, and therefore the political assertion of its right to protest, and, from the other side, we have had the historical justification of that sacrifice.

3. An Inventory

Let us try to examine as concisely as possible which integrating links between North and South actually existed on the eve of Unity and whether or not others appeared in the phase which followed. In so doing, we will also try to bear in mind various opinions expressed in the best-known southern literature concerning the problems inherent in this theme. Firstly, we will consider reciprocal connections between aspects of the factors of production in the North and in the South. Secondly, we will assess some of the implications relative to the more general structure of intersectoral trade between these two areas. The premise which inspires the present discussion is the conviction of the existence of significant ties (in a Leontievian sense) formed between the particular input–output system of a country's industrial capacity and the location of its economic activities. In a country undergoing a process of industrialization, production develops in terms of responses to a series of *appeals* which have a precise location (from abroad, from adjacent areas, from internal peripheral areas): this sequence of appeals can be detailed and elaborated. At the same time, an industrial system, from its first and most archaic phases, implies a series of other demands, this time for the factors of production which also have spatial implications.

4. Natural Resources

By their very nature, of course, natural resources are characterized by lack of mobility; only those primary goods obtainable by extraction from natural resources are transferable. But such resources also enter into a single market between different areas and regions, not only in the sense that they can attract capital from other areas, but also in that they can be mobilized by external demand. It would therefore be limiting to make an inventory of the integrating links between the resources of the North and the South at only those levels concerning the transfer of capital. Rather, one must consider all the possible integrating factors able to encourage – with the application of capital and involvement of a workforce (including that indigenous to the regional, North/South, area) – the mobilization of resources. This is the same as considering the demand for energy sources and for primary products deriving from the productive structure in the respective sections. Therefore, logically, we refer first to the territory's natural resources, but will later discuss the goods resulting from their productive mobilization.

A traditional opinion is that, from its beginnings, the Italian economy has been afflicted by a lack of natural resources. At an inventory level, this is partly true and partly false. The feeling of inferiority started to germinate in the age of iron and coal when paucity of natural resources referred, above all, to a lack of deposits of coal, one of the two products essential to the iron and steel industry. Until almost the end of the last century, coal was not only the main energy source, but also the only one technically flexible enough to meet the evolving demands of industry. Energy from water did not originally have that versatility, but was subject to insurmountable limits of capacity and to seasonal factors. The feeling of under-provision on the basis of lack of coal was successively fed by other shortages, receiving new impetus in the age of oil. But, in this new phase, the idea of inferiority due to a scarcity of prime materials became complicated since no nation could any longer contemplate the ideal of complete self-sufficiency. Consequently, the hope of a development founded on natural endowments had outgrown the restricted confines of national boundaries to range in the more exploitative field of imperial aspirations.

In any case, for the period of Unity and the following decades, a consideration of energy resources cannot be restricted to coal deposits. In addition to hydro power, there are mineral deposits unrelated to energy. What was the distribution of these resources between the two parts of the country? What was the extent of their respective requirements? Were there specific 'demands' from one section, able to stimulate 'answers' from the other which would help mobilize unused factors?

We have described above how, in the North, an industrial core was already indisputably better developed. Let us briefly consider what contributions to this budding industrial system could have come from internal resources.

The first contribution was certainly given by hydroelectric energy which was more abundant in the North than in the Centre or the South. The rivers running from the Alps down the valleys towards the plain were ideal for providing collecting points and were fully exploited. The Strona in Piedmont, the Olona in Lombardy, the Astice in Veneto are three small rivers out of the many to be found in the three major regions of North Italy which have a place in our economic history due to the role they played in the origins of industry.

This energy source, which initially took the place of coal completely but afterwards replaced it only in part (until it became possible to mobilize the richer sources higher up in the mountains which were not directly accessible as electric energy) was available in the North but was not transferable and could not be moved across regions. In any case, when this transfer did become possible thanks to the techniques of long-distance energy transport, the advantage of the availability of energy in the North had apparently already assumed enormous proportions. Thus while in theory it became possible to transfer energy from the North to the South, the cost proved such that it has only recently become economically feasible. It is important constantly to bear in mind all the main possibilities of economic interaction between the North and South in order to verify if and how one part could have been more actively involved in the development of the other. This point must be clarified before judging the advantages and the disadvantages applicable to each from union with the other. On the subject of industry's energy requirements needed by industry, it must be concluded that initially the North was partially self-sufficient but only on a basic technical level which imposed growth limits on industry. Beyond these limits, as solid fuels had to be used which could not be obtained from the South, it became necessary to start importing from abroad. In a third period, the level of self-sufficiency improved. If and when the South needed to make up its energy deficit, it could do so only by importing from abroad, on less favourable economic conditions than were enjoyed by the North. Later it was able to use its own, less accessible, water sources in a hydroelectric form and not import them from the North.

After energy, let us consider the contribution of our materials. Here it will be enough to look at the two groups – textiles and metallurgical–mechanical – which are of most significance to the developing national industry of this period. To use the word 'mechanical' with reference to this era means something rather specific, namely heavy (not highly skilled or qualified) engineering which could make steam boilers or put together imported parts, but not much more than that.

The textile sector was divided into four branches: silk, cotton, wool and linen/hemp. Here we meet, for the first time, the productive factor of 'fertile land' and the natural characteristics determining it. These factors cannot always be separated from those related to historical 'beginnings', although this is a complex question which, for brevity's sake, we have to put aside. Generally one can say that, with the exception of flax, which found favourable natural conditions in the North, and cotton, which enjoyed moderately favourable (but not extensive) conditions for cultivation in the South, the other materials could be grown to advantage in either area. This is in terms of the agricultural possibilities, not the historical ones to which I have just referred, since to take these into account would make the picture much more complex. To complete the picture of opportunities, one could add that the intensive use of land tended to eliminate sheep rearing from the northern regions, whereas in the South one could still find vast districts kept as pasture where sheep raising could prosper. Consequently, linen, hemp and silk could be and were cultivated in the North, silk on a very large scale. In fact, there were productive possibilities for hemp and silk in both areas, thus excluding the possibility of restricting all the required production to the South. It would still have been possible and sensible to localize supplementary, integrative supplies in the South, especially for silk. In fact, silk was a primary material which at that time was largely exported from the North in a raw state. However, an ever-growing proportion was worked as yarn in the spinning mills; at one point, this activity grew to such an extent that it became necessary to resort to the import of raw silk. The complex problems involved in supplying raw silk to the northern spinning mills could have provided a good opening for southern suppliers. Unfortunately, this possibility developed only around 1850 after a severe illness hit the silk cocoons in the West leaving only cocoons from the Far East resistant.[7] The raw silk was therefore imported on advantageous terms from Japan, and this proved fatal for the entire primary sector of the Italian silk industry.

Nevertheless, the South still had the potential to become an exclusive or main supplier of wool and cotton for the industries of the North, but this did not happen. Where there were tentative projects, as in wool, these came to nothing; where actual experiments were set up, as in cotton, these failed.

This is not the place to probe these events or the reasons for the atrophy or failure of these potential integrative links. However, it may be worthwhile mentioning, since it is also relevant later, that the attempt to cultivate cotton in the south of Italy was in large part promoted by the English when the American Civil War curtailed US supplies. Failure or atrophy in terms of integration can be ascribed to three alternative causes. Firstly, the preference which, for reasons of price or quality, northern industry tended to give to foreign suppliers. Secondly, the expansion of northern agricultural output in conditions of increasing productivity. Thirdly, the existence, within southern agriculture, of preferred alternative uses of land and of the pressure of different types of demands. Without doubt, it was foreign demand or lack of demand which overwhelmingly determined the pressure of population on the land.

Thus in all these cases we can identify either internal constraints in the respective economies of the North and South which were not favourable to the formation of reciprocal ties, or a preferential tendency towards external connections which was equally unfavourable.

Let us now consider the case of metallurgy. In spite of the lack of coal deposits ironite was not lacking. The island of Elba, the Aosta valley and the Lombardy valleys had deposits whose use in the past had given rise to significant production within the limits of an iron and steel industry based on charcoal. On the other hand, the South was almost completely lacking in ironite. The change to a modern iron and steel industry using coal called for the import of coal into the northern regions. In the South, coal had to be imported from abroad in any case, though ironite could be shipped from Elba. At this point, the centres on the Tirrenia coast had an advantage over those in the internal valleys in the North which were less easily reached by coal merchants. This was the situation until the Alpine railway tunnels were opened: Fréjus in 1871 and St Gottard in 1880. Once sail fitting had become a thing of the past, the big ports (including Naples) offered good opportunities for external economies, both with regard to the availability of sea transport and to the use of iron and steel products in the boat-yards. Ironite from Elba therefore constituted a potential connection, a centre for the birth of a Tirrenic iron and steel industry. However, as the import of coal meant disadvantageous costs for everyone, only vigorous protectionism allowed this option to be translated into reality. Until the tariff system was imposed in 1887, it is not possible to talk about a modern iron and steel industry in Italy. Until then the industry had to cope somehow by boiling down scrap iron resulting from the substitution of iron railway lines by steel ones which was underway all over Europe.

Insufficient evidence exists to analyse supply links relating to the engineering industry. With no significant internal supplies of iron and with the potential, if protectionism were adopted, for developing this industry both in the North (Genoa) and in the South (Naples), no particular prospects existed to stimulate integrating links in the sense used here.

The question of deposits of non-metalliferous ores remains. But on this point, the only relevant example worth discussing is sulphur, produced in Sicily and destined almost entirely for export. Therefore it did not give rise to trade between the two parts of the country. By the time a chemical industry had started to develop in Italy, the use of sulphur had become largely obsolete compared to that of more competitive pyrites.[8]

Last but not least, fertile land, already mentioned in terms of the contribution of raw materials to manufacturing activities, must always be considered a preeminent natural resource. Let us now concentrate on its essential function – the production of foodstuffs. This is a particularly important focus for our whole discussion. Industrial development always implies a growing movement of the workforce from agriculture to industry, which in turn enlarges that proportion of the population which must buy instead of cultivate its own food. Thus it is necessary for industrialization to be backed up by an agricultural sector capable of providing a growing supply of foodstuffs. Demand can, of course, be satisfied by importing. But in an initial phase in Italy, when exports were primarily agrarian and import requirements were concentrated on manufactured products, it was also necessary to import energy sources. In this initial phase, to resolve the growing need for foodstuffs by substantial imports would thus have been detrimental to the process of industrialization. Therefore an agricultural hinterland with an elastic supply and the ability to increase production was necessary.

Could the mainly agricultural south of Italy, less equipped (as one has seen) for the development of industry, have provided such a hinterland? In all probability, yes. The possibility of intensifying cultivation in a variety of ways certainly existed even though, it would not always have been easy. Unfortunately, however, for the South much more propitious conditions existed in the Lombardy plains which were extensively well-irrigated, associated with successful livestock breeding and laid out in farms with, for the times, good capital investment. On the periphery of this intensive agricultural area were other regions of possible intensification and reclamation as, for example, around Ferrara. As a result, what might have been the best possibility for forging links between the two sections of the country in a combined effort of development did not materialize.

8

On the other hand, as is known, the South did not lack agrarian surpluses for export, nor the possibility of expansion. Some of these products, for instance citrus fruits, even enjoyed conditions of natural monopoly though they were not items of primary necessity. Other exportable agrarian output, like oil and wine, were also produced competitively in areas in the North. In general, therefore, southern agriculture had no choice but to turn to foreign markets to sell its more profitable and growing surpluses. It did this before unification and continued to do so afterwards. When commercial policies cut off these outlets – I particularly allude to the break with France following the tariff reform of 1887 – some products were forced to change direction towards the internal market, towards the North. Using this event as a reason to tour the Puglia region, Luigi Luzzati observed how this demonstrated that the 'North and the South of Italy, in that great free field of national unity, complete each other and together become richer'. The southernist Antonio De Viti De Marco replied that this type of integration, this national market for southern wines, was not useful: it was a negative alternative since the true interests of southern wine producers were with foreign markets.[9]

It may be that, with the perspective of time, this judgement, assumed sound until now, should be reviewed; perhaps the Luzzattians were right because tariff reform initiated commercial exchanges between South and North which then became stable. In any case it is evident that this type of integration, whether positive or negative, was not perceptible before 1887, but only became evident with the success of protectionism. It therefore had an imposed character and was, at least at first, decidedly inconvenient for the South. Therefore, at the level of resources and of trade in primary products, both mineral and agricultural, it must be concluded that the possibilities of an integrating chain joining the two sections of the national economy were almost nil. In the North a situation of self-sufficiency existed; as far as the agrarian and mineral surpluses of the southern economy were concerned, there was a preference for exporting to the international market rather than to the North.

5. The Workforce

The question of the labour market is linked in many ways with the foregoing and therefore is best discussed before exploring the movement of capital.

Industrialization always creates a demand for manpower which, in the first instance, will be aimed at the rural areas. In order not to interrupt or reduce the supply of agricultural products, this requires either the presence of excess labour in the agricultural sector or the possibility of creating such an excess by increases in productivity. Alternatively, there may be a change in land use and in the types of agricultural products cultivated towards crops which are less labour intensive.

However, at the beginning of a process of industrialization, the movement of workers is never a clear-cut occurrence or a sudden and total transfer from one sector to another. Immature and vulnerable industrial development has much to gain from the continuation of workers' links with the land. For example, this permits seasonal or flexible contributions, allowing workers to accept wages below the level of subsistence without serious social consequences. The costs of urbanization, which would otherwise weigh on the process of overall accumulation, are also reduced. Initial industrial development in the northern regions was exactly of this type.[10] There was no frenetic impetus to justify a sudden and massive upheaval. For a long time the textile sector, for instance, was widely manned by female labour and was mainly seasonal.

The statistical data, which show high employment in manufacturing activities in the years near Unification compared to the following years, seem to indicate a phenomenon of stagnation or very slow development of industrial employment. This is explained by one simple fact: of the 382,000 workers employed in industry (measured by Vittorio Ellena in 1876), a good 200,000 worked in the silk industry but, of these, 111,000 – almost exclusively women and children – were employed in the initial phase in the silk-producing process, a short-lived seasonal activity which was closely linked to agriculture. Another 74,000 worked at silk spinning which at that time did not have a year-long productive cycle. Because of technical progress in this sector, employment fell by 14 per cent, as shown in the survey carried out regionally between 1890 and 1900. Later the decline became even more marked, not only because of better productivity, but because of drastic alterations in the structure of the traditional silk industry, from producing mainly raw silk and yarn to producing finished goods. Weaving developed, while those primary and intermediate branches which apparently gave higher employment declined. That is to say, the sector which at the date of the first statistical survey had the largest proportion of employment defined as 'industrial' (52 per cent to be exact) underwent such internal modifications that employment diminished not only relative to the product, but also in an overall sense. The statistical source of this picture does not categorize the effective workforce as we would today, but gives generic social qualifications whose relevance must in some sense be considered arbitrary.

However, we would be mistaken if, in the context of the process of industrialization, we attached no importance to these activities. On the contrary, it prepared the agricultural family to move into the industrial workforce by providing the initial familiarity with the mechanisms of the factory and of factory life without severe dislocation. It started the overall adaptation to a new and different social condition, and made groups of agricultural workers from the foothills between the Alps and the Lombardy plain progressively available for industrial activity. These farmers, for their part, gradually started to modify the cultivation of their land. Mulberry trees and the raising of silk worms, which had formed such a stable part of the productive balance for the farms of the North, tended slowly to disappear wherever industry developed. But, even where this fairly difficult type of cultivation was given up, the land was not necessarily abandoned; thus there was no radical change in the pattern of settlements.

In this first period, other locational reasons helped to prolong the industry's ties with the land; for example, the search for water suitable for use as energy. In short the territorial characteristics of industry in North Italy strongly complemented the original distribution of its labour force. Italian Manchesters with the capacity of providing a large labour market for industry did not exist on a national level. The first centre of this sort was perhaps the city of Turin, at about the time of the First World War when industrialization was at an advanced stage. Milan in the last decades of the 1800s absorbed regional migratory movements (especially from the Veneto area) or from the Lombardy plain, but this was more in relation to a phenomenon of complex urbanization than as a principal centre for industrial recruitment. Thus, for a long time, there existed a phenomenon of self-sufficiency in the socioeconomic structure of the North. As the North had its own reserves of foodstuffs for the new industrial population, for a long initial period, it also had a reserve of labour. Note that this labour force was generally better educated and perhaps more malleable than that offered by the South.

It must be said that the direction of movement of foodstuffs and of the labour force did not strictly correspond. The core agricultural hinterland is found in the south of the Lombardy plain, involving Emilia, while the most relevant demographic hinterland was at the foothills of the Alps and the area towards the delta of the Po River. That 'agricultural dualism' that Romani laid stress on for Lombardy[11] – which can be applied, as a concept, to the entire agriculture of North Italy – thus reveals stimulating backward linkages with industrial development which made it unnecessary to resort to the distant regions of the South for a very long time. Of course, the South also had a large supply of labour and the potential to produce foodstuffs for the national market. It must also be remembered that the North of Italy was not able to ensure adequate prospects and sources of income for the demographic surplus which existed in its own agricultural sector until a number of decades after Unification. It was from the North rather than from the South that the first migratory streams moved abroad. In the decade 1876–86 (the first year for which there are reliable figures), 68 per cent of Italian emigrants came from the northern regions;[12] the possibility of directing this northern demographic surplus towards the badly cultivated South was even discussed, but nothing came of this. And when industrialization plugged the migratory movement from the North and the exodus from the South reached flood-like proportions, the inverse possibility was not raised. Industrialization in the North was still a long way from exhausting its own reservoirs of labour.

6. Capital

If the North of Italy was substantially self-sufficient in contributing natural resources and labour to its industrialization effort (at least compared with the possibilities offered by the South), it is doubtful if the same can be said of capital.

It cannot be disputed that capital is generally scarce at the start of any process of industrialization. Also that while resources and labour should be considered specifically in terms of their natural and historical capacity to meet a given type of demand, capital is, as Cattaneo says, 'free and flying'. And besides, Southern literature has insisted above all on its contributions of this type to the progress of the North.

The most vigorous supporter of this thesis was Francesco Saverio Nitti, in the works he published at the end of the last century.[13] The initial situation that he describes at the moment of Unification is a Keynesian one. State finances in the North were strongly in deficit and financial means were lacking (this applied however only to Piedmont) whereas in the South, a kindhearted Bourbonic fiscal system had allowed the private sector to accumulate money rather freely. This sector, not finding adequate incentives to invest in the stagnant surrounding economy, and because of the traditional Bourbonic hostility to issues of public debt which did not offer secure investments, kept their wealth, according to Nitti, in a liquid state.

In this situation, the sale of ecclesiastical possessions and property by the state was seen as offering vast and advantageous possibilities of investment of a traditionally acceptable kind for the wealth which was being drained by the state. According to Nitti, the effect on the economy of a region of buying ecclesiastical possessions from the state was in reality equal to a tax because, while the general wealth did not increase but decrease, the monetary capital went elsewhere. Greater taxes, in a strict sense, were not lacking, and this added to the transfer of monetary capital to the state. These resources were devoted to more dynamic public spending than in Bourbonic areas. Thus, the central authority was the intermediary between savings and investments, establishing a non-automatic connection in the Keynesian *ante litteram* style.

But to what was this public spending directed? There were the interest payments on a public deficit incurred before Unification (over half was debt contracted by the old state of Piedmont). There were the expenses of the state for its own growth and its defensive armament; there were the public works needed to realize one of the major political tasks that the new Italy had assumed – that of railways. At best, the resources should have been divided proportionately especially as a disproportionate share came from the South. But Nitti wanted to demonstrate that even the division of expenses had given the North unfair advantages. Therefore, there occurred a real transfer of capital from the South to the North, while other circumstances produced further examples of this tendency. For instance, the South entered the financial market as a buyer of public securities during a later period of boom, on terms advantageous to previous buyers from other regions. In short, according to Nitti, the South largely financed the North; the Keynesian connection was established in specific geographical terms.

Independently of the exaggerations and biases which Nitti made and which were challenged by technically qualified people, his is probably not a sustainable premise. In fact, it is doubtful whether the tax bill was really proportionately higher in the South than in the North, relative to its contributory capacity.[14] More important is the fact that, in some sectors such as roads and land reclamation, as moreover Nitti himself noted, public expense was proportionately much higher in the South. In evaluating the division of expenses for the railways, an alternative viewpoint (from Nitti's) is plausible. It can be noted how, although more money was expended in the North, the great inequality which existed at the beginning was reduced.[15] Overall, although a dispute of this kind may refute the impression that the behaviour of the state was deliberately anti-South and although it may put the argument on the contribution of capital from the South to the North in the initial phases of Unification into perspective, it does not address the main question. The most important aspects, I believe, are these: it was perfectly natural that in terms of expenditure on ports, Genoa should be given priority since traffic was concentrated there to the point of being choked. It was likewise natural that an area as densely populated as the Lombardy plain should require greater railway mileage, and that the Alpine tunnels be constructed in the places chosen. It was similarly normal that spending on education was a priority where structures were already working and needing support and where certain standards already existed and had to be maintained.

Today we have a view in which the 'anticipatory' aspects of infrastructure are seen as the most important in any policy aiming for development. This is because we generally debate within the context of a design *ex ante* which shows situations which are stationary or nearly so, and which must be put into motion. But actually, a situation 'in motion' has its own demands, though possibly intermittent, for additional infrastructure; these then become conditions, not of getting underway, but of continuing the process of development.

Therefore, one must differentiate between at least two kinds of infrastructural costs. The first, which we are more used to considering these days, is preliminary to development where this has barely begun, and must be expedited. But there is the second type which follows and accompanies development and which is basically a widening of 'bottlenecks' already evident from the first phase. In short, the latter costs represent a form of intervention *ex post* or subsequent to the main private decision to invest. A phenomenon of indivisibility or, anyway, of linkage does not always allow precise differentiation between these two aspects. Nevertheless, by bearing the difference in mind, we can see that for many decades a large part of Italian public spending was of the second *ex post* type. Not, most certainly, the construction of the great cross-country railway lines, to the extent that the state assumed their cost, which answered the need *ex ante* to create a single great system of communication for the newly-formed nation. And not even the great road-building projects, which were concentrated mainly in the South in obedience to a clear *ex ante* logic. But interventions like those concerning the port of Genoa, the embankment of the Po River, the many short stretches of railway or loop-lines and, I would also add, the Alpine tunnels, all follow operations already underway in the world of production and trade. It is sometimes said that such interventions predominated because the pressures mounted in requesting them were stronger, but this merely makes my point in a different way. In general, it appears that a large part of public spending for infrastructure which benefited the North was of the *ex post* type. In some cases, like that of congestion in the port of Genoa and of the railways at the start of the new century, it even appears that the creation of infrastructure was considerably delayed relative to the requirements of industrial development and trade, delay which inevitably limited the substantial development of the Geolittian era.[16]

Moreover, one must also remember how the need for contributions from the local authorities in all cases considerably restricted the regional division of expenditure. Therefore, the logic which inspired the conduct of the Italian state in this field was, all things considered, fairly neutral with regard to geographical distribution, as Saraceno observed.[17] Other kinds of localized public spending which were criticized for being unequal also obeyed a criterion of neutrality. A neutrality, however, not without some preferential (though inadequate) gestures towards the South. It was, in conclusion, that same neutrality or even a too sporadic and bland preferential treatment that proved disadvantageous to the South. The South needed from the state a non-neutral conduct, or one just slightly sensitive to the greater need of the southern provinces, but vigorously and expressly partisan in its favour.

In order to give the South advantages in public spending, it would have been necessary to give priority to a largely anticipatory type of expenditure, which was precisely what the South requested. This type of expenditure, used for the longitudinal railway network and the roads, was concentrated in the first period following Unification when a large part of public spending was aimed at building the nation. The roads and railways were part of this. But unfortunately in Italy, this expenditure corresponded with a period in which the state sold the ecclesiastic estates and state property, an operation which, according to Nitti, meant a major transfer of wealth from the South to the North. Therefore, even though over a long period of time there could have been an unequal division of regional expenditure, of fiscal contributions and of other securities, it does not seem that there were such unexpected and massive transfers of wealth as could be considered significant in the financing of fixed social capital in the North. In any case, in the North the formation of this capital was not a necessary precondition for general economic development, as it would have had in the South. Though this point of view may have some validity as a criticism of 'southernist' policy, it is insufficient because it does not explain either the origins of Italian dualism, or its first post-unitary consolidation.

Furthermore, as is known, the construction of the railway network did not even create, except in a very limited manner, any demand for the products of the national iron and steel and engineering industries during the period under consideration. It did not attract important investments to this sector, the small amount acquired being divided between Pietrarsa, a plant in Naples, Ansaldo in Genoa and some machine shops in Milan. Not even the secondary effects of railway investment in the South were seen in the North. It can be concluded that in the whole of the first phase following Unification, there did not exist, even at the level of the formation of capital, really substantial links between the North and the South. There were no massive indirect contributions to the formation of capital in the North through fiscal taxation of the South, nor were there, as Nitti himself points out, movements of private capital from the South to the North for the purchase of transferable securities. In the first place, there was still no market worthy of consideration in the whole of Italy, and, in any case, southern diffidence hindered investments of that sort, even for state securities.

On the other hand, in the North the concentration of private capital had just started and was beginning to be organized in such a way as to have considerable effect. The first real example of this was Bastogi, who took on the Southern railways – a case of investment in the South with capital generated elsewhere. But it was not until the third decade after Unification that significant new cases could be found of investments made in the South with capital gathered in the North and of building speculation in the big cities. In the inventory which we are compiling, 'capital' is the most mobile factor, both by its nature and because of the immediate intermediation of the united state. We have shown how, in all cases, this movement of capital was a *sui generis*, with no significantly determining effect on relations between the two areas in the first phase of development. However, it is useful to underline how, in the new century, this relationship was the first to be established in a manner and to an extent which can be defined as essential to the mechanism of development, which by this time was inexorably dualistic and moving with faster rhythms after 1896. Through emigrants' remittances, the South contributed to this acceleration by ensuring the balance of foreign trade which was, at that moment, a fundamental condition for the continuing growth of industrial Italy. Thus we have already moved away from the problem of the 'origins of dualism'. And, once away from it, the relations which were irrelevant in this first period continue to strengthen until the present day and thus establish a goodly part of those integrating links (including the transfer of labour) which were non-existent at the beginning.

7. The Market for Industrial Products

Another theme formerly brought up in southernist literature concerns the presumed formation in the South of an exclusive market for industrial products from the North. That is to say, the creation of a situation which could be defined as colonial. In reality, classic colonialism implies a movement of goods in both directions, with primary products moving from the colonies towards the city and manufactured goods the opposite way. The colonial situation makes sense because the city is one and the colonies many, the sum of the colonial areas giving depth and consistency to a market for manufactured goods which otherwise would not be big enough to support the economies of scale on which industrial concentration is based. Neither of these two conditions were met by the South which, for a fairly long time, had a peripheral and barely significant share of the market of the northern industries, even after the introduction of a protectionist regime. For example, some protected machinery goods did not have a substantial market in the South. To a certain extent the southern consumer had to suffer the consequences of protectionism as its requests for manufactured goods were directed abroad. The large internal market opened up by protectionism was actually that of the northern and central regions. Thus the most important sector in the production of consumer goods – cotton manufacture – filled the needs of the internal market very quickly. It is said that Enrico Dell'Acqua, the merchant prince from Busto Arsizio whose biography was written by the young Luigi Einaudi,[18] initially tried to conquer the Puglia region, but he very soon turned to the more profitable foreign markets of South America. There he found a real possibility of enlarging the market for Italian cotton with sales to consumers who were Italian by nationality though not by residence.

8. Did Italian Industrial Development Really Come About Through a Big Spurt?

At this point one must ask a decisive question. In what way did the South, or rather the dualistic structure of the Italian economy, participate in a 'big spurt' by which, according to Alexander Gerschenkron and Rosario Romeo, the Italian economy was transformed into an industrial one?[19]

As will be remembered, the question of the South or, as it has been called, the question of 'agricultural workers' was at the centre of the picture painted by Romeo concerning the form of industrial development in Italy. However, when faced with the mass of other problems and considerations concerning Italian economic development (which Romeo brought up successively), the question of a big spurt took second place. Rosario Romeo started from the thesis that a contradiction existed between an 'agrarian revolution' (in general terms, granting agricultural workers the right to property) and capitalistic accumulation. An agrarian revolution in the South would have hindered capitalistic development instead of favouring it. In his early writings, by considering the social state of all Italian rural areas as uniform, Romeo rigidly relates the sacrifice of the South to the need to maintain profit and income in agriculture, given that only these could enhance the process of accumulation and stimulate the initial financing of industrial activity.

According to Romeo's reasoning, the difficulty of creating an effective technical-economic basis to an 'agrarian revolution' was undeniable given the structure of southern agriculture and the environmental conditions of the South in Risorgimental times. Likewise the drastic and compulsory nature of a southern sacrifice, which involved much more than an extreme hypothetical alternative to the agrarian revolution, seemed forced.

In successively enlarging his picture, Romeo conveniently abandoned this idea of southern sacrifice, which remained suspended half way between economic and political motivation, and instead concentrated on more accurately evaluating the contribution of agriculture in the initial phases of post-unity economic development.[20] However, in doing this, what might be called the 'financier' agriculture, became even more the agriculture of the advanced regions, as shown in the examples given in Romeo's first writings. This attempt to emphasize the contribution of agriculture to general development and therefore also to industrialization has been criticized.[21] However, I believe that Romeo is quite right in giving weight to the role of northern agriculture in laying the groundwork for industrialization in Italy, even though the strict interdependence he proposes may be debatable. In my opinion, what almost put the whole discussion off course was Romeo's hypothesis that during a crucial period – the initial 20 years of agricultural development (which he documented quantitatively) – resources were harnessed to initiate the big spurt. In fact, no significant accumulation of resources was ever really demonstrated; that which did exist in industry in the 1880s could not be considered a big spurt.

Gerschenkron, Romeo's main critic, also evaluated the modern industrial economy in Italy, but started from partially inadequate assumptions. These assumptions can be summed up as follows: if a country faces the challenge of industrialization from a relatively backward position, the more the effort required calls for the concentration of resources. As a consequence, the gradual course of the first example of industrialization, in England, must be abandoned. Moreover, the ordinary small and medium entrepreneurs who typically accumulate must be replaced by special large 'agents', intermediaries, who have an altogether different capacity for putting together resources and investments. These agents, who historically appeared in underdeveloped countries instead of the small-scale entrepreneurs, are first large banks of industrial credit, then the mixed banks of the German type, and finally the state, in a sort of growing substitution mechanism relative to the degree of backwardness.

This outline is, to my way of thinking, not lacking in usefulness, and contains many well-founded insights. But when examining a specific historical case, there is always something which does not correspond to even the most useful model. In my view, the idea that needs correcting in Gerschenkron's model is not that of the substitute forms of financing, but rather the inevitability of a 'big spurt' which is a complete reversal of the gradual course of the classic English process.

Finally, in evaluating the long controversy between Romeo and Gerschenkron,[22] one must consider the uncertainties that have surrounded the various periods of expansion of industrial activity in Italy and the possibility of ascribing a big spurt to this or that period. It is also necessary to evaluate the findings of other scholars examining another quantitative phenomenon – the relationship between capital and output in the history of the Italian economy.[23] After due consideration, I believe it best to point in another direction. I believe that it is advantageous to jettison the concept of a 'big spurt', and with it Romeo's overburdened thesis of 'primitive accumulation', and to consider the characteristics of the transition to an industrial economy in Italy in terms of a long wait on the threshold of transformation. It is probably more realistic to consider modern economic development in Italy as a mixture of the accumulation of gradual elements of a traditional type (implying, after much consideration, that Romeo's idea of the important contribution of agriculture should be re-thought) together with a number of peaks, none of a really decisive nature, sustained instead of substitute agents for the Gerschenkronian type. Of these peaks I would pick out at least four, adding the period of the First World War which, prior to all these discussions, was commonly considered as the real birth of industry in Italy, to the periods

1880–87 and 1896–1908, and then the period 1922–29. But naturally it is not vital to know whether there were two or four phases; the essential thing to establish is that there was no massive turn of the screw concentrated in a small number of years.

In what sense is a reconsideration of the original characteristics of Italian dualism affected by a view of the type already mentioned relative to the times and the forms of modern development in Italy? In my opinion, it is affected. In one way or another the idea of the decisive sacrificial contribution of the South was always linked to that of a particularly intense turn of the screw; to fiscal accumulation of the Nittian type, to the protectionism of free-traders, to primitive Marxist accumulation under the free-traders' artillery of low prices, described by Sereni, or to primitive accumulation as in Romeo's thesis. In reality, the South has suffered much in Italian history, but not as the result of any particular bloodletting carried out against it, nor by the breaking of any happy pre-existing equilibrium. It was due more to its insistence on its original backwardness, on its substantial alienation from the progressiveness of the northern economy. In this sense, its backwardness has always been a general limiting factor to Italian development, not a condition of it.[24]

One might ask if there was a narrowness of vision or truly insuperable difficulties on the part of the governing class. One could also evaluate differently the objective self-interest which induced the economic and social forces of the North to barricade themselves behind their own problems. It cannot be disputed that the northern economy held back from the enormous job of 'economic unification'. Today we understand the scale of the relevant tasks much better than the southernists did, with their unfortunate emphasis on the virtues of free trade. Therefore we cannot connect the 'distortions' in what is usually considered 'normal' development either with the formation or with the persistence of the dualistic imbalance. Neither can we formulate summary judgements of 'historical incapacity' in the face of tasks which called for plenteous means, concentration of instruments and drastic choices, all of which were impossible or absurd to expect in those times.

The context of a realistic evaluation is therefore rather more restricted than could be expected from a similar kind of controversy elsewhere. In spite of this, such an investigation is certainly not without importance or historical interest. When someone once suggested that the problem of the South was an 'Irish question', he made an analogy that was not, in substance, answered. Quite probably, answering it would not have meant the realization of a miracle, but it might have encouraged a certain type of intervention in the social structure of the rural areas of the South which would have promoted positive effects; even though not economically large, its possible extent must not be undervalued. This was not done. In this respect, the obstacle was northern respect for what was historically southern self-isolation. This aspect must be correctly understood as an expression of 'national' weakness, acceptance of foreignness, not of colonizing aggressiveness; an expression, if one wishes, of a 'European southernism' or 'continentalism', which is the implied doctrine of the economic development of the North of Italy, not of a calculated encroachment. If one does not understand this, one probably runs the risk of not understanding the real limits and the real weaknesses of that part of Italian society which was, after all, the most dynamic. And that which here is called 'middle-European southernism' must not be considered as the more narrow manifestation of our 'south Italian' southernism. But in any case, this is another topic which we do not want to cover here.

The formation of the industrial structure of North Italy, as has been said, was less rapid and concentrated than some theories have led us to believe. And the pressures which accompanied this process, when compared with other countries, make one reflect. These pressures were less clamorously linked to an intense transformation, and therefore were never really reabsorbed by final processes. Instead, they were tied more to those abortive signs that constantly seem to indicate an intermittent evolution but are never wholly decisive.

I think there is an error of omission and undervaluation underlying this misunderstanding which limits the application of models, however important and full of positive elements, of the Gerschenkron and Romeo type. These models rigidly relate to considerations of the *internal* relations of an economy at the beginning of its development. They remain, basically, comparative models even when Gerschenkron introduces the coexistence of economies at different stages of development.

In a later paper, in summarizing the results obtained from his hypothesis explaining the range of cases of European development, Gerschenkron only touched on this point.[25] He observed one case, that of Denmark, that seemed completely to contradict an interpretation using his own criteria. He added that this could be explained if one kept in mind that Denmark could not be considered as an independent unit, but only as complementary to Great Britain. Now *all cases of development are, in some way, complementary to others*, a fact which should be specifically evaluated as cases arise. The initial industrialization of the North of Italy and the preparation of its agriculture, as noted by Romeo, is only understandable in terms of the important trade in silk which for a long time made up a third of total Italian exports. This trade, in raw silk and yarn, was a form of integrating link with those other productive fields of industrial Europe, the weavers of Lyon and Zurich.

The reciprocal feeling of foreignness between the North and the South, before and after Unification, is not a mysterious phenomenon. It is largely connected to the different places held by the two economies in the international markets. 'I do not hesitate to declare,' said Gregorio Sella, an industrialist from Biella who sat in the first Italian Parliament in June 1860, 'that the "Ancient Provinces" [that is to say Piedmont] know the squares of Paris, Lyon and London much better than they know the cities of Florence and of Emilia.' And the South? It was not even mentioned. Similar or opposite arguments would probably have been put by exporters of sulphur, citrus fruit and oil from the South.

The different effects which were (or could have been) produced on North and South by this difference of the markets they occupied remains to be explored: also the question of why an exchange of products, primary in both cases, gave rise to expansion in one and restriction in the other. In the two cases, the dynamism of the respective demands was evidently different. The systems of linkages that could be put in motion were different. The degree of rigidity of the structures in which those demands were made was different. Some of these problems have already been faced in economic historiography (especially the last one); others still wait for more thorough study.

Notes

1. C. Barbagallo (1951), *Le origini della grande industria contemporanea*, Firenze, pp. 451–2; first edition in 1929.
2. F. Milone (1950), 'Le industrie del Mezzogiorno alla unificazione dell'Italia', in *Studi in onore*

di Gino Luzzatto, Milan, Vol. III, pp. 241–65, is probably the most forthright in claiming minimal disparity of development between the industrial structures in the two parts of the country in 1860. Milone defines 'the importance of the cotton textile industry in Campania as more or less the same ... as that of Lombardy' (p. 257), when – again referring to his own data – the production of cotton yarn in Lombardy in 1863–64 seems at least five times greater than that of Campania. In a long chapter entitled 'Il capitalismo e lo Stato' in his (1956) *Storia del Movimento socialista in Italia*, Rome, Vol. III, p. 21, A. Romano speaks of 'common situations of scarce industrial development' between North and South at Unification, maintaining that the disparity appeared afterwards as a direct consequence of government policy.

3. P. Villani (1962), *Mezzogiorno tra riforme e rivoluzione*, Bari, p. 74. By 'aspects', the author means the different economic activities.
4 R. Eckaus (1960), 'L'esistenza di differenze economiche tra Nord e Sud d'Italia al tempo della Unificazione', *Moneta e Credito*, No. 51, pp. 347–72.
5. The balance of all these percentages represents the share of Central Italy.
6. G. Luzzato (1952), 'La vigilia e l'indomani della Unità', in *Orientamenti per la storia d'Italia nel Risorgimento*, Bari, pp. 141–80 (also in *Storia economica dell'eta moderna e contemporanea*, Padova, 1952, Vol. II, pp. 374 and 396) made this point with great precision: a national market effectively starts, not in a free-trade period, but in coincidence with the opening of a protectionist phase. It is understood that free trade would cause greater damage to the weaker productive structures and, pursued *ante litteram*, would cause a preparatory action in favour of less weak structures, with 'the artillery of low prices'. On this, see E. Sereni (1968), *Il capitalismo nelle campagne (1860–1900)*, Turin, 2nd ed., from p. 36. But it must be noted that, in the first place, northern industrial production was also immediately hit by free trade; in the second place, it is obvious that the phenomenon would also have happened with the adoption of a protectionist policy. In that cause the relatively 'low prices' would have been 'shot' by northern industry. In the third place, it was not extraordinary for northern industry (with its internal market prevalently in the less poor regions and with those sectors producing consumer goods) to turn very quickly, for new market shares, to exporting. We are thus taken back to an objective mechanism of the relations of the market in a situation of original dualism, not to a design of pre-constituted interests.
7. There was a very important exception in Italy, in the Marche region, where selective production of national silkworm eggs prospered. See L. Bonnefon-Craponne (1916), *L'Italie au travail*, Paris, p. 48.
8. For this subject see F. Squarzina (1963), *Produzione e commercio dello zolfo in Sicilia nel secolo xix*, Turin.
9. A. De Viti De Marco (1929), *Un trentennio di lotte politiche (1894–1922)*, Rome, p. 42.
10. G. Luzzatto (1923), 'L'evoluzione economica della Lombardia', in *La Cassa di Risparmio delle Province lombarde nelle evoluzione economica della regione*, Milan, shed a great deal of light on this phenomenon.
11. M. Romani (1957), *L'agricoltura in Lombardia dal periodo delle riforme al 1859*, Milan. There are also some important chapters by this author in *Storia di Milano*, edited by the Fondazione Treccani degli Alfieri, and in *Un secolo di vita agricola in Lombardia (1861–1961)*, Milan, 1963.
12. F. Coletti (1911), 'Dell'emigrazione italiana', in *Cinquanta anni di storia italiana*, Milan, Vol. III, p. 45.
13. Now published as F.S. Nitti, *Scritti sulla questione meridionale*, in A. Saitta (ed.) (1958), Vol. II, Bari.
14. This was challenged, as is known, by F. Cini (1914), *L'ammontare e la composizione della ricchezza delle nazioni*, Turin, pp. 241–300.
15. See the observations of P. Saraceno (1963), *L'Italia verso la piena occupazione*, Milan, from p. 14. The author notes, among other things, how the southern railway network which, at the moment of Unification (1861), accounted for only 7 per cent of the national network, had reached one-third of the total in 1886. This author saw, with absolute clarity, the problem which we have put forward at the beginning of these pages. See *op. cit.*, pp. 11–13.

16. On this point, see the articles written by L. Einaudi in the first decade of the century which are now gathered together in *Cronache economiche e politiche di un trentennio (1893–1925)*, Vol. II, Turin 1959, pp. 285–307, 462–8, 568–619.
17. Saraceno, *L'Italia…*, *op. cit.*, p. 21.
18. L. Einaudi (1900), *Un principe mercante*, Turin.
19. R. Romeo (1959), *Risorgimento e capitalismo*, Bari; A. Gerschenkron (1965), *Il problema storico dell'arretratezza economica*, Turin.
20. In any case, as he specified in a courteous argument with the author of this paper, Romeo cannot be considered a supporter of the thesis that the South gave a decisive economic contribution to the development of the North. See *Cultura moderna: Rassegna delle edizioni Laterza*, April 1959.
21. Gerschenkron, *Il problema storico…*, *op. cit.*, p. 107. He does not name Romeo but, in all probability, alludes to him. G. Luzzatto (1963), *L'economia italiana dal 1861 al 1914*, Vol. I (1861–94), Milan, pp. 131–2.
22. A. Caracciolo (ed.) (1969), *La formazione dell'Italia industriale*, Bari, 2nd edition.
23. A. Graziani (1958), 'Il rapporto capitale-prodotto nell'economia italiana: 1861–1957', *Rassegna Economica*, October–December, pp. 686–716, notes how the trend of the capital–output ratio in Italian economic history does not present a very prominent initial peak followed by a decline, but rather a rising tendency starting from 1880 and periodically interrupted by crises (the first started around 1890) or wars.
24. Even the contributions that it has made in various periods – emigrants' remittances in the 'Giolittian era'; absorbing a slowly growing share of the market of northern industry in this century; the contribution of workers, after the Second World War, to the industrial activity of the North through internal migration – have been put in this restricted picture of development more by 'fits and starts' than by 'leaps and bounds'.
25. A. Gerschenkron, in E. Henderson and L. Spaventa (eds) (1962), *Approach to Economic History, Guest Lectures in Economics*, Milan: pp. 3–18.

THE JOURNAL OF ECONOMIC HISTORY

VOL. XX SEPTEMBER 1961 NO. 3

*The North-South Differential In Italian Economic Development**

THOUGH the economy of Italy has been transformed in the one hundred years since its unification, the various regions have experienced quite different degrees of development. Southern Italy, including Sicily and Sardinia, all of which comprises 40 per cent of the land area and, today, about 37 per cent of the population, has lagged far behind the North.

The purpose of this paper is to examine the nature and causes of the economic differentials between North and South Italy as they existed up to 1914. The first problem is to establish the relative economic positions of the North and South at the time of unification in 1861—an issue which must be resolved before the sources of the subsequent differences in development can be determined. The second step will be to trace the divergent economic paths of northern and southern Italy between 1861 and 1914. This requires a survey of the over-all changes which occurred after unification in order to provide a background against which the sectoral patterns can be assessed. After this a synthesis is attempted of the aggregate and sectoral information.

I

The North-South experience has been reviewed many times, and there are a number of *ad hoc* explanations which require testing, as well as hypotheses which can be taken from more generally stated theories of economic development.[1]

*I am particularly indebted to P. N. Rosenstein-Rodan for help and encouragement and to E. Kuh and W. Parker for useful comments on a prior version. The research upon which this paper is based was undertaken as part of the Italy Project of the Center for International Studies.

[1] Francesco Perrone, *Il Problemo del Mezzogiorno* (Naples, 1913), discusses a long list of theories of lack of economic development in the South.

One of the most widely accepted views is that North and South were in roughly equal positions at the time of unification. The subsequent discrepancies in growth patterns are then ascribed mainly to government policy. As examples of a general favoring of the North by the government, it is claimed that it received preferential treatment by concentration of expenditures there and that the national tariff policy discriminated against the South.[2] It has also been claimed that the structure and organization of production in North and South Italy were roughly the same at the middle of the nineteenth century.[3] Of course, in such comparisons the differing significance of handicraft as compared to factory-organized industry and self-supporting as compared to subsidized industry must be appreciated. If these claims are correct, it would be reasonable to conclude that the South's prospects for development were roughly equivalent to those of the North at the time of unification.[4]

The view that the economic differences between North and South antedate the unification of Italy has been argued effectively by a number of authors. It has been suggested that the relative depression of the South has its origin in the ancient world and that the economic changes in the first half of the nineteenth century did not reduce and may even have increased the regional disparities.[5] If the economic differentials antedate unification, identification of the effects of government policy becomes more doubtful, since in absolute terms even equal growth rates would magnify any original regional differences.[6] Original differences in average incomes and income distribution might also indicate unequal potentials for saving and investment and subsequent growth.

In most such discussion there is full recognition of the great disparities within each region. However, Central Italy cannot always be treated separately because data for the Central Italian Papal States of the mid-nineteenth century are particularly inadequate. When possible a threefold distinction of North, Center and South, the latter including Sicily and Sardinia, is presented; it uncovers some crucial factors

[2] For example, F. S. Nitti, *Nord e Sud* (Turin, 1900), and, currently, F. Vochting, "Industrialization or Pre-Industrialization of Southern Italy," Banca Nazionale di Lavoro, *Quarterly Review*, No. 21 (1952), p. 67.

[3] F. Vochting, "Industrialization or Pre-Industrialization," p. 67, and a Molinari, "Southern Italy," Banca Nazionale di Lavoro, *Quarterly Review*, No. 8 (1949), p. 27.

[4] G. Cenzato and S. Guidotti, *Il Problema Industriale del'Mezzagiorno*, Ministero dell'Industria e Commercio.

[5] C. Barbagallo, *La Questione Meridionale* (1948), Chapters 2 and 4; D. Demarco, "Nord e sud nell'economie Italiana preunitaria," *Rassegna Economica*, No. 1 (July–March 1956), p. 34.

[6] See T. Haavelmo, *A Study in the Theory of Economic Evolution* (Amsterdam, 1954), for a discussion of growth models which demonstrate this point.

otherwise concealed by the North-South division. The impression left by a reading of the economic history of the pre-unification period, even by writers favorable to the South, is one of greater differences among the southern than among the northern subregions.

II

Ideally, one would like information on the total income produced in each region, its distribution, its sectoral breakdown and relation to the available capital stock. The indirect indicators which must suffice in any historical work such as this are not always unambiguous.

The occupational distribution of the labor force as given in Table 1 shows a larger percentage of the regional labor force employed in the South than in the North in the 1860's and 1870's. This is often quoted as evidence of the relative economic advancement of the South which balances other evidence less favorable.

In interpreting Table 1 it is useful to jump ahead of the story to Sections IV and V, where it is established that the rate of industrialization in all of Italy went up in the 1880's and 1890's and that the change was concentrated in the North. It is clear then that a simple and direct relation between the proportion of the labor force in industry and the general level of economic development cannot be assumed. It would imply, for example, that the North actually developed more rapidly between 1871 and 1881 than between 1881 and 1901, and was less developed in 1921 than in 1911 or in 1951 as compared to 1931. Central Italy, on this assumption, would have retrogressed between 1881 and 1901 and the South would have declined from 1881 and 1921 and from 1931 to 1951.

Growth of the industrial labor force depends not only on the growth of industrial output but also on the changing distribution of this output between groups of establishments with different labor-output ratios, for example, between artisan and factory establishments.[7] A relative decline in the artisan labor force may be the result of an increase in the role of factory as compared to handicraft labor and thus be consistent with an increase in total industrial output.[8] The data of Table 1, which

[7] Obviously a model is implicit in this analysis which assumes that labor is used in quite different intensities in artisan and factory establishment. This difference is at least one source of cost, and, therefore, returns differentials which may persist over long periods because of market imperfections but which break down during rapid industrialization.

[8] Rosenstein-Rodan reports that investigations in countries of southeastern Europe showed that the percentage of workers in handicraft industries varied first inversely and then directly with higher per capital income.

include both artisan shops and factories in the industry category, thus do not provide a clear indication of the relative economic positions of the regions.[9]

The labor force data of Tables 2, 3 and 4, culled from various sources and collected originally on the basis of quite different definitions and coverages, add a little light. Table 2 seems to confirm the data of Table 1 for 1861 in that the percentage of the labor force in industry, including handicrafts, is higher for the Kingdom of Two Sicilies, which includes most of southern Italy, than for any other region except the Papal States.[10] It is difficult to reconcile Tables 1 and 2 with Tables 3 and 4. The proportions of the labor force in industry in continental southern Italy in 1826 (Table 3) are significantly less than the proportions indicated in Table 1 for 1861, while that proportion in Tuscany in 1841 (Table 4) is much higher.

The stock of social overhead capital available to a region is regarded in current development literature as one of the most important determinants of the growth potentials of a region.[11] Little information is available on this subject for the Italian regions in 1860 other than highway and railway mileage. The superiority of the North in highways is evident in Table 5, where only part of that region can be represented. This superiority would remain even if the mileages were computed relative to occupied and productive land, rather than total area. From Table 6 it appears that, outside the North and Center, railways were virtually a *curiosum* at unification; in the South their mileage was too small to have had a significant effect on economic activity. By the late 1850's some areas within the North must have been benefiting from the advantages of rail transport.[12] Undoubtedly coastal shipping partially made up the inadequacies of land transport both in the South and in the North. But the lack of internal communication

9 It is worth noting that the results of the 1861 census were greeted with surprise at the time. Apparently it was quite generally felt that these results overstated the importance of industry in Italy as a whole and particularly in the South. Other investigators failed to indicate anywhere near the levels of industrial employment shown by the national censuses. There is no doubt that the census methods, putting major responsibility for reporting on the municipal governments, admitted the possibility of gross errors. See R. Tremelloni, "Le Condizione dell'industria italiana al mometo della prima unita," *L'Industria,* 2–3 (1946), 11, and V. Ellena, "La Statistica di alcune industrie italiane," *Annali di Statistica,* ser. 2, Vol. 13 (Rome, 1880).

10 There was a concentration of artisans around Rome attracted by and serving the Papal court.

11 P. N. Rosenstein-Rodan, "Notes on the Theory of the 'Big Push,'" Center for International Studies, M.I.T., March 1957.

12 The substantial differences within the North and Center regions suggest that the North-South comparisons may often be distorted by inclusion of the Center within the North.

in the South suggests relatively more social as well as economic self-sufficiency, so that advances achieved in some areas probably communicated themselves with less speed and impact than in the North. Thus, Tables 5 and 6 tend to confirm the often-remarked-upon isolation of southern Italians in the mid-nineteenth century.

TABLE I

OCCUPATIONAL DISTRIBUTION OF ACTIVE POPULATION IN ITALY, BY REGION AT CENSUS DATES, 1861–1951 [a]

Year	Region[b]	Agriculture Per Cent	Industry Per Cent	Transport Per Cent	Commerce Per Cent	Other Per Cent	Total (thousands)
	N						
1861	C	57.2		25.9		16.9	8,900
	S	57.1		30.4		12.5	5,300
	N	60.3	22.0	1.5	1.3	14.9	6,913
1871	C	60.2	18.5	1.7	1.3	18.3	2,581
	S	54.0	24.0	2.2	1.4	18.6	5,534
	N	56.4	25.4	1.7	2.1	14.4	7,197
1881	C	55.8	23.6	2.0	1.6	17.0	2,555
	S	48.9	30.7	2.2	1.4	16.6	6,362
	N	57.3	26.6	2.3	5.3	8.5	7,562
1901	C	61.3	21.7	2.8	4.3	9.9	2,744
	S	61.4	23.1	2.9	4.3	8.5	5,967
	N	51.8	30.7	3.0	6.0	8.5	7,843
1911	C	55.0	26.6	3.6	4.9	9.9	2,749
	S	60.6	21.9	3.7	5.4	8.3	5,779
	N	50.3	29.5	4.1	7.0	9.1	8,488
1921	C	56.7	22.0	4.7	5.1	11.5	2,969
	S	62.8	20.5	4.3	4.9	7.9	6,193
	N	41.0	35.8	4.1	8.3	10.8	8,295
1931	C	48.8	26.3	4.6	6.9	13.4	3,075
	S	55.3	23.1	5.0	6.4	10.2	5,374
	N	42.2	35.5	3.4	9.0	10.1	8,610
1936	C	50.7	25.3	3.7	7.5	12.8	3,344
	S	57.0	22.4	4.3	7.2	9.2	5,607
	N	33.0	40.3	4.0	13.7	9.0	9,403
1951	C	42.5	28.0	4.3	12.6	12.6	3,611
	S	55.3	22.7	3.9	9.9	8.2	6,563

[a] SVIMEZ, *Statistiche sul Mezzogiorno, 1861–1953* (Rome, 1954), pp. 39–49. These data have their source in the national population censuses taken in Italy since 1861 and have been adjusted to eliminate overlapping of categories and increase comparability.

[b] N—North, C—Center, S—South.

TABLE 2

OCCUPATIONAL DISTRIBUTION IN SOME ITALIAN STATES AROUND 1850[a]

	Proprietors Per Cent	Agriculture Per Cent	Industry and Handicrafts Per Cent	Other Per Cent	Totals Thousands
Piedmont	23.3	60.0	12.2	4.5	2,206
Duchy of Modena	37.6	52.2	6.2	4.0	647
Papal States		60.3	35.8	3.9	1,948
Kingdom of the Two Sicilies	26.9	49.4	14.6	9.1	3,697

[a] P. Maestri, *Annuario Economico-Statistico dell'Italia, 1853* (Turin), pp. 68–69.

TABLE 3

OCCUPATIONAL DISTRIBUTION OF ACTIVE POPULATION, REGIONALLY DISTRIBUTED, OF THE CONTINENTAL PART OF THE KINGDOM OF THE TWO SICILIES, ACCORDING TO THE CENSUS OF 1826[a]

	Agriculture Per Cent	Industry and Handicrafts Per Cent	Other Per Cent	Total Thousands
Capital	4.3	82.0	13.7	125.7
Province of Naples	68.8	27.5	3.7	93.5
Terra di Lavoro	83.8	12.9	3.3	170.9
Principato Citra e Ultra	81.4	15.2	3.4	216.4
Capitanata	91.9	6.2	1.9	133.9
Basilicata	93.0	5.6	1.4	208.6
Molise	92.9	5.9	1.2	145.4
Bari	81.5	15.9	2.6	113.3
Terra d'Otranto	83.7	13.6	2.7	114.8
Abruzzi	88.6	9.1	2.3	307.6
Calabria	83.4	13.6	3.0	286.3
TOTAL	80.4	16.3	3.3	1,915.6

[a] *Censimento ossia Statistica Del Regno delle due Sicilie,* Naples (1826).

TABLE 4

OCCUPATIONAL DISTRIBUTION OF ACTIVE POPULATION REGIONALLY DISTRIBUTED, OF TUSCANY, ACCORDING TO THE CENSUS OF 1841[a]

	Agriculture Per Cent	Artisan Per Cent	Transport Per Cent	Commerce and Services Per Cent	Other Per Cent	Total Thousands
Florence	51.3	29.3	1.4	13.2	4.8	403.4
Pisa	50.7	22.7	4.1	17.1	5.3	181.1
Siena	61.7	19.6	1.2	12.7	4.8	75.6
Arezzo	68.1	18.2	0.5	8.6	4.6	125.0
Grosseto	63.4	15.0	1.7	14.1	5.8	36.1
TOTAL	55.2	24.6	1.9	13.4	4.9	821.3

[a] P. Bandettini, "La popolazione della Toscana alla meta dell'ottocento," *Archivio economico dell'unificazione italiana,* III–IV, Fascicolo I (Rome, 1956), 51–71.

Another type of social overhead capital of a region is the education and skills of its labor force. Primary education, with its effects on productivity and ease of social communication, was more widespread in the North than in the South. Data available for 1871, which reflect the extent of the pre-unification educational systems to a considerable degree, indicate a literacy rate for inhabitants over six years of age in the North almost three times the 15.9 per cent rate of the South, while the Center is intermediate with a 25.3 per cent. The differences are confirmed, though in a somewhat less extreme form, in the literacy rate of army conscripts from the various regions.[13]

Agriculture was far and away the most important sector in both North and South. A fairly complete picture of its relative state can be drawn from the data. Production and available supplies of the major cereal grains in the various regions are shown in Table 7. Apparent per capita availabilities in the North and Center were lower than in the South. This regional pattern of cereal consumption prevails even today and is considered another aspect of the relative depression of the South rather than evidence of its advancement.[14]

TABLE 5

HIGHWAY MILEAGE IN ITALY, 1863 [a]

	Total Mileage (Kilometers)	Per 1000 Inhabitants (Kilometers)	Per Square Kilometer of Land Area (Kilometers)
Piedmont	16,841	4.763	0.487
Lombardy	20,267	6.527	0.909
Emilia, Marche and Umbria	21,660	6.113	0.509
Tuscany	12,359	6.768	0.555
Continental South	11,223	1.653	0.131
Sicily	2,630	1.099	0.090
Sardinia	979	1.655	0.040
TOTAL	85,959	3.947	0.331

[a] L. Bodio, *L'Italia Economica nel 1873* (Rome, 1873), p. 132.

Considerable regional diversity exists in the production of other crops. Potatoes—but not other vegetables—were apparently a more important crop in the continental South than in the Center or North around 1860. The South produced two thirds of the olive oil but only

[13] SVIMEZ, *Statistiche*, pp. 770–72.

[14] In general in Europe higher per capital incomes are associated with lower per capita cereal consumption. As incomes increase, consumption patterns shift to other foods.

TABLE 6

ANNUAL CONSTRUCTION OF RAILROAD MILEAGE IN ITALY TO 1859 (KILOMETERS) [a]

Year	Sardinia	Lombardy-Venice	Tuscany	Papal States	Kingdom of the Two Sicilies	TOTAL
1839		–			8	8
1840		13			–	13
1841		–			–	–
1842		33			–	33
1843		–			33	33
1844		–	19		31	50
1845		–	20		–	20
1846		66	19		12	97
1847			26			26
1848	8	–	72			80
1849	49	80	64			193
1850	56	–	–			56
1851	12	54	16			87
1852	–	3	–			3
1853	107	–	7			114
1854	194	85	–			279
1855	52	72	–			124
1856	146	–	2		15	163
1857	58	50	10	20		138
1858	168	27	–	–		195
1859	–	39	2	81		122
Adjustments	–31					–31
1859 Total	819	522	257	101	99	1,798
Total length per 1,000 Inhabitants	1.92	1.40	0.35	1.10	0.10	
Total length per Millions of Hectares	1.38	1.19	0.24	1.15	0.09	

[a] Isidore Sachs, *L'Italie, ses finances et son développement économique depuis l'unification du royaume 1859–1884* (Paris, 1885), p. 957.

around a fifth of the wine at this time. Fruit crops, particularly citrus, cotton, and, to a lesser extent, tobacco, were also more important in the South. Linen and hemp were produced primarily in the North.

A survey of the animal population at the middle of the nineteenth century in Table 8 shows the very great superiority of the North in cattle of all kinds, while the South had somewhat more of the lighter draft animals, sheep and swine. Part of this difference may be due to soil characteristics imposing different draft requirements. Without more information a conclusion on the relative regional significance of livestock culture and use is difficult, but the North and Center appear to have more of the characteristics of intensive agriculture.

The Italian silk industry, based on silkworm culture in the rural areas, was the major source of foreign exchange earnings at mid-nineteenth century and was, in fact, called Italy's "mine of gold." Although in the 1850's it began to suffer from diseases which reduced output, but raised prices, it remained the principal export for many years. It was more than an agricultural by-product; it was a major source of rural income which could readily be adapted to the varied activities of diversified farming. As Table 9 shows, the North had a strong advantage in this area.

TABLE 7

AVERAGE ANNUAL PRODUCTION, TRADE AND AVAILABILITIES OF CEREAL GRAINS BY REGIONS, 1855–1860 [a]

	North	Center	South
Agricultural Land Area in thousands of Hectares in 1952	8,410	5,559	11,780
Population in thousands in 1861	11,142	4,106	9,768
Wheat Production in thousands of hectoliters	11,008	5,961	18,851
Corn Production in thousands of hectoliters	11,392	2,691	2,818
Total Production, including minor grains	28,767	10,175	32,362
Imports	4,681 (North and Center)		13
Exports	2,334 (North and Center)		1,759
Total Availabilities	41,289 (North and Center)		30,616
Per Capital Availabilities	2.7 (North and Center)		3.1

[a] C. Correnti and P. Maestri, *Annuario statistico italiano* (Turin, 1864), pp. 407, 419.

TABLE 8

AVERAGE ANNUAL ANIMAL POPULATION BY REGIONS, 1855–1860 [a]

	Cattle	Horses, Asses and Mules	Sheep and Goats	Swine
	(thousands of head)			
North and Center	2,906	531	4,017	1,512
South	682	828	6,862	2,168

[a] C. Correnti and P. Maestri, *Annuario statistico italiano*, p. 443.

An over-all regional comparison of agricultural incomes is presented by Correnti and Maestri. The gross estimates seem to have been prepared by valuing the various types of output at some average price. The net estimate involves a subtraction for seed and, perhaps, other adjustments, but appears to have been computed consistently at 40 per cent of gross output. The estimating technique, though crude, probably provides a reasonably reliable index for regional comparisons. These are presented in Table 10; two central states, Umbria and Marche are omitted, thus lowering the total and affecting the relative regional shares. The substantial advantage of the North is clear, however.

The compilers of these estimates themselves warn that they are derived from a variety of sources of varying credibility. Nonetheless, its major conclusions deserve consideration. The North, with roughly 45 per cent of total population and, perhaps, an even smaller share of rural population, appears to have 50 per cent of the gross income earned in agriculture. The agricultural product distributed among all the people in the South was only about 75 per cent of that in the North and about 77 per cent of that of the Center according to these figures. Though apparently behind in grain crop production, the North more than made up the difference by means of livestock and silk worms. The results are about the same if the comparison is made in terms of the per capita product of persons employed in agriculture using the occupational listings in the population census of 1861.

TABLE 9

REGIONAL DISTRIBUTION OF SILK PRODUCTION BY WEIGHT AND VALUE [a]

	Weight (Thousands of Kilograms)	Value (Thousands of Lire)
North [b]	38,989	163,330
	(79.2%)	(78.2%)
Center	2,909	13,160
	(5.9%)	(6.3%)
South [b]	7,320	32,382
	(14.9%)	(15.5%)

[a] C. Correnti and P. Maestri, *Annuario statistico italiano*, pp. 449–50.
[b] The island of Sardinia is included in the Kingdom of Sardinia.

TABLE 10

ESTIMATED AVERAGE ANNUAL AGRICULTURAL OUTPUT, GROSS AND NET, REGIONALLY DISTRIBUTED, 1855–1860 [a]

	Gross Output (millions of lire)	Net Output (millions of lire)
North	1,418 (49.9%)	
Central	506 (17.8%)	
South	918 (32.3%)	
TOTAL	2,842	1,137

[a] C. Correnti and P. Maestri, *Annuario statistico italiano*, p. 451.

Italian industry at mid-century cannot be described with even that limited scope and detail which could be provided for agriculture. Industry, both North and South, was for the most part small and scattered, producing a variety of products and distributing them locally or through traditional foreign trade channels. Our observations will be confined to particular sectors for which a general, but probably adequate, impression can be formed on the basis of the limited information available.

Mining activity in Italy at the time of unification was small in volume, as shown by Table 11, and the most productive mines were concentrated in a few areas. Sulphur—by far the most important mineral product—was mined mainly on Sicily, which had at that time a virtual world monopoly. The average annual value of exports of sulphur, gray and refined, from 1862 to 1866 was about 33.5 million lire,[15] which was, however, not much more than one tenth of the value of Italian silk exports at roughly the same time. Two thirds of the iron was mined on the island of Elba; most of the rest came from Lombardy and Piedmont. A small amount of the high-quality Elba iron ores was exported but imports, mostly for northern Italy, were four times as great. Lack of good coal has been and still is a major handicap to Italian development; of the limited existing coal supplies nearly all were found in North and Central Italy.[16]

Among manufactures, a picture can be obtained of the state of the iron and steel industry in Italy which is relatively good as compared to the information available for other industries. The report by F. Giordano, prepared for the naval ministry in 1864, covers the larger-scale enterprises. Total iron production of all types in Italy at that time was about 29,000 metric tons. Of this around 40 per cent was produced in Lombardy, at least 30 per cent in Tuscany, as much as 25 per cent in the Val d'Osta and the remainder in Calabria and in other small establishments scattered throughout the country. Iron imports into the North were also much larger than in the South.

Another indication of the relative regional development of iron and iron-using industries in Italy at unification is the employment in mechanical establishments—excluding handicraft workers—as shown in Table 12. The employment in metal-using industries in the South in 1864 is much smaller than that in the North. The table also shows

15 C. Correnti and P. Maestri, *Annuario statistico italiano, 1864* (Turin, 1864), p. 231.
16 F. Giordano, *Industria del Ferro in Italia* (Turin, 1864), p. 11.

TABLE 11

OUTPUT OF ITALIAN MINES IN 1868[a]

	Quantity (Thousands of tons)	Value (Thousands of lire)	Number of miners
Iron	148.5	2,033.5	2,212
Copper	16.1	1,593.6	2,412
Lead and Silver	16.0	2,972.7	4,105
Gold	0.1	235.6	642
Mercury	7.6	57.0	288
Zinc	.3	10.0	
Antimony	.1	50.0	
Nickel	.1	1.0	
Iron Pyrites	4.8	26.0	
Manganese	1.9	60.6	
Brown coal and peat	108.4	1,004.0	
Sulphur	181.3	20,059,8	21,000
TOTAL		28,103.8	

[a] P. Maestri, *L'Italia Economica nel 1868* (Florence, 1868), p. 225.

clearly the higher geographical concentration of large metal-using firms within the South, where in each major region they were confined to one city. No other Italian city but Genoa had as many large firms as Naples, but outside Naples there were only two other cities in the South with metal-using firms prominent enough to be included in the compilation.

Not much information can be added to the data of Table 12. Numerous small, artisan ironworking shops scattered widely through the country are not included in this compilation, and their quantitative importance cannot be definitely estimated. It is likely, however, that the South was quite backward in this crucial industry at the time of unification. The descriptive reports of iron-working in the South do not mention as many flourishing areas as the North. Raw materials were a problem in the North, but the South was even more deficient in domestic supplies of iron and coal, and was separated from foreign sources by a higher tariff. The large and advanced firms of Naples, frequently cited to demonstrate the development of the South, were controlled by foreign entrepreneurs—English, French, Swiss, and German, aided by court-conferred privileges. This seems to have been less true in the North, and suggests that the native southern industry was itself less capable of creating the type of firm considered necessary for more modern armaments and railroad equipment. Larger-scale establishments were, at this time, the result of new entrepreneurial activity rather than simple growth in traditional patterns. Presumably, therefore, productivity was higher in the larger firms. If their features in other countries were true of Italy, such firms were also centers of labor training from which skilled workers emerged to seed other establishments.

Information is available for the shipbuilding industry on the number and size of ships constructed in the various shipyards in 1867. In value terms shipbuilding was one of the important industries; the 1867 construction was valued at 22 million lire. Almost 60 per cent of the ships constructed were built along the coast of the continental South and Sicily and Sardinia. But by weight they amounted to less than 18 per cent of the total. Genoa was far and away the most important center of this industry; 60 per cent by weight of the annual production had its source there. Inferences about the pre-unification regional distribution from 1867 data may be incorrect, however. The industry's annual output almost quadrupled from 1860 to 1867 and major regional shifts might have taken place, though there is no reason for supposing they did.[17]

TABLE 12

EMPLOYMENT IN LARGE FIRMS IN METAL-USING INDUSTRIES IN ITALY IN 1864[a]

Regions and Cities	*Workers* *Number*	*Workers* *Per Cent*	*Number of firms*
North			
Piedmont (Cuneo, Novara, Turin)	2,204	18.8	14
Lombardy (Bergamo, Brescia, Como, Milan)	1,522	12.9	11
Venice (Padua, Treviso, Venice, Verona)	1,250	10.6	6
Liguria (Genoa)	2,255	19.2	7
Emilia-Romagna (Bologna, Modena, Piacenza)	203	1.7	4
TOTAL	7,434	63.2	42
Central			
Tuscany (Florence, Livorno, Lucca, Siena)	1,147	9.7	8
Umbria	120	1.0	2
Marche (Ancona)	136	1.2	2
Lazio (Civitavecchia)	400	3.4	1
TOTAL	1,803	15.3	13
South			
Campania (Naples)	2,225	18.9	7
Sicily (Palermo)	275	2.3	1
Sardinia (Cagliari)	40	.3	1
TOTAL	2,540	21.5	9
All Italy	11,777	100.0	64

[a] F. Giordano, *Industria del Ferro*, pp. 354–73. Some rough estimates of employment were made when only information on equipment was given. Metal-using firms were listed only for the regions and provinces specified. Thus, there were no firm reported in Abruzzi, Puglia, Basilicata or Calabria.

[17] P. Maestri, *L'Italia Economica nel 1868*, p. 270.

The "mine of gold" of northern agriculture provided the raw material for silk spinning and weaving, which was probably the sector of Italian industry with highest value of output at the time of unification. The considerable exports and imports of silk at all stages of processing did not shift the overwhelming superiority of the North gained in production of the raw material. Table 13 gives the regional distribution of silk weaving and spinning production.

TABLE 13

SILK SPINNING AND WEAVING IN ITALY BY REGION, 1868 [a]

	Thread Spun from Cocoons		Gray Silk	
	Quantity Per Cent	Value Per Cent	Quantity Per Cent	Value Per Cent
North	89.5	88.9	88.5	88.0
Center [b]	7.7	8.0	8.4	8.7
South	2.8	3.1	3.1	3.3
TOTAL	17,159.0 thousand tons	84,752.3 thousand lire	1,116.6 thousand tons	101,446.7 thousand lire

[a] P. Maestri, *L'Italia Economica nel 1868*, p. 192.
[b] The Roman provinces, mainly Lazio, are omitted.

There is less information available about the woolen industry. However, not only the descriptive reports but the quantitative estimates indicate that the North had a very considerable superiority. The data on the distribution of animal population gives the South more than its proportion of sheep, but apparently somewhat more raw wool was imported than produced domestically, with most of the imports going to the North. Some data on the distribution of looms and their output are given in Table 14.

TABLE 14

REGIONAL DISTRIBUTION OF WOOLEN LOOMS AND WOOL AND LEATHER PRODUCTION IN 1867 [a]

	Number of Woolen Looms	Value of Woolen Output (Thousands of lire)	Leather Quantity (Thousands of tons)	Value of Leather Production (Thousands of lire)
North and Center	5,550	48.0	10,291	45.2
Continental South	1,640	16.0	3,300	14.0
Sicily			783	3.5
TOTAL	7,190	64.0	14,374	62.7

[a] P. Maestri, *L'Italia Economica nel 1868*, p. 199.

The leather industry, from the available data, shows a similar concentration in the North. Table 14 gives some data for 1867.

For the cotton textile industry there are only scattered reports of establishments in different regions. The same is true of linen and hemp, except that the latter industry is generally spoken of as being concentrated in the North.

Evaluation of the relative positions of North and South at time of unification becomes more difficult for industries for which raw material supplies were less specific, and outputs less homogeneous and more scattered. There is no doubt that a variety of products was produced throughout the peninsula in the middle of the nineteenth century, for example, gloves, glass, paper, chemicals, locomotives and firearms. Listing these products and the locations of their production conveys an impression of variety but no idea of relative significance. Without more basic information there is no way to compare the significance of the concentration of glove-making in Naples with that of glass in Venice. It does not seem possible to resolve the problem of lack of data for many sectors, especially those characterized by small and widely dispersed firms. For a few crucial sectors, however, the information is relatively complete.

III

Given the nature of the data, the conclusions to be drawn must inevitably depend to a degree on individual judgment. We cannot add up aggregate regional incomes and compare them on a per capita basis, but must balance the disparate types of evidence as best we can. With only one exception, the bits of evidence point to a clear superiority of the North over the South at the time of unification in terms of per capita output and income. The South had some superiority in wheat and fruit, the North in cattle and the highly lucrative silkworm culture. In industry the South did not approach the North in development in any of those particular sectors for which data were available. In social overhead capital—roads, railroads and educational level of the labor force—the North was strikingly better off.

The one piece of evidence favoring the South is the showing of the occupational censuses at the time of unification. Not only for 1861, but as late as 1881 these still showed a larger percentage of the population employed in "industry" in the South than in the North. Perhaps, however, this "proves" too much. Not only is it at odds with the other information for pre-unification years, but also with the increasingly clear indications of the relative economic advancement of the North in the 1870's and 1880's. The data from this type of census in 1911 disagree strikingly with the results of the first industrial census taken in the same year. The many contemporary criticisms of its procedure also raise doubts. Still, it gives a consistent twenty-year picture and cannot be explained away in a completely satisfactory manner.

It is difficult to put a summary number to the qualitative and quantitative differences observed in the separate sectors. The North had at least a 20 per cent margin over the South in the per capita product in agriculture. The margins in the manufacturing and transport sectors were probably greater, but these sectors were relatively small. In other, less important sectors, the regional differences were probably very small. On the whole, a difference in per capita income between North and South of between 15 and 25 per cent seems plausible.

With respect to the relative abilities of the different regions to undertake development, *a priori* reasoning would lead to greater expectations for the North. The data on social overhead capital and on types as well as amounts of agriculture and industrial production suggest that the transformation from traditional to modern ways of life was well started in the North and hardly begun in the South. The North also had the advantage of producing in silk a substantial earner of foreign exchange. The North also appears in the literature to score higher than the South in terms of the spirit and expectations of the times, while with few exceptions most of the South appears as a backwater. In the North by 1860 economic change seems to have been spreading slowly, but with sureness, through the country-side as well as the cities.

IV

By the early twentieth century, northern Italy's centers of manufacturing produced a wide range of factory goods with modern organization and techniques. Some sectors—autos and certain types of chemical production—compared in the brilliance of their technology with the world's best. Agriculture in the North had also changed; much larger amounts of equipment and fertilizer were used, and the volume and pattern of output had improved. Backwaters in the North continued to exist—remote valleys, lowland centers of agricultural depression, meager hilltop towns and much slow and inefficient production in agriculture and industry. But great and widespread economic changes had occurred.

The exception in the North, however, was the rule in the South, though it was much less backward than it had been at the time of unification fifty years before. New industrial activity and agricultural improvement had taken place. Transport facilities had greatly improved, cities had grown, internal labor mobility had increased. But the region was still a backwater, in touch with the rapid changes occurring elsewhere, but changing only slowly itself. Almost half the new generation had left for the North or foreign countries.

Political unification had not reduced the economic gap between North and South, although it may have reduced the rate at which it widened. The entire experience requires explanation and may suggest general lessons to be drawn for economic development and national policy. The first task is to determine as well as possible the pattern of national development in the fifty years after unification. Against this pattern, differences in the development of the regions can be more clearly perceived.

Italy is relatively well endowed with statistical information on its critical growth period, though income and output series by region and sector are generally lacking. For aggregate output from 1881 to 1913, three major sources of information must be examined critically and reconciled. Over-all economic changes between 1860 and 1881, for which less data are available, can be discussed best after the sources are established in examination of the later period. The official Istituto Centrale di Statistica (ISTAT) has recently published a *Statistical Study on the Development of the National Income of Italy from 1861 to 1956,*[18] with annual gross and net output series in current prices for major sectors, and in constant prices for a few broad sectors. A private net product series and indices of agricultural and industrial output independently calculated by Silvio Golzio are also available starting with 1881.[19] An excellent index of industrial output for the period from 1881 to 1913 has been constructed by A. Gerschenkron.[20] Two older industrial output series [21] and a number of scattered estimates of annual income

[18] *Annali di Statistica,* Anno 86, Serie VIII, Vol. 9 (Rome, 1957). This is, by far, the richest single source of historical economic information now available for Italy.

[19] S. Golzio, *Sulla misura delle variazioni del reddito nazionale Italiano* (Turin, 1951).

[20] A. Gerschenkron, "Notes on the Rate of Industrial Growth in Italy, 1881–1913," *The Journal of Economic History,* XV, No. 4 (December 1955), 360–75, and "Description of an Index of Italian Industrial Output, 1881–1913," unpublished manuscript.

[21] Jean Dessirier, *Bulletin de la Statistique Generale de la France,* XVIII:1 (October–December 1928), 65–110, and G. Tagliacarne in *Rapporto della Commissione Economica presentato all'Assemblea Costituente, L'Industria, I. Relazione,* Vol. 2 (Rome, 1947), Ministero per la Costituente.

and national wealth for various years from 1860 also exist.[22] These aggregate indicators of economic activity which have been constructed for Italy do not tell a uniform story. A careful examination is required to expose and evaluate the differences.

The Golzio and ISTAT net product series, Chart 1, show somewhat different patterns for the period in which they overlap. According to Golzio, net output of the Italian economy grew at an average annual compound rate of 2.05 per cent from 1881 to 1911–1915, and net output per capita grew at 1.38 per cent per annum. The ISTAT series shows an aggregate growth rate of about 1.7 per cent and a per capita growth rate of less than 1 per cent. A major source of the difference lies in the strikingly low Golzio estimate for 1881, and a decline in the early 1890's which has no counterpart in the ISTAT series. Otherwise, when the period 1881–1885 is taken as the basis for comparison, the two series show virtually identical rates over the next thirty years.

CHART I
TWO SERIES OF TOTAL AND PER CAPITA NET NATIONAL PRODUCT (1938 PRICES) IN ITALY.

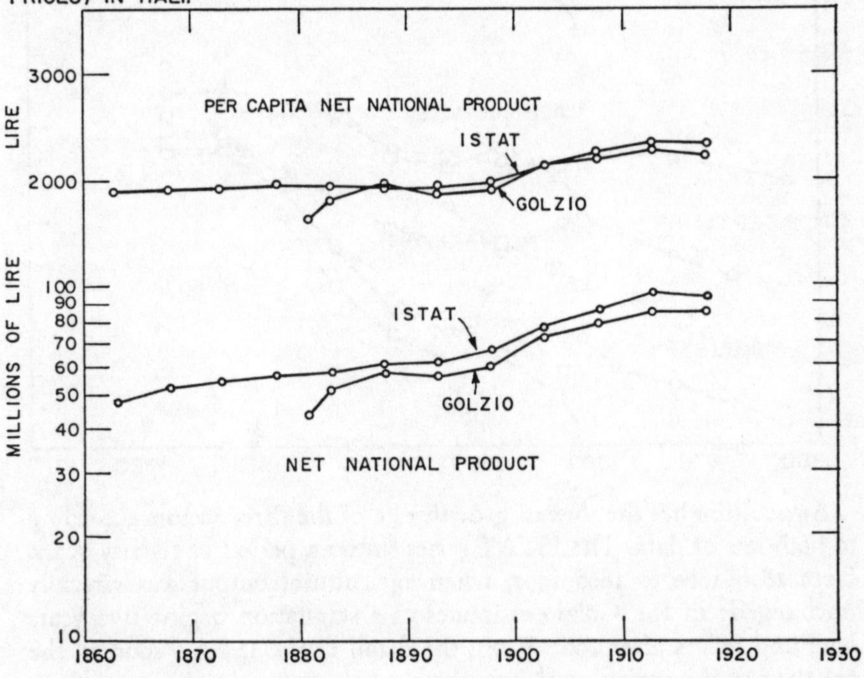

[22] See F. Coppola d'Anna, *Popolazione, reddito e finanze publiche dell'Italia, dal 1860 ad oggi* (Rome, 1946).

The differences between the ISTAT and Golzio national output estimates result from differences in the estimates in the major sectors: agriculture, industry and tertiary services (Chart 2). In each sector, the Golzio estimate is lower than the ISTAT estimate in 1881 and grows more rapidly during the 1880's. The subseries, particularly those for industry, diverge less after 1890, though the Golzio series is more variable. The Golzio series' decline in the early 1890's shows up in the ISTAT series as only a slowing of the rate of growth in all sectors.

CHART 2
TOTAL AND SECTORAL OUTPUTS IN 1938 PRICES.

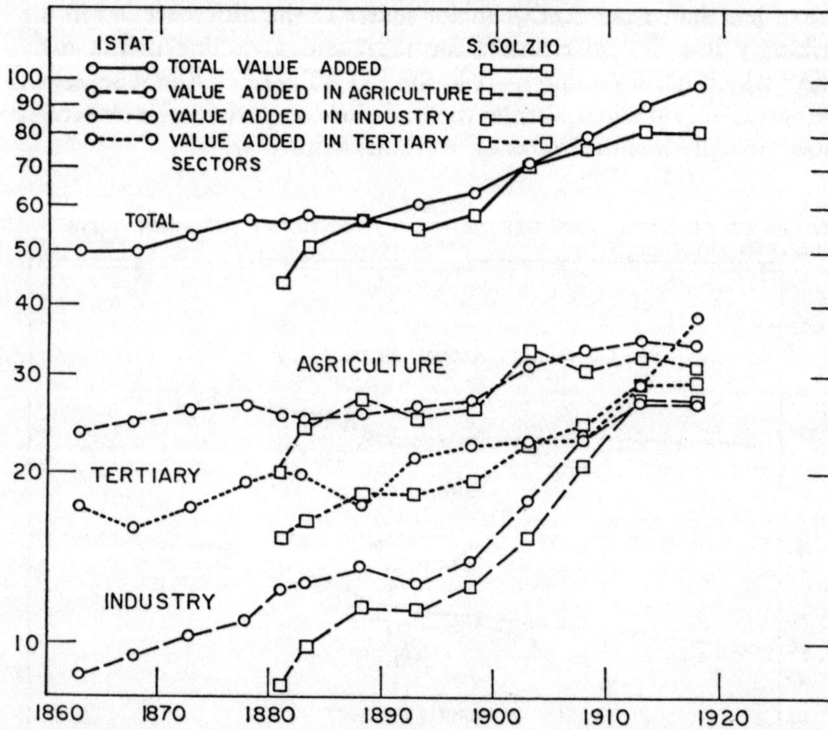

Agriculture has the slowest growth rate of the three sectors according to both sets of data. The ISTAT series shows a period of twenty years, from 1876–1880 to 1896–1901, when agricultural output was virtually unchanged; in the Golzio estimates this stagnation begins five years later and recurs after 1903. From the detail of the ISTAT sources, the behavior of the agricultural sector as a whole appears to be characteristic of the separate products.

For the industrial sector the Golzio and ISTAT studies offer some detail, and we have the valuable independent study by A. Gerschenkron.[23] The three sets of indices are plotted in Chart 3. A visual inspec-

CHART 3
THREE SERIES OF INDUSTRIAL PRODUCTION FOR ITALY.

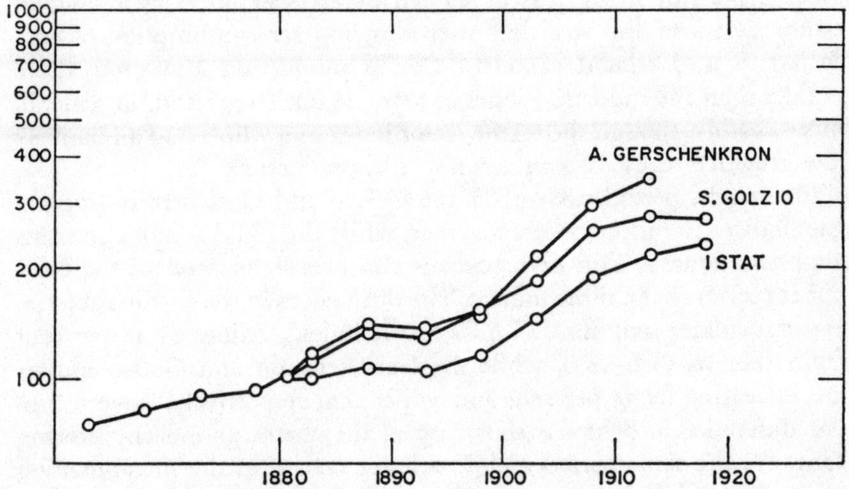

tion shows more agreement between Golzio and Gerschenkron than between either of these two and the ISTAT series. Gerschenkron has distinguished four subperiods as follows:

	Period	*Percentage Rate of Growth*
1)	1881–1888	4.6
2)	1888–1896	0.3
3)	1896–1908	6.7
4)	1908–1913	2.4

The major subsector series for the industrial output index prepared by Gerschenkron (Table 15) show some interesting details. The sectors with rates of growth above the average during the periods of rapid growth according to the Gerschenkron calculations are chemicals, metal-making[24] and engineering. The role of such primary industries in a country notably lacking in raw materials is particularly interesting.

23 Neither Golzio nor the ISTAT survey furnishes basic data for the separate industries used to construct the indices, while all such information is provided by Gerschenkron. For this reason, and because of their intrinsic merit, Gerschenkron's calculations are used here as the reference against which other series are compared.

24 This sector includes both ferrous and non-ferrous metals production.

The chemical sector series is an index of the output of sulphuric acid based mainly on the Sicilian deposits. Since exports expanded relatively little, the growth in this sector indicates increasing domestic usage. Steel output was the fastest growing component of the metal-making series and required increasing imports of scrap and pig iron. The engineering sector index was developed by Gerschenkron as a residual estimate of iron and steel left after allowing for consumption of railroad rails and related products. Cotton production also grew more rapidly than the industrial series as a whole until 1907 and, in general, more steadily, though the textile sector index as a whole had a relatively low growth because of stagnation in silk production.

In the first period, 1881–1888, the Golzio and Gerschenkron aggregate indices rise more or less together, while the ISTAT index remains almost stationary. This divergence is also present in most of the component series of the three indices. The differences in the textile subseries are particularly striking. ISTAT's textile index declines by 14 per cent from 1881 to 1886–1890, while the Gerschenkron and Golzio indices are increasing by 34 per cent and 47 per cent respectively. A very similar difference in behavior shows up in the chemical and engineering series for the same period and, to a lesser extent, in the metal-making series. These differences account for most of the divergences mentioned above in the aggregate series for the period 1881 to 1886–1890.

After 1886–1890 the separate series correspond more closely, with the Gerschenkron series often more buoyant than the other two. This is especially true in metal-making, where the differences account for many of the discrepancies in the aggregate indices. Inspection of the Golzio series not included in the Gerschenkron index brings to light some sectors which played leading roles in the rapid growth at the turn of the century: paper, rubber, electric energy and, for a short time, naval construction.

There are occasionally direct contradictions among the three series. For example, from 1906–1910 to 1911–1915, mining output increased substantially according to the ISTAT and Golzio series, but very slightly according to Gerschenkron. Foodstuff production, in the same period, increased substantially according to the ISTAT and Gerschenkron series, but declined according to Golzio. The ISTAT textile series from 1901–1905 to 1911–1915 shows a steady increase totalling 61 per cent, while the Gerschenkron and Golzio indices moved up and then down for a net increase of only 11 per cent and 25 per cent, respectively.

TABLE 15[a]

AVERAGE ANNUAL RATES OF GROWTH IN THE SIX INDEX INDUSTRIES[b]

	Period						
	1881–1888	*1888–1896*	*1881–1891*	*1891–1896*	*1896–1908*	*1908–1913*	*1881–1913*
Mining	0.0	1.30	0.7	0.8	1.8	0.0	1.0
Metal-making	22.50	−3.24	12.6	−0.5	12.4	6.1	9.3
Textiles	4.40	3.20	3.1	5.2	3.5	−1.2	2.5
Engineering	9.20	−7.40	0.0	0.0	12.2	2.0	4.7
Foodstuffs	0.9	0.0	1.1	0.9	5.5	5.5	3.1
Chemicals	15.1	9.4	12.0	11.8	13.7	4.8	11.3
Aggregate	4.6	0.3	2.1	2.5	6.7	2.4	3.8

[a] Computed on a compound basis using the first and last years of the periods specified.
[b] A. Gerschenkron, *Description of an Index*, pp. 58–59.

Neither the Golzio nor ISTAT publications give basic data on the components or the construction of their indices.[25] In such circumstances the most weight must be given to the series whose detailed composition we know and whose construction can be completely followed.

For the period from unification to 1880, when the Golzio and Gerschenkron indices begin, only the ISTAT series is available, supplemented by bits of data from original sources. In agriculture ISTAT shows an average annual increase in value added from 1861–1865 to 1881 in current prices of 1.96 per cent. Food and industrial field crops production, also in current prices, increased by 62 per cent in the ten years from 1861–1865 to 1871–1875; forest crops and livestock production behave similarly. Price deflation by ISTAT on the total output series removes much of these increases. However, physical output figures which are available from other sources suggest that the deflation may be excessive.[26] For the first ten or twelve years after Italian unity

[25] Since the ISTAT series contradicts results of previous studies, it is particularly unfortunate that ISTAT did not assemble and publish basic price and production data. A compilation of such data would have provided a much-needed tool for students of Italian economic history.

[26] Wheat production, which averaged almost 36 million hectoliters from 1885 to 1860, rose to an average of 51 million hectoliters for the period 1870–1874 and averaged 45.5 million hectoliters from 1879 to 1883. Corn production, on the other hand, almost doubled from 1855–1860 to 1870–1874; the average output then fell about 5 per cent to the 1879–1883 average. Rice production grew rapidly over these years: from a 1.4 million-hectoliter average in 1855–1860 to a 3.8 million-hectoliter average from 1870–1874 and a 7.3 million average from 1879–1883. Measured in hundreds of pieces of fruit, the citrus crop increased by almost 50 per cent from the average output of 1870–1875 to the average for the period from 1879 to 1883. Wine production grew from an average 24.3 million hectoliters in 1855–1860 to a 27.6 million average for 1870–1874 and a 36.8 million-hectoliter average for the period 1879–1883. Olive oil output rose from a 1.6 million-hectoliter average over the period 1855–1860 to a 3.3 million-liter average from 1870–1875 with no further change in the average

was achieved, agricultural output of some types increased at least as rapidly as at any later time. The 1870's were a period of mixed behavior; the growth in output, if there was any, must have been at a much lower rate.

For industry the ISTAT data also show only slow over-all growth for the first ten or twelve years after unification, at about 1.7 per cent per year; this growth slowed in the 1870's and then picked up in the 1880's. From the limited data otherwise available, the impression of a downward bias in the ISTAT series again emerges. Sulphur production increased by almost 240 per cent between 1860 and 1881.[27] Iron ore output increased rapidly during the same period though suffering a setback in the late 1860's; by 1881 it was 500 per cent of the 1861 output. Production of lead and zinc ores increased about 250 per cent to 1881 and copper ore output by 160 per cent.[28] The mining industry may also have grown more rapidly in the first twenty years after unification than at any succeeding time in the century. The 29,000 tons of iron produced in the early 1860's grew by almost 220 per cent to 95,000 tons in 1881. Steel production, which in 1864 was around 650 tons, reached 3,600 tons by 1881.[29] Net cotton imports, the basis for Gerschenkron's cotton textile index, more than doubled during the 1870's after the depressed previous decade. Gray silk output doubled from 1865 to 1871, then fell off again in the 1870's.

Increased use of machinery and steam power after unification is confirmed in many sources, and there was a vast expansion in railroad construction; Italian railroad mileage in 1881 was three and a half times that in 1861. This suggests strongly that the domestic engineering industry was also expanding in the years immediately after Italian unification. Ship construction expanded steadily from 18,290 tons in 1861 to 96,010 tons in 1869; by 1875 it was down to 88,000 tons and fell drastically in the 1880's.[30] Though one of Italy's major industries in the

output for 1879–1883. In livestock raising from an average of 3.6 million during 1855–1860, the number of cows grew to a 4.8 million in 1881. For the 1855–1860 period see C. Correnti and P. Maestri, *Annuario Statistico Italiano, 1864* (Turin, 1865), pp. 407–8; for the 1870–1875 and 1879–1883 periods, *Annuario Statistico Italiano* for 1889 and 1890.

27 E. Corbino, *Annali dell'Economia Italiana,* 1861–1870, p. 72.

28 E. Corbino, *Annali dell'Economia Italiana,* 1861–1870, p. 74; P. Maestri, *L'Italia Economica nel 1868,* p. 225; *Annuario Statistico Italiano* (Rome, 1900), p. 478; V. Ellena, *La Statistica di alcune industrie italiane, Annali di Statistica,* ser. 2, Vol. 13 (Rome, 1880), 136.

29 Statistica Industriale, *Rassunto delle notizie sulle condizioni industriale del Regno, Parte I* (Rome, 1906).

30 *Annuario Statistico Italiano* (Rome, 1886), pp. clxxxviii, 327.

1870's, ship construction did not grow in the last quarter of the nineteenth century.

The scattered and limited data for 1861–1881, and particularly for the 1860's, do not suggest economic stagnation. Mining and naval construction growth was at a higher rate than for succeeding "growth years" distinguished by Gerschenkron. Cotton textiles and metallurgy seem to show slow but accelerating growth, and substantial growth in agricultural output in the 1860's probably occurred. The ISTAT series, which shows little if any growth in the twenty years after unification, thus appears to have a downward bias.

V

Investigation of the regional growth patterns in the fifty years after unification must be based on indirect and partial evidence. One imperfect general indicator of regional activity available for the period 1872–1885, the volume of freight carried on the major railway lines—shows substantial interregional differences. During the fourteen-year period, freight haulage expanded in the Center region by almost 250 per cent, in the North by 230 per cent and in the South by 175 per cent.[31] This evidence is even more significant when it is noted that new railroad construction was actually greatest in the South in this period and least in the Center.[32]

In agriculture, the scattered and discontinuous data present a reasonably consistent picture. For the first fifteen years after unification the increase in output of all the major crops in both the South and Center exceeded that in the North. In the early 1880's cereals production declined sharply outside the North, wine and olive oil output expanded substantially in the South. The years 1896–1898 show further general declines in agricultural output which, however, were more severe in the South than elsewhere. All the regions benefited from the expansion in agriculture after the turn of the century, but in the North, output continued to perform better than in the other two regions, and in the Center better than in the South. Comparing gross agricultural production in 1911 with that just before unification, the expansion in the North was 295 per cent, in the Center 262 per cent and in the

31 *Annuario Statistico Italiano* (Rome, 1897), p. 217.

32 *Annuario Statistico Italiano* (Rome, 1878), Parte II, 86a–89a; *Annuario Statistico Italiano* (Rome, 1884), p. 654; *Annuario Statistico Italiano* (Rome, 1886), pp. 408–9; *Annuario Statistico Italiano* (Rome, 1911), p. 185.

South 228 per cent. Over the entire fifty-year period the South did better than the North in such major items as corn, wine and olive oil production but most of that growth was in the first fifteen years. Though the information is not complete, agriculture appears to have grown fastest and most steadily in the North and least in the South.[33]

Continuous indicators of regional industrial growth are almost completely lacking, forcing reliance on partial and incomplete data. The results of two industrial surveys in 1877 and 1903 and the first industrial census of 1911 are available (Table 16). Each investigation was made on a different basis and presumably with different degrees of accuracy. According to the industrial studies the relative position of the North declined in the first forty or so years after unification and then improved substantially in the next eight years. Separate information on employment in mining is consistent with Table 16.[34] The data for 1911 from the first industrial census show a much larger proportion of miners in the North and Center than previous information.

TABLE 16

DISTRIBUTION OF INDUSTRIAL EMPLOYMENT AND INSTALLED HORSEPOWER

	1877 [a]		1903 [b]		1911 [c]	
	Industrial Employment	Installed Horsepower	Industrial Employment	Installed Horsepower	Industrial Employment	No. of Firms
	(By Per Cent)					
North	78.0	61.5	54.8	60.7	64.1	49.2
Center	10.6	10.3	22.3	22.3	14.9	18.4
South	11.4	28.2	22.9	17.0	21.0	32.4
TOTAL	100.0	100.0	100.0	100.0	100.0	100.0

[a] V. Ellena, *La Statistica di alcune industrie italiane*, p. 35.

[b] Direzione Generale della Statistica, *Statistica Industriale, Riassunto delle Notizie sulle Condizione Industriali del Regno, Parte II* (Rome, 1905), pp. 394–97.

[c] *Annuario Statistico Italiano* (Rome, 1913), pp. 154–55.

Merchant ship construction was always concentrated in the North, but this concentration was reduced in the 1880's, which were, however, a depressed period for the industry. When the output of this sector ex-

[33] C. Correnti and P. Maestri, *Annuario Statistico Italiano*, p. 231; *Annuario Statistico Italiano* (Rome, 1911), p. 102; *Annuario Statistico Italiano* (Rome, 1889), pp. 631–33; *Annuario Statistico Italiano* (Rome, 1900), p. 396; *Annuario Statistico Italiano* (Rome, 1905–07), Vol. 1, 400–2.

[34] *Annuario Statistico Italiano* (Rome, 1881), pp. 623–24; *Annuario Statistico Italiano* (Rome, 1884), p. 95; *Annuario Statistico Italiano* (Rome, 1886), pp. 826–27; *Statistica Industriale* (1906), pp. 5–9; *Annuario Statistico Italiano* (Rome, 1912), pp. 112–13.

panded again after 1900, the North regained its share of the market.[35] The textile industry was likewise concentrated in the North and, on the basis of limited statistics on employment and numbers of looms, appears to have grown most rapidly there while stagnating in the South.[36] The bits of information available on the many, varied smaller industries do not reveal any striking regional developments.

Unfortunately for the interpreter, these regional data do not show any profound and unmistakable trends over the period considered. Therefore, our conclusions must remain tentative. For the first twenty years or so after unification, much of the evidence suggests that the Center experienced an economic growth which in some sectors exceeded and in others equalled the growth in the North. Except in agriculture, the South apparently did not keep pace with either the Center or the North in this early period. However, the data also suggest an accentuation of regional divergences in the last decades of the nineteenth century and after, with the South lagging furthest behind.

With this hypothesis in mind it is useful to examine again the data of Table 1 giving the regional occupational distributions from population censuses. Putting aside the 1861 Census, which omits Rome and the provinces held by the Church, the data appear, with one exception, to confirm the impressions of the relative regional development. The working force in industry in the North grew continuously from 1861 to 1915; growth in the Center and South was more erratic. The industrial working force in the Center grew faster than in the North from 1871 to 1881, and also—although to a lesser degree—from 1901 to 1911. The biggest discrepancy between the data of Table 1 and other information is in the 1881 data for agriculture and industry in the South. They suggest a remarkable, and completely transitory, industrial development which, moreover, has not been borne out by any other information which could be found. If the 1881 data for the South are put aside, the rest of the information for the South up to 1911 is at least broadly consistent with our hypothesis.

[35] P. Maestri, *L'Italia Economica nel 1868* (Florence, 1868), p. 270; *L'Italia Economica nel 1869* (Florence, 1870), p. 262; *L'Italia Economica nel 1870* (Florence, 1871), p. 250; *Annuario Statistico Italiano* (Rome, 1886), pp. clxxxviii, 327; *Annuario Statistico Italiano* (Rome, 1889), p. 514; *Annuario Statistico Italiano* (Rome, 1905–07), p. 636; *Annuario Statistico Italiano* (Rome, 1912), p. 172; *Statistico Industriale*, pp. 14–15.

[36] P. Maestri, *L'Italia Economica nel 1867* (Florence, 1868), p. 199; *L'Italia Economica nel 1868* (Florence, 1869), p. 192; V. Ellena, "La Statistica di Alcune Industria Italiana," p. 41; *Riassunto delle Notizie sulle Condizione Industriali del Regno*, pp. 72–75, 77–79; *Annuario Statistico Italiano* (Rome, 1881), p. 612; *Annuario Statistico Italiano* (Rome, 1905–07), p. 453; *Annuario Statistico Italiano* (Rome, 1913), pp. 156–61.

VI

The data on the sectors and regions of the Italian economy examined in this article throw a little light in two directions. First, certain measures and general propositions relating to economic development may be examined from them. Second, some reasons may be suggested, specifically for the growing economic differences between North and South between 1860 and 1914.

In the first category is the relation between the rate of investment and the rate of growth. Table 17 indicates a net investment rate higher during each of the Gerschenkron-Golzio growth periods than in the stagnant years of the early 1880's and 1890's. Only at the end of the first decade of this century do net domestic investment rates become substantial by modern standards; a lack of dependence on foreign investment is suggested by the fact that the years of most rapid growth were also years of net exports. The incremental capital-output ratio implied by these figures fell during the period of most rapid growth, and was highest just before moderate growth began in the 1880's after a period of stagnation. It was relatively high during the moderate growth in the late 1880's and tended to be low in other periods when growth was relatively low.

The distribution of investment among sectors—a crucial factor in many theories of growth—is shown in Table 18.[37] The connection between changes in the direction of investment and the incremental capital-output ratio is not always clear. During the period from 1885 to 1895, when output was stagnating, the proportion of total investment going into housing and public works was relatively high, and the capital-output ratio was also relatively high. In the succeeding ten-year period when growth was relatively high and the capital-output ratio was low, the proportion of total investment in housing and public works had fallen and the proportion in plant and equipment had risen. This behavior is consistent with the hypothesis that underdeveloped areas must provide a "social overhead capital" base before rapid growth through industrialization can take place. It is less apparent that this process was operative in the preceding growth period of the early

[37] The distribution of investment has two somewhat surprising features. One is the fact that amortization is a larger part of the total than is usual in advanced countries. The other is the high rate which inventory accumulation reached in the fifteen years after unification, a rate achieved only once again in the fifty-year period.

TABLE 17

THE SHARE OF NET INVESTMENT AND NET EXPORTS IN NATIONAL INCOME AND INCREMENTAL CAPITAL-OUTPUT RATIOS 1861–1915 [a]

Period		National Income (millions of lire in 1938 prices)	Inter-Period Growth Per Cent	Net Investment (as a per cent of National Income)	Net Exports (as a per cent of National Income)	Incremental Capital-Output Ratio
1861–1865		48,845		3.9	—4.1	1.01
			0.05			
1866–1870		51,138		4.5	—1.6	
			0.04			0.85
1871–1875		53,403		3.6	—0.1	
			0.05			0.77
1876–1880		55,877		3.4	+0.2	
			0.01			3.44
1881–1885	Moderate Growth	56,665		4.8	—0.5	
			0.04			1.94
1886–1890		58,600		6.4	—2.4	
			0.04			0.93
1891–1895	Stagnation	60,674		3.2	+0.7	
			0.06			0.61
1896–1900	Rapid Growth	64,378		3.5	+2.2	
			0.16			0.50
1901–1905		74,500		6.7	+3.4	
			0.13			0.85
1906–1910	Moderate Growth	84,589		10.2	0	
			0.09			0.86
1911–1915		92,340		7.2	—1.2	

[a] ISTAT, *Annali di Statistica*, pp. 270–71. The division into subperiods is based on the Golzio and Gerschenkron studies previously cited.

1880's, but the early national period was certainly one of great public works construction. The data are also consistent with the hypothesis that industrialization is the high road to rapid economic growth. Of course, the two hypotheses are not necessarily inconsistent and, in this case, it is impossible to choose between them. In the detailed pattern of investment some general trends are clear. The first two periods of relatively rapid over-all expansion identified by Gerschenkron and Golzio, the 1880's and the late 1890's to 1908, were periods of a high rate of railroad construction; the last period of moderate growth was not. The high level of construction in the 1860's tends to confirm that this was also a period of at least moderate growth. Both absolutely and relatively, the South had the largest increase in railroad mileage in the fifty-year period. By 1909, rail mileage in the South was within a few per cent of that of the North both in total length and relative to the land area. The pattern of railroad construction in the Center is consistent with those explanations of economic growth which give causal significance to social overhead capital facilities, but the data for the South do not give any support to that type of hypothesis.

TABLE 18

TOTAL GROSS INVESTMENT AND ITS SECTORAL DISTRIBUTION [a]

	Per Cent of Gross Investment					
	Housing	Public Works	Plant and Equipment	Inventory	Total Amortization	Gross Investment (millions of lire)
1861–1865	17.3	30.8	41.7	10.3	54.4	4,132
1866–1870	16.5	20.5	41.8	21.2	51.5	4,781
1871–1875	15.8	18.9	48.1	17.3	58.7	4,672
1876–1880	21.4	16.8	65.3	−3.5	60.5	4,780
1881–1885	23.9	24.9	60.3	−9.2	54.2	5,924
1886–1890	18.9	26.8	52.2	2.1	49.2	7,374
1891–1895	18.3	26.2	56.4	− .8	66.2	5,664
1896–1900	21.9	12.8	62.5	2.9	63.5	6,197
1901–1905	19.9	9.1	53.6	17.4	49.3	9,900
1906–1910	14.7	7.5	72.0	5.7	41.4	14,688
1911–1915	11.2	12.4	73.9	2.3	52.2	13,877

[a] ISTAT, *Annali di Statistica*, pp. 270–71.

The general effects of tariffs are difficult to isolate in the historical data. The tariff placed on wheat in 1887 had become by 1895 among the highest in Europe.[38] This accounts in part for the fact that in the 1890's, in the bad harvest years of 1892, 1894–1895 and 1897, wheat

[38] *Industrial Growth in Italy*, p. 368.

imports did not rise enough to maintain per capita consumption at levels reached under similar conditions in the 1880's, although per capita income was higher.[39] The effects of the industrial tariffs are more difficult to ascertain. Gerschenkron argues that the textile industry should not have been protected since it was an "old industry with a moderate rate of modern technological progress and accordingly relatively limited possibilities in a backward country on the European continent." [40] Yet according to his own data, textiles were at times a rapidly growing sector supporting the over-all expansion. Over the entire period covered by his index the growth rate of the aggregate index was 3.8 per cent; that of the cotton textile index was 5.82 per cent. Gerschenkron also argues that protection of the iron and steel industry was also mistaken. Yet its growth rates were higher than the average during the periods of "upsurge," and at the turn of the century the relative input of domestic ores actually increased. The engineering and chemical industries were not protected and grew faster than the industrial average during the periods of rapid growth as well as over the entire period covered by Gerschenkron's index. Only if one argues that the protected industries and the unprotected industries together would, on balance, have done even better without protection can one assert that protection hindered Italian development.

The regional effects of the tariff structure were not uniform, but some balancing factors appear. Southern industry may have been checked by exposure to northern and foreign competition with the substitution of the lower Piedmont tariffs after unification. Southern industry was not large, however, and the argument implies it was relatively inefficient. Southern agriculture was probably stimulated immediately after unification with freer access to northern markets. Lower tariffs on manufactures must have benefited the non-manufacturing sectors, including agriculture, as did the later wheat tariffs. The structure of the tariffs does not appear on the whole to have been less favorable to the development of the South than the North.

The regional effects of government fiscal policy, which have been cited as most favorable to the North after unification, cannot be ascertained clearly. The data of Table 19 of F. S. Nitti are not conclusive. Other information, such as that on road construction, shows that in the

39 *Annuario Statistico Italiano* (Rome, 1881), p. 46; *Annuario Statistico Italiano* (Rome, 1905–07), p. 499; *Annuario Statistico Italiano* (Rome, 1911), p. 144.

40 A. Gerschenkron, "Industrial Growth in Italy," p. 369.

decade after unification state expenditures on roads in the South were three times the amount spent in the North.[41]

TABLE 19

EXPENDITURE OF THE STATE FOR EACH TEN LIRE OF TAX (1909) [a]

North		
	Piedmont	8.49
	Liguria	13.49
	Lombardy	8.32
	Venetia	7.50
	Emilia and Romagna	6.48
Center		
	Tuscany	9.97
	Marche	7.57
	Umbria	5.97
	Lazio	12.02
	Abruzzi and Molise	4.82
South		
	Campagna	8.78
	Puglia	4.35
	Basilicata	4.72
	Calabria	6.07
	Sicilia	8.00
	Sardinia	8.10

[a] F. S. Nitti, *Nord e Sud*, pp. 59, 63, 81.

What is left, then, to explain the unsatisfactory over-all performance of the Italian economy in the nineteenth century and the much slower development of its southern provinces? We have no measure of regional income and output, but such regional data as we do have suggest quite different regional growth rates. The North, which did better than the country as a whole, probably showed appreciable development, while the South, with growth below the national average, may hardly have maintained per capita income.

A plausible explanation suggested by the available evidence would run in terms of original differences in development at the time of unification and differences in the agricultural base of the two regions. We have shown that the economic level of the North was distinctly and significantly above that of the South at the time of unification, in its agricultural, industrial, and transportation sectors. With different initial conditions it is not surprising that the disparities increased rather

[41] L. Bodio, *L'Italia Economica nel 1873*, pp. 120–33. Other data which would make it possible to check further the significance of the regional allocation of funds by the national government and the regional development of social overhead capital are not available.

than diminished. Though the South started with a disadvantage in industry, the major difference discernible in the data lay in the agricultural sectors, which composed 50 to 60 per cent of the regional economies. Northern agriculture expanded continually during the last of the nineteenth century. Although silk production became a relatively less important foreign exchange earner, increased output of foodstuffs substituted for food imports. Southern agriculture never provided the surpluses in large enough amounts to make significant growth possible, either by industrial or agricultural investment or as a growing source of demand for manufactured products. Even in land improvement, the concentrated land ownership in the South did not produce significant savings and regional investment. The disparity in this respect, shown in Table 20, indicates one reason for differences in agricultural development.

TABLE 20

RESULTS OF LAND IMPROVEMENT LAWS: 1915[a]

	Area Effectively Improved in Hectares
North	328,669
Center	1,660
South	2,362
TOTAL	332,691

[a] "I Problemi della Bonifiea," *Rapporto della Commissione Economica, Agricultura, I Relazione,* Ministero per la Costituente (Rome, 1947), p. 342.

In per capita wheat production, for example, the North did much better than the Center or the South; in fact, only the North had an upward trend from the 1870's to the 1890's. Since national per capita consumption of wheat was rising over this period, it is not likely that there was enough substitution of other foods in the southern diet to offset completely the lack of growth in wheat production.[42] If southern per capita consumption equalled or exceeded the national average, the South was becoming less and less self-sufficient in wheat. Even if per capita consumption was only maintained in the South, the data suggest that, at best, less and less saving could have been made available

[42] The sharp increases in domestic production at the turn of the century are easily associated with the very large increase in the use of fertilizers which took place at that time.

from agriculture and that there was no per capita increase in effective demand for non-agricultural products.[43]

It would thus appear that the agricultural sector of South Italy in the last of the nineteenth century did not provide a basis of consumption and saving necessary to produce or attract industrial investment. Since the region was too close to the margin of subsistence to require transport for food surpluses in significant quantity, the extensive road and railway construction after unification must have had relatively little impact. The failure of northern or foreign industry to move into the South remains to be explained, but little direct evidence can be adduced. Southern partisans claimed that the South was discriminated against in the location of technical schools; certainly engineering and labor skills were more plentiful in the North. But idfferentials in this respect antedate unification,[44] and from its old and well-established silk industry the North inherited a sizable trained labor group. The nineteenth century was a time of extraordinary emigration, generally heavier in the South, where at some times and places it exceeded the natural increase in population. The concentration of emigrants in the younger, productive ages left the South with a working force of deteriorating quality.

South Italy had relatively cheap labor, adequate rail transport, and was at no disadvantage relative to North Italy with respect to foreign metal and coal supplies. However, its population pressed too hard on its agricultural base to form a market for industrial products sufficiently broad and growing to induce industrialization from the North. Why the savings of the southern middle and upper classes did not turn into industrial investment to supply such markets as did exist is a problem for the social historian.

RICHARD S. ECKAUS, *Brandeis University and Center for International Studies, M. I. T.*

[43] It is true that other sectors of southern agriculture did better than wheat producers. Wine output grew substantially; the citrus fruit crop seems also to have grown considerably. But olive oil, and other products like corn showed little or no improvement.

[44] P. Maestri, *Italia Economica nel 1870* (Florence, 1871), pp. 97–103, gives some indirect evidence.

Name Index